SUMMER PROGRAMS

FOR KIDS & TEENAGERS 2008

PETERSON'S

A nelnet COMPANY

PETERSON'S
A nelnet COMPANY

About Peterson's, a Nelnet company
Peterson's (www.petersons.com) is a leading provider of education information and advice, with books and online resources focusing on education search, test preparation, and financial aid. Its Web site offers searchable databases and interactive tools for contacting educational institutions, online practice tests and instruction, and planning tools for securing financial aid. Peterson's serves 110 million education consumers annually.

For more information, contact Peterson's, 2000 Lenox Drive, Lawrenceville, NJ 08648; 800-338-3282; or find us on the World Wide Web at www.petersons.com/about.

Previous editions published as *Summer Programs for Kids & Teenagers* © 2007 and as *Summer Opportunities for Kids & Teenagers* © 1983, 1984, 1985, 1986, 1987, 1988, 1989, 1990, 1991, 1992, 1993, 1994, 1995, 1996, 1997, 1998, 1999, 2000, 2001, 2002, 2003, 2004, 2005, 2006

Editor: Fern A. Oram; Production Editor: Jill C. Schwartz; Copy Editors: Bret Bollman, Michael Haines, Brooke James, Sally Ross, Pam Sullivan, Valerie Bolus Vaughan; Research Project Manager: Jennifer Fishberg; Research Associate: Helen L. Hannan; Programmer: Phyllis Johnson; Manufacturing Manager: Ray Golaszewski; Composition Manager: Linda M. Williams; Client Relations Representatives: Janet Garwo, Mimi Kaufman, Karen D. Mount, Danielle Vreeland

ISSN 0894-9417
ISBN-13: 978-0-7689-2422-0
ISBN-10: 0-7689-2422-7

Printed in the United States of America

10 9 8 7 6 5 4 3 2 1   10 09 08

Twenty-fifth Edition

CONTENTS

A LETTER

FROM THE PETERSON'S EDITORS

Welcome to the twenty-fifth edition of *Peterson's Summer Programs for Kids & Teenagers*. Our mission: to uncover a mind-boggling array of things to do on your next summer vacation! We'll clue you in on exciting camps, academic options, travel adventures, community service projects, sports clinics, and arts programs throughout the U.S. and around the world.

First off, you'll want to check out **The Inside Scoop**. There you'll uncover all you need to know about finding the summer program that's right for you, questions to ask before you sign on the dotted line, and how to cope with (gulp) homesickness. Next up, the **Quick-Reference Chart** with the fast facts, at-a-glance rundown on who offers what. This chart gives you important information about all the programs listed in this guide, so you can narrow your search to a manageable size in minutes. Who attends— the number of boys and girls, the age range—the day and residential options, the types of activities offered, the availability of financial aid, and job opportunities are found here in an easy-to-use format. You'll also quickly be able to zero in on programs around the U.S. and the globe.

Details, details, details—have we got details for you! Find out who attends, what activities are offered, session dates, costs, financial aid offered, where to go for more information, program history and accreditations, and job opportunities at tons of summer programs. Just turn to the **Profiles of Summer Programs** and let your journey begin! Want even more info? The **In-Depth Descriptions** give you an up close and personal look at select academic programs, camps, and travel adventures. Finally, check out the **Indexes**. With everything from travel programs to special needs accommodations, you'll be able to find the details that are important to you!

Peterson's publishes a full line of resources to help you and your family with any information you need to guide you through the process. Peterson's publications can be found at your local bookstore, library, and high school guidance office—or visit us on the Web at www.petersons.com.

We welcome any comments or suggestions you may have about this publication and invite you to complete our online survey at **www.petersons.com/booksurvey**. Or you can fill out the survey at the back of this book, tear it out, and mail it to us at:

> Publishing Department
> Peterson's, a Nelnet company
> 2000 Lenox Drive
> Lawrenceville, NJ 08648

Your feedback will help us make your educational dreams possible.

Summer camps and programs will be pleased to know that Peterson's helped you in your selection. Staff members are more than happy to answer questions, address specific problems, and help in any way they can. The editors at Peterson's wish you great success in your summer program search. Enjoy the guide and have an awesome summer!

THE INSIDE
Scoop

PERFECT MATCH

There's the kind of summer when you get bored a few weeks after school lets out. When you've listened to all your CDs, aced all your video games, watched one too many soaps, hung out at the same old mall. But summer doesn't have to be this way. You could windsurf on a cool, clear New England lake. Perfect your backhand or golf swing. Horseback ride along breathtaking mountain trails. Trek through spectacular canyonlands or live with a family in Costa Rica, Spain, Switzerland, or Japan. Get a jump on next year's classes. Explore college majors or maybe even careers. Help out on an archeological dig or community service project. And along the way, meet some wonderful people, maybe even make a few lifelong friends.

Interested? Get ready to pack your bags and join the other 5 million kids and teens who'll be having the summer of a lifetime. *Peterson's Summer Programs for Kids & Teenagers* lists terrific camps, academic programs, sports clinics, arts workshops, internships, volunteer opportunities, and travel adventures throughout North America and abroad. Don't have a lump-sum inheritance? Not to worry, there are programs in this guide with costs and fees to meet every budget, from $50 workshops to $4500 world treks, with sessions varying in length from a couple of days to a couple of months.

AND THE CHOICES ARE . . .

Your hardest job will be deciding which one of the summer programs listed in this guide to sign up for. The programs come in many different flavors, but most fit into one of the following categories: traditional, sports, arts, or special-interest camps; academic programs; travel and wilderness adventures; internships; and community service opportunities. Here's a quick rundown on the types of programs described in this guide and what they offer.

CLASSIC CAMPING

Next summer, when 5 million kids enroll in a summer program, most will choose a traditional summer camp. Camps offer a way to learn, grow, have fun, and make friends while enjoying fresh air and sunshine. At a camp, you can learn to skipper a sailboat, ride a horse, master

rock-climbing techniques, develop wilderness survival skills, build a campfire, tell stories, put on a play, and even brush up on computer skills.

Camp is also a place to learn cooperation and leadership, take on a little independence, and leave the pressures of school and everyday stuff behind. Friendships made at camp can be special, too.

You'll find camps in some of America's most spectacular natural settings—from the rugged Atlantic coastline of Maine to the Blue Ridge Mountains of North Carolina to the canyons of Arizona and the temperate rainforests of the Pacific Northwest.

Many camps also offer specialized programs where fun in the great outdoors is supplemented by weight-loss and fitness programs emphasizing nutrition, support, and supervision for happy, health-enhancing results.

For many campers, summer can also be a time of deepening spiritual commitment. For those who'd like to combine the great outdoors with inner growth, there are camps representing a wide range of religious affiliations.

SUMMER ON CAMPUS

If summer school makes you think of kids sweltering in an all-too-familiar classroom while classmates swim and holler at a nearby pool, you're in for a surprise. Whether you're looking for remedial help or a chance to move ahead, the academic programs in this guide offer learning with a difference. When you're studying under the shady trees of a prep school or college campus, attending small classes, and getting individual attention in the company of kids from different parts of the country or around the world, learning takes on a different meaning. The academic programs in this guide are designed to combine a summer of academic study with the chance to make new friends, discover new places, and still have time for summer fun—from swimming, tennis, and horseback riding to trips to nearby amusement parks and cultural attractions.

EXTRA CREDIT?

You can take another stab at course work that you found difficult during the school year or get a challenging course out of the way at a time when you can focus on it—sometimes for high school or even college credit. Take advantage of the rich curricula many private schools and college programs offer by tackling a course you probably won't find in your local school—there are classes in everything from designing a home page on the Internet to studying the masters of the Italian Renaissance.

You may want to get a preview of what college life will be like, and many programs specialize in college preparation. There are programs that can help you improve college entrance test scores and study skills and work with you to build confidence for the coming school year. Others offer older teens a chance to try college on for size for a few days, a week, or longer. Living in a dorm, sampling college-style courses, and talking with current students and professors can be an exciting and useful experience in getting ready for the major transition to come. There are even college tours that visit representative campuses to help you focus your college search.

FOR THE SPORTS FAN

There's a camp for just about every sport imaginable. There are programs for baseball, basketball, biking, golf, gymnastics, hockey, horseback riding, kayaking, sailing, soccer, tennis, and volleyball—to name just a few! Even skiers will find summer spots for expert instruction—some with snow, some without—in the United States, Canada, Switzerland, and even Australia, where our summer is their winter.

FEELING ADVENTUROUS?

Why just sit there when you can hike, bike, sail, paddle, or climb your way through summer? There are adventure programs that will take you trekking through mountain wilderness, down white-water rapids, and over rugged canyons. Others will have you hiking from

village to village. Still others will have you traveling by canoe, raft, or sailboat, meeting people and soaking in scenery and culture along the way. Whether your destination is a Caribbean island, another country, or a famed American national park, there are summer treks to meet a range of abilities and interests. You don't have to be super-fit or experienced, but you should be open to adventure and new challenges.

EXPLORING YOUR ARTISTIC SIDE

Camps may specialize in advanced, preprofessional studies or may open their doors to kids

just beginning to explore the visual or performing arts. This guide has everything from young playwrights' seminars to dance programs to workshops in sculpture, music, architecture, and graphic design. Arts centers, arts camps, or schools provide the setting, often with professional-quality equipment, facilities, and instruction.

CAREER INTERESTS

Summer can be a great time to check out possible career paths before you have to start thinking about choosing colleges or majors. This guide lists internships and volunteer opportunities that let you see up close and personal what it's like to write for a local newspaper, conduct field studies in a marine science center, work in government or a Wall Street investment firm, or teach children, to name a few options. Whatever your career interest, it can be cultivated in any of the special programs offered here.

INTERNATIONAL EXPERIENCES

If languages are your focus, a world of choices awaits. You can sharpen your Spanish skills in Mexico City or Barcelona, learn Japanese in Tokyo, and study

French in Geneva or Paris. You'll find dozens of languages—some common, some less so—represented. But you don't have to travel halfway around the world to study them. Many language programs listed here are held at a campus near you.

If cultural immersion is what you're after, check out the international study and travel programs. International study programs are listed by country under **Opportunities Abroad**. Travel programs, where your itinerary includes stays at more than one site, can be found in the **Travel** section.

WHERE TO GO FROM HERE

Now that we've got your creative juices flowing, make a list of the different activities you'd like to try out. Don't worry if your wish list is all over the place. Eventually, you can focus in on the must-haves. But there's no sense narrowing yourself too soon—you may find a program that has much of what you want. Many summer programs have an incredible variety of activities, spanning a surprising number of interests and ages.

After you've created your list, look it over. Do you see any types of activities again and again? Or is a mix of activities important to you? Depending on your focus, you'll want to stick with either generalized or special-interest offerings. The **Indexes** in this guide let you search by activity or subject area.

You'll have to consider your budget as well. If your funds are limited, you may want to concentrate on short-term programs of a week or less. This guide includes a number of low-cost programs offered by nonprofit groups. In addition, many programs offer financial aid. Availability of aid is listed in the **Quick-Reference Chart** as well as in the **Profiles of Summer Programs** and **In-Depth Descriptions** of the programs themselves.

Another concern will be location—how close to home do you want to stay? After you define your limits, you can look for programs by state or country. If you're hoping to roam in the United States or abroad, head for the **Travel Programs in the United States** section (which is organized alphabetically by program name).

With your list of must-have activities and essential requirements in hand, dive into the **Profiles of Summer Programs** and **In-Depth Descriptions.** You're sure to find a program that's just what you're looking for. Happy hunting (or skiing, or paragliding, or whatever)!

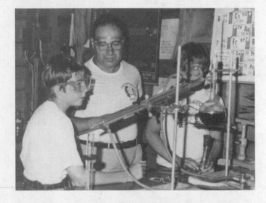

CHECK IT OUT!

Peterson's Law: How happy you are with a summer program is directly proportionate to the number of questions you asked before you signed up. So here's a list of what to check out where you want to check in:

Who is the director? What are his or her credentials or background? What's the director's philosophy about the program? Directors can be hands-on or take on a more administrative role, depending on the size and type of program. Who will be your primary contact?

What is the program's track record? How long has it been in operation? Is it accredited by an outside organization, such as the American Camping Association (ACA)? Not all programs seek accreditation—some programs may not even fall under an accrediting organization's scope, but it is another piece of information you'll want to weigh when making your decision.

Who are the counselors and instructors? What does the director look for when selecting staff members? What training do they receive? What percentage of staff members return each year? As a guideline, look for a counselor return rate of at least 50 percent.

Are family references provided? There's no better way to get the inside scoop about a program than to ask someone who's been there. Most program directors can supply names and phone numbers of satisfied parents and kids who are willing to talk with prospective families. If a program can't supply references, keep looking.

What are the program's goals? If a program's mission is to help polish future athletes for competition and you only like kicking a soccer ball around on the weekend, you're probably not going to be very happy. Read the program's philosophy and make sure its outlook matches your own.

What if discipline problems arise? Make sure you know the program's rules of conduct and its policy for dealing with violations both small and large. Many program directors recommend that parents and teens discuss the rules—and consequences for breaking them—before the program's start.

How safe is the program? When talking with program directors, ask about the ratio of staff members to

xii

DO YOUR HOMEWORK!

Parents worry—they can't help it. It's in their job description. So how do you make sure the summer program you're dying to go to will get their stamp of approval? By doing a little bit of legwork and some reading between the lines, you can tell a lot about a camp, academic program, or travel group before you sign on the dotted line. Here are some tips on making sure a program is everything you hope it will be:

Start looking early. Give yourself plenty of time to ask around, talk to family references (which most programs are happy to provide), and follow up with the programs directly.

Ask around. Your friends, neighbors, and other family members can give you leads on great summer programs. Don't just ask if they liked a particular camp, course, or tour—ask them what they liked and didn't like about it.

Get brochures from a variety of programs. Comparing materials will help you make a more informed decision—and you might even discover an interest you didn't know you had!

Arrange a tour or visit. Many programs invite families to visit their facilities during the session or off-season. Many communities also offer camp fairs where you and your parents can meet with program directors in person.

participants, especially for waterfront and other higher-risk activities. If you'll be living on a campus or traveling, ask about security arrangements and supervision. Less structured, less supervised programs are only appropriate for older teens with a high level of maturity and responsibility.

What provisions are made for medical care and emergencies? Ask about on-site care—is there a nurse or doctor on staff? If you're bound for a wilderness or travel program, ask if counselors have first aid certification and CPR training. Always ask for the distance to the nearest hospital.

How is homesickness handled? Most kids have it, live through it, and are glad that they went away in spite of it. Program directors are more than happy to offer tips for easing the transition to camp and coping with bouts of homesickness.

Who are the other participants? From what areas do they come? What's the age distribution? Nobody wants to find himself or herself in a program that only has a couple of kids in the same grade.

Will I like the food? Most programs offer a variety of food, but if you are a choosy eater, you may want to ask for sample menus. Can substitutions be made? Are special diets accommodated?

HElPiNG KiDS WiTH HoME-SiCKNESS

David G. Richardson
Former Director, Fay School
Southborough, Massachusetts

Everything was unpacked and put away. I was all moved into my new room. We had explored the entire area. What a great place to be! This was so exciting! I was a lucky person. Then Mom and Dad got into the car to go home. It was time for them to leave.

"Have fun!

"Work hard!

"Love you!

"Make us proud, son!

"We'll see you in a few weeks."

All of a sudden it hit me like a ton of bricks. WAIT A MINUTE, my brain screamed, DON'T LEAVE ME! Instead, I choked back the tears, waved, and said, "I will. See you soon."

My parents drove away and the truth became evident. I missed my home and I felt horrible. What had I done?

Homesickness is a part of life. It's a part of growing up and breaking away. Most people experience the nauseating feeling of being homesick at some time in their lives. Some people may even be homesick later in life when they go away to college or get married. However, most people go through this separation experience when they are much younger. Many people learn to cope with homesickness at a summer camp, and camp is a good place to deal with the feeling of homesickness. Camp is a place for children to learn self-confidence. Camp is a place where children learn about responsibility. Camp is a place to have fun with new friends. Camp is a safe, caring environment where nurturing adults are trained to support children through this sometimes difficult growth process. Homesickness is normal and will go away!

As a parent, you can help your child cope with homesickness without actually mentioning it. While preparing to go to camp, talk about the camp experience with your child and tell him or her what to expect. Talk about the routine and how things may seem strange at first but that this is normal in a new situation. Always be positive and upbeat during any discussions about camp. Talk about friendship—how to make new friends and what constitutes a good friend. Discuss how to be flexible in new situations and how to have fun

with change. Point out that you are only a phone call away and explain how the camp can contact you if there is an emergency. Always be honest with your child. Do not leave out important details that will be an unpleasant surprise when your child arrives at camp. If possible, take your child to visit the camp prior to opening day so he or she knows what to expect. In the months leading up to camp, create shorter separation experiences such as an overnight at a friend's house or with another family member to help your child get acclimated to being away from you.

You can expect some letters or telephone calls that sound unhappy. Remember, children can exaggerate quite a bit when they want something. They may not lie, but they may stretch the truth. Sometimes a child will acknowledge his or her homesickness. Although a camper may say, "I miss you" or "I want to come home" or even "I'm homesick," the real message is usually disguised in other statements. For example, you may hear about the bad food or a roommate problem that makes coming home

imperative. Or you may hear that no one is nice and the camp is no fun. Of course, "I want to come home" is a plea that cannot be ignored, but you must remember where the message originates and respond in an appropriate manner. Remember, this is not a logical, intellectually motivated call, it is a call from the heart. You must reassure your child of your love and state the importance of completing the camp experience.

During the camp session, there are several things that can help your child adjust to being away from home. Avoid calling! Nothing is tougher for a homesick child than the sound of Mom's or Dad's voice. Many camps ask parents not to call for the first ten days. This is a great idea. Write letters and send postcards that talk about what is happening in the family. Make the correspondence about news. Avoid mentioning how much you miss your child. Instead, write about how you love your child and look forward to hearing about the fun things at camp. In fact, send a letter or package to arrive before opening day so your child receives something right away. Let the adjustment occur! It is a process, and the timetable varies with each individual. Have faith in your child and in the camp staff. Send care packages and include some items to be shared with the counselors and new friends. Always be positive and upbeat.

Remember that camp staff members are trained and prepared to deal with homesick children. If you hear from your child that he or she is homesick, let the staff know. They are probably aware of the situation, but it will not hurt to make sure. It will probably make you feel better about the situation. In fact, counselors have a more difficult time dealing with campsick parents. Homesick campers are with the staff and simply need some assistance to adjust to this new world without Mom and Dad. Campsick parents are somewhere else and are more difficult to assist in adjusting to this new world without their child. Give the staff a chance and let them do the job you originally trusted them to do. Homesickness causes a little pain in the short run but yields a more self-confident, healthy child in the long run.

Oh—and how did I, the homesick kid in the opening paragraph, do in the horrible place where Mom and Dad left me to suffer by myself? Including time as a staff member, I was only there for twenty years.

HOW TO USE THIS GUIDE

Finding the summer program that best suits your wants and needs can be an exciting—and overwhelming—experience. How you find your way through this guide comes down to one question—Are you a *grazer* or a *digger*? If you're a grazer, you'll just dive in, mull over the program options, and write to a bunch of them. That's okay with us. We're sure you'll find some great summer programs using your own finely tuned grazing system. However, if you're a digger, you probably prefer to search more systematically. You'll want to decide what you're looking for, narrow your list of prospects, and contact the remaining choices.

DETAILS, DETAILS

When you're ready to learn about programs that have piqued your interest, turn to the **Profiles of Summer Programs**. This section concisely describes summer programs in the United States and abroad and provides all the info you'll need to narrow down your list of prospects. Here are some highlights of the information you'll find.

General Information Is the program coed or boys or girls only? Residential or day? When was the program established? Can you earn college credit? What special services are offered? Is there a religious affiliation? Is the program accredited?

Program Focus What's the spotlight on at this program?

Academics/Arts/Special Interest Areas/Sports/Wilderness/Outdoors Whether it's government and politics, arts and crafts, community service, soccer, or mountain biking, all the details are given in these categories.

Excursions/Trips Overnight or day? College tours or cultural?

Program Information How long do the sessions last? What are the dates? What are the age ranges of program participants? What is the cost? Is financial aid available? Is there a religious affiliation? Is the program accredited?

Housing For travel programs, what kind is offered? Tents? Youth hostels? Cabins?

Application Deadline What date do you need to mark on your calendar or is there a continuous deadline?

Jobs Are they available? For high school students? For college students?

Contact/URL Who to talk to and where to go to get more information.

FOR A CLOSER LOOK

Get the lowdown on select summer programs with **In-Depth Descriptions**. Written by program directors exclusively for this guide, the descriptions follow Peterson's own format for easy comparison. These pages give a more complete rundown of program offerings, extra activities, settings, and facilities. You'll learn all the essentials—including enrollment deadlines, staff qualifications, medical care, and transportation arrangements.

FINDING A PERFECT MATCH

If you have a particular interest in mind, check out the **Indexes**. The **Indexes** group programs by seven main search categories: Programs, Primary Activity, Program Sponsors, Specialized Programs, Travel Programs, Special Needs Accommodations, and Religious Affiliation.

ONCE YOU'VE GOT YOUR LIST

Contact the program directly for more information. Keep in mind that it's never too early to start making summer plans. Some programs fill up fast, with many returnees signing up for next year's session at summer's end. So take out your "A" list and mail, phone, fax, or e-mail your favorite programs today!

DATA COLLECTION PROCEDURES

The data contained in *Peterson's Summer Programs for Kids & Teenagers* were collected in the spring and summer of 2007. Questionnaires were sent to directors of summer programs around the globe. Program information included in this edition was submitted by directors of summer programs and supplemented by secondary research when necessary. In addition, most directors were also contacted by Peterson's research and editorial staffs to verify unusual figures, resolve discrepancies, and obtain additional information. All usable information received in time for publication has been included. Because of the editorial review that takes place in our offices, and because most material comes directly from program directors, we have every reason to believe that the information presented in the guide is accurate. However, readers should check with programs to verify costs, fees, venues, and program offerings, which may have changed since the publication of this edition.

Quick-Reference Chart

$\mathcal{S}$ UMMER PROGRAMS AT-A-GLANCE

BY STATE	GENERAL INFORMATION					PROGRAM INFORMATION						
	Profile Page	Boys D/R	Girls D/R	Coed D/R	Age	Acad	Arts	Sports	Wild/ Outdrs	Special Interest	Jobs	Financial Aid
Alaska												
AAVE–Ultimate Alaska	31*				14–18			•	•	•	•	•
Adventure Treks–Alaska Adventures	31				16–18			•	•			•
Putney Student Travel–Community Service–Alaska	31*			R	15–18	•		•	•	•		•
Treetops eXpeditions–Alaska Community Service	32*				14–17				•	•		•
Visions–Alaska	32*				14–18	•	•		•	•	•	•
Westcoast Connection–Community Connections Alaska	32*				14+			•	•	•		•
Wilderness Ventures–Alaska College Leadership	33*				17+			•	•	•	•	•
Wilderness Ventures–Alaska Expedition	33*				14–18	•		•	•	•		•
Wilderness Ventures–Alaska Southcentral	33*				14–18			•	•	•		•
Wilderness Ventures–Alaska Southeast	33*				14–18			•	•	•		•
Wilderness Ventures–Alaska Southeast Community Service	34*				14–18			•	•	•		•
Arizona												
iD Tech Camps–Arizona State University, Tempe, AZ	34*			D	7–17	•	•	•		•		•
Landmark Volunteers: Arizona	34*			R	14–18	•				•	•	
Oak Creek Ranch School–Summer Academic Program	35*			R	12–19	•	•	•	•		•	
Southwestern Adventures–Arizona	35*			R/D	11–18	•	•	•	•	•		
California												
Academic Study Associates–ASA at the University of California, Berkeley	36*			R/D	14–18	•	•	•		•	•	•
Academy by the Sea	37*			R/D	11–17	•	•	•		•	•	
Adventure Treks–California Adventures	37				13–17			•	•			•
American Academy of Dramatic Arts Summer Program at Los Angeles, California	38*			D	14+		•					
Britannia Soccer Camp	38			R/D	4–16			•			•	•
California State Summer School for the Arts/Inner Spark	38*			R	14–18		•	•		•		•
Camp California Fitness	39	R			8–18	•	•	•	•	•		
Camp Pacific's Recreational Camp	39*			R	8–16	•	•	•		•	•	
Camp Pacific's Surf and Bodyboard Camp	39*			R	8–16		•	•		•	•	
Crossroads School–Aquatics	40			D	3+			•		•		•
Crossroads School–Jazz Workshop	40			D	11–18		•					•
Crossroads School–Sports Camps	40			D	5–14			•				
Crossroads School–Summer Educational Journey	40			D	5–18	•	•	•	•	•		•
Cybercamps–Concordia University, Irvine	41*			R/D	7–18	•	•			•	•	
Cybercamps–DeAnza College	41*			R/D	7–18	•	•			•	•	
Cybercamps–Stanford University	42*			R/D	7–18	•	•			•	•	
Cybercamps–UCLA	42*			R/D	7–18	•	•			•	•	
Cybercamps–UC San Diego (UCSD)	42*			R/D	7–18	•	•			•	•	
Cybercamps–University of California at Berkeley	42*			R/D	7–18	•	•			•	•	
Elite Educational Institute Elementary Enrichment	43*			D	9–12	•						
Elite Educational Institute Junior High/PSAT Program	43*			D	12–14	•				•		
Elite Educational Institute SAT and Subject Test Preparation	43*			D	15–18	•				•	•	
Elite Educational Institute SAT Summer Bootcamp	43*			D	15–18	•				•		
Elite Educational Institute–University of Oklahoma College Courses	44*			D	15–18	•				•		
Exploration of Architecture	44*			R	15–18	•					•	•
Harker Summer English Language Institute	44			D	8–15	•	•	•				
The Harker Summer Institute	45			D	12–17	•	•			•		

This program is highlighted by a photograph, special note, or in-depth description; see the profile page for more information.
D = day camp; R = residential camp

	GENERAL INFORMATION					PROGRAM INFORMATION						
	Profile Page	Boys D/R	Girls D/R	Coed D/R	Age	Acad	Arts	Sports	Wild/Outdrs	Special Interest	Jobs	Financial Aid
Harker Summer Programs	45			D	5–14	•	•	•		•	•	
iD Gaming Academy–Stanford University, Palo Alto, CA	45*			R	13–17	•	•	•		•		•
iD Gaming Academy–UC Berkeley, Berkeley, CA	46*			R	13–17	•	•	•		•		•
iD Gaming Academy–UCLA, Westwood, CA	46*			R	13–17	•	•	•		•		•
iD Tech Camps–Cal Lutheran University, Thousand Oaks, CA	47*			D	7–17	•	•	•		•	•	•
iD Tech Camps–Pepperdine University, Malibu, CA	47*			R/D	7–17	•	•	•		•	•	•
iD Tech Camps–St. Mary's College of California, Moraga, CA	47*			D	7–17	•	•	•		•	•	•
iD Tech Camps–Santa Clara University, Santa Clara, CA	48*			D	7–17	•	•	•		•	•	•
iD Tech Camps–Stanford University, Palo Alto, CA	48*			R/D	7–17	•	•	•		•	•	•
iD Tech Camps–Tiger Woods Learning Center, Anaheim, CA	49*			R/D	7–17	•	•	•		•	•	•
iD Tech Camps–UC Berkeley, Berkeley, CA	49*			R/D	7–17	•	•	•		•	•	•
iD Tech Camps–UC Davis, Davis, CA	50*			R/D	7–17	•	•	•		•	•	•
iD Tech Camps–UC Irvine, Irvine, CA	50*			R/D	7–17	•	•	•		•	•	•
iD Tech Camps–UCLA, Westwood, CA	50*			R/D	7–17	•	•	•		•	•	•
iD Tech Camps–UC San Diego, La Jolla, CA	51*			R/D	7–17	•	•	•		•	•	•
iD Tech Camps–UC Santa Cruz, Santa Cruz, CA	51*			R/D	7–17	•	•	•		•	•	•
Idyllwild Arts Summer Program–Children's Center	52*			R/D	5–12		•					
Idyllwild Arts Summer Program–Family Week	52*			R			•	•	•			
Idyllwild Arts Summer Program–Junior Artists' Center	52*			R/D	11–13		•				•	•
Idyllwild Arts Summer Program–Youth Arts Center	53*			R/D	13–18		•				•	•
Junior Statesmen Summer School–Stanford University	53*			R	14–18	•				•		•
Junior Statesmen Symposium on California State Politics and Government	54*			R	14–18	•				•		•
Junior Statesmen Symposium on Los Angeles Politics and Government	54*			R	14–18	•				•		•
Landmark Volunteers: California	54*			R	14–18	•		•	•	•		•
National Student Leadership Conference: Engineering–San Francisco	55*			R	14–18	•				•	•	•
National Student Leadership Conference: Law and Advocacy–San Francisco	55*			R	14–18	•		•		•	•	•
National Student Leadership Conference: Medicine and Health Care–San Francisco	55*			R	14–18	•				•	•	•
Oxbow Summer Art Camp	56*			R/D	14–17	•	•				•	
Science Program for High School Girls	56		R		14–15	•		•		•		•
Science Program for Middle School Boys on Catalina	56	R			11–13	•		•		•		•
Science Program for Middle School Girls on Catalina	56		R		10–13	•		•		•		•
Southwestern Adventures–California	57*			R/D	11–18	•	•	•	•	•	•	
Squaw Valley Academy Summer School	57*			R	11–17	•	•	•	•	•		
Stanford University High School Summer College	58*			R/D	16–18	•	•	•		•		•
The Summer Institute for the Gifted at UCLA	58*			R	8–17	•	•	•		•		•
The Summer Institute for the Gifted at University of California, Berkeley	59*			R	8–17	•	•	•		•		•
UCLA Summer Experience: College Level Courses	59			R/D	15+	•	•					
UCLA Summer Experience: Institutes	60			R/D	14+	•	•					
University of Southern California Summer Seminars	60			R	16–18	•	•	•		•	•	•
Westcoast Connection–California Sprint	60*				13–17		•	•		•		
Westcoast Connection–California Swing Junior Touring Golf Camp	61*				13–17			•		•		
Westcoast Connection Travel–Adventure California	61*				13–17			•	•	•		
Wilderness Ventures–California	61*				14–18			•	•	•		
Wilderness Ventures–High Sierra	61*				14–18			•	•	•		
World Horizons International–Northridge, California	62*			R	14–18			•	•	•	•	

Colorado

AAVE–Colorado Discovery	62*				12–13			•	•	•	•	
AAVE–Rock & Roll	62*				14–18					•	•	
Cheley Colorado Camps	62			R	9–17		•	•	•	•	•	

*This program is highlighted by a photograph, special note, or in-depth description; see the profile page for more information.
D = day camp; R = residential camp

	GENERAL INFORMATION					PROGRAM INFORMATION						
	Profile Page	Boys D/R	Girls D/R	Coed D/R	Age	Acad	Arts	Sports	Wild/ Outdrs	Special Interest	Jobs	Financial Aid
Colorado College Summer Session	63*			R/D	16+	•					•	•
iD Tech Camps–Colorado College, Colorado Springs, CO	63*			R/D	7–17	•	•	•		•	•	•
iD Tech Camps–University of Denver, Denver, CO	64*			R/D	7–17	•	•	•		•	•	•
Landmark Volunteers: Colorado	64*			R	14–18	•		•	•	•	•	•
Perry-Mansfield Performing Arts School and Camp	65*			R/D	8–25		•	•	•	•	•	•
Summer Study at The University of Colorado at Boulder	65*			R	14+	•	•	•	•	•	•	•
Connecticut												
Buck's Rock Performing and Creative Arts Camp	66*			R	11–17	•	•	•	•	•		•
Cheshire Academy Summer Program	67*			R/D	12–19	•	•	•	•	•	•	
Choate Rosemary Hall Beginning Writers Workshop	67*			R/D	10–12	•		•		•		•
Choate Rosemary Hall English Language Institute	67*			R/D	14–19	•	•	•	•			
Choate Rosemary Hall English Language Institute/Focus Program	68*			R/D	12–14	•	•	•	•			•
Choate Rosemary Hall Focus Program	68*			R/D	12–14	•	•	•	•			•
Choate Rosemary Hall Immersion Program	69*			R/D	14–19	•	•			•		•
Choate Rosemary Hall John F. Kennedy Institute in Government	69*			R/D	15–19	•	•			•		•
Choate Rosemary Hall Math and Science Workshops	70*			R/D	13–18	•	•			•		•
Choate Rosemary Hall Math/Science Institute for Girls–CONNECT	70*		R/D		11–14	•	•			•		•
Choate Rosemary Hall Summer Arts Conservatory–Playwriting	70*			R/D	12–18		•			•		•
Choate Rosemary Hall Summer Arts Conservatory–Theater	71*			R/D	12–18		•	•		•		•
Choate Rosemary Hall Summer Arts Conservatory–Visual Arts Program	71*			R/D	12–18		•			•		•
Choate Rosemary Hall Summer Session	71*			R/D	14–19	•	•	•	•	•		•
Choate Rosemary Hall Writing Project	72*			R/D	14–18	•	•	•	•			•
Choate Rosemary Hall Young Writers Workshop	72*			R/D	11–14	•	•	•	•			•
Cybercamps–University of Bridgeport	72*			R/D	7–18	•	•			•		
Cybercamps–University of Hartford	73*			R/D	7–18	•	•			•		•
iD Tech Camps–Sacred Heart University, Fairfield, CT	73*			R/D	7–17	•	•	•		•		•
Junior Statesmen Summer School–Yale University	73*			R	14–18	•				•		•
Kent School Summer Writers Camp	74*			R	10–16	•	•	•	•		•	•
Landmark Volunteers: Connecticut	74*			R	14–18	•			•	•	•	•
Marianapolis Summer Program	75*			R/D	14–18	•	•	•		•		•
Marvelwood Summer Program	75*			R	13–17	•	•	•	•	•		•
Miss Porter's School Arts Alive!	76*		R		12–15	•	•	•		•		•
Miss Porter's School Athletic Experience	76*		R/D		11–15			•				
Miss Porter's School Daoyun Chinese Summer Program	76*		R		11–15	•				•	•	
Miss Porter's School Summer Challenge	77*		R		12–15	•	•	•		•		•
Rumsey Hall School Summer Session	77*			R/D	8–15	•		•	•			
Saint Thomas More School–Summer Academic Camp	78*	R			12+	•	•	•		•	•	•
Salisbury Summer School	78*			R	13–18	•	•	•	•			•
The Sarah Porter Leadership Institute	79*		R		12–15	•				•		
summer@rectory	79*			R/D	9–15	•	•	•		•		•
Summer English Experience	80*			R	13–17	•	•					
The Summer Institute for the Gifted at Fairfield University	80*			D	6–11	•	•	•		•	•	•
Taft Summer School	81*			R/D	12–18	•	•	•			•	•
University of Connecticut Mentor Connection	81*			R	16–17	•	•			•	•	•
World Horizons International–Connecticut	82*			R	14–18		•		•		•	•
District of Columbia												
Cybercamps–American University	82*			R/D	7–18	•	•			•	•	
Georgetown University American Politics and Public Affairs	83*			R/D	15–18	•					•	
Georgetown University College Prep Program	83*			R/D	15–18	•					•	
Georgetown University Gateway to Business Program for High School Students	84*			R	16–18	•						

This program is highlighted by a photograph, special note, or in-depth description; see the profile page for more information.
D = day camp; R = residential camp

	GENERAL INFORMATION					PROGRAM INFORMATION						
	Profile Page	Boys D/R	Girls D/R	Coed D/R	Age	Acad	Arts	Sports	Wild/ Outdrs	Special Interest	Jobs	Financial Aid
Georgetown University International Relations Program for High School Students	84*			R/D	15–18	•						•
Georgetown University Journalism Workshop for High School Students	84*			R/D	15–18	•						•
Georgetown University Summer College for High School Students	85*			R/D	16–18	•						•
George Washington University Summer Scholars Mini-courses	85*			R/D		•						
George Washington University Summer Scholars Pre-college Program	85*			R/D		•	•	•	•			•
iD Tech Camps–Georgetown University, Washington, D.C.	86*			R/D	7–17	•	•	•		•	•	•
Junior Statesmen Summer School–Georgetown University	86*			R	15–18	•				•		•
National Student Leadership Conference: Entrepreneurship and Business–Washington, D.C.	87*			R	14–18	•				•		•
National Student Leadership Conference: Forensic Science	87*			R	14–18	•				•		•
National Student Leadership Conference: Globalization and International Business–Washington, D.C.	87*			R	14–18	•				•		•
National Student Leadership Conference: Intelligence and National Security	88*			R	14–18	•				•		•
National Student Leadership Conference: International Diplomacy–Washington, D.C.	88*			R	14–18	•				•		•
National Student Leadership Conference: Journalism and Mass Communication	89*			R	14–18	•	•			•		•
National Student Leadership Conference: Law and Advocacy–Washington, D.C.	89*			R	14–18	•				•		•
National Student Leadership Conference: U.S. Policy and Politics	89*			R	14–18	•				•		•

Florida

	Profile Page	Boys D/R	Girls D/R	Coed D/R	Age	Acad	Arts	Sports	Wild/ Outdrs	Special Interest	Jobs	Financial Aid
Cybercamps–Barry University	89*			R/D	7–18	•	•			•	•	
Cybercamps–Nova Southeastern University	90*			R/D	7–18	•	•			•		
Cybercamps–University of Central Florida	90*			R/D	7–18	•	•			•		
Cybercamps–University of Miami	90*			R/D	7–18	•	•			•		
iD Tech Camps–University of Central Florida, Orlando, FL	90*			R/D	7–17	•	•	•		•		•
iD Tech Camps–University of Miami, Coral Gables, FL	91*			R/D	7–17	•	•	•		•		•
Seacamp	91*			R	12–17	•	•	•	•	•		
Treetops eXpeditions–Sailing and Marine Ecology	92*				14–17		•			•		
University of Miami Summer Scholar Programs	92*			R	16–17	•	•			•		•
Westcoast Connection–Florida Swing Junior Touring Golf Camp	92*				13–17			•		•		

Georgia

	Profile Page	Boys D/R	Girls D/R	Coed D/R	Age	Acad	Arts	Sports	Wild/ Outdrs	Special Interest	Jobs	Financial Aid
Cybercamps–Georgia State University	92*			R/D	7–18	•	•			•	•	
Cybercamps–Oglethorpe University	93*			R/D	7–18	•	•			•		
Cybercamps–Southern Polytechnic State University	93*			R/D	7–18	•	•			•		
Darlington Summer Programs	93*			R/D	2–18	•	•	•	•	•		
Emagination Computer Camps–Georgia	94*			R/D	8–17	•	•	•		•		•
iD Tech Camps–Emory University, Atlanta, GA	94*			R/D	7–17	•	•	•		•	•	•
The Summer Institute for the Gifted at Emory University	95*			R	8–17	•	•	•		•	•	•

Hawaii

	Profile Page	Boys D/R	Girls D/R	Coed D/R	Age	Acad	Arts	Sports	Wild/ Outdrs	Special Interest	Jobs	Financial Aid
AAVE–Ultimate Hawaii	95*				14–18			•	•	•	•	•
Hawaii Preparatory Academy Summer Session	95*			R/D	12–17	•	•	•	•	•	•	
Putney Student Travel–Community Service–Hawaii	96*			R	15–18	•		•	•	•		•
Rein Teen Tours–Project Hawaii	97*				14–17			•		•	•	•
Weissman Teen Tours–"Aloha–Welcome to Hawaiian Paradise," 2 weeks	97*				14–17			•	•	•		
Westcoast Connection–Community Service Hawaii	97*				14–17		•	•	•	•		
Wilderness Ventures–Hawaii	97*				13–18			•	•	•		•
Wilderness Ventures–Maui/Kauai	98*				14–18			•	•	•		•

This program is highlighted by a photograph, special note, or in-depth description; see the profile page for more information.
D = day camp; R = residential camp

	GENERAL INFORMATION				PROGRAM INFORMATION						
	Profile Page	Boys D/R	Girls D/R	Coed D/R	Age	Acad	Arts	Sports	Wild/ Outdrs	Special Interest	Jobs	Financial Aid

Idaho

Landmark Volunteers: Idaho	98*			R	14–18	•			•	•	•	•

Illinois

Center for Talent Development Summer Academic Program	99*			R/D	4–17	•	•			•	•	•
Cybercamps–Benedictine University	99*			R/D	7–18	•	•			•		•
Cybercamps–Concordia University, Chicago	100*			R/D	7–18	•	•			•		•
Cybercamps–Loyola University	100*			R/D	7–18	•	•			•		•
Emagination Computer Camps–Illinois	100*			R/D	8–17	•	•	•		•		•
iD Tech Camps–Lake Forest College, Evanston, IL	100*			R/D	7–17	•	•	•		•		•
iD Tech Camps–Northwestern University, Chicago, IL	101*			R/D	7–17	•	•	•		•		•
National Student Leadership Conference: State Leadership Workshops	101*			R	14–18					•	•	•
Northwestern University's College Preparation Program	102*			R/D	16–18	•	•	•	•			•
Northwestern University's National High School Institute	102*			R	14–18	•	•					•
University of Chicago–Insight	103*			R/D	15–18	•	•			•		•
University of Chicago–Research in the Biological Sciences	103*			R	15–18	•						•
University of Chicago–Summer Quarter for High School Students	103*			R/D	15–18	•	•					•

Louisiana

RUSTIC PATHWAYS–NEW ORLEANS SUMMER REBUILDING PROGRAM	104*			R	16–18					•		•

Maine

Acadia Institute of Oceanography	105*			R	10–19	•		•	•	•	•	•
Alford Lake Camp	105*		R		8–15		•	•	•	•	•	•
Alford Lake Family Camp	106*			R			•	•	•	•		
Camp Encore-Coda for a Great Summer of Music, Sports, and Friends	106*			R/D	9–17	•	•	•	•	•	•	•
Kamp Kohut	107			R	7–16	•	•	•	•	•	•	
Landmark Volunteers: Maine	107*			R	14–18	•			•	•	•	•
Pine Island Camp	107*	R			9–15		•	•	•	•	•	•

Maryland

Camp Airy	108*	R			7–17	•	•	•	•	•	•	•
Camp Louise	109		R		7–17	•	•	•	•	•	•	•
Cybercamps–Towson University	109*			R/D	7–18	•	•			•		•
Cybercamps–University of Maryland	110*			R/D	7–18	•	•			•		•
Intensive English Language Program	110*			R	13–18	•	•	•	•	•		•
International Leadership Program	110*			R	13–18	•	•	•	•	•		•
Johns Hopkins University Zanvyl Krieger School of Arts and Sciences Summer Programs	111*			R/D	15+	•	•	•		•		•
National Student Leadership Conference: Engineering–Washington, D.C.	111*			R	14–18	•				•		•
National Student Leadership Conference: Mastering Leadership	112*			R	14–18	•				•		•
National Student Leadership Conference: Medicine and Health Care–Washington, D.C.	112*			R	14–18	•				•	•	•
University of Maryland Young Scholars Program	112*			R/D	16–18	•	•			•		•

Massachusetts

Academic Study Associates–ASA at the University of Massachusetts Amherst	113*			R/D	14–18	•	•	•		•	•	•
BAC Summer Academy	113			D	15–18	•	•			•		•
Belvoir Terrace	113		R		8–17	•	•	•			•	
Boston University Tanglewood Institute	114*			R	14–18	•	•		•	•		•
Cape Cod Sea Camps–Monomoy/Wono	114			R/D	8–15		•	•	•	•	•	•
Career Explorations–Boston	115*			R/D	16–18	•	•			•		

*This program is highlighted by a photograph, special note, or in-depth description; see the profile page for more information.
D = day camp; R = residential camp

	GENERAL INFORMATION					PROGRAM INFORMATION						
	Profile Page	Boys D/R	Girls D/R	Coed D/R	Age	Acad	Arts	Sports	Wild/ Outdrs	Special Interest	Jobs	Financial Aid
Cushing Academy Summer Session	115*			R/D	12–18	•	•	•	•	•	•	•
Cybercamps–Bentley College	115*			R/D	7–18	•	•			•	•	
Cybercamps–Dana Hall School	116*			R/D	7–18	•	•			•	•	
Cybercamps–Merrimack College	116*			R/D	7–18	•	•			•	•	
Cybercamps–MIT	116*			R/D	7–18	•	•			•	•	
Eaglebrook Summer Semester	117*			R	11–13	•	•	•	•	•	•	•
Eagle Hill School Summer Session	117*			R/D	10–18	•	•	•	•	•	•	
Emagination Computer Camps–Massachusetts	118*			R/D	8–17	•	•	•		•	•	
Excel at Amherst College	119*			R	15–18	•	•	•		•	•	•
Fenn School Summer Day Camp	119			D	5–15	•	•	•		•	•	•
The Fessenden School Summer ESL Program	120*			R	10–15	•	•	•	•	•	•	
Frontiers Program	120*			R	16–18	•				•		
Harvard University Summer School: Secondary School Program	121*			R/D		•	•			•		•
iD Tech Camps–Merrimack College, North Andover, MA	122*			D	7–17	•	•			•	•	•
iD Tech Camps–MIT, Cambridge, MA	122*			R/D	7–17	•	•			•	•	•
iD Tech Camps–Smith College, Northampton, MA	122*			R/D	7–17	•	•			•	•	•
Internship Connection	123*			D	14–23	•	•	•		•		
Landmark School Summer Academic Program	123*			R/D	7–20	•	•	•	•			
Landmark Volunteers: Massachusetts	124*			R	14–18	•		•		•	•	
Linden Hill Summer Program	124*			R/D	7–17	•	•	•		•	•	•
Massachusetts College of Art/Creative Vacation	125*			D	9–18	•	•			•	•	•
Massachusetts College of Art/Summer Studios	125*			R/D	15–17	•	•			•	•	•
MIT MITES (Minority Introduction to Engineering and Science)	126*			R	16+	•				•	•	
Mount Holyoke College SEARCH (Summer Explorations and Research Collaborations for High School Girls) Program	126*		R/D		15–18	•	•	•	•	•	•	•
Mount Holyoke College SummerMath Program	127*		R/D		13–18	•	•	•	•	•	•	•
Northfield Mount Hermon Summer Session	127*			R/D	12–19	•	•	•		•	•	•
Phillips Academy Summer Session	128*			R/D	13–18	•	•	•	•	•		•
School of the Museum of Fine Arts, Boston–Pre-College Summer Studio	129*			R/D	15–18	•	•			•		•
Smith College Summer Science and Engineering Program	130*		R		13–18	•	•	•		•	•	•
Summer Action–Take the Lead	130*		R		14–17	•	•	•		•		•
The Summer Institute for the Gifted at Amherst College	131*			R	8–17	•	•	•	•	•	•	•
Tabor Academy Summer Program	131*			R/D	6–15	•	•	•		•	•	
Tabor Hockey School	132*			D	7–14			•			•	
The Winchendon School Summer Session	132*			R	13–20	•	•	•	•	•	•	•
Worcester Polytechnic Institute–Launch	133*			D	13–15	•				•		

Michigan

Cybercamps–University of Michigan	133*			R/D	7–18	•	•			•	•	
iD Tech Camps–University of Michigan, Ann Arbor, MI	133*			R/D	7–17	•	•			•	•	•
Interlochen Arts Camp	134*			R	8–18	•	•	•				•
Landmark Volunteers: Michigan	134*			R	14–18	•				•	•	
Michigan Technological University American Indian Workshop	135			R	12+	•				•		•
Michigan Technological University Explorations in Engineering Workshop	135			R	14–18	•				•		•
Michigan Technological University Summer Youth Program	135			R/D	12–18	•	•	•	•	•	•	•
Michigan Technological University Women in Engineering Workshop	136		R		14–18	•				•		•
The Summer Institute for the Gifted at University of Michigan, Ann Arbor	136*			R	8–17	•	•	•		•		•

Minnesota

Camp Lincoln for Boys/Camp Lake Hubert for Girls	136			R	8–16		•	•	•	•	•	•
Camp Lincoln for Boys/Camp Lake Hubert for Girls–Family Camp	137			R	1+		•	•	•	•	•	•
Camp Lincoln for Boys/Camp Lake Hubert for Girls–Golf Camp	137			R	8+			•			•	•

This program is highlighted by a photograph, special note, or in-depth description; see the profile page for more information.
D = day camp; R = residential camp

	GENERAL INFORMATION					PROGRAM INFORMATION						
	Profile Page	Boys D/R	Girls D/R	Coed D/R	Age	Acad	Arts	Sports	Wild/ Outdrs	Special Interest	Jobs	Financial Aid
Camp Lincoln for Boys/Camp Lake Hubert for Girls–Tennis Camp	137			R	8+			•			•	•
Cybercamps–University of Minnesota	137*			R/D	7–18	•	•			•	•	
iD Tech Camps–University of Minnesota, Minneapolis, MN	138*			R/D	7–17	•	•	•		•	•	•
Landmark Volunteers: Minnesota	138*			R	14–18	•				•	•	•

Mississippi

Visions–Mississippi	138*				14–18	•	•	•	•	•	•	•

Missouri

Cybercamps–Webster University	139*			R/D	7–18	•	•			•		
iD Tech Camps–Washington University in St. Louis, St. Louis, MO	139*			D	7–17	•	•	•		•	•	•
Washington University High School Summer Scholars Program	140*			R	16+	•	•					•
Washington University in St. Louis, College of Art–Portfolio Plus	140*			R/D	16–18	•	•			•		•

Montana

Adventure Treks–Montana Adventures	141				15–17				•			•
Landmark Volunteers: Montana	141*			R	14–18	•			•	•	•	•
Visions–Montana	141*				14–18	•	•	•	•	•	•	•

New Hampshire

Brewster Academy Summer Session	142*			R/D	12–17	•	•	•	•	•	•	•
Phillips Exeter Academy Summer School	142*			R/D	13–19	•	•	•	•	•	•	•
Wolfeboro: The Summer Boarding School	143*			R	11–18	•	•	•	•	•		•

New Jersey

Appel Farm Summer Arts Camp	143*			R	9–17	•	•	•	•	•	•	•
Cybercamps–Caldwell College	144*			R/D	7–18	•	•			•	•	
Cybercamps–College of St. Elizabeth	144*			R/D	7–18	•	•			•	•	
Cybercamps–Rutgers University	144*			R/D	7–18	•	•			•		
The Hun School of Princeton American Culture and Language Institute	145*			R/D	13–18	•			•			
The Hun School of Princeton–Summer Academic Session	145*			R/D	11–18	•		•	•	•		
The Hun School of Princeton–Summer Day Camp	146*			D	5–12		•	•	•	•		•
iD Tech Camps–Rider University, Lawrenceville, NJ	146*			R/D	7–17	•	•	•		•	•	•
iD Tech Camps–Seton Hall University, South Orange, NJ	146*			R/D	7–17	•	•	•		•	•	•
Junior Statesmen Summer School–Princeton University	147*			R	14–18	•						•
Junior Statesmen Symposium on New Jersey State Politics and Government	147*			R	14–18	•				•		•
Landmark Volunteers: New Jersey	147*			R	14–18	•				•	•	•
The Summer Institute for the Gifted at Moorestown Friends School	148*			D	6–11	•	•	•	•	•		
The Summer Institute for the Gifted at Princeton University	148*			R	12–17	•	•	•	•	•		

New Mexico

The Experiment in International Living–Navajo Nation	149*				14–19	•	•	•	•	•		•
Landmark Volunteers: New Mexico	149*			R	14–18	•			•	•	•	•

New York

ACTeen August Academy	149*			R/D	13+		•					
ACTeen July Academy	150*			R/D	15+	•	•					
ACTeen June Academy	150*			R/D	13+		•					•
ACTeen Summer Saturday Academy	150*			D	13+		•					
Adirondack Field Ecology	151*			R	16–19	•		•	•	•		•
American Academy of Dramatic Arts Summer Program at New York	151*			D	14+		•					
Applejack Teen Camp	151*			R	13–17	•	•	•	•	•	•	•
Barnard's Summer in New York City: A Pre-College Program	152*			R/D	14–18	•	•			•	•	•

*This program is highlighted by a photograph, special note, or in-depth description; see the profile page for more information.
D = day camp; R = residential camp

	GENERAL INFORMATION					PROGRAM INFORMATION						
	Profile Page	Boys D/R	Girls D/R	Coed D/R	Age	Acad	Arts	Sports	Wild/ Outdrs	Special Interest	Jobs	Financial Aid
Barnard's Summer in New York City: One-Week Liberal Arts Intensive	153*			R/D	14–18	•				•	•	•
Barnard's Summer in New York City: Young Women's Leadership Institute	153*		R		14–18	•				•	•	•
Brant Lake Camp's Dance Centre	153*		R		11–16		•	•	•	•		
Camp Regis	154*			R	6–13	•	•	•	•	•		•
Camp Treetops	154*			R	8–14	•	•	•	•	•	•	•
Career Explorations–New York	155*			R/D	16–18	•	•			•		
Cornell University Summer College Programs for High School Students	155*			R	15–19	•	•	•	•	•		•
Cybercamps–Adelphi University	156*			R/D	7–18	•	•			•		•
Cybercamps–Fordham University	156*			R/D	7–18	•	•			•		•
Cybercamps–The New School	156*			R/D	7–18	•	•			•		
Cybercamps–New York Institute of Technology	157*			R/D	7–18	•	•			•		
Cybercamps–St. John's University	157*			R/D	7–18	•	•			•		
Dunnabeck at Kildonan	157*			R/D	8–16	•					•	
Eastern U.S. Music Camp, Inc. at Colgate University	158*			R/D	10–18	•	•	•		•		•
FivePoints	158*			R	13–18	•	•			•		•
GirlSummer at Emma Willard School	159*		R		11+	•	•	•		•		•
The Gow School Summer Program	160*			R/D	8–16	•	•	•	•	•		•
iD Tech Camps–Columbia University, New York, NY	160*			D	7–17	•	•			•	•	•
iD Tech Camps–Fordham University, Bronx, NY	161*			R/D	7–17	•	•	•		•	•	•
iD Tech Camps–Vassar College, Poughkeepsie, NY	161*			R/D	7–17	•	•	•		•	•	•
Ithaca College Summer College for High School Students: Minicourses	161			R	15–18	•	•	•		•		•
Ithaca College Summer College for High School Students: Session I	162			R	15–18	•	•	•		•		•
Ithaca College Summer College for High School Students: Session II	162			R	15–18	•	•	•	•	•		•
Ithaca College Summer Piano Institute	162			R	12–18		•					
Landmark Volunteers: New York	163*			R	14–18	•		•		•		•
National Student Leadership Conference: Entrepreneurship and Business–New York City	163*			R	14–18	•				•	•	
National Student Leadership Conference: Inside the Arts–New York City	163*			R	14–18	•	•			•	•	
92nd Street Y Camps–Camp Bari Tov	164			D	5–13		•	•		•	•	•
92nd Street Y Camps–Camp Tevah for Science and Nature	164			D	8–11	•	•	•		•	•	•
92nd Street Y Camps–Camp Tova	164			D	6–13		•	•		•	•	•
92nd Street Y Camps–Camp Yaffa for the Arts	164			D	8–11		•			•	•	•
92nd Street Y Camps–Camp Yomi	165			D	5–9		•	•		•	•	•
92nd Street Y Camps–Trailblazers	165				12–14		•	•		•	•	•
Pratt Institute Summer Pre-College Program for High School Students	165*			R/D	16–18	•	•			•		
Sarah Lawrence College Summer High School Programs	166*			R/D	15–18	•	•					
Skidmore College–Pre-College Program in the Liberal & Studio Arts for High School Students	166*			R/D	16+	•	•	•	•	•	•	•
Stagedoor Manor Performing Arts Training Center/Theatre and Dance Camp	167*			R	10–18	•	•	•		•		•
Summer@Rensselaer	168*			R/D	8–18	•	•	•		•		•
The Summer Institute for the Gifted at Manhattanville College	168*			D	6–11	•	•	•		•		•
The Summer Institute for the Gifted at Vassar College	169*			R	8–17	•	•	•		•		•
Summer Theatre Institute–NYC, 2008	169*			R	14+	•	•			•		•
Syracuse University Summer College	170*			R	14–18	•	•	•		•		•
Tisch School of the Arts–Summer High School Programs	171*			R	15+	•	•					•
North Carolina												
Asheville School's Summer Academic Adventures	171*			R	11–17	•	•	•	•	•	•	•

*This program is highlighted by a photograph, special note, or in-depth description; see the profile page for more information.
D = day camp; R = residential camp

	GENERAL INFORMATION					PROGRAM INFORMATION						
	Profile Page	Boys D/R	Girls D/R	Coed D/R	Age	Acad	Arts	Sports	Wild/ Outdrs	Special Interest	Jobs	Financial Aid
Constructing Your College Experience	172*			R/D	16–17	•				•	•	•
Cybercamps–Duke University	173*			R/D	7–18	•	•			•	•	
Cybercamps–UNC, Chapel Hill	173*			R/D	7–18	•	•			•	•	
Duke Action: Science Camp for Young Women	173*		R/D		10–13	•			•		•	•
Duke Creative Writers' Workshop	173*			R/D	15–17	•	•			•	•	•
Duke Drama Workshop	174*			R/D	15–17		•			•	•	•
Duke TIP Institutes	174*			R	14–18	•				•	•	
Duke University PreCollege Program	174*			R	16–18	•	•			•	•	
Duke Young Writers Camp	175*			R/D	12–17	•	•	•		•	•	•
EXPRESSIONS! Duke Fine Arts Camp	175*			R/D	10–13		•			•		•
iD Tech Camps–University of North Carolina at Chapel Hill, Chapel Hill, NC	176*			R/D	7–17	•	•	•		•	•	•
iD Tech Camps–Wake Forest University, Winston-Salem, NC	176*			R/D	7–17	•	•	•		•	•	•
Salem Spotlight	177*		R		13–18	•	•	•		•		
Talisman Summer Camp	177			R	8–17	•	•	•	•	•		
Ohio												
The Grand River Summer Academy	177*			R/D	13–19	•	•	•	•	•	•	
iD Tech Camps–Case Western Reserve University, Cleveland, OH	178*			R/D	7–17	•	•	•		•	•	•
Junior Statesmen Symposium on Ohio State Politics and Government	178*			R	14–18	•				•		•
Miami University Junior Scholars Program	179			R	16–18	•	•	•		•		•
Summerberg at Heidelberg College	179*			R		•	•					
Oregon												
Adventure Treks Oregon Adventures	180				15–16			•	•			•
Cybercamps–Lewis and Clark College	180*			R/D	7–18	•	•			•	•	
Landmark Volunteers: Oregon	180*			R	14–18	•			•	•		•
Summer at Delphi	181*			R/D	5–18	•	•	•	•			•
Wilderness Ventures–Oregon	181*				14–18				•	•	•	•
Pennsylvania												
Academic Camps at Gettysburg College	182*			R	14–18	•	•	•		•		
Bryn Mawr College–Science for College	182*		R/D		15–18	•		•		•	•	•
Bryn Mawr College–Women of Distinction: Personalizing the College Admissions Process	182*		R/D		15–18	•		•		•	•	•
Bryn Mawr College–Writing for College	183*		R/D		15–18	•	•	•		•	•	•
College InSight	183			R/D	15–19	•				•	•	
Cybercamps–Bryn Mawr College	183*			R/D	7–18	•	•			•	•	
Emagination Computer Camps–Pennsylvania	184*			R/D	8–17	•	•	•		•		•
Ensemble Theatre Community School	184*			R	14–18		•	•	•			
iD Gaming Academy–Villanova University, Villanova, PA	185*			R	13–17	•	•	•		•	•	•
iD Tech Camps–Carnegie Mellon University, Pittsburgh, PA	185*			R/D	7–17	•	•	•		•	•	•
iD Tech Camps–Villanova University, Villanova, PA	185*			R/D	7–17	•	•	•		•	•	•
Landmark Volunteers: Pennsylvania	186*			R	14–18	•				•		
92nd Street Y Camps–Camp Kesher	186			R	8–11		•	•		•		•
Pre-College Summer Institute, The University of the Arts	186*			R/D	16–18	•	•			•		
The Summer Institute for the Gifted at Bryn Mawr College	187*			R/D	8–17	•	•	•		•		•
Summer Study at Penn State	188*			R	14+	•	•	•		•	•	•
University of Pennsylvania–Penn Summer Art and Architecture Studios	189*			R/D	15–18	•	•	•	•	•	•	
University of Pennsylvania–Penn Summer Science Academies	189*			R/D	15–18	•	•	•	•	•	•	
University of Pennsylvania–Penn Summer Theatre Workshop	189*			R/D	15–18	•	•	•	•	•	•	
University of Pennsylvania–Pre-College Program	190*			R/D	15–18	•	•	•	•	•	•	
Valley Forge Military Academy Summer Band Camp	190*			R/D	12–17	•		•		•	•	
Valley Forge Military Academy Summer Camp for Boys	191*	R			8–17	•	•	•	•	•		

This program is highlighted by a photograph, special note, or in-depth description; see the profile page for more information.
D = day camp; R = residential camp

	GENERAL INFORMATION					PROGRAM INFORMATION						
	Profile Page	Boys D/R	Girls D/R	Coed D/R	Age	Acad	Arts	Sports	Wild/Outdrs	Special Interest	Jobs	Financial Aid
Valley Forge Military Academy Summer Coed Day Camp	191*			D	6–17	•	•	•	•	•	•	•
Wyoming Seminary–Sem Summer 2008	192*			R/D	12–18	•	•	•			•	•
Rhode Island												
iD Tech Camps–Brown University, Providence, RI	192*			R/D	7–17	•	•	•		•	•	•
Landmark Volunteers: Rhode Island	193*			R	14–18	•		•		•	•	•
Portsmouth Abbey Summer School	193*			R/D	13–15	•	•	•			•	•
Rhode Island School of Design Pre-College Program	194*			R/D	16–18	•	•			•		•
Summer@Brown	194*			R/D		•	•			•		•
Tennessee												
iD Tech Camps–Vanderbilt University, Nashville, TN	195*			R/D	7–17	•	•	•			•	•
Texas												
Camp La Junta	195	R			6–14		•	•	•	•	•	•
Camp Rio Vista for Boys	196	R			6–16		•	•	•	•	•	
Camp Sierra Vista for Girls	196		R		6–16		•	•	•	•	•	
iD Tech Camps–Southern Methodist University, Dallas, TX	196*			R/D	7–17	•	•	•		•	•	
iD Tech Camps–University of Houston, Houston, TX	197*			R/D	7–17	•	•	•		•	•	
iD Tech Camps–UT Austin, Austin, TX	197*			R/D	7–17	•	•	•		•	•	
Junior Statesmen Symposium on Texas Politics and Leadership	198*			R	14–18	•				•		
The Renaissance Scholar Program	198*			R	16–17	•	•	•		•		
Southern Methodist University–College Experience	198*			R/D	15–18	•	•				•	•
Southern Methodist University TAG (Talented and Gifted)	199*			R	12–15	•	•			•	•	•
The Summer Institute for the Gifted at University of Texas, Austin	199*			R	8–17	•	•	•		•	•	•
Utah												
World Horizons International–Kanab, Utah	200*			R	13–18			•	•	•	•	
Vermont												
Future Leader Camp	201*			R	15–18			•	•	•		
Keewaydin Dunmore	201	R			8–16		•	•	•	•		•
Killooleet	202*			R	9–14		•	•	•	•		
Landmark Volunteers: Vermont	202*			R	14–18	•		•		•	•	•
Lochearn Camp for Girls	202		R		8–15	•	•	•	•	•	•	•
Mad River Glen Naturalist Adventure Camp	203			D	8–12	•	•	•	•	•	•	•
The Putney School Summer Arts Program	203*			R/D	14–17	•	•	•	•	•	•	•
The Putney School Summer Program for International Education (ESL)	204*			R	14–17	•	•	•	•	•	•	•
The Putney School Summer Writing Program	204*			R	14–17	•	•	•	•	•	•	•
Roaring Brook Camp for Boys	205	R			9–16		•	•	•	•	•	
Songadeewin of Keewaydin	205		R		8–15		•	•	•	•	•	
University of Vermont Summer Engineering Institute for High School Students	205*			R	15–16	•	•	•		•		
Virginia												
Camp Holiday Trails	206			R	5–17		•	•	•	•	•	
Cybercamps–George Mason University	206*			R/D	7–18	•	•					
Cybercamps–Northern Virginia Community College	206*			R/D	7–18	•	•					
Cybercamps–Oak Marr Rec Center	207*			R/D	7–18	•	•					
Fairfax Collegiate School Summer Enrichment Program	207			D	8–17	•					•	
Girls First	207*		R				•	•		•	•	
Hargrave Summer Leadership Program	208*	R/D			11–18	•		•	•	•		
iD Tech Camps–College of William and Mary, Williamsburg, VA	208*			R/D	7–17	•	•	•		•	•	•
iD Tech Camps–University of Virginia, Charlottesville, VA	209*			R/D	7–17	•	•	•		•	•	
iD Tech Camps–Virginia Tech, Blacksburg, VA	209*			R/D	7–17	•	•	•		•	•	

*This program is highlighted by a photograph, special note, or in-depth description; see the profile page for more information.
D = day camp; R = residential camp

	GENERAL INFORMATION					PROGRAM INFORMATION						
	Profile Page	Boys D/R	Girls D/R	Coed D/R	Age	Acad	Arts	Sports	Wild/ Outdrs	Special Interest	Jobs	Financial Aid
Landmark Volunteers: Virginia	210*			R	14–18	•		•	•	•	•	•
Randolph-Macon Academy Summer Programs	210*			R/D	11–19	•		•	•	•		
Washington												
Adventure Treks–Pacific Northwest Adventures	211				13–16			•	•			•
Camp Berachah Ministries–Camps and Conferences	211			R/D	5–17	•	•	•	•	•	•	•
Canoe Island French Camp	211			R	9–16	•	•	•	•	•		
Cybercamps–Bellevue Community College	211*			R/D	7–18	•	•			•	•	
Cybercamps–Trinity Lutheran College	212*			R/D	7–18	•	•			•		
Cybercamps–University of Washington	212*			R/D	7–18	•	•			•	•	
Cybercamps–University of Washington, Bothell	213*			R/D	7–18	•	•			•	•	
Forest Ridge Summer Program	213			D	4–19	•	•	•	•	•		•
iD Tech Camps University of Washington, Seattle, WA	213*			R/D	7–17	•	•	•		•		•
Junior Statesmen Symposium on Washington State Politics and Government	214*			R	14–18	•				•		
Landmark Volunteers: Washington	214*			R	14–18	•			•	•	•	•
Westcoast Connection–Community Service–Habitat for Humanity	214*				16+		•	•	•			•
Wilderness Ventures–Cascade-Olympic	214*				14–18			•	•	•	•	•
Wilderness Ventures–Puget Sound	215*				13–15			•	•	•	•	•
Wilderness Ventures–Washington Alpine	215*				15–18				•	•	•	•
Wilderness Ventures–Washington Mountaineering	215*				16–18				•	•	•	•
West Virginia												
Camp Greenbrier for Boys	215	R/D			7–18	•	•	•	•	•	•	•
Wisconsin												
Clearwater Camp for Girls	216*		R		8–16		•	•	•	•	•	
Milwaukee School of Engineering (MSOE)–Discover the Possibilities	217			R	13–18	•				•		
Milwaukee School of Engineering (MSOE)–Focus on Business	217			R	13–18	•				•		
Milwaukee School of Engineering (MSOE)–Focus on Nursing	217			R	13–18	•				•		
Milwaukee School of Engineering (MSOE)–Focus on Technical Communication	217			R	13–18	•				•		•
Milwaukee School of Engineering (MSOE)–Focus on the Possibilities	217			R	13–18	•				•		
World Affairs Seminar	218			R	16–18	•	•	•		•	•	•
Wyoming												
Landmark Volunteers: Wyoming	218*			R	14–18	•			•	•	•	•
Teton Valley Ranch Camp–Boys Camp	218	R			11+		•	•	•	•	•	
Teton Valley Ranch Camp–Girls Camp	219		R		11+		•	•	•	•	•	
University of Chicago–Stones and Bones	219*				15–18	•			•			
Wilderness Ventures–Grand Teton	219*				14–18			•	•	•	•	•
Wilderness Ventures–Jackson Hole	220*				13–15			•	•	•	•	•
Wilderness Ventures–Wyoming Mountaineering	220*				15–18				•	•	•	•
Wilderness Ventures–Yellowstone/Teton Adventure	221*				14–18				•	•	•	•
Wilderness Ventures–Yellowstone-Teton Family Adventure	221*				10+			•	•		•	•

BY COUNTRY

Argentina

	Profile Page	Boys D/R	Girls D/R	Coed D/R	Age	Acad	Arts	Sports	Wild/ Outdrs	Special Interest	Jobs	Financial Aid
AFS-USA–Community Service–Argentina	222*			R	15–18	•				•		•
AFS-USA–Homestay–Argentina	222*			R	15–18	•				•		•
Center for Cultural Interchange–Argentina Independent Homestay	222*			R	16+	•				•		•
The Experiment in International Living–Argentina Homestay, Community Service, and Outdoor Ecological Program	223*				14–19	•		•		•		•

*This program is highlighted by a photograph, special note, or in-depth description; see the profile page for more information.
D = day camp; R = residential camp

	GENERAL INFORMATION					PROGRAM INFORMATION						
	Profile Page	Boys D/R	Girls D/R	Coed D/R	Age	Acad	Arts	Sports	Wild/ Outdrs	Special Interest	Jobs	Financial Aid
The Experiment in International Living–Argentina Visual Arts, Photography, and Service	223*				14–19	•	•		•	•		•
GLOBAL WORKS–Language Immersion, Cultural Exchange and Service–Argentina	223*				15–17	•	•	•	•	•	•	•
Putney Student Travel–Community Service–Argentina	224*			R	15–18	•		•	•	•		•
Putney Student Travel–Cultural Exploration–Creative Writing in Argentina	224*			R	15–18	•	•	•	•	•	•	•
Putney Student Travel–Language Learning–Argentina	224*			R	13–18	•		•		•		•

Australia

	Profile Page	Boys D/R	Girls D/R	Coed D/R	Age	Acad	Arts	Sports	Wild/ Outdrs	Special Interest	Jobs	Financial Aid
AAVE–Australia	225*				14–18			•	•	•	•	
ACTIONQUEST: Australian and Great Barrier Reef Adventures	225*				15–18	•		•	•	•		
AFS-USA–Homestay Plus–Australia	225*			R	15–18	•			•	•		•
BROADREACH Adventures Down Under	226*				15–19	•	•	•	•	•		
Center for Cultural Interchange–Australia High School Abroad	226*			R	15–18	•			•	•		•
The Experiment in International Living–Australia Homestay	226*				14–19	•	•	•	•	•		•
LIFEWORKS with the Australian Red Cross	227*				15–19	•	•		•	•		•
RUSTIC PATHWAYS–COMMUNITY SERVICE SCHOOL IN AUSTRALIA	227*				14–18	•		•	•	•	•	•
RUSTIC PATHWAYS–SYDNEY, REEF & RAINFOREST	227*				14–18			•	•	•	•	
Westcoast Connection/On Tour– Australian Outback	227*				14–18			•	•	•		
Wilderness Ventures–Australia	228*				14–18			•	•	•		•

Bahamas

	Profile Page	Boys D/R	Girls D/R	Coed D/R	Age	Acad	Arts	Sports	Wild/ Outdrs	Special Interest	Jobs	Financial Aid
BROADREACH Marine Biology Accredited	228*			R	15–19	•	•	•	•	•		

Belize

	Profile Page	Boys D/R	Girls D/R	Coed D/R	Age	Acad	Arts	Sports	Wild/ Outdrs	Special Interest	Jobs	Financial Aid
ACADEMIC TREKS–Dolphin Studies in Belize	229*				15–19	•		•	•	•		•
ACADEMIC TREKS–Wilderness Emergency Medicine	229*				15–19	•		•	•	•		
The Experiment in International Living–Belize Homestay	229*				14–19	•		•		•		•
Westcoast Connection–Community Service Belize	229*				14+			•	•	•		

Bermuda

	Profile Page	Boys D/R	Girls D/R	Coed D/R	Age	Acad	Arts	Sports	Wild/ Outdrs	Special Interest	Jobs	Financial Aid
ACADEMIC TREKS–Shipwrecks and Underwater Archaeology in Bermuda	230*				15–19	•		•	•	•		•

Botswana

	Profile Page	Boys D/R	Girls D/R	Coed D/R	Age	Acad	Arts	Sports	Wild/ Outdrs	Special Interest	Jobs	Financial Aid
The Experiment in International Living–Botswana Homestay	230*				14–19	•			•	•		•

Brazil

	Profile Page	Boys D/R	Girls D/R	Coed D/R	Age	Acad	Arts	Sports	Wild/ Outdrs	Special Interest	Jobs	Financial Aid
Center for Cultural Interchange–Brazil High School Abroad	230*			R	15–17	•				•		•
The Experiment in International Living–Brazil–Community Service and Soccer	231*				14–19			•	•	•		
The Experiment in International Living–Brazil Homestay, Arts, and Community Service	231*				14–19	•	•			•		•
Global Leadership Adventures–Brazil: Community Service and Leadership	231*				15–18	•			•	•		•

British Virgin Islands

	Profile Page	Boys D/R	Girls D/R	Coed D/R	Age	Acad	Arts	Sports	Wild/ Outdrs	Special Interest	Jobs	Financial Aid
ACTIONQUEST: Advanced PADI Scuba Certification and Specialty Voyages	232*				15–18	•		•	•	•		
ACTIONQUEST: British Virgin Islands–Sailing and Scuba Voyages	232*				13–18	•		•	•	•		
ACTIONQUEST: British Virgin Islands-Sailing Voyages	232*				13–18			•	•	•		•
ACTIONQUEST: Junior Advanced Scuba with Marine Biology	233*				13–15	•		•	•	•		
ACTIONQUEST: PADI Divemaster Voyages	233*				18+			•	•	•		•
ACTIONQUEST: Rescue Diving Voyages	233*				15–19			•	•	•		
ACTIONQUEST: Tropical Marine Biology Voyages	233*				15–19	•		•	•	•		

This program is highlighted by a photograph, special note, or in-depth description; see the profile page for more information.
D = day camp; R = residential camp

	Profile Page	Boys D/R	Girls D/R	Coed D/R	Age	Acad	Arts	Sports	Wild/ Outdrs	Special Interest	Jobs	Financial Aid
LIFEWORKS with the British Virgin Islands Marine Parks and Conservation Department	234*				15–19	•		•	•	•		•
Visions–British Virgin Islands	234*				14–18	•	•	•	•	•	•	•
Cambodia												
Putney Student Travel–Global Awareness in Action–Cambodia	235*			R	15–18			•	•	•		•
Canada												
ACADEMIC TREKS–Pacific Whale Treks	235*				15–19	•		•	•	•		
Adventure Treks–Canadian Rockies Adventures	235				14–16			•	•			•
Camp Chikopi for Boys	235	R			7–17			•	•	•	•	
Keewaydin Temagami	236			R	10–18			•	•		•	
TASC Canadian Wilderness Fishing Camps	236			R	10–17				•			
Westcoast Connection Travel–Canadian Mountain Magic	236*				13–17			•	•	•		•
Westcoast Connection Travel–Quebec Adventure	237*				13–17			•	•	•		•
Westcoast Connection Travel–Western Canadian Adventure	237*				13–17			•	•	•		•
Chile												
AFS-USA–Homestay–Chile	237*			R	16–18	•				•		•
Center for Cultural Interchange–Chile Independent Homestay	238*			R	17+	•				•		•
The Experiment in International Living–Chile North Homestay, Community Service	238*				14–19	•			•	•		•
The Experiment in International Living–Chile South Homestay	238*				14–19	•		•	•	•		•
China												
AAVE–China	238*				15–18	•		•	•	•		•
ACADEMIC TREKS–Immersion China	239*				15–19	•			•	•		•
AFS-USA–China Summer Homestay Language Study Program	239*			R	15–18	•	•			•		•
Choate Rosemary Hall Summer in China	239*			R	14–19	•	•			•		•
EF International Language School–Beijing	240*				16+	•		•		•		•
EF International Language School–Shanghai	240*				16+	•		•		•		•
Excel China	240*			R	15–18	•	•	•	•	•		•
The Experiment in International Living–China North and East Homestay	241*				14–19	•			•	•		•
The Experiment in International Living–China South and West Homestay	241*				14–19	•			•	•		•
LIFEWORKS with the China Little Flower Foundation in China	241*				15–19	•				•		•
Putney Student Travel–Global Awareness–China	241*			R	15–18	•				•		•
Rassias Programs–China	242*				14–18	•		•	•	•		•
RUSTIC PATHWAYS–CHINESE LANGUAGE IMMERSION	242*			R	15–18	•			•	•		•
RUSTIC PATHWAYS–INTENSIVE CHINESE LANGUAGE	242*			R	15–18	•			•	•		•
RUSTIC PATHWAYS–THE WONDERS OF CHINA	243*				16–18					•		
Summer Advantage Study Abroad–Nanjing, China	243*				16–18	•						
Costa Rica												
AAVE–Costa Rica Clásica	243*				14–18	•	•	•	•	•		•
AAVE–Costa Rica Spanish Intensive	243*				14–18	•		•	•	•		•
Academic Study Associates–Costa Rica	244*			R	14–18	•	•	•		•		•
ACADEMIC TREKS–Sea Turtle Studies	244*				15–19	•		•	•	•		•
AFS-USA–Community Service–Costa Rica	244*			R	15–18	•				•		•
AFS-USA–Homestay Language Study–Costa Rica	244*			R	15–18	•				•		•
AFS-USA–Homestay Plus–Costa Rica	245*			R	15–18	•				•		•
BROADREACH Costa Rica Experience	245*				15–19	•		•	•	•		•
Center for Cultural Interchange–Costa Rica Language School	246*			R	13+	•				•		•
Edu-Culture International (ECI)–CPI Costa Rica	246*				15–18	•		•		•		•
Edu-Culture International (ECI)–Grecia Costa Rica	246*				12–15	•		•	•	•	•	•

This program is highlighted by a photograph, special note, or in-depth description; see the profile page for more information.
D = day camp; R = residential camp

	GENERAL INFORMATION					PROGRAM INFORMATION						
	Profile Page	Boys D/R	Girls D/R	Coed D/R	Age	Acad	Arts	Sports	Wild/ Outdrs	Special Interest	Jobs	Financial Aid
EF International Language School–Playa Tamarindo	247*				16+	•		•	•	•		•
The Experiment in International Living–Costa Rica Homestay	247*				14–19	•		•	•	•		•
Global Leadership Adventures–Costa Rica: Community Service and Leadership	247*				15–18	•				•		•
GLOBAL WORKS–Cultural Exchange and Service–Costa Rica-3 weeks	247*				15–17	•	•	•	•	•	•	•
GLOBAL WORKS–Language Immersion, Cultural Exchange and Service–Costa Rica	248*				13–17	•	•	•	•	•	•	•
LIFEWORKS with the Fundación Humanitaria in Costa Rica	248*				15–19	•		•	•	•		•
Putney Student Travel–Community Service–Costa Rica	248*			R	15–18	•		•	•	•		•
Putney Student Travel–Language Learning–Costa Rica	249*			R	13–18	•		•	•	•		•
RUSTIC PATHWAYS–THE CANO NEGRO SERVICE PROJECT	249*			R	14–18	•		•		•	•	
RUSTIC PATHWAYS–COSTA RICA ADVENTURER	249*				14–18			•	•	•		
RUSTIC PATHWAYS–INTENSIVE SPANISH LANGUAGE	250*			R	14–18	•	•	•	•	•		
RUSTIC PATHWAYS–MALEKU TRIBE IMMERSION PROGRAM–COSTA RICA	250*			R	14–18	•		•		•	•	
RUSTIC PATHWAYS–RAMP UP YOUR SPANISH	250*			R	14–18	•		•		•		
RUSTIC PATHWAYS–SOCCER AND SERVICE IN COSTA RICA	250*				14–18	•		•		•		•
RUSTIC PATHWAYS–SPANISH LANGUAGE IMMERSION	251*			R	14–18	•	•	•	•	•		
RUSTIC PATHWAYS–SURF & SERVICE–COSTA RICA	251*				14–18	•		•	•	•		
RUSTIC PATHWAYS–SURF THE SUMMER–COSTA RICA	251*			R	14–18			•	•	•		
RUSTIC PATHWAYS–THE TURTLE CONSERVATION PROJECT	252*			R	14–18			•		•		
RUSTIC PATHWAYS–ULTIMATE JUNGLE ADVENTURE–COSTA RICA	252*				14–18			•	•	•		
RUSTIC PATHWAYS–VOLCANOES AND RAINFORESTS	252*			R	14–18	•		•	•	•		
RUSTIC PATHWAYS–YOUNG ADVENTURERS–COSTA RICA	252*			R	10–14	•		•	•	•		
Visions–Costa Rica	253*				14–18	•	•	•	•	•		•
Westcoast Connection–Community Service Costa Rica	253*				14–17			•	•	•		•
Westcoast Connection–Spanish in Costa Rica	253*				14–17	•		•	•	•		•
Wilderness Ventures–Costa Rica	253*				14–18			•	•	•		•
Wilderness Ventures–Costa Rica Service	254*				14–18			•	•	•		•
Wilderness Ventures–Costa Rica Surfing	254*				14–18			•	•	•		•
World Horizons International–Costa Rica	254*			R	15–18	•		•		•		•
Denmark												
Center for Cultural Interchange–Denmark High School Abroad	255*			R	15–18	•				•		•
Dominica												
Putney Student Travel–Community Service–Dominica, West Indies	255*			R	15–18	•		•	•	•		•
Visions–Dominica	256*				14–18	•	•	•	•	•		•
World Horizons International–Dominica	256*			R	13–15	•		•		•		
Dominican Republic												
Putney Student Travel–Community Service–Dominican Republic	256*			R	15–18	•		•	•	•		•
Visions–Dominican Republic	256*				14–18	•	•	•	•	•		•
Ecuador												
AAVE–Ecuador and Galapagos	257*				15–18	•		•	•	•		•
ACADEMIC TREKS–Spanish Language Immersion in Ecuador	257*				16–20	•		•	•	•		•
ACTIONQUEST: Galapagos Archipelago Expeditions	257*				15–18	•		•	•	•		
AFS-USA–Homestay–Ecuador	258*			R	15–18	•				•		
EF International Language School–Quito	258*				15+	•		•	•	•		•
The Experiment in International Living–Ecuador Homestay	258*				14–19	•		•	•	•		•
GLOBAL WORKS–Language Immersion, Cultural Exchange and Service–Ecuador and the Galapagos-4 weeks	258*				15–17	•	•	•	•	•	•	•
LIFEWORKS with the Galapagos Islands' National Parks	259*				15–19	•		•	•	•		•
Putney Student Travel–Community Service–Ecuador	259*			R	15–18	•		•	•	•		•

*This program is highlighted by a photograph, special note, or in-depth description; see the profile page for more information.
D = day camp; R = residential camp

	GENERAL INFORMATION					PROGRAM INFORMATION						
	Profile Page	Boys D/R	Girls D/R	Coed D/R	Age	Acad	Arts	Sports	Wild/ Outdrs	Special Interest	Jobs	Financial Aid
Visions–Ecuador	259*				16–18	•	•	•	•	•	•	•
Wilderness Ventures–Ecuador and Galapagos Community Service	260*				14–18			•	•	•	•	•
World Horizons International–Cayambe, Ecuador	260*			R	13–18	•			•	•	•	•
Egypt												
AFS-USA–Homestay Language Study–Egypt	260*			R	15–18	•				•		•
BROADREACH Red Sea Scuba Adventure	260*				15–19	•	•	•	•	•		•
El Salvador												
Putney Student Travel–Global Action–El Salvador	261*			R	15 18	•		•	•	•		•
Estonia												
Volunteers for Peace International Voluntary Service–Estonia	261			R	15+	•		•		•		
Fiji												
ACADEMIC TREKS–Shark Studies in Fiji	262*				15–19	•		•	•	•		•
GLOBAL WORKS–Cultural Exchange–Fiji Islands-4 weeks	262*				14–17	•	•	•	•	•	•	•
RUSTIC PATHWAYS–BIG FIJI EXPLORER	262*				14–18			•	•	•	•	
RUSTIC PATHWAYS–ESCAPE TO FIJI	263*			R	14–18			•		•	•	
RUSTIC PATHWAYS–EXTENDED FIJI VILLAGE SERVICE	263*			R	14–18		•	•		•	•	
RUSTIC PATHWAYS–FIJI ISLANDS COMMUNITY SERVICE	263*				14–18			•		•	•	
RUSTIC PATHWAYS–INTRO TO COMMUNITY SERVICE IN FIJI	263*			R	14–18	•		•	•	•	•	
RUSTIC PATHWAYS–REMOTE HIGHLANDS COMMUNITY SERVICE IN FIJI	264*				14–18			•		•	•	
RUSTIC PATHWAYS–SOCCER AND SERVICE IN FIJI	264*				14–18			•	•	•	•	
RUSTIC PATHWAYS–SUN, SAND & INTERNATIONAL SERVICE–FIJI	264*				14–18			•	•	•	•	
Wilderness Ventures–Fiji Community Service	264*				14–18			•	•	•		•
World Horizons International–Fiji	265*			R	14–18			•	•	•		•
Finland												
AFS-USA–Homestay–Finland	265*			R	15–18	•				•		•
Center for Cultural Interchange–Finland High School Abroad	265*			R	15–18	•				•		•
France												
AAVE–France Classique	266*				15–18	•		•	•	•		•
Academic Study Associates–Nice	266*			R	15–18	•		•	•	•		•
Academic Study Associates–Royan	266*			R	15–18	•		•		•	•	
ACADEMIC TREKS–French Immersion in France	266*				15–19	•			•	•		•
AFS-USA–Homestay–France	267*			R	15–18	•				•		•
Barat Foundation Summer Program in Provence	267*				13–19	•	•	•		•		•
Center for Cultural Interchange–France High School Abroad	268*			R	15–18	•				•		•
Center for Cultural Interchange–France Independent Homestay	268*			R	16+	•				•		•
Center for Cultural Interchange–France Language School	268*			R	14+	•		•		•		•
Choate Rosemary Hall Summer in Paris	268*			R	14–18	•		•		•		•
Edu-Culture International (ECI)–Aix-en-Provence/Gap Host Family Immersion	269*				15–18	•		•		•	•	•
Edu-Culture International (ECI)–Lyon Host Family and Travel Program	269*				14–18	•		•		•		•
Edu-Culture International (ECI)–Toulouse/Montpellier Host Family Immersion	269*				15–18	•		•		•		•
EF International Language School–Nice	270*				15+	•				•		•
EF International Language School–Paris	270*				16+	•				•		
Excel at Paris/Provence	271*			R	15–18	•	•	•		•		•
The Experiment in International Living–France, Biking and Homestay	271*				14–19	•		•	•	•		•

This program is highlighted by a photograph, special note, or in-depth description; see the profile page for more information.
D = day camp; R = residential camp

FRANCE

	GENERAL INFORMATION					PROGRAM INFORMATION						
	Profile Page	Boys D/R	Girls D/R	Coed D/R	Age	Acad	Arts	Sports	Wild/ Outdrs	Special Interest	Jobs	Financial Aid
The Experiment in International Living–France, Five-Week Art and Adventure in Provence	271*				14–19	•	•			•		•
The Experiment in International Living–France, Four-Week Brittany Discovery	272*				14–19	•				•		•
The Experiment in International Living–France, Four-Week Homestay and Photography	272*				14–17	•	•			•		•
The Experiment in International Living–France, Four-Week Homestay and Theatre	272*				14–19	•	•			•		•
The Experiment in International Living–France, Four-Week Homestay and Travel–Southern France and Northern Spain	272*				14–19	•			•	•		•
The Experiment in International Living–France, Four-Week Homestay and Travel through Alps	273*				14–19	•			•	•		•
The Experiment in International Living–France, Homestay, Language Training, and Cooking	273*		R		14–19	•				•		•
The Experiment in International Living–France, Three-Week Camargue Homestay	273*				14–19	•				•		•
The Experiment in International Living–France, Three-Week Homestay and Travel–Borders	273*				14–19	•			•	•		•
GLOBAL WORKS–Language Immersion, Cultural Exchange and Service–France-4 weeks	274*				14–17	•	•	•	•	•	•	•
L' Académie de France	274*		R		15–18	•	•	•		•		•
L' Académie de Paris	274*		R		15–18	•	•	•		•		•
Putney Student Travel–Language Learning–France	275*		R		13–18	•		•	•	•		•
Rassias Programs–Arles, France	275*				14–17	•		•		•	•	•
Rassias Programs–Tours, France	276*				14–17	•		•		•	•	•
Service Learning in Paris	276*		R		16+	•	•			•		•
Summer Advantage Study Abroad–Paris, France	277*				16–18	•	•			•		
Summer Study in Paris at The Sorbonne	277*		R		14+	•	•	•		•	•	•
Taft Summer School Abroad–France	278*				14–18	•				•		
TASIS Arts and Architecture in the South of France	278*		R		14–18	•	•	•		•		
Tisch School of the Arts–International High School Program–Paris	278*		R		15+	•	•					•
Volunteers for Peace International Voluntary Service–France	279		R		15+	•				•		
Westcoast Connection–French Language and Touring	279*				14–19	•				•		

French Polynesia

ACTIONQUEST: Tahiti and French Polynesian Island Voyages	279*				15–19	•		•	•	•		

Germany

Center for Cultural Interchange–Germany High School Abroad	279*		R		15–18	•				•		•
Center for Cultural Interchange–Germany Independent Homestay	280*		R		16+	•				•		•
Center for Cultural Interchange–Germany Language School	280*		R		17+	•				•		•
EF International Language School–Munich	280*				16+	•		•		•		•
The Experiment in International Living–Germany, Four-Week Homestay, Travel, Community Service	281*				14–19	•			•	•		•
Volunteers for Peace International Voluntary Service–Germany	281		R		16+	•	•	•	•	•		

Ghana

AFS-USA–Team Mission–Ghana	281*		R		15–18	•	•			•		•
The Experiment in International Living–Ghana Homestay	281*				14–19	•			•	•		•
Global Leadership Adventures–Ghana: Community Service and Leadership	282*				15–18	•				•		

Greece

AAVE–Sail Dive Greece	282*				14–18			•	•	•		•
University of Chicago–The Traveling Academy	282*				15–18	•						•

Guadeloupe

ACADEMIC TREKS–French Immersion in the French West Indies	283*				15–19	•	•	•	•	•		•
Visions–Guadeloupe	283*				14–18	•	•	•	•	•		•

*This program is highlighted by a photograph, special note, or in-depth description; see the profile page for more information.
D = day camp; R = residential camp

	GENERAL INFORMATION					PROGRAM INFORMATION						
	Profile Page	Boys D/R	Girls D/R	Coed D/R	Age	Acad	Arts	Sports	Wild/ Outdrs	Special Interest	Jobs	Financial Aid
Honduras												
BROADREACH Honduras Eco-Adventure	283*				15–19	•	•	•	•	•		
Hungary												
AFS-USA–Homestay Plus–Hungary	284*			R	15–19	•	•		•	•		•
Iceland												
World Horizons International–Iceland	284*			R	13+	•		•	•	•	•	•
India												
Global Leadership Adventures–India: Community Service and Leadership	284*				15–18	•			•	•		•
Putney Student Travel–Community Service–India	285*			R	14–18	•			•	•	•	•
Putney Student Travel–Global Action–India	285*			R	15–18	•			•	•		•
RUSTIC PATHWAYS–THE BUDDHIST CARAVAN	285*				16–18				•	•		•
RUSTIC PATHWAYS–INDIAN HIMALAYA TRAVELER	285*				16–18			•	•			•
RUSTIC PATHWAYS–SERVICE IN THE CLOUDS–INDIA	286*			R	16–18			•	•	•		•
Studies Abroad for Global Education (SAGE), Summer SAGE Program	286				14–18	•	•	•	•	•		•
World Horizons International–Tapovan, Laxman Jhula, India	286*			R	14–18				•	•	•	•
Indonesia												
Putney Student Travel–Community Service–Nusa Penida and Bali	287*			R	14–18	•		•	•	•	•	•
Ireland												
Center for Cultural Interchange–Ireland High School Abroad	287*			R	15–18	•				•		•
Center for Cultural Interchange–Ireland Independent Homestay Program	287*			R	17+	•				•		•
GLOBAL WORKS–Cultural Exchange and Service–Ireland-4 weeks	288*				14–17	•	•	•	•	•		•
Tisch School of the Arts–International High School Program–Dublin	288*			R	15+	•	•					•
Italy												
Academic Study Associates–Florence	289*			R	15–18	•	•	•		•	•	•
AFS-USA–Homestay Plus–Italy	289*			R	15–18	•	•			•		•
Center for Cultural Interchange–Italy High School Abroad	289*			R	15–18	•				•		•
Center for Cultural Interchange–Italy Language School	290*			R	17+	•				•		•
EF International Language School–Rome	290*				16+	•				•		•
The Experiment in International Living–Italy Biodiversity, Cooking, and Culture	290*				14–19	•		•		•		•
The Experiment in International Living–Italy Homestay, Language, Culture, and Travel	291*				14–19	•		•		•		•
Humanities Spring in Assisi	291*				14+	•	•	•		•	•	•
Spoleto Study Abroad	292*			R	15–19	•	•	•	•	•	•	
Summer Advantage Study Abroad–Rome, Italy	292*				16–18	•	•					
TASIS Tuscan Academy of Art and Culture	292*			R	15–19	•	•	•	•			
Volunteers for Peace International Voluntary Service–Italy	293			R	15+	•				•		
Westcoast Connection–Authentic Italy	293*				16–18			•		•	•	
World Horizons International–Rome, Italy	293*			R	14–18				•	•	•	•
Japan												
AFS-USA–Homestay Language Study–Japan	293*			R	15–18	•				•		
Center for Cultural Interchange–Japan High School Abroad	294*			R	15–18	•				•		
The Experiment in International Living–Japan Homestay	294*				14–19	•				•		
Latvia												
AFS-USA–Homestay Language Study–Latvia	294*			R	15–18	•				•		•

*This program is highlighted by a photograph, special note, or in-depth description; see the profile page for more information.
D = day camp; R = residential camp

	GENERAL INFORMATION				PROGRAM INFORMATION						
	Profile Page	Boys D/R	Girls D/R	Coed D/R	Age	Acad	Arts	Sports	Wild/ Outdrs	Special Interest	Jobs	Financial Aid

Madagascar
| Putney Student Travel–Global Awareness–Madagascar | 295* | | | R | 15–18 | • | | | | • | | • |

Malawi
| Putney Student Travel–Global Action–Malawi | 295* | | | R | 15–18 | • | | | | • | | • |

Martinique
| GLOBAL WORKS–Language Immersion, Cultural Exchange and Service–Martinique-4weeks | 295* | | | | 14–17 | • | • | • | • | • | • | • |

Mexico
AAVE–Surf Scuba Safari	296*				14–18	•		•	•	•		•
ACADEMIC TREKS–Immersion Mexico	296*				15–19	•	•		•	•		•
ACADEMIC TREKS–Spanish Immersion in Oaxaca, Mexico	296*				15–19	•			•	•		•
BROADREACH Baja Extreme–Scuba Adventure	297*				15–19	•		•	•			•
BROADREACH Yucatan Adventure	297*				15–19	•	•	•	•			•
Center for Cultural Interchange–Mexico Language School	297*			R	13+	•				•		•
Enforex Residential Youth Summer Camp–Guanajuato, Mexico	297*			R	15–18	•	•	•		•		•
The Experiment in International Living–Mexico–Community Service, Travel, and Homestay	298*				14–19	•				•		•
The Experiment in International Living–Mexico Cooking and Culture	298*				14–19	•				•		•
The Experiment in International Living–Mexico Homestay, Sustainable Development and Fair Trade	298*				14–19	•			•	•		•
The Experiment in International Living–Mexico–Mayan Arts and Culture	298*				14–19	•				•		•
GLOBAL WORKS–Language Immersion, Cultural Exchange and Service–Mexico–3 weeks	299*				15–17	•	•	•	•	•	•	•
GLOBAL WORKS–Language Immersion, Cultural Exchange and Service–Yucatan Peninsula, Mexico-4 weeks	299*				15–18	•	•	•	•	•	•	•

Morocco
| The Experiment in International Living–Morocco Four-Week Arts and Culture Program | 299* | | | | 14–19 | • | • | | | • | | • |

Netherlands
| Center for Cultural Interchange–Netherlands High School Abroad | 300* | | | R | 15–18 | • | | | | • | | • |

New Zealand
AFS-USA–Homestay Plus–New Zealand	300*			R	16–18			•	•	•		•
The Experiment in International Living–New Zealand Homestay	300*				14–19	•			•	•		•
RUSTIC PATHWAYS–NEW ZEALAND NORTH ISLAND ADVENTURE	301*				14–18			•	•	•		•
RUSTIC PATHWAYS–SKI AND SNOWBOARD ADVENTURE IN NEW ZEALAND	301*				14–18			•	•		•	

Nicaragua
| Putney Student Travel–Community Service-Nicaragua | 301* | | | R | 14–18 | • | | • | • | • | | • |
| Visions–Nicaragua | 302* | | | | 16–18 | • | • | • | • | • | | • |

Norway
| Center for Cultural Interchange–Norway High School Abroad | 302* | | | R | 15–18 | • | | | | • | | • |

Panama
AFS-USA–Community Service–Panama	302*			R	16–18	•				•		•
AFS-USA–Homestay Language Study–Panama	303*			R	16–18	•				•		•
AFS-USA–Homestay Plus–Panama	303*			R	16–18	•				•		•

*This program is highlighted by a photograph, special note, or in-depth description; see the profile page for more information.
D = day camp; R = residential camp

	GENERAL INFORMATION					PROGRAM INFORMATION						
	Profile Page	Boys D/R	Girls D/R	Coed D/R	Age	Acad	Arts	Sports	Wild/ Outdrs	Special Interest	Jobs	Financial Aid
Paraguay												
AFS-USA–Community Service–Paraguay	303*			R	16+	•				•		•
AFS-USA–Homestay–Paraguay	303*			R	15–18	•				•		•
AFS-USA–Homestay Plus–Paraguay Soccer	304*			R	16+	•		•		•		•
Peru												
AAVE–Peru and Machu Picchu	304*				14–18	•		•	•	•	•	•
ACADEMIC TREKS–Adventure Peru	304*				15–19	•		•	•	•		•
GLOBAL WORKS–Language Immersion, Cultural Exchange and Service–Peru	305*				15–17	•	•	•	•	•		•
Visions–Peru	305*				14–18	•	•		•	•		•
Wilderness Ventures–Peru Community Service	305*				14–18			•	•	•		•
Poland												
The Experiment in International Living–Poland, Homestay, Community Service, and Travel	306*				14–19	•			•	•		•
Puerto Rico												
GLOBAL WORKS–Cultural Exchange and Service–Puerto Rico-2 or 4 weeks	306*				14–17	•	•	•	•	•		•
GLOBAL WORKS–Language Immersion, Cultural Exchange and Service–Puerto Rico-4 weeks	306*				15–17	•	•	•	•	•	•	•
Republic of Korea												
Elite Educational Institute Elementary Enrichment–Korea	307*			D	9–12	•						
Elite Educational Institute Junior High/PSAT Program–Korea	307*			D	12–14	•				•		
Elite Educational Institute SAT Bootcamp–Korea	307*			D	15–18	•				•		
Elite Educational Institute SAT Preparation–Korea	307*			D	15–18	•				•		
Russian Federation												
Summer Advantage Study Abroad–St. Petersburg, Russia	308*				16–18	•						
Saint Vincent and The Grenadines												
BROADREACH Adventures in the Grenadines–Advanced Scuba	308*				14–19	•	•	•	•	•		•
Senegal												
Putney Student Travel–Community Service–Senegal	308*			R	15–18	•		•	•	•		•
South Africa												
The Experiment in International Living–South Africa Homestay and Community Service	309*				14–19	•	•		•	•		•
Global Leadership Adventures–Cape Town: Community Service and Leadership	309*				15–18	•		•	•	•		•
Putney Student Travel–Global Action–South Africa	309*			R	15–18	•				•		•
Spain												
AAVE–España Clásica	310*				14–18	•		•	•	•		•
Academic Study Associates–Barcelona	310*			R	15–18	•	•	•	•	•		•
Academic Study Associates–Spanish in España	311*			R	15–18	•	•	•	•	•		•
AFS-USA–Homestay Plus–Spain	311*			R	15–18	•				•		•
AFS-USA–Language Study–Spain	311*			R	15–18	•				•		•
Center for Cultural Interchange–Spain High School Abroad	311*			R	15–18	•				•		•
Center for Cultural Interchange–Spain Independent Homestay	312*			R	14+	•				•		•
Center for Cultural Interchange–Spain Language School	312*			R	14+	•	•			•		•
Center for Cultural Interchange–Spain Sports and Language Camp	312*			R	10–17	•	•	•	•	•		•
Choate Rosemary Hall Summer in Spain	312*				14–18	•		•		•		•
Edu-Culture International (ECI)–Andalusion Total Immersion	313*				16–18	•				•	•	•

*This program is highlighted by a photograph, special note, or in-depth description; see the profile page for more information.
D = day camp; R = residential camp

	GENERAL INFORMATION					PROGRAM INFORMATION						
	Profile Page	Boys D/R	Girls D/R	Coed D/R	Age	Acad	Arts	Sports	Wild/ Outdrs	Special Interest	Jobs	Financial Aid
Edu-Culture International (ECI)–Granada Homestay	313*				15–18	•		•		•	•	•
Edu-Culture International (ECI)–Granada Homestay or Dorm Plus Southern Host Family Immersion	313*				15–18	•		•		•		•
Edu-Culture International (ECI)–Granada-Nerja Homestay Combo	314*				15–18	•		•		•		•
Edu-Culture International (ECI)–Nerja Homestay Plus Southern Host Family Immersion	314*				15–18	•		•		•		•
Edu-Culture International (ECI)–Nerja Homestay with Optional Southern Host Family Immersion	314*				15–18	•		•		•	•	•
Edu-Culture International (ECI)–Salamanca Dorm Plus Southern Host Family Immersion	314*				15–18	•		•		•	•	•
Edu-Culture International (ECI)–Salamanca Homestay	315*				15–18	•		•		•	•	•
Edu-Culture International (ECI)–Salamanca Homestay Plus Northern Host Family Immersion	315*				15–18	•		•		•		•
Edu-Culture International (ECI)–Salamanca Homestay (Short Version)	316*				15–18	•		•		•		•
Edu-Culture International (ECI)–San Sebastian Homestay Plus Southern Host Family Immersion	316*				15–18	•		•		•		•
EF International Language School–Barcelona	316*				16+	•		•	•	•		•
EF International Language School–Malaga	317*				15+	•		•	•	•		•
Enforex–General Spanish–Alicante	317*			R	14+	•		•		•		
Enforex–General Spanish–Barcelona	317*			R	14+	•		•		•		
Enforex–General Spanish–Granada	318*			R	14+	•		•		•		
Enforex–General Spanish–Madrid	318*			R	14+	•		•		•		
Enforex–General Spanish–Malaga	318*			R	14+	•		•		•		
Enforex–General Spanish–Marbella	319*			R	14+	•		•		•		
Enforex–General Spanish–Salamanca	319*			R	14+	•		•		•		
Enforex–General Spanish–Sevilla	319*			R	14+	•		•		•		
Enforex–General Spanish–Tenerife	319*			R	14+	•		•		•		
Enforex–General Spanish–Valencia	320*			R	14+	•		•		•		
Enforex Hispanic Culture: Civilization, History, Art, and Literature–Alicante	320*			R	14+	•	•	•		•		
Enforex Hispanic Culture: Civilization, History, Art, and Literature–Barcelona	321*			R	14+	•	•	•		•		•
Enforex Hispanic Culture: Civilization, History, Art, and Literature–Granada	321*			R	14+	•	•	•		•		•
Enforex Hispanic Culture: Civilization, History, Art, and Literature–Madrid	321*			R	14+	•	•	•		•		
Enforex Hispanic Culture: Civilization, History, Art, and Literature–Malaga	322*			R	14+	•	•	•		•		
Enforex Hispanic Culture: Civilization, History, Art, and Literature–Salamanca	322*			R	14+	•	•	•				•
Enforex Hispanic Culture: Civilization, History, Art, and Literature–Sevilla	322*			R	14+	•	•	•		•		
Enforex Hispanic Culture: Civilization, History, Art, and Literature–Tenerife	323*			R	14+	•	•	•		•		
Enforex Hispanic Culture: History, Art, and Literature–Valencia	323*			R	14+	•		•		•		
Enforex Homestay Program–Alicante	324*			R	14+	•	•	•		•		
Enforex Homestay Program–Barcelona	324*			R	14+	•	•	•		•		
Enforex Homestay Program–Granada	324*			R	14+	•	•	•		•		
Enforex Homestay Program–Madrid	325*			R	14+	•	•	•		•		
Enforex Homestay Program–Malaga	325*			R	14+	•	•	•		•		
Enforex Homestay Program–Marbella	325*			R	14+	•	•	•		•		
Enforex Homestay Program–Salamanca	325*			R	14+	•	•	•		•		
Enforex Homestay Program–Sevilla	326*			R	14+	•	•	•		•		
Enforex Homestay Program–Tenerife	326*			R	14+	•	•	•		•		
Enforex Homestay Program–Valencia	326*			R	14+	•	•	•		•		
Enforex Residential Youth Summer Camp–Barcelona	327*			R	14–18	•	•	•		•		•
Enforex Residential Youth Summer Camp–Granada	327*			R	10–18	•	•	•		•		

*This program is highlighted by a photograph, special note, or in-depth description; see the profile page for more information.
D = day camp; R = residential camp

	GENERAL INFORMATION					PROGRAM INFORMATION						
	Profile Page	Boys D/R	Girls D/R	Coed D/R	Age	Acad	Arts	Sports	Wild/ Outdrs	Special Interest	Jobs	Financial Aid
Enforex Residential Youth Summer Camp–Madrid	327*			R	5–18	•	•	•	•	•		
Enforex Residential Youth Summer Camp–Marbella Albergue College	328*			R	15–18	•	•	•	•	•		
Enforex Residential Youth Summer Camp–Marbella Alboran College	328*			R	14–18	•	•	•	•	•		
Enforex Residential Youth Summer Camp–Marbella Aleman College	328*			R	5–14	•	•	•	•	•		
Enforex Residential Youth Summer Camp–Salamanca	329*			R	9–18	•	•	•	•	•		
Enforex Residential Youth Summer Camp–Valencia	329*			R	13–18	•	•	•	•	•		
Enforex Spanish and Golf	329*			R	14+	•		•				
Enforex Spanish and Tennis	330*			R	15+	•		•				
Enforex Study Tour Vacational Program–Alicante	330*			R	14+	•		•		•		
Enforex Study Tour Vacational Program–Barcelona	330*			R	14+	•		•		•		
Enforex Study Tour Vacational Program–Granada	330*			R	14+	•		•		•		
Enforex Study Tour Vacational Program–Madrid	331*			R	14+	•		•		•		
Enforex Study Tour Vacational Program–Malaga	331*			R	14+	•		•		•		
Enforex Study Tour Vacational Program–Marbella	331*			R	14+	•		•		•		
Enforex Study Tour Vacational Program–Salamanca	332*			R	14+	•		•		•		
Enforex Study Tour Vacational Program–Sevilla	332*			R	14+	•		•		•		
Enforex Study Tour Vacational Program–Tenerife	332*			R	14+	•		•		•		
Enforex Study Tour Vacational Program–Valencia	333*			R	14+	•		•		•		
Excel at Madrid/Barcelona	333*			R	15–18	•	•	•	•	•		•
The Experiment in International Living–Spain, Five-Week Homestay, Language Immersion	333*				14–19	•	•			•		•
The Experiment in International Living–Spain, Four-Week Language Training, Travel, and Homestay	334*				14–19	•				•		•
The Experiment in International Living–Spain–Multiculturalism and Service	334*				14–19	•				•		•
The Experiment in International Living–Spain–Spanish Arts and Culture	334*				14–19	•	•		•	•		•
The Experiment in International Living–Spain–The Road to Santiago	334*				14–19	•			•	•		•
The Experiment in International Living–Spanish Culture and Exploration	335*				14–19	•				•		•
GLOBAL WORKS–Language Immersion, Cultural Exchange and Service–Spain–4 weeks	335*				15–17	•	•	•	•	•	•	•
iD Tech Camps–Documentary Filmmaking and Cultural Immersion in Spain	335*				14–17	•	•			•	•	
La Academia de España	336*			R	15–18	•	•	•		•		•
Putney Student Travel–Language Learning–Spain	336*			R	13–18	•		•	•	•		•
Rassias Programs–Gijón, Spain	336*				14–17	•		•	•	•		•
Rassias Programs–Pontevedra, Spain	336*				14–17	•		•	•	•		•
Rassias Programs–Segovia, Spain	337*				14–17	•		•	•	•	•	•
Service Learning in Barcelona	337*			R	16–21	•	•			•		•
Spanish Language and Flamenco Enforex–Granada	337*			R	14+	•	•	•		•		
Spanish Language and Flamenco Enforex–Madrid	338*			R	14+	•	•	•		•		
Spanish Language and Flamenco Enforex–Marbella	338*			R	14+	•	•	•		•		
Spanish Language and Flamenco Enforex–Sevilla	339*			R	14+	•	•	•		•		
Summer Advantage Study Abroad–Granada, Spain	339*				16–18	•	•			•		
Summer Advantage Study Abroad–Salamanca, Spain	339*				16–18	•	•			•		
Taft Summer School Abroad–Spain	339*				14–18	•				•		
TASIS Spanish Summer Program	340*			R	13–17	•	•	•		•		
Westcoast Connection–Spanish Language and Touring	340*				14–19	•				•		
Wilderness Ventures–Spanish Pyrenees	340*				14–18			•	•	•		•
Sweden												
Center for Cultural Interchange–Sweden High School Abroad	341*			R	15–18	•				•		•

*This program is highlighted by a photograph, special note, or in-depth description; see the profile page for more information.
D = day camp; R = residential camp

					GENERAL INFORMATION	PROGRAM INFORMATION						
	Profile Page	Boys D/R	Girls D/R	Coed D/R	Age	Acad	Arts	Sports	Wild/ Outdrs	Special Interest	Jobs	Financial Aid
Switzerland												
Atelier des Arts	341			R	16+	•	•					
The Experiment in International Living–Switzerland French Language Immersion, Homestay, and Alpine Adventure	341*				14–19	•			•	•		•
International Summer Camp Montana, Switzerland	342*			R	8–17	•	•	•	•	•	•	
Les Elfes–International Summer/Winter Camp	342*			R	8–18	•	•	•	•	•	•	
Summer in Switzerland	343*				9–19	•	•	•	•	•		•
TASIS French Language Program in Château–d'Oex, Switzerland	343*			R	13–17	•						
TASIS Le Château des Enfants	343*			R/D	6–10	•	•	•	•	•		
TASIS Middle School Program	344*			R/D	11–13	•	•	•	•	•		
TASIS Summer Program for Languages, Arts, and Outdoor Pursuits	344*			R/D	14–18	•	•	•	•	•		
Taiwan												
Center for Cultural Interchange–Taiwan High School Abroad	345*			R	15–18	•				•		•
Thailand												
AAVE–Thailand	345*				15–18			•	•	•		•
AFS-USA–Community Service–Thailand	345*			R	18+	•		•		•		•
AFS-USA–Homestay–Thailand	346*			R	16–18	•	•			•		•
The Experiment in International Living–Thailand Homestay	346*				14–19	•			•	•		•
LIFEWORKS with the DPF Foundation in Thailand	346*				15–19					•		•
RUSTIC PATHWAYS–THE AMAZING THAILAND ADVENTURE	347*				14–18		•	•	•	•		•
RUSTIC PATHWAYS–THE ART OF MUAY THAI	347*			R	15–18			•		•		•
RUSTIC PATHWAYS–COME WITH NOTHING, GO HOME RICH	347*				16–18					•		•
RUSTIC PATHWAYS–ELEPHANTS & AMAZING THAILAND	347*				14–18			•	•	•		•
RUSTIC PATHWAYS–HILL TRIBE TREKKING ADVENTURE	348*				15–18				•	•		•
RUSTIC PATHWAYS–INTRO TO COMMUNITY SERVICE IN THAILAND	348*			R	14–18		•	•		•		•
RUSTIC PATHWAYS–ISLAND HOPPING AND DIVING–THAILAND	348*				16–18			•	•	•		•
RUSTIC PATHWAYS–RICEFIELDS, MONKS & SMILING CHILDREN	348*			R	14–18		•	•		•		•
RUSTIC PATHWAYS–SOCCER AND SERVICE IN THAILAND	349*			R	14–18			•	•	•		•
RUSTIC PATHWAYS–THE THAI ELEPHANT CONSERVATION PROJECT	349*			R	14–18				•	•		
Turkey												
AFS-USA–Homestay–Turkey	349*			R	15–18	•				•		•
The Experiment in International Living–Turkey Homestay, Community Service, and Travel	350*				14–19	•				•		•
United Kingdom												
Cambridge College Programme	350*				14+	•	•	•		•		
The Cambridge Experience	351*			R	14–18	•	•	•		•	•	
The Cambridge Prep Experience	351*			R	14–15	•	•	•		•		
The Cambridge Tradition	352*			R	15–18	•	•	•		•		
Center for Cultural Interchange–United Kingdom Independent Homestay	352*			R	16+	•				•		
The Experiment in International Living–Scotland	352*				14–19					•		
The Experiment in International Living–United Kingdom Filmmaking Program and Homestay	352*				14–19		•			•		
The Experiment in International Living–United Kingdom Theatre Program	353*				14–19	•	•			•		•
IEI–Fashion and Design Plus Programme	353*			R	16–18	•	•	•		•		
IEI–Photography Plus Programme	353*			R	16–18	•	•	•		•		
IEI–Print and Broadcast Journalism	354*			R	16–18	•	•	•		•		

*This program is highlighted by a photograph, special note, or in-depth description; see the profile page for more information.
D = day camp; R = residential camp

	GENERAL INFORMATION					PROGRAM INFORMATION						
	Profile Page	Boys D/R	Girls D/R	Coed D/R	Age	Acad	Arts	Sports	Wild/ Outdrs	Special Interest	Jobs	Financial Aid
IEI Student Travel–Internship Program in London	354*			R	16–18	•	•	•		•		
IEI–Theatre Plus Programme	354*			R	16–18		•	•		•		
IEI–Video Production Plus Programme	355*			R	16–18	•	•	•		•		
Oxford Advanced Studies Program	355*			R/D	16+	•	•	•		•		
The Oxford Experience	356*			R	14–18	•	•	•		•	•	
Oxford Media School–Film	356*			R	14–18	•	•	•		•		
Oxford Media School–Film Master Class	357*			R	14–18	•	•	•		•		•
Oxford Media School–Newsroom in Europe	357*			R	14–18	•	•	•		•		•
Oxford Media School–Newsroom in Europe, Master Class	357*			R	14–18	•	•	•		•		•
The Oxford Prep Experience	358*			R	14–15	•	•	•		•		•
The Oxford Tradition	358*			R	15–18	•	•	•		•		•
Putney Student Travel–Cultural Exploration–Theatre in Britain	359*			R	15–18		•			•	•	•
Summer Advantage Study Abroad–Cambridge University	359*				16–18	•						
Summer Advantage Study Abroad–London, UK	359*				16–18	•	•	•		•		
TASIS England Summer Program	360*			R	12–18	•	•	•			•	

United Republic of Tanzania

Putney Student Travel–Community Service–Tanzania	360*			R	15–18	•		•	•	•		•
RUSTIC PATHWAYS–CLIMBING KILI	360*				14–18			•	•	•		•
RUSTIC PATHWAYS–SERVICE AND SAFARI IN AFRICA	361*				14–18			•	•	•	•	•

Vanuatu

Treetops eXpeditions–Vanuatu	361*				14–17			•	•	•		•

Vietnam

Putney Student Travel–Community Service–Vietnam	361*			R	15–18	•			•	•		•
RUSTIC PATHWAYS–FACES AND PLACES OF VIETNAM	361*				16–18		•	•	•	•	•	•
Visions–Vietnam	862*				16–18	•	•	•	•	•	•	•

*This program is highlighted by a photograph, special note, or in-depth description; see the profile page for more information.
D = day camp; R = residential camp

Peterson's Summer Programs for Kids & Teenagers 2008   www.petersons.com/summercampsandprograms   25

TRAVEL PROGRAMS IN THE UNITED STATES

	GENERAL INFORMATION		PROGRAM INFORMATION						
	Profile Page	Age	Acad	Arts	Sports	Wild/ Outdrs	Special Interest	Jobs	Financial Aid
AAVE–Bold West	363*	14–18			•	•	•	•	•
AAVE–Boot/Saddle/Paddle	363*	14–18	•		•	•	•	•	•
AAVE–Peak Four	363*	14–18				•	•		
AAVE–Rock & Rapid	364*	14–18			•	•	•	•	•
AAVE–Wild Coast Discovery	364*	13–14			•	•	•	•	•
Adventure Treks–Wilderness Adventures	364	13–18			•	•			•
ATW: Adventure Roads	364*	13–15			•	•	•	•	
ATW: American Horizons	365*	13–17			•	•	•	•	
ATW: California Sunset	365*	13–17			•	•	•		
ATW: Camp Inn 42	365*	13–18			•	•	•	•	
ATW: Discoverer	366*	13–17			•	•	•	•	
ATW: Fire and Ice	366*	14–17			•	•	•	•	
ATW: Mini Tours	366*	12–15			•	•	•		
ATW: Pacific Paradise	366*	13–17			•	•	•	•	
ATW: Skyblazer	367*	14–17			•	•	•	•	
ATW: Sunblazer	367*	13–17			•	•	•	•	
ATW: Wayfarer	367*	13–18			•	•	•	•	
Duke TIP Domestic Field Studies	367*	14–18	•	•		•	•	•	•
92nd Street Y Camps–The TIYUL	368	15–18	•				•	•	•
Rein Teen Tours–California Caper	368*	13–17			•	•	•	•	
Rein Teen Tours–Crossroads	368*	13–17			•	•	•	•	
Rein Teen Tours–Eastern Adventure	368*	13–15			•	•	•	•	
Rein Teen Tours–Grand Adventure	369*	13–17			•	•	•	•	
Rein Teen Tours–Hawaiian/Alaskan Adventure	369*	13–17			•	•	•	•	
Rein Teen Tours–Hawaiian Caper	369*	13–17			•	•	•	•	
Rein Teen Tours–Western Adventure	370*	13–17			•	•	•	•	
Treetops eXpeditions–Glacier/Boundary Waters	370*	14–17			•	•	•		•
Treetops eXpeditions–Horseback Riding	370*	14–17			•		•		•
Weissman Teen Tours–"Aloha–Welcome to Hawaiian Paradise," 3 weeks	370*	14–17			•	•	•	•	
Weissman Teen Tours–U.S. and Western Canada, 40 Days	371*	13–17			•	•	•	•	
Weissman Teen Tours–U.S. and Western Canada, 30 Days	371*	13–17			•	•	•	•	
Westcoast Connection–American Voyageur	372*	13–17			•	•	•	•	•
Westcoast Connection–California Dreaming	372*	13–17			•	•	•	•	•
Westcoast Connection–Californian Extravaganza	372*	13–17			•	•	•	•	
Westcoast Connection–Hawaiian Spirit	372*	14–17			•	•	•	•	
Westcoast Connection–Major League Baseball Tour	373*	13–17			•		•	•	
Westcoast Connection Travel–California and the Canyons	373*	13–17			•	•	•	•	
Westcoast Connection Travel–Eastcoast Encounter	373*	13–16			•	•	•	•	
Westcoast Connection Travel–Great West Challenge	374*	13–17			•	•	•	•	
Westcoast Connection Travel–Northwestern Odyssey	374*	13–17			•	•	•	•	
Westcoast Connection Travel–Ski and Snowboard Sensation	374*	13–17			•	•	•	•	•
Westcoast Connection–U.S. Explorer	374*	13–17			•	•	•	•	•
Wilderness Ventures–Colorado/Utah Mountain Bike	375*	14–18			•	•			•
Wilderness Ventures–Great Divide	375*	14–18			•	•		•	•
Wilderness Ventures–Northwest	375*	14–18			•	•	•		•
Wilderness Ventures–Pacific Northwest	375*	14–18			•	•	•		•
Wilderness Ventures–Rocky Mountain	376*	14–18			•	•		•	•
Wilderness Ventures–Southwest Community Service	376*	14–18			•	•	•	•	•

*This program is highlighted by a photograph, special note, or in-depth description; see the profile page for more information.
D = day camp; R = residential camp

	GENERAL INFORMATION		PROGRAM INFORMATION						
	Profile Page	Age	Acad	Arts	Sports	Wild/ Outdrs	Special Interest	Jobs	Financial Aid
Wilderness Ventures–Teton Crest	376*	14–16				•	•	•	•
Wilderness Ventures–Yellowstone	376*	13–15			•	•	•	•	•
Wilderness Ventures–Yellowstone Fly Fishing	377*	14–18			•	•	•	•	•
Wilderness Ventures–Yellowstone Wilderness	377*	15–18			•	•	•	•	•

TRAVEL PROGRAMS OUTSIDE THE UNITED STATES

	Profile Page	Age	Acad	Arts	Sports	Wild/ Outdrs	Special Interest	Jobs	Financial Aid
AAVE–Africa	378*	15–18	•		•	•	•	•	
AAVE–Bike Amsterdam-Paris	378*	15–18			•	•	•	•	
AAVE–Bold Europe	378*	14–18			•	•	•	•	•
AAVE–Ultimate Alps	379*	14–18			•	•	•	•	•
AAVE–Wild Isles	379*	14–18			•	•	•	•	•
ACADEMIC TREKS–Caribbean Marine Reserves	380*	15–19	•	•	•	•	•		•
ACTIONQUEST: Leeward and French Caribbean Island Voyages	380*	14–19	•		•	•	•		
ACTIONQUEST: Mediterranean Sailing Voyage	380*	15–19	•		•	•	•		
ATW: European Adventures	381*	15–18				•	•		
BROADREACH Adventures in Scuba and Sailing–Underwater Discoveries	381*	13–19	•	•	•	•	•		
BROADREACH Adventures in the Windward Islands–Advanced Scuba	381*	15–19	•	•	•	•	•		•
BROADREACH Adventures Underwater–Advanced Scuba	382*	13–19	•	•	•	•	•		
BROADREACH Arc of the Caribbean Sailing Adventure	382*	15–19	•	•	•	•	•		
BROADREACH Fiji Solomon Quest	382*	15–19	•	•	•	•	•		
Duke TIP International Field Studies	383*	15–18	•			•	•	•	
Excel at Oxford/Tuscany	383*	16–18	•	•		•	•		•
GLOBAL WORKS–Cultural Exchange and Service–New Zealand and Fiji Islands-4 weeks	383*	14–17	•	•	•	•	•		•
GLOBAL WORKS–Language Immersion, Cultural Exchange and Service–Panama/Costa Rica	384*	15–17	•	•		•	•		•
National Student Leadership Conference: Globalization and International Business–Study Abroad	384*	14–18	•				•	•	•
Putney Student Travel–Cultural Exploration–Australia, New Zealand, and Fiji	384*	16–18	•			•	•	•	•
Putney Student Travel–Cultural Exploration–Switzerland, Italy, France, and Holland	385*	16–18	•		•	•	•		•
Putney Student Travel–Cultural Exploration–Thailand and Cambodia	385*	15–18	•			•	•	•	•
Rein Europe	385*	14–17			•		•	•	
RUSTIC PATHWAYS–ASIAN PACIFIC EXTREME	385*	15–18		•	•	•	•		•
RUSTIC PATHWAYS–EDGE OF THE MAP EXTREME	386*	15–18		•	•	•	•		•
RUSTIC PATHWAYS–INTRODUCTION TO PHOTOGRAPHY–SNAPSHOTS IN THE LAND OF SMILES	386*	14–18		•		•	•		•
RUSTIC PATHWAYS–OFF THE MAP BURMA AND CAMBODIA	386*	16–18		•		•	•		
RUSTIC PATHWAYS–PHOTOGRAPHY ADVENTURE IN THAILAND AND ANGKOR WAT	386*	16–18		•			•	•	•
RUSTIC PATHWAYS–PHOTOGRAPHY ADVENTURE IN THAILAND AND BURMA	387*	16–18		•			•	•	•
RUSTIC PATHWAYS–PHOTOGRAPHY ADVENTURE IN THAILAND AND INDIA	387*	16–18		•			•	•	•
RUSTIC PATHWAYS–PHOTOGRAPHY ADVENTURE IN THAILAND AND VIETNAM	387*	16–18		•			•	•	•
RUSTIC PATHWAYS–SERVICE LEARNING EXTREME	387*	15–18	•		•	•	•		•
RUSTIC PATHWAYS–SOCCER AND SERVICE EXTREME	388*	14–18			•		•		•
RUSTIC PATHWAYS–SOUTH PACIFIC EXTREME	388*	15–18	•		•	•	•	•	•
RUSTIC PATHWAYS–THE WONDERS & RICHES OF SOUTHEAST ASIA	388*	14–18			•	•	•	•	
RUSTIC PATHWAYS–WORLD SERVICE EXTREME	389*	15–18	•		•	•	•		•

*This program is highlighted by a photograph, special note, or in-depth description; see the profile page for more information.
D = day camp; R = residential camp

	GENERAL INFORMATION		PROGRAM INFORMATION						
	Profile Page	Age	Acad	Arts	Sports	Wild/ Outdrs	Special Interest	Jobs	Financial Aid
Weissman Teen Tours–European Experience	389*	15–18	•	•	•	•	•		
Westcoast Connection–Australian Outback Plus Hawaii	389*	14–18			•	•	•		
Westcoast Connection–Belize and Costa Rica Water Adventure	390*	14–17			•	•	•	•	
Westcoast Connection–European Escape	390*	14–17			•	•	•		•
Westcoast Connection Travel–European Discovery	390*	14–17			•	•	•	•	
Westcoast Connection Travel/On Tour–European Escapade	390*	16–18			•	•	•		
Westcoast Connection Travel/On Tour–European Experience	391*	16–18			•	•	•		
Wilderness Ventures–Costa Rica/Belize	391*	14–18			•	•	•	•	•
Wilderness Ventures–European Alps	391*	14–18	•			•	•	•	•
Wilderness Ventures–Tahiti, Fiji, and New Zealand	392*				•		•	•	•
World Horizons International–United Kingdom	392*	14–18		•		•	•	•	•

This program is highlighted by a photograph, special note, or in-depth description; see the profile page for more information.
D = day camp; R = residential camp

PROFILES OF SUMMER PROGRAMS

PPORTUNITIES IN THE UNITED STATES

ALASKA

AAVE–Ultimate Alaska

AAVE–Journeys That Matter
Alaska

General Information Coed travel outdoor program, wilderness program, and adventure program established in 1976. Accredited by American Camping Association.
Program Focus Adventure travel.
Special Interest Areas Campcraft, community service, leadership training, team building.
Sports Kayaking, rappelling, sea kayaking, swimming.
Wilderness/Outdoors Backpacking, hiking, ice climbing, mountaineering, orienteering, rafting, survival training, white-water trips, wilderness camping.
Trips Overnight.
Program Information 4–6 sessions per year. Session length: 25 days in June, July, August. Ages: 14–18. 13 participants per session. Cost: $4188. Financial aid available.
Application Deadline Continuous.
Jobs Positions for college students 21 and older.
Contact Mr. Abbott Wallis, Owner, 2308 Fossil Trace Drive, Golden, Colorado 80401. Phone: 800-222-3595. Fax: 303-526-0885. E-mail: info@aave.com.
URL www.aave.com

For more information, see page 394.

Adventure Treks–Alaska Adventures

Adventure Treks, Inc.
Alaska

General Information Coed travel outdoor program, wilderness program, and adventure program established in 1978.
Program Focus Multi-activity adventure programs with a focus on fun, personal growth, leadership, outdoor skills and teamwork.
Sports Sea kayaking.
Wilderness/Outdoors Backpacking, canoe trips, hiking, ice climbing, mountaineering, orienteering, rafting, rock climbing, white-water trips, wilderness camping.
Program Information 1–2 sessions per year. Session length: 4 weeks in June, July, August. Ages: 16–18. 20–24 participants per session. Cost: $4195. Financial aid available.
Application Deadline Continuous.
Contact John Dockendorf, Director, PO Box 1321, Flat Rock, North Carolina 28731. Phone: 888-954-5555. Fax: 828-696-1663. E-mail: info@advtreks.com.
URL www.adventuretreks.com

Putney Student Travel–Community Service–Alaska

Putney Student Travel
Alaska

General Information Coed residential outdoor program, community service program, and wilderness program established in 1951.
Program Focus Community service, cultural

Putney Student Travel–Community Service–Alaska (continued)

exchange, and weekend wilderness excursions from a base in a tiny, exclusively Tlingit native village.
Academics Intercultural studies.
Special Interest Areas Native American culture, community service, construction.
Sports Kayaking.
Wilderness/Outdoors Backpacking, hiking, outdoor adventure, wilderness camping, wilderness/outdoors (general).
Trips Cultural, overnight.
Program Information 2 sessions per year. Session length: 30 days in June, July. Ages: 15–18. 16 participants per session. Boarding program cost: $5390. Financial aid available.
Application Deadline Continuous.
Contact Jeffrey Shumlin, Admissions Director, 345 Hickory Ridge Road, Putney, Vermont 05346. Phone: 802-387-5000. Fax: 802-387-4276. E-mail: info@goputney.com.
URL www.goputney.com
For more information, see page 598.

Treetops eXpeditions–Alaska Community Service

Treetops eXpeditions
Alaska

General Information Coed travel outdoor program, community service program, and cultural program established in 1970.
Program Focus Conservation projects, community service, outdoor living and exploring.
Special Interest Areas Community service, conservation projects, cross-cultural education, nature study, team building.
Wilderness/Outdoors Backpacking, canoe trips, hiking, wilderness camping.
Trips Cultural.
Program Information 1 session per year. Session length: 30 days in July. Ages: 14–17. 6–10 participants per session. Cost: $5500. Financial aid available.
Application Deadline Continuous.
Contact Mr. Chad Jemison, Director, PO Box 187, Lake Placid, New York 12946. Phone: 518-523-9329 Ext.149. Fax: 518-523-4858. E-mail: chad.jemison@nct.org.
URL www.ttexpeditions.org
For more information, see page 672.

Visions–Alaska

Visions
Alaska

General Information Coed travel outdoor program, community service program, and cultural program established in 1989. High school credit may be earned.
Program Focus Community service, cross-cultural experience, and outdoor adventure activities.
Academics Ecology, intercultural studies.
Arts Carpentry.

Special Interest Areas Native American culture, community service, construction, cross-cultural education, field research/expeditions, field trips (arts and culture), leadership training, nature study.
Wilderness/Outdoors Backpacking, hiking, ice climbing, outdoor adventure, rafting, wilderness camping.
Trips Cultural, day, overnight.
Program Information 2 sessions per year. Session length: 3–4 weeks in June, July, August. Ages: 14–18. 20–25 participants per session. Cost: $3200–$4900. Financial aid available.
Application Deadline Continuous.
Jobs Positions for college students 22 and older.
Contact Joanne Pinaire, Director, PO Box 220, Newport, Pennsylvania 17074. Phone: 717-567-7313. Fax: 717-567-7853. E-mail: info@visionsserviceadventures.com.
URL www.visionsserviceadventures.com
For more information, see page 694.

Westcoast Connection–Community Connections Alaska

Westcoast Connection
Alaska

General Information Coed travel community service program established in 1982. Accredited by Ontario Camping Association. High school credit may be earned.
Program Focus Community service plus touring and adventure highlights.
Special Interest Areas Community service, farming, field research/expeditions, touring.
Sports Kayaking.
Wilderness/Outdoors Outdoor adventure, rafting, white-water trips.
Program Information 1–2 sessions per year. Session length: 27 days in July, August. Ages: 14+. 10–20 participants per session. Cost: $4599. Financial aid available.
Application Deadline Continuous.
Contact Mr. Mark Segal, Director, 154 East Boston Post Road, Mamaroneck, New York 10543. Phone: 800-767-0227. Fax: 914-835-0798. E-mail: usa@westcoastconnection.com.
URL www.360studenttravel.com
For more information, see page 702.

WILDERNESS VENTURES–ALASKA COLLEGE LEADERSHIP

Wilderness Ventures
Alaska

General Information Coed travel outdoor program, wilderness program, and adventure program established in 1973.
Program Focus Wilderness travel, wilderness skills, leadership skills.
Special Interest Areas Leadership training.
Sports Sea kayaking.
Wilderness/Outdoors Backpacking, hiking, wilderness camping.
Program Information 2 sessions per year. Session length: 3 weeks in June, July, August. Ages: 17+. Cost: $3990. Financial aid available.
Application Deadline Continuous.
Jobs Positions for college students 21 and older.
Contact Mike Cottingham, Director, PO Box 2768, Jackson Hole, Wyoming 83001. Phone: 800-533-2281. Fax: 307-739-1934. E-mail: info@wildernessventures. com.
URL www.wildernessventures.com
For more information, see page 704.

WILDERNESS VENTURES–ALASKA EXPEDITION

Wilderness Ventures
Alaska

General Information Coed travel outdoor program, wilderness program, and adventure program established in 1973.
Program Focus Wilderness travel, wilderness skills, leadership skills.
Academics Ecology, environmental science, geology/ earth science.
Special Interest Areas Leadership training.
Sports Sea kayaking.
Wilderness/Outdoors Backpacking, hiking, mountaineering, rafting, white-water trips, wilderness camping.
Program Information 1 session per year. Session length: 39 days in June, July, August. Ages: 14–18. 13 participants per session. Cost: $5290. Financial aid available.
Application Deadline Continuous.
Jobs Positions for college students 21 and older.
Contact Mr. Mike Cottingham, Director, PO Box 2768, Jackson Hole, Wyoming 83001. Phone: 800-533-2281. Fax: 307-739-1934. E-mail: info@wildernessventures. com.
URL www.wildernessventures.com
For more information, see page 704.

WILDERNESS VENTURES–ALASKA SOUTHCENTRAL

Wilderness Ventures
Alaska

General Information Coed travel outdoor program, wilderness program, and adventure program established in 1973.
Program Focus Wilderness travel, wilderness skills, leadership skills.
Special Interest Areas Leadership training.
Sports Climbing (wall), sea kayaking.
Wilderness/Outdoors Backpacking, hiking, rafting, wilderness camping.
Trips Overnight.
Program Information 2 sessions per year. Session length: 3 weeks in June, July, August. Ages: 14–18. 13 participants per session. Cost: $3790. Financial aid available.
Application Deadline Continuous.
Jobs Positions for college students 21 and older.
Contact Mike Cottingham, Director, PO Box 2768, Jackson Hole, Wyoming 83001. Phone: 800-533-2281. Fax: 307-739-1934. E-mail: info@wildernessventures. com.
URL www.wildernessventures.com
For more information, see page 704.

WILDERNESS VENTURES–ALASKA SOUTHEAST

Wilderness Ventures
Alaska

General Information Coed travel outdoor program, wilderness program, and adventure program established in 1973.
Program Focus Wilderness travel, wilderness skills, leadership skills.
Special Interest Areas Leadership training.
Sports Climbing (wall), sea kayaking.
Wilderness/Outdoors Backpacking, hiking, mountaineering, rafting, white-water trips, wilderness camping.
Trips Overnight.
Program Information 2 sessions per year. Session length: 3 weeks in June, July, August. Ages: 14–18.

Wilderness Ventures–Alaska Southeast (continued)
13 participants per session. Cost: $3990. Financial aid available.
Application Deadline Continuous.
Jobs Positions for college students 21 and older.
Contact Mr. Mike Cottingham, Director, PO Box 2768, Jackson Hole, Wyoming 83001. Phone: 800-533-2281. Fax: 307-739-1934. E-mail: info@wildernessventures. com.
URL www.wildernessventures.com
For more information, see page 704.

WILDERNESS VENTURES–ALASKA SOUTHEAST COMMUNITY SERVICE

Wilderness Ventures
Alaska

General Information Coed travel community service program established in 1973.
Program Focus Wilderness travel, leadership skills, cultural immersion, community service.
Special Interest Areas Community service, conservation projects, cross-cultural education, leadership training.
Sports Sea kayaking.
Wilderness/Outdoors Hiking, white-water trips, wilderness camping, wilderness/outdoors (general).
Trips Cultural, overnight.
Program Information 2 sessions per year. Session length: 3 weeks in June, July, August. Ages: 14–18. 13 participants per session. Cost: $3890. Financial aid available.
Application Deadline Continuous.
Jobs Positions for college students 21 and older.
Contact Mike Cottingham, Director, PO Box 2768, Jackson Hole, Wyoming 83001. Phone: 800-533-2281. Fax: 307-739-1934. E-mail: info@wildernessventures. com.
URL www.wildernessventures.com
For more information, see page 704.

ARIZONA

iD TECH CAMPS–ARIZONA STATE UNIVERSITY, TEMPE, AZ

iD Tech Camps
Arizona State University
Tempe, Arizona 85287

General Information Coed day academic program established in 1999. Accredited by American Camping Association. Formal opportunities for the academically talented and artistically talented.
Program Focus Students create 2D and 3D video games, build robots to compete, design websites, film and edit digital movies, create their own comic book

with digital photos, learn programming and more. One computer per student and an average of five students per staff member. Campers take home a project at the end of the weeklong course.
Academics Web page design, academics (general), computer programming, computer science (Advanced Placement), computers, precollege program.
Arts Animation, cinematography, digital media, drawing, film, film editing, film production, graphic arts, photography, television/video.
Special Interest Areas Career exploration, computer game design, computer graphics, electronics, leadership training, robotics, team building.
Sports Baseball, basketball, soccer, softball, swimming, volleyball.
Trips College tours.
Program Information 5–9 sessions per year. Session length: 5–7 days in June, July, August. Ages: 7–17. 40–50 participants per session. Day program cost: $729. Financial aid available.
Application Deadline Continuous.
Jobs Positions for college students 18 and older.
Contact Client Services Representatives, 42 West Campbell Avenue, Suite 301, Campbell, California 95008. Phone: 888-709-TECH. Fax: 408-871-2228. E-mail: info@internaldrive.com.
URL www.internaldrive.com
For more information, see page 520.

LANDMARK VOLUNTEERS: ARIZONA

Landmark Volunteers, Inc.
Grand Canyon National Park
Flagstaff, Arizona

General Information Coed residential outdoor program and community service program established in 1992. High school credit may be earned.
Program Focus Opportunity for high school students to earn community service credit while working as a team for two weeks serving Grand Canyon National Park. Similar programs offered through Landmark Volunteers at over 50 locations in 20 states.
Academics Archaeology, botany, environmental science, geology/earth science.
Special Interest Areas Native American culture, career exploration, community service, conservation projects, field research/expeditions, leadership training, nature study, team building, work camp programs.
Wilderness/Outdoors Hiking.
Trips Cultural, day.
Program Information 1 session per year. Session length: 11 days in July. Ages: 14–18. 10–13 participants per session. Boarding program cost: $1250–$1300. Financial aid available.
Application Deadline Continuous.
Jobs Positions for college students.

Contact Ann Barrett, Executive Director, PO Box 455, Sheffield, Massachusetts 01257. Phone: 413-229-0255. Fax: 413-229-2050. E-mail: landmark@volunteers.com. **URL** www.volunteers.com

For more information, see page 542.

OAK CREEK RANCH SCHOOL–SUMMER ACADEMIC PROGRAM

Oak Creek Ranch School
West Sedona, Arizona 86340

General Information Coed residential academic program established in 1972. Specific services available for the learning disabled, participant with ADD, and participant with AD/HD. High school credit may be earned.

Oak Creek Ranch School–Summer Academic Program

Program Focus Summer school studies for academic underachievers and teens with ADD/ADHD.
Academics American literature, English language/literature, Spanish language/literature, academics (general), biology, chemistry, computers, economics, geography, geology/earth science, history, mathematics, reading, science (general), social studies, study skills, writing.
Arts Photography.
Sports Baseball, basketball, bicycling, equestrian

sports, fishing, golf, horseback riding, in-line skating, paintball, ropes course, softball, swimming, tennis, volleyball, weight training.
Wilderness/Outdoors Backpacking, bicycle trips, hiking, mountain biking, mountaineering, pack animal trips, rock climbing, wilderness camping.
Trips Cultural, day, overnight, shopping.
Program Information 3 sessions per year. Session length: 28–30 days in June, July, August. Ages: 12–19. 60–80 participants per session. Boarding program cost: $4100–$4500.
Application Deadline Continuous.
Jobs Positions for college students 22 and older.
Contact Allan Popsack, Director of Admissions, PO Box 4329, West Sedona, Arizona 86340. Phone: 928-634-5571. Fax: 928-634-4915. E-mail: admissions@ocrs.com. **URL** www.ocrs.com

For more information, see page 576.

SOUTHWESTERN ADVENTURES–ARIZONA

Southwestern Academy's Southwestern Adventures
Beaver Creek Ranch Campus
Rimrock, Arizona 86335

General Information Coed residential and day academic program, outdoor program, and cultural program established in 1964. High school credit may be earned.

Southwestern Adventures–Arizona

Program Focus Academic enrichment and outdoor environmental education, college prep credit classes, arts program.
Academics English as a second language, English language/literature, Latin language, SAT/ACT preparation, Spanish language/literature, academics (general), anthropology, archaeology, area studies, astronomy, biology, botany, chemistry, computers, geology/earth science, government and politics, history, mathematics, physics, physiology, reading, science (general), social science, social studies, study skills, writing.
Arts Arts and crafts (general), creative writing, drawing, jewelry making, painting, theater/drama.

Southwestern Adventures–Arizona (continued)

Special Interest Areas Native American culture, career exploration, community service, conservation projects, nature study.

Sports Baseball, basketball, bicycling, bicycling (BMX), climbing (wall), cross-country, equestrian sports, fishing, golf, horseback riding, soccer, softball, swimming, volleyball, weight training.

Wilderness/Outdoors Backpacking, bicycle trips, caving, hiking, mountain biking, orienteering, rock climbing, wilderness camping.

Trips College tours, cultural, day, overnight, shopping.

Program Information 2–6 sessions per year. Session length: 12–40 days in June, July, August. Ages: 11–18. 20–30 participants per session. Boarding program cost: $1950–$5685. Application fee: $100.

Application Deadline Continuous.

Contact Mrs. Terri Rosales, Director of Admissions, Beaver Creek Ranch Campus, HC 64 Box 235, Rimrock, Arizona 86335. Phone: 928-567-4472. Fax: 928-567-5036. E-mail: admissions@southwesternacademy.edu.

URL www.southwesternacademy.edu

For more information, see page 640.

CALIFORNIA

ACADEMIC STUDY ASSOCIATES–ASA AT THE UNIVERSITY OF CALIFORNIA, BERKELEY

Academic Study Associates, Inc. (ASA)
University of California, Berkeley
Berkeley, California

General Information Coed residential and day academic program established in 2001. Formal opportunities for the academically talented and artistically talented. High school or college credit may be earned.

Academic Study Associates–ASA at the University of California, Berkeley

Program Focus Academic enrichment, college credit, SAT preparation, ESL, TOEFL, and professional sports instruction.

Academics American literature, English as a second language, English language/literature, SAT/ACT preparation, TOEFL/TOEIC preparation, academics (general), anthropology, art (Advanced Placement), art history/appreciation, biology, business, chemistry, computer programming, computers, economics, government and politics, history, humanities, intercultural studies, journalism, mathematics, mathematics (Advanced Placement), music (Advanced Placement), philosophy, physics, precollege program, psychology, social science, social studies, speech/debate, writing.

Arts Arts and crafts (general), creative writing, dance, dance (folk), dance (jazz), dance (modern), drawing, film, graphic arts, painting, photography, theater/drama.

Special Interest Areas Field trips (arts and culture).

Sports Aerobics, basketball, soccer, tennis, volleyball, weight training.

Trips College tours, cultural, day, overnight, shopping.

Program Information 1 session per year. Session length: 4 weeks in July, August. Ages: 14–18. 120–140 participants per session. Day program cost: $1250–

$2900. Boarding program cost: $5895. Financial aid available.
Application Deadline Continuous.
Jobs Positions for college students 21 and older.
Contact Mr. David A. Evans, Vice President, 375 West Broadway, Suite 200, New York, New York 10012. Phone: 212-796-8340. Fax: 212-334-4934. E-mail: summer@asaprograms.com.
URL www.asaprograms.com
For more information, see page 398.

ACADEMY BY THE SEA

The Academy by the Sea/Camp Pacific
2605 Carlsbad Boulevard
Carlsbad, California 92008

General Information Coed residential and day academic program established in 1943. Accredited by American Camping Association. Formal opportunities for the academically talented. Specific services available for the participant with ADD and participant with AD/HD. High school credit may be earned.

Academy by the Sea

Program Focus Afternoon water sports, camp activities, weekend excursions, academic enrichment, and credit.
Academics American literature, English as a second language, English language/literature, Spanish language/literature, academics (general), art history/appreciation, biology, communications, computers, history, journalism, marine studies, mathematics, mathematics (Advanced Placement), music, oceanography, precollege program, reading, science (general), social science, social studies, speech/debate, study skills, typing, writing.
Arts Acting, arts and crafts (general), creative writing, dance (folk), drawing, jewelry making, leather working, music, musical productions, painting, photography, pottery, printmaking, radio broadcasting, theater/drama.
Special Interest Areas Campcraft, leadership training.
Sports Baseball, basketball, body boarding, field hockey, football, kayaking, lacrosse, paintball, riflery, scuba diving, sea kayaking, snorkeling, soccer, softball, surfing, swimming, tennis, volleyball, water polo, weight training.
Trips Cultural, day, overnight, shopping.
Program Information 1 session per year. Session length: 5 weeks in July, August. Ages: 11–17. 120–160 participants per session. Boarding program cost: $4725. Application fee: $250.
Application Deadline Continuous.
Jobs Positions for college students 21 and older.
Contact Mrs. Niki Kolb, Associate Director, PO Box 3000, Carlsbad, California 92018-3000. Phone: 760-434-7564. Fax: 760-729-1574. E-mail: summer@abts.com.
URL www.abts.com
For more information, see page 400.

ADVENTURE TREKS–CALIFORNIA ADVENTURES

Adventure Treks, Inc.
California

General Information Coed travel outdoor program, wilderness program, and adventure program established in 1978.
Program Focus Multi-activity outdoor adventure with focus on fun, personal growth, teamwork, leadership, building self-confidence, outdoor skills, and community living.

Adventure Treks–California Adventures (continued)

Sports Sailing, swimming.
Wilderness/Outdoors Backpacking, hiking, mountain biking, mountaineering, orienteering, rafting, rock climbing, white-water trips, wilderness camping.
Program Information 2–4 sessions per year. Session length: 19–25 days in June, July, August. Ages: 13–17. 24 participants per session. Cost: $2995–$3595. Financial aid available.
Application Deadline Continuous.
Contact John Dockendorf, Director, PO Box 1321, Flat Rock, North Carolina 28731. Phone: 888-954-5555. Fax: 828-696-1663. E-mail: info@advtreks.com.
URL www.adventuretreks.com

AMERICAN ACADEMY OF DRAMATIC ARTS SUMMER PROGRAM AT LOS ANGELES, CALIFORNIA

American Academy of Dramatic Arts
1336 North LaBrea Avenue
Hollywood, California 90028

General Information Coed day arts program established in 1974. Formal opportunities for the artistically talented.
Program Focus Acting.
Arts Acting, dance, mime, music (vocal), musical productions, stage movement, television/video, theater/drama, vocal production.
Program Information 1 session per year. Session length: 24–30 days in July, August. Ages: 14+. 100–170 participants per session. Day program cost: $1900–$2000. Application fee: $50. Each elective costs $90; admission by audition only.
Application Deadline Continuous.
Contact Dan Justin, Director of Admissions, main address above. Phone: 800-222-2867.
URL www.aada.org
For more information, see page 414.

BRITANNIA SOCCER CAMP

Ojai Valley School
723 El Paseo Road
Ojai, California 93023

General Information Coed residential and day sports camp established in 1981.
Program Focus Soccer.
Sports Soccer.
Trips Day.
Program Information 1 session per year. Session length: 6 days in July, August. Ages: 4–16. 90–110 participants per session. Day program cost: $180–$415. Boarding program cost: $590. Application fee: $100. Financial aid available.
Application Deadline Continuous.
Jobs Positions for college students.

Contact Mike Hall-Mounsey, Director, main address above. Phone: 805-646-1423. Fax: 805-640-2588. E-mail: mhm@ovs.org.
URL www.ovs.org/britannia

CALIFORNIA STATE SUMMER SCHOOL FOR THE ARTS/INNER SPARK

California State Summer School for the Arts/Inner Spark
24700 McBean Parkway
Valencia, California 91355

General Information Coed residential arts program established in 1987. Formal opportunities for the artistically talented. Specific services available for the emotionally challenged, developmentally challenged, hearing impaired, learning disabled, physically challenged, and visually impaired. College credit may be earned.

California State Summer School for the Arts/Inner Spark

Arts Acting, animation, arts, arts and crafts (general), band, batiking, ceramics, chorus, clowning, creative writing, dance, dance (ballet), dance (folk), dance (jazz), dance (modern), dance (tap), drawing, fabric arts, film, graphic arts, jewelry making, leather working, metalworking, mime, music, music (chamber), music (classical), music (electronic/synthesized), music (ensemble), music (instrumental), music (jazz), music (vocal), music composition/arrangement, painting, photography, pottery, printmaking, puppetry, radio broadcasting, sculpture, television/video, theater/drama, weaving, woodworking.
Special Interest Areas Career exploration, computer graphics.
Sports Baseball, basketball, soccer, softball, swimming, tennis, volleyball.
Trips Cultural.
Program Information 1 session per year. Session length: 4 weeks in July, August. Ages: 14–18. 470–500 participants per session. Boarding program cost: $1400–$4500. Application fee: $20. Financial aid available.
Application Deadline February 28.
Jobs Positions for college students 18 and older.
Summer Contact Neil Brillante, Office Technician,

1010 Hurley, Suite 185, Sacramento, California 95825.
Phone: 916-274-5815. Fax: 916-274-5814. E-mail:
neil@innerspark.us.
Winter Contact Neil Brillante, Office Technician, PO
Box 1077, Sacramento, California 95812-1077. Phone:
916-274-5815. Fax: 916-274-5814. E-mail:
neil@innerspark.us.
URL www.innerspark.us
For more information, see page 438.

CAMP CALIFORNIA FITNESS

1801 Colorado Avenue, Suite 290
Turlock, California 95382

General Information Girls' residential special needs
program established in 2002. Specific services available
for the weight reduction and participant with an eating
disorder. High school credit may be earned.
Program Focus Health and fitness/weight loss
program/self-image development.
Academics Health sciences.
Arts Acting, arts and crafts (general), dance, dance
(modern), jewelry making, music, theater/drama.
Special Interest Areas Community service, culinary
arts, leadership training, nutrition, team building,
weight reduction.
Sports Aerobics, basketball, diving, football, martial
arts, physical fitness, soccer, softball, swimming, tennis,
track and field, volleyball, weight training.
Wilderness/Outdoors Hiking, white-water trips.
Trips Day, shopping.
Program Information 1–4 sessions per year. Session
length: 2–8 weeks in June, July, August. Ages: 8–18.
50–60 participants per session. Boarding program cost:
$3500–$8500.
Application Deadline Continuous.
Jobs Positions for college students 19 and older.
Contact Ms. Shawna Rocha, Executive Camp Director,
main address above. Phone: 877-FIT-KIDS. Fax: 209-
216-3405. E-mail: shawna@campcaliforniafitness.com.
URL www.campcaliforniafitness.com

CAMP PACIFIC'S RECREATIONAL CAMP

The Academy by the Sea/Camp Pacific
2605 Carlsbad Boulevard
Carlsbad, California 92008

General Information Coed residential traditional
camp established in 1943. Accredited by American
Camping Association.
Program Focus Water sports, team sports, traditional
camp activities, team work, sportsmanship.
Academics English as a second language.
Arts Arts and crafts (general), ceramics, dance, dance
(folk), drawing, jewelry making, leather working, music,
painting, pottery, printmaking, radio broadcasting,
theater/drama.
Special Interest Areas Campcraft.
Sports Baseball, basketball, body boarding, football,
kayaking, lacrosse, riflery, sea kayaking, snorkeling,
soccer, softball, surfing, swimming, tennis, volleyball,
water polo, weight training.
Trips Cultural, day, shopping.
Program Information 2 sessions per year. Session
length: 2–3 weeks in June, July, August. Ages: 8–16.
40–70 participants per session. Boarding program cost:
$1690–$2445. Application fee: $150.
Application Deadline Continuous.
Jobs Positions for college students 21 and older.
Contact Mrs. Niki Kolb, Associate Director, PO Box
3000, Carlsbad, California 92018. Phone: 760-434-7564.
Fax: 760-729-1574. E-mail: summer@abts.com.
URL www.abts.com
For more information, see page 400.

CAMP PACIFIC'S SURF AND BODYBOARD CAMP

The Academy by the Sea/Camp Pacific
2605 Carlsbad Boulevard
Carlsbad, California 92008

General Information Coed residential sports camp
established in 1943. Accredited by American Camping
Association.
Program Focus Surf and bodyboard instruction,
sports, recreational activities, field trips, and fun.
Arts Arts and crafts (general), ceramics, dance (folk),
drawing, jewelry making, leather working, music,
painting, pottery, printmaking, radio broadcasting.
Special Interest Areas Campcraft.
Sports Baseball, basketball, body boarding, football,
kayaking, lacrosse, riflery, sea kayaking, snorkeling,
soccer, softball, surfing, swimming, tennis, volleyball,
water polo, weight training.
Trips Day, shopping.
Program Information 1 session per year. Session
length: 1 week in June, July, August. Ages: 8–16. 40–70
participants per session. Boarding program cost: $880.
Application fee: $150.
Application Deadline Continuous.
Jobs Positions for college students 21 and older.

Camp Pacific's Surf and Bodyboard Camp (continued)
Contact Mrs. Niki Kolb, Associate Director, PO Box 3000, Carlsbad, California 92018. Phone: 760-434-7564. Fax: 760-729-1574. E-mail: summer@abts.com.
URL www.abts.com
For more information, see page 400.

CROSSROADS SCHOOL–AQUATICS

Crossroads School for Arts and Sciences
1714 21st Street
Santa Monica, California 90404

General Information Coed day sports camp established in 2000. Specific services available for the physically challenged.
Program Focus Developing swim and water safety skills, 3 years to adult with private lessons.
Special Interest Areas Lifesaving.
Sports Swimming, water aerobics.
Program Information 1–7 sessions per year. Session length: 5–6 days in April, May, June, July, August, September, October. Ages: 3+. 10–200 participants per session. Day program cost: $270. Application fee: $40. Financial aid available.
Application Deadline Continuous.
Jobs Positions for high school students 14 and older and college students.
Contact Angela Smith, Director of Summer Programs, main address above. Phone: 310-829-7391 Ext.506. Fax: 310-828-8147. E-mail: summer@xrds.org.
URL www.xrds.org

CROSSROADS SCHOOL–JAZZ WORKSHOP

Crossroads School for Arts and Sciences
1714 21st Street
Santa Monica, California 90404

General Information Coed day arts program established in 2001. High school credit may be earned.
Program Focus Jazz.
Arts Band, music (ensemble), music (instrumental), music (jazz), music theory, musical performance/recitals.
Trips Day.
Program Information 1 session per year. Session length: 30 days in June, July, August. Ages: 11–18. 100 participants per session. Day program cost: $1300. Application fee: $40. Financial aid available.
Application Deadline Continuous.

Contact Angela Smith, Director, Summer Program, main address above. Phone: 310-829-7391 Ext.506. Fax: 310-828-8147. E-mail: summer@xrds.org.
URL www.xrds.org

CROSSROADS SCHOOL–SPORTS CAMPS

Crossroads School for Arts and Sciences
1714 21st Street
Santa Monica, California 90404

General Information Coed day sports camp established in 2000.
Program Focus Instructional, skill development.
Sports Basketball, football, golf, soccer, softball, sports (general), swimming, volleyball.
Trips Day.
Program Information 1–17 sessions per year. Session length: 5 days in June, July, August. Ages: 5–14. 100 participants per session. Day program cost: $375. Application fee: $40. Financial aid available. Open to participants entering grades 1–6.
Application Deadline Continuous.
Jobs Positions for high school students 14 and older and college students.
Contact Angela Smith, Director of Summer Programs, main address above. Phone: 310-829-7391 Ext.506. Fax: 310-828-8147. E-mail: summer@xrds.org.
URL www.xrds.org

CROSSROADS SCHOOL–SUMMER EDUCATIONAL JOURNEY

Crossroads School for Arts and Sciences
1714 21st Street
Santa Monica, California 90404

General Information Coed day academic program and arts program established in 1980. High school credit may be earned.
Program Focus Academic credit and enrichment; the arts; sports for K-12.
Academics English language/literature, French language/literature, Japanese language/literature, Latin language, SAT/ACT preparation, Spanish language/literature, academics (general), biology, chemistry, computer programming, computers, geology/earth science, history, humanities, mathematics, music, oceanography, physics, reading, science (general), social science, social studies, speech/debate, study skills, typing, writing.
Arts Acting, animation, band, cartooning, ceramics, creative writing, dance, dance (ballet), dance (jazz), dance (modern), drawing, film, graphic arts, jewelry making, music, music (classical), music (ensemble), music (instrumental), music (jazz), music (orchestral), music (vocal), musical productions, painting, photography, pottery, screenwriting, sculpture, studio arts, television/video, theater/drama.
Special Interest Areas Computer game design, culinary arts.
Sports Basketball, climbing (wall), fencing, flag football, football, in-line skating, martial arts, physical

fitness, sailing, sea kayaking, soccer, street/roller hockey, surfing, swimming, volleyball, weight training, yoga.
Wilderness/Outdoors Rock climbing.
Trips Cultural, day, overnight.
Program Information 1–5 sessions per year. Session length: 15–30 days in June, July, August. Ages: 5–18. 300–1,100 participants per session. Day program cost: $375–$1400. Application fee: $40. Financial aid available.
Application Deadline Continuous.
Jobs Positions for high school students 14 and older and college students.
Contact Angela Smith, Director of Summer Programs, Crossroads School, main address above. Phone: 310-829-7391 Ext.506. Fax: 310-828-8147. E-mail: summer@xrds.org.
URL www.xrds.org

Cybercamps–Concordia University, Irvine

Cybercamps–Giant Campus, Inc.
Irvine, California

General Information Coed residential and day academic program established in 1997. Formal opportunities for the academically talented.
Program Focus Computers and technology.
Academics Web page design, academics (general), computer programming, computer science (Advanced Placement), computers.
Arts Animation, digital media, film, graphic arts, musical productions, photography, television/video.
Special Interest Areas Computer game design, electronics, robotics, team building.
Program Information 1–12 sessions per year. Session length: 5 days in June, July, August. Ages: 7–18. 30–50 participants per session. Day program cost: $599–$749. Boarding program cost: $998–$1140.
Application Deadline Continuous.
Jobs Positions for high school students 17 and older and college students 18 and older.

Contact Camp Consultant, 3101 Western Avenue, Suite 100, Seattle, Washington 98121. Phone: 888-904-2267. Fax: 206-442-4501. E-mail: info@cybercamps.com.
URL www.cybercamps.com
For more information, see page 466.

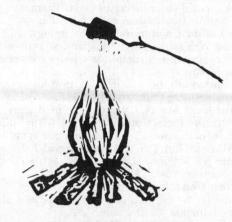

Cybercamps–DeAnza College

Cybercamps–Giant Campus, Inc.
Cupertino, California

General Information Coed residential and day academic program established in 1997. Formal opportunities for the academically talented.
Program Focus Computers and technology.
Academics Web page design, academics (general), computer programming, computer science (Advanced Placement), computers.
Arts Animation, digital media, film, graphic arts, musical productions, photography, television/video.
Special Interest Areas Computer game design, computer graphics, electronics, robotics, team building.
Program Information 1–12 sessions per year. Session length: 5 days in June, July, August. Ages: 7–18. 30–50 participants per session. Day program cost: $599–$749. Boarding program cost: $998–$1148.
Application Deadline Continuous.
Jobs Positions for high school students 17 and older and college students 18 and older.
Contact Camp Consultant, 3101 Western Avenue, Suite 100, Seattle, Washington 98121. Phone: 888-904-2267. Fax: 206-442-4501. E-mail: info@cybercamps.com.
URL www.cybercamps.com
For more information, see page 466.

Cybercamps–Stanford University

Cybercamps–Giant Campus, Inc.
Palo Alto, California

General Information Coed residential and day academic program established in 2004. Formal opportunities for the academically talented.
Program Focus Computers and technology.
Academics Web page design, academics (general), computer programming, computer science (Advanced Placement), computers.
Arts Animation, digital media, film, graphic arts, musical productions, photography, television/video.
Special Interest Areas Computer game design, computer graphics, electronics, robotics, team building.
Program Information 1–12 sessions per year. Session length: 5 days in June, July, August. Ages: 7–18. 30–50 participants per session. Day program cost: $599–$749. Boarding program cost: $998–$1148.
Application Deadline Continuous.
Jobs Positions for high school students 17 and older and college students 18 and older.
Contact Camp Consultant, 3101 Western Avenue, Suite 100, Seattle, Washington 98121. Phone: 888-904-2267. Fax: 206-442-4501. E-mail: info@cybercamps.com.
URL www.cybercamps.com
For more information, see page 466.

Cybercamps–UCLA

Cybercamps–Giant Campus, Inc.
Los Angeles, California

General Information Coed residential and day academic program established in 1997. Formal opportunities for the academically talented.
Program Focus Computers and technology.
Academics Web page design, academics (general), computer programming, computer science (Advanced Placement), computers.
Arts Animation, digital media, film, graphic arts, musical productions, photography, television/video.
Special Interest Areas Computer game design, computer graphics, electronics, robotics, team building.
Program Information 1–12 sessions per year. Session length: 5 days in June, July, August. Ages: 7–18. 30–50 participants per session. Day program cost: $599–$749. Boarding program cost: $998–$1148.
Application Deadline Continuous.
Jobs Positions for high school students 17 and older and college students 18 and older.
Contact Camp Consultant, 3101 Western Avenue, Suite 100, Seattle, Washington 98121. Phone: 888-904-2267. Fax: 206-442-4501. E-mail: info@cybercamps.com.
URL www.cybercamps.com
For more information, see page 466.

Cybercamps–UC San Diego (UCSD)

Cybercamps–Giant Campus, Inc.
La Jolla, California

General Information Coed residential and day academic program established in 1997. Formal opportunities for the academically talented.
Program Focus Computers and technology.
Academics Web page design, academics (general), computer programming, computer science (Advanced Placement), computers.
Arts Animation, digital media, film, graphic arts, musical productions, photography, television/video.
Special Interest Areas Computer game design, computer graphics, electronics, robotics, team building.
Program Information 1–12 sessions per year. Session length: 5 days in June, July, August. Ages: 7–18. 30–50 participants per session. Day program cost: $599–$749. Boarding program cost: $998–$1148.
Application Deadline Continuous.
Jobs Positions for high school students 17 and older and college students 18 and older.
Contact Camp Consultant, 3101 Western Avenue, Suite 100, Seattle, Washington 98121. Phone: 888-904-2267. Fax: 206-442-4501. E-mail: info@cybercamps.com.
URL www.cybercamps.com
For more information, see page 466.

Cybercamps–University of California at Berkeley

Cybercamps–Giant Campus, Inc.
University of California at Berkeley
Berkeley, California

General Information Coed residential and day academic program established in 1997. Formal opportunities for the academically talented.
Program Focus Computers and technology.
Academics Web page design, academics (general), computer programming, computer science (Advanced Placement), computers.
Arts Animation, digital media, film, graphic arts, musical productions, photography, television/video.
Special Interest Areas Computer game design, computer graphics, electronics, robotics, team building.
Program Information 1–12 sessions per year. Session length: 5 days in June, July, August. Ages: 7–18. 30–50

participants per session. Day program cost: $599–$749. Boarding program cost: $998–$1148.
Application Deadline Continuous.
Jobs Positions for high school students 17 and older and college students 18 and older.
Contact Camp Consultant, 3101 Western Avenue, Suite 100, Seattle, Washington 98121. Phone: 888-904-2267. Fax: 206-442-4501. E-mail: info@cybercamps.com.
URL www.cybercamps.com
For more information, see page 466.

ELITE EDUCATIONAL INSTITUTE ELEMENTARY ENRICHMENT

Elite Educational Institute
California

General Information Coed day academic program established in 1987. Formal opportunities for the academically talented.
Program Focus Elementary enrichment: 3rd–6th grade.
Academics English as a second language, English language/literature, SAT/ACT preparation, mathematics, precollege program, reading, social studies, study skills, writing.
Program Information 3 sessions per year. Session length: 100–350 days in January, February, March, April, May, June, July, August, September, October, November, December. Ages: 9–12. 10–40 participants per session. Day program cost: $280–$360. Application fee: $50.
Application Deadline Continuous.
Contact Julian Chou, Program Director, 19735 Colima Road, # 2, Rowland Heights, California 91748. Phone: 909-444-0876. Fax: 909-444-0877. E-mail: julian. chou@eliteprep.com.
URL www.eliteprep.com
For more information, see page 480.

ELITE EDUCATIONAL INSTITUTE JUNIOR HIGH/PSAT PROGRAM

Elite Educational Institute
California

General Information Coed day academic program established in 1987. Formal opportunities for the academically talented.
Academics English as a second language, English language/literature, SAT/ACT preparation, mathematics, reading, study skills, writing.
Special Interest Areas College planning.
Program Information 3 sessions per year. Session length: 100–350 days in January, February, March, April, May, June, July, August, September, October, November, December. Ages: 12–14. 40–80 participants per session. Day program cost: $240–$360. Application fee: $50. Open to participants entering grades 7–9.
Application Deadline Continuous.

Contact Julian Chou, Program Director, 19735 Colima Road, # 2, Rowland Heights, California 91748. Phone: 909-444-0876. Fax: 909-444-0877. E-mail: julian. chou@eliteprep.com.
URL www.eliteprep.com
For more information, see page 480.

ELITE EDUCATIONAL INSTITUTE SAT AND SUBJECT TEST PREPARATION

Elite Educational Institute
California

General Information Coed day academic program established in 1987. Formal opportunities for the academically talented.
Program Focus SAT and Subject Test preparation.
Academics American literature, English language/ literature, SAT/ACT preparation, biology, biology (Advanced Placement), chemistry, history, mathematics, mathematics (Advanced Placement), physics, precollege program, reading, writing.
Special Interest Areas College planning.
Program Information 3 sessions per year. Session length: 100–350 days in January, February, March, April, May, June, July, August, September, October, November, December. Ages: 15–18. 100–300 participants per session. Day program cost: $380–$600. Application fee: $50.
Application Deadline Continuous.
Jobs Positions for college students.
Contact Julian Chou, Program Director, 19735 Colima Road, # 2, Rowland Heights, California 91748. Phone: 909-444-0876. Fax: 909-444-0877. E-mail: Julian. chou@eliteprep.com.
URL www.eliteprep.com
For more information, see page 480.

ELITE EDUCATIONAL INSTITUTE SAT SUMMER BOOTCAMP

Elite Educational Institute
California

General Information Coed day academic program established in 1987. Formal opportunities for the academically talented.

Elite Educational Institute SAT Summer Bootcamp (continued)

Program Focus Intensive SAT preparation program.
Academics English language/literature, SAT/ACT preparation, mathematics, precollege program, reading, writing.
Special Interest Areas College planning.
Program Information 1 session per year. Session length: 40 days in June, July, August. Ages: 15–18. 100–300 participants per session. Day program cost: $2200. Application fee: $50.
Application Deadline June 15.
Contact Julian Chou, Program Director, 19735 Colima Road, # 2, Rowland Heights, California 91748. Phone: 909-444-0876. Fax: 909-444-0877. E-mail: julian. chou@eliteprep.com.
URL www.eliteprep.com
For more information, see page 480.

ELITE EDUCATIONAL INSTITUTE–UNIVERSITY OF OKLAHOMA COLLEGE COURSES

Elite Educational Institute
California

General Information Coed day academic program established in 2006. Formal opportunities for the academically talented. High school or college credit may be earned.
Program Focus College courses for credit.
Academics English language/literature, anthropology, astronomy, economics, geography, geology/earth science, history, mathematics, psychology, social science, social studies.
Special Interest Areas College planning.
Program Information 2–3 sessions per year. Session length: 40–60 days in January, February, March, April, May, June, July, August, September, October, November, December. Ages: 15–18. 20–40 participants per session. Day program cost: $1100–$1300. Application fee: $50.
Application Deadline June 15.
Contact Mr. Julian Chou, Program Director, 19735 Colima Road, # 2, Rowland Heights, California 91748. Phone: 909-444-0876. Fax: 909-444-0877. E-mail: julian.chou@eliteprep.com.
URL www.eliteprep.com
For more information, see page 480.

EXPLORATION OF ARCHITECTURE

University of Southern California, School of Architecture
Watt Hall, Room 204
Los Angeles, California 90089-0291

General Information Coed residential academic program established in 1983. Specific services available for the physically challenged. College credit may be earned.

Exploration of Architecture

Program Focus Architecture and design.
Academics Architecture.
Trips Cultural.
Program Information 2 sessions per year. Session length: 2–4 weeks in July. Ages: 15–18. 60–100 participants per session. Boarding program cost: $2700–$4485. Financial aid available. College credit available for 4-week program only.
Application Deadline Continuous.
Jobs Positions for college students 18 and older.
Contact Ms. Jennifer Park, Director of Undergraduate Admission, USC School of Architecture, Watt Hall 204, Los Angeles, California 90089-0291. Phone: 213-740-2420. Fax: 213-740-8884. E-mail: jenpark@usc.edu.
URL arch.usc.edu
For more information, see page 688.

HARKER SUMMER ENGLISH LANGUAGE INSTITUTE

The Harker School
500 Saratoga Avenue
San Jose, California 95129

General Information Coed day academic program established in 1984.
Program Focus English as a second language.
Academics English as a second language, English language/literature, reading, study skills, vocabulary, writing.

Arts Arts and crafts (general), clowning, dance, music.
Sports Archery, basketball, climbing (wall), flag football, in-line skating, soccer, swimming, tennis, volleyball.
Trips Cultural, day, overnight.
Program Information 1–4 sessions per year. Session length: 15–40 days in June, July, August. Ages: 8–15. 50–80 participants per session. Day program cost: $4500–$8500.
Application Deadline Continuous.
Contact Mr. Joe Rosenthal, Executive Director of Advancement, 500 Saratoga Avenue, San Jose, California 95129. Phone: 408-345-9264. Fax: 408-984-2395. E-mail: eli@harker.org.
URL www.harker.org/eli/index.htm

THE HARKER SUMMER INSTITUTE

The Harker School
500 Saratoga Avenue
San Jose, California 95129

General Information Coed day academic program established in 1999. Formal opportunities for the academically talented and artistically talented. High school credit may be earned.
Program Focus Choose from high school classes for academic credit, language studies abroad, academic enrichment.
Academics SAT/ACT preparation, Spanish language/literature, academics (general), biology, chemistry, computer programming, computers, mathematics, speech/debate, writing.
Arts Drawing, graphic arts.
Special Interest Areas Computer game design.
Program Information 8 sessions per year. Session length: 7–30 days in June, July, August. Ages: 12–17. 200–300 participants per session. Day program cost: $685–$1320.
Application Deadline Continuous.
Contact Jada Burrell, Summer Programs Assistant, main address above. Phone: 408-871-4626. Fax: 408-984-2325. E-mail: campinfo@harker.org.
URL www.harker.org/

HARKER SUMMER PROGRAMS

The Harker School
4300 Bucknall Road
San Jose, California 95130

General Information Coed day traditional camp and academic program established in 1957. Accredited by American Camping Association.
Program Focus Enriched academics in the morning and recreation activities in the afternoon.
Academics English language/literature, academics (general), biology, chemistry, computers, ecology, geology/earth science, health sciences, mathematics, music, reading, science (general), writing.
Arts Arts and crafts (general), clowning, creative writing, dance, drawing, film, graphic arts, music, painting, photography, theater/drama.
Special Interest Areas Leadership training.
Sports Archery, basketball, climbing (wall), football, in-line skating, soccer, softball, street/roller hockey, swimming, tennis, volleyball.
Trips Day.
Program Information 5 sessions per year. Session length: 10–42 days in June, July, August. Ages: 5–14. 200–400 participants per session. Day program cost: $1225–$2550.
Application Deadline Continuous.
Jobs Positions for high school students 16 and older and college students 19 and older.
Contact Kelly Espinosa, Dean Non-Academics/Summer Programs Director, main address above. Phone: 408-871-4611. Fax: 408-871-4320. E-mail: campinfo@harker.org.
URL www.harker.org/

iD GAMING ACADEMY–STANFORD UNIVERSITY, PALO ALTO, CA

iD Tech Camps
Palo Alto, California

General Information Coed residential academic program established in 1999. Accredited by American Camping Association. Formal opportunities for the academically talented and artistically talented.
Program Focus Three weeks of intensive study in video game creation and development. Using industry-standard applications, each student will learn basics of 3D graphics production, including modeling, texturing, and animation, and create their own 3D game level and a personal portfolio of their animated game models.
Academics Web page design, academics (general), computer programming, computer science (Advanced Placement), computers, precollege program.
Arts Animation, cinematography, digital media, drawing, film, film editing, film production, graphic arts, photography, television/video.
Special Interest Areas Career exploration, computer game design, computer graphics, electronics, leadership training, robotics, team building.
Sports Baseball, basketball, soccer, softball, swimming, volleyball.
Trips College tours.
Program Information 4 sessions per year. Session

iD Gaming Academy–Stanford University, Palo Alto, CA (continued)

length: 15–19 days in June, July, August. Ages: 13–17. 40–50 participants per session. Boarding program cost: $3999. Financial aid available. Weekend stays (optional) cost $600 additional for the two weekends during the program.

Application Deadline Continuous.

Contact Client Service Representatives, 42 West Campbell Avenue, Suite 301, Campbell, California 95008. Phone: 888-709-TECH. Fax: 408-871-2228. E-mail: info@internaldrive.com.

URL www.internaldrive.com

For more information, see page 520.

iD Gaming Academy–UC Berkeley, Berkeley, CA

iD Tech Camps
Berkeley, California

General Information Coed residential academic program established in 1999. Accredited by American Camping Association. Formal opportunities for the academically talented and artistically talented.

Program Focus Three weeks of intensive study in video game creation and development. Using industry-standard applications, each student will learn basics of 3D graphics production, including modeling, texturing, and animation, and create their own 3D game level and a personal portfolio of their animated game models.

Academics Web page design, academics (general), computer programming, computer science (Advanced Placement), computers, precollege program.

Arts Animation, cinematography, digital media, drawing, film, film editing, film production, graphic arts, photography, television/video.

Special Interest Areas Career exploration, computer game design, computer graphics, electronics, leadership training, robotics, team building.

Sports Baseball, basketball, soccer, softball, swimming, volleyball.

Trips College tours.

Program Information 4 sessions per year. Session length: 15–19 days in June, July, August. Ages: 13–17. 40–50 participants per session. Boarding program cost: $3999. Financial aid available. Weekend stays (optional) cost $600 additional for the two weekends during the program.

Application Deadline Continuous.

Contact Client Service Representatives, 42 West Campbell Avenue, Suite 301, Campbell, California 95008. Phone: 888-709-TECH. Fax: 408-871-2228. E-mail: info@internaldrive.com.

URL www.internaldrive.com

For more information, see page 520.

iD Gaming Academy–UCLA, Westwood, CA

iD Tech Camps
Westwood, California

General Information Coed residential academic program established in 1999. Accredited by American Camping Association. Formal opportunities for the academically talented and artistically talented.

Program Focus Three weeks of intensive study in video game creation and development. Using industry-standard applications, each student will learn basics of 3D graphics production, including modeling, texturing, and animation, and create their own 3D game level and a personal portfolio of their animated game models.

Academics Web page design, academics (general), computer programming, computer science (Advanced Placement), computers, precollege program.

Arts Animation, cinematography, digital media, drawing, film, film editing, film production, graphic arts, photography, television/video.

Special Interest Areas Career exploration, computer game design, computer graphics, electronics, leadership training, robotics, team building.

Sports Baseball, basketball, soccer, softball, swimming, volleyball.

Trips College tours.

Program Information 4 sessions per year. Session length: 15–19 days in June, July, August. Ages: 13–17. 40–50 participants per session. Boarding program cost: $3999. Financial aid available. Weekend stays (optional) costs $600 additional for the two weekends during the program.

Application Deadline Continuous.

Contact Client Service Representatives, 42 West Campbell Avenue, Suite 301, Campbell, California 95008. Phone: 888-709-TECH. Fax: 408-871-2228. E-mail: info@internaldrive.com.

URL www.internaldrive.com

For more information, see page 520.

iD Tech Camps—Cal Lutheran University, Thousand Oaks, CA

iD Tech Camps
California Lutheran University
Thousand Oaks, California 91360

General Information Coed day academic program established in 1999. Accredited by American Camping Association. Formal opportunities for the academically talented and artistically talented.
Program Focus Students create 2D and 3D video games, build robots to compete, design websites, film and edit digital movies, create their own comic book with digital photos, learn programming and more. One computer per student and an average of five students per staff member. Campers take home a project at the end of the weeklong course.
Academics Web page design, academics (general), computer programming, computer science (Advanced Placement), computers, precollege program.
Arts Animation, cartooning, cinematography, digital media, drawing, film, film editing, film production, graphic arts, photography, television/video.
Special Interest Areas Career exploration, computer game design, computer graphics, electronics, leadership training, robotics, team building.
Sports Baseball, basketball, soccer, softball, swimming, volleyball.
Trips College tours.
Program Information 5–9 sessions per year. Session length: 5–7 days in June, July, August. Ages: 7–17. 40–50 participants per session. Day program cost: $729. Financial aid available.
Application Deadline Continuous.
Jobs Positions for college students 18 and older.
Contact Client Service Representatives, 42 West Campbell Avenue, Suite 301, Campbell, California 95008. Phone: 888-709-TECH. Fax: 408-871-2228. E-mail: info@internaldrive.com.
URL www.internaldrive.com
For more information, see page 520.

iD Tech Camps—Pepperdine University, Malibu, CA

iD Tech Camps
Pepperdine University
Malibu, California 90263

General Information Coed residential and day academic program established in 1999. Accredited by American Camping Association. Formal opportunities for the academically talented and artistically talented.
Program Focus Students create 2D and 3D video games, build robots to compete, design websites, film and edit digital movies, create their own comic book with digital photos, learn programming and more. One computer per student and an average of five students per staff member. Campers take home a project at the end of the weeklong course.
Academics Web page design, academics (general), computer programming, computer science (Advanced

Placement), computers, precollege program.
Arts Animation, cartooning, cinematography, digital media, drawing, film, film editing, film production, graphic arts, photography, television/video.
Special Interest Areas Career exploration, computer game design, computer graphics, electronics, leadership training, robotics, team building.
Sports Baseball, basketball, soccer, softball, swimming, volleyball.
Trips College tours.
Program Information 5–9 sessions per year. Session length: 5–7 days in June, July, August. Ages: 7–17. 40–50 participants per session. Day program cost: $729. Boarding program cost: $1129. Financial aid available.
Application Deadline Continuous.
Jobs Positions for college students 18 and older.
Contact Client Service Representatives, 42 West Campbell Avenue, Suite 301, Campbell, California 95008. Phone: 888-709-TECH. Fax: 408-871-2228. E-mail: info@internaldrive.com.
URL www.internaldrive.com
For more information, see page 520.

iD Tech Camps—St. Mary's College of California, Moraga, CA

iD Tech Camps
St. Mary's College
Moraga, California 94575

General Information Coed day academic program established in 1999. Accredited by American Camping Association. Formal opportunities for the academically talented and artistically talented.
Program Focus Students create 2D and 3D video games, build robots to compete, design websites, film and edit digital movies, create their own comic book with digital photos, learn programming and more. One computer per student and an average of five students per staff member. Campers take home a project at the end of the weeklong course.
Academics Web page design, academics (general), computer programming, computer science (Advanced Placement), computers, precollege program.
Arts Animation, cinematography, digital media, drawing, film, film editing, film production, graphic arts, photography, television/video.
Special Interest Areas Computer game design, computer graphics, electronics, leadership training, robotics, team building.
Sports Baseball, basketball, soccer, softball, swimming, volleyball.
Trips College tours.
Program Information 5–9 sessions per year. Session length: 5–7 days in June, July, August. Ages: 7–17. 40–50 participants per session. Day program cost: $729. Financial aid available.
Application Deadline Continuous.
Jobs Positions for college students 18 and older.

iD Tech Camps–St. Mary's College of California, Moraga, CA (continued)

Contact Client Service Representatives, 42 West Campbell Avenue, Suite 301, Campbell, California 95008. Phone: 888-709-TECH. Fax: 408-871-2228. E-mail: info@internaldrive.com.
URL www.internaldrive.com
For more information, see page 520.

iD Tech Camps–Santa Clara University, Santa Clara, CA

iD Tech Camps
Santa Clara University
Santa Clara, California 95053

General Information Coed day academic program established in 1999. Accredited by American Camping Association. Formal opportunities for the academically talented and artistically talented.
Program Focus Students create 2D and 3D video games, build robots to compete, design websites, film and edit digital movies, create their own comic book with digital photos, learn programming and more. One computer per student and an average of five students per staff member. Campers take home a project at the end of the weeklong course.
Academics Web page design, academics (general), computer programming, computer science (Advanced Placement), computers, precollege program.
Arts Animation, cinematography, digital media, drawing, film, film editing, film production, graphic arts, photography, television/video.
Special Interest Areas Career exploration, computer game design, computer graphics, electronics, leadership training, robotics, team building.
Sports Baseball, basketball, soccer, softball, swimming, volleyball.
Trips College tours.
Program Information 5–9 sessions per year. Session length: 5–7 days in June, July, August. Ages: 7–17. 40–50 participants per session. Day program cost: $729. Financial aid available.
Application Deadline Continuous.
Jobs Positions for college students 18 and older.

Contact Client Service Representatives, 42 West Campbell Avenue, Suite 301, Campbell, California 95008. Phone: 888-709-TECH. Fax: 408-871-2228. E-mail: info@internaldrive.com
URL www.internaldrive.com
For more information, see page 520.

iD Tech Camps–Stanford University, Palo Alto, CA

iD Tech Camps
Stanford University
Palo Alto, California 94305

General Information Coed residential and day academic program and sports camp established in 1999. Accredited by American Camping Association. Formal opportunities for the academically talented and artistically talented.
Program Focus Create 2D/3D video games, build robots, design websites, film and edit digital movies, create their own comic book with digital photos, learn programming. One computer per student, average of five students per staff member. Take home a project at the end of the weeklong course. For an additional fee, Sports & Tech allows campers to spend half the day in the computer lab and the other half working on their skill in taekwondo, tennis, golf, or fencing with University Athletics staff..
Academics Web page design, academics (general), computer programming, computer science (Advanced Placement), computers, precollege program.
Arts Animation, cartooning, cinematography, digital media, drawing, film, film editing, film production, graphic arts, photography, television/video.
Special Interest Areas Career exploration, computer game design, computer graphics, electronics, leadership training, robotics, team building.
Sports Baseball, basketball, fencing, golf, martial arts, soccer, softball, swimming, tennis, volleyball.
Trips College tours.
Program Information 5–9 sessions per year. Session length: 5–7 days in June, July, August. Ages: 7–17. 100–150 participants per session. Day program cost: $729. Boarding program cost: $1129. Financial aid available.
Application Deadline Continuous.
Jobs Positions for college students 18 and older.
Contact Client Service Representatives, 42 West Campbell Avenue, Suite 301, Campbell, California 95008. Phone: 888-709-TECH. Fax: 408-871-2228. E-mail: info@internaldrive.com.
URL www.internaldrive.com
For more information, see page 520.

iD TECH CAMPS–TIGER WOODS LEARNING CENTER, ANAHEIM, CA

iD Tech Camps
Tiger Woods Learning Center
Anaheim, California 92801

General Information Coed residential and day academic program established in 1999. Accredited by American Camping Association. Formal opportunities for the academically talented and artistically talented.

Program Focus Students create 2D and 3D video games, build robots to compete, design websites, film and edit digital movies, create their own comic book with digital photos, learn programming and more. One computer per student and an average of five students per staff member. Campers take home a project at the end of the weeklong course.

Academics Web page design, academics (general), computer programming, computer science (Advanced Placement), computers, precollege program.

Arts Animation, cartooning, cinematography, digital media, drawing, film, film editing, film production, graphic arts, photography, television/video.

Special Interest Areas Career exploration, computer game design, computer graphics, electronics, leadership training, robotics, team building.

Sports Baseball, basketball, soccer, softball, swimming, volleyball.

Trips College tours.

Program Information 5–9 sessions per year. Session length: 5–7 days in June, July, August. Ages: 7–17. 40–50 participants per session. Day program cost: $729. Boarding program cost: $1129. Financial aid available.

Application Deadline Continuous.

Jobs Positions for college students 18 and older.

Contact Client Service Representatives, 42 West Campbell Avenue, Suite 301, Campbell, California 95008. Phone: 888-709-TECH. Fax: 408-871-2228. E-mail: info@internaldrive.com.

URL www.internaldrive.com

For more information, see page 520.

iD TECH CAMPS–UC BERKELEY, BERKELEY, CA

iD Tech Camps
University of California, Berkeley
Berkeley, California 94720

General Information Coed residential and day academic program established in 1999. Accredited by American Camping Association. Formal opportunities for the academically talented and artistically talented.

iD Tech Camps–UC Berkeley, Berkeley, CA

Program Focus Students create 2D and 3D video games, build robots to compete, design websites, film and edit digital movies, create their own comic book with digital photos, learn programming and more. One computer per student and an average of five students per staff member. Campers take home a project at the end of the weeklong course.

Academics Web page design, academics (general), computer programming, computer science (Advanced Placement), computers, precollege program.

Arts Animation, cartooning, cinematography, digital media, drawing, film, film editing, film production, graphic arts, photography, television/video.

Special Interest Areas Career exploration, computer game design, computer graphics, electronics, leadership training, robotics, team building.

Sports Baseball, basketball, soccer, softball, swimming, volleyball.

Trips College tours.

Program Information 5–9 sessions per year. Session length: 5–7 days in June, July, August. Ages: 7–17. 40–50 participants per session. Day program cost: $729. Boarding program cost: $1129. Financial aid available.

Application Deadline Continuous.

Jobs Positions for college students 18 and older.

iD Tech Camps–UC Berkeley, Berkeley, CA (continued)

Contact Client Service Representatives, 42 West Campbell Avenue, Suite 301, Campbell, California 95008. Phone: 888-709-TECH. Fax: 408-871-2228. E-mail: info@internaldrive.com.
URL www.internaldrive.com
For more information, see page 520.

iD Tech Camps–UC Davis, Davis, CA

iD Tech Camps
University of California, Davis
Davis, California

General Information Coed residential and day academic program established in 1999. Accredited by American Camping Association. Formal opportunities for the academically talented and artistically talented.
Program Focus Students create 2D and 3D video games, build robots to compete, design websites, film and edit digital movies, create their own comic book with digital photos, learn programming and more. One computer per student and an average of five students per staff member. Campers take home a project at the end of the weeklong course.
Academics Web page design, academics (general), computer programming, computer science (Advanced Placement), computers, precollege program.
Arts Animation, cinematography, digital media, drawing, film, film editing, film production, graphic arts, television/video.
Special Interest Areas Career exploration, computer game design, computer graphics, electronics, leadership training, robotics, team building.
Sports Baseball, basketball, soccer, softball, swimming, volleyball.
Trips College tours.
Program Information 5–9 sessions per year. Session length: 5–7 days in June, July, August. Ages: 7–17. 40–50 participants per session. Day program cost: $729. Boarding program cost: $1129. Financial aid available.
Application Deadline Continuous.
Jobs Positions for college students 18 and older.
Contact Client Service Representatives, 42 West Campbell Avenue, Suite 301, Campbell, California 95008. Phone: 888-709-TECH. Fax: 408-871-2228. E-mail: info@internaldrive.com.
URL www.internaldrive.com
For more information, see page 520.

iD Tech Camps–UC Irvine, Irvine, CA

iD Tech Camps
University of California at Irvine
Irvine, California 92697

General Information Coed residential and day academic program established in 1999. Accredited by American Camping Association. Formal opportunities for the academically talented and artistically talented.
Program Focus Students create 2D and 3D video games, build robots to compete, design websites, film and edit digital movies, create their own comic book with digital photos, learn programming and more. One computer per student and an average of five students per staff member. Campers take home a project at the end of the weeklong course.
Academics Web page design, academics (general), computer programming, computer science (Advanced Placement), computers, precollege program.
Arts Animation, cinematography, digital media, drawing, film, film editing, film production, graphic arts, photography, television/video.
Special Interest Areas Career exploration, computer game design, computer graphics, electronics, leadership training, robotics, team building.
Sports Baseball, basketball, soccer, softball, swimming, volleyball.
Trips College tours.
Program Information 5–9 sessions per year. Session length: 5–7 days in June, July, August. Ages: 7–17. 40–50 participants per session. Day program cost: $729. Boarding program cost: $1129. Financial aid available.
Application Deadline Continuous.
Jobs Positions for college students 18 and older.
Contact Client Service Representatives, 42 West Campbell Avenue, Suite 301, Campbell, California 95008. Phone: 888-709-TECH. Fax: 408-871-2228. E-mail: info@internaldrive.com.
URL www.internaldrive.com
For more information, see page 520.

iD Tech Camps–UCLA, Westwood, CA

iD Tech Camps
University of California, Los Angeles
Westwood, California 90095

General Information Coed residential and day academic program established in 1999. Accredited by American Camping Association. Formal opportunities for the academically talented and artistically talented.
Program Focus Students create 2D and 3D video games, build robots to compete, design websites, film and edit digital movies, create their own comic book with digital photos, learn programming and more. One computer per student and an average of five students per staff member. Campers take home a project at the end of the weeklong course.
Academics Web page design, academics (general), computer programming, computer science (Advanced

CALIFORNIA

Placement), computers, precollege program.
Arts Animation, cartooning, cinematography, digital media, drawing, film, film editing, film production, graphic arts, photography, television/video.
Special Interest Areas Career exploration, computer game design, computer graphics, electronics, leadership training, robotics, team building.
Sports Baseball, basketball, soccer, softball, swimming, volleyball.
Trips College tours.
Program Information 5–9 sessions per year. Session length: 5–7 days in June, July, August. Ages: 7–17. 40–50 participants per session. Day program cost: $729. Boarding program cost: $1129. Financial aid available.
Application Deadline Continuous.
Jobs Positions for college students 18 and older.
Contact Client Service Representatives, 42 West Campbell Avenue, Suite 301, Campbell, California 95008. Phone: 888-709-TECH. Fax: 408-871-2228. E-mail: info@internaldrive.com.
URL www.internaldrive.com
For more information, see page 520.

iD Tech Camps–UC San Diego, La Jolla, CA

iD Tech Camps
University of California, San Diego
La Jolla, California 92093

General Information Coed residential and day academic program and sports camp established in 1999. Accredited by American Camping Association. Formal opportunities for the academically talented and artistically talented.
Program Focus Students create 2D and 3D video games, build robots to compete, design websites, film and edit digital movies, create their own comic book with digital photos, learn programming and more. One computer per student and an average of five students per staff member. Campers take home a project at the end of the weeklong course. For an additional fee, Surf & Tech option allows campers to spend half the day in the computer lab and the other half working on their surfing skills with Club Ed's Surf Camp.
Academics Web page design, academics (general), computer programming, computer science (Advanced Placement), computers, precollege program.
Arts Animation, cartooning, cinematography, digital media, drawing, film, film editing, film production, graphic arts, photography, television/video.
Special Interest Areas Career exploration, computer game design, computer graphics, electronics, leadership training, robotics, team building.
Sports Baseball, basketball, soccer, softball, surfing, swimming, volleyball.
Trips College tours.
Program Information 5–9 sessions per year. Session length: 5–7 days in June, July, August. Ages: 7–17. 40–50 participants per session. Day program cost: $729. Boarding program cost: $1129. Financial aid available.
Application Deadline Continuous.
Jobs Positions for college students 18 and older.

Contact Client Service Representatives, 42 West Campbell Avenue, Suite 301, Campbell, California 95008. Phone: 888-709-TECH. Fax: 408-871-2228. E-mail: info@internaldrive.com.
URL www.internaldrive.com
For more information, see page 520.

iD Tech Camps–UC Santa Cruz, Santa Cruz, CA

iD Tech Camps
University of California, Santa Cruz
Santa Cruz, California 95064

General Information Coed residential and day academic program and sports camp established in 1999. Accredited by American Camping Association. Formal opportunities for the academically talented and artistically talented.
Program Focus Students create 2D and 3D video games, build robots, design websites, film and edit digital movies, create their own comic book with digital photos, learn programming and more. One computer per student and an average of five students per staff member. Campers take home a project at the end of the weeklong course. For an additional fee, Surf & Tech option allows campers to spend half the day in the computer lab and the other half working on their surfing skills with Club Ed's Surf Camp..
Academics Web page design, academics (general), computer programming, computer science (Advanced Placement), computers, precollege program.
Arts Animation, cinematography, digital media, drawing, film, film editing, film production, graphic arts, photography, television/video.
Special Interest Areas Career exploration, computer game design, computer graphics, electronics, leadership training, robotics, team building.
Sports Baseball, basketball, soccer, softball, surfing, swimming, volleyball.
Trips College tours.
Program Information 5–9 sessions per year. Session length: 5–7 days in June, July, August. Ages: 7–17. 40–50 participants per session. Day program cost: $729. Boarding program cost: $1129. Financial aid available.
Application Deadline Continuous.
Jobs Positions for college students 18 and older.

iD Tech Camps–UC Santa Cruz, Santa Cruz, CA (continued)

Contact Client Service Representatives, 42 West Campbell Avenue, Suite 301, Campbell, California 95008. Phone: 888-709-TECH. Fax: 408-871-2228. E-mail: info@internaldrive.com.
URL www.internaldrive.com

For more information, see page 520.

IDYLLWILD ARTS SUMMER PROGRAM– CHILDREN'S CENTER

Idyllwild Arts Foundation
Idyllwild, California 92549

General Information Coed residential and day arts program established in 1950. Formal opportunities for the artistically talented.
Arts Acting, animation, arts, arts and crafts (general), band, batiking, ceramics, chorus, clowning, creative writing, dance, dance (ballet), dance (jazz), dance (modern), dance (tap), drawing, fabric arts, film, jewelry making, mime, music, music (chamber), music (classical), music (ensemble), music (instrumental), music (jazz), music (orchestral), music (vocal), musical productions, painting, performing arts, photography, pottery, printmaking, sculpture, television/video, theater/drama, visual arts.
Program Information 1–2 sessions per year. Session length: 1–2 weeks in July, August. Ages: 5–12. 75–100 participants per session. Day program cost: $230–$1050. Boarding program cost: $1830. Application fee: $25. Financial aid available. Minimum age for boarding is 9.
Application Deadline Continuous.
Jobs Positions for college students 19 and older.
Contact Ms. Diane Dennis, Summer Program Registrar, PO Box 38, Idyllwild, California 92549. Phone: 951-659-2171 Ext.2365. Fax: 951-659-4552. E-mail: summer@idyllwildarts.org.
URL www.idyllwildarts.org

For more information, see page 522.

IDYLLWILD ARTS SUMMER PROGRAM– FAMILY WEEK

Idyllwild Arts Foundation
Idyllwild, California 92549

General Information Coed residential family program and arts program established in 1950. Formal opportunities for the artistically talented.
Arts Arts, arts and crafts (general), batiking, ceramics, chorus, creative writing, dance, drawing, fabric arts, graphic arts, jewelry making, mime, music, musical productions, painting, performing arts, photography, pottery, printmaking, puppetry, sculpture, theater/drama, visual arts, weaving, woodworking.
Sports Ropes course, sports (general), swimming.
Wilderness/Outdoors Hiking.
Program Information 1–2 sessions per year. Session length: 1 week in June, July. 75–100 participants per session. Boarding program cost: $1580–$3300.

Application Deadline Continuous.
Jobs Positions for college students 19 and older.
Contact Ms. Diane Dennis, Summer Program Registrar, PO Box 38, Idyllwild, California 92549. Phone: 951-659-2171 Ext.2365. Fax: 951-659-4552. E-mail: summer@idyllwildarts.org.
URL www.idyllwildarts.org

For more information, see page 522.

IDYLLWILD ARTS SUMMER PROGRAM– JUNIOR ARTISTS' CENTER

Idyllwild Arts Foundation
Idyllwild, California 92549

General Information Coed residential and day arts program established in 1950. Formal opportunities for the artistically talented.
Arts Acting, arts, band, ceramics, creative writing, dance, dance (ballet), dance (jazz), dance (modern), dance (tap), drawing, fabric arts, jewelry making, mime, music, music (classical), music (ensemble), music (instrumental), music (jazz), music (orchestral), music (vocal), musical productions, painting, performing arts, photography, pottery, printmaking, sculpture, theater/drama, visual arts.
Program Information 1 session per year. Session length: 1–2 weeks in July, August. Ages: 11–13. 75–100 participants per session. Day program cost: $915–$1150. Boarding program cost: $1850–$1950. Application fee: $25. Financial aid available.
Application Deadline Continuous.
Jobs Positions for college students.
Contact Ms. Diane Dennis, Summer Program Registrar, PO Box 38, Idyllwild, California 92549. Phone: 951-659-2171 Ext.2365. Fax: 951-659-4552. E-mail: summer@idyllwildarts.org.
URL www.idyllwildarts.org

For more information, see page 522.

IDYLLWILD ARTS SUMMER PROGRAM-YOUTH ARTS CENTER

Idyllwild Arts Foundation
Idyllwild, California 92549

General Information Coed residential and day arts program established in 1950. Formal opportunities for the artistically talented.

Idyllwild Arts Summer Program-Youth Arts Center

Arts Acting, animation, arts, band, ceramics, chorus, clowning, creative writing, dance, dance (ballet), dance (jazz), dance (modern), dance (tap), drawing, fabric arts, film, graphic arts, jewelry making, mime, music, music (chamber), music (classical), music (ensemble), music (instrumental), music (jazz), music (orchestral), music (vocal), musical productions, musical theater, painting, performing arts, photography, pottery, printmaking, sculpture, television/video, theater/drama, visual arts.
Program Information 3 sessions per year. Session length: 2–3 weeks in July, August. Ages: 13–18. 250–400 participants per session. Day program cost: $915–$1150. Boarding program cost: $1750–$1950. Application fee: $25. Financial aid available.
Application Deadline Continuous.

Jobs Positions for college students 19 and older.
Contact Diane Dennis, Registrar, Summer Program, PO Box 38, Idyllwild, California 92549. Phone: 951-659-2171 Ext.2365. Fax: 951-659-4552. E-mail: summer@idyllwildarts.org.
URL www.idyllwildarts.org
For more information, see page 522.

JUNIOR STATESMEN SUMMER SCHOOL-STANFORD UNIVERSITY

Junior Statesmen Foundation
Stanford University
Stanford, California 94305

General Information Coed residential academic program established in 1941. Formal opportunities for the academically talented. High school credit may be earned.

Junior Statesmen Summer School-Stanford University

Program Focus American government, economics, speech, leadership, political communication, and comparative politics and government.
Academics Communications, economics, government and politics, government and politics (Advanced Placement), journalism, precollege program, social science, social studies, speech/debate.
Special Interest Areas Career exploration, leadership training.
Trips College tours, cultural, day.
Program Information 1 session per year. Session length: 27 days in July. Ages: 14–18. 300–350 participants per session. Boarding program cost: $4150. Financial aid available. Scholarships available to students from West Contra Costa School District.
Application Deadline Continuous.

Junior Statesmen Summer School–Stanford University (continued)

Contact Ms. Jessica Brow, National Summer Programs Director, 400 South El Camino Real, Suite 300, San Mateo, California 94402. Phone: 650-347-1600. Fax: 650-347-7200. E-mail: jsa@jsa.org.
URL summer.jsa.org/summer/stanford.html
For more information, see page 534.

JUNIOR STATESMEN SYMPOSIUM ON CALIFORNIA STATE POLITICS AND GOVERNMENT

Junior Statesmen Foundation
University of California
Davis, California 95616

General Information Coed residential academic program established in 1990. Formal opportunities for the academically talented.
Program Focus State government, politics, debate, and leadership training.
Academics Communications, government and politics, journalism, precollege program, social science, social studies, speech/debate.
Special Interest Areas Career exploration, leadership training.
Trips College tours, day.
Program Information 1 session per year. Session length: 4 days in August. Ages: 14–18. 40–100 participants per session. Boarding program cost: $460. Financial aid available.
Application Deadline Continuous.
Contact Ms. Jessica Brow, National Summer School Director, 400 South El Camino Real, Suite 300, San Mateo, California 94402. Phone: 650-347-1600. Fax: 650-347-7200. E-mail: jsa@jsa.org.
URL summer.jsa.org/symposium/california.html
For more information, see page 534.

JUNIOR STATESMEN SYMPOSIUM ON LOS ANGELES POLITICS AND GOVERNMENT

Junior Statesmen Foundation
University of Southern California
Los Angeles, California 90089

General Information Coed residential academic program established in 1977. Formal opportunities for the academically talented.
Program Focus Local government, politics, debate, and leadership training.
Academics Communications, government and politics, journalism, precollege program, social science, social studies, speech/debate.
Special Interest Areas Career exploration, leadership training.
Trips College tours, day.
Program Information 1 session per year. Session

length: 5 days in August. Ages: 14–18. 40–80 participants per session. Boarding program cost: $460. Financial aid available. Scholarships available to LAUSD inner-city high school students.
Application Deadline Continuous.
Contact Ms. Jessica Brow, National Summer School Director, 400 South El Camino Real, Suite 300, San Mateo, California 94402. Phone: 650-347-1600. Fax: 650-347-7200. E-mail: jsa@jsa.org.
URL summer.jsa.org/
For more information, see page 534.

LANDMARK VOLUNTEERS: CALIFORNIA

Landmark Volunteers, Inc.
California

General Information Coed residential outdoor program and community service program established in 1992. High school credit may be earned.
Program Focus Opportunity for high school students to earn community service credit while working as a team for two weeks serving Henry W. Coe State Park, Golden Gate National Recreation Area. Similar programs offered through Landmark Volunteers at over 50 locations in 20 states.
Academics Biology, ecology, environmental science.
Special Interest Areas Career exploration, community service, conservation projects, field research/expeditions, leadership training, nature study, team building, trail maintenance.
Sports Swimming.
Wilderness/Outdoors Hiking, wilderness camping.
Trips Cultural, day.
Program Information 2 sessions per year. Session length: 2 weeks in July. Ages: 14–18. 10–13 participants per session. Boarding program cost: $1250–$1300. Financial aid available.
Application Deadline Continuous.
Jobs Positions for college students.
Contact Ann Barrett, Executive Director, PO Box 455, Sheffield, Massachusetts 01257. Phone: 413-229-0255. Fax: 413-229-2050. E-mail: landmark@volunteers.com.
URL www.volunteers.com
For more information, see page 542.

NATIONAL STUDENT LEADERSHIP CONFERENCE: ENGINEERING–SAN FRANCISCO

National Student Leadership Conference
University of California, Berkeley
Berkeley, California

General Information Coed residential academic program established in 1989. Formal opportunities for the academically talented. College credit may be earned.
Program Focus Leadership training, engineering and technology, career exploration.
Academics Engineering.
Special Interest Areas Career exploration, leadership training, robotics, team building.
Trips College tours, cultural, shopping.
Program Information 1–4 sessions per year. Session length: 10 days in June, July, August. Ages: 14–18. 150 participants per session. Boarding program cost: $2295. Financial aid available.
Application Deadline Continuous.
Jobs Positions for college students 18 and older.
Contact Director of Admissions, 414 North Orleans Street, Suite LL8, Chicago, Illinois 60610-1087. Phone: 312-322-9999. Fax: 312-765-0081. E-mail: info@nslcleaders.org.
URL www.nslcleaders.org

For more information, see page 564.

NATIONAL STUDENT LEADERSHIP CONFERENCE: LAW AND ADVOCACY–SAN FRANCISCO

National Student Leadership Conference
University of California, Berkeley
Berkeley, California

General Information Coed residential academic program established in 1989. Formal opportunities for the academically talented. College credit may be earned.
Program Focus Leadership, career exploration, law.
Academics Prelaw.
Special Interest Areas Career exploration, leadership training, team building.
Sports Gaelic football, ropes course.
Trips College tours, cultural, shopping.
Program Information 1–4 sessions per year. Session length: 10 days in June, July, August. Ages: 14–18. 150 participants per session. Boarding program cost: $2295. Financial aid available.
Application Deadline Continuous.
Jobs Positions for college students 18 and older.
Contact Director of Admissions, 414 North Orleans Street, Suite LL8, Chicago, Illinois 60610-1087. Phone: 312-322-9999. Fax: 312-765-0081. E-mail: info@nslcleaders.org.
URL www.nslcleaders.org

For more information, see page 564.

NATIONAL STUDENT LEADERSHIP CONFERENCE: MEDICINE AND HEALTH CARE–SAN FRANCISCO

National Student Leadership Conference
University of California, Berkeley
Berkeley, California

General Information Coed residential academic program established in 1989. Formal opportunities for the academically talented. College credit may be earned.
Program Focus Leadership training, medicine and health care, career exploration.
Academics Health sciences, medicine, premed.
Special Interest Areas Career exploration, leadership training, team building.
Trips College tours, cultural, shopping.
Program Information 1–4 sessions per year. Session length: 10 days in June, July, August. Ages: 14–18. 150 participants per session. Boarding program cost: $2295. Financial aid available.
Application Deadline Continuous.
Jobs Positions for college students 18 and older.
Contact Director of Admissions, 414 North Orleans Street, Suite LL8, Chicago, Illinois 60610-1087. Phone: 312-322-9999. Fax: 312-765-0081. E-mail: info@nslcleaders.org.
URL www.nslcleaders.org

For more information, see page 564.

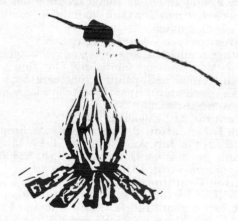

OXBOW SUMMER ART CAMP

The Oxbow School
530 Third Street
Napa, California 94559

General Information Coed residential and day arts program established in 2003.

Oxbow Summer Art Camp

Program Focus Intensive studio art programs focusing on fine art or movie-making, animation, comic, and children's book-making.
Academics Art, art (Advanced Placement).
Arts Acting, animation, arts, arts and crafts (general), creative writing, drawing, fabric arts, film, film production, graphic arts, painting, photography, printmaking, sculpture, studio arts, television/video, visual arts, woodworking.
Trips Cultural, day, shopping.
Program Information 2 sessions per year. Session length: 18 days in July, August. Ages: 14–17. 48 participants per session. Day program cost: $2500. Boarding program cost: $3100.
Application Deadline Continuous.
Jobs Positions for college students 20 and older.
Contact Ms. Barbara Bitner, Oxbow Summer Program Director, main address above. Phone: 707-255-6000. Fax: 707-255-6006. E-mail: summercamp@oxbowschool.org.
URL www.nolanyardscamp.org
For more information, see page 578.

SCIENCE PROGRAM FOR HIGH SCHOOL GIRLS

University of Southern California–Office of Continuing Education and Summer Programs
Wrigley Marine Science Center
Catalina Island, California

General Information Girls' residential academic program established in 2001.

Program Focus Explore the field of oceanography and marine science.
Academics Ecology, environmental science, marine studies, oceanography, science (general).
Special Interest Areas Nature study.
Sports Canoeing, kayaking, snorkeling.
Program Information 1 session per year. Session length: 8 days in July, August. Ages: 14–15. 20–30 participants per session. Boarding program cost: $1645. Financial aid available.
Application Deadline Continuous.
Contact Robin Kaufman, Program Specialist, 979 West Jefferson Boulevard, Los Angeles, California 90089-7009. Phone: 213-740-5679. Fax: 213-740-6417. E-mail: summer@usc.edu.
URL www.usc.edu/summer

SCIENCE PROGRAM FOR MIDDLE SCHOOL BOYS ON CATALINA

University of Southern California–Office of Continuing Education and Summer Programs
Wrigley Marine Science Center
Catalina Island, California

General Information Boys' residential academic program established in 2004.
Program Focus Introduction to oceanography and marine science.
Academics Ecology, environmental science, marine studies, oceanography, science (general).
Special Interest Areas Nature study.
Sports Canoeing, kayaking, snorkeling.
Program Information 1 session per year. Session length: 6–8 days in August. Ages: 11–13. 20–30 participants per session. Boarding program cost: $1645. Financial aid available.
Application Deadline Continuous.
Contact Robin Kaufman, Program Specialist, 979 West Jefferson Boulevard, Los Angeles, California 90089-7009. Phone: 213-740-5679. Fax: 213-740-6417. E-mail: summer@usc.edu.
URL www.usc.edu/summer

SCIENCE PROGRAM FOR MIDDLE SCHOOL GIRLS ON CATALINA

University of Southern California–Office of Continuing Education and Summer Programs
Wrigley Marine Science Center
Catalina Island, California

General Information Girls' residential academic program established in 1999.
Program Focus Introduction to oceanography and marine science.
Academics Ecology, environmental science, marine studies, oceanography, science (general).
Special Interest Areas Nature study.
Sports Canoeing, kayaking, snorkeling.
Program Information 1 session per year. Session length: 8 days in July. Ages: 10–13. 20–30 participants

per session. Boarding program cost: $1645. Financial aid available.

Application Deadline Continuous.

Contact Robin Kaufman, Program Specialist, 979 West Jefferson Boulevard, Los Angeles, California 90089-7009. Phone: 213-740-5679. Fax: 213-740-6417. E-mail: summer@usc.edu.

URL www.usc.edu/summer

SOUTHWESTERN ADVENTURES–CALIFORNIA

Southwestern Academy's Southwestern Adventures
2800 Monterey Road
San Marino, California 91108

General Information Coed residential and day academic program and arts program established in 1924. Formal opportunities for the artistically talented. High school credit may be earned.

Southwestern Adventures–California

Program Focus English as a second language, college prep credit classes, remedial, academic enhancement, and arts program.

Academics English as a second language, English language/literature, SAT/ACT preparation, Spanish language/literature, academics (general), area studies, art history/appreciation, biology, chemistry, computers, economics, environmental science, geography, geology/

earth science, government and politics, history, humanities, intercultural studies, journalism, mathematics, mathematics (Advanced Placement), music, physics, precollege program, psychology, reading, remedial academics, science (general), speech/debate, writing.

Arts Arts, arts and crafts (general), ceramics, chorus, drawing, film, graphic arts, jewelry making, music, music (instrumental), painting, photography, theater/drama.

Special Interest Areas Career exploration, college planning, community service.

Sports Baseball, basketball, golf, soccer, softball, tennis, volleyball, weight training.

Wilderness/Outdoors Hiking.

Trips College tours, cultural, day, overnight, shopping.

Program Information 6–12 sessions per year. Session length: 30–90 days in June, July, August, September. Ages: 11–18. 30–50 participants per session. Boarding program cost: $5500–$16,000. Application fee: $100. Remedial reading and study classes available.

Application Deadline Continuous.

Jobs Positions for college students.

Contact Terri Rosales, Director of Admissions, main address above. Phone: 626-799-5010 Ext.1204. Fax: 626-799-0407. E-mail: admissions@southwesternacademy.edu.

URL www.southwesternacademy.edu

For more information, see page 638.

SQUAW VALLEY ACADEMY SUMMER SCHOOL

Squaw Valley Academy
235 Squaw Valley Road
Olympic Valley, California 96146

General Information Coed residential academic program. High school credit may be earned.

Squaw Valley Academy Summer School

Academics American literature, English as a second language, English language/literature, Spanish language/literature, academics (general), art history/appreciation, biology, chemistry, economics, geography, government and politics, history, humanities,

Squaw Valley Academy Summer School (continued)
mathematics, physics, science (general), social science, social studies, study skills.
Arts Arts, arts and crafts (general), ceramics, painting, photography.
Special Interest Areas Community service.
Sports Bicycling, climbing (wall), fishing, golf, horseback riding, kayaking, ropes course, sea kayaking, skateboarding.
Wilderness/Outdoors Hiking, mountain biking.
Trips Cultural, day.
Program Information 2 sessions per year. Session length: 3 weeks in June, July. Ages: 11–17. 50–60 participants per session. Boarding program cost: $3990.
Application Deadline Continuous.
Contact Donald Rees, Headmaster, PO Box 2667, 235 Squaw Valley Road, Olympic Valley, California 96146. E-mail: enroll@sva.org.
URL www.sva.org

For more information, see page 644.

STANFORD UNIVERSITY HIGH SCHOOL SUMMER COLLEGE

Stanford University Summer Session
482 Galvez Street
Stanford University
Stanford, California 94305-6079

General Information Coed residential and day academic program established in 1960. Formal opportunities for the academically talented. College credit may be earned.

Stanford University High School Summer College

Program Focus Pre-college program through which students earn university credit from Stanford.
Academics American literature, Chinese languages/literature, English language/literature, French language/literature, German language/literature, Greek language/literature, Italian language/literature, Japanese language/literature, Latin language, SAT/ACT preparation, Spanish language/literature, academics (general), aerospace science, anthropology, archaeology, art history/appreciation, astronomy, biology, chemistry,

classical languages/literatures, communications, computer programming, economics, engineering, geology/earth science, government and politics, history, humanities, mathematics, music, philosophy, physics, physiology, precollege program, psychology, religion, speech/debate, study skills, writing.
Arts Acting, chorus, creative writing, music, music (orchestral), painting, photography, theater/drama.
Special Interest Areas College planning, field trips (arts and culture).
Sports Aerobics, basketball, golf, swimming, tennis, yoga.
Trips Cultural, day.
Program Information 1 session per year. Session length: 58 days in June, July, August. Ages: 16–18. 300–350 participants per session. Day program cost: $2670–$8916. Boarding program cost: $9000–$11,000. Application fee: $50. Financial aid available.
Application Deadline May 1.
Contact Patricia Brandt, Associate Dean and Director, main address above. Phone: 650-723-3109. Fax: 650-725-6080. E-mail: summersession@stanford.edu.
URL summer.stanford.edu/

For more information, see page 648.

THE SUMMER INSTITUTE FOR THE GIFTED AT UCLA

Summer Institute for the Gifted
UCLA
Los Angeles, California 90024

General Information Coed residential academic program established in 2004. Formal opportunities for the academically talented and gifted. College credit may be earned.
Academics American literature, English language/literature, French language/literature, SAT/ACT preparation, Spanish language/literature, academics (general), aerospace science, archaeology, architecture, art (Advanced Placement), art history/appreciation, biology, business, chemistry, classical languages/literatures, communications, computer programming, computers, engineering, environmental science, government and politics, history, humanities, marine studies, mathematics, music, oceanography, philosophy, physics, physiology, precollege program, psychology, science (general), social studies, speech/debate, study skills, writing.
Arts Arts and crafts (general), chorus, creative writing, dance, drawing, film, graphic arts, music, music (chamber), music (classical), music (ensemble), music (instrumental), musical productions, painting, photography, sculpture, theater/drama.
Special Interest Areas Animal care, electronics, meditation, model rocketry, robotics.
Sports Archery, baseball, basketball, fencing, field hockey, football, lacrosse, martial arts, soccer, squash, swimming, tennis, track and field, volleyball.
Wilderness/Outdoors Hiking.
Trips Cultural.
Program Information 1 session per year. Session length: 3 weeks in July, August. Ages: 8–17. 150–250 participants per session. Boarding program cost: $4495–

$5000. Application fee: $75. Financial aid available.
Application Deadline May 14.
Jobs Positions for college students 19 and older.
Contact Ms. Barbara Swicord, Director, River Plaza, 9 West Broad Street, Stamford, Connecticut 06902-3788. Phone: 866-303-4744. Fax: 203-399-5598. E-mail: sig.info@aifs.com.
URL www.giftedstudy.com
For more information, see page 654.

THE SUMMER INSTITUTE FOR THE GIFTED AT UNIVERSITY OF CALIFORNIA, BERKELEY

Summer Institute for the Gifted
University of California, Berkeley
Berkeley, California 94720

General Information Coed residential academic program. Formal opportunities for the academically talented and gifted.
Academics American literature, English language/literature, French language/literature, SAT/ACT preparation, Spanish language/literature, academics (general), aerospace science, archaeology, architecture, art history/appreciation, biology, business, chemistry, classical languages/literatures, communications, computers, engineering, government and politics, history, mathematics, music, oceanography, philosophy, physics, precollege program, psychology, science (general), social studies, speech/debate, study skills, writing.
Arts Arts and crafts (general), chorus, creative writing, dance, film, graphic arts, music, music (classical), music (ensemble), music (instrumental), musical productions, painting, photography, sculpture, television/video, theater/drama.
Special Interest Areas Animal care, electronics, meditation, robotics.
Sports Aerobics, archery, baseball, basketball, fencing, field hockey, football, martial arts, soccer, tennis, track and field, volleyball.
Trips Cultural.
Program Information 1 session per year. Session length: 3 weeks in July. Ages: 8–17. 150–250 participants per session. Boarding program cost: $4495–$5000. Application fee: $75. Financial aid available.
Application Deadline May 14.
Jobs Positions for college students 19 and older.

Contact Ms. Barbara Swicord, Director, River Plaza, 9 West Broad Street, Stamford, Connecticut 06902-3788. Phone: 866-303-4744. Fax: 203-399-5598. E-mail: sig.info@aifs.com.
URL www.giftedstudy.com
For more information, see page 654.

UCLA SUMMER EXPERIENCE: COLLEGE LEVEL COURSES

UCLA Summer Sessions and Special Programs
UCLA Westwood
Los Angeles, California 90095

General Information Coed residential and day academic program established in 1970. College credit may be earned.
Program Focus Preparation for college through a real-life college experience.
Academics American literature, Chinese languages/literature, English as a second language, English language/literature, French language/literature, German language/literature, Greek language/literature, Hebrew language, Italian language/literature, Japanese language/literature, Jewish studies, Latin language, Russian language/literature, Spanish language/literature, academics (general), anthropology, archaeology, area studies, art history/appreciation, astronomy, biology, botany, business, chemistry, classical languages/literatures, communications, computer programming, computers, economics, environmental science, geography, geology/earth science, government and politics, health sciences, history, humanities, intercultural studies, linguistics, marine studies, mathematics, music, oceanography, peace education, philosophy, physics, physiology, psychology, religion, science (general), social science, social studies, writing.
Arts Dance, dance (ballet), dance (folk), dance (jazz), dance (modern), film, music, music (ensemble), music (instrumental), music (orchestral), theater/drama.
Trips Cultural, day.
Program Information 1–2 sessions per year. Session length: 40–60 days in June, July, August. Ages: 15+. 400–800 participants per session. Day program cost: $850–$1500. Boarding program cost: $1800–$2500. Application fee: $100.
Application Deadline Continuous.
Contact Ms. Heidi J. Hanzi, Manager, Academic Advising and Student Affairs, Box 951418, Los Angeles, California 90095-1418. Phone: 310-825-4101. Fax: 310-825-1528. E-mail: hhanzi@summer.ucla.edu.
URL www.summer.ucla.edu

UCLA SUMMER EXPERIENCE: INSTITUTES

UCLA Summer Sessions and Special
Programs
UCLA Westwood
Los Angeles, California 90095

General Information Coed residential and day
academic program and arts program established in
1995. College credit may be earned.
Program Focus Opportunity to work with world-
renowned UCLA arts and humanities faculty.
Academics French language/literature, Italian
language/literature, speech/debate.
Arts Acting, band, chorus, dance, dance (ballet), dance
(folk), dance (jazz), dance (modern), dance (tap), digital
media, graphic arts, music, music (chamber), music
(classical), music (ensemble), music (instrumental),
music (orchestral), music (vocal), performing arts,
photography, television/video, theater/drama.
Trips Cultural, day.
Program Information 4–10 sessions per year. Session
length: 7–30 days in June, July, August. Ages: 14+.
50–100 participants per session. Day program cost:
$575–$1000. Boarding program cost: $1000–$1200.
Application fee: $100. Financial aid available.
Application Deadline Continuous.
Contact Dr. Susan Pertel Jain, Director of Academic
Program Development, Box 951418, Los Angeles,
California 90095. Phone: 310-825-4101. Fax: 310-825-
1528. E-mail: spjain@summer.ucla.edu.
URL www.summer.ucla.edu

UNIVERSITY OF SOUTHERN CALIFORNIA SUMMER SEMINARS

University of Southern California–Office of
Continuing Education and Summer Programs
The University of Southern California
Figueroa Street and McCarthy Way
Los Angeles, California 90089-7009

General Information Coed residential academic
program established in 1997. Formal opportunities for
the academically talented and artistically talented.
College credit may be earned.
Academics French language/literature, Spanish
language/literature, academics (general), architecture,
art (Advanced Placement), biology, business,
communications, engineering, journalism, music,
physiology, precollege program, psychology, science
(general), speech/debate, writing.
Arts Acting, animation, creative writing, dance, dance
(jazz), dance (modern), film, graphic arts, guitar, music
(instrumental), painting, photography, theater/drama.
Special Interest Areas Career exploration, field
research/expeditions.
Sports Swimming, tennis, volleyball.
Trips Cultural, day, shopping.
Program Information 1 session per year. Session
length: 4 weeks in July, August. Ages: 16–18. 350–500
participants per session. Boarding program cost: $4485.
Financial aid available.

Application Deadline Continuous.
Jobs Positions for college students 20 and older.
Contact Sonny Hayes, Director of Youth Programs, 979
West Jefferson Boulevard, Los Angeles, California
90089-7009. Phone: 213-740-5679. Fax: 213-740-6417.
E-mail: summer@usc.edu.
URL www.usc.edu/summer

WESTCOAST CONNECTION–CALIFORNIA SPRINT

Westcoast Connection
California

General Information Coed travel adventure program
established in 1982. Accredited by Ontario Camping
Association.
Program Focus A balance of daytime activities, the
sights and sounds of cities, exciting nightly entertainment, and the natural wonders of the great outdoors.
Special Interest Areas Touring.
Sports Bicycling, boating, kayaking, ropes course,
snorkeling, surfing, swimming, tennis, volleyball,
waterskiing.
Wilderness/Outdoors Outdoor adventure, rafting,
white-water trips.
Program Information 1–2 sessions per year. Session
length: 2 weeks in July, August. Ages: 13–17. 20–30
participants per session. Cost: $3799. Financial aid
available.
Application Deadline Continuous.
Contact Mr. Mark Segal, Director, 154 East Boston
Post Road, Mamaroneck, New York 10543. Phone:
800-767-0227. Fax: 914-835-0798. E-mail:
usa@westcoastconnection.com.
URL www.westcoastconnection.com
For more information, see page 702.

WESTCOAST CONNECTION–CALIFORNIA SWING JUNIOR TOURING GOLF CAMP

Westcoast Connection
California

General Information Coed travel sports camp established in 1982. Accredited by Ontario Camping Association.
Program Focus Participants receive professional golf instruction, play top courses, and enjoy recreation and touring highlights.
Special Interest Areas Touring.
Sports Golf.
Program Information 1–2 sessions per year. Session length: 13–19 days in July. Ages: 13–17. 16–28 participants per session. Cost: $3999–$5699.
Application Deadline Continuous.
Jobs Positions for college students 21 and older.
Contact Mr. Ira Solomon, Director, 154 East Boston Post Road, Mamaroneck, New York 10543. Phone: 800-767-0227. Fax: 914-835-0798. E-mail: info@westcoastconnection.com.
URL www.westcoastconnection.com
For more information, see page 702.

WESTCOAST CONNECTION TRAVEL–ADVENTURE CALIFORNIA

Westcoast Connection
California

General Information Coed travel outdoor program and adventure program established in 1982. Accredited by Ontario Camping Association.
Program Focus Outdoor adventure in California.
Special Interest Areas Community service.
Sports Bicycling, kayaking, rappelling, ropes course, sea kayaking, snorkeling, surfing, swimming.
Wilderness/Outdoors Caving, hiking, mountain biking, outdoor adventure, rafting, rock climbing, white-water trips.
Program Information 1–2 sessions per year. Session length: 24 days in June, July, August. Ages: 13–17. 12–20 participants per session. Cost: $4199.
Application Deadline Continuous.
Jobs Positions for college students 21 and older.
Contact Mr. Mark Segal, Director, 154 East Boston Post Road, Mamaroneck, New York 10543. Phone: 800-767-0227. Fax: 914-835-0798. E-mail: usa@westcoastconnection.com.
URL www.360studenttravel.com
For more information, see page 702.

WILDERNESS VENTURES–CALIFORNIA

Wilderness Ventures
California

General Information Coed travel outdoor program, wilderness program, and adventure program established in 1973.

Program Focus Wilderness travel, wilderness skills, leadership skills.
Special Interest Areas Leadership training.
Sports Surfing.
Wilderness/Outdoors Backpacking, hiking, rafting, white-water trips, wilderness camping.
Trips Overnight.
Program Information 2 sessions per year. Session length: 3 weeks in June, July, August. Ages: 14–18. 13 participants per session. Cost: $3690. Financial aid available.
Application Deadline Continuous.
Jobs Positions for college students 21 and older.
Contact Mike Cottingham, Director, PO Box 2768, Jackson Hole, Wyoming 83001. Phone: 800-533-2281. E-mail: info@wildernessventures.com.
URL www.wildernessventures.com
For more information, see page 704.

WILDERNESS VENTURES–HIGH SIERRA

Wilderness Ventures
California

General Information Coed travel outdoor program, wilderness program, and adventure program established in 1973.
Program Focus Wilderness travel, wilderness skills, leadership skills.
Special Interest Areas Leadership training.
Wilderness/Outdoors Backpacking, hiking, mountaineering, rafting, rock climbing, white-water trips, wilderness camping.
Trips Overnight.
Program Information 2 sessions per year. Session length: 25 days in June, July, August. Ages: 14–18. 13 participants per session. Cost: $3990. Financial aid available.
Application Deadline Continuous.
Jobs Positions for college students 21 and older.
Contact Mike Cottingham, Director, PO Box 2768, Jackson Hole, Wyoming 83001. Phone: 800-533-2281. Fax: 307-739-1934. E-mail: info@wildernessventures.com.
URL www.wildernessventures.com
For more information, see page 704.

WORLD HORIZONS INTERNATIONAL–NORTHRIDGE, CALIFORNIA

World Horizons International
Northridge, California

General Information Coed residential community service program established in 2006.
Program Focus Community service; helping disabled riders in a therapeutic riding program.
Special Interest Areas Animal care, community service.
Sports Equestrian sports, horseback riding.
Wilderness/Outdoors Hiking.
Trips Cultural, day, overnight.
Program Information 1 session per year. Session length: 29 days in June, July. Ages: 14–18. 10–12 participants per session. Boarding program cost: $4495. Application fee: $175. Financial aid available.
Application Deadline Continuous.
Jobs Positions for college students 21 and older.
Contact Mr. Stuart L. Rabinowitz, Executive Director, PO Box 662, Bethlehem, Connecticut 06751. Phone: 800-262-5874. Fax: 203-266-6227. E-mail: worldhorizons@att.net.
URL www.world-horizons.com

For more information, see page 714.

COLORADO

AAVE–COLORADO DISCOVERY

AAVE–Journeys That Matter
Colorado

General Information Coed travel outdoor program, wilderness program, and adventure program established in 1976. Accredited by American Camping Association.
Program Focus Adventure travel.
Special Interest Areas Campcraft, community service, leadership training, team building.
Sports Bicycling, horseback riding, rappelling, swimming.
Wilderness/Outdoors Backpacking, bicycle trips, hiking, mountain biking, mountaineering, orienteering, rafting, rock climbing, white-water trips.
Trips Overnight.
Program Information 6–8 sessions per year. Session length: 18 days in June, July, August. Ages: 12–13. 13 participants per session. Cost: $2688. Financial aid available.
Application Deadline Continuous.
Jobs Positions for college students 21 and older.
Contact Mr. Abbott Wallis, Owner, 2308 Fossil Trace Drive, Golden, Colorado 80401. Phone: 800-222-3595. Fax: 303-526-0885. E-mail: info@aave.com.
URL www.aave.com

For more information, see page 394.

AAVE–ROCK & ROLL

AAVE–Journeys That Matter
Colorado

General Information Coed travel outdoor program, community service program, wilderness program, and adventure program established in 1976. Accredited by American Camping Association.
Program Focus Adventure travel.
Special Interest Areas Campcraft, community service, leadership training, team building.
Wilderness/Outdoors Backpacking, hiking, outdoor adventure, rock climbing.
Program Information 3 sessions per year. Session length: 2 weeks. Ages: 14–18. Cost: $2088. Financial aid available.
Application Deadline Continuous.
Contact Mr. Abbott Wallis, Owner, 2308 Fossil Trace Drive, Golden, Colorado 80401. Phone: 800-222-3595. Fax: 303-526-0885. E-mail: info@aave.com.
URL www.aave.com

For more information, see page 394.

CHELEY COLORADO CAMPS

Estes Park, Colorado 80517

General Information Coed residential traditional camp, outdoor program, family program, wilderness program, and adventure program established in 1921. Accredited by American Camping Association. Specific services available for the burn survivor.
Program Focus Youth development and leadership along with horseback riding, wilderness activities, and mountaineering.
Arts Batiking, ceramics, drawing, fabric arts, jewelry making, leather working, painting, pottery, woodworking.
Special Interest Areas Campcraft, leadership training.
Sports Aerobics, archery, basketball, climbing (wall), fishing, horseback riding, rappelling, riflery, ropes course, soccer, weight training.
Wilderness/Outdoors Backpacking, bicycle trips, hiking, mountain biking, mountaineering, orienteering, pack animal trips, rafting, rock climbing, survival training, white-water trips, wilderness camping.
Trips Day, overnight.
Program Information 2 sessions per year. Session

length: 27 days in June, July, August. Ages: 9–17. 480–490 participants per session. Boarding program cost: $4000–$4100. Financial aid available.
Application Deadline Continuous.
Jobs Positions for college students 19 and older.
Summer Contact Ms. Sarah Sanderman, Enrollment Manager, PO Box 1170, Estes Park, Colorado 80517. Phone: 970-586-4244. Fax: 970-586-3020. E-mail: office@cheley.com.
Winter Contact Ms. Sarah Sanderman, Enrollment Manager, PO Box 6525, Denver, Colorado 80206. Phone: 303-377-3616. Fax: 303-377-3605. E-mail: office@cheley.com.
URL www.cheley.com

COLORADO COLLEGE SUMMER SESSION

Colorado College Summer Programs
14 East Cache la Poudre Street
Colorado Springs, Colorado 80903

General Information Coed residential and day academic program. Formal opportunities for the academically talented. Specific services available for the hearing impaired, physically challenged, and visually impaired. College credit may be earned.

Colorado College Summer Session

Academics American literature, Chinese languages/literature, English language/literature, French language/literature, Italian language/literature, Latin language, Spanish language/literature, academics (general), anthropology, archaeology, art (Advanced Placement), art history/appreciation, astronomy, biology, chemistry, classical languages/literatures, ecology, economics, environmental science, government and politics, history, humanities, intercultural studies, mathematics, music, philosophy, physiology, precollege program, psychology, religion, social science.
Trips College tours.
Program Information 3 sessions per year. Session

length: 3 weeks in June, July, August. Ages: 16+. 100–200 participants per session. Day program cost: $2300. Boarding program cost: $3760. Application fee: $50. Financial aid available.
Application Deadline Continuous.
Jobs Positions for college students 18 and older.
Contact Kendra Henry, Director of Summer High School Programs, main address above. Phone: 719-389-6935. Fax: 719-389-6955. E-mail: khenry@coloradocollege.edu.
URL www.coloradocollege.edu

For more information, see page 460.

iD TECH CAMPS—COLORADO COLLEGE, COLORADO SPRINGS, CO

iD Tech Camps
Colorado College
Colorado Springs, Colorado 80903

General Information Coed residential and day academic program established in 1999. Accredited by American Camping Association. Formal opportunities for the academically talented and artistically talented.
Program Focus Students create 2D and 3D video games, build robots to compete, design websites, film and edit digital movies, create their own comic book with digital photos, learn programming and more. One computer per student and an average of five students per staff member. Campers take home a project at the end of the weeklong course.
Academics Web page design, academics (general), computer programming, computer science (Advanced Placement), computers, precollege program.
Arts Animation, cinematography, digital media, drawing, film, film editing, film production, graphic arts, photography, television/video.
Special Interest Areas Career exploration, computer game design, computer graphics, electronics, leadership training, robotics, team building.
Sports Baseball, basketball, soccer, softball, swimming, volleyball.
Trips College tours.
Program Information 5–9 sessions per year. Session length: 5–7 days in June, July, August. Ages: 7–17. 40–50 participants per session. Day program cost: $729. Boarding program cost: $1129. Financial aid available.
Application Deadline Continuous.
Jobs Positions for college students 18 and older.
Contact Client Service Representatives, 42 West Campbell Avenue, Suite 301, Campbell, California 95008. Phone: 888-709-TECH. Fax: 408-871-2228. E-mail: info@internaldrive.com.
URL www.internaldrive.com

For more information, see page 520.

iD Tech Camps–University of Denver, Denver, CO

iD Tech Camps
University of Denver
Denver, Colorado 80208

General Information Coed residential and day academic program established in 1999. Accredited by American Camping Association. Formal opportunities for the academically talented and artistically talented.
Program Focus Students create 2D and 3D video games, build robots to compete, design websites, film and edit digital movies, create their own comic book with digital photos, learn programming and more. One computer per student and an average of five students per staff member. Campers take home a project at the end of the weeklong course.
Academics Web page design, academics (general), computer programming, computer science (Advanced Placement), computers, precollege program.
Arts Animation, cinematography, digital media, drawing, film, film editing, film production, graphic arts, photography, television/video.
Special Interest Areas Career exploration, computer game design, computer graphics, electronics, leadership training, robotics, team building.
Sports Baseball, basketball, soccer, softball, swimming, volleyball.
Trips College tours.
Program Information 5–9 sessions per year. Session length: 5–7 days in June, July, August. Ages: 7–17. 40–50 participants per session. Day program cost: $729. Boarding program cost: $1129. Financial aid available.
Application Deadline Continuous.
Jobs Positions for college students 18 and older.
Contact Client Service Representatives, 42 West Campbell Avenue, Suite 301, Campbell, California 95008. Phone: 888-709-TECH. Fax: 408-871-2228. E-mail: info@internaldrive.com
URL www.internaldrive.com

For more information, see page 520.

Landmark Volunteers: Colorado

Landmark Volunteers, Inc.
Colorado

General Information Coed residential outdoor program and community service program established in 1992. High school credit may be earned.
Program Focus Opportunity for high school students to earn community service credit while working as a team for two weeks serving Chico Basin Ranch, Rocky Mountain Village or Aspen School for the Deaf, Colorado Trail. Similar programs offered through Landmark Volunteers at over 50 locations in 20 states.
Academics Ecology, environmental science, natural resource management, social services.
Special Interest Areas Career exploration, community service, conservation projects, farming, field research/expeditions, leadership training, nature study, team building, trail maintenance, work camp programs.
Sports Swimming.
Wilderness/Outdoors Hiking, wilderness camping.
Trips Cultural, day.
Program Information 3 sessions per year. Session length: 2 weeks in June, July, August. Ages: 14–18. 10–13 participants per session. Boarding program cost: $1250–$1300. Financial aid available.
Application Deadline Continuous.
Jobs Positions for college students.
Contact Ann Barrett, Executive Director, PO Box 455, Sheffield, Massachusetts 01257. Phone: 413-229-0255. Fax: 413-229-2050. E-mail: landmark@volunteers.com.
URL www.volunteers.com

For more information, see page 542.

PERRY-MANSFIELD PERFORMING ARTS SCHOOL AND CAMP

Perry-Mansfield Performing Arts School and Camp
40755 Routt County Road 36
Steamboat Springs, Colorado 80487

General Information Coed residential and day arts program established in 1913. Formal opportunities for the artistically talented and gifted. College credit may be earned.

Perry-Mansfield Performing Arts School and Camp

Program Focus Dance, theater, music, fine arts, horseback riding, and creative writing.
Arts Acting, arts, creative writing, dance, dance (ballet), dance (jazz), dance (modern), dance (tap), drawing, music (vocal), musical productions, painting, performing arts, theater/drama.
Special Interest Areas Field trips (arts and culture).
Sports Equestrian sports, horseback riding.
Wilderness/Outdoors Hiking, rafting, white-water trips.
Trips Cultural.
Program Information 9–10 sessions per year. Session length: 1–6 weeks in June, July, August. Ages: 8–25. 25–100 participants per session. Day program cost: $500–$1310. Boarding program cost: $875–$4000. Application fee: $50. Financial aid available. Work study and scholarships available.
Application Deadline Continuous.
Jobs Positions for college students 21 and older.

Contact June Lindenmayer, Executive Director, main address above. Phone: 800-430-2787. Fax: 970-879-5823. E-mail: p-m@perry-mansfield.org.
URL www.perry-mansfield.org
For more information, see page 586.

SUMMER STUDY AT THE UNIVERSITY OF COLORADO AT BOULDER

Summer Study Programs
Boulder, Colorado 80309

General Information Coed residential academic program established in 2001. Formal opportunities for the academically talented. High school or college credit may be earned.
Program Focus Pre-college experience including college credits, enrichment classes, SAT preparation, sports, special outdoor/wilderness activities and weekend trips amidst the Rocky Mountains.
Academics American literature, English as a second language, English language/literature, French (Advanced Placement), SAT/ACT preparation, Spanish (Advanced Placement), academics (general), anthropology, architecture, art (Advanced Placement), art history/appreciation, astronomy, biology, business, chemistry, classical languages/literatures, communications, computer programming, computers, ecology, economics, engineering, environmental science, geology/earth science, government and politics, health sciences, history, humanities, journalism, mathematics, mathematics (Advanced Placement), music, philosophy, physics, physiology, precollege program, psychology, social science, social studies, speech/debate, study skills, writing
Arts Arts and crafts (general), band, ceramics, creative writing, dance, dance (modern), drawing, graphic arts, jewelry making, music, music (instrumental), music (vocal), painting, photography, pottery, theater/drama
Special Interest Areas Career exploration, community service, nature study, touring.
Sports Aerobics, baseball, basketball, bicycling, canoeing, climbing (wall), cross-country, field hockey, football, golf, horseback riding, lacrosse, racquetball, rappelling, soccer, softball, squash, swimming, tennis, track and field, volleyball, weight training, wrestling.
Wilderness/Outdoors Backpacking, bicycle trips, canoe trips, caving, hiking, mountain biking, rafting, rock climbing, white-water trips, wilderness/outdoors (general).
Trips Cultural, day, overnight, shopping.
Program Information 2 sessions per year. Session length: 25–35 days in July, August. Ages: 14+. 150–200 participants per session. Boarding program cost: $3695–$6195. Application fee: $75. Financial aid available.
Application Deadline Continuous.
Jobs Positions for college students 21 and older.
Contact Mr. Bill Cooperman, Executive Director, 900 Walt Whitman Road, Melville, New York 11747. Phone: 800-666-2556. Fax: 631-424-0567. E-mail: precollegeprograms@summerstudy.com.
URL www.summerstudy.com
For more information, see page 658.

CONNECTICUT

BUCK'S ROCK PERFORMING AND CREATIVE ARTS CAMP

59 Buck's Rock Road
New Milford, Connecticut 06776

General Information Coed residential arts program established in 1943. Accredited by American Camping Association. Formal opportunities for the academically talented and artistically talented.

Buck's Rock Performing and Creative Arts Camp

Program Focus Fine and performing arts, and music, highly motivated participants.

Academics Computer programming, journalism, music, music (Advanced Placement), writing.
Arts Acting, animation, arts, band, batiking, blacksmithing, bookbinding, cartooning, ceramics, chorus, circus arts, clowning, costume design, creative writing, dance, dance (ballet), dance (folk), dance (jazz), dance (modern), dance (tap), digital media, directing, drawing, fabric arts, film, glassblowing, graphic arts, guitar, illustration, jewelry making, juggling, leather working, metalworking, mime, mixed media, music, music (chamber), music (classical), music (ensemble), music (instrumental), music (jazz), music (orchestral), music (rock), music (vocal), music technology/record production, musical performance/recitals, musical productions, musical theater, painting, paper making, performing arts, photography, piano, playwriting, pottery, printmaking, puppetry, quilting, radio broadcasting, sculpture, set design, sewing, silk screening, songwriting, sound design, stage managing, stage movement, studio arts, television/video, theater/drama, visual arts, weaving, woodworking.
Special Interest Areas Animal care, community service, farming.
Sports Archery, badminton, basketball, equestrian sports, fencing, horseback riding, martial arts, soccer, softball, swimming, table tennis/ping-pong, tennis, ultimate frisbee, volleyball.
Wilderness/Outdoors Caving, hiking, orienteering.
Trips Cultural, day, overnight.
Program Information 1–2 sessions per year. Session length: 26–54 days in June, July, August. Ages: 11–17. 350–400 participants per session. Boarding program cost: $5790–$8390. Financial aid available.
Application Deadline Continuous.
Jobs Positions for college students 21 and older.
Contact Ms. Laura Morris, Director, main address above. Phone: 860-354-5030. Fax: 860-354-1355. E-mail: bucksrock@bucksrockcamp.com.
URL www.bucksrockcamp.com

For more information, see page 436.

CHESHIRE ACADEMY SUMMER PROGRAM

Cheshire Academy
10 Main Street
Cheshire, Connecticut 06410

General Information Coed residential and day traditional camp and academic program established in 1911. Specific services available for the learning disabled.

Cheshire Academy Summer Program

Program Focus Academics, arts and athletics, travel, students build their own kayak.
Academics American literature, English as a second language, English language/literature, SAT/ACT preparation, Spanish language/literature, academics (general), art history/appreciation, biology, business, chemistry, computers, ecology, history, journalism, mathematics, music, physics, reading, science (general), study skills, writing.
Arts Arts, arts and crafts (general), ceramics, dance, drawing, fabric arts, graphic arts, jewelry making, metalworking, music, music (instrumental), music (vocal), painting, photography, pottery, printmaking, sculpture, theater/drama.
Special Interest Areas Communication skills, field research/expeditions, field trips (arts and culture), leadership training, model rocketry, nature study, robotics, team building, touring.
Sports Basketball, climbing (wall), fencing, golf, rappelling, ropes course, soccer, softball, swimming, tennis, volleyball, weight training.
Wilderness/Outdoors Hiking.
Trips College tours, cultural, day, overnight, shopping.
Program Information 1 session per year. Session length: 5 weeks in July, August. Ages: 12–19. 125 participants per session. Day program cost: $3080. Boarding program cost: $5660. Application fee: $75.
Application Deadline Continuous.
Jobs Positions for college students.
Contact Mrs. Marisa A. Faleri, Director, main address above. Phone: 203-272-5396. Fax: 203-250-7209. E-mail: summer@cheshireacademy.org.
URL www.cheshireacademy.org

Special Note
Cheshire offers small classes and individual attention. Weekly grade reports are issued to parents in order to monitor progress. The Writing, Reading, and Study Skills Program tests students prior to placement and works to strengthen their skills. The renowned English as a Second Language Program offers four levels of instruction from a caring and experienced faculty. College-prep courses are offered in a variety of subjects. Afternoon activities range from athletics and arts to crime scene investigation, rocketry, ropes course, and fencing. Weekend trips include Boston, New York City, and a long weekend in Washington, D.C. Boarding and day students from all over the United States and more than fifteen countries experience the best of college-preparatory school life with excellent academics, a diverse community, wide-ranging activities, and extensive field trips.

For more information, see page 450.

CHOATE ROSEMARY HALL BEGINNING WRITERS WORKSHOP

Choate Rosemary Hall
333 Christian Street
Wallingford, Connecticut 06492

General Information Coed residential and day academic program established in 2004.
Program Focus Develop and build skills for effective written communication for grades five or six.
Academics English language/literature, reading, speech/debate, writing.
Sports Aerobics, basketball, climbing (wall), field hockey, lacrosse, soccer, softball, squash, swimming, tennis, track and field, volleyball, weight training.
Wilderness/Outdoors Hiking.
Program Information 2 sessions per year. Session length: 13 days in June, July. Ages: 10–12. 10–20 participants per session. Day program cost: $1680. Boarding program cost: $2220. Application fee: $60. Financial aid available.
Application Deadline Continuous.
Contact Mariann Arnold, Director of Admission, main address above. Phone: 203-697-2365. Fax: 203-697-2519. E-mail: marnold@choate.edu.
URL www.choate.edu/summerprograms

For more information, see page 456.

CHOATE ROSEMARY HALL ENGLISH LANGUAGE INSTITUTE

Choate Rosemary Hall
333 Christian Street
Wallingford, Connecticut 06492

General Information Coed residential and day academic program established in 1994. High school credit may be earned.

Choate Rosemary Hall English Language Institute (continued)

Program Focus Strengthening English skills in writing, reading, and speaking.

Academics English as a second language, English language/literature, SAT/ACT preparation, linguistics, mathematics, reading, speech/debate, study skills, typing, writing.

Arts Creative writing, drawing, painting, photography, pottery.

Sports Aerobics, basketball, bicycling, climbing (wall), field hockey, lacrosse, soccer, softball, squash, swimming, tennis, track and field, volleyball, weight training.

Wilderness/Outdoors Hiking.

Trips College tours, cultural, day, overnight, shopping.

Program Information 1 session per year. Session length: 5 weeks in June, July. Ages: 14–19. 75 participants per session. Day program cost: $4500–$4600. Boarding program cost: $5900–$6000. Application fee: $60. Washington D.C. trip: $400.

Application Deadline Continuous.

Contact Mariann Arnold, Director of Admission, main address above. Phone: 203-697-2365. Fax: 203-697-2519. E-mail: marnold@choate.edu.

URL www.choate.edu/summerprograms

For more information, see page 456.

CHOATE ROSEMARY HALL ENGLISH LANGUAGE INSTITUTE/FOCUS PROGRAM

Choate Rosemary Hall
333 Christian Street
Wallingford, Connecticut 06492

General Information Coed residential and day academic program established in 1999.

Program Focus Strengthening English skills in writing, reading, and speaking.

Academics English as a second language, English language/literature, journalism, linguistics, reading, speech/debate, study skills, writing.

Arts Ceramics, creative writing, drawing, painting.

Sports Aerobics, basketball, climbing (wall), field hockey, lacrosse, ropes course, soccer, softball, squash, swimming, tennis, track and field, volleyball, weight training.

Wilderness/Outdoors Hiking.

Trips Cultural, day, overnight, shopping.

Program Information 1 session per year. Session length: 4 weeks in June, July. Ages: 12–14. 35 participants per session. Day program cost: $3520. Boarding program cost: $4800. Application fee: $60. Financial aid available. Washington D.C. trip: $400.

Application Deadline Continuous.

Contact Mariann Arnold, Director of Admission, main address above. Phone: 203-697-2365. Fax: 203-697-2519. E-mail: marnold@choate.edu.

URL www.choate.edu/summerprograms

For more information, see page 456.

CHOATE ROSEMARY HALL FOCUS PROGRAM

Choate Rosemary Hall
333 Christian Street
Wallingford, Connecticut 06492

General Information Coed residential and day academic program established in 1998.

Program Focus Project-based learning.

Academics American literature, Latin language, academics (general), biology, chemistry, computers, economics, environmental science, geology/earth science, government and politics, history, mathematics, physics, reading, social science, social studies, speech/debate, study skills, writing.

Arts Ceramics, drawing.

Sports Aerobics, basketball, climbing (wall), field hockey, lacrosse, soccer, softball, squash, swimming, tennis, track and field, volleyball, weight training.

Wilderness/Outdoors Hiking.

Trips Cultural, day, shopping.

Program Information 1 session per year. Session length: 4 weeks in June, July. Ages: 12–14. 85 participants per session. Day program cost: $3320. Boarding program cost: $4600. Application fee: $60. Financial aid available.

Application Deadline Continuous.

Contact Mariann Arnold, Director of Admission, main address above. Phone: 203-697-2365. Fax: 203-697-2519. E-mail: marnold@choate.edu.

URL www.choate.edu/summerprograms

For more information, see page 456.

CHOATE ROSEMARY HALL IMMERSION PROGRAM

Choate Rosemary Hall
333 Christian Street
Wallingford, Connecticut 06492

General Information Coed residential and day academic program established in 1999. Formal opportunities for the academically talented. High school credit may be earned.

Program Focus Full-year credit courses during five-week summer session.

Academics French language/literature, Latin language, Spanish language/literature, language study, mathematics, physics.

Sports Aerobics, basketball, bicycling, climbing (wall), field hockey, lacrosse, soccer, softball, squash, swimming, tennis, track and field, volleyball, weight training.

Wilderness/Outdoors Hiking.

Trips College tours, cultural, day, shopping.

Program Information 1 session per year. Session length: 5 weeks in June, July. Ages: 14–19. 10–15 participants per session. Day program cost: $3900. Boarding program cost: $5200. Application fee: $60. Financial aid available.

Application Deadline Continuous.

Contact Mariann Arnold, Director of Admission, main address above. Phone: 203-697-2365. Fax: 203-697-2519. E-mail: marnold@choate.edu.

URL www.choate.edu/summerprograms

For more information, see page 456.

CHOATE ROSEMARY HALL JOHN F. KENNEDY INSTITUTE IN GOVERNMENT

Choate Rosemary Hall
333 Christian Street
Wallingford, Connecticut 06492

General Information Coed residential and day academic program established in 1985. Formal opportunities for the academically talented. High school credit may be earned.

Choate Rosemary Hall John F. Kennedy Institute in Government

Program Focus Government and political science.

Academics Economics, government and politics, precollege program, speech/debate, writing.

Sports Aerobics, basketball, climbing (wall), field hockey, lacrosse, soccer, softball, squash, swimming, tennis, track and field, volleyball, weight training.

Wilderness/Outdoors Hiking.

Trips College tours, cultural, day, overnight, shopping.

Program Information 1 session per year. Session length: 5 weeks in June, July. Ages: 15–19. 12–20 participants per session. Day program cost: $4200. Boarding program cost: $5400. Application fee: $60. Financial aid available. Washington D.C. trip: $455.

Application Deadline Continuous.

Contact Mariann Arnold, Director of Admission, main address above. Phone: 203-697-2365. Fax: 203-697-2519. E-mail: marnold@choate.edu.

URL www.choate.edu/summerprograms

For more information, see page 456.

CHOATE ROSEMARY HALL MATH AND SCIENCE WORKSHOPS

Choate Rosemary Hall
333 Christian Street
Wallingford, Connecticut 06492

General Information Coed residential and day academic program established in 2006. Formal opportunities for the academically talented.
Program Focus Enrichment and a stronger understanding of topics in Algebra II, Precalculus, Calculus, Chemistry, and Physics.
Academics Chemistry, mathematics, physics, science (general).
Sports Aerobics, basketball, bicycling, climbing (wall), field hockey, lacrosse, soccer, softball, squash, swimming, tennis, track and field, volleyball, weight training.
Wilderness/Outdoors Hiking.
Trips College tours, cultural, day, shopping.
Program Information 2 sessions per year. Session length: 2 weeks in June, July. Ages: 13–18. 6–12 participants per session. Day program cost: $1680. Boarding program cost: $2220. Application fee: $60. Financial aid available.
Application Deadline Continuous.
Contact Mariann Arnold, Director of Admission, main address above. Phone: 203-697-2365. Fax: 203-697-2519. E-mail: marnold@choate.edu.
URL www.choate.edu/summerprograms
For more information, see page 456.

CHOATE ROSEMARY HALL MATH/ SCIENCE INSTITUTE FOR GIRLS– CONNECT

Choate Rosemary Hall
333 Christian Street
Wallingford, Connecticut 06492

General Information Girls' residential and day academic program established in 1995. Formal opportunities for the academically talented.
Program Focus Mathematics and science project-based group learning.
Academics Biology, chemistry, ecology, environmental science, geology/earth science, health sciences, marine studies, mathematics, physics, science (general), study skills.
Special Interest Areas General camp activities.

Sports Aerobics, basketball, bicycling, climbing (wall), field hockey, lacrosse, soccer, softball, squash, swimming, tennis, track and field, volleyball, weight training.
Wilderness/Outdoors Hiking.
Trips Cultural, day, shopping.
Program Information 1 session per year. Session length: 4 weeks in June, July. Ages: 11–14. 15–30 participants per session. Day program cost: $3320. Boarding program cost: $4600. Application fee: $60. Financial aid available.
Application Deadline Continuous.
Contact Mariann Arnold, Director of Admission, main address above. Phone: 203-697-2365. Fax: 203-697-2519. E-mail: marnold@choate.edu.
URL www.choate.edu/summerprograms
For more information, see page 456.

CHOATE ROSEMARY HALL SUMMER ARTS CONSERVATORY–PLAYWRITING

Choate Rosemary Hall
Paul Mellon Arts Center
333 Christian Street
Wallingford, Connecticut 06492

General Information Coed residential and day arts program established in 1982. Formal opportunities for the artistically talented. High school credit may be earned.
Arts Playwriting, screenwriting.
Sports Racquetball, swimming, tennis.
Trips Cultural, day, overnight, shopping.
Program Information 1 session per year. Session length: 5 weeks in June, July. Ages: 12–18. 12 participants per session. Day program cost: $3975. Boarding program cost: $4975. Application fee: $60. Financial aid available. Optional New York City trip: $595.
Application Deadline May 30.
Jobs Positions for college students 21 and older.
Contact Mrs. Randi J. Brandt, Admissions Director, Arts Conservatory, main address above. Phone: 203-697-2423. Fax: 203-697-2396. E-mail: rbrandt@choate.edu.
URL www.choate.edu/summerprograms
For more information, see page 454.

CHOATE ROSEMARY HALL SUMMER ARTS CONSERVATORY–THEATER

Choate Rosemary Hall
Paul Mellon Arts Center
333 Christian Street
Wallingford, Connecticut 06492

General Information Coed residential and day arts program established in 1982. Formal opportunities for the artistically talented. High school credit may be earned.

Choate Rosemary Hall Summer Arts Conservatory–Theater

Arts Acting, dance, dance (ballet), dance (jazz), dance (tap), music (vocal), musical productions, musical theater, theater/drama, voice and speech.
Sports Racquetball, swimming, tennis.
Trips Cultural, overnight, shopping.
Program Information 1 session per year. Session length: 5 weeks in June, July. Ages: 12–18. 40 participants per session. Day program cost: $3975. Boarding program cost: $4975. Application fee: $60. Financial aid available. Optional New York City trip: $595.
Application Deadline May 30.
Jobs Positions for college students 21 and older.
Contact Mrs. Randi J. Brandt, Admissions Director, Arts Conservatory, main address above. Phone: 203-697-2423. Fax: 203-697-2396. E-mail: rbrandt@choate.edu.
URL www.choate.edu/summerprograms
For more information, see page 454.

CHOATE ROSEMARY HALL SUMMER ARTS CONSERVATORY–VISUAL ARTS PROGRAM

Choate Rosemary Hall
Paul Mellon Arts Center
333 Christian Street
Wallingford, Connecticut 06492

General Information Coed residential and day arts program established in 1982. Formal opportunities for the artistically talented. High school credit may be earned.
Arts Arts, ceramics, drawing, graphic arts, mixed media, painting, photography, pottery, studio arts, visual arts.
Sports Racquetball, swimming, tennis.
Trips Cultural, day, overnight, shopping.
Program Information 1 session per year. Session length: 5 weeks in June, July. Ages: 12–18. 20 participants per session. Day program cost: $3975. Boarding program cost: $4975. Application fee: $60. Financial aid available. Optional New York City trip: $595.
Application Deadline May 30.
Jobs Positions for college students 21 and older.
Contact Mrs. Randi J. Brandt, Admissions Director, Arts Conservatory, main address above. Phone: 203 697-2423. Fax: 203-697-2396. E-mail: rbrandt@choate.edu.
URL www.choate.edu/summerprograms
For more information, see page 454.

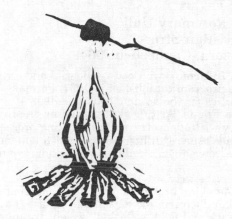

CHOATE ROSEMARY HALL SUMMER SESSION

Choate Rosemary Hall
333 Christian Street
Wallingford, Connecticut 06492

General Information Coed residential and day academic program established in 1916. High school credit may be earned.
Academics American literature, English as a second language, English language/literature, French language/literature, SAT/ACT preparation, Spanish language/literature, academics (general), anthropology, astronomy, biology, chemistry, computers, economics, environmental science, government and politics, history, humanities, journalism, marine studies, mathematics, physics, precollege program, psychology, reading, science (general), speech/debate, study skills, typing, writing.
Arts Ceramics, creative writing, drawing, photography, theater/drama.
Special Interest Areas General camp activities.
Sports Aerobics, baseball, basketball, climbing (wall), field hockey, football, lacrosse, soccer, softball, squash, swimming, tennis, track and field, volleyball, weight training.
Wilderness/Outdoors Hiking.
Trips College tours, cultural, day, shopping.

Choate Rosemary Hall Summer Session (continued)

Program Information 1 session per year. Session length: 5 weeks in June, July. Ages: 14–19. 200 participants per session. Day program cost: $900–$1650. Boarding program cost: $5400–$5500. Application fee: $60. Financial aid available.
Application Deadline Continuous.
Jobs Positions for college students.
Contact Mariann Arnold, Director of Admission, main address above. Phone: 203-697-2365. Fax: 203-697-2519. E-mail: marnold@choate.edu.
URL www.choate.edu/summerprograms
For more information, see page 456.

CHOATE ROSEMARY HALL WRITING PROJECT

Choate Rosemary Hall
333 Christian Street
Wallingford, Connecticut 06492

General Information Coed residential and day academic program established in 1987. Formal opportunities for the academically talented.
Program Focus Writing skills including creative and expository writing, poetry, and the writing process.
Academics American literature, English language/literature, journalism, reading, study skills, typing, writing.
Arts Creative writing.
Sports Aerobics, basketball, bicycling, climbing (wall), field hockey, lacrosse, soccer, softball, squash, swimming, tennis, track and field, volleyball, weight training.
Wilderness/Outdoors Hiking.
Trips College tours, cultural, day, shopping.
Program Information 2 sessions per year. Session length: 2 weeks in June, July. Ages: 14–18. 20–25 participants per session. Day program cost: $1680. Boarding program cost: $2220. Application fee: $60. Financial aid available.
Application Deadline Continuous.
Contact Mariann Arnold, Director of Admission, main address above. Phone: 203-697-2365. Fax: 203-697-2519. E-mail: marnold@choate.edu.
URL www.choate.edu/summerprograms
For more information, see page 456.

CHOATE ROSEMARY HALL YOUNG WRITERS WORKSHOP

Choate Rosemary Hall
333 Christian Street
Wallingford, Connecticut 06492

General Information Coed residential and day academic program established in 1997. Formal opportunities for the academically talented.
Academics American literature, English language/literature, journalism, reading, study skills, typing, writing.
Arts Creative writing.
Sports Aerobics, basketball, climbing (wall), field

hockey, in-line skating, lacrosse, soccer, softball, squash, swimming, tennis, track and field, volleyball, weight training.
Wilderness/Outdoors Hiking.
Trips Cultural, day, shopping.
Program Information 2 sessions per year. Session length: 2 weeks in June, July. Ages: 11–14. 25–30 participants per session. Day program cost: $1680. Boarding program cost: $2220. Application fee: $60. Financial aid available.
Application Deadline Continuous.
Contact Mariann Arnold, Director of Admission, main address above. Phone: 203-697-2365. Fax: 203-697-2519. E-mail: marnold@choate.edu.
URL www.choate.edu/summerprograms
For more information, see page 456.

CYBERCAMPS–UNIVERSITY OF BRIDGEPORT

Cybercamps–Giant Campus, Inc.
Bridgeport, Connecticut

General Information Coed residential and day academic program established in 1997. Formal opportunities for the academically talented.
Program Focus Computers and technology.
Academics Web page design, academics (general), computer programming, computer science (Advanced Placement), computers.
Arts Animation, digital media, film, graphic arts, musical productions, photography, television/video.
Special Interest Areas Computer game design, computer graphics, electronics, robotics, team building.
Program Information 1–12 sessions per year. Session length: 5 days in June, July, August. Ages: 7–18. 30–50 participants per session. Day program cost: $599–$749. Boarding program cost: $998–$1148.
Application Deadline Continuous.
Contact Camp Consultant, 3101 Western Avenue, Suite 100, Seattle, Washington 98121. Phone: 888-904-2267. Fax: 206-442-4501. E-mail: info@cybercamps.com.
URL www.cybercamps.com
For more information, see page 466.

CYBERCAMPS–UNIVERSITY OF HARTFORD

Cybercamps–Giant Campus, Inc.
Hartford, Connecticut

General Information Coed residential and day academic program established in 1997. Formal opportunities for the academically talented.
Program Focus Computers and technology.
Academics Web page design, academics (general), computer programming, computer science (Advanced Placement), computers.
Arts Animation, digital media, film, graphic arts, musical productions, photography, television/video.
Special Interest Areas Computer game design, computer graphics, electronics, robotics, team building.
Program Information 1–12 sessions per year. Session length: 5 days in June, July, August. Ages: 7–18. 30–50 participants per session. Day program cost: $599–$749. Boarding program cost: $998–$1148.
Application Deadline Continuous.
Jobs Positions for high school students 17 and older and college students 18 and older.
Contact Camp Consultant, 3101 Western Avenue, Suite 100, Seattle, Washington 98121. Phone: 888-904-2267. Fax: 206-442-4501. E-mail: info@cybercamps.com.
URL www.cybercamps.com

For more information, see page 466.

ID TECH CAMPS–SACRED HEART UNIVERSITY, FAIRFIELD, CT

iD Tech Camps
Sacred Heart University
Fairfield, Connecticut 06825

General Information Coed residential and day academic program established in 1999. Accredited by American Camping Association. Formal opportunities for the academically talented and artistically talented.
Program Focus Students create 2D and 3D video games, build robots to compete, design websites, film and edit digital movies, create their own comic book with digital photos, learn programming and more. One computer per student and an average of five students per staff member. Campers take home a project at the end of the weeklong course.
Academics Web page design, academics (general), computer programming, computer science (Advanced Placement), computers, precollege program.
Arts Animation, cinematography, digital media, drawing, film, film editing, film production, graphic arts, photography, television/video.
Special Interest Areas Career exploration, computer game design, computer graphics, electronics, leadership training, robotics, team building.
Sports Baseball, basketball, soccer, softball, swimming, volleyball.
Trips College tours.
Program Information 5–9 sessions per year. Session length: 5–7 days in June, July, August. Ages: 7–17. 40–50 participants per session. Day program cost: $729. Boarding program cost: $1129. Financial aid available.
Application Deadline Continuous.

Jobs Positions for college students 18 and older.
Contact Client Service Representatives, 42 West Campbell Avenue, Suite 301, Campbell, California 95008. Phone: 888-709-TECH. Fax: 408-871-2228. E-mail: info@internaldrive.com.
URL www.internaldrive.com

For more information, see page 520.

JUNIOR STATESMEN SUMMER SCHOOL–YALE UNIVERSITY

Junior Statesmen Foundation
Yale University
New Haven, Connecticut 06520

General Information Coed residential academic program established in 1989. Formal opportunities for the academically talented. High school credit may be earned.

Junior Statesmen Summer School–Yale University

Program Focus Constitutional law, American government, speech, debate, and leadership training.
Academics Communications, government and politics, government and politics (Advanced Placement),

Junior Statesmen Summer School–Yale University (continued)

journalism, precollege program, prelaw, social science, social studies, speech/debate.
Special Interest Areas Career exploration, leadership training.
Trips College tours, cultural, day.
Program Information 1 session per year. Session length: 4 weeks in June, July. Ages: 14–18. 200–300 participants per session. Boarding program cost: $4150. Financial aid available.
Application Deadline Continuous.
Contact Ms. Jessica Brow, National Summer School Director, 400 South El Camino Real, Suite 300, San Mateo, California 94402. Phone: 650-347-1600. Fax: 650-347-7200. E-mail: jsa@jsa.org.
URL summer.jsa.org/summer/princeton.html
For more information, see page 534.

KENT SCHOOL SUMMER WRITERS CAMP

Kent School
Route 341
Kent, Connecticut 06757

General Information Coed residential academic program established in 1995. Accredited by American Camping Association. Formal opportunities for the academically talented.

Kent School Summer Writers Camp

Program Focus Creative writing and athletic/recreational activities.
Academics English language/literature, journalism, reading, speech/debate, study skills, writing.
Arts Ceramics, creative writing, dance, drawing, music, painting, theater/drama.
Sports Basketball, boating, canoeing, fishing, in-line skating, rowing (crew/sculling), soccer, swimming, tennis, weight training.
Wilderness/Outdoors Hiking.
Trips Cultural, day.
Program Information 1 session per year. Session length: 3 weeks in July. Ages: 10–16. 50 participants per session. Boarding program cost: $2800. Application fee: $25. Financial aid available.

Application Deadline Continuous.
Jobs Positions for college students 18 and older.
Contact Ms. Meredith Schipani, Summer Camp Admissions Director, PO Box 2006, Kent, Connecticut 06757. Phone: 860-927-6118. Fax: 860-927-6109. E-mail: schipanim@kent-school.edu.
URL www.writerscamp.org
For more information, see page 536.

LANDMARK VOLUNTEERS: CONNECTICUT

Landmark Volunteers, Inc.
Connecticut

General Information Coed residential outdoor program and community service program established in 1992. High school credit may be earned.
Program Focus Opportunity for high school students to earn community service credit while working as a team for one week in the spring serving Hole in the Wall Gang Camp, or two weeks in summer at Sharon Audubon Society. Similar programs offered through Landmark Volunteers at over 50 locations in 20 states.
Academics Ecology, environmental science, social services.
Special Interest Areas Animal care, career exploration, community service, conservation projects, field research/expeditions, leadership training, nature study, team building, trail maintenance, work camp programs.
Wilderness/Outdoors Hiking.
Trips Cultural, day.
Program Information 2 sessions per year. Session length: 14–15 days in April, July, August. Ages: 14–18. 10–13 participants per session. Boarding program cost: $1250–$1300. Financial aid available.
Application Deadline Continuous.
Jobs Positions for college students.
Contact Ann Barrett, Executive Director, PO Box 455, Sheffield, Massachusetts 01257. Phone: 413-229-0255. Fax: 413-229-2050. E-mail: landmark@volunteers.com.
URL www.volunteers.com
For more information, see page 542.

MARIANAPOLIS SUMMER PROGRAM

Marianapolis Preparatory School
26 Chase Road
Thompson, Connecticut 06277-0368

General Information Coed residential and day academic program established in 1975. Formal opportunities for the academically talented and artistically talented. High school credit may be earned.

Marianapolis Summer Program

Program Focus ESL program.
Academics American literature, English as a second language, English language/literature, French language/literature, SAT/ACT preparation, Spanish language/literature, academics (general), art history/appreciation, biology, chemistry, classical languages/literatures, computer programming, computers, ecology, environmental science, geology/earth science, history, humanities, mathematics, religion, science (general), study skills.
Arts Acting, arts and crafts (general), chorus, creative writing, drawing, painting, photography, printmaking, theater/drama.
Special Interest Areas College planning, field trips (arts and culture).
Sports Baseball, basketball, cross-country, soccer, softball, swimming, tennis, volleyball.
Trips College tours, cultural, day, shopping.
Program Information 1 session per year. Session length: 6 weeks in June, July. Ages: 14–18. 60 participants per session. Day program cost: $1000–$2000. Boarding program cost: $6000.
Application Deadline Continuous.
Jobs Positions for college students 20 and older.
Summer Contact Dr. Edward Sembor, Director of Summer Program, 26 Chase Road, PO Box 304, Thompson, Connecticut 06277. Phone: 860-923-9565. Fax: 860-923-3730. E-mail: esembor@marianapolis.org.
Winter Contact Mr. Daniel M. Harrop, Director of Admissions, 26 Chase Road, PO Box 304, Thompson, Connecticut 06277. E-mail: dharrop@marianapolis.org.
URL www.marianapolis.org
For more information, see page 552.

MARVELWOOD SUMMER PROGRAM

The Marvelwood School
476 Skiff Mountain Road
Kent, Connecticut 06757

General Information Coed residential academic program established in 1964. High school credit may be earned.

Marvelwood Summer Program

Program Focus Reading, study skills, math, and English as a second language, outdoor scientific fieldwork.
Academics English as a second language, English language/literature, academics (general), biology, computers, environmental science, history, mathematics, reading, science (general), study skills, writing.
Arts Arts and crafts (general), creative writing, drawing, film, film production, music, painting, photography, studio arts, television/video, theater/drama, woodworking.
Special Interest Areas Community service, conservation projects, field research/expeditions, leadership training, team building.
Sports Bicycling, canoeing, climbing (wall), fishing, rappelling, ropes course, swimming, tennis.
Wilderness/Outdoors Canoe trips, hiking, mountain biking, rock climbing, white-water trips.
Trips Cultural, day, shopping.
Program Information 1 session per year. Session length: 4 weeks in June, July, August. Ages: 13–17. 30–60 participants per session. Boarding program cost: $5150–$6400. Application fee: $50. Financial aid available.
Application Deadline Continuous.
Jobs Positions for college students 21 and older.
Contact Caitlin Lynch, Director of Summer Admission, 476 Skiff Mountain Road, PO Box 3001, Kent, Connecticut 06757-3001. Phone: 800-440-9107. Fax: 860-927-0021. E-mail: caitlin.lynch@marvelwood.org.
URL www.marvelwood.org
For more information, see page 554.

Miss Porter's School Arts Alive!

Miss Porter's School
60 Main Street
Farmington, Connecticut 06032

General Information Girls' residential academic program and arts program established in 2003.
Program Focus Interdisciplinary academic program featuring studio, performing, and literary arts.
Academics English as a second language, English language/literature, academics (general), music, writing.
Arts Acting, arts, arts and crafts (general), ceramics, creative writing, dance, dance (jazz), dance (modern), drawing, fabric arts, graphic arts, jewelry making, mime, music, painting, photography, pottery, printmaking, studio arts, theater/drama, visual arts.
Special Interest Areas Field trips (arts and culture).
Sports Basketball, field hockey, lacrosse, martial arts, soccer, softball, squash, swimming, tennis, volleyball.
Trips Cultural, day.
Program Information 1–2 sessions per year. Session length: 13–28 days in July. Ages: 12–15. 30–60 participants per session. Boarding program cost: $2100–$3600. Application fee: $30. Financial aid available.
Application Deadline Continuous.
Jobs Positions for college students.
Contact Ms. Terry Armington, Director of Summer Programs, main address above. Phone: 860-409-3692. Fax: 860-409-3515. E-mail: summer_programs@missporters.org.
URL www.mpsartsalive.org

For more information, see page 558.

Miss Porter's School Athletic Experience

Miss Porter's School
60 Main Street
Farmington, Connecticut 06032

General Information Girls' residential and day sports camp established in 2005.
Program Focus Multi-sport experience offered as an alternative to one-sport, specialized camps.
Sports Athletic training, basketball, field hockey, lacrosse, physical fitness, soccer, softball, sports (general), squash, volleyball.
Program Information 1 session per year. Session length: 5 days in June, July. Ages: 11–15. 40 participants per session. Day program cost: $675. Boarding program cost: $750.
Application Deadline June 1.
Contact Ms. Terry Armington, Director of Summer Programs, main address above. Phone: 860-409-3692. Fax: 860-409-3515. E-mail: summer_programs@missporters.org.
URL www.mpsvacationprograms.org

For more information, see page 558.

Miss Porter's School Daoyun Chinese Summer Program

Miss Porter's School
60 Main Street
Farmington, Connecticut 06032

General Information Girls' residential academic program established in 2008.
Program Focus Chinese immersion.
Academics Chinese languages/literature.
Special Interest Areas Cross-cultural education.
Trips Cultural, day.
Program Information 1 session per year. Session length: 4 weeks in June, July. Ages: 11–15. 12 participants per session. Boarding program cost: $3000–$4000. Application fee: $30.
Application Deadline June 1.
Jobs Positions for college students.
Contact Ms. Terry Armington, Director of Summer Programs, 60 Main Street, Farmington, Connecticut 06032. Phone: 860-409-3692. Fax: 860-409-3515. E-mail: summer_programs@missporters.org.

For more information, see page 558.

MISS PORTER'S SCHOOL SUMMER CHALLENGE

Miss Porter's School
60 Main Street
Farmington, Connecticut 06032

General Information Girls' residential academic program established in 1995.

Miss Porter's School Summer Challenge

Program Focus An interdisciplinary academic program featuring science, mathematics, and technology.
Academics English as a second language, academics (general), astronomy, biology, chemistry, computers, marine studies, mathematics, physics, science (general).
Arts Arts and crafts (general).
Special Interest Areas Field trips (arts and culture).
Sports Basketball, field hockey, lacrosse, martial arts, soccer, softball, squash, swimming, tennis, volleyball.
Trips Day.
Program Information 1–2 sessions per year. Session length: 13–28 days in July. Ages: 12–15. 30–60 participants per session. Boarding program cost: $2100–$3600. Application fee: $30. Financial aid available.
Application Deadline Continuous.

Jobs Positions for college students.
Contact Ms. Terry Armington, Director of Summer Programs, main address above. Phone: 860-409-3692. Fax: 860-409-3515. E-mail: summer_programs@missporters.org.
URL www.summerchallenge.org
For more information, see page 558.

RUMSEY HALL SCHOOL SUMMER SESSION

Rumsey Hall School
201 Romford Road
Washington Depot, Connecticut 06794

General Information Coed residential and day academic program established in 1975. Formal opportunities for the academically talented. Specific services available for the learning disabled. High school credit may be earned.

Rumsey Hall School Summer Session

Academics American literature, English as a second language, English language/literature, art (Advanced Placement), classical languages/literatures, computers,

Rumsey Hall School Summer Session (continued)
mathematics, mathematics (Advanced Placement), study skills, writing.
Sports Basketball, bicycling, canoeing, equestrian sports, fishing, football, golf, horseback riding, lacrosse, ropes course, soccer, softball, swimming, tennis.
Wilderness/Outdoors Bicycle trips, hiking, mountain biking.
Trips Cultural, day, shopping.
Program Information 1 session per year. Session length: 5 weeks in July, August. Ages: 8–15. 60–70 participants per session. Day program cost: $1300–$2000. Boarding program cost: $5600. Application fee: $40–$100. Financial aid available.
Application Deadline Continuous.
Contact Matthew S. Hoeniger, main address above. Phone: 860-868-0535. Fax: 860-868-7907. E-mail: admiss@rumseyhall.org.
URL www.rumseyhall.org

For more information, see page 610.

SAINT THOMAS MORE SCHOOL–SUMMER ACADEMIC CAMP

Saint Thomas More School
45 Cottage Road
Oakdale, Connecticut 06370

General Information Boys' residential traditional camp and academic program established in 1970. Religious affiliation: Roman Catholic. Accredited by American Camping Association. Specific services available for the learning disabled. High school credit may be earned.
Academics American literature, English as a second language, English language/literature, SAT/ACT preparation, Spanish language/literature, academics (general), art history/appreciation, biology, chemistry, computers, environmental science, geology/earth science, government and politics, history, mathematics, physics, physiology, reading, religion, science (general), social science, social studies, study skills, writing.
Arts Arts and crafts (general).
Sports Baseball, basketball, boating, canoeing, fishing, football, in-line skating, kayaking, lacrosse, sailing, soccer, softball, sports (general), street/roller hockey, swimming, tennis, volleyball, weight training, windsurfing.
Trips Cultural, day, shopping.
Program Information 1 session per year. Session length: 3–5 weeks in June, July, August. Ages: 12+. 80–100 participants per session. Boarding program cost:

$5495–$5995. Application fee: $50–$75. Financial aid available.
Application Deadline Continuous.
Jobs Positions for college students 18 and older.
Contact Mr. Timothy Riordan, Director of Admissions, main address above. Phone: 860-823-3861. Fax: 860-823-3863. E-mail: triordan@stmct.org.
URL www.stmct.org

For more information, see page 614.

SALISBURY SUMMER SCHOOL

Salisbury Summer School
251 Canaan Road
Salisbury, Connecticut 06068

General Information Coed residential academic program established in 1946. Formal opportunities for the academically talented. Specific services available for the learning disabled. High school credit may be earned.

Salisbury Summer School

Program Focus Reading, writing, vocabulary, English, mathematics, and study skills.
Academics English as a second language, English language/literature, SAT/ACT preparation, academics (general), mathematics, reading, study skills, writing.
Arts Band, creative writing, dance, music, theater/drama.
Sports Aerobics, basketball, bicycling, canoeing, cross-country, golf, lacrosse, racquetball, soccer, softball, squash, swimming, tennis, volleyball, weight training, yoga.
Wilderness/Outdoors Bicycle trips, canoe trips, hiking, mountain biking.
Trips Cultural, day, shopping.
Program Information 1 session per year. Session length: 5–6 weeks in June, July, August. Ages: 13–18. 105–110 participants per session. Boarding program cost: $6700–$7000. Application fee: $30–$100. Financial aid available.
Application Deadline Continuous.
Jobs Positions for college students 20 and older.

Contact Peter Gilbert, Director of Admissions, main address above. Phone: 860-435-5700. Fax: 860-435-5750. E-mail: sss@salisburyschool.org.
URL www.salisburysummerschool.org
For more information, see page 620.

THE SARAH PORTER LEADERSHIP INSTITUTE

Miss Porter's School
60 Main Street
Farmington, Connecticut 06032

General Information Girls' residential academic program established in 2003.
Program Focus The knowledge, skills, and resources girls need to develop their leadership potential.
Academics Communications, speech/debate.
Special Interest Areas Leadership training, personal development, team building.
Sports Climbing (wall), martial arts, ropes course, swimming.
Trips Day.
Program Information 1–2 sessions per year. Session length: 1–2 weeks in June, July. Ages: 12–15. 30–50 participants per session. Boarding program cost: $700–$1550. Application fee: $15.
Application Deadline Continuous.
Contact Ms. Terry Armington, Director of Leadership and Summer Programs, main address above. Phone: 860-409-3692. Fax: 860-409-3515. E-mail: summer_programs@missporters.org.
URL www.sarahporterinstitute.org
For more information, see page 558.

SUMMER@RECTORY

The Rectory School
528 Pomfret Street
Pomfret, Connecticut 06258

General Information Coed residential and day academic program established in 1950. Religious affiliation: Episcopal. Formal opportunities for the academically talented and gifted. Specific services available for the learning disabled.
Program Focus English, mathematics, reading, study skills, and optional programs in performing arts and sports.
Academics American literature, English as a second language, English language/literature, academics (general), art (Advanced Placement), computers, history, linguistics, mathematics, mathematics (Advanced Placement), music, music (Advanced Placement), reading, study skills, writing.
Arts Acting, arts and crafts (general), band, batiking, ceramics, chorus, creative writing, drawing, fabric arts, graphic arts, jewelry making, music, music (chamber), music (ensemble), music (instrumental), music (jazz), music (orchestral), music (vocal), musical productions, painting, photography, theater/drama.
Sports Baseball, basketball, bicycling, fishing, football, golf, lacrosse, soccer, softball, street/roller hockey, swimming, tennis, volleyball, weight training.
Trips Cultural, day, overnight.
Program Information 1 session per year. Session length: 5 weeks in June, July. Ages: 9–15. 82 participants per session. Day program cost: $4000. Boarding program cost: $6950. Application fee: $50–$100.
Application Deadline Continuous.
Contact Mr. Vincent Ricci, Assistant Headmaster of Academics and Admissions, PO Box 68, 528 Pomfret Street, Pomfret, Connecticut 06258. Phone: 860-928-1328. Fax: 860-928-4961. E-mail: admissions@rectoryschool.org.
URL www.rectoryschool.org

Special Note
The Rectory School's exciting, coeducational, five-week program, summer@rectory, provides a unique experience for boarding and day students on our beautiful 138-acre campus in northeast Connecticut. We offer an inspiring, customized curriculum. The morning academic program provides choices for exploring an interest, challenging abilities, refreshing academic knowledge, improving study skills, and increasing English language proficiency. Students enroll in four courses for the five-week session. One course is the Individualized Instruction Program. Afternoon offerings include sports clinics, music camps, drama workshops, and recreational activities. Students may elect a different option for each week. Weekend field trips and off-campus excursions add to the enjoyment.

SUMMER ENGLISH EXPERIENCE

University of Connecticut American English Language Institute (UCAELI)
Storrs, Connecticut 06269

General Information Coed residential academic program established in 2006.

Summer English Experience

Program Focus English study.
Academics English as a second language, history, intercultural studies.
Arts Arts and crafts (general).
Special Interest Areas Homestays.
Trips Cultural, day, shopping.
Program Information 2 sessions per year. Session length: 19 days in June, July, August. Ages: 13–17. 15–30 participants per session. Boarding program cost: $2850.
Application Deadline June 1.
Jobs Positions for college students 16 and older.
Contact Mr. Arthur Galinat, Program Coordinator, 843 Bolton Road, U-1198, Storrs, Connecticut 16269. Phone: 860-486-2127. Fax: 860-486-3834. E-mail: arthur.galinat@uconn.edu
URL www.ucaeli.uconn.edu

For more information, see page 678.

THE SUMMER INSTITUTE FOR THE GIFTED AT FAIRFIELD UNIVERSITY

Summer Institute for the Gifted
Fairfield University
Fairfield, Connecticut 06824

General Information Coed day academic program established in 2003. Formal opportunities for the academically talented and gifted.
Academics American literature, English language/literature, French language/literature, SAT/ACT preparation, Spanish language/literature, academics (general), aerospace science, archaeology, architecture, art history/appreciation, biology, botany, business, chemistry, classical languages/literatures, communications, computers, engineering, environmental science, geology/earth science, government and politics, history, marine studies, mathematics, music, oceanography, philosophy, physics, precollege program, psychology, social studies, speech/debate, study skills, writing.
Arts Arts and crafts (general), chorus, creative writing, dance, drawing, music, music (chamber), music (classical), music (ensemble), musical productions, painting, photography, sculpture, theater/drama, weaving.
Special Interest Areas Animal care, chess, electronics, robotics.
Sports Basketball, field hockey, football, lacrosse, martial arts, soccer, squash, swimming, tennis, volleyball.
Program Information 1–2 sessions per year. Session length: 3 weeks in June, July, August. Ages: 6–11. 150–250 participants per session. Day program cost: $1825–$2000. Application fee: $75. Financial aid available.
Application Deadline May 14.
Jobs Positions for college students 19 and older.
Contact Ms. Barbara Swicord, Director, River Plaza, 9 West Broad Street, Stamford, Connecticut 06902-3788. Phone: 866-303-4744. Fax: 203-399-5598. E-mail: sig.info@aifs.com.
URL www.giftedstudy.com

For more information, see page 654.

TAFT SUMMER SCHOOL

The Taft School
110 Woodbury Road
Watertown, Connecticut 06795

General Information Coed residential and day academic program established in 1982. Accredited by American Camping Association. Formal opportunities for the academically talented.

Taft Summer School

Program Focus Academic enrichment courses.
Academics American literature, English as a second language, English language/literature, French language/literature, SAT/ACT preparation, Spanish language/literature, academics (general), art history/appreciation, biology, chemistry, environmental science, history, journalism, mathematics, physics, psychology, reading, speech/debate, study skills, writing.
Arts Acting, creative writing, drawing, painting, photography, printmaking, television/video, theater/drama.
Sports Aerobics, basketball, soccer, softball, sports (general), squash, tennis, track and field, volleyball, weight training.
Trips Cultural, day, shopping.
Program Information 1 session per year. Session length: 35–40 days in June, July. Ages: 12–18. 150–160 participants per session. Day program cost: $3400. Boarding program cost: $5500. Application fee: $50. Financial aid available.
Application Deadline Continuous.
Jobs Positions for college students 21 and older.
Summer Contact Stephen J. McCabe, Jr., Director, main address above. Phone: 860-945-7961. Fax: 860-945-7859. E-mail: summerschool@taftschool.org.
Winter Contact Kristina Kulikauskas, Program Office Manager, main address above. Phone: 860-945-7967.

Fax: 860-945-7859. E-mail: summerschool@taftschool.org.
URL www.taftschool.org/summer
For more information, see page 666.

UNIVERSITY OF CONNECTICUT MENTOR CONNECTION

University of Connecticut Neag Center for Gifted Education and Talent Development
2131 Hillside Road, Unit 3007
Storrs, Connecticut 06269-3007

General Information Coed residential academic program and cultural program established in 1996. Formal opportunities for the academically talented and artistically talented. College credit may be earned.

University of Connecticut Mentor Connection

Program Focus Students work with a university mentor in field of mutual interest.
Academics American literature, English as a second language, English language/literature, academics (general), anthropology, archaeology, astronomy, biology, chemistry, communications, computer programming, engineering, history, humanities, mathematics, physics, physiology, psychology, science (general), social science, social studies, writing.
Arts Creative writing, puppetry.
Special Interest Areas Career exploration, college planning, field research/expeditions, robotics, team building.
Trips Cultural, day.
Program Information 1 session per year. Session length: 3 weeks in July. Ages: 16–17. 75–80 participants per session. Boarding program cost: $3100. Financial aid available. Open to participants entering grades 11–12.
Application Deadline May 1.
Jobs Positions for college students 21 and older.
Contact Heather Spottiswoode, Program Manager, main address above. Phone: 860-486-0283. Fax: 860-486-2900. E-mail: mentorconnection@uconn.edu.
URL www.gifted.uconn.edu/

For more information, see page 680.

WORLD HORIZONS INTERNATIONAL–CONNECTICUT

World Horizons International
Bethlehem, Connecticut

General Information Coed residential arts program established in 2007. Formal opportunities for the artistically talented.
Program Focus Photography, puppetry, mask making, and performing.
Arts Mask making, performing arts, photography, puppetry, sculpture, theater/drama.
Wilderness/Outdoors Hiking.
Trips Day, overnight, shopping.
Program Information 1–5 sessions per year. Session length: 1–2 weeks in July, August. Ages: 14–18. 10–12 participants per session. Boarding program cost: $1200–$6000. Application fee: $175. Financial aid available.
Application Deadline Continuous.
Jobs Positions for college students 21 and older.
Contact Mr. Stuart L. Rabinowitz, Executive Director, PO Box 662, Bethlehem, Connecticut 06751. Phone: 800-262-5874. Fax: 203-266-6227. E-mail: worldhorizons@att.net.
URL www.world-horizons.com

For more information, see page 714.

DISTRICT OF COLUMBIA

CYBERCAMPS–AMERICAN UNIVERSITY

Cybercamps–Giant Campus, Inc.
Washington, District of Columbia

General Information Coed residential and day academic program. Formal opportunities for the academically talented.

Cybercamps–American University

Program Focus Computers and technology.
Academics Web page design, academics (general), computer programming, computer science (Advanced Placement), computers.
Arts Animation, digital media, film, graphic arts, musical productions, photography, television/video.
Special Interest Areas Computer game design, computer graphics, electronics, robotics, team building.
Program Information 1–12 sessions per year. Session length: 5 days in June, July, August. Ages: 7–18. 30–50 participants per session. Day program cost: $599–$749. Boarding program cost: $998–$1148.
Application Deadline Continuous.
Jobs Positions for high school students 17 and older and college students 18 and older.
Contact Camp Consultant, 3101 Western Avenue, Suite 100, Seattle, Washington 98121. Phone: 888-904-2267. Fax: 206-442-4501. E-mail: info@cybercamps.com.
URL www.cybercamps.com

For more information, see page 466.

GEORGETOWN UNIVERSITY AMERICAN POLITICS AND PUBLIC AFFAIRS

Georgetown University
3307 M Street, NW
Suite 202
Washington, District of Columbia 20057

General Information Coed residential and day academic program.
Program Focus Politics and public affairs.
Academics Government and politics.
Trips Cultural, day.
Program Information 1 session per year. Session length: 7–8 days in July. Ages: 15–18. Day program cost: $1100. Boarding program cost: $1575. Application fee: $35. Financial aid available.
Application Deadline Continuous.
Contact Ms. Crystal Hall, Office of Admissions, Georgetown University Special Programs, PO Box 571006, Washington, District of Columbia 20057. Phone: 202-687-8600. Fax: 202-687-8954. E-mail: sscespecialprograms@georgetown.edu.
URL summer.georgetown.edu

For more information, see page 498.

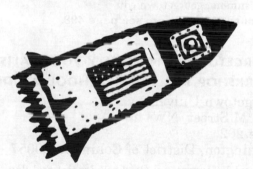

GEORGETOWN UNIVERSITY COLLEGE PREP PROGRAM

Georgetown University
3307 M Street, NW
Suite 202
Washington, District of Columbia 20057

General Information Coed residential and day academic program.

Georgetown University College Prep Program

Program Focus Math, English, and college research/study skills.
Academics English language/literature, SAT/ACT preparation, mathematics, study skills.
Trips Cultural.
Program Information 1 session per year. Session length: 5 weeks in June, July. Ages: 15 18. 55–70 participants per session. Day program cost: $2600–$2800. Boarding program cost: $4325–$4800. Application fee: $35. Financial aid available.
Application Deadline Continuous.

Georgetown University College Prep Program (continued)

Contact Ms. Crystal Hall, Office of Admissions, Georgetown University Special Programs, PO Box 571006, Washington, District of Columbia 20057-1010. Phone: 202-687-8600. Fax: 202-687-8954. E-mail: sscespecialprograms@georgetown.edu.
URL summer.georgetown.edu
For more information, see page 498.

GEORGETOWN UNIVERSITY GATEWAY TO BUSINESS PROGRAM FOR HIGH SCHOOL STUDENTS

Georgetown University
3307 M Street, NW
Suite 202
Washington, District of Columbia 20057

General Information Coed residential academic program. College credit may be earned.
Program Focus Business, finance, marketing, accounting, management, communications, strategy, planning, organizational behavior.
Academics Academics (general), business, communications, management, marketing.
Trips Cultural.
Program Information 1 session per year. Session length: 5 weeks in July, August. Ages: 16–18. 45–95 participants per session. Boarding program cost: $5000–$6700. Application fee: $35. Financial aid available.
Application Deadline Continuous.
Contact Ms. Crystal Hall, Office of Admissions, Georgetown University Special Programs, PO Box 571006, Washington, District of Columbia 20057. Phone: 202-687-8600. Fax: 202-687-8954. E-mail: sscespecialprograms@georgetown.edu.
URL summer.georgetown.edu
For more information, see page 498.

GEORGETOWN UNIVERSITY INTERNATIONAL RELATIONS PROGRAM FOR HIGH SCHOOL STUDENTS

Georgetown University
3307 M Street, NW
Suite 202
Washington, District of Columbia 20057

General Information Coed residential and day academic program. Formal opportunities for the academically talented.
Program Focus International relations and global affairs.
Academics Academics (general), global issues, government and politics, international relations.
Trips Cultural.
Program Information 1 session per year. Session length: 7–8 days in July. Ages: 15–18. 125–150 participants per session. Day program cost: $1100. Boarding program cost: $1575. Application fee: $35. Financial aid available.
Application Deadline Continuous.
Contact Ms. Crystal Hall, Office of Admissions, Georgetown University Special Programs, PO Box 571006, Washington, District of Columbia 20057. Phone: 202-687-8600. Fax: 202-687-8954. E-mail: sscespecialprograms@georgetown.edu.
URL summer.georgetown.edu
For more information, see page 498.

GEORGETOWN UNIVERSITY JOURNALISM WORKSHOP FOR HIGH SCHOOL STUDENTS

Georgetown University
3307 M Street, NW
Suite 202
Washington, District of Columbia 20057

General Information Coed residential and day academic program.
Program Focus Reporting, journalism, media, photo and print fields within journalism.
Academics Web page design, communications, journalism, photojournalism, writing.
Trips Cultural.
Program Information 1 session per year. Session length: 20–21 days in July, August. Ages: 15–18. Day program cost: $3100–$4000. Boarding program cost: $4870–$5770. Application fee: $35. Financial aid available.
Application Deadline Continuous.
Contact Ms. Crystal Hall, Office of Admissions, Georgetown University Special Programs, PO Box 571006, Washington, District of Columbia 20057. Phone: 202-687-8600. Fax: 202-687-8954. E-mail: sscespecialprograms@georgetown.edu.
URL summer.georgetown.edu
For more information, see page 498.

GEORGETOWN UNIVERSITY SUMMER COLLEGE FOR HIGH SCHOOL STUDENTS

Georgetown University
3307 M Street, NW
Suite 202
Washington, District of Columbia 20057

General Information Coed residential and day academic program. Formal opportunities for the academically talented. College credit may be earned.
Academics American literature, English language/literature, French language/literature, German language/literature, Italian language/literature, Spanish language/literature, academics (general), art, art history/appreciation, biology, business, chemistry, computers, economics, government and politics, history, mathematics, music, philosophy, physics, psychology, reading, sociology, writing.
Trips Cultural.
Program Information 2 sessions per year. Session length: 5 weeks in June, July, August. Ages: 16–18. 45–120 participants per session. Day program cost: $5460. Boarding program cost: $7535. Application fee: $35. Financial aid available.
Application Deadline Continuous.
Contact Ms. Crystal Hall, Office of Admissions, Georgetown University Special Programs, PO Box 571006, Washington, District of Columbia 20057. Phone: 202-687-8600. Fax: 202-687-8954. E-mail: sscespecialprograms@georgetown.edu.
URL summer.georgetown.edu

For more information, see page 498.

GEORGE WASHINGTON UNIVERSITY SUMMER SCHOLARS MINI-COURSES

The George Washington University
2100 Foxhall Road, NW
Mount Vernon Campus
Washington, District of Columbia 20007

General Information Coed residential and day academic program. Formal opportunities for the academically talented.
Program Focus Opportunity to explore and analyze complex issues in possible college fields of study.
Academics Academics (general), communications, criminal justice, journalism, law, photojournalism.
Trips Cultural, day.

Program Information 1 session per year. Session length: 10 days in June. 90 participants per session. Day program cost: $1670–$1820. Boarding program cost: $2300–$2450. Application fee: $30. Open to students completing grades 9–11.
Application Deadline Continuous.
Contact Ms. Barbara Frank, Director, main address above. Phone: 202-242-6802. Fax: 202-242-6761. E-mail: scholars@gwu.edu.
URL www.summerscholars.gwu.edu

For more information, see page 500.

GEORGE WASHINGTON UNIVERSITY SUMMER SCHOLARS PRE-COLLEGE PROGRAM

The George Washington University
2100 Foxhall Road, NW
Mount Vernon Campus
Washington, District of Columbia 20007

General Information Coed residential and day academic program. Formal opportunities for the academically talented. College credit may be earned.

George Washington University Summer Scholars Pre-college Program

Program Focus Pre-college/college-prep program.
Academics American literature, English language/literature, French language/literature, Spanish

George Washington University Summer Scholars Pre-college Program (continued)

language/literature, academics (general), anthropology, area studies, art (Advanced Placement), art history/appreciation, biology, chemistry, ecology, economics, engineering, environmental science, geology/earth science, government and politics, history, humanities, mathematics, music, philosophy, precollege program, psychology, religion, social science, study skills, writing.
Arts Dance, music, theater/drama.
Sports Basketball, bicycling, ropes course, swimming, tennis, volleyball.
Wilderness/Outdoors Bicycle trips, hiking, rafting, white-water trips.
Trips College tours, cultural, day, shopping.
Program Information 1 session per year. Session length: 43 days in July, August. 40–60 participants per session. Day program cost: $4189. Boarding program cost: $6100. Application fee: $30. Financial aid available. Open to participants entering grade 12.
Application Deadline Continuous.
Contact Ms. Barbara Frank, Director, main address above. Phone: 202-242-6802. Fax: 202-242-6761. E-mail: scholars@gwu.edu.
URL www.summerscholars.gwu.edu

For more information, see page 500.

iD Tech Camps–Georgetown University, Washington, D.C.

iD Tech Camps
Georgetown University
Washington, District of Columbia 20057

General Information Coed residential and day academic program established in 1999. Accredited by American Camping Association. Formal opportunities for the academically talented and artistically talented.
Program Focus Students create 2D and 3D video games, build robots to compete, design websites, film and edit digital movies, create their own comic book with digital photos, learn programming and more. One computer per student and an average of five students per staff member. Campers take home a project at the end of the weeklong course.
Academics Web page design, academics (general), computer programming, computer science (Advanced Placement), computers, precollege program.
Arts Animation, cartooning, cinematography, digital media, drawing, film, film editing, film production, graphic arts, photography, television/video.
Special Interest Areas Career exploration, computer game design, computer graphics, electronics, leadership training, robotics, team building.
Sports Baseball, basketball, soccer, softball, swimming, volleyball.
Trips College tours.
Program Information 5–9 sessions per year. Session length: 5–7 days in June, July, August. Ages: 7–17. 40–50 participants per session. Day program cost: $729. Boarding program cost: $1129. Financial aid available.
Application Deadline Continuous.
Jobs Positions for college students 18 and older.

Contact Client Service Representatives, 42 West Campbell Avenue, Suite 301, Campbell, California 95008. Phone: 888-709-TECH. Fax: 408-871-2228. E-mail: info@internaldrive.com.
URL www.internaldrive.com

For more information, see page 520.

Junior Statesmen Summer School–Georgetown University

Junior Statesmen Foundation
Georgetown University
Washington, District of Columbia 20057

General Information Coed residential academic program established in 1981. Formal opportunities for the academically talented. High school credit may be earned.

Junior Statesmen Summer School–Georgetown University

Program Focus American government, constitutional law, debate, leadership, and U.S. foreign policy.
Academics Communications, government and politics, government and politics (Advanced Placement), history, international relations, precollege program, prelaw, social science, social studies, speech/debate, writing.
Special Interest Areas Career exploration, leadership training.
Trips College tours, cultural, day.
Program Information 2 sessions per year. Session

length: 3 weeks in June, July, August. Ages: 15–18. 200–300 participants per session. Boarding program cost: $4150. Financial aid available.
Application Deadline Continuous.
Contact Ms. Jessica Brow, National Summer School Director, 400 South El Camino Real, Suite 300, San Mateo, California 94402. Phone: 650-347-1600. Fax: 650-347-7200. E-mail: jsa@jsa.org.
URL summer.jsa.org/summer/georgetown.html
For more information, see page 534.

NATIONAL STUDENT LEADERSHIP CONFERENCE: ENTREPRENEURSHIP AND BUSINESS–WASHINGTON, D.C.

National Student Leadership Conference
American University
Washington, District of Columbia

General Information Coed residential academic program established in 1989. Formal opportunities for the academically talented. College credit may be earned.
Program Focus Leadership, business and entrepreneurship, career exploration.
Academics Business.
Special Interest Areas Career exploration, leadership training, team building.
Trips College tours, cultural, shopping.
Program Information 1–4 sessions per year. Session length: 10 days in June, July, August. Ages: 14–18. 150 participants per session. Boarding program cost: $2295. Financial aid available.
Application Deadline Continuous.
Jobs Positions for college students 18 and older.
Contact Director of Admissions, 414 North Orleans Street, Suite LL8, Chicago, Illinois 60610-1087. Phone: 312-322-9999. Fax: 312-765-0081. E-mail: info@nslcleaders.org.
URL www.nslcleaders.org
For more information, see page 564.

NATIONAL STUDENT LEADERSHIP CONFERENCE: FORENSIC SCIENCE

National Student Leadership Conference
American University
Washington, District of Columbia

General Information Coed residential academic program established in 1989. Formal opportunities for the academically talented. College credit may be earned.
Program Focus Leadership training, forensic science, career exploration.
Academics Academics (general), anatomy, criminal justice, physiology, science (general).
Special Interest Areas Career exploration, leadership training, team building.
Trips College tours, cultural, shopping.
Program Information 1–4 sessions per year. Session length: 10 days in June, July, August. Ages: 14–18. 150 participants per session. Boarding program cost: $2895. Financial aid available.
Application Deadline Continuous.
Jobs Positions for college students 18 and older.
Contact Director of Admissions, 414 North Orleans Street, Suite LL8, Chicago, Illinois 60610-1087. Phone: 312-322-9999. Fax: 312-765-0081. E-mail: info@nslcleaders.org.
URL www.nslcleaders.org
For more information, see page 564.

NATIONAL STUDENT LEADERSHIP CONFERENCE: GLOBALIZATION AND INTERNATIONAL BUSINESS–WASHINGTON, D.C.

National Student Leadership Conference
American University
Washington, District of Columbia

General Information Coed residential academic program established in 1989. Formal opportunities for the academically talented. College credit may be earned.
Program Focus Leadership, career exploration, economics, business, international relations.
Academics Business, economics, government and politics, international relations.
Special Interest Areas Career exploration, leadership training, team building.
Trips College tours, cultural, shopping.
Program Information 1–4 sessions per year. Session length: 10 days in June, July, August. Ages: 14–18. 150 participants per session. Boarding program cost: $2295. Financial aid available.
Application Deadline Continuous.
Jobs Positions for college students 18 and older.
Contact Director of Admissions, 414 North Orleans Street, Suite LL8, Chicago, Illinois 60610-1087. Phone: 312-322-9999. Fax: 312-765-0081. E-mail: info@nslcleaders.org.
URL www.nslcleaders.org
For more information, see page 564.

NATIONAL STUDENT LEADERSHIP CONFERENCE: INTELLIGENCE AND NATIONAL SECURITY

National Student Leadership Conference
American University
Washington, District of Columbia

General Information Coed residential academic program established in 1989. Formal opportunities for the academically talented. College credit may be earned.
Program Focus Leadership, enrichment, and national security career exploration.
Academics Global issues, government and politics.
Special Interest Areas Career exploration, leadership training, team building.
Trips College tours, cultural, shopping.
Program Information 1–4 sessions per year. Session length: 10 days in June, July, August. Ages: 14–18. 150 participants per session. Boarding program cost: $2295. Financial aid available.
Application Deadline Continuous.
Jobs Positions for college students 18 and older.
Contact Director of Admissions, 414 North Orleans Street, Suite LL8, Chicago, Illinois 60610-1087. Phone: 312-322-9999. Fax: 312-765-0081. E-mail: info@nslcleaders.org.
URL www.nslcleaders.org
For more information, see page 564.

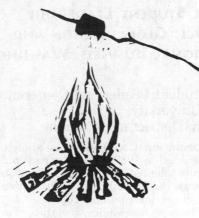

NATIONAL STUDENT LEADERSHIP CONFERENCE: INTERNATIONAL DIPLOMACY–WASHINGTON, D.C.

National Student Leadership Conference
American University
Washington, District of Columbia

General Information Coed residential academic program established in 1989. Formal opportunities for the academically talented. College credit may be earned.

National Student Leadership Conference: International Diplomacy–Washington, D.C.

Program Focus Leadership, career exploration, international relations.
Academics Government and politics, international relations.
Special Interest Areas Career exploration, leadership training, team building.
Trips College tours, cultural, shopping.
Program Information 1–4 sessions per year. Session length: 10 days in June, July, August. Ages: 14–18. 150 participants per session. Boarding program cost: $2295. Financial aid available.
Application Deadline Continuous.
Jobs Positions for college students 18 and older.
Contact Director of Admissions, 414 North Orleans Street, Suite LL8, Chicago, Illinois 60610-1087. Phone: 312-322-9999. Fax: 312-765-0081. E-mail: info@nslcleaders.org
URL www.nslcleaders.org
For more information, see page 564.

NATIONAL STUDENT LEADERSHIP CONFERENCE: JOURNALISM AND MASS COMMUNICATION

National Student Leadership Conference
American University
Washington, District of Columbia

General Information Coed residential academic program established in 1989. Formal opportunities for the academically talented. College credit may be earned.
Program Focus Leadership, career exploration, communication and journalism.
Academics Communications, journalism.
Arts Film, photography, radio broadcasting, television/video.
Special Interest Areas Career exploration, leadership training, team building.
Trips College tours, cultural, shopping.
Program Information 1–4 sessions per year. Session length: 13 days in June, July, August. Ages: 14–18. 150 participants per session. Boarding program cost: $2795. Financial aid available.
Application Deadline Continuous.
Jobs Positions for college students 18 and older.
Contact Director of Admissions, 414 North Orleans Street, Suite LL8, Chicago, Illinois 60610-1087. Phone: 312-322-9999. Fax: 312-765-0081. E-mail: info@nslcleaders.org.
URL www.nslcleaders.org
For more information, see page 564.

NATIONAL STUDENT LEADERSHIP CONFERENCE: LAW AND ADVOCACY–WASHINGTON, D.C.

National Student Leadership Conference
American University
Washington, District of Columbia

General Information Coed residential academic program established in 1989. Formal opportunities for the academically talented. College credit may be earned.
Program Focus Leadership, career exploration, law.
Academics Prelaw.
Special Interest Areas Career exploration, leadership training, team building.
Trips College tours, cultural, shopping.
Program Information 1–4 sessions per year. Session length: 10 days in June, July, August. Ages: 14–18. 150 participants per session. Boarding program cost: $2295. Financial aid available.
Application Deadline Continuous.
Jobs Positions for college students 18 and older.
Contact Director of Admissions, 414 North Orleans Street, Suite LL8, Chicago, Illinois 60610-1087. Phone: 312-322-9999. Fax: 312-765-0081. E-mail: info@nslcleaders.org.
URL www.nslcleaders.org
For more information, see page 564.

NATIONAL STUDENT LEADERSHIP CONFERENCE: U.S. POLICY AND POLITICS

National Student Leadership Conference
American University
Washington, District of Columbia

General Information Coed residential academic program established in 1989. Formal opportunities for the academically talented. College credit may be earned.
Program Focus Leadership, career exploration, political science and American politics.
Academics Government and politics.
Special Interest Areas Career exploration, leadership training, team building.
Trips College tours, cultural, shopping.
Program Information 1–4 sessions per year. Session length: 10 days in June, July, August. Ages: 14–18. 150 participants per session. Boarding program cost: $2295. Financial aid available.
Application Deadline Continuous.
Jobs Positions for college students 18 and older.
Contact Director of Admissions, 414 North Orleans Street, Suite LL8, Chicago, Illinois 60610-1087. Phone: 312-322-9999. Fax: 312-765-0081. E-mail: info@nslcleaders.org.
URL www.nslcleaders.org
For more information, see page 564.

FLORIDA

CYBERCAMPS–BARRY UNIVERSITY

Cybercamps–Giant Campus, Inc.
Miami Shores, Florida

General Information Coed residential and day academic program established in 1997. Formal opportunities for the academically talented.
Program Focus Computers and technology.
Academics Web page design, academics (general), computer programming, computer science (Advanced Placement), computers.
Arts Animation, digital media, film, graphic arts, musical productions, photography, television/video.
Special Interest Areas Computer game design, computer graphics, electronics, robotics, team building.

Cybercamps–Barry University (continued)

Program Information 1–12 sessions per year. Session length: 5 days in June, July, August. Ages: 7–18. 30–50 participants per session. Day program cost: $599–$749. Boarding program cost: $998–$1148.
Application Deadline Continuous.
Jobs Positions for high school students 17 and older and college students 18 and older.
Contact Camp Consultant, 3101 Western Avenue, Suite 100, Seattle, Washington 98121. Phone: 888-904-2267. Fax: 206-442-4501. E-mail: info@cybercamps.com.
URL www.cybercamps.com
For more information, see page 466.

CYBERCAMPS–NOVA SOUTHEASTERN UNIVERSITY

Cybercamps–Giant Campus, Inc.
Fort Lauderdale, Florida

General Information Coed residential and day academic program established in 1997. Formal opportunities for the academically talented.
Program Focus Computers and technology.
Academics Web page design, academics (general), computer programming, computer science (Advanced Placement), computers.
Arts Animation, digital media, film, graphic arts, musical productions, photography, television/video.
Special Interest Areas Computer game design, computer graphics, electronics, robotics, team building.
Program Information 1–12 sessions per year. Session length: 5 days in June, July, August. Ages: 7–18. 30–50 participants per session. Day program cost: $599–$749. Boarding program cost: $998–$1148.
Application Deadline Continuous.
Contact Camp Consultant, 3101 Western Avenue, Suite 100, Seattle, Washington 98121. Phone: 888-904-2267. Fax: 206-442-4501. E-mail: info@cybercamps.com.
URL www.cybercamps.com
For more information, see page 466.

CYBERCAMPS–UNIVERSITY OF CENTRAL FLORIDA

Cybercamps–Giant Campus, Inc.
Orlando, Florida

General Information Coed residential and day academic program established in 1997. Formal opportunities for the academically talented.
Program Focus Computers and technology.
Academics Web page design, academics (general), computer programming, computer science (Advanced Placement), computers.
Arts Animation, digital media, film, graphic arts, musical productions, photography, television/video.
Special Interest Areas Computer game design, computer graphics, electronics, robotics, team building.
Program Information 1–12 sessions per year. Session length: 5 days in June, July, August. Ages: 7–18. 30–50

participants per session. Day program cost: $599–$749. Boarding program cost: $998–$1148.
Application Deadline Continuous.
Contact Camp Consultant, 3101 Western Avenue, Suite 100, Seattle, Washington 98121. Phone: 888-904-2267. Fax: 206-442-4501. E-mail: info@cybercamps.com.
URL www.cybercamps.com
For more information, see page 466.

CYBERCAMPS–UNIVERSITY OF MIAMI

Cybercamps–Giant Campus, Inc.
Coral Gables, Florida

General Information Coed residential and day academic program established in 1997. Formal opportunities for the academically talented.
Program Focus Computers and technology.
Academics Web page design, academics (general), computer programming, computer science (Advanced Placement), computers.
Arts Animation, digital media, film, graphic arts, musical productions, photography, television/video.
Special Interest Areas Computer game design, computer graphics, electronics, robotics, team building.
Program Information 1–12 sessions per year. Session length: 5 days in June, July, August. Ages: 7–18. 30–50 participants per session. Day program cost: $599–$749. Boarding program cost: $998–$1148.
Application Deadline Continuous.
Contact Camp Consultant, 3101 Western Avenue, Suite 100, Seattle, Washington 98121. Phone: 888-904-2267. Fax: 206-442-4501. E-mail: info@cybercamps.com.
URL www.cybercamps.com
For more information, see page 466.

iD TECH CAMPS–UNIVERSITY OF CENTRAL FLORIDA, ORLANDO, FL

iD Tech Camps
Orlando, Florida

General Information Coed residential and day academic program established in 1999. Accredited by American Camping Association. Formal opportunities for the academically talented and artistically talented.
Program Focus Students create 2D and 3D video games, build robots to compete, design websites, film

and edit digital movies, create their own comic book with digital photos, learn programming, and more. One computer per student and an average of five students per staff member. Campers take home a project at the end of the weeklong course.
Academics Web page design, academics (general), computer programming, computer science (Advanced Placement), computers, precollege program.
Arts Animation, cinematography, digital media, drawing, film, film editing, film production, graphic arts, photography, television/video.
Special Interest Areas Career exploration, computer game design, computer graphics, electronics, leadership training, robotics, team building.
Sports Baseball, basketball, soccer, softball, swimming, volleyball.
Trips College tours.
Program Information 5–9 sessions per year. Session length: 5–7 days in June, July, August. Ages: 7–17. 40–50 participants per session. Day program cost: $729. Boarding program cost: $1129. Financial aid available.
Application Deadline Continuous.
Jobs Positions for college students 18 and older.
Contact Client Services Representatives, 42 West Campbell Avenue, Suite 301, Campbell, California 95008. Phone: 888-709-TECH. Fax: 408-871-2228.
E-mail: info@internaldrive.com.
URL www.internaldrive.com
For more information, see page 520.

iD TECH CAMPS–UNIVERSITY OF MIAMI, CORAL GABLES, FL

iD Tech Camps
University of Miami
Coral Gables, Florida 33124

General Information Coed residential and day academic program established in 1999. Accredited by American Camping Association. Formal opportunities for the academically talented and artistically talented.
Program Focus Students create 2D and 3D video games, build robots to compete, design websites, film and edit digital movies, create their own comic book with digital photos, learn programming and more. One computer per student and an average of five students per staff member. Campers take home a project at the end of the weeklong course.
Academics Web page design, academics (general), computer programming, computer science (Advanced Placement), computers, precollege program.
Arts Animation, cinematography, digital media, drawing, film, film editing, film production, graphic arts, photography, television/video.
Special Interest Areas Career exploration, computer game design, computer graphics, electronics, leadership training, robotics, team building.
Sports Baseball, basketball, soccer, softball, swimming, volleyball.
Trips College tours.
Program Information 5–9 sessions per year. Session length: 6–7 days in June, July, August. Ages: 7–17. 40–50 participants per session. Day program cost: $699.

Boarding program cost: $1099. Financial aid available.
Application Deadline Continuous.
Jobs Positions for college students 18 and older.
Contact Client Service Representatives, 42 West Campbell Avenue, Suite 301, Campbell, California 95008. Phone: 888-709-TECH. Fax: 408-871-2228.
E-mail: info@internaldrive.com.
URL www.internaldrive.com
For more information, see page 520.

SEACAMP

1300 Big Pine Avenue
Big Pine Key, Florida 33043-3336

General Information Coed residential academic program and outdoor program established in 1966. Accredited by American Camping Association. Formal opportunities for the academically talented. High school credit may be earned.

Seacamp

Program Focus Marine science, scuba, sailing, snorkeling.
Academics Biology, botany, ecology, environmental science, geology/earth science, journalism, marine studies, oceanography, science (general), writing.
Arts Arts and crafts (general), batiking, ceramics, creative writing, drawing, fabric arts, jewelry making, music, painting, pottery, sculpture, theater/drama.
Special Interest Areas Animal care, career exploration, community service, conservation projects, field research/expeditions, nature study, nautical skills, team building.
Sports Basketball, boating, canoeing, fishing, kayaking, sailing, scuba diving, sea kayaking, snorkeling, swimming, volleyball, water polo, windsurfing.
Wilderness/Outdoors Ocean expeditions, orienteering.
Trips Cultural, day.
Program Information 3 sessions per year. Session length: 18 days in June, July, August. Ages: 12–17. 145–160 participants per session. Boarding program cost: $2990. Extra fee for scuba: $375 per course.
Application Deadline Continuous.
Jobs Positions for college students 19 and older.

Seacamp (continued)

Contact Ms. Grace Upshaw, Director, main address above. Phone: 305-872-2331. Fax: 305-872-2555. E-mail: snorkel&scuba@seacamp.org.
URL www.seacamp.org
For more information, see page 626.

TREETOPS EXPEDITIONS–SAILING AND MARINE ECOLOGY

Treetops eXpeditions
Florida

General Information Coed travel outdoor program and adventure program established in 1970.
Program Focus Sailing.
Special Interest Areas Nautical skills.
Sports Sailing.
Trips Cultural.
Program Information 1 session per year. Session length: 4 weeks in July. Ages: 14–17. 6–10 participants per session. Cost: $5500. Financial aid available.
Application Deadline Continuous.
Contact Mr. Chad Jemison, Director, PO Box 187, Lake Placid, New York 12946. Phone: 518-523-9329 Ext.149. Fax: 518-523-4858. E-mail: chad.jemison@nct.org.
URL www.ttexpeditions.org
For more information, see page 672.

UNIVERSITY OF MIAMI SUMMER SCHOLAR PROGRAMS

University of Miami
111 Allen Hall
Coral Gables, Florida 33124-1610

General Information Coed residential academic program established in 1991. Formal opportunities for the academically talented. College credit may be earned.
Program Focus Research lab projects and field trips.
Academics Academics (general), aerospace science, anthropology, art, art history/appreciation, biology, ecology, engineering, environmental science, forensic science, geology/earth science, government and politics,

health sciences, journalism, management, marine studies, oceanography, precollege program.
Arts Film, television/video.
Special Interest Areas Career exploration.
Sports Aerobics, basketball, racquetball, snorkeling, swimming, tennis, volleyball, weight training.
Trips College tours, cultural, day, shopping.
Program Information 1 session per year. Session length: 3 weeks in July. Ages: 16–17. 100–200 participants per session. Boarding program cost: $4000–$4600. Application fee: $100. Financial aid available.
Application Deadline May 4.
Contact Ms. Dana Render, Assistant Director of High School Programs, 111 Allen Hall, PO Box 248005, Coral Gables, Florida 33124-1610. Phone: 800-788-3986. Fax: 305-284-2620. E-mail: ssp.cstudies@miami.edu.
URL www.miami.edu/summerscholar
For more information, see page 684.

WESTCOAST CONNECTION–FLORIDA SWING JUNIOR TOURING GOLF CAMP

Westcoast Connection
Florida

General Information Coed travel sports camp established in 1982. Accredited by Ontario Camping Association.
Program Focus Participants receive professional golf instruction, play top-rated courses, and enjoy recreation and touring highlights.
Special Interest Areas Touring.
Sports Golf, swimming.
Program Information 1–2 sessions per year. Session length: 2–3 weeks in July, August. Ages: 13–17. 16–28 participants per session. Cost: $4399.
Application Deadline Continuous.
Jobs Positions for college students 21 and older.
Contact Mr. Ira Solomon, Director, 154 East Boston Post Road, Mamaroneck, New York 10543. Phone: 800-767-0227. Fax: 914-835-0798. E-mail: usa@westcoastconnection.com.
URL www.westcoastconnection.com
For more information, see page 702.

GEORGIA

CYBERCAMPS–GEORGIA STATE UNIVERSITY

Cybercamps–Giant Campus, Inc.
Atlanta, Georgia

General Information Coed residential and day academic program established in 1997. Formal opportunities for the academically talented.
Program Focus Computers and technology.
Academics Web page design, academics (general), computer programming, computer science (Advanced Placement), computers.

Arts Animation, digital media, film, graphic arts, musical productions, photography, television/video.
Special Interest Areas Computer game design, computer graphics, electronics, robotics, team building.
Program Information 1–12 sessions per year. Session length: 5 days in June, July, August. Ages: 7–18. 30–50 participants per session. Day program cost: $599–$749. Boarding program cost: $998–$1148.
Application Deadline Continuous.
Jobs Positions for high school students 17 and older and college students 18 and older.
Contact Camp Consultant, 3101 Western Avenue, Suite 100, Seattle, Washington 98121. Phone: 888-904-2267. Fax: 206-442-4501. E-mail: info@cybercamps.com.
URL www.cybercamps.com
For more information, see page 466.

CYBERCAMPS–OGLETHORPE UNIVERSITY

Cybercamps–Giant Campus, Inc.
Atlanta, Georgia

General Information Coed residential and day academic program established in 1997. Formal opportunities for the academically talented.
Program Focus Computers and technology.
Academics Web page design, academics (general), computer programming, computer science (Advanced Placement), computers.
Arts Animation, digital media, film, graphic arts, musical productions, photography, television/video.
Special Interest Areas Computer game design, computer graphics, electronics, robotics, team building.
Program Information 1–12 sessions per year. Session length: 5 days in June, July, August. Ages: 7–18. 30–50 participants per session. Day program cost: $599–$749. Boarding program cost: $998–$1148.
Application Deadline Continuous.
Contact Camp Consultant, 3101 Western Avenue, Suite 100, Seattle, Washington 98121. Phone: 888-904-2267. Fax: 206-442-4501. E-mail: info@cybercamps.com.
URL www.cybercamps.com
For more information, see page 466.

CYBERCAMPS–SOUTHERN POLYTECHNIC STATE UNIVERSITY

Cybercamps–Giant Campus, Inc.
Marietta, Georgia

General Information Coed residential and day academic program established in 1997. Formal opportunities for the academically talented.

Program Focus Computers and technology.
Academics Web page design, academics (general), computer programming, computer science (Advanced Placement), computers.
Arts Animation, digital media, film, graphic arts, musical productions, photography, television/video.
Special Interest Areas Computer game design, computer graphics, electronics, robotics, team building.
Program Information 1–12 sessions per year. Session length: 5 days in June, July, August. Ages: 7–18. 30–50 participants per session. Day program cost: $599–$749. Boarding program cost: $998–$1148.
Application Deadline Continuous.
Contact Camp Consultant, 3101 Western Avenue, Suite 100, Seattle, Washington 98121. Phone: 888-904-2267. Fax: 206-442-4501. E-mail: info@cybercamps.com.
URL www.cybercamps.com
For more information, see page 466.

DARLINGTON SUMMER PROGRAMS

Darlington School
1014 Cave Spring Road
Rome, Georgia 30161-4700

General Information Coed residential and day traditional camp, academic program, outdoor program, and sports camp established in 1905. Formal opportunities for the academically talented.
Academics English as a second language, Spanish (Advanced Placement), Spanish language/literature, academics (general), computers, ecology, environmental science, geology/earth science, health sciences, journalism, marine studies, mathematics, mathematics (Advanced Placement), music, oceanography, science (general), study skills.
Arts Acting, arts and crafts (general), band, creative writing, film, music, music (jazz), pottery, television/video.
Special Interest Areas Career exploration, college planning, community service, leadership training, nature study, robotics, team building.
Sports Basketball, bicycling, canoeing, cheerleading, climbing (wall), football, golf, kayaking, lacrosse, ropes course, soccer, softball, sports (general), swimming, tennis, volleyball.
Wilderness/Outdoors Canoe trips, caving, hiking, mountain biking, rafting, rock climbing, white-water trips, wilderness camping.
Trips Day.
Program Information 1–2 sessions per year. Session length: 6–18 days in June, July. Ages: 2–18. 20–150 participants per session. Day program cost: $85–$365. Boarding program cost: $500–$2600.
Application Deadline May 1.
Contact Ballard Betz, Director of Summer and Extended Programs, main address above. Phone: 706-236-0424. Fax: 706-232-3600. E-mail: bbetz@darlingtonschool.org.
URL www.darlingtonschool.org/summer

Darlington Summer Programs (continued)

Special Note
Exceptional students never stop learning. For the budding intellectual, the pursuit of wisdom means seeking challenges and embracing every opportunity for enrichment. Darlington School's three-week residential Summer Scholars Program (July 8–28) is committed to providing highly motivated students with a unique and rewarding educational experience in a fun-filled summer camp atmosphere. Courses range from Forensic Science and Robotics to Musical Theater, Jazz Exploration, and Creative Writing. Programs details are available online. The competitive application process requires a letter of recommendation from a current math or English teacher as well as a current school transcript. Enrollment is limited to the top 35 residential applicants. In addition to its highly regarded Summer Scholars Program, Darlington Summer Programs also offers high-end specialty sports camps for serious soccer, tennis, lacrosse, and fast pitch softball athletes. Instructors range from Division I coaches to Olympic and professional athletes and coaches. More information is available online.

EMAGINATION COMPUTER CAMPS– GEORGIA

Emagination Computer Camps
Mercer University
Atlanta, Georgia

General Information Coed residential and day academic program. Accredited by American Camping Association. Formal opportunities for the academically talented.
Program Focus Computer science, technology, and art; swimming, tennis, and basketball; web design; computer music, video, photo, and 3-D animation.
Academics Computer programming, computer science (Advanced Placement), computers, technology.
Arts Graphic arts.
Special Interest Areas ADL skills, Internet accessibility, computer graphics, electronics, field trips (arts and culture), model rocketry, robotics.
Sports Basketball, soccer, swimming, tennis.
Trips Day.
Program Information 4 sessions per year. Session length: 2 weeks in June, July, August. Ages: 8–17. 150–250 participants per session. Day program cost: $1235. Boarding program cost: $2245. Financial aid available.
Application Deadline Continuous.
Jobs Positions for college students 18 and older.
Contact Kathi Rigg, Director, 110 Winn Street, Suite 205, Woburn, Massachusetts 01801. Phone: 877-248-0206. Fax: 781-933-0749. E-mail: camp@computercamps.com.
URL www.computercamps.com
For more information, see page 482.

iD TECH CAMPS–EMORY UNIVERSITY, ATLANTA, GA

iD Tech Camps
Emory University
Atlanta, Georgia 30322

General Information Coed residential and day academic program established in 1999. Accredited by American Camping Association. Formal opportunities for the academically talented and artistically talented.
Program Focus Students create 2D and 3D video games, build robots to compete, design websites, film and edit digital movies, create their own comic book with digital photos, learn programming and more. One computer per student and an average of five students per staff member. Campers take home a project at the end of the weeklong course.
Academics Web page design, academics (general), computer programming, computer science (Advanced Placement), computers, precollege program.
Arts Animation, cartooning, cinematography, digital media, drawing, film, film editing, film production, graphic arts, photography, television/video.
Special Interest Areas Career exploration, computer game design, computer graphics, electronics, leadership training, robotics, team building.
Sports Baseball, basketball, soccer, softball, swimming, volleyball.
Trips College tours.
Program Information 5–9 sessions per year. Session length: 5–7 days in June, July, August. Ages: 7–17. 40–50 participants per session. Day program cost: $729. Boarding program cost: $1129. Financial aid available.
Application Deadline Continuous.
Jobs Positions for college students 18 and older.
Contact Client Service Representatives, 42 West Campbell Avenue, Suite 301, Campbell, California 95008. Phone: 888-709-TECH. Fax: 408-871-2228. E-mail: info@internaldrive.com.
URL www.internaldrive.com
For more information, see page 520.

THE SUMMER INSTITUTE FOR THE GIFTED AT EMORY UNIVERSITY

Summer Institute for the Gifted
Emory University
Atlanta, Georgia 30322

General Information Coed residential academic program established in 2006. Formal opportunities for the academically talented and gifted.
Academics American literature, English language/literature, French language/literature, SAT/ACT preparation, Spanish language/literature, academics (general), aerospace science, archaeology, architecture, art history/appreciation, biology, business, chemistry, classical languages/literatures, communications, computers, engineering, environmental science, government and politics, history, marine studies, mathematics, music, oceanography, philosophy, physics, precollege program, psychology, science (general), social studies, speech/debate, study skills, writing.
Arts Band, chorus, creative writing, dance, drawing, film, graphic arts, music, music (chamber), music (classical), music (ensemble), music (instrumental), musical productions, painting, photography, sculpture, theater/drama.
Special Interest Areas Animal care, electronics, meditation, model rocketry, robotics.
Sports Aerobics, archery, baseball, basketball, fencing, field hockey, football, lacrosse, martial arts, soccer, swimming, tennis, track and field, volleyball.
Trips Cultural.
Program Information 1–2 sessions per year. Session length: 3 weeks in June, July, August. Ages: 8–17. 150–250 participants per session. Boarding program cost: $3700–$4200. Application fee: $75. Financial aid available.
Application Deadline May 14.
Jobs Positions for college students 19 and older.
Contact Ms. Barbara Swicord, Director, River Plaza, 9 West Broad Street, Stamford, Connecticut 06902-3788. Phone: 866-303-4744. Fax: 203-399-5598. E-mail: sig.info@aifs.com.
URL www.giftedstudy.com

For more information, see page 654.

HAWAII

AAVE–ULTIMATE HAWAII

AAVE–Journeys That Matter
Hawaii

General Information Coed travel outdoor program, wilderness program, and adventure program established in 1976. Accredited by American Camping Association.
Program Focus Adventure travel.
Special Interest Areas Campcraft, community service, cross-cultural education, leadership training, nautical skills, team building.
Sports Bicycling, boating, sailing, sea kayaking, snorkeling, surfing, swimming.
Wilderness/Outdoors Backpacking, mountain biking, wilderness camping.
Trips Cultural, day, overnight.
Program Information 4–6 sessions per year. Session length: 3 weeks in June, July, August. Ages: 14–18. 13 participants per session. Cost: $3888. Financial aid available.
Application Deadline Continuous.
Jobs Positions for college students 21 and older.
Contact Mr. Abbott Wallis, Owner, 2308 Fossil Trace Drive, Golden, Colorado 80401. Phone: 800-222-3595. Fax: 303-526-0885. E-mail: info@aave.com.
URL www.aave.com

For more information, see page 394.

HAWAII PREPARATORY ACADEMY SUMMER SESSION

Hawai'i Preparatory Academy
65-1692 Kohala Mountain Road
Kamuela, Hawaii 96743

General Information Coed residential and day academic program established in 1971. Formal opportunities for the academically talented. High school credit may be earned.
Program Focus Academic review and enrichment, Hawaiian studies, marine biology, SAT preparation, math and computers.
Academics English as a second language, English language/literature, SAT/ACT preparation, academics (general), area studies, computers, engineering, environmental science, marine studies, mathematics, reading, science (general), speech/debate, study skills, writing.

Hawaii Preparatory Academy Summer Session (continued)

Hawaii Preparatory Academy Summer Session

Arts Arts and crafts (general), ceramics, creative writing, dance, fabric arts, film, music, photography, television/video.
Special Interest Areas College planning, cross-cultural education, driver's education, robotics.
Sports Golf, horseback riding, scuba diving, sea kayaking, snorkeling, soccer, sports (general), swimming, tennis, volleyball, weight training.
Wilderness/Outdoors Hiking, outdoor camping.
Trips Cultural, day, overnight, shopping.

Program Information 1 session per year. Session length: 27–30 days in June, July. Ages: 12–17. 100–120 participants per session. Day program cost: $500–$2000. Boarding program cost: $4000. Application fee: $25–$30.
Application Deadline April 15.
Jobs Positions for high school students 16 and older and college students 19 and older.
Contact Shirley Ann K. Fukumoto, Director of Auxiliary Programs, 65-1692 Kohala Mountain Road, Kamuela, Hawaii 96743. Phone: 808-881-4018. Fax: 808-881-4071. E-mail: summer@hpa.edu.
URL www.hpa.edu

For more information, see page 514.

PUTNEY STUDENT TRAVEL–COMMUNITY SERVICE–HAWAII

Putney Student Travel
Hawaii

General Information Coed residential community service program.
Program Focus Community service focusing on the Habitat for Humanity, cultural exchange, and local excursions in two sessions per year on Oahu and Kauai.
Academics Intercultural studies.
Special Interest Areas Community service, construction.
Sports Kayaking, swimming.
Wilderness/Outdoors Hiking.
Trips Cultural, day.
Program Information 2 sessions per year. Session length: 30 days in June, July. Ages: 15–18. Boarding program cost: $5690. Financial aid available. Airfare from Los Angeles included.
Application Deadline Continuous.
Contact Jeffrey Shumlin, Admissions Director, 345 Hickory Ridge Road, Putney, Vermont 05346. Phone: 802-387-5000. Fax: 802-387-4276. E-mail: excel@goputney.com.
URL www.goputney.com

For more information, see page 598.

REIN TEEN TOURS–PROJECT HAWAII

Rein Teen Tours
Hawaii

General Information Coed travel community service program established in 2007.
Program Focus Community service in Hawaii.
Special Interest Areas Animal care, community service, touring.
Sports Basketball, snorkeling, surfing.
Trips Overnight.
Program Information 1 session per year. Session length: 26 days in July. Ages: 14–17. 60 participants per session. Cost: $6000–$6500. Financial aid available.
Application Deadline Continuous.
Jobs Positions for college students 21 and older.
Summer Contact Norman Rein, President, 30 Galesi Drive, Wayne, New Jersey 07470. Phone: 800-831-1313. Fax: 973-785-4268. E-mail: summer@reinteentours.com.
Winter Contact Norman Rein, President, 30 Galesi Drive, Wayne, New Jersey 07470. Phone: 800-831-1313. Fax: 973-785-4268. E-mail: summer@reinteentours.com.
URL www.reinteentours.com

For more information, see page 604.

WEISSMAN TEEN TOURS–"ALOHA– WELCOME TO HAWAIIAN PARADISE," 2 WEEKS

Weissman Teen Tours
Hawaii

General Information Coed travel outdoor program and cultural program established in 1974.
Program Focus Owner-escorted, personally-supervised, action-packed, culturally-oriented, upscale student travel. All five-star and deluxe beach front hotels; no camping or dormitory accommodations.
Special Interest Areas Native American culture, nature study, team building, touring.
Sports Aerobics, bicycling, boating, golf, parasailing, scuba diving, snorkeling, sports (general), surfing, swimming, tennis, volleyball.
Wilderness/Outdoors Hiking.
Trips Cultural, overnight.
Program Information 1 session per year. Session length: 2 weeks in August. Ages: 14–17. 35 participants per session. Cost: $4799.
Application Deadline Continuous.
Jobs Positions for college students 21 and older.
Contact Ms. Ronee Weissman, Owner/Director, 517 Almena Avenue, Ardsley, New York 10502. Phone: 800-942-8005. Fax: 914-693-4807. E-mail: wtt@cloud9.net.
URL www.weissmantours.com

For more information, see page 700.

WESTCOAST CONNECTION–COMMUNITY SERVICE HAWAII

Westcoast Connection
Hawaii

General Information Coed travel community service program established in 1982. Accredited by Ontario Camping Association. High school credit may be earned.
Arts Photography.
Special Interest Areas Community service, conservation projects.
Sports Rappelling, sailing, snorkeling, surfing.
Wilderness/Outdoors Mountain biking, outdoor adventure.
Program Information 1–2 sessions per year. Session length: 3 weeks in July, August. Ages: 14–17. 10–24 participants per session.
Application Deadline Continuous.
Jobs Positions for college students 21 and older.
Contact Mr. Mark Segal, Director, 154 East Boston Post Road, Mamaroneck, New York 10543. Phone: 800-767-0227. Fax: 914-835-0798. E-mail: usa@westcoastconnection.com.
URL www.360studenttravel.com

For more information, see page 702.

WILDERNESS VENTURES–HAWAII

Wilderness Ventures
Hawaii

General Information Coed travel outdoor program, community service program, wilderness program, and adventure program established in 1973.
Program Focus Wilderness travel, wilderness skills, leadership skills.
Special Interest Areas Community service, leadership training.
Sports Sailing, sea kayaking, snorkeling.
Wilderness/Outdoors Backpacking, hiking, wilderness camping.
Trips Overnight.
Program Information 2 sessions per year. Session length: 3 weeks in June, July, August. Ages: 13–18. 13 participants per session. Cost: $4390. Financial aid available.
Application Deadline Continuous.
Jobs Positions for college students 21 and older.

Wilderness Ventures–Hawaii (continued)

Contact Mike Cottingham, Director, PO Box 2768, Jackson Hole, Wyoming 83001. Phone: 800-533-2281. Fax: 307-739-1934. E-mail: info@wildernessventures. com.
URL www.wildernessventures.com
For more information, see page 704.

WILDERNESS VENTURES–MAUI/KAUAI

Wilderness Ventures
Hawaii

General Information Coed travel outdoor program established in 1973.
Program Focus Outdoor travel, leadership skills.
Special Interest Areas Leadership training.
Sports Scuba diving, sea kayaking, snorkeling, surfing, windsurfing.
Wilderness/Outdoors Hiking.
Trips Overnight.
Program Information 3 sessions per year. Session length: 16 days in June, July, August. Ages: 14–18. 13 participants per session. Cost: $4190. Financial aid available.
Application Deadline Continuous.
Jobs Positions for college students 21 and older.
Contact Mr. Mike Cottingham, Director, PO Box 2768, Jackson Hole, Wyoming 83001. Phone: 800-533-2281. Fax: 307-739-1934. E-mail: info@wildernessventures. com.
URL www.wildernessventures.com
For more information, see page 704.

IDAHO

LANDMARK VOLUNTEERS: IDAHO

Landmark Volunteers, Inc.
Sawtooth National Recreation Area
Stanley, Idaho

General Information Coed residential outdoor program and community service program established in 1992. High school credit may be earned.
Program Focus Opportunity for high school students to earn community service credit while working as a team for two weeks serving Sawtooth National Recreation Area. Similar programs offered through Landmark Volunteers at over 50 locations in 20 states.
Academics Biology, botany, ecology, environmental science.
Special Interest Areas Career exploration, community service, conservation projects, field research/expeditions, leadership training, nature study, team building, trail maintenance, work camp programs.
Wilderness/Outdoors Hiking.
Trips Cultural, day.
Program Information 1 session per year. Session length: 2 weeks in July. Ages: 14–18. 12–13 participants per session. Boarding program cost: $1250–$1300. Financial aid available.
Application Deadline Continuous.
Jobs Positions for college students.
Contact Ann Barrett, Executive Director, PO Box 455, Sheffield, Massachusetts 01257. Phone: 413-229-0255. Fax: 413-229-2050. E-mail: landmark@volunteers.com.
URL www.volunteers.com
For more information, see page 542.

ILLINOIS

CENTER FOR TALENT DEVELOPMENT SUMMER ACADEMIC PROGRAM

Northwestern University's Center for Talent Development
617 Dartmouth Place
Evanston, Illinois 60208

General Information Coed residential and day academic program and community service program established in 1983. Formal opportunities for the academically talented. Specific services available for the physically challenged. High school credit may be earned.

Center for Talent Development Summer Academic Program

Academics American literature, Chinese languages/literature, English language/literature, Latin language, academics (general), archaeology, architecture, art history/appreciation, biology, biology (Advanced Placement), chemistry, classical languages/literatures, computer programming, computer science (Advanced Placement), ecology, economics, engineering, environmental science, geography, geology/earth science, government and politics, government and politics (Advanced Placement), history, humanities, journalism, mathematics, mathematics (Advanced Placement), philosophy, physics, psychology, reading, religion, science (general), social science, social studies, speech/debate, writing.
Arts Arts and crafts (general), creative writing, theater/drama.
Special Interest Areas Community service, model rocketry, robotics.
Trips Cultural, day, shopping.
Program Information 1–3 sessions per year. Session length: 1–3 weeks in June, July, August. Ages: 4–17. 1,000–1,500 participants per session. Day program cost: $220–$1550. Boarding program cost: $2700. Application fee: $50. Financial aid available.
Application Deadline May 15.
Jobs Positions for high school students 17 and older and college students.
Contact Susie Hoffmann, Summer Program Coordinator, main address above. Phone: 847-491-3782. Fax: 847-467-4283. E-mail: ctd@northwestern.edu.
URL www.ctd.northwestern.edu

For more information, see page 570.

CYBERCAMPS–BENEDICTINE UNIVERSITY

Cybercamps–Giant Campus, Inc.
Lisle, Illinois

General Information Coed residential and day academic program established in 1997. Formal opportunities for the academically talented.
Program Focus Computers and technology.
Academics Web page design, academics (general), computer programming, computer science (Advanced Placement), computers.
Arts Animation, digital media, film, graphic arts, musical productions, photography, television/video.
Special Interest Areas Computer game design, computer graphics, electronics, robotics, team building.
Program Information 1–12 sessions per year. Session length: 5 days in June, July, August. Ages: 7–18. 30–50 participants per session. Day program cost: $599–$749. Boarding program cost: $998–$1148.
Application Deadline Continuous.
Jobs Positions for high school students 17 and older and college students 18 and older.
Contact Camp Consultant, 3101 Western Avenue, Suite 100, Seattle, Washington 98121. Phone: 888-904-2267. Fax: 206-442-4501. E-mail: info@cybercamps.com.
URL www.cybercamps.com

For more information, see page 466.

CYBERCAMPS–CONCORDIA UNIVERSITY, CHICAGO

Cybercamps–Giant Campus, Inc.
River Forest, Illinois

General Information Coed residential and day academic program established in 1997. Formal opportunities for the academically talented.
Program Focus Computers and technology.
Academics Web page design, academics (general), computer programming, computer science (Advanced Placement), computers.
Arts Animation, digital media, film, graphic arts, musical productions, photography, television/video.
Special Interest Areas Computer game design, computer graphics, electronics, robotics, team building.
Program Information 1–12 sessions per year. Session length: 5 days in June, July, August. Ages: 7–18. 30–50 participants per session. Day program cost: $599–$749. Boarding program cost: $998–$1148.
Application Deadline Continuous.
Jobs Positions for high school students 17 and older and college students 18 and older.
Contact Camp Consultant, 3101 Western Avenue, Suite 100, Seattle, Washington 98121. Phone: 888-904-2267. Fax: 206-442-4501. E-mail: info@cybercamps..com.
URL www.cybercamps.com

For more information, see page 466.

CYBERCAMPS–LOYOLA UNIVERSITY

Cybercamps–Giant Campus, Inc.
Chicago, Illinois

General Information Coed residential and day academic program established in 1997. Formal opportunities for the academically talented.
Program Focus Computers and technology.
Academics Web page design, academics (general), computer programming, computer science (Advanced Placement), computers.
Arts Animation, digital media, film, graphic arts, musical productions, photography, television/video.
Special Interest Areas Computer game design, computer graphics, electronics, robotics, team building.
Program Information 1–12 sessions per year. Session length: 5 days in June, July, August. Ages: 7–18. 30–50 participants per session. Day program cost: $599–$749. Boarding program cost: $998–$1148.
Application Deadline Continuous.
Jobs Positions for high school students 17 and older and college students 18 and older.
Contact Camp Consultant, 3101 Western Avenue, Suite 100, Seattle, Washington 98121. Phone: 888-904-2267. Fax: 206-442-4501. E-mail: info@cybercamps.com.
URL www.cybercamps.com

For more information, see page 466.

EMAGINATION COMPUTER CAMPS– ILLINOIS

Emagination Computer Camps
Lake Forest Academy
1600 West Kennedy Road
Lake Forest, Illinois 60045

General Information Coed residential and day academic program established in 1982. Accredited by American Camping Association. Formal opportunities for the academically talented.
Program Focus Computer science, technology, and art; swimming, tennis, and basketball clinics; web design, computer music, video, photo, 3-D animation.
Academics Computer programming, computer science (Advanced Placement), computers, technology.
Arts Graphic arts.
Special Interest Areas ADL skills, Internet accessibility, computer graphics, electronics, field trips (arts and culture), model rocketry, robotics.
Sports Basketball, soccer, swimming, tennis.
Trips Day.
Program Information 4 sessions per year. Session length: 2 weeks in June, July, August. Ages: 8–17. 150–250 participants per session. Day program cost: $1235. Boarding program cost: $2245.
Application Deadline Continuous.
Jobs Positions for college students 18 and older.
Contact Ms. Kathi Rigg, Director, 110 Winn Street, Suite 205, Woburn, Massachusetts 01801. Phone: 877-248-0206. Fax: 781-933-0749. E-mail: camp@computercamps.com.
URL www.computercamps.com

For more information, see page 482.

iD TECH CAMPS–LAKE FOREST COLLEGE, EVANSTON, IL

iD Tech Camps
Lake Forest College
Evanston, Illinois 60045

General Information Coed residential and day academic program established in 1999. Accredited by American Camping Association. Formal opportunities for the academically talented and artistically talented.
Program Focus Students create 2D and 3D video games, build robots to compete, design websites, film and edit digital movies, create their own comic book with digital photos, learn programming and more. One computer per student and an average of five students per staff member. Campers take home a project at the end of the weeklong course.
Academics Web page design, academics (general), computer programming, computer science (Advanced Placement), computers, precollege program.
Arts Animation, cinematography, digital media, drawing, film, film editing, film production, graphic arts, photography, television/video.
Special Interest Areas Career exploration, computer

game design, computer graphics, electronics, leadership training, robotics, team building.
Sports Baseball, basketball, soccer, softball, swimming, volleyball.
Trips College tours.
Program Information 5–9 sessions per year. Session length: 5–7 days in June, July, August. Ages: 7–17. 40–50 participants per session. Day program cost: $729. Boarding program cost: $1129. Financial aid available.
Application Deadline Continuous.
Jobs Positions for college students 18 and older.
Contact Client Service Representatives, 42 West Campbell Avenue, Suite 301, Campbell, California 95008. Phone: 888-709-TECH. Fax: 408-871-2228. E-mail: info@internaldrive.com.
URL www.internaldrive.com

For more information, see page 520.

iD Tech Camps–Northwestern University, Chicago, IL

iD Tech Camps
Northwestern University
Chicago, Illinois 60208

General Information Coed residential and day academic program established in 1999. Accredited by American Camping Association. Formal opportunities for the academically talented and artistically talented.
Program Focus Students create 2D and 3D video games, build robots to compete, design websites, film and edit digital movies, create their own comic book with digital photos, learn programming and more. One computer per student and an average of five students per staff member. Campers take home a project at the end of the weeklong course.
Academics Web page design, academics (general), computer programming, computer science (Advanced Placement), computers, precollege program.
Arts Animation, cartooning, cinematography, digital media, drawing, film, film editing, film production, graphic arts, photography, television/video.
Special Interest Areas Career exploration, computer game design, computer graphics, electronics, leadership training, robotics, team building.
Sports Baseball, basketball, soccer, softball, swimming, volleyball.
Trips College tours.
Program Information 5–9 sessions per year. Session length: 5–7 days in June, July, August. Ages: 7–17. 40–50 participants per session. Day program cost: $729.

Boarding program cost: $1129. Financial aid available.
Application Deadline Continuous.
Jobs Positions for college students 18 and older.
Contact Client Service Representatives, 42 West Campbell Avenue, Suite 301, Campbell, California 95008. Phone: 888-709-TECH. Fax: 408-871-2228. E-mail: info@internaldrive.com.
URL www.internaldrive.com

For more information, see page 520.

National Student Leadership Conference: State Leadership Workshops

National Student Leadership Conference
Illinois

General Information Coed residential academic program and community service program established in 1989. Formal opportunities for the academically talented.
Program Focus High school students from around the state attend specialized workshops to develop skills in areas such as: public speaking, goal-setting, team building, project management, conflict resolution, and also plan a statewide community service project. The workshops will take place in colleges and universities in various states. For a list of the states where the program will take place, please go to the Web site: http://www.nslcstates.org.
Special Interest Areas Career exploration, community service, leadership training, team building.
Trips College tours.
Program Information 15 sessions per year. Session length: 5 days in June, July, August. Ages: 14–18. 150 participants per session. Boarding program cost: $1095. Financial aid available.
Application Deadline Continuous.
Jobs Positions for college students 18 and older.
Contact Director of Admissions, 414 North Orleans Street, Suite LL8, Chicago, Illinois 60610-1087. Phone: 312-322-9999. Fax: 312-765-0081. E-mail: info@nslcleaders.org.
URL www.nslcleaders.org

For more information, see page 564.

NORTHWESTERN UNIVERSITY'S COLLEGE PREPARATION PROGRAM

Northwestern University
405 Church Street
Evanston, Illinois 60208

General Information Coed residential and day academic program established in 1987. Formal opportunities for the academically talented. College credit may be earned.

Northwestern University's College Preparation Program

Program Focus Precollege orientation.
Academics American literature, Chinese languages/ literature, English language/literature, French language/ literature, German language/literature, Italian language/literature, Japanese language/literature, Jewish studies, Russian language/literature, Spanish language/literature, academics (general), anthropology, art history/appreciation, astronomy, biology, business, chemistry, classical languages/literatures, communications, computer programming, computers, economics, government and politics, history, humanities, intercultural studies, journalism, linguistics, mathematics, music, philosophy, physics, physiology, precollege program, psychology, religion, science (general), social science, social studies, speech/debate, writing.
Arts Acting, band, chorus, creative writing, dance, drawing, film, graphic arts, music, music (classical), music (ensemble), music (instrumental), music (jazz), music (orchestral), music (vocal), musical productions, painting, photography, television/video, theater/drama.
Sports Aerobics, basketball, canoeing, golf, kayaking, racquetball, sailing, soccer, sports (general), swimming, tennis, volleyball, weight training, windsurfing.
Wilderness/Outdoors Hiking.
Trips College tours, cultural, day, shopping.
Program Information 1 session per year. Session length: 6–8 weeks in June, July, August. Ages: 16–18. 70–100 participants per session. Day program cost: $3500–$8600. Boarding program cost: $5000–$11,000. Application fee: $35–$70. Financial aid available.
Application Deadline Continuous.

Contact Stephanie Teterycz, Director of Summer Sessions, main address above. Phone: 847-467-6703. Fax: 847-491-3660. E-mail: cpp@northwestern.edu. **URL** www.northwestern.edu/collegeprep
For more information, see page 572.

NORTHWESTERN UNIVERSITY'S NATIONAL HIGH SCHOOL INSTITUTE

Northwestern University
617 Noyes Street
Evanston, Illinois 60208

General Information Coed residential academic program and arts program established in 1931. Formal opportunities for the academically talented and artistically talented.

Northwestern University's National High School Institute

Program Focus Six programs in journalism, music, theatre arts, media arts, forensics, and debate.
Academics Academics (general), journalism, music, speech/debate.
Arts Arts, film, music, musical productions, performing arts, radio broadcasting, television/video, theater/drama.
Program Information 1 session per year. Session length: 14–36 days in June, July. Ages: 14–18. 30–200 participants per session. Boarding program cost: $2950–$6200. Application fee: $50. Financial aid available.
Application Deadline April 5.
Jobs Positions for college students.
Contact Nick Kanel, Department Assistant, main address above. Phone: 800-662-NHSI. Fax: 847-467-1057. E-mail: nhsi@northwestern.edu.
URL www.northwestern.edu/nhsi
For more information, see page 574.

UNIVERSITY OF CHICAGO–INSIGHT

University of Chicago
Chicago, Illinois 60637

General Information Coed residential and day academic program established in 1998. Formal opportunities for the academically talented and artistically talented. College credit may be earned.
Program Focus "Hands-on" experiential learning.
Academics English language/literature, academics (general), anthropology, archaeology, biology, government and politics, history, humanities, precollege program, psychology, social science, social studies, speech/debate, writing.
Arts Creative writing.
Special Interest Areas Field research/expeditions.
Trips Cultural, day.
Program Information 2 sessions per year. Session length: 3 weeks in June, July. Ages: 15–18. 10–15 participants per session. Day program cost: $2425–$3017. Boarding program cost: $4125–$4717. Application fee: $40–$55. Financial aid available.
Application Deadline May 15.
Contact Ms. Sarah Lopez, Summer Session Office Administrative Assistant, main address above. Phone: 773-834-3792. Fax: 773-834-0549. E-mail: slopez@uchicago.edu.
URL summer.uchicago.edu/

For more information, see page 676.

UNIVERSITY OF CHICAGO–RESEARCH IN THE BIOLOGICAL SCIENCES

University of Chicago
Chicago, Illinois 60637

General Information Coed residential academic program established in 1999. Formal opportunities for the academically talented. College credit may be earned.
Program Focus Scientific research.
Academics Biology, genetics, microbiology, precollege program, research skills.
Trips Cultural, day.
Program Information 1 session per year. Session length: 4 weeks in June, July. Ages: 15–18. 24–48 participants per session. Boarding program cost: $7206. Application fee: $40–$55. Financial aid available.
Application Deadline May 15.
Contact Ms. Sarah Lopez, Summer Session Office, main address above. Phone: 773-834-3792. Fax: 773-834-0549. E-mail: slopez@uchicago.edu.
URL summer.uchicago.edu/

For more information, see page 676.

UNIVERSITY OF CHICAGO–SUMMER QUARTER FOR HIGH SCHOOL STUDENTS

University of Chicago
Chicago, Illinois 60637

General Information Coed residential and day academic program established in 1999. Formal opportunities for the academically talented. College credit may be earned.
Program Focus College courses for credit.
Academics American literature, Arabic, Chinese languages/literature, English language/literature, French language/literature, German language/literature, Greek language/literature, Hebrew language, Italian language/literature, Japanese language/literature, Jewish studies, Korean, Latin language, Russian language/literature, Sanskrit, Spanish language/literature, academics (general), anthropology, art history/appreciation, biology, business, classical languages/literatures, computer programming, ecology, economics, environmental science, geology/earth science, government and politics, history, humanities, intercultural studies, law, linguistics, mathematics, music, philosophy, precollege program, psychology, religion, social science, sociology.
Arts Drawing, photography, visual arts.
Trips Cultural, day.
Program Information 4 sessions per year. Session length: 3–9 weeks in June, July, August. Ages: 15–18. 100–200 participants per session. Day program cost: $2425–$6957. Boarding program cost: $4022–$10,887. Application fee: $40–$55. Financial aid available.

University of Chicago–Summer Quarter for High School Students (continued)

University of Chicago–Summer Quarter for High School Students

Application Deadline May 15.
Contact Ms. Sarah Lopez, Summer Session Office Administrative Assistant, main address above. Phone: 773-834-3792. Fax: 773-834-0549. E-mail: slopez@uchicago.edu.
URL summer.uchicago.edu/

For more information, see page 676.

LOUISIANA

RUSTIC PATHWAYS–NEW ORLEANS SUMMER REBUILDING PROGRAM

Rustic Pathways
New Orleans, Louisiana

General Information Coed residential community service program and cultural program.
Special Interest Areas Community service, construction, touring.
Trips Cultural, day, shopping.
Program Information 4 sessions per year. Session length: 15 days in June, July, August. Ages: 16–18. 10–15 participants per session. Boarding program cost: $2145. Financial aid available. Airfare not included.
Application Deadline Continuous.
Contact Rustic Pathways, 4121 Erie Street, Willoughby, Ohio 44094. Phone: 800-321-4353. Fax: 440-975-9694. E-mail: rustic@rusticpathways.com.
URL www.rusticpathways.com

For more information, see page 612.

MAINE

ACADIA INSTITUTE OF OCEANOGRAPHY

9 Lower Dunbar Road
Seal Harbor, Maine 04675

General Information Coed residential academic
program established in 1975. Formal opportunities for
the academically talented and gifted. High school credit
may be earned.

Acadia Institute of Oceanography

Program Focus Oceanography.
Academics Biology, botany, chemistry, ecology,
environmental science, geology/earth science, marine
studies, oceanography, science (general).
Special Interest Areas Career exploration, field
research/expeditions, nature study, nautical skills,
navigation.
Sports Basketball, snorkeling, soccer, softball,
swimming, tennis, volleyball.
Wilderness/Outdoors Hiking, orienteering.
Trips College tours, day, shopping.
Program Information 4–5 sessions per year. Session
length: 6–13 days in June, July, August. Ages: 10–19.
42–45 participants per session. Boarding program cost:
$1995. Financial aid available. One-week introductory
session for 10-12 year-olds.
Application Deadline Continuous.
Jobs Positions for college students 19 and older.
Summer Contact Sheryl Christy Gilmore, Director,
PO Box 285, Seal Harbor, Maine 04675. Phone: 207-276-
9825. Fax: 207-276-9825. E-mail: info@acadiainstitute.
com.
Winter Contact Sheryl Christy Gilmore, Executive
Director, PO Box 2220, St. Augustine, Florida 32085-
2220. Phone: 800-375-0058. Fax: 904-461-3331. E-mail:
info@acadiainstitute.com.
URL www.acadiainstitute.com
For more information, see page 402.

ALFORD LAKE CAMP

Alford Lake Camp
258 Alford Lake Road
Hope, Maine 04847

General Information Girls' residential traditional
camp established in 1907. Accredited by American
Camping Association.

Alford Lake Camp

Arts Arts and crafts (general), ceramics, dance
(modern), theater/drama.
Special Interest Areas Campcraft, community service,
leadership training.
Sports Archery, canoeing, climbing (wall), gymnastics,
horseback riding, kayaking, lacrosse, sailing, soccer,
swimming, tennis, windsurfing.
Wilderness/Outdoors Backpacking, canoe trips,
hiking.
Trips Overnight.
Program Information 3 sessions per year. Session
length: 24–49 days in June, July, August. Ages: 8–15.
180–190 participants per session. Boarding program
cost: $4500–$6300. Financial aid available.
Application Deadline Continuous.
Jobs Positions for college students.
Summer Contact Ms. Betsy Brayley, Office Manager/
Assistant Director, main address above. Phone: 207-785-
2400. Fax: 207-785-5290. E-mail: info@alfordlakecamp.
com.
Winter Contact Ms. Betsy Brayley, Office Manager/
Assistant Director, 5 Salt Marsh Way, Cape Elizabeth,
Maine 04107. Phone: 207-799-3005. Fax: 207-799-5044.
E-mail: info@alfordlakecamp.com.

Alford Lake Camp (continued)

Special Note
At Alford Lake, campers experience challenge and fun through a broad, individually elective program. Emphasis is on personal growth and development in a warm, supportive, and values-based community. Living in large, white tents in a simple setting promotes respect for the natural world. In addition, meeting campers and leaders from more than twenty-five states and twenty countries deepens the participants' respect and appreciation for others' differences. The staff-camper ratio of 1:3 allows for individual instruction and encouragement, inspiring tradition, loyalty, and spirit. Established in 1907, Alford Lake is one of the world's oldest girls' camps. Each season brings new friendships and adventures.

For more information, see page 412.

ALFORD LAKE FAMILY CAMP

Alford Lake Camp
258 Alford Lake Road
Hope, Maine 04847

General Information Coed residential traditional camp and family program established in 1980. Accredited by American Camping Association.
Program Focus Camp for all ages.
Arts Arts and crafts (general), ceramics.
Sports Archery, canoeing, horseback riding, kayaking, sailing, swimming, tennis, windsurfing.
Wilderness/Outdoors Canoe trips, hiking.
Trips Day.
Program Information 1 session per year. Session length: 5 days in August. 75–150 participants per session. Cost: $100 per day for adults, $60 per day ages 5–15; no charge for children under 5.
Application Deadline Continuous.
Summer Contact Ms. Sue McMullan, Director, main address above. Phone: 207-785-2400. Fax: 207-785-5290. E-mail: info@alfordlakecamp.com.
Winter Contact Ms. Sue McMullan, Director, 5 Salt Marsh Way, Cape Elizabeth, Maine 04107. Phone: 207-799-3005. Fax: 207-799-5044. E-mail: info@alfordlakecamp.com.

For more information, see page 412.

CAMP ENCORE-CODA FOR A GREAT SUMMER OF MUSIC, SPORTS, AND FRIENDS

Camp Encore-Coda for a Great Summer of Music, Sports, and Friends
50 Encore/Coda Lane
Sweden, Maine 04040

General Information Coed residential and day arts program established in 1950. Accredited by American Camping Association. Formal opportunities for the artistically talented.

Camp Encore-Coda for a Great Summer of Music, Sports, and Friends

Program Focus Music and sports.
Academics Music.
Arts Arts and crafts (general), band, chorus, drawing, jewelry making, music, music (chamber), music (classical), music (ensemble), music (instrumental), music (jazz), music (orchestral), music (vocal), musical productions, painting, photography, theater/drama.
Special Interest Areas Model rocketry.
Sports Basketball, boating, canoeing, kayaking, sailing, soccer, softball, sports (general), swimming, tennis, track and field, volleyball.
Wilderness/Outdoors Hiking.
Trips Day.
Program Information 2 sessions per year. Session length: 25–50 days in July, August. Ages: 9–17. 140–160 participants per session. Day program cost: $1900–$3750. Boarding program cost: $3800–$6500. Financial aid available.
Application Deadline Continuous.
Jobs Positions for high school students and college students 18 and older.

Summer Contact James Saltman, Director, main address above. Phone: 207-647-3947. Fax: 207-647-3259. E-mail: jamie@encore-coda.com.
Winter Contact James Saltman, Director, 32 Grassmere Road, Brookline, Massachusetts 02467. Phone: 617-325-1541. Fax: 617-325-7278. E-mail: jamie@encore-coda.com.
URL www.encore-coda.com

KAMP KOHUT

Kamp Kohut
151 Kohut Road
Oxford, Maine 04270

General Information Coed residential traditional camp established in 1907. Accredited by American Camping Association. High school credit may be earned.
Program Focus Nurturing, non-competitive environment; activities focus on instruction and fun.
Academics Web page design, computer programming, computers, journalism, music, reading.
Arts Acting, animation, arts and crafts (general), band, batiking, ceramics, chorus, creative writing, dance, dance (ballet), dance (folk), dance (jazz), dance (modern), dance (tap), drawing, fabric arts, film, graphic arts, jewelry making, leather working, metalworking, music, music (chamber), music (classical), music (ensemble), music (instrumental), music (jazz), music (orchestral), music (vocal), musical productions, painting, photography, pottery, radio broadcasting, sculpture, television/video, theater/drama, woodworking.
Special Interest Areas Campcraft, community service, conservation projects, field research/expeditions, field trips (arts and culture), leadership training, nature study, team building, yearbook production.
Sports Aerobics, archery, baseball, basketball, bicycling, boating, canoeing, cheerleading, climbing (wall), cross-country, diving, field hockey, fishing, football, golf, gymnastics, horseback riding, in-line skating, kayaking, lacrosse, physical fitness, rappelling, ropes course, rowing (crew/sculling), sailing, snorkeling, soccer, softball, street/roller hockey, swimming, tennis, track and field, volleyball, wakeboarding, water polo, waterskiing, windsurfing.
Wilderness/Outdoors Backpacking, bicycle trips, canoe trips, hiking, mountain biking, orienteering, rafting, rock climbing, white-water trips, wilderness camping.

Trips Day, overnight.
Program Information 2 sessions per year. Session length: 26 days in June, July, August. Ages: 7–16. 175 participants per session. Boarding program cost: $4800.
Application Deadline Continuous.
Jobs Positions for college students 19 and older.
Summer Contact Lisa Tripler, Owner/Director, main address above. Phone: 207-539-0966. Fax: 207-539-4701. E-mail: lisa@kampkohut.com.
Winter Contact Lisa Tripler, Owner / Director, 2 Tall Pine Road, Cape Elizabeth, Maine 04107. Phone: 207-767-2406. Fax: 207-767-0604. E-mail: lisa@kampkohut.com.
URL www.kampkohut.com

LANDMARK VOLUNTEERS: MAINE

Landmark Volunteers, Inc.
Maine

General Information Coed residential outdoor program and community service program established in 1992. High school credit may be earned.
Program Focus Opportunity for high school students to earn community service credit while working as a team for two weeks serving Acadia National Park, Agassiz Village, The Ark, Blue Hill Heritage Trust/Kneisel Hall, Holbrook Island Sanctuary, Island Institute, or Camp Sunshine. Similar programs offered through Landmark Volunteers at over 50 locations in 20 states.
Academics Area studies, botany, ecology, environmental science, music, social services.
Special Interest Areas Animal care, career exploration, community service, conservation projects, field research/expeditions, leadership training, nature study, team building, work camp programs.
Wilderness/Outdoors Hiking.
Trips Cultural, day.
Program Information 7 sessions per year. Session length: 14–15 days in June, July, August. Ages: 14–18. 10–13 participants per session. Boarding program cost: $1250–$1300. Financial aid available.
Application Deadline Continuous.
Jobs Positions for college students.
Contact Ann Barrett, Executive Director, PO Box 455, Sheffield, Massachusetts 01257. Phone: 413-229-0255. Fax: 413-229-2050. E-mail: landmark@volunteers.com.
URL www.volunteers.com

For more information, see page 542.

PINE ISLAND CAMP

Pine Island Camp
Belgrade Lakes, Maine 04918

General Information Boys' residential traditional camp and outdoor program established in 1902.
Arts Woodworking.
Special Interest Areas Campcraft, conservation projects.
Sports Archery, boating, canoeing, fishing, kayaking, riflery, rowing (crew/sculling), sailing, swimming, tennis.
Wilderness/Outdoors Backpacking, canoe trips,

Pine Island Camp (continued)
hiking, wilderness camping, wilderness/outdoors (general).
Trips Overnight.
Program Information 1 session per year. Session length: 44 days in June, July, August. Ages: 9–15. 75–85 participants per session. Boarding program cost: $6600. Financial aid available.
Application Deadline Continuous.
Jobs Positions for college students 18 and older.
Summer Contact Benjamin B. Swan, Director, Water Route 200, Belgrade Lakes, Maine 04918. Phone: 207-465-3031.
Winter Contact Benjamin B. Swan, Director, PO Box 242, Brunswick, Maine 04011. Phone: 207-729-7714. Fax: 207-725-1241. E-mail: benswan@pineisland.org.
URL pineisland.org

Special Note
Founded in 1902, Pine Island remains true to the mission described in the 1904 catalog: "To give boys a healthful and beneficial summer outing, to clarify their minds and reinvigorate their bodies, to give them new life and new strength—in a word, to afford them an opportunity for re-creation, not merely recreation." Boys live without electricity in platform tents, each of which houses 4 boys and a counselor. An absence of competitive sports and the island setting make Pine Island unique. Eleven in-camp activities are offered daily, including canoeing, sailing, rowing, kayaking, swimming, workshop, archery, riflery, tennis, and fly-fishing. More than forty camping trips leave the island each summer, including hiking, canoeing, and kayaking trips and excursions to the camp's 90-acre saltwater island. In addition, there is a campfire every night by the lake.

MARYLAND

CAMP AIRY
Camp Airy and Camp Louise Foundation, Inc.
14938 Old Camp Airy Road
Thurmont, Maryland 21788

General Information Boys' residential traditional camp established in 1924. Religious affiliation: Jewish. Accredited by American Camping Association.
Program Focus Athletics, outdoor living, swimming, performing arts, fine arts.
Academics Journalism.
Arts Acting, arts and crafts (general), band, ceramics, creative writing, dance, fabric arts, jewelry making, leather working, mime, music, music (chamber), music (classical), music (ensemble), music (instrumental), music (jazz), music (orchestral), music (vocal), musical productions, painting, performing arts, photography, pottery, printmaking, radio broadcasting, television/video, theater/drama, woodworking.
Special Interest Areas Campcraft, leadership training, model rocketry, nature study, robotics.
Sports Archery, baseball, basketball, bicycling, canoeing, climbing (wall), cross-country, fencing, field hockey, fishing, football, golf, in-line skating, lacrosse, martial arts, mountain boarding, rappelling, riflery, ropes course, scuba diving, skateboarding, soccer, softball, street/roller hockey, swimming, tennis, track and field, volleyball, weight training, wrestling.
Wilderness/Outdoors Backpacking, canoe trips, caving, hiking, mountain biking, mountaineering, orienteering, rafting, rock climbing, survival training, white-water trips, wilderness camping.
Trips Cultural, day, overnight.
Program Information 6 sessions per year. Session length: 2–4 weeks in June, July, August. Ages: 7–17. 400 participants per session. Boarding program cost: $1600–$3200. Financial aid available. Financial aid available for Jewish residents of Maryland.
Application Deadline Continuous.
Jobs Positions for college students 18 and older.
Summer Contact Mike Schneider, Executive Director, main address above. Phone: 301-271-4636. Fax: 301-271-1766. E-mail: airlou@airylouise.org.
Winter Contact Mike Schneider, Executive Director, 5750 Park Heights Avenue, Baltimore, Maryland 21215. Phone: 410-466-9010. Fax: 410-466-0560. E-mail: airlou@airylouise.org.
URL www.airylouise.org

Special Note

More than eighty-two summers of full enrollment say Camp Airy and Camp Louise are doing something right. In addition, more than two thirds of participants are returning campers. Camp Airy (for boys) and Camp Louise (for girls) are brother/sister camps for Jewish children and are located in the beautiful mountains of western Maryland, only an hour from Baltimore and Washington, D.C. With outstanding and varied programs, top-notch facilities, and a warm, caring, fun-loving staff (college students and educators), parents are assured their camper is in the best of hands at the best of all places. Four 2-week sessions and two 4-week sessions ensure a time frame to fit almost any summer schedule. These camps are traditional summer camps that provide many choices for campers and are liberally sprinkled with an abundance of special guests and activities. Our daily program offers a wide variety of activities that include swimming (Red Cross program); athletics (softball, basketball, beach volleyball, tennis, soccer, wrestling, boxing, archery, golf, lacrosse, weight training and conditioning, and more); mountain boarding; mountain biking; dance; crafts; ceramics; music; drama; photography; radio; video production; DJ'ing; outdoor living (ropes, zip lines, climbing wall, caving, orienteering, camping, rafting, kayaking, etc.); nature study; robotics; and much more. Summer has never looked better at Airy and Louise!

CAMP LOUISE

Camp Airy and Camp Louise Foundation, Inc.
24959 Pen Mar Road
Cascade, Maryland 21719

General Information Girls' residential traditional camp established in 1922. Religious affiliation: Jewish. Accredited by American Camping Association.
Program Focus Performing arts, fine arts, athletics, and outdoor living.
Academics Journalism.
Arts Acting, arts, arts and crafts (general), band, batiking, ceramics, chorus, creative writing, dance,

dance (ballet), dance (folk), dance (jazz), dance (modern), dance (tap), drawing, fabric arts, film, jewelry making, leather working, mime, music, music (chamber), music (classical), music (ensemble), music (instrumental), music (jazz), music (orchestral), music (vocal), musical productions, painting, photography, pottery, printmaking, puppetry, radio broadcasting, sculpture, television/video, theater/drama.
Special Interest Areas Culinary arts, leadership training, nature study.
Sports Aerobics, archery, basketball, boxing, canoeing, cheerleading, climbing (wall), fencing, field hockey, football, gymnastics, in-line skating, kayaking, lacrosse, martial arts, rappelling, ropes course, scuba diving, soccer, softball, sports (general), swimming, tennis, volleyball, water polo, weight training.
Wilderness/Outdoors Backpacking, canoe trips, caving, hiking, orienteering, rafting, rock climbing, survival training, white-water trips.
Trips Cultural, day, overnight.
Program Information 6 sessions per year. Session length: 2–4 weeks in June, July, August. Ages: 7–17. 430–440 participants per session. Boarding program cost: $1600–$3200. Financial aid available.
Application Deadline Continuous.
Jobs Positions for college students 18 and older.
Summer Contact Roberta Miller, Director, main address above. Phone: 301-241-3661. Fax: 301-241-5030. E-mail: airlou@airylouise.org.
Winter Contact Mike Schneider, Executive Director, 5750 Park Heights Avenue, Baltimore, Maryland 21215. Phone: 410-466-9010. Fax: 410-466-0560. E-mail: airlou@airylouise.org.
URL www.airylouise.org

CYBERCAMPS–TOWSON UNIVERSITY

Cybercamps–Giant Campus, Inc.
Baltimore, Maryland

General Information Coed residential and day academic program established in 1997. Formal opportunities for the academically talented.
Program Focus Computers and technology.
Academics Web page design, academics (general), computer programming, computer science (Advanced Placement), computers.
Arts Animation, digital media, film, graphic arts, musical productions, photography, television/video.
Special Interest Areas Computer game design, computer graphics, electronics, robotics, team building.
Program Information 1–12 sessions per year. Session length: 5 days in June, July, August. Ages: 7–18. 30–50 participants per session. Day program cost: $599–$749. Boarding program cost: $998–$1148.
Application Deadline Continuous.
Jobs Positions for high school students 17 and older and college students 18 and older.
Contact Camp Consultant, 3101 Western Avenue, Suite 100, Seattle, Washington 98121. Phone: 888-904-2267. Fax: 206-442-4501. E-mail: info@cybercamps.com.
URL www.cybercamps.com
For more information, see page 466.

CYBERCAMPS–UNIVERSITY OF MARYLAND

Cybercamps–Giant Campus, Inc.
College Park, Maryland

General Information Coed residential and day academic program established in 1997. Formal opportunities for the academically talented.
Program Focus Computers and technology.
Academics Web page design, academics (general), computer programming, computer science (Advanced Placement), computers.
Arts Animation, digital media, film, graphic arts, musical productions, photography, television/video.
Special Interest Areas Computer game design, computer graphics, electronics, robotics, team building.
Program Information 1–12 sessions per year. Session length: 5 days in June, July, August. Ages: 7–18. 30–50 participants per session. Day program cost: $599–$749. Boarding program cost: $998–$1148.
Application Deadline Continuous.
Jobs Positions for high school students 17 and older and college students 18 and older.
Contact Camp Consultant, 3101 Western Avenue, Suite 100, Seattle, Washington 98121. Phone: 888-904-2267. Fax: 206-442-4501. E-mail: info@cybercamps.com.
URL www.cybercamps.com
For more information, see page 466.

INTENSIVE ENGLISH LANGUAGE PROGRAM

St. Timothy's School
8400 Greenspring Avenue
Stevenson, Maryland 21153

General Information Coed residential academic program established in 2007.
Academics English as a second language, TOEFL/ TOEIC preparation, history, intercultural studies, reading, writing.
Arts Arts and crafts (general), ceramics.
Special Interest Areas Cross-cultural education, field trips (arts and culture).
Sports Basketball, miniature golf, soccer, swimming, ultimate frisbee, weight training.
Wilderness/Outdoors Hiking.
Trips Cultural, day.
Program Information 1 session per year. Session length: 4 weeks in July. Ages: 13–18. 20–40 participants per session. Boarding program cost: $5000.
Application Deadline Continuous.
Jobs Positions for college students 21 and older.
Contact Anne Esposito, Business Manager, main address above. Phone: 410-486-7400 Ext. 3036. Fax: 410-486-1167. E-mail: sttsummerprog@stt.org.
URL www.stt.org
For more information, see page 616.

INTERNATIONAL LEADERSHIP PROGRAM

St. Timothy's School
8400 Greenspring Avenue
Stevenson, Maryland 21153

General Information Coed residential academic program established in 2006.

International Leadership Program

Academics Current events, economics, global issues, government and politics, history, intercultural studies, international relations, peace education, research skills, speech/debate.
Arts Arts and crafts (general).
Special Interest Areas Communication skills, community service, field research/expeditions, field trips (arts and culture), leadership training, political organizing, problem solving, team building, touring.
Sports Basketball, miniature golf, soccer, swimming, ultimate frisbee, weight training.
Wilderness/Outdoors Hiking.
Trips Cultural, day.
Program Information 1 session per year. Session length: 4 weeks in July. Ages: 13–18. 20–40 participants per session. Boarding program cost: $4500.
Application Deadline Continuous.

Jobs Positions for college students 20 and older.
Contact Anne Esposito, Business Manager, main address above. Phone: 410-486-7400 Ext. 3036. Fax: 410-486-1167. E-mail: sstsummerprog@stt.org.
URL www.stt.org
For more information, see page 616.

JOHNS HOPKINS UNIVERSITY ZANVYL KRIEGER SCHOOL OF ARTS AND SCIENCES SUMMER PROGRAMS

The Johns Hopkins University
3400 North Charles Street
Whitehead Hall, Suite 100
Baltimore, Maryland 21218-2685

General Information Coed residential and day academic program. Formal opportunities for the academically talented. Specific services available for the hearing impaired, learning disabled, physically challenged, and visually impaired. College credit may be earned.

Johns Hopkins University Zanvyl Krieger School of Arts and Sciences Summer Programs

Program Focus Pre-college program offers a choice of college-level courses offered during a 5-week term and Discover Hopkins programs offer short-term one-credit theme based programs.
Academics American literature, English as a second language, English language/literature, French (Advanced Placement), French language/literature, German language/literature, Greek language/literature, Italian language/literature, Spanish (Advanced Placement), Spanish language/literature, academics (general), anthropology, art history/appreciation, astronomy, biology, biology (Advanced Placement), business, chemistry, classical languages/literatures, communications, computer programming, computer science (Advanced Placement), computers, economics, engineering, environmental science, geology/earth science, government and politics, government and politics (Advanced Placement), health sciences, history, humanities, mathematics, mathematics (Advanced Placement), music, oceanography, philosophy, physics,

physiology, precollege program, psychology, religion, science (general), social science, social studies, writing.
Arts Band, creative writing, drawing, film, music (chamber), music (classical), music (instrumental), painting, photography.
Special Interest Areas Community service.
Sports Baseball, basketball, climbing (wall), racquetball, squash, swimming, tennis, volleyball.
Trips Cultural, day, shopping.
Program Information 3–7 sessions per year. Session length: 1–5 weeks in May, June, July, August. Ages: 15+. 250–300 participants per session. Boarding program cost: $1595–$5990. Application fee: $50. Financial aid available. Cost for precollege day program: $590 per credit.
Application Deadline Continuous.
Contact Summer Programs Office, main address above. Phone: 800-548-0548. Fax: 410-516-5585. E-mail: summer@jhu.edu.
URL www.jhu.edu/summer
For more information, see page 532.

NATIONAL STUDENT LEADERSHIP CONFERENCE: ENGINEERING– WASHINGTON, D.C.

National Student Leadership Conference
University of Maryland, College Park
College Park, Maryland

General Information Coed residential academic program established in 1989. Formal opportunities for the academically talented. College credit may be earned.
Program Focus Leadership training, engineering and technology, career exploration.
Academics Engineering.
Special Interest Areas Career exploration, leadership training, robotics, team building.
Trips College tours, cultural, shopping.
Program Information 1–4 sessions per year. Session length: 10 days in June, July, August. Ages: 14–18. 150 participants per session. Boarding program cost: $2295. Financial aid available.
Application Deadline Continuous.
Jobs Positions for college students 18 and older.
Contact Director of Admissions, 414 North Orleans Street, Suite LL8, Chicago, Illinois 60610-1087. Phone: 312-322-9999. Fax: 312-765-0081. E-mail: info@nslcleaders.org.
URL www.nslcleaders.org
For more information, see page 564.

NATIONAL STUDENT LEADERSHIP CONFERENCE: MASTERING LEADERSHIP

National Student Leadership Conference
University of Maryland, College Park
College Park, Maryland

General Information Coed residential academic program and community service program established in 1989. Formal opportunities for the academically talented. College credit may be earned.
Program Focus Leadership training, career exploration, community service.
Academics Precollege program.
Special Interest Areas Career exploration, community service, leadership training, team building.
Trips College tours, cultural, shopping.
Program Information 1–4 sessions per year. Session length: 10 days in June, July, August. Ages: 14–18. 150 participants per session. Boarding program cost: $2295. Financial aid available.
Application Deadline Continuous.
Jobs Positions for college students 18 and older.
Contact Director of Admissions, 414 North Orleans Street, Suite LL8, Chicago, Illinois 60610-1087. Phone: 312-322-9999. Fax: 312-765-0081. E-mail: info@nslcleaders.org.
URL www.nslcleaders.org

For more information, see page 564.

NATIONAL STUDENT LEADERSHIP CONFERENCE: MEDICINE AND HEALTH CARE–WASHINGTON, D.C.

National Student Leadership Conference
University of Maryland, College Park
College Park, Maryland

General Information Coed residential academic program established in 1989. Formal opportunities for the academically talented. College credit may be earned.
Program Focus Leadership training, medicine and health care career exploration.
Academics Health sciences, medicine, premed.
Special Interest Areas Career exploration, leadership training, team building.
Trips College tours, cultural, shopping.
Program Information 1–4 sessions per year. Session length: 10 days in June, July, August. Ages: 14–18. 150 participants per session. Boarding program cost: $2295. Financial aid available.
Application Deadline Continuous.
Jobs Positions for college students 18 and older.

Contact Director of Admissions, 414 North Orleans Street, Suite LL8, Chicago, Illinois 60610-1087. Phone: 312-322-9999. Fax: 312-765-0081. E-mail: info@nslcleaders.org.
URL www.nslcleaders.org

For more information, see page 564.

UNIVERSITY OF MARYLAND YOUNG SCHOLARS PROGRAM

University of Maryland, Office of Extended Studies
College Park, Maryland 20742

General Information Coed residential and day academic program established in 2002. Formal opportunities for the academically talented and artistically talented. College credit may be earned.

University of Maryland Young Scholars Program

Academics English language/literature, academics (general), architecture, biology, business, communications, computers, engineering, environmental science, government and politics, government and politics (Advanced Placement), health sciences, humanities, journalism, mathematics (Advanced Placement), music, precollege program, science (general), social science.
Arts Creative writing, music.
Special Interest Areas Career exploration.
Trips Cultural, day.
Program Information 1 session per year. Session length: 15 days in July. Ages: 16–18. 25–350

participants per session. Day program cost: $1650–$1700. Boarding program cost: $2650–$2750. Application fee: $55. Financial aid available. Open to participants entering grades 11–12.
Application Deadline Continuous.
Contact Eric Johnson, Program Coordinator, Office of Extended Studies, main address above. Phone: 301-405-1027. Fax: 301-314-1282. E-mail: summer@umd.edu.
URL www.summer.umd.edu

For more information, see page 682.

MASSACHUSETTS

ACADEMIC STUDY ASSOCIATES–ASA AT THE UNIVERSITY OF MASSACHUSETTS AMHERST

Academic Study Associates, Inc. (ASA)
University of Massachusetts Amherst
Amherst, Massachusetts 01002

General Information Coed residential and day academic program and arts program established in 1987. Formal opportunities for the academically talented and artistically talented. High school or college credit may be earned.
Program Focus Academic enrichment, college credit, SAT preparation, creative and performing arts, and sports instruction, including professional tennis program.
Academics American literature, English as a second language, English language/literature, French language/literature, SAT/ACT preparation, Spanish language/literature, academics (general), art (Advanced Placement), art history/appreciation, biology (Advanced Placement), business, chemistry, college tours, communications, computer programming, computers, economics, government and politics, history, humanities, journalism, mathematics, music, philosophy, physics, precollege program, psychology, social science, speech/debate, writing.
Arts Arts and crafts (general), creative writing, dance, dance (jazz), dance (modern), drawing, film, graphic arts, music, music (ensemble), music (jazz), music (vocal), musical productions, painting, photography, pottery, radio broadcasting, sculpture, television/video, theater/drama.
Special Interest Areas Community service, field trips (arts and culture).
Sports Aerobics, basketball, golf, horseback riding, soccer, softball, sports (general), swimming, tennis, volleyball, weight training.
Wilderness/Outdoors Hiking, white-water trips.
Trips College tours, cultural, day, overnight, shopping.
Program Information 1 session per year. Session length: 4 weeks in July. Ages: 14–18. 100–150 participants per session. Day program cost: $1250–$2900. Boarding program cost: $5895. Financial aid available.

Application Deadline Continuous.
Jobs Positions for college students 21 and older.
Contact Mr. David A. Evans, Vice President, 375 West Broadway, Suite 200, New York, New York 10012. Phone: 212-796-8340. Fax: 212-334-4934. E-mail: summer@asaprograms.com.
URL www.asaprograms.com

For more information, see page 398.

BAC SUMMER ACADEMY

Boston Architectural College
320 Newbury Street
Boston, Massachusetts 02115

General Information Coed day academic program established in 1973. Formal opportunities for the academically talented and artistically talented.
Program Focus Architecture, interior design, and landscape architecture.
Academics Architecture, art (Advanced Placement), art history/appreciation, computers.
Arts Design, drawing, graphic arts, photography, studio arts.
Special Interest Areas Career exploration, field trips (arts and culture).
Trips Day.
Program Information 1 session per year. Session length: 20 days in July, August. Ages: 15–18. 60–75 participants per session. Day program cost: $1290. Financial aid available.
Application Deadline Continuous.
Contact Continuing Education at BAC, main address above. Phone: 617-585-0101. Fax: 617-585-0121. E-mail: summer@the-bac.edu.
URL www.the-bac.edu/summer

BELVOIR TERRACE

80 Cliffwood Street
Lenox, Massachusetts 01240

General Information Girls' residential arts program established in 1954. Accredited by American Camping Association. Formal opportunities for the academically talented, artistically talented, and gifted. High school credit may be earned.
Program Focus Fine and performing arts.
Academics English as a second language, art (Advanced Placement), music, writing.
Arts Acting, animation, arts, band, ceramics, chorus, creative writing, dance, dance (ballet), dance (jazz), dance (modern), dance (tap), drawing, fabric arts, film, jewelry making, metalworking, music, music (chamber), music (classical), music (ensemble), music (instrumental), music (jazz), music (orchestral), music (vocal), musical productions, painting, performing arts, photography, pottery, printmaking, sculpture, television/video, theater/drama, weaving.
Sports Aerobics, archery, basketball, bicycling, canoeing, equestrian sports, horseback riding, soccer, swimming, tennis.
Trips Cultural.
Program Information 1 session per year. Session

Belvoir Terrace (continued)

length: 7 weeks in June, July, August. Ages: 8–17. 180 participants per session. Boarding program cost: $9100–$9600. Application fee: $250. Financial aid available. Art studio classes are $50–$100 extra.
Application Deadline Continuous.
Jobs Positions for college students 21 and older.
Summer Contact Ms. Nancy S. Goldberg, Director, 80 Cliffwood Street, Lenox, Massachusetts 01240. Phone: 413-637-0555. Fax: 413-637-4651. E-mail: belvoirt@aol.com.
Winter Contact Ms. Nancy S. Goldberg, Director, 101 West 79th Street, New York, New York 10024. Phone: 212-580-3398. Fax: 212-579-7282. E-mail: info@belvoirterrace.
URL www.belvoirterrace.com

BOSTON UNIVERSITY TANGLEWOOD INSTITUTE

Boston University Tanglewood Institute
45 West Street
Lenox, Massachusetts 01240

General Information Coed residential arts program established in 1966. Formal opportunities for the artistically talented. College credit may be earned.

Boston University Tanglewood Institute

Program Focus Classical music.
Academics Music, music (Advanced Placement).

Arts Band, chorus, music, music (chamber), music (classical), music (ensemble), music (instrumental), music (orchestral), music (vocal).
Sports Basketball, soccer, softball, swimming, tennis, volleyball.
Wilderness/Outdoors Hiking.
Trips Cultural.
Program Information 1–3 sessions per year. Session length: 2–8 weeks in June, July, August. Ages: 14–18. 100–350 participants per session. Boarding program cost: $2300–$6100. Application fee: $65. Financial aid available.
Application Deadline February 15.
Jobs Positions for college students.
Contact Shirley Leiphon, Administrative Director, 855 Commonwealth Avenue, Boston, Massachusetts 02215. Phone: 800-643-4796. Fax: 617-353-7455. E-mail: tanglewd@bu.edu.
URL www.bu.edu/tanglewood

CAPE COD SEA CAMPS–MONOMOY/WONO

Cape Cod Sea Camps, Inc.
3057 Main Street
Brewster, Massachusetts 02631

General Information Coed residential and day traditional camp established in 1922. Accredited by American Camping Association.
Program Focus Sailing and traditional activities.
Arts Arts and crafts (general), batiking, ceramics, creative writing, dance, drawing, graphic arts, painting, photography, pottery, printmaking, theater/drama, woodworking.
Special Interest Areas Leadership training, nature study.
Sports Aerobics, archery, baseball, basketball, bicycling, canoeing, field hockey, fishing, gymnastics, kayaking, lacrosse, riflery, sailing, snorkeling, soccer, softball, swimming, tennis, track and field, volleyball, waterskiing, windsurfing.
Wilderness/Outdoors Bicycle trips, canoe trips.
Trips Day.
Program Information 2 sessions per year. Session length: 10–49 days in July, August. Ages: 8–15. 350–380 participants per session. Day program cost: $550. Boarding program cost: $4300–$7700. Financial aid available. Financial aid deadline is January 1.
Application Deadline Continuous.
Jobs Positions for college students 19 and older.
Contact David Peterson, Director, Box 1880, Brewster, Massachusetts 02631. Phone: 508-896-3451. Fax: 508-896-8272. E-mail: info@capecodseacamps.com.
URL www.capecodseacamps.com

CAREER EXPLORATIONS—BOSTON

Career Explorations, LLC
Boston, Massachusetts

General Information Coed residential and day academic program established in 2006.
Program Focus Career exploration through an internship in a field of personal interest. Optional college tours and SAT preparation.
Academics Architecture, business, communications, computers, economics, engineering, environmental science, government and politics, health sciences, journalism, music, psychology, social science.
Arts Photography.
Special Interest Areas Animal care, career exploration, college planning, community service, culinary arts, internships.
Trips College tours, cultural, day.
Program Information 1 session per year. Session length: 4 weeks in June, July. Ages: 16–18. 45–60 participants per session. Boarding program cost: $5795. Application fee: $50.
Application Deadline Continuous.
Contact Todd Aronson, Boston Director, 18 Exeter Lane, Morristown, New Jersey 07960. Phone: 781-559-3261. E-mail: todd@ceinternships.com.
URL www.ceinternships.com

For more information, see page 446.

CUSHING ACADEMY SUMMER SESSION

Cushing Academy
39 School Street
Ashburnham, Massachusetts 01430-8000

General Information Coed residential and day academic program and arts program established in 1976. Formal opportunities for the academically talented and artistically talented. Specific services available for the learning disabled. High school credit may be earned.

Cushing Academy Summer Session

Program Focus Academic coursework, review, and enrichment.

Academics American literature, English as a second language, English language/literature, SAT/ACT preparation, academics (general), art (Advanced Placement), art history/appreciation, biology, chemistry, computers, history, mathematics, mathematics (Advanced Placement), physics, reading, research skills, science (general), study skills, writing.
Arts Acting, ceramics, creative writing, dance, drawing, film, graphic arts, jewelry making, metalworking, music, music (instrumental), painting, photography, pottery, radio broadcasting, sculpture, television/video, theater/drama.
Special Interest Areas College planning, community service, field research/expeditions.
Sports Aerobics, basketball, figure skating, golf, ice hockey, martial arts, soccer, swimming, tennis, volleyball.
Wilderness/Outdoors Hiking.
Trips College tours, cultural, day, overnight, shopping.
Program Information 1–2 sessions per year. Session length: 20–40 days in July, August. Ages: 12–18. 300 participants per session. Day program cost: $2800. Boarding program cost: $5650. Application fee: $60. Financial aid available.
Application Deadline Continuous.
Jobs Positions for college students 20 and older.
Contact Mr. Dan Frank, Director of Summer Session, 39 School Street, PO Box 8000, Ashburnham, Massachusetts 01430-8000. Phone: 978-827-7700. Fax: 978-827-6927. E-mail: summersession@cushing.org.
URL www.cushing.org

For more information, see page 464.

CYBERCAMPS—BENTLEY COLLEGE

Cybercamps—Giant Campus, Inc.
Waltham, Massachusetts

General Information Coed residential and day academic program established in 1997. Formal opportunities for the academically talented.
Program Focus Computers and technology.
Academics Web page design, academics (general), computer programming, computer science (Advanced Placement), computers.
Arts Animation, digital media, film, graphic arts, musical productions, photography, television/video.
Special Interest Areas Computer game design, computer graphics, electronics, robotics, team building.
Program Information 1–12 sessions per year. Session length: 5 days in June, July, August. Ages: 7–18. 30–50 participants per session. Day program cost: $599–$749. Boarding program cost: $998–$1148.
Application Deadline Continuous.

Cybercamps–Bentley College (continued)

Jobs Positions for high school students 17 and older and college students 18 and older.
Contact Camp Consultant, 3101 Western Avenue, Suite 100, Seattle, Washington 98121. Phone: 888-904-2267. Fax: 206-442-4501. E-mail: info@cybercamps.com. **URL** www.cybercamps.com
For more information, see page 466.

CYBERCAMPS–DANA HALL SCHOOL

Cybercamps–Giant Campus, Inc.
Wellesley, Massachusetts

General Information Coed residential and day academic program established in 1997. Formal opportunities for the academically talented.
Program Focus Computers and technology.
Academics Web page design, academics (general), computer programming, computer science (Advanced Placement), computers.
Arts Animation, digital media, film, graphic arts, musical productions, photography, television/video.
Special Interest Areas Computer game design, computer graphics, electronics, robotics, team building.
Program Information 1–12 sessions per year. Session length: 5 days in June, July, August. Ages: 7–18. 30–50 participants per session. Day program cost: $599–$749. Boarding program cost: $998–$1148.
Application Deadline Continuous.
Jobs Positions for high school students 17 and older and college students 18 and older.
Contact Camp Consultant, 3101 Western Avenue, Suite 100, Seattle, Washington 98121. Phone: 888-904-2267. Fax: 206-442-4501. E-mail: info@cybercamps.com. **URL** www.cybercamps.com
For more information, see page 466.

CYBERCAMPS–MERRIMACK COLLEGE

Cybercamps–Giant Campus, Inc.
North Andover, Massachusetts

General Information Coed residential and day academic program. Formal opportunities for the academically talented.
Program Focus Computers and technology.
Academics Web page design, academics (general), computer programming, computer science (Advanced Placement), computers.
Arts Animation, digital media, film, graphic arts, musical productions, photography, television/video.
Special Interest Areas Computer game design, computer graphics, electronics, robotics, team building.
Program Information 1–12 sessions per year. Session length: 5 days in June, July, August. Ages: 7–18. 30–50 participants per session. Day program cost: $599–$749. Boarding program cost: $998–$1148.
Application Deadline Continuous.
Jobs Positions for high school students 17 and older and college students 18 and older.

Contact Camp Consultant, 3101 Western Avenue, Suite 100, Seattle, Washington 98121. Phone: 888-904-2267. Fax: 206-442-4501. E-mail: info@cybercamps.com. **URL** www.cybercamps.com
For more information, see page 466.

CYBERCAMPS–MIT

Cybercamps–Giant Campus, Inc.
Cambridge, Massachusetts

General Information Coed residential and day academic program. Formal opportunities for the academically talented.
Program Focus Computers and technology.
Academics Web page design, academics (general), computer programming, computer science (Advanced Placement), computers.
Arts Animation, digital media, film, graphic arts, musical productions, photography, television/video.
Special Interest Areas Computer game design, computer graphics, electronics, robotics, team building.
Program Information 1–12 sessions per year. Session length: 5 days in June, July, August. Ages: 7–18. 30–50 participants per session. Day program cost: $599–$749. Boarding program cost: $998–$1148.
Application Deadline Continuous.
Jobs Positions for high school students 17 and older and college students 18 and older.
Contact Camp Consultant, 3101 Western Avenue, Suite 100, Seattle, Washington 98121. Phone: 888-904-2267. Fax: 206-442-4501. E-mail: info@cybercamps.com. **URL** www.cybercamps.com
For more information, see page 466.

EAGLEBROOK SUMMER SEMESTER

Eaglebrook School
271 Pine Nook Road
Deerfield, Massachusetts 01342

General Information Coed residential academic program established in 1996. Formal opportunities for the academically talented.

Academics American literature, English as a second language, English language/literature, French language/literature, Japanese language/literature, Spanish language/literature, academics (general), area studies, computers, environmental science, history, journalism, mathematics, reading, science (general), study skills, writing.

Arts Acting, ceramics, creative writing, drawing, film, jewelry making, painting, photography, pottery, printmaking, sculpture, theater/drama, woodworking.

Special Interest Areas Field trips (arts and culture), leadership training.

Sports Baseball, basketball, canoeing, fishing, golf, lacrosse, soccer, softball, sports (general), squash, swimming, tennis, volleyball, water polo, weight training.

Wilderness/Outdoors Canoe trips, hiking, wilderness camping.

Trips Cultural, day, shopping.

Program Information 1 session per year. Session length: 4 weeks in July. Ages: 11–13. 50–60 participants per session. Boarding program cost: $5100. Application fee: $35–$75. Financial aid available.

Application Deadline Continuous.

Jobs Positions for college students 19 and older.

Contact Mr. Karl J. Koenigsbauer, Director, main address above. Phone: 413-774-7411. Fax: 413-772-2394. URL www.eaglebrook.org

Special Note
Eaglebrook's campus is located on 680 wooded acres in western Massachusetts on a hillside that overlooks the village of historic Deerfield. The program offers opportunities for classes in English and math. The Summer Semester relies on the same resources that have already earned Eaglebrook a reputation for excellence: the beauty of its natural setting, family life in the dorms and dining room, the excellence of its faculty members, and the variety of classes. The Summer Semester is a four-week boarding adventure for boys and girls ages 11–13. The program is designed to build confidence through achievement and to foster leadership skills in the classroom, on the playing field, and within the school community. Children from every ethnic, racial, economic, and geographic background are welcome. Working and playing together, they discover inner strengths while they expand their knowledge, develop artistic talents, gain physical coordination and strength, and make friends in a multicultural community that encourages shared common interests and respect for differences.

EAGLE HILL SCHOOL SUMMER SESSION

Eagle Hill School
242 Old Petersham Road
Hardwick, Massachusetts 01037

General Information Coed residential and day academic program established in 1967. Specific services available for the learning disabled and participant with AD/HD.

Eagle Hill School Summer Session

Program Focus Academic course work, social skills building, camp activities.

Eagle Hill School Summer Session (continued)

Academics English language/literature, academics (general), computers, history, mathematics, philosophy, psychology, reading, science (general), social studies, study skills, typing, writing.

Arts Arts and crafts (general), ceramics, creative writing, drawing, graphic arts, painting, photography, pottery, printmaking, sculpture, theater/drama, weaving, woodworking.

Special Interest Areas Culinary arts, field trips (arts and culture), gardening, leadership training, model rocketry.

Sports Aerobics, basketball, bicycling, climbing (wall), equestrian sports, fishing, golf, horseback riding, ropes course, soccer, softball, sports (general), swimming, tennis, volleyball, weight training.

Wilderness/Outdoors Bicycle trips, canoe trips, hiking, mountain biking, rafting, white-water trips, wilderness camping.

Trips Cultural, day, overnight, shopping.

Program Information 1 session per year. Session length: 40 days in July, August. Ages: 10–18. 60–70 participants per session. Day program cost: $6888. Boarding program cost: $6888. Application fee: $50.

Application Deadline Continuous.

Jobs Positions for college students.

Contact Mr. Dana M. Harbert, Director of Admission, PO Box 116, 242 Old Petersham Road, Hardwick, Massachusetts 01037. Phone: 413-477-6000. Fax: 413-477-6837. E-mail: admission@ehs1.org.

URL www.ehs1.org

Special Note

Eagle Hill School runs a six-week summer session for students with learning differences, ages 10 to 18, who have been diagnosed with specific learning (dis)abilities and/or attention deficit disorder. The summer session is primarily designed to remediate academic and social deficits while maintaining progress achieved during the school year. Arts and sports-based electives are combined with academic courses to address the needs of the whole person in a camp-like atmosphere. This structured and individualized environment gives bright students the opportunity to flourish. Evening clubs and weekend trips round out the summer session's offerings and provide for a fun-filled camp experience.

EMAGINATION COMPUTER CAMPS–MASSACHUSETTS

Emagination Computer Camps
Bentley College
Waltham, Massachusetts

General Information Coed residential and day academic program established in 1982. Accredited by American Camping Association. Formal opportunities for the academically talented.

Emagination Computer Camps–Massachusetts

Program Focus Computer science, technology, and art, swimming, tennis, and basketball clinics; web design; computer music, video, photo, 3-D animation.

Academics Computer programming, computer science (Advanced Placement), computers, technology.

Arts Graphic arts.

Special Interest Areas ADL skills, Internet accessibility, computer graphics, electronics, field trips (arts and culture), model rocketry, robotics.

Sports Basketball, soccer, swimming, tennis.

Trips Day.

Program Information 4 sessions per year. Session length: 2 weeks in June, July, August. Ages: 8–17. 150–250 participants per session. Day program cost: $1235. Boarding program cost: $2245.

Application Deadline Continuous.

Jobs Positions for college students 18 and older.

Contact Ms. Kathi Rigg, Director, 110 Winn Street, Suite 205, Woburn, Massachusetts 01801. Phone: 877-248-0206. Fax: 781-933-0749. E-mail: camp@computercamps.com.

URL www.computercamps.com

For more information, see page 482.

EXCEL AT AMHERST COLLEGE

Putney Student Travel
Amherst College
Amherst, Massachusetts 01002

General Information Coed residential academic program and arts program established in 1951. Formal opportunities for the academically talented and artistically talented. Specific services available for the learning disabled.

Excel at Amherst College

Program Focus Precollege program emphasizing small classes and creative interaction among students and faculty. Excursions available to sites of interest in the Northeast and Canada.

Academics American literature, English as a second language, English language/literature, French language/literature, SAT/ACT preparation, Spanish language/literature, academics (general), anthropology, archaeology, architecture, area studies, art history/appreciation, astronomy, biology, business, college tours, communications, computers, ecology, economics, environmental science, geology/earth science, government and politics, history, humanities, intercultural studies, journalism, mathematics, music, philosophy, physics, physiology, precollege program, psychology, science (general), social science, social studies, speech/debate, study skills, writing.

Arts Arts, arts and crafts (general), batiking, creative writing, dance, dance (jazz), dance (modern), drawing, fabric arts, film, jewelry making, music, music (ensemble), music (instrumental), music (vocal), musical productions, painting, photography, puppetry, sculpture, television/video, theater/drama.

Special Interest Areas Career exploration, community service, field research/expeditions, nature study.

Sports Aerobics, baseball, basketball, bicycling, canoeing, climbing (wall), cross-country, fishing, football, golf, in-line skating, lacrosse, rappelling, sea kayaking, soccer, softball, sports (general), squash, swimming, tennis, volleyball, weight training.

Wilderness/Outdoors Bicycle trips, canoe trips, caving, hiking, mountain biking, rafting, rock climbing, white-water trips.

Trips College tours, cultural, day, overnight.

Program Information 3 sessions per year. Session length: 21–45 days in June, July, August. Ages: 15–18. 90–150 participants per session. Boarding program cost: $4290–$5090. Financial aid available.

Application Deadline Continuous.

Jobs Positions for college students 20 and older.

Summer Contact Patrick Noyes, Director, 345 Hickory Ridge Road, Putney, Vermont 05346. Phone: 802-387-5000. Fax: 802-387-4276. E-mail: excel@goputney.com.

Winter Contact Patrick Noyes, main address above.

URL www.goputney.com

For more information, see page 490.

FENN SCHOOL SUMMER DAY CAMP

The Fenn School
516 Monument Street
Concord, Massachusetts 01742-1894

General Information Coed day traditional camp, outdoor program, and arts program established in 1999. Accredited by American Camping Association.

Program Focus Summer fun and learning.

Academics American literature, Spanish language/literature, academics (general), computer programming, computers, ecology, environmental science, geology/earth science, history, journalism, mathematics, music, reading, science (general), writing.

Arts Acting, arts, arts and crafts (general), ceramics, circus arts, clowning, creative writing, drawing, film, jewelry making, music, musical productions, painting, photography, pottery, television/video, theater/drama, woodworking.

Special Interest Areas Campcraft, community service, leadership training, nature study.

Sports Baseball, basketball, bicycling, canoeing, climbing (wall), rappelling, ropes course, soccer, softball, swimming, volleyball.

Wilderness/Outdoors Bicycle trips, canoe trips, hiking, mountain biking, orienteering, outdoor adventure, rock climbing, white-water trips.

Fenn School Summer Day Camp (continued)

Trips Cultural, day, overnight.
Program Information 8 sessions per year. Session length: 5–10 days in June, July, August. Ages: 5–15. 200–350 participants per session. Day program cost: $300–$595. Financial aid available.
Application Deadline Continuous.
Jobs Positions for high school students 18 and older and college students 18 and older.
Contact Mr. David A. Platt, Director of Summer Programs, main address above. Phone: 978-318-3614. Fax: 978-318-3683. E-mail: summercamp@fenn.org.
URL www.summerfenn.org

THE FESSENDEN SCHOOL SUMMER ESL PROGRAM

The Fessenden School
250 Waltham Street
West Newton, Massachusetts 02465

General Information Coed residential academic program, outdoor program, and cultural program established in 1992. Formal opportunities for the academically talented.

The Fessenden School Summer ESL Program

Program Focus English as a Second Language instruction.
Academics English as a second language, computers, history, intercultural studies, reading, science (general), study skills, writing.
Arts Arts and crafts (general), creative writing, photography, television/video, theater/drama.
Special Interest Areas Field trips (arts and culture), touring.
Sports Baseball, basketball, canoeing, soccer, softball, swimming, tennis, volleyball.
Wilderness/Outdoors Hiking, wilderness camping.
Trips Cultural, day, overnight, shopping.
Program Information 1 session per year. Session length: 5 weeks in June, July. Ages: 10–15. 35–45 participants per session. Boarding program cost: $5800–$5975. Application fee: $75.
Application Deadline Continuous.
Jobs Positions for college students 17 and older.

Contact Mr. Mark Hansen, Director, main address above. Phone: 617-678-2978. Fax: 617-630-2317. E-mail: esl@fessenden.org.
URL www.fessenden.org
For more information, see page 494.

FRONTIERS PROGRAM

Worcester Polytechnic Institute
100 Institute Road
Worcester, Massachusetts 01609-2280

General Information Coed residential academic program established in 1982. Formal opportunities for the academically talented.

Frontiers Program

Program Focus Science, math, technology and engineering.
Academics Aerospace science, biology, chemistry, computer programming, computers, engineering, history, mathematics, music, physics, precollege program, science (general), speech/debate, writing.
Arts Acting, band, creative writing, music, music

(instrumental), music (jazz), music (orchestral), theater/drama.

Special Interest Areas Computer game design, robotics.
Sports Basketball, bowling, tennis, volleyball.
Trips Day, shopping.
Program Information 1 session per year. Session length: 13 days in July. Ages: 16–18. 120–140 participants per session. Boarding program cost: $2100. Application fee: $50. Open to participants entering grades 11–12.
Contact Julie Chapman, Frontiers Program/Associate Director of Admissions, Student Affairs Office, 100 Institute Road, Worcester, Massachusetts 01609-2280. Phone: 508-831-5286. Fax: 508-831-5875. E-mail: frontiers@wpi.edu.
URL www.wpi.edu/+frontiers

For more information, see page 710.

HARVARD UNIVERSITY SUMMER SCHOOL: SECONDARY SCHOOL PROGRAM

Harvard University Summer School:
Secondary School Program
51 Brattle Street
Cambridge, Massachusetts 02138

General Information Coed residential and day academic program established in 1975. Formal opportunities for the academically talented. Specific services available for the hearing impaired, learning disabled, physically challenged, and visually impaired. College credit may be earned.
Program Focus College prep.
Academics American literature, Chinese languages/literature, English as a second language, English language/literature, French language/literature, German language/literature, Greek language/literature, Hebrew language, Italian language/literature, Japanese language/literature, Latin language, Russian language/literature, Spanish language/literature, academics (general), anthropology, archaeology, art history/appreciation, astronomy, biology, botany, business, chemistry, classical languages/literatures, college tours, communications, computer programming, computers, economics, environmental science, geography, geology/earth science, government and politics, health sciences, history, humanities, journalism, linguistics, marine studies, mathematics, music, philosophy, physics, precollege program, psychology, religion, science (general), social science, study skills, writing.
Arts Acting, band, chorus, creative writing, film, graphic arts, music, music (classical), music (ensemble), music (instrumental), music (orchestral), music (vocal), painting, photography, theater/drama.
Special Interest Areas College planning, community service, touring.
Sports Aerobics, basketball, rowing (crew/sculling), soccer, softball, squash, swimming, tennis, volleyball, weight training.
Trips College tours, cultural, day, shopping.

Harvard University Summer School: Secondary School Program

Program Information 1–2 sessions per year. Session length: 4–8 weeks in June, July, August. 1,000–1,100 participants per session. Day program cost: $2125–$4250. Boarding program cost: $7275–$8500. Application fee: $50. Financial aid available. Participants need to be at least sophomore level.
Application Deadline Continuous.
Contact Mr. William Holinger, Director of Secondary School Programs, main address above. Phone: 617-495-3192. Fax: 617-495-9176. E-mail: ssp@hudce.harvard.edu.
URL www.ssp.harvard.edu

For more information, see page 512.

iD Tech Camps–Merrimack College, North Andover, MA

iD Tech Camps
Merrimack College
North Andover, Massachusetts 01845

General Information Coed day academic program established in 1999. Accredited by American Camping Association. Formal opportunities for the academically talented and artistically talented.
Program Focus Students create 2D and 3D video games, build robots to compete, design websites, film and edit digital movies, create their own comic book with digital photos, learn programming and more. One computer per student and an average of five students per staff member. Campers take home a project at the end of the weeklong course.
Academics Web page design, academics (general), computer programming, computer science (Advanced Placement), computers, precollege program.
Arts Animation, cinematography, digital media, drawing, film, film editing, film production, graphic arts, photography, television/video.
Special Interest Areas Career exploration, computer game design, computer graphics, electronics, leadership training, robotics, team building.
Sports Baseball, basketball, soccer, softball, swimming, volleyball.
Trips College tours.
Program Information 5–9 sessions per year. Session length: 5–7 days in June, July, August. Ages: 7–17. 40–50 participants per session. Day program cost: $729. Financial aid available.
Application Deadline Continuous.
Jobs Positions for college students 18 and older.
Contact Client Service Representatives, 42 West Campbell Avenue, Suite 301, Campbell, California 95008. Phone: 888-709-TECH. Fax: 408-871-2228. E-mail: info@internaldrive.com
URL www.internaldrive.com
For more information, see page 520.

iD Tech Camps–MIT, Cambridge, MA

iD Tech Camps
Massachusetts Institute of Technology
Cambridge, Massachusetts 02139

General Information Coed residential and day academic program established in 1999. Accredited by American Camping Association. Formal opportunities for the academically talented and artistically talented.
Program Focus Students create 2D and 3D video games, build robots to compete, design websites, film and edit digital movies, create their own comic book with digital photos, learn programming and more. One computer per student and an average of five students per staff member. Campers take home a project at the end of the weeklong course.
Academics Web page design, academics (general), computer programming, computer science (Advanced Placement), computers, precollege program.

Arts Animation, cartooning, cinematography, digital media, drawing, film, film editing, film production, graphic arts, photography, television/video.
Special Interest Areas Career exploration, computer game design, computer graphics, electronics, leadership training, robotics, team building.
Sports Baseball, basketball, soccer, softball, swimming, volleyball.
Trips College tours.
Program Information 5–9 sessions per year. Session length: 5–7 days in June, July, August. Ages: 7–17. 40–50 participants per session. Day program cost: $729. Boarding program cost: $1129. Financial aid available.
Application Deadline Continuous.
Jobs Positions for college students 18 and older.
Contact Client Service Representatives, 42 West Campbell Avenue, Suite 301, Campbell, California 95008. Phone: 888-709-TECH. Fax: 408-871-2228. E-mail: info@internaldrive.com
URL www.internaldrive.com
For more information, see page 520.

iD Tech Camps–Smith College, Northampton, MA

iD Tech Camps
Smith College
Northampton, Massachusetts 01063

General Information Coed residential and day academic program established in 1999. Accredited by American Camping Association. Formal opportunities for the academically talented and artistically talented.
Program Focus Students create 2D and 3D video games, build robots to compete, design websites, film and edit digital movies, create their own comic book with digital photos, learn programming and more. One computer per student and an average of five students per staff member. Campers take home a project at the end of the weeklong course.
Academics Web page design, academics (general), computer programming, computer science (Advanced Placement), computers, precollege program.
Arts Animation, cartooning, cinematography, digital media, drawing, film, film editing, film production, graphic arts, photography, television/video.
Special Interest Areas Career exploration, computer game design, computer graphics, electronics, leadership training, robotics, team building.
Sports Baseball, basketball, soccer, softball, swimming, volleyball.
Trips College tours.
Program Information 5–9 sessions per year. Session length: 5–7 days in June, July, August. Ages: 7–17. 40–50 participants per session. Day program cost: $729. Boarding program cost: $1129. Financial aid available.
Application Deadline Continuous.
Jobs Positions for college students 18 and older.

Contact Client Service Representatives, 42 West Campbell Avenue, Suite 301, Campbell, California 95008. Phone: 888-709-TECH. Fax: 408-871-2228. E-mail: info@internaldrive.com.
URL www.internaldrive.com
For more information, see page 520.

INTERNSHIP CONNECTION
Internship Connection
Boston, Massachusetts

General Information Coed day academic program established in 2003.

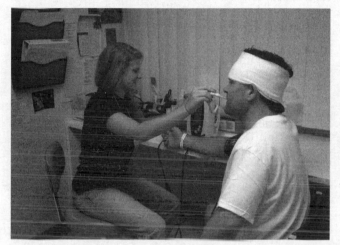

Internship Connection

Program Focus Summer internships in the Greater Boston Area for high school and college students.
Academics French language/literature, Spanish language/literature, Web page design, academics (general), advertising, architecture, art history/appreciation, banking/finance, biology, biotechnology, business, communications, computers, ecology, economics, engineering, environmental science, geology/earth science, global issues, government and politics, health sciences, journalism, law, marketing, medicine, music, prelaw, premed, psychology, science (general), social services, technology, writing.
Arts Animation, arts, arts business, ceramics, costume design, creative writing, design, digital media, fashion design/production, graphic arts, photography, puppetry, set design, television/video, theater/drama.
Special Interest Areas Native American culture, animal care, career exploration, college planning, communication skills, community service, computer graphics, conservation projects, culinary arts, field research/expeditions, gardening, health education, internships, leadership training, nature study.
Sports Sports (general).
Program Information 1 session per year. Session length: 28–60 days in June, July, August. Ages: 14–23. 60–80 participants per session. Day program cost: $1500.
Application Deadline Continuous.

Contact Dr. Carole Jabbawy, Director, 17 Countryside Road, Newton, Massachusetts 02459. Phone: 617-796-9283. Fax: 617-796-9283. E-mail: carole@internshipconnection.com.
URL www.internshipconnection.com
For more information, see page 530.

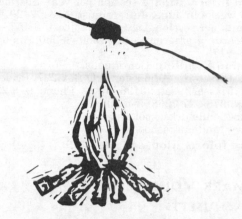

LANDMARK SCHOOL SUMMER ACADEMIC PROGRAM
Landmark School
Prides Crossing, Massachusetts 01965-0227

General Information Coed residential and day academic program and special needs program established in 1971. Specific services available for the learning disabled. High school credit may be earned.

Landmark School Summer Academic Program

Program Focus Customized academic instruction for students with language-based learning disabilities or dyslexia.
Academics English language/literature, marine studies, mathematics, reading, remedial academics, study skills, writing.
Arts Arts and crafts (general), musical productions, theater/drama.
Sports Baseball, basketball, bicycling, canoeing,

Landmark School Summer Academic Program (continued)

fishing, kayaking, ropes course, soccer, softball, swimming, tennis, volleyball.

Wilderness/Outdoors Backpacking, hiking.

Trips Day, overnight.

Program Information 1 session per year. Session length: 6 weeks in June, July, August. Ages: 7–20. 170 participants per session. Day program cost: $3975–$6050. Boarding program cost: $7950–$8350. Application fee: $150–$175.

Application Deadline Continuous.

Contact Director of Admission, PO Box 227, Prides Crossing, Massachusetts 01965-0227. Phone: 978-236-3000. Fax: 978-927-7268. E-mail: admission@landmarkschool.org.

URL www.landmarkschool.org

For more information, see page 540.

LANDMARK VOLUNTEERS: MASSACHUSETTS

Landmark Volunteers, Inc.
Massachusetts

General Information Coed residential outdoor program and community service program established in 1992. High school credit may be earned.

Landmark Volunteers: Massachusetts

Program Focus Opportunity for high school students to earn community service credit while working as a team for two weeks serving Boston Symphony at Tanglewood, Perkins School for the Blind, Gould Farm, Cape Cod National Seashore, Norman Rockwell Museum, Plimoth Plantation, Bartholomew's Cobble, Hancock Shaker Village, or Berkshire Scenic Railway. Similar programs offered through Landmark Volunteers at over 50 locations in 20 states.

Academics Area studies, college tours, ecology, environmental science, history, music, science (general), social science, social services.

Arts Music (orchestral), theater/drama.

Special Interest Areas Animal care, career exploration, community service, conservation projects, farming, field research/expeditions, gardening, leadership training, nature study, team building, trail maintenance, work camp programs.

Sports Swimming.

Wilderness/Outdoors Hiking.

Trips Cultural, day.

Program Information 11 sessions per year. Session length: 2 weeks in June, July, August. Ages: 14–18. 10–13 participants per session. Boarding program cost: $1250–$1300. Financial aid available.

Application Deadline Continuous.

Jobs Positions for college students.

Contact Ann Barrett, Executive Director, PO Box 455, Sheffield, Massachusetts 01257. Phone: 413-229-0255. Fax: 413-229-2050. E-mail: landmark@volunteers.com.

URL www.volunteers.com

For more information, see page 542.

LINDEN HILL SUMMER PROGRAM

Linden Hill School
154 South Mountain Road
Northfield, Massachusetts 01360-9681

General Information Coed residential and day traditional camp, academic program, and special needs program established in 1998. Specific services available for the learning disabled. High school credit may be earned.

Program Focus Program offers additional academic support for dyslexia or language-based learning differences as well as attention issues.

Academics English as a second language, English language/literature, SAT/ACT preparation, academics (general), communications, computers, environmental science, journalism, mathematics, music, reading, science (general), study skills, writing.

Arts Acting, arts and crafts (general), creative writing, dance, drawing, music, painting, photography, pottery, sculpture, theater/drama, woodworking.

Special Interest Areas Animal care, community service, culinary arts, field trips (arts and culture), leadership training, speech therapy, touring.

Sports Aerobics, archery, basketball, bicycling, climbing (wall), fishing, golf, horseback riding, in-line skating, soccer, softball, street/roller hockey, swimming, tennis, volleyball.

Wilderness/Outdoors Backpacking, bicycle trips,

canoe trips, hiking, mountain biking, orienteering, white-water trips.
Trips Cultural, day, overnight.

Linden Hill Summer Program

Program Information 1 session per year. Session length: 31 days in July. Ages: 7–17. 35–45 participants per session. Day program cost: $3200. Boarding program cost: $5350. Application fee: $60. Financial aid available.
Application Deadline Continuous.
Jobs Positions for college students 19 and older.
Contact James A. McDaniel, Headmaster and Summer Program Director, main address above. Phone: 413-498-2906. Fax: 413-498-2908. E-mail: admissions@lindenhs.org.
URL www.lindenhs.org
For more information, see page 550.

MASSACHUSETTS COLLEGE OF ART/ CREATIVE VACATION

Massachusetts College of Art
621 Huntington Avenue
Boston, Massachusetts 02115

General Information Coed day arts program established in 1994. Formal opportunities for the artistically talented.
Academics Art (Advanced Placement), art history/appreciation.
Arts Animation, arts, ceramics, drawing, film, graphic arts, painting, photography, pottery, printmaking, sculpture.
Special Interest Areas Career exploration.
Trips College tours, cultural.
Program Information 1 session per year. Session length: 10 days in July. Ages: 9–18. 100–120 participants per session. Day program cost: $560–$1120. Financial aid available. Scholarship deadline is May 6.
Application Deadline May 20.
Jobs Positions for college students.
Contact Lin Lufkin, Program Administrative Assistant, main address above. Phone: 617-879-7170. Fax: 617-879-7171. E-mail: llufkin@massart.edu.
URL www.massartplus.org
For more information, see page 556.

MASSACHUSETTS COLLEGE OF ART/ SUMMER STUDIOS

Massachusetts College of Art
621 Huntington Avenue
Boston, Massachusetts 02115

General Information Coed residential and day arts program established in 1990. Formal opportunities for the artistically talented.

Massachusetts College of Art / Summer Studios

Academics Architecture, art (Advanced Placement), art history/appreciation.
Arts Animation, arts, ceramics, design, drawing, fashion design/production, film, graphic arts, jewelry making, metalworking, painting, photography, pottery, printmaking, sculpture.
Special Interest Areas Career exploration, computer graphics.
Trips College tours, cultural.
Program Information 1 session per year. Session length: 26 days in July, August. Ages: 15–17. 100 participants per session. Day program cost: $1970.

Massachusetts College of Art/Summer Studios (continued)

Boarding program cost: $4335. Financial aid available. Scholarship deadline is June 3.
Application Deadline Continuous.
Jobs Positions for college students 19 and older.
Contact Lin Lufkin, Program Administrative Assistant, main address above. Phone: 617-879-7170. Fax: 617-879-7171. E-mail: llufkin@massart.edu.
URL www.massartplus.org
For more information, see page 556.

MIT MITES (MINORITY INTRODUCTION TO ENGINEERING AND SCIENCE)

Massachusetts Institute of Technology
77 Massachusetts Avenue, Room 11-123
Cambridge, Massachusetts 02139

General Information Coed residential academic program established in 1975. Formal opportunities for the academically talented and gifted.
Program Focus Science and engineering.
Academics Chemistry, computer programming, engineering, humanities, mathematics, physics, precollege program, science (general), study skills, writing.
Special Interest Areas Career exploration, robotics.
Trips College tours, cultural, day.
Program Information 1 session per year. Session length: 42–46 days in June, July, August. Ages: 16+. 60–80 participants per session. No cost for program, students responsible for cost of travel to and from program.
Application Deadline February 1.
Jobs Positions for college students 19 and older.
Contact Dr. Dedric A. Carter, Executive Director, Engineering Outreach Programs, main address above. Phone: 617-253-3298. Fax: 617-253-8549. E-mail: dedric@mit.edu.
URL web.mit.edu/mites/www/

Special Note
Now in its thirty-third year, the MIT Minority Introduction to Engineering and Science (MITES) Program offers a rigorous 6½-week residential, academic-enrichment summer experience to promising rising high school seniors, many of whom are from racial and ethnic groups underrepresented in the fields of engineering and science. The goal is to prepare gifted young men and women for careers in engineering and science by reinforcing the value and reward of pursuing advanced technical degrees, the academic preparation and skills necessary to achieve success in these disciplines, and the national importance of increasing the representation of underrepresented groups pursuing higher education and careers in science and engineering. MITES gives selected students the opportunity to experience MIT's demanding academic atmosphere and helps them to build the self-confidence necessary for success. The MITES Program is supported by corporations, foundations, individuals, and a grant from the federal government. With additional support from MIT, the program provides each admitted student with full coverage of program living and educational expenses.

MOUNT HOLYOKE COLLEGE SEARCH (SUMMER EXPLORATIONS AND RESEARCH COLLABORATIONS FOR HIGH SCHOOL GIRLS) PROGRAM

Mount Holyoke College
50 College Street
South Hadley, Massachusetts 01075-1441

General Information Girls' residential and day academic program established in 2004. Formal opportunities for the academically talented.
Program Focus Mathematics, collaborative research.
Academics Computer programming, computers, mathematics.
Arts Arts and crafts (general), dance, jewelry making, photography.
Special Interest Areas Career exploration, college planning, robotics.
Sports Basketball, cross-country, racquetball, soccer, swimming, tennis, track and field, volleyball, weight training.
Wilderness/Outdoors Hiking.
Trips College tours, cultural, day, shopping.
Program Information 1 session per year. Session length: 28–30 days in July. Ages: 15–18. 12–16 participants per session. Day program cost: $3500. Boarding program cost: $4500. Application fee: $25. Financial aid available.
Application Deadline Continuous.
Jobs Positions for college students 19 and older.

Contact Dr. James Morrow, Director, SEARCH, main address above. Phone: 413-538-2608. Fax: 413-538-2002. E-mail: search@mtholyoke.edu.
URL www.mtholyoke.edu/proj/search/
For more information, see page 562.

MOUNT HOLYOKE COLLEGE SUMMERMATH PROGRAM

Mount Holyoke College
50 College Street
South Hadley, Massachusetts 01075-1441

General Information Girls' residential and day academic program established in 1982.

Mount Holyoke College SummerMath Program

Program Focus Mathematics, computer programming, applied workshops.
Academics Architecture, art history/appreciation, biology, computer programming, computers, economics, engineering, mathematics, social science, study skills.
Arts Arts and crafts (general), dance, film, music, photography.
Special Interest Areas Career exploration, college planning, robotics.
Sports Basketball, bicycling, cross-country, racquetball, soccer, swimming, tennis, volleyball, weight training.
Wilderness/Outdoors Hiking.
Trips College tours, cultural, day, shopping.
Program Information 1–2 sessions per year. Session length: 28–30 days in July. Ages: 13–18. 50–70 participants per session. Day program cost: $3500. Boarding program cost: $4500. Application fee: $25. Financial aid available.

Application Deadline May 2.
Jobs Positions for college students 19 and older.
Contact Dr. Charlene Morrow, Director, main address above. Phone: 413-538-2608. Fax: 413-538-2002. E-mail: summermath@mtholyoke.edu.
URL www.mtholyoke.edu/proj/summermath/smhome.html
For more information, see page 562.

NORTHFIELD MOUNT HERMON SUMMER SESSION

Northfield Mount Hermon School
One Lamplighter Way
Mount Hermon, Massachusetts 01354

General Information Coed residential and day academic program established in 1961. Formal opportunities for the academically talented. High school credit may be earned.

Northfield Mount Hermon Summer Session

Academics American literature, English as a second language, English language/literature, French language/literature, SAT/ACT preparation, Spanish language/

Northfield Mount Hermon Summer Session (continued)

literature, academics (general), biology, chemistry, economics, history, humanities, journalism, mathematics, music, philosophy, physics, precollege program, psychology, reading, science (general), speech/ debate, study skills, writing.

Arts Acting, arts and crafts (general), creative writing, dance, dance (jazz), dance (modern), drawing, music (instrumental), painting, photography, printmaking, television/video, theater/drama.

Special Interest Areas Community service.

Sports Basketball, bicycling, soccer, swimming, tennis, volleyball, weight training.

Trips College tours, cultural, day, shopping.

Program Information 1 session per year. Session length: 5 weeks in July, August. Ages: 12–19. 300 participants per session. Day program cost: $3300. Boarding program cost: $5700–$5800. Application fee: $50–$100. Financial aid available. Apply for financial aid by April 1.

Application Deadline Continuous.

Jobs Positions for college students 21 and older.

Contact Debra J. Frank, Dean of Admission, NMH Summer Session, main address above. Phone: 413-498-3290. Fax: 413-498-3112. E-mail: summer_school@nmhschool.org.

URL www.nmhschool.org/summer

For more information, see page 568.

PHILLIPS ACADEMY SUMMER SESSION

Phillips Academy (Andover)
180 Main Street
Andover, Massachusetts 01810

General Information Coed residential and day academic program established in 1942. Formal opportunities for the academically talented and artistically talented.

Phillips Academy Summer Session

Program Focus Academic enrichment within a nurturing pre-college environment.

Academics American literature, Chinese languages/ literature, English as a second language, English language/literature, French language/literature, Japanese language/literature, Latin language, SAT/ACT preparation, Spanish language/literature, academics (general), anthropology, archaeology, art (Advanced Placement), art history/appreciation, astronomy, biology, chemistry, college tours, computer programming, computers, economics, government and politics, history, journalism, linguistics, marine studies, mathematics, music, philosophy, physics, physiology, precollege

program, psychology, reading, social science, speech/debate, study skills, writing.
Arts Acting, animation, band, ceramics, chorus, creative writing, dance, drawing, film, graphic arts, jewelry making, music (chamber), music (classical), music (instrumental), music (jazz), painting, photography, pottery, theater/drama, visual arts.
Special Interest Areas College planning.
Sports Aerobics, badminton, basketball, figure skating, martial arts, physical fitness, power walking, running/jogging, soccer, softball, squash, swimming, tennis, ultimate frisbee, volleyball, weight training, yoga.
Wilderness/Outdoors Outdoor adventure.
Trips College tours, cultural, day, shopping.
Program Information 1 session per year. Session length: 38 days in June, July, August. Ages: 13–18. 500–600 participants per session. Day program cost: $3700–$4200. Boarding program cost: $5500–$6000. Application fee: $50–$100. Financial aid available. Apply for financial aid by March 1.
Application Deadline Continuous.
Jobs Positions for college students 21 and older.
Contact Ms. Maxine S. Grogan, Dean of Admission, Phillips Academy Summer Session, 180 Main Street, Andover, Massachusetts 01810. Phone: 978-749-4400. Fax: 978-749-4414. E-mail: summersession@andover.edu.
URL www.andover.edu/summersession

Special Note
The nation's oldest incorporated boarding school, situated 25 miles north of Boston, opens a five-week summer session from the beginning of July through early August to students from all over the world. Students choose from more than sixty courses, including literature, languages, writing, natural sciences, computer science, mathematics, SAT prep, philosophy, social science, speech and debate, English as a second language, music, and the visual arts. Summer Session students represent an extraordinary diversity of geographic, religious, racial, and economic circumstances. They are students who have strong school records and a serious desire to spend the summer in challenging, disciplined study. With a student-faculty ratio of 7:1 and an average class size of 14, the Phillips Academy Summer Session provides a highly individualized and intensive precollege experience, including an extensive college counseling program, on a beautiful campus with excellent facilities.

For more information, see page 588.

SCHOOL OF THE MUSEUM OF FINE ARTS, BOSTON–PRE-COLLEGE SUMMER STUDIO

School of the Museum of Fine Arts, Boston
230 The Fenway
Boston, Massachusetts 02115

General Information Coed residential and day arts program established in 2000. College credit may be earned.

School of the Museum of Fine Arts, Boston–Pre-College Summer Studio

Academics Art.
Arts Arts, digital media, drawing, film, graphic arts, mixed media, painting, performing arts, photography, printmaking, sculpture, sound design, television/video, visual arts.
Special Interest Areas Career exploration, team building.
Trips Cultural, day.
Program Information 1 session per year. Session length: 5 weeks in June, July. Ages: 15–18. 60–75 participants per session. Day program cost: $3700. Boarding program cost: $6600. Application fee: $50. Financial aid available.
Application Deadline Continuous.
Contact Debra Samdperil, Director of Continuing Education and the Artist's Resource Center, main address above. Phone: 617-369-3644. Fax: 617-369-3679. E-mail: coned@smfa.edu.
URL www.smfa.edu/precollege

For more information, see page 624.

SMITH COLLEGE SUMMER SCIENCE AND ENGINEERING PROGRAM

Smith College
Clark Hall
Northampton, Massachusetts 01063

General Information Girls' residential academic program established in 1990. Formal opportunities for the academically talented. Specific services available for the hearing impaired, physically challenged, and visually impaired.

Smith College Summer Science and Engineering Program

Program Focus Hands-on research and science and engineering enrichment program for girls.
Academics Architecture, astronomy, biology, botany, chemistry, computer programming, computers, ecology, engineering, environmental science, geology/earth science, health sciences, mathematics, physics, psychology, science (general), writing.
Arts Arts and crafts (general), creative writing, dance, film, jewelry making, music, music (classical), music (jazz), theater/drama.
Special Interest Areas Career exploration, field research/expeditions, leadership training, robotics.
Sports Basketball, bicycling, climbing (wall), racquetball, soccer, softball, sports (general), squash, swimming, tennis, track and field, volleyball, weight training.
Trips College tours, cultural, day.
Program Information 1 session per year. Session length: 4 weeks in July. Ages: 13–18. 100–110 participants per session. Boarding program cost: $4250. Financial aid available.
Application Deadline Continuous.
Jobs Positions for college students 20 and older.

Contact Dr. Gail E. Scordilis, Director of Educational Outreach, main address above. Phone: 413-585-3060. Fax: 413-585-3068. E-mail: edoutreach@smith.edu.
URL www.smith.edu/summerprograms/ssep/
For more information, see page 634.

SUMMER ACTION–TAKE THE LEAD

Mount Holyoke College
South Hadley, Massachusetts

General Information Girls' residential academic program and community service program established in 2008.

Summer Action–Take the Lead

Program Focus Leadership development.
Academics Communications, writing.
Arts Acting, dance, film, jewelry making, television/video.
Special Interest Areas College planning, community service, conservation projects, leadership training, team building.
Sports Aerobics, basketball, golf, racquetball, swimming, tennis, weight training.
Trips College tours, cultural, day, shopping.
Program Information 1 session per year. Session length: 2 weeks in June, July. Ages: 14–17. 80

participants per session. Boarding program cost: $2950. Financial aid available.
Application Deadline Continuous.
Contact Ms. Rosita Nunez, Associate Director, 4 Mary Woolley Hall, 50 College Street, South Hadley, Massachusetts 01075-1441. Phone: 413-538-3500. Fax: 413-538-2691. E-mail: summeraction-web@mtholyoke.edu.
URL www.mtholyoke.edu/summeraction
For more information, see page 560.

THE SUMMER INSTITUTE FOR THE GIFTED AT AMHERST COLLEGE

Summer Institute for the Gifted
Amherst College
Amherst, Massachusetts 01002

General Information Coed residential academic program established in 2000. Formal opportunities for the academically talented and gifted. High school or college credit may be earned.
Academics American literature, English language/literature, French language/literature, SAT/ACT preparation, Spanish language/literature, academics (general), aerospace science, archaeology, architecture, art (Advanced Placement), art history/appreciation, biology, business, chemistry, classical languages/literatures, communications, computer programming, computers, engineering, environmental science, government and politics, history, humanities, marine studies, mathematics, music, oceanography, philosophy, physics, physiology, precollege program, psychology, science (general), social studies, speech/debate, study skills, writing.
Arts Arts and crafts (general), ceramics, chorus, creative writing, dance, drawing, film, graphic arts, music, music (chamber), music (classical), music (ensemble), musical productions, painting, photography, puppetry, sculpture, theater/drama.
Special Interest Areas Electronics, meditation, model rocketry, robotics.
Sports Aerobics, archery, baseball, basketball, fencing, field hockey, football, lacrosse, martial arts, soccer, softball, squash, swimming, tennis, track and field, volleyball.
Wilderness/Outdoors Hiking.
Trips Cultural.
Program Information 1–2 sessions per year. Session length: 3 weeks in July, August. Ages: 8–17. 150–250 participants per session. Boarding program cost: $3700–$4200. Application fee: $75. Financial aid available.
Jobs Positions for college students 19 and older.
Contact Ms. Barbara Swicord, Director, River Plaza, 9 West Broad Street, Stamford, Connecticut 06902-3788. Phone: 866-303-4744. Fax: 203-399-5598. E-mail: sig.info@aifs.com.
URL www.giftedstudy.com
For more information, see page 654.

TABOR ACADEMY SUMMER PROGRAM

Tabor Academy
66 Spring Street
Marion, Massachusetts 02738

General Information Coed residential and day traditional camp and academic program established in 1917.

Tabor Academy Summer Program

Academics English as a second language, English language/literature, French language/literature, Latin language, SAT/ACT preparation, Spanish language/literature, academics (general), biology, computer programming, computer science (Advanced Placement), computers, environmental science, marine studies, mathematics, oceanography, reading, science (general), study skills, writing.
Arts Acting, arts and crafts (general), ceramics, creative writing, drawing, painting, photography, pottery, theater/drama.
Special Interest Areas Nautical skills.
Sports Baseball, basketball, field hockey, golf, kayaking, lacrosse, sailing, soccer, softball, squash, swimming, tennis, volleyball.
Trips Cultural, day, shopping.
Program Information 3 sessions per year. Session length: 1–6 weeks in June, July, August. Ages: 6–15. 160–200 participants per session. Day program cost: $560–$2600. Boarding program cost: $4700–$6000. Campers 6–8 participate in day program only.
Application Deadline Continuous.
Jobs Positions for college students 18 and older.
Summer Contact Noel Pardo, Director, main address above. Phone: 508-748-2000 Ext.2292. Fax: 508-291-2242. E-mail: summer@taboracademy.org.
Winter Contact Rachel Habicht, Assistant Director, main address above. Phone: 508-748-2000 Ext.2242. Fax: 508-291-8392. E-mail: summer@taboracademy.org.
URL www.taborsummer.org
For more information, see page 664.

TABOR HOCKEY SCHOOL

Tabor Academy
66 Spring Street
Marion, Massachusetts 02738

General Information Coed day sports camp established in 1996.
Program Focus Ice hockey.
Sports Ice hockey.
Program Information 2–3 sessions per year. Session length: 5 days in June, July. Ages: 7–14. 26–46 participants per session. Day program cost: $575.
Application Deadline Continuous.
Jobs Positions for college students 19 and older.
Contact Mr. Dick Muther, Co-Director, main address above. Phone: 508-748-2000 Ext.2315. E-mail: dmuther@taboracademy.org.
URL www.taboracademy.org/summer/hockeycamp.asp

For more information, see page 664.

THE WINCHENDON SCHOOL SUMMER SESSION

The Winchendon School
172 Ash Street
Winchendon, Massachusetts 01475

General Information Coed residential academic program established in 1985. Specific services available for the learning disabled, participant with ADD, and participant with AD/HD. High school credit may be earned.
Program Focus ESL, learning style differences, and ADD/ADHD, study skills.
Academics American literature, Bible study, English as a second language, English language/literature, French (Advanced Placement), French language/literature, Latin language, SAT/ACT preparation, Spanish (Advanced Placement), Spanish language/literature, TOEFL/TOEIC preparation, academics (general), biology, biology (Advanced Placement), computer programming, computers, health sciences, history, humanities, mathematics, mathematics (Advanced Placement), music, physics, physiology, precollege program, psychology, reading, science (general), social science, social studies, speech/debate, study skills, typing, writing.
Arts Arts and crafts (general), ceramics, creative writing, drawing, graphic arts, music, music (classical), music (instrumental), painting, photography, pottery.
Special Interest Areas College planning, driver's education, homestays.

Sports Basketball, bicycling, bicycling (BMX), cross-country, equestrian sports, fishing, golf, horseback riding, soccer, softball, sports (general), swimming, tennis, volleyball, weight training.
Wilderness/Outdoors Backpacking, bicycle trips, canoe trips, hiking, mountain biking, orienteering, rafting, rock climbing, white-water trips.
Trips College tours, cultural, day, overnight, shopping.
Program Information 1 session per year. Session length: 6 weeks in June, July, August. Ages: 13–20. 50–70 participants per session. Boarding program cost: $5900. Application fee: $50–$100. Financial aid available.
Application Deadline Continuous.

The Winchendon School Summer Session

Jobs Positions for high school students 16 and older.
Contact Mr. J. William LaBelle, Headmaster, main address above. Phone: 978-297-1223. Fax: 978-297-0911. E-mail: admissions@winchendon.org.
URL www.winchendon.org

For more information, see page 706.

WORCESTER POLYTECHNIC INSTITUTE– LAUNCH

Worcester Polytechnic Institute
100 Institute Road
Worcester, Massachusetts 01609

General Information Coed day academic program established in 2006.

Worcester Polytechnic Institute–Launch

Program Focus Science, technology and engineering.
Academics Biology, biotechnology, computers, engineering, science (general), technology.
Special Interest Areas Computer game design, robotics.
Program Information 1 session per year. Session length: 5 days in July. Ages: 13–15. 60 participants per session. Day program cost: $495. Application fee: $50.
Application Deadline July 15.
Contact Julie Chapman, Associate Director of Admissions/Launch Program, main address above. Phone: 508-831-5286. Fax: 508-831-5875. E-mail: launch@wpi.edu.
URL www.wpi.edu/+launch

For more information, see page 712.

MICHIGAN

CYBERCAMPS–UNIVERSITY OF MICHIGAN

Cybercamps–Giant Campus, Inc.
Ann Arbor, Michigan

General Information Coed residential and day academic program established in 1997. Formal opportunities for the academically talented.
Program Focus Computers and technology.
Academics Web page design, academics (general), computer programming, computer science (Advanced Placement), computers.
Arts Animation, digital media, film, graphic arts, musical productions, photography, television/video.
Special Interest Areas Computer graphics, electronics, robotics, team building.
Program Information 1–12 sessions per year. Session length: 5 days in June, July, August. Ages: 7–18. 30–50 participants per session. Day program cost: $599–$749. Boarding program cost: $998–$1148.
Application Deadline Continuous.
Jobs Positions for high school students 17 and older and college students 18 and older.
Contact Camp Consultant, 3101 Western Avenue, Suite 100, Seattle, Washington 98121. Phone: 888-904-2267. Fax: 206-442-4501. E-mail: info@cybercamps.com.
URL www.cybercamps.com

For more information, see page 466.

iD TECH CAMPS–UNIVERSITY OF MICHIGAN, ANN ARBOR, MI

iD Tech Camps
University of Michigan
Ann Arbor, Michigan 48109

General Information Coed residential and day academic program established in 1999. Accredited by American Camping Association. Formal opportunities for the academically talented and artistically talented.
Program Focus Students create 2D and 3D video games, build robots to compete, design websites, film and edit digital movies, create their own comic book with digital photos, learn programming and more. One computer per student and an average of five students per staff member. Campers take home a project at the end of the weeklong course.
Academics Web page design, academics (general), computer programming, computer science (Advanced Placement), computers, precollege program.
Arts Animation, cinematography, digital media, drawing, film, film editing, film production, graphic arts, television/video.
Special Interest Areas Career exploration, computer game design, computer graphics, electronics, leadership training, robotics, team building.
Sports Baseball, basketball, soccer, softball, swimming, volleyball.
Trips College tours.
Program Information 5–9 sessions per year. Session

iD Tech Camps–University of Michigan, Ann Arbor, MI (continued)

length: 5–7 days in June, July, August. Ages: 7–17. 40–50 participants per session. Day program cost: $729. Boarding program cost: $1129. Financial aid available.
Application Deadline Continuous.
Jobs Positions for college students 18 and older.
Contact Client Service Representatives, 42 West Campbell Avenue, Suite 301, Campbell, California 95008. Phone: 888-709-TECH. Fax: 408-871-2228. E-mail: info@internaldrive.com.
URL www.internaldrive.com
For more information, see page 520.

INTERLOCHEN ARTS CAMP

Interlochen Center for the Arts
4000 Highway M-137
Interlochen, Michigan 49643

General Information Coed residential arts program established in 1928. Formal opportunities for the artistically talented.

Interlochen Arts Camp

Program Focus Fine arts, visual arts, theatre arts, dance, music, and creative writing, motion picture arts.
Academics Art (Advanced Placement), environmental science, music, music (Advanced Placement), writing.
Arts Arts, arts and crafts (general), band, ceramics, chorus, creative writing, dance, dance (ballet), dance (jazz), dance (modern), drawing, fabric arts, film, jewelry making, metalworking, music, music (chamber), music (classical), music (ensemble), music (instrumental), music (jazz), music (orchestral), music (vocal), musical productions, painting, photography, pottery, printmaking, puppetry, radio broadcasting, sculpture, theater/drama, weaving.
Sports Aerobics, archery, basketball, boating, canoeing, football, ropes course, sailing, soccer, softball, swimming, tennis, volleyball.
Trips Cultural, day, overnight, shopping.
Program Information 1–3 sessions per year. Session length: 1–6 weeks in June, July, August. Ages: 8–18. 1,000–1,700 participants per session. Boarding program

cost: $775–$6162. Application fee: $50. Financial aid available.
Application Deadline February 1.
Jobs Positions for college students 18 and older.
Contact Kelye Modarelli, Director of Admissions, PO Box 199, Interlochen, Michigan 49643. Phone: 800-681-5912. Fax: 231-276-7464. E-mail: admission@interlochen.org.
URL www.interlochen.org
For more information, see page 524.

LANDMARK VOLUNTEERS: MICHIGAN

Landmark Volunteers, Inc.
Monising, Michigan

General Information Coed residential outdoor program and community service program established in 1992. High school credit may be earned.
Program Focus Opportunity for high school students to earn community service credit while working as a team for two weeks serving The Nature Conservancy at the Lakes of the Upper Peninsula. Similar programs offered through Landmark Volunteers at over 50 locations in 20 states.
Academics Ecology, environmental science.
Special Interest Areas Career exploration, community service, conservation projects, field research/expeditions, leadership training, nature study, team building, trail maintenance, work camp programs.
Wilderness/Outdoors Hiking.
Trips Cultural, day.
Program Information 1 session per year. Session length: 2 weeks in June, July. Ages: 14–18. 10–13 participants per session. Boarding program cost: $1250–$1300. Financial aid available.
Application Deadline Continuous.
Jobs Positions for college students.
Contact Ann Barrett, Executive Director, PO Box 455, Sheffield, Massachusetts 01257. Phone: 413-229-0255. Fax: 413-229-2050. E-mail: landmark@volunteers.com.
URL www.volunteers.com
For more information, see page 542.

MICHIGAN TECHNOLOGICAL UNIVERSITY AMERICAN INDIAN WORKSHOP

Michigan Technological University
1400 Townsend Drive
Houghton, Michigan 49931-1295

General Information Coed residential academic program established in 1988.
Program Focus Native American study, computers, math, biology, physiology, and ecology.
Academics Biology, computers, ecology, environmental science, health sciences, mathematics, physiology, precollege program, science (general), technology.
Special Interest Areas Native American culture, career exploration, college planning, field research/expeditions, team building.
Trips College tours, cultural, day.
Program Information 1 session per year. Session length: 5–7 days in June, July. Ages: 12+. 50–70 participants per session. Financial aid available. No cost for Michigan residents; $575 for out-of-state residents.
Application Deadline April 30.
Jobs Positions for college students 18 and older.
Contact Ms. Lynn L. Heil, Youth Programs Coordinator, main address above. Phone: 888-PRECOLLEGE. Fax: 906-487-3101. E-mail: yp@mtu.edu.
URL youthprograms.mtu.edu/aiw

MICHIGAN TECHNOLOGICAL UNIVERSITY EXPLORATIONS IN ENGINEERING WORKSHOP

Michigan Technological University
1400 Townsend Drive
Houghton, Michigan 49931-1295

General Information Coed residential academic program established in 1988. Formal opportunities for the academically talented.
Program Focus Engineering, science, mathematics, and associated career explorations.
Academics Computers, engineering, geology/earth science, mathematics, physics, science (general).
Special Interest Areas Career exploration, electronics, robotics, team building.
Trips College tours, cultural, day.
Program Information 1 session per year. Session length: 1 week in June, July. Ages: 14–18. 80–100 participants per session. Financial aid available. Cost (excluding travel and $100 registration fee) covered by scholarship.
Application Deadline April 9.
Jobs Positions for college students 18 and older.

Contact Ms. Lynn L. Heil, Youth Programs Coordinator, main address above. Phone: 906-487-2219. Fax: 906-487-3101. E-mail: yp@mtu.edu.
URL youthprograms.mtu.edu/eie

MICHIGAN TECHNOLOGICAL UNIVERSITY SUMMER YOUTH PROGRAM

Michigan Technological University
1400 Townsend Drive
Houghton, Michigan 49931

General Information Coed residential and day academic program, outdoor program, arts program, and wilderness program established in 1973.
Program Focus Explorations in careers and knowledge; university residential living.
Academics Academics (general), aerospace science, astronomy, biology, business, chemistry, computer programming, computer science (Advanced Placement), computers, ecology, engineering, environmental science, geology/earth science, health sciences, journalism, physiology, precollege program, psychology, science (general), writing.
Arts Acting, arts, arts and crafts (general), creative writing, dance (folk), drawing, fabric arts, painting, performing arts, photography, pottery, television/video, theater/drama.
Special Interest Areas College planning, electronics, field research/expeditions, model rocketry, nature study, robotics.
Sports Rappelling.
Wilderness/Outdoors Backpacking, hiking, mountaineering, orienteering, outdoor adventure, outdoor camping, rock climbing, wilderness/outdoors (general).
Trips College tours, cultural, day, overnight.
Program Information 70–90 sessions per year. Session length: 1 week in July, August. Ages: 12–18. 10–20 participants per session. Day program cost: $375. Boarding program cost: $575–$755. Financial aid available.
Application Deadline Continuous.
Jobs Positions for college students 18 and older.
Contact Ms. Lynn L. Heil, Youth Programs Coordinator, main address above. Phone: 906-487-2219. Fax: 906-487-3101. E-mail: yp@mtu.edu.
URL youthprograms.mtu.edu

MICHIGAN TECHNOLOGICAL UNIVERSITY WOMEN IN ENGINEERING WORKSHOP

Michigan Technological University
1400 Townsend Drive
Houghton, Michigan 49931-1295

General Information Girls' residential academic program established in 1973. Formal opportunities for the academically talented.
Program Focus Engineering, science, and mathematics, and associated career explorations.
Academics Computers, engineering, geology/earth science, mathematics, physics, science (general).
Special Interest Areas Career exploration, electronics, robotics, team building.
Trips College tours, cultural, day.
Program Information 1 session per year. Session length: 1 week in June, July. Ages: 14–18. 100–120 participants per session. Boarding program cost: $100. Financial aid available. Cost (excluding travel and $100 registration fee) covered by scholarship.
Application Deadline April 9.
Jobs Positions for college students 18 and older.
Contact Ms. Lynn L. Heil, Youth Programs Coordinator, main address above. Phone: 906-487-2219. Fax: 906-487-3101. E-mail: yp@mtu.edu.
URL youthprograms.mtu.edu

THE SUMMER INSTITUTE FOR THE GIFTED AT UNIVERSITY OF MICHIGAN, ANN ARBOR

Summer Institute for the Gifted
University of Michigan
Ann Arbor, Michigan 48103

General Information Coed residential academic program established in 2006. Formal opportunities for the academically talented and gifted.
Academics American literature, English language/literature, French language/literature, SAT/ACT preparation, Spanish language/literature, academics (general), aerospace science, archaeology, architecture, biology, business, chemistry, classical languages/literatures, communications, computers, engineering, government and politics, history, marine studies, mathematics, music, oceanography, philosophy, physics, precollege program, psychology, science (general), social studies, speech/debate, study skills, writing.
Arts Chorus, creative writing, dance, film, graphic arts, music, music (ensemble), music (instrumental), musical productions, painting, photography, sculpture, theater/drama.
Special Interest Areas Animal care, electronics, meditation, robotics.
Sports Aerobics, baseball, basketball, fencing, football, martial arts, soccer, swimming, tennis, track and field, volleyball.
Trips Cultural.
Program Information 1–2 sessions per year. Session length: 3 weeks in June, July. Ages: 8–17. 150–250

participants per session. Boarding program cost: $3700–$4200. Application fee: $75. Financial aid available.
Application Deadline May 14.
Jobs Positions for college students 19 and older.
Contact Ms. Barbara Swicord, Director, River Plaza, 9 West Broad Street, Stamford, Connecticut 06902-3788. Phone: 866-303-4744. Fax: 203-399-5598. E-mail: sig.info@aifs.com.
URL www.giftedstudy.com
For more information, see page 654.

MINNESOTA

CAMP LINCOLN FOR BOYS/CAMP LAKE HUBERT FOR GIRLS

Camp Lincoln/Camp Lake Hubert
Lake Hubert, Minnesota 56459

General Information Coed residential traditional camp established in 1909. Accredited by American Camping Association.
Arts Arts and crafts (general), ceramics, dance, dance (jazz), dance (modern), leather working, painting, photography, pottery, theater/drama, weaving, woodworking.
Special Interest Areas Campcraft, leadership training, model rocketry, nature study.
Sports Aerobics, archery, baseball, basketball, bicycling, canoeing, cheerleading, climbing (wall), fishing, frisbee golf, golf, gymnastics, horseback riding, kayaking, lacrosse, martial arts, riflery, ropes course, rowing (crew/sculling), sailing, snorkeling, soccer, softball, sports (general), swimming, tennis, volleyball, water polo, windsurfing, wrestling.
Wilderness/Outdoors Backpacking, bicycle trips, canoe trips, hiking, mountain biking, orienteering, rock climbing, white-water trips.
Trips Overnight.
Program Information 13 sessions per year. Session length: 12–27 days in June, July, August. Ages: 8–16. 200 participants per session. Boarding program cost: $1875–$3495. Financial aid available.
Application Deadline Continuous.
Jobs Positions for college students 19 and older.
Summer Contact Sam Cote, Director, Box 1308, Lake Hubert, Minnesota 56459. Phone: 218-963-2339. Fax: 218-963-2447. E-mail: home@lincoln-lakehubert.com.
Winter Contact Bill Jones, Director, 10179 Crosstown Circle, Eden Prairie, Minnesota 55344. Phone: 800-242-1909. Fax: 952-922-7149. E-mail: home@lincoln-lakehubert.com.
URL www.lincoln-lakehubert.com

CAMP LINCOLN FOR BOYS/CAMP LAKE HUBERT FOR GIRLS–FAMILY CAMP

Camp Lincoln/Camp Lake Hubert
Lake Hubert, Minnesota 56459

General Information Coed residential family program established in 1909. Accredited by American Camping Association.
Arts Arts and crafts (general), ceramics, fabric arts, leather working, photography, pottery.
Sports Archery, basketball, bicycling, boating, canoeing, fishing, golf, horseback riding, kayaking, riflery, ropes course, sailing, soccer, softball, swimming, tennis, volleyball, water polo, windsurfing.
Wilderness/Outdoors Hiking.
Program Information 1 session per year. Session length: 5–6 days in August. Ages: 1+. 120 participants per session. Boarding program cost: $600–$800. Financial aid available.
Application Deadline Continuous.
Jobs Positions for college students 19 and older.
Summer Contact Sam Cote, Director, Box 1308, Lake Hubert, Minnesota 56459. Phone: 218-963-2339. Fax: 218-963-2447. E-mail: home@lincoln-lakehubert.com.
Winter Contact Bill Jones, Director, 10179 Crosstown Circle, Eden Prairie, Minnesota 55344. Phone: 800-242-1909. Fax: 952-922-7149. E-mail: home@lincoln-lakehubert.com.
URL www.lincoln-lakehubert.com

CAMP LINCOLN FOR BOYS/CAMP LAKE HUBERT FOR GIRLS–GOLF CAMP

Camp Lincoln/Camp Lake Hubert
Lake Hubert, Minnesota 56459

General Information Coed residential sports camp established in 1990. Accredited by American Camping Association.
Program Focus Golf.
Sports Archery, bicycling, canoeing, fishing, golf, horseback riding, riflery, sailing, soccer, swimming, windsurfing.
Program Information 3–4 sessions per year. Session length: 5–6 days in June, July, August. Ages: 8+. 18–28 participants per session. Boarding program cost: $925. Financial aid available.
Application Deadline Continuous.

Jobs Positions for college students 19 and older.
Summer Contact Sam Cote, Director, Box 1308, Lake Hubert, Minnesota 56459. Phone: 218-963-2339. Fax: 218-963-2447. E-mail: home@lincoln-lakehubert.com.
Winter Contact Sam Cote, Director, 10179 Crosstown Circle, Eden Prairie, Minnesota 55344. Phone: 800-242-1909. Fax: 952-922-7149. E-mail: home@lincoln-lakehubert.com.
URL www.lincoln-lakehubert.com

CAMP LINCOLN FOR BOYS/CAMP LAKE HUBERT FOR GIRLS–TENNIS CAMP

Camp Lincoln/Camp Lake Hubert
Lake Hubert, Minnesota 56459

General Information Coed residential sports camp established in 1972. Accredited by American Camping Association.
Program Focus Tennis.
Sports Archery, basketball, bicycling, canoeing, horseback riding, kayaking, riflery, ropes course, sailing, soccer, swimming, tennis, volleyball, water polo, windsurfing.
Program Information 2 sessions per year. Session length: 6–7 days in August. Ages: 8+. 40 participants per session. Boarding program cost: $875. Financial aid available.
Application Deadline Continuous.
Jobs Positions for college students 19 and older.
Summer Contact Sam Cote, Director, Box 1308, Lake Hubert, Minnesota 56459. Phone: 218-963-2339. Fax: 218-963-2447. E-mail: home@lincoln-lakehubert.com.
Winter Contact Sam Cote, Director, 10179 Crosstown Circle, Eden Prairie, Minnesota 55344. Phone: 800-242-1909. Fax: 952-922-7149. E-mail: home@lincoln-lakehubert.com.
URL www.lincoln-lakehubert.com

CYBERCAMPS–UNIVERSITY OF MINNESOTA

Cybercamps–Giant Campus, Inc.
Minneapolis, Minnesota

General Information Coed residential and day academic program established in 1997. Formal opportunities for the academically talented.
Program Focus Computers and technology.
Academics Web page design, academics (general), computer programming, computer science (Advanced Placement), computers.
Arts Animation, digital media, film, graphic arts, musical productions, photography, television/video.
Special Interest Areas Computer game design, computer graphics, electronics, robotics, team building.
Program Information 1–12 sessions per year. Session length: 5 days in June, July, August. Ages: 7–18. 30–50 participants per session. Day program cost: $599–$749. Boarding program cost: $998–$1148.

Cybercamps–University of Minnesota (continued)

Application Deadline Continuous.
Jobs Positions for high school students 17 and older and college students 18 and older.
Contact Camp Consultant, 3101 Western Avenue, Suite 100, Seattle, Washington 98121. Phone: 888-904-2267. Fax: 206-442-4501. E-mail: info@cybercamps.com.
URL www.cybercamps.com

For more information, see page 466.

iD Tech Camps–University of Minnesota, Minneapolis, MN

iD Tech Camps
University of Minnesota
Minneapolis, Minnesota

General Information Coed residential and day academic program established in 1999. Formal opportunities for the academically talented and artistically talented.
Program Focus Students create 2D and 3D video games, build robots to compete, design websites, film and edit digital movies, create their own comic book with digital photos, learn programming and more. One computer per student and an average of five students per staff member. Campers take home a project at the end of the weeklong course.
Academics Web page design, academics (general), computer programming, computer science (Advanced Placement), computers, precollege program.
Arts Animation, cinematography, digital media, drawing, film, film editing, film production, graphic arts, photography, television/video.
Special Interest Areas Career exploration, computer game design, computer graphics, electronics, leadership training, robotics, team building.
Sports Baseball, basketball, soccer, softball, swimming, volleyball.
Trips College tours.
Program Information 5–9 sessions per year. Session length: 5–7 days in June, July, August. Ages: 7–17. 40–50 participants per session. Day program cost: $729. Boarding program cost: $1129. Financial aid available.
Application Deadline Continuous.
Jobs Positions for college students 18 and older.

Contact Client Service Representatives, 42 West Campbell Avenue, Suite 301, Campbell, California 95008. Phone: 888-709-TECH. Fax: 408-871-2228. E-mail: info@internaldrive.com.
URL www.internaldrive.com

For more information, see page 520.

Landmark Volunteers: Minnesota

Landmark Volunteers, Inc.
Minnesota

General Information Coed residential outdoor program and community service program established in 1992. High school credit may be earned.
Program Focus Opportunity for high school students to earn community service credit while working as a team for two weeks serving Friendship Ventures at Eden Wood Camp. Similar programs offered through Landmark Volunteers at over 50 locations in 20 states.
Academics Social services.
Special Interest Areas Career exploration, community service, leadership training, team building, work camp programs.
Trips Cultural, day.
Program Information 1 session per year. Session length: 14–16 days in July. Ages: 14–18. 10–12 participants per session. Boarding program cost: $1250–$1300. Financial aid available.
Application Deadline Continuous.
Jobs Positions for college students.
Contact Ann Barrett, Executive Director, PO Box 455, Sheffield, Massachusetts 01257. Phone: 413-229-0255. Fax: 413-229-2050. E-mail: landmark@volunteers.com.
URL www.volunteers.com

For more information, see page 542.

MISSISSIPPI

Visions–Mississippi

Visions
Mississippi

General Information Coed travel outdoor program, community service program, and cultural program established in 1989. High school credit may be earned.
Program Focus Community service, cross-cultural experience, and outdoor adventure activities.
Academics Intercultural studies.
Arts Carpentry.
Special Interest Areas Community service, construction, cross-cultural education, field research/expeditions, field trips (arts and culture), leadership training, nature study.
Sports Swimming.
Wilderness/Outdoors Hiking, outdoor adventure.
Trips Cultural, day, overnight.
Program Information 1–2 sessions per year. Session length: 3–4 weeks in June, July, August. Ages: 14–18.

20–25 participants per session. Cost: $3200–$4900. Financial aid available.
Application Deadline Continuous.
Jobs Positions for college students 22 and older.
Contact Joanne Pinaire, Director, PO Box 220, Newport, Pennsylvania 17074. Phone: 717-567-7313. Fax: 717-567-7853. E-mail: info@visionsserviceadventures.com.
URL www.visionsserviceadventures.com

For more information, see page 694.

MISSOURI

CYBERCAMPS–WEBSTER UNIVERSITY

Cybercamps–Giant Campus, Inc.
St. Louis, Missouri

General Information Coed residential and day academic program established in 1997. Formal opportunities for the academically talented.
Program Focus Computers and technology.
Academics Web page design, academics (general), computer programming, computer science (Advanced Placement), computers.
Arts Animation, digital media, film, graphic arts, musical productions, photography, television/video.
Special Interest Areas Computer game design, computer graphics, electronics, robotics, team building.
Program Information 1–12 sessions per year. Session length: 5 days in June, July, August. Ages: 7–18. 30–50 participants per session. Day program cost: $599–$749. Boarding program cost: $998–$1148.
Application Deadline Continuous.
Contact Camp Consultant, 3101 Western Avenue, Suite 100, Seattle, Washington 98121. Phone: 888-904-2267. Fax: 206-442-4501. E-mail: info@cybercamps.com.
URL www.cybercamps.com

For more information, see page 466.

iD TECH CAMPS–WASHINGTON UNIVERSITY IN ST. LOUIS, ST. LOUIS, MO

iD Tech Camps
Washington University in St. Louis
St. Louis, Missouri 63130

General Information Coed day academic program established in 1999. Accredited by American Camping Association. Formal opportunities for the academically talented and artistically talented.
Program Focus Students create 2D and 3D video games, build robots to compete, design websites, film and edit digital movies, create their own comic book with digital photos, learn programming and more. One computer per student and an average of five students per staff member. Campers take home a project at the end of the weeklong course.
Academics Web page design, academics (general), computer programming, computer science (Advanced Placement), computers, precollege program.
Arts Animation, cinematography, digital media, drawing, film, film editing, film production, graphic arts, television/video.
Special Interest Areas Career exploration, computer game design, computer graphics, electronics, leadership training, robotics, team building.
Sports Baseball, basketball, soccer, softball, swimming, volleyball
Trips College tours.
Program Information 5–9 sessions per year. Session length: 5–7 days in June, July, August. Ages: 7–17. 40–50 participants per session. Day program cost: $729. Boarding program cost: $1129. Financial aid available.
Application Deadline Continuous.
Jobs Positions for college students 18 and older.
Contact Client Service Representatives, 42 West Campbell Avenue, Suite 301, Campbell, California 95008. Phone: 888-709-TECH. Fax: 408-871-2228. E-mail: info@internaldrive.com.
URL www.internaldrive.com

For more information, see page 520.

WASHINGTON UNIVERSITY HIGH SCHOOL SUMMER SCHOLARS PROGRAM

Washington University in St. Louis
1 Brookings Drive
St. Louis, Missouri 63130-4899

General Information Coed residential academic program established in 1988. Formal opportunities for the academically talented. College credit may be earned.

Washington University High School Summer Scholars Program

Program Focus Pre-college academic enrichment.
Academics English language/literature, French language/literature, German language/literature, Italian language/literature, Russian language/literature, Spanish (Advanced Placement), archaeology, art history/appreciation, biology, chemistry, economics, environmental science, geology/earth science, government and politics, history, humanities, mathematics, music, philosophy, physics, precollege program, psychology, science (general), social science, social studies, writing.
Arts Dance, music, theater/drama.
Trips Day.
Program Information 2 sessions per year. Session length: 5 weeks in June, July, August. Ages: 16+. 70–80 participants per session. Boarding program cost: $5365. Application fee: $35–$70. Financial aid available. Up to 7 units of college credit may be earned.
Application Deadline Continuous.
Contact Ms. Marsha Hussung, Director, High School Summer Scholars Program, Campus Box 1145, 1 Brookings Drive, St. Louis, Missouri 63130. Phone: 866-209-0691. Fax: 314-935-4847. E-mail: mhussung@wustl.edu.
URL summerscholars.wustl.edu

For more information, see page 696.

WASHINGTON UNIVERSITY IN ST. LOUIS, COLLEGE OF ART–PORTFOLIO PLUS

Washington University in St. Louis, College of Art
One Brookings Drive
St. Louis, Missouri 63130

General Information Coed residential and day arts program established in 2004. Formal opportunities for the academically talented and artistically talented. College credit may be earned.

Washington University in St. Louis, College of Art–Portfolio Plus

Program Focus Portfolio preparation, visual arts studies.
Academics Art (Advanced Placement).
Arts Arts, design, drawing, fashion design/production, painting, photography, printmaking, sculpture, visual arts.
Special Interest Areas Career exploration, college planning.
Trips College tours, cultural, day.
Program Information 1 session per year. Session length: 25–30 days in June, July. Ages: 16–18. 30–50 participants per session. Day program cost: $2373–$2500. Boarding program cost: $4500–$5000. Application fee: $25–$30. Financial aid available.
Application Deadline April 1.

Contact Mauricio Bruce, Senior Coordinator Special Programs, Washington University in St. Louis, College of Art, Box 1031, One Brookings Drive, St. Louis, Missouri 63130. Phone: 314-935-6500. Fax: 314-935-4643. E-mail: mbruce@wustl.edu.
URL www.artsci.wustl.edu/~artweb/washUSoa/
For more information, see page 698.

MONTANA

ADVENTURE TREKS–MONTANA ADVENTURES

Adventure Treks, Inc.
Montana

General Information Coed travel outdoor program, wilderness program, and adventure program established in 1978.
Program Focus Multi-activity outdoor adventures with a focus on fun, personal growth, teamwork, leadership, building self-confidence, outdoor skills, and community living.
Wilderness/Outdoors Backpacking, hiking, mountain biking, mountaineering, orienteering, rafting, rock climbing, white-water trips, wilderness camping.
Program Information 2 sessions per year. Session length: 24 days in June, July, August. Ages: 15–17. 24 participants per session. Cost: $3595. Financial aid available.
Application Deadline Continuous.
Contact John Dockendorf, Director, PO Box 1321, Flat Rock, North Carolina 28731. Phone: 888-954-5555. Fax: 828-696-1663. E-mail: info@advtreks.com
URL www.adventuretreks.com

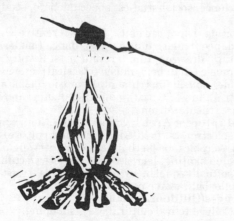

LANDMARK VOLUNTEERS: MONTANA

Landmark Volunteers, Inc.
Montana

General Information Coed residential outdoor program and community service program established in 1992. High school credit may be earned.
Program Focus Opportunity for high school students to earn community service credit while working as a team for two weeks serving Glacier National Park or Spotted Bear Ranger District. Similar programs offered through Landmark Volunteers at over 50 locations in 21 states.
Academics Ecology, environmental science, geology/earth science, natural resource management, science (general).
Special Interest Areas Career exploration, community service, conservation projects, field research/expeditions, leadership training, nature study, team building, trail maintenance, work camp programs.
Wilderness/Outdoors Hiking.
Trips Cultural, day.
Program Information 2 sessions per year. Session length: 2 weeks in July, August. Ages: 14–18. 10–13 participants per session. Boarding program cost: $1250–$1300. Financial aid available.
Application Deadline Continuous.
Jobs Positions for college students.
Contact Ann Barrett, Executive Director, PO Box 455, Sheffield, Massachusetts 01257. Phone: 413-229-0255. Fax: 413-229-2050. E-mail: landmark@volunteers.com.
URL www.volunteers.com
For more information, see page 542.

VISIONS–MONTANA

Visions
Montana

General Information Coed travel outdoor program, community service program, and cultural program established in 1989. High school credit may be earned.
Program Focus Community service, cross-cultural experience, outdoor adventure activities.
Academics Intercultural studies.
Arts Carpentry.
Special Interest Areas Native American culture, community service, construction, cross-cultural education, field research/expeditions, field trips (arts and culture), leadership training, nature study.
Sports Horseback riding, swimming.
Wilderness/Outdoors Backpacking, hiking, outdoor adventure, rafting, rock climbing, wilderness camping.
Trips Cultural, day, overnight.
Program Information 2 sessions per year. Session length: 3–4 weeks in June, July, August. Ages: 14–18. 20–25 participants per session. Cost: $3200–$4900. Financial aid available.
Application Deadline Continuous.

Visions–Montana (continued)

Contact Joanne Pinaire, Director, PO Box 220, Newport, Pennsylvania 17074. Phone: 717-567-7313. Fax: 717-567-7853. E-mail: info@visionsserviceadventures.com. **URL** www.visionsserviceadventures.com **For more information, see page 694.**

NEW HAMPSHIRE

BREWSTER ACADEMY SUMMER SESSION

Brewster Academy
80 Academy Drive
Wolfeboro, New Hampshire 03894

General Information Coed residential and day academic program and outdoor program established in 1994. Formal opportunities for the academically talented. Specific services available for the learning disabled. High school credit may be earned.

Brewster Academy Summer Session

Program Focus Academics (including for-credit courses in English and math), ESL, science, computer graphics and design, video editing, technology, instructional skills (organization, study, time management, reading/writing, etc.), and mentored study halls.
Academics English as a second language, English language/literature, computers, environmental science, humanities, language study, mathematics, reading, research skills, science (general), study skills, writing.
Arts Digital media, film, film editing, graphic arts, photography, studio arts, television/video.
Sports Aerobics, baseball, basketball, boating, canoeing, climbing (wall), kayaking, rappelling, ropes course, sea kayaking, soccer, softball, swimming, tennis, volleyball, weight training.
Wilderness/Outdoors Backpacking, canoe trips, hiking, mountaineering, orienteering, rock climbing, survival training, wilderness camping.
Trips Cultural, day, shopping.

Program Information 1 session per year. Session length: 6 weeks in June, July, August. Ages: 12–17. 50–70 participants per session. Day program cost: $3600–$3700. Boarding program cost: $6100–$6500. Application fee: $35–$75.
Application Deadline Continuous.
Jobs Positions for college students 21 and older.
Contact Ms. Christine Brown, Summer Programs Manager, main address above. Phone: 603-569-7155. Fax: 603-569-7050. E-mail: summer@brewsteracademy. org.
URL www.brewsteracademy.org
For more information, see page 430.

PHILLIPS EXETER ACADEMY SUMMER SCHOOL

Phillips Exeter Academy
20 Main Street
Exeter, New Hampshire 03833-2460

General Information Coed residential and day academic program established in 1919. Formal opportunities for the academically talented and artistically talented.
Academics American literature, Chinese languages/literature, English as a second language, English language/literature, French language/literature, German language/literature, Italian language/literature, Japanese language/literature, Latin language, Russian language/literature, SAT/ACT preparation, Spanish language/literature, academics (general), archaeology, architecture, art history/appreciation, astronomy, biology, chemistry, classical languages/literatures, computer programming, computers, ecology, economics, environmental science, government and politics, government and politics (Advanced Placement), history, humanities, journalism, marine studies, mathematics, music, physics, physiology, psychology, science (general), social science, social studies, speech/debate, study skills, writing.
Arts Acting, band, ceramics, chorus, creative writing, dance, dance (ballet), dance (jazz), dance (modern), dance (tap), drawing, film, graphic arts, jewelry making, music, music (chamber), music (classical), music (ensemble), music (instrumental), music (jazz), music (orchestral), music (vocal), painting, photography, sculpture, theater/drama.
Special Interest Areas Career exploration, community service, electronics, field trips (arts and culture).
Sports Aerobics, basketball, cross-country, field hockey, golf, in-line skating, lacrosse, rowing (crew/sculling), soccer, softball, squash, swimming, tennis, track and field, volleyball, water polo, weight training.
Wilderness/Outdoors Hiking.
Trips College tours, cultural, day, shopping.
Program Information 1 session per year. Session length: 5 weeks in July, August. Ages: 13–19. 700 participants per session. Day program cost: $995–$3995. Boarding program cost: $5995–$6195. Application fee: $65–$95. Financial aid available. March 1 deadline for financial aid applicants.
Application Deadline Continuous.
Jobs Positions for college students.

Contact Douglas G. Rogers, Director, main address above. Phone: 603-777-3488. Fax: 603-777-4385. E-mail: summer@exeter.edu

URL www.exeter.edu/summer

For more information, see page 590.

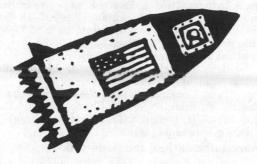

WOLFEBORO: THE SUMMER BOARDING SCHOOL

93 Camp School Road
Wolfeboro, New Hampshire 03894

General Information Coed residential academic program and outdoor program established in 1910. High school credit may be earned.

Wolfeboro: The Summer Boarding School

Program Focus Wolfeboro emphasizes the development of student confidence, study skills, accountability, and academic success.

Academics American literature, English as a second language, English language/literature, French language/literature, Greek language/literature, Latin language, SAT/ACT preparation, Spanish language/literature, academics (general), biology, chemistry, ecology, history, mathematics, physics, reading, science (general), social studies, study skills, vocabulary, writing.

Arts Ceramics, drawing, painting, pottery, sculpture.

Sports Aerobics, baseball, basketball, boating, canoeing, cross-country, fishing, horseback riding,

lacrosse, sailing, soccer, softball, swimming, tennis, volleyball, weight training.

Wilderness/Outdoors Backpacking, hiking, wilderness camping.

Trips Day, overnight.

Program Information 1 session per year. Session length: 45 days in June, July, August. Ages: 11–18. 200 participants per session. Boarding program cost: $10,100.

Application Deadline Continuous.

Jobs Positions for college students 20 and older.

Contact Edward A. Cooper, Head of School, main address above. Phone: 603-569-3451. Fax: 603-569-4080. E-mail: school@wolfeboro.org

URL www.wolfeboro.org

For more information, see page 708.

NEW JERSEY

APPEL FARM SUMMER ARTS CAMP

Appel Farm Arts and Music Center
457 Shirley Road
Elmer, New Jersey 08318-0888

General Information Coed residential arts program established in 1959. Accredited by American Camping Association. Formal opportunities for the artistically talented.

Appel Farm Summer Arts Camp

Academics Art (Advanced Placement), art history/appreciation, environmental science, journalism, music, music (Advanced Placement), writing.

Arts Acting, animation, arts, arts and crafts (general), band, batiking, ceramics, chorus, creative writing, dance, dance (ballet), dance (folk), dance (jazz), dance (modern), dance (tap), directing, drawing, fabric arts, film, glassblowing, graphic arts, jewelry making, metalworking, mime, music, music (chamber), music (classical), music (ensemble), music (instrumental), music (jazz), music (orchestral), music (rock), music

Appel Farm Summer Arts Camp (continued)

(vocal), music technology/record production, musical productions, painting, photography, pottery, printmaking, puppetry, sculpture, stage managing, television/video, theater/drama.
Special Interest Areas Campcraft, community service, conservation projects, gardening, leadership training, nature study.
Sports Aerobics, basketball, soccer, softball, swimming, tennis, volleyball.
Wilderness/Outdoors Wilderness camping.
Trips Cultural, day.
Program Information 4 sessions per year. Session length: 2–8 weeks in June, July, August. Ages: 9–17. 190–220 participants per session. Boarding program cost: $2450–$7200. Financial aid available.
Application Deadline Continuous.
Jobs Positions for college students 20 and older.
Contact Ms. Jennie Quinn, Camp Director, PO Box 888, Elmer, New Jersey 08318-0888. Phone: 856-358-2472. Fax: 856-358-6513. E-mail: appelcamp@aol.com.
URL www.appelfarm.org

For more information, see page 418.

Cybercamps–Caldwell College

Cybercamps–Giant Campus, Inc.
Caldwell, New Jersey

General Information Coed residential and day academic program established in 1997. Formal opportunities for the academically talented.
Program Focus Computers and technology.
Academics Web page design, academics (general), computer programming, computer science (Advanced Placement), computers.
Arts Animation, digital media, film, graphic arts, musical productions, photography, television/video.
Special Interest Areas Computer game design, computer graphics, electronics, robotics, team building.
Program Information 1–12 sessions per year. Session length: 5 days in June, July, August. Ages: 7–18. 30–50 participants per session. Day program cost: $599–$749. Boarding program cost: $998–$1148.
Application Deadline Continuous.
Jobs Positions for high school students 17 and older and college students 18 and older.
Contact Camp Consultant, 3101 Western Avenue, Suite 100, Seattle, Washington 98121. Phone: 888-904-2267. Fax: 206-442-4501. E-mail: info@cybercamps.com.
URL www.cybercamps.com

For more information, see page 466.

Cybercamps–College of St. Elizabeth

Cybercamps–Giant Campus, Inc.
Morristown, New Jersey

General Information Coed residential and day academic program established in 2004. Formal opportunities for the academically talented.
Program Focus Computers and technology.
Academics Web page design, academics (general),

computer programming, computer science (Advanced Placement), computers.
Arts Animation, digital media, film, graphic arts, musical productions, photography, television/video.
Special Interest Areas Computer game design, computer graphics, electronics, robotics, team building.
Program Information 1–12 sessions per year. Session length: 5 days in June, July, August. Ages: 7–18. 30–50 participants per session. Day program cost: $599–$749. Boarding program cost: $998–$1148.
Application Deadline Continuous.
Jobs Positions for high school students 17 and older and college students 18 and older.
Contact Camp Consultant, 3101 Western Avenue, Suite 100, Seattle, Washington 98121. Phone: 888-904-2267. Fax: 206-442-4501. E-mail: info@cybercamps.com.
URL www.cybercamps.com

For more information, see page 466.

Cybercamps–Rutgers University

Cybercamps–Giant Campus, Inc.
New Brunswick, New Jersey

General Information Coed residential and day academic program established in 1997. Formal opportunities for the academically talented.
Program Focus Computers and technology.
Academics Web page design, academics (general), computer programming, computer science (Advanced Placement), computers.
Arts Animation, digital media, film, graphic arts, musical productions, photography, television/video.
Special Interest Areas Computer game design, computer graphics, electronics, robotics, team building.
Program Information 1–12 sessions per year. Session length: 5 days in June, July, August. Ages: 7–18. 30–50 participants per session. Day program cost: $599–$749. Boarding program cost: $998–$1148.
Application Deadline Continuous.
Contact Camp Consultant, 3101 Western Avenue, Suite 100, Seattle, Washington 98121. Phone: 888-904-2267. Fax: 206-442-4501. E-mail: info@cybercamps.com.
URL www.cybercamps.com

For more information, see page 466.

THE HUN SCHOOL OF PRINCETON AMERICAN CULTURE AND LANGUAGE INSTITUTE

The Hun School of Princeton
176 Edgerstoune Road
Princeton, New Jersey 08540

General Information Coed residential and day academic program and cultural program established in 1994. Formal opportunities for the academically talented.

Program Focus English as a second language and TOEFL preparation.

Academics English as a second language, computers, reading, writing.

Sports Basketball, bicycling, canoeing, soccer, softball, swimming, tennis, volleyball.

Trips Cultural, day, overnight.

Program Information 1 session per year. Session length: 25 days in July. Ages: 13–18. 20–25 participants per session. Day program cost: $2000–$2955. Boarding program cost: $6540. Application fee: $100–$250. Residential student minimum age: 13.

Application Deadline Continuous.

Summer Contact Ms. Dianne Somers, Director, main address above. Phone: 609-921-7600. Fax: 609-683-4410. E-mail: summer@hunschool.org.

Winter Contact Ms. Donna O'Sullivan, Director of Auxiliary Services, main address above. Phone: 609-921-7600 Ext.2265. Fax: 609-924-2170. E-mail: summer@hunschool.org.

URL www.hunschool.org

For more information, see page 518.

THE HUN SCHOOL OF PRINCETON– SUMMER ACADEMIC SESSION

The Hun School of Princeton
176 Edgerstoune Road
Princeton, New Jersey 08540

General Information Coed residential and day academic program established in 1990. Formal opportunities for the academically talented. High school credit may be earned.

The Hun School of Princeton–Summer Academic Session

Academics American literature, English as a second language, English language/literature, SAT/ACT preparation, academics (general), biology, chemistry, computers, mathematics, physics, reading, writing.

Sports Basketball, bicycling, canoeing, in-line skating, soccer, softball, sports (general), swimming, tennis, volleyball.

Wilderness/Outdoors Canoe trips.

Trips Cultural, shopping.

Program Information 1 session per year. Session length: 5 weeks in July, August. Ages: 11–18. 115–125 participants per session. Day program cost: $1248–$2165. Boarding program cost: $5023. Application fee: $100–$250. Open to participants entering grades 6–12.

Application Deadline Continuous.

Jobs Positions for college students 21 and older.

Summer Contact Ms. LeRhonda Greats, Summer Academic Director, main address above. Phone: 609-921-7600 Ext.2258. Fax: 609-683-4410. E-mail: summer@hunschool.org.

Winter Contact Ms. Donna O'Sullivan, Director of Auxiliary Services, main address above. Phone: 609-921-7600 Ext.2265. Fax: 609-924-2170. E-mail: summer@hunschool.org.

URL www.hunschool.org

For more information, see page 518.

THE HUN SCHOOL OF PRINCETON–SUMMER DAY CAMP

The Hun School of Princeton
176 Edgerstoune Road
Princeton, New Jersey 08540

General Information Coed day traditional camp.
Arts Acting, arts and crafts (general), dance, fabric arts, theater/drama.
Special Interest Areas Culinary arts, nature study.
Sports Archery, basketball, fishing, golf, soccer, swimming.
Program Information 3 sessions per year. Session length: 10–30 days in June, July, August. Ages: 5–12. 140–145 participants per session. Day program cost: $796–$1908. Financial aid available.
Application Deadline Continuous.
Jobs Positions for college students 21 and older.
Contact Ms. Donna O'Sullivan, Director of Auxiliary Services, main address above. Phone: 609-921-7600 Ext.2265. Fax: 609-924-2170. E-mail: summer@hunschool.org.
URL www.hunschool.org

For more information, see page 518.

iD TECH CAMPS–RIDER UNIVERSITY, LAWRENCEVILLE, NJ

iD Tech Camps
Rider University
Lawrenceville, New Jersey 08648

General Information Coed residential and day academic program established in 1999. Accredited by American Camping Association. Formal opportunities for the academically talented and artistically talented.
Program Focus Students create 2D and 3D video games, build robots to compete, design websites, film and edit digital movies, create their own comic book with digital photos, learn programming and more. One computer per student and an average of five students per staff member. Campers take home a project at the end of the weeklong course.
Academics Web page design, academics (general),
computer programming, computer science (Advanced Placement), computers, precollege program.
Arts Animation, cinematography, digital media, drawing, film, film editing, film production, graphic arts, photography, television/video.
Special Interest Areas Career exploration, computer game design, computer graphics, electronics, leadership training, robotics, team building.
Sports Baseball, basketball, soccer, softball, swimming, volleyball.
Trips College tours.
Program Information 5–9 sessions per year. Session length: 5–7 days in June, July, August. Ages: 7–17. 100–150 participants per session. Day program cost: $729. Boarding program cost: $1129. Financial aid available.
Application Deadline Continuous.
Jobs Positions for college students 18 and older.
Contact Client Service Representatives, 42 West Campbell Avenue, Suite 301, Campbell, California 95008. Phone: 888-709-TECH. Fax: 408-871-2228. E-mail: info@internaldrive.com.
URL www.internaldrive.com

For more information, see page 520.

iD TECH CAMPS–SETON HALL UNIVERSITY, SOUTH ORANGE, NJ

iD Tech Camps
South Orange, New Jersey

General Information Coed residential and day academic program established in 1999. Accredited by American Camping Association. Formal opportunities for the academically talented and artistically talented.
Program Focus Students create 2D and 3D video games, build robots to compete, design websites, film and edit digital movies, create their own comic book with digital photos, learn programming, and more. One computer per student and an average of five students per staff member. Campers take home a project at the end of the weeklong course.
Academics Web page design, academics (general), computer programming, computer science (Advanced Placement), computers, precollege program.
Arts Animation, cinematography, digital media, drawing, film, film editing, film production, graphic arts, photography, television/video.
Special Interest Areas Career exploration, computer game design, computer graphics, electronics, leadership training, robotics, team building.
Sports Baseball, basketball, soccer, softball, swimming, volleyball.
Trips College tours.
Program Information 5–9 sessions per year. Session length: 5–7 days in June, July, August. Ages: 7–17. 40–50 participants per session. Day program cost: $729. Boarding program cost: $1129. Financial aid available.
Application Deadline Continuous.
Jobs Positions for college students 18 and older.

Contact Client Service Representatives, 42 West Campbell Avenue, Suite 301, Campbell, California 95008. Phone: 888-709-TECH. Fax: 408-871-2228. E-mail: info@internaldrive.com. **URL** www.internaldrive.com

For more information, see page 520.

JUNIOR STATESMEN SUMMER SCHOOL– PRINCETON UNIVERSITY

Junior Statesmen Foundation
Princeton University
Princeton, New Jersey 08544

General Information Coed residential academic program established in 1997. Formal opportunities for the academically talented. High school credit may be earned.

Junior Statesmen Summer School–Princeton University

Program Focus American government and politics, debate, leadership, speech, economics.
Academics Communications, economics, government and politics, government and politics (Advanced Placement), history, journalism, precollege program, social science, social studies, speech/debate.
Special Interest Areas Career exploration, leadership training.

Trips College tours, cultural, day.
Program Information 1 session per year. Session length: 27 days in June, July. Ages: 14–18. 200–300 participants per session. Boarding program cost: $4150. Financial aid available.
Application Deadline Continuous.
Contact Ms. Jessica Brow, National Summer School Director, 400 South El Camino Real, Suite 300, San Mateo, California 94402. Phone: 650-347-1600. Fax: 650-347-7200. E-mail: jsa@jsa.org.
URL www.jsa.org/summer

For more information, see page 534.

JUNIOR STATESMEN SYMPOSIUM ON NEW JERSEY STATE POLITICS AND GOVERNMENT

Junior Statesmen Foundation
Princeton University
Princeton, New Jersey 08544

General Information Coed residential academic program established in 1996. Formal opportunities for the academically talented.
Program Focus State government, politics, debate, and leadership training.
Academics Communications, government and politics, journalism, precollege program, social science, social studies, speech/debate.
Special Interest Areas Career exploration, leadership training.
Trips College tours, day.
Program Information 1 session per year. Session length: 4 days in August. Ages: 14–18. 100–150 participants per session. Boarding program cost: $480. Financial aid available.
Application Deadline Continuous.
Contact Ms. Jessica Brow, National Summer School Director, 400 South El Camino Real, Suite 300, San Mateo, California 94402. Phone: 650-347-1600. Fax: 650-347-7200. E-mail: jsa@jsa.org.
URL summer.jsa.org/

For more information, see page 534.

LANDMARK VOLUNTEERS: NEW JERSEY

Landmark Volunteers, Inc.
Wall Township
New Jersey

General Information Coed residential outdoor program and community service program established in 1992. High school credit may be earned.

Landmark Volunteers: New Jersey (continued)

Program Focus Opportunity for high school students to earn community service credit while working as a team for two weeks serving InfoAge Science-History Center. Similar programs offered through Landmark Volunteers at over 50 locations in 20 states.

Academics Meteorology, science (general).

Special Interest Areas Career exploration, community service, electronics, leadership training, nature study, team building.

Trips Cultural, day.

Program Information 1 session per year. Session length: 2 weeks in July. Ages: 14–18. 10–13 participants per session. Boarding program cost: $1250–$1300. Financial aid available.

Application Deadline Continuous.

Jobs Positions for college students.

Contact Ann Barrett, Executive Director, PO Box 455, Sheffield, Massachusetts 01257. Phone: 413-229-0255. Fax: 413-229-2050. E-mail: landmark@volunteers.com.

URL www.volunteers.com

For more information, see page 542.

THE SUMMER INSTITUTE FOR THE GIFTED AT MOORESTOWN FRIENDS SCHOOL

Summer Institute for the Gifted
Moorestown Friends School
Moorestown, New Jersey 08057

General Information Coed day academic program established in 2003. Formal opportunities for the academically talented and gifted.

Academics American literature, English language/literature, French language/literature, SAT/ACT preparation, Spanish language/literature, academics (general), aerospace science, archaeology, architecture, art (Advanced Placement), art history/appreciation, biology (Advanced Placement), botany, business, chemistry, classical languages/literatures, communications, computer programming, computers, engineering, environmental science, geology/earth science, government and politics, history, humanities, marine studies, mathematics, music, oceanography, philosophy, physics, physiology, precollege program, psychology, science (general), social studies, speech/debate, study skills, writing.

Arts Arts and crafts (general), ceramics, chorus, creative writing, dance, drawing, graphic arts, music, music (chamber), music (classical), music (ensemble), musical productions, painting, photography, puppetry, sculpture, theater/drama, weaving.

Special Interest Areas Animal care, chess, electronics, model rocketry, robotics.

Sports Aerobics, baseball, basketball, field hockey, football, lacrosse, martial arts, soccer, softball, squash, swimming, tennis, volleyball.

Wilderness/Outdoors Hiking.

Program Information 1 session per year. Session length: 3 weeks in June, July. Ages: 6–11. 150–250 participants per session. Day program cost: $1825–$2000. Application fee: $75. Financial aid available.

Application Deadline May 14.

Jobs Positions for college students 19 and older.

Contact Ms. Barbara Swicord, Director, River Plaza, 9 West Broad Street, Stamford, Connecticut 06902-3788. Phone: 866-303-4744. Fax: 203-399-5598. E-mail: sig.info@aifs.com.

URL www.giftedstudy.com

For more information, see page 654.

THE SUMMER INSTITUTE FOR THE GIFTED AT PRINCETON UNIVERSITY

Summer Institute for the Gifted
Princeton University
Princeton, New Jersey 08544

General Information Coed residential academic program. Formal opportunities for the academically talented and gifted.

Academics English language/literature, French language/literature, SAT/ACT preparation, Spanish language/literature, academics (general), aerospace science, biology, business, chemistry, classical languages/literatures, communications, computers, engineering, government and politics, history, mathematics, music, oceanography, philosophy, physics, precollege program, psychology, science (general), social studies, speech/debate, study skills, writing.

Arts Band, chorus, creative writing, dance, film, graphic arts, music, music (classical), music (ensemble), music (instrumental), musical productions, photography, sculpture, theater/drama.

Special Interest Areas Animal care, electronics, meditation, robotics.

Sports Aerobics, baseball, basketball, fencing, football, martial arts, soccer, tennis, track and field, volleyball.

Trips Cultural.

Program Information 1–2 sessions per year. Session length: 3 weeks in July, August. Ages: 12–17. 150–250 participants per session. Boarding program cost: $4495–$5000. Application fee: $75. Financial aid available.

Application Deadline May 14.

Jobs Positions for college students 19 and older.

Contact Ms. Barbara Swicord, Director, River Plaza, 9 West Broad Street, Stamford, Connecticut 06902-3788. Phone: 866-303-4744. Fax: 203-399-5598. E-mail: sig.info@aifs.com.

URL www.giftedstudy.com

For more information, see page 654.

NEW MEXICO

THE EXPERIMENT IN INTERNATIONAL LIVING-NAVAJO NATION

The Experiment in International Living
Farmington, New Mexico

General Information Coed travel outdoor program, community service program, cultural program, and adventure program established in 1932.
Program Focus Youth travel, homestay, Navajo culture.
Academics Navajo language, ecology.
Arts Arts and crafts (general), jewelry making.
Special Interest Areas Native American culture, community service, cross-cultural education, homestays, nature study, touring.
Sports Horseback riding.
Wilderness/Outdoors Backpacking, hiking, outdoor camping, white-water trips.
Trips Cultural, day, overnight.
Program Information 1 session per year. Session length: 4 weeks in June, July. Ages: 14–19. 10–15 participants per session. Cost: $4250. Financial aid available.
Application Deadline May 1.
Contact Annie Thompson, Enrollment Director, Summer Abroad, Kipling Road, PO Box 676, Brattleboro, Vermont 05302-0676. Phone: 800-345-2929. Fax: 802-258-3428. E-mail: eil@worldlearning.org.
URL www.usexperiment.org

For more information, see page 492.

LANDMARK VOLUNTEERS: NEW MEXICO

Landmark Volunteers, Inc.
New Mexico

General Information Coed residential outdoor program, community service program, and wilderness program established in 1992. High school credit may be earned.
Program Focus Opportunity for high school students to earn community service credit while working as a team for two weeks serving Chaco Culture/Salmon Ruins Heritage Park, or Continental Divide Trail.

Similar programs offered through Landmark Volunteers at over 50 locations in 20 states.
Academics Archaeology, environmental science.
Special Interest Areas Native American culture, career exploration, community service, conservation projects, field research/expeditions, nature study, team building, trail maintenance.
Wilderness/Outdoors Hiking, wilderness camping.
Trips Cultural, day.
Program Information 2 sessions per year. Session length: 2 weeks in July, August. Ages: 14–18. 10–13 participants per session. Boarding program cost: $1250–$1300. Financial aid available.
Application Deadline Continuous.
Jobs Positions for college students.
Contact Ann Barrett, Executive Director, PO Box 455, Sheffield, Massachusetts 01257. Phone: 413-229-0255. Fax: 413-229-2050. E-mail: landmark@volunteers.com.
URL www.volunteers.com

For more information, see page 542.

NEW YORK

ACTEEN AUGUST ACADEMY

ACTeen
35 West 45th Street, 6th Floor
New York, New York 10036

General Information Coed residential and day arts program established in 1978. Formal opportunities for the artistically talented.

ACTeen August Academy

Program Focus Film and television acting, videotape camera work.
Arts Acting, audition technique, film, music (vocal), musical theater, performing arts, stage movement, television/video, theater/drama, voice and speech.
Trips Cultural.
Program Information 1 session per year. Session

ACTeen August Academy (continued)

length: 17–18 days in August. Ages: 13+. 20–30 participants per session. Day program cost: $300–$2250. Boarding program cost: $1300–$3500. Application fee: $25.
Application Deadline Continuous.
Contact Rita Litton, ACTeen Director, main address above. Phone: 212-391-5915. Fax: 212-768-8918. E-mail: rita@acteen.com.
URL www.acteen.com
For more information, see page 404.

ACTEEN JULY ACADEMY

ACTeen
35 West 45th Street, 6th Floor
New York, New York 10036

General Information Coed residential and day arts program established in 1978. Formal opportunities for the artistically talented.
Program Focus Film and television acting, Shakespeare, theater, playwriting, screenwriting.
Academics Writing.
Arts Acting, creative writing, directing, film, music (vocal), musical theater, playwriting, screenwriting, stage movement, television/video, theater/drama, voice and speech.
Trips Cultural.
Program Information 1 session per year. Session length: 4 weeks in July. Ages: 15+. 40–60 participants per session. Day program cost: $350–$2700. Boarding program cost: $1600–$4500. Application fee: $25.
Application Deadline Continuous.
Contact Rita Litton, ACTeen Director, main address above. Phone: 212-391-5915. Fax: 212-768-8918. E-mail: rita@acteen.com.
URL www.acteen.com
For more information, see page 404.

ACTEEN JUNE ACADEMY

ACTeen
35 West 45th Street, 6th Floor
New York, New York 10036

General Information Coed residential and day arts program established in 1978. Formal opportunities for the artistically talented.
Program Focus Film and television acting, videotape camera work.
Arts Acting, audition technique, film, stage movement, television/video, theater/drama, voice and speech.
Program Information 1 session per year. Session length: 11 days in June. Ages: 13+. 12–24 participants per session. Day program cost: $1450–$1600. Boarding program cost: $2050–$2300. Application fee: $25. Financial aid available.
Application Deadline Continuous.

Contact Rita Litton, ACTeen Director, main address above. Phone: 212-391-5915. Fax: 212-768-8918. E-mail: rita@acteen.com.
URL www.acteen.com
For more information, see page 404.

ACTEEN SUMMER SATURDAY ACADEMY

ACTeen
35 West 45th Street, 6th Floor
New York, New York 10036

General Information Coed day arts program established in 1978. Formal opportunities for the artistically talented.
Program Focus Film and television acting, improvisation.
Arts Acting, audition technique, film, performing arts, television/video, theater/drama, voice and speech.
Program Information 1 session per year. Session length: 6 weeks in July, August. Ages: 13+. 30–50 participants per session. Day program cost: $325–$1250. Application fee: $25.
Application Deadline Continuous.
Contact Rita Litton, ACTeen Director, main address above. Phone: 212-391-5915. Fax: 212-768-8918. E-mail: rita@acteen.com.
URL www.acteen.com
For more information, see page 404.

ADIRONDACK FIELD ECOLOGY

Adirondack Field Ecology
Adirondack Park
Lake Placid, New York

General Information Coed residential academic program, outdoor program, and wilderness program established in 2004. Formal opportunities for the academically talented. College credit may be earned.

Adirondack Field Ecology

Program Focus Academic, introductory college-level field ecology (bio 232) that includes camping and wilderness travel.
Academics Academics (general), astronomy, biology, biology (Advanced Placement), botany, ecology, environmental science, geology/earth science, natural resource management, precollege program, science (general).
Special Interest Areas Field research/expeditions, nature study.
Sports Canoeing, fishing.
Wilderness/Outdoors Backpacking, canoe trips, hiking, wilderness camping.
Trips College tours, overnight.
Program Information 1 session per year. Session length: 4 weeks in July. Ages: 16–19. 16–20 participants per session. Boarding program cost: $4800. Financial aid available.
Application Deadline Continuous.
Contact Chad Jemison, Director, PO Box 187, Lake Placid, New York 12946. Phone: 518-523-9329 Ext.149. Fax: 518-523-4858. E-mail: chad.jemison@nct.org.
URL www.adkecology.org

For more information, see page 672.

AMERICAN ACADEMY OF DRAMATIC ARTS SUMMER PROGRAM AT NEW YORK

American Academy of Dramatic Arts
120 Madison Avenue
New York, New York 10016

General Information Coed day arts program established in 1884. Formal opportunities for the artistically talented.

American Academy of Dramatic Arts Summer Program at New York

Program Focus Acting.
Arts Acting, dance, music (vocal), musical productions, stage movement, television/video, theater/drama, vocal production, voice and speech.
Program Information 1 session per year. Session length: 24–30 days in July, August. Ages: 14+. 100–170 participants per session. Day program cost: $1900–$2000. Application fee: $50. Each elective costs $90; admission by audition only.
Application Deadline Continuous.
Contact Ms. Karen Higginbotham, Director of Admissions, main address above. Phone: 800-463-8990. Fax: 212-685-8093. E-mail: admissions-ny@aada.org.
URL www.aada.org

For more information, see page 414.

APPLEJACK TEEN CAMP

Camp Regis, Inc.
Paul Smiths, New York 12970

General Information Coed residential traditional camp established in 1946. Religious affiliation: Society of Friends. Accredited by American Camping Association.
Program Focus Waterfront activities, sports, and wilderness experiences.
Academics English as a second language.
Arts Acting, arts and crafts (general), band, batiking, ceramics, chorus, creative writing, dance, dance (ballet), dance (folk), dance (jazz), dance (modern), drawing, guitar, jewelry making, leather working, music, music (classical), music (ensemble), music (instrumental),

Applejack Teen Camp (continued)

music (jazz), music (vocal), musical productions, painting, photography, piano, pottery, sculpture, theater/ drama, weaving, woodworking.

Special Interest Areas Native American culture, animal care, campcraft, community service, culinary arts, field trips (arts and culture), leadership training, nature study, touring.

Sports Aerobics, archery, baseball, basketball, bicycling, boating, canoeing, cross-country, diving, equestrian sports, field hockey, fishing, football, golf, gymnastics, horseback riding, kayaking, lacrosse, sailing, snorkeling, soccer, softball, street/roller hockey, swimming, tennis, track and field, volleyball, water polo, waterskiing, windsurfing.

Wilderness/Outdoors Backpacking, bicycle trips, canoe trips, hiking, mountain biking, mountaineering, orienteering, rafting, wilderness camping.

Trips Cultural, day, overnight.

Program Information 3 sessions per year. Session length: 4–8 weeks in June, July, August. Ages: 13–17. 280 participants per session. Boarding program cost: $4000–$7000. Financial aid available. Deposit of $600 required. Applications accepted during winter and spring.

Application Deadline Continuous.

Jobs Positions for college students 19 and older.

Summer Contact Michael P. Humes, Director, PO Box 245, Paul Smiths, New York 12970. Phone: 518-327-3117. Fax: 518-327-3193. E-mail: campregis@aol.com.

Winter Contact Michael P. Humes, Director, 60 Lafayette Road West, Princeton, New Jersey 08540-2428. Phone: 609-688-0368. Fax: 609-688-0369. E-mail: campregis@aol.com.

URL www.campregis-applejack.com

For more information, see page 442.

Barnard's Summer in New York City: A Pre-College Program

Barnard College/Columbia University
3009 Broadway
112 Hewitt Hall
New York, New York 10027-6598

General Information Coed residential and day academic program established in 1985. Formal opportunities for the academically talented. Specific services available for the learning disabled. High school credit may be earned.

Barnard's Summer in New York City: A Pre-College Program

Program Focus Exploring New York City.

Academics American literature, English language/ literature, academics (general), architecture, art history/ appreciation, history, humanities, intercultural studies, philosophy, precollege program, psychology, religion, social science, writing.

Arts Acting, creative writing, dance, dance (ballet), dance (modern), film, theater/drama.

Special Interest Areas Career exploration, community service, field trips (arts and culture), leadership training.

Trips Cultural, day.

Program Information 1–3 sessions per year. Session length: 6–35 days in June, July. Ages: 14–18. 40–170 participants per session. Day program cost: $1030–$2900. Boarding program cost: $1400–$4400. Application fee: $40–$65. Financial aid available.

Application Deadline May 1.

Jobs Positions for college students.

Contact Alexandra Nestoras, Director of Pre-College Programs, Barnard College, 3009 Broadway, New York, New York 10027. Phone: 212-854-8866. Fax: 212-854-8867. E-mail: pcp@barnard.edu.

URL www.barnard.edu/pcp

For more information, see page 424.

BARNARD'S SUMMER IN NEW YORK CITY: ONE-WEEK LIBERAL ARTS INTENSIVE

Barnard College/Columbia University
3009 Broadway
New York, New York 10027

General Information Coed residential and day academic program established in 1985. Formal opportunities for the academically talented. Specific services available for the learning disabled. High school credit may be earned.
Program Focus Exploring New York City.
Academics American literature, English language/literature, academics (general), architecture, art history/appreciation, history, humanities, intercultural studies, precollege program, psychology, social science, writing.
Special Interest Areas Career exploration, field trips (arts and culture), leadership training.
Trips Cultural, day.
Program Information 1 session per year. Session length: 1 week in June. Ages: 14–18. 42–52 participants per session. Day program cost: $1030. Boarding program cost: $1650. Application fee: $40–$65. Financial aid available.
Application Deadline May 1.
Jobs Positions for college students.
Contact Alexandra Nestoras, Director of Pre-College Programs, main address above. Phone: 212-854-8866. Fax: 212-854-8867. E-mail: pcp@barnard.edu.
URL www.barnard.edu/pcp
For more information, see page 424.

BARNARD'S SUMMER IN NEW YORK CITY: YOUNG WOMEN'S LEADERSHIP INSTITUTE

Barnard College/Columbia University
3009 Broadway
New York, New York 10027

General Information Girls' residential academic program established in 2003. Formal opportunities for the academically talented. Specific services available for the learning disabled. High school credit may be earned.
Program Focus Leadership training.
Academics Academics (general), area studies, humanities, intercultural studies, precollege program, social science, social studies, speech/debate, writing.
Special Interest Areas Career exploration, community service, field research/expeditions, field trips (arts and culture), leadership training.
Trips Cultural, day.
Program Information 1 session per year. Session length: 1 week in July. Ages: 14–18. 35–45 participants per session. Boarding program cost: $1400. Application fee: $40–$65. Financial aid available.
Application Deadline May 1.
Jobs Positions for college students.
Contact Alexandra Nestoras, Director of Pre-College Programs, main address above. Phone: 212-854-8866. Fax: 212-854-8867. E-mail: pcp@barnard.edu.
URL www.barnard.edu/pcp
For more information, see page 424.

BRANT LAKE CAMP'S DANCE CENTRE

Brant Lake Camp
7586 State Route 8
Brant Lake, New York 12815

General Information Girls' residential arts program established in 1980. Accredited by American Camping Association.

Brant Lake Camp's Dance Centre

Program Focus Professional dance classes in a camp environment.
Arts Arts and crafts (general), ceramics, dance, dance (ballet), dance (jazz), dance (modern), dance (tap), drawing, music (vocal), painting, photography, pottery, television/video, theater/drama, weaving, woodworking.
Sports Aerobics, bicycling, boating, canoeing, climbing (wall), golf, ropes course, sailing, swimming, tennis, volleyball, waterskiing, weight training.
Wilderness/Outdoors Bicycle trips, canoe trips, hiking.
Trips Cultural, day, overnight.
Program Information 2 sessions per year. Session length: 21–43 days in June, July, August. Ages: 11–16. 45–60 participants per session. Boarding program cost: $4000–$7400.
Application Deadline Continuous.
Jobs Positions for college students 19 and older.
Contact Ms. Kirstin Been Spielman, Director, main address above. Phone: 518-494-2406. Fax: 518-494-7372. E-mail: brantlakec@aol.com.
URL www.blcdance.com
For more information, see page 428.

CAMP REGIS

Camp Regis, Inc.
Paul Smiths, New York 12970

General Information Coed residential traditional camp established in 1946. Religious affiliation: Society of Friends. Accredited by American Camping Association.

Camp Regis

Program Focus Sports, wilderness experiences, and waterfront activities.
Academics English as a second language.
Arts Acting, arts and crafts (general), band, batiking, ceramics, chorus, creative writing, dance, dance (ballet), dance (folk), dance (jazz), dance (modern), drawing, guitar, jewelry making, leather working, music, music (classical), music (ensemble), music (jazz), music (vocal), musical productions, painting, photography, piano, pottery, sculpture, theater/drama, weaving, woodworking.
Special Interest Areas Native American culture, animal care, campcraft, culinary arts, field trips (arts and culture), leadership training, nature study.
Sports Archery, baseball, basketball, bicycling, boating, canoeing, cross-country, diving, equestrian sports, field hockey, fishing, football, golf, gymnastics, horseback riding, kayaking, lacrosse, sailing, snorkeling, soccer, softball, street/roller hockey, swimming, tennis, track and field, volleyball, water polo, waterskiing, windsurfing.
Wilderness/Outdoors Backpacking, bicycle trips, canoe trips, hiking, mountain biking, mountaineering, orienteering, rafting, wilderness camping.
Trips Cultural, day, overnight.
Program Information 3 sessions per year. Session length: 4–8 weeks in June, July, August. Ages: 6–13. 280 participants per session. Boarding program cost: $4000–$7000. Financial aid available. Deposit of $600 required. Applications accepted during winter and spring.
Application Deadline Continuous.

Jobs Positions for college students 19 and older.
Summer Contact Michael P. Humes, Director, PO Box 245, Paul Smiths, New York 12970. Phone: 518-327-3117. Fax: 518-327-3193. E-mail: campregis@aol.com.
Winter Contact Michael P. Humes, Director, 60 Lafayette Road West, Princeton, New Jersey 08540-2428. Phone: 609-688-0368. Fax: 609-688-0369. E-mail: campregis@aol.com.
URL www.campregis-applejack.com
For more information, see page 442.

CAMP TREETOPS

Cascade Road, Route 73
Lake Placid, New York 12946

General Information Coed residential traditional camp and outdoor program established in 1921. Accredited by American Camping Association. Formal opportunities for the artistically talented.

Camp Treetops

Program Focus Organic farming, wilderness program, and the arts.
Academics Astronomy, ecology, environmental science, music.
Arts Arts, arts and crafts (general), batiking, ceramics, creative writing, dance, dance (ballet), dance (folk),

drawing, fabric arts, jewelry making, leather working, music, musical productions, painting, photography, pottery, printmaking, puppetry, sculpture, theater/drama, weaving, woodworking.

Special Interest Areas Native American culture, animal care, campcraft, community service, culinary arts, farming, field trips (arts and culture), gardening, nature study, nautical skills.

Sports Baseball, basketball, boating, canoeing, climbing (wall), diving, equestrian sports, fishing, gymnastics, horseback riding, kayaking, rappelling, rowing (crew/sculling), sailing, snorkeling, soccer, softball, swimming, tennis, water polo.

Wilderness/Outdoors Backpacking, canoe trips, hiking, mountaineering, orienteering, pack animal trips, rock climbing, wilderness camping.

Trips Cultural, day, overnight.

Program Information 2 sessions per year. Session length: 7 weeks in June, July, August. Ages: 8–14. 150–160 participants per session. Boarding program cost: $6400. Financial aid available.

Application Deadline Continuous.

Jobs Positions for high school students 17 and older and college students 18 and older.

Contact Karen Culpepper, Director, PO Box 187, Lake Placid, New York 12946. Phone: 518-523-9329 Ext.112. Fax: 518-523-4858. E-mail: karenc@nct.org.

URL www.camptreetops.org

For more information, see page 444.

CAREER EXPLORATIONS–NEW YORK

Career Explorations, LLC
The Juilliard School, Samuel B. and David Rose Building
60 Lincoln Center Plaza
New York, New York 10023-6588

General Information Coed residential and day academic program established in 2003.

Career Explorations–New York

Program Focus Career exploration through an intern-

ship in a field of personal interest. Optional college tours and SAT preparation.

Academics Architecture, art history/appreciation, business, communications, computers, economics, engineering, environmental science, government and politics, health sciences, intercultural studies, journalism, music, psychology, social science, writing.

Arts Fabric arts, fashion design/production, photography.

Special Interest Areas Animal care, career exploration, college planning, community service, culinary arts, internships, leadership training, touring.

Trips College tours, cultural, day

Program Information 1 session per year. Session length: 28–30 days in July. Ages: 16–18. 55–70 participants per session. Boarding program cost: $5795. Application fee: $50.

Application Deadline Continuous.

Contact Todd Aronson, Boston Director, 18 Exeter Lane, Morristown, New Jersey 07960. Phone: 781-559-3261. E-mail: todd@ceinternships.com.

URL www.ceinternships.com

For more information, see page 446.

CORNELL UNIVERSITY SUMMER COLLEGE PROGRAMS FOR HIGH SCHOOL STUDENTS

Cornell University
B20 Day Hall
Ithaca, New York 14853-2801

General Information Coed residential academic program established in 1962. Formal opportunities for the academically talented. Specific services available for the emotionally challenged, hearing impaired, learning disabled, physically challenged, and visually impaired. College credit may be earned.

Cornell University Summer College Programs for High School Students

Academics English as a second language, English language/literature, French language/literature, Russian language/literature, Spanish language/literature, academics (general), anthropology, architecture, art history/appreciation, astronomy, biology, botany, business, chemistry, classical languages/literatures,

Cornell University Summer College Programs for High School Students (continued)

communications, computer programming, economics, engineering, government and politics, history, humanities, mathematics, music, philosophy, physics, precollege program, psychology, speech/debate, study skills.

Arts Chorus, dance, drawing, film, painting.
Special Interest Areas Animal care, career exploration.
Sports Basketball, bicycling, climbing (wall), equestrian sports, golf, sailing, swimming, tennis, volleyball, weight training, windsurfing.
Wilderness/Outdoors Hiking.
Program Information 2 sessions per year. Session length: 3–6 weeks in June, July, August. Ages: 15–19. 150–600 participants per session. Boarding program cost: $4810–$8025. Application fee: $50–$100. Financial aid available.
Application Deadline Continuous.
Contact Abby H. Eller, Director, main address above. Phone: 607-255-6203. Fax: 607-255-6665. E-mail: summer_college@cornell.edu.
URL www.summercollege.cornell.edu

For more information, see page 462.

CYBERCAMPS–ADELPHI UNIVERSITY

Cybercamps–Giant Campus, Inc.
Garden City, New York

General Information Coed residential and day academic program established in 1996. Formal opportunities for the academically talented. Specific services available for the emotionally challenged.
Program Focus Computers and technology.
Academics Web page design, academics (general), computer programming, computer science (Advanced Placement), computers.
Arts Animation, digital media, film, graphic arts, musical productions, photography, television/video.
Special Interest Areas Computer game design, computer graphics, electronics, robotics, team building.
Program Information 1–12 sessions per year. Session length: 5 days in June, July, August. Ages: 7–18. 30–50 participants per session. Day program cost: $599–$749. Boarding program cost: $998–$1148.
Application Deadline Continuous.
Jobs Positions for high school students 17 and older and college students 18 and older.

Contact Camp Consultant, 3101 Western Avenue, Suite 100, Seattle, Washington 98121. Phone: 888-904-2267. Fax: 206-442-4501. E-mail: info@cybercamps.com.
URL www.cybercamps.com

For more information, see page 466.

CYBERCAMPS–FORDHAM UNIVERSITY

Cybercamps–Giant Campus, Inc.
Tarrytown, New York

General Information Coed residential and day academic program established in 1996. Formal opportunities for the academically talented.
Program Focus Computers and technology.
Academics Web page design, academics (general), computer programming, computer science (Advanced Placement), computers.
Arts Animation, digital media, film, graphic arts, musical productions, photography, television/video.
Special Interest Areas Computer game design, computer graphics, electronics, robotics, team building.
Program Information 1–12 sessions per year. Session length: 5 days in June, July, August. Ages: 7–18. 30–50 participants per session. Day program cost: $599–$749. Boarding program cost: $998–$1148.
Application Deadline Continuous.
Jobs Positions for high school students 17 and older and college students 18 and older.
Contact Camp Consultant, 3101 Western Avenue, Suite 100, Seattle, Washington 98121. Phone: 888-904-2267. Fax: 206-442-4501. E-mail: info@cybercamps.com.
URL www.cybercamps.com

For more information, see page 466.

CYBERCAMPS–THE NEW SCHOOL

Cybercamps–Giant Campus, Inc.
New York, New York

General Information Coed residential and day academic program established in 1997. Formal opportunities for the academically talented.
Program Focus Computers and technology.
Academics Web page design, academics (general), computer programming, computer science (Advanced Placement), computers.
Arts Animation, digital media, film, graphic arts, musical productions, photography, television/video.
Special Interest Areas Computer game design, computer graphics, electronics, robotics, team building.
Program Information 1–12 sessions per year. Session length: 5 days in June, July, August. Ages: 7–18. 30–50 participants per session. Day program cost: $599–$749. Boarding program cost: $998–$1148.
Application Deadline Continuous.
Contact Camp Consultant, 3101 Western Avenue, Suite 100, Seattle, Washington 98121. Phone: 888-904-2267. Fax: 206-442-4501. E-mail: info@cybercamps.com.
URL www.cybercamps.com

For more information, see page 466.

CYBERCAMPS–NEW YORK INSTITUTE OF TECHNOLOGY

Cybercamps–Giant Campus, Inc.
New York, New York

General Information Coed residential and day academic program established in 1997. Formal opportunities for the academically talented.
Program Focus Computers and technology.
Academics Web page design, academics (general), computer programming, computer science (Advanced Placement), computers.
Arts Animation, digital media, film, graphic arts, musical productions, photography, television/video.
Special Interest Areas Computer game design, computer graphics, electronics, robotics, team building.
Program Information 1–12 sessions per year. Session length: 5 days in June, July, August. Ages: 7–18. 30–50 participants per session. Day program cost: $599–$749. Boarding program cost: $998–$1148.
Application Deadline Continuous.
Jobs Positions for high school students 17 and older and college students 18 and older.
Contact Camp Consultant, 3101 Western Avenue, Suite 100, Seattle, Washington 98121. Phone: 888-904-2267. Fax: 206-442-4501. E-mail: info@cybercamps.com.
URL www.cybercamps.com
For more information, see page 466.

CYBERCAMPS–ST. JOHN'S UNIVERSITY

Cybercamps–Giant Campus, Inc.
Queens, New York

General Information Coed residential and day academic program established in 1997. Formal opportunities for the academically talented.
Program Focus Computers and technology.
Academics Web page design, academics (general), computer programming, computer science (Advanced Placement), computers.
Arts Animation, digital media, film, graphic arts, musical productions, photography, television/video.
Special Interest Areas Computer game design, computer graphics, electronics, robotics, team building.

Program Information 1–12 sessions per year. Session length: 5 days in June, July, August. Ages: 7–18. 30–50 participants per session. Day program cost: $599–$749. Boarding program cost: $998–$1148.
Application Deadline Continuous.
Contact Camp Consultant, 3101 Western Avenue, Suite 100, Seattle, Washington 98121. Phone: 888-904-2267. Fax: 206-442-4501. E-mail: info@cybercamps.com.
URL www.cybercamps.com
For more information, see page 466.

DUNNABECK AT KILDONAN

Kildonan School
425 Morse Hill Road
Amenia, New York 12501

General Information Coed residential and day academic program and special needs program established in 1955. Specific services available for the learning disabled.

Dunnabeck at Kildonan

Program Focus Language training for dyslexic students.

Dunnabeck at Kildonan (continued)

Academics Academics (general), computers, reading, study skills, writing.

Arts Arts and crafts (general), ceramics, drawing, painting, woodworking.

Sports Archery, baseball, basketball, bicycling, boating, canoeing, equestrian sports, fishing, horseback riding, sailing, soccer, swimming, tennis, waterskiing, windsurfing.

Wilderness/Outdoors Rock climbing.

Trips Cultural, day, overnight.

Program Information 1 session per year. Session length: 42–50 days in June, July, August. Ages: 8–16. 75–100 participants per session. Day program cost: $4350–$6600. Boarding program cost: $8350. Application fee: $50. Financial aid available.

Application Deadline Continuous.

Jobs Positions for college students 21 and older.

Contact Ronald A. Wilson, Headmaster, main address above. Phone: 845-373-8111. Fax: 845-373-9793. E-mail: bsattler@kildonan.org.

URL www.kildonan.org

For more information, see page 472.

EASTERN U.S. MUSIC CAMP, INC. AT COLGATE UNIVERSITY

Dana Arts Center
Hamilton, New York 13346-1398

General Information Coed residential and day arts program established in 1976. Accredited by American Camping Association. Formal opportunities for the artistically talented and gifted. High school credit may be earned.

Eastern U.S. Music Camp, Inc. at Colgate University

Program Focus Concert band, wind ensemble, jazz ensembles, jazz combos, orchestras, chamber ensemble, string quartets, woodwind ensemble, choirs, private lessons; piano, voice, guitar, organ, harp, string, percussion, woodwind, brass; music theory, harmony, improvisation, composition, arranging, conducting; recitals, concerts, recreation, trip, and guest artists.

Academics Computers, music, music (Advanced Placement).

Arts Arts and crafts (general), band, chorus, guitar, harp, music, music (chamber), music (classical), music (ensemble), music (instrumental), music (jazz), music (orchestral), music (vocal), music composition/arrangement, music conducting, music theory, musical performance/recitals, organ, performing arts, piano.

Special Interest Areas Career exploration, leadership training, weight reduction.

Sports Basketball, climbing (wall), diving, golf, racquetball, softball, sports (general), swimming, tennis, track and field, volleyball.

Trips Day.

Program Information 1–3 sessions per year. Session length: 2–4 weeks in June, July. Ages: 10–18. 150–180 participants per session. Day program cost: $635–$952. Boarding program cost: $1760–$2640. Financial aid available.

Application Deadline Continuous.

Jobs Positions for high school students 16 and older and college students 18 and older.

Summer Contact Dr. Thomas A. Brown, Director, main address above. Phone: 315-228-7041. Fax: 315-228-7557. E-mail: summer@EasternUSMusicCamp.com.

Winter Contact Dr. Thomas A. Brown, Director, 7 Brook Hollow Road, Ballston Lake, New York 12019. Phone: 866-777-7841. Fax: 518-877-4943. E-mail: summer@EasternUSMusicCamp.com.

URL www.EasternUSMusicCamp.com

For more information, see page 474.

FIVEPOINTS

Union College
Schenectady, New York 12308

General Information Coed residential academic program and arts program established in 2005.

FivePoints

Academics English language/literature, academics (general), anthropology, archaeology, area studies, art

history/appreciation, biology, business, chemistry, communications, computers, economics, forensic science, geology/earth science, government and politics, history, humanities, intercultural studies, journalism, linguistics, physics, precollege program, psychology, science (general), social science, social studies, speech/debate, study skills, writing.
Arts Animation, arts, creative writing, digital media, drawing, film, graphic arts, music, photography, radio broadcasting, television/video.
Special Interest Areas Career exploration, team building.
Sports Basketball, swimming, tennis, track and field.
Trips Cultural, day, shopping.
Program Information 2–3 sessions per year. Session length: 13 days in June, July, August. Ages: 13–18. 50–100 participants per session. Boarding program cost: $2395.
Application Deadline Continuous.
Jobs Positions for college students.
Contact Douglas Murphy, Program Coordinator, Office of Special Events, 807 Union Street, Schenectady, New York 12308. Phone: 800-883-2540. E-mail: fivepoints@union.edu.
URL www.union.edu/fivepoints

For more information, see page 674.

GIRLSUMMER AT EMMA WILLARD SCHOOL

Emma Willard School
285 Pawling Avenue
Troy, New York 12180

General Information Girls' residential academic program and arts program established in 2003.

GirlSummer at Emma Willard School

Program Focus Students choose from one of nine academic tracks: college prep; Spanish; French; computers, writer's workshop; performing arts; fine arts; mock trial; and model U.N. All students visit Manhattan at least once on a program-specific field trip.
Academics English language/literature, French language/literature, SAT/ACT preparation, Spanish language/literature, academics (general), computer programming, computers, journalism, precollege program, writing.
Arts Acting, arts, arts and crafts (general), creative writing, painting, photography, theater/drama.
Special Interest Areas College planning, culinary arts, robotics.
Sports Aerobics, basketball, field hockey, soccer, softball, swimming, tennis, volleyball, weight training.
Trips College tours, cultural, day, shopping.
Program Information 3 sessions per year. Session length: 13 days in July, August. Ages: 11+. 40–100 participants per session. Boarding program cost: $2395. Open to participants entering grades 7–12.
Application Deadline Continuous.
Jobs Positions for college students.
Summer Contact Doug Murphy, Director, main address above. Phone: 866-EWS-CAMP. Fax: 718-237-8862. E-mail: girlsummer@emmawillard.org.
Winter Contact Doug Murphy, Director, 285 Pawling Avenue, Troy, New York 12180. Phone: 866-EWS-CAMP. Fax: 718-237-8862. E-mail: girlsummer@emmawillard.org.
URL www.emmawillard.org/summer/residential
For more information, see page 484.

THE GOW SCHOOL SUMMER PROGRAM

The Gow School
2491 Emery Road
South Wales, New York 14139

General Information Coed residential and day traditional camp and academic program established in 1990. Accredited by American Camping Association. Specific services available for the learning disabled.

The Gow School Summer Program

Program Focus Camping, academics, sports, arts, and weekend overnight trips. Offering a curriculum designed for students with language-based learning disabilities, including dyslexia, ADHD and ADD.
Academics English language/literature, academics (general), communications, computers, humanities, journalism, mathematics, music, reading, science (general), speech/debate, study skills, writing.
Arts Acting, arts and crafts (general), ceramics, chorus, creative writing, dance, drawing, fabric arts, film, graphic arts, jewelry making, leather working, music, musical productions, painting, photography, pottery, printmaking, television/video, theater/drama.
Special Interest Areas Leadership training.
Sports Aerobics, archery, baseball, basketball, bicycling, canoeing, climbing (wall), cross-country, equestrian sports, fishing, football, golf, gymnastics, horseback riding, in-line skating, lacrosse, rappelling, ropes course, soccer, softball, squash, street/roller hockey, swimming, tennis, track and field, volleyball, weight training, wrestling.
Wilderness/Outdoors Backpacking, bicycle trips, canoe trips, hiking, mountain biking, orienteering, rock climbing, white-water trips, wilderness camping.
Trips Day, overnight.
Program Information 1 session per year. Session length: 5 weeks in June, July. Ages: 8–16. 115–120 participants per session. Day program cost: $2850–$3900. Boarding program cost: $5700–$5975. Application fee: $50. Financial aid available.
Application Deadline Continuous.
Jobs Positions for college students 18 and older.

Contact Mr. Robert Garcia, Director of Admissions, 2491 Emery Road, PO Box 85, South Wales, New York 14139. Phone: 716-652-3450. Fax: 716-687-2003. E-mail: summer@gow.org.
URL www.gow.org

Special Note
The Gow School Summer Program was created for girls and boys who have experienced academic difficulties or have learning differences but possess the potential for success. The program is composed of a carefully considered balance between academics, traditional camp activities, and weekend overnight trips. In short, the program balances learning and fun. The Summer Program provides the camper-students with the academic growth they need and the fun that all kids deserve in the summer. The goal is for camper-students to go home at the end of the summer feeling confident, relaxed, and prepared for the coming school year. The Gow School is accredited by the New York State Association of Independent Schools.

For more information, see page 508.

iD TECH CAMPS–COLUMBIA UNIVERSITY, NEW YORK, NY

iD Tech Camps
Columbia University
New York, New York 10027

General Information Coed day academic program established in 1999. Accredited by American Camping Association. Formal opportunities for the academically talented and artistically talented.
Program Focus Students create 2D and 3D video games, build robots to compete, design websites, film and edit digital movies, create their own comic book with digital photos, learn programming and more. One computer per student and an average of five students per staff member. Campers take home a project at the end of the weeklong course.
Academics Web page design, academics (general), computer programming, computer science (Advanced Placement), computers, precollege program.
Arts Animation, cinematography, digital media, drawing, film, film editing, film production, graphic arts, photography, television/video.
Special Interest Areas Career exploration, computer game design, computer graphics, electronics, leadership training, robotics, team building.
Sports Baseball, basketball, soccer, softball, swimming, volleyball.
Trips College tours.
Program Information 5–9 sessions per year. Session length: 5–7 days in June, July, August. Ages: 7–17. 40–50 participants per session. Day program cost: $729. Financial aid available.
Application Deadline Continuous.
Jobs Positions for college students 18 and older.

Contact Client Service Representatives, 42 West Campbell Avenue, Suite 301, Campbell, California 95008. Phone: 888-709-TECH. Fax: 408-871-2228. E-mail: info@internaldrive.com. **URL** www.internaldrive.com

For more information, see page 520.

iD TECH CAMPS–FORDHAM UNIVERSITY, BRONX, NY

iD Tech Camps
Bronx, New York

General Information Coed residential and day academic program established in 1999. Accredited by American Camping Association. Formal opportunities for the academically talented and artistically talented. **Program Focus** Students create 2D and 3D video games, build robots to compete, design websites, film and edit digital movies, create their own comic book with digital photos, learn programming, and more. One computer per student and an average of five students per staff member. Campers take home a project at the end of the weeklong course. **Academics** Web page design, academics (general), computer programming, computer science (Advanced Placement), computers, precollege program. **Arts** Animation, cinematography, digital media, drawing, film, film editing, film production, graphic arts, photography, television/video. **Special Interest Areas** Career exploration, computer game design, computer graphics, electronics, leadership training, robotics, team building. **Sports** Baseball, basketball, soccer, softball, swimming, volleyball. **Trips** College tours. **Program Information** 5–9 sessions per year. Session length: 5–7 days in June, July, August. Ages: 7–17. 40–50 participants per session. Day program cost: $729. Boarding program cost: $1129. Financial aid available. **Application Deadline** Continuous. **Jobs** Positions for college students 18 and older. **Contact** Client Service Representatives, 42 West Campbell Avenue, Suite 301, Campbell, California 95008. Phone: 888-709-TECH. Fax: 408-871-2228. E-mail: info@internaldrive.com. **URL** www.internaldrive.com

For more information, see page 520.

iD TECH CAMPS–VASSAR COLLEGE, POUGHKEEPSIE, NY

iD Tech Camps
Vassar College
Poughkeepsie, New York 12604

General Information Coed residential and day academic program established in 1999. Accredited by American Camping Association. Formal opportunities for the academically talented and artistically talented. **Program Focus** Students create 2D and 3D video games, build robots to compete, design websites, film and edit digital movies, create their own comic book with digital photos, learn programming and more. One computer per student and an average of five students per staff member. Campers take home a project at the end of the weeklong course. **Academics** Web page design, academics (general), computer programming, computer science (Advanced Placement), computers, precollege program. **Arts** Animation, cartooning, cinematography, digital media, drawing, film, film editing, film production, graphic arts, photography, television/video. **Special Interest Areas** Career exploration, computer game design, computer graphics, electronics, leadership training, robotics, team building. **Sports** Baseball, basketball, soccer, softball, swimming, volleyball. **Trips** College tours. **Program Information** 5–9 sessions per year. Session length: 5–7 days in June, July, August. Ages: 7–17. 40–50 participants per session. Day program cost: $729. Boarding program cost: $1129. Financial aid available. **Application Deadline** Continuous. **Jobs** Positions for college students 18 and older. **Contact** Client Service Representatives, 42 West Campbell Avenue, Suite 301, Campbell, California 95008. Phone: 888-709-TECH. Fax: 408-871-2228. E-mail: info@internaldrive.com. **URL** www.internaldrive.com

For more information, see page 520.

ITHACA COLLEGE SUMMER COLLEGE FOR HIGH SCHOOL STUDENTS: MINICOURSES

Ithaca College Division of Continuing Education and Summer Sessions
Ithaca, New York 14850-7141

General Information Coed residential academic program established in 2002. Formal opportunities for the academically talented and artistically talented. College credit may be earned. **Program Focus** Students participate in noncredit college preparatory workshops. **Academics** English language/literature, biology, communications, government and politics, health sciences, humanities, journalism, philosophy, precollege program, psychology, science (general), social science, speech/debate, writing. **Arts** Acting, music (instrumental), photography, television/video, theater/drama.

Ithaca College Summer College for High School Students: Minicourses (continued)

Sports Climbing (wall), soccer, swimming, tennis, volleyball.
Wilderness/Outdoors Hiking.
Trips Day, shopping.
Program Information 2 sessions per year. Session length: 6 days in July. Ages: 15–18. 25–40 participants per session. Boarding program cost: $1100–$1200. Application fee: $25. Financial aid available.
Application Deadline May 1.
Jobs Positions for college students 18 and older.
Contact Mr. E. Kimball Milling, Director of Continuing Education and Summer Sessions, 120 Towers Concourse, Ithaca, New York 14850-7141. Phone: 607-274-3143. Fax: 607-274-1263. E-mail: cess@ithaca.edu.
URL www.ithaca.edu/summercollege

ITHACA COLLEGE SUMMER COLLEGE FOR HIGH SCHOOL STUDENTS: SESSION I

Ithaca College Division of Continuing Education and Summer Sessions
Ithaca, New York 14850-7141

General Information Coed residential academic program established in 1997. Formal opportunities for the academically talented. College credit may be earned.
Program Focus Participants earn three college credits.
Academics English language/literature, biology, communications, health sciences, humanities, precollege program, psychology, science (general), social science, social studies, writing.
Arts Acting, theater/drama.
Special Interest Areas Community service.
Sports Basketball, soccer, swimming, tennis.
Wilderness/Outdoors Hiking.
Trips Day, shopping.
Program Information 1 session per year. Session length: 20 days in July. Ages: 15–18. 40–60 participants per session. Boarding program cost: $3500–$3650. Application fee: $40. Financial aid available.
Application Deadline May 1.
Jobs Positions for college students 18 and older.
Contact Mr. E. Kimball Milling, Director of Continuing Education and Summer Sessions, 120 Towers Concourse, Ithaca, New York 14850-7141. Phone: 607-274-3143. Fax: 607-274-1263. E-mail: cess@ithaca.edu.
URL www.ithaca.edu/summercollege

ITHACA COLLEGE SUMMER COLLEGE FOR HIGH SCHOOL STUDENTS: SESSION II

Ithaca College Division of Continuing Education and Summer Sessions
Ithaca, New York 14850-7141

General Information Coed residential academic program established in 1998. Formal opportunities for the academically talented and artistically talented. College credit may be earned.

Program Focus Participants earn six freshman level college credits.
Academics English language/literature, communications, health sciences, humanities, journalism, philosophy, precollege program, psychology, science (general), social science, writing.
Arts Acting, film, musical productions, television/video, theater/drama.
Special Interest Areas Community service.
Sports Basketball, soccer, swimming, tennis.
Wilderness/Outdoors Hiking.
Trips Day, shopping.
Program Information 1 session per year. Session length: 34 days in June, July. Ages: 15–18. 25–40 participants per session. Boarding program cost: $6400–$6600. Application fee: $40. Financial aid available.
Application Deadline May 1.
Jobs Positions for college students 18 and older.
Contact Mr. E. Kimball Milling, Director of Continuing Education and Summer Sessions, 120 Towers Concourse, Ithaca, New York 14850-7141. Phone: 607-274-3143. Fax: 607-274-1263. E-mail: cess@ithaca.edu.
URL www.ithaca.edu/summercollege

ITHACA COLLEGE SUMMER PIANO INSTITUTE

Ithaca College Division of Continuing Education and Summer Sessions
Ithaca, New York 14850-7141

General Information Coed residential arts program established in 2000. Formal opportunities for the artistically talented.
Program Focus A comprehensive and intensive week and-a-half of varied musical experiences for young pianists.
Arts Music (ensemble), music (instrumental), music (piano), piano.
Trips Day.
Program Information 1 session per year. Session length: 10 days in July. Ages: 12–18. 30–40 participants per session. Boarding program cost: $1200–$1400. Application fee: $25. Financial aid available.
Application Deadline April 1.
Jobs Positions for college students 18 and older.

Contact Mr. E. Kimball Milling, Director of Continuing Education and Summer Sessions, 120 Towers Concourse, Ithaca, New York 14850-7141. Phone: 607-274-3143. Fax: 607-274-1263. E-mail: cess@ithaca.edu. **URL** www.ithaca.edu/cess

LANDMARK VOLUNTEERS: NEW YORK

Landmark Volunteers, Inc.
New York

General Information Coed residential outdoor program and community service program established in 1992. High school credit may be earned.
Program Focus High school students may earn community service credit while working as a team for two weeks serving Adirondack Mountain Club, Clearpool, Cooperstown, Adaptive Sports, Fort Ticonderoga, Pathfinder Village, Farmers' Museum, Santanoni, Mohonk Preserve, Wagon Road Camp, or Wilderstein Preservation. Similar programs offered through Landmark Volunteers at over 50 locations in 20 states.
Academics Area studies, ecology, environmental science, history, science (general), social science, social services.
Special Interest Areas Career exploration, community service, conservation projects, field research/expeditions, leadership training, nature study, team building, trail maintenance, work camp programs.
Sports Swimming.
Wilderness/Outdoors Hiking, wilderness camping.
Trips Cultural, day.
Program Information 10 sessions per year. Session length: 14–18 days in June, July, August. Ages: 14–18. 10–13 participants per session. Boarding program cost: $1250–$1300. Financial aid available.
Application Deadline Continuous.
Jobs Positions for college students.
Contact Ann Burrett, Executive Director, PO Box 455, Sheffield, Massachusetts 01257. Phone: 413-229-0255. Fax: 413-229-2050. E-mail: landmark@volunteers.com. **URL** www.volunteers.com

For more information, see page 542.

NATIONAL STUDENT LEADERSHIP CONFERENCE: ENTREPRENEURSHIP AND BUSINESS–NEW YORK CITY

National Student Leadership Conference
Fordham University
New York, New York

General Information Coed residential academic program established in 1989. Formal opportunities for the academically talented. College credit may be earned.
Program Focus Leadership, business and entrepreneurship, career exploration.
Academics Business.
Special Interest Areas Career exploration, leadership training, team building.
Trips College tours, cultural, shopping.
Program Information 1–4 sessions per year. Session length: 10 days in June, July, August. Ages: 14–18. 150 participants per session. Boarding program cost: $2295. Financial aid available.
Application Deadline Continuous.
Jobs Positions for college students 18 and older.
Contact Director of Admissions, 414 North Orleans Street, Suite LL8, Chicago, Illinois 60610-1087. Phone: 312-322-9999. Fax: 312-765-0081. E-mail: info@nslcleaders.org. **URL** www.nslcleaders.org

For more information, see page 564.

NATIONAL STUDENT LEADERSHIP CONFERENCE: INSIDE THE ARTS–NEW YORK CITY

National Student Leadership Conference
Fordham University
New York, New York

General Information Coed residential academic program and arts program established in 1989. Formal opportunities for the academically talented and artistically talented. College credit may be earned.
Program Focus Leadership training, exploring careers in the arts.
Academics Architecture, art history/appreciation.
Arts Arts, arts business.
Special Interest Areas Career exploration, leadership training, team building.
Trips College tours, cultural, shopping.
Program Information 1–4 sessions per year. Session length: 10 days in June, July, August. Ages: 14–18. 150 participants per session. Boarding program cost: $2295. Financial aid available.
Application Deadline Continuous.
Jobs Positions for college students 18 and older.
Contact Director of Admissions, 414 North Orleans Street, Suite LL8, Chicago, Illinois 60610-1087. Phone: 312-322-9999. Fax: 312-765-0081. E-mail: info@nslcleaders.org. **URL** www.nslcleaders.org

For more information, see page 564.

92ND STREET Y CAMPS–CAMP BARI TOV

92nd Street YM–YWHA
1395 Lexington Avenue
New York, New York 10128

General Information Coed day traditional camp and special needs program established in 1955. Religious affiliation: Jewish. Accredited by American Camping Association. Specific services available for the developmentally challenged.
Program Focus For children with developmental disabilities who require one-to-one supervision.
Arts Arts and crafts (general), music.
Special Interest Areas Campcraft, nature study.
Sports Swimming.
Trips Day.
Program Information 1 session per year. Session length: 39 days in June, July, August. Ages: 5–13. 15–20 participants per session. Financial aid available.
Application Deadline Continuous.
Jobs Positions for high school students 18 and older and college students.
Contact Steve Levin, Director of Camp Programs, main address above. Phone: 212-415-5600. Fax: 212-415-5668. E-mail: camps@92y.org.
URL www.92y.org/camps

92ND STREET Y CAMPS–CAMP TEVAH FOR SCIENCE AND NATURE

92nd Street YM–YWHA
New York

General Information Coed day traditional camp and outdoor program established in 1955. Religious affiliation: Jewish. Accredited by American Camping Association.
Program Focus Exploring science and nature.
Academics Science (general).
Arts Arts and crafts (general).
Special Interest Areas Campcraft, nature study.
Sports Archery, baseball, basketball, boating, climbing (wall), football, golf, in-line skating, martial arts, ropes course, soccer, softball, swimming, tennis, volleyball.
Trips Day.
Program Information 1 session per year. Session length: 30 days in June, July, August. Ages: 8–11. 35–45 participants per session. Day program cost: $4350. Financial aid available.
Application Deadline Continuous.
Jobs Positions for high school students 18 and older and college students.
Contact Steve Levin, Director of Camp Programs, 1395 Lexington Avenue, New York, New York 10128. Phone: 212-415-5573. Fax: 212-415-5668. E-mail: camps@92y.org.
URL www.92y.org/camps

92ND STREET Y CAMPS–CAMP TOVA

92nd Street YM–YWHA
New York

General Information Coed day traditional camp and special needs program established in 1955. Religious affiliation: Jewish. Accredited by American Camping Association. Specific services available for the emotionally challenged, developmentally challenged, and learning disabled.
Program Focus Designed to foster each child's emotional, social, and physical growth.
Arts Arts and crafts (general), music, painting, sculpture.
Special Interest Areas Campcraft, nature study.
Sports Archery, basketball, ropes course, soccer, softball, sports (general), swimming.
Program Information 1 session per year. Session length: 40 days in June, July, August. Ages: 6–13. 60–75 participants per session. Day program cost: $4800. Financial aid available.
Application Deadline Continuous.
Jobs Positions for high school students 18 and older and college students.
Contact Steve Levin, Director of Camp Programs, 1395 Lexington Avenue, New York, New York 10128. Phone: 212-415-5573. Fax: 212-415-5668. E-mail: camps@92y.org.
URL www.92y.org/camps

92ND STREET Y CAMPS–CAMP YAFFA FOR THE ARTS

92nd Street YM–YWHA
1395 Lexington Avenue
New York, New York 10128

General Information Coed day traditional camp and arts program established in 1955. Religious affiliation: Jewish. Accredited by American Camping Association. Formal opportunities for the artistically talented.
Program Focus Workshops in dance, visual arts, and drama; multidisciplinary performance and exhibition.
Arts Arts, arts and crafts (general), ceramics, chorus, dance, drawing, jewelry making, music, painting, performing arts, pottery, theater/drama.
Special Interest Areas Campcraft, model rocketry.
Sports Archery, baseball, basketball, boating, climbing (wall), football, golf, horseback riding, in-line skating, martial arts, ropes course, soccer, softball, swimming, tennis, volleyball.
Trips Day.
Program Information 1 session per year. Session length: 30 days in June, July, August. Ages: 8–11. 35–45 participants per session. Day program cost: $4000. Financial aid available.
Application Deadline Continuous.
Jobs Positions for high school students 18 and older and college students.

Contact Steven Levin, Director of Camp Programs, main address above. Phone: 212-415-5573. Fax: 212-415-5668. E-mail: camps@92y.org.
URL www.92y.org/camps

92ND STREET Y CAMPS–CAMP YOMI

92nd Street YM–YWHA
1395 Lexington Avenue
New York, New York 10128

General Information Coed day traditional camp established in 1955. Religious affiliation: Jewish. Accredited by American Camping Association.
Arts Animation, arts and crafts (general), ceramics, chorus, clowning, dance, drawing, film, jewelry making, music, painting, photography, pottery, sculpture, television/video, theater/drama
Special Interest Areas Campcraft, model rocketry, nature study.
Sports Archery, baseball, basketball, boating, football, golf, gymnastics, horseback riding, in-line skating, martial arts, ropes course, soccer, softball, swimming, tennis, volleyball.
Trips Overnight.
Program Information 2 sessions per year. Session length: 20–40 days in June, July, August. Ages: 5–9. 600–800 participants per session. Day program cost: $3000–$4800. Application fee: $50. Financial aid available. Open to participants entering grades K–4.
Application Deadline Continuous.
Jobs Positions for high school students 16 and older and college students.
Contact Steve Levin, Director of Camp Programs, main address above. Phone: 212-415-5573. Fax: 212-415-5668. E-mail: camps@92y.org.
URL www.campyomi.com

92ND STREET Y CAMPS–TRAILBLAZERS

92nd Street YM–YWHA
New York

General Information Coed travel traditional camp established in 1955. Religious affiliation: Jewish. Accredited by American Camping Association.
Program Focus Day-travel program where campers go on a diverse range of one-day trips to various destinations.

Arts Arts and crafts (general).
Special Interest Areas Campcraft, touring.
Sports Archery, baseball, basketball, boating, football, in-line skating, ropes course, soccer, softball, swimming, tennis, volleyball.
Wilderness/Outdoors Bicycle trips, rafting, rock climbing.
Trips Day, overnight.
Program Information 2 sessions per year. Session length: 20–40 days in June, July, August. Ages: 12–14. 60–90 participants per session. Cost: $3300–$4900. Financial aid available. Open to participants entering grades 7–9.
Application Deadline Continuous.
Jobs Positions for college students 19 and older.
Contact Steve Levin, Director of Camp Programs, 1395 Lexington Avenue, New York, New York 10128. Phone: 212-415-5573. Fax: 212-415-5668. E-mail: camps@92y.org.
URL www.92y.org/camps

PRATT INSTITUTE SUMMER PRE-COLLEGE PROGRAM FOR HIGH SCHOOL STUDENTS

Pratt Institute
200 Willoughby Avenue
ISC Building, Room 205
Brooklyn, New York 11205

General Information Coed residential and day academic program and arts program. Formal opportunities for the academically talented and artistically talented. College credit may be earned.

Pratt Institute Summer Pre-College Program for High School Students

Program Focus The development of a portfolio and academic skills in art, design, and architecture.
Academics Architecture, art (Advanced Placement), art

Pratt Institute Summer Pre-College Program for High School Students (continued)

history/appreciation, intercultural studies, precollege program, writing.

Arts Arts, arts and crafts (general), creative writing, design, fabric arts, fashion design/production, film, graphic arts, illustration, photography, sculpture.

Special Interest Areas Career exploration, industrial arts.

Trips Cultural, day, shopping.

Program Information 1 session per year. Session length: 25 days in July, August. Ages: 16–18. 300–400 participants per session. Day program cost: $2345. Boarding program cost: $3635. Application fee: $25. Tuition scholarship available by competitive application.

Application Deadline April 30.

Contact Ms. Johndell Wilson, Program Assistant, main address above. Phone: 718-636-3453. Fax: 718-399-4410. E-mail: precollege@pratt.edu.

URL www.pratt.edu/ccps-precollege

For more information, see page 594.

SARAH LAWRENCE COLLEGE SUMMER HIGH SCHOOL PROGRAMS

Sarah Lawrence College
1 Mead Way
Bronxville, New York 10708

General Information Coed residential and day academic program and arts program established in 2005.

Sarah Lawrence College Summer High School Programs

Academics History, writing.

Arts Acting, creative writing, drawing, film, music, painting, screenwriting, sculpture, theater/drama.

Trips College tours, day.

Program Information 6–8 sessions per year. Session

length: 6–42 days in June, July, August. Ages: 15–18. 12–15 participants per session. Day program cost: $425–$2150. Boarding program cost: $4950–$7750. Application fee: $25.

Application Deadline Continuous.

Contact Liz Irmiter, Director of Special Programs, main address above. Phone: 914-395-2693. Fax: 914-395-2694. E-mail: specialprograms@sarahlawrence.edu.

URL www.sarahlawrence.edu/highschool

For more information, see page 622.

SKIDMORE COLLEGE–PRE-COLLEGE PROGRAM IN THE LIBERAL & STUDIO ARTS FOR HIGH SCHOOL STUDENTS

Skidmore College
815 North Broadway
Saratoga Springs, New York 12866

General Information Coed residential and day academic program and arts program established in 1978. Formal opportunities for the academically talented and artistically talented. High school or college credit may be earned.

Skidmore College–Pre-College Program in the Liberal & Studio Arts for High School Students

Program Focus College credit-bearing courses offered in the liberal and studio arts.

Academics American literature, English language/literature, French language/literature, Spanish language/literature, academics (general), anthropology, archaeology, area studies, art (Advanced Placement), biology, business, chemistry, ecology, economics, environmental science, geology/earth science, government and politics, history, humanities, intercultural studies, mathematics, music, oceanography, philosophy, physics, precollege program, psychology, religion, science (general), social science, writing.

Arts Arts and crafts (general), ceramics, creative writing, drawing, fabric arts, film, graphic arts, music, painting, photography, pottery, sculpture, studio arts, television/video, weaving.

Special Interest Areas Career exploration, college planning, field trips (arts and culture).

Sports Basketball, cross-country, diving, equestrian sports, horseback riding, racquetball, soccer, softball, sports (general), squash, swimming, tennis, volleyball, weight training.

Wilderness/Outdoors Hiking.

Trips Cultural, day.

Program Information 1 session per year. Session length: 37 days in July, August. Ages: 16+. 110–120 participants per session. Day program cost: $1380–$3680. Boarding program cost: $4800–$5600. Application fee: $30. Financial aid available.

Application Deadline Continuous.

Jobs Positions for college students 19 and older.

Contact Dr. James Chansky, Director of Summer Special Programs, main address above. Phone: 518-580-5590. Fax: 518-580-5548. E-mail: jchansky@skidmore.edu.

URL www.skidmore.edu/summer

For more information, see page 632.

STAGEDOOR MANOR PERFORMING ARTS TRAINING CENTER/THEATRE AND DANCE CAMP

116 Karmel Road
Loch Sheldrake, New York 12759-5308

General Information Coed residential arts program established in 1975. Formal opportunities for the artistically talented and gifted. High school credit may be earned.

Stagedoor Manor Performing Arts Training Center/Theatre and Dance Camp

Program Focus Theater, dance, voice, television, film, and modeling.

Academics Music, precollege program, speech/debate, writing.

Arts Acting, arts and crafts (general), batiking, chorus, creative writing, dance, dance (ballet), dance (folk), dance (jazz), dance (modern), dance (tap), film, film production, mime, modeling, music, music (vocal), musical productions, performing arts, television/video, theater/drama, voice and speech.

Special Interest Areas Career exploration.

Sports Aerobics, basketball, soccer, softball, swimming, tennis, volleyball.

Trips Day.

Program Information 3 sessions per year. Session length: 3–9 weeks in June, July, August. Ages: 10–18. 245 participants per session. Boarding program cost: $4295–$9595.

Application Deadline Continuous.

Jobs Positions for college students 21 and older.

Summer Contact Barbara Martin, Director, main address above. Phone: 888-STAGE 88. Fax: 888-STAGE 88.

Winter Contact Barbara Martin, Director, 3658 Churchville Avenue, Churchville, Virginia 24421. Phone: 888-STAGE 88. Fax: 888-STAGE 88. E-mail: stagedoormanor@aol.com.

URL www.stagedoormanor.com

For more information, see page 646.

SUMMER@RENSSELAER

Rensselaer Polytechnic Institute–Outreach
Programs
110 8th Street
Troy, New York 12180

General Information Coed residential and day
academic program, outdoor program, arts program, and
sports camp. Formal opportunities for the academically
talented and artistically talented. College credit may be
earned.

Summer@Rensselaer

Academics American literature, academics (general),
aerospace science, architecture, art (Advanced
Placement), art history/appreciation, biology, chemistry,
communications, computer programming, computer
science (Advanced Placement), computers, ecology,
economics, engineering, environmental science,
geography, geology/earth science, humanities,
mathematics, physics, precollege program, psychology,
science (general).

Arts Acting, animation, arts and crafts (general), dance,
drawing, film, graphic arts, music, painting, television/
video, theater/drama.
Special Interest Areas Career exploration, college
planning, computer game design, electronics, field
research/expeditions, model rocketry, nature study,
navigation, robotics.
Sports Football, ice hockey.
Trips Day.
Program Information 1–3 sessions per year. Session
length: 5–258 days in May, June, July, August. Ages:
8–18.
Application Deadline Continuous.
Jobs Positions for college students.
Contact Mr. Michael L. Gunther, Program Manager for
Recruitment, 110 8th Street, CII Low Center, Suite
4011, Troy, New York 12180-3590. Phone: 518-276-8351.
Fax: 518-276-8738. E-mail: gunthm@rpi.edu.
URL summer.rpi.edu

For more information, see page 606.

THE SUMMER INSTITUTE FOR THE GIFTED AT MANHATTANVILLE COLLEGE

Summer Institute for the Gifted
Manhattanville College
Purchase, New York 10577

General Information Coed day academic program.
Formal opportunities for the academically talented and
gifted.
Academics American literature, English language/
literature, French (Advanced Placement), SAT/ACT
preparation, Spanish language/literature, academics
(general), aerospace science, archaeology, architecture,
art (Advanced Placement), art history/appreciation,
biology, botany, business, chemistry, classical languages/
literatures, communications, computers, engineering,
geology/earth science, government and politics, history,
humanities, marine studies, mathematics, music,

oceanography, philosophy, physics, precollege program, social studies, study skills, writing.
Arts Arts and crafts (general), creative writing, dance, drawing, graphic arts, music, music (chamber), music (classical), music (ensemble), music (instrumental), musical productions, painting, sculpture, theater/drama, weaving.
Special Interest Areas Animal care, chess, electronics, model rocketry, robotics.
Sports Aerobics, baseball, basketball, field hockey, football, lacrosse, martial arts, soccer, softball, squash, swimming, tennis, volleyball.
Program Information 1 session per year. Session length: 3 weeks in June, July. Ages: 6–11. 150–250 participants per session. Day program cost: $1825–$2000. Application fee: $75. Financial aid available.
Application Deadline May 14.
Jobs Positions for college students 19 and older.
Contact Ms. Barbara Swicord, Director, River Plaza, 9 West Broad Street, Stamford, Connecticut 06902-3788. Phone: 866-303-4744. Fax: 203-399-5598. E-mail: sig.info@aifs.com.
URL www.giftedstudy.com
For more information, see page 654.

THE SUMMER INSTITUTE FOR THE GIFTED AT VASSAR COLLEGE

Summer Institute for the Gifted
Vassar College
Poughkeepsie, New York 12603

General Information Coed residential academic program established in 1992. Formal opportunities for the academically talented and gifted. College credit may be earned.
Academics American literature, English language/literature, French language/literature, SAT/ACT preparation, Spanish language/literature, academics (general), aerospace science, archaeology, architecture, art history/appreciation, astronomy, biology, business, chemistry, classical languages/literatures, communications, computers, engineering, environmental science, government and politics, history, marine studies, mathematics, music, oceanography, philosophy, physics, physiology, precollege program, psychology, science (general), social studies, speech/debate, study skills, writing.
Arts Band, ceramics, chorus, creative writing, dance,

drawing, film, graphic arts, music, music (chamber), music (classical), music (ensemble), music (instrumental), musical productions, painting, photography, sculpture, television/video, theater/drama.
Special Interest Areas Animal care, electronics, meditation, robotics.
Sports Baseball, basketball, fencing, field hockey, football, lacrosse, martial arts, soccer, squash, swimming, tennis, track and field, volleyball.
Trips Cultural.
Program Information 1–2 sessions per year. Session length: 3 weeks in June, July, August. Ages: 8–17. 150–250 participants per session. Boarding program cost: $3700–$4200. Application fee: $75. Financial aid available.
Application Deadline May 14.
Jobs Positions for college students 19 and older.
Contact Ms. Barbara Swicord, Director, River Plaza, 9 West Broad Street, Stamford, Connecticut 06902-3788. Phone: 866-303-4744. Fax: 203-399-5598. E-mail: sig.info@aifs.com.
URL www.giftedstudy.com
For more information, see page 654.

SUMMER THEATRE INSTITUTE–NYC, 2008

Summer Theatre Institute New York City
New York, New York

General Information Coed residential arts program established in 1989. Formal opportunities for the artistically talented.

Summer Theatre Institute–NYC, 2008

Program Focus Professional theater training program for teens.
Academics Communications, music.
Arts Acting, chorus, clowning, creative writing, dance, dance (ballet), dance (jazz), dance (modern), dance (tap), directing, mime, music (vocal), musical productions, musical theater, performing arts, playwriting, puppetry, stage movement, theater/drama, voice and speech.

Summer Theatre Institute–NYC, 2008 (continued)

Special Interest Areas Career exploration, team building.
Trips Cultural, day, shopping.
Program Information 1 session per year. Session length: 27 days in June, July. Ages: 14+. 25–32 participants per session. Boarding program cost: $5100–$5500. Application fee: $60. Financial aid available. Discounts available if enrolled before May 20.
Application Deadline June 15.
Jobs Positions for college students 22 and older.
Contact Ms. Allyn Sitjar, Artistic Director, 23 Tomahawk Trail, Sparta, New Jersey 07871. Phone: 201-415-5329. Fax: 973-726-8926. E-mail: youththeatreallyn@yahoo.com.
URL www.youththeatreinstitutes.org

For more information, see page 660.

Syracuse University Summer College

Syracuse University
111 Waverly Avenue
Suite 240
Syracuse, New York 13244-1270

General Information Coed residential academic program and arts program established in 1961. Formal opportunities for the academically talented and artistically talented. College credit may be earned.
Program Focus General academic, earn college credits.
Academics American literature, English language/literature, academics (general), aerospace science, anthropology, architecture, art history/appreciation, biology, business, chemistry, communications, computer programming, computers, economics, engineering, environmental science, forensic science, geography, geology/earth science, government and politics, history, humanities, journalism, law, mathematics, philosophy, physics, precollege program, psychology, reading, religion, science (general), social science, social studies, speech/debate, study skills, writing.
Arts Acting, chorus, dance, dance (ballet), dance (folk), dance (jazz), dance (modern), dance (tap), drawing, fabric arts, fashion design/production, graphic arts, music, music (vocal), musical productions, painting, printmaking, radio broadcasting, sculpture, stage managing, television/video, theater/drama, weaving.
Special Interest Areas Career exploration, college planning, community service, field research/expeditions, leadership training, model rocketry, robotics.
Sports Aerobics, basketball, racquetball, soccer, softball, sports (general), squash, swimming, tennis, volleyball, weight training.
Wilderness/Outdoors Hiking.

Syracuse University Summer College

Trips College tours, cultural, day, shopping.
Program Information 1 session per year. Session length: 6 weeks in July, August. Ages: 14–18. 175–225 participants per session. Boarding program cost: $5800–$6245. Application fee: $50. Financial aid available. Non-credit program costs range from $750 for 1-week music workshop to $1400 for 2-week art studio.
Application Deadline May 15.
Contact Dr. Anne Shelly, Executive Director, main address above. Phone: 315-443-5297. Fax: 315-443-3976. E-mail: sumcoll@syr.edu.
URL www.summercollege.syr.edu/

For more information, see page 662.

TISCH SCHOOL OF THE ARTS–SUMMER HIGH SCHOOL PROGRAMS

New York University, Tisch School of the Arts
721 Broadway
New York, New York 10003

General Information Coed residential academic program and arts program established in 2001. Formal opportunities for the academically talented and artistically talented. College credit may be earned.

Tisch School of the Arts–Summer High School Programs

Program Focus College-level training in the performing and media arts.
Academics Classical languages/literatures, communications, precollege program, writing.
Arts Acting, animation, creative writing, dance, dance (jazz), dance (modern), dance (tap), drawing, film, music (vocal), musical productions, musical theater, performing arts, photography, television/video, theater/drama.
Trips Cultural, day.
Program Information 1 session per year. Session length: 28–30 days in July, August. Ages: 15+. 8–20 participants per session. Boarding program cost: $7900–$9200. Application fee: $60. Financial aid available. Open to participants entering grade 12.
Application Deadline February 1.

Contact Mariangela Lardaro, Assistant Director of Recruitment, main address above. Phone: 212-998-1517. Fax: 212-995-4578. E-mail: tisch.special.info@nyu.edu. **URL** specialprograms.tisch.nyu.edu
For more information, see page 566.

NORTH CAROLINA

ASHEVILLE SCHOOL'S SUMMER ACADEMIC ADVENTURES

Asheville School
360 Asheville School Road
Asheville, North Carolina 28806

General Information Coed residential academic program, outdoor program, and community service program established in 1982. Formal opportunities for the academically talented and artistically talented.
Program Focus Academic enrichment and English as a second language.
Academics American literature, English as a second language, English language/literature, academics (general), architecture, area studies, art, art history/appreciation, biology, botany, chemistry, computer programming, computers, ecology, economics, environmental science, government and politics, history, humanities, intercultural studies, journalism, mathematics, philosophy, physics, psychology, reading, science (general), social science, social studies, speech/debate, study skills, writing.
Arts Acting, arts and crafts (general), creative writing, drawing, film, graphic arts, painting, pottery, studio arts, theater/drama.
Special Interest Areas Campcraft, community service, conservation projects, field research/expeditions, field trips (arts and culture), leadership training, nature study, robotics, team building.

Asheville School's Summer Academic Adventures (continued)

Sports Basketball, bicycling, climbing (wall), kayaking, rappelling, ropes course, soccer, swimming, tennis, volleyball, water polo, weight training.

Wilderness/Outdoors Backpacking, canoe trips, caving, hiking, mountain biking, mountaineering, orienteering, rafting, rock climbing, survival training, white-water trips, wilderness camping.

Trips College tours, cultural, day, overnight.

Program Information 2 sessions per year. Session length: 3–6 weeks in June, July. Ages: 11–17. 70 participants per session. Boarding program cost: $3150–$6000. Application fee: $30. Financial aid available. Open to participants entering grades 6–10.

Application Deadline Continuous.

Asheville School's Summer Academic Adventures

Jobs Positions for college students 18 and older.

Contact Ms. Emily Johns, Director, main address above. Phone: 828-254-6345. Fax: 828-210-6109. E-mail: saa@ashevilleschool.org.

URL www.ashevilleschool.org

For more information, see page 420.

CONSTRUCTING YOUR COLLEGE EXPERIENCE

Duke Youth Programs–Duke University Continuing Studies
Duke University
Durham, North Carolina 27708

General Information Coed residential and day academic program established in 1998.

Constructing Your College Experience

Program Focus Exploration of the college selection process and navigation of the college admissions process.

Academics SAT/ACT preparation, writing.

Special Interest Areas Career exploration, college planning, leadership training.

Trips College tours, day.

Program Information 1 session per year. Session length: 1 week in July, August. Ages: 16–17. 50–65 participants per session. Day program cost: $900–$1000. Boarding program cost: $1150–$1200. Financial aid available.

Application Deadline Continuous.

Jobs Positions for college students 18 and older.

Contact Youth Program Director, 203 Bishop's House, Box 90702, Durham, North Carolina 27708. Phone: 919-684-6259. Fax: 919-681-8235. E-mail: youth@duke.edu.
URL www.learnmore.duke.edu/youth
For more information, see page 470.

CYBERCAMPS–DUKE UNIVERSITY

Cybercamps–Giant Campus, Inc.
Durham, North Carolina

General Information Coed residential and day academic program established in 2004. Formal opportunities for the academically talented.
Program Focus Computers and technology.
Academics Web page design, academics (general), computer programming, computer science (Advanced Placement), computers.
Arts Animation, digital media, film, graphic arts, musical productions, photography, television/video.
Special Interest Areas Computer game design, computer graphics, electronics, robotics, team building.
Program Information 1–12 sessions per year. Session length: 5 days in June, July, August. Ages: 7–18. 30–50 participants per session. Day program cost: $599–$749. Boarding program cost: $998–$1148.
Application Deadline Continuous.
Jobs Positions for high school students 17 and older and college students 18 and older.
Contact Camp Consultant, 3101 Western Avenue, Suite 100, Seattle, Washington 98121. Phone: 888-904-2267. Fax: 206-442-4501. E-mail: info@cybercamps.com.
URL www.cybercamps.com
For more information, see page 466.

CYBERCAMPS–UNC, CHAPEL HILL

Cybercamps–Giant Campus, Inc.
Chapel Hill, North Carolina

General Information Coed residential and day academic program established in 1997. Formal opportunities for the academically talented.
Program Focus Computers and technology.
Academics Web page design, academics (general), computer programming, computer science (Advanced Placement), computers.
Arts Animation, digital media, film, graphic arts, musical productions, photography, television/video.
Special Interest Areas Computer game design, computer graphics, electronics, robotics, team building.
Program Information 1–12 sessions per year. Session length: 5 days in June, July, August. Ages: 7–18. 30–50 participants per session. Day program cost: $599–$749. Boarding program cost: $998–$1148.
Application Deadline Continuous.
Jobs Positions for high school students 17 and older and college students 18 and older.

Contact Camp Consultant, 3101 Western Avenue, Suite 100, Seattle, Washington 98121. Phone: 888-904-2267. Fax: 206-442-4501. E-mail: info@cybercamps.com.
URL www.cybercamps.com
For more information, see page 466.

DUKE ACTION: SCIENCE CAMP FOR YOUNG WOMEN

Duke Youth Programs–Duke University
Continuing Studies
Duke University
Durham, North Carolina 27708

General Information Girls' residential and day academic program established in 1991.
Program Focus Scientific discovery through field and laboratory experiences.
Academics Biology, botany, chemistry, ecology, environmental science, geology/earth science, health sciences, science (general).
Wilderness/Outdoors Canoe trips, hiking.
Trips Cultural, day.
Program Information 1 session per year. Session length: 12 days in June, July. Ages: 10–13. 40–60 participants per session. Day program cost: $865–$875. Boarding program cost: $1655–$1700. Financial aid available.
Application Deadline Continuous.
Jobs Positions for college students 18 and older.
Contact Youth Program Director, 203 Bishop's House, Box 90702, Durham, North Carolina 27708. Phone: 919-684-6259. Fax: 919-681-8235. E-mail: youth@duke.edu.
URL www.learnmore.duke.edu/youth
For more information, see page 470.

DUKE CREATIVE WRITERS' WORKSHOP

Duke Youth Programs–Duke University
Continuing Studies
Duke University
Durham, North Carolina 27708

General Information Coed residential and day academic program established in 1993. Formal opportunities for the academically talented and artistically talented.

Duke Creative Writers' Workshop (continued)

Program Focus Creative writing in all genres for advanced writers.
Academics Writing.
Arts Creative writing.
Special Interest Areas Field trips (arts and culture).
Trips Cultural, day.
Program Information 1 session per year. Session length: 12 days in July. Ages: 15–17. 38–48 participants per session. Day program cost: $1025. Boarding program cost: $1565–$1600. Financial aid available.
Application Deadline Continuous.
Jobs Positions for college students 18 and older.
Contact Youth Program Director, 203 Bishop's House, Box 90702, Durham, North Carolina 27708. Phone: 919-684-6259. Fax: 919-681 8235. E-mail: youth@duke.edu.
URL www.learnmore.duke.edu/youth

For more information, see page 470.

DUKE DRAMA WORKSHOP

Duke Youth Programs–Duke University
Continuing Studies
Duke University
Durham, North Carolina 27708

General Information Coed residential and day arts program established in 1996. Formal opportunities for the academically talented and artistically talented.
Program Focus Intense experience in acting and other aspects of theater.
Arts Acting, dance, music (vocal), musical productions, theater/drama.
Special Interest Areas Field trips (arts and culture).
Trips Cultural, day.
Program Information 1 session per year. Session length: 12 days in July. Ages: 15–17. 36–50 participants per session. Day program cost: $1025. Boarding program cost: $1565–$1600. Financial aid available.
Application Deadline Continuous.
Jobs Positions for college students 18 and older.
Contact Program Director, 203 Bishop's House, Box 90702, Durham, North Carolina 27708. Phone: 919-684-6259. Fax: 919-681-8235. E-mail: youth@duke.edu.
URL www.learnmore.duke.edu/youth

For more information, see page 470.

DUKE TIP INSTITUTES

Duke University Talent Identification
Program (Duke TIP)
Duke University
Durham, North Carolina

General Information Coed residential academic program. Formal opportunities for the academically talented.
Program Focus Institutes include: International Affairs, Great Debates, and Leadership.
Academics Academics (general).

Special Interest Areas Community service, leadership training, team building.
Trips College tours, cultural, day.
Program Information 3 sessions per year. Session length: 14–16 days in June, July. Ages: 14–18. 28–34 participants per session. Boarding program cost: $2500–$3200. Application fee: $35.
Application Deadline March 23.
Jobs Positions for college students 21 and older.
Contact Dr. Nicki Charles, Coordinator of Educational Programs, Duke TIP, 1121 West Main Street, Durham, North Carolina 27701. Phone: 919-681-6519. Fax: 919-681-7921.
URL www.tip.duke.edu

For more information, see page 468.

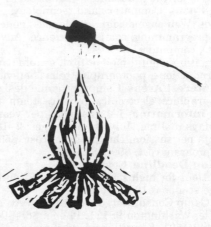

DUKE UNIVERSITY PRECOLLEGE PROGRAM

Duke University Talent Identification
Program (Duke TIP)
Duke University West Campus
Durham, North Carolina 27708

General Information Coed residential academic program. Formal opportunities for the academically talented. College credit may be earned.
Program Focus Participants enroll in Duke University summer courses for credit.
Academics American literature, Chinese languages/literature, English language/literature, Japanese language/literature, Spanish language/literature, academics (general), anthropology, architecture, art history/appreciation, astronomy, biology, business, chemistry, classical languages/literatures, computer programming, computer science (Advanced Placement), ecology, economics, geology/earth science, government and politics, history, humanities, intercultural studies, journalism, mathematics, philosophy, physics, precollege program, psychology, religion, social science, speech/debate.
Arts Creative writing.
Special Interest Areas Career exploration, college planning, community service, team building.
Trips College tours, cultural, day, shopping.
Program Information 1 session per year. Session length: 6 weeks in July, August. Ages: 16–18. 50–100

participants per session. Boarding program cost: $7000. Application fee: $35.
Application Deadline Continuous.

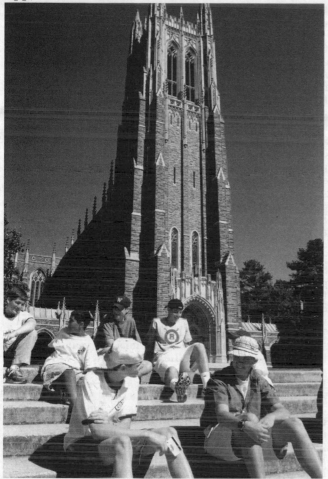

Duke University PreCollege Program

Jobs Positions for college students 21 and older.
Contact Brian Denton, Coordinator of Educational Programs, 1121 West Main Street, Durham, North Carolina 27701. Phone: 919-668-9100. Fax: 919-681-7921.
URL www.tip.duke.edu

For more information, see page 468.

DUKE YOUNG WRITERS CAMP

Duke Youth Programs–Duke University
Continuing Studies
Duke University
Durham, North Carolina 27708

General Information Coed residential and day academic program established in 1983. Formal opportunities for the academically talented and artistically talented.
Program Focus The development of creative and analytical processes of writing.

Academics Communications, journalism, strategy games, writing.
Arts Acting, arts and crafts (general), creative writing, dance, theater/drama.
Special Interest Areas Community service.
Sports Basketball, soccer, sports (general), tennis, volleyball.
Trips Cultural.
Program Information 3 sessions per year. Session length: 11–12 days in June, July. Ages: 12–17. 140–160 participants per session. Day program cost: $775–$800. Boarding program cost: $1565–$1600. Financial aid available.
Application Deadline Continuous.
Jobs Positions for college students 18 and older.
Contact Youth Program Director, 203 Bishop's House, Box 90702, Durham, North Carolina 27708. Phone: 919-684-6259. Fax: 919-681-8235. E-mail: youth@duke.edu.
URL www.learnmore.duke.edu/youth

For more information, see page 470.

EXPRESSIONS! DUKE FINE ARTS CAMP

Duke Youth Programs–Duke University
Continuing Studies
Duke University
Durham, North Carolina 27708

General Information Coed residential and day arts program established in 1995. Formal opportunities for the artistically talented.
Program Focus A fine arts experience that explores: dance, drama, visual art, and musical theatre.
Arts Acting, arts, arts and crafts (general), dance, drawing, fabric arts, music (vocal), musical productions, painting, performing arts, sculpture, theater/drama.
Program Information 1 session per year. Session length: 10 days in June. Ages: 10–13. 40 participants per session. Day program cost: $825–$850. Boarding program cost: $1565–$1600. Financial aid available.
Application Deadline Continuous.
Jobs Positions for college students 18 and older.
Contact Youth Program Director, 203 Bishop's House, Box 90702, Durham, North Carolina 27708. Phone: 919-684-6259. Fax: 919-681-8235. E-mail: youth@duke.edu.
URL www.learnmore.duke.edu/youth

For more information, see page 470.

iD Tech Camps–University of North Carolina at Chapel Hill, Chapel Hill, NC

iD Tech Camps
University of North Carolina at Chapel Hill
Chapel Hill, North Carolina 27599

General Information Coed residential and day academic program established in 1999. Accredited by American Camping Association. Formal opportunities for the academically talented and artistically talented.
Program Focus Students create 2D and 3D video games, build robots to compete, design websites, film and edit digital movies, create their own comic book with digital photos, learn programming and more. One computer per student and an average of five students per staff member. Campers take home a project at the end of the weeklong course.
Academics Web page design, academics (general), computer programming, computer science (Advanced Placement), computers, precollege program.
Arts Animation, cinematography, digital media, drawing, film, film editing, film production, graphic arts, photography, television/video.
Special Interest Areas Career exploration, computer game design, computer graphics, electronics, leadership training, robotics, team building.
Sports Baseball, basketball, soccer, softball, swimming, volleyball.
Trips College tours.
Program Information 5–9 sessions per year. Session length: 6–7 days in June, July, August. Ages: 7–17. 40–50 participants per session. Day program cost: $729. Boarding program cost: $1129. Financial aid available.
Application Deadline Continuous.
Jobs Positions for college students 18 and older.
Contact Client Service Representatives, 42 West Campbell Avenue, Suite 301, Campbell, California 95008. Phone: 888-709-TECH. Fax: 408-871-2228. E-mail: info@internaldrive.com
URL www.internaldrive.com

For more information, see page 520.

iD Tech Camps–Wake Forest University, Winston-Salem, NC

iD Tech Camps
Winston-Salem, North Carolina

General Information Coed residential and day academic program established in 1999. Accredited by American Camping Association. Formal opportunities for the academically talented and artistically talented.
Program Focus Students create 2D and 3D video games, build robots to compete, design websites, film and edit digital movies, create their own comic book with digital photos, learn programming, and more. One computer per student and an average of five students per staff member. Campers take home a project at the end of the weeklong course.
Academics Web page design, academics (general), computer programming, computer science (Advanced Placement), computers, precollege program.
Arts Animation, cinematography, digital media, drawing, film, film editing, film production, graphic arts, photography, television/video.
Special Interest Areas Career exploration, computer game design, computer graphics, electronics, leadership training, robotics, team building.
Sports Baseball, basketball, soccer, softball, swimming, volleyball.
Trips College tours.
Program Information 5–9 sessions per year. Session length: 5–7 days in June, July, August. Ages: 7–17. 40–50 participants per session. Day program cost: $729. Boarding program cost: $1127. Financial aid available.
Application Deadline Continuous.
Jobs Positions for college students 18 and older.
Contact Client Service Representatives, 42 West Campbell Avenue, Suite 301, Campbell, California 95008. Phone: 888-709-TECH. Fax: 408-871-2228. E-mail: info@internaldrive.com
URL www.internaldrive.com

For more information, see page 520.

SALEM SPOTLIGHT

Salem Academy and College
Winston-Salem, North Carolina 27108-0578

General Information Girls' residential academic program and arts program established in 2005.

Salem Spotlight

Academics American literature, English language/literature, Spanish language/literature, academics (general), area studies, art history/appreciation, business, chemistry, economics, forensic science, history, humanities, journalism, peace education, psychology, reading, science (general), social science, social studies, writing.
Arts Acting, arts, arts and crafts (general), creative writing, drawing, graphic arts, musical productions, painting, photography, studio arts, theater/drama.
Special Interest Areas Leadership training.
Sports Swimming.
Trips Cultural, day, shopping.
Program Information 2 sessions per year. Session length: 13 days in July. Ages: 13–18. 50–100 participants per session. Boarding program cost: $2395.
Application Deadline Continuous.
Contact Douglas Murphy, Executive Director, PO Box 10578, Winston-Salem, North Carolina 27108-1753. Phone: 800-883-1753. E-mail: spotlight@salem.edu.
URL spotlight.salem.edu

For more information, see page 618.

TALISMAN SUMMER CAMP

Talisman Summer Programs
64 Gap Creek Road
Zirconia, North Carolina 28790

General Information Coed residential traditional camp, academic program, outdoor program, and special needs program established in 1980. Accredited by American Camping Association. Specific services available for the emotionally challenged, learning disabled, and participant with AD/HD.
Program Focus Self-esteem and decision-making skills.

Academics Academics (general).
Arts Arts and crafts (general), music, theater/drama.
Special Interest Areas Native American culture, campcraft, leadership training, nature study, team building.
Sports Canoeing, climbing (wall), fishing, rappelling, ropes course, sailing, swimming.
Wilderness/Outdoors Backpacking, canoe trips, hiking, orienteering, rafting, rock climbing, wilderness camping.
Trips Day, overnight.
Program Information 3 sessions per year. Session length: 2–3 weeks in June, July, August. Ages: 8–17. 100 participants per session. Boarding program cost: $1400–$4100.
Application Deadline Continuous.
Jobs Positions for high school students 16 and older and college students 18 and older.
Summer Contact Ms. Linda Tatsapaugh, Director, main address above. Phone: 888-458-8226. Fax: 828-697-6249. E-mail: summer@talismancamps.com.
Winter Contact Ms. Linda Tatsapaugh, Director, 64 Gap Creek Road, Zirconia, North Carolina 28790. Phone: 888-458-8226. Fax: 828-697-6249. E-mail: summer@talismancamps.com.
URL www.talismancamps.com

OHIO

THE GRAND RIVER SUMMER ACADEMY

The Grand River Academy
3042 College Street
Austinburg, Ohio 44010

General Information Coed residential and day academic program established in 1990. High school credit may be earned.

The Grand River Summer Academy

The Grand River Summer Academy (continued)

Program Focus Remedial and advanced academics with full afternoon activity program and Ohio Graduation Test prep.

Academics English as a second language, English language/literature, French language/literature, SAT/ACT preparation, Spanish language/literature, academics (general), art history/appreciation, biology, chemistry, computers, economics, environmental science, geography, geology/earth science, government and politics, health sciences, history, journalism, mathematics, physics, reading, science (general), social science, social studies, study skills, typing, writing.

Arts Arts and crafts (general), ceramics, creative writing, drawing, film, painting, photography, pottery, printmaking, sculpture.

Special Interest Areas Community service, driver's education, field trips (arts and culture).

Sports Baseball, basketball, bicycling, canoeing, cross-country, equestrian sports, fishing, football, golf, horseback riding, in-line skating, kayaking, paintball, soccer, softball, sports (general), swimming, tennis, volleyball, weight training.

Wilderness/Outdoors Bicycle trips, canoe trips, hiking, wilderness camping.

Trips Cultural, day.

Program Information 1 session per year. Session length: 30 days in June, July, August. Ages: 13–19. 80–100 participants per session. Day program cost: $1200. Boarding program cost: $3300–$3500. Application fee: $25. Open to participants entering grades 9–12.

Application Deadline Continuous.

Jobs Positions for college students 18 and older.

Contact Sam Corabi, Director of Admission, main address above. Phone: 440-275-2811 Ext.25. Fax: 440-275-1825. E-mail: academy@grandriver.org.

URL www.grandriver.org

For more information, see page 510.

iD Tech Camps–Case Western Reserve University, Cleveland, OH

iD Tech Camps
Cleveland, Ohio

General Information Coed residential and day academic program established in 1999. Accredited by American Camping Association. Formal opportunities for the academically talented and artistically talented.

Program Focus Students create 2D and 3D video games, build robots to compete, design websites, film and edit digital movies, create their own comic book with digital photos, learn programming, and more. One computer per student and an average of five students per staff member. Campers take home a project at the end of the weeklong course.

Academics Web page design, academics (general), computer programming, computer science (Advanced Placement), computers, precollege program.

Arts Animation, cinematography, digital media, drawing, film, film editing, film production, graphic arts, photography, television/video.

Special Interest Areas Career exploration, computer game design, computer graphics, electronics, leadership training, robotics, team building.

Sports Baseball, basketball, soccer, softball, swimming, volleyball.

Trips College tours.

Program Information 5–9 sessions per year. Session length: 5–7 days in June, July, August. Ages: 7–17. 40–50 participants per session. Day program cost: $729. Boarding program cost: $1129. Financial aid available.

Application Deadline Continuous.

Jobs Positions for college students 18 and older.

Contact Client Service Representatives, 42 West Campbell Avenue, Suite 301, Campbell, California 95008. Phone: 888-700-TECH. Fax: 408-871-2228. E-mail: info@internaldrive.com.

URL www.internaldrive.com

For more information, see page 520.

Junior Statesmen Symposium on Ohio State Politics and Government

Junior Statesmen Foundation
Ohio State University
Columbus, Ohio

General Information Coed residential academic program established in 1998. Formal opportunities for the academically talented.

Program Focus State government, politics, debate, and leadership training.

Academics Communications, government and politics, journalism, precollege program, social science, social studies, speech/debate.

Special Interest Areas Career exploration, leadership training.

Trips College tours, day.

Program Information 1 session per year. Session length: 4 days in August. Ages: 14–18. 50–80

participants per session. Boarding program cost: $360.
Financial aid available.
Application Deadline Continuous.
Contact Ms. Jessica Brow, National Summer School
Director, 400 South El Camino Real, Suite 300, San
Mateo, California 94402. Phone: 650-347-1600. Fax:
650-347-7200. E-mail: jsa@jsa.org.
URL summer.jsa.org/

For more information, see page 534.

MIAMI UNIVERSITY JUNIOR SCHOLARS PROGRAM

Miami University
301 South Patterson Avenue
Room 202
Oxford, Ohio 45056-3414

General Information Coed residential academic
program established in 1982. Formal opportunities for
the academically talented. College credit may be earned.
Program Focus College credit for academically
talented rising high school seniors.
Academics American literature, English language/
literature, French language/literature, German
language/literature, Russian language/literature,
Spanish language/literature, academics (general),
anthropology, architecture, art, art history/appreciation,
astronomy, biology, botany, business, classical languages/
literatures, communications, computer programming,
computers, ecology, economics, environmental science,
geography, government and politics, history, humanities,
international relations, journalism, mathematics,
philosophy, physics, physiology, precollege program,
psychology, religion, science (general), social science,
speech/debate, women's studies, writing.
Arts Drawing, film, painting.
Special Interest Areas College planning.
Sports Aerobics, basketball, climbing (wall), diving,
figure skating, golf, racquetball, soccer, softball, squash,
street/roller hockey, swimming, tennis, volleyball.
Trips Cultural, day, shopping.
Program Information 1 session per year. Session
length: 6 weeks in June, July, August. Ages: 16–18.
60–85 participants per session. Boarding program cost:
$2200–$3400. Financial aid available. Each qualified
applicant receives a scholarship.
Application Deadline May 15.
Contact Dr. Robert S. Smith, Director, main address
above. Phone: 513-529-5825. Fax: 513-529-1498. E-mail:
juniorscholars@muohio.edu.
URL www.muohio.edu/JuniorScholars/

SUMMERBERG AT HEIDELBERG COLLEGE

Heidelberg College
Tiffin, Ohio

General Information Coed residential academic
program.

Summerberg at Heidelberg College

Academics Chinese languages/literature, German
language/literature, Spanish language/literature,
criminal justice, forensic science, journalism, language
study, law, management, prelaw, writing.
Arts Creative writing, film.
Program Information 2 sessions per year. Session
length: 2 weeks in July, August. Boarding program cost:
$2395. Open to rising 8th thru 12th grade students.
Application Deadline Continuous.
Contact SummerBerg, 310 East Market Street, Tiffin,
Ohio 44883. Phone: 866-686-3012. E-mail:
summerberg@heidelberg.edu.
URL www.heidelberg.edu/summerberg

For more information, see page 652.

OREGON

ADVENTURE TREKS–OREGON ADVENTURES

Adventure Treks, Inc.
Oregon

General Information Coed travel outdoor program, wilderness program, and adventure program established in 1978.
Program Focus Multi-activity outdoor adventure program with an emphasis on fun, personal growth, leadership, teamwork, and outdoor skills.
Sports Sailing, swimming.
Wilderness/Outdoors Backpacking, hiking, mountain biking, mountaineering, orienteering, rafting, rock climbing, white-water trips, wilderness camping.
Program Information 1–2 sessions per year. Session length: 22 days in June, July, August. Ages: 15–16. 20–24 participants per session. Cost: $2995. Financial aid available.
Application Deadline Continuous.
Contact John Dockendorf, Director, PO Box 1321, Flat Rock, North Carolina 28731. Phone: 888-954-5555. Fax: 828-696-1663. E-mail: info@advtreks.com.
URL www.adventuretreks.com

CYBERCAMPS–LEWIS AND CLARK COLLEGE

Cybercamps–Giant Campus, Inc.
Lewis and Clark College
Portland, Oregon

General Information Coed residential and day academic program established in 1997. Formal opportunities for the academically talented.
Program Focus Computers and technology.
Academics Web page design, academics (general), computer programming, computer science (Advanced Placement), computers.
Arts Animation, digital media, film, graphic arts, musical productions, photography, television/video.
Special Interest Areas Computer game design, computer graphics, electronics, robotics, team building.
Program Information 1–12 sessions per year. Session length: 5 days in June, July, August. Ages: 7–18. 30–50 participants per session. Day program cost: $599–$749. Boarding program cost: $998–$1148.
Application Deadline Continuous.
Jobs Positions for high school students 17 and older and college students 18 and older.
Contact Camp Consultant, 3101 Western Avenue, Suite 100, Seattle, Washington 98121. Phone: 888-904-2267. Fax: 206-442-4501. E-mail: info@cybercamps.com.
URL www.cybercamps.com
For more information, see page 466.

LANDMARK VOLUNTEERS: OREGON

Landmark Volunteers, Inc.
Oregon

General Information Coed residential outdoor program, community service program, and wilderness program established in 1992.
Program Focus Opportunity for high school students to earn community service credit while working as a team for two weeks serving the Pacific Crest Trail. Similar programs offered through Landmark Volunteers at over 50 locations in 20 states.
Academics Area studies, biology, botany, environmental science, history, science (general), social science.
Special Interest Areas Campcraft, career exploration, community service, conservation projects, field research/expeditions, nature study, trail maintenance, work camp programs.
Wilderness/Outdoors Canoe trips, hiking.
Trips Day.
Program Information 1 session per year. Session length: 2 weeks in July, August. Ages: 14–18. 10–13 participants per session. Boarding program cost: $1250–$1300. Financial aid available.
Application Deadline Continuous.
Contact Ann Barrett, Executive Director, PO Box 455, Sheffield, Massachusetts 01257. Phone: 413-229-0255. Fax: 413-229-2050. E-mail: landmark@volunteers.com.
URL www.volunteers.com

For more information, see page 542.

SUMMER AT DELPHI

The Delphian School
20950 Southwest Rock Creek Road
Sheridan, Oregon 97378

General Information Coed residential and day traditional camp and academic program established in 1976. Formal opportunities for the academically talented and gifted. High school credit may be earned.

Summer at Delphi

Program Focus Challenge young people in and out of the classroom and help them discover that their potential for success is unlimited.

Academics American literature, English as a second language, English language/literature, academics (general), art history/appreciation, biology, business, chemistry, communications, computer programming, computers, economics, geography, geology/earth science, government and politics, health sciences, history, humanities, journalism, linguistics, mathematics, meteorology, music, philosophy, physics, physiology, reading, religion, science (general), social science, social studies, study skills, typing, writing.

Arts Arts and crafts (general), ceramics, creative writing, dance (modern), drawing, music, music (classical), music (instrumental), music (jazz), music (orchestral), music (vocal), painting, photography, pottery, television/video, theater/drama, woodworking.

Sports Archery, baseball, basketball, equestrian sports, golf, horseback riding, soccer, softball, swimming, tennis, volleyball, weight training.

Wilderness/Outdoors Hiking, outdoor camping, rafting, white-water trips.

Trips Cultural, day, overnight, shopping.

Program Information 1–2 sessions per year. Session length: 4–6 weeks in June, July, August. Ages: 5–18. 300 participants per session. Financial aid available. Contact school for costs.

Application Deadline Continuous.

Contact Sharon Fry, Director of Admissions, 20950 Southwest Rock Creek Road, Sheridan, Oregon 97378. Phone: 800-626-6610. Fax: 503-843-4158. E-mail: summer@delphian.org.

URL www.SummerAtDelphi.org

For more information, see page 650.

WILDERNESS VENTURES–OREGON

Wilderness Ventures
Oregon

General Information Coed travel outdoor program, wilderness program, and adventure program established in 1973.

Program Focus Wilderness travel, wilderness skills, leadership skills.

Special Interest Areas Leadership training.

Wilderness/Outdoors Backpacking, hiking, rafting, rock climbing, white-water trips, wilderness camping.

Trips Overnight.

Program Information 3 sessions per year. Session length: 16 days in June, July, August. Ages: 14–18. 10 participants per session. Cost: $2990. Financial aid available.

Application Deadline Continuous.

Jobs Positions for college students 21 and older.

Contact Mike Cottingham, Director, PO Box 2768, Jackson Hole, Wyoming 83001. Phone: 800-533-2281. Fax: 307-739-1934. E-mail: info@wildernessventures.com.

URL www.wildernessventures.com

For more information, see page 704.

PENNSYLVANIA

ACADEMIC CAMPS AT GETTYSBURG COLLEGE

Gettysburg College
300 North Washington Street
Gettysburg, Pennsylvania 17325

General Information Coed residential academic program established in 2004.

Academic Camps at Gettysburg College

Program Focus Experiential summer learning with choice of academic tracks including astronomy, psychology, creative writing, Spanish, and U.S. Civil War.
Academics Spanish language/literature, academics (general), astronomy, history, psychology.
Arts Creative writing, theater/drama.
Special Interest Areas College planning, community service.
Sports Baseball, basketball, ropes course, softball, track and field.
Trips College tours, cultural, day, shopping.
Program Information 2 sessions per year. Session length: 12 days in June, July. Ages: 14–18. 100 participants per session. Boarding program cost: $2395.
Application Deadline Continuous.
Contact Doug Murphy, Director, 300 North Washington Street, Box 2994, Gettysburg, Pennsylvania 17325. Phone: 800-289-7029. Fax: 718-237-8862. E-mail: academiccamps@gettysburg.edu.
URL www.gettysburg.edu/academiccamps
For more information, see page 396.

BRYN MAWR COLLEGE–SCIENCE FOR COLLEGE

Bryn Mawr College
101 North Merion Avenue
Bryn Mawr, Pennsylvania 19010-2899

General Information Girls' residential and day academic program established in 2005. Formal opportunities for the academically talented.
Program Focus Hands-on preparation for college science.
Academics Precollege program, science (general), study skills, writing.
Special Interest Areas Field research/expeditions.
Sports Swimming, tennis, weight training.
Trips College tours, cultural, day, shopping.
Program Information 1 session per year. Session length: 3 weeks in June, July. Ages: 15–18. 10–15 participants per session. Day program cost: $2200. Boarding program cost: $3000. Application fee: $30. Financial aid available.
Application Deadline Continuous.
Jobs Positions for college students 20 and older.
Contact Ms. Jean Lacovara, Coordinator, main address above. Phone: 610-526-5274. Fax: 610-526-6569. E-mail: scienceforcollege@brynmawr.edu.
URL www.brynmawr.edu/summerprograms
For more information, see page 656.

BRYN MAWR COLLEGE–WOMEN OF DISTINCTION: PERSONALIZING THE COLLEGE ADMISSIONS PROCESS

Bryn Mawr College
101 North Merion Avenue
Bryn Mawr, Pennsylvania 19010-2899

General Information Girls' residential and day academic program established in 2004. Formal opportunities for the academically talented.
Program Focus Through interactive workshops and personality assessment, students gain a better understanding of themselves and what is important to them in selecting a college.
Academics Precollege program.
Special Interest Areas College planning.
Sports Swimming, tennis, weight training.
Trips College tours.
Program Information 1 session per year. Session length: 6 days in July. Ages: 15–18. 20–40 participants per session. Day program cost: $900. Boarding program cost: $1100. Financial aid available.
Application Deadline Continuous.
Jobs Positions for college students 20 and older.

Contact Ms. Sue Joceville, Administrative Assistant, Undergraduate Admissions, main address above. Phone: 610-526-5154. Fax: 610-526-7471. E-mail: sjocevil@brynmawr.edu.
URL www.brynmawr.edu/summerprograms
For more information, see page 656.

BRYN MAWR COLLEGE–WRITING FOR COLLEGE

Bryn Mawr College
101 North Merion Avenue
Bryn Mawr, Pennsylvania 19010-2899

General Information Girls' residential and day academic program established in 1993. Formal opportunities for the academically talented.

Bryn Mawr College–Writing for College

Program Focus College-level writing offered in two writing-intensive strands: creative writing and urban studies.
Academics English language/literature, college tours, humanities, precollege program, social science, study skills, writing.
Arts Creative writing.

Special Interest Areas Field trips (arts and culture).
Sports Swimming, tennis, weight training.
Trips College tours, cultural, day, shopping.
Program Information 1 session per year. Session length: 3 weeks in June, July. Ages: 15–18. 45–50 participants per session. Day program cost: $2200. Boarding program cost: $3000. Application fee: $30. Financial aid available.
Application Deadline Continuous.
Jobs Positions for college students 20 and older.
Contact Ms. Ann Brown, Coordinator, main address above. Phone: 610-526-5376. Fax: 610-526-7476. E-mail: summer@brynmawr.edu.
URL www.brynmawr.edu/summerprograms
For more information, see page 656.

COLLEGE INSIGHT

The Phelps School
583 Sugartown Road
Malvern, Pennsylvania 19355

General Information Coed residential and day academic program established in 2007. Formal opportunities for the academically talented and artistically talented. Specific services available for the learning disabled.
Program Focus College admissions.
Academics SAT/ACT preparation, academics (general), college tours, writing.
Special Interest Areas Career exploration, college planning, personal development.
Trips College tours, cultural, day.
Program Information 2 sessions per year. Session length: 8 days in July. Ages: 15–19.
Application Deadline Continuous.
Jobs Positions for college students 20 and older.
Contact Ms. Emily A. Shaker, 583 Sugartown Road, Malvern, Pennsylvania 19355. Phone: 610-644-1754. Fax: 610-644-6679. E-mail: emily@theadmissionsauthority.com.
URL www.theadmissionsauthority.com

CYBERCAMPS–BRYN MAWR COLLEGE

Cybercamps–Giant Campus, Inc.
Bryn Mawr, Pennsylvania

General Information Coed residential and day academic program established in 1997. Formal opportunities for the academically talented.
Program Focus Computers and technology.
Academics Web page design, academics (general), computer programming, computer science (Advanced Placement), computers.
Arts Animation, digital media, film, graphic arts, musical productions, photography, television/video.
Special Interest Areas Computer game design, computer graphics, electronics, robotics, team building.
Program Information 1–12 sessions per year. Session length: 5 days in June, July, August. Ages: 7–18. 30 participants per session. Day program cost: $599–$749. Boarding program cost: $998–$1148.
Application Deadline Continuous.

Cybercamps–Bryn Mawr College (continued)

Jobs Positions for high school students 17 and older and college students 18 and older.
Contact Camp Consultant, 3101 Western Avenue, Suite 100, Seattle, Washington 98121. Phone: 888-904-2267. Fax: 206-442-4501. E-mail: info@cybercamps.com.
URL www.cybercamps.com
For more information, see page 466.

EMAGINATION COMPUTER CAMPS–PENNSYLVANIA

Emagination Computer Camps
Rosemont College
Rosemont, Pennsylvania

General Information Coed residential and day academic program. Accredited by American Camping Association. Formal opportunities for the academically talented.
Program Focus Computer science, technology, and art; swimming, tennis, and basketball; web design; computer music, video, photo, and 3-D animation.
Academics Computer programming, computer science (Advanced Placement), computers, technology.
Arts Graphic arts.
Special Interest Areas ADL skills, Internet accessibility, computer graphics, electronics, field trips (arts and culture), model rocketry, robotics.
Sports Basketball, soccer, swimming, tennis.
Trips Day.
Program Information 4 sessions per year. Session length: 2 weeks in June, July, August. Ages: 8–17. 150–250 participants per session. Day program cost: $1235. Boarding program cost: $2245. Financial aid available.
Application Deadline Continuous.
Jobs Positions for college students 18 and older.
Contact Kathi Rigg, Director, 110 Winn Street, Suite 205, Woburn, Massachusetts 01801. Phone: 877-248-0206. Fax: 781-933-0749. E-mail: camp@computercamps.com
URL www.computercamps.com
For more information, see page 482.

ENSEMBLE THEATRE COMMUNITY SCHOOL

Player's Lodge, Pennsylvania Avenue
Eagles Mere, Pennsylvania 17731

General Information Coed residential arts program established in 1984. Formal opportunities for the artistically talented. High school or college credit may be earned.

Ensemble Theatre Community School

Program Focus Theater, acting, movement, and music.
Arts Acting, clowning, costume design, creative writing, dance, dance (jazz), dance (modern), film, mime, music, music (instrumental), music (vocal), musical productions, painting, performing arts, puppetry, set design, television/video, theater/drama.
Sports Basketball, bicycling, fencing, swimming, tennis.
Wilderness/Outdoors Hiking.
Trips Cultural, day.
Program Information 1 session per year. Session length: 40–42 days in June, July, August. Ages: 14–18. 18–22 participants per session. Boarding program cost: $4000–$4500. Financial aid available.
Application Deadline Continuous.
Jobs Positions for college students 19 and older.
Summer Contact Seth Orbach, Director, PO Box 188, Eagles Mere, Pennsylvania 17731. Phone: 570-525-3043. Fax: 570-525-3548. E-mail: info@etcschool.org.
Winter Contact Seth Orbach, Director, 43 Lyman Circle, Shaker Heights, Ohio 44122. Phone: 216-464-1688. E-mail: info@etcschool.org.
URL www.etcschool.org
For more information, see page 488.

iD GAMING ACADEMY–VILLANOVA UNIVERSITY, VILLANOVA, PA

iD Tech Camps
Villanova, Pennsylvania

General Information Coed residential academic program established in 1999. Accredited by American Camping Association. Formal opportunities for the academically talented and artistically talented.
Program Focus Three weeks of intensive study in video game creation and development. Using industry-standard applications, each student will learn basics of 3D graphics production, including modeling, texturing, and animation, and create their own 3D game level and a personal portfolio of their animated game models.
Academics Web page design, academics (general), computer programming, computer science (Advanced Placement), computers, precollege program.
Arts Animation, cinematography, digital media, drawing, film, film editing, film production, graphic arts, photography, television/video.
Special Interest Areas Career exploration, computer game design, computer graphics, electronics, leadership training, robotics, team building.
Sports Baseball, basketball, soccer, softball, swimming, volleyball.
Trips College tours.
Program Information 4 sessions per year. Session length: 15–19 days in June, July, August. Ages: 13–17. 40–50 participants per session. Boarding program cost: $3999. Financial aid available. Weekend stays (optional) cost $600 additional for the two weekends during the program.
Application Deadline Continuous.
Contact Client Service Representatives, 42 West Campbell Avenue, Suite 301, Campbell, California 95008. Phone: 888-709-TECH. Fax: 408-871-2228. E-mail: info@internaldrive.com.
URL www.internaldrive.com

For more information, see page 520.

iD TECH CAMPS–CARNEGIE MELLON UNIVERSITY, PITTSBURGH, PA

iD Tech Camps
Carnegie Mellon University
Pittsburgh, Pennsylvania 15213

General Information Coed residential and day academic program established in 1999. Accredited by American Camping Association. Formal opportunities for the academically talented and artistically talented.
Program Focus Students create 2D and 3D video games, build robots to compete, design websites, film and edit digital movies, create their own comic book with digital photos, learn programming and more. One computer per student and an average of five students per staff member. Campers take home a project at the end of the weeklong course.
Academics Web page design, academics (general), computer programming, computer science (Advanced Placement), computers, precollege program.

Arts Animation, cinematography, digital media, drawing, film, film editing, film production, graphic arts, photography, television/video.
Special Interest Areas Career exploration, computer game design, computer graphics, electronics, leadership training, robotics, team building.
Sports Baseball, basketball, soccer, softball, swimming, volleyball.
Trips College tours.
Program Information 5–9 sessions per year. Session length: 5–7 days in June, July, August. Ages: 7–17. 40–50 participants per session. Day program cost: $729. Boarding program cost: $1129. Financial aid available.
Application Deadline Continuous.
Jobs Positions for college students 18 and older.
Contact Client Service Representatives, 42 West Campbell Avenue, Suite 301, Campbell, California 95008. Phone: 888-709-TECH. Fax: 408-871-2228. E-mail: info@internaldrive.com
URL www.internaldrive.com

For more information, see page 520.

iD TECH CAMPS–VILLANOVA UNIVERSITY, VILLANOVA, PA

iD Tech Camps
Villanova University
Villanova, Pennsylvania 19085

General Information Coed residential and day academic program established in 1999. Accredited by American Camping Association. Formal opportunities for the academically talented and artistically talented.
Program Focus Students create 2D and 3D video games, build robots to compete, design websites, film and edit digital movies, create their own comic book with digital photos, learn programming and more. One computer per student and an average of five students per staff member. Campers take home a project at the end of the weeklong course.
Academics Web page design, academics (general), computer programming, computer science (Advanced Placement), computers, precollege program.
Arts Animation, cinematography, digital media, drawing, film, film editing, film production, graphic arts, photography, television/video.
Special Interest Areas Career exploration, computer game design, computer graphics, electronics, leadership training, robotics, team building.
Sports Baseball, basketball, soccer, softball, swimming, volleyball.
Trips College tours.
Program Information 5–9 sessions per year. Session length: 5–7 days in June, July, August. Ages: 7–17. 40–50 participants per session. Day program cost: $729. Boarding program cost: $1129. Financial aid available.
Application Deadline Continuous.
Jobs Positions for college students 18 and older.

iD Tech Camps–Villanova University, Villanova, PA (continued)

Contact Client Service Representatives, 42 West Campbell Avenue, Suite 301, Campbell, California 95008. Phone: 888-709-TECH. Fax: 408-871-2228. E-mail: info@internaldrive.com. **URL** www.internaldrive.com

For more information, see page 520.

LANDMARK VOLUNTEERS: PENNSYLVANIA

Landmark Volunteers, Inc.
Pennsylvania

General Information Coed residential community service program established in 1992.
Program Focus Opportunity for high school students to earn community service credit while working as a team for two weeks serving the Pocono Environmental Education Center at the Delaware Water Gap. Similar programs offered through Landmark Volunteers at over 50 locations in 20 states.
Academics Biology, ecology, environmental science, landscape architecture, marine studies.
Special Interest Areas Animal care, career exploration, community service, conservation projects, field research/expeditions, gardening, nature study, nautical skills, team building, trail maintenance, work camp programs.
Trips Day.
Program Information 1 session per year. Session length: 2 weeks in July. Ages: 14–18. 10–12 participants per session.
Application Deadline Continuous.
Contact Ann Barrett, Executive Director, PO Box 455, Sheffield, Massachusetts 01257. Phone: 413-229-0255. Fax: 413-229-2050.

For more information, see page 542.

92ND STREET Y CAMPS–CAMP KESHER

92nd Street YM–YWHA
Milford, Pennsylvania

General Information Coed residential traditional camp established in 1955. Religious affiliation: Jewish. Accredited by American Camping Association.
Program Focus Tailored for campers who may struggle while being away from home.
Arts Arts and crafts (general), ceramics, dance, music, painting, photography, pottery, woodworking.
Special Interest Areas Campcraft, model rocketry, nature study, team building.
Sports Archery, baseball, basketball, bicycling, boating, climbing (wall), gymnastics, in-line skating, ropes course, soccer, softball, sports (general), street/roller hockey, swimming.
Program Information 1 session per year. Session length: 13 days in July, August. Ages: 8–11. 90–100 participants per session. Boarding program cost: $1900. Financial aid available. Open to participants entering grades 3–6.
Application Deadline Continuous.
Jobs Positions for college students 18 and older.
Contact Steve Levin, Director of Camp Programs, 1395 Lexington Avenue, New York, New York 10128. Phone: 212-415-5573. Fax: 212-415-5668. E-mail: camps@92y.org.
URL www.92y.org/camps

PRE-COLLEGE SUMMER INSTITUTE, THE UNIVERSITY OF THE ARTS

The University of the Arts
320 South Broad Street
Philadelphia, Pennsylvania 19102

General Information Coed residential and day arts program established in 1981. Formal opportunities for the artistically talented and gifted. High school credit may be earned.
Program Focus Four week visual and performing arts (musical theater and acting) and media and communication program, a two-week jazz performance: instrumental and voice program, and a two-week dance program.
Academics Art (Advanced Placement), art history/appreciation, communications, computers, music, precollege program, writing.

Pre-College Summer Institute, The University of the Arts

Arts Acting, animation, arts and crafts (general), band, ceramics, creative writing, dance, dance (ballet), dance (jazz), dance (modern), drawing, fabric arts, film, graphic arts, jewelry making, metalworking, music, music (ensemble), music (instrumental), music (jazz), music (vocal), musical productions, painting, photography, pottery, printmaking, sculpture, television/video, theater/drama, weaving.
Special Interest Areas College planning.
Trips Cultural.
Program Information 1 session per year. Session length: 14–20 days in July, August. Ages: 16–18. 300–400 participants per session. Day program cost: $2400. Boarding program cost: $3450. Application fee: $100. Contact the Pre-College Department for tuition information.
Application Deadline Continuous.

Contact Erin Elman, Director, Pre-College Programs, main address above. Phone: 215-717-6430. Fax: 215-717-6433. E-mail: precollege@uarts.edu.
URL www.uarts.edu/precollege
For more information, see page 690.

THE SUMMER INSTITUTE FOR THE GIFTED AT BRYN MAWR COLLEGE

Summer Institute for the Gifted
Bryn Mawr College
Bryn Mawr, Pennsylvania 19010

General Information Coed residential and day academic program established in 1991. Formal opportunities for the academically talented and gifted. College credit may be earned.
Academics American literature, English language/literature, French language/literature, SAT/ACT preparation, Spanish language/literature, academics (general), aerospace science, archaeology, architecture, art (Advanced Placement), art history/appreciation, biology, botany, business, chemistry, classical languages/literatures, communications, computer programming, computers, engineering, environmental science, geology/earth science, government and politics, history, humanities, marine studies, mathematics, music, oceanography, philosophy, physics, physiology, precollege program, psychology, science (general), social studies, speech/debate, study skills, writing.
Arts Arts and crafts (general), chorus, creative writing, dance, drawing, film, graphic arts, music, music (chamber), music (classical), music (ensemble), musical productions, painting, photography, sculpture, theater/drama, weaving.
Special Interest Areas Animal care, electronics, meditation, model rocketry, robotics.
Sports Aerobics, archery, baseball, basketball, fencing, field hockey, football, lacrosse, martial arts, soccer, squash, swimming, tennis, volleyball.
Wilderness/Outdoors Hiking.
Trips Cultural.

The Summer Institute for the Gifted at Bryn Mawr College (continued)

Program Information 1–2 sessions per year. Session length: 3 weeks in June, July, August. Ages: 8–17. 150–250 participants per session. Day program cost: $1825–$2000. Boarding program cost: $3700–$4200. Application fee: $75. Financial aid available.
Application Deadline May 14.

The Summer Institute for the Gifted at Bryn Mawr College

Jobs Positions for college students 19 and older.
Contact Ms. Barbara Swicord, Director, River Plaza, 9 West Broad Street, Stamford, Connecticut 06902-3788. Phone: 866-303-4744. Fax: 203-399-5598. E-mail: sig.info@aifs.com.
URL www.giftedstudy.com
For more information, see page 654.

SUMMER STUDY AT PENN STATE

Summer Study Programs
University Park, Pennsylvania 16802

General Information Coed residential academic program established in 1991. Formal opportunities for the academically talented and artistically talented. High school or college credit may be earned.

Summer Study at Penn State

Program Focus Pre-college experience including college credit courses, enrichment classes, SAT preparation, sports, and touring of different college campuses.
Academics American literature, English as a second language, English language/literature, French (Advanced Placement), French language/literature, German language/literature, Russian language/literature, SAT/ACT preparation, Spanish (Advanced Placement), Spanish language/literature, academics (general), anthropology, architecture, art (Advanced Placement), art history/appreciation, astronomy, biology, business, chemistry, classical languages/literatures, college tours, communications, computer programming, computers, ecology, economics, engineering, environmental science, geography, geology/earth science, government and politics, government and

politics (Advanced Placement), health sciences, history, humanities, journalism, mathematics, mathematics (Advanced Placement), music, philosophy, physics, physiology, precollege program, psychology, religion, science (general), social science, social studies, study skills, writing.
Arts Acting, arts and crafts (general), band, ceramics, creative writing, dance, dance (modern), drawing, graphic arts, jewelry making, music, music (instrumental), music (vocal), painting, photography, pottery, theater/drama.
Special Interest Areas Career exploration, community service, touring.
Sports Aerobics, baseball, basketball, bicycling, boating, canoeing, climbing (wall), diving, field hockey, football, golf, gymnastics, ice hockey, in-line skating, lacrosse, martial arts, racquetball, soccer, softball, sports (general), squash, street/roller hockey, swimming, tennis, track and field, volleyball, water polo, weight training.
Wilderness/Outdoors Hiking, rock climbing.
Trips College tours, cultural, day, overnight.
Program Information 2 sessions per year. Session length: 25–46 days in June, July, August. Ages: 14+. 300–400 participants per session. Boarding program cost: $4195–$6495. Application fee: $75. Financial aid available.
Application Deadline Continuous.
Jobs Positions for college students 21 and older.
Contact Mr. Bill Cooperman, Executive Director, 900 Walt Whitman Road, Melville, New York 11747. Phone: 800-666-2556. Fax: 631-424-0567. E-mail: precollegeprograms@summerstudy.com.
URL www.summerstudy.com
For more information, see page 658.

UNIVERSITY OF PENNSYLVANIA–PENN SUMMER ART AND ARCHITECTURE STUDIOS

University of Pennsylvania
3440 Market Street, Suite 100
Philadelphia, Pennsylvania 19104-3335

General Information Coed residential and day arts program established in 2002. Formal opportunities for the academically talented and artistically talented.
Academics SAT/ACT preparation, architecture, study skills.
Arts Animation, ceramics, dance, digital media, drawing, film, graphic arts, painting, photography, printmaking.
Special Interest Areas Career exploration, college planning, community service.
Sports Aerobics, basketball, bicycling, climbing (wall), paintball, soccer, swimming, tennis, weight training.
Wilderness/Outdoors Rafting.
Trips College tours, cultural, day, shopping.
Program Information 1 session per year. Session length: 4 weeks in June, July. Ages: 15–18. 50–100 participants per session. Day program cost: $3045. Boarding program cost: $5105. Application fee: $70. Financial aid available.

Application Deadline April 15.
Jobs Positions for college students 18 and older.
Contact Ms. Heather Haseley, Youth Programs Coordinator, main address above. Phone: 215-746-6901. Fax: 215-573-2053. E-mail: hsprogs@sas.upenn.edu.
URL www.upenn.edu/summer/highschool
For more information, see page 686.

UNIVERSITY OF PENNSYLVANIA–PENN SUMMER SCIENCE ACADEMIES

University of Pennsylvania
3440 Market Street, Suite 100
Philadelphia, Pennsylvania 19104-3335

General Information Coed residential and day academic program. Formal opportunities for the academically talented.
Academics SAT/ACT preparation, astronomy, biology, biology (Advanced Placement), biomedical research, ecology, forensic science, physics, study skills.
Arts Dance.
Special Interest Areas Career exploration, college planning, community service.
Sports Aerobics, baseball, basketball, climbing (wall), paintball, soccer, swimming, tennis, weight training.
Wilderness/Outdoors Rafting.
Trips College tours, cultural, day, shopping.
Program Information 1 session per year. Session length: 4 weeks in June, July. Ages: 15–18. 150–200 participants per session. Day program cost: $3045. Boarding program cost: $5105. Application fee: $70. Financial aid available.
Application Deadline April 15.
Jobs Positions for college students 18 and older.
Contact Ms. Heather Haseley, Youth Programs Coordinator, main address above. Phone: 215-746-6901. Fax: 215-573-2053. E-mail: hsprogs@sas.upenn.edu.
URL www.upenn.edu/summer/highschool
For more information, see page 686.

UNIVERSITY OF PENNSYLVANIA–PENN SUMMER THEATRE WORKSHOP

University of Pennsylvania
3440 Market Street, Suite 100
Philadelphia, Pennsylvania 19104-3335

General Information Coed residential and day arts program established in 2005. Formal opportunities for the artistically talented.
Academics SAT/ACT preparation, study skills.
Arts Acting, dance, musical productions, theater/drama.
Special Interest Areas Career exploration, college planning, community service.
Sports Aerobics, baseball, basketball, climbing (wall), paintball, soccer, swimming, tennis, weight training.
Wilderness/Outdoors Rafting.
Trips College tours, cultural, day.
Program Information 1 session per year. Session length: 4 weeks in June, July. Ages: 15–18. 20–30 participants per session. Day program cost: $3500.

University of Pennsylvania–Penn Summer Theatre Workshop (continued)

Boarding program cost: $5105. Application fee: $70. Financial aid available.
Application Deadline April 15.
Jobs Positions for college students 18 and older.
Contact Ms. Heather Haseley, Youth Programs Coordinator, main address above. Phone: 215-746-6901. Fax: 215-573-2053. E-mail: hsprogs@sas.upenn.edu.
URL www.upenn.edu/summer/highschool
For more information, see page 686.

UNIVERSITY OF PENNSYLVANIA–PRE-COLLEGE PROGRAM

University of Pennsylvania
3440 Market Street, Suite 100
Philadelphia, Pennsylvania 19104-3335

General Information Coed residential and day academic program established in 1981. Formal opportunities for the academically talented. College credit may be earned.
Academics American literature, Chinese languages/literature, English language/literature, Italian language/literature, Japanese language/literature, Jewish studies, SAT/ACT preparation, Spanish language/literature, anthropology, archaeology, architecture, art history/appreciation, astronomy, biology, business, chemistry, classical languages/literatures, communications, computer programming, economics, engineering, geology/earth science, government and politics, government and politics (Advanced Placement), health sciences, history, humanities, intercultural studies, linguistics, mathematics, music, philosophy, physics, precollege program, psychology, religion, social science, study skills, writing.
Arts Creative writing, dance.
Special Interest Areas Career exploration, college planning, community service.
Sports Aerobics, basketball, bicycling, climbing (wall), paintball, soccer, swimming, tennis, weight training.
Wilderness/Outdoors Rafting.
Trips College tours, cultural, day, shopping.
Program Information 1 session per year. Session length: 6 weeks in June, July, August. Ages: 15–18. 200–300 participants per session. Day program cost: $2600–$5400. Boarding program cost: $6150–$8700. Application fee: $70. Financial aid available.
Application Deadline April 15.

University of Pennsylvania–Pre-College Program

Jobs Positions for college students 18 and older.
Contact Ms. Heather Haseley, Youth Programs Coordinator, main address above. Phone: 215-746-6901. Fax: 215-573-2053. E-mail: hsprogs@sas.upenn.edu.
URL www.upenn.edu/summer/highschool
For more information, see page 686.

VALLEY FORGE MILITARY ACADEMY SUMMER BAND CAMP

Valley Forge Military Academy and College
1001 Eagle Road
Wayne, Pennsylvania 19087-3695

General Information Coed residential and day traditional camp and arts program established in 1945.
Program Focus Day and overnight coed band camp.
Academics Music.
Arts Arts and crafts (general), band, music (instrumental), musical productions.
Special Interest Areas Leadership training.
Sports Archery, baseball, basketball, canoeing, climbing

(wall), equestrian sports, go-carts, golf, horseback riding, in-line skating, martial arts, paintball, rappelling, riflery, ropes course, scuba diving, soccer, softball, sports (general), street/roller hockey, swimming, tennis, track and field, volleyball, water polo, weight training.
Trips Cultural, day, overnight.
Program Information 1 session per year. Session length: 4 weeks in June, July. Ages: 12–17. 25–75 participants per session. Day program cost: $2000. Boarding program cost: $3300. Application fee: $125. Financial aid available.
Application Deadline Continuous.
Jobs Positions for high school students 18 and older and college students 18 and older.
Contact Maj. Jeffrey Bond, Director of Summer Camps, main address above. Phone: 610-989-1253. Fax: 610-688-1260. E-mail: summercamp@vfmac.edu.
URL www.vfmac.edu
For more information, see page 692.

VALLEY FORGE MILITARY ACADEMY SUMMER CAMP FOR BOYS

Valley Forge Military Academy and College
1001 Eagle Road
Wayne, Pennsylvania 19087-3695

General Information Boys' residential traditional camp and outdoor program established in 1945.

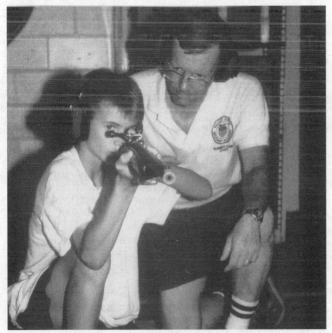

Valley Forge Military Academy Summer Camp for Boys

Academics Bible study, English language/literature, mathematics, music, reading.
Arts Arts and crafts (general), band, music (instrumental).
Special Interest Areas Campcraft, leadership training, team building.

Sports Archery, baseball, basketball, boating, canoeing, climbing (wall), equestrian sports, go-carts, golf, horseback riding, in-line skating, martial arts, paintball, physical fitness, rappelling, riflery, ropes course, running/jogging, scuba diving, soccer, softball, sports (general), street/roller hockey, swimming, tennis, volleyball, water polo, weight training.
Wilderness/Outdoors Canoe trips, hiking, orienteering, survival training, wilderness camping.
Trips Cultural, day, overnight.
Program Information 1 session per year. Session length: 4 weeks in June, July. Ages: 8–17. 320–400 participants per session. Boarding program cost: $3300. Application fee: $125. $175 spending allowance required; additional classes and activities: $250–$900.
Application Deadline Continuous.
Jobs Positions for high school students 18 and older and college students 18 and older.
Contact Maj. Jeffrey Bond, Director of Summer Camps, main address above. Phone: 610-989-1253. Fax: 610-688-1260. E-mail: summercamp@vfmac.edu.
URL www.vfmac.edu
For more information, see page 692.

VALLEY FORGE MILITARY ACADEMY SUMMER COED DAY CAMP

Valley Forge Military Academy and College
1001 Eagle Road
Wayne, Pennsylvania 19087-3695

General Information Coed day traditional camp and outdoor program established in 2004.
Academics English language/literature, mathematics, music, reading.
Arts Arts and crafts (general), band, music (instrumental).
Special Interest Areas Field trips (arts and culture), leadership training.
Sports Archery, baseball, basketball, canoeing, climbing (wall), equestrian sports, go-carts, golf, horseback riding, in-line skating, martial arts, paintball, physical fitness, rappelling, riflery, ropes course, running/jogging, scuba diving, soccer, softball, sports (general), street/roller hockey, swimming, tennis, volleyball, water polo, weight training.
Wilderness/Outdoors Canoe trips, hiking, orienteering, survival training, wilderness camping.
Trips Cultural, day, overnight.
Program Information 1–6 sessions per year. Session length: 5–30 days in June, July. Ages: 6–17. 150–200 participants per session. Day program cost: $350–$2100. Application fee: $125. Financial aid available. $175 spending allowance required; additional classes and activities for 6-week participants only: $350–$900.
Application Deadline Continuous.
Jobs Positions for high school students 18 and older and college students 18 and older.

Valley Forge Military Academy Summer Coed Day Camp (continued)

Contact Maj. Jeffrey Bond, Director of Summer Camps, main address above. Phone: 610-989-1253. Fax: 610-688-1260. E-mail: summercamp@vfmac.edu. **URL** www.vfmac.edu

For more information, see page 692.

WYOMING SEMINARY– SEM SUMMER 2008

Wyoming Seminary College Preparatory School
Wyoming Seminary
201 North Sprague Avenue
Kingston, Pennsylvania 18704

General Information Coed residential and day academic program and arts program established in 1991. Religious affiliation: United Methodist. Formal opportunities for the academically talented and artistically talented. High school credit may be earned.

Wyoming Seminary–Sem Summer 2008

Program Focus Academic enrichment, English as a Second Language, performing arts.
Academics Bible study, English as a second language,

academics (general), art history/appreciation, communications, computers, health sciences, humanities, mathematics, music, precollege program, reading, religion, speech/debate, study skills, writing.
Arts Arts and crafts (general), band, chorus, dance, dance (ballet), dance (jazz), dance (modern), drawing, music, music (chamber), music (classical), music (ensemble), music (instrumental), music (jazz), music (orchestral), music (vocal), musical productions, painting, performing arts, photography, pottery, theater/drama.
Sports Basketball, climbing (wall), swimming, tennis, volleyball.
Trips Cultural, day, overnight, shopping.
Program Information 1–2 sessions per year. Session length: 21–60 days in June, July, August. Ages: 12–18. 325–425 participants per session. Day program cost: $900–$1800. Boarding program cost: $2425–$9100. Application fee: $50–$100. Financial aid available.
Application Deadline Continuous.
Jobs Positions for high school students 17 and older and college students 19 and older.
Contact John R. Eidam, Dean of Admissions/Director of International and Summer Programs, main address above. Phone: 570-270-2186. Fax: 570-270-2198. E-mail: summeratsem@wyomingseminary.org.
URL www.wyomingseminary.org/summer

For more information, see page 716.

RHODE ISLAND

iD TECH CAMPS–BROWN UNIVERSITY, PROVIDENCE, RI

iD Tech Camps
Providence, Rhode Island

General Information Coed residential and day academic program established in 1999. Accredited by American Camping Association. Formal opportunities for the academically talented and artistically talented.
Program Focus Students create 2D and 3D video games, build robots to compete, design websites, film and edit digital movies, create their own comic book with digital photos, learn programming, and more. One computer per student and an average of five students per staff member. Campers take home a project at the end of the weeklong course.
Academics Web page design, academics (general), computer programming, computer science (Advanced Placement), computers, precollege program.
Arts Animation, cinematography, digital media, drawing, film, film editing, film production, graphic arts, photography, television/video.
Special Interest Areas Career exploration, computer game design, computer graphics, electronics, leadership training, robotics, team building.
Sports Baseball, basketball, soccer, swimming, volleyball.
Trips College tours.

Program Information 5–9 sessions per year. Session length: 5–7 days in June, July, August. Ages: 7–17. 40–50 participants per session. Day program cost: $729. Boarding program cost: $1129. Financial aid available.
Application Deadline Continuous.
Jobs Positions for college students 18 and older.
Contact Client Service Representatives, 42 West Campbell Avenue, Suite 301, Campbell, California 95008. Phone: 888-709-TECH. Fax: 408-871-2228. E-mail: info@internaldrive.com.
URL www.internaldrive.com

For more information, see page 520.

LANDMARK VOLUNTEERS: RHODE ISLAND

Landmark Volunteers, Inc.
Tennis Hall of Fame
Newport, Rhode Island

General Information Coed residential community service program established in 1992. High school credit may be earned.
Program Focus Opportunity for high school students to earn community service credit while working as a team for two weeks serving Tennis Hall of Fame. Similar programs offered through Landmark Volunteers at over 50 locations in 20 states.
Academics Area studies, history.
Special Interest Areas Career exploration, community service, leadership training, team building.
Sports Tennis.
Trips Cultural, day.
Program Information 1 session per year. Session length: 14–17 days in July. Ages: 14–18. 10–13 participants per session. Boarding program cost: $1250–$1300. Financial aid available.
Application Deadline Continuous.
Jobs Positions for college students.
Contact Ann Barrett, Executive Director, PO Box 455, Sheffield, Massachusetts 01257. Phone: 413-229-0255. Fax: 413-229-2050. E-mail: landmark@volunteers.com.
URL www.volunteers.com

For more information, see page 542.

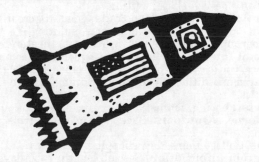

PORTSMOUTH ABBEY SUMMER SCHOOL

Portsmouth Abbey School
285 Corys Lane
Portsmouth, Rhode Island 02871-1352

General Information Coed residential and day academic program established in 1943. Religious affiliation: Roman Catholic.

Portsmouth Abbey Summer School

Program Focus Academic enrichment.
Academics English as a second language, English language/literature, academics (general), speech/debate, writing.
Arts Ceramics, creative writing, drawing, painting, photography.
Sports Basketball, equestrian sports, horseback riding, lacrosse, sailing, soccer, softball, squash, tennis, track and field, volleyball, weight training.
Trips Cultural, day, shopping.
Program Information 1 session per year. Session length: 30 days in July. Ages: 13–15. 60–70 participants per session. Day program cost: $2500. Boarding program cost: $4800. Application fee: $55. Financial aid available.
Application Deadline Continuous.
Jobs Positions for college students 21 and older.
Contact Director of Summer School, Portsmouth Abbey School, Portsmouth, Rhode Island 02871. Phone: 401-683-2000 Ext.225. Fax: 401-683-5888. E-mail: summer@portsmouthabbey.org.
URL www.portsmouthabbey.org

For more information, see page 592.

RHODE ISLAND SCHOOL OF DESIGN PRE-COLLEGE PROGRAM

Rhode Island School of Design
2 College Street
Providence, Rhode Island 02903-2787

General Information Coed residential and day arts program established in 1970. Formal opportunities for the artistically talented.

Rhode Island School of Design Pre-College Program

Program Focus Art and design.
Academics Web page design, architecture, art, art (Advanced Placement), art history/appreciation, precollege program.
Arts Animation, arts, ceramics, design, drawing, fabric arts, fashion design/production, film, graphic arts, illustration, jewelry making, painting, photography, pottery, printmaking, sculpture, television/video, weaving.
Special Interest Areas Computer game design, field trips (arts and culture).
Trips Cultural, day, shopping.
Program Information 1 session per year. Session length: 6 weeks in June, July, August. Ages: 16–18. 400–600 participants per session. Day program cost: $3825. Boarding program cost: $5900. Financial aid available. Rhode Island Resident Scholarships, Balfour Minority Scholarship.
Application Deadline Continuous.
Contact Mr. Marc Torick, Continuing Education Office/Summer Programs, main address above. Phone: 401-454-6200. Fax: 401-454-6218. E-mail: cemail@risd. edu.
URL www.risd.edu/precollege

For more information, see page 608.

SUMMER@BROWN

Brown University
Providence, Rhode Island 02912

General Information Coed residential and day academic program. Formal opportunities for the academically talented. College credit may be earned.

Summer@Brown

Academics American literature, Bible study, Chinese languages/literature, English as a second language, English language/literature, French language/literature, Greek language/literature, Italian language/literature, Japanese language/literature, Jewish studies, Latin language, Russian language/literature, Spanish language/literature, academics (general), archaeology, architecture, area studies, art history/appreciation, astronomy, biology, biology (Advanced Placement), business, chemistry, classical languages/literatures, computer programming, computers, ecology, economics, engineering, environmental science, geography, geology/earth science, government and politics, health sciences, history, humanities, intercultural studies, journalism, marine studies, mathematics, mathematics (Advanced Placement), music, peace education, philosophy, physics, physiology, precollege program, psychology, reading, religion, speech/debate, writing.
Arts Acting, arts, arts and crafts (general), creative writing, drawing, film, graphic arts, painting, photography, sculpture, television/video, theater/drama.
Special Interest Areas Career exploration, community service, conservation projects, electronics, farming, field research/expeditions, leadership training, nature study, robotics.
Sports Fencing, tennis.
Wilderness/Outdoors Backpacking, canoe trips, hiking.
Trips College tours, day, shopping.
Program Information Session length: 7–50 days in June, July, August. Day program cost: $1415–$2936. Boarding program cost: $1975–$8500. Financial aid available. Open to students in grades 7-12.
Application Deadline Continuous.
Jobs Positions for college students.

Contact Ms. Allie Mills, Office of Summer & Continuing Studies, 42 Charlesfield Street, Box T, Providence, Rhode Island 02912. Phone: 401-863-7900. Fax: 401-863-3916. E-mail: summer@brown.edu. **URL** brown.edu/Administration/Continuing_Studies/

For more information, see page 434.

TENNESSEE

iD TECH CAMPS–VANDERBILT UNIVERSITY, NASHVILLE, TN

iD Tech Camps
Nashville, Tennessee

General Information Coed residential and day academic program established in 1999. Accredited by American Camping Association. Formal opportunities for the academically talented and artistically talented.
Program Focus Students create 2D and 3D video games, build robots to compete, design websites, film and edit digital movies, create their own comic book with digital photos, learn programming, and more. One computer per student and an average of five students per staff member. Campers take home a project at the end of the weeklong course.
Academics Web page design, computer programming, computer science (Advanced Placement), computers, precollege program.
Arts Animation, cinematography, digital media, drawing, film, film editing, film production, graphic arts, photography, television/video.
Special Interest Areas Career exploration, computer game design, computer graphics, electronics, leadership training, robotics, team building.
Sports Baseball, basketball, soccer, softball, swimming, volleyball.
Trips College tours.
Program Information 5–9 sessions per year. Session length: 5–7 days in June, July, August. Ages: 7–17. 40–50 participants per session. Day program cost: $729. Boarding program cost: $1129. Financial aid available.
Application Deadline Continuous.
Jobs Positions for college students 18 and older.
Contact Client Service Representatives, 42 West Campbell Avenue, Suite 301, Campbell, California 95008. Phone: 888-709-TECH. Fax: 408-871-2228. E-mail: info@internaldrive.com
URL www.internaldrive.com

For more information, see page 520.

TEXAS

CAMP LA JUNTA

Camp La Junta
1585 Highway 39
Hunt, Texas 78024

General Information Boys' residential traditional camp established in 1928.
Program Focus Individualized programs and recreation.
Arts Arts and crafts (general).
Special Interest Areas Campcraft, driver's education, flight instruction, leadership training, model rocketry, nature study, team building.
Sports Archery, baseball, basketball, bicycling, boating, canoeing, climbing (wall), equestrian sports, fishing, football, golf, horseback riding, kayaking, rappelling, riflery, ropes course, sailing, scuba diving, snorkeling, soccer, softball, swimming, tennis, volleyball, waterskiing.
Wilderness/Outdoors Canoe trips, hiking, mountain biking, orienteering, pack animal trips, rock climbing, survival training, wilderness camping.
Trips Day, overnight.
Program Information 6 sessions per year. Session length: 13–26 days in June, July. Ages: 6–14. 100–200 participants per session. Boarding program cost: $1750–$3200. Financial aid available.
Application Deadline Continuous.
Jobs Positions for college students 18 and older.
Contact Blake W. Smith, Camp Director, PO Box 139, Hunt, Texas 78024. Phone: 830-238-4621. Fax: 830-238-4888. E-mail: lajunta@ktc.com.
URL www.lajunta.com

CAMP RIO VISTA FOR BOYS

Vista Camps
175 Rio Vista Road
Ingram, Texas 78025

General Information Boys' residential traditional camp established in 1921.
Program Focus Providing safe, wholesome, fun-filled learning camp experiences.
Arts Arts and crafts (general), jewelry making, leather working, music (instrumental), photography, television/video, theater/drama.
Special Interest Areas Animal care, campcraft, leadership training, nature study.
Sports Archery, basketball, canoeing, climbing (wall), equestrian sports, fencing, fishing, football, golf, horseback riding, kayaking, lacrosse, martial arts, rappelling, riflery, ropes course, sailing, soccer, softball, sports (general), swimming, tennis, track and field, volleyball, waterskiing, weight training, wrestling.
Wilderness/Outdoors Hiking, hunter safety, orienteering.
Program Information 4 sessions per year. Session length: 12–26 days in June, July, August. Ages: 6–16. 50–150 participants per session. Boarding program cost: $1700–$3100. Application fee: $25. Payment plans available.
Application Deadline Continuous.
Jobs Positions for high school students 18 and older and college students 18 and older.
Contact Mr. Mike Roberts, Camp Director, 175 Rio Vista Road, Ingram, Texas 78025. Phone: 830-367-5353. Fax: 830-367-4044. E-mail: riovista@ktc.com.
URL www.vistacamps.com

CAMP SIERRA VISTA FOR GIRLS

Vista Camps
175 Rio Vista Road
Ingram, Texas 78025

General Information Girls' residential traditional camp established in 1982.
Program Focus Providing safe, wholesome, fun-filled learning camp experiences.
Arts Arts and crafts (general), dance, fabric arts, jewelry making, leather working, music (instrumental), photography, television/video, theater/drama.
Special Interest Areas Animal care, campcraft, leadership training, nature study.
Sports Aerobics, archery, basketball, canoeing, cheerleading, climbing (wall), equestrian sports, fencing, fishing, golf, horseback riding, kayaking, lacrosse, martial arts, rappelling, riflery, ropes course, sailing, soccer, softball, sports (general), swimming, tennis, track and field, volleyball, waterskiing, weight training.
Wilderness/Outdoors Hiking, hunter safety, orienteering.
Program Information 4 sessions per year. Session length: 12–26 days in June, July, August. Ages: 6–16. 50–105 participants per session. Boarding program cost: $1700–$3100. Application fee: $25. Payment plans available.
Application Deadline Continuous.
Jobs Positions for high school students 18 and older and college students 18 and older.
Contact Ms. Joanne Kovac-Roberts, Camp Director, 175 Rio Vista Road, Ingram, Texas 78025. Phone: 830-367-5353. Fax: 830-367-4044. E-mail: riovista@ktc.com.
URL www.vistacamps.com

iD TECH CAMPS–SOUTHERN METHODIST UNIVERSITY, DALLAS, TX

iD Tech Camps
Southern Methodist University
Dallas, Texas 75205

General Information Coed residential and day academic program established in 1999. Accredited by American Camping Association. Formal opportunities for the academically talented and artistically talented.
Program Focus Students create 2D and 3D video games, build robots to compete, design websites, film and edit digital movies, create their own comic book with digital photos, learn programming and more. One computer per student and an average of five students per staff member. Campers take home a project at the end of the weeklong course.
Academics Web page design, academics (general), computer programming, computer science (Advanced Placement), computers, precollege program.
Arts Animation, cinematography, digital media, drawing, film, film editing, film production, graphic arts, photography, television/video.
Special Interest Areas Career exploration, computer game design, computer graphics, electronics, leadership training, robotics, team building.

Sports Baseball, basketball, soccer, softball, swimming, volleyball.
Trips College tours.
Program Information 5–9 sessions per year. Session length: 5–7 days in June, July, August. Ages: 7–17. 40–50 participants per session. Day program cost: $729. Boarding program cost: $1129. Financial aid available.
Application Deadline Continuous.
Jobs Positions for college students 18 and older.
Contact Client Service Representatives, 42 West Campbell Avenue, Suite 301, Campbell, California 95008. Phone: 888-709-TECH. Fax: 408-871-2228. E-mail: info@internaldrive.com.
URL www.internaldrive.com
For more information, see page 520.

iD Tech Camps–University of Houston, Houston, TX

iD Tech Camps
University of Houston
Houston, Texas 77204

General Information Coed residential and day academic program established in 1999. Accredited by American Camping Association. Formal opportunities for the academically talented and artistically talented.
Program Focus Students create 2D and 3D video games, build robots to compete, design websites, film and edit digital movies, create their own comic book with digital photos, learn programming and more. One computer per student and an average of five students per staff member. Campers take home a project at the end of the weeklong course.
Academics Web page design, academics (general), computer programming, computer science (Advanced Placement), computers, precollege program.
Arts Animation, cinematography, digital media, drawing, film, film editing, film production, graphic arts, photography, television/video.
Special Interest Areas Career exploration, computer game design, computer graphics, electronics, leadership training, robotics, team building.
Sports Baseball, basketball, soccer, softball, swimming, volleyball.
Trips College tours.
Program Information 5–9 sessions per year. Session length: 5–7 days in June, July, August. Ages: 7–17. 40–50 participants per session. Day program cost: $729. Boarding program cost: $1129. Financial aid available.
Application Deadline Continuous.
Jobs Positions for college students 18 and older.

Contact Client Service Representatives, 42 West Campbell Avenue, Suite 301, Campbell, California 95008. Phone: 888-709-TECH. Fax: 408-871-2228. E-mail: info@internaldrive.com.
URL www.internaldrive.com
For more information, see page 520.

iD Tech Camps–UT Austin, Austin, TX

iD Tech Camps
The University of Texas at Austin
Austin, Texas 78712

General Information Coed residential and day academic program established in 1999. Accredited by American Camping Association. Formal opportunities for the academically talented and artistically talented.
Program Focus Students create 2D and 3D video games, build robots to compete, design websites, film and edit digital movies, create their own comic book with digital photos, learn programming and more. One computer per student and an average of five students per staff member. Campers take home a project at the end of the weeklong course.
Academics Web page design, academics (general), computer programming, computer science (Advanced Placement), computers, precollege program.
Arts Animation, cinematography, digital media, drawing, film, film editing, film production, graphic arts, photography, television/video.
Special Interest Areas Career exploration, computer game design, computer graphics, electronics, leadership training, robotics, team building.
Sports Baseball, basketball, soccer, softball, swimming, volleyball.
Trips College tours.
Program Information 5–9 sessions per year. Session length: 5–7 days in June, July, August. Ages: 7–17. 40–50 participants per session. Day program cost: $729. Boarding program cost: $1129. Financial aid available.
Application Deadline Continuous.
Jobs Positions for college students 18 and older.

iD Tech Camps–UT Austin, Austin, TX (continued)

Contact Client Service Representatives, 42 West Campbell Avenue, Suite 301, Campbell, California 95008. Phone: 888-709-TECH. Fax: 408-871-2228. E-mail: info@internaldrive.com.
URL www.internaldrive.com
For more information, see page 520.

JUNIOR STATESMEN SYMPOSIUM ON TEXAS POLITICS AND LEADERSHIP

Junior Statesmen Foundation
The University of Texas at Austin
Austin, Texas 78712-1157

General Information Coed residential academic program established in 1999. Formal opportunities for the academically talented.

Junior Statesmen Symposium on Texas Politics and Leadership

Program Focus Leadership at the national, state, and high school level.
Academics Communications, government and politics, journalism, social science, social studies, speech/debate.
Special Interest Areas Career exploration, leadership training.
Trips College tours, cultural, day.
Program Information 1 session per year. Session length: 4 days in June. Ages: 14–18. 100–130 participants per session. Boarding program cost: $370.
Application Deadline Continuous.
Contact Ms. Jessica Brow, National Summer School Director, 400 South El Camino Real, Suite 300, San Mateo, California 94402. Phone: 800-334-5353. Fax: 650-347-7200. E-mail: jsa@jsa.org.
URL summer.jsa.org/symposium/texas.html
For more information, see page 534.

THE RENAISSANCE SCHOLAR PROGRAM

Baylor University Honors College and School of Engineering/Computer Science
1 Bear Place, #97181
Waco, Texas 76798-7181

General Information Coed residential academic program established in 2006. Formal opportunities for the academically talented. College credit may be earned.

The Renaissance Scholar Program

Program Focus Interdisciplinary study of science, technology, literature, philosophy, theology, and contemporary film.
Academics American literature, English language/literature, Greek language/literature, academics (general), aerospace science, classical languages/literatures, computer programming, computer science (Advanced Placement), computers, engineering, environmental science, history, humanities, philosophy, precollege program, reading.
Arts Arts and crafts (general), film.
Special Interest Areas Career exploration, college planning.
Sports Climbing (wall), racquetball.
Program Information 3 sessions per year. Session length: 6 days in June. Ages: 16–17. 30 participants per session. Boarding program cost: $1800. Financial aid available.
Application Deadline Continuous.
Contact Ms. Petra Carey, Coordinator of Summer Programs, Communications, & External Relations, main address above. Phone: 254-710-1523. Fax: 254-710-7782. E-mail: petra_carey@baylor.edu.
URL www.baylor.edu/renaissancescholar
For more information, see page 426.

SOUTHERN METHODIST UNIVERSITY– COLLEGE EXPERIENCE

Southern Methodist University
Dallas, Texas 75275

General Information Coed residential and day academic program established in 1978. Formal opportunities for the academically talented and gifted. College credit may be earned.

Academics American literature, English language/ literature, academics (general), anthropology, art history/appreciation, chemistry, computer programming, computers, economics, engineering, geology/earth science, government and politics, history, journalism, mathematics, philosophy, precollege program, psychology, social science, writing.
Arts Creative writing, film.
Trips Cultural.
Program Information 1 session per year. Session length: 25–30 days in July, August. Ages: 15–18. 70 participants per session. Day program cost: $2200. Boarding program cost: $3500. Application fee: $35. Financial aid available.
Application Deadline Continuous.
Jobs Positions for college students 21 and older.
Contact Marilyn Swanson, Director of Programming, PO Box 750383, Dallas, Texas 75275. Phone: 214-768-0123. Fax: 214-768-3147. E-mail: gifted@smu.edu.
URL www.smu.edu/ce
For more information, see page 636.

SOUTHERN METHODIST UNIVERSITY TAG (TALENTED AND GIFTED)

Southern Methodist University
Dallas, Texas 75275

General Information Coed residential academic program established in 1978. Formal opportunities for the academically talented and gifted. College credit may be earned.

Southern Methodist University TAG (Talented and Gifted)

Academics American literature, English language/ literature, academics (general), art history/appreciation, engineering, geography, government and politics, humanities, mathematics, philosophy, precollege program, psychology, science (general), social science, writing.
Arts Creative writing, music, photography, theater/ drama.
Special Interest Areas Leadership training, model rocketry.
Trips Cultural, day.
Program Information 1 session per year. Session length: 3 weeks in July. Ages: 12–15. 75–100 participants per session. Boarding program cost: $2500. Application fee: $35. Financial aid available.
Application Deadline Continuous.
Jobs Positions for college students 19 and older.
Contact Ms. Marilyn Swanson, Director of Programming, PO Box 750383, Dallas, Texas 75275. Phone: 214-768-0123. Fax: 214-768-3147. E-mail: gifted@smu.edu.
URL www.smu.edu/tag
For more information, see page 636.

THE SUMMER INSTITUTE FOR THE GIFTED AT UNIVERSITY OF TEXAS, AUSTIN

Summer Institute for the Gifted
University of Texas, Austin
Austin, Texas 78705

General Information Coed residential academic program established in 2007. Formal opportunities for the academically talented and gifted. College credit may be earned.
Academics American literature, English language/ literature, French language/literature, SAT/ACT preparation, Spanish language/literature, academics (general), aerospace science, archaeology, architecture, art history/appreciation, biology, business, chemistry, classical languages/literatures, communications, computers, engineering, environmental science, government and politics, history, marine studies, mathematics, music, oceanography, philosophy, physics, physiology, precollege program, psychology, science (general), social studies, speech/debate, study skills, writing.
Arts Band, chorus, creative writing, dance, drawing, film, graphic arts, music, music (chamber), music (classical), music (ensemble), music (instrumental), musical productions, painting, photography, sculpture, theater/drama.
Special Interest Areas Animal care, electronics, meditation, robotics.
Sports Aerobics, archery, baseball, basketball, fencing, field hockey, football, lacrosse, martial arts, soccer, squash, swimming, tennis, track and field, volleyball.
Trips Cultural.
Program Information 1–2 sessions per year. Session length: 3 weeks in June, July, August. Ages: 8–17. 150–250 participants per session. Boarding program cost: $3700–$4200. Application fee: $75. Financial aid available.
Application Deadline May 14.

The Summer Institute for the Gifted at University of Texas, Austin (continued)

Jobs Positions for college students 19 and older.
Contact Barbara Swicord, Director, River Plaza, 9 West Broad Street, Stamford, Connecticut 06902-3788. Phone: 866-303-4744. Fax: 203-399-5598. E-mail: sig.info@aifs.com.
URL www.giftedstudy.com
For more information, see page 654.

UTAH

WORLD HORIZONS INTERNATIONAL-KANAB, UTAH

World Horizons International
Kanab, Utah

General Information Coed residential outdoor program and community service program established in 1996.
Program Focus Working with abused and abandoned animals in conjunction with "Best Friends Animal Sanctuary".
Special Interest Areas Animal care, career exploration, community service.
Sports Horseback riding, swimming.
Wilderness/Outdoors Backpacking, hiking.
Trips Cultural, day, overnight.
Program Information 1–2 sessions per year. Session length: 10–21 days in June, July, August. Ages: 13–18. 10–12 participants per session. Boarding program cost: $2595–$4195. Application fee: $175. Financial aid available.
Application Deadline Continuous.
Jobs Positions for college students 21 and older.
Contact Mr. Stuart L. Rabinowitz, Executive Director, PO Box 662, Bethlehem, Connecticut 06751. Phone: 800-262-5874. Fax: 203-266-6227. E-mail: worldhorizons@att.net.
URL www.world-horizons.com
For more information, see page 714.

VERMONT

FUTURE LEADER CAMP

Norwich University
27 I. D. White Avenue
Northfield, Vermont 05663

General Information Coed residential outdoor
program and adventure program established in 1998.

Future Leader Camp

Program Focus Leadership and team skills development for active participants in community service,
sports, scouting and youth groups.
Special Interest Areas Career exploration, college
planning, community service, first aid, leadership
training, lifesaving, nature study, team building.
Sports Archery, climbing (wall), martial arts, physical
fitness, rappelling, riflery, ropes course, swimming, track
and field.
Wilderness/Outdoors Backpacking, hiking,
orienteering, outdoor adventure, rock climbing, survival
training, wilderness camping.
Trips College tours, day, overnight.
Program Information 2 sessions per year. Session
length: 2 weeks in June, July. Ages: 15–18. 80
participants per session. Boarding program cost: $1455.
Application fee: $25. Open to participants entering
grades 10–12.
Application Deadline Continuous.

Contact Maj. Guy Boucher, Operations Officer, 27 I.D.
White Avenue, Northfield, Vermont 05663. Phone:
802-485-2531. Fax: 802-485-2739. E-mail: flc@norwich.
edu.
URL www.norwich.edu/flc
For more information, see page 496.

KEEWAYDIN DUNMORE

Keewaydin Foundation
10 Keewaydin Road
Salisbury, Vermont 05769

General Information Boys' residential traditional
camp and outdoor program established in 1910.
Accredited by American Camping Association.
Program Focus Canoeing and backpacking trips plus
full in-camp program.
Arts Arts and crafts (general), photography, theater/
drama, woodworking.
Special Interest Areas Campcraft, nature study.
Sports Archery, baseball, basketball, boxing, canoeing,
climbing (wall), diving, fencing, fishing, golf, kayaking,
martial arts, rappelling, riflery, sailing, snorkeling,
soccer, softball, swimming, tennis, windsurfing,
wrestling.
Wilderness/Outdoors Backpacking, canoe trips,
caving, hiking, mountaineering, orienteering, rock
climbing, white-water trips, wilderness camping.
Trips Cultural, day, overnight.
Program Information 1–2 sessions per year. Session
length: 4–8 weeks in June, July, August. Ages: 8–16. 215
participants per session. Boarding program cost: $5150–
$6750. Financial aid available.
Application Deadline Continuous.
Jobs Positions for college students 18 and older.
Contact Mr. Peter Hare, Director, main address above.
Phone: 802-352-4770. Fax: 802-352-4772. E-mail:
pete@keewaydin.org.
URL www.keewaydin.org

KILLOOLEET

Route 100
Hancock, Vermont 05748-0070

General Information Coed residential traditional camp established in 1927. Accredited by American Camping Association. Formal opportunities for the artistically talented.

Killooleet

Program Focus Personal development and leadership skills.
Arts Acting, arts, arts and crafts (general), band, batiking, ceramics, creative writing, dance, drawing, fabric arts, graphic arts, guitar, jewelry making, metalworking, music, music (folk), music (jazz), music (rock), music (vocal), musical productions, painting, photography, pottery, stained glass, television/video, theater/drama, weaving, woodworking.
Special Interest Areas Campcraft, electronics, gardening, leadership training, model rocketry, nature study, team building.
Sports Archery, basketball, bicycling, boating, canoeing, diving, fencing, fishing, horseback riding, kayaking, martial arts, rappelling, riflery, sailing, soccer, softball, swimming, tennis, ultimate frisbee, volleyball, windsurfing.
Wilderness/Outdoors Backpacking, bicycle trips, canoe trips, caving, hiking, mountain biking, mountaineering, rock climbing, wilderness/outdoors (general).
Trips Day, overnight.
Program Information 1 session per year. Session length: 50–55 days in June, July, August. Ages: 9–14. 100–105 participants per session. Boarding program cost: $6600. Financial aid available.
Application Deadline Continuous.
Jobs Positions for college students 19 and older.
Summer Contact Ms. Kate Seeger, Director, PO Box 70, Hancock, Vermont 05748. Phone: 802-767-3152.
Winter Contact Ms. Kate Seeger, Director, 70 Trull Street, Somerville, Massachusetts 02145. Phone: 617-666-1484. Fax: 617-666-0378. E-mail: kseeger@killooleet.com.
URL www.killooleet.com
For more information, see page 538.

LANDMARK VOLUNTEERS: VERMONT

Landmark Volunteers, Inc.
Vermont

General Information Coed residential outdoor program and community service program established in 1992. High school credit may be earned.
Program Focus Opportunity for high school students to earn community service credit while working as a team for two weeks serving Merck Forest, Morgan Horse farm, and Eddy Farm School. Similar programs offered through Landmark Volunteers at over 50 locations in 20 states.
Academics Ecology, environmental science.
Special Interest Areas Career exploration, community service, conservation projects, farming, leadership training, team building, trail maintenance, work camp programs.
Sports Swimming.
Wilderness/Outdoors Hiking.
Trips Cultural, day.
Program Information 2 sessions per year. Session length: 2 weeks in July, August. Ages: 14–18. 10–13 participants per session. Boarding program cost: $1250–$1300. Financial aid available.
Application Deadline Continuous.
Jobs Positions for college students.
Contact Ann Barrett, Executive Director, PO Box 455, Sheffield, Massachusetts 01257. Phone: 413-229-0255. Fax: 413-229-2050. E-mail: landmark@volunteers.com.
URL www.volunteers.com
For more information, see page 542.

LOCHEARN CAMP FOR GIRLS

Lake Fairlee
1061 Robinson Hill Road
Post Mills, Vermont 05058

General Information Girls' residential traditional camp established in 1916. Accredited by American Camping Association.
Academics Reading.
Arts Acting, arts and crafts (general), basketry, ceramics, chorus, creative writing, dance, dance (jazz), drawing, jewelry making, musical productions, painting, pottery, quilting, set design, theater/drama.
Special Interest Areas Leadership training.
Sports Aerobics, archery, basketball, canoeing, cross-country, diving, equestrian sports, field hockey, gymnastics, horseback riding, lacrosse, sailing, snorkeling, soccer, softball, swimming, tennis, volleyball, waterskiing.
Wilderness/Outdoors Hiking.
Trips Day, overnight.
Program Information 2 sessions per year. Session length: 27 days in June, July, August. Ages: 8–15. 170 participants per session. Boarding program cost: $4550. Financial aid available.
Application Deadline Continuous.
Jobs Positions for college students 18 and older.

Contact Ginny Maxson, Director, Lake Fairlee, PO Box 400, Post Mills, Vermont 05058. Phone: 802-333-4211. Fax: 802-333-4856. E-mail: ginny@lochearncamp.com. **URL** www.lochearncamp.com

MAD RIVER GLEN NATURALIST ADVENTURE CAMP

Mad River Glen Cooperative
Route 17 West, 62 Mad River Resort Road
Waitsfield, Vermont 05673

General Information Coed day traditional camp and outdoor program established in 1998.
Program Focus Adventure activities and naturalist skills, plus environmental education in a day camp setting.
Academics Biology, botany, ecology, environmental science, geology/earth science, science (general).
Arts Arts and crafts (general).
Special Interest Areas Field research/expeditions, nature study, team building.
Sports Bicycling, canoeing, climbing (wall), fishing, kayaking, rappelling, ropes course.
Wilderness/Outdoors Backpacking, canoe trips, hiking, mountain biking, rock climbing, wilderness camping.
Trips Day, overnight.
Program Information 10 sessions per year. Session length: 1–5 days in June, July, August. Ages: 8–12. 6–13 participants per session. Day program cost: $47–$282. Application fee: $25. Financial aid available.
Application Deadline Continuous.
Jobs Positions for college students 18 and older.
Contact Mr. Sean T. Lawson, Naturalist Program Director, PO Box 1089, Waitsfield, Vermont 05673. Phone: 802-496-3551 Ext.117. Fax: 802-496-3562. E-mail: sean@madriverglen.com.
URL www.madriverglen.com/naturalist

THE PUTNEY SCHOOL SUMMER ARTS PROGRAM

The Putney School
Elm Lea Farm
418 Houghton Brook Road
Putney, Vermont 05346

General Information Coed residential and day arts program established in 1987. Formal opportunities for the artistically talented.

The Putney School Summer Arts Program

Program Focus Visual and performing arts, music, and theater.
Academics English as a second language, art (Advanced Placement), music, music (Advanced Placement), writing.
Arts Acting, animation, arts, ceramics, chorus, creative writing, dance, dance (jazz), dance (modern), drawing, fabric arts, film, jewelry making, metalworking, music, music (chamber), music (classical), music (ensemble), music (instrumental), music (jazz), music (orchestral), music (vocal), music composition/arrangement, painting, performing arts, photography, playwriting, pottery, printmaking, sculpture, songwriting, stained glass, studio arts, theater/drama, visual arts, weaving, woodworking.
Special Interest Areas Animal care, community service, farming, gardening.
Sports Basketball, bicycling, canoeing, fencing,

The Putney School Summer Arts Program (continued)

horseback riding, running/jogging, soccer, softball, swimming, volleyball.
Wilderness/Outdoors Backpacking, canoe trips, hiking, mountain biking.
Trips Cultural, day, overnight.
Program Information 2 sessions per year. Session length: 18 days in June, July, August. Ages: 14–17. 110–140 participants per session. Day program cost: $1150–$2000. Boarding program cost: $3100–$5800. Application fee: $50. Financial aid available.
Application Deadline Continuous.
Jobs Positions for college students 21 and older.
Contact Maria Ogden, Administrative Coordinator, main address above. Phone: 802-387-6297. Fax: 802-387-6216. E-mail: summer@putneyschool.org.
URL www.putneyschool.org/summer
For more information, see page 596.

THE PUTNEY SCHOOL SUMMER PROGRAM FOR INTERNATIONAL EDUCATION (ESL)

The Putney School
Elm Lea Farm
418 Houghton Brook Road
Putney, Vermont 05346

General Information Coed residential academic program established in 1987. Formal opportunities for the artistically talented.
Program Focus English as a second language, cultural exchange.
Academics English as a second language, English language/literature, intercultural studies, reading, social studies, speech/debate, study skills, writing.
Arts Animation, batiking, ceramics, chorus, creative writing, dance, drawing, fabric arts, graphic arts, jewelry making, metalworking, music, painting, photography, printmaking, sculpture, theater/drama, weaving, woodworking.
Special Interest Areas Animal care, community service, cross-cultural education, farming, field trips (arts and culture), gardening.
Sports Basketball, canoeing, fencing, horseback riding, running/jogging, soccer, softball, swimming, volleyball.
Wilderness/Outdoors Backpacking, canoe trips, hiking.
Trips Cultural, day, overnight.
Program Information 2 sessions per year. Session length: 18 days in June, July, August. Ages: 14–17. 20–30 participants per session. Boarding program cost: $3300–$6150. Application fee: $50. Financial aid available.
Application Deadline Continuous.
Jobs Positions for college students 21 and older.
Contact Maria Ogden, Administrative Coordinator, main address above. Phone: 802-387-6297. Fax: 802-387-6216. E-mail: summer@putneyschool.org.
URL www.putneyschool.org/summer
For more information, see page 596.

THE PUTNEY SCHOOL SUMMER WRITING PROGRAM

The Putney School
Elm Lea Farm
418 Houghton Brook Road
Putney, Vermont 05346

General Information Coed residential academic program and arts program established in 1987. Formal opportunities for the academically talented, artistically talented, and gifted.
Program Focus Creative writing, fiction, playwriting, and poetry.
Academics English language/literature, writing.
Arts Animation, arts, batiking, ceramics, chorus, creative writing, dance, drawing, fabric arts, graphic arts, jewelry making, metalworking, music, music (chamber), music (classical), music (jazz), music (orchestral), music (vocal), painting, photography, playwriting, pottery, printmaking, sculpture, theater/drama, weaving, woodworking.
Special Interest Areas Animal care, community service, field trips (arts and culture), gardening.
Sports Basketball, bicycling, canoeing, fencing, horseback riding, soccer, softball, swimming, volleyball.
Wilderness/Outdoors Backpacking, canoe trips, hiking.
Trips Cultural, day, overnight.
Program Information 2 sessions per year. Session length: 18 days in June, July, August. Ages: 14–17. 12–15 participants per session. Boarding program cost: $3100–$5800. Application fee: $50. Financial aid available.
Application Deadline Continuous.
Jobs Positions for college students 21 and older.
Contact Maria Ogden, Administrative Coordinator, main address above. Phone: 802-387-6297. Fax: 802-387-6216. E-mail: summer@putneyschool.org.
URL www.putneyschool.org/summer
For more information, see page 596.

ROARING BROOK CAMP FOR BOYS

480 Roaring Brook Road
Bradford, Vermont 05033

General Information Boys' residential outdoor
program established in 1965. Accredited by American
Camping Association.
Program Focus Outdoor sports, Vermont crafts, and
wilderness backpack/canoe trips.
Arts Blacksmithing, fly-tying, leather working,
metalworking, woodworking.
Special Interest Areas Campcraft, leadership
training, nature study.
Sports Archery, canoeing, fishing, kayaking, rappelling,
riflery, ropes course, swimming.
Wilderness/Outdoors Backpacking, canoe trips,
hiking, mountain biking, mountaineering, orienteering,
outdoor living skills, rafting, rock climbing, survival
training, white-water trips, wilderness camping,
wilderness/outdoors (general).
Trips Day, overnight.
Program Information 3 sessions per year. Session
length: 2–6 weeks in June, July, August. Ages: 9–16. 45
participants per session. Boarding program cost: $1900–
$5200.
Application Deadline Continuous.
Jobs Positions for college students 21 and older.
Summer Contact Dr. Candice L. Raines, Director/
Owner, main address above. Phone: 802-222-5702.
Winter Contact Dr. Candice L. Raines, Director/
Owner, 300 Grove Street, #4, Rutland, Vermont 05701.
Phone: 800-832-4295. Fax: 802-786-0653. E-mail:
rainest@sover.net.
URL www.roaringbrookcamp.com

SONGADEEWIN OF KEEWAYDIN

Keewaydin Foundation
500 Rustic Lane
Salisbury, Vermont 05769

General Information Girls' residential traditional
camp and outdoor program established in 1999.
Accredited by American Camping Association.
Program Focus Canoeing and backpacking trip plus
full in-camp program.
Arts Arts and crafts (general), dance, music (vocal),
photography.
Special Interest Areas Campcraft, nature study.
Sports Archery, basketball, canoeing, climbing (wall),
field hockey, golf, kayaking, lacrosse, riflery, sailing,
soccer, softball, swimming, tennis, volleyball.
Wilderness/Outdoors Backpacking, canoe trips,
hiking, rock climbing, white-water trips, wilderness
camping.
Trips Cultural, day, overnight.
Program Information 1–2 sessions per year. Session
length: 4–8 weeks in June, July, August. Ages: 8–15.
110–112 participants per session. Boarding program
cost: $5150–$6750. Financial aid available.
Application Deadline Continuous.
Jobs Positions for college students.

Contact Ellen Flight, Director, 500 Rustic Lane,
Salisbury, Vermont 05769. Phone: 802-352-9860. Fax:
802-352-4772. E-mail: ellen@keewaydin.org.
URL www.keewaydin.org

UNIVERSITY OF VERMONT SUMMER ENGINEERING INSTITUTE FOR HIGH SCHOOL STUDENTS

University of Vermont, College of Engineering
and Mathematical Sciences
101 Votey Building
Burlington, Vermont 05405

General Information Coed residential academic
program established in 1990. Formal opportunities for
the academically talented. Specific services available for
the physically challenged.
Program Focus Firsthand insight into civil, electrical,
mechanical, environmental, aerospace, and biomedical
engineering, computer science, and mathematical
sciences. Hands-on projects include: aeronautical, biom-
ass, robotics, and wind energy. Students will do
research, create a poster presentation and create a
working device during the Institute.
Academics English language/literature, aerospace
science, computer science (Advanced Placement),
computers, engineering, mathematics, music, writing.
Arts Music.
Special Interest Areas Career exploration, robotics,
team building.
Sports Volleyball.
Trips Day.
Program Information 1 session per year. Session
length: 9 days in June. Ages: 15–16. 90–115 participants
per session. Boarding program cost: $980. Financial aid
available.
Application Deadline Continuous.
Contact Ms. Dawn Densmore, Director, College of
Engineering and Mathematical Sciences, 101 Votey
Building, Burlington, Vermont 05405. Phone: 802-656-
8748. Fax: 802-656-8802.
URL www.cems.uvm.edu/summer

Special Note
Discover the Power of Engineering Thought! The
UVM/GIV Engineering Summer Institute is packed with
projects that stretch students' creativity and challenge
the way they see the world! Learn how to think outside
the box with hands-on activities, laboratory experiences,
faculty presentations, and enlightening tours. See the
links between technology and the human experience.
Consider a career that could impact the twenty-first
century with global environmental solutions. Experience
the thrill of creating sand arches, and become part of a
team to design, construct, and build prototype projects.
For pictures and more information on this program,
students should visit http://www.cems.uvm.edu/summer/.

VIRGINIA

CAMP HOLIDAY TRAILS

Holiday Trails, Inc.
400 Holiday Trails Lane
Charlottesville, Virginia 22903

General Information Coed residential special needs program established in 1973. Accredited by American Camping Association. Specific services available for the hearing impaired, physically challenged, visually impaired, diabetic, participant with heart defects, participant with cancer, participant with HIV/AIDS, organ transplant recipient, participant with asthma, epileptic, participant with kidney disorders, participant with hemophilia, participant with Sickle Cell Anemia, participant with Cystic Fibrosis, and participant with arthritis.
Program Focus Children with chronic illness and special medical needs.
Arts Aboriginal arts, acting, arts and crafts (general), ceramics, creative writing, dance, drawing, fabric arts, jewelry making, leather working, music, painting, photography, pottery, puppetry, theater/drama, woodworking.
Special Interest Areas Campcraft, community service, conservation projects, culinary arts, gardening, leadership training, nature study, team building, weight reduction.
Sports Archery, basketball, canoeing, challenge course, climbing (wall), equestrian sports, fishing, horseback riding, rappelling, ropes course, swimming, tennis, volleyball.
Wilderness/Outdoors Hiking, orienteering.
Trips Day, overnight.
Program Information 3–5 sessions per year. Session length: 6–13 days in January, February, March, April, May, June, July, August, September, October, November, December. Ages: 5–17. 50–70 participants per session. Boarding program cost: $670–$1120. Application fee: $60. Financial aid available.
Application Deadline Continuous.
Jobs Positions for high school students 18 and older and college students 18 and older.
Contact Ashleigh Suthers, Program Director, main address above. Phone: 434-977-3781. Fax: 434-977-8814. E-mail: ashleigh@campholidaytrails.org.
URL www.campholidaytrails.org

CYBERCAMPS–GEORGE MASON UNIVERSITY

Cybercamps–Giant Campus, Inc.
Fairfax, Virginia

General Information Coed residential and day academic program established in 1997. Formal opportunities for the academically talented.
Program Focus Computers and technology.
Academics Web page design, academics (general), computer programming, computer science (Advanced Placement), computers.
Arts Animation, digital media, film, graphic arts, musical productions, photography, television/video.
Special Interest Areas Computer game design, computer graphics, electronics, robotics, team building.
Program Information 1–12 sessions per year. Session length: 5 days in June, July, August. Ages: 7–18. 30–50 participants per session. Day program cost: $599–$749. Boarding program cost: $998–$1148.
Application Deadline Continuous.
Jobs Positions for high school students 17 and older and college students 18 and older.
Contact Camp Consultant, 3101 Western Avenue, Suite 100, Seattle, Washington 98121. Phone: 888-904-2267. Fax: 206-442-4501. E-mail: info@cybercamps.com.
URL www.cybercamps.com
For more information, see page 466.

CYBERCAMPS–NORTHERN VIRGINIA COMMUNITY COLLEGE

Cybercamps–Giant Campus, Inc.
Alexandria, Virginia

General Information Coed residential and day academic program established in 1997. Formal opportunities for the academically talented.
Program Focus Computers and technology.
Academics Web page design, academics (general), computer programming, computer science (Advanced Placement), computers.
Arts Animation, digital media, film, graphic arts, musical productions, photography, television/video.
Special Interest Areas Computer game design, computer graphics, electronics, robotics, team building.
Program Information 1–12 sessions per year. Session length: 5 days in June, July, August. Ages: 7–18. 30–50 participants per session. Day program cost: $599–$749. Boarding program cost: $998–$1148.
Application Deadline Continuous.
Contact Camp Consultant, 3101 Western Avenue, Suite 100, Seattle, Washington 98121. Phone: 888-904-2267. Fax: 206-442-4501. E-mail: info@cybercamps.com.
URL www.cybercamps.com
For more information, see page 466.

CYBERCAMPS–OAK MARR REC CENTER

Cybercamps–Giant Campus, Inc.
Oakton, Virginia

General Information Coed residential and day academic program established in 1997. Formal opportunities for the academically talented.
Program Focus Computers and technology.
Academics Web page design, academics (general), computer programming, computer science (Advanced Placement), computers.
Arts Animation, digital media, film, graphic arts, musical productions, photography, television/video.
Special Interest Areas Computer game design, computer graphics, electronics, robotics, team building.
Program Information 1–12 sessions per year. Session length: 5 days in June, July, August. Ages: 7–18. 30–50 participants per session. Day program cost: $599–$749. Boarding program cost: $998–$1148.
Application Deadline Continuous.
Contact Camp Consultant, 3101 Western Avenue, Suite 100, Seattle, Washington 98121. Phone: 888-904-2267. Fax: 206-442-4501. E-mail: info@cybercamps.com.
URL www.cybercamps.com

For more information, see page 466.

FAIRFAX COLLEGIATE SCHOOL SUMMER ENRICHMENT PROGRAM

Fairfax Collegiate School
St. Katherine's Greek Orthodox Church, Falls Church
St. Joseph's Church, Herndon
Virginia

General Information Coed day academic program established in 1993. Formal opportunities for the academically talented.
Academics SAT/ACT preparation, Spanish language/literature, academics (general), computer programming, computers, journalism, mathematics, typing, writing.
Arts Acting, creative writing, film, television/video, theater/drama.
Program Information 5 sessions per year. Session length: 9–10 days in June, July, August. Ages: 8–17. 100 participants per session. Day program cost: $410–$655. Cost: $410 per 10-day course, $655 for 2 courses; 5% discount for multiple siblings or multiple sessions, and also for early registration.
Application Deadline Continuous.
Jobs Positions for high school students 16 and older and college students 18 and older.

Contact Jennifer Nossal, Director, PO Box 8473, Reston, Virginia 20195. Phone: 703-481-3080. Fax: 703-481-3081. E-mail: jennifer_nossal@fairfaxcollegiate.com.
URL www.fairfaxcollegiate.com

GIRLS FIRST

The Madeira School
8328 Georgetown Pike
McLean, Virginia 22102

General Information Girls' residential academic program established in 2006.

Girls First

Academics Chinese languages/literature, English language/literature, academics (general), architecture, biology, chemistry, forensic science, global issues, government and politics, veterinary science.
Arts Acting, arts, arts and crafts (general), creative writing, fashion design/production, jewelry making, performing arts, theater/drama.
Special Interest Areas Animal care.
Sports Aerobics, basketball, ropes course, swimming, tennis, volleyball.
Trips Cultural, day, shopping.
Program Information 2 sessions per year. Session length: 13 days in July, August. 25–50 participants per session. Boarding program cost: $2395. Open to rising 7th–11th graders.
Application Deadline Continuous.
Jobs Positions for college students 18 and older.

Girls First (continued)

Contact Douglas Murphy, Program Director, main address above. Phone: 800-883-4159. E-mail: girlsfirst@madeira.org.
URL www.madeira.org/girlsfirst
For more information, see page 502.

HARGRAVE SUMMER LEADERSHIP PROGRAM

Hargrave Military Academy
Chatham, Virginia 24531

General Information Boys' residential and day academic program and outdoor program established in 1923. Religious affiliation: Christian. Formal opportunities for the academically talented. High school credit may be earned.
Program Focus All students are required to choose at least one sports camp to attend in the afternoon session.
Academics Bible study, English as a second language, English language/literature, SAT/ACT preparation, Spanish language/literature, academics (general), biology, computers, geography, government and politics, history, mathematics, mathematics (Advanced Placement), reading, religion, science (general), social studies, study skills, writing.
Special Interest Areas Leadership training, team building.
Sports Baseball, basketball, canoeing, climbing (wall), football, kayaking, lacrosse, rappelling, riflery, ropes course, soccer, sports (general), swimming, tennis, weight training.
Wilderness/Outdoors Canoe trips, hiking, rock climbing, white-water trips.
Trips Day, overnight, shopping.
Program Information 1 session per year. Session length: 27 days in June, July. Ages: 11–18. 140–160 participants per session. Day program cost: $850–$2400. Boarding program cost: $3750–$4000. Application fee: $75.
Application Deadline Continuous.
Contact Frank L. Martin, III, Director of Admissions, main address above. Phone: 434-432-2585. Fax: 434-432-3129. E-mail: martinf@grave.edu.
URL www.hargrave.edu

Special Note
Hargrave Military Academy is located in a beautiful setting of hills and valleys in southern Virginia. The campus is in proximity to historic battlefields and museums. The 214-acre campus is located within the town limits of Chatham. Chatham is 65 miles north of Greensboro, North Carolina, and 40 miles south of Lynchburg, Virginia, on U.S. Highway 29. The Academy opened its doors in 1909. The summer school was established in 1923. The summer school provides the opportunity for students to accelerate an academic program, strengthen weak areas, improve reading skills, learn study skills, and enjoy recreational and athletic experiences through the Academy's sports camp. It also gives the fall school applicant the opportunity to familiarize himself with school routine and the life of a boarding student and to spend a profitable and enjoyable summer. Hargrave also has a mandatory study period in the evening in order to enhance students' organizational and study habits.

iD TECH CAMPS–COLLEGE OF WILLIAM AND MARY, WILLIAMSBURG, VA

iD Tech Camps
College of William and Mary
Williamsburg, Virginia 23187

General Information Coed residential and day academic program established in 1999. Accredited by American Camping Association. Formal opportunities for the academically talented and artistically talented.
Program Focus Students create 2D and 3D video games, build robots to compete, design websites, film and edit digital movies, create their own comic book with digital photos, learn programming and more. One computer per student and an average of five students per staff member. Campers take home a project at the end of the weeklong course.
Academics Web page design, academics (general), computer programming, computer science (Advanced Placement), computers, precollege program.
Arts Animation, cinematography, digital media, drawing, film, film editing, film production, graphic arts, photography, television/video.
Special Interest Areas Career exploration, computer game design, computer graphics, electronics, leadership training, robotics, team building.
Sports Baseball, basketball, soccer, softball, swimming, volleyball.
Trips College tours.
Program Information 5–9 sessions per year. Session length: 5–7 days in June, July, August. Ages: 7–17. 40–50 participants per session. Day program cost: $729. Boarding program cost: $1129. Financial aid available.
Application Deadline Continuous.
Jobs Positions for college students 18 and older.

Contact Client Service Representatives, 42 West Campbell Avenue, Suite 301, Campbell, California 95008. Phone: 888-709-TECH. Fax: 408-871-2228. E-mail: info@internaldrive.com
URL www.internaldrive.com
For more information, see page 520.

iD Tech Camps—University of Virginia, Charlottesville, VA

iD Tech Camps
University of Virginia
Charlottesville, Virginia 22904

General Information Coed residential and day academic program established in 1999. Accredited by American Camping Association. Formal opportunities for the academically talented and artistically talented.
Program Focus Students create 2D and 3D video games, build robots to compete, design websites, film and edit digital movies, create their own comic book with digital photos, learn programming and more. One computer per student and an average of five students per staff member. Campers take home a project at the end of the weeklong course.
Academics Web page design, academics (general), computer programming, computer science (Advanced Placement), computers, precollege program.
Arts Animation, cartooning, cinematography, digital media, drawing, film, film editing, film production, graphic arts, photography, television/video.
Special Interest Areas Career exploration, computer game design, computer graphics, electronics, leadership training, robotics, team building.
Sports Baseball, basketball, soccer, softball, swimming, volleyball.
Trips College tours.
Program Information 5–9 sessions per year. Session length: 5–7 days in June, July, August. Ages: 7–17. 40–50 participants per session. Day program cost: $729. Boarding program cost: $1129. Financial aid available.
Application Deadline Continuous.
Jobs Positions for college students 18 and older.

Contact Client Service Representatives, 42 West Campbell Avenue, Suite 301, Campbell, California 95008. Phone: 888-709-TECH. Fax: 408-871-2228. E-mail: info@internaldrive.com
URL www.internaldrive.com
For more information, see page 520.

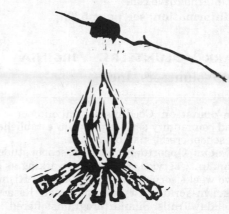

iD Tech Camps—Virginia Tech, Blacksburg, VA

iD Tech Camps
Blacksburg, Virginia

General Information Coed residential and day academic program established in 1999. Accredited by American Camping Association. Formal opportunities for the academically talented and artistically talented.
Program Focus Students create 2D and 3D video games, build robots to compete, design websites, film and edit digital movies, create their own comic book with digital photos, learn programming, and more. One computer per student and an average of five students per staff member. Campers take home a project at the end of the weeklong course.
Academics Web page design, academics (general), computer programming, computer science (Advanced Placement), computers, precollege program.
Arts Animation, cinematography, digital media, drawing, film, film editing, film production, graphic arts, photography, television/video.
Special Interest Areas Career exploration, computer game design, computer graphics, electronics, leadership training, robotics, team building.
Sports Baseball, basketball, soccer, softball, swimming, volleyball.
Trips College tours.
Program Information 5–9 sessions per year. Session length: 5–7 days in June, July, August. Ages: 7–17. 40–50 participants per session. Day program cost: $729. Boarding program cost: $1129. Financial aid available.
Application Deadline Continuous.
Jobs Positions for college students 18 and older.

iD Tech Camps–Virginia Tech, Blacksburg, VA
(continued)

Contact Client Service Representatives, 42 West Campbell Avenue, Suite 301, Campbell, California 95008. Phone: 888-709-TECH. Fax: 408-871-2228. E-mail: info@internaldrive.com. **URL** www.internaldrive.com

For more information, see page 520.

For more information, see page 520.

LANDMARK VOLUNTEERS: VIRGINIA

Landmark Volunteers, Inc.
Virginia

General Information Coed residential outdoor program and community service program established in 1992. High school credit may be earned.
Program Focus Opportunity for high school students to earn community service credit while working as a team for two weeks serving Colonial National Historic Park/Jamestown-Yorktown Foundation, Kerr Reservoir or Camp Holiday Trails. Similar programs offered through Landmark Volunteers at over 50 locations in 20 states.
Academics Art (Advanced Placement), biology, ecology, environmental science, history, social services.
Special Interest Areas Community service, conservation projects, field research/expeditions, leadership training, nature study, team building, trail maintenance.
Sports Swimming.
Wilderness/Outdoors Hiking.
Trips Cultural, day.
Program Information 3 sessions per year. Session length: 2 weeks in June, July, August. Ages: 14–18. 10–13 participants per session. Boarding program cost: $1250–$1300. Financial aid available.
Application Deadline Continuous.
Jobs Positions for college students.
Contact Ann Barrett, Executive Director, PO Box 455, Sheffield, Massachusetts 01257. Phone: 413-229-0255. Fax: 413-229-2050. E-mail: landmark@volunteers.com. **URL** www.volunteers.com

For more information, see page 542.

For more information, see page 542.

RANDOLPH-MACON ACADEMY SUMMER PROGRAMS

Randolph-Macon Academy
200 Academy Drive
Front Royal, Virginia 22630

General Information Coed residential and day academic program established in 1966. Religious affiliation: United Methodist. Formal opportunities for the academically talented. High school credit may be earned.

Randolph-Macon Academy Summer Programs

Academics English as a second language, English language/literature, French language/literature, Latin language, Spanish language/literature, academics (general), biology, chemistry, computers, government and politics, history, mathematics, science (general), social studies, study skills, writing.
Special Interest Areas Flight instruction, team building.
Sports Baseball, basketball, soccer, softball, swimming, tennis, volleyball, weight training.
Wilderness/Outdoors Hiking.
Trips Day.
Program Information 1 session per year. Session length: 27 days in June, July. Ages: 11–19. 180–200 participants per session. Day program cost: $1050–$1395. Boarding program cost: $3239–$4630. Application fee: $75–$200.
Application Deadline Continuous.
Contact Mrs. Paula Brady, Admissions Coordinator, main address above. Phone: 800-272-1172. Fax: 540-636-5419. E-mail: admissions@rma.edu.
URL www.rma.edu

For more information, see page 600.

For more information, see page 600.

WASHINGTON

ADVENTURE TREKS–PACIFIC NORTHWEST ADVENTURES

Adventure Treks, Inc.
Washington

General Information Coed travel outdoor program, wilderness program, and adventure program established in 1978.
Program Focus Multi-activity outdoor adventure program with an emphasis on fun, personal growth, leadership, teamwork, and outdoor skills.
Sports Sea kayaking.
Wilderness/Outdoors Backpacking, hiking, mountaineering, orienteering, rafting, rock climbing, white-water trips, wilderness camping.
Program Information 4–5 sessions per year. Session length: 16–20 days in June, July, August. Ages: 13–16. 24 participants per session. Cost: $2395–$2995. Financial aid available.
Application Deadline Continuous.
Contact John Dockendorf, Director, PO Box 1321, Flat Rock, North Carolina 28731. Phone: 888-954-5555. Fax: 828-696-1663. E-mail: info@advtreks.com.
URL www.adventuretreks.com

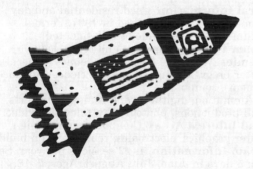

CAMP BERACHAH MINISTRIES–CAMPS AND CONFERENCES

Camp Berachah Ministries Christian Camps and Conferences
19830 South East 328th Place
Auburn, Washington 98092

General Information Coed residential and day traditional camp, outdoor program, sports camp, bible camp, and special needs program established in 1973. Religious affiliation: Christian. Specific services available for the developmentally challenged, hearing impaired, learning disabled, physically challenged, and visually impaired.
Academics Bible study, religion.
Arts Arts and crafts (general).
Special Interest Areas Leadership training.
Sports Archery, bicycling, canoeing, challenge course, climbing (wall), equestrian sports, horseback riding, riflery, ropes course, soccer, swimming, volleyball.
Wilderness/Outdoors Backpacking, hiking, mountain biking, orienteering, outdoor adventure, rafting, rock climbing, wilderness camping.
Trips Day, overnight.
Program Information 25 sessions per year. Session length: 3–6 days in June, July, August. Ages: 5–17. Day program cost: $135–$190. Boarding program cost: $126–$345. Application fee: $30. Financial aid available. Open to participants entering grade 8–college freshmen.
Application Deadline Continuous.
Jobs Positions for high school students 16 and older and college students 18 and older.
Contact Melissa Walker, Human Resources, main address above. Phone: 800-859-CAMP. Fax: 253-833-7027. E-mail: hr@campberachah.org.
URL www.campberachah.org

CANOE ISLAND FRENCH CAMP

Canoe Island French Camp
Canoe Island, San Juan Islands
Washington 98280

General Information Coed residential traditional camp, family program, and cultural program established in 1969. Accredited by American Camping Association. Formal opportunities for the academically talented and artistically talented.
Program Focus French language and culture.
Academics French language/literature, art history/appreciation, astronomy, ecology, marine studies.
Arts Arts and crafts (general), ceramics, creative writing, dance (folk), drawing, film, music, painting, photography, pottery, puppetry, theater/drama.
Special Interest Areas Native American culture, culinary arts, nature study.
Sports Archery, basketball, canoeing, fencing, kayaking, rappelling, sailing, sea kayaking, snorkeling, soccer, swimming, tennis, volleyball.
Wilderness/Outdoors Bicycle trips, rock climbing.
Trips Day, overnight.
Program Information 5 sessions per year. Session length: 2–3 weeks in June, July, August, September. Ages: 9–16. 35–40 participants per session. Boarding program cost: $1885–$2585. Financial aid available.
Application Deadline Continuous.
Jobs Positions for college students 18 and older.
Contact Connie Jones, Camp Director, PO Box 370, Orcas, Washington 98280. Phone: 360-468-2329. Fax: 360-468-3027. E-mail: connie@canoeisland.org.
URL www.canoeisland.org

CYBERCAMPS–BELLEVUE COMMUNITY COLLEGE

Cybercamps–Giant Campus, Inc.
Bellevue, Washington

General Information Coed residential and day academic program established in 1997. Formal opportunities for the academically talented.

Cybercamps–Bellevue Community College (continued)

Program Focus Computers and technology.
Academics Web page design, academics (general), computer programming, computer science (Advanced Placement), computers.
Arts Animation, digital media, film, graphic arts, musical productions, photography, television/video.
Special Interest Areas Computer game design, computer graphics, electronics, robotics, team building.
Program Information 1–12 sessions per year. Session length: 5 days in June, July, August. Ages: 7–18. 30–50 participants per session. Day program cost: $599–$749. Boarding program cost: $998–$1148.
Application Deadline Continuous.
Jobs Positions for high school students 17 and older and college students 18 and older.
Contact Camp Consultant, 3101 Western Avenue, Suite 100, Seattle, Washington 98121. Phone: 888-904-2267. Fax: 206-442-4501. E-mail: info@cybercamps.com.
URL www.cybercamps.com
For more information, see page 466.

CYBERCAMPS–TRINITY LUTHERAN COLLEGE

Cybercamps–Giant Campus, Inc.
Sammamish, Washington

General Information Coed residential and day academic program established in 1997. Formal opportunities for the academically talented.
Program Focus Computers and technology.
Academics Web page design, academics (general), computer programming, computer science (Advanced Placement), computers.
Arts Animation, digital media, film, graphic arts, musical productions, photography, television/video.
Special Interest Areas Computer game design, computer graphics, electronics, robotics, team building.
Program Information 1–12 sessions per year. Session length: 5 days in June, July, August. Ages: 7–18. 30–50 participants per session. Day program cost: $599–$749. Boarding program cost: $998–$1148.
Application Deadline Continuous.

Contact Camp Consultant, 3101 Western Avenue, Suite 100, Seattle, Washington 98121. Phone: 888-904-2267. Fax: 206-442-4501. E-mail: info@cybercamps.com.
URL www.cybercamps.com
For more information, see page 466.

CYBERCAMPS–UNIVERSITY OF WASHINGTON

Cybercamps–Giant Campus, Inc.
University of Washington
Seattle, Washington

General Information Coed residential and day academic program established in 1997. Formal opportunities for the academically talented.
Program Focus Computers and technology.
Academics Web page design, academics (general), computer programming, computer science (Advanced Placement), computers.
Arts Animation, digital media, film, graphic arts, musical productions, photography, television/video.
Special Interest Areas Computer game design, computer graphics, electronics, robotics, team building.
Program Information 1–12 sessions per year. Session length: 5 days in June, July, August. Ages: 7–18. 30–50 participants per session. Day program cost: $599–$749. Boarding program cost: $998–$1148.
Application Deadline Continuous.
Jobs Positions for high school students 17 and older and college students 18 and older.
Contact Camp Consultant, 3101 Western Avenue, Suite 100, Seattle, Washington 98121. Phone: 888-904-2267. Fax: 206-442-4501. E-mail: info@cybercamps.com.
URL www.cybercamps.com
For more information, see page 466.

CYBERCAMPS—UNIVERSITY OF WASHINGTON, BOTHELL

Cybercamps–Giant Campus, Inc.
Bothell, Washington

General Information Coed residential and day academic program established in 1997. Formal opportunities for the academically talented.
Program Focus Computers and technology.
Academics Web page design, academics (general), computer programming, computer science (Advanced Placement), computers.
Arts Animation, digital media, film, graphic arts, musical productions, photography, television/video.
Special Interest Areas Computer game design, computer graphics, electronics, robotics, team building.
Program Information 1–12 sessions per year. Session length: 5 days in June, July, August. Ages: 7–18. 30–50 participants per session. Day program cost: $599–$749. Boarding program cost: $998–$1148.
Application Deadline Continuous.
Jobs Positions for high school students 17 and older and college students 18 and older.
Contact Camp Consultant, 3101 Western Avenue, Suite 100, Seattle, Washington 98121. Phone: 888-904-2267. Fax: 206-442-4501. E-mail: info@cybercamps.com.
URL www.cybercamps.com

For more information, see page 466.

FOREST RIDGE SUMMER PROGRAM

Forest Ridge School of the Sacred Heart
4800 139th Avenue, SE
Bellevue, Washington 98006

General Information Coed day traditional camp established in 2002.
Program Focus Sports, technology, and arts as well as traditional camp offerings.
Academics English language/literature, SAT/ACT preparation, academics (general), business, computers, intercultural studies, mathematics, science (general), study skills, writing.
Arts Acting, animation, arts and crafts (general), creative writing, dance, drawing, film, painting, photography, television/video, theater/drama.
Special Interest Areas Culinary arts.
Sports Basketball, climbing (wall), soccer, sports (general), tennis, volleyball, weight training.
Wilderness/Outdoors Rock climbing.
Trips Cultural, day.
Program Information 4–6 sessions per year. Session length: 5–10 days in June, July, August. Ages: 4–19. 30–100 participants per session. Day program cost: $125–$600. Financial aid available.
Application Deadline Continuous.
Jobs Positions for high school students 16 and older and college students 18 and older.
Contact Ms. Melissa Miller, Summer Program Director, main address above. Phone: 425-201-2446. Fax: 425-643-3881. E-mail: melissami@forestridge.org.
URL www.forestridge.org

iD TECH CAMPS—UNIVERSITY OF WASHINGTON, SEATTLE, WA

iD Tech Camps
University of Washington
Seattle, Washington 98195

General Information Coed residential and day academic program established in 1999. Accredited by American Camping Association. Formal opportunities for the academically talented and artistically talented.
Program Focus Students create 2D and 3D video games, build robots to compete, design websites, film and edit digital movies, create their own comic book with digital photos, learn programming and more. One computer per student and an average of five students per staff member. Campers take home a project at the end of the weeklong course.
Academics Web page design, academics (general), computer programming, computer science (Advanced Placement), computers, precollege program.
Arts Animation, cinematography, digital media, drawing, film, film editing, film production, graphic arts, photography, television/video.
Special Interest Areas Career exploration, computer game design, computer graphics, electronics, leadership training, robotics, team building.
Sports Baseball, basketball, soccer, softball, swimming, volleyball.
Trips College tours.
Program Information 5–9 sessions per year. Session length: 5–7 days in June, July, August. Ages: 7–17. 40–50 participants per session. Day program cost: $729. Boarding program cost: $1129. Financial aid available.
Application Deadline Continuous.
Jobs Positions for college students 18 and older.
Contact Client Service Representatives, 42 West Campbell Avenue, Suite 301, Campbell, California 95008. Phone: 888-709-TECH. Fax: 408-871-2228. E-mail: info@internaldrive.com.
URL www.internaldrive.com

For more information, see page 520.

JUNIOR STATESMEN SYMPOSIUM ON WASHINGTON STATE POLITICS AND GOVERNMENT

Junior Statesmen Foundation
University of Washington
Seattle, Washington 98195

General Information Coed residential academic program established in 1979. Formal opportunities for the academically talented.
Program Focus State government, politics, debate, and leadership training.
Academics Communications, government and politics, journalism, precollege program, social science, social studies, speech/debate.
Special Interest Areas Career exploration, leadership training.
Trips College tours, day.
Program Information 1 session per year. Session length: 4 days in August. Ages: 14–18. 40–75 participants per session. Boarding program cost: $350.
Application Deadline Continuous.
Contact Ms. Jessica Brow, National Summer School Director, 400 South El Camino Real, Suite 300, San Mateo, California 94402. Phone: 650-347-1600. Fax: 650-347-7200. E-mail: jsa@jsa.org.
URL summer.jsa.org/symposium/washington.html
For more information, see page 534.

LANDMARK VOLUNTEERS: WASHINGTON

Landmark Volunteers, Inc.
Washington

General Information Coed residential outdoor program and community service program established in 1992. High school credit may be earned.
Program Focus Opportunity for high school students to earn community service credit while working as a team for two weeks in Washington State serving Washington Trails Association or Olympic National Park. Similar programs offered through Landmark Volunteers at over 60 locations in 21 states.
Academics Botany, ecology, environmental science, history.
Special Interest Areas Native American culture, career exploration, community service, conservation projects, construction, field research/expeditions, leadership training, nature study, team building, trail maintenance, work camp programs.
Wilderness/Outdoors Hiking.
Trips Cultural, day.
Program Information 2 sessions per year. Session length: 2 weeks in July, August. Ages: 14–18. 12–14 participants per session. Boarding program cost: $1250–$1300. Financial aid available.
Application Deadline Continuous.
Jobs Positions for college students.

Contact Ann Barrett, Executive Director, PO Box 455, Sheffield, Massachusetts 01257. Phone: 413-229-0255. Fax: 413-229-2050. E-mail: landmark@volunteers.com. **URL** www.volunteers.com
For more information, see page 542.

WESTCOAST CONNECTION–COMMUNITY SERVICE–HABITAT FOR HUMANITY

Westcoast Connection
Washington

General Information Coed travel community service program established in 1982. Accredited by Ontario Camping Association. High school credit may be earned.
Program Focus Community service including Habitat for Humanity combined with touring and adventure highlights.
Special Interest Areas Community service, construction, touring.
Sports Sea kayaking.
Wilderness/Outdoors Hiking, outdoor adventure, rafting.
Program Information 1–2 sessions per year. Session length: 3 weeks in July, August. Ages: 16+. 10–20 participants per session. Cost: $4399. Financial aid available.
Application Deadline Continuous.
Contact Mr. Mark Segal, Director, 154 East Boston Post Road, Mamaroneck, New York 10543. Phone: 800-767-0227. Fax: 914-835-0798. E-mail: usa@westcoastconnection.com.
URL www.360studenttravel.com
For more information, see page 702.

WILDERNESS VENTURES–CASCADE-OLYMPIC

Wilderness Ventures
Washington

General Information Coed travel outdoor program, wilderness program, and adventure program established in 1973.
Program Focus Wilderness travel, wilderness skills, leadership skills.
Special Interest Areas Leadership training.
Sports Sea kayaking.
Wilderness/Outdoors Backpacking, hiking, mountaineering, rafting, wilderness camping.
Trips Overnight.
Program Information 2 sessions per year. Session length: 25 days in June, July, August. Ages: 14–18. 10 participants per session. Cost: $4090. Financial aid available.
Application Deadline Continuous.
Jobs Positions for college students 21 and older.

Contact Mike Cottingham, Director, PO Box 2768, Jackson Hole, Wyoming 83001. Phone: 800-533-2281. Fax: 307-739-1934. E-mail: info@wildernessventures. com.
URL www.wildernessventures.com
For more information, see page 704.

WILDERNESS VENTURES—PUGET SOUND

Wilderness Ventures
Washington

General Information Coed travel outdoor program, wilderness program, and adventure program established in 1973.
Program Focus Wilderness travel, wilderness skills, leadership skills.
Special Interest Areas Leadership training.
Sports Sea kayaking.
Wilderness/Outdoors Backpacking, hiking, rafting, white-water trips, wilderness camping.
Trips Overnight.
Program Information 2 sessions per year. Session length: 25 days in June, July, August. Ages: 13–15. 10 participants per session. Cost: $3690. Financial aid available.
Application Deadline Continuous.
Jobs Positions for college students 21 and older.
Contact Mike Cottingham, Director, PO Box 2768, Jackson Hole, Wyoming 83001. Phone: 800-533-2281. Fax: 307-739-1934. E-mail: info@wildernessventures. com.
URL www.wildernessventures.com
For more information, see page 704.

WILDERNESS VENTURES—WASHINGTON ALPINE

Wilderness Ventures
Washington

General Information Coed travel outdoor program, wilderness program, and adventure program established in 1973.
Program Focus Wilderness travel, wilderness skills, leadership skills.
Special Interest Areas Leadership training.
Wilderness/Outdoors Backpacking, rafting, white-water trips, wilderness camping.
Trips Overnight.
Program Information 2 sessions per year. Session length: 16 days in June, July, August. Ages: 15–18.

10 participants per session. Cost: $2790. Financial aid available.
Application Deadline Continuous.
Jobs Positions for college students 21 and older.
Contact Mike Cottingham, Director, PO Box 2768, Jackson Hole, Wyoming 83001. Phone: 800-533-2281. Fax: 307-739-1934. E-mail: info@wildernessventures. com.
URL www.wildernessventures.com
For more information, see page 704.

WILDERNESS VENTURES—WASHINGTON MOUNTAINEERING

Wilderness Ventures
Washington

General Information Coed travel outdoor program, wilderness program, and adventure program established in 1973.
Program Focus Wilderness travel, wilderness skills, leadership skills.
Special Interest Areas Leadership training.
Wilderness/Outdoors Backpacking, hiking, mountaineering, wilderness camping.
Trips Overnight.
Program Information 2 sessions per year. Session length: 22 days in June, July, August. Ages: 16–18. 10 participants per session. Cost: $4190. Financial aid available.
Application Deadline Continuous.
Jobs Positions for college students 21 and older.
Contact Mike Cottingham, Director, PO Box 2768, Jackson Hole, Wyoming 83001. Phone: 800-533-2281. Fax: 307-739-1934. E-mail: info@wildernessventures. com.
URL www.wildernessventures.com
For more information, see page 704.

WEST VIRGINIA

CAMP GREENBRIER FOR BOYS

Camp Greenbrier for Boys
Route 12
Alderson, West Virginia 24910

General Information Boys' residential and day traditional camp established in 1898. Accredited by American Camping Association.
Program Focus A tradition of fun since 1898 for 7 to 15 year olds. For rising 11th and 12th grades (and for those who are 16 by July 1), the Leadership Academy provides the best in leadership training.
Academics English as a second language, English language/literature, mathematics, reading, writing.
Arts Arts and crafts (general), creative writing, drawing, leather working, painting, pottery, sculpture, theater/drama, weaving, woodworking.

Camp Greenbrier for Boys (continued)

Special Interest Areas Campcraft, leadership training, nature study, team building.

Sports Archery, baseball, basketball, canoeing, climbing (wall), cross-country, fishing, golf, kayaking, lacrosse, rappelling, riflery, snorkeling, soccer, softball, sports (general), swimming, tennis, track and field, volleyball, wrestling.

Wilderness/Outdoors Backpacking, canoe trips, caving, hiking, orienteering, rafting, rock climbing, white-water trips.

Trips Day, overnight.

Program Information 3 sessions per year. Session length: 3–6 weeks in June, July, August. Ages: 7–18. 140 participants per session. Day program cost: $800. Boarding program cost: $1631–$3850. Financial aid available.

Application Deadline Continuous.

Jobs Positions for high school students 17 and older and college students 18 and older.

Summer Contact Mr. William J. Harvie, Director, Route 2, Box 5A, Alderson, West Virginia 24910. Phone: 304-445-7168. Fax: 304-445-7168. E-mail: woofus@juno.com.

Winter Contact Mr. William J. Harvie, Director, PO Box 585, Exmore, Virginia 23350. Phone: 888-226-7427. Fax: 757-789-3477. E-mail: woofus@juno.com.

URL www.campgreenbrier.com

WISCONSIN

CLEARWATER CAMP FOR GIRLS

Clearwater Camp, Inc.
7490 Clearwater Road
Minocqua, Wisconsin 54548

General Information Girls' residential traditional camp established in 1933. Accredited by American Camping Association.

Clearwater Camp for Girls

Arts Arts and crafts (general), ceramics, creative writing, dance, photography, pottery, theater/drama.

Special Interest Areas Campcraft, general camp activities, leadership training, nature study.

Sports Archery, basketball, bicycling, boating, canoeing, climbing (wall), diving, equestrian sports, fishing, gymnastics, horseback riding, kayaking, ropes course, swimming, tennis, volleyball, waterskiing, windsurfing.

Wilderness/Outdoors Backpacking, canoe trips, hiking, white-water trips, wilderness camping.

Trips Day, overnight.

Program Information 1–2 sessions per year. Session length: 25–49 days in June, July, August. Ages: 8–16. 100–125 participants per session. Boarding program cost: $3200–$5900.

Application Deadline Continuous.

Jobs Positions for high school students 16 and older and college students 19 and older.

Summer Contact Sunny Moore, Executive Director, main address above. Phone: 715-356-5030. Fax: 715-356-3124. E-mail: clearwatercamp@newnorth.net.

Winter Contact Sunny Moore, Director, main address above. Phone: 800-399-5030.

URL www.clearwatercamp.com

For more information, see page 458.

MILWAUKEE SCHOOL OF ENGINEERING (MSOE)–DISCOVER THE POSSIBILITIES

Milwaukee School of Engineering
1025 North Broadway
Milwaukee, Wisconsin 53202

General Information Coed residential academic program established in 1999.
Program Focus Explores the exciting field of engineering through lab experiments, expos, and industry visits.
Academics Communications, computers, engineering.
Special Interest Areas Career exploration, college planning.
Trips Cultural, day.
Program Information 2 sessions per year. Session length: 5 days in July. Ages: 13–18. 50–90 participants per session. Boarding program cost: $650.
Application Deadline Continuous.
Contact Ms. Linda Levandowski, Special Events Coordinator, MSOE, main address above. Phone: 800-332-6763. Fax: 414-277-7475. E-mail: levandow@msoe.edu.
URL www.msoe.edu/high_school_students/summer_programs

MILWAUKEE SCHOOL OF ENGINEERING (MSOE)–FOCUS ON BUSINESS

Milwaukee School of Engineering
1025 North Broadway
Milwaukee, Wisconsin 53202

General Information Coed residential academic program established in 2006.
Program Focus Explore a career in business.
Academics Business, computers.
Special Interest Areas Career exploration.
Trips Cultural.
Program Information 1 session per year. Session length: 5 days in July. Ages: 13–18. 10–25 participants per session. Boarding program cost: $650.
Application Deadline Continuous.
Contact Linda Levandowski, Special Events Coordinator, MSOE, main address above. Phone: 800-332-6763. Fax: 414-277-7475. E-mail: levandow@msoe.edu.
URL www.msoe.edu/high_school_students/summer_programs

MILWAUKEE SCHOOL OF ENGINEERING (MSOE)–FOCUS ON NURSING

Milwaukee School of Engineering
1025 North Broadway
Milwaukee, Wisconsin 53202

General Information Coed residential academic program established in 2004.
Program Focus Explore the field of nursing.
Academics Health sciences, medicine.
Special Interest Areas Career exploration.

Trips Cultural, day.
Program Information 1 session per year. Session length: 5 days in July. Ages: 13–18. 15–24 participants per session. Boarding program cost: $650.
Application Deadline Continuous.
Contact Ms. Linda Levandowski, Special Events Coordinator, MSOE, main address above. Phone: 800-332-6763. Fax: 414-277-7475. E-mail: levandow@msoe.edu.
URL www.msoe.edu/high_school_students/summer_programs

MILWAUKEE SCHOOL OF ENGINEERING (MSOE)–FOCUS ON TECHNICAL COMMUNICATION

Milwaukee School of Engineering
1025 North Broadway
Milwaukee, Wisconsin 53202

General Information Coed residential academic program established in 2005.
Program Focus Develop electronic and interpersonal media.
Academics Communications, computer programming, computers, engineering.
Special Interest Areas Career exploration.
Trips Cultural, day.
Program Information 1 session per year. Session length: 5 days in July. Ages: 13–18. 10–25 participants per session. Boarding program cost: $650. Financial aid available.
Application Deadline Continuous.
Contact Ms. Linda Levandowski, Special Events Coordinator, MSOE, main address above. Phone: 800-332-6763. Fax: 414-277-7475. E-mail: levandow@msoe.edu.
URL www.msoe.edu/high_school_students/summer_programs

MILWAUKEE SCHOOL OF ENGINEERING (MSOE)–FOCUS ON THE POSSIBILITIES

Milwaukee School of Engineering
1025 North Broadway
Milwaukee, Wisconsin 53202

General Information Coed residential academic program established in 1999.
Program Focus Participant pursues a track of activity in one area of engineering: biomedical, architectural/

Milwaukee School of Engineering (MSOE)–Focus on the Possibilities (continued)

construction management, electrical, mechanical, or computer/software.

Academics Architecture, computers, engineering.
Special Interest Areas Career exploration.
Trips Cultural, day.
Program Information 6 sessions per year. Session length: 5 days in July. Ages: 13–18. 10–25 participants per session. Boarding program cost: $650.
Application Deadline Continuous.
Contact Ms. Linda Levandowski, Special Events Coordinator, MSOE, main address above. Phone: 800-332-6763. Fax: 414-277-7475. E-mail: levandow@msoe.edu.
URL www.msoe.edu/high_school_students/summer_programs

WORLD AFFAIRS SEMINAR

Wisconsin World Affairs Council, Inc.
University of Wisconsin–Whitewater
800 West Main Street
Whitewater, Wisconsin 53190

General Information Coed residential academic program and cultural program established in 1977. Formal opportunities for the academically talented. Specific services available for the physically challenged. College credit may be earned.
Program Focus In association with University of Wisconsin-Whitewater and District 6270 of Rotary International, seminar deals with issues and events shaping world affairs. Program approved by National Association of Secondary School Principals.
Academics Area studies, economics, government and politics, intercultural studies, peace education, social studies.
Arts Acting, dance (folk), music, music (ensemble), music (vocal).
Special Interest Areas Career exploration, community service, team building.
Sports Baseball, basketball, cross-country, diving, field hockey, football, gymnastics, in-line skating, lacrosse, racquetball, soccer, softball, squash, swimming, tennis, track and field, volleyball, water polo, weight training.
Trips College tours.
Program Information 1 session per year. Session length: 1 week in June. Ages: 16–18. 900–1,200 participants per session. Boarding program cost: $465–$495. Financial aid available.
Application Deadline Continuous.
Jobs Positions for college students 19 and older.
Contact Mr. Frederick R. Luedke, General Manager, 800 West Main Street, University of Wisconsin-Whitewater, Whitewater, Wisconsin 53190. Phone: 888-404-4049. Fax: 262-472-5210. E-mail: was@uww.edu.
URL www.worldaffairsseminar.org

WYOMING

LANDMARK VOLUNTEERS: WYOMING

Landmark Volunteers, Inc.
Wyoming

General Information Coed residential outdoor program and community service program established in 1992. High school credit may be earned.
Program Focus Opportunity for high school students to earn community service credit while working as a team for two weeks serving Jackson Hole Land Trust or National Elk Refuge. Similar programs offered through Landmark Volunteers at over 50 locations in 20 states.
Academics Ecology, environmental science.
Special Interest Areas Career exploration, community service, conservation projects, construction, field research/expeditions, leadership training, nature study, team building, trail maintenance, work camp programs.
Wilderness/Outdoors Hiking.
Trips Cultural, day.
Program Information 2 sessions per year. Session length: 2 weeks in July, August. Ages: 14–18. 10–12 participants per session. Boarding program cost: $1250–$1300. Financial aid available.
Application Deadline Continuous.
Jobs Positions for college students.
Contact Ann Barrett, Executive Director, PO Box 455, Sheffield, Massachusetts 01257. Phone: 413-229-0255. Fax: 413-229-2050. E-mail: landmark@volunteers.com.
URL www.volunteers.com

For more information, see page 542.

TETON VALLEY RANCH CAMP–BOYS CAMP

Teton Valley Ranch Camp Education Foundation
Dubois, Wyoming 82513

General Information Boys' residential traditional camp, outdoor program, and wilderness program established in 1939. Accredited by American Camping Association.
Program Focus Western mountain adventures in a

great ranch community with wilderness trips on foot and horseback.

Arts Arts and crafts (general), drawing, jewelry making, leather working, painting, photography.
Special Interest Areas Animal care, campcraft, community service, field trips (arts and culture), gold panning, leadership training, nature study, rodeo arts, stone carving.
Sports Archery, equestrian sports, fishing, horseback riding, riflery, swimming.
Wilderness/Outdoors Backpacking, hiking, orienteering, outdoor adventure, pack animal trips, wilderness camping, wilderness/outdoors (general).
Trips Day, overnight, shopping.
Program Information 1 session per year. Session length: 31 days in June, July. Ages: 11+. 130 participants per session. Boarding program cost: $4600. Financial aid available.
Application Deadline Continuous.
Jobs Positions for high school students 18 and older and college students 18 and older.
Contact Mr. Jim Walter, Director, PO Box 3968, Jackson, Wyoming 83001. Phone: 307-733-2958. Fax: 307-733-0258. E-mail: mailbag@tvrcamp.org.
URL www.tvrcamp.org

TETON VALLEY RANCH CAMP–GIRLS CAMP

Teton Valley Ranch Camp Education Foundation
Dubois, Wyoming 82513

General Information Girls' residential traditional camp, outdoor program, and wilderness program established in 1939. Accredited by American Camping Association.
Program Focus Western mountain adventures in a great ranch community with wilderness trips on foot and horseback.
Arts Arts and crafts (general), drawing, jewelry making, leather working, painting, photography.
Special Interest Areas Animal care, campcraft, community service, field trips (arts and culture), gold panning, leadership training, nature study, rodeo arts, stone carving.
Sports Archery, equestrian sports, fishing, horseback riding, riflery, swimming.
Wilderness/Outdoors Backpacking, hiking, orienteering, outdoor adventure, pack animal trips, wilderness camping, wilderness/outdoors (general).
Trips Day, overnight, shopping.
Program Information 1 session per year. Session length: 31 days in July, August. Ages: 11+. 130 participants per session. Boarding program cost: $4600. Financial aid available.
Application Deadline Continuous.
Jobs Positions for high school students 18 and older and college students 18 and older.
Contact Mr. Jim Walter, Director, PO Box 3968, Jackson, Wyoming 83001. Phone: 307-733-2958. Fax: 307-733-0258. E-mail: mailbag@tvrcamp.org.
URL www.tvrcamp.org

UNIVERSITY OF CHICAGO–STONES AND BONES

University of Chicago
Wyoming

General Information Coed travel academic program and outdoor program established in 2001. Formal opportunities for the academically talented. College credit may be earned.
Program Focus Paleontology, field work.
Academics Biology, geology/earth science, precollege program.
Special Interest Areas Field research/expeditions.
Wilderness/Outdoors Outdoor camping.
Trips Cultural, day.
Program Information 1 session per year. Session length: 4 weeks in June, July. Ages: 15–18. 15–20 participants per session. Cost: $8075. Application fee: $40–$55. Financial aid available. Airfare from Chicago to Wyoming included.
Application Deadline May 15.
Contact Ms. Sarah Lopez, Summer Session Office Administrative Assistant, Graham School of General Studies, The University of Chicago, 1427 East 60th Street, Chicago, Illinois 60637. Phone: 773-834-3792. Fax: 773-834-0549. E-mail: slopez@uchicago.edu.
URL summer.uchicago.edu/

For more information, see page 676.

WILDERNESS VENTURES–GRAND TETON

Wilderness Ventures
Wyoming

General Information Coed travel outdoor program, wilderness program, and adventure program established in 1973.
Program Focus Wilderness travel, wilderness skills, leadership skills.
Special Interest Areas Leadership training.
Sports Sea kayaking.
Wilderness/Outdoors Backpacking, hiking, rafting, rock climbing, wilderness camping.
Trips Overnight.

Wilderness Ventures–Grand Teton (continued)

Program Information 4 sessions per year. Session length: 22 days in June, July, August. Ages: 14–18. 13 participants per session. Cost: $3890. Financial aid available.

Wilderness Ventures–Grand Teton

Jobs Positions for college students 21 and older.
Contact Mike Cottingham, Director, PO Box 2768, Jackson Hole, Wyoming 83001. Phone: 800-533-2281. Fax: 307-739-1934. E-mail: info@wildernessventures. com.
URL www.wildernessventures.com
For more information, see page 704.

WILDERNESS VENTURES–JACKSON HOLE

Wilderness Ventures
Wyoming

General Information Coed travel outdoor program, wilderness program, and adventure program established in 1973.
Program Focus Wilderness travel, wilderness skills, leadership skills.
Special Interest Areas Leadership training.
Sports Sea kayaking.
Wilderness/Outdoors Backpacking, canoe trips, hiking, rafting, rock climbing, wilderness camping.
Trips Overnight.
Program Information 2 sessions per year. Session length: 22 days in June, July, August. Ages: 13–15. 13 participants per session. Cost: $3790. Financial aid available.
Application Deadline Continuous.
Jobs Positions for college students 21 and older.
Contact Mike Cottingham, Director, PO Box 2768, Jackson Hole, Wyoming 83001. Phone: 800-533-2281. Fax: 307-739-1934. E-mail: info@wildernessventures. com.
URL www.wildernessventures.com
For more information, see page 704.

WILDERNESS VENTURES–WYOMING MOUNTAINEERING

Wilderness Ventures
Wyoming

General Information Coed travel outdoor program, wilderness program, and adventure program established in 1973.
Program Focus Wilderness travel, wilderness skills, leadership skills.
Special Interest Areas Leadership training.
Wilderness/Outdoors Backpacking, hiking, mountaineering, rock climbing, wilderness camping.
Trips Overnight.

Program Information 2 sessions per year. Session length: 22 days in July, August. Ages: 15–18. 10 participants per session. Cost: $3990. Financial aid available.
Application Deadline Continuous.
Jobs Positions for college students 21 and older.
Contact Mike Cottingham, Director, PO Box 2768, Jackson Hole, Wyoming 83001. Phone: 800-533-2281. Fax: 307-739-1934. E-mail: info@wildernessventures. com.
URL www.wildernessventures.com

Special Note
For more than thirty-five years, Wilderness Ventures has been conducting exciting expeditions for beginners and experienced young adults, ages 13–20. Expeditions visit a variety of wilderness environments in the western United States, Hawaii, Alaska, Canada, Europe, Australia, Central America, and the South Pacific for extended periods. Students learn outdoor and group leadership skills as well as gain an appreciation for America's varied wilderness environments. The professional staff consists of outdoor educators, whose ages range from 21 to 32. Participants come from nearly every state and several countries. Enrollment is limited and applicants must submit school references prior to admission. Previous wilderness experience is not necessary.

For more information, see page 704.

WILDERNESS VENTURES—YELLOWSTONE/ TETON ADVENTURE

Wilderness Ventures
Wyoming

General Information Coed travel outdoor program, wilderness program, and adventure program established in 1973.
Program Focus Wilderness travel, wilderness skills, leadership skills.
Sports Kayaking, sea kayaking.

Wilderness/Outdoors Hiking, rafting, rock climbing, white-water trips.
Trips Overnight.
Program Information 3 sessions per year. Session length: 16 days in June, July, August. Ages: 14–18. 12 participants per session. Cost: $3090. Financial aid available.
Application Deadline Continuous.
Jobs Positions for college students 21 and older.
Contact Mike Cottingham, Director, PO Box 2768, Jackson Hole, Wyoming 83001. Phone: 800-533-2281. Fax: 307-739-1934. E-mail: info@wildernessventures. com.
URL www.wildernessventures.com
For more information, see page 704.

WILDERNESS VENTURES—YELLOWSTONE-TETON FAMILY ADVENTURE

Wilderness Ventures
Wyoming

General Information Coed travel outdoor program, family program, wilderness program, and adventure program established in 1973.
Program Focus Wilderness travel, wilderness skills, leadership skills.
Sports Bicycling, horseback riding, sea kayaking.
Wilderness/Outdoors Hiking, rafting, white-water trips.
Trips Day, overnight.
Program Information 5 sessions per year. Session length: 6 days in July, August. Ages: 10+. Cost: $2100–$2590. Financial aid available.
Application Deadline Continuous.
Jobs Positions for college students 21 and older.
Contact Mike Cottingham, Director, PO Box 2768, Jackson Hole, Wyoming 83001. Phone: 800-533-2281. Fax: 307-739-1934. E-mail: info@wildernessventures. com.
URL www.wildernessventures.com
For more information, see page 704.

OPPORTUNITIES ABROAD

ARGENTINA

AFS-USA–COMMUNITY SERVICE–ARGENTINA

AFS-USA
Argentina

General Information Coed residential community service program and cultural program. High school credit may be earned.
Program Focus Participants spend a summer doing community service, and live with a host family to gain a better understanding of the culture and improve their Spanish. They might volunteer in an orphanage, help teach soccer to children with disabilities, or work on environmental projects restoring parks.
Academics Spanish language/literature.
Special Interest Areas Community service, cross-cultural education, homestays.
Trips Cultural, day.
Program Information 1 session per year. Session length: 30–45 days in July. Ages: 15–18. Boarding program cost: $4000–$6000. Application fee: $75. Financial aid available. International airfare and volunteer homestay support included.
Application Deadline Continuous.
Contact Manager, AFS Info Center, 506 Southwest 6th Avenue, 2nd Floor, Portland, Oregon 97204. Phone: 800-AFS-INFO. Fax: 503-299-0753. E-mail: afsinfo@afs.org.
URL www.afs.org/usa
For more information, see page 408.

AFS-USA–HOMESTAY–ARGENTINA

AFS-USA
Argentina

General Information Coed residential academic program and cultural program.
Program Focus Living with a host family while attending school.
Academics Spanish language/literature.
Special Interest Areas Homestays.
Trips Cultural, day, overnight.
Program Information 1 session per year. Session length: 30–45 days in June, July, August. Ages: 15–18. Boarding program cost: $4000–$6000. Application fee: $75. Financial aid available. International airfare and volunteer homestay support included.
Application Deadline Continuous.
Jobs Positions for college students.
Contact Manager, AFS Info Center, 506 Southwest 6th Avenue, 2nd Floor, Portland, Oregon 97204. Phone: 800-AFS-INFO. Fax: 503-299-0753. E-mail: afsinfo@afs.org.
URL www.afs.org/usa
For more information, see page 408.

CENTER FOR CULTURAL INTERCHANGE–ARGENTINA INDEPENDENT HOMESTAY

Center for Cultural Interchange
Argentina

General Information Coed residential cultural program established in 1985.
Program Focus Homestay program.
Academics Independent study, language study.

Special Interest Areas Homestays.
Trips Cultural, day, shopping.
Program Information Session length: 1–6 weeks in January, February, March, April, May, June, July, August, September, October, November, December. Ages: 16+. Boarding program cost: $1000–$1230. Financial aid available.
Application Deadline Continuous.
Contact Ms. Juliet Jones, Outbound Programs Director, 746 North LaSalle Drive, Chicago, Illinois 60610-3617. Phone: 866-684-9675. Fax: 312-944-2644. E-mail: info@cci-exchange.com.
URL www.cci-exchange.com

For more information, see page 448.

THE EXPERIMENT IN INTERNATIONAL LIVING–ARGENTINA HOMESTAY, COMMUNITY SERVICE, AND OUTDOOR ECOLOGICAL PROGRAM

The Experiment in International Living
Argentina

General Information Coed travel outdoor program, community service program, cultural program, and adventure program established in 1932.
Program Focus International youth travel, homestays, ecological trek.
Academics Spanish language/literature.
Special Interest Areas Community service, homestays, nature study, touring.
Sports Horseback riding.
Trips Cultural, day, overnight.
Program Information 1 session per year. Session length: 4 weeks in June, July. Ages: 14–19. 10–15 participants per session. Cost: $5200. Financial aid available. Airfare included.
Application Deadline May 1.
Contact Annie Thompson, Enrollment Director, Summer Abroad, Kipling Road, PO Box 676, Brattleboro, Vermont 05302-0676. Phone: 800-345-2929. Fax: 802-258-3428. E-mail: eil@worldlearning.org.
URL www.usexperiment.org

For more information, see page 492.

THE EXPERIMENT IN INTERNATIONAL LIVING–ARGENTINA VISUAL ARTS, PHOTOGRAPHY, AND SERVICE

The Experiment in International Living
Argentina

General Information Coed travel outdoor program, community service program, cultural program, and adventure program established in 1932.
Program Focus International youth travel, homestays, ecological trek.
Academics Spanish language/literature.
Arts Arts, dance (Latin), photography.
Special Interest Areas Community service, culinary arts, homestays, touring.

Wilderness/Outdoors Hiking.
Trips Cultural, day, overnight.
Program Information 1 session per year. Session length: 4 weeks in July, August. Ages: 14–19. 10–15 participants per session. Cost: $5200. Financial aid available. Airfare included.
Application Deadline May 1.
Contact Annie Thompson, Enrollment Director, Summer Abroad, Kipling Road, PO Box 676, Brattleboro, Vermont 05302-0676. Phone: 800-345-2929. Fax: 802-258-3428. E-mail: eil@worldlearning.org.
URL www.usexperiment.org

For more information, see page 492.

GLOBAL WORKS–LANGUAGE IMMERSION, CULTURAL EXCHANGE AND SERVICE–ARGENTINA

GLOBAL WORKS
Argentina

General Information Coed travel community service program, cultural program, and adventure program established in 1988. College credit may be earned.
Program Focus Community service, cultural exchange, and outdoor adventure in the Andes and the Pampas.
Academics Biology, ecology, environmental science, intercultural studies.
Arts Arts and crafts (general), dance (Latin), music.
Special Interest Areas Community service, conservation projects, construction, homestays, team building.
Sports Sea kayaking, snorkeling, soccer, swimming, volleyball.
Wilderness/Outdoors Hiking, outdoor adventure, rafting.
Trips Cultural, day, overnight.
Program Information 1 session per year. Session length: 4 weeks in June, July. Ages: 15–17. 16–18 participants per session. Cost: $4695. Application fee: $100. Financial aid available. Airfare not included.
Application Deadline Continuous.
Jobs Positions for college students 23 and older.
Contact Mr. Erik Werner, Director, 1113 South Allen Street, State College, Pennsylvania 16801. Phone: 814-867-7000. Fax: 814-867-2717. E-mail: info@globalworksinc.com.
URL www.globalworksinc.com

For more information, see page 506.

PUTNEY STUDENT TRAVEL–COMMUNITY SERVICE–ARGENTINA

Putney Student Travel
Argentina

General Information Coed residential community service program and cultural program established in 1951.
Program Focus Community service cultural exchange, and weekend excursions from a base in a small rural community.
Academics Intercultural studies.
Special Interest Areas Community service, construction.
Sports Soccer, swimming.
Wilderness/Outdoors Hiking.
Trips Cultural, day.
Program Information 1 session per year. Session length: 28–30 days in June, July, August. Ages: 15–18. 16 participants per session. Boarding program cost: $5790. Financial aid available.
Application Deadline Continuous.
Contact Jeffrey Shumlin, Admissions Director, 345 Hickory Ridge Road, Putney, Vermont 05346. Phone: 802-387-5000. Fax: 802-387-4276. E-mail: info@goputney.com.
URL www.goputney.com
For more information, see page 598.

PUTNEY STUDENT TRAVEL–CULTURAL EXPLORATION–CREATIVE WRITING IN ARGENTINA

Putney Student Travel
Argentina

General Information Coed residential arts program established in 1951.
Program Focus A group of aspiring writers hone their skills while experiencing the unique life and culture of Sicily.
Academics Writing.
Arts Creative writing.
Special Interest Areas Cross-cultural education.
Sports Bicycling, snorkeling, swimming.
Wilderness/Outdoors Hiking.
Trips Cultural, day, overnight.
Program Information 1 session per year. Session length: 28–34 days in June, July, August. Ages: 15–18. 25 participants per session. Boarding program cost: $8690. Financial aid available.
Application Deadline Continuous.
Jobs Positions for college students 21 and older.
Contact Jeffrey Shumlin, Admissions Director, 345 Hickory Ridge Road, Putney, Vermont 05346. Phone: 802-387-5000. Fax: 802-387-4276. E-mail: info@goputney.com.
URL www.goputney.com
For more information, see page 598.

PUTNEY STUDENT TRAVEL–LANGUAGE LEARNING–ARGENTINA

Putney Student Travel
Argentina

General Information Coed residential academic program and cultural program established in 1951. Formal opportunities for the academically talented.
Program Focus Spanish language immersion in the context of community service. Participants housed in host-family homes and community buildings. Enrollment limited to those who are studying Spanish.
Academics Spanish (Advanced Placement), Spanish language/literature, art history/appreciation, intercultural studies.
Special Interest Areas Community service, homestays, touring.
Sports Horseback riding, soccer, swimming.
Wilderness/Outdoors Hiking, rafting.
Trips Cultural, day, overnight.
Program Information 1 session per year. Session length: 28–30 days in June, July. Ages: 13–18. 16–18 participants per session. Boarding program cost: $5690. Financial aid available. Airfare included.
Application Deadline Continuous.
Contact Jeffrey Shumlin, Admissions Director, 345 Hickory Ridge Road, Putney, Vermont 05346. Phone: 802-387-5000. Fax: 802-387-4276. E-mail: info@goputney.com.
URL www.goputney.com
For more information, see page 598.

AUSTRALIA

AAVE–Australia

AAVE–Journeys That Matter
Australia

General Information Coed travel outdoor program, wilderness program, and adventure program established in 1976. Accredited by American Camping Association.

AAVE–Australia

Program Focus Watersports.
Special Interest Areas Campcraft, cattle driving, leadership training, nautical skills, touring.
Sports Sailing, scuba diving, snorkeling, surfing, swimming.
Wilderness/Outdoors Backpacking, hiking, orienteering, wilderness camping.
Trips Cultural, day, overnight.
Program Information 2–4 sessions per year. Session length: 3 weeks in June, July, August. Ages: 14–18. 14

participants per session. Cost: $5188. Financial aid available.
Application Deadline Continuous.
Jobs Positions for college students 21 and older.
Contact Mr. Abbott Wallis, Owner, 2308 Fossil Trace Drive, Golden, Colorado 80401. Phone: 800-222-3595. Fax: 303-526-0885. E-mail: info@aave.com.
URL www.aave.com

For more information, see page 394.

ACTIONQUEST: Australian and Great Barrier Reef Adventures

ActionQuest
Australia

General Information Coed travel outdoor program, cultural program, and adventure program established in 1986.
Program Focus Sailing and land exploration of Sydney, Great Barrier Reef, Whitsunday Islands, and Queensland. Voyage includes PADI scuba certifications, sail training, community service, and shore adventures.
Academics Intercultural studies, marine studies.
Special Interest Areas Aboriginal studies, community service, leadership training, nautical skills, team building, touring.
Sports Sailing, scuba diving, snorkeling, surfing.
Wilderness/Outdoors Hiking, white-water trips.
Trips Cultural, day, overnight.
Program Information 3 sessions per year. Session length: 22 days in June, July, August. Ages: 15–18. 10–20 participants per session. Cost: $4970.
Application Deadline Continuous.
Contact Mike Meighan, Director, PO Box 5517, Sarasota, Florida 34277. Phone: 800-317-6789. Fax: 941-924-6075. E-mail: info@actionquest.com.
URL www.actionquest.com

For more information, see page 406.

AFS-USA–Homestay Plus–Australia

AFS-USA
Australia

General Information Coed residential outdoor program and cultural program.
Program Focus Living with a host family, participating in outdoor activities and doing valuable volunteer work in the local community.
Academics Area studies.
Special Interest Areas Campcraft, career exploration, homestays.
Wilderness/Outdoors Backpacking, hiking, mountaineering, outdoor adventure, rock climbing, wilderness camping.
Trips Cultural, day, overnight.
Program Information 1 session per year. Session length: 30–45 days in June, July, August. Ages: 15–18. Boarding program cost: $6100. Application fee: $75. Financial aid available. International airfare and volunteer homestay support included.
Application Deadline Continuous.

AFS-USA–Homestay Plus–Australia (continued)

Contact Manager, AFS Info Center, 506 Southwest 6th Avenue, 2nd Floor, Portland, Oregon 97204. Phone: 800-AFS-INFO. Fax: 503-299-0753. E-mail: afsinfo@afs.org.
URL www.afs.org/usa
For more information, see page 408.

BROADREACH ADVENTURES DOWN UNDER

Broadreach
Australia

General Information Coed travel outdoor program, wilderness program, and adventure program established in 1992.
Program Focus Coed program exploring the "Land Down Under" including the Great Barrier Reef, rain forests, coastline, rivers, and the Outback. A week of live-aboard scuba diving includes scuba certification and hands-on marine research.
Academics Environmental science, intercultural studies, marine studies.
Arts Photography.
Special Interest Areas Aboriginal studies, community service, field research/expeditions, leadership training, nature study.
Sports Canoeing, rappelling, sailing, scuba diving, sea kayaking, snorkeling, surfing.
Wilderness/Outdoors Backpacking, canoe trips, hiking, ocean expeditions, outdoor adventure, rafting, rock climbing, white-water trips, wilderness camping, wilderness/outdoors (general).
Trips Cultural.
Program Information 2 sessions per year. Session length: 25 days in June, July, August. Ages: 15–19. 10–14 participants per session. Cost: $5380.
Application Deadline Continuous.
Contact Carlton Goldthwaite, Director, 806 McCulloch Street, Suite 102, Raleigh, North Carolina 27603. Phone: 888-833-1907. Fax: 919-833-2129. E-mail: info@gobroadreach.com.
URL www.gobroadreach.com
For more information, see page 432.

CENTER FOR CULTURAL INTERCHANGE–AUSTRALIA HIGH SCHOOL ABROAD

Center for Cultural Interchange
Australia

General Information Coed residential academic program and cultural program established in 1985. High school credit may be earned.
Program Focus High school abroad, homestay and adventure program.
Academics Academics (general), independent study, precollege program.
Special Interest Areas Cross-cultural education, homestays.
Wilderness/Outdoors Hiking.
Trips Cultural, day, overnight.
Program Information 2 sessions per year. Session length: 150–300 days in January, February, March, April, May, June, July, August, September, October, November, December. Ages: 15–18. Boarding program cost: $9300–$16,000. Financial aid available. Early Bird discount.
Application Deadline Continuous.
Contact Ms. Juliet Jones, Outbound Programs Director, 746 North LaSalle Drive, Chicago, Illinois 60610-3617. Phone: 866-684-9675. Fax: 312-944-2644. E-mail: info@cci-exchange.com.
URL www.cci-exchange.com
For more information, see page 448.

THE EXPERIMENT IN INTERNATIONAL LIVING–AUSTRALIA HOMESTAY

The Experiment in International Living
Australia

General Information Coed travel outdoor program, cultural program, and adventure program established in 1932. Specific services available for the hearing impaired and visually impaired.
Program Focus International youth travel, homestay, ecology.
Academics Ecology, environmental science.
Arts Woodworking.
Special Interest Areas Homestays.
Sports Snorkeling, swimming.
Wilderness/Outdoors Backpacking, hiking, wilderness camping.
Trips Cultural, day, overnight.
Program Information 1 session per year. Session length: 5 weeks in June, July. Ages: 14–19. 10–15 participants per session. Cost: $6200. Application fee: $100. Financial aid available. Airfare included.
Application Deadline May 1.
Contact Annie Thompson, Enrollment Director, Summer Abroad, Kipling Road, PO Box 676, Brattleboro, Vermont 05302-0676. Phone: 800-345-2929. Fax: 802-258-3428. E-mail: eil@worldlearning.org.
URL www.usexperiment.org
For more information, see page 492.

LIFEWORKS WITH THE AUSTRALIAN RED CROSS

LIFEWORKS International
Australia

General Information Coed travel outdoor program, community service program, cultural program, and adventure program established in 1986. High school credit may be earned.
Program Focus Working with the Australian Red Cross, students participate primarily in aboriginal community projects. During the program, students travel to Sydney, Queensland, and the Northern Territories.
Academics Intercultural studies.
Arts Aboriginal arts.
Special Interest Areas Aboriginal studies, community service, leadership training, team building, touring.
Sports Snorkeling, swimming.
Wilderness/Outdoors Hiking, wilderness camping.
Trips Cultural, day, overnight.
Program Information 1 session per year. Session length: 22 days in June, July. Ages: 15–19. 8–12 participants per session. Cost: $4370. Financial aid available.
Application Deadline Continuous.
Contact James Stoll, Director, PO Box 5517, Sarasota, Florida 34277. Phone: 800-808-2115. Fax: 941-924-6075. E-mail: info@lifeworks-international.com.
URL www.lifeworks-international.com
For more information, see page 548.

RUSTIC PATHWAYS–COMMUNITY SERVICE SCHOOL IN AUSTRALIA

Rustic Pathways
Australia

General Information Coed travel cultural program and adventure program established in 2005.
Academics Ecology, environmental science, global issues, marine studies, natural resource management, social studies.
Special Interest Areas Aboriginal studies, community service, conservation projects, construction, cross-cultural education, first aid.
Sports Boating, sailing, snorkeling, surfing, swimming.
Wilderness/Outdoors Hiking, outdoor adventure, wilderness camping.
Trips Cultural, day, overnight, shopping.
Program Information 4 sessions per year. Session length: 17 days in June, July. Ages: 14–18. 10–15 participants per session. Cost: $2995. Financial aid available.
Application Deadline Continuous.
Jobs Positions for college students 21 and older.

Contact Rustic Pathways, 4121 Erie Street, Willoughby, Ohio 44094. Phone: 800-321-4353. Fax: 440-975-9694. E-mail: rustic@rusticpathways.com.
URL www.rusticpathways.com
For more information, see page 612.

RUSTIC PATHWAYS–SYDNEY, REEF & RAINFOREST

Rustic Pathways
Brisbane, Cairns
Australia

General Information Coed travel cultural program and adventure program established in 1982.
Special Interest Areas Cross-cultural education, touring.
Sports Horseback riding, sailing, scuba diving, snorkeling, swimming.
Wilderness/Outdoors Hiking, outdoor adventure, rafting, white-water trips.
Trips Cultural, day, overnight, shopping.
Program Information 2 sessions per year. Session length: 17 days in June, July, August. Ages: 14–18. 10–15 participants per session. Cost: $3995. Application fee: $100–$200.
Application Deadline Continuous.
Jobs Positions for college students 21 and older.
Contact Rustic Pathways, 4121 Erie Street, Willoughby, Ohio 44094. Phone: 800-321-4353. Fax: 440-975-9694. E-mail: rustic@rusticpathways.com.
URL www.rusticpathways.com
For more information, see page 612.

WESTCOAST CONNECTION/ON TOUR–AUSTRALIAN OUTBACK

Westcoast Connection
Australia

General Information Coed travel adventure program established in 1982. Accredited by Ontario Camping Association.
Program Focus A balance of touring, recreation, and adventure; visiting Fraser Island, Gold Coast, Cairns, Ayers Rock, Sydney, and the Great Barrier Reef.
Special Interest Areas Touring.

Westcoast Connection/On Tour– Australian Outback (continued)

Sports Boating, kayaking, scuba diving, sea kayaking, snorkeling, surfing, swimming.
Wilderness/Outdoors Hiking, mountain biking, outdoor adventure, rafting, white-water trips.
Program Information 1–2 sessions per year. Session length: 23–28 days in July. Ages: 14–18. 30–40 participants per session. Cost: $6599–$7699.
Application Deadline Continuous.
Contact Mr. Mark Segal, Director, 154 East Boston Post Road, Mamaroneck, New York 10543. Phone: 800-767-0227. Fax: 914-835-0798. E-mail: usa@westcoastconnection.com.
URL www.westcoastconnection.com

For more information, see page 702.

WILDERNESS VENTURES–AUSTRALIA

Wilderness Ventures
Australia

General Information Coed travel outdoor program, wilderness program, cultural program, and adventure program established in 1973.
Program Focus Wilderness travel, cultural immersion, leadership skills.
Special Interest Areas Aboriginal studies, leadership training.
Sports Boating, scuba diving, snorkeling.
Wilderness/Outdoors Backpacking, hiking, rafting, white-water trips.
Trips Cultural, overnight.
Program Information 1 session per year. Session length: 32 days in June, July, August. Ages: 14–18. 15 participants per session. Cost: $6690. Financial aid available.
Application Deadline Continuous.
Jobs Positions for college students 21 and older.
Contact Mike Cottingham, Director, PO Box 2768, Jackson Hole, Wyoming 83001. Phone: 800-533-2281. Fax: 307-739-1934. E-mail: info@wildernessventures.com.
URL www.wildernessventures.com

For more information, see page 704.

BAHAMAS

BROADREACH MARINE BIOLOGY
ACCREDITED

Broadreach
The Gerace Research Center on San Salvador Island
Bahamas

General Information Coed residential academic program and outdoor program established in 1992. High school or college credit may be earned.
Program Focus Coed program focusing on marine biology, marine studies, scuba, advanced and specialty dive certifications as well as high school and college credit.
Academics Biology, ecology, environmental science, marine studies, oceanography.
Arts Photography.
Special Interest Areas Community service, conservation projects, field research/expeditions, nature study.
Sports Bicycling, boating, fishing, sailing, scuba diving, sea kayaking, snorkeling, volleyball, waterskiing.
Wilderness/Outdoors Hiking, outdoor adventure, wilderness/outdoors (general).
Trips Cultural, day.
Program Information 2 sessions per year. Session length: 3 weeks in June, July, August. Ages: 15–19. 14–18 participants per session. Boarding program cost: $4780.
Application Deadline Continuous.
Contact Carlton Goldthwaite, Director, 806 McCulloch Street, Suite 102, Raleigh, North Carolina 27603. Phone: 888-833-1907. Fax: 919-833-2129. E-mail: info@gobroadreach.com.
URL www.gobroadreach.com

For more information, see page 432.

BELIZE

ACADEMIC TREKS–DOLPHIN
STUDIES IN BELIZE

Academic Treks, the academic adventure and community service division of Broadreach
Oceanic Society's Belize Field Station
Blackbird Caye
Belize

General Information Coed travel academic program, outdoor program, community service program, and adventure program established in 1992. High school or college credit may be earned.
Program Focus Academic adventure program focusing on dolphin field studies and research, community service, marine ecology, scuba diving, sailing voyage, sea kayaking, high school and college credit.
Academics Academics (general), biology, ecology, environmental science, marine studies.
Special Interest Areas Community service, conservation projects, field research/expeditions, leadership training.
Sports Sailing, scuba diving, sea kayaking, snorkeling, swimming.
Wilderness/Outdoors Hiking, outdoor adventure, wilderness camping, wilderness/outdoors (general).
Trips Cultural, day, overnight.
Program Information 2 sessions per year. Session length: 3 weeks in June, July, August. Ages: 15–19. 10–12 participants per session. Cost: $4680. Financial aid available.
Application Deadline Continuous.
Contact Carlton Goldthwaite, Director, 806 McCulloch Street, Suite 102, Raleigh, North Carolina 27603. Phone: 888-833-1907. E-mail: info@academictreks.com.
URL www.academictreks.com

For more information, see page 432.

ACADEMIC TREKS–WILDERNESS
EMERGENCY MEDICINE

Academic Treks, the academic adventure and community service division of Broadreach
Belize

General Information Coed travel academic program, outdoor program, community service program, and cultural program established in 1992. High school or college credit may be earned.
Program Focus Program focuses on Wilderness First Responder (WFR) certification, traditional medicine, clinic and hospital service work, cultural immersion; hiking.
Academics Academics (general), area studies, health sciences, intercultural studies, medicine.
Special Interest Areas Career exploration, community service, cross-cultural education, first aid, leadership training.

Sports Canoeing.
Wilderness/Outdoors Caving, hiking, outdoor adventure, wilderness camping, wilderness/outdoors (general).
Trips Cultural.
Program Information 2 sessions per year. Session length: 22 days in June, July, August. Ages: 15–19. 10–14 participants per session. Cost: $3990.
Application Deadline Continuous.
Contact Carlton Goldthwaite, Director, 806 McCulloch Street, Suite 102, Raleigh, North Carolina 27603. Phone: 888-833-1907. Fax: 919-833-2129. E-mail: info@academictreks.com.
URL www.academictreks.com

For more information, see page 432.

THE EXPERIMENT IN INTERNATIONAL LIVING–BELIZE HOMESTAY

The Experiment in International Living
Belize

General Information Coed travel outdoor program, community service program, cultural program, and adventure program established in 1932. Specific services available for the hearing impaired and visually impaired.
Program Focus International youth travel, homestay, community service, ecology.
Academics Ecology, environmental science.
Special Interest Areas Community service, homestays, team building.
Sports Canoeing, fishing, snorkeling, swimming.
Trips Cultural, day, overnight.
Program Information 1 session per year. Session length: 4 weeks in June, July. Ages: 14–19. 10–15 participants per session. Cost: $4700. Financial aid available. Airfare included.
Application Deadline May 1.
Contact Annie Thompson, Enrollment Director, Summer Abroad, Kipling Road, PO Box 676, Brattleboro, Vermont 05302-0676. Phone: 800-345-2929. Fax: 802-258-3428. E-mail: eil@worldlearning.org.
URL www.usexperiment.org

For more information, see page 492.

WESTCOAST CONNECTION–COMMUNITY SERVICE BELIZE

Westcoast Connection
Belize

General Information Coed travel community service program established in 1982. Accredited by Ontario Camping Association. High school credit may be earned.
Special Interest Areas Community service, field research/expeditions, touring.
Sports Snorkeling.
Wilderness/Outdoors Hiking, outdoor adventure, rafting.
Trips Cultural, day.
Program Information 1–2 sessions per year. Session

Westcoast Connection–Community Service Belize (continued)

length: 3 weeks in July. Ages: 14+. 10–24 participants per session. Cost: $3999.
Application Deadline Continuous.
Contact Mr. Mark Segal, Director, 154 East Boston Post Road, Mamaroneck, New York 10543. Phone: 800-767-0227. Fax: 914-835-0798. E-mail: info@westcoastconnection.com.
URL www.360studenttravel.com

For more information, see page 702.

BERMUDA

ACADEMIC TREKS–SHIPWRECKS AND UNDERWATER ARCHAEOLOGY IN BERMUDA

Academic Treks, the academic adventure and community service division of Broadreach
Bermuda Biological Station for Research (BBSR)
Bermuda

General Information Coed travel academic program, outdoor program, community service program, and adventure program established in 1992. High school or college credit may be earned.
Program Focus Academic program focusing on scuba diving and studying Bermuda's historical shipwrecks, community service, island exploration, marine science, and college credit.
Academics Academics (general), archaeology, history, marine studies.
Special Interest Areas Community service, conservation projects, field research/expeditions, leadership training.
Sports Scuba diving, snorkeling, swimming.
Wilderness/Outdoors Hiking.
Trips Cultural.
Program Information 2 sessions per year. Session length: 16 days in June, July, August. Ages: 15–19. 10–12 participants per session. Cost: $4380. Financial aid available.
Application Deadline Continuous.

Contact Carlton Goldthwaite, Director, 806 McCulloch Street, Suite 102, Raleigh, North Carolina 27603. Phone: 919-833-1907. Fax: 919-833-2129. E-mail: info@academictreks.com.
URL www.academictreks.com

For more information, see page 432.

BOTSWANA

THE EXPERIMENT IN INTERNATIONAL LIVING–BOTSWANA HOMESTAY

The Experiment in International Living
Botswana

General Information Coed travel outdoor program, community service program, cultural program, and adventure program established in 1932. Specific services available for the hearing impaired and visually impaired.
Program Focus International youth travel, homestay, community service.
Academics Setswana language.
Special Interest Areas Community service, homestays.
Wilderness/Outdoors Backpacking, safari, wilderness/outdoors (general).
Trips Cultural, day, overnight.
Program Information 1 session per year. Session length: 5 weeks in June, July, August. Ages: 14–19. 10–15 participants per session. Cost: $5900. Application fee: $100. Financial aid available. Airfare included.
Application Deadline May 1.
Contact Annie Thompson, Enrollment Director, Summer Abroad, Kipling Road, PO Box 676, Brattleboro, Vermont 05302-0676. Phone: 800-345-2929. Fax: 802-258-3428. E-mail: eil@worldlearning.org.
URL www.usexperiment.org

For more information, see page 492.

BRAZIL

CENTER FOR CULTURAL INTERCHANGE–BRAZIL HIGH SCHOOL ABROAD

Center for Cultural Interchange
Brazil

General Information Coed residential academic program and cultural program established in 1985. High school credit may be earned.
Program Focus High school abroad, homestay program, cultural immersion.
Academics Academics (general), precollege program.

Special Interest Areas Cross-cultural education, homestays.
Trips Cultural, day.
Program Information 2 sessions per year. Session length: 150–300 days in January, February, March, April, May, June, July, August, September, October, November, December. Ages: 15–17. Boarding program cost: $4500–$5500. Financial aid available.
Application Deadline Continuous.
Contact Ms. Juliet Jones, Outbound Programs Director, 746 North LaSalle Drive, Chicago, Illinois 60610-3617. Phone: 866-684-9675. Fax: 312-944-2644. E-mail: info@cci-exchange.com.
URL www.cci-exchange.com

For more information, see page 448.

THE EXPERIMENT IN INTERNATIONAL LIVING–BRAZIL–COMMUNITY SERVICE AND SOCCER

The Experiment in International Living
Brazil

General Information Coed travel outdoor program, community service program, cultural program, and adventure program established in 1932.
Program Focus International youth travel, homestay, community service, and soccer.
Special Interest Areas Community service, homestays, touring.
Sports Soccer.
Wilderness/Outdoors Backpacking, hiking, white-water trips.
Trips Cultural, day, overnight.
Program Information 1 session per year. Session length: 5 weeks in June, July, August. Ages: 14–19. 10–15 participants per session. Cost: $5800. Application fee: $100. Financial aid available. Airfare included.
Application Deadline May 1.
Contact Ms. Annie Thompson, Enrollment Director, Summer Abroad, Kipling Road, PO Box 676, Brattleboro, Vermont 05302-0676. Phone: 800-345-2929. Fax: 802-258-3428. E-mail: eil@worldlearning.org.
URL www.usexperiment.org

For more information, see page 492.

THE EXPERIMENT IN INTERNATIONAL LIVING–BRAZIL HOMESTAY, ARTS, AND COMMUNITY SERVICE

The Experiment in International Living
Brazil

General Information Coed travel arts program, community service program, and cultural program established in 1932. Specific services available for the hearing impaired and visually impaired.
Program Focus International youth travel, homestay, community service, and arts including traditional music and dance (Capoeira).
Academics Portuguese language/literature, music.
Arts Dance, dance (folk), music, music (folk).
Special Interest Areas Community service, homestays, touring.
Trips Cultural, day, overnight.
Program Information 1 session per year. Session length: 5 weeks in June, July, August. Ages: 14–19. 10–15 participants per session. Cost: $5900. Financial aid available. Airfare included.
Application Deadline May 1.
Contact Ms. Annie Thompson, Enrollment Director, Summer Abroad, Kipling Road, PO Box 676, Brattleboro, Vermont 05302-0676. Phone: 800-345-2929. Fax: 802-258-3428. E-mail: eil@worldlearning.org.
URL www.usexperiment.org

For more information, see page 492.

GLOBAL LEADERSHIP ADVENTURES–BRAZIL: COMMUNITY SERVICE AND LEADERSHIP

Global Leadership Adventures
Brazil

General Information Coed travel academic program, community service program, and cultural program established in 2004. High school credit may be earned.
Program Focus Learning about a country and its culture through community service, classes, and adventures.
Academics Spanish language/literature, intercultural studies, social studies.
Special Interest Areas Community service, leadership training.
Wilderness/Outdoors Hiking.
Trips Cultural, day.
Program Information 1–2 sessions per year. Session length: 3 weeks in June, July, August. Ages: 15–18. 40–60 participants per session. Cost: $4395–$4595. Financial aid available.
Application Deadline Continuous.
Contact Mr. Andrew Motiwalla, Executive Director, 2633 Lincoln Boulevard, #427, Santa Monica, California 90405. Phone: 888-358-4321. Fax: 866-612-3697. E-mail: info@globalleadershipadventures.com.
URL www.globalleadershipadventures.com/main/home.asp

For more information, see page 504.

BRITISH VIRGIN ISLANDS

ACTIONQUEST: ADVANCED PADI SCUBA CERTIFICATION AND SPECIALTY VOYAGES

ActionQuest
British Virgin Islands

General Information Coed travel outdoor program and adventure program established in 1986.
Program Focus Live-aboard program offering PADI advanced and specialty scuba certifications.
Academics Marine studies, oceanography.
Special Interest Areas Field research/expeditions, leadership training, nature study, nautical skills, team building.
Sports Sailing, scuba diving, snorkeling, wakeboarding, waterskiing.
Wilderness/Outdoors Hiking.
Trips Cultural, day.
Program Information 3 sessions per year. Session length: 17–21 days in June, July, August. Ages: 15–18. 12–24 participants per session. Cost: $3970–$4870.
Application Deadline Continuous.
Contact Mike Meighan, Director, PO Box 5517, Sarasota, Florida 34277. Phone: 800-317-6789. Fax: 941-924-6075. E-mail: info@actionquest.com.
URL www.actionquest.com

For more information, see page 406.

ACTIONQUEST: BRITISH VIRGIN ISLANDS–SAILING AND SCUBA VOYAGES

ActionQuest
British Virgin Islands

General Information Coed travel outdoor program and adventure program established in 1986.

ACTIONQUEST: British Virgin Islands–Sailing and Scuba Voyages

Program Focus Live-aboard adventures for teenagers offering sailing and scuba diving certifications with associated watersports.
Academics Marine studies.
Special Interest Areas Leadership training, nature study, nautical skills, team building.
Sports Sailing, scuba diving, snorkeling, wakeboarding, waterskiing, windsurfing.
Wilderness/Outdoors Hiking, outdoor adventure, sailing trips.
Trips Day.
Program Information 3 sessions per year. Session length: 17–21 days in June, July, August. Ages: 13–18. 66–84 participants per session. Cost: $3870–$4770. No experience necessary.
Application Deadline Continuous.
Contact Mike Meighan, Director, PO Box 5517, Sarasota, Florida 34277. Phone: 800-317-6789. Fax: 941-924-6075. E-mail: info@actionquest.com.
URL www.actionquest.com

For more information, see page 406.

ACTIONQUEST: BRITISH VIRGIN ISLANDS–SAILING VOYAGES

ActionQuest
British Virgin Islands

General Information Coed travel outdoor program, community service program, and adventure program established in 1986.
Program Focus Live-aboard adventures for teenagers offering sailing and American Red Cross certifications with community service and associated watersports.
Special Interest Areas Community service, conservation projects, leadership training, lifesaving, nature study, nautical skills, team building.
Sports Sailing, snorkeling, wakeboarding, waterskiing, windsurfing.
Wilderness/Outdoors Hiking, outdoor adventure, sailing trips.
Trips Day.
Program Information 3–4 sessions per year. Session length: 10–21 days in June, July, August. Ages: 13–18. 12–48 participants per session. Cost: $2570–$4670. Financial aid available.
Application Deadline Continuous.
Contact Mike Meighan, Director, PO Box 5517, Sarasota, Florida 34277. Phone: 800-317-6789. Fax: 941-924-6075. E-mail: info@actionquest.com.
URL www.actionquest.com

For more information, see page 406.

ACTIONQUEST: JUNIOR ADVANCED SCUBA WITH MARINE BIOLOGY

ActionQuest
British Virgin Islands

General Information Coed travel outdoor program and adventure program established in 1986.
Program Focus Live-aboard program focusing on PADI junior advanced scuba and specialty certifications with introduction to marine biology.
Academics Ecology, marine studies, oceanography.
Special Interest Areas Field research/expeditions, leadership training, nature study, nautical skills, team building.
Sports Sailing, scuba diving, snorkeling, wakeboarding, waterskiing.
Wilderness/Outdoors Hiking.
Trips Cultural, day.
Program Information 3 sessions per year. Session length: 3 weeks in June, July, August. Ages: 13–15. 12 participants per session. Cost: $3970–$4870.
Application Deadline Continuous.
Contact Mike Meighan, Director, PO Box 5517, Sarasota, Florida 34277. Phone: 800-317-6789. Fax: 941-924-6075. E-mail: info@actionquest.com.
URL www.actionquest.com
For more information, see page 106.

ACTIONQUEST: PADI DIVEMASTER VOYAGES

ActionQuest
British Virgin Islands

General Information Coed travel outdoor program and adventure program established in 1986.
Program Focus Liveaboard program offering professional PADI Divemaster course taught as an internship program.
Special Interest Areas Leadership training, nautical skills, team building.
Sports Sailing, scuba diving, snorkeling, wakeboarding, waterskiing, windsurfing.
Wilderness/Outdoors Hiking.
Trips Day, overnight.
Program Information 3 sessions per year. Session length: 17–21 days in June, July, August. Ages: 18+. 8 participants per session. Cost: $3670–$4470. Financial aid available.
Application Deadline Continuous.
Contact Mike Meighan, Director, PO Box 5517, Sarasota, Florida 34277. Phone: 800-317-6789. Fax: 941-924-6075. E-mail: info@actionquest.com.
URL www.actionquest.com
For more information, see page 406.

ACTIONQUEST: RESCUE DIVING VOYAGES

ActionQuest
British Virgin Islands

General Information Coed travel outdoor program and adventure program established in 1986.
Program Focus Live-aboard program focusing on PADI Rescue certification and diver safety, search and recovery, and underwater navigation.
Special Interest Areas Cardiac education, first aid, leadership training, nature study, nautical skills, team building.
Sports Sailing, scuba diving, snorkeling, wakeboarding, waterskiing.
Wilderness/Outdoors Hiking.
Trips Day.
Program Information 3 sessions per year. Session length: 3 weeks in June, July, August. Ages: 15–19. 12 participants per session. Cost: $3970–$4870.
Application Deadline Continuous.
Contact Mike Meighan, Director, PO Box 5517, Sarasota, Florida 34277. Phone: 800-317-6789. Fax: 941-924-6075. E-mail: info@actionquest.com.
URL www.actionquest.com
For more information, see page 406.

ACTIONQUEST: TROPICAL MARINE BIOLOGY VOYAGES

ActionQuest
British Virgin Islands

General Information Coed travel academic program, outdoor program, and adventure program established in 1986. High school credit may be earned.
Program Focus Live-aboard program focusing on PADI specialty certifications and marine biology with research scuba diving.
Academics Biology, ecology, environmental science, marine studies, oceanography.
Special Interest Areas Field research/expeditions, leadership training, nature study, nautical skills, team building.
Sports Sailing, scuba diving, snorkeling, wakeboarding, waterskiing.
Wilderness/Outdoors Hiking.
Trips Cultural, day.

ACTIONQUEST: Tropical Marine Biology Voyages (continued)

Program Information 3 sessions per year. Session length: 3 weeks in June, July, August. Ages: 15–19. 10–16 participants per session. Cost: $3970–$4870.
Application Deadline Continuous.
Contact Mike Meighan, Director, PO Box 5517, Sarasota, Florida 34277. Phone: 800-317-6789. Fax: 941-924-6075. E-mail: info@actionquest.com.
URL www.actionquest.com

For more information, see page 406.

LIFEWORKS WITH THE BRITISH VIRGIN ISLANDS MARINE PARKS AND CONSERVATION DEPARTMENT

LIFEWORKS International
British Virgin Islands

General Information Coed travel outdoor program, community service program, cultural program, and adventure program established in 1986. High school credit may be earned.

LIFEWORKS with the British Virgin Islands Marine Parks and Conservation Department

Program Focus Live-aboard program sailing throughout British Virgin Islands, working on both marine and land-based service projects.
Academics Ecology, marine studies.
Special Interest Areas Community service, conservation projects, field research/expeditions, leadership training, nautical skills, team building.
Sports Sailing, snorkeling.
Wilderness/Outdoors Hiking, sailing trips.
Trips Cultural, day.
Program Information 3 sessions per year. Session length: 17–21 days in June, July, August. Ages: 15–19. 8–26 participants per session. Cost: $3670–$4170. Financial aid available.
Application Deadline Continuous.

Contact James Stoll, Director, PO Box 5517, Sarasota, Florida 34277. Phone: 800-808-2115. Fax: 941-924-6075. E-mail: info@lifeworks-international.com.
URL www.lifeworks-international.com

For more information, see page 548.

VISIONS–BRITISH VIRGIN ISLANDS

Visions
British Virgin Islands

General Information Coed travel outdoor program, community service program, and cultural program established in 1989. High school credit may be earned.

Visions–British Virgin Islands

Program Focus Community service, cross-cultural experience, and outdoor adventure activities.
Academics Intercultural studies.
Arts Carpentry.
Special Interest Areas Community service, construction, cross-cultural education, field research/expeditions, field trips (arts and culture), leadership training, nature study.
Sports Scuba diving, sea kayaking, snorkeling, swimming.
Wilderness/Outdoors Hiking, outdoor adventure.
Trips Cultural, day, overnight.
Program Information 2–3 sessions per year. Session length: 3–4 weeks in June, July, August. Ages: 14–18. 20–25 participants per session. Cost: $3200–$4900. Financial aid available.
Application Deadline Continuous.
Jobs Positions for college students 22 and older.
Contact Joanne Pinaire, Director, PO Box 220, Newport, Pennsylvania 17074. Phone: 717-567-7313. Fax: 717-567-7853. E-mail: info@visionsserviceadventures.com.
URL www.visionsserviceadventures.com

For more information, see page 694.

CAMBODIA

PUTNEY STUDENT TRAVEL–GLOBAL AWARENESS IN ACTION–CAMBODIA

Putney Student Travel
Cambodia

General Information Coed residential cultural program and adventure program established in 1951.
Program Focus Students spend three weeks pursuing research in Cambodia.
Special Interest Areas Community service, cross-cultural education, field research/expeditions.
Sports Bicycling, snorkeling, swimming.
Wilderness/Outdoors Hiking.
Trips Cultural, day, overnight.
Program Information 1 session per year. Session length: 28–34 days in June, July, August. Ages: 15–18. 25 participants per session. Boarding program cost: $6990. Financial aid available. Airfare included.
Application Deadline Continuous.
Jobs Positions for college students 21 and older.
Contact Jeffrey Shumlin, Admissions Director, 345 Hickory Ridge Road, Putney, Vermont 05346. Phone: 802-387-5000. Fax: 802-387-4276. E-mail: info@goputney.com.
URL www.goputney.com
For more information, see page 598.

CANADA

ACADEMIC TREKS–PACIFIC WHALE TREKS

Academic Treks, the academic adventure and community service division of Broadreach
Vancouver Island
British Columbia
Canada

General Information Coed travel academic program, outdoor program, and adventure program established in 1992. High school or college credit may be earned.
Program Focus Academic adventure program focusing on whale and dolphin studies, community service, sea kayaking, hiking, exploration and high school/college credit.
Academics Academics (general), area studies, biology, ecology, environmental science, marine studies.
Special Interest Areas Native American culture, career exploration, community service, conservation projects, field research/expeditions, leadership training.
Sports Sea kayaking, swimming.
Wilderness/Outdoors Backpacking, hiking, ocean expeditions, outdoor adventure, wilderness camping, wilderness/outdoors (general).
Trips Cultural.
Program Information 2 sessions per year. Session length: 22 days in June, July, August. Ages: 15–19. 10–14 participants per session. Cost: $4180.
Application Deadline Continuous.
Contact Carlton Goldthwaite, Director, 806 McCulloch Street, Suite 102, Raleigh, North Carolina 27603. Phone: 888-833-1907. Fax: 919-833-2129. E-mail: info@academictreks.com.
URL www.academictreks.com
For more information, see page 432.

ADVENTURE TREKS–CANADIAN ROCKIES ADVENTURES

Adventure Treks, Inc.
British Columbia
Canada

General Information Coed travel outdoor program, wilderness program, and adventure program established in 1978.
Program Focus Multi-activity outdoor adventure programs with a focus on fun, personal growth, leadership, outdoor skills, and teamwork.
Sports Canoeing, swimming.
Wilderness/Outdoors Backpacking, canoe trips, hiking, mountaineering, orienteering, rafting, rock climbing, white-water trips, wilderness camping.
Program Information 3–4 sessions per year. Session length: 21–22 days in June, July, August. Ages: 14–16. 24 participants per session. Cost: $3295. Financial aid available.
Application Deadline Continuous.
Contact John Dockendorf, Director, PO Box 1321, Flat Rock, North Carolina 28731. Phone: 888-954-5555. Fax: 828-696-1663. E-mail: info@advtreks.com.
URL www.adventuretreks.com

CAMP CHIKOPI FOR BOYS

Camp Chikopi
373 Chikopi Road
Ahmic Harbour, Ontario P0A 1A0
Canada

General Information Boys' residential traditional camp and outdoor program established in 1920. Accredited by Ontario Camping Association.

Camp Chikopi for Boys (continued)

Program Focus Provides the setting for campers to improve self-confidence and think more positively in every challenge that arises.

Special Interest Areas Leadership training, nautical skills, weight reduction.

Sports Aerobics, archery, badminton, baseball, basketball, bicycling, boules, canoeing, climbing (wall), cricket, croquet, cross-country, diving, field hockey, fishing, football, golf, gymnastics, horseback riding, kayaking, lacrosse, martial arts, ropes course, rowing (crew/sculling), rugby, sailing, soccer, softball, sports (general), swimming, tennis, track and field, volleyball, water polo, weight training, windsurfing, wrestling.

Wilderness/Outdoors Backpacking, canoe trips, hiking, mountain biking, mountaineering, orienteering, survival training, wilderness camping, wilderness/outdoors (general).

Trips Day, overnight.

Program Information 4 sessions per year. Session length: 2–7 weeks in June, July, August. Ages: 7–17. 100 participants per session. Boarding program cost: 425–695 Canadian dollars.

Application Deadline Continuous.

Jobs Positions for college students 20 and older.

Summer Contact Mr. Bob Duenkel, Director, main address above. Phone: 705-387-3811. Fax: 705-387-4747. E-mail: campchikopi@aol.com.

Winter Contact Mr. Bob Duenkel, Director, 2132 Northeast 17 Terrace, Ft. Lauderdale, Florida 33305. Phone: 954-566-8235. Fax: 954-525-4031. E-mail: campchikopi@aol.com.

URL www.campchikopi.com

KEEWAYDIN TEMAGAMI

Keewaydin Foundation
Lake Temagami
Temagami, Ontario P0H 2H0
Canada

General Information Coed residential outdoor program, wilderness program, and adventure program established in 1893. Accredited by Ontario Camping Association.

Program Focus To develop independence, self confidence and leadership skills.

Sports Canoeing, fishing, swimming.

Wilderness/Outdoors Canoe trips, hiking, orienteering, white-water trips, wilderness camping.

Trips Overnight.

Program Information 3 sessions per year. Session length: 3–6 weeks in June, July, August. Ages: 10–18. 40–60 participants per session. Boarding program cost: $3500–$5800. Financial aid available.

Application Deadline Continuous.

Jobs Positions for high school students 18 and older and college students 18 and older.

Contact Mr. Bruce Ingersoll, Director, 10 Keewaydin Road, Salisbury, Vermont 05769. Phone: 802-352-4709. Fax: 802-352-4772. E-mail: bruce@keewaydin.org. **URL** www.keewaydin.org

TASC CANADIAN WILDERNESS FISHING CAMPS

TASC for Teens, Inc.
Tatachikapika Lake
Gogama, Ontario
Canada

General Information Coed residential outdoor program, wilderness program, and adventure program established in 1976.

Program Focus Fishing camp.

Sports Boating, fishing, swimming.

Trips Day, overnight.

Program Information 2 sessions per year. Session length: 2 weeks in June, July, August. Ages: 10–17. 10–16 participants per session. Boarding program cost: $2395.

Application Deadline Continuous.

Contact Mr. Paul Oesterreicher, Director, 5439 Countryside Circle, Jeffersonton, Virginia 22724. Phone: 800-296-8272. Fax: 540-937-8272. E-mail: tasc@peoplepc.com.

URL www.tascforteens.com

WESTCOAST CONNECTION TRAVEL–CANADIAN MOUNTAIN MAGIC

Westcoast Connection
Canada

General Information Coed travel outdoor program and adventure program established in 1982. Accredited by Ontario Camping Association.

Program Focus A challenging outdoor adventure in Whistler and the Canadian Rockies with visits to Vancouver and Calgary.

Special Interest Areas Community service.

Sports Bicycling, canoeing, kayaking, rappelling, ropes course, sea kayaking, skiing (downhill), snowboarding, swimming.

Wilderness/Outdoors Caving, hiking, mountain biking, mountaineering, outdoor adventure, rafting, rock climbing, white-water trips.

Program Information 4–7 sessions per year. Session

length: 8–40 days in July, August. Ages: 13–17. 12–20 participants per session. Cost: $1400–$5499.
Application Deadline Continuous.
Jobs Positions for college students 21 and older.
Contact Mr. Mark Segal, Director, 154 East Boston Post Road, Mamaroneck, New York 10543. Phone: 800-767-0227. Fax: 914-835-0798. E-mail: usa@westcoastconnection.com.
URL www.360studenttravel.com
For more information, see page 702.

WESTCOAST CONNECTION TRAVEL– QUEBEC ADVENTURE

Westcoast Connection
Quebec
Canada

General Information Coed travel outdoor program and adventure program established in 1982. Accredited by Ontario Camping Association.
Program Focus A challenging outdoor adventure with whitewater rafting, canoeing, rock climbing, kayaking, and mountain biking with visits to Quebec City and Montreal.
Special Interest Areas Community service.
Sports Bicycling, canoeing, horseback riding, kayaking, rappelling, ropes course, swimming, windsurfing.
Wilderness/Outdoors Bicycle trips, canoe trips, hiking, mountain biking, outdoor adventure, rafting, rock climbing, white-water trips, wilderness camping, wilderness/outdoors (general).
Program Information 2–3 sessions per year. Session length: 20 days in July, August. Ages: 13–17. 12–20 participants per session. Cost: $2999.
Application Deadline Continuous.
Jobs Positions for college students 21 and older.
Contact Mr. Mark Segal, Director, 154 East Boston Post Road, Mamaroneck, New York 10543. Phone: 800-767-0227. Fax: 914-835-0798. E-mail: usa@westcoastconnection.com.
URL www.360studenttravel.com
For more information, see page 702.

WESTCOAST CONNECTION TRAVEL– WESTERN CANADIAN ADVENTURE

Westcoast Connection
Alberta
Canada

General Information Coed travel outdoor program and adventure program established in 1982. Accredited by Ontario Camping Association.
Program Focus A challenging outdoor adventure in Whistler and the Canadian Rockies, with a visit to Vancouver, British Columbia.
Special Interest Areas Community service.
Sports Bicycling, canoeing, horseback riding, rappelling, ropes course, sea kayaking, skiing (downhill), snowboarding, swimming.
Wilderness/Outdoors Caving, hiking, mountain

biking, mountaineering, outdoor adventure, rafting, rock climbing, white-water trips, wilderness/outdoors (general).
Program Information 4–6 sessions per year. Session length: 8–40 days in July, August. Ages: 13–17. 12–20 participants per session. Cost: $1400–$5499.
Application Deadline Continuous.
Jobs Positions for college students 21 and older.
Contact Mr. Mark Segal, Director, 154 East Boston Post Road, Mamaroneck, New York 10543. Phone: 800-767-0227. Fax: 914-835-0798. E-mail: usa@westcoastconnection.com.
URL www.360studenttravel.com
For more information, see page 702.

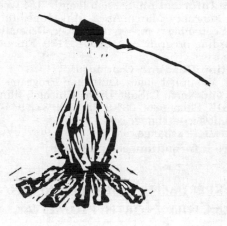

CHILE

AFS-USA–HOMESTAY–CHILE

AFS-USA
Chile

General Information Coed residential academic program and cultural program.
Program Focus Living with a host family while attending school.
Academics Spanish language/literature.
Special Interest Areas Homestays.
Trips Cultural, day, overnight.
Program Information 1 session per year. Session length: 30–45 days in June, July, August. Ages: 16–18. Boarding program cost: $4000–$6000. Application fee: $75. Financial aid available. International airfare and volunteer homestay support included.
Application Deadline Continuous.
Jobs Positions for college students.
Contact Manager, AFS Info Center, 506 Southwest 6th Avenue, 2nd Floor, Portland, Oregon 97204. Phone: 800-AFS-INFO. Fax: 503-299-0753. E-mail: afsinfo@afs.org.
URL www.afs.org/usa
For more information, see page 408.

CENTER FOR CULTURAL INTERCHANGE–CHILE INDEPENDENT HOMESTAY

Center for Cultural Interchange
Chile

General Information Coed residential cultural program established in 1985.
Program Focus Cultural immersion, independent homestay program.
Academics Spanish language/literature, area studies, independent study.
Special Interest Areas Homestays.
Trips Cultural, day.
Program Information Session length: 1–4 weeks in January, February, March, April, May, June, July, August, September, October, November, December. Ages: 17+. Boarding program cost: $890–$1190. Financial aid available.
Application Deadline Continuous.
Contact Ms. Juliet Jones, Outbound Programs Director, 746 North LaSalle Drive, Chicago, Illinois 60610-3617. Phone: 866-684-9675. Fax: 312-944-2644. E-mail: info@cci-exchange.com.
URL www.cci-exchange.com

For more information, see page 448.

THE EXPERIMENT IN INTERNATIONAL LIVING–CHILE NORTH HOMESTAY, COMMUNITY SERVICE

The Experiment in International Living
Chile

General Information Coed travel outdoor program, community service program, cultural program, and adventure program established in 1932. Specific services available for the hearing impaired and visually impaired.
Program Focus International youth travel, homestay, community service.
Academics Spanish language/literature.
Special Interest Areas Community service, homestays, touring.
Wilderness/Outdoors Hiking.
Trips Cultural, day, overnight.
Program Information 1 session per year. Session length: 4 weeks in June, July. Ages: 14–19. 10–15 participants per session. Cost: $5000. Financial aid available. Airfare included.
Application Deadline May 1.
Contact Ms. Annie Thompson, Enrollment Director, Summer Abroad, Kipling Road, PO Box 676, Brattleboro, Vermont 05302-0676. Phone: 800-345-2929. Fax: 802-258-3428. E-mail: eil@worldlearning.org.
URL www.usexperiment.org

For more information, see page 492.

THE EXPERIMENT IN INTERNATIONAL LIVING–CHILE SOUTH HOMESTAY

The Experiment in International Living
Chile

General Information Coed travel outdoor program, community service program, and cultural program established in 1932. Specific services available for the hearing impaired and visually impaired.
Program Focus International youth travel, homestay, community service.
Academics Spanish language/literature.
Special Interest Areas Community service, homestays, touring.
Sports Horseback riding.
Wilderness/Outdoors Canoe trips, hiking.
Trips Cultural, day, overnight.
Program Information 1 session per year. Session length: 4 weeks in June, July. Ages: 14–19. 10–15 participants per session. Cost: $5000. Financial aid available. Airfare included.
Application Deadline May 1.
Contact Annie Thompson, Enrollment Director, Summer Abroad, Kipling Road, PO Box 676, Brattleboro, Vermont 05302-0676. Phone: 800-345-2929. Fax: 802-258-3428. E-mail: eil@worldlearning.org.
URL www.usexperiment.org

For more information, see page 492.

CHINA

AAVE–CHINA

AAVE–Journeys That Matter
China

General Information Coed travel outdoor program, cultural program, and adventure program established in 1976. Accredited by American Camping Association.
Program Focus Adventure travel and culture.
Academics Area studies, intercultural studies.
Special Interest Areas Community service, cross-cultural education, culinary arts, leadership training, touring.
Sports Bicycling.

Wilderness/Outdoors Bicycle trips, hiking, rock climbing.
Trips Cultural, day, overnight.
Program Information 2–4 sessions per year. Session length: 3 weeks in June, July, August. Ages: 15–18. 13 participants per session. Cost: $4888. Financial aid available.
Application Deadline Continuous.
Jobs Positions for college students 21 and older.
Contact Mr. Abbott Wallis, Owner, 2308 Fossil Trace Drive, Golden, Colorado 80401. Phone: 800-222-3595. Fax: 303-526-0885. E-mail: info@aave.com.
URL www.aave.com

For more information, see page 394.

ACADEMIC TREKS–IMMERSION CHINA

Academic Treks, the academic adventure and community service division of Broadreach
Beijing, Kunming, Zhongdian, Lijiang, Tiger Leaping Gorge
China

General Information Coed travel academic program, community service program, and adventure program established in 1992. High school or college credit may be earned.
Program Focus Academic adventure and community service program focusing on Chinese language, weeklong home stay community service projects, cultural immersion, adventure travel, hiking and college credit.
Academics Chinese languages/literature, academics (general), area studies, history, intercultural studies.
Special Interest Areas Community service, cross-cultural education, homestays, leadership training.
Wilderness/Outdoors Hiking.
Trips Cultural, day, overnight.
Program Information 2 sessions per year. Session length: 25 days in June, July, August. Ages: 15–19. 10–12 participants per session. Cost: $5180. Financial aid available.
Application Deadline Continuous.
Contact Carlton Goldthwaite, Director, 806 McCulloch Street, Suite 102, Raleigh, North Carolina 27603. Phone: 888-833-1907. Fax: 919-833-2129. E-mail: info@academictreks.com.
URL www.academictreks.com

For more information, see page 432.

AFS-USA–CHINA SUMMER HOMESTAY LANGUAGE STUDY PROGRAM

AFS-USA
China

General Information Coed residential academic program and cultural program established in 1995. High school credit may be earned.
Program Focus Live with a host family and join other students at a local school attending classes to learn Mandarin and calligraphy as well as lectures on Chinese culture and society.
Academics Chinese languages/literature, intercultural studies.
Arts Calligraphy.
Special Interest Areas Homestays.
Trips Cultural, day.
Program Information 1 session per year. Session length: 30–45 days in June, July, August. Ages: 15–18. Boarding program cost: $6100. Application fee: $75. Financial aid available. International airfare and volunteer homestay support included.
Application Deadline Continuous.
Contact Manager, AFS Info Center, 506 Southwest 6th Avenue, 2nd Floor, Portland, Oregon 97204. Phone: 800-AFS-INFO. Fax: 503-299-0753. E-mail: afsinfo@afs.org.
URL www.afs.org/usa

For more information, see page 408.

CHOATE ROSEMARY HALL SUMMER IN CHINA

Choate Rosemary Hall
China

General Information Coed residential academic program and cultural program established in 2000. High school credit may be earned.

Choate Rosemary Hall Summer in China

Program Focus Chinese culture and language.
Academics Chinese languages/literature, art history/appreciation.
Arts Calligraphy, painting.
Special Interest Areas Cross-cultural education, homestays, touring.
Trips Cultural, day, overnight.
Program Information 1 session per year. Session length: 5 weeks in June, July. Ages: 14–19. 20–35 participants per session. Boarding program cost: $6499. Application fee: $60. Financial aid available. Airfare from USA to China included. Participants housed in college dormitories and hotels.
Application Deadline Continuous.

Choate Rosemary Hall Summer in China (continued)

Contact Dr. Carol S. Chen-Lin, Director Summer in China, 333 Christian Street, Wallingford, Connecticut 06492. Phone: 203-697-2080. Fax: 203-697-2519. E-mail: cchen@choate.edu.
URL www.choate.edu/summerprograms
For more information, see page 452.

EF INTERNATIONAL LANGUAGE SCHOOL- BEIJING

EF International Language Schools
Beijing
China

General Information Coed travel academic program and cultural program established in 2007.
Program Focus Language and cultural immersion.
Academics Chinese languages/literature.
Special Interest Areas Field trips (arts and culture), homestays, touring.
Sports Sports (general).
Trips Cultural, day, overnight.
Program Information 2–52 sessions per year. Session length: 14–365 days in January, February, March, April, May, June, July, August, September, October, November, December. Ages: 16+. 100–150 participants per session. Cost: $790–$8280. Application fee: $145. Financial aid available. Call for costs.
Application Deadline Continuous.
Contact Margaret Kelly, Director of Admissions, One Education Street, Cambridge, Massachusetts 02141. Phone: 800-992-1892. Fax: 800-590-1125. E-mail: ils@ef.com.
URL www.ef.com
For more information, see page 478.

EF INTERNATIONAL LANGUAGE SCHOOL- SHANGHAI

EF International Language Schools
218 South Xi Zang Road
19th Floor, Silver Tower
Shanghai
China

General Information Coed travel academic program and cultural program established in 2004.
Program Focus Language and cultural immersion.
Academics Chinese languages/literature.
Special Interest Areas Field trips (arts and culture), homestays.
Sports Sports (general).
Trips Cultural, day, overnight.
Program Information 2–52 sessions per year. Session length: 2–52 weeks in January, February, March, April, May, June, July, August, September, October, November, December. Ages: 16+. 50–100 participants per session. Application fee: $145. Financial aid available. Call for costs.
Application Deadline Continuous.
Contact Ms. Margaret Kelly, Director of Admissions, One Education Street, Cambridge, Massachusetts 02141. Phone: 800-992-1892. Fax: 800-590-1125. E-mail: ils@ef.com.
URL www.ef.com
For more information, see page 478.

EXCEL CHINA

Putney Student Travel
China

General Information Coed residential academic program and cultural program established in 1951. Formal opportunities for the academically talented and artistically talented.
Program Focus Precollege program that emphasizes small classes, creative interactions among students and faculty, and cultural exchange.
Academics Chinese languages/literature, academics (general), architecture, area studies, art history/appreciation, government and politics, history, humanities, intercultural studies, precollege program, social science, writing.
Arts Creative writing, drawing, film, music, painting, theater/drama.
Special Interest Areas Field research/expeditions, touring.
Sports Basketball, bicycling, soccer, swimming.
Wilderness/Outdoors Hiking.
Trips Cultural, day.
Program Information 1 session per year. Session length: 4 weeks in July, August. Ages: 15–18. 60–70 participants per session. Boarding program cost: $5590. Financial aid available. Airfare included.
Application Deadline Continuous.

Contact Patrick Noyes, Director, 345 Hickory Ridge Road, Putney, Vermont 05346. Phone: 802-387-5000. Fax: 802-387-4276. E-mail: info@goputney.com. **URL** www.goputney.com

For more information, see page 490.

THE EXPERIMENT IN INTERNATIONAL LIVING–CHINA NORTH AND EAST HOMESTAY

The Experiment in International Living
China

General Information Coed travel outdoor program, cultural program, and adventure program established in 1932.
Program Focus International youth travel, homestay, travel with Chinese high school students.
Academics Chinese languages/literature.
Special Interest Areas Homestays, touring.
Wilderness/Outdoors Hiking.
Trips Cultural, day, overnight.
Program Information 1 session per year. Session length: 4 weeks in June, July. Ages: 14–19. 10–20 participants per session. Cost: $5600. Financial aid available. Airfare included.
Application Deadline May 1.
Contact Annie Thompson, Enrollment Director, Summer Abroad, Kipling Road, PO Box 676, Brattleboro, Vermont 05302-0676. Phone: 800-345-2929. Fax: 802-258-3428. E-mail: eil@worldlearning.org. **URL** www.usexperiment.org

For more information, see page 492.

THE EXPERIMENT IN INTERNATIONAL LIVING–CHINA SOUTH AND WEST HOMESTAY

The Experiment in International Living
China

General Information Coed travel cultural program and adventure program established in 1932.
Program Focus International youth travel, homestays, travel with Chinese high school students.
Academics Chinese languages/literature.
Special Interest Areas Homestays, touring.
Wilderness/Outdoors Hiking.
Trips Cultural, day, overnight.
Program Information 1 session per year. Session length: 4 weeks in June, July. Ages: 14–19. 10–20 participants per session. Cost: $5600. Financial aid available. Airfare included.
Application Deadline May 1.
Contact Annie Thompson, Enrollment Director, Summer Abroad, Kipling Road, PO Box 676, Brattleboro, Vermont 05302-0676. Phone: 800-345-2929. Fax: 802-258-3428. E-mail: eil@worldlearning.org. **URL** www.usexperiment.org

For more information, see page 492.

LIFEWORKS WITH THE CHINA LITTLE FLOWER FOUNDATION IN CHINA

LIFEWORKS International
China

General Information Coed travel community service program, cultural program, and adventure program established in 1986. High school credit may be earned.
Program Focus Participants work primarily with physically disabled children in the China Little Flower foundation orphanages. Students will experience this unique culture and visit many of the historical sites for which China is famous.
Academics Chinese languages/literature, intercultural studies.
Special Interest Areas Childcare, community service, leadership training, team building, touring.
Trips Cultural, day, overnight, shopping.
Program Information 1 session per year. Session length: 3 weeks in June, July. Ages: 15–19. 12 participants per session. Cost: $4370. Financial aid available.
Application Deadline Continuous.
Contact James Stoll, Director, PO Box 5517, Sarasota, Florida 34277. Phone: 800-808-2115. Fax: 941-924-6075. E-mail: info@lifeworks-international.com. **URL** www.lifeworks-international.com

For more information, see page 548.

PUTNEY STUDENT TRAVEL–GLOBAL AWARENESS–CHINA

Putney Student Travel
China

General Information Coed residential cultural program established in 1951.
Program Focus Students spend three weeks pursuing research in relation to the effects of economic transformation.
Academics Economics, intercultural studies.
Special Interest Areas Cross-cultural education, field research/expeditions.
Trips Cultural, day.

Putney Student Travel–Global Awareness–China (continued)

Program Information 1 session per year. Session length: 25–32 days in June, July, August. Ages: 15–18. 16 participants per session. Boarding program cost: $6790. Financial aid available.
Application Deadline Continuous.
Contact Jeffrey Shumlin, Admissions Director, 345 Hickory Ridge Road, Putney, Vermont 05346. Phone: 802-387-5000. Fax: 802-387-4276. E-mail: info@goputney.com.
URL www.goputney.com
For more information, see page 598.

RASSIAS PROGRAMS–CHINA

Rassias Programs
Gyalthang
China

General Information Coed travel academic program and cultural program established in 1986.
Program Focus Chinese language and culture, community service.
Academics Chinese languages/literature.
Special Interest Areas Campcraft, community service, conservation projects, cross-cultural education, farming, field research/expeditions, homestays, nature study, touring.
Sports Bicycling.
Wilderness/Outdoors Backpacking, bicycle trips, hiking, outdoor camping.
Trips Cultural, day, overnight.
Program Information 1 session per year. Session length: 40 days in June, July, August. Ages: 14–18. 15 participants per session. Cost: $8375. Financial aid available. Airfare included.
Application Deadline Continuous.
Jobs Positions for college students 21 and older.
Contact Bill Miles, President, PO Box 5456, Hanover, New Hampshire 03755. Phone: 603-643-3007. Fax: 603-643-4249. E-mail: wmiles@rassias.com.
URL www.rassias.com
For more information, see page 602.

RUSTIC PATHWAYS–CHINESE LANGUAGE IMMERSION

Rustic Pathways
Dali University
Dali
China

General Information Coed residential.
Program Focus Mandarin Chinese.
Academics Chinese languages/literature.
Special Interest Areas Cross-cultural education, touring.
Wilderness/Outdoors Bicycle trips, hiking.
Trips Cultural, day, shopping.
Program Information 3 sessions per year. Session length: 17–45 days in June, July, August. Ages: 15–18. 10–15 participants per session. Boarding program cost: $2495–$6895. Financial aid available. Airfare not included.
Application Deadline Continuous.
Contact Rustic Pathways, 4121 Erie Street, Willoughby, Ohio 44094. Phone: 800-321-4353. E-mail: rustic@rusticpathways.com.
URL www.rusticpathways.com
For more information, see page 612.

RUSTIC PATHWAYS–INTENSIVE CHINESE LANGUAGE

Rustic Pathways
Dali University
Dali
China

General Information Coed residential academic program and cultural program.
Program Focus Private, one-on-one Chinese language instruction.
Academics Chinese languages/literature.
Special Interest Areas Cross-cultural education, touring.
Wilderness/Outdoors Bicycle trips, hiking.
Trips Cultural, day, shopping.
Program Information 3 sessions per year. Session length: 17–45 days in June, July, August. Ages: 15–18. 10–15 participants per session. Boarding program cost: $2995–$8395. Financial aid available. Airfare not included.
Application Deadline Continuous.
Contact Rustic Pathways, 4121 Erie Street, Willoughby, Ohio 44094. Phone: 800-321-4353. Fax: 440-975-9694. E-mail: rustic@rusticpathways.com.
URL www.rusticpathways.com
For more information, see page 612.

RUSTIC PATHWAYS–THE WONDERS OF CHINA

Rustic Pathways
China

General Information Coed travel cultural program.
Special Interest Areas Cross-cultural education, touring.
Trips Cultural, day, overnight, shopping.
Program Information 1 session per year. Session length: 17 days in July. Ages: 16–18. 10–15 participants per session. Cost: $3895. Financial aid available. Airfare not included.
Application Deadline Continuous.
Contact Rustic Pathways, 4121 Erie Street, Willoughby, Ohio 44094. Phone: 800-231-4353. Fax: 440-975-9694. E-mail: rustic@rusticpathways.com.
URL www.rusticpathways.com

For more information, see page 612.

SUMMER ADVANTAGE STUDY ABROAD– NANJING, CHINA

American Institute for Foreign Study (AIFS)
Nanjing University
Nanjing
China

General Information Coed travel academic program and cultural program established in 2006. College credit may be earned.
Program Focus Study abroad for college credit.
Academics Chinese languages/literature, history, intercultural studies, social studies.
Trips Cultural, day, overnight, shopping.
Program Information 1 session per year. Session length: 29–34 days in June, July. Ages: 16–18. 10–15 participants per session. Cost: $5095. Application fee: $95.
Application Deadline April 15.
Contact Mrs. Amy Van Stone, Director of Admissions, Summer Advantage, 9 West Broad Street, River Plaza, Stamford, Connecticut 06902. Phone: 800-913-7151. Fax: 203-399-5463. E-mail: summeradvantage@aifs.com.
URL www.summeradvantage.com

For more information, see page 410.

COSTA RICA

AAVE–COSTA RICA CLÁSICA

AAVE–Journeys That Matter
Costa Rica

General Information Coed travel academic program, outdoor program, community service program, cultural program, and adventure program established in 1976. Accredited by American Camping Association.
Program Focus One week of academic Spanish language study/3 weeks Spanish immersion.
Academics Latin language, Spanish language/ literature.
Arts Dance.
Special Interest Areas Community service, homestays, leadership training, nature study.
Sports Bicycling, horseback riding, sailing, snorkeling, surfing, swimming.
Wilderness/Outdoors Hiking, mountain biking, rafting, white-water trips.
Trips Cultural, day, overnight.
Program Information 4 sessions per year. Session length: 3 weeks in June, July, August. Ages: 14–18. 13–15 participants per session. Cost: $4088. Financial aid available.
Application Deadline Continuous.
Jobs Positions for college students 21 and older.
Contact Mr. Abbott Wallis, Owner, 2308 Fossil Trace Drive, Golden, Colorado 80401. Phone: 800-222-3595. Fax: 303-526-0806. E-mail: info@aave.com.
URL www.aave.com

For more information, see page 394.

AAVE–COSTA RICA SPANISH INTENSIVE

AAVE–Journeys That Matter
Costa Rica

General Information Coed travel academic program and adventure program established in 1976. Accredited by American Camping Association.
Program Focus Three weeks of Spanish language immersion study.
Academics Latin language, Spanish language/literature, area studies, intercultural studies.
Special Interest Areas Community service, leadership training, touring.
Sports Snorkeling, surfing.
Wilderness/Outdoors Hiking, mountain biking.
Trips Cultural, day, overnight.
Program Information 2–4 sessions per year. Session length: 3 weeks in June, July, August. Ages: 14–18. 14 participants per session. Cost: $4088. Financial aid available.
Application Deadline Continuous.
Jobs Positions for college students 21 and older.
Contact Mr. Abbott Wallis, Owner, 2308 Fossil Trace Drive, Golden, Colorado 80401. Phone: 800-222-3595. Fax: 303-526-0885. E-mail: info@aave.com.
URL www.aave.com

For more information, see page 394.

ACADEMIC STUDY ASSOCIATES– COSTA RICA

Academic Study Associates, Inc. (ASA)
Heredia
Costa Rica

General Information Coed residential academic program, community service program, and cultural program established in 2007. Formal opportunities for the academically talented.
Program Focus Spanish language, community service, culture.
Academics Spanish language/literature, academics (general).
Arts Arts and crafts (general), dance (folk).
Special Interest Areas Community service, conservation projects, homestays, touring.
Sports Soccer.
Wilderness/Outdoors Hiking, rafting.
Trips Cultural, day, overnight.
Program Information 1 session per year. Session length: 30 days in July. Ages: 14–18. 25–35 participants per session. Boarding program cost: $5295. Financial aid available.
Application Deadline Continuous.
Jobs Positions for college students 21 and older.
Contact Marcia Evans, President, 375 West Broadway, Suite 200, New York, New York 10012. Phone: 212-796-8340. Fax: 212-334-4934.
URL www.asaprograms.com
For more information, see page 398.

ACADEMIC TREKS–SEA TURTLE STUDIES

Academic Treks, the academic adventure and community service division of Broadreach
Tortuguero and Drake Bay
Costa Rica

General Information Coed travel academic program, outdoor program, community service program, and adventure program established in 1992. High school or college credit may be earned.
Program Focus Academic adventure program focusing on sea turtle ecology, conservation and research, community service, marine science, hiking, high school and college credit.
Academics Academics (general), biology, ecology, environmental science, marine studies.
Special Interest Areas Community service, conservation projects, field research/expeditions, leadership training, nature study.
Sports Sea kayaking, snorkeling, swimming.
Wilderness/Outdoors Hiking, outdoor adventure, wilderness/outdoors (general).
Trips Cultural, day.
Program Information 2 sessions per year. Session length: 20 days in June, July, August. Ages: 15–19. 10–14 participants per session. Cost: $4480. Financial aid available.
Application Deadline Continuous.

Contact Carlton Goldthwaite, Director, 806 McCulloch Street, Suite 102, Raleigh, North Carolina 27603. Phone: 888-833-1907. Fax: 919-833-2129. E-mail: info@academictreks.com.
URL www.academictreks.com
For more information, see page 432.

AFS-USA–COMMUNITY SERVICE– COSTA RICA

AFS-USA
Costa Rica

General Information Coed residential community service program and cultural program. High school credit may be earned.
Program Focus Community service program with an ecological focus and a short homestay experience.
Academics Spanish language/literature.
Special Interest Areas Community service, homestays, nature study, touring.
Wilderness/Outdoors Hiking.
Trips Cultural, day, overnight.
Program Information 1 session per year. Session length: 30–45 days in June, July, August. Ages: 15–18. Boarding program cost: $4000–$6000. Application fee: $75. Financial aid available. International airfare and volunteer homestay support included.
Application Deadline Continuous.
Contact Manager, AFS Info Center, 506 Southwest 6th Avenue, 2nd Floor, Portland, Oregon 97204. Phone: 800-AFS-INFO. Fax: 503-299-0753. E-mail: afsinfo@afs. org.
URL www.afs.org/usa
For more information, see page 408.

AFS-USA–HOMESTAY LANGUAGE STUDY–COSTA RICA

AFS-USA
Costa Rica

General Information Coed residential cultural program.
Program Focus Language study program.
Academics Spanish language/literature.
Special Interest Areas Homestays, touring.
Trips Cultural, day, overnight.
Program Information 1 session per year. Session length: 30–45 days in June, July. Ages: 15–18. Boarding program cost: $5000–$6000. Application fee: $75. Financial aid available. International airfare and volunteer homestay support included.

Application Deadline Continuous.
Contact Manager, AFS Info Center, 506 Southwest 6th Avenue, 2nd Floor, Portland, Oregon 97204. Phone: 800-AFS-INFO. Fax: 503-299-0753. E-mail: afsinfo@afs.org.
URL www.afs.org/usa

For more information, see page 408.

AFS-USA–HOMESTAY PLUS–COSTA RICA

AFS-USA
Costa Rica

General Information Coed residential cultural program.
Program Focus Live with a host family, perform community service and go on nature bus trips with expert guides.
Academics Spanish language/literature.
Special Interest Areas Community service, homestays, nature study.
Trips Cultural, day, overnight.
Program Information 1 session per year. Session length: 30–45 days in June, July, August. Ages: 15–18. Boarding program cost: $4000–$6000. Application fee: $75. Financial aid available. International airfare and volunteer homestay support included.
Application Deadline Continuous.
Contact Manager, AFS Info Center, 506 Southwest 6th Avenue, 2nd Floor, Portland, Oregon 97204. Phone: 800-AFS-INFO. Fax: 503-299-0753. E-mail: afsinfo@afs.org.
URL www.afs.org/usa

For more information, see page 408.

BROADREACH COSTA RICA EXPERIENCE

Broadreach
Costa Rica

General Information Coed travel outdoor program, wilderness program, and adventure program established in 1992.

BROADREACH Costa Rica Experience

Academics Ecology, environmental science, geology/earth science, intercultural studies.
Arts Photography.
Special Interest Areas Community service, conservation projects, field research/expeditions, leadership training, nature study.
Sports Horseback riding, rappelling, sea kayaking, snorkeling, surfing.
Wilderness/Outdoors Backpacking, hiking, kayaking trips, outdoor adventure, rafting, white-water trips, wilderness camping, wilderness/outdoors (general).
Trips Cultural.
Program Information 2 sessions per year. Session length: 3 weeks in June, July, August. Ages: 15–19. 12 participants per session. Cost: $3990.
Application Deadline Continuous.

BROADREACH *Costa Rica Experience (continued)*

Contact Carlton Goldthwaite, Director, 806 McCulloch Street, Suite 102, Raleigh, North Carolina 27603. Phone: 888-833-1907. Fax: 919-833-2129. E-mail: info@gobroadreach.com.
URL www.gobroadreach.com
For more information, see page 432.

CENTER FOR CULTURAL INTERCHANGE—COSTA RICA LANGUAGE SCHOOL

Center for Cultural Interchange
San Jose
Costa Rica

General Information Coed residential academic program and cultural program established in 1985. High school or college credit may be earned.
Program Focus Cultural immersion and language study.
Academics Spanish language/literature.
Special Interest Areas Homestays.
Trips Cultural, day.
Program Information 1–50 sessions per year. Session length: 14–90 days in January, February, March, April, May, June, July, August, September, October, November, December. Ages: 13+. Boarding program cost: $2000–$2500. Financial aid available.
Application Deadline Continuous.
Contact Ms. Juliet Jones, Outbound Programs Director, 746 North LaSalle Drive, Chicago, Illinois 60610-3617. Phone: 866-684-9675. Fax: 312-944-2644. E-mail: info@cci-exchange.com.
URL www.cci-exchange.com
For more information, see page 448.

EDU-CULTURE INTERNATIONAL (ECI)—CPI COSTA RICA

Edu-Culture International (ECI)
Costa Rica

General Information Coed travel academic program and cultural program established in 2006. College credit may be earned.
Program Focus Pre-college experience including intensive Spanish classes and homestay in Heredia (1 week) and Monteverde (1 week). Spanish Classes and hotel accommodation at Flamingo Beach for 1 week. Spanish language immersion, daily activities and excursions, weekend travel.
Academics Spanish language/literature, intercultural studies, precollege program.
Special Interest Areas Community service, cross-cultural education, homestays, nature study, touring.
Sports Boating, horseback riding, snorkeling, soccer, swimming.
Wilderness/Outdoors Hiking, zip line.
Trips Cultural, day, overnight, shopping.
Program Information 1 session per year. Session length: 24 days in June, July. Ages: 15–18. 25–30 participants per session. Cost: $4400. Application fee: $95. Financial aid available. Airfare from San Francisco, CA to San Jose, Costa Rica included in cost.
Application Deadline Continuous.
Jobs Positions for college students 22 and older.
Contact Ms. Phyllis O'Neill, Director, PO Box 2692, Berkeley, California 94702. Phone: 866-343-8990. Fax: 510-845-2231. E-mail: info@educulture.org.
URL www.educulture.org
For more information, see page 476.

EDU-CULTURE INTERNATIONAL (ECI)—GRECIA COSTA RICA

Edu-Culture International (ECI)
Costa Rica

General Information Coed travel academic program and cultural program established in 2006.
Program Focus Intensive Spanish classes and accommodation in a small cozy dormitory. Designed for 7th, 8th and 9th grade students. Spanish language immersion, daily activities and excursions, sports, weekend travel.
Academics Spanish language/literature, intercultural studies.
Special Interest Areas Community service, cross-cultural education, nature study, touring.
Sports Horseback riding, soccer, swimming.
Wilderness/Outdoors Hiking, zip line.
Trips Cultural, day, overnight, shopping.
Program Information 1 session per year. Session length: 17 days in June, July. Ages: 12–15. 20–22 participants per session. Cost: $3750. Application fee: $95. Financial aid available. Airfare from San Francisco, CA to San Jose, Costa Rica included in cost.
Application Deadline Continuous.
Jobs Positions for college students 22 and older.
Contact Ms. Phyllis O'Neill, Director, PO Box 2692, Berkeley, California 94702. Phone: 866-343-8990. Fax: 510-845-2231. E-mail: info@educulture.org.
URL www.educulture.org
For more information, see page 476.

EF International Language School–Playa Tamarindo

EF International Language Schools
Playa Tamarindo
Costa Rica

General Information Coed travel academic program and cultural program established in 2007.
Program Focus Spanish language and cultural immersion.
Academics Spanish (Advanced Placement), Spanish language/literature, social science.
Special Interest Areas Homestays, touring.
Sports Sports (general).
Wilderness/Outdoors Wilderness/outdoors (general).
Trips Cultural, day, overnight.
Program Information 2–52 sessions per year. Session length: 14–365 days in January, February, March, April, May, June, July, August, September, October, November, December. Ages: 16+. 100–150 participants per session. Cost: $790–$8600. Application fee: $145. Financial aid available. Call for costs.
Application Deadline Continuous.
Contact Margaret Kelly, Director of Admissions, One Education Street, Cambridge, Massachusetts 02141. Phone: 800-992-1892. Fax: 800-590-1125. E-mail: ils@ef.com.
URL www.ef.com

For more information, see page 478.

The Experiment in International Living–Costa Rica Homestay

The Experiment in International Living
Costa Rica

General Information Coed travel outdoor program, community service program, cultural program, and adventure program established in 1932.
Program Focus International youth travel, homestay, ecology.
Academics Spanish language/literature, ecology.
Special Interest Areas Community service, homestays.
Sports Snorkeling, swimming.
Wilderness/Outdoors Hiking, white-water trips.
Trips Cultural, day, overnight.
Program Information 1 session per year. Session length: 4 weeks in June, July. Ages: 14–19. 10–15

participants per session. Cost: $5000. Financial aid available. Airfare included.
Application Deadline May 1.
Contact Annie Thompson, Enrollment Director, Summer Abroad, Kipling Road, PO Box 676, Brattleboro, Vermont 05302-0676. Phone: 800-345-2929. Fax: 802-258-3428. E-mail: eil@worldlearning.org.
URL www.usexperiment.org

For more information, see page 492.

Global Leadership Adventures–Costa Rica: Community Service and Leadership

Global Leadership Adventures
Costa Rica

General Information Coed travel academic program, community service program, and cultural program established in 2004. High school credit may be earned.
Program Focus Learning about a country and its culture through community service, classes and adventure.
Academics Spanish language/literature, intercultural studies, social studies.
Special Interest Areas Community service, leadership training.
Trips Cultural, day.
Program Information 1–2 sessions per year. Session length: 3 weeks in June, July, August. Ages: 15–18. 40–60 participants per session. Cost: $4395–$4595. Financial aid available.
Application Deadline Continuous.
Contact Mr. Andrew Motiwalla, Executive Director, 2633 Lincoln Boulevard, #427, Santa Monica, California 90405. Phone: 888-358-4321. Fax: 866-612-3697. E-mail: info@globalleadershipadventures.com.

For more information, see page 504.

Global Works–Cultural Exchange and Service–Costa Rica–3 weeks

GLOBAL WORKS
Costa Rica

General Information Coed travel community service program, cultural program, and adventure program established in 1988. High school credit may be earned.
Program Focus Environmental and community service, language exposure and cultural exchange.
Academics Spanish language/literature, environmental science, intercultural studies.
Arts Arts and crafts (general), dance (Latin), painting.
Special Interest Areas Community service, conservation projects, construction, cross-cultural education, field trips (arts and culture), homestays.
Sports Basketball, horseback riding, rappelling, soccer, surfing, swimming, volleyball.
Wilderness/Outdoors Backpacking, hiking, outdoor adventure, rafting, white-water trips.

GLOBAL WORKS–Cultural Exchange and Service–Costa Rica-3 weeks (continued)

Trips Cultural, day, overnight.
Program Information 2 sessions per year. Session length: 21–24 days in June, July, August. Ages: 15–17. 16–18 participants per session. Cost: $3595–$3995. Application fee: $100. Financial aid available. Airfare not included.
Application Deadline Continuous.
Jobs Positions for college students 23 and older.
Contact Mr. Erik Werner, Director, 1113 South Allen Street, State College, Pennsylvania 16801. Phone: 814-867-7000. Fax: 814-867-2717. E-mail: info@globalworksinc.com.
URL www.globalworksinc.com
For more information, see page 506.

GLOBAL WORKS–LANGUAGE IMMERSION, CULTURAL EXCHANGE AND SERVICE–COSTA RICA

GLOBAL WORKS
Costa Rica

General Information Coed travel community service program, cultural program, and adventure program established in 1988. High school credit may be earned.
Program Focus Environmental and community service, language immersion, and cultural exchange.
Academics Spanish language/literature, ecology, intercultural studies.
Arts Arts and crafts (general), dance (Latin), painting.
Special Interest Areas Community service, conservation projects, construction, field trips (arts and culture), homestays.
Sports Horseback riding, ropes course, soccer, sports (general), surfing, swimming, volleyball.
Wilderness/Outdoors Backpacking, hiking, outdoor adventure, rafting, white-water trips.
Trips Cultural, day, overnight.
Program Information 5 sessions per year. Session length: 3–4 weeks in June, July, August. Ages: 13–17. 16–18 participants per session. Cost: $3595–$4295. Application fee: $100. Financial aid available. Airfare not included.
Application Deadline Continuous.
Jobs Positions for college students 23 and older.

Contact Mr. Erik Werner, Director, 1113 South Allen Street, State College, Pennsylvania 16801. Phone: 814-867-7000. Fax: 814-867-2717. E-mail: info@globalworksinc.com.
URL www.globalworksinc.com
For more information, see page 506.

LIFEWORKS WITH THE FUNDACIÓN HUMANITARIA IN COSTA RICA

LIFEWORKS International
Costa Rica

General Information Coed travel academic program, outdoor program, community service program, cultural program, and adventure program established in 1986. High school credit may be earned.
Program Focus Students work on different humanitarian projects, primarily for children. The program includes a formal language component and travel to Tortuguero and the Monteverde Rainforest.
Academics Spanish language/literature, intercultural studies.
Special Interest Areas Community service, conservation projects, homestays, leadership training, nature study, team building, touring.
Sports Swimming.
Wilderness/Outdoors Hiking.
Trips Cultural, day, overnight.
Program Information 2 sessions per year. Session length: 3 weeks in June, July, August. Ages: 15–19. 18 participants per session. Cost: $3970. Financial aid available.
Application Deadline Continuous.
Contact James Stoll, Director, PO Box 5517, Sarasota, Florida 34277. Phone: 800-808-2115. Fax: 941-924-6075. E-mail: info@lifeworks-international.com.
URL www.lifeworks-international.com
For more information, see page 548.

PUTNEY STUDENT TRAVEL–COMMUNITY SERVICE–COSTA RICA

Putney Student Travel
Costa Rica

General Information Coed residential community service program and cultural program established in 1951.
Program Focus Community service, cultural

exchange, and weekend excursions from a base in a small, rural community.
Academics Intercultural studies.
Special Interest Areas Community service, construction.
Sports Horseback riding, soccer, swimming.
Wilderness/Outdoors Hiking, white-water trips.
Trips Cultural, day.
Program Information 4–5 sessions per year. Session length: 28–30 days in June, July, August. Ages: 15–18. 16 participants per session. Boarding program cost: $5290. Financial aid available. Airfare from Miami included.
Application Deadline Continuous.
Contact Jeffrey Shumlin, Admissions Director, 345 Hickory Ridge Road, Putney, Vermont 05346. Phone: 802-387-5000. Fax: 802-387-4276. E-mail: info@goputney.com.
URL www.goputney.com

For more information, see page 598.

PUTNEY STUDENT TRAVEL–LANGUAGE LEARNING–COSTA RICA

Putney Student Travel
Costa Rica

General Information Coed residential academic program and cultural program. Formal opportunities for the academically talented.
Program Focus Spanish language immersion in the context of community service. Participants housed in host-family homes and hotels. Enrollment limited to those who are studying Spanish.
Academics Spanish (Advanced Placement), Spanish language/literature, art history/appreciation, intercultural studies.
Special Interest Areas Homestays.
Sports Horseback riding, rappelling, sailing, soccer, swimming, windsurfing.
Wilderness/Outdoors Bicycle trips, hiking, mountaineering, rock climbing.
Trips Cultural, day, overnight.
Program Information 2 sessions per year. Session length: 28–30 days in June, July, August. Ages: 13–18. 16–18 participants per session. Boarding program cost: $5890. Financial aid available. Airfare from Miami included.
Application Deadline Continuous.
Contact Jeffrey Shumlin, Admissions Director, 345 Hickory Ridge Road, Putney, Vermont 05346. Phone: 802-387-5000. Fax: 802-387-4276. E-mail: info@goputney.com.
URL www.goputney.com

For more information, see page 598.

RUSTIC PATHWAYS–THE CANO NEGRO SERVICE PROJECT

Rustic Pathways
Caño Negro
Costa Rica

General Information Coed residential community service program and cultural program established in 2003.
Academics Biology.
Special Interest Areas Animal care, community service, construction, cross-cultural education.
Sports Bicycling, horseback riding, sea kayaking.
Trips Cultural, day, overnight.
Program Information 9 sessions per year. Session length: 8 days in June, July, August. Ages: 14–18. 10–15 participants per session. Boarding program cost: $985.
Application Deadline Continuous.
Jobs Positions for college students 21 and older.
Contact Rustic Pathways, 4121 Erie Street, Willoughby, Ohio 44094. Phone: 800-321-4353. Fax: 440-975-9694. E-mail: rustic@rusticpathways.com.
URL www.rusticpathways.com

For more information, see page 612.

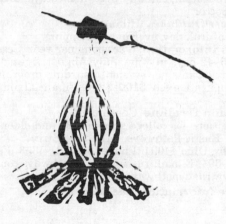

RUSTIC PATHWAYS–COSTA RICA ADVENTURER

Rustic Pathways
Costa Rica

General Information Coed travel outdoor program, wilderness program, cultural program, and adventure program established in 2002.
Program Focus Cultural immersion.
Special Interest Areas Cross-cultural education, touring.
Sports Bicycling, horseback riding, kayaking, rappelling, sailing, snorkeling, soccer, swimming.
Wilderness/Outdoors Hiking, outdoor adventure, rafting, white-water trips.
Trips Cultural, day, overnight, shopping.
Program Information 7 sessions per year. Session length: 15 days in June, July, August. Ages: 14–18.

RUSTIC PATHWAYS–COSTA RICA ADVENTURER (continued)

10–15 participants per session. Cost: $2495. Application fee: $100–$200.
Application Deadline Continuous.
Jobs Positions for college students 21 and older.
Contact Rustic Pathways, 4121 Erie Street, Willoughby, Ohio 44094. Phone: 800-321-4353. Fax: 440-975-9694. E-mail: rustic@rusticpathways.com.
URL www.rusticpathways.com
For more information, see page 612.

RUSTIC PATHWAYS–INTENSIVE SPANISH LANGUAGE

Rustic Pathways
Costa Rica

General Information Coed residential academic program and cultural program established in 2005.
Academics Spanish (Advanced Placement), Spanish language/literature, academics (general).
Arts Dance (folk).
Special Interest Areas Community service, cross-cultural education, culinary arts, homestays, touring.
Sports Soccer.
Wilderness/Outdoors Hiking.
Trips Cultural, day, overnight, shopping.
Program Information 8 sessions per year. Session length: 15–42 days in June, July, August. Ages: 14–18. 10–20 participants per session. Boarding program cost: $2695. Application fee: $100–$200. Financial aid available.
Application Deadline Continuous.
Jobs Positions for college students 21 and older.
Contact Rustic Pathways, 4121 Erie Street, Willoughby, Ohio 44094. Phone: 800-321-4353. Fax: 440-975-9694. E-mail: rustic@rusticpathways.com.
URL www.rusticpathways.com
For more information, see page 612.

RUSTIC PATHWAYS–MALEKU TRIBE IMMERSION PROGRAM–COSTA RICA

Rustic Pathways
Costa Rica

General Information Coed residential academic program and cultural program.
Program Focus Live and work with indigenous tribe and practice Spanish.
Academics Spanish (Advanced Placement), Spanish language/literature.
Arts Dance.
Special Interest Areas Community service, cross-cultural education, homestays, touring.
Sports Soccer.
Wilderness/Outdoors Hiking.
Trips Cultural, day, overnight, shopping.
Program Information 10 sessions per year. Session length: 8 days in June, July, August. Ages: 14–18. 15–20

participants per session. Boarding program cost: $945.
Application Deadline Continuous.
Jobs Positions for college students 21 and older.
Contact Rustic Pathways, 4121 Erie Street, Willoughby, Ohio 44094. Phone: 800-321-4353. Fax: 440-975-9694. E-mail: rustic@rusticpathways.com.
URL www.rusticpathways.com
For more information, see page 612.

RUSTIC PATHWAYS–RAMP UP YOUR SPANISH

Rustic Pathways
Escazu, Alajuela
Costa Rica

General Information Coed residential academic program and cultural program established in 2002.
Academics Spanish (Advanced Placement), Spanish language/literature.
Arts Dance.
Special Interest Areas Homestays.
Sports Bicycling, soccer.
Trips Cultural, day, overnight, shopping.
Program Information 9 sessions per year. Session length: 8 days in June, July, August. Ages: 14–18. 15–20 participants per session. Boarding program cost: $995.
Jobs Positions for college students 21 and older.
Contact Rustic Pathways, 4121 Erie Street, Willoughby, Ohio 44094. Phone: 800-321-4353. Fax: 440-975-9694. E-mail: rustic@rusticpathways.com.
URL www.rusticpathways.com
For more information, see page 612.

RUSTIC PATHWAYS–SOCCER AND SERVICE IN COSTA RICA

Rustic Pathways
Costa Rica

General Information Coed travel sports camp, community service program, cultural program, and adventure program established in 2005.
Academics Spanish language/literature.
Special Interest Areas Community service, cross-cultural education, homestays, touring.
Sports Soccer, surfing, tennis.
Trips Cultural, day, overnight.

Program Information 9 sessions per year. Session length: 8–15 days in June, July, August. Ages: 14–18. 10–15 participants per session. Cost: $945–$2495. Financial aid available.
Application Deadline Continuous.
Contact Rustic Pathways, 4121 Erie Street, Willoughby, Ohio 44094. Phone: 800-321-4353. Fax: 440-975-9694. E-mail: rustic@rusticpathways.com.
URL www.rusticpathways.com

For more information, see page 612.

RUSTIC PATHWAYS–SPANISH LANGUAGE IMMERSION

Rustic Pathways
Turrialba, Cartago
Costa Rica

General Information Coed residential academic program and cultural program established in 2002.
Program Focus Spanish language class, homestay, cultural immersion.
Academics Spanish (Advanced Placement), Spanish language/literature, academics (general).
Arts Dance.
Special Interest Areas Cross-cultural education, homestays, touring.
Sports Soccer.
Wilderness/Outdoors Hiking, rafting, white-water trips.
Trips Cultural, day, overnight, shopping.
Program Information 8 sessions per year. Session length: 15 days in June, July, August. Ages: 14–18. 5–10 participants per session. Boarding program cost: $1895. Application fee: $100–$200.
Application Deadline Continuous.
Jobs Positions for college students 21 and older.
Contact Rustic Pathways, 4121 Erie Street, Willoughby, Ohio 44094. Phone: 800-321-4353. Fax: 440-975-9694. E-mail: rustic@rusticpathways.com.
URL www.rusticpathways.com

For more information, see page 612.

RUSTIC PATHWAYS–SURF & SERVICE–COSTA RICA

Rustic Pathways
Costa Rica

General Information Coed travel sports camp established in 2005.
Program Focus Live and surf in a beach community while working on a variety of projects.
Academics Spanish language/literature.
Special Interest Areas Community service, cross-cultural education, touring.
Sports Snorkeling, soccer, surfing, swimming.
Wilderness/Outdoors Hiking.
Trips Cultural, day, overnight, shopping.
Program Information 10 sessions per year. Session length: 8 days in June, July, August. Ages: 14–18. 10–20

participants per session. Cost: $1295. Application fee: $100–$200. Financial aid available.
Application Deadline Continuous.
Jobs Positions for college students 21 and older.
Contact Rustic Pathways, 4121 Erie Street, Willoughby, Ohio 44094. Phone: 800-321-4353. Fax: 440-975-9694. E-mail: rustic@rusticpathways.com.
URL www.rusticpathways.com

For more information, see page 612.

RUSTIC PATHWAYS–SURF THE SUMMER–COSTA RICA

Rustic Pathways
Costa Rica

General Information Coed residential sports camp and adventure program established in 2002.
Special Interest Areas Touring.
Sports Bicycling, horseback riding, kayaking, sailing, sea kayaking, snorkeling, soccer, surfing, swimming, volleyball.
Wilderness/Outdoors Hiking.
Trips Cultural, day, overnight, shopping.
Program Information 9 sessions per year. Session length: 8–15 days in June, July, August. Ages: 14–18. 10–15 participants per session. Boarding program cost: $995–$1985. Financial aid available.
Application Deadline Continuous.
Jobs Positions for college students 21 and older.
Contact Rustic Pathways, 4121 Erie Street, Willoughby, Ohio 44094. Phone: 800-321-4353. Fax: 440-975-9694. E-mail: rustic@rusticpathways.com.
URL www.rusticpathways.com

For more information, see page 612.

RUSTIC PATHWAYS–THE TURTLE CONSERVATION PROJECT

Rustic Pathways
Punta Judas
Costa Rica

General Information Coed residential outdoor program and community service program established in 2002.
Academics Biology, ecology, marine studies.
Special Interest Areas Animal care, community service, conservation projects, construction, cross-cultural education.
Sports Horseback riding, soccer, swimming, volleyball.
Trips Cultural, day, overnight, shopping.
Program Information 8 sessions per year. Session length: 8 days in June, July, August. Ages: 14–18. 10–15 participants per session. Boarding program cost: $985.
Application Deadline Continuous.
Jobs Positions for college students 21 and older.
Contact Rustic Pathways, 4121 Erie Street, Willoughby, Ohio 44094. Phone: 800-321-4353. Fax: 440-975-9694. E-mail: rustic@rusticpathways.com.
URL www.rusticpathways.com

For more information, see page 612.

RUSTIC PATHWAYS–ULTIMATE JUNGLE ADVENTURE–COSTA RICA

Rustic Pathways
Costa Rica

General Information Coed travel outdoor program, wilderness program, cultural program, and adventure program established in 2002.
Special Interest Areas Native American culture, leadership training, nature study, team building, touring.
Sports Bicycling, fishing, horseback riding, kayaking, rappelling, sailing, sea kayaking, snorkeling, soccer, surfing, swimming.
Wilderness/Outdoors Hiking, outdoor adventure, rafting, white-water trips.
Trips Cultural, day, overnight, shopping.
Program Information 2 sessions per year. Session length: 15 days in June, July, August. Ages: 14–18. 10–15 participants per session. Cost: $2895.
Application Deadline Continuous.
Jobs Positions for college students 21 and older.
Contact Rustic Pathways, 4121 Erie Street, Willoughby, Ohio 44094. Phone: 800-321-4353. Fax: 440-975-9694. E-mail: rustic@rusticpathways.com.
URL www.rusticpathways.com

For more information, see page 612.

RUSTIC PATHWAYS–VOLCANOES AND RAINFORESTS

Rustic Pathways
Arenal Volcano Park Station
Fortuna
Costa Rica

General Information Coed residential outdoor program and community service program established in 2002.
Academics Environmental science, geology/earth science.
Special Interest Areas Community service, conservation projects, construction, gardening, nature study, trail maintenance.
Sports Soccer, swimming.
Wilderness/Outdoors Hiking.
Trips Cultural, day, overnight, shopping.
Program Information 9 sessions per year. Session length: 8 days in June, July, August. Ages: 14–18. 10–15 participants per session. Boarding program cost: $1095.
Application Deadline Continuous.
Jobs Positions for college students 21 and older.
Contact Rustic Pathways, 4121 Erie Street, Willoughby, Ohio 44094. Phone: 800-321-4353. Fax: 440-975-9694. E-mail: rustic@rusticpathways.com.
URL www.rusticpathways.com

For more information, see page 612.

RUSTIC PATHWAYS–YOUNG ADVENTURERS–COSTA RICA

Rustic Pathways
Costa Rica

General Information Coed residential cultural program and adventure program established in 2006.
Program Focus Combining community service, learning Spanish, fostering international travel, learning about other cultures, and outdoor adventures.
Academics Spanish language/literature, environmental science.
Special Interest Areas Community service, nature study, touring.
Sports Soccer, swimming, volleyball.
Wilderness/Outdoors Hiking, rafting, wilderness camping.
Trips Cultural, day, shopping.
Program Information 2 sessions per year. Session length: 15 days in June, July. Ages: 10–14. 30 participants per session. Boarding program cost: $2495. Application fee: $100–$200.
Application Deadline Continuous.
Jobs Positions for college students 21 and older.

Contact Rustic Pathways, 4121 Erie Street, Willoughby, Ohio 44094. Phone: 800-321-4353. Fax: 440-975-9694. E-mail: rustic@rusticpathways.com. **URL** www.rusticpathways.com

For more information, see page 612.

VISIONS–COSTA RICA

Visions
Costa Rica

General Information Coed travel outdoor program, community service program, and cultural program established in 1989. High school credit may be earned.
Program Focus Community service, cross-cultural experience, and outdoor adventure activities.
Academics Spanish language/literature, intercultural studies.
Arts Carpentry.
Special Interest Areas Community service, construction, cross-cultural education, field research/expeditions, field trips (arts and culture), leadership training, nature study.
Sports Scuba diving, sea kayaking, snorkeling, swimming.
Wilderness/Outdoors Hiking, outdoor adventure.
Trips Cultural, day, overnight.
Program Information 1–2 sessions per year. Session length: 3–4 weeks in June, July, August. Ages: 14–18. 15–17 participants per session. Cost: $3200–$4900. Financial aid available.
Application Deadline Continuous.
Jobs Positions for college students 22 and older.
Contact Joanne Pinaire, Director, PO Box 220, Newport, Pennsylvania 17074. Phone: 717-567-7313. Fax: 717-567-7853. E-mail: info@visionsserviceadventures.com
URL www.visionsserviceadventures.com

For more information, see page 694.

WESTCOAST CONNECTION–COMMUNITY SERVICE COSTA RICA

Westcoast Connection
Costa Rica

General Information Coed travel community service program, cultural program, and adventure program established in 1982. Accredited by Ontario Camping Association. High school credit may be earned.
Special Interest Areas Community service, conservation projects, construction, farming, touring.
Sports Ropes course.
Wilderness/Outdoors Hiking, outdoor adventure.
Program Information 1–2 sessions per year. Session length: 3–4 weeks in July, August. Ages: 14–17. 10–24 participants per session. Financial aid available.
Application Deadline Continuous.
Jobs Positions for college students 21 and older.
Contact Mr. Mark Segal, Director, 154 East Boston Post Road, Mamaroneck, New York 10543. Phone: 800-767-0227. Fax: 914-835-0798. E-mail: usa@westcoastconnection.com
URL www.360studenttravel.com

For more information, see page 702.

WESTCOAST CONNECTION–SPANISH IN COSTA RICA

Westcoast Connection
Costa Rica

General Information Coed travel academic program and cultural program established in 1982. Accredited by Ontario Camping Association. High school or college credit may be earned.
Program Focus Explore Costa Rica while studying Spanish, and taking part in adventure activities.
Academics Spanish language/literature.
Special Interest Areas Touring.
Sports Snorkeling.
Wilderness/Outdoors Outdoor adventure.
Program Information 1–3 sessions per year. Session length: 2–4 weeks in July, August. Ages: 14–17. 10–30 participants per session. Financial aid available.
Application Deadline Continuous.
Jobs Positions for college students 21 and older.
Contact Mr. Ira Solomon, Director, 154 East Boston Post Road, Mamaroneck, New York 10543. Phone: 800-767-0227. Fax: 914-835-0798. E-mail: usa@westcoastconnection.com
URL www.360studenttravel.com

For more information, see page 702.

WILDERNESS VENTURES–COSTA RICA

Wilderness Ventures
Costa Rica

General Information Coed travel outdoor program, wilderness program, cultural program, and adventure program established in 1973.

Wilderness Ventures–Costa Rica (continued)

Program Focus Wilderness travel, cultural immersion, leadership skills.

Special Interest Areas Community service, leadership training.

Sports Rappelling, sea kayaking.

Wilderness/Outdoors Backpacking, hiking, rafting, white-water trips, wilderness camping.

Trips Cultural, overnight.

Program Information 2 sessions per year. Session length: 3 weeks in June, July, August. Ages: 14–18. 15 participants per session. Cost: $4290. Financial aid available.

Application Deadline Continuous.

Jobs Positions for college students 21 and older.

Contact Mike Cottingham, Director, PO Box 2768, Jackson Hole, Wyoming 83001. Phone: 800-533-2281. Fax: 307-739-1934. E-mail: info@wildernessventures. com.

URL www.wildernessventures.com

For more information, see page 704.

WILDERNESS VENTURES–COSTA RICA SERVICE

Wilderness Ventures
Costa Rica

General Information Coed travel outdoor program, community service program, cultural program, and adventure program established in 1973.

Program Focus Wilderness travel, wilderness skills, leadership skills, community service.

Special Interest Areas Community service, conservation projects, leadership training.

Sports Sea kayaking.

Wilderness/Outdoors Hiking, rafting, white-water trips.

Trips Overnight.

Program Information 2 sessions per year. Session length: 3 weeks in June, July, August. Ages: 14–18. 15 participants per session. Cost: $4920. Financial aid available.

Application Deadline Continuous.

Jobs Positions for college students 21 and older.

Contact Mike Cottingham, Director, PO Box 2768, Jackson Hole, Wyoming 83001. Phone: 800-533-2281. Fax: 307-739-1934. E-mail: info@wildernessventures. com.

URL www.wildernessventures.com

For more information, see page 704.

WILDERNESS VENTURES–COSTA RICA SURFING

Wilderness Ventures
Costa Rica

General Information Coed travel outdoor program, wilderness program, and adventure program established in 1973.

Program Focus Adventure travel, cultural immersion, leadership skills.

Special Interest Areas Leadership training.

Sports Surfing.

Wilderness/Outdoors Rafting, white-water trips, wilderness camping.

Trips Overnight.

Program Information 3 sessions per year. Session length: 16 days in June, July, August. Ages: 14–18. 15 participants per session. Cost: $3290. Financial aid available.

Application Deadline Continuous.

Jobs Positions for college students 21 and older.

Contact Mr. Mike Cottingham, Director, PO Box 2768, Jackson Hole, Wyoming 83001. Phone: 800-533-2281. Fax: 307-739-1934. E-mail: info@wildernessventures. com.

URL www.wildernessventures.com

For more information, see page 704.

WORLD HORIZONS INTERNATIONAL– COSTA RICA

World Horizons International
Palmares
Costa Rica

General Information Coed residential community service program and cultural program established in 1988.

World Horizons International–Costa Rica

Program Focus Community service, intercultural travel abroad, and foreign language immersion.

Academics Spanish language/literature.
Special Interest Areas Community service, cross-cultural education, work camp programs.
Sports Horseback riding, snorkeling.
Wilderness/Outdoors Hiking.
Trips Cultural, day, overnight.
Program Information 1–2 sessions per year. Session length: 2–4 weeks in June, July, August. Ages: 15–18. 10–12 participants per session. Boarding program cost: $3900–$4600. Application fee: $175. Financial aid available. Airfare from Miami to San Jose included.
Application Deadline Continuous.
Jobs Positions for college students 21 and older.
Contact Mr. Stuart L. Rabinowitz, Executive Director, PO Box 662, Bethlehem, Connecticut 06751. Phone: 800-262-5874. Fax: 203-266-6227. E-mail: worldhorizons@att.net.
URL www.world-horizons.com

For more information, see page 714.

DENMARK

CENTER FOR CULTURAL INTERCHANGE– DENMARK HIGH SCHOOL ABROAD

Center for Cultural Interchange
Denmark

General Information Coed residential academic program and cultural program established in 1985. High school credit may be earned.
Program Focus High school abroad.
Academics Danish language/literature, academics (general).
Special Interest Areas Cross-cultural education, homestays.
Trips Cultural, day.
Program Information 2 sessions per year. Session length: 90–300 days in January, February, March, April, May, June, July, August, September, October, November, December. Ages: 15–18. Boarding program cost: $5900–$7700. Financial aid available. Early Bird discount.
Application Deadline Continuous.

Contact Ms. Juliet Jones, Outbound Programs Director, 746 North LaSalle Drive, Chicago, Illinois 60610-3617. Phone: 866-684-9675. Fax: 312-944-2644. E-mail: info@cci-exchange.com.
URL www.cci-exchange.com

For more information, see page 448.

DOMINICA

PUTNEY STUDENT TRAVEL–COMMUNITY SERVICE–DOMINICA, WEST INDIES

Putney Student Travel
Dominica

General Information Coed residential community service program and cultural program established in 1951.
Program Focus Community service, cultural exchange, and weekend excursions from a small rural community.
Academics Intercultural studies.
Special Interest Areas Community service, construction, farming.
Sports Sailing, snorkeling, soccer, swimming.
Wilderness/Outdoors Canoe trips, hiking.
Trips Cultural, day.
Program Information 1 session per year. Session length: 4 weeks in June, July. Ages: 15–18. 16 participants per session. Boarding program cost: $5290. Financial aid available. Airfare included.
Application Deadline Continuous.
Contact Jeffrey Shumlin, Admissions Director, 345 Hickory Ridge Road, Putney, Vermont 05346. Phone: 802-387-5000. Fax: 802-387-4276. E-mail: info@goputney.com.
URL www.goputney.com

For more information, see page 598.

Visions–Dominica

Visions
Dominica

General Information Coed travel outdoor program, community service program, and cultural program established in 1989. High school credit may be earned.
Program Focus Community service, cross-cultural experience, and outdoor adventure activities.
Academics Intercultural studies.
Arts Carpentry, painting.
Special Interest Areas Community service, construction, cross-cultural education, field research/ expeditions, field trips (arts and culture), leadership training, nature study, whale watching.
Sports Canoeing, snorkeling, swimming.
Wilderness/Outdoors Backpacking, hiking, outdoor adventure.
Trips Cultural, day, overnight.
Program Information 1 session per year. Session length: 4 weeks in June, July. Ages: 14–18. 18–21 participants per session. Cost: $3200–$4900. Financial aid available.
Application Deadline Continuous.
Jobs Positions for college students 22 and older.
Contact Joanne Pinaire, Director, PO Box 220, Newport, Pennsylvania 17074. Phone: 717-567-7313. Fax: 717-567-7853. E-mail: info@visionsserviceadventures.com.
URL www.visionsserviceadventures.com
For more information, see page 694.

World Horizons International– Dominica

World Horizons International
Dominica

General Information Coed residential community service program and cultural program established in 1988.
Program Focus Community service and intercultural travel abroad.
Special Interest Areas Community service, conservation projects, construction, cross-cultural education, gardening, work camp programs.
Sports Snorkeling, swimming.
Wilderness/Outdoors Backpacking, hiking.
Trips Cultural, day, overnight.
Program Information 1 session per year. Session length: 3–4 weeks in June, July. Ages: 13–15. 10–12 participants per session. Boarding program cost: $3900– $4600. Application fee: $175. Financial aid available. Airfare from Miami to Dominica included.
Application Deadline Continuous.
Jobs Positions for college students 21 and older.
Contact Mr. Stuart L. Rabinowitz, Executive Director, PO Box 662, Bethlehem, Connecticut 06751. Phone: 800-262-5874. Fax: 203-266-6227. E-mail: worldhorizons@att.net.
URL www.world-horizons.com
For more information, see page 714.

DOMINICAN REPUBLIC

Putney Student Travel–Community Service–Dominican Republic

Putney Student Travel
Dominican Republic

General Information Coed residential community service program and cultural program established in 1951.
Program Focus Community service, cultural exchange, and weekend excursions from a base in a small, rural community.
Academics Intercultural studies.
Special Interest Areas Community service, construction, farming.
Sports Baseball, soccer, swimming.
Wilderness/Outdoors Caving, hiking.
Trips Cultural, day.
Program Information 2 sessions per year. Session length: 28–29 days in June, July. Ages: 15–18. 16 participants per session. Boarding program cost: $5290. Financial aid available. Airfare from Miami included.
Application Deadline Continuous.
Contact Jeffrey Shumlin, Admissions Director, 345 Hickory Ridge Road, Putney, Vermont 05346. Phone: 802-387-5000. Fax: 802-387-4276. E-mail: info@goputney.com.
URL www.goputney.com
For more information, see page 598.

Visions–Dominican Republic

Visions
Santo Domingo
Dominican Republic

General Information Coed travel outdoor program, community service program, and cultural program established in 1989. High school credit may be earned.
Program Focus Community service, cross-cultural experience, language immersion, and outdoor adventure activities.
Academics Spanish language/literature, intercultural studies, language study.
Arts Carpentry.
Special Interest Areas Community service, construction, cross-cultural education, field trips (arts and culture), homestays, leadership training, nature study.
Sports Snorkeling, swimming.

Wilderness/Outdoors Backpacking, hiking.
Trips Cultural, day, overnight, shopping.
Program Information 2 sessions per year. Session length: 3–4 weeks in June, July, August. Ages: 14–18. 20–25 participants per session. Cost: $3200–$4900. Financial aid available.
Application Deadline Continuous.
Jobs Positions for college students 22 and older.
Contact Joanne Pinaire, Director, PO Box 220, Newport, Pennsylvania 17074. Phone: 717-567-7313. Fax: 717-567-7853. E-mail: info@visionsserviceadventures.com.
URL www.visionsserviceadventures.com

For more information, see page 694.

ECUADOR

AAVE–ECUADOR AND GALAPAGOS

AAVE–Journeys That Matter
Ecuador

General Information Coed travel outdoor program, cultural program, and adventure program established in 1976. Accredited by American Camping Association.
Program Focus Cultural and outdoor experience; travel to Galapagos Islands and the Amazon Basin.
Academics Area studies, ecology, intercultural studies.
Special Interest Areas Community service, leadership training, nature study, touring.
Sports Bicycling, boating, horseback riding, sailing, snorkeling, swimming.
Wilderness/Outdoors Bicycle trips, hiking, rafting, white-water trips.
Trips Cultural, day, overnight.
Program Information 2–4 sessions per year. Session length: 3 weeks in June, July, August. Ages: 15–18. 12 participants per session. Cost: $5188. Financial aid available.
Application Deadline Continuous.
Jobs Positions for college students 21 and older.
Contact Mr. Abbott Wallis, Owner, 2308 Fossil Trace Drive, Golden, Colorado 80401. Phone: 800-222-3595. Fax: 303-526-0885. E-mail: info@aave.com.
URL www.aave.com

For more information, see page 394.

ACADEMIC TREKS–SPANISH LANGUAGE IMMERSION IN ECUADOR

Academic Treks, the academic adventure and community service division of Broadreach
Quito, Cotopaxi, Tosagua, Cuenca
Ecuador

General Information Coed travel academic program, outdoor program, community service program, cultural program, and adventure program established in 1992. High school or college credit may be earned.

Program Focus Academic adventure and community service program focusing on language study, cultural exchange, service learning, hiking in the Andes, homestay, and high school and college credit.
Academics Spanish language/literature, academics (general), area studies, intercultural studies.
Special Interest Areas Community service, conservation projects, cross-cultural education, homestays, leadership training.
Sports Horseback riding.
Wilderness/Outdoors Backpacking, hiking, outdoor adventure, wilderness camping, wilderness/outdoors (general).
Trips Cultural, day.
Program Information 2 sessions per year. Session length: 30 days in June, July, August. Ages: 16–20. 10–14 participants per session. Cost: $5280.
Application Deadline Continuous.
Contact Carlton Goldthwaite, Director, 806 McCulloch Street, Suite 102, Raleigh, North Carolina 27603. Phone: 888-833-1907. Fax: 919-833-2129. E-mail: info@academictreks.com.
URL www.academictreks.com

For more information, see page 432.

ACTIONQUEST: GALAPAGOS ARCHIPELAGO EXPEDITIONS

ActionQuest
Ecuador

General Information Coed travel outdoor program, community service program, cultural program, and adventure program established in 1986.
Program Focus Live-aboard; land exploration of the Galapagos Islands, with emphasis on ecology and nature study with community service. Voyage includes a three-day Amazon rainforest trek.
Academics Ecology, environmental science, geology/earth science, intercultural studies, marine studies, oceanography.
Special Interest Areas Community service, conservation projects, field research/expeditions, leadership training, nature study, team building, touring.
Sports Snorkeling.
Wilderness/Outdoors Hiking, white-water trips.
Trips Cultural, day, overnight.
Program Information 2 sessions per year. Session length: 22 days in June, July, August. Ages: 15–18. 14 participants per session. Cost: $4870.
Application Deadline Continuous.

ACTIONQUEST: Galapagos Archipelago Expeditions (continued)

Contact Mike Meighan, Director, PO Box 5517, Sarasota, Florida 34277. Phone: 800-317-6789. Fax: 941-924-6075. E-mail: info@actionquest.com.
URL www.actionquest.com

For more information, see page 406.

AFS–USA–HOMESTAY–ECUADOR

AFS-USA
Ecuador

General Information Coed residential cultural program.
Program Focus Living with a host family and taking part in activities with other teenagers.
Academics Spanish language/literature.
Special Interest Areas Homestays, touring.
Trips Cultural, day, overnight.
Program Information 1 session per year. Session length: 30–45 days in June, July, August. Ages: 15–18. Boarding program cost: $4000–$6000. Application fee: $75. Financial aid available. International airfare and volunteer homestay support included.
Application Deadline Continuous.
Contact Manager, AFS Info Center, 506 Southwest 6th Avenue, 2nd Floor, Portland, Oregon 97204. Phone: 800-AFS-INFO. Fax: 503-299-0753. E-mail: afsinfo@afs.org.
URL www.afs.org/usa

For more information, see page 408.

EF INTERNATIONAL LANGUAGE SCHOOL–QUITO

EF International Language Schools
Catalina Alda Z #263 y Avenida Portugal
Quito
Ecuador

General Information Coed travel academic program and cultural program established in 1996. High school or college credit may be earned.
Program Focus Language and cultural immersion.
Academics Spanish (Advanced Placement), Spanish language/literature.

Special Interest Areas Community service, field trips (arts and culture), homestays, touring.
Sports Horseback riding, soccer, sports (general).
Wilderness/Outdoors Wilderness/outdoors (general).
Trips Cultural, day, overnight.
Program Information 2–52 sessions per year. Session length: 2–52 weeks in January, February, March, April, May, June, July, August, September, October, November, December. Ages: 15+. 100–150 participants per session. Application fee: $145. Financial aid available. Call for costs.
Application Deadline Continuous.
Contact Ms. Margaret Kelly, Director of Admissions, One Education Street, Cambridge, Massachusetts 02141. Phone: 800-992-1892. Fax: 800-590-1125. E-mail: ils@ef.com.
URL www.ef.com

For more information, see page 478.

THE EXPERIMENT IN INTERNATIONAL LIVING–ECUADOR HOMESTAY

The Experiment in International Living
Ecuador

General Information Coed travel outdoor program, cultural program, and adventure program established in 1932.
Program Focus International youth travel, Galapagos trip/animal observation, homestay.
Academics Spanish language/literature, ecology.
Special Interest Areas Community service, homestays, nature study.
Sports Snorkeling, swimming.
Wilderness/Outdoors Hiking, rafting, white-water trips.
Trips Cultural, day, overnight.
Program Information 1 session per year. Session length: 5 weeks in June, July, August. Ages: 14–19. 10–15 participants per session. Cost: $5300. Financial aid available. Airfare included.
Application Deadline May 1.
Contact Annie Thompson, Enrollment Director, Summer Abroad, Kipling Road, PO Box 676, Brattleboro, Vermont 05302-0676. Phone: 800-345-2929. Fax: 802-258-3428. E-mail: eil@worldlearning.org.
URL www.usexperiment.org

For more information, see page 492.

GLOBAL WORKS–LANGUAGE IMMERSION, CULTURAL EXCHANGE AND SERVICE–ECUADOR AND THE GALAPAGOS–4 WEEKS

GLOBAL WORKS
Ecuador

General Information Coed travel community service program, cultural program, and adventure program established in 1988. High school credit may be earned.
Program Focus Environmental and community

service, language immersion, and cultural exchange.
Academics Spanish language/literature, intercultural studies.
Arts Arts and crafts (general), dance, music.
Special Interest Areas Community service, conservation projects, construction, field trips (arts and culture), homestays.
Sports Bicycling, boating, sea kayaking, snorkeling, soccer, sports (general), surfing, swimming, volleyball.
Wilderness/Outdoors Hiking, rafting.
Trips Cultural, day, overnight.
Program Information 2 sessions per year. Session length: 4 weeks in June, July. Ages: 15–17. 16–18 participants per session. Cost: $4795. Application fee: $100. Financial aid available. Airfare not included.
Application Deadline Continuous.
Jobs Positions for college students 23 and older.
Contact Mr. Erik Werner, Director, 1113 South Allen Street, State College, Pennsylvania 16801. Phone: 814-867-7000. Fax: 814-867-2717. E-mail: info@globalworksinc.com.
URL www.globalworksinc.com
For more information, see page 506.

LIFEWORKS WITH THE GALAPAGOS ISLANDS' NATIONAL PARKS

LIFEWORKS International
Ecuador

General Information Coed travel outdoor program, community service program, cultural program, and adventure program established in 1986. High school credit may be earned.
Program Focus Service-learning travel program with cultural immersion and outdoor adventure activities with a focus on the Galapagos ecosystem.
Academics Ecology.
Special Interest Areas Community service, conservation projects, field research/expeditions, leadership training, nature study, team building, touring.
Sports Snorkeling.
Wilderness/Outdoors Hiking.
Trips Cultural, day, overnight.
Program Information 1 session per year. Session length: 22 days in July, August. Ages: 15–19. 8–15 participants per session. Cost: $4370–$4770. Financial aid available.
Application Deadline Continuous.

Contact James Stoll, Director, PO Box 5517, Sarasota, Florida 34277. Phone: 800-808-2115. Fax: 941-924-6075. E-mail: info@lifeworks-international.com.
URL www.lifeworks-international.com
For more information, see page 548.

PUTNEY STUDENT TRAVEL–COMMUNITY SERVICE–ECUADOR

Putney Student Travel
Ecuador

General Information Coed residential community service program and cultural program established in 1951.
Program Focus Community service, cultural exchange, and weekend excursions from a base in a small, rural community.
Academics Intercultural studies.
Special Interest Areas Community service, construction.
Sports Horseback riding, soccer.
Wilderness/Outdoors Hiking.
Trips Cultural, day.
Program Information 2 sessions per year. Session length: 28–30 days in June, July, August. Ages: 15–18. 16 participants per session. Boarding program cost: $5290. Financial aid available. Airfare from Miami included.
Application Deadline Continuous.
Contact Jeffrey Shumlin, Admissions Director, 345 Hickory Ridge Road, Putney, Vermont 05346. Phone: 802-387-5000. Fax: 802-387-4276. E-mail: info@goputney.com.
URL www.goputney.com
For more information, see page 598.

VISIONS–ECUADOR

Visions
Quito
Ecuador

General Information Coed travel community service program and cultural program established in 1989. High school credit may be earned.
Academics Spanish language/literature, intercultural studies, language study, writing.
Arts Arts and crafts (general), basketry, creative writing, jewelry making.
Special Interest Areas Community service, construction, cross-cultural education, farming, field research/expeditions, homestays, leadership training, nature study.
Sports Bicycling, fishing, snorkeling, swimming.
Wilderness/Outdoors Hiking.
Trips Cultural, day, overnight.
Program Information 1 session per year. Session length: 4 weeks in July. Ages: 16–18. 15–17 participants per session. Cost: $3200–$4900. Financial aid available.
Application Deadline Continuous.
Jobs Positions for college students 22 and older.

Visions–Ecuador (continued)

Contact Joanne Pinaire, Director, PO Box 220, Newport, Pennsylvania 17074-0220. Phone: 717-567-7313. Fax: 717-567-7853. E-mail: info@visionsserviceadventures.com. **URL** www.visionsserviceadventures.com **For more information, see page 694.**

WILDERNESS VENTURES–ECUADOR AND GALAPAGOS COMMUNITY SERVICE

Wilderness Ventures
Ecuador

General Information Coed travel outdoor program, cultural program, and adventure program established in 1973.
Program Focus Wilderness travel, cultural immersion, leadership skills.
Special Interest Areas Community service, conservation projects, leadership training, touring.
Sports Boating.
Wilderness/Outdoors Backpacking, hiking, rafting, white-water trips, wilderness camping.
Trips Cultural, overnight.
Program Information 3 sessions per year. Session length: 24 days in June, July, August. Ages: 14–18. 14 participants per session. Cost: $5290. Financial aid available. Participants tour the Galapagos Islands.
Application Deadline Continuous.
Jobs Positions for college students 21 and older.
Contact Mike Cottingham, Director, PO Box 2768, Jackson Hole, Wyoming 83001. Phone: 800-533-2281. Fax: 307-739-1934. E-mail: info@wildernessventures.com.
URL www.wildernessventures.com
For more information, see page 704.

WORLD HORIZONS INTERNATIONAL–CAYAMBE, ECUADOR

World Horizons International
Cayambe
Ecuador

General Information Coed residential community service program and cultural program established in 1990.

Program Focus Working with teaching children in schools in the Andes Mountains.
Academics Spanish language/literature.
Special Interest Areas Community service, cross-cultural education.
Wilderness/Outdoors Backpacking, hiking.
Trips Cultural, day, overnight.
Program Information 1–2 sessions per year. Session length: 2–4 weeks in March, April, June, July, August, December. Ages: 13–18. 10–12 participants per session. Boarding program cost: $2500–$4800. Application fee: $175. Financial aid available.
Application Deadline Continuous.
Jobs Positions for college students 21 and older.
Contact Mr. Stuart L. Rabinowitz, Executive Director, PO Box 662, Bethlehem, Connecticut 06751. Phone: 800-262-5874. Fax: 203-266-6227. E-mail: worldhorizons@att.net.
URL www.world-horizons.com

For more information, see page 714.

EGYPT

AFS-USA–HOMESTAY LANGUAGE STUDY–EGYPT

AFS-USA
Egypt

General Information Coed residential academic program and cultural program.
Program Focus Language study program.
Academics Arabic.
Special Interest Areas Cross-cultural education, homestays, touring.
Trips Cultural, day, overnight.
Program Information 1 session per year. Session length: 30 days in July. Ages: 15–18. Boarding program cost: $6000. Application fee: $75. Financial aid available. International airfare and volunteer homestay support included.
Application Deadline Continuous.
Contact Manager, AFS Info Center, 506 Southwest 6th Avenue, 2nd Floor, Portland, Oregon 97204. Phone: 800-AFS-INFO. Fax: 503-299-0753. E-mail: afsinfo@afs.org.
URL www.afs.org/usa

For more information, see page 408.

BROADREACH RED SEA SCUBA ADVENTURE

Broadreach
Egypt

General Information Coed travel outdoor program, cultural program, and adventure program established in 1992.
Program Focus Coed program focusing on scuba

diving, advanced and specialty dive training, marine biology, wilderness desert experience, cultural immersion and exploration.
Academics Area studies, environmental science, marine studies.
Arts Photography.
Special Interest Areas Community service, cross-cultural education, field research/expeditions, leadership training, nature study.
Sports Boating, fishing, scuba diving, snorkeling.
Wilderness/Outdoors Hiking, ocean expeditions, outdoor adventure, pack animal trips, safari, wilderness camping, wilderness/outdoors (general).
Trips Cultural, overnight.
Program Information 4 sessions per year. Session length: 3 weeks in June, July, August. Ages: 15–19. 12–14 participants per session. Cost: $4880.
Application Deadline Continuous.
Contact Carlton Goldthwaite, Director, 806 McCulloch Street, Suite 102, Raleigh, North Carolina 27603. Phone: 888-833-1907. Fax: 919-833-2129. E-mail: info@gobroadreach.com
URL www.gobroadreach.com

For more information, see page 432.

EL SALVADOR

PUTNEY STUDENT TRAVEL–GLOBAL ACTION–EL SALVADOR

Putney Student Travel
El Salvador

General Information Coed residential cultural program established in 1951.
Program Focus Students spend three weeks pursuing research in relation to grassroots community development.
Academics Intercultural studies.
Special Interest Areas Community service, cross-cultural education, field research/expeditions.
Sports Soccer.
Wilderness/Outdoors Hiking.
Trips Cultural, day.
Program Information 1 session per year. Session length: 25–32 days in June, July, August. Ages: 15–18. 16 participants per session. Boarding program cost: $5690. Financial aid available. Airfare included.
Application Deadline Continuous.

Contact Jeffrey Shumlin, Admissions Director, 345 Hickory Ridge Road, Putney, Vermont 05346. Phone: 802-387-5000. Fax: 802-387-4276. E-mail: info@goputney.com.
URL www.goputney.com

For more information, see page 598.

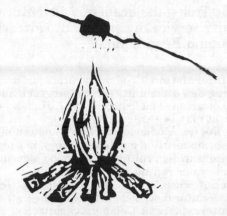

ESTONIA

VOLUNTEERS FOR PEACE INTERNATIONAL VOLUNTARY SERVICE–ESTONIA

Volunteers for Peace International Voluntary Service
Tallin
Estonia

General Information Coed residential community service program established in 1981. Specific services available for the hearing impaired and physically challenged. College credit may be earned.
Program Focus International voluntary service projects or workcamps.
Academics Intercultural studies, peace education.
Special Interest Areas Community service, farming, work camp programs.
Sports Swimming.
Trips Cultural, day, overnight.
Program Information 8 sessions per year. Session length: 2–3 weeks in June, July, August, September. Ages: 15+. 12–20 participants per session. Boarding program cost: $500–$800.
Application Deadline Continuous.
Contact Peter Coldwell, Director, 1034 Tiffany Road, Belmont, Vermont 05730. Phone: 802-259-2759. Fax: 802-259-2922. E-mail: vfp@vfp.org.
URL www.vfp.org

FIJI

ACADEMIC TREKS–Shark Studies in Fiji

Academic Treks, the academic adventure and community service division of Broadreach
Viti Levu and Beqa Island
Fiji

General Information Coed travel academic program, outdoor program, community service program, and adventure program established in 1992. High school or college credit may be earned.
Program Focus Academic adventure and community service program focusing on shark ecology, marine science, service learning, cultural immersion, adventure travel, whitewater rafting and college credit.
Academics Academics (general), area studies, ecology, history, intercultural studies, marine studies.
Special Interest Areas Community service, conservation projects, cross-cultural education, field research/expeditions, homestays, leadership training.
Sports Scuba diving, sea kayaking, snorkeling, swimming.
Wilderness/Outdoors Hiking, white-water trips, wilderness camping.
Trips Cultural, day, overnight.
Program Information 2 sessions per year. Session length: 24 days in June, July, August. Ages: 15–19. 10–12 participants per session. Cost: $5180. Financial aid available.
Application Deadline Continuous.
Contact Carlton Goldthwaite, Director, 806 McCulloch Street, Suite 102, Raleigh, North Carolina 27603. Phone: 888-833-1907. Fax: 919-833-2129. E-mail: info@academictreks.com.
URL www.academictreks.com

For more information, see page 432.

GLOBAL WORKS–Cultural Exchange–Fiji Islands–4 weeks

GLOBAL WORKS
Fiji

General Information Coed travel community service program, cultural program, and adventure program established in 1988. High school credit may be earned.
Program Focus Environmental and community service and cultural exchange.
Academics Intercultural studies.
Arts Arts and crafts (general), dance, music.
Special Interest Areas Community service, conservation projects, construction, field trips (arts and culture).
Sports Fishing, rugby, scuba diving, sea kayaking, snorkeling, soccer, sports (general), swimming, volleyball.
Wilderness/Outdoors Hiking.
Trips Cultural, day, overnight.

Program Information 2 sessions per year. Session length: 28–30 days in June, July. Ages: 14–17. 16–18 participants per session. Cost: $4295. Application fee: $100. Financial aid available. Airfare not included.
Application Deadline Continuous.
Jobs Positions for college students 23 and older.
Contact Mr. Erik Werner, Director, 1113 South Allen Street, State College, Pennsylvania 16801. Phone: 814-867-7000. Fax: 814-867-2717. E-mail: info@globalworksinc.com.
URL www.globalworksinc.com

For more information, see page 506.

RUSTIC PATHWAYS–BIG FIJI EXPLORER

Rustic Pathways
Fiji

General Information Coed travel outdoor program, wilderness program, cultural program, and adventure program established in 1994.
Program Focus Cultural immersion.
Special Interest Areas Conservation projects, construction, cross-cultural education, homestays, touring.
Sports Boating, fishing, horseback riding, kayaking, sailing, scuba diving, sea kayaking, snorkeling, swimming.
Wilderness/Outdoors Hiking, outdoor adventure, white-water trips, wilderness camping.
Trips Cultural, day, overnight, shopping.
Program Information 2 sessions per year. Session length: 17 days in July, August. Ages: 14–18. 10–15 participants per session. Cost: $2495. Application fee: $100–$200.
Application Deadline Continuous.
Jobs Positions for college students 21 and older.
Contact Rustic Pathways, 4121 Erie Street, Willoughby, Ohio 44094. Phone: 800-321-4353. Fax: 440-975-9694. E-mail: rustic@rusticpathways.com.
URL www.rusticpathways.com

For more information, see page 612.

RUSTIC PATHWAYS–ESCAPE TO FIJI

Rustic Pathways
Fiji

General Information Coed residential sports camp established in 1994.
Special Interest Areas Cross-cultural education.
Sports Sailing, scuba diving, snorkeling, surfing.
Program Information 8 sessions per year. Session length: 10 days in June, July, August. Ages: 14–18. 10–15 participants per session. Boarding program cost: $1295.
Application Deadline Continuous.
Jobs Positions for college students 21 and older.
Contact Rustic Pathways, 4121 Erie Street, Willoughby, Ohio 44094. Phone: 800-321-4353. Fax: 440-975-9694. E-mail: rustic@rusticpathways.com.
URL www.rusticpathways.com
For more information, see page 612.

RUSTIC PATHWAYS–EXTENDED FIJI VILLAGE SERVICE

Rustic Pathways
Nasivikoso, Nakuku
Fiji

General Information Coed residential community service program and cultural program established in 1994. High school credit may be earned.
Arts Dance.
Special Interest Areas Community service, construction, cross-cultural education, farming, gardening, homestays, nature study.
Sports Boating, horseback riding, sailing, swimming.
Trips Cultural, day, overnight, shopping.
Program Information 4 sessions per year. Session length: 31 days in June, July, August. Ages: 14–18. 15–20 participants per session. Boarding program cost: $3895.
Application Deadline Continuous.
Jobs Positions for college students 21 and older.
Contact Rustic Pathways, 4121 Erie Street, Willoughby, Ohio 44094. Phone: 800-321-4353. Fax: 440-975-9694. E-mail: rustic@rusticpathways.com.
URL www.rusticpathways.com
For more information, see page 612.

RUSTIC PATHWAYS–FIJI ISLANDS COMMUNITY SERVICE

Rustic Pathways
Fiji

General Information Coed travel outdoor program, community service program, and cultural program established in 1994.
Special Interest Areas Community service, construction, cross-cultural education, farming, homestays.

Sports Boating, swimming.
Trips Day, overnight, shopping.
Program Information 3 sessions per year. Session length: 17 days in June, July, August. Ages: 14–18. 5–10 participants per session. Cost: $2295.
Application Deadline Continuous.
Jobs Positions for college students 21 and older.
Contact Rustic Pathways, 4121 Erie Street, Willoughby, Ohio 44094. Phone: 800-321-4353. Fax: 440-975-9694. E-mail: rustic@rusticpathways.com.
URL www.rusticpathways.com
For more information, see page 612.

RUSTIC PATHWAYS–INTRO TO COMMUNITY SERVICE IN FIJI

Rustic Pathways
Vanua Levu, Nausori Highlands
Fiji

General Information Coed residential community service program and cultural program established in 1994.
Arts Dance.
Special Interest Areas Community service, construction, cross-cultural education, farming, gardening, homestays, touring.
Sports Boating, swimming.
Wilderness/Outdoors Hiking.
Trips Cultural, day, overnight, shopping.
Program Information 10 sessions per year. Session length: 10 days in June, July, August. Ages: 14–18. 15–20 participants per session. Boarding program cost: $965. Application fee: $100–$200.
Application Deadline Continuous.
Jobs Positions for college students 21 and older.
Contact Rustic Pathways, 4121 Erie Street, Willoughby, Ohio 44094. Phone: 800-321-4353. Fax: 440-975-9694. E-mail: rustic@rusticpathways.com.
URL www.rusticpathways.com
For more information, see page 612.

RUSTIC PATHWAYS–REMOTE HIGHLANDS COMMUNITY SERVICE IN FIJI

Rustic Pathways
Vanua Levu, Nausori Highlands
Fiji

General Information Coed travel community service program and cultural program established in 1994. High school credit may be earned.
Special Interest Areas Community service, construction, cross-cultural education, farming, gardening, homestays, nature study, touring.
Sports Boating, swimming.
Trips Cultural, day, overnight, shopping.
Program Information 5 sessions per year. Session length: 17 days in June, July, August. Ages: 14–18. 10–15 participants per session. Cost: $1895. Application fee: $100–$200.
Application Deadline Continuous.
Jobs Positions for college students 21 and older.
Contact Rustic Pathways, 4121 Erie Street, Willoughby, Ohio 44094. Phone: 800-321-4353. Fax: 440-975-9694. E-mail: rustic@rusticpathways.com.
URL www.rusticpathways.com

For more information, see page 612.

RUSTIC PATHWAYS–SOCCER AND SERVICE IN FIJI

Rustic Pathways
Fiji

General Information Coed travel outdoor program, community service program, and cultural program established in 2005.
Special Interest Areas Community service, cross-cultural education, homestays.
Sports Sailing, snorkeling, soccer, swimming.
Wilderness/Outdoors Hiking.
Trips Day, overnight, shopping.
Program Information 2 sessions per year. Session length: 17 days in June, July. Ages: 14–18. 8–10 participants per session. Cost: $2195. Application fee: $100–$200.
Application Deadline Continuous.
Jobs Positions for college students 21 and older.
Contact Rustic Pathways, 4121 Erie Street, Willoughby, Ohio 44094. Phone: 800-321-4353. Fax: 440-975-9694. E-mail: rustic@rusticpathways.com.
URL www.rusticpathways.com

For more information, see page 612.

RUSTIC PATHWAYS–SUN, SAND & INTERNATIONAL SERVICE–FIJI

Rustic Pathways
Fiji

General Information Coed travel cultural program and adventure program established in 1994.
Special Interest Areas Cross-cultural education, touring.
Sports Boating, canoeing, fishing, kayaking, sailing, scuba diving, snorkeling, swimming.
Wilderness/Outdoors Outdoor adventure, white-water trips, wilderness camping.
Trips Cultural, day, overnight, shopping.
Program Information 9 sessions per year. Session length: 17–73 days in June, July, August. Ages: 14–18. 10–15 participants per session. Cost: $1895–$9095.
Application Deadline Continuous.
Jobs Positions for college students 21 and older.
Contact Rustic Pathways, 4121 Erie Street, Willoughby, Ohio 44094. Phone: 800-321-4353. Fax: 440-975-9694. E-mail: rustic@rusticpathways.com.
URL www.rusticpathways.com

For more information, see page 612.

WILDERNESS VENTURES–FIJI COMMUNITY SERVICE

Wilderness Ventures
Fiji

General Information Coed travel outdoor program, community service program, cultural program, and adventure program established in 1973.
Program Focus Community service, cultural immersion, leadership skills.
Special Interest Areas Community service, conservation projects, leadership training.
Sports Sailing, scuba diving.
Wilderness/Outdoors White-water trips.
Trips Overnight.
Program Information 2 sessions per year. Session length: 22 days in June, July, August. Ages: 14–18. 15 participants per session. Cost: $5490. Financial aid available.
Application Deadline Continuous.
Jobs Positions for college students 21 and older.

Contact Mr. Mike Cottingham, Director, PO Box 2768, Jackson Hole, Wyoming 83001. Phone: 800-533-2281. Fax: 307-739-1934. E-mail: info@wildernessventures.com.
URL www.wildernessventures.com
For more information, see page 704.

WORLD HORIZONS INTERNATIONAL-FIJI

World Horizons International
Nokoru Kula
Fiji

General Information Coed residential community service program and cultural program established in 2003.
Program Focus Community service and cross-cultural education.
Special Interest Areas Community service, conservation projects, construction, cross-cultural education.
Sports Scuba diving, snorkeling, swimming.
Wilderness/Outdoors Hiking.
Trips Cultural, day, overnight.
Program Information 1–2 sessions per year. Session length: 3–5 weeks in June, July, August. Ages: 14–18. 10–12 participants per session. Boarding program cost: $4250–$5500. Application fee: $175. Financial aid available. Round trip airfare from Los Angeles included.
Application Deadline Continuous.
Jobs Positions for college students 21 and older.
Contact Mr. Stuart L. Rabinowitz, Executive Director, PO Box 662, Bethlehem, Connecticut 06751. Phone: 800-262-5874. Fax: 203-266-6227. E-mail: worldhorizons@att.net.
URL www.world-horizons.com
For more information, see page 714.

FINLAND

AFS-USA–HOMESTAY–FINLAND

AFS-USA
Finland

General Information Coed residential cultural program.
Program Focus Living with a host family, taking part in activities with other teenagers, and a 2-day cruise to Sweden.
Academics Finnish language/literature.
Special Interest Areas Homestays, touring.
Trips Cultural, day, overnight.
Program Information 1 session per year. Session length: 30–45 days in June, July, August. Ages: 15–18. Boarding program cost: $4000–$6000. Application fee: $75. Financial aid available. International airfare and volunteer homestay support included.
Application Deadline Continuous.
Contact Manager, AFS Info Center, 506 Southwest 6th Avenue, 2nd Floor, Portland, Oregon 97204. Phone: 800-AFS-INFO. Fax: 503-299-0753. E-mail: afsinfo@afs.org.
URL www.afs.org/usa
For more information, see page 408.

CENTER FOR CULTURAL INTERCHANGE–FINLAND HIGH SCHOOL ABROAD

Center for Cultural Interchange
Finland

General Information Coed residential academic program and cultural program established in 1985. High school credit may be earned.
Program Focus High school abroad.
Academics Finnish language/literature, academics (general).
Special Interest Areas Cross-cultural education, homestays.
Trips Cultural, day.
Program Information 2 sessions per year. Session length: 90–300 days in January, February, March, April, May, June, July, August, September, October, November, December. Ages: 15–18. Boarding program cost: $5900–$7700. Financial aid available. Early Bird discount.
Application Deadline Continuous.
Contact Ms. Juliet Jones, Outbound Programs Director, 746 North LaSalle Drive, Chicago, Illinois 60610-3617. Phone: 866-684-9675. Fax: 312-944-2644. E-mail: info@cci-exchange.com.
URL www.cci-exchange.com
For more information, see page 448.

FRANCE

AAVE–France Classique

AAVE–Journeys That Matter
Nice
France

General Information Coed travel academic program, outdoor program, cultural program, and adventure program established in 1976. Accredited by American Camping Association.
Program Focus Language immersion and culture and adventure travel.
Academics French language/literature, area studies, intercultural studies.
Special Interest Areas Leadership training, touring.
Sports Horseback riding, snorkeling, swimming.
Wilderness/Outdoors Backpacking, canyoneering, rafting, rock climbing, wilderness camping.
Trips Cultural, day, overnight.
Program Information 2–3 sessions per year. Session length: 3 weeks in July, August. Ages: 15–18. 13–16 participants per session. Cost: $5388. Financial aid available.
Application Deadline Continuous.
Jobs Positions for college students 21 and older.
Contact Mr. Abbott Wallis, Owner, 2308 Fossil Trace Drive, Golden, Colorado 80401. Phone: 800-222-3595. Fax: 303-526-0885. E-mail: info@aave.com.
URL www.aave.com

For more information, see page 394.

Academic Study Associates–Nice

Academic Study Associates, Inc. (ASA)
Nice
France

General Information Coed residential academic program and cultural program established in 1984. Formal opportunities for the academically talented. High school credit may be earned.
Program Focus Coed program focusing on academic enrichment, French language and culture, art history, literature, and European travel.
Academics French (Advanced Placement), French language/literature, academics (general), art history/appreciation, history, intercultural studies, precollege program, writing.
Arts Film.
Special Interest Areas Culinary arts, touring.

Sports Basketball, canoeing, parasailing, soccer, swimming, tennis, volleyball.
Wilderness/Outdoors Hiking, white-water trips.
Trips Cultural, day.
Program Information 1 session per year. Session length: 27–31 days in July. Ages: 15–18. 80 participants per session. Boarding program cost: $6495. Paris extension: $1595.
Application Deadline Continuous.
Jobs Positions for college students 21 and older.
Contact Marcia Evans, President, 375 West Broadway, Suite 200, New York, New York 10012. Phone: 212-796-8340. Fax: 212-334-4934. E-mail: summer@asaprograms.com.
URL www.asaprograms.com

For more information, see page 398.

Academic Study Associates–Royan

Academic Study Associates, Inc. (ASA)
Royan
France

General Information Coed residential academic program and cultural program established in 1998. Formal opportunities for the academically talented. High school credit may be earned.
Program Focus Cultural and linguistic immersion through daily language instruction and homestay.
Academics French (Advanced Placement), French language/literature, academics (general), intercultural studies, precollege program, writing.
Special Interest Areas Culinary arts, touring.
Sports Aerobics, archery, body boarding, horseback riding, sailing, surfing, swimming, tennis, volleyball, windsurfing.
Trips Cultural, day, overnight.
Program Information 1 session per year. Session length: 4 weeks in June, July. Ages: 15–18. 35–40 participants per session. Boarding program cost: $6295.
Application Deadline Continuous.
Jobs Positions for college students 21 and older.
Contact Marcia Evans, President, 375 West Broadway, Suite 200, New York, New York 10012. Phone: 212-796-8340. Fax: 212-334-4934. E-mail: summer@asaprograms.com.
URL www.asaprograms.com

For more information, see page 398.

ACADEMIC TREKS–French Immersion in France

Academic Treks, the academic adventure and community service division of Broadreach
Paris, Chamonix, Mont Blanc, Amboise, Montpellier
France

General Information Coed travel academic program, community service program, and adventure program established in 1992. High school or college credit may be earned.

Program Focus Academic adventure and community service program focusing on French language immersion, adventure travel, cultural exchange, hiking, homestay, college credit.

Academics French (Advanced Placement), French language/literature, academics (general), area studies, history, intercultural studies.

Special Interest Areas Community service, cross-cultural education, homestays, leadership training, touring.

Sports Bicycling.

Wilderness/Outdoors Backpacking, bicycle trips, hiking.

Trips Cultural, overnight.

Program Information 2 sessions per year. Session length: 25 days in June, July, August. Ages: 15–19. 10–12 participants per session. Cost: $6180. Financial aid available.

Application Deadline Continuous.

Contact Carlton Goldthwaite, Director, 806 McCulloch Street, Suite 102, Raleigh, North Carolina 27603. Phone: 888-833-1907. Fax: 919-833-2129. E-mail: info@academictreks.com.

URL www.academictreks.com

For more information, see page 432.

AFS-USA–HOMESTAY–FRANCE

AFS-USA
France

General Information Coed residential academic program and cultural program

Program Focus 4-week homestay

Academics French language/literature.

Special Interest Areas Homestays, touring.

Trips Cultural, day.

Program Information 1 session per year. Session length: 30–45 days in June, July. Ages: 15–18. Boarding program cost: $6100. Application fee: $75. Financial aid available. International airfare and volunteer homestay support included.

Application Deadline Continuous.

Contact Manager, AFS Info Center, 506 Southwest 6th Avenue, 2nd Floor, Portland, Oregon 97204. Phone: 800-AFS-INFO. Fax: 503-299-0753. E-mail: afsinfo@afs.org.

URL www.afs.org/usa

For more information, see page 408.

BARAT FOUNDATION SUMMER PROGRAM IN PROVENCE

Barat Foundation
Provence
France

General Information Coed travel academic program, arts program, community service program, and cultural program established in 1997. Formal opportunities for the academically talented.

Barat Foundation Summer Program in Provence

Program Focus French language and cultural immersion with emphasis on the arts and an international group of participants and instructors.

Academics French (Advanced Placement), French language/literature, architecture, art history/appreciation, humanities, intercultural studies, music.

Arts Arts, arts and crafts (general), drawing, film, graphic arts, music, painting, photography, television/video, theater/drama.

Special Interest Areas Cross-cultural education, culinary arts, field trips (arts and culture).

Sports Aerobics, basketball, bicycling, canoeing, equestrian sports, horseback riding, kayaking, swimming, tennis, volleyball.

Wilderness/Outdoors Bicycle trips, canoe trips, hiking, mountain biking.

Trips Cultural, day, shopping.

Program Information 1–2 sessions per year. Session length: 4–6 weeks in June, July, August. Ages: 13–19. 30–35 participants per session. Cost: $5700–$10,700. Application fee: $100. Financial aid available. Scholarships available for qualified students in the arts.

Barat Foundation Summer Program in Provence (continued)

Application Deadline Continuous.
Jobs Positions for college students 21 and older.
Contact Chandri Barat, Executive Director, main address above. Phone: 973-263-1013. E-mail: info@baratfoundation.org.
URL www.baratfoundation.org
For more information, see page 422.

CENTER FOR CULTURAL INTERCHANGE–FRANCE HIGH SCHOOL ABROAD

Center for Cultural Interchange
France

General Information Coed residential academic program and cultural program established in 1985. High school credit may be earned.
Program Focus High school abroad.
Academics French language/literature, academics (general).
Special Interest Areas Cross-cultural education, homestays.
Trips Cultural, day.
Program Information 2 sessions per year. Session length: 90–300 days in January, February, March, April, May, June, July, August, September, October, November, December. Ages: 15–18. Boarding program cost: $5900–$7700. Financial aid available. Early Bird discount.
Application Deadline Continuous.
Contact Ms. Juliet Jones, Outbound Programs Director, 746 North LaSalle Drive, Chicago, Illinois 60610-3617. Phone: 866-684-9675. Fax: 312-944-2644. E-mail: info@cci-exchange.com.
URL www.cci-exchange.com
For more information, see page 448.

CENTER FOR CULTURAL INTERCHANGE–FRANCE INDEPENDENT HOMESTAY

Center for Cultural Interchange
France

General Information Coed residential cultural program established in 1985.
Program Focus Independent homestay program.
Academics French language/literature, independent study.
Special Interest Areas Homestays.
Trips Cultural, day.
Program Information Session length: 1–4 weeks in January, February, March, April, May, June, July, August, September, October, November, December. Ages: 16+. Boarding program cost: $950–$1550. Financial aid available.
Application Deadline Continuous.

Contact Ms. Juliet Jones, Outbound Programs Director, 746 North LaSalle Drive, Chicago, Illinois 60610-3617. Phone: 866-684-9675. Fax: 312-944-2644. E-mail: info@cci-exchange.com.
URL www.cci-exchange.com
For more information, see page 448.

CENTER FOR CULTURAL INTERCHANGE–FRANCE LANGUAGE SCHOOL

Center for Cultural Interchange
France

General Information Coed residential academic program and cultural program established in 1985. High school or college credit may be earned.
Program Focus Cultural immersion and language study.
Academics French language/literature.
Special Interest Areas Homestays.
Sports Swimming.
Trips Cultural, day.
Program Information 1–50 sessions per year. Session length: 14–90 days in January, February, March, April, May, June, July, August, September, October, November, December. Ages: 14+. Boarding program cost: $2590–$3290. Financial aid available.
Application Deadline Continuous.
Contact Ms. Juliet Jones, Outbound Programs Director, 746 North LaSalle Drive, Chicago, Illinois 60610-3617. Phone: 866-684-9675. Fax: 312-944-2644. E-mail: info@cci-exchange.com.
URL www.cci-exchange.com
For more information, see page 448.

CHOATE ROSEMARY HALL SUMMER IN PARIS

Choate Rosemary Hall
Paris
France

General Information Coed residential academic program and cultural program established in 1975. High school credit may be earned.
Program Focus French language and culture immersion.
Academics French language/literature, art history/appreciation, history, social studies.
Special Interest Areas Cross-cultural education, homestays, touring.
Sports Swimming.

Trips Cultural, day, overnight.
Program Information 1 session per year. Session length: 36 days in June, July. Ages: 14–18. 28 participants per session. Boarding program cost: $6499. Application fee: $60. Financial aid available. Airfare from New York to Paris included.
Application Deadline Continuous.
Contact Mr. Carl Hermey, Co-Director, Summer Program in Paris, 333 Christian Street, Wallingford, Connecticut 06492. Phone: 203-697-2365. Fax: 203-697-2519. E-mail: chermey@choate.edu.
URL www.choate.edu/summerprograms
For more information, see page 452.

EDU-CULTURE INTERNATIONAL (ECI)– AIX-EN-PROVENCE/GAP HOST FAMILY IMMERSION

Edu-Culture International (ECI)
France

General Information Coed travel academic program and cultural program established in 2001. College credit may be earned.
Program Focus Pre-college experience including 2 weeks of intensive French classes in Aix-en-Provence with daily excursions and activities, 1 week of French language and culture immersion with host families in the alpine town of Gap, and 3 days/nights in Paris.
Academics French language/literature, intercultural studies, precollege program.
Special Interest Areas Cross-cultural education, homestays, touring.
Sports Bicycling, boating, kayaking, swimming.
Trips Cultural, day, overnight, shopping.
Program Information 1 session per year. Session length: 27 days in June, July. Ages: 15–18. 25–30 participants per session. Cost: $5495. Application fee: $95. Financial aid available. Airfare from San Francisco, CA to Marseille, France included in cost.
Application Deadline Continuous.
Jobs Positions for college students 22 and older.
Contact Ms. Phyllis O'Neill, Director, PO Box 2692, Berkeley, California 94702. Phone: 866-343-8990. Fax: 510-845-2231. E-mail: info@educulture.org.
URL www.educulture.org
For more information, see page 476.

EDU-CULTURE INTERNATIONAL (ECI)– LYON HOST FAMILY AND TRAVEL PROGRAM

Edu-Culture International (ECI)
France

General Information Coed travel cultural program established in 1999.
Program Focus 2 weeks of French language and culture immersion with host families in Lyon, daily activities and excursions, 3 days/nights in Nice, 3 days/nights in Paris.

Academics French language/literature, intercultural studies, precollege program.
Special Interest Areas Cross-cultural education, homestays, touring.
Sports Boating, kayaking, swimming.
Trips Cultural, day, overnight, shopping.
Program Information 1 session per year. Session length: 3 weeks in June, July. Ages: 14–18. 25–30 participants per session. Cost: $3850. Application fee: $95. Financial aid available. Airfare from San Francisco, CA to Nice, France included in cost.
Application Deadline Continuous.
Jobs Positions for college students 22 and older.
Contact Ms. Phyllis O'Neill, Director, PO Box 2692, Berkeley, California 94702. Phone: 866-343-8990. Fax: 510-845-2231. E-mail: info@educulture.org.
URL www.educulture.org
For more information, see page 476.

EDU-CULTURE INTERNATIONAL (ECI)– TOULOUSE/MONTPELLIER HOST FAMILY IMMERSION

Edu-Culture International (ECI)
France

General Information Coed travel academic program and cultural program established in 2006. College credit may be earned.
Program Focus Pre-college experience including 2 weeks of intensive French classes in Toulouse with daily excursions and activities, 1 week of French language and culture immersion with host families in the Mediterranean town of Montpellier, and 3 days/nights in Paris.
Academics French language/literature, intercultural studies, precollege program.
Special Interest Areas Cross-cultural education, homestays, touring.
Sports Bicycling, canoeing, kayaking, swimming.
Trips Cultural, day, overnight, shopping.
Program Information 1 session per year. Session length: 4 weeks in July, August. Ages: 15–18. 25–30 participants per session. Cost: $5425. Application fee: $95. Financial aid available. Airfare from San Francisco, CA to Toulouse, France included in cost.
Application Deadline Continuous.
Jobs Positions for college students 22 and older.
Contact Ms. Phyllis O'Neill, Director, PO Box 2692, Berkeley, California 94702. Phone: 866-343-8990. Fax: 510-845-2231. E-mail: info@educulture.org.
URL www.educulture.org
For more information, see page 476.

EF INTERNATIONAL LANGUAGE SCHOOL– NICE

EF International Language Schools
21, Rue Meyerbeer
Nice 06000
France

General Information Coed travel academic program and cultural program established in 1984. High school or college credit may be earned.

EF International Language School–Nice

Program Focus Language and cultural immersion.
Academics French (Advanced Placement), French language/literature.
Special Interest Areas Field trips (arts and culture), homestays, internships.
Sports Sports (general).
Wilderness/Outdoors Wilderness/outdoors (general).
Trips Cultural, day, overnight.
Program Information 2–52 sessions per year. Session length: 14–365 days in January, February, March, April, May, June, July, August, September, October, November, December. Ages: 15+. 300–350 participants per session. Application fee: $145. Financial aid available. Call for costs.
Application Deadline Continuous.

Contact Ms. Margaret Kelly, Director of Admissions, One Education Street, Cambridge, Massachusetts 02141. Phone: 800-992-1892. Fax: 800-590-1125. E-mail: ils@ef.com.
URL www.ef.com
For more information, see page 478.

EF INTERNATIONAL LANGUAGE SCHOOL– PARIS

EF International Language Schools
41, rue de L'Echiquier
Paris
France

General Information Coed travel academic program and cultural program established in 2007. High school or college credit may be earned.
Program Focus Language and cultural immersion.
Academics French (Advanced Placement), French language/literature.
Special Interest Areas Field trips (arts and culture), homestays.
Trips Cultural, overnight.
Program Information 2–52 sessions per year. Session length: 2–52 weeks in January, February, March, April, May, June, July, August, September, October, November, December. Ages: 16+. 200–250 participants per session. Application fee: $145. Financial aid available. Call for costs.
Application Deadline Continuous.
Contact Ms. Margaret Kelly, Director of Admissions, One Education Street, Cambridge, Massachusetts 02141. Phone: 800-992-1892. Fax: 800-590-1125. E-mail: ils@ef.com.
URL www.ef.com
For more information, see page 478.

EXCEL AT PARIS/PROVENCE

Putney Student Travel
Paris, Provence
France

General Information Coed residential academic
program and cultural program established in 1951.
Formal opportunities for the academically talented and
artistically talented.
Program Focus Precollege program that emphasizes
small classes, creative interactions among student and
faculty, and cultural exchange.
Academics French language/literature, academics
(general), architecture, area studies, art
history/appreciation, government and politics, history,
humanities, intercultural studies, precollege program,
writing.
Arts Creative writing, drawing, film, music, painting,
theater/drama.
Special Interest Areas Field research/expeditions,
touring.
Sports Basketball, bicycling, soccer, swimming.
Wilderness/Outdoors Hiking.
Trips Cultural, day.
Program Information 1 session per year. Session
length: 4 weeks in July, August. Ages: 15–18. 60–70
participants per session. Boarding program cost: $7290.
Financial aid available.
Application Deadline Continuous.
Contact Patrick Noyes, Director, 345 Hickory Ridge
Road, Putney, Vermont 05346. Phone: 802-387-5000.
Fax: 802-387-4276. E-mail: info@goputney.com.
URL www.goputney.com

For more information, see page 490.

THE EXPERIMENT IN INTERNATIONAL LIVING–FRANCE, BIKING AND HOMESTAY

The Experiment in International Living
France

General Information Coed travel outdoor program,
cultural program, and adventure program established in
1932.
Program Focus International youth travel, homestay,
biking in Brittany.
Academics French language/literature.
Special Interest Areas Homestays, touring.
Sports Bicycling.
Wilderness/Outdoors Bicycle trips.
Trips Cultural, day, overnight.
Program Information 1 session per year. Session
length: 4 weeks in June, July. Ages: 14–19. 10–15
participants per session. Cost: $4950. Financial aid
available. Airfare included.
Application Deadline May 1.

Contact Annie Thompson, Enrollment Director,
Summer Abroad, Kipling Road, PO Box 676,
Brattleboro, Vermont 05302-0676. Phone: 800-345-2929.
Fax: 802-258-3428. E-mail: eil@worldlearning.org.
URL www.usexperiment.org

For more information, see page 492.

THE EXPERIMENT IN INTERNATIONAL LIVING–FRANCE, FIVE-WEEK ART AND ADVENTURE IN PROVENCE

The Experiment in International Living
France

General Information Coed travel arts program and
cultural program established in 1932.

*The Experiment in International Living–France, Five-Week Art
and Adventure in Provence*

Program Focus International youth travel, homestay,
exploration of Provence through the arts.
Academics French language/literature, art history/
appreciation.
Arts Arts, arts and crafts (general), drawing, painting,
pottery, sculpture.
Special Interest Areas Homestays, touring.
Trips Cultural, day, overnight.
Program Information 1 session per year. Session
length: 5 weeks in June, July, August. Ages: 14–19.
10–15 participants per session. Cost: $6200. Financial
aid available. Airfare included.
Application Deadline May 1.

The Experiment in International Living–France, Five-Week Art and Adventure in Provence (continued)

Contact Annie Thompson, Enrollment Director, Summer Abroad, Kipling Road, PO Box 676, Brattleboro, Vermont 05302-0676. Phone: 800-345-2929. Fax: 802-258-3428. E-mail: eil@worldlearning.org. **URL** www.usexperiment.org

For more information, see page 492.

THE EXPERIMENT IN INTERNATIONAL LIVING–FRANCE, FOUR-WEEK BRITTANY DISCOVERY

The Experiment in International Living France

General Information Coed travel cultural program established in 1932.
Program Focus International youth travel, Brittany culture, homestay.
Academics French language/literature.
Special Interest Areas Homestays, touring.
Trips Cultural, day, overnight.
Program Information 1 session per year. Session length: 4 weeks in June, July. Ages: 14–19. 10–15 participants per session. Cost: $5100. Financial aid available. Airfare included.
Application Deadline May 1.
Contact Annie Thompson, Enrollment Director, Summer Abroad, Kipling Road, PO Box 676, Brattleboro, Vermont 05302-0676. Phone: 800-345-2929. Fax: 802-258-3428. E-mail: eil@worldlearning.org. **URL** www.usexperiment.org

For more information, see page 492.

THE EXPERIMENT IN INTERNATIONAL LIVING–FRANCE, FOUR-WEEK HOMESTAY AND PHOTOGRAPHY

The Experiment in International Living France

General Information Coed travel arts program, cultural program, and adventure program established in 1932.
Program Focus International youth travel, homestay.
Academics French language/literature.
Arts Photography.
Special Interest Areas Homestays, touring.
Trips Cultural, day, overnight.
Program Information 1 session per year. Session length: 4 weeks in June, July. Ages: 14–17. 10–15 participants per session. Cost: $5700. Application fee: $75. Financial aid available. Airfare included.
Application Deadline May 1.
Contact Chris Frantz, Deputy Director, EIL–World Learning, PO Box 676, Kipling Road, Brattleboro, Vermont 05302-0676. Phone: 800-345-2929. Fax: 802-258-3428. E-mail: eil@worldlearning.org. **URL** www.usexperiment.org

For more information, see page 492.

THE EXPERIMENT IN INTERNATIONAL LIVING–FRANCE, FOUR-WEEK HOMESTAY AND THEATRE

The Experiment in International Living France

General Information Coed travel arts program, cultural program, and adventure program established in 1932.
Program Focus International youth travel, homestay.
Academics French language/literature.
Arts Clowning, dance, mime, theater/drama.
Special Interest Areas Homestays, touring.
Trips Cultural, day, overnight.
Program Information 1 session per year. Session length: 4 weeks in June, July. Ages: 14–19. 10–15 participants per session. Cost: $5700. Application fee: $75. Financial aid available. Airfare included.
Application Deadline May 1.
Contact Chris Frantz, Deputy Director, EIL–World Learning, PO Box 676, Kipling Road, Brattleboro, Vermont 05302-0676. Phone: 800-345-2929. Fax: 802-258-3428. E-mail: eil@worldlearning.org. **URL** www.usexperiment.org

For more information, see page 492.

THE EXPERIMENT IN INTERNATIONAL LIVING–FRANCE, FOUR-WEEK HOMESTAY AND TRAVEL–SOUTHERN FRANCE AND NORTHERN SPAIN

The Experiment in International Living France

General Information Coed travel outdoor program and cultural program established in 1932.
Program Focus International youth travel, homestay, travel in the Pyrenees.
Academics French language/literature.
Special Interest Areas Homestays, touring.
Wilderness/Outdoors Hiking.
Trips Cultural, day, overnight.
Program Information 1 session per year. Session length: 4 weeks in June, July. Ages: 14–19. 10–15 participants per session. Cost: $5800. Financial aid available. Airfare included.
Application Deadline May 1.
Contact Annie Thompson, Enrollment Director, Summer Abroad, Kipling Road, PO Box 676, Brattleboro, Vermont 05302-0676. Phone: 800-345-2929. Fax: 802-258-3428. E-mail: eil@worldlearning.org. **URL** www.usexperiment.org

For more information, see page 492.

THE EXPERIMENT IN INTERNATIONAL LIVING–FRANCE, FOUR-WEEK HOMESTAY AND TRAVEL THROUGH ALPS

The Experiment in International Living
France

General Information Coed travel outdoor program, cultural program, and adventure program established in 1932.
Program Focus International youth travel, homestay.
Academics French language/literature.
Special Interest Areas Homestays, touring.
Wilderness/Outdoors Hiking, wilderness camping.
Trips Cultural, day, overnight.
Program Information 1 session per year. Session length: 4 weeks in June, July. Ages: 14–19. 10–15 participants per session. Cost: $5200. Application fee: $75. Financial aid available. Airfare included.
Application Deadline May 1.
Contact Chris Frantz, Deputy Director, EIL–World Learning, PO Box 676, Kipling Road, Brattleboro, Vermont 05302-0676. Phone: 800-345-2929. Fax: 802-258 3428. E-mail: eil@worldlearning.org
URL www.usexperiment.org
For more information, see page 492.

THE EXPERIMENT IN INTERNATIONAL LIVING–FRANCE, HOMESTAY, LANGUAGE TRAINING, AND COOKING

The Experiment in International Living
France

General Information Coed residential academic program and cultural program established in 1932.
Program Focus International youth travel, homestay, language classes, cooking.
Academics French language/literature.
Special Interest Areas Culinary arts, homestays, touring.
Trips Cultural, day, overnight.
Program Information 1 session per year. Session length: 5 weeks in June, July, August. Ages: 14–19. 10–15 participants per session. Boarding program cost: $6200. Financial aid available. Airfare included.
Application Deadline May 1.
Contact Annie Thompson, Enrollment Director, Summer Abroad, Kipling Road, PO Box 676, Brattleboro, Vermont 05302-0676. Phone: 800-345-2929. Fax: 802-258-3428. E-mail: eil@worldlearning.org.
URL www.usexperiment.org
For more information, see page 492.

THE EXPERIMENT IN INTERNATIONAL LIVING–FRANCE, THREE-WEEK CAMARGUE HOMESTAY

The Experiment in International Living
France

General Information Coed travel cultural program established in 1932.
Program Focus International youth travel, homestay, Camargue travel.
Academics French language/literature.
Special Interest Areas Homestays.
Trips Cultural, day, overnight.
Program Information 1 session per year. Session length: 3 weeks in June, July. Ages: 14–19. 10–15 participants per session. Cost: $4800. Financial aid available. Airfare included.
Application Deadline May 1.
Contact Annie Thompson, Enrollment Director, Summer Abroad, Kipling Road, PO Box 676, Brattleboro, Vermont 05302-0676. Phone: 800-345-2929. Fax: 802-258-3428. E-mail: eil@worldlearning.org.
URL www.usexperiment.org
For more information, see page 492.

THE EXPERIMENT IN INTERNATIONAL LIVING–FRANCE, THREE-WEEK HOMESTAY AND TRAVEL–BORDERS

The Experiment in International Living
France

General Information Coed travel cultural program and adventure program established in 1932.
Program Focus International youth travel, homestay.
Academics French language/literature.
Special Interest Areas Homestays, touring.
Wilderness/Outdoors Hiking.
Trips Cultural, day, overnight.
Program Information 1 session per year. Session length: 3 weeks in June, July. Ages: 14–19. 10–15 participants per session. Cost: $4700. Application fee: $75. Financial aid available. Airfare included.
Application Deadline May 1.
Contact Chris Frantz, Deputy Director, EIL–World Learning, PO Box 676, Kipling Road, Brattleboro, Vermont 05302-0676. Phone: 800-345-2929. Fax: 802-258-3428. E-mail: eil@worldlearning.org
URL www.usexperiment.org
For more information, see page 492.

GLOBAL WORKS–Language Immersion, Cultural Exchange and Service–France–4 weeks

GLOBAL WORKS
Carcassonne/Corsica
France

General Information Coed travel community service program, cultural program, and adventure program established in 1988. High school credit may be earned.
Program Focus Environmental and community service, language immersion, and cultural exchange.
Academics French language/literature, archaeology, intercultural studies.
Arts Arts and crafts (general).
Special Interest Areas Community service, conservation projects, construction, field trips (arts and culture), homestays.
Sports Bicycling, soccer, sports (general), swimming.
Wilderness/Outdoors Caving, hiking, rafting, rock climbing, white-water trips.
Trips Cultural, day, overnight.
Program Information 1 session per year. Session length: 27 days in June, July. Ages: 14–17. 16–18 participants per session. Cost: $4995. Application fee: $100. Financial aid available. Airfare not included.
Application Deadline Continuous.
Jobs Positions for college students 23 and older.
Contact Mr. Erik Werner, Director, 1113 South Allen Street, State College, Pennsylvania 16801. Phone: 814-867-7000. Fax: 814-867-2717. E-mail: info@globalworksinc.com.
URL www.globalworksinc.com

For more information, see page 506.

L' ACADÉMIE DE FRANCE

Oxbridge Academic Programs
Notre Dame de la Merci
Montpellier
France

General Information Coed residential academic program and arts program established in 2005. Formal opportunities for the academically talented and artistically talented.
Program Focus Academic and cultural enrichment.
Academics English language/literature, French language/literature, academics (general), criminal justice, history, humanities, law, mathematics, medicine, philosophy, psychology, science (general), speech/debate, writing.
Arts Arts, drawing, painting, theater/drama.
Special Interest Areas Field trips (arts and culture).
Sports Aerobics, baseball, basketball, rowing (crew/sculling), soccer, sports (general), tennis.
Trips Cultural, day.
Program Information 1 session per year. Session length: 25 days in July. Ages: 15–18. 90 participants per session. Boarding program cost: $6695. Financial aid available. Airfare not included.
Application Deadline Continuous.
Contact Ms. Andrea Mardon, Executive Director, Oxbridge Academic Programs, 601 West 110th Street, Suite 7R, New York, New York 10025-2186. Phone: 800-828-8349. Fax: 212-663-8169. E-mail: info@oxbridgeprograms.com.
URL www.oxbridgeprograms.com

For more information, see page 580.

L' ACADÉMIE DE PARIS

Oxbridge Academic Programs
Lycée Notre-Dame de Sion
Paris
France

General Information Coed residential academic program and arts program established in 1989. Formal opportunities for the academically talented and artistically talented. High school credit may be earned.
Program Focus Academic and cultural enrichment.
Academics English language/literature, French (Advanced Placement), French language/literature, academics (general), architecture, art history/appreciation, business, government and politics, health sciences, history, humanities, law, medicine, philosophy, precollege program, social studies, writing.
Arts Arts, creative writing, drawing, painting, photography, theater/drama.
Special Interest Areas Field trips (arts and culture).
Sports Aerobics, basketball, cross-country, soccer, sports (general), tennis.
Trips Cultural, day.
Program Information 1 session per year. Session length: 4 weeks in July. Ages: 15–18. 160–170 participants per session. Boarding program cost: $6695. Financial aid available.
Application Deadline Continuous.

Jobs Positions for college students 20 and older.
Contact Ms. Andrea Mardon, Executive Director, Oxbridge Academic Programs, 601 West 110th Street, Suite 7R, New York, New York 10025-2186. Phone: 800-828-8349. Fax: 212-663-8169. E-mail: info@oxbridgeprograms.com.
URL www.oxbridgeprograms.com
For more information, see page 580.

PUTNEY STUDENT TRAVEL–LANGUAGE LEARNING–FRANCE

Putney Student Travel
France

General Information Coed residential academic program and cultural program established in 1951.
Program Focus French language immersion. Participants housed in host-family homes and hotels. Enrollment limited to those who are studying French.
Academics French (Advanced Placement), French language/literature, area studies, art history/appreciation, intercultural studies, linguistics.
Special Interest Areas Homestays.
Sports Bicycling, canoeing, fishing, horseback riding, kayaking, rappelling, skiing (downhill), snorkeling, soccer, swimming, tennis, windsurfing.
Wilderness/Outdoors Bicycle trips, hiking, mountaineering, rock climbing.
Trips Cultural, day, overnight.
Program Information 2–5 sessions per year. Session length: 35–45 days in June, July, August. Ages: 13–18. 16–18 participants per session. Boarding program cost: $8690. Financial aid available. Airfare from New York included.
Application Deadline Continuous.
Contact Jeffrey Shumlin, Admissions Director, 345 Hickory Ridge Road, Putney, Vermont 05346. Phone: 802-387-5000. Fax: 802-387-4276. E-mail: info@goputney.com.
URL www.goputney.com
For more information, see page 598.

RASSIAS PROGRAMS–ARLES, FRANCE

Rassias Programs
Arles
France

General Information Coed travel academic program and cultural program established in 1985.
Program Focus French Language studies taught in the Rassias method, homestay, and travel in France.
Academics French (Advanced Placement), French language/literature.
Special Interest Areas Homestays, touring.
Sports Bicycling, kayaking, sailing, swimming, tennis.
Trips Cultural, overnight.
Program Information 1 session per year. Session length: 36 days in June, July. Ages: 14–17, 20–22 participants per session. Cost: $7750–$8000. Financial aid available. Airfare included.
Application Deadline Continuous.
Jobs Positions for college students 21 and older.
Contact Bill Miles, Director, PO Box 5456, Hanover, New Hampshire 03755. Phone: 603-643-3007. Fax: 603-643-4249. E-mail: wmiles@rassias.com.
URL www.rassias.com
For more information, see page 602.

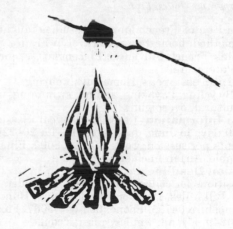

RASSIAS PROGRAMS–TOURS, FRANCE

Rassias Programs
Tours
France

General Information Coed travel academic program and cultural program established in 1985.

Rassias Programs–Tours, France

Program Focus French language studies taught in the Rassias method, homestay, and travel in France.
Academics French (Advanced Placement), French language/literature.
Special Interest Areas Homestays, touring.
Sports Bicycling, kayaking, sailing, swimming, tennis.
Trips Cultural, overnight.
Program Information 1 session per year. Session length: 30 days in June, July. Ages: 14–17. 20–22 participants per session. Cost: $7475–$8000. Financial aid available. Airfare included.
Application Deadline Continuous.
Jobs Positions for college students 21 and older.
Contact Bill Miles, Director, PO Box 5456, Hanover, New Hampshire 03755. Phone: 603-643-3007. Fax: 603-643-4249. E-mail: wmiles@rassias.com.
URL www.rassias.com

For more information, see page 602.

SERVICE LEARNING IN PARIS

International Seminar Series
Paris
France

General Information Coed residential academic program, community service program, and cultural program established in 1998. High school credit may be earned.

Service Learning in Paris

Program Focus Participants fluent in French, or having strong competencies in French may complete their community service, academic course work, and cultural visits in the native language.
Academics French language/literature, architecture, art history/appreciation, government and politics, writing.
Arts Creative writing.
Special Interest Areas Community service, cross-cultural education, field trips (arts and culture).
Trips Cultural, day.
Program Information 1 session per year. Session length: 25–31 days in July. Ages: 16+. 40–50 participants per session. Boarding program cost: $6500. Application fee: $50. Financial aid available.
Application Deadline April 15.
Contact John Nissen, Director, PO Box 1212, Manchester, Vermont 05254-1212. Phone: 802-362-5855. Fax: 802-362-5855. E-mail: iss@study-serve.org.
URL www.study-serve.org

For more information, see page 630.

SUMMER ADVANTAGE STUDY ABROAD– PARIS, FRANCE

American Institute for Foreign Study (AIFS)
Université Paris Sorbonne–Paris IV
1 rue Victor Cousin 75005
Paris
France

General Information Coed travel academic program and cultural program established in 2004. College credit may be earned.

Summer Advantage Study Abroad–Paris, France

Program Focus Study abroad for college credit.
Academics French (Advanced Placement), French language/literature, art history/appreciation.
Arts Fashion design/production.
Special Interest Areas Culinary arts, field trips (arts and culture), touring.
Trips Cultural, day, overnight, shopping.
Program Information 1 session per year. Session length: 29–34 days in June, July. Ages: 16–18. 35–45 participants per session. Cost: $6275. Application fee: $95.
Application Deadline April 15.
Contact Mrs. Amy Van Stone, Director of Admissions, Summer Advantage, 9 West Broad Street, River Plaza, Stamford, Connecticut 06902. Phone: 800-913-7151. Fax: 203-399-5463. E-mail: summeradvantage@aifs.com.
URL www.summeradvantage.com

For more information, see page 410.

SUMMER STUDY IN PARIS AT THE SORBONNE

Summer Study Programs
Paris
France

General Information Coed residential academic program and cultural program established in 1995. Formal opportunities for the academically talented. College credit may be earned.
Program Focus Pre-college experience including college credit classes, enrichment classes, SAT preparation, daily cultural excursions and sightseeing in Paris, weekend excursions in France and London, French immersion (for interested students).
Academics English language/literature, French (Advanced Placement), French language/literature, Hausa, SAT/ACT preparation, academics (general), architecture, art (Advanced Placement), art history/ appreciation, business, communications, economics, government and politics, government and politics (Advanced Placement), history, humanities, journalism, music, precollege program, psychology, social science, social studies, writing.
Arts Creative writing, drawing, fabric arts, film, graphic arts, painting, photography, theater/drama.
Special Interest Areas Field trips (arts and culture), touring.
Sports Aerobics, baseball, basketball, bicycling, football, lacrosse, racquetball, soccer, softball, sports (general), swimming, tennis, volleyball, weight training.
Trips Cultural, day, overnight, shopping.
Program Information 2 sessions per year. Session length: 3–5 weeks in July, August. Ages: 14+. 150–200 participants per session. Boarding program cost: $4795– $6695. Application fee: $75. Financial aid available.
Application Deadline Continuous.
Jobs Positions for college students 21 and older.
Contact Mr. Bill Cooperman, Executive Director, 900 Walt Whitman Road, Melville, New York 11747. Phone: 800-666-2556. Fax: 631-424-0567. E-mail: precollegeprograms@summerstudy.com.
URL www.summerstudy.com

For more information, see page 658.

TAFT SUMMER SCHOOL ABROAD–FRANCE

The Taft School
Tours
France

General Information Coed travel academic program established in 1982. Accredited by American Camping Association.
Program Focus The program is designed to completely immerse the student in the people, language, and culture of the country.
Academics French language/literature, art history/ appreciation, history, intercultural studies.
Special Interest Areas Homestays, touring.
Trips Cultural, day, overnight, shopping.
Program Information 1 session per year. Session length: 35–40 days in June, July. Ages: 14–18. 10–20 participants per session. Cost: $5950. Application fee: $50. Airfare from New York to Paris included.
Application Deadline April 15.
Contact Mr. Brian Denyer, Director, Taft Summer in France, 110 Woodbury Road, Watertown, Connecticut 06795. Phone: 860-945-7955. Fax: 860-945-7859. E-mail: denyerb@taftschool.org.
URL www.taftschool.org/summer

For more information, see page 666.

TASIS ARTS AND ARCHITECTURE IN THE SOUTH OF FRANCE

TASIS The American School in England
Les Tapies, The Ardeche
France

General Information Coed residential arts program established in 2003. Formal opportunities for the artistically talented. High school credit may be earned.
Program Focus Intensive drawing, painting, photography, and architecture.
Academics Architecture, art, art (Advanced Placement).
Arts Arts, drawing, painting, photography, printmaking.
Sports Kayaking, swimming.
Trips Cultural, day.
Program Information 1 session per year. Session length: 3 weeks in June, July. Ages: 14–18. 16–20 participants per session. Boarding program cost: $4600.
Application Deadline Continuous.
Contact W. Thomas Fleming, US Director, 1640 Wisconsin Avenue, NW, Washington, District of Columbia 20007. Phone: 202-965-5800. Fax: 202-965-5816. E-mail: usadmissions@tasis.com.
URL www.tasis.com

For more information, see page 668.

TISCH SCHOOL OF THE ARTS– INTERNATIONAL HIGH SCHOOL PROGRAM–PARIS

New York University, Tisch School of the Arts
Paris
France

General Information Coed residential academic program, arts program, and cultural program established in 2001. Formal opportunities for the artistically talented. College credit may be earned.
Program Focus Drama/theater, writing, art studies.
Academics French language/literature, intercultural studies.
Arts Acting, creative writing, music, theater/drama.
Trips Cultural, day.
Program Information 1 session per year. Session length: 28–30 days in July, August. Ages: 15+. 8–20 participants per session. Boarding program cost: $7900–$9200. Application fee: $60. Financial aid available.
Application Deadline February 1.
Contact Mariangela Lardaro, Assistant Director of Recruitment, Special Programs, 721 Broadway, 12th Floor, New York, New York 10003. Phone: 212-998-1517. Fax: 212-995-4578. E-mail: tisch.special.info@nyu.edu.
URL specialprograms.tisch.nyu.edu

For more information, see page 566.

VOLUNTEERS FOR PEACE INTERNATIONAL VOLUNTARY SERVICE–FRANCE

Volunteers for Peace International Voluntary
Service
Paris
France

General Information Coed residential community
service program established in 1981. Specific services
available for the hearing impaired and physically
challenged. College credit may be earned.
Program Focus International voluntary service
projects or work camps.
Academics Intercultural studies, peace education.
Special Interest Areas Community service,
construction, gardening, work camp programs.
Trips Cultural, day, overnight.
Program Information 60 sessions per year. Session
length: 2–3 weeks in May, June, July, August,
September. Ages: 15+. 12–20 participants per session.
Boarding program cost: $500–$800.
Application Deadline Continuous.
Contact Peter Coldwell, Director, 1034 Tiffany Road,
Belmont, Vermont 05730. Phone: 802-259-2759. Fax:
802-259-2922. E-mail: vfp@vfp.org.
URL www.vfp.org

WESTCOAST CONNECTION–FRENCH LANGUAGE AND TOURING

Westcoast Connection
France

General Information Coed travel academic program
and cultural program established in 1982. Accredited by
Ontario Camping Association. High school or college
credit may be earned.
Program Focus French study program combining
study in three centers: Paris, Loire Valley, and French
Rivera; plus many touring highlights.
Academics French (Advanced Placement), French
language/literature.
Special Interest Areas Touring.
Trips Cultural, day, shopping.
Program Information 1–2 sessions per year. Session
length: 23–28 days in July. Ages: 14–19. 20–40
participants per session. Cost: $3999.
Application Deadline Continuous.
Contact Mr. Mark Segal, Director, 154 East Boston
Post Road, Mamaroneck, New York 10543. Phone:
800-767-0227. Fax: 914-835-0798. E-mail:
info@westcoastconnection.com.
URL www.360studenttravel.com
For more information, see page 702.

FRENCH POLYNESIA

ACTIONQUEST: TAHITI AND FRENCH POLYNESIAN ISLAND VOYAGES

ActionQuest
French Polynesia

General Information Coed travel outdoor program,
cultural program, and adventure program established in
1986.
Program Focus Sailing and land exploration of Tahiti
and the surrounding French Polynesian Islands.
Academics Intercultural studies, marine studies.
Special Interest Areas Community service, leadership
training, nature study, nautical skills, team building,
touring.
Sports Bicycling, horseback riding, sailing, scuba
diving, snorkeling.
Wilderness/Outdoors Hiking, sailing trips.
Trips Cultural, day, overnight.
Program Information 1 session per year. Session
length: 22 days in June, July, August. Ages: 15–19. 10
participants per session. Cost: $4870.
Application Deadline Continuous.
Contact Mike Meighan, Director, PO Box 5517,
Sarasota, Florida 34277. Phone: 800-317-6789. Fax:
941-924-6075. E-mail: info@actionquest.com.
URL www.actionquest.com
For more information, see page 406.

GERMANY

CENTER FOR CULTURAL INTERCHANGE– GERMANY HIGH SCHOOL ABROAD

Center for Cultural Interchange
Germany

General Information Coed residential academic
program and cultural program established in 1985. High
school credit may be earned.
Program Focus High school abroad in Germany,
cultural immersion.
Academics German language/literature, academics
(general), mathematics, music, philosophy, physics,
science (general), social science.
Special Interest Areas Cross-cultural education,
homestays.
Trips Cultural, day.
Program Information 2 sessions per year. Session
length: 90–300 days in January, February, March, April,
May, June, July, August, September, October, November,
December. Ages: 15–18. Boarding program cost: $4900–
$6200. Financial aid available. Early Bird discount.
Application Deadline Continuous.

Center for Cultural Interchange–Germany High School Abroad (continued)

Contact Ms. Juliet Jones, Outbound Programs Director, 746 North LaSalle Drive, Chicago, Illinois 60610-3617. Phone: 866-684-9675. Fax: 312-944-2644. E-mail: info@cci-exchange.com. **URL** www.cci-exchange.com

For more information, see page 448.

CENTER FOR CULTURAL INTERCHANGE–GERMANY INDEPENDENT HOMESTAY

Center for Cultural Interchange
Germany

General Information Coed residential cultural program established in 1985.
Program Focus Cultural immersion.
Academics German language/literature, independent study.
Special Interest Areas Homestays.
Trips Cultural, day.
Program Information Session length: 7–30 days in January, February, March, April, May, June, July, August, September, October, November, December. Ages: 16+. Boarding program cost: $890–$1390. Financial aid available.
Application Deadline Continuous.
Contact Ms. Juliet Jones, Outbound Programs Director, 746 North LaSalle Drive, Chicago, Illinois 60610-3617. Phone: 866-684-9675. Fax: 312-944-2644. E-mail: info@cci-exchange.com. **URL** www.cci-exchange.com

For more information, see page 448.

CENTER FOR CULTURAL INTERCHANGE–GERMANY LANGUAGE SCHOOL

Center for Cultural Interchange
Germany

General Information Coed residential academic program and cultural program established in 1985. High school or college credit may be earned.

Program Focus Cultural immersion and language study.
Academics German language/literature.
Special Interest Areas Homestays.
Trips Cultural, day.
Program Information 1–50 sessions per year. Session length: 14–90 days in January, February, March, April, May, June, July, August, September, October, November, December. Ages: 17+. Boarding program cost: $2350–$2890. Financial aid available.
Application Deadline Continuous.
Contact Ms. Juliet Jones, Outbound Programs Director, 746 North LaSalle Drive, Chicago, Illinois 60610-3617. Phone: 866-684-9675. Fax: 312-944-2644. E-mail: info@cci-exchange.com. **URL** www.cci-exchange.com

For more information, see page 448.

EF INTERNATIONAL LANGUAGE SCHOOL–MUNICH

EF International Language Schools
Herzogstrasse 36
Munich 80803
Germany

General Information Coed travel academic program and cultural program established in 1987. High school or college credit may be earned.
Program Focus Language and cultural immersion.
Academics German (Advanced Placement), German language/literature.
Special Interest Areas Field trips (arts and culture), homestays, touring.
Sports Sports (general).
Wilderness/Outdoors Wilderness/outdoors (general).
Trips Cultural, day, overnight.
Program Information 2–52 sessions per year. Session length: 2–52 weeks in January, February, March, April, May, June, July, August, September, October, November, December. Ages: 16+. 100–150 participants per session. Application fee: $145. Financial aid available. Call for costs.
Application Deadline Continuous.
Contact Ms. Margaret Kelly, Director of Admissions, One Education Street, Cambridge, Massachusetts 02141. Phone: 800-992-1892. Fax: 800-590-1125. E-mail: ils@ef.com. **URL** www.ef.com

For more information, see page 478.

THE EXPERIMENT IN INTERNATIONAL LIVING–GERMANY, FOUR-WEEK HOMESTAY, TRAVEL, COMMUNITY SERVICE

The Experiment in International Living
Germany

General Information Coed travel community service program, cultural program, and adventure program established in 1932. Specific services available for the hearing impaired and visually impaired.
Program Focus International youth travel, homestay.
Academics German language/literature.
Special Interest Areas Community service, homestays, touring.
Wilderness/Outdoors Hiking.
Trips Cultural, day, overnight.
Program Information 1 session per year. Session length: 4 weeks in June, July. Ages: 14–19. 10–15 participants per session. Cost: $5700. Application fee: $75. Financial aid available. Airfare included.
Application Deadline May 1.
Contact Mr. Chris Frantz, Deputy Director, EIL–World Learning, PO Box 676, Kipling Road, Brattleboro, Vermont 05302-0676. Phone: 800-345-2929. Fax: 802-258-3428. E-mail: eil@worldlearning.org.
URL www.usexperiment.org
For more information, see page 492.

VOLUNTEERS FOR PEACE INTERNATIONAL VOLUNTARY SERVICE–GERMANY

Volunteers for Peace International Voluntary Service
Berlin
Germany

General Information Coed residential community service program established in 1981. Specific services available for the hearing impaired and physically challenged. College credit may be earned.
Program Focus International voluntary service projects or work camps.
Academics History, intercultural studies, peace education.
Arts Film, theater/drama.
Special Interest Areas Community service, construction, work camp programs.
Sports Swimming.
Wilderness/Outdoors Hiking.
Trips Cultural, day, overnight.
Program Information 100 sessions per year. Session

length: 2–3 weeks in May, June, July, August, September, October. Ages: 16+. 12–20 participants per session. Boarding program cost: $500–$800.
Application Deadline Continuous.
Contact Peter Coldwell, Director, 1034 Tiffany Road, Belmont, Vermont 05730. Phone: 802-259-2759. Fax: 802-259-2922. E-mail: vfp@vfp.org.
URL www.vfp.org

GHANA

AFS-USA–TEAM MISSION–GHANA

AFS-USA
Ghana

General Information Coed residential community service program and cultural program established in 1995. High school credit may be earned.
Program Focus Learn about Ghanaian history, tribal culture and modern life. Sightsee, visit a tribal village, take language lessons and stay with a host family. Participants may also work in a Ghanaian foster home or be involved with a community service program with an adult team leader.
Academics Intercultural studies.
Arts Dance (folk), music.
Special Interest Areas Community service, cross-cultural education, homestays.
Trips Cultural, day, overnight.
Program Information 1 session per year. Session length: 30–45 days in June, July. Ages: 15–18. Boarding program cost: $6000. Application fee: $75. Financial aid available. International airfare and volunteer homestay support included.
Application Deadline Continuous.
Contact Manager, AFS Info Center, 506 Southwest 6th Avenue, 2nd Floor, Portland, Oregon 97204. Phone: 800-AFS-INFO. Fax: 503-299-0753. E-mail: afsinfo@afs.org.
URL www.afs.org/usa
For more information, see page 408.

THE EXPERIMENT IN INTERNATIONAL LIVING–GHANA HOMESTAY

The Experiment in International Living
Ghana

General Information Coed travel community service program and cultural program established in 1932.
Program Focus International youth travel, homestay, community service.
Academics Language study.
Special Interest Areas Community service, homestays, touring.
Wilderness/Outdoors Hiking.
Trips Cultural, day, overnight.
Program Information 1 session per year. Session

The Experiment in International Living–Ghana Homestay (continued)

length: 5 weeks in June, July, August. Ages: 14–19. 10–15 participants per session. Cost: $5950. Financial aid available. Airfare included.
Application Deadline May 1.
Contact Annie Thompson, Enrollment Director, Summer Abroad, Kipling Road, PO Box 676, Brattleboro, Vermont 05302-0676. Phone: 800-345-2929. Fax: 802-258-3428. E-mail: eil@worldlearning.org.
URL www.usexperiment.org
For more information, see page 492.

GLOBAL LEADERSHIP ADVENTURES–GHANA: COMMUNITY SERVICE AND LEADERSHIP

Global Leadership Adventures
Ghana

General Information Coed travel academic program, community service program, and cultural program established in 2004. High school credit may be earned.
Program Focus Learning about a country and its culture through community service, classes and adventure.
Academics Spanish language/literature, intercultural studies, social studies.
Special Interest Areas Community service, leadership training.
Wilderness/Outdoors Hiking.
Trips Cultural, day.
Program Information 1–2 sessions per year. Session length: 3 weeks in June, July, August. Ages: 15–18. 40–60 participants per session. Cost: $4395–$4595. Financial aid available.
Application Deadline Continuous.
Contact Mr. Andrew Motiwalla, Executive Director, 2633 Lincoln Boulevard, #427, Santa Monica, California 90405. Phone: 888-358-4321. Fax: 866-612-3697. E-mail: info@globalleadershipadventures.com.
URL www.globalleadershipadventures.com/main/home.asp
For more information, see page 504.

GREECE

AAVE–SAIL DIVE GREECE

AAVE–Journeys That Matter
Greece

General Information Coed travel outdoor program, cultural program, and adventure program established in 1976. Accredited by American Camping Association.
Program Focus Sail and scuba diving certification.
Special Interest Areas Leadership training, team building, touring.
Sports Boating, sailing, scuba diving, snorkeling.
Wilderness/Outdoors Orienteering.
Trips Cultural, day, overnight.
Program Information 2–4 sessions per year. Session length: 18 days in June, July, August. Ages: 14–18. 15 participants per session. Cost: $5288. Financial aid available.
Application Deadline Continuous.
Jobs Positions for college students 21 and older.
Contact Mr. Abbott Wallis, Owner, 2308 Fossil Trace Drive, Golden, Colorado 80401. Phone: 800-222-3595. Fax: 303-526-0885. E-mail: info@aave.com.
URL www.aave.com
For more information, see page 394.

UNIVERSITY OF CHICAGO–THE TRAVELING ACADEMY

University of Chicago
Spetses
Greece

General Information Coed travel academic program and cultural program established in 1999. Formal opportunities for the academically talented. College credit may be earned.
Program Focus Interdisciplinary civilization studies.
Academics French language/literature, Greek language/literature, anthropology, archaeology, architecture, art history/appreciation, classical languages/literatures, geography, history, humanities, intercultural studies, philosophy, religion, social studies, writing.
Trips Cultural, day.
Program Information 1 session per year. Session length: 3 weeks in July. Ages: 15–18. 10–15 participants per session. Cost: $7101. Application fee: $40–$55. Financial aid available. Airfare from Chicago to Athens included.
Application Deadline April 15.
Contact Ms. Sarah Lopez, Summer Session Office Administrative Assistant, Graham School of General Studies, The University of Chicago, 1427 East 60th Street, Chicago, Illinois 60637. Phone: 773-834-3792. Fax: 773-834-0549. E-mail: slopez@uchicago.edu.
URL summer.uchicago.edu/
For more information, see page 676.

GUADELOUPE

ACADEMIC TREKS–French Immersion in the French West Indies

Academic Treks, the academic adventure and community service division of Broadreach
Guadeloupe

General Information Coed travel academic program, community service program, and adventure program established in 1992. High school or college credit may be earned.
Program Focus Academic adventure and community service program focusing on French language immersion, cultural exchange, hiking, island exploration, water sports, college credit.
Academics French (Advanced Placement), French language/literature, academics (general), area studies, intercultural studies.
Arts Dance (folk).
Special Interest Areas Community service, cross-cultural education, culinary arts, homestays, leadership training.
Sports Sailing, sea kayaking, snorkeling, surfing, swimming, waterskiing.
Wilderness/Outdoors Hiking, ocean expeditions, wilderness camping, zip line.
Trips Cultural, day, overnight.
Program Information 2 sessions per year. Session length: 3 weeks in June, July, August. Ages: 15–19. 10–12 participants per session. Cost: $4680. Financial aid available.
Application Deadline Continuous.
Contact Carlton Goldthwaite, Director, 806 McCulloch Street, Suite 102, Raleigh, North Carolina 27603. Phone: 888-833-1907 Fax: 919-833-2129. E-mail: info@academictreks.com.
URL www.academictreks.com
For more information, see page 432.

VISIONS–GUADELOUPE

Visions
Guadeloupe

General Information Coed travel outdoor program, community service program, and cultural program established in 1989. High school credit may be earned.
Program Focus Community service, cross-cultural experience, and outdoor adventure activities, language immersion.
Academics French language/literature, intercultural studies, language study.
Arts Carpentry, painting.
Special Interest Areas Community service, construction, cross-cultural education, field research/expeditions, field trips (arts and culture), leadership training, nature study.
Sports Scuba diving, snorkeling, swimming.
Wilderness/Outdoors Backpacking, hiking.
Trips Cultural, day, overnight.

Program Information 1 session per year. Session length: 4 weeks in June, July. Ages: 14–18. 20–25 participants per session. Cost: $3200–$4900. Financial aid available.
Application Deadline Continuous.
Jobs Positions for college students 22 and older.
Contact Joanne Pinaire, Director, PO Box 220, Newport, Pennsylvania 17074. Phone: 717-567-7313. Fax: 717-567-7853. E-mail: info@visionsserviceadventures.com.
URL www.visionsserviceadventures.com
For more information, see page 694.

HONDURAS

BROADREACH Honduras Eco-Adventure

Broadreach
mainland and islands of Roatan and Utila
Honduras

General Information Coed travel academic program, outdoor program, wilderness program, and adventure program established in 1992.
Program Focus Coed program focusing on adventure travel, marine biology, scuba diving, dolphin and whale shark studies, cultural exploration whitewater rafting, and rainforest ecology.
Academics Botany, ecology, environmental science, marine studies, oceanography.
Arts Photography.
Special Interest Areas Mayan studies, community service, conservation projects, field research/expeditions, nature study.
Sports Boating, horseback riding, scuba diving, snorkeling, waterskiing, windsurfing.
Wilderness/Outdoors Backpacking, canoe trips, hiking, outdoor adventure, rafting, white-water trips, wilderness camping, wilderness/outdoors (general).
Trips Cultural.
Program Information 2 sessions per year. Session length: 3 weeks in June, July, August. Ages: 15–19. 12–14 participants per session. Cost: $4180.
Application Deadline Continuous.

BROADREACH *Honduras Eco-Adventure (continued)*

Contact Carlton Goldthwaite, Director, 806 McCulloch Street, Suite 102, Raleigh, North Carolina 27603. Phone: 888-833-1907. Fax: 919-833-2129. E-mail: info@gobroadreach.com.
URL www.gobroadreach.com

For more information, see page 432.

HUNGARY

AFS-USA–Homestay Plus–Hungary

AFS-USA
Hungary

General Information Coed residential arts program and cultural program established in 1995.
Program Focus Traditional crafts from local artisans, multiple day trips to cultural and historical sites.
Academics Hungarian language/literature, history, intercultural studies.
Arts Art (folk), arts and crafts (general), dance (folk), fabric arts, jewelry making, leather working, music, pottery, weaving, woodworking.
Special Interest Areas Cross-cultural education, homestays.
Wilderness/Outdoors Hiking.
Trips Cultural, day, overnight.
Program Information 1 session per year. Session length: 30–45 days in July. Ages: 15–19. Boarding program cost: $4000–$6000. Application fee: $75. Financial aid available. International airfare and volunteer homestay support included.
Application Deadline Continuous.
Contact Manager, AFS Info Center, 506 Southwest 6th Avenue, 2nd Floor, Portland, Oregon 97204. Phone: 800-AFS-INFO. Fax: 503-299-0753. E-mail: afsinfo@afs.org.
URL www.afs.org/usa

For more information, see page 408.

ICELAND

World Horizons International–Iceland

World Horizons International
Reykjavik
Iceland

General Information Coed residential outdoor program, community service program, and cultural program established in 2001.
Program Focus Reforestation project with the government of Iceland.

Academics Environmental science.
Special Interest Areas Community service, conservation projects, cross-cultural education, work camp programs.
Sports Horseback riding.
Wilderness/Outdoors Hiking.
Trips Cultural, day, overnight.
Program Information 1 session per year. Session length: 4 weeks in June, July, August. Ages: 13+. 10–12 participants per session. Boarding program cost: $5250–$5600. Application fee: $175. Financial aid available. Airfare from New York included.
Application Deadline Continuous.
Jobs Positions for college students 21 and older.
Contact Mr. Stuart L. Rabinowitz, Executive Director, PO Box 662, Bethlehem, Connecticut 06751. Phone: 800-262-5874. Fax: 203-266-6227. E-mail: worldhorizons@att.net.
URL www.world-horizons.com

For more information, see page 714.

INDIA

Global Leadership Adventures–India: Community Service and Leadership

Global Leadership Adventures
India

General Information Coed travel academic program, community service program, and cultural program established in 2004. High school credit may be earned.
Program Focus Learning about a country and its' culture through community service, classes and adventure.
Academics Spanish language/literature, intercultural studies, social studies.
Special Interest Areas Community service, leadership training.
Wilderness/Outdoors Hiking.
Trips Cultural, day.
Program Information 1–2 sessions per year. Session length: 3 weeks in June, July, August. Ages: 15–18. 40–60 participants per session. Cost: $4395–$4595. Financial aid available.
Application Deadline Continuous.
Contact Mr. Andrew Motiwalla, Executive Director, 2633 Lincoln Boulevard, #427, Santa Monica, California 90405. Phone: 888-358-4321. Fax: 866-612-3697. E-mail: info@globalleadershipadventures.com.
URL www.globalleadershipadventures.com/main/home.asp

For more information, see page 504.

PUTNEY STUDENT TRAVEL–COMMUNITY SERVICE–INDIA

Putney Student Travel
Rajasthan
India

General Information Coed residential community service program and cultural program established in 1951.
Program Focus Community service, cultural exchange, and weekend excursions from a base in a small, rural village.
Academics Intercultural studies.
Special Interest Areas Community service, construction, team building.
Wilderness/Outdoors Hiking, pack animal trips.
Trips Cultural, day, overnight.
Program Information 1 session per year. Session length: 28–30 days in June, July. Ages: 14–18. 16 participants per session. Boarding program cost: $6490. Financial aid available.
Application Deadline Continuous.
Jobs Positions for college students 21 and older.
Contact Jeffrey Shumlin, Admissions Director, 345 Hickory Ridge Road, Putney, Vermont 05346. Phone: 802-387-5000. Fax: 802-387-4276. E-mail: info@goputney.com
URL www.goputney.com
For more information, see page 598.

PUTNEY STUDENT TRAVEL–GLOBAL ACTION–INDIA

Putney Student Travel
India

General Information Coed residential cultural program established in 1951.

Putney Student Travel–Global Action–India

Program Focus Students spend three weeks pursuing research in relation to community and building and sustainable development.
Academics Intercultural studies.

Special Interest Areas Cross-cultural education, field research/expeditions.
Trips Cultural, day, overnight.
Program Information 1 session per year. Session length: 25–32 days in June, July, August. Ages: 15–18. 16 participants per session. Boarding program cost: $7390. Financial aid available.
Application Deadline Continuous.
Contact Jeffrey Shumlin, Admissions Director, 345 Hickory Ridge Road, Putney, Vermont 05346. Phone: 802-387-5000. Fax: 802-387-4276. E-mail: info@goputney.com.
URL www.goputney.com

For more information, see page 598.

RUSTIC PATHWAYS–THE BUDDHIST CARAVAN

Rustic Pathways
Ladakh
India

General Information Coed travel outdoor program, community service program, and cultural program established in 1998.
Special Interest Areas Community service, conservation projects, cross-cultural education, nature study, touring.
Wilderness/Outdoors Backpacking, hiking, wilderness camping.
Trips Cultural, day, shopping.
Program Information 2 sessions per year. Session length: 17 days in July, August. Ages: 16–18. 10–15 participants per session. Cost: $2695. Airfare not included.
Application Deadline Continuous.
Jobs Positions for college students 21 and older.
Contact Rustic Pathways, 4121 Erie Street, Willoughby, Ohio 44094. Phone: 800-321-4353. Fax: 440-975-9694. E-mail: rustic@rusticpathways.com.
URL www.rusticpathways.com

For more information, see page 612.

RUSTIC PATHWAYS–INDIAN HIMALAYA TRAVELER

Rustic Pathways
India

General Information Coed travel outdoor program and cultural program established in 2005.
Special Interest Areas Cross-cultural education, touring.
Sports Mountain boarding.
Wilderness/Outdoors Hiking, outdoor adventure, rafting, rock climbing.
Trips Cultural, day, overnight, shopping.
Program Information 2 sessions per year. Session

RUSTIC PATHWAYS–INDIAN HIMALAYA TRAVELER (continued)

length: 17 days in June, July. Ages: 16–18. 10–20 participants per session. Cost: $2195. Application fee: $100–$200. Financial aid available.
Application Deadline Continuous.
Jobs Positions for college students 21 and older.
Contact Rustic Pathways, 4121 Erie Street, Willoughby, Ohio 44094. Phone: 800-321-4353. Fax: 440-975-9694. E-mail: rustic@rusticpathways.com.
URL www.rusticpathways.com

For more information, see page 612.

RUSTIC PATHWAYS–SERVICE IN THE CLOUDS–INDIA

Rustic Pathways
India

General Information Coed residential community service program and cultural program established in 2005.
Special Interest Areas Community service, cross-cultural education, culinary arts, homestays, massage therapy training, meditation, touring.
Sports Yoga.
Wilderness/Outdoors Hiking.
Trips Cultural, day, overnight, shopping.
Program Information 2 sessions per year. Session length: 17 days in June, July. Ages: 16–18. 10–20 participants per session. Boarding program cost: $1995. Application fee: $100–$200. Financial aid available.
Application Deadline Continuous.
Jobs Positions for college students 21 and older.
Contact Rustic Pathways, 4121 Erie Street, Willoughby, Ohio 44094. Phone: 800-321-4353. Fax: 440-975-9694. E-mail: rustic@rusticpathways.com.
URL www.rusticpathways.com

For more information, see page 612.

STUDIES ABROAD FOR GLOBAL EDUCATION (SAGE), SUMMER SAGE PROGRAM

Studies Abroad for Global Education (SAGE), Summer SAGE Program
India

General Information Coed travel academic program, outdoor program, arts program, community service program, cultural program, and adventure program established in 2005. Formal opportunities for the academically talented and artistically talented.
Program Focus Study Indian art and culture, Hindi and Tamil languages, volunteer at a school or refugee camp, experience outdoor adventures in India.
Academics Hindi language, Tamil language, anthropology, area studies, art history/appreciation, ecology, environmental science, geology/earth science, government and politics, history, humanities, intercultural studies, international relations, music, peace education, religion, social studies.
Arts Arts and crafts (general), dance, music, painting, theater/drama.
Special Interest Areas Community service, conservation projects, cross-cultural education, culinary arts, homestays, touring.
Sports Martial arts, yoga.
Wilderness/Outdoors Backpacking, hiking, outdoor adventure, wilderness camping.
Trips Cultural, day, overnight, shopping.
Program Information 2–3 sessions per year. Session length: 23 days in June, July. Ages: 14–18. 10–15 participants per session. Cost: $4000; including airfare. Application fee: $50.
Application Deadline March 1.
Jobs Positions for college students 25 and older.
Contact Serena Leland, Director, Project Manager, Summer SAGE, SAGE Program, 19 Old Town Square, Suite 238, Fort Collins, Colorado 80524. Phone: 888-997-7243. Fax: 970-482-0251. E-mail: info@sageprogram.org.
URL www.sageprogram.org

WORLD HORIZONS INTERNATIONAL–TAPOVAN, LAXMAN JHULA, INDIA

World Horizons International
Tapovan, Laxman Jhula
India

General Information Coed residential community service program and cultural program established in 2007.
Program Focus Community service, cross cultural immersion, working with children at an orphanage.
Special Interest Areas Childcare, community service, cross-cultural education.
Wilderness/Outdoors Hiking.
Trips Cultural, day, overnight.
Program Information 1 session per year. Session length: 29 days in June, July. Ages: 14–18. 10–12 participants per session. Boarding program cost: $5295–

$5595. Application fee: $175. Financial aid available. Airfare from New York is included.
Application Deadline Continuous.
Jobs Positions for college students 21 and older.
Contact Mr. Stuart L. Rabinowitz, Executive Director, PO Box 662, Bethlehem, Connecticut 06751. Phone: 800-262-5874. Fax: 203-266-6227. E-mail: worldhorizons@att.net.
URL www.world-horizons.com

For more information, see page 714.

INDONESIA

PUTNEY STUDENT TRAVEL–COMMUNITY SERVICE–NUSA PENIDA AND BALI
Putney Student Travel
Indonesia

General Information Coed residential community service program established in 1951.
Program Focus Community service, cultural exchange, and excursions (including to Bali) from a base in a small, rural community on the remote, unspoiled island of Nusa Penida.
Academics Intercultural studies.
Special Interest Areas Community service, construction, team building.
Sports Scuba diving, snorkeling, swimming.
Wilderness/Outdoors Bicycle trips, hiking.
Trips Cultural, day, overnight.
Program Information 1 session per year. Session length: 30–32 days in July, August. Ages: 14–18. 16 participants per session. Boarding program cost: $6490. Financial aid available.
Application Deadline Continuous.
Jobs Positions for college students 21 and older.
Contact Jeffrey Shumlin, Admissions Director, 345 Hickory Ridge Road, Putney, Vermont 05346. Phone: 802-387-5000. Fax: 802-387-4276. E-mail: info@goputney.com.
URL www.goputney.com

For more information, see page 598.

IRELAND

CENTER FOR CULTURAL INTERCHANGE–IRELAND HIGH SCHOOL ABROAD
Center for Cultural Interchange
Ireland

General Information Coed residential academic program and cultural program established in 1985. High school credit may be earned.
Program Focus Cultural immersion, high school in Ireland.
Academics Irish studies, academics (general).
Special Interest Areas Cross-cultural education, homestays.
Trips Cultural, day.
Program Information 3 sessions per year. Session length: 90–300 days in January, February, March, April, May, June, July, August, September, October, November, December. Ages: 15–18. Boarding program cost: $6500–$11,300. Financial aid available. Early Bird discount.
Application Deadline Continuous.
Contact Ms. Juliet Jones, Outbound Programs Director, 746 North LaSalle Drive, Chicago, Illinois 60610-3617. Phone: 866-684-9675. Fax: 312-944-2644. E-mail: info@cci-exchange.com.
URL www.cci-exchange.com

For more information, see page 448.

CENTER FOR CULTURAL INTERCHANGE–IRELAND INDEPENDENT HOMESTAY PROGRAM
Center for Cultural Interchange
Ireland

General Information Coed residential cultural program established in 1985.
Program Focus Cultural immersion; independent homestay.
Academics Irish studies, independent study.
Special Interest Areas Homestays.
Trips Cultural, day.
Program Information Session length: 7–90 days in January, February, March, April, May, June, July, August, September, October, November, December. Ages: 17+. Boarding program cost: $900–$1790. Financial aid available.
Application Deadline Continuous.
Contact Ms. Juliet Jones, Outbound Programs Director, 746 North LaSalle Drive, Chicago, Illinois 60610-3617. Phone: 866-684-9675. Fax: 312-944-2644. E-mail: info@cci-exchange.com.
URL www.cci-exchange.com

For more information, see page 448.

GLOBAL WORKS–CULTURAL EXCHANGE AND SERVICE–IRELAND– 4 WEEKS

GLOBAL WORKS
Ireland

General Information Coed travel community service program, cultural program, and adventure program established in 1988. High school credit may be earned.

GLOBAL WORKS–Cultural Exchange and Service–Ireland-4 weeks

Program Focus Environmental and community service and cultural exchange.
Academics Intercultural studies, peace education.
Arts Arts and crafts (general), creative writing, dance, music, theater/drama.
Special Interest Areas Community service, conservation projects, construction, cross-cultural education, field trips (arts and culture).
Sports Gaelic football, ropes course, rugby, sea kayaking, sports (general), ultimate frisbee, volleyball.
Wilderness/Outdoors Hiking, outdoor adventure.
Trips Cultural, day, overnight.
Program Information 1 session per year. Session length: 27 days in June, July. Ages: 14–17. 16–18 participants per session. Cost: $4995. Application fee: $100. Financial aid available. Airfare not included.
Application Deadline Continuous.
Jobs Positions for college students 23 and older.

Contact Mr. Erik Werner, Director, 1113 South Allen Street, State College, Pennsylvania 16801. Phone: 814-867-7000. Fax: 814-867-2717. E-mail: info@globalworksinc.com.
URL www.globalworksinc.com
For more information, see page 506.

TISCH SCHOOL OF THE ARTS– INTERNATIONAL HIGH SCHOOL PROGRAM–DUBLIN

New York University, Tisch School of the Arts
Dublin
Ireland

General Information Coed residential academic program, arts program, and cultural program established in 2001. Formal opportunities for the artistically talented. College credit may be earned.
Program Focus Filmmaking, drama/theater, writing, art studies.
Academics Irish language/literature, Irish studies, intercultural studies.
Arts Acting, creative writing, film, music, theater/drama.
Trips Cultural, day.
Program Information 1 session per year. Session length: 28–30 days in July, August. Ages: 15+. 8–20 participants per session. Boarding program cost: $7900–$9200. Application fee: $60. Financial aid available.
Application Deadline February 1.
Contact Mariangela Lardaro, Assistant Director of Recruitment, Special Programs, 721 Broadway, 12th Floor, New York, New York 10003. Phone: 212-998-1517. Fax: 212-995-4578. E-mail: tisch.special.info@nyu.edu.
URL specialprograms.tisch.nyu.edu
For more information, see page 566.

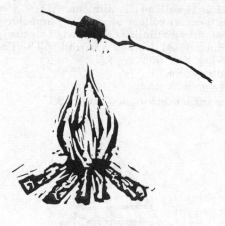

ITALY

ACADEMIC STUDY ASSOCIATES–FLORENCE

Academic Study Associates, Inc. (ASA)
Florence
Italy

General Information Coed residential academic program and cultural program established in 2004. Formal opportunities for the academically talented and artistically talented. High school credit may be earned.
Program Focus Academic enrichment, study abroad in the Arts, Humanities, cultural studies. Daily activities and weekend excursions.
Academics Italian language/literature, academics (general), archaeology, architecture, art (Advanced Placement), art history/appreciation, government and politics, history, humanities, intercultural studies, precollege program, writing.
Arts Arts and crafts (general), creative writing, drawing, painting, photography.
Special Interest Areas Culinary arts, touring.
Sports Aerobics, basketball, soccer, swimming, tennis, volleyball.
Trips Cultural, day, overnight, shopping.
Program Information 1 session per year. Session length: 30 days in July. Ages: 15–18. 50–60 participants per session. Boarding program cost: $6695. Financial aid available.
Application Deadline Continuous.
Jobs Positions for college students 21 and older.
Contact Mr. David Evans, Vice President, 375 West Broadway, Suite 200, New York, New York 10012. Phone: 212-796-8340. Fax: 212-334-4934. E-mail: summer@asaprograms.com.
URL www.asaprograms.com

For more information, see page 398.

AFS-USA–HOMESTAY PLUS–ITALY

AFS-USA
Italy

General Information Coed residential cultural program.
Program Focus Italian language and culture camp, with additional home-stay experience and day trips.
Academics Italian language/literature.
Arts Arts and crafts (general), music.
Special Interest Areas Culinary arts, homestays, touring.
Trips Cultural, day.
Program Information 1 session per year. Session length: 30–45 days in June, July, August. Ages: 15–18. Boarding program cost: $6100. Application fee: $75. Financial aid available. International airfare and volunteer homestay support included.
Application Deadline Continuous.

Contact Manager, AFS Info Center, 506 Southwest 6th Avenue, 2nd Floor, Portland, Oregon 97204. Phone: 800-AFS-INFO. Fax: 503-299-0753. E-mail: afsinfo@afs.org.
URL www.afs.org/usa

For more information, see page 408.

CENTER FOR CULTURAL INTERCHANGE– ITALY HIGH SCHOOL ABROAD

Center for Cultural Interchange
Italy

General Information Coed residential academic program and cultural program established in 1985. High school credit may be earned.
Program Focus High school in Italy, cultural immersion.
Academics Italian language/literature, academics (general).
Special Interest Areas Cross-cultural education, homestays.
Trips Cultural, day, overnight.
Program Information 2 sessions per year. Session length: 90–300 days in January, February, March, April, May, June, July, August, September, October, November, December. Ages: 15–18. Boarding program cost: $5900–$7500. Financial aid available.
Application Deadline Continuous.
Contact Ms. Juliet Jones, Outbound Programs Director, 746 North LaSalle Drive, Chicago, Illinois 60610-3617. Phone: 866-684-9675. Fax: 312-944-2644. E-mail: info@cci-exchange.com.
URL www.cci-exchange.com

For more information, see page 448.

CENTER FOR CULTURAL INTERCHANGE–ITALY LANGUAGE SCHOOL

Center for Cultural Interchange
Florence
Italy

General Information Coed residential academic program and cultural program established in 1985. High school or college credit may be earned.

Center for Cultural Interchange–Italy Language School

Program Focus Cultural immersion and language study.
Academics Italian language/literature.
Special Interest Areas Homestays.
Trips Cultural, day.
Program Information Session length: 3–4 weeks in January, February, March, April, May, June, July, August, September, October, November, December. Ages: 17+. Boarding program cost: $2150–$2590. Financial aid available.
Application Deadline Continuous.
Contact Ms. Juliet Jones, Outbound Programs Director, 746 North LaSalle Drive, Chicago, Illinois 60610-3617. Phone: 866-684-9675. Fax: 312-944-2644. E-mail: info@cci-exchange.com.
URL www.cci-exchange.com

For more information, see page 448.

EF INTERNATIONAL LANGUAGE SCHOOL–ROME

EF International Language Schools
EF International School of Italian in Rome (DILIT)
Via Marghera, 22
Rome 00105
Italy

General Information Coed travel academic program and cultural program established in 1974. High school or college credit may be earned.
Program Focus Language and cultural immersion.
Academics Italian language/literature.
Special Interest Areas Culinary arts, field trips (arts and culture), homestays, touring.
Trips Cultural, day, overnight.
Program Information 2–52 sessions per year. Session length: 2–52 weeks in January, February, March, April, May, June, July, August, September, October, November, December. Ages: 16+. 200–250 participants per session. Application fee: $145. Financial aid available. Call for costs.
Application Deadline Continuous.
Contact Ms. Margaret Kelly, Director of Admissions, One Education Street, Cambridge, Massachusetts 02141. Phone: 800-992-1892. Fax: 800-590-1125. E-mail: ils@ef.com.
URL www.ef.com

For more information, see page 478.

THE EXPERIMENT IN INTERNATIONAL LIVING–ITALY BIODIVERSITY, COOKING, AND CULTURE

The Experiment in International Living
Italy

General Information Coed travel cultural program established in 1932.
Program Focus International youth travel, homestay, Italian language, travel.
Academics Italian language/literature, global issues, natural resource management.
Special Interest Areas Culinary arts, field trips (arts and culture), homestays, touring.
Sports Boating.
Trips Cultural, day, overnight.
Program Information 1 session per year. Session length: 5 weeks in June, July. Ages: 14–19. 10–15 participants per session. Cost: $6200. Financial aid available. Airfare included.
Application Deadline May 1.
Contact Annie Thompson, Enrollment Director, Summer Abroad, Kipling Road, PO Box 676, Brattleboro, Vermont 05302-0676. Phone: 800-345-2929. Fax: 802-258-3428. E-mail: eil@worldlearning.org.
URL www.usexperiment.org

For more information, see page 492.

THE EXPERIMENT IN INTERNATIONAL LIVING–ITALY HOMESTAY, LANGUAGE, CULTURE, AND TRAVEL

The Experiment in International Living
Italy

General Information Coed travel cultural program established in 1932.
Program Focus International youth travel, homestay, Italian language, travel.
Academics Italian language/literature.
Special Interest Areas Homestays, touring.
Sports Boating.
Trips Cultural, day, overnight.
Program Information 1 session per year. Session length: 5 weeks in June, July, August. Ages: 14–19. 10–15 participants per session. Cost: $6100. Financial aid available. Airfare included.
Application Deadline May 1.
Contact Annie Thompson, Enrollment Director, Summer Abroad, Kipling Road, PO Box 676, Brattleboro, Vermont 05302-0676. Phone: 800-345-2929. Fax: 802-258-3428. E-mail: eil@worldlearning.org.
URL www.usexperiment.org

For more information, see page 492.

HUMANITIES SPRING IN ASSISI

Humanities Spring in Assisi
Santa Maria di Lignano, 2
Assisi, (PG) 06081
Italy

General Information Coed travel academic program, arts program, and cultural program established in 1991. Formal opportunities for the academically talented and artistically talented. High school credit may be earned.

Humanities Spring in Assisi

Program Focus Teaches students to engage individually and constructively with great works of art and literature, from classical to contemporary.

Academics English language/literature, Greek language/literature, Italian language/literature, Latin language, archaeology, architecture, art history/appreciation, botany, classical languages/literatures, humanities, writing.
Arts Arts and crafts (general), creative writing, drawing, painting, photography.
Special Interest Areas Culinary arts, gardening, nature study.
Sports Bicycling, swimming.
Trips Cultural, day, overnight.
Program Information 1 session per year. Session length: 28–31 days in June, July. Ages: 14+. 10–12 participants per session. Cost: $2850–$3200. Application fee: $25. Financial aid available. Includes trips to Venice, Pompeii, Florence, Paestum, Ravenna, Spoleto Festival, and Umbria Jazz.
Application Deadline Continuous.
Jobs Positions for high school students 16 and older and college students.
Contact Ms. Jane R. Oliensis, Director, main address above. Phone: 39-075-802400. Fax: 39-075-802400. E-mail: info@humanitiesspring.com.
URL www.humanitiesspring.com

For more information, see page 516.

SPOLETO STUDY ABROAD

Spoleto Study Abroad
Spoletino Valley
Spoleto
Italy

General Information Coed residential academic program, arts program, and cultural program established in 1997. Formal opportunities for the academically talented and artistically talented.

Spoleto Study Abroad

Program Focus An intensive interdisciplinary program for high school students interested in visual arts, photography, film studies, dance, and vocal music in the Spoleto Valley of Central Italy.
Academics Italian language/literature, architecture, art (Advanced Placement), art history/appreciation, history, humanities, music, writing.
Arts Acting, chorus, creative writing, dance, drawing, film, music, music (chamber), music (classical), music (ensemble), music (instrumental), music (jazz), music (orchestral), music (vocal), painting, performing arts, photography, visual arts.
Special Interest Areas Touring.
Sports Soccer, swimming, tennis.
Wilderness/Outdoors Hiking.
Trips Cultural, day.
Program Information 1–2 sessions per year. Session length: 25–27 days in June, July, August. Ages: 15–19. 50–70 participants per session. Boarding program cost: $5550. Application fee: $75. Participants housed in renovated 15th-century Italian convents.
Application Deadline February 1.
Jobs Positions for college students 21 and older.

Contact Nancy Langston, Marketing Director, PO Box 13389, Charleston, South Carolina 29422-3389. Phone: 843-822-1248. E-mail: spoleto@mindspring.com.
URL www.spoletostudyabroad.com
For more information, see page 642.

SUMMER ADVANTAGE STUDY ABROAD–ROME, ITALY

American Institute for Foreign Study (AIFS)
DILIT International House
Via Marghera, 22
Rome 00185
Italy

General Information Coed travel academic program and cultural program established in 2002. College credit may be earned.
Program Focus Study abroad for college credit.
Academics Italian language/literature, architecture, art history/appreciation, history.
Arts Photography, studio arts.
Trips Cultural, day, overnight, shopping.
Program Information 1 session per year. Session length: 29–34 days in June, July. Ages: 16–18. 35–45 participants per session. Cost: $6175. Application fee: $95.
Application Deadline April 15.
Contact Mrs. Amy Van Stone, Director of Admissions, Summer Advantage, 9 West Broad Street, River Plaza, Stamford, Connecticut 06902. Phone: 800-913-7151. Fax: 203-399-5463. E-mail: summeradvantage@aifs.com.
URL www.summeradvantage.com
For more information, see page 410.

TASIS TUSCAN ACADEMY OF ART AND CULTURE

TASIS The American School in Switzerland
Capitignano-San Cresci
Borgo San Lorenzo
Italy

General Information Coed residential arts program and cultural program established in 2002.
Program Focus Art and art history.
Academics Art history/appreciation.
Arts Arts, arts and crafts (general), drawing, painting.
Sports Basketball, swimming, tennis.
Wilderness/Outdoors Hiking.
Trips Cultural, day.
Program Information 1 session per year. Session length: 3 weeks in July, August. Ages: 15–19. 25 participants per session. Boarding program cost: $3900. Offered every two years.
Application Deadline Continuous.

Contact Mrs. Toni Soule, US TASIS Representative, 1640 Wisconsin Avenue, NW, Washington, District of Columbia 20007. Phone: 202-965-5800. Fax: 202-965-5816. E-mail: usadmissions@tasis.com.
URL www.tasis.com
For more information, see page 670.

VOLUNTEERS FOR PEACE INTERNATIONAL VOLUNTARY SERVICE–ITALY

Volunteers for Peace International Voluntary Service
Rome
Italy

General Information Coed residential community service program established in 1999. Specific services available for the hearing impaired and physically challenged. College credit may be earned.
Program Focus International voluntary service projects or work camps.
Academics Intercultural studies, peace education.
Special Interest Areas Community service, work camp programs.
Trips Cultural, day, overnight.
Program Information 4 sessions per year. Session length: 2–3 weeks in July, August, September. Ages: 15+. 12–20 participants per session. Boarding program cost: $500–$800.
Application Deadline Continuous.
Contact Peter Coldwell, Director, 1034 Tiffany Road, Belmont, Vermont 05730. Phone: 802-259-2759. Fax: 802-259-2922. E-mail: vfp@vfp.org.
URL www.vfp.org

WESTCOAST CONNECTION–AUTHENTIC ITALY

Westcoast Connection
Italy

General Information Coed travel cultural program established in 1982. Accredited by Ontario Camping Association.

Program Focus A two-week trip capturing the best highlights and experiences in Italy.
Special Interest Areas Culinary arts, touring.
Sports Swimming.
Program Information 1–2 sessions per year. Session length: 2 weeks in July, August. Ages: 16–18. 20–30 participants per session. Cost: $4199.
Application Deadline Continuous.
Jobs Positions for college students 21 and older.
Contact Mr. Mark Segal, Director, 154 East Boston Post Road, Mamaroneck, New York 10543. Phone: 800-767-0227. Fax: 914-835-0798. E-mail: usa@westcoastconnection.com.
URL www.westcoastconnection.com
For more information, see page 702.

WORLD HORIZONS INTERNATIONAL– ROME, ITALY

World Horizons International
Rome
Italy

General Information Coed residential community service program and cultural program established in 2007.
Program Focus Community service, cross cultural immersion, working with children and handicapped individuals.
Special Interest Areas Childcare, community service, cross-cultural education.
Wilderness/Outdoors Hiking.
Trips Cultural, day, overnight.
Program Information 1 session per year. Session length: 29 days in July, August. Ages: 14–18. 10–12 participants per session. Boarding program cost: $4995–$5495. Application fee: $175. Financial aid available. Airfare from New York is included.
Application Deadline Continuous.
Jobs Positions for college students 21 and older.
Contact Mr. Stuart L. Rabinowitz, Executive Director, PO Box 662, Bethlehem, Connecticut 06751. Phone: 800-262-5874. Fax: 203-266-6227. E-mail: worldhorizons@att.net.
URL www.world-horizons.com
For more information, see page 714.

JAPAN

AFS-USA–HOMESTAY LANGUAGE STUDY–JAPAN

AFS-USA
Japan

General Information Coed residential cultural program.

AFS-USA–Homestay Language Study–Japan (continued)

Program Focus Living with a host family and attending language school.

Academics Japanese language/literature.

Special Interest Areas Homestays.

Trips Cultural, day, overnight.

Program Information 1 session per year. Session length: 30–45 days in June, July, August. Ages: 15–18. Boarding program cost: $6100. Application fee: $75. Financial aid available. International airfare and volunteer homestay support included.

Application Deadline Continuous.

Contact Manager, AFS Info Center, 506 Southwest 6th Avenue, 2nd Floor, Portland, Oregon 97204. Phone: 800-AFS-INFO. Fax: 503-299-0753. E-mail: afsinfo@afs.org.

URL www.afs.org/usa

For more information, see page 408.

CENTER FOR CULTURAL INTERCHANGE– JAPAN HIGH SCHOOL ABROAD

Center for Cultural Interchange
Japan

General Information Coed residential academic program and cultural program established in 1985. High school credit may be earned.

Program Focus High school abroad, homestay program, cultural immersion.

Academics Japanese language/literature, academics (general), precollege program.

Special Interest Areas Cross-cultural education, homestays.

Trips Cultural, day.

Program Information 2 sessions per year. Session length: 150–300 days in January, February, March, April, May, June, July, August, September, October, November, December. Ages: 15–18. Boarding program cost: $4700–$5900. Financial aid available.

Application Deadline Continuous.

Contact Ms. Juliet Jones, Outbound Programs Director, 746 North LaSalle Drive, Chicago, Illinois 60610-3617. Phone: 866-684-9675. Fax: 312-944-2644. E-mail: info@cci-exchange.com.

URL www.cci-exchange.com

For more information, see page 448.

THE EXPERIMENT IN INTERNATIONAL LIVING–JAPAN HOMESTAY

The Experiment in International Living
Japan

General Information Coed travel cultural program established in 1932. Specific services available for the hearing impaired and visually impaired.

Program Focus International youth travel, homestay, Japanese language.

Academics Japanese language/literature.

Special Interest Areas Homestays, touring.

Trips Cultural, day, overnight.

Program Information 1 session per year. Session length: 4 weeks in June, July. Ages: 14–19. 10–15 participants per session. Cost: $5800. Application fee: $100. Financial aid available. Airfare included.

Application Deadline May 1.

Contact Annie Thompson, Enrollment Director, Summer Abroad, Kipling Road, PO Box 676, Brattleboro, Vermont 05302-0676. Phone: 800-345-2929. Fax: 802-258-3428. E-mail: eil@worldlearning.org.

URL www.usexperiment.org

For more information, see page 492.

LATVIA

AFS-USA–HOMESTAY LANGUAGE STUDY–LATVIA

AFS-USA
Latvia

General Information Coed residential academic program and cultural program.

Program Focus Living with a host family and studying Russian.

Academics Russian language/literature.

Special Interest Areas Homestays, touring.

Trips Cultural, day, overnight.

Program Information 1 session per year. Session length: 30–45 days in June, July. Ages: 15–18. Boarding program cost: $5000–$6000. Application fee: $75. Financial aid available. International airfare and volunteer homestay support included.

Application Deadline Continuous.

Contact Manager, AFS Info Center, 506 Southwest 6th Avenue, 2nd Floor, Portland, Oregon 97204. Phone: 800-AFS-INFO. Fax: 503-299-0753. E-mail: afsinfo@afs.org.

URL www.afs.org/usa

For more information, see page 408.

MADAGASCAR

PUTNEY STUDENT TRAVEL–GLOBAL AWARENESS–MADAGASCAR

Putney Student Travel
Madagascar

General Information Coed residential outdoor program and cultural program established in 1951.
Program Focus Students spend four weeks researching and working in relation to conservation of endangered flora and fauna and working with the community.
Academics Ecology.
Special Interest Areas Community service, conservation projects, cross-cultural education, field research/expeditions.
Trips Cultural, day, overnight.
Program Information 1 session per year. Session length: 33 days in July, August. Ages: 15–18. 16 participants per session. Boarding program cost: $7390. Financial aid available.
Application Deadline Continuous.
Contact Jeffrey Shumlin, Admissions Director, 345 Hickory Ridge Road, Putney, Vermont 05346. Phone: 802-387-5000. Fax: 802-387-4276. E-mail: info@goputney.com.
URL www.goputney.com
For more information, see page 598.

MALAWI

PUTNEY STUDENT TRAVEL–GLOBAL ACTION–MALAWI

Putney Student Travel
Malawi

General Information Coed residential cultural program established in 1951.
Program Focus Students spend three weeks pursuing research in relation to community building and sustainable development.
Academics Intercultural studies.
Special Interest Areas Cross-cultural education, field research/expeditions.
Trips Cultural, day, overnight.
Program Information 1 session per year. Session length: 25–32 days in June, July, August. Ages: 15–18. 16 participants per session. Boarding program cost: $6990. Financial aid available.
Application Deadline Continuous.

Contact Jeffrey Shumlin, Admissions Director, 345 Hickory Ridge Road, Putney, Vermont 05346. Phone: 802-387-5000. Fax: 802-387-4276. E-mail: info@goputney.com.
URL www.goputney.com
For more information, see page 598.

MARTINIQUE

GLOBAL WORKS–LANGUAGE IMMERSION, CULTURAL EXCHANGE AND SERVICE–MARTINIQUE–4WEEKS

GLOBAL WORKS
Martinique

General Information Coed travel community service program, cultural program, and adventure program established in 1988. High school credit may be earned.
Program Focus Environmental and community service, language immersion, and cultural exchange.
Academics French language/literature, archaeology, ecology, intercultural studies.
Arts Arts and crafts (general), dance (Latin), painting.
Special Interest Areas Community service, conservation projects, construction, field research/expeditions, field trips (arts and culture), homestays.
Sports Horseback riding, ropes course, scuba diving, sea kayaking, soccer, swimming, volleyball.
Wilderness/Outdoors Backpacking, hiking, outdoor adventure, rafting, white-water trips.
Trips Cultural, day, overnight.
Program Information 1 session per year. Session length: 27 days in June, July. Ages: 14–17. 16–18 participants per session. Cost: $4695. Application fee: $100. Financial aid available. Airfare not included.
Application Deadline Continuous.
Jobs Positions for college students 23 and older.
Contact Mr. Erik Werner, Director, 1113 South Allen Street, State College, Pennsylvania 16801. Phone: 814-867-7000. Fax: 814-867-2717. E-mail: info@globalworksinc.com.
URL www.globalworksinc.com
For more information, see page 506.

MEXICO

AAVE–Surf Scuba Safari

AAVE–Journeys That Matter
Baja
Mexico

General Information Coed travel outdoor program, community service program, wilderness program, cultural program, and adventure program established in 1976. Accredited by American Camping Association.
Program Focus Adventure travel, surfing and scuba diving certification.
Academics Area studies, intercultural studies.
Special Interest Areas Community service, leadership training.
Sports Fishing, scuba diving, sea kayaking, snorkeling, surfing, swimming.
Wilderness/Outdoors Hiking, rock climbing, wilderness camping.
Trips Cultural, day, overnight.
Program Information 3–5 sessions per year. Session length: 18 days in June, July, August. Ages: 14–18. 13–15 participants per session. Cost: $4288. Financial aid available.
Application Deadline Continuous.
Jobs Positions for college students 21 and older.
Contact Mr. Abbott Wallis, Owner, 2308 Fossil Trace Drive, Golden, Colorado 80401. Phone: 800-222-3595. Fax: 303-526-0885. E-mail: info@aave.com.
URL www.aave.com

For more information, see page 394.

ACADEMIC TREKS–Immersion Mexico

Academic Treks, the academic adventure and community service division of Broadreach
Guanajuato
Mexico

General Information Coed travel academic program, outdoor program, cultural program, and adventure program established in 1992. High school or college credit may be earned.
Program Focus Academic adventure and community services program focusing on Spanish language immersion, cultural exchange, hiking, rafting, week long homestay, college credit.
Academics Spanish language/literature, academics (general), area studies, history, intercultural studies.
Arts Dance (Latin).
Special Interest Areas Native American culture, community service, cross-cultural education, culinary arts, homestays, leadership training.
Wilderness/Outdoors Backpacking, hiking, white-water trips, wilderness camping.
Trips Cultural, day, overnight.
Program Information 2 sessions per year. Session length: 3 weeks in June, July, August. Ages: 15–19.

10–14 participants per session. Cost: $3990. Financial aid available.
Application Deadline Continuous.
Contact Carlton Goldthwaite, Director, 806 McCulloch Street, Suite 102, Raleigh, North Carolina 27603. Phone: 888-833-1908. Fax: 919-833-2129. E-mail: info@academictreks.com.
URL www.academictreks.com

For more information, see page 432.

ACADEMIC TREKS–Spanish Immersion in Oaxaca, Mexico

Academic Treks, the academic adventure and community service division of Broadreach
Oaxaca
Mexico

General Information Coed travel academic program, outdoor program, cultural program, and adventure program established in 1992. High school or college credit may be earned.
Program Focus Academic adventure community service program focusing on Spanish language immersion, adventure travel, cultural exchange, hiking, 10-weeklong homestay, college credit, no pre-requisites.
Academics Spanish language/literature, academics (general), area studies, intercultural studies.
Arts Dance (folk), pottery.
Special Interest Areas Native American culture, community service, cross-cultural education, culinary arts, homestays, leadership training.
Wilderness/Outdoors Hiking, outdoor adventure.
Trips Cultural, day.
Program Information 2 sessions per year. Session length: 3 weeks in June, July, August. Ages: 15–19. 10–14 participants per session. Cost: $3990.
Application Deadline Continuous.
Contact Carlton Goldthwaite, Director, 806 McCulloch Street, Suite 102, Raleigh, North Carolina 27603. Phone: 888-833-1907. Fax: 919-833-2129. E-mail: info@academictreks.com.
URL www.academictreks.com

For more information, see page 432.

BROADREACH BAJA EXTREME–SCUBA ADVENTURE

Broadreach
Baja California Sur
Mexico

General Information Coed travel outdoor program and adventure program established in 1992.
Program Focus Coed program focusing on intensive scuba diving, advanced and specialty dive training, marine ecology, sea kayaking, surfing, adventure travel and exploration.
Academics Area studies, environmental science, marine studies.
Arts Photography.
Special Interest Areas Community service, leadership training, nature study.
Sports Boating, fishing, scuba diving, sea kayaking, snorkeling, surfing.
Wilderness/Outdoors Hiking, ocean expeditions, outdoor adventure, outdoor camping, wilderness/outdoors (general).
Trips Cultural, overnight.
Program Information 2 sessions per year. Session length: 19 days in June, July, August. Ages: 15–19. 12–14 participants per session. Cost: $4680. Financial aid available.
Application Deadline Continuous.
Contact Carlton Goldthwaite, Director, 806 McCulloch Street, Suite 102, Raleigh, North Carolina 27603. Phone: 888-833-1907. Fax: 919-833-2129. E-mail: info@gobroadreach.com.
URL www.gobroadreach.com
For more information, see page 432.

BROADREACH YUCATAN ADVENTURE

Broadreach
Yucatan Peninsula
Mexico

General Information Coed travel outdoor program and adventure program established in 1992.
Program Focus Coed program focusing on intensive scuba diving in both the ocean and freshwater cenotes or caves, snorkeling with whale sharks, cultural exchange, Mayan ruins, tropical rainforest exploration.
Academics Area studies, ecology, marine studies.
Arts Photography.
Special Interest Areas Mayan studies, community service, conservation projects, leadership training, nature study.
Sports Scuba diving, sea kayaking, snorkeling.
Wilderness/Outdoors Caving, hiking, ocean expeditions, wilderness/outdoors (general).
Trips Cultural, day.
Program Information 2 sessions per year. Session length: 3 weeks in June, July, August. Ages: 15–19. 10–14 participants per session. Cost: $4990. Financial aid available.
Application Deadline Continuous.

Contact Carlton Goldthwaite, Director, 806 McCulloch Street, Suite 102, Raleigh, North Carolina 27603. Phone: 919-256-8200. Fax: 919-833-2129. E-mail: info@gobroadreach.com.
URL www.gobroadreach.com
For more information, see page 432.

CENTER FOR CULTURAL INTERCHANGE–MEXICO LANGUAGE SCHOOL

Center for Cultural Interchange
Cuernavaca
Mexico

General Information Coed residential academic program and cultural program established in 1985. High school or college credit may be earned.
Program Focus Cultural immersion and language study.
Academics Spanish language/literature.
Special Interest Areas Homestays.
Trips Cultural, day.
Program Information 1–50 sessions per year. Session length: 14–90 days in January, February, March, April, May, June, July, August, September, October, November, December. Ages: 13+. Boarding program cost: $1750–$2050. Financial aid available.
Application Deadline Continuous.
Contact Ms. Juliet Jones, Outbound Programs Director, 746 North LaSalle Drive, Chicago, Illinois 60610-3617. Phone: 866-684-9675. Fax: 312-944-2644. E-mail: info@cci-exchange.com.
URL www.cci-exchange.com
For more information, see page 448.

ENFOREX RESIDENTIAL YOUTH SUMMER CAMP–GUANAJUATO, MEXICO

Enforex Spanish in the Spanish World
Calle Pastita 76
Colonia Barrio Pastita
Guanajuato 36090
Mexico

General Information Coed residential traditional camp established in 1989.
Program Focus Excursions cultural activities, workshops.
Academics Spanish language/literature, academics (general), communications, study skills, writing.
Arts Acting, arts and crafts (general), drawing, leather working, music, painting, radio broadcasting, television/video, theater/drama.
Special Interest Areas Farming, field research/expeditions, general camp activities, work camp programs.
Sports Aerobics, archery, baseball, soccer.
Trips Cultural, day.
Program Information 4 sessions per year. Session length: 2–8 weeks in July, August. Ages: 15–18. 100 participants per session. Boarding program cost: 1100

Enforex Residential Youth Summer Camp–Guanajuato, Mexico (continued)

euros. Application fee: 65 euros. Financial aid available.
Application Deadline Continuous.
Contact Antonio Anadón, Director, Alberto Aguilera 26, Madrid 28015, Spain. E-mail: info@enforex.es.
URL www.enforex.com

For more information, see page 486.

THE EXPERIMENT IN INTERNATIONAL LIVING–MEXICO–COMMUNITY SERVICE, TRAVEL, AND HOMESTAY

The Experiment in International Living
Mexico

General Information Coed travel community service program and cultural program established in 1932.
Program Focus International youth travel, homestay, Spanish language, community service.
Academics Spanish language/literature.
Special Interest Areas Community service, homestays, touring.
Trips Cultural, day, overnight.
Program Information 1 session per year. Session length: 5 weeks in June, July, August. Ages: 14–19. 10–15 participants per session. Cost: $3900. Financial aid available.
Application Deadline May 1.
Contact Annie Thompson, Enrollment Director, Summer Abroad, Kipling Road, PO Box 676, Brattleboro, Vermont 05302-0676. Phone: 800-345-2929. Fax: 802-258-3428. E-mail: eil@worldlearning.org.
URL www.usexperiment.org

For more information, see page 492.

THE EXPERIMENT IN INTERNATIONAL LIVING–MEXICO COOKING AND CULTURE

The Experiment in International Living
Mexico

General Information Coed travel cultural program established in 1932.
Program Focus International youth travel, homestay, Spanish language, cooking.
Academics Spanish language/literature.

Special Interest Areas Culinary arts, field research/expeditions, homestays, touring.
Trips Cultural, day, overnight.
Program Information 1 session per year. Session length: 5 weeks in June, July. Ages: 14–19. 10–15 participants per session. Cost: $3900. Financial aid available.
Application Deadline May 1.
Contact Annie Thompson, Enrollment Director, Summer Abroad, Kipling Road, PO Box 676, Brattleboro, Vermont 05302-0676. Phone: 800-345-2929. Fax: 802-258-3428. E-mail: eil@worldlearning.org.
URL www.usexperiment.org

For more information, see page 492.

THE EXPERIMENT IN INTERNATIONAL LIVING–MEXICO HOMESTAY, SUSTAINABLE DEVELOPMENT AND FAIR TRADE

The Experiment in International Living
Mexico

General Information Coed travel cultural program established in 1932.
Program Focus International youth travel, homestay, Spanish language.
Academics Spanish language/literature, global issues, natural resource management.
Special Interest Areas Community service, cross-cultural education, culinary arts, farming, field research/expeditions, homestays, touring.
Wilderness/Outdoors Hiking, rafting.
Trips Cultural, day, overnight.
Program Information 1 session per year. Session length: 5 weeks in June, July. Ages: 14–19. 10–15 participants per session. Cost: $3800. Financial aid available.
Application Deadline May 1.
Contact Annie Thompson, Enrollment Director, Summer Abroad, Kipling Road, PO Box 676, Brattleboro, Vermont 05302-0676. Phone: 800-345-2929. Fax: 802-258-3428. E-mail: eil@worldlearning.org.
URL www.usexperiment.org

For more information, see page 492.

THE EXPERIMENT IN INTERNATIONAL LIVING–MEXICO–MAYAN ARTS AND CULTURE

The Experiment in International Living
Mexico

General Information Coed travel cultural program established in 1932.
Program Focus International youth travel, homestay, Spanish language, Mayan arts and culture.
Academics Spanish language/literature.
Special Interest Areas Mayan studies, culinary arts, field research/expeditions, homestays, touring.
Wilderness/Outdoors Hiking.

Trips Cultural, day, overnight.
Program Information 1 session per year. Session length: 4 weeks in June, July. Ages: 14–19. 10–15 participants per session. Cost: $3700. Financial aid available.
Application Deadline May 1.
Contact Annie Thompson, Enrollment Director, Summer Abroad, Kipling Road, PO Box 676, Brattleboro, Vermont 05302-0676. Phone: 800-345-2929. Fax: 802-258-3428. E-mail: eil@worldlearning.org.
URL www.usexperiment.org
For more information, see page 492.

GLOBAL WORKS–Language Immersion, Cultural Exchange and Service–Mexico–3 weeks

GLOBAL WORKS
Mexico

General Information Coed travel community service program, cultural program, and adventure program established in 1988. High school credit may be earned.
Program Focus Community service, language learning and travel.
Academics Spanish language/literature, archaeology, intercultural studies.
Arts Arts and crafts (general), dance (Latin), painting.
Special Interest Areas Community service, conservation projects, construction, homestays.
Sports Basketball, snorkeling, surfing, swimming, ultimate frisbee.
Wilderness/Outdoors Hiking, outdoor adventure, rafting.
Trips Cultural, day, overnight.
Program Information 2 sessions per year. Session length: 3 weeks in June, July, August. Ages: 15–17. 16–18 participants per session. Cost: $3895. Application fee: $100. Financial aid available. Airfare not included.
Application Deadline Continuous.
Jobs Positions for college students 23 and older.
Contact Mr. Erik Werner, Director, 1113 South Allen Street, State College, Pennsylvania 16801. Phone: 814-867-7000. Fax: 814-867-2717. E-mail: info@globalworksinc.com.
URL www.globalworksinc.com
For more information, see page 506.

GLOBAL WORKS–Language Immersion, Cultural Exchange and Service–Yucatan Peninsula, Mexico– 4 weeks

GLOBAL WORKS
Mexico

General Information Coed travel community service program, cultural program, and adventure program established in 1988. High school credit may be earned.
Program Focus Community service, language learning and travel.
Academics Latin language, Spanish (Advanced Placement), archaeology, intercultural studies, language study.
Arts Arts and crafts (general), dance (Latin), painting.
Special Interest Areas Community service, conservation projects, construction, field research/ expeditions, homestays.
Sports Basketball, snorkeling, swimming, ultimate frisbee.
Wilderness/Outdoors Hiking, outdoor adventure.
Trips Cultural, day, overnight.
Program Information 1 session per year. Session length: 28–30 days in June, July. Ages: 15–18. 16–18 participants per session. Cost: $4295. Application fee: $100. Financial aid available. Airfare not included.
Application Deadline Continuous.
Jobs Positions for college students 23 and older.
Contact Mr. Erik Werner, Director, 1113 South Allen Street, State College, Pennsylvania 16801. Phone: 814-867-7000. Fax: 814-867-2717. E-mail: info@globalworksinc.com.
URL www.globalworksinc.com
For more information, see page 506.

MOROCCO

The Experiment in International Living–Morocco Four-Week Arts and Culture Program

The Experiment in International Living
Morocco

General Information Coed travel community service program, cultural program, and adventure program established in 1932.
Program Focus International youth travel, homestay, community service, arts.
Academics Arabic, language study.
Arts Arts, ceramics, dance (folk), fabric arts, music, weaving.
Special Interest Areas Community service, homestays, nature study, touring.
Trips Cultural, day, overnight.
Program Information 1 session per year. Session

The Experiment in International Living–Morocco Four-Week Arts and Culture Program (continued)

length: 4 weeks in June, July. Ages: 14–19. 15–20 participants per session. Cost: $5200. Financial aid available. Airfare included.
Application Deadline May 1.
Contact Annie Thompson, Enrollment Director, Summer Abroad, Kipling Road, PO Box 676, Brattleboro, Vermont 05302-0676. Phone: 800-345-2929. Fax: 802-258-3428. E-mail: eil@worldlearning.org.
URL www.usexperiment.org

For more information, see page 492.

NETHERLANDS

CENTER FOR CULTURAL INTERCHANGE– NETHERLANDS HIGH SCHOOL ABROAD

Center for Cultural Interchange
Netherlands

General Information Coed residential academic program and cultural program established in 1985. High school credit may be earned.
Program Focus Cultural immersion, high school in Holland.
Academics Dutch language, academics (general), independent study.
Special Interest Areas Cross-cultural education, homestays.
Trips Cultural, day.
Program Information 2 sessions per year. Session length: 150–300 days in January, February, March, April, May, June, August, September, October, November, December. Ages: 15–18. Boarding program cost: $6000–$6700. Financial aid available.
Application Deadline Continuous.
Contact Ms. Juliet Jones, Outbound Programs Director, 746 North LaSalle Drive, Chicago, Illinois 60610-3617. Phone: 866-684-9675. Fax: 312-944-2644. E-mail: info@cci-exchange.com.
URL www.cci-exchange.com

For more information, see page 448.

NEW ZEALAND

AFS-USA–HOMESTAY PLUS– NEW ZEALAND

AFS-USA
New Zealand

General Information Coed residential outdoor program and cultural program.
Program Focus Camp experience with fun and rigorous outdoor activities which will develop leadership, decision-making, and teamwork skills. Then living with a host family, participating in volunteer projects, learning what it's like to live as a member of a family and community in New Zealand.
Special Interest Areas Career exploration, community service, homestays.
Sports Kayaking.
Wilderness/Outdoors Backpacking, canoe trips, caving, hiking, mountaineering, orienteering, outdoor adventure, rafting, rock climbing, wilderness camping.
Trips Cultural, day, overnight.
Program Information 1 session per year. Session length: 30–45 days in June, July, August. Ages: 16–18. Boarding program cost: $6100. Application fee: $75. Financial aid available. International airfare and volunteer homestay support included.
Application Deadline Continuous.
Contact Manager, AFS Info Center, 506 Southwest 6th Avenue, 2nd Floor, Portland, Oregon 97204. Phone: 800-AFS-INFO. Fax: 503-299-0753. E-mail: afsinfo@afs.org.
URL www.afs.org/usa

For more information, see page 408.

THE EXPERIMENT IN INTERNATIONAL LIVING–NEW ZEALAND HOMESTAY

The Experiment in International Living
New Zealand

General Information Coed travel outdoor program, community service program, and cultural program established in 1932.
Program Focus International youth travel, homestay, community service.
Academics Ecology, intercultural studies.
Special Interest Areas Community service, field research/expeditions, homestays, nature study, touring.
Wilderness/Outdoors Backpacking, hiking, mountaineering.
Trips Cultural, day, overnight.
Program Information 1 session per year. Session length: 5 weeks in June, July, August. Ages: 14–19. 10–15 participants per session. Cost: $5600. Financial aid available. Airfare included.
Application Deadline May 1.

Contact Annie Thompson, Enrollment Director, Summer Abroad, Kipling Road, PO Box 676, Brattleboro, Vermont 05302-0676. Phone: 800-345-2929. Fax: 802-258-3428. E-mail: eil@worldlearning.org. **URL** www.usexperiment.org

For more information, see page 492.

RUSTIC PATHWAYS–NEW ZEALAND NORTH ISLAND ADVENTURE

Rustic Pathways
Bay of Islands, Waitomo Caves
Auckland, Rotoura
New Zealand

General Information Coed travel cultural program and adventure program established in 2005.
Special Interest Areas Cross-cultural education, touring.
Sports Hang gliding, sailing, snorkeling, swimming.
Wilderness/Outdoors Caving, hiking, outdoor adventure, white-water trips.
Trips Cultural, day, overnight.
Program Information 2 sessions per year. Session length: 10 days in June, July. Ages: 14–18. 10–15 participants per session. Cost: $1495. Financial aid available.
Application Deadline Continuous.
Contact Rustic Pathways, 4121 Erie Street, Willoughby, Ohio 44094. Phone: 800-321-4353. Fax: 440-975-9694. E-mail: rustic@rusticpathways.com. **URL** www.rusticpathways.com

For more information, see page 612.

RUSTIC PATHWAYS–SKI AND SNOWBOARD ADVENTURE IN NEW ZEALAND

Rustic Pathways
New Zealand

General Information Coed travel adventure program established in 1994.
Sports Bungee jumping, skiing (downhill), snowboarding.
Wilderness/Outdoors Glacier travel, hiking.
Trips Day.
Program Information 6 sessions per year. Session length: 10–24 days in July, August. Ages: 14–18. 15–20 participants per session. Cost: $1495–$3875.
Application Deadline Continuous.
Jobs Positions for college students 21 and older.

Contact Rustic Pathways, 4121 Erie Street, Willoughby, Ohio 44094. Phone: 800-321-4353. Fax: 440-975-9694. E-mail: rustic@rusticpathways.com. **URL** www.rusticpathways.com

For more information, see page 612.

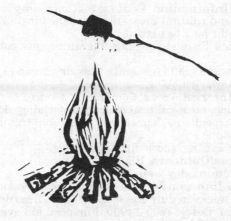

NICARAGUA

PUTNEY STUDENT TRAVEL–COMMUNITY SERVICE–NICARAGUA

Putney Student Travel
Ometepe
Nicaragua

General Information Coed residential community service program established in 1951.
Program Focus Community service, cultural exchange, and weekend excursions from a base in a small, rural community.
Academics Intercultural studies.
Special Interest Areas Community service, construction, team building.
Sports Snorkeling, swimming.
Wilderness/Outdoors Hiking, mountain biking.
Trips Cultural, day, overnight.
Program Information 1 session per year. Session length: 28–30 days in June, July. Ages: 14–18. 16 participants per session. Boarding program cost: $5290. Financial aid available.
Application Deadline Continuous.
Jobs Positions for college students 21 and older.
Contact Jeffrey Shumlin, Admissions Director, 345 Hickory Ridge Road, Putney, Vermont 05346. Phone: 802-387-5000. Fax: 802-387-4276. E-mail: info@goputney.com. **URL** www.goputney.com

For more information, see page 598.

VISIONS–NICARAGUA

Visions
Jinotega
Nicaragua

General Information Coed travel community service program and cultural program established in 1989. High school credit may be earned.
Academics Spanish language/literature, intercultural studies.
Arts Arts and crafts (general), basketry, creative writing, jewelry making.
Special Interest Areas Community service, construction, cross-cultural education, farming, field research/expeditions, homestays, leadership training, nature study.
Sports Bicycling, snorkeling, swimming.
Wilderness/Outdoors Hiking.
Trips Cultural, day, overnight.
Program Information 1 session per year. Session length: 4 weeks in July. Ages: 16–18. 15–17 participants per session. Cost: $3200–$4900. Financial aid available.
Application Deadline Continuous.
Jobs Positions for college students 22 and older.
Contact Joanne Pinaire, Director, PO Box 220, Newport, Pennsylvania 17074-0220. Phone: 717-567-7313. Fax: 717-567-7853. E-mail: info@visionsserviceadventures.com.
URL www.visionsserviceadventures.com

For more information, see page 694.

NORWAY

CENTER FOR CULTURAL INTERCHANGE– NORWAY HIGH SCHOOL ABROAD

Center for Cultural Interchange
Norway

General Information Coed residential academic program and cultural program established in 1985. High school credit may be earned.
Program Focus High school abroad.
Academics Norwegian language/literature, academics (general).
Special Interest Areas Cross-cultural education, homestays.
Trips Cultural, day.
Program Information 2 sessions per year. Session length: 90–300 days in January, February, March, April, May, June, July, August, September, October, November, December. Ages: 15–18. Boarding program cost: $5900–$7700. Financial aid available. Early Bird discount.
Application Deadline Continuous.

Contact Ms. Juliet Jones, Outbound Programs Director, 746 North LaSalle Drive, Chicago, Illinois 60610-3617. Phone: 866-684-9675. Fax: 312-944-2644. E-mail: info@cci-exchange.com.
URL www.cci-exchange.com

For more information, see page 448.

PANAMA

AFS-USA–COMMUNITY SERVICE– PANAMA

AFS-USA
Panama

General Information Coed residential community service program and cultural program. High school credit may be earned.
Program Focus After a two-day orientation in Panama City, participants are placed in host communities in groups of eight to ten. Individuals stay with a host family and perform community service at local elementary schools in the morning, and attend Spanish class in the afternoon.
Academics Spanish language/literature.
Special Interest Areas Community service.
Trips Cultural, day.
Program Information 1 session per year. Session length: 30–45 days in June, July. Ages: 16–18. Boarding program cost: $4000–$6000. Application fee: $75. Financial aid available. International airfare and volunteer homestay support included.
Application Deadline Continuous.
Contact Manager, AFS Info Center, 506 Southwest 6th Avenue, 2nd Floor, Portland, Oregon 97204. Phone: 800-AFS-INFO. Fax: 503-299-0753. E-mail: afsinfo@afs.org.
URL www.afs.org/usa

For more information, see page 408.

1

AFS-USA–HOMESTAY LANGUAGE STUDY–PANAMA

AFS-USA
Panama

General Information Coed residential cultural program.
Program Focus Language study program.
Academics Spanish language/literature.
Special Interest Areas Homestays, touring.
Trips Cultural, day, overnight.
Program Information 1 session per year. Session length: 30–45 days in June, July. Ages: 16–18. Boarding program cost: $4000–$6000. Application fee: $75. Financial aid available. International airfare and volunteer homestay support included.
Application Deadline Continuous.
Contact Manager, AFS Info Center, 506 Southwest 6th Avenue, 2nd Floor, Portland, Oregon 97204. Phone: 800-AFS-INFO. Fax: 03-299-0753. E-mail: afsinfo@afs.org.
URL www.afs.org/usa

For more information, see page 408.

AFS-USA–HOMESTAY PLUS–PANAMA

AFS-USA
Panama

General Information Coed residential community service program and cultural program. High school credit may be earned.
Academics Spanish language/literature.
Special Interest Areas Community service, homestays.
Trips Cultural, day, overnight.
Program Information 1 session per year. Session length: 30 days in June, July. Ages: 16–18. 10–25 participants per session. Boarding program cost: $4000–$5000. Application fee: $75. Financial aid available. International airfare and volunteer homestay support included.
Application Deadline Continuous.
Contact Manager, AFS Info Center, 506 Southwest 6th Avenue, 2nd Floor, Portland, Oregon 97204. Phone: 800-AFS-INFO. Fax: 503-248-4076. E-mail: afsinfo@afs.org.
URL www.afs.org/usa

For more information, see page 408.

PARAGUAY

AFS-USA–COMMUNITY SERVICE–PARAGUAY

AFS-USA
Paraguay

General Information Coed residential community service program and cultural program established in 1995. High school credit may be earned.
Program Focus Volunteer in a nature preserve or with indigenous people.
Academics Spanish language/literature, ecology, intercultural studies.
Special Interest Areas Community service, conservation projects, homestays, trail maintenance.
Trips Cultural, day, overnight.
Program Information 1 session per year. Session length: 30–45 days in July, August. Ages: 16+. Boarding program cost: $4000–$6000. Application fee: $75. Financial aid available. International airfare and volunteer homestay support included.
Application Deadline Continuous.
Contact Manager, AFS Info Center, 506 Southwest 6th Avenue, 2nd Floor, Portland, Oregon 97204. Phone: 800-AFS-INFO. Fax: 503-299-0753. E-mail: afsinfo@afs.org.
URL www.afs.org/usa

For more information, see page 408.

AFS-USA–HOMESTAY–PARAGUAY

AFS-USA
Paraguay

General Information Coed residential academic program and cultural program.
Program Focus Living with a host family, taking part in activities with other teenagers, and attending high school in Paraguay.
Academics Spanish language/literature, academics (general).
Special Interest Areas Homestays, touring.
Trips Cultural, day.
Program Information 1 session per year. Session length: 30–45 days in June, July, August. Ages: 15–18. Boarding program cost: $4000–$6000. Application fee: $75. Financial aid available. International airfare and volunteer homestay support included.
Application Deadline Continuous.

AFS-USA–Homestay–Paraguay (continued)

Contact Manager, AFS Info Center, 506 Southwest 6th Avenue, 2nd Floor, Portland, Oregon 97204. Phone: 800-AFS-INFO. Fax: 503-299-0753. E-mail: afsinfo@afs.org.
URL www.afs.org/usa

For more information, see page 408.

AFS-USA–HOMESTAY PLUS–PARAGUAY
SOCCER

AFS-USA
Paraguay

General Information Coed residential sports camp established in 2005.
Program Focus Practicing soccer with professional Paraguayan soccer players.
Academics Spanish language/literature.
Special Interest Areas Homestays, team building.
Sports Soccer.
Program Information 1 session per year. Session length: 30–50 days in June, July, August. Ages: 16+. Boarding program cost: $4000–$6000. Application fee: $75. Financial aid available.
Application Deadline Continuous.
Contact Manager, AFS Information Center, 506 Southwest 6th Avenue, 2nd Floor, Portland, Oregon 97204. Phone: 800-AFS-INFO. Fax: 503-299-0753. E-mail: afsinfo@afs.org.
URL www.afs.org/usa

For more information, see page 408.

PERU

AAVE–PERU AND MACHU PICCHU

AAVE–Journeys That Matter
Peru

General Information Coed travel outdoor program, community service program, wilderness program, cultural program, and adventure program established in 1976. Accredited by American Camping Association.
Program Focus Cultural and outdoor experience.
Academics Area studies, intercultural studies.
Special Interest Areas Community service, cross-cultural education, leadership training, touring.
Sports Horseback riding.
Wilderness/Outdoors Backpacking, bicycle trips, hiking, rafting, white-water trips.
Trips Cultural, day, overnight.
Program Information 2–4 sessions per year. Session length: 3 weeks in June, July, August. Ages: 14–18. 12 participants per session. Cost: $4288. Financial aid available.
Jobs Positions for college students 21 and older.
Contact Mr. Abbott Wallis, Owner, 2308 Fossil Trace Drive, Golden, Colorado 80401. Phone: 800-222-3595. Fax: 303-526-0885. E-mail: info@aave.com.
URL www.aave.com

For more information, see page 394.

ACADEMIC TREKS–ADVENTURE PERU

Academic Treks, the academic adventure and community service division of Broadreach
Cusco, Machu Picchu, Urubamba, Caraz
Peru

General Information Coed travel academic program, outdoor program, community service program, cultural program, and adventure program established in 1992. High school or college credit may be earned.
Program Focus Academic adventure and community service program focusing on language exposure, service learning, cultural immersion, and trekking the Inca Trail in Peru.
Academics Spanish language/literature, academics (general), archaeology, area studies, history, intercultural studies.
Special Interest Areas Community service, conservation projects, cross-cultural education, leadership training.
Wilderness/Outdoors Hiking, outdoor adventure, wilderness camping, wilderness/outdoors (general).
Trips Cultural.
Program Information 2 sessions per year. Session length: 23 days in June, July, August. Ages: 15–19. 12–14 participants per session. Cost: $4580. Financial aid available.
Application Deadline Continuous.

Contact Carlton Goldthwaite, Director, 806 McCulloch Street, Suite 102, Raleigh, North Carolina 27603. Phone: 888-833-1907. Fax: 919-833-2129. E-mail: info@academictreks.com.
URL www.academictreks.com
For more information, see page 432.

GLOBAL WORKS–Language Immersion, Cultural Exchange and Service–Peru

GLOBAL WORKS
Peru

General Information Coed travel community service program, cultural program, and adventure program established in 1988. High school credit may be earned.
Program Focus Environmental and community service, language immersion, and cultural exchange.
Academics Spanish language/literature, intercultural studies.
Arts Arts and crafts (general), dance, music.
Special Interest Areas Community service, conservation projects, construction, field research/expeditions, field trips (arts and culture), homestays.
Sports Bicycling, snorkeling, soccer, volleyball.
Wilderness/Outdoors Hiking, rafting, white-water trips.
Trips Cultural, day, overnight.
Program Information 1 session per year. Session length: 24 days in June, July. Ages: 15–17. 16–18 participants per session. Cost: $3995. Application fee: $100. Financial aid available. Airfare not included.
Application Deadline Continuous.
Jobs Positions for college students 23 and older.
Contact Mr. Erik Werner, Director, 1113 South Allen Street, State College, Pennsylvania 16801. Phone: 814-867-7000. Fax: 814-867-2717. E-mail: info@globalworksinc.com.
URL www.globalworksinc.com
For more information, see page 506.

VISIONS–PERU

Visions
Peru

General Information Coed travel outdoor program, community service program, and cultural program established in 1989. High school credit may be earned.
Program Focus Community service, cross-cultural experience, language immersion, and outdoor adventure activities.
Academics Spanish language/literature, intercultural studies, language study.
Arts Carpentry, painting, pottery.
Special Interest Areas Community service, construction, cross-cultural education, field trips (arts and culture), leadership training, nature study.
Wilderness/Outdoors Backpacking, hiking, rafting.
Trips Cultural, day, overnight.
Program Information 1–2 sessions per year. Session length: 3–4 weeks in June, July, August. Ages: 14–18. 20–25 participants per session. Cost: $3200–$4900. Financial aid available.
Application Deadline Continuous.
Jobs Positions for college students 22 and older.
Contact Joanne Pinaire, Director, PO Box 220, Newport, Pennsylvania 17074. Phone: 717-567-7313. Fax: 717-567-7853. E-mail: info@visionsserviceadventures.com.
URL www.visionsserviceadventures.com
For more information, see page 694.

WILDERNESS VENTURES–PERU COMMUNITY SERVICE

Wilderness Ventures
Peru

General Information Coed travel outdoor program, community service program, wilderness program, and adventure program established in 1973.
Program Focus Wilderness travel, wilderness skills, leadership skills, community service.
Special Interest Areas Community service, homestays, nature study.
Sports Sea kayaking.
Wilderness/Outdoors Hiking, rafting, white-water trips, wilderness camping.
Trips Cultural, day, overnight.
Program Information 2 sessions per year. Session length: 3 weeks in June, July, August. Ages: 14–18. 13 participants per session. Cost: $4990. Financial aid available.
Application Deadline Continuous.
Jobs Positions for college students 21 and older.
Contact Mike Cottingham, Director, PO Box 2768, Jackson Hole, Wyoming 83001. Phone: 800-533-2281. Fax: 307-739-1934. E-mail: info@wildernessventures.com.
URL www.wildernessventures.com
For more information, see page 704.

POLAND

THE EXPERIMENT IN INTERNATIONAL LIVING–POLAND, HOMESTAY, COMMUNITY SERVICE, AND TRAVEL

The Experiment in International Living
Poland

General Information Coed travel community service program, cultural program, and adventure program established in 1932.
Program Focus International youth travel, homestay, public policy.
Academics Polish language/literature, government and politics.
Special Interest Areas Community service, homestays, touring.
Wilderness/Outdoors Hiking.
Trips Cultural, day, overnight.
Program Information 1 session per year. Session length: 5 weeks in June, July, August. Ages: 14–19. 10–15 participants per session. Cost: $5300. Application fee: $75. Financial aid available. Airfare included.
Application Deadline May 1.
Contact Ms. Annie Thompson, Enrollment Director, Summer Abroad, Kipling Road, PO Box 676, Brattleboro, Vermont 05302-0676. Phone: 800-345-2929. Fax: 802-258-3428. E-mail: eil@worldlearning.org.
URL www.usexperiment.org

For more information, see page 492.

PUERTO RICO

GLOBAL WORKS–CULTURAL EXCHANGE AND SERVICE–PUERTO RICO– 2 OR 4 WEEKS

GLOBAL WORKS
Puerto Rico

General Information Coed travel community service program, cultural program, and adventure program established in 1988. High school credit may be earned.
Academics Spanish language/literature, intercultural studies, language study.
Arts Arts and crafts (general), dance (Latin).
Special Interest Areas Community service, conservation projects, construction, team building.
Sports Basketball, scuba diving, sea kayaking, snorkeling, soccer, swimming, volleyball.
Wilderness/Outdoors Hiking, outdoor adventure.
Trips Cultural, day, overnight.
Program Information 3 sessions per year. Session length: 2–4 weeks in June, July, August. Ages: 14–17. 16–18 participants per session. Cost: $2995–$4695. Application fee: $100. Financial aid available. Airfare

not included; sessions 1 and 2 may be combined for a 28-day program.
Application Deadline Continuous.
Jobs Positions for college students 23 and older.
Contact Mr. Erik Werner, Director, 1113 South Allen Street, State College, Pennsylvania 16801. Phone: 814-867-7000. Fax: 814-867-2717. E-mail: info@globalworksinc.com.
URL www.globalworksinc.com

For more information, see page 506.

GLOBAL WORKS–LANGUAGE IMMERSION, CULTURAL EXCHANGE AND SERVICE–PUERTO RICO-4 WEEKS

GLOBAL WORKS
Puerto Rico

General Information Coed travel community service program, cultural program, and adventure program established in 1988. High school credit may be earned.
Program Focus Environmental and community service, language learning, and cultural exchange.
Academics Spanish language/literature, intercultural studies.
Arts Arts and crafts (general), creative writing, dance.
Special Interest Areas Community service, conservation projects, construction, field trips (arts and culture), homestays.
Sports Basketball, scuba diving, sea kayaking, snorkeling, soccer, sports (general), swimming, volleyball.
Wilderness/Outdoors Hiking.
Trips Cultural, day, overnight.
Program Information 1 session per year. Session length: 4 weeks in June, July. Ages: 15–17. 16–18 participants per session. Cost: $4495. Application fee: $100. Financial aid available. Airfare not included.
Application Deadline Continuous.
Jobs Positions for college students 23 and older.
Contact Mr. Erik Werner, Director, 1113 South Allen Street, State College, Pennsylvania 16801. Phone: 814-867-7000. Fax: 814-867-2717. E-mail: info@globalworksinc.com.
URL www.globalworksinc.com

For more information, see page 506.

REPUBLIC OF KOREA

ELITE EDUCATIONAL INSTITUTE ELEMENTARY ENRICHMENT–KOREA

Elite Educational Institute
Seoul
Republic of Korea

General Information Coed day academic program established in 1987. Formal opportunities for the academically talented.
Program Focus Elementary education: 2nd–6th grade.
Academics English as a second language, English language/literature, SAT/ACT preparation, mathematics, precollege program, reading, social studies, study skills, writing.
Program Information 3 sessions per year. Session length: 100–350 days in January, February, March, April, May, June, July, August, September, October, November, December. Ages: 9–12. 10–40 participants per session. Day program cost: $280–$360. Application fee: $50.
Application Deadline Continuous.
Contact Mr. Min, Director, Kangnam-Gu Shinsa Dong 595-1, Ahnkook Building 5F, Seoul, Republic of Korea. Phone: 02-3444-6886. Fax: 02-3444-6887. E-mail: apgujung@eliteprep.com.
URL www.eliteprep.com

For more information, see page 480.

ELITE EDUCATIONAL INSTITUTE JUNIOR HIGH/PSAT PROGRAM–KOREA

Elite Educational Institute
Seoul
Republic of Korea

General Information Coed day academic program established in 1987. Formal opportunities for the academically talented.
Academics English as a second language, English language/literature, SAT/ACT preparation, mathematics, reading, study skills, writing.
Special Interest Areas College planning.
Program Information 3 sessions per year. Session length: 100–350 days in January, February, March, April, May, June, July, August, September, October, November, December. Ages: 12–14. 40–80 participants per session. Day program cost: $240–$360. Application fee: $50.
Application Deadline Continuous.
Contact Mr. Min, Director, Kangnam-Gu Shinsa Dong 595-1, Ahnkook Building 5F, Seoul, Republic of Korea. Phone: 02-3444-6886. Fax: 02-3444-6887. E-mail: apgujung@eliteprep.com.
URL www.eliteprep.com

For more information, see page 480.

ELITE EDUCATIONAL INSTITUTE SAT BOOTCAMP–KOREA

Elite Educational Institute
Seoul
Republic of Korea

General Information Coed day academic program established in 1987. Formal opportunities for the academically talented.
Program Focus Intensive SAT preparation program.
Academics English language/literature, SAT/ACT preparation, mathematics, precollege program, reading, writing.
Special Interest Areas College planning.
Program Information 1 session per year. Session length: 40 days in June, July, August. Ages: 15–18. 100–300 participants per session. Day program cost: $2200. Application fee: $50.
Application Deadline June 15.
Contact Mr. Min, Director, Kangnam-Gu Shinsa Dong 595-1, Ahnkook Building 5F, Seoul, Republic of Korea. Phone: 02-3444-6886. Fax: 02-3444-6887. E-mail: apgujung@eliteprep.com.
URL www.eliteprep.com

For more information, see page 480.

ELITE EDUCATIONAL INSTITUTE SAT PREPARATION–KOREA

Elite Educational Institute
Seoul
Republic of Korea

General Information Coed day academic program established in 1987. Formal opportunities for the academically talented.
Program Focus SAT and subject test preparation.
Academics American literature, English language/literature, SAT/ACT preparation, biology, biology (Advanced Placement), chemistry, history, mathematics, mathematics (Advanced Placement), physics, precollege program, reading, writing.
Special Interest Areas College planning.
Program Information 3 sessions per year. Session length: 100–350 days in January, February, March, April, May, June, July, August, September, October, November, December. Ages: 15–18. 100–300 participants

Elite Educational Institute SAT Preparation–Korea (continued)

per session. Day program cost: $380–$600. Application fee: $50.

Application Deadline Continuous.

Contact Mr. Min, Director, Kangnam-Gu Shinsa Dong 595-1, Ahnkook Building 5F, Seoul, Republic of Korea. Phone: 02-3444-6886. Fax: 02-3444-6887. E-mail: apgujung@eliteprep.com.

URL www.eliteprep.com

For more information, see page 480.

RUSSIAN FEDERATION

SUMMER ADVANTAGE STUDY ABROAD–ST. PETERSBURG, RUSSIA

American Institute for Foreign Study (AIFS)
St. Petersburg State Polytechnic University
29 Politekhnitcheskaya Str.
St. Petersburg 195251
Russian Federation

General Information Coed travel academic program and cultural program established in 1984. College credit may be earned.

Program Focus Study abroad for college credit.

Academics Russian language/literature, art history/appreciation, government and politics, history, social science, sociology.

Trips Cultural, day, overnight, shopping.

Program Information 1 session per year. Session length: 30–42 days in June, July. Ages: 16–18. 10–20 participants per session. Cost: $6295. Application fee: $95.

Application Deadline April 15.

Contact Mrs. Amy Van Stone, Director of Admissions, Summer Advantage, 9 West Broad Street, River Plaza, Stamford, Connecticut 06902. Phone: 800-913-7151. Fax: 203-399-5463. E-mail: summeradvantage@aifs.com.

URL www.summeradvantage.com

For more information, see page 410.

SAINT VINCENT AND THE GRENADINES

BROADREACH ADVENTURES IN THE GRENADINES–ADVANCED SCUBA

Broadreach
Saint Vincent and The Grenadines

General Information Coed travel outdoor program and adventure program established in 1992.

Program Focus Coed program focusing on advanced PADI scuba certification, PADI rescue certification, sail training, marine biology, island exploration.

Academics Ecology, environmental science, marine studies.

Arts Photography.

Special Interest Areas Community service, conservation projects, field research/expeditions, leadership training, nature study.

Sports Boating, fishing, sailing, scuba diving, snorkeling, waterskiing.

Wilderness/Outdoors Hiking, ocean expeditions, outdoor adventure, sailing trips, wilderness/outdoors (general).

Trips Cultural.

Program Information 2 sessions per year. Session length: 3 weeks in June, July, August. Ages: 14–19. 10–12 participants per session. Cost: $4940. Financial aid available.

Application Deadline Continuous.

Contact Carlton Goldthwaite, Director, 806 McCulloch Street, Suite 102, Raleigh, North Carolina 27603. Phone: 888-833-1907. Fax: 919-833-2129. E-mail: info@gobroadreach.com.

URL www.gobroadreach.com

For more information, see page 432.

SENEGAL

PUTNEY STUDENT TRAVEL–COMMUNITY SERVICE–SENEGAL

Putney Student Travel
Senegal

General Information Coed residential community service program and cultural program established in 1951.

Program Focus Community service and cultural exchange and weekend excursions from a base in a small rural community.

Academics Intercultural studies.

Special Interest Areas Community service, construction, cross-cultural education, field research/expeditions.

Sports Swimming.
Wilderness/Outdoors Hiking, pack animal trips.
Trips Cultural, day, overnight.
Program Information 1–2 sessions per year. Session length: 28–30 days in June, July, August. Ages: 15–18. 16 participants per session. Boarding program cost: $6790. Financial aid available. Airfare included.
Application Deadline Continuous.
Contact Jeffrey Shumlin, Admissions Director, 345 Hickory Ridge Road, Putney, Vermont 05346. Phone: 802-387-5000. Fax: 802-387-4276. E-mail: info@goputney.com.
URL www.goputney.com

For more information, see page 598.

SOUTH AFRICA

THE EXPERIMENT IN INTERNATIONAL LIVING–SOUTH AFRICA HOMESTAY AND COMMUNITY SERVICE

The Experiment in International Living
South Africa

General Information Coed travel outdoor program, arts program, community service program, cultural program, and adventure program established in 1932.
Program Focus International youth travel, homestays, community service, arts.
Academics Language study.
Arts Arts, arts and crafts (general), dance, music, theater/drama.
Special Interest Areas Community service, homestays, touring.
Wilderness/Outdoors Safari.
Trips Cultural, day, overnight.
Program Information 1 session per year. Session length: 5 weeks in June, July, August. Ages: 14–19. 10–20 participants per session. Cost: $6200. Application fee: $75. Financial aid available. Airfare included.
Application Deadline May 1.
Contact Annie Thompson, Enrollment Director, Summer Abroad, Kipling Road, PO Box 676, Brattleboro, Vermont 05302-0676. Phone: 800-345-2929. Fax: 802-258-3428. E-mail: eil@worldlearning.org.
URL www.usexperiment.org

For more information, see page 492.

GLOBAL LEADERSHIP ADVENTURES–CAPE TOWN: COMMUNITY SERVICE AND LEADERSHIP

Global Leadership Adventures
Cape Town
South Africa

General Information Coed travel academic program, community service program, and cultural program established in 2004. High school credit may be earned.

Global Leadership Adventures–Cape Town: Community Service and Leadership

Academics African languages, academics (general), art history/appreciation, ecology, geology/earth science, history, intercultural studies, international relations, music, zoology.
Special Interest Areas Community service.
Sports Football, soccer.
Wilderness/Outdoors Hiking.
Trips Cultural, day, overnight.
Program Information 1–2 sessions per year. Session length: 3 weeks in June, July, August. Ages: 15–18. Cost: $4395. Financial aid available.
Application Deadline February 28.
Contact Admissions, 2633 Lincoln Boulevard, #427, Santa Monica, California 90405. Phone: 888-358-4321. Fax: 866-612-3697. E-mail: admissions@globalleadershipadventures.com.
URL www.globalleadershipadventures.com/main/home.asp

For more information, see page 504.

PUTNEY STUDENT TRAVEL–GLOBAL ACTION–SOUTH AFRICA

Putney Student Travel
South Africa

General Information Coed residential cultural program established in 1951.
Program Focus Students spend three weeks pursuing

Putney Student Travel–Global Action–South Africa (continued)

research in relation to community building and sustainable development.

Academics Intercultural studies.

Special Interest Areas Cross-cultural education, field research/expeditions.

Trips Cultural, day, overnight.

Program Information 1 session per year. Session length: 25–32 days in June, July, August. Ages: 15–18. 16 participants per session. Boarding program cost: $6990. Financial aid available.

Application Deadline Continuous.

Contact Jeffrey Shumlin, Admissions Director, 345 Hickory Ridge Road, Putney, Vermont 05346. Phone: 802-387-5000. Fax: 802-387-4276. E-mail: info@goputney.com.

URL www.goputney.com

For more information, see page 598.

SPAIN

AAVE–España Clásica

AAVE–Journeys That Matter
Spain

General Information Coed travel academic program, outdoor program, wilderness program, cultural program, and adventure program established in 1976. Accredited by American Camping Association.

Program Focus Language immersion and adventure travel.

Academics Spanish language/literature, intercultural studies.

Special Interest Areas Community service, cross-cultural education, homestays, leadership training, touring.

Sports Bicycling, horseback riding, sailing, surfing, swimming.

Wilderness/Outdoors Backpacking, bicycle trips, hiking, rafting, white-water trips.

Trips Cultural, day, overnight.

Program Information 2–4 sessions per year. Session length: 3 weeks in June, July, August. Ages: 14–18. 13–15 participants per session. Cost: $5388. Financial aid available.

Application Deadline Continuous.

Jobs Positions for college students 21 and older.

Contact Mr. Abbott Wallis, Owner, 2308 Fossil Trace Drive, Golden, Colorado 80401. Phone: 800-222-3595. Fax: 303-526-0885. E-mail: info@aave.com.

URL www.aave.com

For more information, see page 394.

Academic Study Associates–Barcelona

Academic Study Associates, Inc. (ASA)
Barcelona
Spain

General Information Coed residential academic program and cultural program established in 2001. Formal opportunities for the academically talented. High school credit may be earned.

Program Focus Language and cultural immersion program combining language, activities, and excursions.

Academics Spanish (Advanced Placement), Spanish language/literature, architecture, intercultural studies, precollege program, writing.

Arts Film.

Special Interest Areas Touring.

Sports Basketball, soccer, swimming, tennis, volleyball.

Trips Cultural, day.

Program Information 1 session per year. Session length: 4 weeks in July. Ages: 15–18. 100 participants per session. Boarding program cost: $6495. Financial aid available.

Application Deadline Continuous.

Jobs Positions for college students 21 and older.

Contact Marcia Evans, President, 375 West Broadway, Suite 200, New York, New York 10012. Phone: 212-796-8340. Fax: 212-334-4934. E-mail: summer@asaprograms.com.

URL www.asaprograms.com

For more information, see page 398.

ACADEMIC STUDY ASSOCIATES–SPANISH IN ESPAÑA

Academic Study Associates, Inc. (ASA)
Andalucia
Spain

General Information Coed residential academic program and cultural program established in 1984. Formal opportunities for the academically talented. High school credit may be earned.
Program Focus Spanish language, art history, culture.
Academics Spanish language/literature, academics (general), art history/appreciation, history, intercultural studies.
Arts Arts and crafts (general), ceramics, dance, dance (folk), drawing, painting, photography, pottery.
Special Interest Areas Culinary arts, field trips (arts and culture), homestays, touring.
Sports Basketball, boating, canoeing, equestrian sports, horseback riding, sailing, scuba diving, soccer, sports (general), swimming, tennis, volleyball.
Wilderness/Outdoors Wilderness camping.
Trips Cultural, day, overnight.
Program Information 1 session per year. Session length: 30 days in June, July. Ages: 15–18. 130–150 participants per session. Boarding program cost: $6995. Participant may study in Cadiz, Conil, Tarifa or Nerja. Cost includes airfare from New York City.
Application Deadline Continuous.
Jobs Positions for college students 21 and older.
Contact Marcia E. Evans, President, 375 West Broadway, Suite 200, New York, New York 10012. Phone: 212-796-8340. Fax: 212-334-4934. E-mail: summer@asaprograms.com.
URL www.asaprograms.com

For more information, see page 398.

AFS-USA–HOMESTAY PLUS–SPAIN

AFS-USA
Spain

General Information Coed residential outdoor program and cultural program.
Program Focus Homestay with outdoor education.
Academics Spanish language/literature.
Special Interest Areas Homestays, touring.
Wilderness/Outdoors Hiking.
Trips Cultural, day, overnight.
Program Information 1 session per year. Session length: 30–45 days in June, July. Ages: 15–18. Boarding program cost: $6100. Application fee: $75. Financial aid available. International airfare and volunteer homestay support included.
Application Deadline Continuous.
Contact Manager, AFS Info Center, 506 Southwest 6th Avenue, 2nd Floor, Portland, Oregon 97204. Phone: 800-AFS-INFO. Fax: 503-299-0753. E-mail: afsinfo@afs.org.
URL www.afs.org/usa

For more information, see page 408.

AFS-USA–LANGUAGE STUDY–SPAIN

AFS-USA
Spain

General Information Coed residential cultural program.
Program Focus Living in Salamanca and attending a language school.
Academics Spanish language/literature.
Special Interest Areas Touring.
Trips Cultural, day, overnight.
Program Information 1 session per year. Session length: 4 weeks in June, July. Ages: 15–18. 35 participants per session. Boarding program cost: $6000. Application fee: $75. Financial aid available. International airfare and volunteer homestay support included.
Application Deadline Continuous.
Contact Manager, AFS Info Center, 506 Southwest 6th Avenue, 2nd Floor, Portland, Oregon 97204. Phone: 800-AFS-INFO. Fax: 503-248-4076. E-mail: afsinfo@afs.org.
URL www.afs.org/usa

For more information, see page 408.

CENTER FOR CULTURAL INTERCHANGE–SPAIN HIGH SCHOOL ABROAD

Center for Cultural Interchange
Spain

General Information Coed residential academic program and cultural program established in 1985. High school credit may be earned.
Program Focus High school in Spain, cultural immersion.
Academics Spanish language/literature, academics (general).
Special Interest Areas Cross-cultural education, homestays.
Trips Cultural, day, overnight.
Program Information 2 sessions per year. Session length: 90–300 days in January, February, March, April, May, June, July, August, September, October, November, December. Ages: 15–18. Boarding program cost: $7200–$9100. Financial aid available.
Application Deadline Continuous.

Center for Cultural Interchange–Spain High School Abroad (continued)

Contact Ms. Juliet Jones, Outbound Programs Director, 746 North LaSalle Drive, Chicago, Illinois 60610-3617. Phone: 866-684-9675. Fax: 312-944-2644. E-mail: info@cci-exchange.com.
URL www.cci-exchange.com
For more information, see page 448.

CENTER FOR CULTURAL INTERCHANGE–SPAIN INDEPENDENT HOMESTAY

Center for Cultural Interchange
Spain

General Information Coed residential cultural program established in 1985.
Program Focus Cultural immersion, homestay in Spain.
Academics Spanish language/literature, independent study.
Special Interest Areas Homestays.
Trips Cultural, day.
Program Information Session length: 14–90 days in January, February, March, April, May, June, July, August, September, October, November, December. Ages: 14+. Boarding program cost: $1250–$1990. Financial aid available.
Application Deadline Continuous.
Contact Ms. Juliet Jones, Outbound Programs Director, 746 North LaSalle Drive, Chicago, Illinois 60610-3617. Phone: 866-684-9675. Fax: 312-944-2644. E-mail: info@cci-exchange.com.
URL www.cci-exchange.com
For more information, see page 448.

CENTER FOR CULTURAL INTERCHANGE–SPAIN LANGUAGE SCHOOL

Center for Cultural Interchange
Spain

General Information Coed residential academic program and cultural program established in 1985. High school or college credit may be earned.
Program Focus Cultural immersion; language study.
Academics Spanish language/literature.
Arts Arts and crafts (general), dance (folk).
Special Interest Areas Homestays.
Trips Cultural, day.
Program Information 1–50 sessions per year. Session length: 2–6 weeks in January, February, March, April, May, June, July, August, September, October, November, December. Ages: 14+. Boarding program cost: $2100–$3050. Financial aid available.
Application Deadline Continuous.
Contact Ms. Juliet Jones, Outbound Programs Director, 746 North LaSalle Drive, Chicago, Illinois 60610-3617. Phone: 866-684-9675. Fax: 312-944-2644. E-mail: info@cci-exchange.com.
URL www.cci-exchange.com
For more information, see page 448.

CENTER FOR CULTURAL INTERCHANGE–SPAIN SPORTS AND LANGUAGE CAMP

Center for Cultural Interchange
Granada
Spain

General Information Coed residential academic program, outdoor program, sports camp, and cultural program established in 1985.
Program Focus Language and sports camp.
Academics Spanish language/literature.
Arts Arts and crafts (general).
Special Interest Areas Cross-cultural education.
Sports Archery, basketball, canoeing, equestrian sports, horseback riding, soccer, swimming, tennis, volleyball.
Wilderness/Outdoors Hiking, mountain biking, outdoor adventure.
Trips Cultural, day.
Program Information 1 session per year. Session length: 3 weeks in July. Ages: 10–17. Boarding program cost: $2950. Financial aid available.
Application Deadline Continuous.
Contact Ms. Juliet Jones, Outbound Programs Director, 746 North LaSalle Drive, Chicago, Illinois 60610-3617. Phone: 866-684-9675. Fax: 312-944-2644. E-mail: info@cci-exchange.com.
URL www.cci-exchange.com
For more information, see page 448.

CHOATE ROSEMARY HALL SUMMER IN SPAIN

Choate Rosemary Hall
Santander/La Coruña
Spain

General Information Coed travel academic program and cultural program established in 1973. High school credit may be earned.
Program Focus Spanish language and culture immersion.
Academics Spanish language/literature, art history/appreciation, history, social studies.
Special Interest Areas Cross-cultural education, homestays, touring.
Sports Swimming.
Trips Cultural, day, overnight.
Program Information 1 session per year. Session length: 40 days in June, July. Ages: 14–18. 45–52 participants per session. Cost: $6499. Application fee:

$60. Financial aid available. Airfare from New York to Madrid included.
Application Deadline Continuous.
Contact Ms. Nancy Burress, Director, Summer Programs in Spain, 333 Christian Street, Wallingford, Connecticut 06492. Phone: 203-697-2365. Fax: 203-697-2519. E-mail: nburress@choate.edu.
URL www.choate.edu/summerprograms

For more information, see page 452.

EDU-CULTURE INTERNATIONAL (ECI)– ANDALUSION TOTAL IMMERSION

Edu-Culture International (ECI)
Spain

General Information Coed travel cultural program established in 2007.
Program Focus Total Spanish language and culture immersion with host families in Southern Spain for 18 days (no classes), 1 week of travel throughout Spain.
Academics Spanish language/literature, intercultural studies, precollege program.
Special Interest Areas Cross-cultural education, homestays, touring.
Trips Cultural, overnight, shopping.
Program Information 1 session per year. Session length: 4 weeks in June, July. Ages: 16–18. 25–30 participants per session. Cost: $4300. Application fee: $95. Financial aid available. Airfare from San Francisco, CA to Madrid, Spain included in cost.
Application Deadline Continuous.
Jobs Positions for college students 22 and older.
Contact Ms. Phyllis O'Neill, Director, PO Box 2692, Berkeley, California 94702. Phone: 866-343-8990. Fax: 510-845-2231. E-mail: info@educulture.org.
URL www.educulture.org

For more information, see page 476.

EDU-CULTURE INTERNATIONAL (ECI)– GRANADA HOMESTAY

Edu-Culture International (ECI)
Spain

General Information Coed travel academic program and cultural program established in 2001. College credit may be earned.
Program Focus Pre-college experience including 3 weeks of intensive Spanish classes and homestay in Granada with daily excursions and activities, 1 week travel throughout Spain.
Academics Spanish language/literature, intercultural studies, precollege program.
Special Interest Areas Cross-cultural education, homestays, touring.
Sports Swimming.
Trips Cultural, day, overnight, shopping.
Program Information 1 session per year. Session length: 4 weeks in June, July. Ages: 15–18. 25–30 participants per session. Cost: $5700. Application fee:

$95. Financial aid available. Airfare from San Francisco, CA to Malaga, Spain included in cost.
Application Deadline Continuous.
Jobs Positions for college students 22 and older.
Contact Ms. Phyllis O'Neill, Director, PO Box 2692, Berkeley, California 94702. Phone: 866-343-8990. Fax: 510-845-2231. E-mail: info@educulture.org.
URL www.educulture.org

For more information, see page 476.

EDU-CULTURE INTERNATIONAL (ECI)– GRANADA HOMESTAY OR DORM PLUS SOUTHERN HOST FAMILY IMMERSION

Edu-Culture International (ECI)
Spain

General Information Coed travel academic program and cultural program established in 2001. College credit may be earned.
Program Focus Pre-college experience including 2 weeks of intensive Spanish classes in Granada (dorm or homestay) with daily excursions and activities, 1 week Spanish language and culture immersion with host families in Southern Spain, 1 week travel throughout Spain.
Academics Spanish language/literature, intercultural studies, precollege program.
Special Interest Areas Cross-cultural education, homestays, touring.
Sports Swimming.
Trips Cultural, day, overnight, shopping.
Program Information 1 session per year. Session length: 27 days in July, August. Ages: 15–18. 25–30 participants per session. Cost: $5700. Application fee: $95. Financial aid available. Airfare from San Francisco, CA to Malaga, Spain included in cost.
Application Deadline Continuous.
Jobs Positions for college students 22 and older.
Contact Ms. Phyllis O'Neill, Director, PO Box 2692, Berkeley, California 94702. Phone: 866-343-8990. Fax: 510-845-2231. E-mail: info@educulture.org.
URL www.educulture.org

For more information, see page 476.

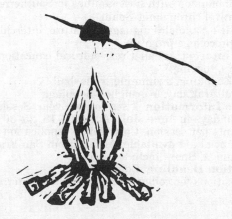

EDU-CULTURE INTERNATIONAL (ECI)– GRANADA-NERJA HOMESTAY COMBO

Edu-Culture International (ECI)
Spain

General Information Coed travel academic program and cultural program established in 2007.
Program Focus Pre-college 3-week experience including intensive Spanish classes and homestay in Granada for 1 week and in Nerja for 1 week. Daily excursions and activities, travel throughout Spain for 1 week.
Academics Spanish language/literature, intercultural studies, precollege program.
Special Interest Areas Cross-cultural education, homestays, touring.
Sports Swimming, volleyball.
Trips Cultural, day, overnight, shopping.
Program Information 1 session per year. Session length: 22 days in July, August. Ages: 15–18. 25–30 participants per session. Cost: $5300. Application fee: $95. Financial aid available. Airfare from San Francisco, CA to Malaga, Spain included in cost.
Application Deadline Continuous.
Jobs Positions for college students 22 and older.
Contact Ms. Phyllis O'Neill, Director, PO Box 2692, Berkeley, California 94702. Phone: 866-343-8990. Fax: 510-845-2231. E-mail: info@educulture.org
URL www.educulture.org
For more information, see page 476.

EDU-CULTURE INTERNATIONAL (ECI)– NERJA HOMESTAY PLUS SOUTHERN HOST FAMILY IMMERSION

Edu-Culture International (ECI)
Spain

General Information Coed travel academic program and cultural program established in 2003. College credit may be earned.
Program Focus Pre-college experience including 2 weeks of intensive Spanish classes in Nerja with daily excursions and activities, 1 week Spanish language and culture immersion with host families in Southern Spain, 1 week travel throughout Spain.
Academics Spanish language/literature, intercultural studies, precollege program.
Special Interest Areas Cross-cultural education, homestays, touring.
Sports Kayaking, swimming, volleyball.
Trips Cultural, day, overnight, shopping.
Program Information 1 session per year. Session length: 29 days in June, July. Ages: 15–18. 25–30 participants per session. Cost: $5950. Application fee: $95. Financial aid available. Airfare from San Francisco, CA to Malaga, Spain included in cost.
Application Deadline Continuous.
Jobs Positions for college students 22 and older.

Contact Ms. Phyllis O'Neill, Director, PO Box 2692, Berkeley, California 94702. Phone: 866-343-8990. Fax: 510-845-2231. E-mail: info@educulture.org
URL www.educulture.org
For more information, see page 476.

EDU-CULTURE INTERNATIONAL (ECI)– NERJA HOMESTAY WITH OPTIONAL SOUTHERN HOST FAMILY IMMERSION

Edu-Culture International (ECI)
Spain

General Information Coed travel academic program and cultural program established in 2003. College credit may be earned.
Program Focus Pre-college experience including 2 weeks of intensive Spanish classes in Nerja with daily excursions and activities, optional 1 week Spanish language and culture immersion with host families in Southern Spain, travel in Spain for 4 days.
Academics Spanish language/literature, intercultural studies, precollege program.
Special Interest Areas Cross-cultural education, homestays, touring.
Sports Kayaking, swimming, volleyball.
Trips Cultural, day, overnight, shopping.
Program Information 1 session per year. Session length: 24 days in July, August. Ages: 15–18. 25–30 participants per session. Cost: $5300. Application fee: $95. Financial aid available. Airfare from Los Angeles, CA to Malaga, Spain included in cost.
Application Deadline Continuous.
Jobs Positions for college students 22 and older.
Contact Ms. Phyllis O'Neill, Director, PO Box 2692, Berkeley, California 94702. Phone: 866-343-8990. Fax: 510-845-2231. E-mail: info@educulture.org
URL www.educulture.org
For more information, see page 476.

EDU-CULTURE INTERNATIONAL (ECI)– SALAMANCA DORM PLUS SOUTHERN HOST FAMILY IMMERSION

Edu-Culture International (ECI)
Spain

General Information Coed travel academic program and cultural program established in 2005. College credit may be earned.
Program Focus Pre-college experience including intensive Spanish classes for 2 weeks in Salamanca with daily excursions and activities, Spanish language and culture immersion with host families in Southern Spain for 1 week, travel throughout Spain for 1 week.
Academics Spanish language/literature, intercultural studies, precollege program.
Special Interest Areas Cross-cultural education, homestays, touring.
Sports Horseback riding, soccer, swimming.
Trips Cultural, day, overnight, shopping.

Program Information 1 session per year. Session length: 30 days in June, July. Ages: 15–18. 25–30 participants per session. Cost: $5950. Application fee: $95. Financial aid available. Airfare from San Francisco, CA to Madrid, Spain included in cost.
Application Deadline Continuous.
Jobs Positions for college students 22 and older.
Contact Ms. Phyllis O'Neill, Director, PO Box 2692, Berkeley, California 94702. Phone: 866-343-8990. Fax: 510-845-2231. E-mail: info@educulture.org.
URL www.educulture.org

For more information, see page 476.

EDU-CULTURE INTERNATIONAL (ECI)– SALAMANCA HOMESTAY

Edu-Culture International (ECI)
Spain

General Information Coed travel academic program and cultural program established in 2000. College credit may be earned.
Program Focus Pre-college experience including intensive Spanish classes and homestay in Salamanca for 3 weeks with daily excursions and activities, travel throughout Spain for 1 week.
Academics Spanish language/literature, intercultural studies, precollege program.
Special Interest Areas Cross-cultural education, homestays, touring.
Sports Horseback riding, soccer, swimming.
Trips Cultural, day, overnight, shopping.
Program Information 1 session per year. Session length: 4 weeks in June, July. Ages: 15–18. 25–30 participants per session. Cost: $5700. Application fee: $95. Financial aid available. Airfare from San Francisco, CA to Malaga, Spain included in cost.
Application Deadline Continuous.
Jobs Positions for college students 22 and older.
Contact Ms. Phyllis O'Neill, Director, PO Box 2692, Berkeley, California 94702. Phone: 866-343-8990. Fax: 510-845-2231. E-mail: info@educulture.org.
URL www.educulture.org

For more information, see page 476.

EDU-CULTURE INTERNATIONAL (ECI)– SALAMANCA HOMESTAY PLUS NORTHERN HOST FAMILY IMMERSION

Edu-Culture International (ECI)
Spain

General Information Coed travel academic program and cultural program established in 2001. College credit may be earned.

Edu-Culture International (ECI)–Salamanca Homestay Plus Northern Host Family Immersion

Program Focus Pre-college experience including intensive Spanish classes for 2 weeks in Salamanca with daily excursions and activities, Spanish language and culture immersion with host families in Northern Spain for 1 week, travel throughout Spain for 1 week.
Academics Spanish language/literature, intercultural studies, precollege program.
Special Interest Areas Cross-cultural education, homestays, touring.
Sports Horseback riding, soccer, swimming.
Trips Cultural, day, overnight, shopping.
Program Information 2 sessions per year. Session length: 30 days in June, July. Ages: 15–18. 25–30 participants per session. Cost: $5850. Application fee: $95. Financial aid available. Airfare from San Francisco, CA to Madrid, Spain.
Application Deadline Continuous.
Jobs Positions for college students 22 and older.
Contact Ms. Phyllis O'Neill, Director, PO Box 2692, Berkeley, California 94702. Phone: 866-343-8990. Fax: 510-845-2231. E-mail: info@educulture.org.
URL www.educulture.org

For more information, see page 476.

EDU-CULTURE INTERNATIONAL (ECI)– SALAMANCA HOMESTAY (SHORT VERSION)

Edu-Culture International (ECI)
Spain

General Information Coed travel academic program and cultural program established in 2000.
Program Focus Pre-college experience including intensive Spanish classes and homestay in Salamanca for 2 weeks with daily excursions and activities, 3 days/nights in Madrid.
Academics Spanish language/literature, intercultural studies, precollege program.
Special Interest Areas Cross-cultural education, homestays, touring.
Sports Horseback riding, soccer, swimming.
Trips Cultural, day, overnight, shopping.
Program Information 1 session per year. Session length: 19 days in July, August. Ages: 15–18. 25–30 participants per session. Cost: $3950. Application fee: $95. Financial aid available. Airfare from San Francisco, CA to Madrid, Spain included in cost.
Application Deadline Continuous.
Jobs Positions for college students 22 and older.
Contact Ms. Phyllis O'Neill, Director, PO Box 2692, Berkeley, California 94702. Phone: 866-343-8990. Fax: 510-845-2231. E-mail: info@educulture.org.
URL www.educulture.org
For more information, see page 476.

EDU-CULTURE INTERNATIONAL (ECI)– SAN SEBASTIAN HOMESTAY PLUS SOUTHERN HOST FAMILY IMMERSION

Edu-Culture International (ECI)
Spain

General Information Coed travel academic program and cultural program established in 2004. College credit may be earned.
Program Focus Pre-college experience including 2 weeks of intensive Spanish classes in San Sebastian with daily excursions and activities, 1 week of Spanish language and culture immersion with host families in Southern Spain, and 1 week of travel throughout Spain.
Academics Spanish language/literature, intercultural studies, precollege program.
Special Interest Areas Cross-cultural education, homestays, touring.
Sports Surfing, swimming, tennis.
Trips Cultural, day, overnight, shopping.
Program Information 1 session per year. Session length: 30 days in July, August. Ages: 15–18. 25–30 participants per session. Cost: $6400. Application fee: $95. Financial aid available. Airfare from San Francisco, CA to Barcelona, Spain included in cost.
Application Deadline Continuous.
Jobs Positions for college students 22 and older.

Contact Ms. Phyllis O'Neill, Director, PO Box 2692, Berkeley, California 94702. Phone: 866-343-8990. Fax: 510-845-2231. E-mail: info@educulture.org.
URL www.educulture.org
For more information, see page 476.

EF INTERNATIONAL LANGUAGE SCHOOL– BARCELONA

EF International Language Schools
Calle Calvet 68-70
2nd Floor
Barcelona 08021
Spain

General Information Coed travel academic program and cultural program established in 1988. High school or college credit may be earned.
Program Focus Language and cultural immersion.
Academics Spanish (Advanced Placement), Spanish language/literature.
Special Interest Areas Field trips (arts and culture), homestays, internships, touring.
Sports Sports (general).
Wilderness/Outdoors Outdoor adventure.
Trips Cultural, day, overnight.
Program Information 2–52 sessions per year. Session length: 14–365 days in January, February, March, April, May, June, July, August, September, October, November, December. Ages: 16+. 200–250 participants per session. Application fee: $145. Financial aid available. Call for costs.
Application Deadline Continuous.
Contact Ms. Margaret Kelly, Director of Admissions, One Education Street, Cambridge, Massachusetts 02141. Phone: 800-992-1892. Fax: 800-590-1125. E-mail: ils@ef.com.
URL www.ef.com
For more information, see page 478.

EF International Language School–Malaga

EF International Language Schools
Avenida Juan Sebastian Elcano, 117
Malaga 29017
Spain

General Information Coed travel academic program and cultural program established in 2004. High school or college credit may be earned.
Program Focus Language and cultural immersion.
Academics Spanish (Advanced Placement), Spanish language/literature.
Special Interest Areas Field trips (arts and culture).
Sports Horseback riding, sailing, scuba diving, snorkeling, sports (general), swimming, waterskiing, windsurfing.
Wilderness/Outdoors Wilderness/outdoors (general).
Trips Cultural, day, overnight.
Program Information 2–52 sessions per year. Session length: 2–52 weeks in January, February, March, April, May, June, July, August, September, October, November, December. Ages: 15+. 100–150 participants per session. Application fee: $145. Financial aid available. Call for costs.
Application Deadline Continuous.
Contact Ms. Margaret Kelly, Director of Admissions, One Education Street, Cambridge, Massachusetts 02141. Phone: 800-992-1892. Fax: 800-590-1125. E-mail: ils@ef.com.
URL www.ef.com

For more information, see page 478.

Enforex–General Spanish–Alicante

Enforex Spanish in the Spanish World
Paseo Explanada de España
Alicante 03001
Spain

General Information Coed residential academic program established in 1989. High school or college credit may be earned.
Program Focus Language program with optional cultural and sport activities. Course offerings include part-time, intensive, super-intensive.
Academics Spanish (Advanced Placement), Spanish language/literature, classical languages/literatures, computers, intercultural studies.
Special Interest Areas Homestays, nautical skills.
Sports Canoeing, climbing (wall), cross-country, football, golf, gymnastics, soccer, swimming, volleyball.
Trips Cultural, day, overnight, shopping.
Program Information 48 sessions per year. Session length: 1–52 weeks in January, February, March, April, May, June, July, August, September, October, November, December. Ages: 14+. 50 participants per session. Boarding program cost: 280 euros. Application fee: 65 euros. Prices are per week, including accommodation.
Application Deadline Continuous.

Contact Antonio Anadón, Director, Alberto Aguilera 26, Madrid 28015, Spain. Phone: 34-91-594-3776. Fax: 34-91-594-5159. E-mail: info@enforex.es.
URL www.enforex.com

For more information, see page 486.

Enforex–General Spanish–Barcelona

Enforex Spanish in the Spanish World
Diputacion 92
Barcelona 08015
Spain

General Information Coed residential academic program established in 1989. High school or college credit may be earned.
Program Focus Language program with optional cultural and sport activities. Course offerings include part-time, intensive, super-intensive.
Academics Spanish (Advanced Placement), Spanish language/literature, classical languages/literatures, computers, intercultural studies.
Special Interest Areas Homestays, nautical skills.
Sports Canoeing, climbing (wall), cross-country, football, golf, gymnastics, soccer, swimming, volleyball.
Trips Cultural, day, overnight, shopping.
Program Information 48 sessions per year. Session length: 1–52 weeks in January, February, March, April, May, June, July, August, September, October, November, December. Ages: 14+. 500 participants per session. Boarding program cost: 305–390 euros. Application fee: 65 euros. Prices are per week, including accommodation.
Application Deadline Continuous.
Contact Antonio Anadón, Director, Alberto Aguilera 26, Madrid 28015, Spain. Phone: 34-91-594-3776. Fax: 34-91-594-5159. E-mail: info@enforex.es.
URL www.enforex.com

For more information, see page 486.

ENFOREX–GENERAL SPANISH–GRANADA

Enforex Spanish in the Spanish World
Santa Teresa 20
Granada 18002
Spain

General Information Coed residential academic program established in 1989. High school or college credit may be earned.
Program Focus Language program with optional cultural and sport activities. Course offerings include part-time, intensive, super-intensive.
Academics Spanish (Advanced Placement), Spanish language/literature, classical languages/literatures, computers, intercultural studies.
Special Interest Areas Homestays, nautical skills.
Sports Canoeing, climbing (wall), cross-country, football, golf, gymnastics, soccer, swimming, volleyball.
Trips Cultural, day, overnight, shopping.
Program Information 48 sessions per year. Session length: 1–52 weeks in January, February, March, April, May, June, July, August, September, October, November, December. Ages: 14+. 120 participants per session. Boarding program cost: 280–330 euros. Application fee: 65 euros. Prices are per week, including accommodation.
Application Deadline Continuous.
Contact Antonio Anadón, Director, Alberto Aguilera 26, Madrid 28015, Spain. Phone: 34-91-594-3776. Fax: 34-91-594-5159. E-mail: info@enforex.es.
URL www.enforex.com

For more information, see page 486.

ENFOREX–GENERAL SPANISH–MADRID

Enforex Spanish in the Spanish World
Calle Baltasar Gracian 4
Madrid 28015
Spain

General Information Coed residential academic program established in 1989. High school or college credit may be earned.

Enforex–General Spanish–Madrid

Program Focus Language program with optional

cultural and sport activities. Course offerings include part-time, intensive, super-intensive.
Academics Spanish (Advanced Placement), Spanish language/literature, classical languages/literatures, computers, intercultural studies.
Special Interest Areas Homestays, nautical skills.
Sports Canoeing, climbing (wall), cross-country, football, golf, gymnastics, soccer, swimming, volleyball.
Trips Cultural, day, overnight, shopping.
Program Information 48 sessions per year. Session length: 1–52 weeks in January, February, March, April, May, June, July, August, September, October, November, December. Ages: 14+. 350 participants per session. Boarding program cost: 305–390 euros. Application fee: 65 euros. Prices are per week, including accommodation.
Application Deadline Continuous.
Contact Antonio Anadón, Director, Alberto Aguilera 26, Madrid 28015, Spain. Phone: 34-91-594-3776. Fax: 34-91-594-5159. E-mail: info@enforex.es.
URL www.enforex.com

For more information, see page 486.

ENFOREX–GENERAL SPANISH–MALAGA

Enforex Spanish in the Spanish World
Avenida Juan Sebastian Elcano 23
Malaga 29017
Spain

General Information Coed residential academic program established in 1989. High school or college credit may be earned.
Program Focus Language program with optional cultural and sport activities. Course offerings include part-time, intensive, super-intensive.
Academics Spanish (Advanced Placement), Spanish language/literature, classical languages/literatures, computers.
Sports Canoeing, climbing (wall), cross-country, football, golf, gymnastics, sailing, soccer, swimming, volleyball.
Trips Cultural, day, overnight, shopping.
Program Information 48 sessions per year. Session length: 1–52 weeks in January, February, March, April, May, June, July, August, September, October, November, December. Ages: 14+. 120 participants per session. Boarding program cost: 305–390 euros. Application fee: 65 euros. Prices are per week, including accommodation.
Application Deadline Continuous.
Contact Antonio Anadón, Director, Alberto Aguilera 26, Madrid 28015, Spain. Phone: 34-91-594-3776. Fax: 34-91-594-5159. E-mail: info@enforex.es.
URL www.enforex.com

For more information, see page 486.

ENFOREX–GENERAL SPANISH–MARBELLA

Enforex Spanish in the Spanish World
Avenida Ricardo Soriano 43
Marbella 29600
Spain

General Information Coed residential academic program established in 1989. High school or college credit may be earned.
Program Focus Language program with optional cultural and sport activities. Course offerings include part-time, intensive, super-intensive.
Academics Spanish (Advanced Placement), Spanish language/literature, classical languages/literatures, computers, intercultural studies.
Special Interest Areas Homestays, nautical skills.
Sports Climbing (wall), cross-country, football, golf, gymnastics, horseback riding, sailing, soccer, swimming, volleyball.
Trips Cultural, day, overnight, shopping.
Program Information 48 sessions per year. Session length: 1–52 weeks in January, February, March, April, May, June, July, August, September, October, November, December. Ages: 14+. 140 participants per session. Boarding program cost: 305–390 euros. Application fee: 65 euros. Prices are per week, including accommodation.
Application Deadline Continuous.
Contact Antonio Anadón, Director, Alberto Aguilera 26, Madrid 28015, Spain. Phone: 34-91-594-3776. Fax: 34-91-594-5159. E-mail: info@enforex.es.
URL www.enforex.com

For more information, see page 486.

ENFOREX–GENERAL SPANISH–SALAMANCA

Enforex Spanish in the Spanish World
Marquesa de Almarza 1
Salamanca 37001
Spain

General Information Coed residential academic program established in 1989. High school or college credit may be earned.
Program Focus Language program with optional cultural and sport activities. Course offerings include part-time, intensive, super-intensive.
Academics Spanish (Advanced Placement), Spanish language/literature, classical languages/literatures, computers, intercultural studies.
Special Interest Areas Homestays, nautical skills.
Sports Canoeing, climbing (wall), cross-country, football, golf, gymnastics, soccer, swimming, volleyball.

Trips Cultural, day, overnight, shopping.
Program Information 48 sessions per year. Session length: 1–52 weeks in January, February, March, April, May, June, July, August, September, October, November, December. Ages: 14+. 280 participants per session. Boarding program cost: 280–330 euros. Application fee: 65 euros. Prices are per week, including accommodation.
Application Deadline Continuous.
Contact Antonio Anadón, Director, Alberto Aguilera 26, Madrid 28015, Spain. Phone: 34-91-594-3776. Fax: 34-91-594-5159. E-mail: info@enforex.es.
URL www.enforex.com

For more information, see page 486.

ENFOREX–GENERAL SPANISH–SEVILLA

Enforex Spanish in the Spanish World
Conde de Ibarra 2
Sevilla 41004
Spain

General Information Coed residential academic program established in 1989. High school or college credit may be earned.
Program Focus Language program with optional cultural and sport activities. Course offerings include part-time, intensive, super-intensive.
Academics Spanish (Advanced Placement), Spanish language/literature, classical languages/literatures, computers, intercultural studies.
Special Interest Areas Homestays, nautical skills.
Sports Canoeing, climbing (wall), cross-country, football, golf, gymnastics, soccer, swimming, volleyball.
Trips Cultural, day, overnight, shopping.
Program Information 48 sessions per year. Session length: 1–52 weeks in January, February, March, April, May, June, July, August, September, October, November, December. Ages: 14+. 100 participants per session. Boarding program cost: 280–330 euros. Application fee: 65 euros. Prices are per week, including accommodation.
Application Deadline Continuous.
Contact Antonio Anadón, Director, Alberto Aguilera 26, Madrid 28015, Spain. Phone: 34-91-594-3776. Fax: 34-91-594-5159. E-mail: info@enforex.es.
URL www.enforex.com

For more information, see page 486.

ENFOREX–GENERAL SPANISH–TENERIFE

Enforex Spanish in the Spanish World
Avenida de Colon 14
Edificio Belgica
Puerto de la Cruz 38400
Spain

General Information Coed residential academic program established in 1989.
Program Focus Language program with optional cultural and sport activities. Course offerings include part-time, intensive, super-intensive.
Academics Spanish (Advanced Placement), Spanish language/literature, classical languages/literatures,

Enforex–General Spanish–Tenerife (continued)

communications, computers, intercultural studies.
Special Interest Areas Homestays, nautical skills.
Sports Canoeing, climbing (wall), cross-country, football, gymnastics, soccer, swimming, volleyball.
Trips Cultural, day, overnight, shopping.
Program Information 48 sessions per year. Session length: 1–52 weeks in January, February, March, April, May, June, July, August, September, October, November, December. Ages: 14+. 50 participants per session. Boarding program cost: 285–380 euros. Application fee: 65 euros. Prices are per week, including accommodation.
Application Deadline Continuous.
Contact Antonio Anadón, Director, Alberto Aguilera 26, Madrid 28015, Spain. Phone: 34-91-594-3776. Fax: 34-91-594-5159. E-mail: info@enforex.es.
URL www.enforex.com
For more information, see page 486.

ENFOREX–GENERAL SPANISH–VALENCIA

Enforex Spanish in the Spanish World
Paseo de Facultades 3, local
Valencia 46021
Spain

General Information Coed residential academic program established in 1989. High school or college credit may be earned.
Program Focus Language program with optional cultural and sports activities. Course offerings include part-time, intensive, super-intensive.
Academics Spanish (Advanced Placement), Spanish language/literature, classical languages/literatures, computers, intercultural studies.
Special Interest Areas Homestays, nautical skills.
Sports Canoeing, climbing (wall), cross-country, football, golf, gymnastics, soccer, swimming, volleyball.
Trips Cultural, day, overnight, shopping.
Program Information 48 sessions per year. Session length: 1–52 weeks in January, February, March, April, May, June, July, August, September, October, November, December. Ages: 14+. 200 participants per session. Boarding program cost: 280–330 euros. Application fee: 65 euros. Prices are per week, including accommodation.
Application Deadline Continuous.

Contact Antonio Anadón, Director, Alberto Aguilera 26, Madrid 28015, Spain. Phone: 34-91-594-3776. Fax: 34-91-594-5159. E-mail: info@enforex.es.
URL www.enforex.com
For more information, see page 486.

ENFOREX HISPANIC CULTURE: CIVILIZATION, HISTORY, ART, AND LITERATURE–ALICANTE

Enforex Spanish in the Spanish World
Paseo Explanada de España
Alicante 03001
Spain

General Information Coed residential academic program established in 1989. High school or college credit may be earned.
Program Focus Language program with special focus on Spanish history, art and literature.
Academics Spanish (Advanced Placement), Spanish language/literature, architecture, area studies, art (Advanced Placement), art history/appreciation, business, classical languages/literatures, computers, history, history (Advanced Placement), humanities, intercultural studies.
Arts Film.
Special Interest Areas Field trips (arts and culture), homestays, nautical skills.
Sports Aerobics, archery, baseball, basketball, canoeing, climbing (wall), football, golf, gymnastics, horseback riding, soccer, sports (general), swimming, volleyball, waterskiing.
Trips College tours, cultural, day, overnight, shopping.
Program Information 12 sessions per year. Session length: 4 weeks in January, February, March, April, May, June, July, August, September, October, November, December. Ages: 14+. 5–10 participants per session. Boarding program cost: 920–1520 euros. Application fee: 65 euros.
Application Deadline Continuous.
Contact Antonio Anadón, Director, Alberto Aguilera 26, Madrid 28015, Spain. Phone: 34-91-594-3776. Fax: 34-91-594-5159. E-mail: info@enforex.es.
URL www.enforex.com
For more information, see page 486.

ENFOREX HISPANIC CULTURE: CIVILIZATION, HISTORY, ART, AND LITERATURE—BARCELONA

Enforex Spanish in the Spanish World
Diputacion 92
Barcelona 08015
Spain

General Information Coed residential academic program established in 1989. High school or college credit may be earned.
Program Focus Language program with special focus on Spanish history, art and literature.
Academics Spanish (Advanced Placement), Spanish language/literature, architecture, area studies, art (Advanced Placement), art history/appreciation, business, classical languages/literatures, computers, history, history (Advanced Placement), humanities, intercultural studies.
Arts Film.
Special Interest Areas Field trips (arts and culture), homestays, nautical skills.
Sports Aerobics, archery, baseball, basketball, canoeing, climbing (wall), cross-country, football, golf, gymnastics, horseback riding, sailing, soccer, sports (general), swimming, volleyball, waterskiing.
Trips College tours, cultural, day, overnight, shopping.
Program Information 12 sessions per year. Session length: 4 weeks in January, February, March, April, May, June, July, August, September, October, November, December. Ages: 14+. 5–10 participants per session. Boarding program cost: 920–1920 euros. Application fee: 65 euros. Financial aid available.
Application Deadline Continuous.
Contact Antonio Anadón, Director, Alberto Aguilera 26, Madrid 28015, Spain. Phone: 34-91-594-3776. Fax: 34-91-594-5159. E-mail: info@enforex.es.
URL www.enforex.com
For more information, see page 486.

ENFOREX HISPANIC CULTURE: CIVILIZATION, HISTORY, ART, AND LITERATURE—GRANADA

Enforex Spanish in the Spanish World
Santa Teresa 20
Granada 18002
Spain

General Information Coed residential academic program established in 1989. High school or college credit may be earned.
Program Focus Language program with optional sport and cultural activities.
Academics Spanish (Advanced Placement), Spanish language/literature, architecture, area studies, art (Advanced Placement), art history/appreciation, business, classical languages/literatures, computers, history, history (Advanced Placement), humanities, intercultural studies.

Special Interest Areas Field trips (arts and culture), homestays, nautical skills.
Sports Aerobics, archery, baseball, basketball, canoeing, climbing (wall), cross-country, football, golf, gymnastics, horseback riding, sailing, soccer, sports (general), swimming, volleyball.
Trips College tours, cultural, day, overnight, shopping.
Program Information 12 sessions per year. Session length: 4 weeks in January, February, March, April, May, June, July, August, September, October, November, December. Ages: 14+. 5–10 participants per session. Boarding program cost: 920–1520 euros. Application fee: 65 euros. Financial aid available.
Application Deadline Continuous.
Contact Antonio Anadón, Director, Alberto Aguilera 26, Madrid 28015, Spain. Phone: 34-91-594-3776. Fax: 34-34-91-594-5159. E-mail: info@enforex.es.
URL www.enforex.com
For more information, see page 486.

ENFOREX HISPANIC CULTURE: CIVILIZATION, HISTORY, ART, AND LITERATURE—MADRID

Enforex Spanish in the Spanish World
Alberto Aguilera 26
Madrid 28015
Spain

General Information Coed residential academic program established in 1989. High school or college credit may be earned.
Program Focus Language program with optional sport and cultural activities.
Academics Spanish (Advanced Placement), Spanish language/literature, architecture, area studies, art (Advanced Placement), art history/appreciation, business, classical languages/literatures, computers, history, history (Advanced Placement), humanities, intercultural studies.
Special Interest Areas Field trips (arts and culture), homestays, nautical skills.
Sports Aerobics, archery, baseball, basketball, canoeing, climbing (wall), cross-country, football, golf, gymnastics, horseback riding, sailing, soccer, sports (general), swimming, volleyball.
Trips College tours, cultural, day, overnight, shopping.
Program Information 12 sessions per year. Session length: 4 weeks in January, April, May, July, October. Ages: 14+. 5–10 participants per session. Boarding program cost: 920–1920 euros. Application fee: 65 euros.
Application Deadline Continuous.

Enforex Hispanic Culture: Civilization, History, Art, and Literature–Madrid (continued)

Contact Antonio Anadón, Director, Alberto Aguilera 26, Madrid 28015, Spain. Phone: 34-91-594-3776. Fax: 34-91-594-5159. E-mail: info@enforex.es.
URL www.enforex.com
For more information, see page 486.

ENFOREX HISPANIC CULTURE: CIVILIZATION, HISTORY, ART, AND LITERATURE–MALAGA

Enforex Spanish in the Spanish World
Avenida Juan Sebastian Elcano 23
Malaga 29017
Spain

General Information Coed residential academic program established in 1989. High school or college credit may be earned.
Program Focus Language program with special focus on Spanish history, art and literature.
Academics Spanish (Advanced Placement), Spanish language/literature, architecture, area studies, art (Advanced Placement), art history/appreciation, business, classical languages/literatures, computers, history, history (Advanced Placement), humanities, intercultural studies.
Arts Film.
Special Interest Areas Field trips (arts and culture), homestays, nautical skills.
Sports Aerobics, archery, baseball, basketball, canoeing, climbing (wall), football, golf, gymnastics, horseback riding, soccer, sports (general), swimming, volleyball, waterskiing.
Trips College tours, cultural, day, overnight, shopping.
Program Information 12 sessions per year. Session length: 4 weeks in January, February, March, April, May, June, July, August, September, October, November, December. Ages: 14+. 5–10 participants per session. Boarding program cost: 920–1920 euros. Application fee: 65 euros.
Application Deadline Continuous.
Contact Antonio Anadón, Director, Alberto Aguilera 26, Madrid 28015, Spain. Phone: 34-91-594-3776. Fax: 34-91-594-5159. E-mail: info@enforex.es.
URL www.enforex.com
For more information, see page 486.

ENFOREX HISPANIC CULTURE: CIVILIZATION, HISTORY, ART, AND LITERATURE–SALAMANCA

Enforex Spanish in the Spanish World
Marquesa de Almarza 1
Salamanca 37001
Spain

General Information Coed residential academic program established in 1989. High school or college credit may be earned.
Program Focus Language program with optional sport and cultural activities.
Academics Spanish (Advanced Placement), Spanish language/literature, architecture, area studies, art (Advanced Placement), art history/appreciation, business, classical languages/literatures, computers, history, history (Advanced Placement), humanities, intercultural studies.
Special Interest Areas Field trips (arts and culture), homestays, nautical skills.
Sports Aerobics, archery, baseball, basketball, canoeing, climbing (wall), football, golf, gymnastics, horseback riding, sailing, soccer, sports (general), swimming, volleyball.
Trips College tours, cultural, day, overnight, shopping.
Program Information 12 sessions per year. Session length: 4 weeks in January, February, March, April, May, June, July, August, September, October, November, December. Ages: 14+. 5–10 participants per session. Boarding program cost: 920–1520 euros. Application fee: 65 euros. Financial aid available.
Application Deadline Continuous.
Contact Antonio Anadón, Director, Alberto Aguilera 26, Madrid 28015, Spain. Phone: 34-91-594-3776. Fax: 34-91-594-5159. E-mail: info@enforex.es.
URL www.enforex.com
For more information, see page 486.

ENFOREX HISPANIC CULTURE: CIVILIZATION, HISTORY, ART, AND LITERATURE–SEVILLA

Enforex Spanish in the Spanish World
Conde de Ibarra 2
Sevilla 41004
Spain

General Information Coed residential academic program established in 1989.
Program Focus Language program with optional sport and cultural activities.
Academics Spanish (Advanced Placement), Spanish language/literature, architecture, area studies, art (Advanced Placement), art history/appreciation, business, classical languages/literatures, computers, history, history (Advanced Placement), humanities, intercultural studies.
Arts Film.
Special Interest Areas Homestays.

Sports Aerobics, archery, baseball, basketball, canoeing, football, golf, gymnastics, horseback riding, soccer, sports (general), swimming, volleyball.
Program Information 12 sessions per year. Session length: 4 weeks in January, February, March, April, May, June, July, August, September, October, November, December. Ages: 14+. 5–10 participants per session. Boarding program cost: 920–1520 euros. Application fee: 65 euros.
Application Deadline Continuous.
Contact Antonio Anadón, Director, Alberto Aguilera 26, Madrid 28015, Spain. Phone: 34-91-594-3776. Fax: 34-91-594-5159. E-mail: info@enforex.es.
URL www.enforex.com
For more information, see page 486.

ENFOREX HISPANIC CULTURE: CIVILIZATION, HISTORY, ART, AND LITERATURE–TENERIFE

Enforex Spanish in the Spanish World
Avenida de Colon 14
Edificio Belgica
Puerto de la Cruz 38400
Spain

General Information Coed residential academic program. High school or college credit may be earned.
Program Focus Language program with optional sport and cultural activities.
Academics Spanish (Advanced Placement), Spanish language/literature, architecture, area studies, art (Advanced Placement), art history/appreciation, classical languages/literatures, computers, history, history (Advanced Placement), humanities, intercultural studies.
Arts Film.
Special Interest Areas Field trips (arts and culture), homestays, nautical skills.
Sports Aerobics, archery, baseball, basketball, canoeing, climbing (wall), football, golf, gymnastics, horseback riding, soccer, sports (general), swimming, volleyball, waterskiing.
Trips College tours, cultural, day, overnight, shopping.
Program Information 12 sessions per year. Session length: 4 weeks in January, February, March, April, May, June, July, August, September, October, November, December. Ages: 14+. 5–10 participants per session. Boarding program cost: 920–1884 euros. Application fee: 65 euros.
Application Deadline Continuous.

Contact Antonio Anadón, Director, Alberto Aguilera 26, Madrid 28015, Spain. Phone: 34-91-594-3776. Fax: 34-91-594-5159. E-mail: info@enforex.es.
URL www.enforex.com
For more information, see page 486.

ENFOREX HISPANIC CULTURE: HISTORY, ART, AND LITERATURE–VALENCIA

Enforex Spanish in the Spanish World
Paseo de Facultades 3, local
Valencia 46021
Spain

General Information Coed residential academic program established in 1989. High school or college credit may be earned.
Program Focus Language program with optional sport and cultural activities.
Academics Spanish (Advanced Placement), Spanish language/literature, architecture, area studies, art (Advanced Placement), art history/appreciation, business, classical languages/literatures, computers, history, history (Advanced Placement), humanities, intercultural studies.
Special Interest Areas Field trips (arts and culture), homestays, nautical skills.
Sports Aerobics, archery, baseball, basketball, canoeing, climbing (wall), football, golf, gymnastics, horseback riding, sailing, soccer, sports (general), swimming, volleyball, waterskiing.
Trips College tours, cultural, day, overnight, shopping.
Program Information 12 sessions per year. Session length: 4 weeks in January, February, March, April, May, June, July, August, September, October, November, December. Ages: 14+. 5–10 participants per session. Boarding program cost: 920–1520 euros. Application fee: 65 euros.
Application Deadline Continuous.
Contact Antonio Anadón, Director, Alberto Aguilera 26, Madrid 28015, Spain. Phone: 34-91-594-3776. Fax: 34-91-594-5159. E-mail: info@enforex.es.
URL www.enforex.com
For more information, see page 486.

ENFOREX HOMESTAY PROGRAM— ALICANTE

Enforex Spanish in the Spanish World
Paseo Explanada de España
Alicante 03001
Spain

General Information Coed residential academic program established in 1989. High school or college credit may be earned.
Program Focus Experience living with a Spanish family.
Academics Spanish (Advanced Placement), Spanish language/literature.
Arts Film.
Special Interest Areas Homestays, nautical skills.
Sports Aerobics, archery, baseball, basketball, canoeing, climbing (wall), cross-country, football, golf, gymnastics, horseback riding, sailing, soccer, swimming, tennis, volleyball.
Trips College tours, cultural, day, overnight, shopping.
Program Information 12 sessions per year. Session length: 4 weeks in January, February, March, April, May, June, July, August, September, October, November, December. Ages: 14+. 5–10 participants per session. Boarding program cost: 1440–1520 euros. Application fee: 65 euros.
Application Deadline Continuous.
Contact Antonio Anadón, Director, Alberto Aguilera 26, Madrid 28015, Spain. Phone: 34-91-594-3776. Fax: 34-91-594-5159. E-mail: info@enforex.es.
URL www.enforex.com

For more information, see page 486.

ENFOREX HOMESTAY PROGRAM— BARCELONA

Enforex Spanish in the Spanish World
Diputacion 92
Barcelona
Spain

General Information Coed residential academic program established in 1989. High school or college credit may be earned.
Program Focus Experience living with a Spanish family.
Academics Spanish (Advanced Placement), Spanish language/literature.
Arts Film.
Special Interest Areas Homestays, nautical skills.
Sports Aerobics, archery, baseball, basketball, canoeing, climbing (wall), cross-country, football, golf, gymnastics, horseback riding, sailing, soccer, swimming, tennis, volleyball.
Trips College tours, cultural, day, overnight, shopping.
Program Information 12 sessions per year. Session length: 4 weeks in January, February, March, April, May, June, July, August, September, October, November, December. Ages: 14+. 5–10 participants per session. Boarding program cost: 1580–1800 euros. Application fee: 65 euros.

Application Deadline Continuous.
Contact Antonio Anadón, Director, Alberto Aguilera 26, Madrid 28015, Spain. Phone: 34-91-594-3776. Fax: 34-91-594-5159. E-mail: info@enforex.es.
URL www.enforex.com

For more information, see page 486.

ENFOREX HOMESTAY PROGRAM— GRANADA

Enforex Spanish in the Spanish World
Santa Teresa 20
Granada 18002
Spain

General Information Coed residential academic program established in 1989. High school or college credit may be earned.
Program Focus Experience living with a Spanish family.
Academics Spanish (Advanced Placement), Spanish language/literature.
Arts Film.
Special Interest Areas Homestays, nautical skills.
Sports Aerobics, archery, baseball, basketball, canoeing, climbing (wall), cross-country, football, golf, gymnastics, horseback riding, sailing, soccer, swimming, tennis, volleyball.
Trips College tours, cultural, day, overnight, shopping.
Program Information 12 sessions per year. Session length: 4 weeks in January, February, March, April, May, June, July, August, September, October, November, December. Ages: 14+. 5–10 participants per session. Boarding program cost: 1440–1520 euros. Application fee: 65 euros.
Application Deadline Continuous.
Contact Antonio Anadón, Director, Alberto Aguilera 26, Madrid 28015, Spain. Phone: 34-91-594-3776. Fax: 34-91-594-5159. E-mail: info@enforex.es.
URL www.enforex.com

For more information, see page 486.

ENFOREX HOMESTAY PROGRAM–MADRID

Enforex Spanish in the Spanish World
Calle Baltasar Gracian 4
Madrid 28015
Spain

General Information Coed residential academic program established in 1989. High school or college credit may be earned.
Program Focus Experience living with a Spanish family.
Academics Spanish (Advanced Placement), Spanish language/literature.
Arts Film.
Special Interest Areas Homestays, nautical skills.
Sports Aerobics, archery, baseball, basketball, canoeing, climbing (wall), cross-country, football, golf, gymnastics, horseback riding, sailing, soccer, swimming, tennis, volleyball, waterskiing.
Trips College tours, cultural, day, overnight, shopping.
Program Information 12 sessions per year. Session length: 4 weeks in January, February, March, April, May, June, July, August, September, October, November, December. Ages: 14+. 5–10 participants per session. Boarding program cost: 1580–1800 euros. Application fee: 65 euros.
Application Deadline Continuous.
Contact Antonio Anadón, Director, Alberto Aguilera 26, Madrid 28015, Spain. Phone: 34-91-594-3776. Fax: 34-91-594-5159. E-mail: info@enforex.es.
URL www.enforex.com
For more information, see page 486.

ENFOREX HOMESTAY PROGRAM–MALAGA

Enforex Spanish in the Spanish World
Avenida Juan Sebastian Elcano 23
Malaga 29017
Spain

General Information Coed residential academic program established in 1989. High school or college credit may be earned.
Program Focus Experience living with a Spanish family.
Academics Spanish (Advanced Placement), Spanish language/literature.
Arts Film.
Special Interest Areas Homestays, nautical skills.
Sports Aerobics, archery, baseball, basketball, canoeing, climbing (wall), cross-country, football, golf, gymnastics, horseback riding, sailing, soccer, swimming, tennis, volleyball.
Trips College tours, cultural, day, overnight, shopping.
Program Information 12 sessions per year. Session length: 4 weeks in January, February, March, April, May, June, July, August, September, October, November, December. Ages: 14+. 5–10 participants per session. Boarding program cost: 1580–1800 euros. Application fee: 65 euros.
Application Deadline Continuous.

Contact Antonio Anadón, Director, Alberto Aguilera 26, Madrid 28015, Spain. Phone: 34-91-594-3776. Fax: 34-91-594-5159. E-mail: info@enforex.es.
URL www.enforex.com
For more information, see page 486.

ENFOREX HOMESTAY PROGRAM–MARBELLA

Enforex Spanish in the Spanish World
Avenida Ricardo Soriano 43
Marbella 29600
Spain

General Information Coed residential academic program established in 1989. High school or college credit may be earned.
Program Focus Experience living with a Spanish family.
Academics Spanish (Advanced Placement), Spanish language/literature.
Arts Film.
Special Interest Areas Homestays, nautical skills.
Sports Aerobics, archery, baseball, basketball, canoeing, climbing (wall), cross-country, football, golf, gymnastics, horseback riding, sailing, soccer, swimming, tennis, volleyball.
Trips College tours, cultural, day, overnight, shopping.
Program Information 12 sessions per year. Session length: 4 weeks in January, February, March, April, May, June, July, August, September, October, November, December. Ages: 14+. 5–10 participants per session. Boarding program cost: 1580–1800 euros. Application fee: 65 euros.
Application Deadline Continuous.
Contact Antonio Anadón, Director, Alberto Aguilera 26, Madrid 28015, Spain. Phone: 34-91-594-3776. Fax: 34-91-594-5159. E-mail: info@enforex.es.
URL www.enforex.com
For more information, see page 486.

ENFOREX HOMESTAY PROGRAM–SALAMANCA

Enforex Spanish in the Spanish World
Marquesa de Almarza 1
Salamanca 37001
Spain

General Information Coed residential academic program established in 1989. High school or college credit may be earned.
Program Focus Experience living with a Spanish family.
Academics Spanish (Advanced Placement), Spanish language/literature.
Arts Film.
Special Interest Areas Homestays, nautical skills.
Sports Aerobics, archery, baseball, basketball, canoeing, climbing (wall), cross-country, football, golf,

Enforex Homestay Program–Salamanca (continued)
gymnastics, horseback riding, soccer, swimming, tennis, volleyball.
Trips College tours, cultural, day, overnight, shopping.
Program Information 12 sessions per year. Session length: 4 weeks in January, February, March, April, May, June, July, August, September, October, November, December. Ages: 14+. 5–10 participants per session. Boarding program cost: 1440–1520 euros. Application fee: 65 euros.
Application Deadline Continuous.
Contact Antonio Anadón, Director, Alberto Aguilera 26, Madrid 28015, Spain. Phone: 34-91-594-3776. Fax: 34-91-594-5159. E-mail: info@enforex.es.
URL www.enforex.com

For more information, see page 486.

ENFOREX HOMESTAY PROGRAM–SEVILLA

Enforex Spanish in the Spanish World
Conde de Ibarra 2
Sevilla 41004
Spain

General Information Coed residential academic program established in 1989. High school or college credit may be earned.
Program Focus Experience living with a Spanish family.
Academics Spanish (Advanced Placement), Spanish language/literature.
Arts Film.
Special Interest Areas Homestays, nautical skills.
Sports Aerobics, archery, baseball, basketball, canoeing, climbing (wall), cross-country, football, golf, gymnastics, horseback riding, sailing, soccer, tennis, volleyball.
Trips College tours, cultural, day, overnight, shopping.
Program Information 12 sessions per year. Session length: 4 weeks in January, February, March, April, May, June, July, August, September, October, November, December. Ages: 14+. 5–10 participants per session. Boarding program cost: 1440–1520 euros. Application fee: 65 euros.
Application Deadline Continuous.
Contact Antonio Anadón, Director, Alberto Aguilera 26, Madrid 28015, Spain. Phone: 34-91-594-3776. Fax: 34-91-594-5159. E-mail: info@enforex.es.
URL www.enforex.com

For more information, see page 486.

ENFOREX HOMESTAY PROGRAM–TENERIFE

Enforex Spanish in the Spanish World
Avenida de Colon 14
Edificio Belgica
Puerto de la Cruz 38400
Spain

General Information Coed residential academic program.
Program Focus Experience living with a Spanish family.
Academics Spanish (Advanced Placement), Spanish language/literature.
Arts Film.
Special Interest Areas Homestays, nautical skills.
Sports Aerobics, archery, baseball, basketball, canoeing, climbing (wall), cross-country, football, golf, gymnastics, horseback riding, sailing, soccer, swimming, tennis, volleyball.
Trips College tours, cultural, day, overnight, shopping.
Program Information 12 sessions per year. Session length: 4 weeks in January, February, March, April, May, June, July, August, September, October, November, December. Ages: 14+. 5–10 participants per session. Boarding program cost: 1500–1880 euros. Application fee: 65 euros.
Application Deadline Continuous.
Contact Antonio Anadón, Director, Alberto Aguilera 26, Madrid 28015, Spain. Phone: 34-91-594-3776. Fax: 34-91-594-5159. E-mail: info@enforex.es.
URL www.enforex.com

For more information, see page 486.

ENFOREX HOMESTAY PROGRAM– VALENCIA

Enforex Spanish in the Spanish World
Paseo de Facultades 3, local
Valencia 46021
Spain

General Information Coed residential academic program established in 1989. High school or college credit may be earned.
Program Focus Experience living with a Spanish family.
Academics Spanish (Advanced Placement), Spanish language/literature.
Arts Film.
Special Interest Areas Homestays, nautical skills.
Sports Aerobics, archery, baseball, basketball, canoeing, climbing (wall), cross-country, football, golf, gymnastics, horseback riding, sailing, soccer, swimming, tennis, volleyball.
Trips College tours, cultural, day, overnight, shopping.
Program Information 12 sessions per year. Session length: 4 weeks in January, February, March, April, May, June, July, August, September, October, November, December. Ages: 14+. 5–10 participants per session. Boarding program cost: 1440–1520 euros. Application fee: 65 euros.
Application Deadline Continuous.

Contact Antonio Anadón, Director, Alberto Aguilera 26, Madrid 28015, Spain. Phone: 34-91-594-3776. Fax: 34-91-594-5159. E-mail: info@enforex.es.
URL www.enforex.com
For more information, see page 486.

ENFOREX RESIDENTIAL YOUTH SUMMER CAMP–BARCELONA

Enforex Spanish in the Spanish World
Colegio Residencial "Sil"
Avenida Tibidabo, 28
Barcelona 08022
Spain

General Information Coed residential traditional camp established in 1989.
Program Focus Sports, excursions, workshops, trips to the beach.
Academics Spanish language/literature, academics (general), communications, study skills, writing.
Arts Acting, animation, arts and crafts (general), dance, drawing, leather working, music, painting, radio broadcasting, television/video.
Special Interest Areas Farming, field research/expeditions, general camp activities, work camp programs.
Sports Aerobics, archery, baseball, basketball, soccer, swimming, tennis, volleyball.
Trips Cultural, day.
Program Information 4 sessions per year. Session length: 2–8 weeks in July, August. Ages: 14–18. 180 participants per session. Boarding program cost: 1100 euros. Application fee: 65 euros. Financial aid available.
Application Deadline Continuous.
Contact Antonio Anadón, Director, Alberto Aguilera 26, Madrid 28015, Spain. E-mail: info@enforex.es.
URL www.enforex.com
For more information, see page 486.

ENFOREX RESIDENTIAL YOUTH SUMMER CAMP–GRANADA

Enforex Spanish in the Spanish World
Camino de Fuente Grande s/n
Viznar 18179
Spain

General Information Coed residential traditional camp established in 1989.
Program Focus Sports, workshops, excursions.
Academics Spanish language/literature, academics (general), communications, writing.
Arts Acting, arts and crafts (general), dance, dance (folk), drawing, leather working, music, printmaking, theater/drama.
Special Interest Areas Work camp programs.
Sports Aerobics, archery, baseball, basketball, climbing (wall), cross-country, gymnastics, soccer, swimming, volleyball.
Trips Cultural, day.
Program Information 4 sessions per year. Session length: 2–8 weeks in July, August. Ages: 10–18. 100 participants per session. Boarding program cost: 1095–3955 euros. Application fee: 65 euros.
Application Deadline Continuous.
Contact Antonio Anadón, Director, Alberto Aguilera 26, Madrid 28015, Spain. Phone: 34-91-594-3776. Fax: 34-91-594-5159. E-mail: info@enforex.es.
URL www.enforex.com
For more information, see page 486.

ENFOREX RESIDENTIAL YOUTH SUMMER CAMP–MADRID

Enforex Spanish in the Spanish World
Avenida de Seneca 18
Ciudad Universitaria
Madrid 28040
Spain

General Information Coed residential traditional camp established in 1989.
Program Focus Sports, workshops, excursions.
Academics Spanish (Advanced Placement), Spanish language/literature, academics (general), communications, writing.
Arts Acting, arts and crafts (general), dance, dance (jazz), drawing, leather working, music, television/video, theater/drama.
Special Interest Areas Field research/expeditions, work camp programs.
Sports Aerobics, archery, baseball, basketball, climbing (wall), cross-country, football, soccer, swimming, volleyball.
Wilderness/Outdoors Canoe trips.
Trips Cultural, day.
Program Information 4 sessions per year. Session length: 2–8 weeks in July, August. Ages: 5–18. 280 participants per session. Boarding program cost: 1095–3955 euros. Application fee: 65 euros.
Application Deadline Continuous.

Enforex Residential Youth Summer Camp–Madrid (continued)

Contact Antonio Anadón, Director, Alberto Aguilera 26, Madrid 28015, Spain. Phone: 34-91-594-3776. Fax: 34-91-594-5159. E-mail: info@enforex.es.
URL www.enforex.com
For more information, see page 486.

ENFOREX RESIDENTIAL YOUTH SUMMER CAMP–MARBELLA ALBERGUE COLLEGE

Enforex Spanish in the Spanish World
Colegio Albergue
Calle Trapiche 2
Marbella 29600
Spain

General Information Coed residential traditional camp established in 1989.
Program Focus Sports, horseback riding, and trips to the beach and farms, workshops, excursions.
Academics Spanish language/literature, academics (general), communications.
Arts Acting, arts and crafts (general), dance, dance (jazz), drawing, leather working, music, painting, television/video, theater/drama.
Special Interest Areas Farming, field research/expeditions, work camp programs.
Sports Aerobics, archery, baseball, basketball, football, golf, horseback riding, soccer, swimming, tennis, volleyball.
Wilderness/Outdoors Canoe trips.
Trips Cultural, day.
Program Information 4 sessions per year. Session length: 2–8 weeks in July, August. Ages: 15–18. 120 participants per session. Boarding program cost: 1095–3955 euros. Application fee: 65 euros.
Application Deadline Continuous.
Contact Antonio Anadón, Director, Alberto Aguilera 26, Madrid 28015, Spain. Phone: 34-91-594-3776. Fax: 34-91-594-5159. E-mail: info@enforex.es.
URL www.enforex.com
For more information, see page 486.

ENFOREX RESIDENTIAL YOUTH SUMMER CAMP–MARBELLA ALBORAN COLLEGE

Enforex Spanish in the Spanish World
Alboran College
Urbanizacion Ric-Mar, S/N (KM 188-189)
Marbella 29600
Spain

General Information Coed residential traditional camp established in 1989.
Program Focus Sports, horseback riding, and trips to the beach and farms, workshops, excursions.
Academics Spanish language/literature, academics (general), communications, writing.
Arts Acting, arts and crafts (general), dance, dance (jazz), drawing, leather working, music, painting, radio

broadcasting, television/video, theater/drama.
Special Interest Areas Farming, field research/expeditions, work camp programs.
Sports Aerobics, archery, baseball, basketball, football, golf, horseback riding, soccer, swimming, tennis, volleyball.
Wilderness/Outdoors Canoe trips.
Trips Cultural, day.
Program Information 4 sessions per year. Session length: 2–8 weeks in July, August. Ages: 14–18. 220 participants per session. Boarding program cost: 1095–3955 euros. Application fee: 65 euros.
Application Deadline Continuous.
Contact Antonio Anadón, Director, Alberto Aguilera 26, Madrid 28015, Spain. Phone: 34-91-594-3776. Fax: 34-91-594-5159. E-mail: info@enforex.es.
URL www.enforex.com
For more information, see page 486.

ENFOREX RESIDENTIAL YOUTH SUMMER CAMP–MARBELLA ALEMAN COLLEGE

Enforex Spanish in the Spanish World
Aleman College Urb. Elviria S/N
Apto de Correos 318
Marbella 29600
Spain

General Information Coed residential traditional camp established in 1989.
Program Focus Sports, horseback riding, and trips to the beach and farms, workshops, excursions.
Academics Spanish language/literature, academics (general), communications, writing.
Arts Acting, arts and crafts (general), dance, dance (jazz), drawing, leather working, music, painting, television/video.
Special Interest Areas Farming, field research/expeditions, work camp programs.
Sports Aerobics, archery, baseball, basketball, climbing (wall), cross-country, football, golf, horseback riding, soccer, swimming, tennis, volleyball.
Wilderness/Outdoors Canoe trips.
Trips Cultural, day.
Program Information 4 sessions per year. Session length: 2–8 weeks in July, August. Ages: 5–14. 220 participants per session. Boarding program cost: 1095–3955 euros. Application fee: 65 euros.
Application Deadline Continuous.

Contact Antonio Anadón, Director, Alberto Aguilera 26, Madrid 28015, Spain. Phone: 34-91-594-3776. Fax: 34-91-594-5159. E-mail: info@enforex.es.
URL www.enforex.com

For more information, see page 486.

ENFOREX RESIDENTIAL YOUTH SUMMER CAMP–SALAMANCA

Enforex Spanish in the Spanish World
Paseo Canalejas 139-159
Salamanca 37001
Spain

General Information Coed residential traditional camp established in 1989.
Program Focus Sports, horseback riding, and trips to the beach and farms, workshops, excursions.
Academics Spanish language/literature, academics (general), communications, writing.
Arts Acting, arts and crafts (general), dance, dance (jazz), drawing, leather working, music, painting, television/video, theater/drama.
Special Interest Areas Field research/expeditions, work camp programs.
Sports Aerobics, archery, baseball, basketball, climbing (wall), cross-country, soccer, swimming, volleyball.
Wilderness/Outdoors Canoe trips.
Trips Cultural, day.
Program Information 4 sessions per year. Session length: 2–8 weeks in July, August. Ages: 9–18. 210 participants per session. Boarding program cost: 1095–3955 euros. Application fee: 65 euros.
Application Deadline Continuous.
Contact Antonio Anadón, Director, Alberto Aguilera 26, Madrid 28015, Spain. Phone: 34-91-594-3776. Fax: 34-91-594-5159. E-mail: info@enforex.es.
URL www.enforex.com

For more information, see page 486.

ENFOREX RESIDENTIAL YOUTH SUMMER CAMP–VALENCIA

Enforex Spanish in the Spanish World
Avenida los Naranjos s/n
Valencia 46022
Spain

General Information Coed residential traditional camp established in 1989.
Program Focus Sports, trips to the beach, workshops, excursions.
Academics Spanish (Advanced Placement), Spanish language/literature, academics (general), communications, writing.
Arts Acting, arts and crafts (general), dance, drawing, leather working, music, theater/drama.
Special Interest Areas Field research/expeditions, work camp programs.
Sports Aerobics, archery, baseball, basketball, climbing (wall), cross-country, soccer, swimming, volleyball.

Wilderness/Outdoors Canoe trips.
Trips Cultural, day.
Program Information 4 sessions per year. Session length: 2–8 weeks in July, August. Ages: 13–18. 110 participants per session. Boarding program cost: 1095–3955 euros. Application fee: 65 euros.
Application Deadline Continuous.
Contact Antonio Anadón, Director, Alberto Aguilera 26, Madrid 28015, Spain. Phone: 34-91-594-3776. Fax: 34-91-594-5159. E-mail: info@enforex.es.
URL www.enforex.com

For more information, see page 486.

ENFOREX SPANISH AND GOLF

Enforex Spanish in the Spanish World
Avenida Ricardo Soriano 43
Marbella 29600
Spain

General Information Coed residential academic program established in 1989. High school or college credit may be earned.
Program Focus Course includes 20 classes of Spanish and 10 classes of golf.
Academics Spanish (Advanced Placement), Spanish language/literature.
Sports Football, golf, horseback riding, sailing, swimming, tennis, volleyball.
Trips Cultural, day, overnight, shopping.
Program Information 48 sessions per year. Session length: 1–52 weeks in January, February, March, April, May, June, July, August, September, October, November, December. Ages: 14+. 170 participants per session. Boarding program cost: 630–655 euros. Application fee: 65 euros. Prices are for one week, including accommodation.
Application Deadline Continuous.
Contact Antonio Anadón, Director, Alberto Aguilera 26, Madrid 28015, Spain. Phone: 34-91-594-3776. Fax: 34-91-594-5159. E-mail: info@enforex.es.
URL www.enforex.com

For more information, see page 486.

ENFOREX SPANISH AND TENNIS

Enforex Spanish in the Spanish World
Avenida Ricardo Soriano 43
Marbella 29600
Spain

General Information Coed residential academic program established in 1989. High school or college credit may be earned.
Program Focus Course offers 20 classes of Spanish and 10 classes of tennis.
Academics Spanish (Advanced Placement), Spanish language/literature.
Sports Football, golf, horseback riding, sailing, swimming, tennis, volleyball.
Trips Cultural, day, overnight, shopping.
Program Information 48 sessions per year. Session length: 1–52 weeks in January, February, March, April, May, June, July, August, September, October, November, December. Ages: 15+. 150 participants per session. Boarding program cost: 630–655 euros. Application fee: 65 euros. Minimum age for participants is 15 in non-summer months; cost is per week, including accommodation.
Application Deadline Continuous.
Contact Antonio Anadón, Director, Alberto Aguilera 26, Madrid 28015, Spain. Phone: 34-91-594-3776. Fax: 34-91-594-5159. E-mail: info@enforex.es.
URL www.enforex.com
For more information, see page 486.

ENFOREX STUDY TOUR VACATIONAL PROGRAM–ALICANTE

Enforex Spanish in the Spanish World
Paseo Explanada de España
Alicante 03001
Spain

General Information Coed residential academic program established in 1989. High school or college credit may be earned.
Program Focus Language program with optional cultural activities.
Academics Spanish (Advanced Placement), Spanish language/literature, art history/appreciation, communications, history, intercultural studies.
Special Interest Areas Field trips (arts and culture), homestays, touring.
Sports Football, gymnastics, soccer, swimming, volleyball.
Trips Cultural, day, overnight, shopping.
Program Information 50 sessions per year. Session length: 1–52 weeks in January, February, March, April, May, June, July, August, September, October, November, December. Ages: 14+. 50 participants per session. Boarding program cost: 285–400 euros. Application fee: 65 euros. Prices are per week, including accommodation.
Application Deadline Continuous.

Contact Antonio Anadón, Director, Alberto Aguilera 26, Madrid 28015, Spain. Phone: 34-91-594-3776. Fax: 34-91-594-5159. E-mail: info@enforex.es.
URL www.enforex.com
For more information, see page 486.

ENFOREX STUDY TOUR VACATIONAL PROGRAM–BARCELONA

Enforex Spanish in the Spanish World
Diputacion 92
Barcelona 08015
Spain

General Information Coed residential academic program established in 1989. High school or college credit may be earned.
Program Focus Language program with optional cultural activities.
Academics Spanish (Advanced Placement), Spanish language/literature, art history/appreciation, communications, history, intercultural studies.
Special Interest Areas Homestays, touring.
Sports Football, soccer, swimming, volleyball.
Trips Cultural, day, overnight, shopping.
Program Information 50 sessions per year. Session length: 1–52 weeks in January, February, March, April, May, June, July, August, September, October, November, December. Ages: 14+. 500 participants per session. Boarding program cost: 310–400 euros. Application fee: 65 euros. Prices are per week, including accommodation.
Application Deadline Continuous.
Contact Antonio Anadón, Director, Alberto Aguilera 26, Madrid 28015, Spain. Phone: 34-91-594-3776. Fax: 34-91-594-5159. E-mail: info@enforex.es.
URL www.enforex.com
For more information, see page 486.

ENFOREX STUDY TOUR VACATIONAL PROGRAM–GRANADA

Enforex Spanish in the Spanish World
Calle Santa Teresa 20
Granada 18002
Spain

General Information Coed residential academic program established in 1989. High school or college credit may be earned.
Program Focus Language program with optional cultural activities.
Academics Spanish (Advanced Placement), Spanish language/literature, art history/appreciation, communications, history, intercultural studies.
Special Interest Areas Field trips (arts and culture), homestays, touring.
Sports Football, gymnastics, soccer, swimming, volleyball.
Trips Cultural, day, overnight, shopping.
Program Information 50 sessions per year. Session length: 1–52 weeks in January, February, March, April,

May, June, July, August, September, October, November, December. Ages: 14+. 120 participants per session. Boarding program cost: 285–340 euros. Application fee: 65 euros. Prices are per week, including accommodation.
Application Deadline Continuous.
Contact Antonio Anadón, Director, Alberto Aguilera 26, Madrid 28015, Spain. Phone: 34-91-594-3776. Fax: 34-91-594-5159. E-mail: info@enforex.es.
URL www.enforex.com
For more information, see page 486.

ENFOREX STUDY TOUR VACATIONAL PROGRAM–MADRID

Enforex Spanish in the Spanish World
Calle Baltasar Gracian 4
Madrid 28015
Spain

General Information Coed residential academic program established in 1989. High school or college credit may be earned.
Program Focus Language program with optional cultural activities.
Academics Spanish (Advanced Placement), Spanish language/literature, art history/appreciation, communications, history, intercultural studies.
Special Interest Areas Field trips (arts and culture), homestays, touring.
Sports Football, gymnastics, soccer, swimming, volleyball.
Trips Cultural, day, overnight, shopping.
Program Information 50 sessions per year. Session length: 1–52 weeks in January, February, March, April, May, June, July, August, September, October, November, December. Ages: 14+. 350 participants per session. Boarding program cost: 310–400 euros. Application fee: 65 euros. Prices are per week, including accommodation.
Application Deadline Continuous.
Contact Antonio Anadón, Director, Alberto Aguilera 26, Madrid 28015, Spain. Phone: 34-91-594-3776. Fax: 34-91-594-5159. E-mail: info@enforex.es.
URL www.enforex.com
For more information, see page 486.

ENFOREX STUDY TOUR VACATIONAL PROGRAM–MALAGA

Enforex Spanish in the Spanish World
Avenida Juan Sebastian Elcano, 23
Malaga 29017
Spain

General Information Coed residential academic program established in 1989.
Program Focus Language program with optional cultural activities.
Academics Spanish (Advanced Placement), Spanish language/literature, art history/appreciation, communications, history, intercultural studies.
Special Interest Areas Field trips (arts and culture), homestays, touring.
Sports Football, gymnastics, soccer, swimming, volleyball.
Trips Cultural, day, overnight, shopping.
Program Information 50 sessions per year. Session length: 1–52 weeks in January, February, March, April, May, June, July, August, September, October, November, December. Ages: 14+. 10–120 participants per session. Boarding program cost: 310–400 euros. Application fee: 65 euros. Prices are per week, including accommodation.
Application Deadline Continuous.
Contact Antonio Anadón, Director, Alberto Aguilera 26, Madrid 28015, Spain. Phone: 34-91-594-3776. Fax: 34-91-594-5159. E-mail: info@enforex.es.
URL www.enforex.com
For more information, see page 486.

ENFOREX STUDY TOUR VACATIONAL PROGRAM–MARBELLA

Enforex Spanish in the Spanish World
Avenida Ricardo Soriano 43
Marbella 29600
Spain

General Information Coed residential academic program established in 1989. High school or college credit may be earned.
Program Focus Language program with optional cultural activities.
Academics Spanish (Advanced Placement), Spanish language/literature, art history/appreciation, communications, history, intercultural studies.
Special Interest Areas Field trips (arts and culture), homestays, touring.
Sports Football, gymnastics, soccer, swimming, volleyball.
Trips Cultural, day, overnight, shopping.
Program Information 50 sessions per year. Session length: 1–52 weeks in January, February, March, April, May, June, July, August, September, October, November, December. Ages: 14+. 120 participants per session. Boarding program cost: 310–400 euros. Application fee: 65 euros. Prices are per week, including accommodation.
Application Deadline Continuous.

Enforex Study Tour Vacational Program–Marbella (continued)

Contact Antonio Anadón, Director, Alberto Aguilera 26, Madrid 28015, Spain. Phone: 34-91-594-3776. Fax: 34-91-594-5159. E-mail: info@enforex.es.
URL www.enforex.com

For more information, see page 486.

ENFOREX STUDY TOUR VACATIONAL PROGRAM–SALAMANCA

Enforex Spanish in the Spanish World
Calle Marquesa de Almarza 1
Salamanca 37001
Spain

General Information Coed residential academic program established in 1989. High school or college credit may be earned.
Program Focus Language program with optional cultural activities.
Academics Spanish (Advanced Placement), Spanish language/literature, art history/appreciation, communications, history, intercultural studies.
Special Interest Areas Field trips (arts and culture), homestays, touring.
Sports Football, gymnastics, soccer, swimming, volleyball.
Trips Cultural, day, overnight, shopping.
Program Information 50 sessions per year. Session length: 1–52 weeks in January, February, March, April, May, June, July, August, September, October, November, December. Ages: 14+. 280 participants per session. Boarding program cost: 285–340 euros. Application fee: 65 euros. Prices are per week, including accommodation.
Application Deadline Continuous.
Contact Antonio Anadón, Director, Alberto Aguilera 26, Madrid 28015, Spain. Phone: 34-91-594-3776. Fax: 34-91-594-5159. E-mail: info@enforex.es.
URL www.enforex.com

For more information, see page 486.

ENFOREX STUDY TOUR VACATIONAL PROGRAM–SEVILLA

Enforex Spanish in the Spanish World
Sevilla
Spain

General Information Coed residential academic program established in 1989. High school or college credit may be earned.
Program Focus Language program with optional cultural activities.
Academics Spanish (Advanced Placement), Spanish language/literature, art history/appreciation, communications, history, intercultural studies.
Special Interest Areas Field trips (arts and culture), homestays, touring.
Sports Football, gymnastics, soccer, swimming, volleyball.
Trips Cultural, day, overnight, shopping.
Program Information 50 sessions per year. Session length: 1–52 weeks in January, February, March, April, May, June, July, August, September, October, November, December. Ages: 14+. 10–50 participants per session. Boarding program cost: 285–340 euros. Application fee: 65 euros. Prices are per week, including accommodation.
Application Deadline Continuous.
Contact Antonio Anadón, Director, Alberto Aguilera 26, Madrid 28015, Spain. Phone: 34-91-594-3776. Fax: 34-91-594-5159. E-mail: info@enforex.es.
URL www.enforex.com

For more information, see page 486.

ENFOREX STUDY TOUR VACATIONAL PROGRAM–TENERIFE

Enforex Spanish in the Spanish World
Avenida de Colon 14
Edificio Belgica
Puerta de la Cruz 38400
Spain

General Information Coed residential academic program established in 1989. High school or college credit may be earned.
Program Focus Language program with optional cultural activities.
Academics Spanish (Advanced Placement), Spanish language/literature, art history/appreciation, communications, history, intercultural studies.
Special Interest Areas Field trips (arts and culture), homestays, touring.
Sports Football, gymnastics, soccer, swimming, volleyball.
Trips Cultural, day, overnight, shopping.
Program Information 50 sessions per year. Session length: 1–52 weeks in January, February, March, April, May, June, July, August, September, October, November, December. Ages: 14+. 10–50 participants per session. Boarding program cost: 290–390 euros. Application fee: 65 euros. Prices are per week, including accommodation.
Application Deadline Continuous.

Contact Antonio Anadón, Director, Alberto Aguilera 26, Madrid 28015, Spain. Phone: 34-91-594-3776. Fax: 34-91-594-5159. E-mail: info@enforex.es.
URL www.enforex.com

For more information, see page 486.

Enforex Study Tour Vacational Program–Valencia

Enforex Spanish in the Spanish World
Paseo De Facultades 3, local
Valencia 46021
Spain

General Information Coed residential academic program established in 1989. High school or college credit may be earned.
Program Focus Language program with optional cultural activities.
Academics Spanish (Advanced Placement), Spanish language/literature, art history/appreciation, communications, history, intercultural studies.
Special Interest Areas Field trips (arts and culture), homestays, touring.
Sports Football, gymnastics, soccer, swimming, volleyball.
Trips Cultural, day, overnight, shopping.
Program Information 50 sessions per year. Session length: 1–52 weeks in January, February, March, April, May, June, July, August, September, October, November, December. Ages: 14+. 200 participants per session. Boarding program cost: 285–400 euros. Application fee: 65 euros. Prices are per week, including accommodation.
Application Deadline Continuous.
Contact Antonio Anadón, Director, Alberto Aguilera 26, Madrid 28015, Spain. Phone: 34-91-594-3776. Fax: 34-91-594-5159. E-mail: info@enforex.es.
URL www.enforex.com

For more information, see page 486.

Excel at Madrid/Barcelona

Putney Student Travel
Spain

General Information Coed residential academic program and cultural program established in 1951. Formal opportunities for the academically talented and artistically talented.
Program Focus Precollege program that emphasizes small classes, creative interactions among student and faculty, and cultural exchange.
Academics Spanish language/literature, academics (general), architecture, area studies, art history/appreciation, government and politics, history, humanities, intercultural studies, precollege program, writing.
Arts Creative writing, drawing, film, music, painting, theater/drama.
Special Interest Areas Field research/expeditions, touring.
Sports Basketball, bicycling, soccer, swimming.

Wilderness/Outdoors Hiking.
Trips Cultural, day.
Program Information 1 session per year. Session length: 4 weeks in July, August. Ages: 15–18. 60–70 participants per session. Boarding program cost: $6990. Financial aid available. Airfare included.
Application Deadline Continuous.
Contact Patrick Noyes, Director, 345 Hickory Ridge Road, Putney, Vermont 05346. Phone: 802-387-5000. Fax: 802-387-4276. E-mail: info@goputney.com.
URL www.goputney.com

For more information, see page 490.

The Experiment in International Living–Spain, Five-Week Homestay, Language Immersion

The Experiment in International Living
Spain

General Information Coed travel outdoor program, cultural program, and adventure program established in 1932.
Program Focus International youth travel, homestay, language immersion.
Academics Spanish language/literature.
Arts Dance (folk), music.
Special Interest Areas Field trips (arts and culture), homestays, touring.
Trips Cultural, day, overnight.
Program Information 1 session per year. Session length: 5 weeks in June, July, August. Ages: 14–19. 10–15 participants per session. Cost: $5950. Application fee: $75. Financial aid available. Airfare included.
Application Deadline May 1.
Contact Chris Frantz, Deputy Director, EIL–World Learning, PO Box 676, Kipling Road, Brattleboro, Vermont 05302-0676. Phone: 800-345-2929. Fax: 802-258-3428. E-mail: eil@worldlearning.org.
URL www.usexperiment.org

For more information, see page 492.

THE EXPERIMENT IN INTERNATIONAL LIVING–SPAIN, FOUR-WEEK LANGUAGE TRAINING, TRAVEL, AND HOMESTAY

The Experiment in International Living
Spain

General Information Coed travel academic program and cultural program established in 1932.
Program Focus International youth travel, homestay, language training.
Academics Spanish language/literature.
Special Interest Areas Homestays, touring.
Trips Cultural, day, overnight.
Program Information 1 session per year. Session length: 5 weeks in June, July. Ages: 14–19. 10–15 participants per session. Cost: $5300. Financial aid available. Airfare included.
Application Deadline May 1.
Contact Annie Thompson, Enrollment Director, Summer Abroad, Kipling Road, PO Box 676, Brattleboro, Vermont 05302-0676. Phone: 800-345-2929. Fax: 802-258-3428. E-mail: eil@worldlearning.org.
URL www.usexperiment.org
For more information, see page 492.

THE EXPERIMENT IN INTERNATIONAL LIVING–SPAIN–MULTICULTURALISM AND SERVICE

The Experiment in International Living
Spain

General Information Coed travel academic program, community service program, and cultural program established in 1932.
Program Focus International youth travel, homestay, Spanish language study, community service.
Academics Spanish language/literature, social science.
Special Interest Areas Community service, cross-cultural education, homestays, touring.
Trips Cultural, day, overnight.
Program Information 1 session per year. Session length: 4 weeks in June, July. Ages: 14–19. 10–15 participants per session. Cost: $5500. Financial aid available. Airfare included.
Application Deadline May 1.
Contact Annie Thompson, Enrollment Director, Summer Abroad, Kipling Road, PO Box 676, Brattleboro, Vermont 05302-0676. Phone: 800-345-2929. Fax: 802-258-3428. E-mail: eil@worldlearning.org.
URL www.usexperiment.org
For more information, see page 492.

THE EXPERIMENT IN INTERNATIONAL LIVING–SPAIN–SPANISH ARTS AND CULTURE

The Experiment in International Living
Spain

General Information Coed travel arts program and cultural program established in 1932.
Program Focus International youth travel, arts and culture study.
Academics Spanish language/literature, intercultural studies.
Arts Ceramics, dance (folk), music (folk), theater/drama.
Special Interest Areas Cross-cultural education, homestays, touring.
Wilderness/Outdoors Hiking.
Trips Cultural, day, overnight.
Program Information 1 session per year. Session length: 5 weeks in June, July, August. Ages: 14–19. 10–15 participants per session. Cost: $5950. Financial aid available. Airfare included.
Application Deadline May 1.
Contact Annie Thompson, Enrollment Director, Summer Abroad, Kipling Road, PO Box 676, Brattleboro, Vermont 05302-0676. Phone: 800-345-2929. Fax: 802-258-3428. E-mail: eil@worldlearning.org.
URL www.usexperiment.org
For more information, see page 492.

THE EXPERIMENT IN INTERNATIONAL LIVING–SPAIN–THE ROAD TO SANTIAGO

The Experiment in International Living
Spain

General Information Coed travel outdoor program, cultural program, and adventure program established in 1932.
Program Focus International youth travel, homestay, pilgrimage to Santiago de Compostela.
Academics Spanish language/literature.
Special Interest Areas Homestays, touring.
Wilderness/Outdoors Hiking.
Trips Cultural, day, overnight.
Program Information 1 session per year. Session length: 4 weeks in June, July. Ages: 14–19. 10–15 participants per session. Cost: $5200. Application fee: $75. Financial aid available. Airfare included.
Application Deadline May 1.

Contact Ms. Annie Thompson, Enrollment Director, Summer Abroad, Kipling Road, PO Box 676, Brattleboro, Vermont 05302-0676. Phone: 800-345-2929. Fax: 802-258-3428. E-mail: eil@worldlearning.org. **URL** www.usexperiment.org

For more information, see page 492.

THE EXPERIMENT IN INTERNATIONAL LIVING–SPANISH CULTURE AND EXPLORATION

The Experiment in International Living
Spain

General Information Coed travel cultural program established in 1932.
Program Focus International youth travel, homestay, Spanish language.
Academics Spanish language/literature.
Special Interest Areas Homestays, touring.
Trips Cultural, day, overnight.
Program Information 1 session per year. Session length: 3 weeks in June, July. Ages: 14–19. 10–15 participants per session. Cost: $4750. Financial aid available. Airfare included.
Application Deadline May 1.
Contact Annie Thompson, Enrollment Director, Summer Abroad, Kipling Road, PO Box 676, Brattleboro, Vermont 05302-0676. Phone: 800-345-2929. Fax: 802-258-3428. E-mail: eil@worldlearning.org. **URL** www.usexperiment.org

For more information, see page 492.

GLOBAL WORKS–LANGUAGE IMMERSION, CULTURAL EXCHANGE AND SERVICE–SPAIN–4 WEEKS

GLOBAL WORKS
Spain

General Information Coed travel community service program, cultural program, and adventure program established in 1988. High school credit may be earned.
Program Focus Environmental and community service, language immersion, and cultural exchange.
Academics Spanish language/literature, intercultural studies.
Arts Arts and crafts (general), dance (Latin).
Special Interest Areas Community service, construction, field trips (arts and culture), homestays.
Sports Basketball, soccer, sports (general), swimming, volleyball.
Wilderness/Outdoors Hiking, rafting.
Trips Cultural, day, overnight.
Program Information 2 sessions per year. Session length: 27 days in June, July, August. Ages: 15–17. 16–18 participants per session. Cost: $4995. Application fee: $100. Financial aid available. Airfare not included.
Application Deadline Continuous.
Jobs Positions for college students 23 and older.

Contact Mr. Erik Werner, Director, 1113 South Allen Street, State College, Pennsylvania 16801. Phone: 814-867-7000. Fax: 814-867-2717. E-mail: info@globalworksinc.com. **URL** www.globalworksinc.com

For more information, see page 506.

iD TECH CAMPS–DOCUMENTARY FILMMAKING AND CULTURAL IMMERSION IN SPAIN

iD Tech Camps
Andalucia
Spain

General Information Coed travel academic program and cultural program established in 1999. Formal opportunities for the academically talented and artistically talented.
Program Focus Documentary filmmaking and cultural immersion.
Academics Spanish (Advanced Placement), Spanish language/literature, computers, precollege program.
Arts Digital media, photography, television/video.
Special Interest Areas Career exploration, homestays, leadership training, team building, touring.
Trips Cultural, day, overnight.
Program Information 1–2 sessions per year. Session length: 14–20 days in June, July, August. Ages: 14–17. 20–50 participants per session. Cost: $3999.
Application Deadline Continuous.
Jobs Positions for college students 18 and older.
Contact Kendra Lundgaard, Spain Regional Manager, 42 West Campbell Avenue, Suite 301, Campbell, California 95008. Phone: 408-871-3734. Fax: 408-871-2228. E-mail: kendra@internaldrive.com. **URL** spain.internaldrive.com

For more information, see page 520.

LA ACADEMIA DE ESPAÑA

Oxbridge Academic Programs
Barcelona
Spain

General Information Coed residential academic program and arts program established in 2006. Formal opportunities for the academically talented and artistically talented. High school credit may be earned.
Program Focus Academic and cultural enrichment.
Academics Spanish language/literature, academics (general), architecture, art history/appreciation, government and politics, history, humanities, international relations, journalism, medicine, philosophy, precollege program, psychology, social science, social studies, speech/debate, writing.
Arts Acting, arts, creative writing, drawing, film, music, painting, performing arts, photography, theater/drama.
Special Interest Areas Field trips (arts and culture).
Sports Aerobics, basketball, cross-country, soccer, sports (general), tennis.
Trips Cultural, day.
Program Information 1 session per year. Session length: 4 weeks in July. Ages: 15–18. 150 participants per session. Boarding program cost: $6695. Financial aid available. Airfare not included.
Application Deadline Continuous.
Contact Ms. Andrea Mardon, Executive Director, Oxbridge Academic Programs, 601 West 110th Street, Suite 7R, New York, New York 10025-2186. Phone: 800-828-8349. Fax: 212-663-8169. E-mail: info@oxbridgeprograms.com.
URL www.oxbridgeprograms.com
For more information, see page 580.

PUTNEY STUDENT TRAVEL–LANGUAGE LEARNING–SPAIN

Putney Student Travel
Spain

General Information Coed residential academic program and cultural program established in 1951.
Program Focus Spanish language immersion. Participants housed in host-family homes and hotels. Enrollment limited to those who are studying Spanish.
Academics Spanish (Advanced Placement), Spanish language/literature, art history/appreciation, intercultural studies.
Special Interest Areas Homestays.
Sports Horseback riding, rappelling, sailing, soccer, swimming, windsurfing.
Wilderness/Outdoors Bicycle trips, hiking, mountaineering, rock climbing.
Trips Cultural, day, overnight.
Program Information 3–6 sessions per year. Session length: 38–40 days in June, July, August. Ages: 13–18. 16–18 participants per session. Boarding program cost: $8590. Financial aid available. Airfare from New York included.
Application Deadline Continuous.

Contact Jeffrey Shumlin, Admissions Director, 345 Hickory Ridge Road, Putney, Vermont 05346. Phone: 802-387-5000. Fax: 802-387-4276. E-mail: info@goputney.com.
URL www.goputney.com
For more information, see page 598.

RASSIAS PROGRAMS–GIJÓN, SPAIN

Rassias Programs
Gijón
Spain

General Information Coed travel academic program and cultural program established in 1985.
Program Focus Spanish language studies taught in the Rassias method, homestays, and travel in Spain.
Academics Spanish (Advanced Placement), Spanish language/literature.
Special Interest Areas Homestays, touring.
Sports Aerobics, basketball, kayaking, squash, swimming, tennis, weight training.
Wilderness/Outdoors Hiking.
Trips Cultural, overnight.
Program Information 1 session per year. Session length: 30 days in June, July. Ages: 14–17. 20–22 participants per session. Cost: $7475–$8000. Financial aid available. Airfare included.
Application Deadline Continuous.
Jobs Positions for college students 21 and older.
Contact Bill Miles, Director, PO Box 5456, Hanover, New Hampshire 03755. Phone: 603-643-3007. Fax: 603-643-4249. E-mail: wmiles@rassias.com.
URL www.rassias.com
For more information, see page 602.

RASSIAS PROGRAMS–PONTEVEDRA, SPAIN

Rassias Programs
Pontevedra
Spain

General Information Coed travel academic program and cultural program established in 1985.
Program Focus Spanish language studies taught in the Rassias method, homestays, and travel in Spain.
Academics Spanish (Advanced Placement), Spanish language/literature.
Special Interest Areas Homestays, touring.
Sports Basketball, swimming, tennis.
Wilderness/Outdoors Hiking.
Trips Cultural, overnight.
Program Information 1 session per year. Session length: 30 days in June, July. Ages: 14–17. 20–22 participants per session. Cost: $7475–$8000. Financial aid available. Airfare included.
Application Deadline Continuous.
Jobs Positions for college students 21 and older.

Contact Bill Miles, Director, PO Box 5456, Hanover, New Hampshire 03755. Phone: 603-643-3007. Fax: 603-643-4249. E-mail: wmiles@rassias.com. **URL** www.rassias.com

For more information, see page 602.

RASSIAS PROGRAMS–SEGOVIA, SPAIN

Rassias Programs
Segovia
Spain

General Information Coed travel academic program and cultural program established in 1985.
Program Focus Spanish language studies taught in the Rassias method, homestays and travel in Spain.
Academics Spanish (Advanced Placement), Spanish language/literature.
Special Interest Areas Homestays, touring.
Sports Basketball, kayaking, swimming, tennis, weight training.
Wilderness/Outdoors Hiking.
Trips Cultural, overnight.
Program Information 1 session per year. Session length: 30 days in June, July. Ages: 14–17. 20–22 participants per session. Cost: $7475–$8000. Financial aid available. Airfare included.
Application Deadline Continuous.
Jobs Positions for college students 21 and older.
Contact Bill Miles, Director, PO Box 5456, Hanover, New Hampshire 03755. Phone: 603-643-3007. Fax: 603-643-4249. E-mail: wmiles@rassias.com. **URL** www.rassias.com

For more information, see page 602.

SERVICE LEARNING IN BARCELONA

International Seminar Series
Barcelona
Spain

General Information Coed residential academic program, community service program, and cultural program established in 2005.

Service Learning in Barcelona

Academics Spanish language/literature, academics (general), architecture, art history/appreciation, history, writing.
Arts Creative writing.
Special Interest Areas Community service, cross-cultural education, homestays.
Trips Cultural, day.
Program Information 1 session per year. Session length: 4 weeks in July. Ages: 16–21. 15–30 participants per session. Boarding program cost: $7000. Application fee: $50. Financial aid available.
Application Deadline April 15.
Contact Mr. John Nissen, Director, PO Box 1212, Manchester, Vermont 05254-1212. Phone: 802-362-5855. Fax: 802-362-5855. E-mail: iss@study-serve.org. **URL** www.study-serve.org

For more information, see page 628.

SPANISH LANGUAGE AND FLAMENCO ENFOREX–GRANADA

Enforex Spanish in the Spanish World
Santa Teresa 20
Granada 18002
Spain

General Information Coed residential academic program established in 1989. High school or college credit may be earned.
Program Focus Language program with Flamenco lessons.
Academics Spanish (Advanced Placement), Spanish language/literature, communications, computers, intercultural studies.

Spanish Language and Flamenco Enforex–Granada (continued)

Arts Dance (folk), flamenco.
Special Interest Areas Homestays.
Sports Football, gymnastics, soccer, swimming, volleyball.
Trips Cultural, day, overnight, shopping.
Program Information 48 sessions per year. Session length: 1–52 weeks in January, February, March, April, May, June, July, August, September, October, November, December. Ages: 14+. 100 participants per session. Boarding program cost: 535–585 euros. Application fee: 65 euros. Prices are per week, including accommodation.
Application Deadline Continuous.
Contact Antonio Anadón, Director, Alberto Aguilera 26, Madrid 28015, Spain. Phone: 34-91-594-3776. Fax: 34-91-594-5159. E-mail: info@enforex.es.
URL www.enforex.com
For more information, see page 486.

Spanish Language and Flamenco Enforex–Madrid

Enforex Spanish in the Spanish World
Baltasar Gracián 4
Madrid 28015
Spain

General Information Coed residential academic program established in 1989. High school or college credit may be earned.
Program Focus Language program with Flamenco lessons.
Academics Spanish (Advanced Placement), Spanish language/literature, communications, computers, intercultural studies.
Arts Dance (folk), flamenco.
Special Interest Areas Homestays.
Sports Football, gymnastics, soccer, swimming, volleyball.
Trips Cultural, day, overnight, shopping.
Program Information 48 sessions per year. Session length: 1–52 weeks in January, February, March, April, May, June, July, August, September, October, November, December. Ages: 14+. 300 participants per session. Boarding program cost: 560–645 euros. Application fee: 65 euros. Prices are per week, including accommodation.
Application Deadline Continuous.

Contact Antonio Anadón, Director, Alberto Aguilera 26, Madrid 28015, Spain. Phone: 34-91-594-3776. Fax: 34-91-594-5159. E-mail: info@enforex.es.
URL www.enforex.com
For more information, see page 486.

Spanish Language and Flamenco Enforex–Marbella

Enforex Spanish in the Spanish World
Avenida Ricardo Soriano 43
Marbella 29600
Spain

General Information Coed residential academic program established in 1989. High school or college credit may be earned.
Program Focus Language program with Flamenco lessons.
Academics Spanish (Advanced Placement), Spanish language/literature, communications, computers, intercultural studies.
Arts Dance (folk), flamenco.
Special Interest Areas Homestays.
Sports Football, gymnastics, soccer, swimming, volleyball.
Trips Cultural, day, overnight, shopping.
Program Information 48 sessions per year. Session length: 1–52 weeks in January, February, March, April, May, June, July, August, September, October, November, December. Ages: 14+. 100 participants per session. Boarding program cost: 560–645 euros. Application fee: 65 euros. Prices are per week, including accommodation.
Application Deadline Continuous.
Contact Antonio Anadón, Director, Alberto Aguilera 26, Madrid 28015, Spain. Phone: 34-91-594-3776. Fax: 34-91-594-5159. E-mail: info@enforex.es.
URL www.enforex.com
For more information, see page 486.

SPANISH LANGUAGE AND FLAMENCO ENFOREX–SEVILLA

Enforex Spanish in the Spanish World
Conde de Ibarra 2
Sevilla 41004
Spain

General Information Coed residential academic program established in 1989. High school or college credit may be earned.
Program Focus Language program with Flamenco lessons.
Academics Spanish (Advanced Placement), Spanish language/literature, communications, computers, intercultural studies.
Arts Dance (folk), flamenco.
Special Interest Areas Homestays.
Sports Football, gymnastics, soccer, swimming, volleyball.
Trips Cultural, day, overnight, shopping.
Program Information 48 sessions per year. Session length: 1–52 weeks in January, February, March, April, May, June, July, August, September, October, November, December. Ages: 14+. 100 participants per session. Boarding program cost: 535–585 euros. Application fee: 65 euros. Prices are per week, including accommodation.
Application Deadline Continuous.
Contact Antonio Anadón, Director, Alberto Aguilera 26, Madrid 28015, Spain. Phone: 34-91-594-3776. Fax: 34-91-594-5159. E-mail: info@enforex.es.
URL www.enforex.com

For more information, see page 486.

SUMMER ADVANTAGE STUDY ABROAD– GRANADA, SPAIN

American Institute for Foreign Study (AIFS)
University of Granada
Grenada
Spain

General Information Coed travel academic program and cultural program established in 2007. College credit may be earned.
Academics Spanish (Advanced Placement), Spanish language/literature, art history/appreciation, history, social studies.
Arts Dance (folk), theater/drama.
Special Interest Areas Touring.
Trips Cultural, day, overnight, shopping.
Program Information 1 session per year. Session length: 29–34 days in June, July. Ages: 16–18. Cost: $5115. Application fee: $95.
Application Deadline April 15.
Contact Mrs. Amy Van Stone, Director of Admissions, Summer Advantage, 9 West Broad Street, River Plaza, Stamford, Connecticut 06902. Phone: 800-913-7151. Fax: 203-399-5463. E-mail: summeradvantage@aifs.com.
URL www.summeradvantage.com

For more information, see page 410.

SUMMER ADVANTAGE STUDY ABROAD– SALAMANCA, SPAIN

American Institute for Foreign Study (AIFS)
University of Salamanca
Patio de Escuelas
Salamanca 37071
Spain

General Information Coed travel academic program and cultural program established in 1984. College credit may be earned.
Program Focus Study abroad for college credit.
Academics Spanish (Advanced Placement), Spanish language/literature, art history/appreciation, business, history, music.
Arts Dance (folk), music (folk), music (instrumental).
Special Interest Areas Culinary arts, homestays.
Trips Cultural, day, overnight, shopping.
Program Information 1 session per year. Session length: 29–34 days in June, July. Ages: 16–18. 60 participants per session. Cost: $5115. Application fee: $95.
Application Deadline April 15.
Contact Mrs. Amy Van Stone, Director of Admissions, Summer Advantage, 9 West Broad Street, River Plaza, Stamford, Connecticut 06902. Phone: 800-913-7151. Fax: 203-399-5463. E-mail: summeradvantage@aifs.com.
URL www.summeradvantage.com

For more information, see page 410.

TAFT SUMMER SCHOOL ABROAD–SPAIN

The Taft School
Madrid
Spain

General Information Coed travel academic program established in 1982. Accredited by American Camping Association.
Program Focus The program is designed to completely immerse the student in the people, language, and culture of the country.
Academics Spanish language/literature, art history/ appreciation, history, intercultural studies.

Taft Summer School Abroad–Spain (continued)

Special Interest Areas Homestays, touring.
Trips Cultural, day, overnight, shopping.
Program Information 1 session per year. Session length: 35–40 days in June, July. Ages: 14–18. 10–20 participants per session. Cost: $5150. Application fee: $50. Airfare from New York to Madrid included.
Application Deadline April 15.
Contact Kevin Conroy, Coordinator, Taft Summer in Spain, 110 Woodbury Road, Watertown, Connecticut 06795. Phone: 860-945-7894. Fax: 860-945-7859. E-mail: conroyk@taftschool.org.
URL www.taftschool.org/summer

For more information, see page 666.

TASIS SPANISH SUMMER PROGRAM

TASIS The American School in England
Colegio Internacional
Salamanca
Spain

General Information Coed residential academic program and cultural program established in 1993. High school credit may be earned.
Program Focus Intensive Spanish instruction combined with cultural experiences. The city of Salamanca is the School's classroom, with the last week of the program spent on the Costa del Sol.
Academics Spanish language/literature.
Arts Dance, dance (folk), flamenco.
Sports Aerobics, basketball, gymnastics, soccer, swimming, tennis, weight training.
Trips Cultural, day, overnight, shopping.
Program Information 1 session per year. Session length: 30 days in July. Ages: 13–17. 75 participants per session. Boarding program cost: $5400.
Application Deadline Continuous.
Jobs Positions for college students.
Contact W. Thomas Fleming, US Director, 1640 Wisconsin Avenue, NW, Washington, District of Columbia 20007. Phone: 202-965-5800. Fax: 202-965-5816. E-mail: usadmissions@tasis.com.
URL www.tasis.com

For more information, see page 668.

WESTCOAST CONNECTION–SPANISH LANGUAGE AND TOURING

Westcoast Connection
Spain

General Information Coed travel academic program and cultural program established in 1982. Accredited by Ontario Camping Association. High school or college credit may be earned.
Program Focus Spanish study program featuring study in three locations: Barcelona, Valencia, and Marbella plus touring Seville and Madrid.
Academics Spanish (Advanced Placement), Spanish language/literature.
Special Interest Areas Touring.

Trips Cultural, day, shopping.
Program Information 2–3 sessions per year. Session length: 4 weeks in July. Ages: 14–19. 20–40 participants per session. Cost: $5999.
Application Deadline Continuous.
Contact Mr. Ira Solomon, Director, 154 East Boston Post Road, Mamaroneck, New York 10543. Phone: 800-767-0227. Fax: 914-835-0798. E-mail: info@westcoastconnection.com.
URL www.360studenttravel.com

For more information, see page 702.

WILDERNESS VENTURES–SPANISH PYRENEES

Wilderness Ventures
Spain

General Information Coed travel outdoor program, wilderness program, cultural program, and adventure program established in 1973.
Program Focus Wilderness travel, cultural immersion, leadership skills.
Special Interest Areas Leadership training.
Sports Sea kayaking.
Wilderness/Outdoors Backpacking, rafting, whitewater trips, wilderness camping.
Trips Cultural, overnight.
Program Information 2 sessions per year. Session length: 3 weeks in June, July, August. Ages: 14–18. 15 participants per session. Cost: $4490. Financial aid available.
Application Deadline Continuous.
Jobs Positions for college students 21 and older.
Contact Mike Cottingham, Director, PO Box 2768, Jackson Hole, Wyoming 83001. Phone: 800-533-2281. Fax: 307-739-1934. E-mail: info@wildernessventures.com.
URL www.wildernessventures.com

For more information, see page 704.

SWEDEN

CENTER FOR CULTURAL INTERCHANGE– SWEDEN HIGH SCHOOL ABROAD

Center for Cultural Interchange
Sweden

General Information Coed residential academic program and cultural program established in 1985. High school credit may be earned.
Program Focus Cultural immersion, high school in Sweden.
Academics Swedish language/literature, academics (general), independent study.
Special Interest Areas Cross-cultural education, homestays.
Trips Cultural, day.
Program Information 2 sessions per year. Session length: 150–300 days in January, February, March, April, May, June, August, September, October, November, December. Ages: 15–18. Boarding program cost: $4530–$5550. Financial aid available.
Application Deadline Continuous.
Contact Ms. Juliet Jones, Outbound Programs Director, 746 North LaSalle Drive, Chicago, Illinois 60610-3617. Phone: 866-684-9675. Fax: 312-944-2644. E-mail: info@cci-exchange.com.
URL www.cci-exchange.com

For more information, see page 448.

SWITZERLAND

ATELIER DES ARTS

Atelier des Arts
La-Chaux-de-Fonds
Switzerland

General Information Coed residential arts program established in 1995. Formal opportunities for the artistically talented. College credit may be earned.
Program Focus Jazz, fine arts, studio work, travel, exhibitions, and concerts.
Academics Art history/appreciation, music.
Arts Drawing, music (ensemble), music (jazz), painting, performing arts, photography, printmaking, sculpture, visual arts.
Trips Cultural, day.
Program Information 2 sessions per year. Session length: 2–4 weeks in July, August. Ages: 16+. 20–30 participants per session. Boarding program cost: $3550. Second session in Umbria, Italy.
Application Deadline Continuous.

Contact Ms. Francia Tobacman, Director, 55 Bethune Street, B645, New York, New York 10014. Phone: 212-727-1756. Fax: 212-691-0631. E-mail: info@atelierdesarts.org.
URL www.atelierdesarts.org

THE EXPERIMENT IN INTERNATIONAL LIVING–SWITZERLAND FRENCH LANGUAGE IMMERSION, HOMESTAY, AND ALPINE ADVENTURE

The Experiment in International Living
Switzerland

General Information Coed travel outdoor program, cultural program, and adventure program established in 1932.
Program Focus International youth travel, homestay, French language, outdoor adventure.
Academics French language/literature.
Special Interest Areas Homestays, touring.
Wilderness/Outdoors Backpacking, hiking.
Trips Cultural, day, overnight.
Program Information 1 session per year. Session length: 4 weeks in June, July. Ages: 14–19. 10–15 participants per session. Cost: $5400. Financial aid available. Airfare included.
Application Deadline May 1.
Contact Annie Thompson, Enrollment Director, Summer Abroad, Kipling Road, PO Box 676, Brattleboro, Vermont 05302-0676. Phone: 800-345-2929. Fax: 802-258-3428. E-mail: eil@worldlearning.org.
URL www.usexperiment.org

For more information, see page 492.

INTERNATIONAL SUMMER CAMP MONTANA, SWITZERLAND

International Summer Camp Montana,
Switzerland
La Moubra
Crans-Montana CH-3963
Switzerland

General Information Coed residential outdoor
program and cultural program established in 1961.

International Summer Camp Montana, Switzerland

Program Focus All outdoor sports including horseback
riding. Language courses.
Academics English as a second language, French
language/literature, German language/literature,
Spanish language/literature.
Arts Arts and crafts (general), ceramics, circus arts,
dance, drawing, jewelry making, leather working,
macramé, modeling, music, musical productions,
painting, performing arts, photography, pottery,
sculpture, weaving.
Special Interest Areas Nature study.
Sports Aerobics, archery, baseball, basketball,
bicycling, boating, canoeing, climbing (wall), equestrian
sports, fencing, field hockey, golf, gymnastics, horseback
riding, martial arts, physical fitness, sailing, skiing
(downhill), snowboarding, soccer, softball, sports
(general), swimming, tennis, track and field,
trampolining, volleyball.
Wilderness/Outdoors Hiking, mountain biking,
mountaineering, rafting, rock climbing.
Trips Cultural, day, overnight, shopping.
Program Information 3 sessions per year. Session
length: 3 weeks in June, July, August. Ages: 8–17. 280
participants per session. Boarding program cost: 4667
Swiss francs.
Application Deadline Continuous.
Jobs Positions for college students 20 and older.

Contact Philippe Studer, Director, La Moubra, CH-
3963, Crans-Montana 1, Switzerland. Phone: 41-27-486-
8686. Fax: 41-27-486-8687. E-mail: info@campmontana.
ch.
URL www.campmontana.ch
For more information, see page 526.

LES ELFES–INTERNATIONAL SUMMER/ WINTER CAMP

Les Elfes International Summer/Winter Camp
Verbier 1936
Switzerland

General Information Coed residential traditional
camp, academic program, and outdoor program
established in 1987.

Les Elfes–International Summer/Winter Camp

Program Focus Language training: English, French,
German, Spanish.
Academics English as a second language, English
language/literature, French language/literature, German
language/literature, Spanish language/literature,
computers.
Arts Arts and crafts (general).
Special Interest Areas Counselor-in-training program,
leadership training, team building.
Sports Basketball, bicycling, boating, climbing (wall),
equestrian sports, figure skating, football, golf,
horseback riding, ice hockey, ropes course, skiing

(downhill), soccer, sports (general), squash, swimming, tennis, volleyball, waterskiing.
Wilderness/Outdoors Bicycle trips, hiking, mountain biking, mountaineering, rock climbing.
Trips Cultural, day, overnight.
Program Information 18–20 sessions per year. Session length: 14–20 days in January, February, March, April, May, June, July, August, December. Ages: 8–18. 120–130 participants per session. Boarding program cost: 3070–5300 Swiss francs.
Application Deadline Continuous.
Jobs Positions for college students 21 and older.
Contact Mr. Philippe Stettler, Director, PO Box 174, 1936 Verbier, Switzerland. Phone: 41-27-775-35-90. Fax: 41-27-775-35-99. E-mail: info@leselfes.ch.
URL www.leselfes.com
For more information, see page 544.

SUMMER IN SWITZERLAND

Leysin American School in Switzerland
Leysin 1854
Switzerland

General Information Coed travel traditional camp, academic program, outdoor program, arts program, and cultural program established in 1982. High school credit may be earned.

Summer in Switzerland

Program Focus Academic enrichment, ESL, theater, leadership, chamber music, sports and recreation, travel, language study, SAT preparation.
Academics American literature, English as a second language, English language/literature, French language/literature, SAT/ACT preparation, Spanish language/literature, TOEFL/TOEIC preparation, academics (general), art history/appreciation, computers, intercultural studies, mathematics, music, writing.
Arts Acting, arts and crafts (general), ceramics, chorus, creative writing, dance, drawing, music, music (chamber), music (instrumental), music (vocal), musical productions, performing arts, photography, pottery, stage combat, stage managing, theater/drama.
Special Interest Areas Field trips (arts and culture), general camp activities, leadership training.

Sports Aerobics, basketball, bicycling, climbing (wall), equestrian sports, golf, horseback riding, ice hockey, paragliding, rappelling, ropes course, skiing (downhill), soccer, squash, street/roller hockey, swimming, tennis, volleyball, weight training.
Wilderness/Outdoors Hiking, mountain biking, mountaineering, orienteering, rafting, rock climbing, white-water trips.
Trips Cultural, day, overnight, shopping.
Program Information 2 sessions per year. Session length: 3 weeks in June, July, August. Ages: 9–19. 250–300 participants per session. Cost: 3350–8800 euros. Financial aid available. Airfare not included.
Application Deadline Continuous.
Jobs Positions for college students 22 and older.
Contact Mr. Tim Sloman, Director of Summer in Switzerland, Admissions Office, Leysin American School, Leysin 1854, Switzerland. Phone: 41-24-493-3777. Fax: 41-24-494-1585. E-mail: admissions@las.ch.
URL www.las.ch/summer
For more information, see page 546.

TASIS FRENCH LANGUAGE PROGRAM IN CHÂTEAU-D'OEX, SWITZERLAND

TASIS The American School in Switzerland
Le Vieux Chalet
Château–d'Oex 1660
Switzerland

General Information Coed residential academic program and outdoor program established in 1986. High school credit may be earned.
Program Focus Intensive French language study.
Academics French (Advanced Placement), French language/literature.
Sports Bicycling, soccer, swimming, tennis, volleyball.
Wilderness/Outdoors Hiking, mountain biking, rafting, rock climbing, white-water trips.
Trips Cultural, day, overnight.
Program Information 1 session per year. Session length: 4–5 weeks in June, July. Ages: 13–17. 60 participants per session. Boarding program cost: $5000–$6200.
Application Deadline Continuous.
Contact Mrs. Toni Soule, US TASIS Representative, 1640 Wisconsin Avenue, NW, Washington, District of Columbia 20007. Phone: 202-965-5800. Fax: 202-965-5816. E-mail: usadmissions@tasis.com.
URL www.tasis.com
For more information, see page 670.

TASIS LE CHÂTEAU DES ENFANTS

TASIS The American School in Switzerland
Montagnola-Lugano, Ticino 6926
Switzerland

General Information Coed residential and day traditional camp, academic program, and cultural program established in 1969.
Program Focus Bilingual experiences. The program

TASIS Le Château des Enfants (continued)

offers many excursions and field trips in neighboring northern Italy as well as southern Switzerland.

Academics English as a second language, French language/literature.

Arts Arts and crafts (general), chorus, drawing, mime, music, music (vocal), musical productions, painting, puppetry, theater/drama.

Special Interest Areas Campcraft, cross-cultural education, nature study.

Sports Basketball, bicycling, soccer, softball, swimming, tennis, volleyball.

Wilderness/Outdoors Hiking.

Trips Cultural, day, overnight.

Program Information 2 sessions per year. Session length: 3–4 weeks in June, July, August. Ages: 6–10. 50–55 participants per session. Day program cost: $1950–$2400. Boarding program cost: $4100–$5000.

Application Deadline Continuous.

Jobs Positions for college students.

Contact Mrs. Toni Soule, US TASIS Representative, 1640 Wisconsin Avenue, NW, Washington, District of Columbia 20007. Phone: 202-965-5800. Fax: 202-965-5816. E-mail: usadmissions@tasis.com.

URL www.tasis.com

For more information, see page 670.

TASIS MIDDLE SCHOOL PROGRAM

TASIS The American School in Switzerland
Montagnola-Lugano, Ticino 6926
Switzerland

General Information Coed residential and day traditional camp, academic program, and cultural program established in 1976.

Program Focus Language study combined with local excursion and travel to places of interest.

Academics English as a second language, French language/literature.

Arts Acting, arts and crafts (general), ceramics, chorus, dance, graphic arts, jewelry making, music (vocal), musical productions, painting, puppetry, theater/drama.

Special Interest Areas Cross-cultural education.

Sports Archery, basketball, bicycling, bicycling (BMX), canoeing, horseback riding, martial arts, sailing, soccer,

swimming, tennis, track and field, volleyball, waterskiing, windsurfing.

Wilderness/Outdoors Hiking, mountain biking, mountaineering, rafting, rock climbing.

Trips Cultural, day, overnight.

Program Information 2 sessions per year. Session length: 3–4 weeks in June, July, August. Ages: 11–13. 80 participants per session. Day program cost: $2500–$3000. Boarding program cost: $4100–$5000.

Application Deadline Continuous.

Jobs Positions for college students.

Contact Mrs. Toni Soule, US TASIS Representative, 1640 Wisconsin Avenue, NW, Washington, District of Columbia 20007. Phone: 202-965-5800. Fax: 202-965-5816. E-mail: usadmissions@tasis.com.

URL www.tasis.com

For more information, see page 670.

TASIS SUMMER PROGRAM FOR LANGUAGES, ARTS, AND OUTDOOR PURSUITS

TASIS The American School in Switzerland
Montagnola-Lugano, Ticino 6926
Switzerland

General Information Coed residential and day traditional camp, academic program, and cultural program established in 1955. High school credit may be earned.

TASIS Summer Program for Languages, Arts, and Outdoor Pursuits

Program Focus Language study, photography, painting, engineering, or art history. Frequent trips to visit French and northern Italian cities.

Academics English as a second language, French language/literature, Italian language/literature, TOEFL/TOEIC preparation, art history/appreciation, engineering.

Arts Arts and crafts (general), dance, drawing, film, music (vocal), painting, photography.

Special Interest Areas Touring.

Sports Aerobics, basketball, bicycling, canoeing, sailing, soccer, swimming, tennis, track and field, volleyball, windsurfing.

Wilderness/Outdoors Bicycle trips, canyoneering, hiking, mountain biking, rafting, rock climbing.

Trips Cultural, day, overnight.

Program Information 2 sessions per year. Session length: 3–4 weeks in June, July, August. Ages: 14–18. 150–160 participants per session. Day program cost: $2500–$3000. Boarding program cost: $4100–$5000.

Application Deadline Continuous.

Jobs Positions for college students 21 and older.

Contact Mrs. Toni Soule, US TASIS Representative, 1640 Wisconsin Avenue, NW, Washington, District of Columbia 20007. Phone: 202-965-5800. Fax: 202-965-5816. E-mail: usadmissions@tasis.com.

URL www.tasis.com

For more information, see page 670.

TAIWAN

CENTER FOR CULTURAL INTERCHANGE–TAIWAN HIGH SCHOOL ABROAD

Center for Cultural Interchange
Taiwan

General Information Coed residential academic program and cultural program established in 1985. High school credit may be earned.

Program Focus High school abroad.

Academics Chinese languages/literature, academics (general).

Special Interest Areas Cross-cultural education, homestays.

Trips Cultural, day.

Program Information 2 sessions per year. Session length: 90–300 days in January, February, March, April, May, June, July, August, September, October, November, December. Ages: 15–18. Boarding program cost: $5900–$7700. Financial aid available. Early Bird discount.

Application Deadline Continuous.

Contact Ms. Juliet Jones, Outbound Programs Director, 746 North LaSalle Drive, Chicago, Illinois 60610-3617. Phone: 866-684-9675. Fax: 312-944-2644. E-mail: info@cci-exchange.com.

URL www.cci-exchange.com

For more information, see page 448.

THAILAND

AAVE–THAILAND

AAVE–Journeys That Matter
Thailand

General Information Coed travel outdoor program, cultural program, and adventure program established in 1976. Accredited by American Camping Association.

Program Focus Cultural and outdoor experience.

Special Interest Areas Community service, cross-cultural education, culinary arts, leadership training, touring.

Sports Bicycling, kayaking, sea kayaking, snorkeling.

Wilderness/Outdoors Bicycle trips, hiking, rafting.

Trips Cultural, day, overnight.

Program Information 2–4 sessions per year. Session length: 3 weeks in June, July, August. Ages: 15–18. 12 participants per session. Cost: $4088. Financial aid available.

Application Deadline Continuous.

Jobs Positions for college students 21 and older.

Contact Mr. Abbott Wallis, Owner, 2308 Fossil Trace Drive, Golden, Colorado 80401. Phone: 800-222-3595. Fax: 303-526-0885. E-mail: info@aave.com.

URL www.aave.com

For more information, see page 394.

AFS-USA–COMMUNITY SERVICE–THAILAND

AFS-USA
Thailand

General Information Coed residential community service program and cultural program. High school credit may be earned.

Program Focus Community service activities centered around the teaching of English as a second language.

Academics English as a second language, Thai language.

Special Interest Areas Community service, homestays.

Sports Martial arts.

Trips Cultural, day, overnight.

Program Information 1 session per year. Session length: 30–45 days in July, August. Ages: 18+. Boarding program cost: $4000–$6000. Application fee: $75. Financial aid available. International airfare and volunteer homestay support included.

Application Deadline Continuous.

AFS-USA–Community Service–Thailand (continued)

AFS-USA–Community Service–Thailand

Contact Manager, AFS Info Center, 506 Southwest 6th Avenue, 2nd Floor, Portland, Oregon 97204. Phone: 800-AFS-INFO. Fax: 503-299-0753. E-mail: afsinfo@afs.org.
URL www.afs.org/usa
For more information, see page 408.

AFS-USA–HOMESTAY–THAILAND
AFS-USA
Thailand

General Information Coed residential academic program and cultural program.
Program Focus Living with a host family while attending school.
Academics English as a second language, Thai language.
Arts Arts and crafts (general).
Special Interest Areas Homestays.
Trips Cultural, day.
Program Information 1 session per year. Session length: 30–45 days in July, August. Ages: 16–18.

Boarding program cost: $4000–$6000. Application fee: $75. Financial aid available. International airfare and volunteer homestay support included.
Application Deadline Continuous.
Contact Manager, AFS Info Center, 506 Southwest 6th Avenue, 2nd Floor, Portland, Oregon 97204. Phone: 800-AFS-INFO. Fax: 503-299-0753. E-mail: afsinfo@afs.org.
URL www.afs.org/usa
For more information, see page 408.

THE EXPERIMENT IN INTERNATIONAL LIVING–THAILAND HOMESTAY
The Experiment in International Living
Thailand

General Information Coed travel outdoor program, community service program, cultural program, and adventure program established in 1932.
Program Focus International youth travel, homestay, community service.
Academics Thai language, intercultural studies.
Arts Pottery.
Special Interest Areas Community service, homestays, touring.
Wilderness/Outdoors Backpacking, hiking, rafting.
Trips Cultural, day, overnight.
Program Information 1 session per year. Session length: 5 weeks in June, July, August. Ages: 14–19. 10–15 participants per session. Cost: $4600. Financial aid available. Airfare included.
Application Deadline May 1.
Contact Annie Thompson, Enrollment Director, Summer Abroad, Kipling Road, PO Box 676, Brattleboro, Vermont 05302-0676. Phone: 800-345-2929. Fax: 802-258-3428. E-mail: eil@worldlearning.org.
URL www.usexperiment.org
For more information, see page 492.

LIFEWORKS WITH THE DPF FOUNDATION IN THAILAND
LIFEWORKS International
Thailand

General Information Coed travel community service program, cultural program, and adventure program established in 1986. High school credit may be earned.
Program Focus Service-learning travel program with cultural immersion working with underprivileged children associated with the DPF Foundation.
Academics Thai language, intercultural studies.
Special Interest Areas Community service, leadership training, team building, touring.
Trips Cultural, day, overnight.
Program Information 2 sessions per year. Session length: 3 weeks in July, August. Ages: 15–19. 8–15 participants per session. Cost: $3970. Financial aid available.
Application Deadline Continuous.

Contact Mr. James Stoll, Director, PO Box 5517, Sarasota, Florida 34277. Phone: 800-808-2115. Fax: 941-924-6075. E-mail: info@lifeworks-international.com. **URL** www.lifeworks-international.com

For more information, see page 548.

RUSTIC PATHWAYS–THE AMAZING THAILAND ADVENTURE

Rustic Pathways
Thailand

General Information Coed travel cultural program and adventure program established in 2003.
Arts Arts and crafts (general).
Special Interest Areas Cross-cultural education, touring.
Sports Boating.
Wilderness/Outdoors Outdoor adventure.
Trips Cultural, day, overnight, shopping.
Program Information 5 sessions per year. Session length: 10 days in June, July, August. Ages: 14–18. 10–15 participants per session. Cost: $1295.
Application Deadline Continuous.
Jobs Positions for college students 21 and older.
Contact Rustic Pathways, 4121 Erie Street, Willoughby, Ohio 44094. Phone: 800-321-4353. Fax: 440-975-9694. E-mail: rustic@rusticpathways.com.
URL www.rusticpathways.com

For more information, see page 612.

RUSTIC PATHWAYS–THE ART OF MUAY THAI

Rustic Pathways
Thailand

General Information Coed residential sports camp established in 2005.
Special Interest Areas Cross-cultural education, touring.
Sports Martial arts.
Trips Cultural, day, overnight, shopping.
Program Information 9 sessions per year. Session length: 1–6 weeks in June, July, August. Ages: 15–18. 10–20 participants per session. Boarding program cost:

$995–$5495. Application fee: $100–$200. Financial aid available.
Application Deadline Continuous.
Jobs Positions for college students 21 and older.
Contact Rustic Pathways, 4121 Erie Street, Willoughby, Ohio 44094. Phone: 800-321-4353. Fax: 440-975-9694. E-mail: rustic@rusticpathways.com.
URL www.rusticpathways.com

For more information, see page 612.

RUSTIC PATHWAYS–COME WITH NOTHING, GO HOME RICH

Rustic Pathways
Thailand

General Information Coed travel community service program and cultural program established in 2005.
Special Interest Areas Community service, cross-cultural education, homestays, touring.
Trips Cultural, day, overnight, shopping.
Program Information 5 sessions per year. Session length: 24 days in June, July, August. Ages: 16–18. 10–20 participants per session. Cost: $2995. Application fee: $100–$200. Financial aid available.
Application Deadline Continuous.
Jobs Positions for college students 21 and older.
Contact Rustic Pathways, 4121 Erie Street, Willoughby, Ohio 44094. Phone: 800-321-4353. Fax: 440-975-9694. E-mail: rustic@rusticpathways.com.
URL www.rusticpathways.com

For more information, see page 612.

RUSTIC PATHWAYS–ELEPHANTS & AMAZING THAILAND

Rustic Pathways
Thailand

General Information Coed travel community service program, cultural program, and adventure program established in 1998. High school credit may be earned.
Program Focus Travel through northern Thailand: Bangkok, Chiang Mai, Mae Hong Song.
Special Interest Areas Animal care, community service, construction, cross-cultural education, homestays, nature study, touring.
Sports Boating, soccer, swimming.
Wilderness/Outdoors Hiking, outdoor adventure, pack animal trips.
Trips Cultural, day, overnight, shopping.
Program Information 5 sessions per year. Session length: 17 days in June, July, August. Ages: 14–18. 10–15 participants per session. Cost: $2295. Application fee: $100–$200.
Application Deadline Continuous.
Jobs Positions for college students 21 and older.

RUSTIC PATHWAYS–ELEPHANTS & AMAZING THAILAND (continued)

Contact Rustic Pathways, 4121 Erie Street, Willoughby, Ohio 44094. Phone: 800-321-4353. Fax: 440-975-9694. E-mail: rustic@rusticpathways.com.
URL www.rusticpathways.com
For more information, see page 612.

RUSTIC PATHWAYS–HILL TRIBE TREKKING ADVENTURE

Rustic Pathways
Thailand

General Information Coed travel outdoor program and cultural program.
Special Interest Areas Homestays, nature study, touring.
Wilderness/Outdoors Hiking, outdoor adventure, rafting, white-water trips, wilderness camping.
Trips Cultural, day.
Program Information 1 session per year. Session length: 17 days in July. Ages: 15–18. 10–15 participants per session. Cost: $2195. Financial aid available. Airfare not included.
Application Deadline Continuous.
Jobs Positions for college students 21 and older.
Contact Rustic Pathways, 4121 Erie Street, Willoughby, Ohio 44094. Phone: 800-321-4353. Fax: 440-975-9694. E-mail: rustic@rusticpathways.com.
URL www.rusticpathways.com
For more information, see page 612.

RUSTIC PATHWAYS–INTRO TO COMMUNITY SERVICE IN THAILAND

Rustic Pathways
Udon Thani
Thailand

General Information Coed residential community service program and cultural program established in 1998. High school credit may be earned.
Arts Arts and crafts (general), painting.
Special Interest Areas Community service, construction, cross-cultural education, farming, gardening, homestays, touring.
Sports Swimming.
Trips Cultural, day, overnight, shopping.
Program Information 10 sessions per year. Session length: 10 days in June, July, August. Ages: 14–18.

15–30 participants per session. Boarding program cost: $965. Application fee: $100–$200.
Application Deadline Continuous.
Jobs Positions for college students 21 and older.
Contact Rustic Pathways, 4121 Erie Street, Willoughby, Ohio 44094. Phone: 800-321-4353. Fax: 440-975-9694. E-mail: rustic@rusticpathways.com.
URL www.rusticpathways.com
For more information, see page 612.

RUSTIC PATHWAYS–ISLAND HOPPING AND DIVING–THAILAND

Rustic Pathways
Thailand

General Information Coed travel outdoor program, cultural program, and adventure program.
Special Interest Areas Nature study, touring.
Sports Scuba diving, sea kayaking, snorkeling.
Wilderness/Outdoors Hiking, outdoor adventure, rafting, rock climbing.
Trips Cultural, day.
Program Information 1 session per year. Session length: 17 days in July, August. Ages: 16–18. 10–15 participants per session. Cost: $2895. Financial aid available.
Application Deadline Continuous.
Jobs Positions for college students 21 and older.
Contact Rustic Pathways, 4121 Erie Street, Willoughby, Ohio 44094. Phone: 800-321-4353. Fax: 440-975-9694. E-mail: rustic@rusticpathways.com.
URL www.rusticpathways.com
For more information, see page 612.

RUSTIC PATHWAYS–RICEFIELDS, MONKS & SMILING CHILDREN

Rustic Pathways
Udon Thani
Thailand

General Information Coed residential community service program and cultural program established in 1998.
Arts Arts and crafts (general), painting.
Special Interest Areas Community service, construction, cross-cultural education, farming, gardening, homestays, touring.
Sports Swimming.
Trips Cultural, day, overnight, shopping.
Program Information 9 sessions per year. Session length: 17–73 days in June, July, August. Ages: 14–18. 15–20 participants per session. Boarding program cost: $1895–$8095.
Application Deadline Continuous.
Jobs Positions for college students 21 and older.

Contact Rustic Pathways, 4121 Erie Street, Willoughby, Ohio 44094. Phone: 800-321-4353. Fax: 440-975-9694. E-mail: rustic@rusticpathways.com. **URL** www.rusticpathways.com

For more information, see page 612.

RUSTIC PATHWAYS–SOCCER AND SERVICE IN THAILAND

Rustic Pathways
Thailand

General Information Coed residential community service program and cultural program established in 2005.
Special Interest Areas Community service, cross-cultural education, homestays, touring.
Sports Soccer.
Wilderness/Outdoors Outdoor adventure, rafting.
Trips Cultural, day, overnight, shopping.
Program Information 1 session per year. Session length: 17 days in June, July. Ages: 14–18. 10–20 participants per session. Boarding program cost: $2195. Application fee: $100–$200. Financial aid available.
Application Deadline Continuous.
Jobs Positions for college students 21 and older.
Contact Rustic Pathways, 4121 Erie Street, Willoughby, Ohio 44094. Phone: 800-321-4353. Fax: 440-975-9694. E-mail: rustic@rusticpathways.com. **URL** www.rusticpathways.com

For more information, see page 612.

RUSTIC PATHWAYS–THE THAI ELEPHANT CONSERVATION PROJECT

Rustic Pathways
Royal Thai Elephant Reserve
Chiang Mai
Thailand

General Information Coed residential community service program and cultural program established in 2003.
Special Interest Areas Animal care, community service, nature study, touring.
Wilderness/Outdoors Hiking.
Trips Cultural, day.
Program Information 10 sessions per year. Session length: 10 days in June, July, August. Ages: 14–18. 10–15 participants per session. Boarding program cost: $1095.
Application Deadline Continuous.
Jobs Positions for college students 21 and older.
Contact Rustic Pathways, 4121 Erie Street, Willoughby, Ohio 44094. Phone: 800-321-4353. Fax: 440-975-9694. E-mail: rustic@rusticpathways.com. **URL** www.rusticpathways.com

For more information, see page 612.

TURKEY

AFS-USA–HOMESTAY–TURKEY

AFS-USA
Turkey

General Information Coed residential cultural program.
Program Focus Living with a host family and taking part in activities with other teenagers.
Academics Turkish language/literature.
Special Interest Areas Homestays.
Trips Cultural, day.
Program Information 1 session per year. Session length: 30–45 days in June, July, August. Ages: 15–18. Boarding program cost: $4000–$6000. Application fee: $75. Financial aid available. International airfare and volunteer homestay support included.
Application Deadline Continuous.
Contact Manager, AFS Info Center, 506 Southwest 6th Avenue, 2nd Floor, Portland, Oregon 97204. Phone: 800-AFS-INFO. Fax: 503-299-0753. E-mail: afsinfo@afs.org.
URL www.afs.org/usa

For more information, see page 408.

THE EXPERIMENT IN INTERNATIONAL LIVING–TURKEY HOMESTAY, COMMUNITY SERVICE, AND TRAVEL

The Experiment in International Living Turkey

General Information Coed travel community service program and cultural program established in 1932.
Program Focus International youth travel, homestay, community service.
Academics Turkish language/literature.
Special Interest Areas Community service, homestays, touring.
Trips Cultural, day, overnight.
Program Information 1 session per year. Session length: 5 weeks in June, July. Ages: 14–19. 10–15 participants per session. Cost: $5000. Financial aid available. Airfare included.
Application Deadline May 1.
Contact Annie Thompson, Enrollment Director, Summer Abroad, Kipling Road, PO Box 676, Brattleboro, Vermont 05302-0676. Phone: 800-345-2929. Fax: 802-258-3426. E-mail: eil@worldlearning.org.
URL www.usexperiment.org

For more information, see page 492.

UNITED KINGDOM

CAMBRIDGE COLLEGE PROGRAMME

Cambridge College Programme
Cambridge University
Cambridge, England
United Kingdom

General Information Coed travel academic program and cultural program established in 1986. Formal opportunities for the academically talented. High school or college credit may be earned.

Cambridge College Programme

Program Focus Academic and cultural enrichment in England. Optional one-week trip to Paris.
Academics Bible study, English language/literature, French language/literature, Jewish studies, Latin language, SAT/ACT preparation, academics (general), anthropology, archaeology, architecture, area studies, art history/appreciation, astronomy, biology, business, chemistry, classical languages/literatures, computer programming, computers, ecology, economics, environmental science, geology/earth science, government and politics, history, humanities, journalism, marine studies, mathematics, medicine, meteorology, music, oceanography, philosophy, physics, physiology, precollege program, psychology, religion, science (general), social science, social studies, speech/debate, writing.
Arts Acting, band, chorus, creative writing, dance, drawing, film, music, music (ensemble), music (orchestral), music (vocal), painting, photography, theater/drama.

Special Interest Areas Field trips (arts and culture), leadership training.
Sports Aerobics, baseball, basketball, boating, cricket, croquet, cross-country, equestrian sports, fencing, football, golf, gymnastics, lacrosse, racquetball, rowing (crew/sculling), rugby, soccer, squash, swimming, tennis, volleyball, water polo, weight training.
Trips College tours, cultural, day, shopping.
Program Information 1 session per year. Session length: 3 weeks in July, August. Ages: 14+. Cost: $5795.
Application Deadline Continuous.
Contact Ms. Taryn Edwards, Director, John Hancock Building, 175 East Delaware Place, Suite 5518, Chicago, Illinois 60611. Phone: 800-922-3552. Fax: 312-988-7268. E-mail: info@cambridgeuk.org.
URL www.cambridgeuk.org
For more information, see page 440.

THE CAMBRIDGE EXPERIENCE

Academic Study Associates, Inc. (ASA)
Corpus Christi College
Cambridge University
Cambridge
United Kingdom

General Information Coed residential academic program and cultural program established in 2006. Formal opportunities for the academically talented. High school credit may be earned.
Program Focus Academic enrichment in humanities, arts, social sciences, and SAT preparation. Optional travel extension to Paris.
Academics Chinese languages/literature, English language/literature, SAT/ACT preparation, academics (general), anthropology, archaeology, architecture, art history/appreciation, biology, business, communications, economics, government and politics, health sciences, history, humanities, journalism, mathematics, music, philosophy, physics, precollege program, psychology, science (general), social science, writing.
Arts Arts and crafts (general), creative writing, dance (modern), drawing, film, painting, photography, screenwriting, theater/drama.
Special Interest Areas Touring.
Sports Aerobics, basketball, boating, soccer, softball, sports (general), tennis, volleyball.
Trips Cultural, day, overnight, shopping.
Program Information 1 session per year. Session length: 4 weeks in June, July. Ages: 14–18. 45 participants per session. Boarding program cost: $6695. Financial aid available.
Application Deadline Continuous.
Jobs Positions for college students 21 and older.
Contact Mr. David A. Evans, Vice President, 375 West Broadway, Suite 200, New York, New York 10012. Phone: 212-796-8340. Fax: 212-334-4934. E-mail: summer@asaprograms.com.
URL www.asaprograms.com
For more information, see page 398.

THE CAMBRIDGE PREP EXPERIENCE

Oxbridge Academic Programs
Cambridge University
Cambridge
United Kingdom

General Information Coed residential academic program and arts program established in 1995. Formal opportunities for the academically talented and artistically talented.

The Cambridge Prep Experience

Program Focus Academic and cultural enrichment.
Academics English language/literature, academics (general), criminal justice, history, humanities, law, mathematics, medicine, philosophy, psychology, science (general), speech/debate, writing.
Arts Arts, creative writing, drawing, painting, theater/drama.
Special Interest Areas Field trips (arts and culture).
Sports Aerobics, baseball, basketball, rowing (crew/sculling), soccer, sports (general), tennis.
Trips Cultural, day.
Program Information 1 session per year. Session length: 25 days in July. Ages: 14–15. 170 participants per session. Boarding program cost: $6395. Financial aid available. Airfare not included.
Application Deadline Continuous.
Contact Ms. Andrea Mardon, Executive Director, Oxbridge Academic Programs, 601 West 110th Street, Suite 7R, New York, New York 10025-2186. Phone: 800-828-8349. Fax: 212-663-8169. E-mail: info@oxbridgeprograms.com.
URL www.oxbridgeprograms.com
For more information, see page 580.

THE CAMBRIDGE TRADITION

Oxbridge Academic Programs
Cambridge University
Cambridge
United Kingdom

General Information Coed residential academic program and arts program established in 1999. Formal opportunities for the academically talented and artistically talented. High school credit may be earned.
Program Focus Academic and cultural enrichment.
Academics English language/literature, Latin language, academics (general), architecture, art history/appreciation, classical languages/literatures, computers, criminal justice, economics, government and politics, history, humanities, journalism, medicine, music, philosophy, precollege program, psychology, religion, social science, social studies.
Arts Arts, creative writing, drawing, music, music (ensemble), painting, photography, television/video, theater/drama.
Special Interest Areas Field trips (arts and culture).
Sports Aerobics, basketball, cross-country, soccer, sports (general), squash, tennis.
Trips Cultural, day.
Program Information 1 session per year. Session length: 4 weeks in July. Ages: 15–18. 265 participants per session. Boarding program cost: $6695. Financial aid available.
Application Deadline Continuous.
Contact Ms. Andrea Mardon, Executive Director, Oxbridge Academic Programs, 601 West 110th Street, Suite 7R, New York, New York 10025-2186. Phone: 800-828-8349. Fax: 212-663-8169. E-mail: info@oxbridgeprograms.com.
URL www.oxbridgeprograms.com

For more information, see page 580.

CENTER FOR CULTURAL INTERCHANGE–UNITED KINGDOM INDEPENDENT HOMESTAY

Center for Cultural Interchange
United Kingdom

General Information Coed residential cultural program established in 1985.
Program Focus Independent homestay in the United Kingdom.
Academics Independent study.

Special Interest Areas Cross-cultural education, homestays.
Trips Cultural, day.
Program Information Session length: 1–4 weeks in January, February, March, April, May, June, July, August, September, October, November, December. Ages: 16+. Boarding program cost: $990–$1790. Financial aid available.
Application Deadline Continuous.
Contact Ms. Juliet Jones, Outbound Programs Director, 746 North LaSalle Drive, Chicago, Illinois 60610-3617. Phone: 866-684-9675. Fax: 312-944-2644. E-mail: info@cci-exchange.com.
URL www.cci-exchange.com

For more information, see page 448.

THE EXPERIMENT IN INTERNATIONAL LIVING–SCOTLAND

The Experiment in International Living
United Kingdom

General Information Coed travel outdoor program, cultural program, and adventure program established in 1932.
Program Focus International youth travel, Celtic culture.
Academics Intercultural studies, language study.
Special Interest Areas Community service, conservation projects, homestays, touring.
Sports Fishing, sea kayaking.
Wilderness/Outdoors Hiking, wilderness camping.
Trips Cultural, day, overnight.
Program Information 1 session per year. Session length: 4 weeks in June, July. Ages: 14–19. 10–15 participants per session. Cost: $5900. Financial aid available. Airfare included.
Application Deadline May 1.
Contact Annie Thompson, Enrollment Director, Summer Abroad, Kipling Road, PO Box 676, Brattleboro, Vermont 05302-0676. Phone: 800-345-2929. Fax: 802-258-3428. E-mail: eil@worldlearning.org.
URL www.usexperiment.org

For more information, see page 492.

THE EXPERIMENT IN INTERNATIONAL LIVING–UNITED KINGDOM FILMMAKING PROGRAM AND HOMESTAY

The Experiment in International Living
United Kingdom

General Information Coed travel arts program, cultural program, and adventure program established in 1932.
Program Focus International youth travel, homestays, filmmaking, travel.
Arts Film.
Special Interest Areas Homestays, touring.
Trips Cultural, day, overnight.
Program Information 1 session per year. Session length: 4 weeks in June, July. Ages: 14–19. 10–15

participants per session. Cost: $5900. Financial aid available. Airfare included.
Application Deadline May 1.
Contact Annie Thompson, Enrollment Director, Summer Abroad, Kipling Road, PO Box 676, Brattleboro, Vermont 05302-0676. Phone: 800-345-2929. Fax: 802-258-3428. E-mail: eil@worldlearning.org.
URL www.usexperiment.org
For more information, see page 492.

THE EXPERIMENT IN INTERNATIONAL LIVING–UNITED KINGDOM THEATRE PROGRAM

The Experiment in International Living
United Kingdom

General Information Coed travel arts program and cultural program established in 1932.
Program Focus International youth travel, homestay, theatre.
Academics Intercultural studies.
Arts Theater/drama.
Special Interest Areas Homestays, touring.
Trips Cultural, day, overnight.
Program Information 1 session per year. Session length: 4 weeks in June, July. Ages: 14–19. 10–15 participants per session. Cost: $5900. Financial aid available. Airfare included.
Application Deadline May 1.
Contact Annie Thompson, Enrollment Director, Summer Abroad, Kipling Road, PO Box 676, Brattleboro, Vermont 05302-0676. Phone: 800-345-2929. Fax: 802-258-3428. E-mail: eil@worldlearning.org.
URL www.usexperiment.org
For more information, see page 492.

IEI–FASHION AND DESIGN PLUS PROGRAMME

Intern Exchange International, Ltd.
London
United Kingdom

General Information Coed residential arts program established in 1987. High school or college credit may be earned.
Program Focus Fashion theory, fashion drawing, and production of a fashion design project.
Academics Business, marketing.
Arts Drawing, fabric arts, fashion design/production, illustration, printmaking.
Special Interest Areas Career exploration, college planning, field trips (arts and culture).
Sports Basketball, squash, tennis.
Trips Cultural, day.
Program Information 1 session per year. Session length: 31 days in June, July. Ages: 16–18. 20–30 participants per session. Boarding program cost: $6945. Application fee: $100.
Application Deadline Continuous.
Contact Nina Miller Glickman, Director, 1858 Mallard Lane, Villanova, Pennsylvania 19085. Phone: 610-527-6066. Fax: 610-527-5499. E-mail: info@internexchange. com.
URL www.internexchange.com
For more information, see page 528.

IEI–PHOTOGRAPHY PLUS PROGRAMME

Intern Exchange International, Ltd.
London
United Kingdom

General Information Coed residential arts program established in 1987. High school or college credit may be earned.
Program Focus Documentary photography, special processes and experimental imaging photography, and digital photography.
Academics Computers.
Arts Design, graphic arts, photography.
Special Interest Areas Career exploration, college planning, computer graphics, field trips (arts and culture).
Sports Basketball, squash, tennis.
Trips Cultural, day.
Program Information 1 session per year. Session length: 31 days in June, July. Ages: 16–18. 15–36 participants per session. Boarding program cost: $6945. Application fee: $100.
Application Deadline Continuous.
Contact Nina Miller Glickman, Director, 1858 Mallard Lane, Villanova, Pennsylvania 19085. Phone: 610-527-6066. Fax: 610-527-5499. E-mail: info@internexchange. com.
URL www.internexchange.com
For more information, see page 528.

IEI—PRINT AND BROADCAST JOURNALISM

Intern Exchange International, Ltd.
London
United Kingdom

General Information Coed residential academic program established in 1987. High school or college credit may be earned.
Program Focus To learn and sharpen journalistic skills, cover and report on politics, art, music, sports and current events while creating a publication.
Academics Computers, journalism, writing.
Arts Design, graphic arts.
Special Interest Areas Career exploration, college planning, computer graphics, field trips (arts and culture).
Sports Basketball, squash, tennis.
Trips Cultural, day.
Program Information 1 session per year. Session length: 31 days in June, July. Ages: 16–18. 10–20 participants per session. Boarding program cost: $6945. Application fee: $100.
Application Deadline Continuous.
Contact Nina Miller Glickman, Director, 1858 Mallard Lane, Villanova, Pennsylvania 19085. Phone: 610-527-6066. Fax: 610-527-5499. E-mail: info@internexchange. com
URL www.internexchange.com
For more information, see page 528.

IEI STUDENT TRAVEL—INTERNSHIP PROGRAM IN LONDON

Intern Exchange International, Ltd.
London
United Kingdom

General Information Coed residential academic program established in 1987. High school credit may be earned.

IEI Student Travel–Internship Program in London

Program Focus Career internships in archaeology, art gallery and auction house, business/finance, community service, culinary arts, hotel management, information technology, law, medical research, public relations, publishing, retail sales, strategic studies, and veterinary medicine.
Academics Advertising, archaeology, art history/appreciation, banking/finance, business, communications, computers, government and politics, health sciences, journalism, marketing, prelaw, premed, psychology, social services, writing.
Arts Acting, drawing, fabric arts, fashion design/production, film, music (vocal), painting, photography, printmaking, sculpture, television/video, theater/drama.
Special Interest Areas Animal care, career exploration, college planning, community service, culinary arts, field trips (arts and culture), internships.
Sports Basketball, squash, tennis.
Trips Cultural, day.
Program Information 1 session per year. Session length: 31 days in June, July. Ages: 16–18. 150–200 participants per session. Boarding program cost: $6945. Application fee: $100.
Application Deadline Continuous.
Contact Nina Miller Glickman, Director, 1858 Mallard Lane, Villanova, Pennsylvania 19085. Phone: 610-527-6066. Fax: 610-527-5499. E-mail: info@internexchange. com
URL www.internexchange.com
For more information, see page 528.

IEI—THEATRE PLUS PROGRAMME

Intern Exchange International, Ltd.
London
United Kingdom

General Information Coed residential arts program established in 1987. High school or college credit may be earned.
Program Focus Designed for students interested in theatre and in exploring the nature of the acting process.
Arts Acting, dance, stage movement, theater/drama, voice and speech.
Special Interest Areas Career exploration, college planning, field trips (arts and culture).
Sports Basketball, squash, tennis.
Trips Cultural, day.
Program Information 1 session per year. Session

length: 31 days in June, July. Ages: 16–18. 10–18 participants per session. Boarding program cost: $6945. Application fee: $100.
Application Deadline Continuous.
Contact Nina Miller Glickman, Director, 1858 Mallard Lane, Villanova, Pennsylvania 19085. Phone: 610-527-6066. Fax: 610-527-5499. E-mail: info@internexchange.com.
URL www.internexchange.com
For more information, see page 528.

IEI–VIDEO PRODUCTION PLUS PROGRAMME

Intern Exchange International, Ltd.
London
United Kingdom

General Information Coed residential arts program established in 1987. High school or college credit may be earned.
Program Focus To give students first-hand knowledge of video production.
Academics Computers, music, writing.
Arts Acting, film, film editing, film production, graphic arts, television/video.
Special Interest Areas Career exploration, college planning, field trips (arts and culture).
Sports Basketball, squash, tennis.
Trips Cultural, day.
Program Information 1 session per year. Session length: 31 days in June, July. Ages: 16–18. 30–40 participants per session. Boarding program cost: $6945. Application fee: $100.
Application Deadline Continuous.
Contact Nina Miller Glickman, Director, 1858 Mallard Lane, Villanova, Pennsylvania 19085. Phone: 610-527-6066. Fax: 610-527-5499. E-mail: info@internexchange.com.
URL www.internexchange.com
For more information, see page 528.

OXFORD ADVANCED STUDIES PROGRAM

Oxford Tutorial College
12 King Edward Street
Oxford OX1 4HT
United Kingdom

General Information Coed residential and day academic program and cultural program established in 1984. Formal opportunities for the academically talented and gifted. High school credit may be earned.

Oxford Advanced Studies Program

Program Focus Academic courses and cultural visits.
Academics English language/literature, French (Advanced Placement), French language/literature, German language/literature, Italian language/literature, Russian language/literature, SAT/ACT preparation, Spanish (Advanced Placement), Spanish language/literature, academics (general), architecture, art history/appreciation, biology, biology (Advanced Placement), business, chemistry, communications, economics, government and politics, government and politics (Advanced Placement), history, humanities, intercultural studies, journalism, mathematics, mathematics (Advanced Placement), philosophy, physics, precollege program, psychology, science (general), social science, speech/debate, writing.
Arts Acting, band, clowning, creative writing, dance, dance (modern), film, mime, music (classical), music (instrumental), photography, television/video, theater/drama.
Special Interest Areas Community service, field trips (arts and culture).
Sports Aerobics, baseball, basketball, football, gymnastics, rowing (crew/sculling), soccer, softball, squash, swimming, tennis, ultimate frisbee, volleyball, weight training.
Trips College tours, cultural, day, shopping.
Program Information 1 session per year. Session length: 25 days in July. Ages: 16+. 90–120 participants per session. Day program cost: $6000–$6900. Boarding program cost: $8500–$9400. Application fee: $350. Airfare not included.
Application Deadline June 1.
Summer Contact Ms. Joan Ives, Program Registrar,

Oxford Advanced Studies Program (continued)

PO Box 2043, Darien, Connecticut 06820. Phone: 203-966-2886. Fax: 203-966-0015. E-mail: oxedge@aol. com.
Winter Contact Mr. Charles Duncan, Admissions Tutor, 12 King Edward Street, Oxford, Oxon OX1 4HT, United Kingdom. Phone: 44-1865-793333. Fax: 44-1865-793233. E-mail: charles.duncan@oasp.ac.uk.
URL www.oasp.ac.uk

Special Note
Each year in July, a group of talented young people gather in Oxford to take part in a unique experience that combines the Oxbridge mode of tutorial-style learning with a wide range of academic and cultural activities and visits. This is a stimulating and maturing four weeks, both academically and personally, that many previous participants have described as the most wonderful and rewarding experience of their lives. The course is intended for high school students who have completed sophomore year and who have an academic curiosity and ability well above average.

For more information, see page 582.

THE OXFORD EXPERIENCE

Academic Study Associates, Inc. (ASA)
Lady Margaret Hall College
Oxford University
Oxford
United Kingdom

General Information Coed residential academic program and cultural program established in 1984. Formal opportunities for the academically talented. High school credit may be earned.
Program Focus Academic enrichment in humanities, arts, social sciences, and SAT preparation. Optional travel extension to Paris.
Academics Chinese languages/literature, English language/literature, French language/literature, SAT/ACT preparation, academics (general), anthropology, archaeology, architecture, art history/appreciation, biology, business, communications, economics, government and politics, health sciences, history, humanities, intercultural studies, journalism, mathematics, music, philosophy, physics, precollege program, psychology, social science, speech/debate, writing.
Arts Arts and crafts (general), creative writing, dance (modern), drawing, film, painting, photography, screenwriting, theater/drama.
Special Interest Areas Touring.
Sports Aerobics, basketball, boating, soccer, softball, sports (general), tennis, volleyball.
Trips Cultural, day, overnight, shopping.
Program Information 2 sessions per year. Session length: 3–4 weeks in June, July, August. Ages: 14–18. 100–200 participants per session. Boarding program cost: $5695–$6695. Paris extension: $1695.
Application Deadline Continuous.
Jobs Positions for college students 21 and older.

Contact Mr. David A. Evans, Vice President, 375 West Broadway, Suite 200, New York, New York 10012. Phone: 212-796-8340. Fax: 212-334-4934. E-mail: summer@asaprograms.com.
URL www.asaprograms.com
For more information, see page 398.

OXFORD MEDIA SCHOOL–FILM

Oxford Media School
New College, Oxford University
Oxford OX1 3BN
United Kingdom

General Information Coed residential academic program and arts program established in 1992. Formal opportunities for the artistically talented.
Program Focus Film, drama, and video.
Academics English language/literature, communications, history, journalism, reading, writing.
Arts Acting, cinematography, creative writing, film, film editing, film lighting, film production, radio broadcasting, screenwriting, sound design, television/video, theater/drama.
Special Interest Areas Field research/expeditions, touring.
Sports Boating, soccer, sports (general), tennis, ultimate frisbee.
Trips College tours, cultural, day, shopping.
Program Information 1 session per year. Session length: 4 weeks in July. Ages: 14–18. 20–35 participants per session. Boarding program cost: $6500–$6845.
Application Deadline Continuous.
Contact Mr. Desmond Smith, Director, 110 Pricefield Road, Toronto, Ontario M4W 1Z9, Canada. Phone: 416-964-0746. Fax: 416-929-4230. E-mail: newsco@sympatico.ca.
URL www.oxfordmediaschool.com
For more information, see page 584.

Oxford Media School Film

OXFORD MEDIA SCHOOL–FILM MASTER CLASS

Oxford Media School
New College, Oxford University
Oxford OX1 3BN
United Kingdom

General Information Coed residential academic program and arts program. Formal opportunities for the artistically talented.
Program Focus Advanced film production.
Academics English language/literature, communications, history, journalism, reading, writing.
Arts Acting, cinematography, creative writing, film, film editing, film lighting, film production, radio broadcasting, screenwriting, sound design, television/video, theater/drama.
Special Interest Areas Field research/expeditions, touring.
Sports Boating, soccer, sports (general), tennis, ultimate frisbee.
Trips College tours, cultural, day, shopping.
Program Information 1 session per year. Session length: 4 weeks in July. Ages: 14–18. 10 participants per session. Boarding program cost: $7000–$7045. Financial aid available.
Application Deadline Continuous.
Contact Mr. Desmond Smith, Director, 110 Pricefield Road, Toronto, Ontario M4W 1Z9, Canada. Phone: 416-964-0746. Fax: 416-929-4230. E-mail: newsco@sympatico.ca.
URL www.oxfordmediaschool.com
For more information, see page 584.

OXFORD MEDIA SCHOOL–NEWSROOM IN EUROPE

Oxford Media School
New College, Oxford University
Oxford OX1 3BN
United Kingdom

General Information Coed residential academic program and arts program. Formal opportunities for the artistically talented.
Program Focus Introduction to the basics of documentary making and television journalism.
Academics English language/literature, communications, history, journalism, reading, writing.
Arts Acting, creative writing, film, film editing, film production, radio broadcasting, television/video, theater/drama.
Special Interest Areas Field research/expeditions, touring.
Sports Boating, soccer, sports (general), tennis, ultimate frisbee.
Trips College tours, cultural, day, shopping.
Program Information 1 session per year. Session length: 4 weeks in July. Ages: 14–18. 20–35 participants per session. Boarding program cost: $6500–$6845. Financial aid available.
Application Deadline Continuous.
Contact Mr. Desmond Smith, Director, 110 Pricefield Road, Toronto, Ontario M4W 1Z9, Canada. Phone: 416-964-0746. Fax: 416-929-4230. E-mail: newsco@sympatico.ca.
URL www.oxfordmediaschool.com
For more information, see page 584.

OXFORD MEDIA SCHOOL–NEWSROOM IN EUROPE, MASTER CLASS

Oxford Media School
New College, Oxford University
Oxford OX1 3BN
United Kingdom

General Information Coed residential academic program and arts program. Formal opportunities for the artistically talented.
Program Focus Advanced documentary making and television journalism.
Academics English language/literature, communications, history, journalism, reading, writing.

Oxford Media School–Newsroom in Europe, Master Class (continued)

Arts Creative writing, film, film editing, film production, radio broadcasting, television/video, theater/drama.
Special Interest Areas Field research/expeditions, touring.
Sports Boating, soccer, sports (general), tennis, ultimate frisbee.
Trips College tours, cultural, day, shopping.
Program Information 1 session per year. Session length: 4 weeks in July. Ages: 14–18. 10–20 participants per session. Boarding program cost: $7000–$7045. Financial aid available.
Application Deadline Continuous.
Contact Mr. Desmond Smith, Director, 110 Pricefield Road, Toronto, Ontario M4W 1Z9, Canada. Phone: 416-964-0746. Fax: 416-929-4230. E-mail: newsco@sympatico.ca.
URL www.oxfordmediaschool.com

For more information, see page 584.

THE OXFORD PREP EXPERIENCE

Oxbridge Academic Programs
Oxford University
Oxford
United Kingdom

General Information Coed residential academic program and arts program established in 2004. Formal opportunities for the academically talented and artistically talented.
Program Focus Academic and cultural enrichment.
Academics English language/literature, academics (general), art history/appreciation, government and politics, health sciences, history, humanities, precollege program, social science, social studies, speech/debate, writing.
Arts Acting, arts, creative writing, painting, theater/drama.
Special Interest Areas Field trips (arts and culture).
Sports Aerobics, basketball, cross-country, soccer, sports (general), tennis.
Trips Cultural, day.
Program Information 1 session per year. Session

length: 25 days in July. Ages: 14–15. 141 participants per session. Boarding program cost: $6395. Financial aid available.
Application Deadline Continuous.
Contact Ms. Andrea Mardon, Executive Director, Oxbridge Academic Programs, 601 West 110th Street, Suite 7R, New York, New York 10025-2186. Phone: 800-828-8349. Fax: 212-663-8169. E-mail: info@oxbridgeprograms.com.
URL www.oxbridgeprograms.com

For more information, see page 580.

THE OXFORD TRADITION

Oxbridge Academic Programs
Oxford University
Oxford
United Kingdom

General Information Coed residential academic program and arts program established in 1983. Formal opportunities for the academically talented and artistically talented. High school credit may be earned.

The Oxford Tradition

Program Focus Academic and cultural enrichment.
Academics English language/literature, academics (general), anthropology, archaeology, architecture, art history/appreciation, classical languages/literatures, economics, environmental science, government and politics, history, humanities, international relations, journalism, law, medicine, music, philosophy, precollege program, psychology, social science, social studies, speech/debate, writing.
Arts Acting, arts, creative writing, drawing, film, music, painting, performing arts, photography, theater/drama.
Special Interest Areas Field trips (arts and culture).
Sports Aerobics, basketball, cross-country, soccer, sports (general), tennis.
Trips Cultural, day.
Program Information 1 session per year. Session length: 29 days in July. Ages: 15–18. 400 participants per session. Boarding program cost: $6695. Financial aid available. Airfare not included.
Application Deadline Continuous.

Contact Ms. Andrea Mardon, Executive Director, Oxbridge Academic Programs, 601 West 110th Street, Suite 7R, New York, New York 10025-2186. Phone: 800-828-8349. Fax: 212-663-8169. E-mail: info@oxbridgeprograms.com.
URL www.oxbridgeprograms.com
For more information, see page 580.

PUTNEY STUDENT TRAVEL—CULTURAL EXPLORATION—THEATRE IN BRITAIN

Putney Student Travel
United Kingdom

General Information Coed residential arts program established in 1951.
Program Focus Working in a small group, students create a theatrical production and perform it at the Edinburgh Fringe Festival.
Arts Theater/drama.
Special Interest Areas Team building.
Trips Cultural, day, overnight.
Program Information 1 session per year. Session length: 28–30 days in July, August. Ages: 15–18. 16 participants per session. Boarding program cost: $8090. Financial aid available.
Application Deadline Continuous.
Jobs Positions for college students 21 and older.
Contact Jeffrey Shumlin, Admissions Director, 345 Hickory Ridge Road, Putney, Vermont 05346. Phone: 802-387-5000. Fax: 802-387-4276. E-mail: info@goputney.com.
URL www.goputney.com
For more information, see page 598.

SUMMER ADVANTAGE STUDY ABROAD— CAMBRIDGE UNIVERSITY

American Institute for Foreign Study (AIFS)
Newnham College
Cambridge
United Kingdom

General Information Coed travel academic program and cultural program established in 2006. College credit may be earned.
Program Focus Study abroad for college credit.
Academics English language/literature, architecture, art history/appreciation, government and politics, history, intercultural studies, social studies, study skills.
Trips Cultural, day, overnight, shopping.
Program Information 1 session per year. Session length: 29–34 days in July, August. Ages: 16–18. 45–55 participants per session. Cost: $6395. Application fee: $95.
Application Deadline April 15.

Contact Mrs. Amy Van Stone, Director of Admissions, Summer Advantage, 9 West Broad Street, River Plaza, Stamford, Connecticut 06902. Phone: 800-913-7151. Fax: 203-399-5463. E-mail: summeradvantage@aifs.com.
URL www.summeradvantage.com
For more information, see page 410.

SUMMER ADVANTAGE STUDY ABROAD— LONDON, UK

American Institute for Foreign Study (AIFS)
Richmond—The American International University in London
Queens Road
Richmond upon Thames TW10 6JP
United Kingdom

General Information Coed travel academic program and cultural program established in 1984. College credit may be earned.
Program Focus Study abroad for college credit.
Academics English language/literature, SAT/ACT preparation, architecture, art history/appreciation, government and politics, history, intercultural studies, international relations, music, social science, study skills, writing.
Arts Creative writing, music, theater/drama.
Special Interest Areas Field trips (arts and culture).
Sports Soccer.
Trips Cultural, day, overnight, shopping.
Program Information 1 session per year. Session length: 29–34 days in June, July. Ages: 16–18. 25–35 participants per session. Cost: $6395. Application fee: $95.
Application Deadline April 15.
Contact Mrs. Amy Van Stone, Director of Admissions, Summer Advantage, 9 West Broad Street, River Plaza, Stamford, Connecticut 06902. Phone: 800-913-7151. Fax: 203-399-5463. E-mail: summeradvantage@aifs.com.
URL www.summeradvantage.com
For more information, see page 410.

TASIS England Summer Program

TASIS The American School in England
Coldharbour Lane
Thorpe, Surrey TW20 8TE
United Kingdom

General Information Coed residential academic program and arts program established in 1976. High school credit may be earned.
Program Focus Enrichment, theatre, acting, film making, Shakespeare, and academic summer school courses for credit.
Academics English as a second language, English language/literature, SAT/ACT preparation, TOEFL/TOEIC preparation, academics (general), archaeology, architecture, art history/appreciation, biology, chemistry, computers, history, humanities, journalism, mathematics, music, study skills, writing.
Arts Acting, arts and crafts (general), creative writing, dance, dance (jazz), dance (modern), drawing, film, music, music (instrumental), musical productions, painting, photography, theater/drama.
Sports Aerobics, baseball, basketball, bicycling, equestrian sports, golf, horseback riding, soccer, softball, swimming, tennis, volleyball, waterskiing, weight training.
Trips Cultural, day, overnight, shopping.
Program Information 2 sessions per year. Session length: 3–6 weeks in June, July, August. Ages: 12–18. 150–220 participants per session. Boarding program cost: $4200–$7100. Airfare not included.
Application Deadline Continuous.
Jobs Positions for college students 21 and older.
Contact W. Thomas Fleming, US Director, 1640 Wisconsin Avenue, NW, Washington, District of Columbia 20007. Phone: 202-965-5800. Fax: 202-965-5816. E-mail: usadmissions@tasis.com.
URL www.tasis.com

For more information, see page 668.

UNITED REPUBLIC OF TANZANIA

Putney Student Travel–Community Service–Tanzania

Putney Student Travel
United Republic of Tanzania

General Information Coed residential community service program and cultural program established in 1951.
Program Focus Community service, cultural exchange, and weekend excursions from a base in a small, rural community, and a week-long safari.
Academics Intercultural studies.
Special Interest Areas Community service, construction, farming.

Sports Soccer.
Wilderness/Outdoors Hiking, safari.
Trips Cultural, day.
Program Information 1 session per year. Session length: 4 weeks in June, July. Ages: 15–18. 16 participants per session. Boarding program cost: $7190. Financial aid available. Airfare from New York included.
Application Deadline Continuous.
Contact Jeffrey Shumlin, Admissions Director, 345 Hickory Ridge Road, Putney, Vermont 05346. Phone: 802-387-5000. Fax: 802-387-4276. E-mail: info@goputney.com.
URL www.goputney.com

For more information, see page 598.

RUSTIC PATHWAYS–CLIMBING KILI

Rustic Pathways
Mount Kilimanjaro
United Republic of Tanzania

General Information Coed travel outdoor program and wilderness program established in 2005.
Special Interest Areas Cross-cultural education, nature study, touring.
Wilderness/Outdoors Hiking, mountaineering, outdoor adventure, wilderness camping.
Trips Cultural, day, overnight, shopping.
Program Information 2 sessions per year. Session length: 10 days in June, July. Ages: 14–18. 10–20 participants per session. Cost: $2195. Application fee: $100–$200. Financial aid available.
Application Deadline Continuous.
Jobs Positions for college students 21 and older.
Contact Rustic Pathways, 4121 Erie Street, Willoughby, Ohio 44094. Phone: 800-321-4353. Fax: 440-975-9694. E-mail: rustic@rusticpathways.com.
URL www.rusticpathways.com

For more information, see page 612.

RUSTIC PATHWAYS–SERVICE AND SAFARI IN AFRICA

Rustic Pathways
United Republic of Tanzania

General Information Coed travel outdoor program, wilderness program, and cultural program established in 2005.
Special Interest Areas Cross-cultural education, nature study, touring.
Sports Sandboarding.
Wilderness/Outdoors Caving, hiking, safari, wilderness/outdoors (general).
Trips Cultural, day, overnight, shopping.
Program Information 3 sessions per year. Session length: 17 days in June, July, August. Ages: 14–18. 10–20 participants per session. Cost: $3495. Application fee: $100–$200. Financial aid available.
Application Deadline Continuous.
Jobs Positions for college students 21 and older.
Contact Rustic Pathways, 4121 Erie Street, Willoughby, Ohio 44094. Phone: 800-321-4353. Fax: 440-975-9694. E-mail: rustic@rusticpathways.com.
URL www.rusticpathways.com

For more information, see page 612.

VANUATU

TREETOPS EXPEDITIONS–VANUATU

Treetops eXpeditions
Vanuatu

General Information Coed travel outdoor program, community service program, cultural program, and adventure program established in 1970.
Special Interest Areas Community service, cross-cultural education.
Sports Sailing, sea kayaking.
Wilderness/Outdoors Canoe trips, hiking, wilderness camping.
Trips Cultural.
Program Information 1 session per year. Session length: 30 days in July. Ages: 14–17. 6–10 participants per session. Cost: $5900. Financial aid available.
Application Deadline Continuous.
Contact Mr. Chad Jemison, Director, PO Box 187, Lake Placid, New York 12946. Phone: 518-523-9329 Ext.149. Fax: 518-523-4858. E-mail: chad.jemison@nct.org.
URL www.ttexpeditions.org

For more information, see page 672.

VIETNAM

PUTNEY STUDENT TRAVEL–COMMUNITY SERVICE–VIETNAM

Putney Student Travel
Vietnam

General Information Coed residential community service program and cultural program established in 1951.
Program Focus Community service, cultural exchange and weekend excursions from a base in a small rural community.
Academics Intercultural studies.
Special Interest Areas Community service, construction.
Wilderness/Outdoors Hiking.
Trips Cultural, day.
Program Information 1–2 sessions per year. Session length: 28–30 days in June, July, August. Ages: 15–18. 16 participants per session. Boarding program cost: $6790. Financial aid available.
Application Deadline Continuous.
Contact Jeffrey Shumlin, Admissions Director, 345 Hickory Ridge Road, Putney, Vermont 05346. Phone: 802-387-5000. Fax: 802-387-4276. E-mail: info@goputney.com.
URL www.goputney.com

For more information, see page 598.

RUSTIC PATHWAYS–FACES AND PLACES OF VIETNAM

Rustic Pathways
Vietnam

General Information Coed travel cultural program established in 2005.
Arts Photography.
Special Interest Areas Cross-cultural education, touring.
Sports Boating.
Wilderness/Outdoors Hiking.
Trips Cultural, day, overnight, shopping.
Program Information 2 sessions per year. Session length: 17 days in July, August. Ages: 16–18. 10–20 participants per session. Cost: $2195. Application fee: $100–$200. Financial aid available.
Application Deadline Continuous.
Jobs Positions for college students 21 and older.

RUSTIC PATHWAYS–FACES AND PLACES OF VIETNAM (continued)

Contact Rustic Pathways, 4121 Erie Street, Willoughby, Ohio 44094. Phone: 800-321-4353. Fax: 440-975-9694. E-mail: rustic@rusticpathways.com. **URL** www.rusticpathways.com

For more information, see page 612.

VISIONS–VIETNAM

Visions
Hanoi
Vietnam

General Information Coed travel community service program and cultural program established in 1989. High school credit may be earned.

Academics Intercultural studies.
Arts Arts and crafts (general), basketry, creative writing, jewelry making.
Special Interest Areas Community service, construction, cross-cultural education, farming, field research/expeditions, homestays, leadership training, nature study.
Sports Bicycling, fishing, snorkeling, swimming.
Wilderness/Outdoors Hiking.
Trips Cultural, day, overnight.
Program Information 1 session per year. Session length: 4 weeks in July. Ages: 16–18. 15–20 participants per session. Cost: $3200–$4900. Financial aid available.
Application Deadline Continuous.
Jobs Positions for college students 22 and older.
Contact Joanne Pinaire, Director, PO Box 220, Newport, Pennsylvania 17074-0220. Phone: 717-567-7313. Fax: 717-567-7853. E-mail: info@visionsserviceadventures.com.
URL www.visionsserviceadventures.com

For more information, see page 694.

Travel Programs in the United States

AAVE–Bold West

AAVE–Journeys That Matter
Locations California, Nevada, Utah.

General Information Coed travel outdoor program, community service program, wilderness program, and adventure program established in 1976. Accredited by American Camping Association.
Program Focus Adventure travel.
Special Interest Areas Community service, leadership training, touring.
Sports Rappelling, surfing, swimming.
Wilderness/Outdoors Hiking, mountaineering, orienteering, rafting, rock climbing, white-water trips, wilderness camping.
Excursions Overnight.
Program Information 3–6 sessions per year. Session length: 26 days in June, July, August. Ages: 14–18. 13 participants per session. Cost: $3888. Financial aid available.
Housing Tents and youth hostels.
Application Deadline Continuous.
Jobs Positions for college students 21 and older.
Contact Mr. Abbott Wallis, Owner, 2308 Fossil Trace Drive, Golden, Colorado 80401. Phone: 800-222-3595. Fax: 303-526-0885. E-mail: info@aave.com.
URL www.aave.com

For more information, see page 394.

AAVE–Boot/Saddle/Paddle

AAVE–Journeys That Matter
Locations Arizona, Colorado.

General Information Coed travel outdoor program, wilderness program, and adventure program established

in 1976. Accredited by American Camping Association.
Program Focus Adventure travel.
Academics Intercultural studies.
Special Interest Areas Native American culture, campcraft, community service, leadership training, team building, touring.
Sports Horseback riding, swimming.
Wilderness/Outdoors Backpacking, hiking, mountaineering, orienteering, pack animal trips, rafting, white-water trips, wilderness camping.
Excursions Cultural, overnight.
Program Information 4 sessions per year. Session length: 24 days in June, July, August. Ages: 14–18. 13 participants per session. Cost: $4088. Financial aid available.
Housing Tents.
Application Deadline Continuous.
Jobs Positions for college students 21 and older.
Contact Mr. Abbott Wallis, Owner, 2308 Fossil Trace Drive, Golden, Colorado 80401. Phone: 800-222-3595. Fax: 303-526-0885. E-mail: info@aave.com.
URL www.aave.com

For more information, see page 394.

AAVE–Peak Four

AAVE–Journeys That Matter
Locations Colorado, Utah.

General Information Coed travel outdoor program, community service program, wilderness program, and adventure program established in 1976. Accredited by American Camping Association.
Program Focus Adventure travel.
Special Interest Areas Campcraft, community service, leadership training.

AAVE–Peak Four (continued)

Wilderness/Outdoors Backpacking, hiking, outdoor adventure, rock climbing.
Program Information 2 sessions per year. Session length: 3 weeks. Ages: 14–18. Cost: $3288.
Application Deadline Continuous.
Contact Mr. Abbott Wallis, Owner, 2308 Fossil Trace Drive, Golden, Colorado 80401. E-mail: info@aave.com.
URL www.aave.com

For more information, see page 394.

AAVE–Rock & Rapid

AAVE–Journeys That Matter
Locations Colorado, Utah.

General Information Coed travel outdoor program, wilderness program, and adventure program established in 1976. Accredited by American Camping Association.
Program Focus Adventure travel.
Special Interest Areas Campcraft, community service, leadership training, team building.
Sports Rappelling, swimming.
Wilderness/Outdoors Backpacking, hiking, orienteering, rafting, rock climbing, white-water trips, wilderness camping.
Excursions Cultural, day, overnight.
Program Information 5–8 sessions per year. Session length: 3 weeks in June, July, August. Ages: 14–18. 13 participants per session. Cost: $3388. Financial aid available.
Housing Tents.
Application Deadline Continuous.
Jobs Positions for college students 21 and older.
Contact Mr. Abbott Wallis, Owner, 2308 Fossil Trace Drive, Golden, Colorado 80401. Phone: 800-222-3595. Fax: 303-526-0885. E-mail: info@aave.com.
URL www.aave.com

For more information, see page 394.

AAVE–Wild Coast Discovery

AAVE–Journeys That Matter
Locations Canada, Washington.

General Information Coed travel outdoor program, community service program, wilderness program, and adventure program established in 1976. Accredited by American Camping Association.

Program Focus Adventure travel.
Special Interest Areas Community service, leadership training, nautical skills, team building, touring.
Sports Bicycling, rappelling, sea kayaking, skiing (downhill), snowboarding, swimming.
Wilderness/Outdoors Backpacking, bicycle trips, hiking, mountain biking, mountaineering, orienteering, rock climbing, wilderness camping.
Excursions Overnight.
Program Information 3–4 sessions per year. Session length: 3 weeks in June, July, August. Ages: 13–14. 13 participants per session. Cost: $3188. Financial aid available.
Housing Tents.
Application Deadline Continuous.
Jobs Positions for college students 21 and older.
Contact Mr. Abbott Wallis, Owner, 2308 Fossil Trace Drive, Golden, Colorado 80401. Phone: 800-222-3595. Fax: 303-526-0885. E-mail: info@aave.com.
URL www.aave.com

For more information, see page 394.

Adventure Treks–Wilderness Adventures

Adventure Treks, Inc.
Locations Alaska, California, Canada, Montana, Oregon, Washington.

General Information Coed travel outdoor program, wilderness program, and adventure program established in 1978.
Program Focus Multi-activity outdoor adventures with focus on fun, personal growth, teamwork, leadership, building self-confidence, outdoor skills, and community living.
Sports Sailing, swimming.
Wilderness/Outdoors Backpacking, mountain biking, mountaineering, orienteering, rafting, rock climbing, white-water trips, wilderness camping.
Program Information 12–14 sessions per year. Session length: 16–28 days in June, July, August. Ages: 13–18. 24 participants per session. Cost: $2395–$4195. Financial aid available.
Housing Tents.
Application Deadline Continuous.
Contact John Dockendorf, Director, PO Box 1321, Flat Rock, North Carolina 28731. Phone: 888-954-5555. Fax: 828-696-1663. E-mail: info@advtreks.com.
URL www.adventuretreks.com

ATW: Adventure Roads

American Trails West
Locations Canada, District of Columbia, Florida, Georgia, Massachusetts, Pennsylvania, South Carolina, Virginia.

General Information Coed travel adventure program established in 1966.
Special Interest Areas Touring.
Sports Bicycling, boating, horseback riding, in-line skating, swimming, tennis.

Wilderness/Outdoors Hiking, mountain biking, rafting.
Excursions College tours.
Program Information 1–2 sessions per year. Session length: 4 weeks in July, August. Ages: 13–15. 40–45 participants per session. Cost: $5795.
Housing Hotels.
Application Deadline Continuous.
Jobs Positions for college students 20 and older.
Contact Director, 92 Middle Neck Road, Great Neck, New York 11021. Phone: 800-645-6260. Fax: 516-487-2855. E-mail: info@atwteentours.com.
URL www.atwteentours.com

For more information, see page 416.

ATW: American Horizons

American Trails West

Locations Arizona, California, Colorado, Illinois, Michigan, Minnesota, Missouri, Nevada, New York, Ohio, Pennsylvania, South Dakota, Utah, Wisconsin, Wyoming.

General Information Coed travel adventure program established in 1966.
Special Interest Areas Touring.
Sports Bicycling, boating, horseback riding, in-line skating, swimming, tennis, waterskiing.
Wilderness/Outdoors Hiking, mountain biking, rafting.
Excursions College tours.
Program Information 2–3 sessions per year. Session length: 45 days in July, August. Ages: 13–17. 40–45 participants per session. Cost: $8095.
Housing College dormitories, hotels, and tents.
Application Deadline Continuous.
Jobs Positions for college students 20 and older.
Contact Director, 92 Middle Neck Road, Great Neck, New York 11021. Phone: 800-645-6260. Fax: 516-487-2855. E-mail: info@atwteentours.com.
URL www.atwteentours.com

For more information, see page 416.

ATW: California Sunset

American Trails West
Locations Arizona, California, Nevada.

General Information Coed travel adventure program established in 1966.
Special Interest Areas Touring.
Sports Bicycling, boating, horseback riding, in-line skating, swimming, tennis, waterskiing.
Wilderness/Outdoors Hiking, mountain biking, rafting.
Excursions College tours.
Program Information 1–3 sessions per year. Session length: 3 weeks in July, August. Ages: 13–17. 40–45 participants per session. Cost: $5695.
Housing College dormitories and hotels.
Application Deadline Continuous.
Jobs Positions for college students 20 and older.
Contact Director, 92 Middle Neck Road, Great Neck, New York 11021. Phone: 800-645-6260. Fax: 516-487-2855. E-mail: info@atwteentours.com.
URL www.atwteentours.com

For more information, see page 416.

ATW: Camp Inn 42

American Trails West
Locations Arizona, California, Canada, Hawaii, Montana, Nevada, Utah, Washington, Wyoming.

General Information Coed travel adventure program established in 1966.
Special Interest Areas Touring.
Sports Bicycling, boating, horseback riding, in-line skating, skiing (downhill), snorkeling, swimming, tennis, waterskiing.
Wilderness/Outdoors Hiking, mountain biking, rafting.
Excursions College tours.
Program Information 3–4 sessions per year. Session length: 6 weeks in July, August. Ages: 13–18. 40–45 participants per session. Cost: $8595.
Housing College dormitories, hotels, and tents.
Application Deadline Continuous.
Jobs Positions for college students 20 and older.
Contact Director, 92 Middle Neck Road, Great Neck, New York 11021. Phone: 800-645-6260. Fax: 516-487-2855. E-mail: info@atwteentours.com.
URL www.atwteentours.com

For more information, see page 416.

ATW: Discoverer

American Trails West

Locations Arizona, California, Colorado, Nevada, South Dakota, Utah, Wyoming.

General Information Coed travel adventure program established in 1966.

ATW: Discoverer

Special Interest Areas Touring.
Sports Bicycling, boating, horseback riding, in-line skating, swimming, tennis, waterskiing.
Wilderness/Outdoors Hiking, mountain biking, rafting.
Excursions College tours.
Program Information 2–3 sessions per year. Session length: 4 weeks in July, August. Ages: 13–17. 40–45 participants per session. Cost: $6195.
Housing College dormitories, hotels, and tents.
Application Deadline Continuous.
Jobs Positions for college students 20 and older.
Contact Director, 92 Middle Neck Road, Great Neck, New York 11021. Phone: 800-645-6260. Fax: 516-487-2855. E-mail: info@atwteentours.com.
URL www.atwteentours.com

For more information, see page 416.

ATW: Fire and Ice

American Trails West

Locations Alaska, California, Canada, Hawaii, Washington.

General Information Coed travel adventure program established in 1966.
Special Interest Areas Touring.
Sports Bicycling, boating, horseback riding, in-line skating, skiing (downhill), snorkeling, swimming, tennis, waterskiing.
Wilderness/Outdoors Rafting.
Excursions College tours.
Program Information 1–2 sessions per year. Session length: 5 weeks in July, August. Ages: 14–17. 40–45 participants per session. Cost: $8795.
Housing Hotels.
Application Deadline Continuous.

Jobs Positions for college students 20 and older.
Contact Director, 92 Middle Neck Road, Great Neck, New York 11021. Phone: 800-645-6260. Fax: 516-487-2855. E-mail: info@atwteentours.com.
URL www.atwteentours.com

For more information, see page 416.

ATW: Mini Tours

American Trails West

Locations Canada, Florida, Maine, Maryland, Massachusetts, New Hampshire, New York, Pennsylvania, Virginia.

General Information Coed travel cultural program and adventure program established in 1966.
Program Focus Travel Monday through Friday, home on the weekends.
Special Interest Areas Touring.
Sports Bicycling, boating, horseback riding, in-line skating, swimming, tennis, waterskiing.
Wilderness/Outdoors Hiking, mountain biking, rafting.
Program Information 4–6 sessions per year. Session length: 3–7 weeks in July, August. Ages: 12–15. 40–45 participants per session. Cost: $3295–$7790.
Housing Hotels.
Application Deadline Continuous.
Jobs Positions for college students 20 and older.
Contact Director, 92 Middle Neck Road, Great Neck, New York 11021. Phone: 800-645-6260. Fax: 516-487-2855. E-mail: info@atwteentours.com.
URL www.atwteentours.com

For more information, see page 416.

ATW: Pacific Paradise

American Trails West

Locations Arizona, California, Canada, Nevada, Oregon, Washington.

General Information Coed travel adventure program established in 1966.
Special Interest Areas Touring.
Sports Bicycling, boating, horseback riding, in-line skating, swimming, tennis, waterskiing.
Wilderness/Outdoors Hiking, mountain biking, rafting.
Excursions College tours.
Program Information 1–2 sessions per year. Session length: 4 weeks in July, August. Ages: 13–17. 40–45 participants per session. Cost: $6995.
Housing College dormitories and hotels.
Application Deadline Continuous.
Jobs Positions for college students 20 and older.

Contact Director, 92 Middle Neck Road, Great Neck, New York 11021. Phone: 800-645-6260. Fax: 516-487-2855. E-mail: info@atwteentours.com.
URL www.atwteentours.com
For more information, see page 416.

ATW: SKYBLAZER

American Trails West

Locations Arizona, California, Canada, Colorado, Montana, Nevada, Oregon, South Dakota, Utah, Washington, Wyoming.

General Information Coed travel adventure program established in 1966.
Special Interest Areas Touring.
Sports Bicycling, boating, horseback riding, in-line skating, skiing (downhill), swimming, tennis, waterskiing.
Wilderness/Outdoors Hiking, mountain biking, rafting.
Excursions College tours.
Program Information 1–2 sessions per year. Session length: 40 days in July, August. Ages: 14–17. 40–45 participants per session. Cost: $7995.
Housing College dormitories, hotels, and tents.
Application Deadline Continuous.
Jobs Positions for college students 20 and older.
Contact Director, 92 Middle Neck Road, Great Neck, New York 11021. Phone: 800-645-6260. Fax: 516-487-2855. E-mail: info@atwteentours.com.
URL www.atwteentours.com
For more information, see page 416.

ATW: SUNBLAZER

American Trails West

Locations Arizona, California, Nevada, Utah.

General Information Coed travel adventure program established in 1966.
Special Interest Areas Touring.
Sports Bicycling, boating, horseback riding, in-line skating, swimming, tennis, waterskiing.
Wilderness/Outdoors Hiking, mountain biking, rafting.

Excursions College tours.
Program Information 2–3 sessions per year. Session length: 3 weeks in July, August. Ages: 13–17. 40–45 participants per session. Cost: $5195.
Housing College dormitories, hotels, and tents.
Application Deadline Continuous.
Jobs Positions for college students 20 and older.
Contact Director, 92 Middle Neck Road, Great Neck, New York 11021. Phone: 800-645-6260. Fax: 516-487-2855. E-mail: info@atwteentours.com.
URL www.atwteentours.com
For more information, see page 416.

ATW: WAYFARER

American Trails West

Locations Arizona, California, Colorado, Illinois, Michigan, Minnesota, Nevada, New York, Ohio, South Dakota, Utah, Wisconsin, Wyoming.

General Information Coed travel adventure program established in 1966.
Special Interest Areas Touring.
Sports Bicycling, boating, horseback riding, in-line skating, swimming, tennis, waterskiing.
Wilderness/Outdoors Hiking, mountain biking, rafting.
Excursions College tours.
Program Information 5–6 sessions per year. Session length: 40 days in July, August. Ages: 13–18. 40–45 participants per session. Cost: $7095.
Housing College dormitories, hotels, and tents.
Application Deadline Continuous.
Jobs Positions for college students 20 and older.
Contact Director, 92 Middle Neck Road, Great Neck, New York 11021. Phone: 800-645-6260. Fax: 516-487-2855. E-mail: info@atwteentours.com.
URL www.atwteentours.com
For more information, see page 416.

DUKE TIP DOMESTIC FIELD STUDIES

Duke University Talent Identification Program (Duke TIP)
Locations California, New Mexico, North Carolina.

General Information Coed travel academic program. Formal opportunities for the academically talented.
Program Focus Specific topics include: astronomy, ecology/geology, filmmaking, creative writing, marine biology and neuroscience. Sites vary by program topic, see Web site for details.
Academics Academics (general), astronomy, biology, ecology, marine studies, physics, science (general), writing.
Arts Creative writing, film, film production, television/video.
Special Interest Areas Field research/expeditions.
Wilderness/Outdoors Canoe trips, hiking.
Excursions Cultural, day.
Program Information 4–6 sessions per year. Session length: 14–16 days in June, July. Ages: 14–18. 18–22 participants per session. Cost: $2600–$3600. Application fee: $35. Financial aid available.

Duke TIP Domestic Field Studies (continued)

Housing College dormitories and hotels.
Application Deadline March 23.
Jobs Positions for college students 20 and older.
Contact Dr. Nicki Charles, Coordinator of Educational Programs, Duke TIP, 1121 West Main Street, Durham, North Carolina 27701. Phone: 919-681-6519. Fax: 919-681-7921.
URL www.tip.duke.edu
For more information, see page 468.

92ND STREET Y CAMPS–THE TIYUL

92nd Street YM–YWHA
Locations Connecticut, Georgia, Maine, Massachusetts, New York, West Virginia.

General Information Coed travel outdoor program and community service program established in 1955. Religious affiliation: Jewish. Accredited by American Camping Association.
Program Focus Community service, travel, Jewish.
Academics Jewish studies, environmental science.
Special Interest Areas Community service, farming, gardening, leadership training, nature study, touring.
Excursions Overnight.
Program Information 1 session per year. Session length: 6 weeks in July, August. Ages: 15–18. 30–40 participants per session. Cost: $5000. Financial aid available.
Housing College dormitories, host-family homes, and hotels.
Application Deadline Continuous.
Jobs Positions for college students 21 and older.
Contact Steve Levin, Director of Camp Programs, 1395 Lexington Avenue, New York, New York 10128. Phone: 212-415-5614. Fax: 212-415-5668. E-mail: camps@92y.org.
URL www.92y.org/camps

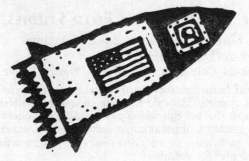

REIN TEEN TOURS–CALIFORNIA CAPER

Rein Teen Tours
Locations Arizona, California, Nevada, Utah.

General Information Coed travel outdoor program and adventure program established in 1985.
Program Focus Travel in the United States.
Special Interest Areas Touring.
Sports Basketball, bicycling, canoeing, climbing (wall),

in-line skating, ropes course, sea kayaking, snorkeling, softball, surfing, swimming, tennis, waterskiing, windsurfing.
Wilderness/Outdoors Canoe trips, mountain biking, outdoor adventure, rafting, rock climbing, white-water trips, wilderness camping.
Program Information 3–4 sessions per year. Session length: 3 weeks in June, July, August. Ages: 13–17. 40 participants per session. Cost: $5000–$5500.
Housing College dormitories, hotels, and tents.
Application Deadline Continuous.
Jobs Positions for college students 21 and older.
Contact Norman Rein, President, 30 Galesi Drive, Wayne, New Jersey 07470. Phone: 800-831-1313. Fax: 973-785-4268. E-mail: summer@reinteentours.com.
URL www.reinteentours.com
For more information, see page 604.

REIN TEEN TOURS–CROSSROADS

Rein Teen Tours
Locations Arizona, California, Canada, Illinois, Michigan, Minnesota, Nevada, New York, Ohio, South Dakota, Utah, Wyoming.

General Information Coed travel outdoor program and adventure program established in 1985.
Program Focus Travel in the United States and Canada.
Special Interest Areas Touring.
Sports Basketball, bicycling, canoeing, climbing (wall), in-line skating, ropes course, sea kayaking, snorkeling, softball, surfing, swimming, tennis, waterskiing, windsurfing.
Wilderness/Outdoors Canoe trips, hiking, mountain biking, outdoor adventure, rafting, rock climbing, white-water trips, wilderness camping.
Program Information 4 sessions per year. Session length: 40 days in June, July, August. Ages: 13–17. 40 participants per session. Cost: $6500–$7000.
Housing College dormitories, hotels, and tents.
Application Deadline Continuous.
Jobs Positions for college students 21 and older.
Contact Norman Rein, President, 30 Galesi Drive, Wayne, New Jersey 07470. Phone: 800-831-1313. Fax: 973-785-4268. E-mail: summer@reinteentours.com.
URL www.reinteentours.com
For more information, see page 604.

REIN TEEN TOURS–EASTERN ADVENTURE

Rein Teen Tours
Locations Canada, Florida, Maine, Massachusetts, New Hampshire, New York, Pennsylvania, South Carolina, Virginia.

General Information Coed travel outdoor program and adventure program established in 1985.
Program Focus Travel in the United States and Canada.
Special Interest Areas Touring.
Sports Basketball, bicycling, canoeing, climbing (wall), in-line skating, ropes course, sea kayaking, snorkeling, softball, swimming, tennis, waterskiing, windsurfing.

Wilderness/Outdoors Canoe trips, hiking, mountain biking, outdoor adventure, rafting, rock climbing, white-water trips, wilderness camping.
Program Information 1–2 sessions per year. Session length: 4 weeks in June, July, August. Ages: 13–15. 40 participants per session. Cost: $5000–$5500.
Housing College dormitories, hotels, and tents.
Application Deadline Continuous.
Jobs Positions for college students 21 and older.
Contact Norman Rein, President, 30 Galesi Drive, Wayne, New Jersey 07470. Phone: 800-831-1313. Fax: 973-785-4268. E-mail: summer@reinteentours.com.
URL www.reinteentours.com
For more information, see page 604.

REIN TEEN TOURS–GRAND ADVENTURE

Rein Teen Tours

Locations Arizona, California, Canada, Montana, Nevada, South Dakota, Utah, Washington, Wyoming.

General Information Coed travel outdoor program and adventure program established in 1985.

Rein Teen Tours–Grand Adventure

Program Focus Travel in the United States and Canada.
Special Interest Areas Touring.
Sports Basketball, bicycling, canoeing, climbing (wall), in-line skating, ropes course, sea kayaking, skiing (downhill), snorkeling, softball, surfing, swimming, tennis, waterskiing, windsurfing.
Wilderness/Outdoors Canoe trips, hiking, mountain biking, outdoor adventure, rafting, rock climbing, white-water trips, wilderness camping.
Program Information 6 sessions per year. Session length: 40 days in June, July, August. Ages: 13–17. 40 participants per session. Cost: $8000–$8500.
Housing College dormitories, hotels, and tents.
Application Deadline Continuous.
Jobs Positions for college students 21 and older.

Contact Norman Rein, President, 30 Galesi Drive, Wayne, New Jersey 07470. Phone: 800-831-1313. Fax: 973-785-4268. E-mail: summer@reinteentours.com.
URL www.reinteentours.com
For more information, see page 604.

REIN TEEN TOURS–HAWAIIAN/ALASKAN ADVENTURE

Rein Teen Tours

Locations Alaska, California, Canada, Hawaii, Oregon, Washington.

General Information Coed travel outdoor program and adventure program established in 1985.
Program Focus Travel in the United States and Canada.
Special Interest Areas Touring.
Sports Basketball, bicycling, canoeing, climbing (wall), in-line skating, ropes course, sea kayaking, skiing (downhill), snorkeling, softball, surfing, swimming, tennis, waterskiing, windsurfing.
Wilderness/Outdoors Canoe trips, hiking, mountain biking, outdoor adventure, rafting, rock climbing, white-water trips, wilderness camping.
Program Information 4 sessions per year. Session length: 34 days in June, July, August. Ages: 13–17. 40 participants per session. Cost: $8000–$8500.
Housing College dormitories, cruise ships, and hotels.
Application Deadline Continuous.
Jobs Positions for college students 24 and older.
Contact Norman Rein, President, 30 Galesi Drive, Wayne, New Jersey 07470. Phone: 800-831-1313. Fax: 973-785-4268. E-mail: summer@reinteentours.com.
URL www.reinteentours.com
For more information, see page 604.

REIN TEEN TOURS–HAWAIIAN CAPER

Rein Teen Tours
Locations California, Hawaii, Oregon, Washington.

General Information Coed travel outdoor program and adventure program established in 2004.
Program Focus Travel in the United States.
Special Interest Areas Touring.
Sports Basketball, bicycling, boating, ropes course,

Rein Teen Tours–Hawaiian Caper (continued)
skiing (downhill), snorkeling, tennis, waterskiing, windsurfing.
Wilderness/Outdoors Outdoor adventure, white-water trips.
Program Information 2 sessions per year. Session length: 3 weeks in July. Ages: 13–17. 40 participants per session. Cost: $6000–$6500.
Housing Hotels.
Application Deadline Continuous.
Jobs Positions for college students 21 and older.
Contact Norman Rein, President, 30 Galesi Drive, Wayne, New Jersey 07470. Phone: 800-831-1313. Fax: 973-785-4268. E-mail: summer@reinteentours.com.
URL www.reinteentours.com

For more information, see page 604.

REIN TEEN TOURS–WESTERN ADVENTURE

Rein Teen Tours
Locations Arizona, California, Nevada, South Dakota, Utah, Wyoming.

General Information Coed travel outdoor program and adventure program established in 1985.
Program Focus Travel in the United States.
Special Interest Areas Touring.
Sports Basketball, bicycling, canoeing, climbing (wall), in-line skating, ropes course, sea kayaking, snorkeling, softball, surfing, swimming, tennis, waterskiing, windsurfing.
Wilderness/Outdoors Canoe trips, hiking, mountain biking, outdoor adventure, rafting, rock climbing, white-water trips, wilderness camping.
Program Information 4 sessions per year. Session length: 4 weeks in June, July, August. Ages: 13–17. 40 participants per session. Cost: $6000–$6500.
Housing College dormitories, hotels, and tents.
Application Deadline Continuous.
Jobs Positions for college students 21 and older.
Contact Norman Rein, President, 30 Galesi Drive, Wayne, New Jersey 07470. Phone: 800-831-1313. Fax: 973-785-4268. E-mail: summer@reinteentours.com.
URL www.reinteentours.com

For more information, see page 604.

TREETOPS EXPEDITIONS–GLACIER/ BOUNDARY WATERS

Treetops eXpeditions
Locations Minnesota, Montana, South Dakota.

General Information Coed travel outdoor program, wilderness program, and adventure program established in 1970.
Program Focus Two weeks canoeing in Boundary Waters wilderness, one week in the Badlands of South Dakota, and two weeks backpacking in Glacier National Park.
Special Interest Areas Nature study.
Sports Canoeing, fishing.
Wilderness/Outdoors Backpacking, canoe trips, hiking, rock climbing, wilderness camping.

Excursions Cultural.
Program Information 1 session per year. Session length: 5 weeks in July. Ages: 14–17. 6–10 participants per session. Cost: $6000. Financial aid available.
Application Deadline Continuous.
Contact Mr. Chad Jemison, Director, PO Box 187, Lake Placid, New York 12946. Phone: 518-523-9329 Ext.149. Fax: 518-523-4858. E-mail: chad.jemison@nct.org.
URL www.ttexpeditions.org

For more information, see page 672.

TREETOPS EXPEDITIONS–HORSEBACK RIDING

Treetops eXpeditions
Locations Colorado, Wyoming.

General Information Coed travel outdoor program established in 1970.
Program Focus Intermediate level horseback riding in Colorado and Wyoming.
Special Interest Areas Animal care.
Sports Equestrian sports, horseback riding.
Excursions Overnight.
Program Information 1 session per year. Session length: 4 weeks in July. Ages: 14–17. 6–10 participants per session. Cost: $6000. Financial aid available.
Application Deadline Continuous.
Contact Mr. Chad Jemison, Director, PO Box 187, Lake Placid, New York 12946. Phone: 518-523-9329 Ext.149. Fax: 518-523-4858. E-mail: chad.jemison@nct.org.
URL www.ttexpeditions.org

For more information, see page 672.

WEISSMAN TEEN TOURS–"ALOHA– WELCOME TO HAWAIIAN PARADISE," 3 WEEKS

Weissman Teen Tours
Locations California, Hawaii, Mexico.

General Information Coed travel outdoor program and cultural program established in 1974.
Program Focus Owner-escorted, personally-supervised, action-packed, culturally-oriented, upscale

student travel. All five-star resorts and ocean front hotels; no camping or dormitory accommodations.

Special Interest Areas Native American culture, nature study, team building, touring.

Sports Aerobics, basketball, bicycling, boating, body boarding, diving, football, golf, parasailing, scuba diving, sea kayaking, snorkeling, soccer, sports (general), surfing, swimming, tennis, volleyball, waterskiing, weight training.

Wilderness/Outdoors Hiking.

Excursions College tours, cultural, day, overnight, shopping.

Program Information 1 session per year. Session length: 3 weeks in July, August. Ages: 14–17. 30–40 participants per session. Cost: $6699.

Housing Hotels.

Application Deadline Continuous.

Jobs Positions for college students 21 and older.

Contact Ms. Ronee Weissman, Owner/Director, 517 Almena Avenue, Ardsley, New York 10502. Phone: 800-942-8005. Fax: 914-693-4807. E-mail: wtt@cloud9. net.

URL www.weissmantours.com

For more information, see page 700.

WEISSMAN TEEN TOURS–U.S. AND WESTERN CANADA, 40 DAYS

Weissman Teen Tours

Locations Arizona, California, Canada, Colorado, Mexico, Montana, Nevada, Utah, Washington, Wyoming.

General Information Coed travel outdoor program and cultural program established in 1974.

Weissman Teen Tours–U.S. and Western Canada, 40 Days

Program Focus Owner-escorted, personally-supervised, action-packed, sports-oriented, upscale travel program in the U.S. and western Canada. No camping or dormitory accommodations.

Special Interest Areas Native American culture, field trips (arts and culture), nature study, nautical skills, touring.

Sports Aerobics, basketball, bicycling, bicycling (BMX), boating, climbing (wall), cross-country, football, golf, horseback riding, in-line skating, kayaking, parasailing,

skiing (downhill), snorkeling, snowboarding, soccer, sports (general), surfing, swimming, tennis, volleyball, waterskiing, weight training.

Wilderness/Outdoors Hiking, mountain biking, outdoor adventure, rafting, rock climbing, white-water trips.

Excursions College tours, day, overnight.

Program Information 2 sessions per year. Session length: 40 days in July, August. Ages: 13–17. 35 participants per session. Cost: $9299.

Housing National Park lodges and resorts and hotels.

Application Deadline Continuous.

Jobs Positions for college students 21 and older.

Contact Mr. Eugene Weissman, Owner/Director, 517 Almena Avenue, Ardsley, New York 10502. Phone: 800-942-8005. Fax: 914-693-4807. E-mail: wtt@cloud9. net.

URL www.weissmantours.com

For more information, see page 700.

WEISSMAN TEEN TOURS–U.S. AND WESTERN CANADA, 30 DAYS

Weissman Teen Tours

Locations California, Canada, Colorado, Mexico, Montana, Utah, Washington, Wyoming.

General Information Coed travel outdoor program and cultural program established in 1974.

Program Focus Owner-escorted, personally-supervised, action-packed, sports-oriented, upscale travel program in the U.S. and Western Canada. No camping or dormitory accommodations.

Special Interest Areas Native American culture, field trips (arts and culture), nature study, nautical skills, team building, touring.

Sports Aerobics, basketball, bicycling, bicycling (BMX), boating, climbing (wall), cross-country, football, golf, horseback riding, in-line skating, kayaking, parasailing, sailing, scuba diving, skiing (downhill), snorkeling, snowboarding, soccer, sports (general), surfing, swimming, tennis, volleyball, waterskiing, weight training.

Wilderness/Outdoors Hiking, mountain biking, outdoor adventure, rafting, rock climbing, white-water trips.

Excursions College tours, day, overnight.

Program Information 2 sessions per year. Session length: 30 days in July, August. Ages: 13–17. 35 participants per session. Cost: $7599.

Housing National Park lodges and resorts, cruise ships, and hotels.

Application Deadline Continuous.

Jobs Positions for college students 21 and older.

Weissman Teen Tours–U.S. and Western Canada, 30 Days (continued)

Contact Mr. Eugene Weissman, Owner/Director, 517 Almena Avenue, Ardsley, New York 10502. Phone: 800-942-8005. Fax: 914-693-4807. E-mail: wtt@cloud9.net.
URL www.weissmantours.com
For more information, see page 700.

WESTCOAST CONNECTION–AMERICAN VOYAGEUR

Westcoast Connection

Locations Arizona, California, Canada, Montana, Nevada, Oregon, Utah, Washington, Wyoming.

General Information Coed travel outdoor program and adventure program established in 1982. Accredited by Ontario Camping Association.
Program Focus A balance of daytime activities, the sights and sounds of cities, exciting nightly entertainment, and natural wonders of the great outdoors.
Special Interest Areas Touring.
Sports Bicycling, boating, canoeing, horseback riding, kayaking, ropes course, sea kayaking, skiing (downhill), snorkeling, snowboarding, surfing, swimming, tennis, waterskiing.
Wilderness/Outdoors Hiking, mountain biking, outdoor adventure, rafting, white-water trips.
Program Information 2–3 sessions per year. Session length: 6 weeks in July, August. Ages: 13–17. 40–50 participants per session. Cost: $7699. Financial aid available.
Housing College dormitories, hotels, and tents.
Application Deadline Continuous.
Jobs Positions for college students 21 and older.
Contact Mr. Mark Segal, Director, 154 East Boston Post Road, Mamaroneck, New York 10543. Phone: 800-767-0227. Fax: 914-835-0798. E-mail: usa@westcoastconnection.com.
URL www.westcoastconnection.com
For more information, see page 702.

WESTCOAST CONNECTION–CALIFORNIA DREAMING

Westcoast Connection

Locations Arizona, California, Nevada, Utah.

General Information Coed travel adventure program established in 1982. Accredited by Ontario Camping Association.

Program Focus A balance of daytime activities, the sights and sounds of cities, exciting nightly entertainment, and the natural wonders of the great outdoors.
Special Interest Areas Touring.
Sports Bicycling, boating, horseback riding, kayaking, ropes course, sea kayaking, snorkeling, surfing, swimming, tennis, volleyball, waterskiing.
Wilderness/Outdoors Hiking, mountain biking, rafting, white-water trips.
Program Information 1–2 sessions per year. Session length: 3 weeks in July, August. Ages: 13–17. 35–45 participants per session. Cost: $5499. Financial aid available.
Housing College dormitories and hotels.
Application Deadline Continuous.
Jobs Positions for college students 21 and older.
Contact Mr. Mark Segal, Director, 154 East Boston Post Road, Mamaroneck, New York 10543. Phone: 800-767-0227. Fax: 914-835-0798. E-mail: usa@westcoastconnection.com.
URL www.westcoastconnection.com
For more information, see page 702.

WESTCOAST CONNECTION–CALIFORNIAN EXTRAVAGANZA

Westcoast Connection

Locations Arizona, California, Colorado, Nevada, Utah, Wyoming.

General Information Coed travel outdoor program and adventure program established in 1982. Accredited by Ontario Camping Association.
Program Focus A balance of daytime activities, the sights and sounds of cities, exciting nightly entertainment, and the natural wonders of the great outdoors.
Special Interest Areas Touring.
Sports Bicycling, boating, horseback riding, kayaking, ropes course, sea kayaking, snorkeling, surfing, swimming, tennis, volleyball, waterskiing.
Wilderness/Outdoors Hiking, mountain biking, outdoor adventure, rafting, white-water trips.
Program Information 3–4 sessions per year. Session length: 4 weeks in July, August. Ages: 13–17. 40–50 participants per session. Cost: $5999.
Housing College dormitories, hotels, and tents.
Application Deadline Continuous.
Jobs Positions for college students 21 and older.
Contact Mr. Mark Segal, Director, 154 East Boston Post Road, Mamaroneck, New York 10543. Phone: 800-767-0227. Fax: 914-835-0798. E-mail: usa@westcoastconnection.com.
URL www.westcoastconnection.com
For more information, see page 702.

WESTCOAST CONNECTION–HAWAIIAN SPIRIT

Westcoast Connection

Locations California, Hawaii.

General Information Coed travel adventure program

established in 1982. Accredited by Ontario Camping Association.

Program Focus Touring and recreational activities on the Pacific coast and the Hawaiian Islands.

Special Interest Areas Touring.

Sports Bicycling, boating, ropes course, sea kayaking, skiing (downhill), snorkeling, snowboarding, surfing.

Wilderness/Outdoors Hiking, mountain biking, outdoor adventure, rafting, white-water trips.

Program Information 1–2 sessions per year. Session length: 18 days in July. Ages: 14–17. 25–45 participants per session. Cost: $5999.

Housing College dormitories and hotels.

Application Deadline Continuous.

Jobs Positions for college students 21 and older.

Contact Mr. Mark Segal, Director, 154 East Boston Post Road, Mamaroneck, New York 10543. Phone: 800-767-0227. Fax: 914-835-0798. E-mail: usa@westcoastconnection.com.

URL www.westcoastconnection.com

For more information, see page 702.

WESTCOAST CONNECTION–MAJOR LEAGUE BASEBALL TOUR

Westcoast Connection

Locations District of Columbia, Illinois, Maryland, Michigan, Missouri, New York, Ohio, Pennsylvania.

General Information Coed travel sports camp established in 1982. Accredited by Ontario Camping Association.

Program Focus Baseball fanatics get the chance to visit up to 12 stadiums, watch 15 games, and attend Hall of Fame induction ceremony.

Special Interest Areas Touring.

Sports Baseball.

Program Information 1 session per year. Session length: 3 weeks in July, August. Ages: 13–17. 20–40 participants per session. Cost: $5399.

Housing College dormitories and hotels.

Application Deadline Continuous.

Jobs Positions for college students 21 and older.

Contact Mr. Mark Segal, Director, 154 East Boston Post Road, Mamaroneck, New York 10543. Phone: 800-767-0227. Fax: 914-835-0798. E-mail: usa@westcoastconnection.com.

URL www.westcoastconnection.com

For more information, see page 702.

WESTCOAST CONNECTION TRAVEL–CALIFORNIA AND THE CANYONS

Westcoast Connection

Locations Arizona, California, Nevada, Utah.

General Information Coed travel adventure program established in 1982. Accredited by Ontario Camping Association.

Program Focus A balance of daytime activities, the sights and sounds of cities, exciting nightly entertainment, and the natural wonders of the great outdoors.

Special Interest Areas Touring.

Sports Bicycling, boating, horseback riding, kayaking, ropes course, sea kayaking, snorkeling, surfing, swimming, tennis, volleyball, waterskiing.

Wilderness/Outdoors Hiking, mountain biking, outdoor adventure, rafting, white-water trips, wilderness/outdoors (general).

Program Information 3–6 sessions per year. Session length: 3 weeks in July, August. Ages: 13–17. 40–50 participants per session. Cost: $4999.

Housing College dormitories, hotels, and tents.

Application Deadline Continuous.

Jobs Positions for college students 21 and older.

Contact Mr. Mark Segal, Director, 154 East Boston Post Road, Mamaroneck, New York 10543. Phone: 800-767-0227. Fax: 914-835-0798. E-mail: usa@westcoastconnection.com.

URL www.westcoastconnection.com

For more information, see page 702.

WESTCOAST CONNECTION TRAVEL–EASTCOAST ENCOUNTER

Westcoast Connection

Locations Canada, District of Columbia, Florida, Maine, Massachusetts, New Hampshire, Ohio, Virginia.

General Information Coed travel adventure program established in 1982. Accredited by Ontario Camping Association.

Program Focus A balance of daytime activities, the sights and sounds of cities, exciting nightly entertainment, and the natural wonders of the great outdoors.

Special Interest Areas Touring.

Sports Bicycling, boating, canoeing, rappelling, ropes course, sea kayaking, snorkeling, surfing, swimming, tennis, waterskiing, windsurfing.

Wilderness/Outdoors Hiking, mountain biking, outdoor adventure, rafting, white-water trips.

Program Information 1–2 sessions per year. Session length: 21–26 days in July. Ages: 13–16. 30–50 participants per session. Cost: $4399–$5399.

Housing College dormitories, hotels, and tents.

Application Deadline Continuous.

Jobs Positions for college students 21 and older.

Contact Mr. Mark Segal, Director, 154 East Boston Post Road, Mamaroneck, New York 10543. Phone: 800-767-0227. Fax: 914-835-0798. E-mail: usa@westcoastconnection.com.

URL www.westcoastconnection.com

For more information, see page 702.

WESTCOAST CONNECTION TRAVEL–GREAT WEST CHALLENGE

Westcoast Connection

Locations California, Canada, Oregon, Washington.

General Information Coed travel outdoor program and adventure program established in 1982. Accredited by Ontario Camping Association.
Program Focus A challenging outdoor adventure in Whistler, the Canadian Rockies, Mt. Rainier, the San Juan Islands and Mt. Hood.
Special Interest Areas Community service.
Sports Bicycling, canoeing, kayaking, rappelling, ropes course, sailing, sea kayaking, skiing (downhill), snowboarding, swimming.
Wilderness/Outdoors Caving, hiking, mountain biking, mountaineering, outdoor adventure, rafting, rock climbing, white-water trips, wilderness camping, wilderness/outdoors (general).
Program Information 2–3 sessions per year. Session length: 8–40 days in July, August. Ages: 13–17. 10–20 participants per session. Cost: $1400–$5400.
Housing College dormitories and tents.
Application Deadline Continuous.
Jobs Positions for college students 21 and older.
Contact Mr. Mark Segal, Director, 154 East Boston Post Road, Mamaroneck, New York 10543. Phone: 800-767-0227. Fax: 914-835-0798. E-mail: usa@westcoastconnection.com.
URL www.360studenttravel.com

For more information, see page 702.

WESTCOAST CONNECTION TRAVEL–NORTHWESTERN ODYSSEY

Westcoast Connection

Locations Canada, Montana, Oregon, Washington, Wyoming.

General Information Coed travel outdoor program and adventure program established in 1982. Accredited by Ontario Camping Association.
Program Focus A balanced variety of daytime activities, the sights and sounds of cities, exciting nightly entertainment, and the natural wonders of the great outdoors.
Special Interest Areas Touring.
Sports Bicycling, boating, canoeing, horseback riding, in-line skating, ropes course, skiing (downhill), snowboarding, swimming, tennis.
Wilderness/Outdoors Hiking, outdoor adventure, rafting, white-water trips.
Program Information 2–3 sessions per year. Session

length: 25 days in July, August. Ages: 13–17. 40–50 participants per session. Cost: $4999.
Housing College dormitories, hotels, and tents.
Application Deadline Continuous.
Jobs Positions for college students 21 and older.
Contact Mr. Mark Segal, Director, 154 East Boston Post Road, Mamaroneck, New York 10543. Phone: 800-767-0227. Fax: 914-835-0798. E-mail: usa@westcoastconnection.com.
URL www.westcoastconnection.com

For more information, see page 702.

WESTCOAST CONNECTION TRAVEL–SKI AND SNOWBOARD SENSATION

Westcoast Connection

Locations Canada, Oregon, Washington.

General Information Coed travel sports camp established in 1982. Accredited by Ontario Camping Association.
Program Focus Participants receive professional instruction in skiing and/or snowboarding combined with other recreational activities and touring Western USA and Canada.
Special Interest Areas Touring.
Sports Skiing (downhill), snowboarding, swimming.
Wilderness/Outdoors Mountain biking, rafting.
Program Information 1–2 sessions per year. Session length: 12–20 days in July. Ages: 13–17. 21–28 participants per session. Cost: $4999; including airfare. Financial aid available.
Housing College dormitories and hotels.
Application Deadline Continuous.
Jobs Positions for college students 21 and older.
Contact Mr. Mark Segal, Director, 154 East Boston Post Road, Mamaroneck, New York 10543. Phone: 800-767-0227. Fax: 914-835-0798. E-mail: usa@westcoastconnection.com.
URL www.westcoastconnection.com

For more information, see page 702.

WESTCOAST CONNECTION–U.S. EXPLORER

Westcoast Connection

Locations Arizona, California, Canada, Illinois, Michigan, Minnesota, Nevada, New York, South Dakota, Utah, Wyoming.

General Information Coed travel outdoor program and adventure program established in 1982. Accredited by Ontario Camping Association.
Program Focus A balance of daytime activities, the sights and sounds of cities, exciting nightly entertainment, and the natural wonders of the great outdoors.
Special Interest Areas Touring.
Sports Bicycling, boating, horseback riding, kayaking, ropes course, sea kayaking, snorkeling, surfing, swimming, tennis, volleyball, waterskiing.
Wilderness/Outdoors Hiking, mountain biking, outdoor adventure, rafting, white-water trips.
Program Information 1–2 sessions per year. Session length: 40 days in July, August. Ages: 13–17. 40–50

participants per session. Cost: $6799. Financial aid available.
Housing College dormitories, hotels, and tents.
Application Deadline Continuous.
Jobs Positions for college students 21 and older.
Contact Mr. Mark Segal, Director, 154 East Boston Post Road, Mamaroneck, New York 10543. Phone: 800-767-0227. Fax: 914-835-0798. E-mail: usa@westcoastconnection.com.
URL www.westcoastconnection.com

For more information, see page 702.

WILDERNESS VENTURES–COLORADO/ UTAH MOUNTAIN BIKE

Wilderness Ventures
Locations Colorado, Utah.

General Information Coed travel outdoor program and adventure program established in 1973.
Program Focus Bike program, leadership training.
Sports Bicycling.
Wilderness/Outdoors Bicycle trips, mountain biking, rafting, white-water trips.
Excursions Overnight.
Program Information 3 sessions per year. Session length: 16 days in June, July, August. Ages: 14–18. 13 participants per session. Cost: $3190. Financial aid available.
Housing Tents.
Application Deadline Continuous.
Jobs Positions for college students 21 and older.
Contact Mike Cottingham, Director, PO Box 2768, Jackson Hole, Wyoming 83001. Phone: 800-533-2281. Fax: 307-739-1934. E-mail: info@wildernessventures.com.
URL www.wildernessventures.com

For more information, see page 704.

WILDERNESS VENTURES–GREAT DIVIDE

Wilderness Ventures
Locations Idaho, Montana, Oregon, Wyoming.

General Information Coed travel outdoor program, wilderness program, and adventure program established in 1973.
Program Focus Wilderness travel, wilderness skills, leadership skills.

Special Interest Areas Leadership training.
Sports Sea kayaking.
Wilderness/Outdoors Backpacking, hiking, mountaineering, rafting, rock climbing, white-water trips, wilderness camping.
Excursions Overnight.
Program Information 2 sessions per year. Session length: 26 days in June, July, August. Ages: 14–18. 13 participants per session. Cost: $4090. Financial aid available.
Housing Tents.
Application Deadline Continuous.
Jobs Positions for college students 21 and older.
Contact Mike Cottingham, Director, PO Box 2768, Jackson Hole, Wyoming 83001. Phone: 800-533-2281. Fax: 307-739-1934. E-mail: info@wildernessventures.com
URL www.wildernessventures.com

For more information, see page 704.

WILDERNESS VENTURES–NORTHWEST

Wilderness Ventures
Locations Oregon, Washington.

General Information Coed travel outdoor program, wilderness program, and adventure program established in 1973.
Program Focus Wilderness travel, wilderness skills, leadership skills.
Special Interest Areas Leadership training.
Sports Sea kayaking.
Wilderness/Outdoors Backpacking, hiking, mountaineering, rafting, rock climbing, wilderness camping.
Excursions Overnight.
Program Information 1 session per year. Session length: 36 days in June, July, August. Ages: 14–18. 10 participants per session. Cost: $5290. Financial aid available.
Housing Tents.
Application Deadline Continuous.
Jobs Positions for college students 21 and older.
Contact Mike Cottingham, Director, PO Box 2768, Jackson Hole, Wyoming 83001. Phone: 800-533-2281. Fax: 307-739-1934. E-mail: info@wildernessventures.com
URL www.wildernessventures.com

For more information, see page 704.

WILDERNESS VENTURES–PACIFIC NORTHWEST

Wilderness Ventures
Locations Oregon, Washington.

General Information Coed travel outdoor program, wilderness program, and adventure program established in 1973.
Program Focus Wilderness travel, wilderness skills, leadership skills.
Special Interest Areas Leadership training.
Sports Sea kayaking.
Wilderness/Outdoors Backpacking, hiking, rafting,

Wilderness Ventures–Pacific Northwest (continued)
rock climbing, white-water trips, wilderness camping.
Excursions Overnight.
Program Information 2 sessions per year. Session length: 25 days in June, July, August. Ages: 14–18. 10 participants per session. Cost: $3690. Financial aid available.
Housing Tents.
Application Deadline Continuous.
Jobs Positions for college students 21 and older.
Contact Mike Cottingham, Director, PO Box 2768, Jackson Hole, Wyoming 83001. Phone: 800-533-2281. Fax: 307-739-1934. E-mail: info@wildernessventures. com.
URL www.wildernessventures.com
For more information, see page 704.

WILDERNESS VENTURES–ROCKY MOUNTAIN

Wilderness Ventures
Locations Idaho, Montana, Wyoming.

General Information Coed travel outdoor program, wilderness program, and adventure program established in 1973.
Program Focus Wilderness travel, wilderness skills, leadership skills.
Special Interest Areas Leadership training.
Sports Sea kayaking.
Wilderness/Outdoors Backpacking, hiking, mountain biking, rafting, white-water trips, wilderness camping.
Excursions Overnight.
Program Information 2 sessions per year. Session length: 22 days in June, July, August. Ages: 14–18. 13 participants per session. Cost: $3690. Financial aid available.
Housing Tents.
Application Deadline Continuous.
Jobs Positions for college students 21 and older.
Contact Mike Cottingham, Director, PO Box 2768, Jackson Hole, Wyoming 83001. Phone: 800-533-2281. Fax: 307-739-1934. E-mail: info@wildernessventures. com.
URL www.wildernessventures.com
For more information, see page 704.

WILDERNESS VENTURES–SOUTHWEST COMMUNITY SERVICE

Wilderness Ventures
Locations Arizona, Colorado, New Mexico, Utah.

General Information Coed travel outdoor program, community service program, and adventure program established in 1973.
Program Focus Wilderness travel, wilderness skills, leadership skills, community service.
Special Interest Areas Native American culture, community service, conservation projects, leadership training, touring.
Sports Kayaking, rappelling.
Wilderness/Outdoors Hiking, rafting, white-water trips.
Excursions Cultural, day, overnight.
Program Information 2 sessions per year. Session length: 3 weeks in July, August. Ages: 14–18. 13 participants per session. Cost: $3790. Financial aid available.
Application Deadline Continuous.
Jobs Positions for college students 21 and older.
Contact Mike Cottingham, Director, PO Box 2768, Jackson Hole, Wyoming 83001. Phone: 800-533-2281. Fax: 307-739-1934. E-mail: info@wildernessventures. com.
URL www.wildernessventures.com
For more information, see page 704.

WILDERNESS VENTURES–TETON CREST

Wilderness Ventures
Locations Idaho, Wyoming.

General Information Coed travel outdoor program, wilderness program, and adventure program established in 1973.
Program Focus Wilderness travel, wilderness skills, leadership skills.
Special Interest Areas Leadership training.
Wilderness/Outdoors Backpacking, rafting, rock climbing, white-water trips.
Excursions Overnight.
Program Information 3 sessions per year. Session length: 2 weeks in June, July, August. Ages: 14–16. 13 participants per session. Cost: $2590. Financial aid available.
Application Deadline Continuous.
Jobs Positions for college students 21 and older.
Contact Mike Cottingham, Director, PO Box 2768, Jackson Hole, Wyoming 83001. Phone: 800-533-2281. Fax: 307-739-1934. E-mail: info@wildernessventures. com.
URL www.wildernessventures.com
For more information, see page 704.

WILDERNESS VENTURES–YELLOWSTONE

Wilderness Ventures
Locations Montana, Wyoming.

General Information Coed travel outdoor program,

wilderness program, and adventure program established in 1973.

Program Focus Wilderness travel, wilderness skills, leadership skills.

Special Interest Areas Leadership training.

Sports Sea kayaking.

Wilderness/Outdoors Backpacking, rafting, white-water trips.

Excursions Overnight.

Program Information 3 sessions per year. Session length: 16 days in June, July, August. Ages: 13–15. 13 participants per session. Cost: $2990. Financial aid available.

Application Deadline Continuous.

Jobs Positions for college students 21 and older.

Contact Mike Cottingham, Director, PO Box 2768, Jackson Hole, Wyoming 83001. Phone: 800-533-2281. Fax: 307-739-1934. E-mail: info@wildernessventures. com.

URL www.wildernessventures.com

For more information, see page 704.

WILDERNESS VENTURES–YELLOWSTONE FLY FISHING

Wilderness Ventures

Locations Idaho, Montana, Wyoming.

General Information Boys' travel outdoor program, wilderness program, and adventure program established in 1973.

Program Focus Wilderness travel, wilderness skills, leadership skills.

Special Interest Areas Leadership training.

Sports Fishing.

Wilderness/Outdoors Backpacking, fly fishing, rafting, white-water trips.

Excursions Overnight.

Program Information 3 sessions per year. Session length: 16 days in June, July, August. Ages: 14–18. 13 participants per session. Cost: $2890. Financial aid available.

Application Deadline Continuous.

Jobs Positions for college students 21 and older.

Contact Mike Cottingham, Director, PO Box 2768, Jackson Hole, Wyoming 83001. Phone: 800-533-2281. Fax: 307-739-1934. E-mail: info@wildernessventures. com.

URL www.wildernessventures.com

For more information, see page 704.

WILDERNESS VENTURES–YELLOWSTONE WILDERNESS

Wilderness Ventures

Locations Montana, Wyoming.

General Information Coed travel outdoor program, wilderness program, and adventure program established in 1973.

Program Focus Wilderness travel, wilderness skills, leadership skills.

Special Interest Areas Leadership training.

Sports Sea kayaking.

Wilderness/Outdoors Backpacking.

Excursions Overnight.

Program Information 1 session per year. Session length: 22 days in June, July, August. Ages: 15–18. 10 participants per session. Cost: $3190. Financial aid available.

Application Deadline Continuous.

Jobs Positions for college students 21 and older.

Contact Mike Cottingham, Director, PO Box 2768, Jackson Hole, Wyoming 83001. Phone: 800-533-2281. Fax: 307-739-1934. E-mail: info@wildernessventures. com.

URL www.wildernessventures.com

For more information, see page 704.

RAVEL PROGRAMS ABROAD

AAVE–Africa

AAVE–Journeys That Matter

Locations Namibia, South Africa.

General Information Coed travel outdoor program, community service program, wilderness program, cultural program, and adventure program established in 1976. Accredited by American Camping Association.

Program Focus Adventure travel, including wildlife viewing and service project.

Academics Area studies, intercultural studies.

Special Interest Areas Campcraft, community service, conservation projects, cross-cultural education, leadership training, nature study, team building, touring.

Sports Bicycling, dune buggies, horseback riding, kayaking, sandboarding.

Wilderness/Outdoors Hiking, mountain biking, rafting, safari, white-water trips, wilderness camping.

Excursions Cultural, day, overnight.

Program Information 2–4 sessions per year. Session length: 3 weeks in June, July, August. Ages: 15–18. 15 participants per session. Cost: $4988.

Housing Cabins, hotels, and tents.

Application Deadline Continuous.

Jobs Positions for college students 21 and older.

Contact Mr. Abbott Wallis, Owner, 2308 Fossil Trace Drive, Golden, Colorado 80401. Phone: 800-222-3595. Fax: 303-526-0885. E-mail: info@aave.com.

URL www.aave.com

For more information, see page 394.

AAVE–Bike Amsterdam-Paris

AAVE–Journeys That Matter

Locations Belgium, France, Netherlands.

General Information Coed travel outdoor program, cultural program, and adventure program established in 1976. Accredited by American Camping Association.

Program Focus Adventure travel.

Special Interest Areas Leadership training, touring.

Sports Bicycling.

Wilderness/Outdoors Bicycle trips, hiking.

Excursions Cultural, day, overnight.

Program Information 2–4 sessions per year. Session length: 2 weeks in June, July, August. Ages: 15–18. 12 participants per session. Cost: $3388.

Housing Tents and youth hostels.

Application Deadline Continuous.

Jobs Positions for college students 21 and older.

Contact Mr. Abbott Wallis, Owner, 2308 Fossil Trace Drive, Golden, Colorado 80401. Phone: 800-222-3595. Fax: 303-526-0885. E-mail: info@aave.com.

URL www.aave.com

For more information, see page 394.

AAVE–Bold Europe

AAVE–Journeys That Matter

Locations France, Italy, Spain.

General Information Coed travel outdoor program, wilderness program, cultural program, and adventure program established in 1976. Accredited by American Camping Association.

Program Focus Adventure travel.

Special Interest Areas Cross-cultural education, leadership training, touring.

Sports Bicycling, climbing (wall), rappelling, ropes course, snorkeling, swimming.

Wilderness/Outdoors Bicycle trips, hiking, mountain biking, outdoor adventure, outdoor camping, rafting, rock climbing, white-water trips.

AAVE–Bold Europe

Excursions Cultural, day, overnight.
Program Information 4–6 sessions per year. Session length: 4 weeks in June, July, August. Ages: 14–18. 13–15 participants per session. Cost: $5788. Financial aid available.
Housing Tents and youth hostels.
Application Deadline Continuous.
Jobs Positions for college students 21 and older.
Contact Mr. Abbott Wallis, Owner, 2308 Fossil Trace Drive, Golden, Colorado 80401. Phone: 800-222-3595. Fax: 303-526-0885. E-mail: info@aave.com.
URL www.aave.com

For more information, see page 394.

AAVE–Ultimate Alps

AAVE–Journeys That Matter
Locations France, Italy, Switzerland.

General Information Coed travel outdoor program, wilderness program, cultural program, and adventure program established in 1976. Accredited by American Camping Association.
Program Focus Adventure travel.
Special Interest Areas Campcraft, leadership training, team building.
Sports Bicycling, rappelling, skiing (downhill), snowboarding, swimming, waterskiing.
Wilderness/Outdoors Backpacking, hiking, mountain biking, mountaineering, orienteering, rock climbing, wilderness camping.
Program Information 4–6 sessions per year. Session length: 3 weeks in June, July, August. Ages: 14–18. 13–15 participants per session. Cost: $5288. Financial aid available.
Housing Cabins and tents.
Application Deadline Continuous.
Jobs Positions for college students 21 and older.
Contact Mr. Abbott Wallis, Owner, 2308 Fossil Trace Drive, Golden, Colorado 80401. Phone: 800-222-3595. Fax: 303-526-0885. E-mail: info@aave.com.
URL www.aave.com

For more information, see page 394.

AAVE–Wild Isles

AAVE–Journeys That Matter
Locations Ireland, United Kingdom.

General Information Coed travel outdoor program, wilderness program, cultural program, and adventure program established in 1976. Accredited by American Camping Association.
Program Focus Adventure travel.
Special Interest Areas Campcraft, cross-cultural education, leadership training, touring.
Sports Bicycling, horseback riding, kayaking, rappelling, sea kayaking, surfing, swimming.
Wilderness/Outdoors Bicycle trips, hiking, mountain biking, outdoor adventure, rock climbing.
Excursions Cultural, day, overnight.
Program Information 2–4 sessions per year. Session length: 22 days in June, July, August. Ages: 14–18. 16 participants per session. Cost: $5288. Financial aid available.
Housing Tents and youth hostels.
Application Deadline Continuous.
Jobs Positions for college students 21 and older.
Contact Mr. Abbott Wallis, Owner, 2308 Fossil Trace Drive, Golden, Colorado 80401. Phone: 800-222-3595. Fax: 303-526-0885. E-mail: info@aave.com.
URL www.aave.com

For more information, see page 394.

ACADEMIC TREKS–Caribbean Marine Reserves

Academic Treks, the academic adventure and community service division of Broadreach

Locations Guadeloupe, Netherlands Antilles, Saint Kitts and Nevis.

General Information Coed travel academic program, outdoor program, community service program, and adventure program established in 1992. High school or college credit may be earned.

Program Focus Academic adventure program focusing on marine resource management and underwater marine parks, scuba diving, community service, island exploration, sailing, and school credit. Travel to Saba, Statia, St. Kitts, and St. Barts.

Academics Academics (general), ecology, environmental science, marine studies.

Arts Photography.

Special Interest Areas Community service, conservation projects, field research/expeditions, leadership training.

Sports Sailing, scuba diving, snorkeling, swimming, waterskiing.

Wilderness/Outdoors Hiking, ocean expeditions, outdoor adventure, sailing trips, wilderness/outdoors (general).

Excursions Cultural, day.

Program Information 2 sessions per year. Session length: 22 days in June, July, August. Ages: 15–19. 10–14 participants per session. Cost: $4580. Financial aid available.

Housing Hotels and yachts.

Application Deadline Continuous.

Contact Carlton Goldthwaite, Director, 806 McCulloch Street, Suite 102, Raleigh, North Carolina 27603. Phone: 888-833-1907. Fax: 919-833-1907. E-mail: info@academictreks.com

URL www.academictreks.com

For more information, see page 432.

ACTIONQUEST: Leeward and French Caribbean Island Voyages

ActionQuest

Locations Antigua and Barbuda, British Virgin Islands, Guadeloupe, Netherlands Antilles, Saint Kitts and Nevis.

General Information Coed travel outdoor program, cultural program, and adventure program established in 1970.

Program Focus Sailing voyage throughout the Leeward Islands, with emphasis on seamanship, sailing certifications, water sports, and island exploration.

Academics Astronomy, intercultural studies.

Special Interest Areas Cross-cultural education, leadership training, nature study, nautical skills, team building, touring.

Sports Sailing, scuba diving, snorkeling, waterskiing, windsurfing.

Wilderness/Outdoors Hiking, ocean expeditions, sailing trips.

Excursions Cultural, day.

Program Information 2 sessions per year. Session length: 3 weeks in June, July. Ages: 14–19. 10–20 participants per session. Cost: $4770.

Housing Yachts.

Application Deadline Continuous.

Contact Mike Meighan, Director, PO Box 5517, Sarasota, Florida 34277. Phone: 800-317-6789. Fax: 941-924-6075. E-mail: info@actionquest.com.

URL www.actionquest.com

For more information, see page 406.

ACTIONQUEST: Mediterranean Sailing Voyage

ActionQuest

Locations France, Italy, Monaco.

General Information Coed travel outdoor program, cultural program, and adventure program established in 1986.

ACTIONQUEST: Mediterranean Sailing Voyage

Program Focus Live-aboard voyage throughout French and Italian Rivieras. Ports of call include Rome, Corsica, Sardinia, Elba, and Monaco. Emphasis on sailing certifications, history, and culture, with numerous shore excursions.

Academics Astronomy, geography, history, intercultural studies.

Special Interest Areas Field trips (arts and culture),

leadership training, nautical skills, team building, touring.
Sports Sailing, swimming.
Wilderness/Outdoors Hiking, sailing trips.
Excursions Cultural, day.
Program Information 1 session per year. Session length: 3 weeks in June, July. Ages: 15–19. 10 participants per session. Cost: $4970.
Housing Yachts.
Application Deadline Continuous.
Contact Mike Meighan, Director, PO Box 5517, Sarasota, Florida 34277. Phone: 800-317-6789. Fax: 941-924-6075. E-mail: info@actionquest.com.
URL www.actionquest.com

For more information, see page 406.

ATW: EUROPEAN ADVENTURES

American Trails West
Locations France, Greece, Italy, Switzerland, United Kingdom.

General Information Coed travel cultural program and adventure program established in 1966.
Special Interest Areas Touring.
Sports Bicycling, boating, horseback riding, in-line skating, skiing (downhill), snorkeling, swimming, tennis, waterskiing.
Wilderness/Outdoors Hiking, mountain biking, rafting.
Excursions College tours, cultural.
Program Information 1–2 sessions per year. Session length: 4 weeks in July, August. Ages: 15–18. 40–45 participants per session. Cost: $8995.
Housing Hotels.
Application Deadline Continuous.
Jobs Positions for college students 20 and older.
Contact Director, 92 Middle Neck Road, Great Neck, New York 11021. Phone: 800-645-6260. Fax: 516-487-2855. E-mail: info@atwteentours.com.
URL www.atwteentours.com

For more information, see page 416.

BROADREACH ADVENTURES IN SCUBA AND SAILING–UNDERWATER DISCOVERIES

Broadreach
Locations Antigua and Barbuda, Guadeloupe, Netherlands Antilles, Saint Kitts and Nevis.

General Information Coed travel outdoor program and adventure program established in 1992.
Program Focus Coed program focusing on PADI scuba certification, sail training, marine biology, island exploration, and travel to St. Barts and St. Marten and throughout the Leeward Islands.
Academics Environmental science, marine studies.
Arts Photography.
Special Interest Areas Community service, conservation projects, field research/expeditions, leadership training, nature study.

Sports Boating, fishing, sailing, scuba diving, snorkeling, waterskiing.
Wilderness/Outdoors Hiking, ocean expeditions, outdoor adventure, sailing trips, wilderness/outdoors (general).
Excursions Cultural.
Program Information 3 sessions per year. Session length: 2–3 weeks in June, July, August. Ages: 13–19. 10–12 participants per session. Cost: $3540–$4980.
Housing Yachts.
Application Deadline Continuous.
Contact Carlton Goldthwaite, Director, 806 McCulloch Street, Suite 102, Raleigh, North Carolina 27603. Phone: 888-833-1907. Fax: 919-833-2129. E-mail: info@gobroadreach.com.
URL www.gobroadreach.com

For more information, see page 432.

BROADREACH ADVENTURES IN THE WINDWARD ISLANDS–ADVANCED SCUBA

Broadreach
Locations Grenada, Saint Lucia, Saint Vincent and The Grenadines.

General Information Coed travel outdoor program and adventure program established in 1992.
Program Focus Coed program focusing on advanced PADI scuba certification, PADI specialty and rescue certifications, sail training and certification, marine science, and island exploration.
Academics Ecology, marine studies.
Arts Photography.
Special Interest Areas Community service, conservation projects, field research/expeditions, leadership training, nature study.
Sports Boating, fishing, sailing, scuba diving, snorkeling, waterskiing.
Wilderness/Outdoors Hiking, ocean expeditions, outdoor adventure, sailing trips, wilderness/outdoors (general).
Excursions Cultural, day.
Program Information 2 sessions per year. Session length: 3 weeks in June, July, August. Ages: 15–19. 10–12 participants per session. Cost: $4940. Financial aid available.
Housing Yachts.
Application Deadline Continuous.

BROADREACH Adventures in the Windward Islands–Advanced Scuba (continued)

Contact Carlton Goldthwaite, Director, 806 McCulloch Street, Suite 102, Raleigh, North Carolina 27603. Phone: 888-833-1907. Fax: 919-833-2129. E-mail: info@gobroadreach.com.
URL www.gobroadreach.com
For more information, see page 432.

BROADREACH ADVENTURES UNDERWATER–ADVANCED SCUBA

Broadreach

Locations Antigua and Barbuda, Guadeloupe, Netherlands Antilles, Saint Kitts and Nevis.

General Information Coed travel outdoor program and adventure program established in 1992.
Program Focus Coed program focusing on advanced PADI scuba certification, PADI rescue certification, sail training, marine biology, underwater community service and island exploration, travel to St. Barts and St. Marten and throughout the Leeward Islands.
Academics Ecology, environmental science, marine studies.
Arts Photography.
Special Interest Areas Community service, conservation projects, field research/expeditions, leadership training, nature study.
Sports Boating, fishing, sailing, scuba diving, snorkeling, waterskiing.
Wilderness/Outdoors Hiking, ocean expeditions, outdoor adventure, sailing trips, wilderness/outdoors (general).
Excursions Cultural.
Program Information 3 sessions per year. Session length: 2–3 weeks in June, July, August. Ages: 13–19. 10–12 participants per session. Cost: $3190–$4980.
Housing Yachts.
Application Deadline Continuous.
Contact Carlton Goldthwaite, Director, 806 McCulloch Street, Suite 102, Raleigh, North Carolina 27603. Phone: 888-833-1907. Fax: 919-833-2129. E-mail: info@gobroadreach.com.
URL www.gobroadreach.com
For more information, see page 432.

BROADREACH ARC OF THE CARIBBEAN SAILING ADVENTURE

Broadreach

Locations Antigua and Barbuda, Dominica, Guadeloupe, Martinique, Netherlands Antilles, Saint Kitts and Nevis, Saint Lucia, Saint Vincent and The Grenadines, Trinidad and Tobago.

General Information Coed travel outdoor program, cultural program, and adventure program established in 1992.
Program Focus 32-day sailing voyage focusing on intensive sail training, IYT sailing certification, seamanship, island exploration, optional scuba, and leadership course.
Academics Ecology, environmental science, intercultural studies, marine studies.
Arts Photography.
Special Interest Areas Community service, conservation projects, leadership training.
Sports Boating, fishing, sailing, scuba diving, snorkeling, waterskiing.
Wilderness/Outdoors Hiking, ocean expeditions, outdoor adventure, sailing trips, wilderness camping, wilderness/outdoors (general).
Excursions Cultural.
Program Information 3 sessions per year. Session length: 32 days in June, July, August. Ages: 15–19. 8–10 participants per session. Cost: $5540.
Housing Yachts.
Application Deadline Continuous.
Contact Carlton Goldthwaite, Director, 806 McCulloch Street, Suite 102, Raleigh, North Carolina 27603. Phone: 888-833-1907. Fax: 919-833-2129. E-mail: info@gobroadreach.com.
URL www.gobroadreach.com
For more information, see page 432.

BROADREACH FIJI SOLOMON QUEST

Broadreach

Locations Fiji, Solomon Islands, Vanuatu.

General Information Coed travel outdoor program, cultural program, and adventure program established in 1992.
Program Focus Coed program focusing on scuba diving, cultural immersion, adventure travel, and exploration in Fiji, Vanuatu, and the Solomon Islands in the South Pacific.
Academics Area studies, environmental science, history, marine studies.
Arts Photography.
Special Interest Areas Community service, cross-cultural education, field research/expeditions, leadership training, nature study.
Sports Fishing, scuba diving, sea kayaking, snorkeling, swimming.
Wilderness/Outdoors Hiking, ocean expeditions, outdoor adventure, wilderness camping, wilderness/outdoors (general).
Excursions Cultural.
Program Information 2 sessions per year. Session

length: 24 days in June, July, August. Ages: 15–19.
10–12 participants per session. Cost: $4980.
Housing Tents and youth hostels.
Application Deadline Continuous.
Contact Carlton Goldthwaite, Director, 806 McCulloch
Street, Suite 102, Raleigh, North Carolina 27603.
Phone: 888-833-1907. Fax: 919-833-2129. E-mail:
info@gobroadreach.com.
URL www.gobroadreach.com
For more information, see page 432.

DUKE TIP INTERNATIONAL FIELD STUDIES

Duke University Talent Identification Program (Duke TIP)

Locations China, Costa Rica, France, Italy, United
Kingdom.

General Information Coed travel academic program.
Formal opportunities for the academically talented.
Program Focus Specific topics include: world politics,
global economics, art history, philosophy, tropical ecology, and tropical medicine.
Academics French language/literature, academics
(general), architecture, art history/appreciation, biology,
business, ecology, economics, global issues, government
and politics, health sciences, intercultural studies,
medicine, philosophy, physiology, science (general).
Special Interest Areas Cross-cultural education, field
research/expeditions, nature study, touring.
Wilderness/Outdoors Hiking.
Excursions Cultural, day, shopping.
Program Information 5 sessions per year. Session
length: 16–18 days in June, July, August. Ages: 15–18.
18–22 participants per session. Cost: $3200–$3900.
Application fee: $35.
Housing College dormitories and hotels.
Application Deadline March 23.
Jobs Positions for college students 21 and older.
Contact Dr. Nicki Charles, Coordinator of Educational
Programs, Duke TIP, 1121 West Main Street, Durham,
North Carolina 27701. Phone: 919-681-6519. Fax:
919-681-7921.
URL www.tip.duke.edu
For more information, see page 468.

EXCEL AT OXFORD/TUSCANY

Putney Student Travel

Locations France, Italy, United Kingdom.

General Information Coed travel academic program
and cultural program established in 1951. Formal
opportunities for the academically talented and
artistically talented.
Program Focus Two weeks at Oxford University, two
weeks in Tuscany, and a weekend in France.
Academics Italian language/literature, academics
(general), archaeology, architecture, art
history/appreciation, government and politics, history,
intercultural studies, international relations, precollege
program, social science, writing.
Arts Creative writing, drawing, painting, television/
video, theater/drama.
Special Interest Areas Field research/expeditions.
Sports Basketball, bicycling, boating, soccer,
swimming, tennis.
Wilderness/Outdoors Hiking.
Excursions Cultural, day, overnight.
Program Information 1 session per year. Session
length: 29–32 days in July, August. Ages: 16–18. 70
participants per session. Cost: $7290. Financial aid
available.
Housing College dormitories.
Application Deadline Continuous.
Contact Patrick Noyes, Director, 345 Hickory Ridge
Road, Putney, Vermont 05346. Phone: 802-387-5000.
Fax: 802-387-4276. E-mail: excel@goputney.com.
URL www.goputney.com
For more information, see page 490.

GLOBAL WORKS–CULTURAL EXCHANGE AND SERVICE–NEW ZEALAND AND FIJI ISLANDS–4 WEEKS

GLOBAL WORKS

Locations Fiji, New Zealand.

General Information Coed travel community service
program, cultural program, and adventure program
established in 1988. High school credit may be earned.
Program Focus Environmental and community
service and cultural exchange.
Academics Intercultural studies.
Arts Arts and crafts (general), dance, music
(instrumental), music (vocal), weaving.
Special Interest Areas Community service,
conservation projects, construction, field trips (arts and
culture), homestays, nature study.
Sports Kayaking, rappelling, rugby, scuba diving, sea
kayaking, snorkeling, soccer, swimming, volleyball.
Wilderness/Outdoors Hiking.
Excursions Cultural, day, overnight.
Program Information 1 session per year. Session
length: 28–30 days in June, July. Ages: 14–17. 16–18
participants per session. Cost: $4495. Application fee:
$100. Financial aid available. Airfare not included.
Housing Host-family homes and youth hostels.
Application Deadline Continuous.
Jobs Positions for college students 23 and older.

GLOBAL WORKS–Cultural Exchange and Service–New Zealand and Fiji Islands-4 weeks (continued)

Contact Mr. Erik Werner, Director, 1113 South Allen Street, State College, Pennsylvania 16801. Phone: 814-867-7000. Fax: 814-867-2717. E-mail: info@globalworksinc.com.
URL www.globalworksinc.com
For more information, see page 506.

GLOBAL WORKS–LANGUAGE IMMERSION, CULTURAL EXCHANGE AND SERVICE–PANAMA/COSTA RICA

GLOBAL WORKS
Locations Costa Rica, Panama.

General Information Coed travel community service program, cultural program, and adventure program established in 1988. High school credit may be earned.
Program Focus Environmental and community service, Spanish language immersion, and cultural exchange.
Academics Spanish language/literature, ecology, environmental science, intercultural studies.
Arts Arts and crafts (general).
Special Interest Areas Community service, conservation projects, construction, field trips (arts and culture), homestays.
Sports Boating, sea kayaking, snorkeling, soccer, swimming.
Wilderness/Outdoors Hiking, outdoor adventure, rafting, white-water trips.
Excursions Cultural, day, overnight.
Program Information 1 session per year. Session length: 28–29 days in July. Ages: 15–17. 16–18 participants per session. Cost: $4395. Application fee: $100. Financial aid available. Airfare not included.
Housing Host-family homes.
Application Deadline Continuous.
Jobs Positions for college students 23 and older.
Contact Mr. Erik Werner, Director, 1113 South Allen Street, State College, Pennsylvania 16801. Phone: 814-867-7000. Fax: 814-867-2717. E-mail: info@globalworksinc.com.
URL www.globalworksinc.com
For more information, see page 506.

NATIONAL STUDENT LEADERSHIP CONFERENCE: GLOBALIZATION AND INTERNATIONAL BUSINESS–STUDY ABROAD

National Student Leadership Conference
Locations France, Switzerland.

General Information Coed travel academic program established in 1989. Formal opportunities for the academically talented. College credit may be earned.
Program Focus Leadership training, global economics, career exploration.
Academics Academics (general), business, economics,

government and politics, international relations.
Special Interest Areas Career exploration, leadership training, team building, touring.
Excursions College tours, cultural, day, shopping.
Program Information 1–4 sessions per year. Session length: 12 days in June, July, August. Ages: 14–18. 150 participants per session. Cost: $4295; including airfare from Newark, NJ, USA to Geneva, Switzerland. Financial aid available.
Housing Hotels.
Application Deadline Continuous.
Jobs Positions for college students 18 and older.
Contact Director of Admissions, 414 North Orleans Street, Suite LL8, Chicago, Illinois 60610-1087. Phone: 312-322-9999. Fax: 312-765-0081. E-mail: info@nslcleaders.org.
URL www.nslcleaders.org
For more information, see page 564.

PUTNEY STUDENT TRAVEL–CULTURAL EXPLORATION–AUSTRALIA, NEW ZEALAND, AND FIJI

Putney Student Travel
Locations Australia, Fiji, New Zealand.

General Information Coed travel cultural program and adventure program established in 1951.
Program Focus Active exploration of the cultures and landscapes of the region through direct interaction with local people, and sailing and skiing adventures.
Academics Intercultural studies.
Special Interest Areas Homestays.
Sports Canoeing, rappelling, sailing, scuba diving, skiing (downhill), snorkeling, swimming.
Wilderness/Outdoors Hiking, outdoor adventure, rock climbing.
Excursions Cultural, day.
Program Information 1–2 sessions per year. Session length: 5–6 weeks in June, July. Ages: 16–18. 16–18 participants per session. Cost: $9690; including airfare. Financial aid available. Airfare from Los Angeles included.
Housing Host-family homes, hotels, and yachts.
Application Deadline Continuous.
Contact Jeffrey Shumlin, Admissions Director, 345 Hickory Ridge Road, Putney, Vermont 05346. Phone: 802-387-5000. Fax: 802-387-4276. E-mail: info@goputney.com.
URL www.goputney.com
For more information, see page 598.

PUTNEY STUDENT TRAVEL–CULTURAL EXPLORATION–SWITZERLAND, ITALY, FRANCE, AND HOLLAND

Putney Student Travel

Locations France, Italy, Netherlands, Switzerland.

General Information Coed travel cultural program and adventure program established in 1951.

Program Focus Active exploration of the cultures and landscapes of Europe in both major cities and rural areas.

Academics Art history/appreciation, intercultural studies.

Special Interest Areas Homestays.

Sports Bicycling, horseback riding, skiing (downhill), soccer, swimming.

Wilderness/Outdoors Bicycle trips, hiking, mountaineering, outdoor adventure.

Excursions Cultural, day.

Program Information 2 sessions per year. Session length: 5–6 weeks in June, July, August. Ages: 16–18. 16 participants per session. Cost: $8690; including airfare from New York to Geneva. Financial aid available.

Housing Host-family homes and hotels.

Application Deadline Continuous.

Contact Jeffrey Shumlin, Admissions Director, 345 Hickory Ridge Road, Putney, Vermont 05346. Phone: 802-387-5000. Fax: 802-387-4276. E-mail: info@goputney.com.

URL www.goputney.com

For more information, see page 598.

PUTNEY STUDENT TRAVEL–CULTURAL EXPLORATION–THAILAND AND CAMBODIA

Putney Student Travel

Locations Cambodia, Thailand.

General Information Coed residential cultural program established in 1951.

Program Focus Active exploration of the culture and history of Thailand and Cambodia through direct contact with local people.

Academics Intercultural studies.

Special Interest Areas Community service, cross-cultural education.

Wilderness/Outdoors Hiking, pack animal trips.

Excursions Cultural, day, overnight.

Program Information 1 session per year. Session length: 28–30 days in June, July. Ages: 15–18. 16 participants per session. Cost: $6000–$7000; including airfare from Los Angeles. Financial aid available.

Housing Hotels.

Application Deadline Continuous.

Jobs Positions for college students 21 and older.

Contact Jeffrey Shumlin, Admissions Director, 345 Hickory Ridge Road, Putney, Vermont 05346. Phone: 802-387-5000. Fax: 802-387-4276. E-mail: info@goputney.com.

URL www.goputney.com

For more information, see page 598.

REIN EUROPE

Rein Teen Tours

Locations France, Italy, Spain, Switzerland, United Kingdom.

General Information Coed travel outdoor program, cultural program, and adventure program established in 2005.

Special Interest Areas Cross-cultural education, touring.

Sports Skiing (downhill).

Excursions Cultural, overnight.

Program Information 1–2 sessions per year. Session length: 32 days in July, August. Ages: 14–17. 45 participants per session. Cost: $8999–$9499.

Housing Hotels.

Application Deadline Continuous.

Jobs Positions for college students 21 and older.

Contact Norman Rein, President, 30 Galesi Drive, Wayne, New Jersey 07470. Phone: 800-831-1313. Fax: 973-785-4268. E-mail: summer@reinteentours.com.

URL www.reinteentours.com

For more information, see page 604.

RUSTIC PATHWAYS–ASIAN PACIFIC EXTREME

Rustic Pathways

Locations Cambodia, China, Fiji, India, Myanmar, Thailand, Vietnam.

General Information Coed travel outdoor program, cultural program, and adventure program. High school credit may be earned.

Arts Photography.

Special Interest Areas Field research/expeditions, homestays, nature study, touring.

Sports Boating, kayaking, sailing, scuba diving, sea kayaking, snorkeling, soccer, surfing, swimming.

Wilderness/Outdoors Backpacking, bicycle trips, hiking, outdoor adventure, rafting.

Excursions Cultural, day, overnight, shopping.

Program Information 1 session per year. Session length: 58 days in June, July, August. Ages: 15–18. 10–15 participants per session. Cost: $12,895. Application fee: $100–$200. Financial aid available. Airfare not included.

Housing Host-family homes, hotels, tents, and youth hostels.

RUSTIC PATHWAYS–ASIAN PACIFIC EXTREME (continued)

Application Deadline Continuous.
Jobs Positions for college students 21 and older.
Contact Rustic Pathways, 4121 Erie Street, Willoughby, Ohio 44094. Phone: 800-321-4353. Fax: 440-975-9694. E-mail: rustic@rusticpathways.com.
URL www.rusticpathways.com
For more information, see page 612.

RUSTIC PATHWAYS–EDGE OF THE MAP EXTREME

Rustic Pathways

Locations Cambodia, India, Myanmar, Thailand, United Republic of Tanzania.

General Information Coed travel.
Arts Photography.
Special Interest Areas Animal care, community service, conservation projects, field research/expeditions, homestays, nature study, touring.
Sports Boating, fishing, kayaking, rappelling, soccer, swimming.
Wilderness/Outdoors Backpacking, hiking, mountaineering, outdoor adventure, rafting, safari, white-water trips, wilderness camping.
Program Information 1 session per year. Session length: 58 days in June, July, August. Ages: 15–18. 10–15 participants per session. Cost: $11,995. Application fee: $100–$200. Financial aid available. Airfare not included.
Application Deadline Continuous.
Jobs Positions for college students 21 and older.
Contact Rustic Pathways, 4121 Erie Street, Willoughby, Ohio 44094. Phone: 800-321-4353. Fax: 440-975-9694. E-mail: rustic@rusticpathways.com.
URL www.rusticpathways.com
For more information, see page 612.

RUSTIC PATHWAYS–INTRODUCTION TO PHOTOGRAPHY–SNAPSHOTS IN THE LAND OF SMILES

Rustic Pathways

Locations Cambodia, Lao People's Democratic Republic, Myanmar, Thailand.

General Information Coed travel outdoor program, arts program, cultural program, and adventure program.
Program Focus Photography.
Arts Photography.
Special Interest Areas Nature study, touring.
Wilderness/Outdoors Hiking.
Excursions Cultural, day.
Program Information 1 session per year. Session length: 17 days in June, July. Ages: 14–18. 10–15 participants per session. Cost: $2895. Financial aid available.
Application Deadline Continuous.
Jobs Positions for college students 21 and older.

Contact Rustic Pathways, 4121 Erie Street, Willoughby, Ohio 44094. Phone: 800-321-4353. Fax: 440-975-9694. E-mail: rustic@rusticpathways.com.
URL www.rusticpathways.com
For more information, see page 612.

RUSTIC PATHWAYS–OFF THE MAP BURMA AND CAMBODIA

Rustic Pathways

Locations Cambodia, Myanmar.

General Information Coed travel cultural program and adventure program.
Program Focus Rugged travel to exotic, isolated locations for experienced travelers.
Arts Photography.
Special Interest Areas Cross-cultural education, touring.
Wilderness/Outdoors Hiking.
Excursions Cultural, day, overnight, shopping.
Program Information 1 session per year. Session length: 17 days in June. Ages: 16–18. 10–15 participants per session. Cost: $2995. Financial aid available. Airfare not included.
Housing Host-family homes, hotels, and houses.
Application Deadline Continuous.
Jobs Positions for college students 21 and older.
Contact Mr., Rustic Pathways, 4121 Erie Street, Willoughby, Ohio 44094. Phone: 440-975-9691. Fax: 440-975-9694. E-mail: rustic@rusticpathways.com.
URL www.rusticpathways.com
For more information, see page 612.

RUSTIC PATHWAYS–PHOTOGRAPHY ADVENTURE IN THAILAND AND ANGKOR WAT

Rustic Pathways

Locations Cambodia, Thailand.

General Information Coed travel arts program and cultural program established in 2005.
Arts Photography.
Special Interest Areas Cross-cultural education, touring.
Excursions Cultural, day, overnight, shopping.
Program Information 1 session per year. Session length: 17 days in August. Ages: 16–18. 10–20 participants per session. Cost: $2995. Application fee: $100–$200. Financial aid available.

Application Deadline Continuous.
Jobs Positions for college students 21 and older.
Contact Rustic Pathways, 4121 Erie Street,
Willoughby, Ohio 44094. Phone: 800-321-4353. Fax:
440-975-9694. E-mail: rustic@rusticpathways.com.
URL www.rusticpathways.com

For more information, see page 612.

RUSTIC PATHWAYS– PHOTOGRAPHY ADVENTURE IN THAILAND AND BURMA

Rustic Pathways
Locations Myanmar, Thailand.

General Information Coed travel arts program and
cultural program established in 2005.
Arts Photography.
Special Interest Areas Cross-cultural education,
touring.
Excursions Cultural, day, overnight, shopping.
Program Information 1 session per year. Session
length: 17 days in June, July. Ages: 16–18. 10–20
participants per session. Cost: $2995. Application fee:
$100–$200. Financial aid available.
Application Deadline Continuous.
Jobs Positions for college students 21 and older.
Contact Rustic Pathways, 4121 Erie Street,
Willoughby, Ohio 44094. Phone: 800-321-4353. Fax:
440-975-9694. E-mail: rustic@rusticpathways.com.
URL www.rusticpathways.com

For more information, see page 612.

RUSTIC PATHWAYS– PHOTOGRAPHY ADVENTURE IN THAILAND AND INDIA

Rustic Pathways
Locations India, Thailand.

General Information Coed travel arts program and
cultural program established in 1998.
Arts Photography.
Special Interest Areas Cross-cultural education,
touring.
Wilderness/Outdoors Hiking.
Excursions Cultural, day, overnight, shopping.
Program Information 1 session per year. Session
length: 17 days in June, July, August. Ages: 16–18.
10–15 participants per session. Cost: $2995. Airfare not
included.
Application Deadline Continuous.
Jobs Positions for college students 21 and older.
Contact Rustic Pathways, 4121 Erie Street,
Willoughby, Ohio 44094. Phone: 800-321-4353. Fax:
440-975-9694. E-mail: rustic@rusticpathways.com.
URL www.rusticpathways.com

For more information, see page 612.

RUSTIC PATHWAYS– PHOTOGRAPHY ADVENTURE IN THAILAND AND VIETNAM

Rustic Pathways
Locations Thailand, Vietnam.

General Information Coed travel arts program and
cultural program established in 2005.
Arts Photography.
Special Interest Areas Cross-cultural education,
touring.
Excursions Cultural, day, overnight, shopping.
Program Information 1 session per year. Session
length: 17 days in July, August. Ages: 16–18. 10–20
participants per session. Cost: $2995. Application fee:
$100–$200. Financial aid available.
Application Deadline Continuous.
Jobs Positions for college students 21 and older.
Contact Rustic Pathways, 4121 Erie Street,
Willoughby, Ohio 44094. Phone: 800-321-4353. Fax:
440-975-9694. E-mail: rustic@rusticpathways.com.
URL www.rusticpathways.com

For more information, see page 612.

RUSTIC PATHWAYS–SERVICE LEARNING EXTREME

Rustic Pathways
Locations Australia, Fiji, Thailand.

General Information Coed travel community service
program, cultural program, and adventure program
established in 1994. High school credit may be earned.
Program Focus Combined programs in Fiji, Thailand
and Australia offering practical service opportunities
and real life service learning.
Academics Latin language, environmental science,
geology/earth science, marine studies, oceanography,
science (general).
Special Interest Areas Animal care, community
service, conservation projects, field research/expeditions,
homestays, nature study, touring.
Sports Boating, climbing (wall), fishing, horseback
riding, kayaking, rappelling, sailing, scuba diving, sea
kayaking, skiing (cross-country), skiing (downhill),
snorkeling, soccer, surfing, swimming.

RUSTIC PATHWAYS–SERVICE LEARNING EXTREME
(continued)

RUSTIC PATHWAYS–SERVICE LEARNING EXTREME

Wilderness/Outdoors Backpacking, bicycle trips, hiking, mountain biking, outdoor adventure, rafting, white-water trips, wilderness camping.
Excursions Cultural, day, overnight, shopping.
Program Information 1 session per year. Session length: 7 weeks in June, July, August. Ages: 15–18. 10–15 participants per session. Cost: $7495. Application fee: $100–$200.
Housing Host-family homes, hotels, tents, and youth hostels.
Application Deadline Continuous.
Jobs Positions for college students 21 and older.
Contact Rustic Pathways, 4121 Erie Street, Willoughby, Ohio 44094. Phone: 800-321-4353. Fax: 440-975-9694. E-mail: rustic@rusticpathways.com.
URL www.rusticpathways.com

For more information, see page 612.

RUSTIC PATHWAYS–SOCCER AND SERVICE EXTREME

Rustic Pathways

Locations Costa Rica, Fiji, Thailand.

General Information Coed travel outdoor program, community service program, and cultural program established in 2005.
Program Focus Cultural immersion, community service, and playing soccer in towns and villages in Fiji, Thailand, and Costa Rica.
Special Interest Areas Animal care, community service, conservation projects, construction, cross-cultural education, homestays, touring.
Sports Soccer.
Excursions Cultural, day, overnight, shopping.
Program Information 1 session per year. Session length: 51 days in June, July, August. Ages: 14–18. 10–15 participants per session. Cost: $7495. Application fee: $100–$200. Financial aid available.
Application Deadline Continuous.
Jobs Positions for college students 21 and older.

Contact Rustic Pathways, 4121 Erie Street, Willoughby, Ohio 44094. Phone: 800-321-4353. Fax: 440-975-9694. E-mail: rustic@rusticpathways.com.
URL www.rusticpathways.com

For more information, see page 612.

RUSTIC PATHWAYS–SOUTH PACIFIC EXTREME

Rustic Pathways

Locations Australia, Fiji, New Zealand.

General Information Coed travel.
Academics Marine studies, oceanography.
Special Interest Areas Field research/expeditions, homestays, nature study, touring.
Sports Boating, climbing (wall), fishing, horseback riding, kayaking, rappelling, sailing, scuba diving, sea kayaking, skiing (cross-country), skiing (downhill), snorkeling, snowboarding, soccer, surfing, swimming.
Wilderness/Outdoors Backpacking, bicycle trips, hiking, mountain biking, outdoor adventure, rafting, white-water trips, wilderness camping.
Program Information 1 session per year. Session length: 51 days in June, July, August. Ages: 15–18. 10–15 participants per session. Cost: $9985. Application fee: $100–$200. Financial aid available. Airfare not included.
Housing Host-family homes, hotels, tents, and youth hostels.
Application Deadline Continuous.
Jobs Positions for college students 21 and older.
Contact Rustic Pathways, 4121 Erie Street, Willoughby, Ohio 44094. Phone: 800-321-4353. Fax: 440-975-9694. E-mail: rustic@rusticpathways.com.
URL www.rusticpathways.com

For more information, see page 612.

RUSTIC PATHWAYS–THE WONDERS & RICHES OF SOUTHEAST ASIA

Rustic Pathways

Locations Cambodia, Myanmar, Thailand, Vietnam.

General Information Coed travel cultural program and adventure program established in 2003.
Special Interest Areas Cross-cultural education, culinary arts, massage therapy training, touring.
Sports Boating.
Wilderness/Outdoors Outdoor adventure.
Excursions Cultural, day, overnight, shopping.
Program Information 1 session per year. Session length: 17 days in July. Ages: 14–18. 10–15 participants per session. Cost: $5860. Cost includes internal Asian flights only.
Application Deadline Continuous.
Jobs Positions for college students 21 and older.

Contact Rustic Pathways, 4121 Erie Street, Willoughby, Ohio 44094. Phone: 800-321-4353. Fax: 440-975-9694. E-mail: rustic@rusticpathways.com. **URL** www.rusticpathways.com

For more information, see page 612.

RUSTIC PATHWAYS–WORLD SERVICE EXTREME

Rustic Pathways

Locations India, Thailand, United Republic of Tanzania.

General Information Coed travel community service program, cultural program, and adventure program. High school credit may be earned.
Program Focus Combining village service initiatives in India, Thailand and Tanzania.
Academics Environmental science, geology/earth science, science (general).
Special Interest Areas Animal care, community service, conservation projects, construction, field research/expeditions, homestays, nature study, touring.
Sports Boating, climbing (wall), fishing, horseback riding, kayaking, rappelling, soccer, swimming.
Wilderness/Outdoors Backpacking, bicycle trips, hiking, mountain biking, outdoor adventure, rafting, safari, white-water trips, wilderness camping.
Excursions Cultural, day, overnight, shopping.
Program Information 1 session per year. Session length: 58 days in June, July, August. Ages: 15–18. 10–15 participants per session. Cost: $8995. Application fee: $100–$200. Financial aid available. Airfare not included.
Housing Host-family homes, hotels, tents, and youth hostels.
Application Deadline Continuous.
Contact Rustic Pathways, 4121 Erie Street, Willoughby, Ohio 44094. Phone: 800-321-4353. Fax: 440-975-9694. E-mail: rustic@rusticpathways.com. **URL** www.rusticpathways.com

For more information, see page 612.

WEISSMAN TEEN TOURS–EUROPEAN EXPERIENCE

Weissman Teen Tours

Locations Belgium, France, Italy, Netherlands, Switzerland, United Kingdom.

General Information Coed travel outdoor program and cultural program established in 1974.
Program Focus Owner-escorted, action-packed, culturally-oriented, upscale European travel program. All deluxe four- and five-star hotels and resorts; no camping or dormitory accommodations.
Academics Architecture, art history/appreciation, college tours, history, intercultural studies.
Arts Theater/drama.
Special Interest Areas Team building, touring.
Sports Aerobics, bicycling, boating, parasailing, skiing (downhill), snowboarding, swimming, tennis, volleyball, weight training.

Wilderness/Outdoors Bicycle trips, hiking, white-water trips.
Excursions College tours, cultural, day, overnight, shopping.
Program Information 2 sessions per year. Session length: 34 days in June, July, August. Ages: 15–18. 45 participants per session. Cost: $10,699.
Housing Hotels.
Application Deadline Continuous.
Jobs Positions for college students 21 and older.
Contact Ms. Ronee Weissman, Owner/Director, 517 Almena Avenue, Ardsley, New York 10502. Phone: 800-942-8005. Fax: 914-693-4807. E-mail: wtt@cloud9.net.
URL www.weissmantours.com

For more information, see page 700.

WESTCOAST CONNECTION–AUSTRALIAN OUTBACK PLUS HAWAII

Westcoast Connection
Locations Australia, Hawaii.

General Information Coed travel adventure program established in 1982. Accredited by Ontario Camping Association.

Westcoast Connection–Australian Outback Plus Hawaii

Program Focus A balance of touring, recreation, and adventure visiting Fraser Island, Gold Coast, Cairns, Ayers Rock, Sydney and Hawaii.
Special Interest Areas Touring.
Sports Boating, kayaking, scuba diving, sea kayaking, snorkeling, surfing, swimming.
Wilderness/Outdoors Hiking, outdoor adventure, rafting, white-water trips.
Program Information 1–2 sessions per year. Session length: 23–28 days in July. Ages: 14–18. 30–40 participants per session. Cost: $6599–$7699.
Housing Hotels.
Application Deadline Continuous.

Westcoast Connection–Australian Outback Plus Hawaii (continued)

Contact Mr. Mark Segal, Director, 154 East Boston Post Road, Mamaroneck, New York 10543. Phone: 800-767-0227. Fax: 914-835-0798. E-mail: usa@westcoastconnection.com.
URL www.westcoastconnection.com
For more information, see page 702.

WESTCOAST CONNECTION–BELIZE AND COSTA RICA WATER ADVENTURE

Westcoast Connection
Locations Belize, Costa Rica.

General Information Coed travel adventure program established in 1982. Accredited by Ontario Camping Association.
Program Focus An adventure program with emphasis on sailing, surfing and scuba diving-PADI certification available.
Special Interest Areas Community service, conservation projects.
Sports Sailing, scuba diving, snorkeling, surfing.
Wilderness/Outdoors Outdoor adventure, rafting, white-water trips.
Program Information 1–2 sessions per year. Session length: 3 weeks in July, August. Ages: 14–17. 10–21 participants per session. Cost: $4999.
Housing Hotels and sailboats.
Application Deadline Continuous.
Jobs Positions for college students 21 and older.
Contact Mr. Mark Segal, Director, 154 East Boston Post Road, Mamaroneck, New York 10543. Phone: 800-767-0227. Fax: 914-835-0798. E-mail: usa@westcoastconnection.com.
URL www.360studenttravel.com
For more information, see page 702.

WESTCOAST CONNECTION–EUROPEAN ESCAPE

Westcoast Connection
Locations France, Italy, Monaco, Switzerland.

General Information Coed travel cultural program established in 1982. Accredited by Ontario Camping Association.
Program Focus A touring program balancing big city highlights and nightlife with adventure in the Swiss Alps and recreation on the French and Adriatic Rivieras.
Special Interest Areas Culinary arts, touring.
Sports Bicycling (BMX), boating, skiing (downhill), snowboarding, swimming.
Wilderness/Outdoors Rafting, white-water trips.
Program Information 1–2 sessions per year. Session length: 3 weeks in July, August. Ages: 14–17. 20–35 participants per session. Cost: $6999. Financial aid available.
Application Deadline Continuous.

Contact Mr. Mark Segal, Director, 154 East Boston Post Road, Mamaroneck, New York 10543. Phone: 800-767-0227. Fax: 914-835-0798. E-mail: usa@westcoastconnection.com.
URL www.westcoastconnection.com
For more information, see page 702.

WESTCOAST CONNECTION TRAVEL–EUROPEAN DISCOVERY

Westcoast Connection
Locations Belgium, France, Italy, Monaco, Netherlands, Switzerland, United Kingdom.

General Information Coed travel cultural program established in 1982. Accredited by Ontario Camping Association.
Program Focus A touring program balancing big city highlights and nightlife with adventure in the Swiss Alps and recreation on the French and Adriatic Rivieras.
Special Interest Areas Culinary arts, touring.
Sports Bicycling, boating, skiing (downhill), snowboarding, swimming, windsurfing.
Wilderness/Outdoors Mountain biking, rafting, white-water trips.
Program Information 1–2 sessions per year. Session length: 32 days in July, August. Ages: 14–17. 35–45 participants per session. Cost: $8900.
Housing Hotels.
Application Deadline Continuous.
Jobs Positions for college students 21 and older.
Contact Mr. Mark Segal, Director, 154 East Boston Post Road, Mamaroneck, New York 10543. Phone: 800-767-0227. Fax: 914-835-0798. E-mail: usa@westcoastconnection.com.
URL www.westcoastconnection.com
For more information, see page 702.

WESTCOAST CONNECTION TRAVEL/ON TOUR–EUROPEAN ESCAPADE

Westcoast Connection
Locations France, Italy, Monaco, Switzerland.

General Information Coed travel cultural program established in 1982. Accredited by Ontario Camping Association.
Program Focus A program balancing big city (Paris, Rome, Geneva and others) highlights and nightlife, with adventure in the Swiss Alps and recreation on the

French and Adriatic Rivieras; designed with more independence for ages 17–18.
Special Interest Areas Culinary arts, touring.
Sports Boating, skiing (downhill), snowboarding, swimming, windsurfing.
Wilderness/Outdoors Mountain biking, rafting, white-water trips.
Program Information 1–2 sessions per year. Session length: 3 weeks in July. Ages: 16–18. 40–48 participants per session. Cost: $5799–$6899.
Housing Hotels.
Application Deadline Continuous.
Contact Mr. Mark Segal, Director, 154 East Boston Post Road, Mamaroneck, New York 10543. Phone: 800-767-0227. Fax: 914-835-0798. E-mail: usa@westcoastconnection.com.
URL www.westcoastconnection.com
For more information, see page 702.

WESTCOAST CONNECTION TRAVEL/ON TOUR–EUROPEAN EXPERIENCE

Westcoast Connection
Locations France, Italy, Monaco, Switzerland, United Kingdom.

General Information Coed travel cultural program established in 1982. Accredited by Ontario Camping Association.
Program Focus This program is designed for greater independence for ages 17 to 18. A tour balancing big city highlights and nightlife with adventure in the French and Swiss Alps, and recreation on the French and Adriatic Rivieras.
Special Interest Areas Culinary arts, touring.
Sports Bicycling, skiing (downhill), snowboarding, swimming, windsurfing.
Wilderness/Outdoors Mountain biking, rafting, white-water trips.
Program Information 2–4 sessions per year. Session length: 4 weeks in July, August. Ages: 16–18. 40–48 participants per session. Cost: $5799–$6899.
Housing Hotels.
Application Deadline Continuous.
Contact Mr. Mark Segal, Director, 154 East Boston Post Road, Mamaroneck, New York 10543. Phone: 800-767-0227. Fax: 914-835-0798. E-mail: usa@westcoastconnection.com.
URL www.westcoastconnection.com
For more information, see page 702.

WILDERNESS VENTURES–COSTA RICA/ BELIZE

Wilderness Ventures
Locations Belize, Costa Rica.

General Information Coed travel adventure program established in 1973.
Program Focus Wilderness travel, wilderness skills, leadership skills.
Special Interest Areas Nature study.
Sports Sailing, scuba diving, snorkeling, surfing.

Wilderness/Outdoors Hiking, rafting, white-water trips, wilderness camping, zip line.
Program Information 2 sessions per year. Session length: 24 days in June, July, August. Ages: 14–18. 13 participants per session. Cost: $5290. Financial aid available.
Application Deadline Continuous.
Jobs Positions for college students 21 and older.
Contact Mike Cottingham, Director, PO Box 2768, Jackson Hole, Wyoming 83001. Phone: 800-533-2281. Fax: 307-739-1934. E-mail: info@wildernessventures. com.
URL www.wildernessventures.com
For more information, see page 704.

WILDERNESS VENTURES–EUROPEAN ALPS

Wilderness Ventures
Locations France, Italy, Switzerland.

General Information Coed travel outdoor program, wilderness program, cultural program, and adventure program established in 1973.
Program Focus Wilderness travel, cultural immersion, leadership skills.
Academics Intercultural studies.
Special Interest Areas Leadership training.
Wilderness/Outdoors Backpacking, hiking, mountaineering.
Excursions Cultural, overnight.
Program Information 1 session per year. Session length: 29 days in June, July, August. Ages: 14–18. 15 participants per session. Cost: $5090. Financial aid available.
Housing Youth hostels.
Application Deadline Continuous.
Jobs Positions for college students 21 and older.
Contact Mike Cottingham, Director, PO Box 2768, Jackson Hole, Wyoming 83001. Phone: 800-533-2281. Fax: 307-739-1934. E-mail: info@wildernessventures. com.
URL www.wildernessventures.com
For more information, see page 704.

WILDERNESS VENTURES–TAHITI, FIJI, AND NEW ZEALAND

Wilderness Ventures

Locations Fiji, French Polynesia, New Zealand.

General Information Coed travel outdoor program, wilderness program, and adventure program established in 1973.
Program Focus Wilderness travel, cultural immersion, leadership skills.
Special Interest Areas Animal care, community service, farming, homestays, nature study.
Sports Sailing, scuba diving, snorkeling, surfing.
Excursions Cultural, overnight.
Program Information 1 session per year. Session length: 29 days in June, July. 13 participants per session. Cost: $6690. Financial aid available.
Application Deadline Continuous.
Jobs Positions for college students 21 and older.
Contact Mike Cottingham, Director, PO Box 2768, Jackson Hole, Wyoming 83001. Phone: 800-533-2281. Fax: 307-739-1934. E-mail: info@wildernessventures.com.
URL www.wildernessventures.com

For more information, see page 704.

WORLD HORIZONS INTERNATIONAL– UNITED KINGDOM

World Horizons International

Locations Iceland, United Kingdom.

General Information Coed travel academic program, arts program, and cultural program established in 2005. Formal opportunities for the artistically talented.
Program Focus Learning photography in Yorkshire, London, and Iceland, plus sightseeing.

Arts Photography.
Special Interest Areas Community service, cross-cultural education.
Wilderness/Outdoors Hiking.
Excursions Cultural, day, overnight.
Program Information 1–2 sessions per year. Session length: 10–14 days in March, April, August. Ages: 14–18. 10–12 participants per session. Cost: $3995–$4595; including airfare from New York, NY to Longona nd Reykjavik. Application fee: $175. Financial aid available. Program cost includes airfare from New York.
Housing Hotels and youth hostels.
Application Deadline Continuous.
Jobs Positions for college students 21 and older.
Contact Mr. Stuart L. Rabinowitz, Executive Director, PO Box 662, Bethlehem, Connecticut 06751. Phone: 800-262-5874. Fax: 203-266-6227. E-mail: worldhorizons@att.net.
URL www.world-horizons.com

For more information, see page 714.

IN-DEPTH DESCRIPTIONS

AAVE TEEN ADVENTURES

aave Teen Adventure Travel Since 1976

GOLDEN, COLORADO

TYPE OF PROGRAM: Adventure, wilderness, community service and culture, travel, and French and Spanish language immersion

PARTICIPANTS: Coeducational and international; grades 6–12, ages 11–18, separated by age

ENROLLMENT: 800 participants per summer in independent groups of 13 to 15 teenagers

PROGRAM DATES: Two-, three-, four-, and six-week trips from June through August

HEAD OF PROGRAM: Abbott Wallis, Owner

LOCATION

AAVE Teen Adventures has its year-round base in Colorado. Trips include adventure travel in Colorado, Utah, Arizona, Alaska, Washington, California, Africa, Hawaii, Costa Rica, Australia, Thailand, China, Canada, South America, Mexico, and Europe with no base facility.

BACKGROUND AND PHILOSOPHY

Since 1976, AAVE Teen Adventures has been about feeling alive, competent, and part of a highly motivated team of teenagers having fun. The hallmark of AAVE has been to combine inspirational leaders, innovative adventures, and a high level of individual responsibility and commitment. An interview and two references are required prior to acceptance. All groups include 13 to 15 teenagers and 2 or 3 adults; the small group size results in an honest experience in which each participant's contribution makes a difference. AAVE Teen Adventures is accredited by the American Camp Association.

PROGRAM OFFERINGS

Australia (twenty-one days, Australia) Beach activities down under include scuba certification, diving the Great Barrier Reef, sailing, surfing, the Great Northern Walk, and sightseeing in Sydney.

Thailand (twenty-one days, Thailand) Thailand is the ultimate adventure off the beaten tourist path. Participants learn about Asian culture as they go elephant trekking and exploring.

Ultimate Hawaii (twenty-one days, Hawaii) Hawaii is a rugged adventure, including tropical backpacking, three days of surfing, mountain biking around Hawaii's Volcano National Park, and a seven-day water sport and Pacific sailing experience, including instruction in navigation, windsurfing, outrigger canoeing, and sea kayaking.

Boot•Saddle•Paddle (twenty-four days, Colorado, Utah, and Arizona) Boot•Saddle•Paddle, in the southwestern United States, includes two backpacking trips, including the southern rim of the Grand Canyon; a horseback-riding adventure in Colorado; Native American intercultural experiences and community service projects; and a class III–IV white-water rafting trip.

Bold Europe (twenty-eight days, Spain, France, and Italy) Bold Europe is an exploration of three distinct European regions. Activities include hiking, mountain biking, rafting, canyoning, rock climbing, and visits to Mediterranean beaches, museums, Barcelona, Florence, Siena, and Paris.

Bold West (twenty-six days, Utah, Nevada, and California) Bold West is an active way to explore the western United States. Itineraries include hiking in national parks, rafting, rock climbing, surfing, and exploring western towns and cities.

Rock and Rapid (twenty-one days, Colorado) Rock and Rapid offers the best of Colorado and includes five days of rock climbing, action-packed white-water rafting, and two backpacking trips in the high country of Colorado.

Colorado Discovery (eighteen days, Colorado) Colorado Discovery is designed exclusively for 12- and 13-year-olds and is a challenging introductory sampler of wilderness sports, including backpacking, white-water rafting, mountain biking, rock climbing, horseback riding, and adventure camping.

Ultimate Alaska (twenty-two days, Alaska) Alaska requires previous backcountry experience. This rugged Alaskan adventure includes a five-day backpacking trip in the Chugach Mountain Range, a sea-kayaking trip in Resurrection Bay, a five-day technical glacier-climbing school on the Matanuska Glacier, a two-day river trip on the Matanuska River, and a final backpacking trip in Denali State Park.

Ultimate Alps (twenty-one days, France, Italy, and Switzerland) Alps is an exciting adventure in the alpine center of Europe. Glacier skiing and snowboarding, white-water rafting, klettersteig, canyoning, mountain biking, and backpacking complete this high-powered international mountaineering trip.

Costa Rica Clasica (twenty-one days, Costa Rica) Costa Rica Clasica combines Spanish language, adventure, and community service in a wondrous, friendly, and safe Central American country. Basic knowledge of Spanish (a minimum of one year) is required.

Costa Rica Spanish Intensive (twenty-one days, Costa Rica) Costa Rica Spanish Intensive is a challenging Spanish-language immersion program. The program includes three weeks of language classes and living with a host family. A minimum of two years of Spanish study is required.

France Classique (twenty-one days, France) France Classique is an aggressive French-language immersion program that combines university study, cultural excursions, and outdoor adventure. Basic knowledge of French (a minimum of one year) is required.

España Clasica (twenty-one days, Spain) España Clasica is an aggressive Spanish-language immersion program combining university study, homestays, and outdoor adventure in Madrid and Santander. Basic knowledge of Spanish (a minimum of one year) is required.

Wild Coast Discovery (twenty-one days, Washington and British Columbia, Canada) Wild Coast Discovery is designed for teens 13 and 14 years old and explores Washington and British Columbia. It features two days of skiing or snowboarding in Whistler, sea kayaking on Puget Sound, biking in the San Juan Islands, rock climbing in Canada, and backpacking trips in the Olympic and Cascade Mountains.

Wild Isles (twenty-two days, Ireland, Wales, and England) Wild Isles takes place in the wilderness and culture of Ireland, Wales, and England. Activities include two days of horseback riding, two days of surfing, two days of mountain biking, and plenty of sightseeing.

Bike Amsterdam/Paris (fourteen days, Holland, Belgium, and France) Participants bike some of Europe's best trails and experience some of Europe's most fascinating cities. Whether bicycle novices or fanatics, riders see culture and beauty on this 350-mile ride spread over eleven days.

Sail Dive Greece (nineteen days, Greece) The Greek passion for culture, adventure, sport, food, and life is contagious as participants sail, scuba dive, and experience the very best of Greece.

Surf Scuba Safari (eighteen days, Baja, Mexico) Participants in this program ride the waves by day, camp on the beach by night, and scuba dive along the coast of Mexico. Surf Scuba Safari also includes a zip-line canopy tour, a survival skills safari, and a service project.

Peru and Machu Picchu (twenty-one days, Peru) Students explore the legacy of the Incas as they explore ancient cities, hike the Peruvian Andes, and visit Machu Picchu, the most beautiful and mysterious of the Incan ruins. This trip also includes rafting class III rapids, surfing the Pacific, visiting the largest lake in the world, service work with local villages, and enjoying the wonders of the Amazon.

Ecuador and Galapagos (twenty-one days, Ecuador and Galapagos Islands) This trip gives students the best of mainland Ecuador, a trip to the Galapagos Islands, and a rare glimpse of the cloud forest. A naturalist teaches students about the surrounding ecosystems. Participants explore, snorkel, hike, swim, bike, and work with local schoolchildren.

Africa (twenty-one days, South Africa, Namibia, Zambia, and Botswana) This program is a combination of high-adrenaline activities in some of the world's largest desert sand dunes, first-rate rapids, and rugged trails, with unique exposure to diverse cultures and wildlife.

China (twenty-one days, China) Teens crisscross centuries and cultures in this intriguing country as they experience China's vast expanses up close and adventurous. Participants hike the Great Wall, visit a panda breeding center, participate in community service projects, and explore the history and mystery of China. The trip includes two overnight trains and no camping.

Rock & Roll (fourteen days, Colorado) Rock & Roll includes five days of white-water kayak school on the Arkansas River, three days of rock climbing, a two-day service project with the Colorado Fourteeners Initiative, and a final summit of a 14,000-foot peak. The scenery is beautiful and the challenge is intense; this trip is geared toward both first-timers and experienced paddlers and climbers.

ENROLLMENT

Each coed group of 13 to 15 participants and 2 or 3 trip leaders is carefully grouped by age. Participants from forty-two states and twenty-six countries have joined AAVE. The small group size promotes strong friendships and one-on-one instruction and responsibility. AAVE trips feature service projects and intercultural exchanges with an international staff, group, and locale. No previous experience is needed for most trips.

DAILY SCHEDULE

Each day, participants have a variety of responsibilities that may include leadership, grocery shopping, cooking, cleaning, environmental service projects, and orienteering.

STAFF

AAVE Teen Adventures requires staff members to have Wilderness First Responder, Adult CPR, and Lifeguard Training certifications; extensive experience with teenagers; backcountry travel knowledge; and proven leadership skills. The minimum age of staff members is 21, and the average age is 26. Each trip includes a female leader and a male leader.

COSTS

Tuition ranges from $2088 to $6088. AAVE recommends $50 per week for personal expenses.

FINANCIAL AID

Scholarships are based on financial need. Interested participants should call for an application. Scholarships are offered only for trips in the United States.

TRANSPORTATION

Round-trip airfare to all trip locations is the participant's responsibility. All participants are met at the airport on arrival and departure days.

APPLICATION TIMETABLE

Interested participants should call for more information. Applications are processed in the order in which they are received.

FOR MORE INFORMATION, CONTACT

AAVE Teen Adventures
2308 Fossil Trace Drive
Golden, Colorado 80401
Phone: 303-526-0806
      800-222-3595 (toll-free)
Fax: 303-526-0885
E-mail: info@aave.com
Web site: http://www.aave.com

PARTICIPANT/FAMILY COMMENTS

"I saw my first shooting star, slept on beaches, planned and cooked meals, had plenty of water fights, and climbed a 14,000-foot peak."

"Not only do I recommend AAVE, I think it should be required for all!"

ACADEMIC CAMPS AT GETTYSBURG COLLEGE

Gettysburg COLLEGE

SUMMER ACADEMIC CAMPS

GETTYSBURG, PENNSYLVANIA

TYPE OF PROGRAM: Academic enrichment
PARTICIPANTS: Coeducational, students entering grades 9–12
ENROLLMENT: 50–100 students each session
PROGRAM DATES: Multiple two-week sessions in June and July
HEAD OF PROGRAM: Douglas Murphy, Executive Director

LOCATION
Academic Camps at Gettysburg College (ACGC) is located in Gettysburg, Pennsylvania, on the campus of the nationally recognized, coeducational residential college of liberal arts and sciences. Just 80 minutes by car from Washington, D.C., the campus lies on 200 acres in a historic town that is home to an array of stores, restaurants, and cultural and historical attractions, including Gettysburg National Military Park.

BACKGROUND AND PHILOSOPHY
The ACGC experience is a two-week-long immersion in a stimulating and fun on-campus academic environment. Designed to further its participants' scholastic aptitude and broaden their academic interests within a dynamic, structured environment, the program's unique curricular approach was developed specifically to pique the students' interests and challenge their abilities. Academic Camps at Gettysburg combines rigorous yet interesting academic endeavors during the day with great evening and weekend activities.

PROGRAM OFFERINGS
Astronomy Gettysburg's summer astronomy students have full use of all of the College's state-of-the-art facilities, including the Hayden Planetarium, a radio telescope, 8-inch Celestron and Meade telescopes, computer labs, and bright night skies. Program activities include charting stars and solar systems, observing solar flares, and building spectroscopes and sundials. In addition, all students visit the National Air and Space Museum, the Naval Observatory (where students receive privileged access to areas that are otherwise restricted), and the Maryland Science Center.

College Prep and Preview ACGC's College Prep and Preview gives high school students a head start on the college admission process. By the end of the session, each student has developed her or his own college plan. Classes include SAT Prep; Writing for College–Applications and Essays; Writing for College–Academic Papers, Clubs, and Volunteerism; Choosing a College; The College Admissions Process; and Social Life at College. Off-campus field trips might include visits to local colleges for tours and visits with admissions officers.

Service and Leadership In this program, students learn to set service-oriented goals for improving the well-being of a population, an environment, or a way of life. The satisfaction that comes from guiding a plan through to fruition is deeply rewarding. Throughout this two-week workshop, students develop their leadership skills and the ability to work effectively in teams. They engage in hands-on projects and off-campus mini-internship experiences. All instruction is geared toward the creation of new skills to effect change, both interpersonally and within the local community. Gettysburg College's proximity to Washington, D.C., is invaluable in learning about and addressing service issues.

Spanish Language and Culture The program is designed for any ability level and is based not on rote memorization, but rather

on conversation. Offering a unique linguistic learning environment, the program provides students with the opportunity to speak their selected language in a real-life setting. Cultural awareness is learned through teaching traditional geographic areas, traditions, customs, and foods. In addition, campers enjoy an exploration of cultures, which might include learning folk dances, cooking dishes from specific regions, or taking a field trip to Manhattan for foreign language–themed productions on or off Broadway.

U.S. Civil War This program takes advantage of the amazing resources offered by the College, including teachers and teachings from the Civil War Institute (CWI) and its surroundings. Whether students are Civil War buffs or they simply have an interest in history, this program enhances their understanding of the Civil War and how it shaped the nation. Topics include the events that led to war (a broad introduction that explores the issues of slavery, economics, and the cultural clash between North and South in the antebellum period and the decade of crisis that began in 1850), the conflict (an examination of the lives of soldiers, civilians, and leaders as well as the details and consequences of military operations), and Reconstruction (a study of the Civil War's aftermath from social, economic, and political perspectives).

Creative Writing Workshop Students who love to write and students who want to improve their writing abilities get the opportunity to work in intensive writing workshops of limited size; discussion and ideas abound. This program is a comprehensive education in the craft of writing, and it outlines the lessons students need in order to be good writers. Main topics covered by the students include an introduction to writing, the mechanics of creative writing, journaling, poetry, and fiction writing. Off-campus field trips might include a visit to a major publishing house and talks with writers, editors, and others in the field.

Psychology The study of consciousness, the subconscious, and behavior is a favorite among college students everywhere. This intensive course, which was designed by a member of Gettysburg's faculty, utilizes the College's resources. The curriculum revolves around the core philosophies of the Psychology Department. Students experience class work at a level that demands focus and concentration. This is a great opportunity to survey the major areas of study in psychology today. The program features hands-on studies and compelling lectures that touch on the many ways students can contribute to the field. Some of the areas of study that are currently producing exciting results are human interaction, mental illness, infant development, personality, adolescent behavior, the brain and the mind, chemicals and drugs as they impact human experiences, and detailed examination of emotional and cognitive processing on a biological level.

Performing Arts Beginning with the building blocks of acting, students learn the tools professional actors use to create believable performances by working on scenes, monologues, and speeches. ACGC builds on this by allowing campers to study improv and musical theater. Students are asked if they are comfortable in front of an audience, if they can be put on the spot, and what improv games they have tried. The weeks are then rounded out with dramatic acting, when everything the students have learned is brought together. They can practice dialogue, monologue, emotional expression, voice, and more.

DAILY SCHEDULE

Though actual schedules may vary, the following is a typical schedule for program participants.

7:30	Rise and shine
8:00	Breakfast
9:00	Announcements
9:15–10:30	Classroom session I
10:30–10:45	Morning break
10:45–12:00	Classroom session II
12:00– 1:00	Lunch
1:15– 2:30	Classroom session III
2:30– 2:45	Afternoon break
2:45– 4:00	Classroom session IV
4:00– 5:30	Sports, activities, free time
5:30– 6:30	Dinner
7:00– 8:00	Special events
8:00–11:00	Movies, games, free time
11:00	Students in rooms (most nights)

ENROLLMENT

To allow for small classes with individual attention, ACGC enrolls a maximum of 100 campers each session.

EXTRA OPPORTUNITIES AND ACTIVITIES

Each two-week session incorporates a Saturday excursion, which is known as SuperSaturday, to Hersheypark. Session 1 students get to see Civil War reenactments.

Each academic camp goes on unique and exciting field trip adventures. Depending on the program, participants might visit a major college or university in the area, science centers or planetariums, Spanish-themed events or restaurants, or a major publishing house to meet authors and editors.

FACILITIES

All students stay overnight in the College's spectacular dormitory facilities and enjoy the first-rate services and amenities that full-time Gettysburg students experience during the school year. Campers are supervised by adult and junior counselors who live in the dorms with them.

STAFF

Intelligent and energetic, the staff is the heart of the ACGC experience. From professional teachers to talented graduate and undergraduate students, all staff members participate in safety and training sessions. The maximum student-teacher ratio is 8:1.

MEDICAL CARE

Medical care is available 24 hours a day at nearby hospital facilities. All participants must submit comprehensive medical forms and proof of insurance.

COSTS

The tuition for each two-week session is $2395. This includes all instruction; instructional materials; breakfast, lunch, and dinner each day; a dorm room with linens; self-service laundry facilities; all sports and recreational activities; transportation for sponsored trips; admission tickets to excursion destinations; and total 24-hour supervision for the duration of each camp session. In addition, there is a $100 field trip account, which allocates spending money to each student for field trips.

FINANCIAL AID

No financial aid is available at this time.

TRANSPORTATION

Transportation to and from Baltimore/Washington International Airport is available for an additional fee.

APPLICATION TIMETABLE

Inquiries are welcome at any time. Applications are accepted until June 1. After June 1, acceptance to the program is based on availability, and applications must include a late fee of $100.

FOR MORE INFORMATION, CONTACT

Academic Camps at Gettysburg College
300 North Washington Street, Box 2994
Gettysburg, Pennsylvania 17325

Phone: 800-289-7029 (toll-free)
Web site: http://www.gettysburg.edu/academiccamps/

ACADEMIC STUDY ASSOCIATES SUMMER PROGRAMS

ASA
ACADEMIC
STUDY
ASSOCIATES

PRECOLLEGE, STUDY ABROAD, LANGUAGE IMMERSION, AND COLLEGE ADMISSIONS PREP PROGRAMS IN THE U.S., EUROPE, AND COSTA RICA

AMHERST AND BOSTON, MASSACHUSETTS; BERKELEY, CALIFORNIA; AND NEW YORK, NEW YORK
OXFORD AND CAMBRIDGE, ENGLAND; ITALY; FRANCE; SPAIN; AND COSTA RICA

TYPE OF PROGRAM: Academic enrichment, language immersion, and college admissions prep
PARTICIPANTS: Coeducational, students completing grades 9–12
ENROLLMENT: Varies by program, rolling admissions
PROGRAM DATES: Most programs run during the month of July; for detailed information, students should visit http://www.asaprograms.com
HEAD OF PROGRAM: Marcia E. Evans, President

LOCATION
Academic Study Associates (ASA) uses four of the world's most magnificent college campuses and several of the hottest international destinations as backdrops for their summer programs.

BACKGROUND AND PHILOSOPHY
Since 1984, ASA has offered the finest educational opportunities for students in both the United States and Europe. ASA's academic enrichment programs have an excellent reputation for providing students with an exciting and challenging educational experience as well as an environment in which they can sample the academic, social, and recreational aspects of college life and immerse themselves in an international culture.

PROGRAM OFFERINGS
Precollege Full access to the extensive academic, sports, and recreational facilities make the ASA U.S. precollege summer program at either the University of California, Berkeley, or the University of Massachusetts Amherst a perfect way to study, make new friends, and enjoy an unforgettable summer. College credit courses are available at UMass. Students select one major and one elective from a large variety of courses in many academic disciplines, from math and writing to marketing and psychology. Courses are held in the format of a college seminar and incorporate interactive exchange between teachers and students. In addition to enrichment courses, students at all ASA campuses have the opportunity to take SAT Preparation, which is designed and taught by the Princeton Review. SAT classes are small and are tailored to students' individual needs.

Study Abroad Three- to four-week summer study-abroad programs in England (Oxford or Cambridge) and Italy (Florence) combine a taste of college life with exploration of another culture. There are excellent classes in exciting subjects, a wide range of activities to choose from, and guided excursions to all the best sights in the area.

Language Immersion Monthlong language and cultural immersion programs include dorm living and homestays in France (Nice and Royan) and Spain (Barcelona and Andalusia) and homestays with community service in Costa Rica. Daily language classes are taught by native speakers, and there are

electives and activities in everything from surfing and Flamenco guitar to French cinema and cooking plus excursions to all the best sights in the area.

College Admissions Prep (CAP) Students improve their SAT scores, write a personal statement, and get prepared to apply for college. They choose from three unique campuses—from West Coast to East, public and private, large or small. Each two-week ASA College Admissions Prep experience provides the same curriculum, along with visits to three other campuses.

ENROLLMENT
Enrollment varies by program. Precollege programs accept students in grades 9–12; language immersion programs welcome applicants in grades 10–12; CAP programs accept students in grades 10–11. Students should contact ASA directly for specific program information.

EXTRA OPPORTUNITIES AND ACTIVITIES
ASA programs take full advantage of local areas of interest and cultural attractions. In all programs, a wide range of optional recreational and social activities are organized in the afternoon and evening. These vary by location and include team sports such as soccer, softball, basketball, tennis, and volleyball; intramural competitions; working on the yearbook; or working on

a community service project. Evening activities include dances, movies, theater performances, ice skating, bowling, concerts, talent shows, and games.

Weekends are reserved for fully supervised excursions that allow students an opportunity to visit area attractions. Students can often take advantage of guided tours and independent time to shop, eat, and explore.

At several locations, optional excursions to New York City, Rome, Paris, Seville, Granada, and the Loire Valley are open to students. (Some trips require an additional fee.) For a detailed list of activities and excursions, students should visit http://www.asaprograms.com.

DAILY SCHEDULE

7:30– 8:30 . . .	Breakfast
9:00–12:00 . . .	Major course
12:15– 1:15 . . .	Lunch
1:30– 4:30 . . .	Recreation, activities, and mini-courses
4:30– 6:00 . . .	Elective
6:00– 7:00 . . .	Dinner
7:30–10:30 . . .	Evening activities
11:00 . . .	Students in dormitories (weekdays)
12:00 . . .	Weekend curfew

FACILITIES

Residential Programs: All students are housed in residence halls at each campus and have access to many campus amenities, such as libraries, art rooms, athletic facilities, swimming pools, and coffee bars. Staff members live on each floor, and the dorms are the hub of many activities. Meals are provided in the dining rooms of the colleges.

Homestay Programs: The utmost care is given to selecting host families for ASA's homestay programs. Most families have many years' experience hosting international students, and all are carefully screened. Homes are often modest but comfortable, and ASA students live relatively close to their classes and to each other.

STAFF

Marcia Evans, ASA's founder and president, has a noteworthy educational background and wide professional experience as a teacher and educational consultant in England and the United States. The administrative and supervisory staff members are all professional educators and graduate students from the finest schools in the United States and abroad. The program's academic courses are taught by professors, teachers, and teaching assistants from leading colleges and schools. The residen-

tial and recreational components of the program are under the supervision of carefully selected college students who attend an extensive training program before the summer begins.

MEDICAL CARE

There are medical facilities within easy reach of all the program sites. Each student submits a medical form and release form before joining the program. Staff members accompany students to medical facilities.

COSTS

Program fees vary by location. Students should visit http://www.asaprograms.com for detailed information about tuition and supplemental fees.

Fees include tuition, accommodations, three meals daily (two meals a day at Oxford, Cambridge, and Florence), use of most college facilities, all scheduled excursions (except optional trips), the scheduled afternoon and evening recreational program, and transportation from and to the local airports. Courses that carry supplemental fees are noted on ASA's Web site. The fee for Spanish in Espana includes airfare.

APPLICATION TIMETABLE

Initial inquiries are welcome at any time. Students should visit http://www.asaprograms.com to request a brochure or complete an application. ASA representatives are always available by phone to answer questions. Applications are accepted on a rolling basis starting in September, but students are advised to apply early to ensure placement in their first-choice courses, as class size is limited. In addition to the application, ASA requires a teacher recommendation before acceptance can be confirmed. A phone interview is required of homestay applicants. Students are notified of acceptance within fourteen days of receipt of all application materials.

FOR MORE INFORMATION, CONTACT

Academic Study Associates
375 West Broadway, Suite 200
New York, New York 10012
Phone: 212-796-8340
          800-752-2250 (toll-free outside New York State)
Fax: 212-334-4934
E-mail: summer@asaprograms.com
Web site: http://www.asaprograms.com

PARTICIPANT/FAMILY COMMENTS

"This program was fun, exciting, and challenging. I took great classes and made friends from all over the world. Thank you ASA!"

"I got a great taste of college life and feel better prepared academically and socially for when I go to college."

ACADEMY BY THE SEA/ CAMP PACIFIC

SUMMER PROGRAMS

CARLSBAD, CALIFORNIA

TYPE OF PROGRAM: Academic program (grades 7–10), recreational camp (ages 8–16), and Surf and Body-board Camp (ages 8–16)

PARTICIPANTS: All programs are coeducational

ENROLLMENT: Academic program: 150–180, Camp Pacific: 50–80, Surf and Bodyboard Camp: 50–80

PROGRAM DATES: Academic Program: approximately five weeks in July and August; Camp Pacific: two- and three-week sessions in June and July; Surf and Bodyboard Camp: one-week session, June–August

HEAD OF PROGRAM: Mr. Jeffrey Barton, Director of Summer Programs

LOCATION

The Academy by the Sea/Camp Pacific is held on the Army and Navy Academy campus in the beautiful coastal town of Carlsbad, California. The campus is located on 16 acres of prime oceanfront property. The average temperature in Carlsbad from June to August is 75 degrees. Students and campers stay in dormitories (2–3 per room) and eat at the on-campus dining facility.

BACKGROUND AND PHILOSOPHY

The Camp Pacific program was founded in 1943 as an all-boys' surfing camp. Since then, the program has grown to offer a wide variety of sessions for both boys and girls. The camp's philosophy is to provide a safe and fun environment in which young people can learn and grow.

PROGRAM OFFERINGS

Academic Programs The Academy by the Sea's summer session offers a coeducational program that balances academics and recreation for a fulfilling educational experience. The Academy offers a variety of class subjects, and students are expected to pick the four classes to comprise their summer schedules. Students have the option of being boarding or day students. Boarding is encouraged, as the dormitory experience is an important part of a student's overall learning and enjoyment. Boarding students also have the benefit of participating in a mandatory evening study hall and afternoon activities. The summer academic session classes are small (generally 6–10 students), and individual participation is required. Subjects offered include math, English, science, oceanography, creative writing, computers, history, Spanish, English as a second language, and various electives. Designated courses may be taken for a semester of high school credit. Afternoon activities, special events, and weekend excursions allow each student the opportunity to take a break from scholastic responsibilities and experience lasting friendships and fun.

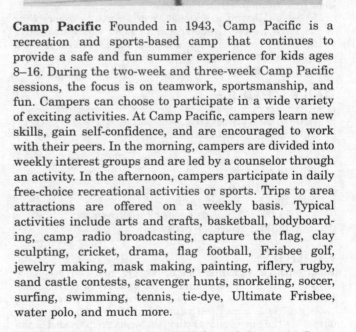

Camp Pacific Founded in 1943, Camp Pacific is a recreation and sports-based camp that continues to provide a safe and fun summer experience for kids ages 8–16. During the two-week and three-week Camp Pacific sessions, the focus is on teamwork, sportsmanship, and fun. Campers can choose to participate in a wide variety of exciting activities. At Camp Pacific, campers learn new skills, gain self-confidence, and are encouraged to work with their peers. In the morning, campers are divided into weekly interest groups and are led by a counselor through an activity. In the afternoon, campers participate in daily free-choice recreational activities or sports. Trips to area attractions are offered on a weekly basis. Typical activities include arts and crafts, basketball, bodyboarding, camp radio broadcasting, capture the flag, clay sculpting, cricket, drama, flag football, Frisbee golf, jewelry making, mask making, painting, riflery, rugby, sand castle contests, scavenger hunts, snorkeling, soccer, surfing, swimming, tennis, tie-dye, Ultimate Frisbee, water polo, and much more.

Camp Pacific's Surf and Bodyboard Camp At Camp Pacific's Surf and Bodyboard Camp, the goal is to provide each camper with an unforgettable experience. The Surf and Bodyboard Camp is designed for all skill levels, from beginner to intermediate. The session is one week in duration and is full of activities. Group beach instruction, classroom instruction, independent practice, and field trips all combine for a very exciting week of learning. Campers are taught skills in equipment options, wave selection, and basic surf techniques. All activities are supervised by counselors, certified lifeguards, and experienced surfing and bodyboarding instructors. In the afternoons, campers can continue their practice at the beach or participate in the variety of activities enjoyed by participants in the three-week Camp Pacific, listed above. Surfers and bodyboarders from the ages of 8 to 16 are eligible.

ENROLLMENT

The academic program enrolls between 150 and 180 students. Camp Pacific enrolls between 50 and 80 campers. The Surf and Bodyboard Camp enrolls between 50 and 80 campers.

EXTRA OPPORTUNITIES AND ACTIVITIES

Each program offers a wide variety of fun and educational activities. On weekends, the five-week and three-week groups participate in outings to popular southern California destinations such as theme parks, sporting events, museums, and beaches.

FACILITIES

Boarding students and campers live in dormitories that house 2–3 people per room. Dormitories are important centers of activity where friendships with peers and counselors are formed. Each dormitory is supervised by resident faculty members and counselors who serve as advisers to students and campers, ensuring that an adult is always available for assistance and guidance. Boys and girls are housed in separate dormitories. Rooms are furnished with beds, desks, and bureaus. Each student or camper is responsible for the condition of his or her room. Although the basic organization of the dormitories is informal, constant faculty presence is essential to develop an atmosphere of learning and safety. Students and campers receive three meals each day, served at the dining hall. Security personnel are on campus 24 hours a day. Campus facilities include tennis courts, private beach access, a swimming pool, athletic fields, an on-campus dining facility, an oceanfront recreation hall, a chapel, a library, a radio station, health center, and an indoor gymnasium and weight room.

STAFF

For the academic session, experienced teachers and administrators provide classroom instruction and overall supervision of academics, dormitories, and campus life. For Camp Pacific sessions, college and university students, selected for their demonstrated responsibility and experience, live in the dormitories and serve as counselors and resident assistants. All staff members successfully complete a thorough background check and drug test.

MEDICAL CARE

Medical personnel are on campus, and a physician is on call 24 hours a day. Due to the high cost of hospitalization, it is required that all students enroll in a medical insurance program prior to arriving at The Academy by the Sea/Camp Pacific. All international campers must have a temporary U.S. medical insurance policy, for which an additional fee is charged.

COSTS

Costs vary according to the program. Costs for the 2007 season are as follows: Academic Session, $4725; Camp Pacific recreational camp, $1690 for a two-week session or $2445 for a three-week session; and Surf and Bodyboard Camp, $880. An incidental account of between $200 and $450 is required for academic and recreational sessions. For any inquiries, prospective campers and their families should contact the camp's office or visit the Web site at http://www.abts.com.

TRANSPORTATION

With advance notice, students and campers can be transported to and from San Diego International Airport, Los Angeles International Airport, Carlsbad Airport, or Oceanside Amtrak Train Station for a nominal fee.

APPLICATION TIMETABLE

Applications are preferred before May 15; however, they are accepted until enrollment is full.

FOR MORE INFORMATION, CONTACT

Academy by the Sea/Camp Pacific
P.O. Box 3000
Carlsbad, California 92018-3000
Phone: 760-434-7564
        877-581-9283 (toll-free)
Fax: 760-729-1574
E-mail: summer@abts.com
Web site: http://www.abts.com

ACADIA INSTITUTE OF OCEANOGRAPHY

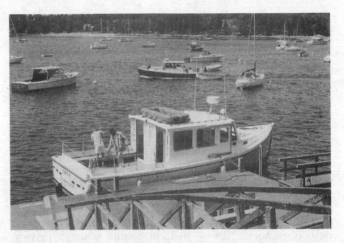

MARINE SCIENCE PROGRAM

MOUNT DESERT ISLAND, MAINE

TYPE OF PROGRAM: Educational camping program in marine science and oceanography

PARTICIPANTS: Coeducational, ages 10–18

ENROLLMENT: 45 students per session

PROGRAM DATES: Five sessions per summer, mid-June to mid-August

HEAD OF PROGRAM: Sheryl Christy Gilmore, Executive Director

LOCATION

The Acadia Institute of Oceanography (AIO) is based in the picturesque village of Seal Harbor on the southern end of Mount Desert Island, Maine, approximately 5 hours north of Boston along one of the most beautiful coastlines in the United States. Located adjacent to Acadia National Park, the program is housed three blocks from the harbor in a vintage schoolhouse that serves as the base of operations for this field-oriented program.

BACKGROUND AND PHILOSOPHY

The Acadia Institute of Oceanography is a one-of-a-kind educational experience for students ages 10 to 18. Since 1975, AIO has introduced young people to the world of marine science through a curriculum that combines the basic elements of biological, physical, and chemical oceanography with field, classroom, offshore, and laboratory work.

AIO seeks highly motivated students for participation in the program. All are expected to arrive with a curious mind and a commitment to learn. A science teacher's recommendation is required for admission.

PROGRAM OFFERINGS

Mount Desert Island is the perfect location to study marine ecology. Waters are rich in plankton, and there are many species of fish. Rocky tidal pools shelter invertebrates, rivers and estuaries serve as ocean nurseries, and offshore dredges yield sediments full of benthic life. The AIO program makes full use of the natural environment. Sample activities include tidal pool study; beach profiles; coastal transects; geologic profiles; algal study; seabirds, seals, and cetacean observations; chemical study of a fjord (Somes Sound); island ecology; plankton collection and study; dissections; developmental biology; fishing; navigation; and whale watching.

Over the course of a summer, AIO offers a one-week introductory session and four 2-week sessions. Two of these are basic sessions and two are advanced.

The introductory session is for students (ages 10 to 12) who have a strong interest in ocean life and wish to begin their lifelong study of marine concepts. The basic sessions are designed for students, ages 12 to 15. These courses present a solid natural-history approach to oceanography and introduce students to marine concepts and laboratory procedures. Many students who attend a basic session return another year for an advanced session.

The advanced sessions are precollege courses offered to students, ages 15 to 18, who have completed a minimum of high school–level biology or chemistry. These students are expected to prepare laboratory reports and do analysis of their field work.

ENROLLMENT

Each summer, students come to AIO from all over North America and around the world. Individual sessions are limited to 45 students.

DAILY SCHEDULE

The edge of the sea is AIO's classroom, and academic activities follow the tides. While one group of student oceanographers might finish a transect of the beach, another group collects specimens for the cold water tanks in the wet lab. Others may have focused their binoculars on the seabirds and cetaceans that swim offshore.

Mini-seminars are offered before dinner for those students interested in pursuing more specialized topics. For early risers, AIO offers optional morning laboratory activities. Evenings are devoted to more traditional classroom academics. Each night, students attend a lecture to provide background

Collecting water samples and mud in Somes Sound.

information and prepare them for upcoming field activities. All students design and maintain a saltwater aquarium.

Despite the busy academic schedule, AIO leaves a block of time each day for recreational activities, such as hiking, swimming, group games, and visits to local laboratories and museums. There is plenty of free time for students to read, write letters, and relax.

EXTRA OPPORTUNITIES AND ACTIVITIES
Graduates of advanced sessions are eligible to apply for one of the programs offered by AIO during school vacations. A Marine Biology Career Seminar is scheduled to take place in Florida for nine days in November 2006. Students go behind the scenes to meet and work with rangers, scientists, and marine mammal trainers to explore potential careers in the field. AIO's ninth Tropical program is scheduled to take place at the Belize Marine Tropical Research and Education Center during Thanksgiving week of 2007. Students are chosen for these programs based on the quality of their past work and social maturity. Information is available during summer orientation meetings.

FACILITIES
The program is housed in the vintage Dunham Schoolhouse, built in 1931 by John D. Rockefeller. The building was acquired by AIO in 1976 and has been carefully restored. Accommodations are clean and comfortable. Three of the large classrooms have been converted into dormitories, and students sleep on bunk beds. The facility includes a lecture hall, a recreation room, a research wet laboratory, a library, a nurse's office, a dining room, bathrooms, and showers.

STAFF
At the heart of the program is an experienced and qualified core of educators trained in the field of oceanography. These are classroom teachers, practicing scientists, and researchers,

many with advanced graduate degrees. Each faculty member brings his or her own unique background to the program. The student-instructor ratio is approximately 4:1.

Other staff members include a nurse, a professional chef, and interns. Internships are offered to college students who have attended AIO previously and are seriously considering a career in marine studies and education.

MEDICAL CARE
A full-time registered nurse is on staff. There is a fully equipped hospital 8 miles away in Bar Harbor, and Eastern Maine Medical Center, a regional state-of-the-art medical facility, is located 1 hour away in the city of Bangor.

All students must have a health form completed by a physician before final acceptance into the program.

COSTS
For 2007, the cost was $1995 per two week session and $995 for the one-week session. The price includes tuition, room, board, and all program costs except for transportation to the site.

A small amount of spending money ($60–$70) is recommended for trips into Bar Harbor.

FINANCIAL AID
A limited number of partial scholarships are available at the discretion of the executive director. Students are asked for additional references and to provide written material in support of their application.

TRANSPORTATION
Transportation is available from the Bar Harbor-Hancock County Regional Airport or the Vermont/Greyhound terminal in Bar Harbor. Students can also be picked up at the Bangor International Airport for an additional fee.

APPLICATION TIMETABLE
Student registration begins in the fall and continues until all available slots are filled. Sessions typically begin filling by March, and most slots are filled by Memorial Day.

A $300 deposit and completed registration form are required at the time of application. Health and teacher recommendation forms are sent upon receipt of deposit. Notification of acceptance is given upon the return of a satisfactory recommendation.

FOR MORE INFORMATION, CONTACT
Sheryl Christy Gilmore, Executive Director
Acadia Institute of Oceanography
P.O. Box 2220
St. Augustine, Florida 32085
Phone: 800-375-0058 (toll-free)
      207-276-9825 (June 10–September 1 only)
E-mail: info@acadiainstitute.com
Web site: http://www.acadiainstitute.com

PARTICIPANT/FAMILY COMMENTS

"There is a wealth of knowledge to be gained at AIO; in the field, in the lecture hall and in discussions with other students and faculty."—Michael Harmon, student, Baltimore, Maryland

"Heather spent two great summers (at AIO) and was motivated beyond all expectations. She is very excited about her future in the Marine Sciences and AIO was the catalyst for sure."—Steve and Mary McRae, parents, Temple, New Hampshire

ACTEEN
ACTing for Teens

SUMMER PROGRAMS

NEW YORK, NEW YORK

TYPE OF PROGRAM: Acting conservatory with a film and television concentration
PARTICIPANTS: Coeducational, ages 13–15 and 16–20
ENROLLMENT: Limited to 20–30 students per session
PROGRAM DATES: June 23 to July 3, July 7 to July 31, August 4 to August 20, or July 12 to August 16 (Saturdays)
HEAD OF PROGRAM: Rita Litton, Director

LOCATION

ACTeen is located in New York City's Broadway theater district, near Rockefeller Center and Radio City Music Hall. ACTeen occupies the entire sixth floor of a midtown office building.

BACKGROUND AND PHILOSOPHY

ACTeen was created in 1978 by successful theater and commercial actress Rita Litton as the first on-camera acting curriculum for teenagers. Stories about ACTeen have appeared in the *New York Times, New York Magazine, Cosmopolitan,* and the *Wall Street Journal;* on television and news broadcasts; and in various acting books, including praise in *How to Be a Working Actor* by Mari Lyn Henry (former head of East Coast casting for ABC-TV) and *Acting Like a Pro* by Mary McTigue. ACTeen is consistently recommended to clients and prospective clients by more than 30 New York City talent agents and managers. Hundreds of ACTeen graduates have achieved successful careers in film, television, and the theater. Many ACTeen graduates have starred on TV series *(One Tree Hill, Related, Third Watch, That 70's Show, Charmed, The Sopranos, According to Jim, Boston Public, Sabrina the Teenage Witch, The Guardian, Homicide,* and *Freaks & Geeks)* each of the last nine seasons. Many alumni acquired their overall professionalism and first representation through ACTeen's industry showcases.

The ACTeen Summer Academy accepts dedicated beginners and preprofessionals, developing them into technically proficient, versatile, and marketable actors. ACTeen combines theatrical discipline with spontaneous, effective on-camera acting techniques, so students learn to successfully navigate both film and theater media with skill and professionalism. ACTeen believes that acting is action oriented and that emotions are the result of intentions successfully or unsuccessfully achieved. Therefore, various acting techniques are incorporated to offer more than one path to characterization. Students learn to function among diverse directors and actors with varying acting approaches. In addition, students benefit enormously from video playbacks (the "one picture is worth a thousand words" theory), which are an integral part of the on-camera acting classes and may be utilized in elective courses.

PROGRAM OFFERINGS

While ACTeen offers courses during the fall and spring, its summer academies are more extensive. ACTeen offers six different courses in the June academy, sixteen in the four-week July academy, and nine in the three-week August academy. Students may attend full-time or part-time. There is also a four-course, six-week Saturday-only summer session. A typical 29-hour week for students who attend ACTeen's July full-time summer academy includes 8 hours of on-camera acting technique and scene study, 4 hours of commercial audition skills, 3 hours of speech and voice, 3 hours of movement, 3 hours of improvisation, 4 hours of auditioning skills, and 4 hours of musical theater or Shakespeare. Various electives include directing and script writing. Students may choose from several course offerings, including those listed below.

Film Acting Technique Exercises involving intention, motivation, relationship, obstacles, and actions are tied to assigned film and television scripts to better relate process with result. All exercises and scenes are videotaped in a two-camera setup, and playback critiques are an essential part of class time.

Film Scene Study In multicamera studios, students explore the technique and emotional depth required for successful film acting. Emphasis is on creating characters common or unique to television and film—situation comedy, episodic TV, feature films, and daytime dramas.

Commercial Audition Technique Successful on-camera commercial audition techniques are taught while encouraging the actor's natural delivery and unique personality. Students perform all work on videotape and audition privately for a guest casting director. Copyrighted text includes valuable information on agents, unions, photos, and getting started professionally.

Improvisation Using the wonderful theater games of Viola Spolin and Keith Johnstone, actors learn to listen, work creatively and physically, and channel fears into actions.

Movement for Actors Work includes centers, rotations, transformations, posture, and Alexander Technique.

Musical Theater An audition workshop is taught by an established New York City vocal coach and musical director.

Script Writing Students learn to refine plot structure, character, dialogue, and conflict while creating a short one-act script. This workshop is taught by an award-winning playwright/screenwriter.

Shakespeare Students explore the wonderful challenges and vocal demands of Shakespeare's characters and text.

Speech and Voice This workshop develops the flexibility and musicality of the actor's speaking voice. Speech exercises on phonetics develop standardized American speech, while voice work develops breath control, resonance, and tone.

ENROLLMENT

Previous students have come to ACTeen from all over the world. Class size for each workshop is extremely limited—6 to 12 students maximum—for utmost personal attention. ACTeen seeks bright, dedicated teens who love to act. Prior experience is recommended but not required. Students requiring housing must be at least 17 years old by the summer to qualify for suggested off-site housing.

DAILY SCHEDULE

Classes meet Monday through Thursday from 9 to 5 and Friday from 10 to 3 (June), Monday through Thursday from 9 to 5 (July), or Monday through Friday from 9:30 to 5 (August), with appropriate lunch breaks. Students have the option of attending part-time. Beyond the classroom, students must devote time to homework preparation.

EXTRA OPPORTUNITIES AND ACTIVITIES

ACTeen has a special VIP guest series on selected evenings, during which visiting professionals share their insights and expertise. In addition, students enrolled in the Audition Workshop work closely with New York City industry guests, including a Broadway director, a film/theater casting director, a commercial casting director, a monologue coach, and guest professional actors.

FACILITIES

ACTeen has seven air-conditioned on-camera video studios. Three studios are equipped with double cameras and simultaneous editing equipment. There are three lounges and office space.

STAFF

The staff is exemplary and includes adults from professional acting, directing, and casting backgrounds. Many also teach in colleges, universities, and other acting conservatories, and the majority hold advanced degrees. Full-time academy students work with 6 to 8 different experienced instructors as well as special guest artists. The small class size enables a close personal relationship between students and faculty members. Teachers work creatively to tailor scenes and exercises to best stimulate each student.

COSTS

Tuition for full-time programs ranges from $1450 to $1600 in June, $1950 to $2700 in July, and $1300 to $2250 in August. Individual courses cost $300 to $350, with discounts for mul-

tiple course selection. Limited scholarships are available for male actors via the Will Sears Scholarship Fund. ACTeen does not maintain housing or off-studio supervision for its out-of-state academy participants. However, affordable dormitory or apartment-style rooms are available at discounted rates for accepted ACTeen registrants (over age 17 only) through May 1. Fees range from $1000 to $2000 per month. Students may request a housing list after they submit their applications.

TRANSPORTATION

ACTeen's midtown location is ideally situated so that all public transportation is accessible. ACTeen is within walking distance of all the suburban transportation hubs, including Grand Central Station, Penn Station, and the Port Authority Bus Terminal.

APPLICATION TIMETABLE

ACTeen prefers on-site auditions and interviews, if possible. Long-distance applicants should request a registration packet. Completed summer applications (available online, under Download Forms) are accepted November through June, but Summer Academy students are advised to apply early, preferably by April 1, for the best housing opportunities. Tuition discounts are typically available through April 15.

FOR MORE INFORMATION, CONTACT

Rita Litton, ACTeen Director
ACTeen
35 West 45th Street, 6th Floor
New York, New York 10036
Phone: 212-391-5915
Fax: 212-768-8918
E-mail: rita@acteen.com
Web site: http://www.acteen.com

PARTICIPANT/FAMILY COMMENTS

"ACTeen gave me great training and audition confidence."—Daniella Alonso (WB's *One Tree Hill, As the World Turns*)

"I went from knowing nothing about the business to booking a soap opera thanks to ACTeen. They prepared me totally for auditions."—Jordana Brewster (*Annapolis, Fast and the Furious, The Faculty*)

"ACTeen was definitely the best decision I made that summer! Rita Litton is great at making teenagers feel confident—a gargantuan task."—Jenna Lamia (*Without a Trace, Law & Order SVU, NYPD Blue*)

ACTIONQUEST

WORLDWIDE ADVENTURES IN SAILING, SCUBA DIVING, AND MARINE SCIENCE

![ActionQuest logo]

SUMMER PROGRAMS

CARIBBEAN, MEDITERRANEAN, GALAPAGOS, AUSTRALIA, AND TAHITI VOYAGES

TYPE OF PROGRAM: Live-aboard sailing and diving global expeditions: beginner and advanced sail training, all levels of scuba diving certifications, marine science, water sports, cultural and historical shore exploration, and community service. Participants are challenged with high action, life-changing adventures that promote personal growth, team-work, and leadership. No previous experience necessary.

PARTICIPANTS: Coed, ages 13–18, grouped by grade.

ENROLLMENT: More than 400 shipmates in seventeen different voyage programs grouped by age and grade. Group size ranges from 10 to 60.

PROGRAM DATES: Two-, three-, five-, and six-week programs from June through August.

HEADS OF PROGRAM: Mike Meighan, B.Sc.; James Stoll, Master Mariner

LOCATION

ActionQuest offers programs for students of all levels, beginner through advanced, in the British Virgin Islands, the Leeward Islands, the Mediterranean, Galapagos, Australia, and Tahiti. Participants in all programs live aboard 50-foot sailing yachts and catamarans while voyaging from island to island.

BACKGROUND AND PHILOSOPHY

For over thirty years, ActionQuest has consistently delivered high-quality expedition-based summer programs for teenagers. Through hands-on experiential learning and adventure travel throughout the world, AQ has successfully ignited the inherent leadership skills within thousands of young adults. The AQ path offers action-packed adventures that focus on sailing, scuba diving, cultural immersion, marine biology, and global exploration—all in a "live-aboard" environment unlike any other. Centered on small, coed, age-appropriate groups of 8 to 20 teenagers, the experience is complemented by a committed, professional staff whose main goal is to support their shipmates' discovery. The individual attention and camaraderie between staff and shipmates makes each voyage unique, as the entire team unites to accomplish the AQ mission of high action, real-world learning.

PROGRAM OFFERINGS

British Virgin Islands Vega and Quest voyages are designed for shipmates with little or no previous experience and offer the broadest adventure activities. Shipmates earn sailing and diving certifications through International Yachtmaster Training (IYT) and the Professional Association of Diving Instructors (PADI). Waterskiing, windsurfing, small-boat sailing, and nautical training round out the program. For the more seasoned sailor or diver, programs are available for shipmates to build on their skills and earn IYT sailing certifications up to and including the Basic Flotilla Skipper Certificate and PADI Advanced and Specialty certifications. ActionQuest is the only fully accredited PADI International Five-Star Gold Palm Facility dedicated entirely to teenagers. For those already dive-certified, distinctive voyages offer participants multiple certifications while living aboard sailing yachts and diving to explore

the rich coral reefs of the British Virgin Islands (BVI). Students receive training in safe diving practices from Advanced levels through to professional Divemaster level. These voyages are designed for teens ages 13–18 who have already been certified by any organization. Program offerings include PADI Advanced and Junior Advanced Open Water, Rescue Diver, Master Scuba Diver, and Divemaster as well as ten different PADI specialties.

Tropical Marine Biology voyages, conducted by staff marine biologists, are live-aboard programs combining diving and field studies with marine sciences. This program is designed for participants interested in studying the coral reefs and participating in underwater research to build knowledge in this dynamic area of environmental science. High school credit documentation is available on request.

The Leeward Islands Voyage is a fast-paced sailing, hiking, and shore exploration adventure that visits ten different islands on a voyage that stretches from the BVI to the island of Antigua and back. Depending on previous experience, shipmates may earn IYT sailing certifications from International Crew Certificate to Basic Flotilla Skipper Certificate. Hiking the hand-carved steps to Mt. Scenery at Saba, exploring the rain forest and volcanic terrain of Nevis, and snorkeling the reefs of Ile Forche are some of the highlights.

The Mediterranean Voyage sails the French and Italian rivieras to ports of call that include Nice, Cannes, Corsica, Sardinia, Rome, Elba, Portofino, and Monte Carlo. This voyage combines offshore sailing skills with cultural and historical exploration.

The Galapagos Archipelago Experience combines snorkeling and hiking the main islands of the Galapagos with an expedition to Ecuador. Nature study, rain-forest trekking, white-water rafting, community service, and cultural exploration are part of the voyage.

The Australia and Great Barrier Reef Adventure encompasses exploration of Sydney, live-aboard sailing and diving in the Whitsunday Islands, and action-packed touring in Queensland—an incredible way to experience the land down under.

The Tahiti Voyage is an experience set in the exotic tropical South Seas. These volcanic islands offer lush rain forests, blue lagoons, and dazzling reefs and have a history rich with tradition. Activities include interisland sailing, snorkeling, trekking, and community service.

ENROLLMENT
Every year, more than 400 shipmates and staff members from at least thirty-three different states and fifteen other countries participate. Coed crew members are grouped according to age and grade. Shipmates live together on yachts while sailing in a fleet in the BVIs. Other locations are single- or two-boat programs. Small groups and close working relationships help build lasting friendships and allow for a strongly beneficial experience in teamwork.

DAILY SCHEDULE
About the only thing typical of the ActionQuest day is that there is no such thing as a typical day. The days are as varied as the activities pursued. A rotation of positions aboard allows shipmates to develop diverse skills—whether as skipper of the day or chef. Regardless of prior experience, the first time the yachts sail from the dock, it is a shipmate who takes the helm under the guidance of licensed sailing masters. Whether participants are sailing, scuba diving, trekking, or simply taking in the local sights and sounds, each day is another opportunity to make life extraordinary.

EXTRA OPPORTUNITIES AND ACTIVITIES
Although all shipmates participate in most of the core certification programs, the optional Action Credit program is designed to quantify what is learned and accomplished during the voyage. The program encompasses forty-five skills useful both on and off the water. ActionQuest also offers Sea|mester programs (global semester-at-sea voyages for college students) and Lifeworks international service-learning programs (http://www.lifeworks-international.com).

FACILITIES
All shipmates live aboard modern, fully equipped 50-foot sailing yachts or catamarans, each containing five cabins with four

bathrooms and showers. Ninety sets of dive gear are carried with more than 120 tanks and nine ski boats. Laser sailboats, Mistral windsurfers, wake boards, water skis, and all other training equipment are provided.

STAFF
Sailing and diving instructors are fully licensed and certified men and women eager to share their areas of expertise. They come from a variety of backgrounds. Many have been with ActionQuest for years. Among the more than 40 staff members are 15 USCG-licensed Sailing Masters, 15 PADI-certified dive instructors, and those assisting in other activities. No other U.S.-based program can offer their combined level of certification and experience. The staff-shipmate ratio is 1:4, and the average staff age is 27.

COSTS
Program costs for two- and three-week voyages in 2007 ranged from $3670 to $4970. Five- and six-week program costs vary, depending upon courses chosen.

TRANSPORTATION
Shipmates fly in small groups, and staff assistance is available at arrival airports.

APPLICATION TIMETABLE
Applications are accepted at any time. Some programs fill up faster in certain age groups than in others. Some fill up in February, but most are full by April. Students should call for information on availability if applying late.

FOR MORE INFORMATION, CONTACT
ActionQuest
P.O. Box 5517
Sarasota, Florida 34277
Phone: 941-924-6789
        800-317-6789 (toll-free)
Fax: 941-924-6075
E-mail: info@actionquest.com
Web site: http://www.actionquest.com

PARTICIPANT/FAMILY COMMENTS

"In three weeks, I made the best of friends, had the best times, and learned things I will never ever forget. Thank you for everything you taught me."

"We had high expectations and they were exceeded. The increase in self-confidence and the motivation and skills learned were most valuable."

AFS INTERCULTURAL PROGRAMS/USA

SUMMER PROGRAMS

AFRICA, ASIA AND THE PACIFIC, EUROPE, AND LATIN AMERICA

TYPE OF PROGRAM: Summer Homestay: Language Study, Homestay Plus, Soccer, or Community Service/Team Mission

PARTICIPANTS: Coeducational, ages 15–18

ENROLLMENT: Varies, depending on program

PROGRAM DATES: Four- to eight-week sessions

LOCATION

AFS offers summer exchange programs for young people, ages 15–18 in more than twenty countries, such as Argentina, Australia, Brazil, Chile, China, Costa Rica, Ecuador, Finland, France, Ghana, Hungary, Italy, Japan, Latvia, New Zealand, Panama, Paraguay, Spain, Thailand, Turkey, and the United Kingdom.

BACKGROUND AND PHILOSOPHY

With sixty years of proven success, AFS Intercultural Programs has been leading international high school student exchange as a worldwide, volunteer-based, nonprofit organization. In the U.S., AFS-USA provides summer, semester, and year-long study-abroad opportunities to high school students and young adults in more than forty countries around the world. The mission of AFS is to help build a more just and peaceful world by providing international and intercultural learning experiences to individuals, families, schools, and communities through a global volunteer partnership. Each year, more than 11,000 young people are exchanged throughout the world with AFS Intercultural Programs.

The international exchange program was founded in 1947 by volunteer ambulance drivers from World Wars I and II, who believed that the way to ensure future peace among nations was to educate a generation of enlightened future world leaders through international student exchanges.

PROGRAM OFFERINGS

Nothing compares to the life-changing experience of living and studying abroad with AFS. Students discover a world of new experiences and gain self-confidence, resourcefulness, and self-reliance. AFS programs are, above all, about learning through active participation and immersion in the culture. Most students live with host families to learn what it is like to live as a member of a family, school, and community in another country and culture. Previous foreign language experience is desirable but not required for all programs. Many AFS programs offer some language training as part of orientation.

Summer Homestay As members of AFS host families and communities, participants, ages 15–18, discover what it really means to live in another culture. Students make new friends, learn a second language or improve their language skills, and discover firsthand what it is like to live as a member of a family in Argentina, Chile, Ecuador, Finland, Paraguay, Thailand, or Turkey.

Summer Homestay: Language Study This program offers students, ages 15–18, at all language levels, a total immersion experience through formal instruction and daily informal conversation with the host family or dorm mates. Students are placed in small classes according to their proficiency. Programs last four to eight weeks and are offered in Costa Rica, Japan, Latvia, and Panama.

Summer Homestay Plus Participants, ages 15–18, enjoy all the benefits of a homestay. In addition, they participate in group activities, such as studying the arts in Hungary, mountain hiking in New Zealand, playing soccer in Paraguay, or studying the Amazon in Brazil. Programs are offered in Australia, Brazil, Costa Rica, Hungary, Italy, New Zealand, and Paraguay.

Summer Community Service and Team Mission Participants make a difference and learn new skills through four weeks of volunteer work that might include helping physically challenged children in Argentina or working in an orphanage and learning about tribal culture in Ghana. Community Service programs are for students aged 15–21. Team Mission students in China and Ghana travel in groups with adult leaders for three to four weeks. Community Service programs are available in Argentina, Costa Rica, Panama, Paraguay, Thailand, and the United Kingdom.

ENROLLMENT

Students ages 15–18 (some programs are for students up to age 21) are eligible to enroll. Previous foreign language experience is desirable but not required for all programs.

STAFF

The AFS network includes more than 4,500 experienced, international volunteers in the U.S. and more than 30,000 worldwide, making AFS one of the largest community-based volunteer organizations of its kind in the world. Local volunteers recruit and screen host families and student candidates. They also provide orientation, counseling, and enrichment for AFS exchange students and their natural and host families.

COSTS

Program fees range from $4000 to $6000. All fees include international travel with the AFS group and transportation to and from the host family, placement with a carefully selected family who provides room and board, predeparture and post-arrival orientations, 24-hour worldwide emergency numbers, a tuition waiver from the host school, and visa information.

MEDICAL CARE

Secondary medical coverage is required so that immediate assistance can be provided.

FINANCIAL AID

AFS is actively committed to making its programs available to all qualified students, irrespective of their financial situation, with many need-based and merit-based scholarships available. Examples of some of the financial aid and scholarships awarded nationally are Local AFS Chapter Awards, DeWitt Scholars Diversity Award, AFS Awards for Excellence, and Global Scholars.

To qualify for financial aid, candidates must demonstrate strong financial need, a willingness to allow AFS to help select country placements, interest in community service, and/or a strong academic record. Financial aid is limited; applicants are advised to apply early. Merit scholarships are awarded to applicants who exemplify the qualities promoted and valued by AFS. These include, but are not limited to, academic excellence, strong community involvement, and an interest in intercultural learning.

AFS staff members and volunteers can help participants with financial planning for study abroad. Ways to raise funds to cover remaining program costs are described in *Financing Your AFS Experience,* a free booklet.

TRANSPORTATION

International transportation is provided with the participation fee, and students fly together through a gateway city. Transportation to and from the host community is also provided. AFS volunteers and staff members meet students at the airport upon arrival in the host country and upon their return to the U.S. Assistance in arranging affordable domestic flights to gateway cities is available from AFS Travel.

APPLICATION TIMETABLE

AFS has a rolling admissions policy. Because popular programs fill quickly, students are advised to apply early.

FOR MORE INFORMATION, CONTACT

AFS Info Center
506 SW Sixth Avenue, Second Floor
Portland, Oregon 97204

Phone: 800-AFS-INFO (toll-free)
Fax: 503-229-0753
E-mail: afsinfo@afs.org
Web site: http://www.afs.org/usa

PARTICIPANT/FAMILY COMMENTS

"As I walked by some of the Americans, I knew they were wondering if I was a local. It was one of the best feelings—being on the "inside" in the local lifestyle instead of watching from the outside."—Angela, Costa Rica

"This international experience will considerably broaden my horizons and make me a more open, wise, and worldly human being."—Tziah, Ghana Team Mission

"Enjoy every minute of it and really try to connect with your family . . . Australians are amazing, friendly, and accepting people."—Ashley, Australia

AIFS SUMMER ADVANTAGE

STUDY-ABROAD FOR HIGH SCHOOL STUDENTS

NANJING, CHINA;
CAMBRIDGE AND LONDON, ENGLAND;
PARIS, FRANCE; ROME, ITALY;
ST. PETERSBURG, RUSSIA;
GRANADA AND SALAMANCA, SPAIN

TYPE OF PROGRAM: International precollege campus study (for college credit)

PARTICIPANTS: Coeducational: Students at least 16 years of age who have completed their sophomore year of high school

ENROLLMENT: 300 students, rolling admission

PROGRAM DATES: Vary depending on program, four to five weeks in late June through early August

HEAD OF PROGRAM: Amy Van Stone, Director of Admissions

LOCATION
AIF Summer Advantage programs are offered at eight different campus locations around the world: Nanjing University, China; Cambridge University, England; Richmond, the American International University in London, England; University of Paris IV de la Sorbonne, France; Richmond in Rome, Italy; St. Petersburg State Polytechnic University, Russia; University of Granada, Spain; and University of Salamanca, Spain.

BACKGROUND AND PHILOSOPHY
Summer Advantage is a division of The American Institute For Foreign Study®, Inc. AIFS and its family of companies organize cultural exchange, educational, and travel programs of the highest quality throughout the world for more than 50,000 participants each year. Its highest priority is the safety and security of its participants; all of the programs provide exceptional support services and comprehensive insurance policies. Since its founding in 1964, more than 1.2 million people have participated in AIFS programs worldwide. *We bring the world together®.*

PROGRAM OFFERINGS
Summer Advantage programs offer high school students a unique opportunity to take for-credit college classes through campus-based academic programs, while providing exceptional opportunities for students to combine learning and fun.

These four- to five-week summer programs provide a great opportunity for students to get a head start on one or more of the subjects they wish to study in college, in an exciting international setting. In a typical program, AIFS Summer Advantage participants learn about art by studying original masterpieces, visit the places where history was actually made, and immerse themselves in another language and culture.

A typical day could include classes taught on the campus or at museums and historical sites, professional guided tours, and social activities organized by AIFS Summer Advantage staff members. Students spend an average of 15 hours per week in class. In addition, program coordinators organize numerous cultural outings, and students have time to explore independently. AIFS Summer Advantage programs are carefully designed to give participants a balance of classroom lectures, experiential learning, and social and recreational activities.

Those applying to college may submit transcripts from summer course work along with their high school records, and many colleges grant advanced standing or transfer credit for campus-based programs. All students are issued transcripts for completed course work by the host institution.

ENROLLMENT
More than 300 students from across the United States and abroad participate in these study and travel programs, creating an exciting, diverse community in which ideas and cultural experiences are shared. For most of the Summer Advantage programs, students must be at least 16 years old; have completed their sophomore, junior, or senior years of high school; and have a minimum 2.75 GPA.

EXTRA OPPORTUNITIES AND ACTIVITIES
With AIFS Summer Advantage, there is little that can be added on, because so much has already been included in the program; one fee covers everything. AIFS programs provide an educational and economical way to experience a new culture. The programs provide superior value for affordable fees and cost less than if students made arrangements on their own.

FACILITIES
With programs all around the world, Summer Advantage facilities vary by location. Students are generally housed in twin or triple rooms in university residence halls or hotels or with local families. To see the type of accommodations for each program, the student should visit http://www. summeradvantage.com and select a location.

STAFF

Summer Advantage programs have full-time AIFS staff members responsible for the supervision, welfare, and counseling of the students on campus, with 1 staff person for every 15 students. The Resident Directors have extensive experience working with visiting young Americans on AIFS programs and are available 24 hours a day.

The AIFS staff members organize excursions and field trips and arrange a social and cultural program that introduces students to the local community. Their local knowledge, familiarity, and skills help students adjust to their new environment and get the most out of their time abroad.

Resident Directors work closely with the host university and its professors for the welfare of AIFS students. The Resident Director and staff are always available to help. The AIFS staff members make every effort to enable the students to have a good time under safe and supervised conditions.

MEDICAL CARE

All participants are required to purchase program medical insurance. Students should contact their doctor or local Board of Health to see if immunizations are needed.

With AIFS, families can also rest assured that students' safety and security are top priority. The program offers the most comprehensive insurance coverage available, on-site resident staff to provide support and assistance, and a 24-hour emergency service both in the U.S. and abroad.

COSTS

For a complete listing of Summer Advantage fees, students should visit http://www.summeradvantage.com. All costs are guaranteed not to fluctuate with changes in foreign currency and are payable in U.S. dollars before leaving. With AIFS, there are no worries and no additional bills.

AIFS Summer Advantage programs are comprehensive and include air fare (if selected), ground transportation (if selected), a London stopover (not available for all programs), tuition, housing, most meals, special services, 24-hour supervision, many entrance fees to museums and places of interest, cultural events, most weekend excursions, and transferable college credit. Some programs offer optional weekend excursions at an additional cost.

Summer Advantage offers up to ten scholarships of $750 each for candidates who demonstrate leadership potential and involvement in multicultural and international activities. Scholarship applications are available on request and must be submitted with the campus program application and deposit, along with a 1,000-word essay, Why Study Abroad Will Change My Life. Completed scholarship applications must be postmarked by March 15.

APPLICATION TIMETABLE

The application deadline is April 15; Russia is April 1. The scholarship deadline is March 15.

FOR MORE INFORMATION, CONTACT

Summer Advantage
American Institute For Foreign Study (AIFS)
River Plaza
9 West Broad Street
Stamford, Connecticut 06902

Phone: 800-913-7151 (toll-free)
E-mail: summeradvantage@aifs.com
Web site: http://www.summeradvantage.com

ALFORD LAKE CAMP

Celebrating
Over 100 Summers
of Community!

SUMMER PROGRAMS

HOPE, MAINE

TYPE OF PROGRAM: Multi-activity camping, lifetime sports, arts, and wilderness trips, as well as challenge trips for teens

PARTICIPANTS: Seven-week resident camp and 3½-week resident camp: girls, grades 2–9; counselor training: girls completing grades 10–12; 7-week backpacking trip: coed, grades 8–10; 7-week trip to Great Britain: girls, grades 8–10; 7-week sailing trip to Nova Scotia, coed, grades 8–9; 5-week trip to Mexico: coed, grades 8–9

ENROLLMENT: In-camp, 175; counselor trainees, 20; extended trips, 40

PROGRAM DATES: Resident camp: June 24 to August 11 (full season), June 24 to July 18 or July 20 to August 11 (half season); other program dates vary

HEADS OF PROGRAM: Suzanne McMullan, Director, Betsy Brayley, Assistant Director, and Jean McMullan, Consulting Director

LOCATION
Located 10 miles inland from the picturesque seacoast towns of Camden and Rockport, Maine, Alford Lake has extensive freshwater lake frontage and 400 acres of woods and blueberry fields. The camp area is beautiful and secluded. It is close to Maine's Penobscot Bay and is only a 2-hour trip from Bar Harbor and Acadia National Park.

BACKGROUND AND PHILOSOPHY
Alford Lake Camp was founded in 1907 and will be 101 years old, making it one of the oldest girls' camps in the world. Three generations of McMullans are involved with the camp.

Alford Lake believes that campers should experience challenge and adventure through a largely elective program, that they should be relaxed and able to enjoy any activity without self-consciousness or fear, and that they should feel warmly accepted and be steadily encouraged.

The simple outdoor setting gives campers the opportunity to enjoy their natural surroundings and to gain awareness of the importance of environmental responsibility. The community also practices and promotes responsibility in health and nutrition.

Challenge trips are offered to capable and deserving campers, grades 8–10, by invitation. These trips include a coed backpacking/hiking trip on the Appalachian Trail, a coed sailing trip to Nova Scotia, a coed trip to Mexico, and trips for girls to Great Britain and Italy.

One of the camp goals is to nurture international friendships and to foster attitudes of greater global understanding.

PROGRAM OFFERINGS
Resident Camp Lifetime sports, arts, and outdoor living skills are offered to 180 campers. Activities chosen daily may include swimming, sailing, tennis, kayaking, sailboarding, field sports, archery, challenge course with a climbing wall, gymnastics, and riding. Creative arts choices are art and ceramics, dance, drama, and a library program. Music and singing are also a part of camp life. A variety of traditional and origi-

nal camp songs are sung throughout the day. The outdoor camping skills portion of the program encompasses campcraft skills (including environmental and nature exploration), canoeing, overnight trips, trips geared toward community service, and two- to five-day trips on Maine's rivers, mountains, lakes, and islands. These trips are arranged according to age and skill.

Junior Counselor Training Program Approximately 15 girls completing grades 10 and 11 are invited to join this program, which includes courses in American Red Cross first aid and lifeguard training, camping philosophy, advanced wilderness skills, camper development, and communication skills. The program includes a six- to seven-day canoe or mountain trip. Junior trainees join the teaching staff for six days of orientation before campers arrive.

Leadership Training Internship Three to 6 girls completing grades 11 and 12 are invited to join this program. Senior trainees assist in two activities throughout the summer and have counselor privileges, including days off each week. Senior trainees join the teaching staff for six days of orientation before campers arrive.

Appalachian Mountain Trail Trip A highly challenging backpacking trip, from Maine's Mount Katahdin to the New Hampshire border, is provided for 10 coed campers (grades 8–10) and 2 leaders. (June 24–August 11)

Alford Lake Abroad Ten girls (grades 8–10) and 2 leaders explore Great Britain, staying in prearranged youth hostels. The group visits sites and explores the countryside of England (including London), Scotland, Wales, and perhaps Ireland. (June 24–August 11)

Alford Lake Camp/Nova Scotia Up to 9 coed campers (grades 8 and 9) experience seven weeks of travel, sailing, and wilderness adventure in Nova Scotia. (June 24–August 11)

Exchange Trip to Mexico A coed group (grades 8–9) travels to Camp Pipiol in Valle de Bravo for five weeks. (July 5–August 11)

Family Camp After the resident camp ends, Family Camp begins. ALC leaders facilitate activities for adults and children of all ages. This is a wonderful way to introduce children to camping or for adults and families to enjoy a low-cost vacation. (August 13–17)

ENROLLMENT

Alford Lake enrolls approximately 175 resident campers at any one time, about 40 in the extended trip programs, and about 20 counselor-trainees.

Although the number varies from year to year, the total camp community may represent upwards of twenty-five states and twenty countries in a season.

FACILITIES

There are fifteen small cabins for activities and staff living quarters as well as seven large buildings that house the dining hall, kitchen, offices, and a large recreational area; the Camp House, which is a meeting hall and theater building; a large stable with stalls for fourteen horses and jodhpur and boot storage; a health center; a library; an art complex of three buildings with five studio areas; and a staff recreation building. The campers, counselor-trainees, and tent counselors live in forty-one large platform tents with double roofs, permanent superstructures, and floors. Toilet buildings are located at each end of the tent line, with one containing shower facilities. Four hardtop tennis courts, a nature building, thirty canoes, ten sailboats, six sailboards, twelve kayaks, archery facilities, gymnastics equipment, a 26-foot climbing wall, and an activities building are also extensively used. With more than a mile of lakefront, Alford Lakers are blessed with privacy and a clear, sandy-bottomed swim area on a 550-acre lake.

STAFF

The teaching staff, which includes the directors, key staff members, and 2 nurses, consists of about 70 women and a few men, not including the counselor-trainees. The maintenance, office, and kitchen staff add another 15 persons to the community. The leader-camper ratio is 1.9. Teaching staff members are college students or older. They are selected for their interest and experience in teaching children, their enthusiasm and energy, and their ability to be positive role models for campers. Alford Lake employs only nonsmokers.

MEDICAL CARE

There are 2 registered nurses in residence. Within 10 miles of camp are excellent physicians, specialists, and the Pen Bay Medical Center.

RELIGIOUS LIFE

Sunday-in-the-Pines is a weekly gathering of the entire camp that celebrates its community values. The gathering is coordinated by counselors with camper/counselor participation.

COSTS

For the seven-week resident camp, the all-inclusive 2008 tuition is $6600; the shorter sessions, lasting 3½ weeks, cost $4500. Costs for the Junior Counselor Training Program are $5750, with suggested spending money being $300. The Appalachian Mountain Trail Trip is $7550. Alford Lake Abroad and the trip to Mexico cost $7550, including airfare; the Nova Scotia sailing trip is $7550. Additional spending money is suggested for each of the international trips. Cost information on Family Camp is supplied upon request.

TRANSPORTATION

On June 24, transportation is available from New York City; Connecticut; Boston, Massachusetts (airport); and Portland, Maine (airport). Similar arrangements for the trip home are provided on August 11. Campers leaving on July 18 or arriving on July 20 may travel by car or plane with service only to the Portland airport.

APPLICATION TIMETABLE

Early enrollment is encouraged as most camp registrations are received before November for the following June. No cost reduction is given for late arrival or early departure of a camper. In the event a camper must withdraw before camp opens, half of the tuition deposit is refundable until February 1; after February 1, the full tuition deposit will be retained.

FOR MORE INFORMATION, CONTACT
Suzanne McMullan

Winter:
Alford Lake Camp
5 Salt Marsh Way
Cape Elizabeth, Maine 04107

Phone: 207-799-3005
Fax: 207-799-5044
E-mail: alc@alfordlake.com
Web site: http://www.alfordlakecamp.com

Summer:
Alford Lake Camp
258 Alford Lake Road
Hope, Maine 04847

Phone: 207-785-2400
Fax: 207-785-5290
E-mail: alc@alfordlake.com
Web site: http://www.alfordlakecamp.com

AMERICAN ACADEMY OF DRAMATIC ARTS

The American Academy of Dramatic Arts

SUMMER PROGRAM

NEW YORK CITY, NEW YORK, AND LOS ANGELES, CALIFORNIA

TYPE OF PROGRAM: Dramatic arts conservatory

PARTICIPANTS: Coeducational; teenagers (ages 14 and older), college students, and adults

ENROLLMENT: Approximately 100 students at each campus

PROGRAM DATES: Six weeks in July and August

HEADS OF PROGRAM: Roger Croucher, President; New York City: Constantine Scopas, Director; Hollywood: Dr. Nina LeNoir, Director

LOCATION

The Academy's New York home, an outstanding example of the architecture of Stanford White, is an official New York City Landmark and is on the National Register of Historic Places. The six-story building is centrally located in midtown Manhattan.

The Academy's West Coast home is set on a 2½-acre campus in the heart of Hollywood.

BACKGROUND AND PHILOSOPHY

Founded in New York in 1884, the Academy was the first school in America to provide professional education for actors. The soundness of the Academy's approach is reflected in the achievements of its alumni, a body of professionals unmatched by any other institution of actor training.

In 1974, a west coast campus was established in the Los Angeles area.

The six-week Summer Program was established for those who want to test their interest and ability in an environment of professional training. It provides an opportunity to evaluate educational goals and to assist the student in choosing a profession. Academy training involves the student intellectually, physically, and emotionally, while stressing self-discovery and self-discipline and cherishing individuality.

The Academy is accredited in New York by the Middle States Association of Colleges and Schools and in California by the Western Association of Schools and Colleges. The Academy is accredited at both locations by the National Association of Schools of Theatre.

PROGRAM OFFERINGS

Summer students take classes in acting, voice and speech, vocal production, and movement.

Acting Through exercises, improvisations, and scene study, students learn the importance of relaxation, concentration, involvement, contact, and sense memory and gain a sense of truthful behavior.

Voice and speech Starting with basic principles of vocal production, placement, and control, students develop the speaking voice as an instrument of better communication both on and off the stage.

Vocal production This course augments the Academy's emphasis on the development of an expressive and flexible speaking voice through singing.

Movement Students are exposed to a variety of dance and movement techniques for the development of the imagination, coordination, and body awareness necessary to an actor.

At the conclusion of the six-week program, each student performs in a presentation of scenes.

ENROLLMENT

Students attending the Academy come from all over the world, united by their shared commitment to acting and the challenge of working to become the best actors they can be. Students are grouped in sections that are carefully selected to ensure as much similarity of background, maturity, and objectives as possible. Teenagers are grouped separately.

DAILY SCHEDULE

At both schools, summer classes take place Monday through Thursday, from 9 to 1 for morning students and from 2 to 6 for afternoon students. Electives are scheduled between 1 and 2 Monday through Thursday and all day on Friday.

EXTRA OPPORTUNITIES AND ACTIVITIES

Depending on the interests expressed by applicants, electives such as Fencing, Improvisation, Camera Technique, Dancing for the Actor, Alexander Technique, and Musical Theatre may be offered.

FACILITIES

The Academy's New York building includes classrooms, rehearsal halls, dance studios, a student lounge, locker areas, dressing rooms, a prop department/production workshop, a costume department, a library/audiovisual learning center, and three theaters.

The Hollywood campus has similar facilities, including classrooms, dance studios, a theater, a library, full production facilities, and ample parking.

The Academy offers off-campus housing options.

STAFF

Most of the Summer Program faculty members also staff the full-time two-year program. Others are distinguished professionals who are available to the Academy only in the summer. The Academy's faculty comprises alumni of the most esteemed acting schools in the world. Their professional experience encompasses Broadway, off-Broadway, stock, regional theater, film, and television in a variety of positions. In both New York and Hollywood, the Summer Program is staffed by faculties of 12 or more instructors.

COSTS

The 2007 Summer Program fee was $1900 for six weeks. A nonrefundable $50 application fee was also required. Each elective cost an additional $90. No refunds are granted after classes have begun. There is limited financial aid available for the Summer Program.

TRANSPORTATION

Students at the New York school generally travel to and from classes by public transportation. The Academy is a short distance from the Port Authority Bus Terminal and both Grand Central and Pennsylvania Stations and is within walking distance of PATH trains to New Jersey.

California students generally rely on cars to get them to and from class every day, although some use bicycles or public transportation.

APPLICATION TIMETABLE

Applications are accepted year-round on a rolling timetable, but applicants should confirm their plans well before the program begins in early July. All applicants must audition. An audition is scheduled after the completed application, health forms, and $50 application fee have been received. An audition consists of the delivery from memory of two contrasting monologues (one comic, one serious) of up to 2 minutes each from published plays. Auditions can take place at either the New York or California school for acceptance at either school; the audition, however, must be scheduled through the school to which the student is applying. For those students unable to get to New York or Hollywood for an audition, a regional audition may be arranged.

FOR MORE INFORMATION, CONTACT

Ms. Karen Higginbotham, Director of Admissions
AADA/New York
120 Madison Avenue
New York, New York 10016

Phone: 212-686-0620
        800-463-8990 (toll-free)

Mr. Dan Justin, Director of Admissions
AADA/Hollywood
1336 North La Brea Avenue
Hollywood, California 90028

Phone: 323-464-2777
        800-222-2867 (toll-free)

PARTICIPANT/FAMILY COMMENTS

"This summer has been one of the most fulfilling, inspiring, and most fun summers and times of my life so far."

"Through the professional atmosphere at AADA, I learned about the hard work and creative rewards that are the life of the actor. Whether you are an actor-in-training or a student testing your curiosity further, I can honestly say that the summer program won't let you down. For me personally, it was one of the best and most positive choices I have ever made. (P.S.—It was a lot of fun!)"

"The experience I had over the summer was so amazing. The teachers were excellent, and I grew tremendously."

"I was astounded by how much I learned in only six weeks."

AMERICAN TRAILS WEST

SUMMER TRAVEL PROGRAMS

UNITED STATES, CANADA, HAWAII, ALASKA, AND EUROPE

TYPE OF PROGRAM: Active student travel
PARTICIPANTS: Coeducational, ages 12–18, grouped by age
ENROLLMENT: Approximately 40 per group
PROGRAM DATES: End of June through August, twenty-one to forty-two days
HEADS OF PROGRAM: Howie Fox, Jeff Gass, Howard Gorchov, Josh Miller, and Will Thompson, directors

BACKGROUND AND PHILOSOPHY

Since 1965, the American Trails West (ATW) family has been the originator and innovator in the field of student travel. From the first camping trip to the first combination trip to the exciting itineraries for the summer of 2008, American Trails West has led the way. ATW's years of experience in working with young people, as well as their expertise in the field of travel, can be seen in every aspect of their program. Student travel is a specialized field, and the ATW family devotes its full-time efforts year-round solely to the preparation of their summer programs.

A summer of travel with American Trails West is a broadening experience in discovering new places and an opportunity to make friends with fellow travelers from across the United States, Canada, and Europe. Many teenagers come on their own, and compatible age groupings and a wide geographic mix assure that each one feels comfortable. Traveling on an American Trails West trip means being part of the group, a member of the ATW family. ATW's philosophy, staff, and activities make that goal a reality.

PROGRAM OFFERINGS

North, South, East, and West, American Trails West takes students to the most exciting destinations. ATW is the only student travel program that features so many great itineraries. Across the **U.S.**, through **Canada**, north to **Alaska**, west to **Hawaii**, or around **Europe**, travelers experience the best that each has to offer. From the natural beauty of National Parks to the high energy of great cities, students are always in the very center of the action on American Trails West.

Students may choose exciting combination camping/hotel/dorm trips or hotel/dorm trips. Each one offers a skillful blend of outdoor adventures, sightseeing, sports, and evening entertainment. During the day campers raft the best rivers, hike the most exciting canyon trails, or ski down awesome Alpine mountains. Campers do everything from in-line skating, mountain biking, and snorkeling to dog sledding, inner tubing, and waterskiing, depending on the itinerary. At night, it is comedy clubs and campfires, light shows and dance clubs, go-carts, theme parks, and much more.

ATW is the only student travel program whose itineraries have no one-night stops. Every location visited is for two nights or more. No one-night stops means more time for activities, more time for nightlife, and more time to make friends. It provides more time for breaking the ice, learning the ropes, and feeling at home. Everyone can use a little help during the first few days of a new experience. Meeting new people, adjusting to new routines, and being in new locations can be overwhelming if the itinerary rushes from place to place. All ATW camping and dorm trips start with a special two-day group orientation. Travelers learn all they need to know, meet the staff, and begin to make those friends for a lifetime in a relaxed, unpressured atmosphere.

For families located in the New York metropolitan area, ATW offers its unique **MINI TOURS.** Specially designed for middle school students, MINI TOURS feature travel from Monday to Friday, with weekends at home. Destinations range from Virginia Beach to Niagara Falls and from Maine to Orlando. Pickups and drop-offs each week are conveniently located in both the Greater New York/New Jersey metropolitan area as well as the Philadelphia/Cherry Hill area.

ENROLLMENT

Each summer, American Trails West attracts students from across the United States and from around the world. Through the years, campers from forty states and more than a dozen countries have traveled with American Trails West. Living together, learning from each other, and having fun with students from all over is what makes an American Trails West summer so special.

EXTRA OPPORTUNITIES AND ACTIVITIES

American Trails West itineraries are planned to maximize action, fun, and excitement, while minimizing bus riding. ATW's unique blend of great activities, both day and night, guarantees each traveler the greatest summer ever. These include everything from waterskiing to snow skiing, London theater to laser tag, jet boating to river rafting, and Planet Hollywood to the Hard Rock Café. Nonetheless, ATW directors have the flexibility, as well as the experience, to find new and exciting, up-to-the-minute surprises while traveling, and to incorporate them into the itinerary.

FACILITIES

American Trails West pioneered cross-country camping in 1965. Over the next four decades, continual innovation and improvement have culminated in ATW's Five-Star Camping. Personally selected National Park and private campgrounds, custom-designed walk-in cabin tents, comfortable cots with mattresses, three delicious and nutritious meals each day plus snacks, and meticulous year-round maintenance of all camping equipment are hallmarks of ATW's commitment to the comfort and safety of its travelers. Each trip travels with everything it needs, right down to its own spotless picnic tables, so it never has to depend on equipment used by the general public.

All dorms, hotels, and resorts are chosen for security, comfort, and outstanding facilities. Every camper sleeps in an individual bed each night. Whether it's shooting hoops on a college campus, playing tennis at the Hyatt Regency, or working out in the state-of-the-art fitness center at a mountain resort, American Trails West campers enjoy the finest accommodations and facilities.

STAFF

Each American Trails West trip is personally supervised by an experienced director returning for another summer of leadership. These directors and their specially selected staff members—all college graduates over the age of 21—offer youthful participation in all facets of the ATW program. The ratio of campers to staff members is 6:1. All senior staff members (directors, co-directors, and returning counselors) are CPR and first aid certified. Every staff member takes part in ongoing training sessions at the American Trails West office over the winter months. In the spring, these culminate in a five-day orientation program of workshops, seminars, and hands-on training.

Each trip staff combines many summers of ATW experience with the unique ability to understand and relate to their campers. This combination guarantees each trip the finest in responsible supervision. The ATW family is very proud of the large number of past campers who return as staff members each year.

MEDICAL CARE

The health, safety, and security of each trip member is the number one priority of the ATW family. The senior staff of each trip is certified in CPR and first aid. Over the years, American Trails West has developed a wide network of doctors, hospitals, and 24-hour emergency facilities in every part of the country to whom the staff turns should medical attention be necessary. A sick traveler is accompanied by an ATW staff member at all times, and parents are always contacted when a traveler sees a doctor.

COSTS

Costs vary by program depending on length, location, and accommodations. For 2007, prices ranged from $3295 to $8995. Three meals daily and all entertainment, recreation, lodging, gratuities, and taxes are included. Airfare to and from home is not included.

TRANSPORTATION

All air travel on American Trails West is by regularly scheduled jet. American Trails West arranges round-trip transportation for all travelers. Each camper is met at the airport upon arrival and accompanied to their flight on the day of departure.

ATW's deluxe motorcoach and professional driver remain with each trip for the entire summer. ATW's ultramodern motorcoaches are air conditioned and restroom equipped. They feature reclining seats, video and stereo sound systems, and panoramic windows for the greatest view on the road.

APPLICATION TIMETABLE

Inquiries are welcomed year-round. Admissions are on a rolling basis starting in the fall. Because the number of seats is limited, early enrollment is encouraged. A deposit of $300 is required (fully refundable until February 1).

FOR MORE INFORMATION, CONTACT

American Trails West
92 Middle Neck Road
Great Neck, New York 11021-1243
Phone: 516-487-2800 (in New York State)
      800-645-6260 (toll-free)
Fax: 516 487 2855
E-mail: info@atwteentours.com
Web site: http://www.atwteentours.com

PARTICIPANT/FAMILY COMMENTS

"Alex had an unbelievably fantastic summer. She has not stopped talking about the trip, and especially about Doug, the director, and his staff. It sounds like they really put everything into making it a fun and one-of-a-kind experience. Thank you for providing the wonderful staff, director, bus driver and summer experience."—Debbie and Owen Kassimir, East Hills, New York

"Ask Abbie how her trip was and she'll answer 'amazing.' Her description of the staff: caring, really nice, enthusiastic, respectful . . . let's just say 'amazing.' She has not stopped talking about all the places she saw and all the activities, from the majesty of the National Parks to the glitz of Las Vegas, the food, the bus rides . . . in short, it was all 'amazing.' You have truly provided her with an unforgettable experience. So ATW, 'Amazing Trails West,' thank you . . . you are indeed 'amazing'."—Rebecca and Art Strichman, Orange, Connecticut

APPEL FARM ARTS AND MUSIC CENTER

▼▲▼▲▼▲▼▲▼▲▼▲▼▲▼▲▼▲▼▲▼▲▼▲▼▲▼▲

SUMMER ARTS CAMP

ELMER, NEW JERSEY

TYPE OF PROGRAM: Community of caring and creative artists exploring the visual and performing arts
PARTICIPANTS: Coeducational, ages 9–17
ENROLLMENT: Limited to 220 per session
PROGRAM DATES: Two, four-, and eight-week programs
HEAD OF PROGRAM: Jennie Quinn, Camp Director

LOCATION
Appel Farm's 176-acre site is nestled in the fields and woods of Salem County in southern New Jersey. The New Jersey shore, Philadelphia, New York City, and Washington, D.C., are all close by.

BACKGROUND AND PHILOSOPHY
Appel Farm Arts and Music Center is a multidisciplinary regional arts center offering the Summer Arts Camp, a performing arts series, the Arts Classes at Appel Farm program, and a wide range of community arts outreach programs. Albert and Clare Appel founded Appel Farm in 1960 as a private summer residential arts camp for children. Based on their belief that all young people have artistic talent, the camp has provided an atmosphere where all children, from beginner through the most advanced, are welcomed into a nurturing, supportive, cooperative environment in which to explore the visual and performing arts. In 1978, Appel Farm Arts and Music Center was incorporated as a nonprofit charitable organization.

PROGRAM OFFERINGS
Structured classes are balanced with workshops, performances, games and sports, group projects, trips, and all kinds of fun and outdoor activities. Campers design a dynamic program centered on one major and two minors studied six days a week for the entire session. Majors meet each morning for 2½ hours, and minors are held in 75-minute sessions each afternoon.

Theater Performance Theater majors learn and/or refine their acting skills, study theater techniques and theory, and work with instructors and cast through a combination of acting classes, rehearsals, and performances. At the same time, the theoretical and historical background of theater as an art form is taught to increase each student's appreciation of the field. Theater performance majors are cast in one of six plays performed at the end of each session. Theater minors make in-depth explorations of focused areas of theater. The emphasis is on teaching processes and skills and may lead to the development of a short, informal performance piece. A minor can be designed around disciplines such as scene-based acting, playwriting, an introduction to directing, stage combat, audition techniques, musical theater skills, or comedy sketch techniques.

Technical Theater Technical theater students study the fundamentals of theatrical design, including lighting, sound, sets, props, costumes, and stage management.

Music Campers selecting music as a major or minor can focus on vocal or instrumental music in a wide variety of forms ranging from classical to contemporary. Music majors should be at an intermediate or advanced level and be able to read and play music at a middle school level or higher. Each camper in the music program receives a half hour of private instruction per week. Groups are formed to work in small ensembles that range from rock bands to string ensembles, choruses, jazz combos, and chamber groups. Larger ensembles include the concert band, jazz band, all-major choir, and the orchestra. Classes can also be taken in music theory, conducting, sight reading, music history, appreciation, and song writing and composition classes.

Dance Ballet, jazz, and modern dance form the core of the dance program. Form, spatial awareness, breathing, choreography, and role-playing exercises help students understand the creative context for different styles, and campers often work on several long and short works that are presented for the camp community at the end of each session. Dance minors learn and practice basic dance skills and techniques while focusing on a specialized area or dance form. In each session, there are at least two minors that draw on the special talents and interests of individual instructors. Recent dance minor areas have included choreography, beginning ballet, pointe ballet, tap, hip hop, and folk dance. The emphasis is placed on teaching process, though there are many small ensembles formed that also give dancers opportunities for performing.

Visual Arts Campers can select majors or minors in painting, drawing, illustration, printmaking, ceramics, sculpture, glass art, fiber art, beading, and crafts. They learn about the history and qualities of their chosen medium and study the work of its master artists. A spacious new art building houses large, open studio spaces; a gallery; and a wide array of equipment, including ceramics kilns, pottery wheels, welding equipment, a printing press, and a host of other tools and artists' supplies.

Photography Campers can major or minor in photography and learn the fundamentals of black-and-white photography, including developing film, making high-quality prints, and finishing and presenting their work. They become familiar with darkroom set-up, equipment, and chemistry and develop technical skills, including composition, framing, lighting, time, and sequence.

Video Video majors study the many roles, skills, and techniques necessary for producing, screenwriting, directing, designing, filming, editing, scoring, and sound engineering. Campers play key roles in the production of several short films presented to the camp community at the end of each session. Video minors focus on a single aspect of filmmaking, such as cinematography, editing, or sound design. Video minors may also have opportunities to work on short films and collaborative projects.

Recording Arts Campers in all departments have opportunities to work in the recording studio and may record original music with a band, design sound effects for a play, create a soundtrack for a video, combine poetry and music as part of a dance piece, or incorporate sound into a photography or art exhibition. Students gain a hands-on knowledge of the skills necessary to record, edit, and mix audio on a basic level.

Creative Writing and Journalism Minors Campers interested in poetry, creative nonfiction, and short story writing explore these art forms as they learn about choices of style, point of view, structure, use of language, and characterization. Journalism minors follow a similar program while focusing on publishing *The Appel Core,* the camp newsletter, and learn about creating content and giving structure to a publication as they become staff writers and editors, conduct interviews, report news, write editorial columns, and design and edit the newsletter for publication.

Sports and Swim programs are offered as minors. Tennis minors participate in daily skill-building exercises focused on stroke development and tactical strategy and the etiquette of the game in set and match play. The swim minor provides instruction to develop swimming and water safety skills. Aquatic and safety skills are based on the American Red Cross Learn-to-Swim Program. Group games include soccer, basketball, street hockey, softball, cricket, volleyball, and Ultimate Frisbee, among many others.

ENROLLMENT
Young artists ages 9–17 come from all over the world to participate in two-, four-, and eight-week sessions. Sessions are limited to 220 participants.

DAILY SCHEDULE

Majors meet each morning for 2½ hours. Two minors are held in 75-minute sessions each afternoon. Each evening there is a different activity at 7:30.

7:30	Early bird activities
8:30	Breakfast
9:00	Bunk cleanup
9:30	Major
12:00	Free time
12:30	Lunch
1:15	Rest hour
2:15	Minor I
3:30	Snack
3:45	Minor II
5:00	Free choice
6:30	Dinner
7:30	Evening activity
8:30	Snack
9:00	Free time
10:00–11:00	Lights out (based on age)

EXTRA OPPORTUNITIES AND ACTIVITIES

Campers may choose the free-choice period (after minors each day) to take part in a structured activity such as afternoon art or the actor's studio. Others may prefer exercise with aerobics, yoga, free swim, tennis, or basketball.

The entire camp community gathers every evening to enjoy an entertaining and/or educational evening activity, which may be a performance by campers, staff members, or guest artists; a dinner dance; a Fourth of July Parade; or a carnival. During international week, campers celebrate the diversity of Appel Farm's community by participating in special workshops, enjoying meals that reflect the cuisines of many cultures, watching films from around the world, and discovering other cultures from people who have a wealth of interesting backgrounds, art forms, customs, and perspectives to share.

Hour-long workshops on Tuesday evenings and Sundays consists of demonstrations, hands-on projects, or lessons. Past workshops have included The History of Rock Music, Screen Printing, Papermaking, Capoeira, Haiku, Cooking and Baking, Jazz Improvisation, Rocket Making, Building a Campfire, World Events, Debating, Basic Spanish, Polaroid Transfer, and Video Animation.

Friday night concerts feature a dynamic and ever-changing, camper-driven, program of exhibition and performances that are a highlight of each week. Performance week, the last week of each session, celebrates campers' hard work throughout the session with performances and exhibitions in all program areas.

Each program area is enhanced with field trips tailored to that group's special interests. Trips to concerts by the Philadelphia orchestra, special exhibitions at the Philadelphia Museum of Art, glassblowing demonstrations at Wheaton Village, filmmaking workshops at Drexel University, and photography shoots at the Salem County Fair are only part of the picture. Recreational trips to the beach, berry picking at a local farm, and bowling or miniature golf outings offer fun for everyone.

Outreach programs offer an opportunity for sharing a wealth of talent with children and adults in the region, including programs ranging from concerts, skits, and dance performances to hands-on arts workshops for young and old.

The Counselor-in-Training Program is designed for campers ages 16 and 17 or campers who are entering eleventh grade. Students can work with younger children, complete an apprenticeship, lead an all-camp event, and organize a camp community service project.

FACILITIES

Campers stay with 8 to 10 other campers and 2 bunk counselors in a dorm-style bunk that includes electricity, hot water, and a private bathroom. Other facilities include a 250-seat theater; an outdoor stage; a digital piano lab; a variety of indoor and outdoor performance and practice facilities; a new art building with large, well-ventilated studios; electric, gas, and unique wood-fired Nob-origama kilns; a fully equipped darkroom for 35mm black-and-white developing and printing; a media arts center; a digital recording studio; a beautiful, air-conditioned dance studio; and sports facilities that include a basketball court, two tennis courts, three athletic fields, and a 25-meter swimming pool.

STAFF

Under the mature leadership of the full-time camp directors, veteran staff members at Appel Farm possess years of training and/or advanced degrees and significant accomplishments in their chosen artistic fields. Above all, each staff member is totally dedicated to the daily care of campers—physically, socially, and emotionally as well as artistically—and they accept responsibility for helping each camper develop a sense of belonging and respect for one another within the Appel Farm community.

MEDICAL CARE

Two registered nurses provide health care in a comfortable, air-conditioned health center. At least one nurse is at the camp at all times. A licensed physician visits daily and is on call 24 hours a day, and a fully accredited hospital is less than 1 mile away.

COSTS

Tuition is $2450 for the two-week program, $4900 for the four-week program, and $7200 for the eight-week program, with significant discounts for early registration. Tuition is all-inclusive. Payment plans are available.

FINANCIAL AID

The Appel Farm Scholarship and Tuition Assistance Program provides financial support, such as scholarships and tuition assistance, based on financial need, potential for growth and development through the Appel Farm experience, interest and involvement in one or more of the arts offered at Appel Farm, background and experience that will broaden the cultural diversity of Appel Farm, and space availability. Awards are made on a rolling basis beginning in January.

TRANSPORTATION

Appel Farm is easily accessible from the New Jersey Turnpike, Interstate 95, and Routes 40 and 76 and is just 30 minutes from the Philadelphia Airport, 2 hours from the Newark Airport, and 3 hours from New York City airports. Appel Farm staff members pick up campers from the Philadelphia airport, train station, or bus station for no additional fee. Bus service from New York City is provided each way.

APPLICATION TIMETABLE

Campers are accepted on a first-come, first-served basis. There is no application deadline, but prospective campers are encouraged to apply early. Applications may be submitted via mail or phone and must be accompanied by an $800 deposit.

FOR MORE INFORMATION, CONTACT

Jennie Quinn, Camp Director
Appel Farm Arts and Music Center
P.O. Box 888
Elmer, New Jersey 08318-0888
Phone: 856-358-2472
     800-394-8478 (toll-free)
Fax: 856-358-6513
E-mail: camp@appelfarm.org
Web site: http://www.appelfarm.org

PARTICIPANT/FAMILY COMMENTS

Appel Farm is my dream place. It is a place of love, kindness and respect. This is a place where everyone is accepted."—Siona Stone, Camper

ASHEVILLE SCHOOL SUMMER ACADEMIC ADVENTURES

SUMMER ACADEMIC ADVENTURES

ASHEVILLE, NORTH CAROLINA

TYPE OF PROGRAM: Experiential academics and outdoor adventure

PARTICIPANTS: Coed; residential students entering grades 6–8 (Chart Your Own Course) and grades 9–11 (Immersion Adventures in Leadership, Art, Film, and the American Landscape)

ENROLLMENT: 80 students per session

PROGRAM DATES: First session, June 15–July 5, 2008; second session, July 6–July 26, 2008

HEAD OF PROGRAM: Jenny Wallace

LOCATION

Situated on nearly 300 wooded acres at Asheville's city limits, Asheville School is minutes from downtown, yet a stone's throw from the surrounding Blue Ridge Mountains. Such a setting offers many resources: Pisgah National Forest, the Pigeon and French Broad Rivers, and Blue Ridge Parkway.

BACKGROUND AND PHILOSOPHY

Summer opportunities were introduced at the School in the early 1900s, but it was not until 1954 that its first summer school was established, offering only two courses. Now the summer program offers a wider variety of courses and activities. Summer Academic Adventures' (SAA) mission is to provide an atmosphere in which all members of the community appreciate and strive for excellence of mind, body, and spirit. SAA has grown to include new programs and goals that serve academically gifted and high-achieving students who want to get ahead or who consider themselves aspiring writers, artists, scientists, historians, and leaders. In addition, there is a chance for exposure to new languages and cultures from around the world. Students who would like to experience boarding school life have the perfect short-term opportunity to do so.

PROGRAM OFFERINGS

The Summer Academic Adventures curriculum offers two program options: Chart Your Own Course (rising sixth to eighth graders) and Immersion Adventures (rising ninth to eleventh graders). Students in the Chart Your Own Course option select three courses out of a range of options, including art, drama, creative writing, history, Web publishing, film, problem-solving strategies, physics, chemistry, and more. The average class size is 9 students. Rising ninth to eleventh graders select one Immersion Adventure each session. All Immersion Adventures are interdisciplinary and experiential and include community service. Instead of a traditional exam, all students produce a final project or presentation for the project fair at the end of the session.

The program embraces Dewey's concept that experience and education are one and also touches on Grant Wiggins' writings on project-based assessment. Students study literature, science, math, art, drama, or technology in an academic setting and then go out into the field to find or make connections. For example, students from the forensic science, mysteries, and real life logic courses work together to solve a "murder mystery," gathering evidence, interviewing witnesses, and holding a mock trial.

International students are immersed in the English language through course work and social interaction. They participate in all afternoon and weekend activities and live in the dormitories with the other students. This is a very special opportunity for developing conversational English and creating lasting friendships.

Everyone enjoys the opportunity to learn about different places and languages. On top of the casual learning of a different language, students have a chance to learn Spanish in the classroom. This new class gives a basic introduction to the language, along with an overview of Hispanic cultures, histories, and literature.

ENROLLMENT

Summer Academic Adventures draws participants from all around the country and the globe. Last year, participants represented twenty-five states and eleven countries.

DAILY SCHEDULE

After breakfast, participants gather for a brief morning assembly or chapel. Morning classes follow, and all summer participants spend three 60-minute periods in class each morning. Despite its demanding academic schedule, Asheville School realizes the importance of allowing time for recreation and friendly competition. In the afternoon, students participate in a wide variety of athletic activities of their choosing. Each Monday, students sign up for a different sport or activity for the week. Mountaineering, which takes full advantage of Asheville's unique location, is especially popular among the students, who learn basic rock-climbing, kayaking, and mountain-biking skills. Students return to the dining hall for dinner before settling in for study hall. After study hall, students enjoy some free time in the dorms or the student center before lights-out.

EXTRA OPPORTUNITIES AND ACTIVITIES

Wednesday and Saturday afternoons and Sundays allow for extensive activities both on and off campus. These are organized by a full-time activities director, interns, and the director of mountaineering. Included in the tuition are activities such as white-water rafting, tours of historic Asheville, a visit to Sliding Rock, and many mountaineering opportunities (equipment is provided) such as hiking, camping, backpacking, rock climbing, kayaking, and use of the campus ropes course and alpine tower. Greater understanding of teamwork and trust, the development of new friendships, and a renewed appreciation for the environment are just some of the benefits of participating in the mountaineering program.

FACILITIES

Campus facilities for academic work and social interaction are superior. Many buildings are nearly a century old, while others are quite modern, providing a mix of historical value and up-to-date amenities. Traditional classrooms, a state-of-the-art media center, and computer labs complement each other. The student center includes a game room, snack bar, post office, TV room, and art gallery. Campus activities abound, with tennis courts, a state-of-the-art athletic center, an Olympic-size pool, a fitness center, a gymnasium, a wooded trail for hiking, an alpine tower, a ropes course, and several playing fields. Students reside in Anderson Hall and meals are served in Sharp Dining Hall.

STAFF

Learning is interactive, so there is a friendly spirit of give-and-take between teachers and students. With a student-faculty ratio of 3:1 and an average class size of 9 students, every student receives individual attention. Each is assigned a faculty adviser, who serves as a mentor and friend. Interns are college students who have demonstrated leadership skills, responsibility, and an eagerness to teach. Interns live in the residence halls with the students and provide support and guidance. Mountaineering is led by skilled outdoor enthusiasts who are part of the year-round mountaineering staff. An Activities Director coordinates all School-wide activities and supports interns in planning and leading activities.

The Summer Academic Adventures Director works throughout the year to prepare for the summer, ensuring first-rate faculty and staff members, high quality in programming, and a well-rounded campus life.

MEDICAL CARE

A full-time nurse lives on campus and is available 24 hours a day. The campus infirmary is located in the dormitory, and an urgent-care center is within 2 miles of the School. In emergencies, students are transported to one of two Asheville hospitals. Participants are required to have a complete physical examination within one year prior to registration; they must also have health insurance against major illnesses and accidents. Students who do not have such coverage with an American carrier may purchase temporary insurance.

RELIGIOUS LIFE

Though Asheville School embraces a Judeo-Christian heritage, chapel services are designed to be a time for all students of many faiths to feel comfortable and spiritually uplifted. Chapel "talks" are values-based and are typically given by the interns and faculty members. Twice weekly, students, faculty members, and interns gather in the chapel for these brief services.

COSTS

In 2007, the application fee was $30. Tuition was $3150 for one 3-week session or $6000 for a six-week term. Tuition includes fees for all courses, textbooks, room, board, and activities.

There are merit scholarships that cover either full or partial tuition. A limited amount of need-based financial aid is available.

TRANSPORTATION

The Asheville Regional Airport (AVL) is located approximately 9 miles from the School. Transportation to Asheville is not included in tuition; however, students are transported to and from the airport at no charge.

APPLICATION TIMETABLE

Inquires are welcome at any time throughout the year. Campus visits are available but are not required for admission. Applicants are selected on the basis of teacher recommendations and school transcripts. Admission decisions are made on a rolling basis until the program fills. Notification of acceptance takes place within two weeks of receipt of all application materials. It is advisable to begin the application process early.

FOR MORE INFORMATION, CONTACT

Director of Summer Programs
Asheville School
Asheville, North Carolina 28806

Phone: 828-254-6345
Fax: 828-252-8666
E-mail: summer@ashevilleschool.org
Web site: http://www.ashevilleschool.org

PARTICIPANT/FAMILY COMMENTS

"My son came home a changed child (for the better). He said more than once it was so fun to be around other kids who love to learn and to have fun teachers who are really smart. He said it was nice being around kids who weren't constantly 'putting others down' or who were solely focused on being in a clique. Whatever you all did, you successfully built the team spirit and the mutual respect in your learning community this summer. Successful educational institutions do exactly that: offer challenging academic experiences as well as build a mutually respectful learning community... For that we say thank you so very much."

"The Film Program at SAA opened my eyes to what filmmakers have to go through when making a film. It takes creativity, intelligence, patience, and a lot of hard work to make a film of any kind."

"Age is not measured in years or numbers, but by experience, and the experiences I have had at SAA these past two years are worth generations. I have made lifelong friends, better even than those I have at home, and I have felt the joy of independence, coupled with the support of the SAA community; it is an experience not to be missed."

"It is hard for me to put into words how great my experience with the Leadership program was. I learned so much about myself and the world around me, gained a sense of being a part of an amazing community, and made lifelong friends."

THE BARAT FOUNDATION
SUMMER IN PROVENCE

‹‹‹‹‹‹‹‹‹‹‹‹‹‹‹‹‹‹‹‹‹‹‹‹‹‹‹‹‹

SUMMER PROGRAM

PROVENCE, FRANCE

TYPE OF PROGRAM: Academic enrichment
PARTICIPANTS: Students who have completed grades 8 through 12
ENROLLMENT: Varies
PROGRAM DATES: June 23–August 4, 2007
HEAD OF PROGRAM: Chandri and Gary Barat, founders, the Barat Foundation

LOCATION
This program takes place in the village of L'Isle sur la Sorgue, in the heart of Provence. Located on the islands of five branches of the Sorgue River, L'Isle-sur-la-Sorgue is the antiques capital of the region, hosting an open market every Sunday that features more than 200 permanent art and antique dealers. The village is a short walk from many of Provence's other attractions, including the vineyards of Chateauneuf-du-Pape, Paul Cezanne's studio in Aix-en-Provence, and the Mediterranean shore.

BACKGROUND AND PHILOSOPHY
The Barat Foundation, a nonprofit educational corporation dedicated to expanding creative opportunities through immersion programs, was founded in 1997 by Chandri and Gary Barat, who decided to pursue their lifelong dreams of exploring new educational concepts and returning to their creative roots after twenty years as entrepreneurs and business people. The Foundation's summer program in Provence has established itself as one of the premier high school foreign language and cultural immersion programs abroad, attracting students from all over the world who want to experience total immersion in French language and culture.

Unlike more traditional academic settings in which learning stops at the end of the session, the Barat Method incorporates learning 24 hours a day. The curriculum is taught within the context of a threefold learning method. First, the student is exposed to new material in classes and workshops, including French conversation and art, literature, dance, and music. Second, the student experiences the material in the form of field excursions to the many natural and manmade wonders of the region. Third, each student creates his or her own individual expression of the new material through workshops, creative projects, and journal writing.

Students live in Provence not as tourists but as locals, attending the same attractions and enjoying the same activities that are enjoyed by year-round residents. The award-winning teaching staff provides a personal introduction to French language, culture, history, and art, working together with students in and out of the classroom to create a fully rounded immersion program. The teacher-student ratio is 1:3.

PROGRAM OFFERINGS
Students are grouped according to French language experience into beginner, intermediate, and advanced French sections.

All classes focus on conversational French and often include preparation for the day's itinerary and excursion.

Beginner classes concentrate on basic conversational skills, basic vocabulary, and, specifically, the needs of everyday life in France. Students prepare to order in a restaurant or café; visit shops, bakeries, and markets; ask directions; and generally move around France with confidence.

In addition to the basic foundation, intermediate sections also stress conversational skills, with added support in vocabulary and grammar. Intermediate students are introduced to classics of French literature appropriate to their level of comprehension.

Advanced classes include lively discussion of current events from *Le Monde,* a French daily newspaper. Advanced students are introduced to French philosophy and literature, including the reading of a play they will later see performed at the world famous Avignon Theatre Festival, schedules permitting.

All students are required to maintain a journal documenting their stay in Provence. The journal is submitted to and corrected by the student's French language teacher, in order for students to optimize written language skills as well as their oral communication skills. Time is allotted each day for journal writing. The journal is a personal memoir that will become a lifetime treasure of writing, sketches, photographs, postcards, and other mementos of the summer experience in France.

ENROLLMENT

The program enrolls students from throughout the United States and around the world who have completed grades 8 through 12.

DAILY SCHEDULE

```
 9:00–10:00 . . . Breakfast
10:00–11:30 . . . French language classes
11:30–12:30 . . . Cultural enrichment classes
12:30– 1:00 . . . Journal
 1:00– 2:00 . . . Lunch
 2:00– 7:00 . . . Excursions, activities, and free time
 7:00– 8:00 . . . Dinner
 8:00–11:00 . . . Evening activities
       12:00 . . . Lights out
```

EXTRA OPPORTUNITIES AND ACTIVITIES

Students travel around Provence to explore and enjoy its natural beauty, history, culture, and art. Accompanied by their French teachers, they are given the opportunity to immediately apply what they learn in class as they explore ancient Roman ruins, medieval castles, cafés, festivals, beaches, nature preserves, vineyards, and open-air markets.

Cultural ateliers are included in the curriculum, including a wine tasting and culinary workshops in which students learn to make French dishes and regional craft workshops, where students create Provencal artifacts, such as sachets made of lavender. Every atelier works toward a cumulative project to be presented by the end of the session, be it a performance, a photo exhibition, an art installation, a short story, or a dance.

FACILITIES

Students stay in suites or apartments at a beautiful, fully equipped French compound that includes several houses, a large outdoor swimming pool, lavender fields, indoor and outdoor kitchens, arts workshops, and dining facilities. Towels and sheets are provided.

STAFF

The award-winning staff comprises young and talented French nationals from esteemed academic institutions, prestigious contemporary art schools, and the leading edge of the European artistic community. They specialize in a range of artistic and academic disciplines, and their work has been featured in exhibitions and performances in leading capitals of the world as well as in leading European periodicals. A chef is on site to prepare meals that reflect the culinary offerings of Provence.

MEDICAL CARE

A local doctor is available in case of illness, and the facility is located within a 15-minute drive of a hospital should an emergency arrive.

RELIGIOUS LIFE

Participation in religious services is not mandatory, but students may take part in religious services in the region.

COSTS

The cost is $5695 for one session (June 23–July 14 or July 14– August 4) and $10,695 for both sessions. The cost includes lodging and two meals per day (breakfast and dinner) plus classes, instruction, planned excursions, and weekend activities. A payment of $1100, which includes the $1000 deposit plus a $100 nonrefundable application fee, must accompany the application, with the balance due on or before April 1.

FINANCIAL AID

The Barat Foundation offers limited need- and merit-based scholarships to gifted and talented students from all over the world. Interested students must first apply to the program. Upon receiving all materials, the Foundation contacts the student regarding further requirements.

TRANSPORTATION

Participants may choose to travel on Barat group flights or find alternative transportation. In any case, all students are encouraged to contact the foundation's travel agent, Gil Travel, at 215-568-6655 Ext. 244. On acceptance into the program, students receive group flight information. Travel insurance is available on request.

APPLICATION TIMETABLE

Applicants must submit an application form, a teacher recommendation form from a teacher or guidance counselor, a school transcript, and a payment of $1100. The teacher recommendation form and transcript may be sent separately. Admissions are on a rolling basis, so applicants are encouraged to apply as early as possible. A decision is made within one to two days of receiving all materials, and applicants are notified by mail about acceptance.

FOR MORE INFORMATION, CONTACT

Barat Foundation
121 Hawkins Place #222
Boonton, New Jersey 07005

Phone: 973-263-1013
Fax: 254-710-7782
E-mail: info@baratfoundation.org
Web site: http://www.baratfoundation.org/summer/index.
     html

PARTICIPANT/FAMILY COMMENTS

"I just wanted to thank you for providing the girls with such an incredible summer. They absolutely loved Provence and loved the program. It was the best summer they've ever had. What an enriching experience! The pictures were beautiful and next summer we want to travel there with them—they can't say enough about how beautiful the entire trip was."

"Thank you for this experience. Thank you for the excursions, and thank you for this magnificent summer. This summer was truly the best summer of my life. You have shown me a new and remarkable path. You have changed me forever, and forever I will be grateful."

"It was a really good experience to live like a family with people from all over the world and have close contact with all of them. I could confirm that everybody, without any exception, has something wonderful to teach. And in this point, I broke a barrier that existed in my mind that separated people because of different cultures."

BARNARD'S SUMMER IN NEW YORK CITY

PRE-COLLEGE PROGRAM

NEW YORK, NEW YORK

TYPE OF PROGRAM: College-level academic enrichment and leadership development

PARTICIPANTS: Coeducational, students who have completed grade 10 or 11

ENROLLMENT: 170

PROGRAM DATES: Four-week Liberal Arts Program: June 29–July 26; one-week Liberal Arts Intensive: June 29–July 5; Young Women's Leadership Institute: July 13–19 (program dates are tentative; students should visit the program's Web site for current information)

HEAD OF PROGRAM: Director of Pre-College Programs

LOCATION

The 4-acre Barnard College campus on Morningside Heights in Manhattan is adjacent to the Columbia University campus. Barnard's Summer in New York City makes full use of New York City's exceptional educational, cultural, and recreational resources.

BACKGROUND AND PHILOSOPHY

The Barnard Pre-College Program was established in 1985 as a program for high school students with substantial academic commitment and interest as well as the ability to handle college-level work. As a selective liberal arts college affiliated with Columbia University, Barnard offers an unusual educational opportunity for coeducational life on a university campus, enriched by the unparalleled offerings of New York City. The city often becomes an extension of the classroom. The Metropolitan Museum of Art and Broadway are used extensively, for example. Each week, students have the opportunity to shadow professionals at some of the city's major businesses and organizations. Evening and weekend programs provide students with additional exposure to New York City's cultural, historical, and international attractions.

PROGRAM OFFERINGS

Course offerings are varied, and classes are limited in size so that students can receive individual attention, engage in lively discussion, and work on independent projects.

The city plays an important role in the design of courses. Resources such as the Bronx Zoo, the Museum of Television and Radio, Ellis Island, the Hayden Planetarium, the Cathedral of St. John the Divine, and the Museum of Modern Art are used extensively. Guest lecturers, artists, and performers are invited to participate. Students are graded on a pass/fail basis and receive reports from each of their professors, who evaluate their participation, performance, and academic promise. Official course credit is not granted.

The Young Women's Leadership Institute combines academic learning, skill-building workshops, and student-run sessions to train young women leaders in an intensive weeklong program.

ENROLLMENT

Approximately 170 young men and women attend each summer, coming from more than thirty states and several other countries. More than 80 percent are residential, but students whose families live within the New York metropolitan area may choose to commute.

DAILY SCHEDULE

Students in the four-week program attend morning and afternoon classes four days per week, while students in the one-week program take a morning course in writing or theater and complete intensive assignments each afternoon. Young Women's Leadership Institute students learn from college staff members, alumnae, and professional facilitators in a series of workshops, discussions, and seminars. On Wednesdays, students in the four-week program participate in the Life After College career-exploration series. Organized evening and weekend programs include supervised trips to famous New York City attractions as well as to lesser-known venues. Coffeehouses featuring local entertainers, talent shows, dances, parties, sports activities, and workshops on current issues are available on campus. Students may also volunteer for community service programs.

Students are expected to observe sign-out procedures and curfews and to comply with regulations designed to protect the health and safety of all participants. The social policy is sent to each admitted applicant and is available on request.

EXTRA OPPORTUNITIES AND ACTIVITIES

The Life After College series gives students a taste of both the occupational and the neighborhood diversity that make New York such an exciting place. Each week, small escorted groups visit leading institutions and businesses, meet with professionals, take "inside" tours, and learn about career opportunities. Elective workshops on applying to college, interviewing strategies, and study skills are also offered.

FACILITIES

Residential students live in an air-conditioned residence hall and eat in the student cafeteria. Classes meet in air-conditioned classrooms, and students have access to all the modern campus facilities, including Wollman Library, the Academic Computer Center, and the campus gym.

STAFF

Courses are taught by Barnard faculty members, visiting faculty members, and graduate students who have adapted their undergraduate courses for the program. Students are supervised by the professional staff, including 14 specially selected and trained undergraduate assistants and 3 graduate assistants. The entire staff offers support and guidance to all.

MEDICAL CARE

The Columbia University Health Service provides medical care, low-cost prescriptions, and routine lab tests. St. Luke's–Roosevelt Hospital, three blocks from the campus, is available for emergency medical care. All students must provide themselves with health insurance coverage, including benefits for emergency care and hospitalization.

RELIGIOUS LIFE

Barnard College has no religious affiliation. Religious services for all denominations are available close to the campus. The meal plan accommodates religious dietary restrictions.

COSTS

The 2007 comprehensive charge for the four-week program was $4400 for residential students, including tuition, fees, room and board, and some evening and weekend programs. For commuting students, the charge was $2900 for tuition, weekday lunches, and fees. The one-week Liberal Arts Intensive fee was $1650 for residential students and $1030 for commuting students. The Young Women's Leadership Institute is a residential program only, and the fee was $1500. Transportation, books, course supplies, weekend dinners, optional trips, personal laundry, and incidentals are not included.

FINANCIAL AID

A limited number of partial financial grants are available.

TRANSPORTATION

Barnard is accessible from all area airports and train and bus stations as well as by car. Buses and subways make campus stops.

APPLICATION TIMETABLE

Admission is selective and based upon receipt of the completed application, including the $40 application fee. For those living outside the United States, the application fee is $65. Applicants must be completing grade 10 or 11 and must demonstrate academic strength. High motivation, emotional stability, and social maturity are expected. Admission decisions are made on a rolling basis beginning March 1. The application deadline is May 1. Course enrollment and housing are limited, so early application is advised.

FOR MORE INFORMATION, CONTACT

Director of Pre-College Programs
Barnard College
Columbia University
3009 Broadway
New York, New York 10027-6598

Phone: 212-854-8866
Fax: 212-854-8867
E-mail: pcp@barnard.edu
Web site: http://www.barnard.edu/pcp

BAYLOR UNIVERSITY
THE RENAISSANCE SCHOLAR PROGRAM

▽△▽△▽△▽△▽△▽△▽△▽△▽△▽△▽△▽△▽△▽△▽△▽△▽△▽

SUMMER PROGRAM

WACO, TEXAS

TYPE OF PROGRAM: Precollege academic program, 1 hour of college credit possible

PARTICIPANTS: Coeducational, for current high school juniors

ENROLLMENT: 90 students total, 30 maximum for each course week

PROGRAM DATES: Three 1-week sessions: June 10–15, June 17–22, June 24–29

HEAD OF PROGRAM: Petra Carey, Coordinator of Summer Programs, Communications, and External Relations

LOCATION

The Renaissance Scholar Program is conducted at Baylor University's 735-acre campus, located on the banks of the Brazos River in Waco, Texas, a metropolitan area of 200,000. The one-week summer session complements and follows the curriculum, standards, and philosophy of Baylor University.

BACKGROUND AND PHILOSOPHY

From Plato and Augustine through Pascal, Shakespeare, and Leonardo da Vinci and on up to Einstein, the greatest thinkers have bridged the gap between the sciences and the humanities, technology and art, philosophy, and theology.

At the Baylor University Renaissance Scholar Program, high school juniors embark on a journey of intellectual discovery that sets them on a path to becoming a person of universal education, someone conversant with all of human learning.

Sponsored by Baylor's nationally acclaimed School of Engineering & Computer Science and its esteemed Honors College, The Renaissance Scholar Program offers students an integrated introduction to topics in engineering/technology, with complementary readings in history, art, literature, philosophy, and theology.

This precollege academic program awards 1 hour of transferable college credit upon successful completion. It presents an integrated introduction to topics in engineering/technology, with complementary readings in history, art, literature, philosophy, and theology. The contemporary relevance of these classroom discussions is brought out through evening viewings and group discussions of films such as *The Matrix* and *The Lord of the Rings*—films that highlight issues regarding technology, human nature, the philosophy of the quest, and the role of classical myth and theology in the contemporary world. Students spend a week with Baylor faculty members, who are experts in the fields of technology, art, philosophy, theology, and literature.

PROGRAM OFFERINGS

During the course of one week, participants have the opportunity to gain college life experience; study, dine, and debate with the best faculty members; and earn 1 hour of college credit.

In addition, participants are given priority consideration for admission to Baylor University following their senior year in high school. Students must successfully complete the program and submit the Baylor University Undergraduate Application. Application decisions are made at the discretion of the Admissions Committee.

More than just an ordinary summer camp, The Renaissance Scholar Program opens the door for students to take a real college course, get to know real faculty members, and earn real college credit.

ENROLLMENT

Consistent with Baylor University's commitment to increased student-faculty interaction, one-on-one mentoring, and small distinctive classes, enrollment for each week of the program is capped at 30 students.

DAILY SCHEDULE

Sunday

4:00– 6:00 . . . Check-in	
6:00– 9:00 . . . Mixer	

Monday through Thursday

7:00– 7:45 . . . Breakfast	
8:10–10:50 . . . Engineering/Computer Science class	
11:00–12:20 . . . Lab	
12:30– 1:30 . . . Lunch	
2:00– 3:50 . . . Great Texts class	
4:30– 6:15 . . . Group study	
6:30– 7:30 . . . Dinner	
8:00–10:00 . . . Scheduled event: Monday, activities at Student Life Center; Tuesday, *The Lord of the Rings* discussion; Wednesday, *The Matrix* discussion; Thursday, bowling	

Friday

7:00– 7:45 . . . Breakfast	
8:00–12:20 . . . Wrap-up	
12:30– 1:30 . . . Lunch	
3:00– 4:15 . . . Check-out	
5:00– 6:00 . . . Scholarly presentations	

EXTRA OPPORTUNITIES AND ACTIVITIES

Renaissance Scholars have the opportunity to get ahead of their peers, experience college life, and meet other high-achieving students from around the nation. Participants also enjoy an introductory mixer with fun and games as well as coordinate and present a group project at week's end displaying what they have learned.

FACILITIES

Classes are conducted in the Rogers Engineering and Computer Science Building and in Morrison Hall, site of the Honors College.

Participants reside in respective men's and women's on-campus residence halls that feature reading rooms, study rooms, lounges, and computer labs.

Meals are served in the Memorial Dining Hall. Participants also may dine at the on-site Chili's Too and Starbucks.

Baylor University's Student Life Center is open to program participants and features a 10,000-square-foot fitness center, racquetball/squash courts, an indoor jogging track, leisure pool, a 2,400-square-foot aerobics room with sound system and dance lights, and indoor/outdoor volleyball and basketball courts.

Baylor University's Bowling Alley and Game Room is open to participants and has six automated bowling lanes with above-ground ball returns, four billiards tables, foosball, dart boards, and a shuffleboard table.

STAFF

Baylor University's most admired professors teach the course work—those professors highly respected by students and peers alike and known for their surpassing ability to communicate, motivate, and evoke in students a love for learning.

There is adult supervision, including Baylor professors and staff members, who are on hand and involved with the participants at all occasions.

Baylor University's Campus Living & Learning Department is proud to support students while they live at Baylor. Residence halls are operated by highly talented and trained staff members who live on site and work diligently to build community and support students in all aspects of their college lives. In addition, Community Leaders (CLs) reside in each hall. Employed by Baylor's Campus Living & Learning Department, CLs are current Baylor students who are committed to providing leadership by fostering community and cultivating relationships as well as mentoring residents and facilitating learning through efforts that integrate aspects of diversity, faith, development, academics, and relationships.

MEDICAL CARE

Participants have access to the Baylor University Medical Clinic for diagnosis and treatment of injuries and illnesses. In addition, Hillcrest Baptist Medical Center is approximately 4 miles from the Baylor campus.

RELIGIOUS LIFE

Students from all faiths and religions are welcome.

COSTS

The cost of The Renaissance Scholar Program is $1800. This fee includes the $500 nonrefundable deposit, tuition, books and student fees, room for the entire stay, meal plan for the entire

stay, money for Starbucks and Chili's Too (located on the campus), all special events for students, and use of Baylor University's Student Life Center.

The $500 nonrefundable deposit is due on admission. All monies for the remaining balance should be postmarked by May 25, 2007.

FINANCIAL AID

Students should apply early while scholarships in the amount of $500 are still available.

TRANSPORTATION

Parents or guardians of participants who reside beyond driving distance must arrange transportation from nearby airports (Dallas/Fort Worth International Airport and Waco Regional Airport) to Baylor University on the day of registration—Sunday, June 10; Sunday, June 17; or Sunday, June 24, 2007. Others arrive by car.

APPLICATION TIMETABLE

The Renaissance Scholar Program accepts applicants on a rolling admission basis beginning in December and continuing until the start of the program. Applicants are urged to apply early while scholarships are available and to ensure placement in the program. Applications are available on the program's Web site; http://www.baylor.edu/renaissancescholar.

FOR MORE INFORMATION, CONTACT

Petra Carey
Honors College
Baylor University
One Bear Place #97181
Waco, Texas 76798-7181

Phone: 254-710-1523
Fax: 254-710-7782
E-mail: petra_carey@baylor.edu
Web site: http://www.baylor.edu/renaissancescholar

Adam Ecklund
School of Engineering & Computer Science
Baylor University
One Bear Place #97356
Waco, Texas 76798-7356

Phone: 254-710-3890
Fax: 254-710-3839
E-mail: adam_ecklund@baylor.edu
Web site: http://www.baylor.edu/renaissancescholar

BRANT LAKE DANCE CENTRE

SUMMER PROGRAMS

BRANT LAKE, NEW YORK

TYPE OF PROGRAM: Dance for girls in a coeducational setting
PARTICIPANTS: Girls, ages 11–16
ENROLLMENT: 60
PROGRAM DATES: June 24–August 4
HEAD OF PROGRAM: Kirstin Been Spielman, Director

LOCATION

The Dance Centre is located adjacent to Brant Lake Camp for Boys, with which it is affiliated. The campus is on Brant Lake, a 6-mile-long, crystal-clear lake in the foothills of the Adirondack Mountains, within the Adirondack Park.

BACKGROUND AND PHILOSOPHY

The goal is to provide a high-quality experience for girls with an interest in dance. The Dance Centre helps the girls plan a fun program while ensuring that they can broaden and strengthen their skills in dance. When they are not dancing, there are many activities from which campers may choose. The staff is well aware that teenagers need freedom of choice coupled with close, warm guidance and supervision. Brant Lake is a wonderful place for an active teenage girl. She does not have to be headed for a lifelong pursuit of dance, although Brant Lake does have some noted alumni, and superb instruction is offered at all levels.

The girls are asked to set goals for their stay at camp, and they design their own schedules each day. Kirstin Been Spielman, the Dance Centre's director, helps guide each girl to achieve those goals as needed. Brant Lake's experienced and mature staff members provide guidance that leads to a safe, healthy, rewarding, and memorable summer.

Brant Lake Camp for Boys, part of one family since 1917, has enjoyed an outstanding reputation, not just for its beauty and fine facilities but also because of its guidance and fine supervision. The same high standards have been upheld for the Dance Centre since its inception in 1980.

PROGRAM OFFERINGS

Dance: The girls choose from top-quality professional teachers in the disciplines of ballet, modern, tap, and jazz. The program offers beginner through advanced classes. Girls can take up to 5 hours of dance a day if they wish, with a required minimum of 1 hour a day. Hip-hop, yoga, Pilates, improvisation, and choreography are also offered as workshops for the girls.

Brant Lake hires dance teachers who not only are wonderful professional dancers but also know how to teach dance, especially to teenagers.

Sharon Gersten Luckman, founder of Brant Lake's Dance Centre, has created an intensive, professional dance program where teens get guidance, have lots of fun, and socialize in a healthy atmosphere. Sharon is currently the Executive Director of the Alvin Ailey American Dance Theater and was formerly the Director of Dance at the 92nd Street Y.

Tennis: All lessons are ability grouped. There are clinics, group lessons (with a maximum of 4 per court), and intensives (with 1 pro per 2 girls). Court time is available throughout the day and evening.

Brant Lake has more than 20 tennis instructors (varsity players with teaching experience) and 5 tennis pros. The thirteen clay and three hard courts are beautifully maintained in picturesque settings.

Waterfront: Few camps in the United States offer as extensive a waterfront program as Brant Lake. The girls receive excellent instruction and supervision in swimming, sailing, boating, waterskiing, canoeing, and kayaking. Brant Lake, which is crystal clear with a lovely sand bottom, is ideally suited to learning and participating in these water sports.

Fine arts: There is a choice of wood crafts, papermaking, leathercraft, weaving, painting, drawing, sculpture, jewelry, photography, and video in the arts facility.

Performing arts: There are Wednesday and Saturday variety shows that include singing, dancing, and drama. There is a "works-in-progress" performance at the end of each session. This performance is a culmination of the work that has taken place in the various dance classes.

Sports: The sports program provides both instruction and games to those who are interested. Land sports include tennis, basketball, golf, wall climbing, volleyball, jogging, and fitness training. Water sports include swimming, waterskiing, sailing, canoeing, and boating. Brant Lake Camp's wonderful boys' instructors and fields enrich and strengthen the sports program.

ENROLLMENT
Girls ages 11–16 come from all over the country and all around the world. Sessions are three or six weeks.

EXTRA OPPORTUNITIES AND ACTIVITIES
Evening activities vary daily. Once a week, the group travels to the Saratoga Performing Arts Center to enjoy a dance performance, a rock concert, or a play. On other evenings, girls may choose from movies, coed activities, dance, or art electives, or they may rehearse for the weekly musical or talent show. On certain evenings, bunks have campfires or run their own separate activities. Coed events are casual, supervised, and fun.

The Sunday program provides for a change of pace, a time for relaxation after a busy week. Brunch is followed by a schedule of special workshops and classes that are taught by experienced and talented dance teachers. The late afternoon offers coed waterfront and other activities, a barbecue, and an evening movie.

Trip day is one day each week. Girls may go to such local attractions as Lake George, Saratoga, Lake Placid, or Great Escape theme park. They may also choose a bicycling trip through the countryside, a mountain hike, or an overnight camping trip on a private mountain nearby.

FACILITIES
The Centre's dance and lodging facilities are beautifully designed to fit the special needs of its campers. The upper level of the Dance Lodge contains a spacious, professional studio overlooking peaceful woods. A second studio for tap is housed in a beautifully restored barn. A third dance studio in the field house has a professional vinyl floor. On the main level of the lodge is a lovely living room that serves as a communal lounge for the girls, two large dormitory-style bunks, and two bathrooms (each with sinks, showers, and toilets). Three other bunks provide the same homey atmosphere and facilities. Here the girls live with others their own age and 2 counselors per bunk. The girls eat breakfast and lunch in a beautiful new pine-paneled, Adirondack-style dining room, which was completed in 2005. Healthy snacks and juice are available there throughout the day. Dinner is served in the dining hall on the boys' campus.

In addition to this, the Dance Centre shares many of the numerous outstanding indoor and outdoor facilities with Brant Lake Camp for Boys.

STAFF
In addition to the professional dance staff, the camp hires experienced, mature counselors. Brant Lake looks for experienced women who can guide teenage girls in making appropriate decisions in a fun, safe, and compassionate way. Each staff member is personally interviewed; the average age of the staff is 22. At all times, the girls are supervised by these mature counselors, who understand that teenagers are ready to make many of their own decisions and able to set their own goals.

MEDICAL CARE
The Health Center is fully equipped and has 4 nurses and 1 doctor in residence throughout the season. In addition, most counselors are certified in first aid and CPR.

COSTS
Tuition in 2007 is approximately $4000 for three weeks and $7400 for six weeks. Extra costs are incurred for transportation and spending money.

TRANSPORTATION
Girls may take the chartered bus (from New York City) or fly to the Albany airport, where they are met by a staff member, or parents may drive them to camp.

FOR MORE INFORMATION, CONTACT
Kirstin Been Spielman
Brant Lake Dance Centre
7586 State Route 8
Brant Lake, New York 12815

Phone: 518-494-2406
Fax: 518-494-7372
E-mail: brantlakec@aol.com
Web site: http://www.blcdance.com

PARTICIPANT/FAMILY COMMENTS

"I learned new techniques at Brant Lake Dance Centre. My dancing improved and I had a great time. It is not a competitive environment."—Rebecca (age 15), New York

"I feel as if I have joined a family at Brant Lake. It is a close-knit community. The counselors and teachers are warm and approachable. I made lifelong friends."—Stephanie (age 13), Florida

BREWSTER ACADEMY SUMMER SESSION

THE PERFECT SUMMER

WOLFEBORO, NEW HAMPSHIRE

TYPE OF PROGRAM: Academics, instructional support, English as a second language (ESL), adventure education, and technology enrichment
PARTICIPANTS: Coeducational, ages 12–18
PROGRAM DATES: Six weeks in June through August
HEAD OF PROGRAM: Bill Lee, Director

LOCATION

Brewster Academy, on Lake Winnipesaukee, is located where the lakes meet the mountains in one of New England's most picturesque areas. The campus, adjacent to the safe and quaint village of Wolfeboro, is on 80 acres of playing fields and rolling hillside overlooking miles of waterfront on New Hampshire's largest lake.

BACKGROUND AND PHILOSOPHY

The Brewster Academy Summer Session provides summer fun while teaching important skills that serve students well in school and in life. Brewster takes full advantage of its beautiful site and the extraordinary resources that serve both academics and athletics on its campus. In the outdoor adventure program, participants climb, hike, paddle, and play in one of the most spectacular geographic regions of New Hampshire. Brewster has high expectations concerning the amount of academic material that can be covered in a six-week summer program. There are similarly high expectations for having fun in the beautiful New Hampshire summer. Everyone works hard when they work and plays hard when they play.

Brewster's Summer Session is designed with the belief that there are things that every successful and happy person needs to know and be able to do. In addition to the skills of reading and writing and/or mathematics, there is an emphasis on study, organization, and time-management skills. There are three other skill areas that are essential for success in secondary school, college, the workplace, and life: the skills of critical thinking and problem solving, the skills of collaborative teamwork, and the skills that lead to technological literacy and fluency. The first two are taught both indoors and outdoors; the third is taught on Brewster's technologically sophisticated campus, where students are able to access the network from anywhere on the campus using laptop computers that are provided as part of the program.

PROGRAM OFFERINGS

Core Courses Everyone takes one core course: English (reading and writing), math (prealgebra, algebra I, algebra II, or geometry), or English as a second language (ESL), level one through five (level five is identical to the English course for American students). These courses meet for 2 hours each morning, Monday through Friday, supported by daily 90-minute study sessions conducted by qualified teaching assistants who work collaboratively with the core classroom teachers. These courses can be taken either as accelerated classes or as makeup for those seeking or requiring remedial work. Up to a full year's academic credit can be granted to those who demonstrate mastery. These courses are intensive; the primary purpose is not issuing credit but rather to teach important concepts and to meaningfully advance student knowledge, especially about themselves as learners, in the six short weeks available.

English In this course, students learn, practice, and master some of the essential skills needed to succeed in the study of English. These skills break down into two major areas—reading and writing—but Brewster's approach also includes the promotion of critical thinking. In terms of writing skills, students learn how writers use language to communicate human experiences. Students learn elements of descriptive, analytical, and persuasive writing and practice these skills by producing multiple forms of essays. In terms of reading, students add several powerful tools to their tool kit of reading skills, including the ability to locate clues in a text, distinguish the explicit from the implicit, make predictions, comprehend factual and inferential information, and locate and draw conclusions from character clues. These are taught in small classes in the context of an intentional, sequential skills-building curriculum and focus on the relevance of reading and writing to the lives of the students.

Mathematics The summer math courses are prealgebra, algebra I, algebra II, and geometry. The classes are intensive, but they have an individualized tutorial aspect as well. A great deal of material is covered, and no one gets left behind. Instructors change the pace, the approaches, and the perspective often to keep things interesting and to make sure that everyone really understands what are, sometimes, abstract principles.

English as a Second Language The summer ESL program is an integrated system of learning where students participate in various classes and activities that are intricately connected. An unusually rich and intensive set of daily offerings is provided, resulting in as many as 4 to 6 hours a day of directed English learning as well as a full immersion in English-only classes, recreational activities, and dorm life for the remainder of each day. The ESL academic program includes three courses: ESL language, ESL communication, and an innovative ESL video-editing course. Each student also takes an elective class with native English speakers.

Photo courtesy of Eric Poggenpohl

Non-Core Courses Everyone takes two elective courses, choosing from computer graphic art and design, experiential science, video production, and/or instructional support (IS). IS, a program for which Brewster is renowned, offers one-on-one instruction that focuses on the learning needs of each student (see details below). These courses meet for 1 hour each morning.

Instructional Support A very popular option, instructional support employs a tutorial approach to guide students to better understand how they best learn and to develop improved study, organization, and time-management skills. The IS program is directly linked to the student's core curriculum (reading/writing or math skills) as a collaboration between the teacher, the IS teacher, and the student.

Science This course, taken for enrichment and enjoyment, provides students with a refreshing new way to approach the discipline of science. There are no boring "stand-and-deliver" lectures. It is a get-involved, hands-on, experiential class in which the basic principles of scientific investigation are learned by doing.

Computer Graphics Led by an energetic, popular, and experienced teacher, the computer graphics program consists of the manipulation of student-generated digital images using a variety of sophisticated software applications in several challenging and engaging projects.

Adventure Recreation These courses are fun, but they are also purposeful and important and are not just for recreation. Adventure recreation courses are designed to build skills. Confidence, critical thinking, judgment, precision, teamwork, and leadership skills are just some of the benefits derived from engaging in outdoor adventure. The courses include rock and wall climbing, rappelling, flat and white-water canoeing, kayaking, hiking/camping, and a few surprises.

Technology Enrichment "Brewster is probably the most innovative and successful school using (information technology) on this planet... The success of their students has been enormous," says Steve Kessell of Curtin University of Technology. Summer session students use laptops, provided by Brewster, in every class and learn firsthand how powerful technology can be when purposefully integrated into the curriculum.

ENROLLMENT

Students from throughout the United States and many other countries attend Summer Session. Brewster does not discriminate on the basis of race, color, or national or ethnic origin in administering its programs. Demonstrations of motivation are criteria for inclusion.

DAILY SCHEDULE

Classes and study halls meet five days per week until 2:30 p.m. Adventure recreation lasts until 5:30. Adventure trips, with some overnight stays beginning on Friday, are scheduled on Saturdays.

EXTRA OPPORTUNITIES AND ACTIVITIES

Three nights a week, everyone goes to the spectacular Athletics and Wellness Center for games and to learn fitness regimens. Sundays are set aside for trips that take advantage of New England's scenic, recreational, and cultural opportunities, including the mountains, the seacoast, and Boston.

FACILITIES

Brewster enjoys modern dormitory and dining facilities, innovative classrooms, a campuswide network that provides network and Internet access from every dorm room, a multipurpose boathouse, and a modern fitness center.

STAFF

All classes are taught by teachers who have many years of experience. Teacher interns, who are recruited from America's top universities, oversee study halls, adventure activities, and dorms. All are American Red Cross–certified in CPR and first aid and in basic water safety and rescue. Rock-climbing instructors are qualified, certified, and experienced.

MEDICAL CARE

There is an on-campus infirmary, and a hospital is ¼ mile from the campus.

COSTS

The 2007 tuition was $6195. Instructional support fees are additional.

TRANSPORTATION

Transportation from air and rail centers is included.

APPLICATION TIMETABLE

The admissions process is rolling and ongoing.

FOR MORE INFORMATION, CONTACT

Brewster Academy Summer Session
80 Academy Drive
Wolfeboro, New Hampshire 03894
Phone: 603-569-7155
Fax: 603-569-7050
E-mail: summer@brewsteracademy.org
Web site: http://www.brewsteracademy.org

BROADREACH AND ACADEMIC TREKS

broadreach

SCUBA, SAILING, MARINE BIOLOGY, LANGUAGE IMMERSION, AND COMMUNITY SERVICE ADVENTURES FOR TEENAGERS

CARIBBEAN, AUSTRALIA, COSTA RICA, HONDURAS, CHINA, BAHAMAS, CANADA, MEXICO, BELIZE, BRAZIL, PERU, ECUADOR, FRANCE, BERMUDA, AND FIJI

TYPE OF PROGRAM: International adventure and experiential education programs in more than fifteen countries, including live-aboard scuba- and sail-training voyages in the Caribbean from beginner to advanced, wilderness adventures, advanced scuba training, marine biology studies, community service, language immersion, and academic expeditions. All trips are designed to maximize fun, learning, and adventure. Additional adventure activities include whitewater rafting, sea kayaking, backpacking, surfing, cultural immersion, and island and rainforest exploration, with hands-on skill building, cultural immersion, and leadership training. No experience is necessary for many trips. High school and college academic credit is offered, as well as community service credit (up to 55 hours).

PARTICIPANTS: Coed, grouped by ages 13–14, 15–18 or 19

ENROLLMENT: 10–14 participants per trip

PROGRAM DATES: Two-, three-, four-, and six-week programs, June through August

LOCATION
Each BROADREACH and ACADEMIC TREKS location offers its own special blend of discovery and challenge. Destinations are selected to maximize cultural, educational, and adventure opportunities and provide participants with exceptional personal growth experiences.

BACKGROUND AND PHILOSOPHY
BROADREACH goes beyond the traditional structure of other summer programs. Each trip is designed to take advantage of the unique opportunities in regions traveled by combining the thrill of discovery, the pride of accomplishment, and the excitement of exploring the wilderness and sea. BROADREACH participants learn and grow together in an active, hands-on environment that is both fun and educational. Whether the activity is sailing, sea kayaking, or scuba diving, expertise is built sensibly through a step-by-step, learn-by-doing approach. No experience is necessary on most programs, only a desire to try new things and broaden experiences.

BROADREACH's ACADEMIC TREKS offers academic and community service adventures in some of the world's most extraordinary environments and cultures. Programs blend the hands-on study of marine science, language, or cultures with community service, wilderness adventure, and international travel. On each dynamic journey, students are fully immersed in an educational experience in a real-world setting, gaining a global perspective and a hands-on understanding of the topics studied. They also get a head-start on college by earning college credit and up to 55 hours of community service credit and by building a host of skills they are likely to use both in school and beyond.

A small group size is one of the key ingredients in BROADREACH's ability to offer the highest caliber summer experience. Limiting the group size to 10 to 14 participants encourages strong friendships in an atmosphere of teamwork, support, and accomplishment. The small group permits individual attention, preserves the sense of discovery, and allows the staff to cater to the specific dynamics of each group.

PROGRAM OFFERINGS
CARIBBEAN ADVENTURES Discover the magic of the underwater world, feel the freedom of life aboard a yacht, hike through lush rain forests, experience rich cultures, and water ski in a paradise cove. No experience is required for **Adventures in Scuba and Sailing/Underwater Discoveries,** an incredible live-aboard voyage through the Caribbean's Leeward Islands that offers scuba instruction, sail training, and island exploration. Certified divers take this adventure to the next level on **Adventures Underwater–Advanced Scuba** (St. Martin, St. Barts, Saba, Nevis, and Statia) and **Adventures in the Grenadines–Advanced Scuba** (St. Lucia, St. Vincent, and the Grenadines), extraordinary dive-training and sail-training adventures. Participants live aboard and crew fully equipped yachts while working toward multiple scuba and sailing certifications. They also learn about marine biology while exploring flourishing coral gardens, mysterious wrecks, dramatic pinnacles, and world-renowned marine parks. **Arc of the Caribbean** is an adventure-filled, intensive thirty-one-day sail-training voyage from St. Martin to the coast of South America.

WORLD ADVENTURES Explore the world with BROADREACH on scuba diving and multisport wilderness expeditions that span the globe. On **Adventures Down Under,** participants dive the spectacular Great Barrier Reef and explore Australia's diverse terrain—beautiful beaches, lush rain forests, thrilling white water, and the Outback. On the **Costa Rica Experience,** Broadreachers experience the ultimate ecological adventure by backpacking, rafting, horseback riding, surfing, and sea kayaking in this wilderness wonderland. Participants on **Baja Extreme** experience amazing diving, with an abundance of big marine life, surfing, beach camping, hiking, sea kayaking, and a festive culture on this journey to the Sea of Cortez. Broadreachers on **Fiji Solomon Quest** encounter the magnificent scuba diving, beautiful islands, lush rain forests, rich history, and unique cultures of the South Pacific. What Jacques Cousteau rated as the best diving in the world is the heart of the **Sinai Experience**—a spectacular odyssey combining scuba training in the hypnotic Red Sea, cultural immersion, and a desert camel safari. **Honduras Eco-Adventure** combines scuba diving, marine biology studies, dolphin research, rain-forest ecology, whitewater rafting, and cultural exploration from Mayan ruins to Garafuna dancing.

MARINE BIOLOGY ADVENTURES BROADREACH and ACADEMIC TREKS offer a wide variety of hands-on marine biology adventures that qualify for high school and college credit. Students on **Marine Biology Accredited** scuba dive with professional marine biologists and study tropical marine biology with the Bahamas' thriving reefs as their classrooms. On **Sea Turtle Studies,** students travel to Costa Rica to learn about sea turtles and assist in research and protection efforts, trek through lush rain forests, and snorkel with a wealth of marine mammals. Participants on **Dolphin Studies** travel to the beautiful cayes of Belize to learn about dolphins up close with expert researchers as their guides, monitoring dolphin behavior, scuba diving, and gathering data that contributes to ongoing research projects. Participants on **Caribbean Marine Reserves** scuba dive and study the marine parks in Saba, Statia, and St. Barts, designed to safeguard endangered marine resources while allowing for their sustainable use. On **Pacific Whale Treks,** students study the awe-inspiring whales, sea lions, seals, and dolphins that congregate off the coast of British Columbia each summer, work alongside professional scientists, and sea kayak through breathtaking vistas. On **Shipwreck Archaeology** in Bermuda, participants learn to locate, identify, document, and research the Atlantic's most intriguing wrecks under the guidance of professional underwater archaeologists.

COMMUNITY SERVICE ADVENTURES Although every program includes a community service component, these trips have a much stronger focus on service. Participants work on fun and rewarding community service projects while exploring unique cultures and spectacular environments. Participants on **Adventure Peru** trek to Macchu Picchu, explore historical cities, learn about Incan and colonial traditions, and do service work with Quechua Indians in the magnificent Peruvian Andes. On **Amazon Community Service Expedition,** students travel to Brazil to learn basic Portuguese, do service work alongside Brazilians, and explore—from the carnival city of Rio to colonial Salvador to the remote corners of the Amazon. Students interested in medicine travel to Belize for **Wilderness and Traditional Medicine** to become Wilderness First Responders (WFR) and then put their knowledge and skills to use volunteering in medical clinics and villages.

LANGUAGE IMMERSION ADVENTURES There is no better way to learn a language than to live and work among native speakers. ACADEMIC TREKS offers several adventure-filled immersion trips that qualify for college credit and up to 40 hours of community service credit. Participants on **Immersion Ecuador, Immersion Oaxaca (Mexico),** and **Immersion Costa Rica/Nicaragua** build their conversational Spanish-language skills experientially while hiking through beautiful mountains and magnificent landscapes, exploring villages, living with families, and working on community service projects with locals. Students on **Immersion France** and **Immersion Guadeloupe** develop their French-language skills through formal instruction, cultural exploration, adventure activities, and community service work. Students on **Immersion China** learn basic language skills and do service work while exploring the intriguing history and culture of one of the world's oldest civilizations in transformation.

DAILY SCHEDULE

Days are energizing, challenging, and fun, with participants fully involved in all aspects of the trip. There are goals for each day, but the schedule is flexible, and the group decides how the adventure will unfold.

STAFF

BROADREACH staff members are as diverse as its programs. Program leaders include experiential education professionals, PADI scuba instructors, marine biologists, Coast Guard–licensed sailing masters, teachers, and graduate students. On ACADEMIC TREKS adventures, the primary academic instructors have a master's degree or Ph.D. in their program's field of study. At various points in the programs, marine scientists, naturalists, and native culturalists join the group to enhance the educational experience.

COSTS

Tuition is between $3540 and $6180, depending on the program and is all-inclusive except for airfare. Sibling discounts are available.

FOR MORE INFORMATION, CONTACT

BROADREACH/ACADEMIC TREKS
806 McCulloch Street, Suite 102
Raleigh, North Carolina 27603
Phone: 919-256-8200
        888-833-1907 (toll-free)
E-mail: info@gobroadreach.com
Web site: http://www.gobroadreach.com
            http://www.academictreks.com

PARTICIPANT/FAMILY COMMENTS

"I learned more, did more, and had more fun than on any other summer program I've done. I made best friends, saw new places, and learned more about myself. . . . Having only 10 people in the group was the best. I took more responsibility and gained confidence."

"Katherine had an outstanding experience! The teaching was of the highest caliber and beyond our expectations. The staff listened to her goals and helped her reach them. My daughter's adventure was unforgettable . . . enriching . . . Broadreaching. You live up to your name."

"Broadreach surpasses all other summer programs I've seen for the right balance of fun, challenge, skill building, responsibility, and independence. Thanks for another wonderful summer."

"Emily had the experience of a lifetime. It was well-rounded with a wonderful combination of experiential learning, environment, classroom, and culture. What I liked best is the opportunity for such a unique experience combined with college credit."

BROWN UNIVERSITY

BROWN

SUMMER@BROWN

PROVIDENCE, RHODE ISLAND

TYPE OF PROGRAM: Academic enrichment
PARTICIPANTS: Boys and girls, grades 7–12
PROGRAM DATES: Late June through early August

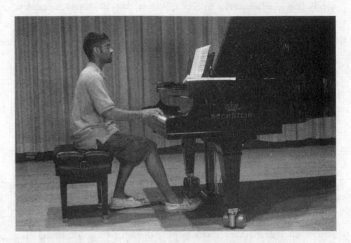

LOCATION

Providence, by virtue of its size, location, and diversity, offers many advantages. A city large enough to support a convention center and a large, active Civic Center that draws top entertainment and sports events, Providence is still small enough to offer involvement in local politics, community service, and cultural activities. Providence also offers an excellent repertory company and a major performing arts center as well as museums, concert halls, and a good commercial transportation system. It does not overwhelm the newcomer.

BACKGROUND AND PHILOSOPHY

Summer@Brown is about learning to succeed on a competitive college campus like Brown's. For many students, the greatest challenge in transition from high school to college is balancing the competing demands of increased responsibility, increased personal freedom, and increased opportunity. Year after year, students report that the primary benefit of Summer@Brown is that they are better prepared, more confident, and better positioned to succeed during one of the biggest transitions of their lives. Academics are the core of the Summer@Brown experience. The program strives to ignite a passion for learning while providing the tools students need to succeed in college. A diverse roster of courses is available—everything from the cutting edge of arts and science to practical, career-oriented courses. Many students report that Summer@Brown is their first taste of a participatory academic environment in which students are encouraged to debate, question, challenge, and explore rather than simply absorb information. This give-and-take is a cornerstone of the Brown academic experience and a key component to success.

PROGRAM OFFERINGS

Summer@Brown allows exceptional high school students to experience what life is like on an Ivy League campus. A number of precollege programs are offered from late June through early August each year. A full description of each program, including dates and fees, is available online (http://www.brown.edu/Administration/Continuing_Studies/pc/index/php).

Seven-week credit courses are for seniors and exceptional juniors who want to challenge themselves in full-credit Brown University courses. Seven-week students share the classroom and study side-by-side with Brown University undergraduates. They are given ample freedom to make decisions and are challenged to meet rigorous academic standards. The standard work load for the program is two courses, and all residential students are expected to be enrolled as full-time students. Seven-week students are tested both emotionally and intellectually, and successful completion of any course demonstrates a student is ready for rigorous Ivy-level academic work.

Mini-courses vary in duration from one to five weeks and allow students to delve deeper into subjects they enjoy or explore new topics they may not have experienced in high school. The short-term, intensive summer courses show students what it means to be completely absorbed in the learning process. As part of their learning, students do such things as shadow a physician, hone their writing skills, map the stars, seek answers to human behavior, examine international affairs, or analyze their own DNA.

Intensive English Language Program is designed for high-achieving international high school students who do not speak English as their native language. The program immerses students in English language and college life through a combination of classroom meetings, trips, social activities, and interactions with American students. Students improve their ability to speak, read, write, and understand English while enjoying all the benefits of Summer@Brown and making lasting friendships with people from all over the world.

The Leadership Institute teaches leadership skills in the context of environmental issues, trade, health, security, human rights, conflict, and diversity. The program brings together students who desire to understand complex issues and develops the knowledge, skills, and attitudes associated with positive, socially responsible leadership. Participants learn to pair new skills with their own strengths as they are educated, inspired, and encouraged to engage in their local communities and the world at large. The Leadership Institute also runs the BELL program for environmental leadership.

TheatreBridge is a unique, six-week hands-on professional theater program that offers a connecting link between high school and college theater and encourages a commitment to a life of creative engagement. Rising high school juniors and seniors have a unique opportunity to stretch their imaginations and skills as they create new work under the mentorship of established theater professionals and develop their acting, directing, and writing skills.

Language and Culture courses are intensive four-week classes that combine the study of language with the study of culture. In a unique approach that combines the study of language, culture, customs, and media, participants build a base from which they can begin to understand a chosen language and its associated culture. These courses allow high school students to get a head start on studying foreign languages and cultures that are often outside the normal high school curriculum.

SPARK is a one-week summer residential program for rising seventh and eighth grade students who have demonstrated outstanding ability in science. The program nurtures students' love of science in a challenging but noncompetitive, stress-free environment with no tests or grades. SPARK brings together groups of students with similar abilities and diverse backgrounds and gives them access to the ideas, resources, and tools they need to nurture their academic gifts in the sciences. They grow as individuals and cultivate their academic gifts in an environment that is safe, challenging, and, most of all, fun.

ENROLLMENT
Programs are open to highly motivated high school students.

DAILY SCHEDULE
Students enrolled in the seven-week credit-bearing summer session take two classes with Brown undergraduates. Those enrolled in noncredit mini-course programs take one class that meets in the morning or afternoon. When students are not in class, they can take advantage of a wide range of college-success workshops that occur during the day and evening.

EXTRA OPPORTUNITIES AND ACTIVITIES
Students can take trips to Boston, Newport, area beaches, and shopping outlets. Other activities include ultimate Frisbee on the Campus Green, documentary films viewing, yoga, karaoke, talent shows, dances, a speaker series, and performances at the Brown/Trinity Playwrights Repertory Theatre. Most (but not all) events and activities are free. College visits and trips to popular destinations have limited space. Students are strongly encouraged to sign up early in the dining halls.

FACILITIES
Students have access to a variety of excellent nonacademic facilities and services. Public computer clusters allow access to the Internet and laser printers. In addition, all students have broadband network connections in the dorm rooms for their personal computers. The Writing Center offers writing experts to review paper and to show students how to be better writers. Brown's excellent air-conditioned libraries offer study spaces where students can obtain ready assistance from resource specialists. There are seven libraries on the Brown campus, each with a different specialty. Brown has a range of world-class athletic facilities—from outdoor tennis courts, to

indoor weight and cardio-training equipment and a track, to an Olympic-sized swimming pool. The main campus dining hall, known among Brown students as "the Ratty," serves all-you-can-eat breakfasts, lunches, and dinners.

STAFF
At Brown, students enjoy a world-class faculty. Brown University Public Safety personnel are on duty twenty-four hours a day, seven days a week. The department comprises more than 70 men and women, including police officers, security officers, communications control officers, and building guards.

MEDICAL CARE
Brown University Health Services is available to all students during business hours, Monday through Friday, for medical problems such as colds, cuts, sprains, or infections. Situations involving medical attention are referred to local hospitals, and parents/guardians are notified. Limited pharmacy and X-ray hours are offered. Brown University maintains its own Emergency Medical Services (EMS). EMTs are equipped to respond immediately to medical emergencies twenty-four hours a day.

COSTS
The cost for each program is available online. Course fees range between $1400 for day students taking one-week classes to $8500 for residential students enrolled in a seven-week credit class.

FINANCIAL AID
Dean's Scholarships are awarded, on a first-come, first-served basis, to high school students who have demonstrated financial need. Applicants must be citizens or permanent residents of the United States. Scholarship funding is limited.

APPLICATION TIMETABLE
Students should check the Web site for specific information regarding application requirements and deadlines. In general, students must submit the completed application, the application fee (which varies depending on when the application is sent in), an official school transcript, and a teacher's recommendation

FOR MORE INFORMATION, CONTACT
Office of Summer and Continuing Studies
Brown University
42 Charlesfield Street
Providence, Rhode Island 02912

Phone: 401-863-7900
Fax: 401-863-3916
E-mail: summer@brown.edu
Web site: http://www.brown.edu/Administration/Continuing_
        Studies/pc/index/php

BUCK'S ROCK PERFORMING AND CREATIVE ARTS CAMP

▼▲▼▲▼▲▼▲▼▲▼▲▼▲▼▲▼▲▼▲▼▲▼▲▼▲▼▲▼▲▼▲▼▲

SUMMER CAMP

NEW MILFORD, CONNECTICUT

TYPE OF PROGRAM: Creative and performing arts
PARTICIPANTS: Coeducational, ages 11–16
ENROLLMENT: 350–400
PROGRAM DATES: June 25 to August 16, 2008
HEADS OF PROGRAM: Mickey and Laura Morris

LOCATION
Situated on 125 acres of deeply wooded forest, only 85 miles from New York City (1½ hours by car), Buck's Rock Performing and Creative Arts Camp is located in the heart of many cultural facilities.

BACKGROUND AND PHILOSOPHY
The challenge to create, to strive, and to know the triumph of achievement: this is the challenge that Buck's Rock Performing and Creative Arts Camp offers teens. Buck's Rock provides campers with the freedom of choice—the ability to choose their own activities and spend as much time at them as they need. Campers are thus able to commit themselves wholeheartedly to their chosen activities, gaining self-confidence and, in the process, developing a better sense of purpose and direction.

Ernst and Ilse Bulova, European educators who studied under Maria Montessori, founded Buck's Rock in 1942. Dr. and Mrs. Bulova left Nazi Germany for England and then came to the United States. They chose a camp setting to apply their convictions about how young people learn. At a time when camps were highly regimented, their approach was daring. In its early years, Buck's Rock emphasized farming, crafts, music, and drama. Gradually, fine arts and additional crafts were introduced, and studios and workshops were built to house them. The performing arts—music, drama, dance, clowning, and improvisation—flourished, as did programs in science, technology, sports, and creative and journalistic writing.

PROGRAM OFFERINGS
Buck's Rock is extremely proud of its performing arts program. The Theater Department produces eight to ten fully mounted plays each summer at one of the many performance stages. Campers may choose to participate not only as actors, but also as stage lighting, sound system, costume, and set design crew members. At the Actor's Studio, daily classes in improvisation, movement, scene study, and characterization are also offered. Clowning workshops include improvisation, standup and sketch comedy, pantomime, slapstick, and juggling. The Music program features many wonderful concerts and houses the orchestra, chorus, a cappella chorus, madrigals, jazz band, and chamber ensembles. Private lessons are available for most instruments. The extensive guitar program includes folk, rock, jazz, and alternative music and is a large part of camp life. Buck's Rock's own recording studio has state-of-the-art professional recording and mixing equipment, a full music-sequencing keyboard workstation, a digital keyboard and drum kit, a sound booth, a band room, and a vocal/drum room. Dance classes are offered at all levels in modern, jazz, tap, ballet, hip-hop, and swing. Campers may also choose to perform in the Dance Recital, which features pieces choreographed by both campers and instructors.

The high level of instruction in the studio arts includes painting and drawing using various techniques and paints; printmaking, in which students may create posters, cards, hand-printed fabrics for clothing, quilts, or three-dimensional pieces using silkscreen, intaglio, monotype, etching, linoleum, and woodcuts; and sculpture, in which campers use plaster, wood, steel, aluminum, and various combinations of these materials, in addition to casting in bronze. Campers interested in photography are encouraged to explore Buck's Rock's beautiful surroundings using a 35-mm format and are taught developing and printing techniques; studio photography and photojournalism workshops are also available. Other fine arts include woodworking, ceramics, metalsmithing, glass blowing, lamp work, and a variety of other glass techniques. The fiber arts feature batik, sewing, weaving, book arts, and papermaking.

Superb opportunities in communications are offered. The publications shop produces newspapers, literary art magazines, a yearbook, programs for Buck's Rock's many performing arts productions, and many other items using word processors, commercial art facilities, offset presses, and digital photography. Creative writing groups, journalism workshops, and poetry and short story seminars meet regularly to produce materials for publication. Campers work on the layout, design, graphics, and art for all projects. WBBC, the camp's radio voice, broadcasts news, reviews, talk shows, radio plays, forums, documentaries, and music seven days a week on its own FM frequency; campers are announcers, performers, DJs, script writers, commentators, and panelists. The digital video program is used as a teaching device, as a recorder of special programs and events, and as an opportunity for creative endeavors in acting and cinematography.

The computer program provides instruction using state-of-the-art equipment. Campers may work on a variety of projects, including the design and implementation of personal programs, HTML, graphics, animation, and games.

Campers may also enjoy working on the animal farm. The animal farm offers an alternative experience to many of the other studios. Campers may choose to adopt an animal, which then becomes their responsibility and playmate during their stay. Opportunities are available to groom and care for the animals, learning much about basic biology and animal care.

Augmenting these excellent programs is a noncompetitive yet comprehensive sports program in which fun and recreation are emphasized. Sports include tennis, fencing, martial arts, basketball, swimming, softball, archery, horseback riding, volleyball, and spelunking.

ENROLLMENT
Many talented children attend camp each summer, but talent is not a prerequisite, since it is at Buck's Rock that many first discover their talents and potential.

DAILY SCHEDULE

7:30 . . . Wake-up (8:30 on Sundays)
8:00 . . . Breakfast (9:00 on Sundays)
9:00 . . . Open shop time, morning activities begin
12:00 . . . Lunch
2:00 . . . Open shop time, afternoon activities begin
6:00 . . . Dinner
. . . After dinner
      Team sports/early evening activities
7:30 . . . Shops and studios reopen on an alternating
      schedule
8:30 . . . Evening activities
10:30 . . . Bedtime (lights-out 20–30 minutes later)

EXTRA OPPORTUNITIES AND ACTIVITIES

Evenings are for relaxation, recreation, and entertainment. In the early evening, campers may choose to participate in a team sport or engage in a choice of other activities, such as guest lectures, workshops, and speak-outs. The featured evening activity includes theater and dance performances, coffee houses, talent nights, poetry slams, weekly movies, concerts, carnivals, and more.

Buck's Rock holds many workshops throughout the summer. Visiting artists lecture and demonstrate their own methods, and trips are taken to nearby museums and galleries. Because the camp believes that an appreciation of the performing arts enriches the lives of young people, trips are made to the Shakespeare Theater, the Berkshire Music Festival at Tanglewood, and Jacob's Pillow for dance. Professional musicians perform concerts during the summer, as do professional comedians.

The main event of the summer is Buck's Rock's Festival, when parents, friends, and alumni are invited to see what campers have accomplished. Displays of fine arts and crafts, demonstrations in the studios, poetry readings, a fashion show, and performances by the orchestra, chorus, jazz band, Actor's Studio, clowns, and dancers are enjoyed by all.

Campers who have reached the age of 15½ are eligible to apply for the Counselor-in-Training (CIT) program, in which they serve an apprentice internship in a specialty area of their choice.

FACILITIES

Dormitory rooms, most occupied by 4 campers, are well planned, practical, and comfortable. Each dormitory and house contains bathrooms with running hot and cold water and showers. The housekeeping staff cleans bathroom facilities daily; campers are responsible for cleaning their own living areas.

Many large buildings house workshops and studios. Buck's Rock's Summer Theater compares favorably with professional theaters in both size and equipment; the music shed and dance studio permit camper concerts, and the recreation hall provides ample room for an actor's studio. The dining hall includes a thoroughly modern kitchen, a bakery, a large dining room where meals are served buffet-style, and a full salad bar. The camp also has a fully stocked canteen, which is open daily.

STAFF

The camper-staff ratio is 2:1, ensuring individualized attention in every area of interest. The large number of staff members who return to the program year after year ensures the stability and continuity of camp programs. Staff members are all college trained and are either teachers in leading schools or universities or talented young artists. All are selected based on their proven abilities in working successfully with teens.

Guidance or house counselors supervise each camper living area. Similar to surrogate parents, these counselors provide leadership for the campers, stimulate initiative, and encourage participation in camp activities.

MEDICAL CARE

Every effort is made to protect the health and safety of campers. Buck's Rock is equipped with an infirmary/dispensary. The camp physicians supervise medical care. Two to three nurses and a nurse's aide are in residence throughout the summer.

COSTS

For 2008, tuition is $8390 for the full season, $7290 for the six-week option, $5990 for the first half session, and $5790 for the second half session. Fees include laundry, short trips, and most shop materials. Fees do not include optional items such as horseback riding, the canteen, long trips, and some shop materials. CITs receive a $500 reduction in tuition for the full season.

TRANSPORTATION

Campers arriving at New York City airports and local bus and rail terminals can be met and picked up by Buck's Rock staff members.

APPLICATION TIMETABLE

Initial inquiry is welcome year-round. An open house is held in the spring. Tours are available during the summer. There is no application deadline or fee, space permitting.

FOR MORE INFORMATION, CONTACT

Mickey and Laura Morris, Directors
Buck's Rock Camp
59 Buck's Rock Road
New Milford, Connecticut 06776
Phone: 860-354-5030
Fax: 860-354-1355
E-mail: bucksrock@bucksrockcamp.com
Web site: http://bucksrockcamp.com

CALIFORNIA STATE SUMMER SCHOOL FOR THE ARTS– INNERSPARK

SUMMER PROGRAM

VALENCIA, CALIFORNIA

TYPE OF PROGRAM: Arts program
PARTICIPANTS: Coeducational, grades 9–12
ENROLLMENT: More than 520
PROGRAM DATES: July 12 through August 8
HEAD OF PROGRAM: Robert M. Jaffe, Director

LOCATION

The California State Summer School for the Arts–InnerSpark is held at the California Institute of the Arts (CalArts), a fully accredited degree-granting institution of higher learning for students of the visual, cinematic, and performing arts. Established through the vision and generosity of Walt Disney in 1961, CalArts is located in Valencia, a residential community situated 25 miles north of Hollywood in the Santa Clarita Valley.

BACKGROUND AND PHILOSOPHY

The California State Summer School for the Arts–InnerSpark is a rigorous preprofessional training program in the visual and performing arts, creative writing, animation, and film for talented artists of high school age. InnerSpark provides a supportive environment in which students hone acquired skills and explore new techniques and ideas for an intense and exciting learning experience. The School was created by the California Legislature and held its first session in 1987. Its purpose is to provide a training ground for future artists who wish to pursue careers in the arts and entertainment industries in California. The California State Summer School for the Arts–InnerSpark is a state agency funded through a unique public-private partnership.

PROGRAM OFFERINGS

Students apply for the opportunity to study in one of the School's seven departments. They receive 3 units of California State University elective credit for successful participation.

Animation students explore the theories and techniques of animation in studio workshops conducted by leading artists in the field. Course work in two-dimensional animation, figure drawing, and conceptual issues in art is augmented by visits from guest animators and tours of Hollywood animation studios. Students attend screenings of animations that demonstrate the history and breadth of the art form.

Students in the **Creative Writing** Program receive individualized instruction in poetry, fiction, and scriptwriting. They work with an award-winning faculty in small groups and have opportunities to learn from visiting writers, literary agents, journalists, and poets. Students and faculty members share their work with the School community in weekly open readings and publish an anthology at the end of the session.

InnerSpark's **Dance** Program provides a rigorous course of dance instruction. The curriculum includes intensive training in ballet, modern, body conditioning mat technique, choreography, dance history, and jazz. Students have the option of taking classes in improvisation and modern repertory or pointe and ballet repertory.

Film and Video students receive instruction and experience in film and video production techniques. They work with Super-8 and 16-mm film and a variety of video media to create short works individually and in collaboration with other students. They attend film screenings, meet filmmakers and producers, and go on field trips to film studios and locations of interest in the Los Angeles area.

InnerSpark's **Music** Program for vocalists, instrumentalists, and composers is designed to develop each student's creativity, fundamental musicianship, and understanding of contemporary musical history and styles. Courses include musicianship and theory, twentieth-century musical styles, improvisation, world music, composition, electro-acoustic computer music, piano, and voice. Students receive private lessons and participate in student ensembles. The School presents leading professionals in concerts and master classes.

The **Theatre** Program is an intensive acting course that emphasizes the development of physical and vocal awareness and control as essential elements of the actor's craft. Classes are held in tai chi chu'an, acting, movement, voice, story, stage combat, physical comedy, stage acrobatics, and musical theater. There are special forums, workshops, and guest lecturers. Students perform works-in-progress throughout the summer.

InnerSpark's **Visual Arts** Program offers studio classes in figure drawing, design, painting, digital art, printmaking, sculpture, ceramics, and digital and traditional photography. Lectures on topics of importance to visual artists are given by guest artists and others. Workshops are conducted by visiting artists, and students go on field trips to local museums and galleries.

ENROLLMENT

California residents enrolled in grades 9 through 12 may attend InnerSpark. Students from outside of California may also apply; a limited number are admitted each year. Participants are selected in the spring on the basis of their talent and creativity, as demonstrated through assignments and teacher recommendations. InnerSpark's student body is representative of the ethnic and socioeconomic diversity of the state. The admissions process is highly competitive; in 2007, approximately half of all applicants were accepted. Students who attend the School are named California Arts Scholars.

DAILY SCHEDULE
On Monday through Saturday, breakfast is available in the cafeteria beginning at 7 a.m. Regular classes are held between 8 a.m. and 4 p.m. and generally last about 3 hours each. One hour is set aside for lunch. Students have opportunities to participate in special interdisciplinary classes and other activities from 4 to 6 p.m. Dinner is served from 5 to 7 p.m. Evenings are devoted to rehearsals, self-paced studio work, film screenings, collaborative projects, concerts, lectures, sports activities, and informal student performances and poetry readings in the student coffeehouse.

EXTRA OPPORTUNITIES AND ACTIVITIES
There is a full schedule of recreational opportunities available on weekdays and Saturdays after class and all day on Sundays. Optional field trips to California attractions such as Disneyland, the Los Angeles Music Center, and the Getty Museum are offered on Sundays at cost.

FACILITIES
The main building on the 60-acre campus is a five-level multiwinged structure of 500,000 square feet that houses art and electronic music studios, classrooms, dance spaces, rehearsal rooms, theaters, galleries, film editing laboratories, sound and video stages, animation studios, libraries, the bookstore, and the cafeteria. All students reside in Chouinard Hall, the student dormitory. Tennis courts and a large swimming pool are located adjacent to the facility. Spacious lawns with shade trees, open fields, and large hillside areas provide room for sports and relaxation.

STAFF
InnerSpark faculty members are accomplished practicing professional artists, musicians, writers, dancers, actors, and filmmakers. Many are distinguished college and university instructors. The teacher-student ratio is roughly 1:9. The School employs a registered nurse and assistants, a licensed counselor, and a recreation director. The CalArts Residential Life staff, supervised by an experienced professional director, includes 18 graduate student resident assistants. CalArts security personnel are on campus at all times.

MEDICAL CARE
A registered nurse is on duty Monday through Friday from 8:30 a.m. to 8:30 p.m. Emergency and after-hours care and medical referrals are available through Santa Clarita Valley Quality Care (medical walk-in center), Kaiser-Permanente (HMO), and the Henry Mayo Newhall Memorial Hospital, all of which are located within 4 miles of the campus.

RELIGIOUS LIFE
InnerSpark is a nonsectarian institution. Students with parental permission and prearranged transportation may leave the campus to attend religious services.

COSTS
The comprehensive fee covering room, board, and tuition for California residents is $1400; for out-of-state attendees, it is $4400. Students must pay a $60 credit registration fee if they wish to receive California State University credit. Animation, Film and Video, and Visual Arts students pay additional materials fees of $120. The nonrefundable application fee is $20. A small amount of pocket money for laundry, postage, and souvenirs is recommended. Optional Sunday field trips are offered at cost. A nonrefundable deposit of 30 percent of the comprehensive fee is required upon acceptance. Payment plans are available.

FINANCIAL AID
InnerSpark provides financial aid for applicants based on demonstrated need. Nearly 40 percent of the students who attend InnerSpark have from 20 percent to 90 percent of their tuition paid by the California State Summer School for the Arts (CSSSA) Foundation. A financial aid request form is included in the InnerSpark application flyer. A request for financial aid does not affect a student's chances of being accepted. Financial aid is available only to California residents.

TRANSPORTATION
The Hollywood/Burbank airport is located 20 miles south of CalArts and is served by major domestic airlines. InnerSpark provides transportation to and from this airport on the first and last day with prior reservation. Those who come by car should take Interstate 5 to the McBean Parkway exit and head east. The campus entrance is on the immediate right.

APPLICATION TIMETABLE
Inquiries are welcome throughout the year. The application postmark deadline is February 29, 2008. Letters of acceptance are sent out by the first week in May. The application assignments require careful preparation, so interested students should download the application forms as early as possible.

FOR MORE INFORMATION, CONTACT
California State Summer School for the Arts–InnerSpark
Phone: 916-274-5815
Fax: 916-274-5814
E-mail: application@innerspark.us
Web site: http://www.innerspark.us

CAMBRIDGE COLLEGE PROGRAMME

―――――――――――――――――――――――――――――

PRECOLLEGE SUMMER PROGRAMME AT UNIVERSITY OF CAMBRIDGE, ENGLAND

CAMBRIDGE, ENGLAND

TYPE OF PROGRAM: Precollege academic and cultural enrichment
PARTICIPANTS: Coeducational, high school ages
ENROLLMENT: Limited
PROGRAM DATES: Three-week session during July and August; optional one-week Paris trip afterward
HEAD OF PROGRAM: Ms. Taryn Edwards, Director

LOCATION

The University of Cambridge is made up of more than thirty colleges located in the city centre and its environs. The programme is held at several of these colleges. Headquarters is at Queens' College, one of the most beautiful of all the colleges, which is located on the banks of the River Cam in the historic centre of Cambridge.

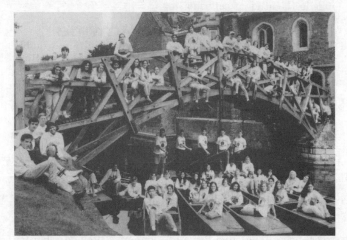

BACKGROUND AND PHILOSOPHY

This programme is the oldest established teen program at Cambridge. It is the only program at either Oxford or Cambridge where students are lectured only by faculty members associated with the University of Cambridge. Founded in 1986, the programme provides a stimulating and rigorous course of study for qualified and well-motivated students. It stresses the needs of the individual student and provides an opportunity to explore subjects on the skill-building level where no prerequisites are required.

Faculty members guide students to master skills, to acquire knowledge, and to think critically, creatively, and independently. The programme's structure fosters close association between staff and students for personal, social, and intellectual development.

The director and staff live at the colleges with the students to supervise and ensure their safety and well-being. Academics are enriched with both field trips and day trips to historic sites, plus trips to London, Bath, Stratford-upon-Avon, and Stonehenge. Cultural enrichment is achieved through visits to London museums, a workshop for Shakespeare and Drama classes at Shakespeare's Globe Theatre in London, and theatre performances in the West End.

PROGRAM OFFERINGS

The programme offers a choice of academic study in courses. Last year they included History of Chemistry, Criminal Law, English Literary Villains, Veterinary Medicine, Philosophy of Mind, The British Monarchy, History of Calculus, Tibetan Buddhism, Jane Austen, Marine Biology, Special Relativity, Superstrings, A Hitchhiker's Guide to 20th-Century Physics, Comparative Law, Psychology of War, Sociology, International Relations and Terrorism, Astrophysics, British Intelligence and the Art of Espionage, War and Chivalry, Biomedical Ethics, Photography, Scriptwriting, Moot Court, Archaeology, Philosophy, Shakespeare, *Hamlet,* Cambridge Scientific Discoveries, Studio Art, Saxons, Saints and Scholars, Psychology, Creative Writing, Debate, History of Art, Latin, Quantum Physics, Major World Religions, DNA Fingerprinting, Evolutionary Biology, Economics, Alfred Hitchcock, Journalism, Psy-

chology and Law, World War II, Egyptology, Drama, Architecture and History, and Political Theory. In addition, there are daily group lectures and field trips on British cultural history. Supplemental lectures by distinguished professors enrich the curriculum on a variety of subjects, such as Roman Britain, the mysteries of Stonehenge, and much more. The large variety of evening activities includes tennis, punting, rowing, volleyball, croquet, basketball, lacrosse, squash, soccer, rugby, cricket, aerobics, swimming, field hockey, golf, running, chess, movies, salsa dancing, concerts, choir, plays on the College lawns, polo, fencing, ice skating, a James Bond party, and barbeques.

Most students participate in the programme to broaden their knowledge and strengthen their skills rather than to gain academic credits. Each student receives an evaluation of performance for classwork, including detailed comments by their instructor, a syllabus of each course, and a certificate of attendance. Many students include these in their applications to colleges and universities, and many high schools and colleges give credit to students on the basis of these reports.

ENROLLMENT

One of the most pleasant and beneficial experiences of the Cambridge College Programme is living and working with other students who represent diverse geographic locations, religions, races, and economic circumstances.

DAILY SCHEDULE

The day begins with a self-service breakfast, followed by the first course, freely elected, which meets from 9 to 10:30 a.m. Field trips are scheduled in conjunction with the lectures. The second course, British Cultural History, meets from 11 a.m. to 12:30 p.m. and is structured for the whole group, with lectures and field trips planned to enrich students' knowledge of England. The afternoon course, also elected, meets from 2 to 3:30 and is followed by free time for exploring Cambridge or studying. Or students may use this time to rehearse for a play, orchestra, or choir, or take golf lessons or an SAT Review. Dinner is taken between 4:30 and 7:15 p.m., with 2 hours reserved afterward for the evening activities described above. Study hours are from 9 to 11 p.m.

EXTRA OPPORTUNITIES AND ACTIVITIES

Excursions are supervised by the director and staff members. Four trips are taken to London for museums, sightseeing, shopping, and two plays, such as *The Lion King* or *My Fair Lady*, in the West End. Sites visited in London include the British Museum, the Tower of London, the National Gallery and Portrait Gallery, the new Tate Modern, Churchill's War Rooms, Covent Garden, and Harrod's. Sites viewed on day trips are Big Ben, the Houses of Parliament, Trafalgar Square, St. Paul's Cathedral, Hyde Park, Buckingham Palace, Westminster Abbey, and 10 Downing Street. Day trips are to Warwick Castle, Stonehenge, Bath, Ely Cathedral, and Stratford-upon-Avon for a Royal Shakespeare Company play such as *Richard III*.

Though the daily schedule is a full one, there is ample free time to walk into town for lunch, relax with friends, play tennis, or punt on the River Cam. Cambridge is one of the most beautiful cities in England. Its college quadrangles of ancient stone buildings along the river surround gardens of trees, flowers, and manicured lawns. The city has an active cultural life during the summer, including concerts, plays, and special events during the Cambridge Festival, the annual historic fair, and the annual Shakespeare Festival. Museums, theatres, and shops are within a short walk of the colleges.

All students have the option to participate in sports, which are scheduled in the early evening. The programme aims to provide practical experience in traditional British sports. Each year an exhibition and opportunity to play real tennis are offered, and the programme also offers daily supervised use of the weight and fitness gym at Queens' College.

There is an optional 10-hour workshop to coach students in how to mentally prepare for the PSAT/SAT exams, how to approach each section, and how to manage time during the test. Practice tests are taken, timed, and results discussed.

There is also an optional one-week trip to Paris with the director and staff after the regular program, for a cultural feast of French history. This includes visits to the Eiffel Tower, the Louvre, the Arc de Triomphe, the Tuileries Garden, the Sacré Coeur, Notre Dame, Versailles, Claude Monet's home, Vincent Van Gogh's village, Rodin's studio, a boat tour on the Seine, shopping, and more.

FACILITIES

Students have a private room in a college dormitory with daily maid service. The sexes are segregated, and all supervision and curfew enforcement is undertaken by the live-in director and staff.

STAFF

The founder and director, Ms. Taryn Edwards, is Fmr. Honorary Senior Member of Staff at a college of the university, and a member of the College Board of Appeals. She has served on the Board of Trustees at the Putney School of Vermont and on the Board of Directors at the Chicago Academy. Ms. Edwards and staff are present throughout the programme.

The faculty members are British lecturers and educators distinguished in their fields. The motivating faculty members care about their students and are available to them both in and out of class, creating an atmosphere in which learning is a positive experience.

MEDICAL CARE

Addenbrooke's Hospital is available for emergencies on a 24-hour basis. Students are accompanied to these facilities by the director or a member of the staff.

RELIGIOUS LIFE

The programme is nondenominational, but schedules of church and synagogue services are made available.

COSTS

The 2006 resident-student charge, which included a private room in a college dormitory, breakfast and dinners while on campus (vegetarian meals available), theatre, excursions, scheduled transportation to and from London airports, entrance fees, linen, and daily maid service, was $5795. This fee excluded airfare, lunches, any dinners off campus, and tickets for some optional evening activities. A fee of $595 was required with each application. Optional costs included golf lessons, $250; Cambridge SAT Review fee, $500; and Paris trip, $2200, including all fees and excursions, room and breakfast, and transportation to Paris and to the airport for departure. It did not include lunch, dinner, or airfare home. Enrollment was limited to 75 students and the fee must have been paid in full immediately upon acceptance. Students can write or call the programme for a brochure that reflects 2008 costs.

TRANSPORTATION

The director organizes a group for departure with her from Chicago to London. All students departing from other cities will be met by staff and private coaches at both London's Heathrow and Gatwick Airports.

APPLICATION TIMETABLE

Enrollment is limited, and there is a rolling admission policy.

FOR MORE INFORMATION, CONTACT

Ms. Taryn Edwards, Director
Cambridge College Programme, U.S. Office
175 East Delaware Place, Suite 5518
Chicago, Illinois 60611
Phone: 312-787-7477
      800-922-3552 (toll-free)
Fax: 312-988-7268

CAMP REGIS–APPLEJACK

SUMMER CAMP

PAUL SMITHS, NEW YORK

TYPE OF PROGRAM: Traditional camping, land sports, water sports, and wilderness experiences

PARTICIPANTS: Coeducational, ages 6–16

ENROLLMENT: 225

PROGRAM DATES: Late June through mid-August: one 8-week and two 4-week sessions (two-week sessions available for younger, first-time campers)

HEAD OF PROGRAM: Michael P. Humes

LOCATION

Camp Regis–Applejack occupies its own protected cove with a ¾-mile shoreline on one of the most treasured lakes in the pristine Adirondack Park, Upper St. Regis Lake. Access to wilderness canoeing and hiking is at the camp's doorstep. Within the 6-million-acre park are forty-six high peaks and thousands of lakes, streams, and rivers. Regis–Applejack is 2½ hours south of Montreal, 5 hours from New York City, and 1½ hours from Burlington, Vermont.

BACKGROUND AND PHILOSOPHY

Much of the feeling and spirit at Regis–Applejack can be attributed to its location and philosophy. Upper St. Regis Lake puts campers in touch with the wild every day. They see, hear, and touch nature, whether watching a sunset across the water, listening to the call of loons, or feeling the wind in their faces while sailing. This closeness to nature is a profound counterpoint to an often-crowded urban environment and to the pressures of today's busy lifestyle. Here campers learn about nature and themselves by observing and by doing—a refreshing change from the academic climate of a student's school year.

The camp philosophy has been established through the years by the Humes family, who founded Regis–Applejack in 1946. The family's background is in education. The Humes believe that camping is best when it strives for excellence and brings together a variety of religions and races, as is the tradition in the Society of Friends (Quakers), of which the Humes are members. Each camper is made to feel accepted as an individual. To help implement this philosophy, a mature staff is employed, including many couples who are skilled in making campers feel at home and at ease.

Because the boys' and girls' sections are on the same campus, meals and many activities are routinely shared, creating a comfortable climate and avoiding the often-forced situations where boys and girls meet only on formal occasions. Both sexes are encouraged to try all the activities at camp without preconceptions about what they "should" enjoy.

PROGRAM OFFERINGS

Regis–Applejack offers an extensive water sports program. Three separate docks support the small-craft and waterskiing programs; a fourth Olympic-regulation dock and sand beach support the swimming program. One of the highlights of a Regis–Applejack summer is sailing the length of the lake aboard a variety of boats, from small craft to full-size sloops.

Campers can water-ski, windsurf, sail, fish, dive, earn American Red Cross swim certificates, canoe, and kayak.

Land sport facilities include seven all-weather tennis courts, handball and basketball courts, and four large playing fields. Regis–Applejack offers a wide range of land sports, including basketball, field hockey, street hockey, football, lacrosse, soccer, softball, tennis, volleyball, and track and field. Instruction in all athletics is patient and thorough; emphasis is put on learning the proper technique through individual instruction from experienced coaches who know how to focus on the special abilities of each camper. Thus the shy beginner and the natural athlete can both learn and have fun.

The Adirondack Park offers splendid opportunities to explore the natural world. All campers participate in outings, which vary in length from overnight to a week, depending on age, experience, and interest. Campers study campcraft and pioneering in a setting that lends substance to what is taught. Camp Applejack, the teen division, makes available optional weeklong canoeing and hiking trips in the wilderness as well as "teen tour" excursions to such places as Montreal, Cape Cod, and Maine.

ENROLLMENT

Campers come from different racial and ethnic backgrounds as well as from other countries.

EXTRA OPPORTUNITIES AND ACTIVITIES

The athletics and outing programs are balanced by a wide choice of arts and crafts, performing arts, special interest activities, hobbies, and field trips. During the summer, every group in camp puts on a play or musical and takes part in theater workshops, including ones on stagecraft, lighting, and makeup. The arts and crafts building offers classes in everything from batik to woodworking. Special interests include club nights, the small farm and animal center, photography, the yearbook, and cooking. For those interested in more sports, there are active competitive programs.

FACILITIES

Regis–Applejack, on 70 acres, was originally a private estate, and many of the "Adirondack rustic" buildings have been carefully restored to keep their original spirit. The camp's forty-

five buildings include the playhouse and recreation and dining halls. Campers are housed approximately 12–16 to a cabin. All cabins have their own inside bathrooms, three or four bedrooms, and rustic "Adirondack-style" recreation rooms with fireplaces. Girls' cabins are near the boating area, and boys' cabins are near the swimming dock; most have views of the lake.

DAILY SCHEDULE

```
8:00 . . . Breakfast
9:15 . . . Free-choice activities
10:30 . . . Group activities or swim
11:45 . . . Free-choice activities
1:00 . . . Lunch
2:00 . . . Quiet time
2:45 . . . Free-choice activities
4:00 . . . Group activities
5:15 . . . General swim or free time
6:00 . . . Dinner
7:00 . . . Evening activities
8:30 . . . Special teen programs
```

Thursday is set aside for field trips in the Lake George–Lake Placid area or for occasional trips to Montreal. On Saturday, there are picnics in the afternoon and skits and plays in the evening. Sunday afternoon is devoted to all-camp activities and programs, and Sunday evening is Buffet Night in the dining hall.

STAFF

The highly qualified and mature counselors include many married couples. Bunk counselors and program leaders do not double as athletics coaches; coaches are specialists and teachers. All staff members spend a week on campus familiarizing themselves with camp philosophy and programs and learning about each camper in their group.

MEDICAL CARE

The infirmary is staffed by 2 nurses. A doctor is on call, and a hospital is 12 miles away in Saranac Lake.

RELIGIOUS LIFE

The camp has always been nonsectarian, although its origins are loosely tied with the Society of Friends and Unitarians. Catholic campers have the option of attending Mass nearby. There is a nondenominational Sunday meeting on campus at which topics relating to ethics, values, and the environment are discussed.

COSTS

The 2008 costs are $4000 to $7500. A registration deposit of $600 is required.

FINANCIAL AID

A limited number of scholarships are available based on need. Work-study positions for college students ages 19 and older are available.

TRANSPORTATION

Staff members escort campers from the New York tristate area, Philadelphia, and central New Jersey aboard the camp's chartered overland buses, and group flights are arranged out of the Baltimore/Washington, Atlanta, and Miami airports. The camp also provides group transportation from Boston, Syracuse, and Montreal. Campers may also be met at the

Plattsburgh, Albany, Burlington, and Montreal, Canada, airports. Travel details are worked out with each camper.

APPLICATION TIMETABLE

Applications are accepted beginning in early October. The director visits prospective campers in their homes in fall and winter. Parents are welcome to visit camp during summer.

FOR MORE INFORMATION, CONTACT

Summer
Michael Humes
Camp Regis–Applejack
P.O. Box 245
Paul Smiths, New York 12970

Phone: 518-327-3117
Fax: 518-327-3193

Fall, Winter, Spring
Michael Humes
Camp Regis–Applejack
60 Lafayette Road West
Princeton, New Jersey 08540

Phone: 609-688-0368
Fax: 609-688-0369
E-mail: campregis@aol.com
Web site: http://www.campregis-applejack.com

PARTICIPANT/FAMILY COMMENTS

"Yesterday I climbed a nearby mountain and sat on the top for a couple of hours. As I sat there, I thought about all the fun times I have had at camp. I have so many memories from the last six summers. . . . many of the happiest days of my life took place at Camp Regis–Applejack. Within only two months a year, I made some of my closest friends—both campers and staff. The conditions at camp force people to learn to live together, accept each other, and understand each other. I think I owe a lot of my good qualities to the summers at camp."

"Hank and I want to thank you for providing another successful summer for our daughter Katherine. Each summer we have seen a big leap in her independence and development of social skills. Thanks for your diligence in providing a safe atmosphere in which learning and childhood joys appear to be intertwined and flourish."

CAMP TREETOPS

CAMP
Treetops
A time and place for wonder

SUMMER PROGRAM

LAKE PLACID, NEW YORK

TYPE OF PROGRAM: Residential summer camp offering diverse traditional activities with a progressive philosophy; integral farm and garden program, including horseback riding and animal care; studio and performing arts; day and overnight wilderness trips; waterfront activities, including swimming, canoeing, kayaking, and sailing; emphasis on community as well as individual growth

PARTICIPANTS: Coeducational, ages 8–14; Junior Camp, ages 8–11; Senior Camp, ages 12–14

ENROLLMENT: Junior Camp, 75; Senior Camp, 90

PROGRAM DATES: Full seven-week session: June 28–August 16, 2008; four-week option for first-time 8- to 11-year-olds: June 28–July 27, 2008

HEAD OF PROGRAM: Karen Culpepper, Camp Director

LOCATION

Camp Treetops is located on beautiful Round Lake in the High Peaks region of the Adirondack Mountains, just outside the village of Lake Placid, New York. Its 225-acre campus is charming yet rugged and includes a working organic farm, providing fresh produce for meals and opportunities for interaction with farm animals.

BACKGROUND AND PHILOSOPHY

Established in 1921, Camp Treetops pioneered the concept of the coeducational, culturally diverse summer camp for children. Directors Helen and Doug Haskell were informed by the progressive values of educator John Dewey, and the Treetops philosophy is still the same as it was more than eighty-five years ago: to provide an environment where children have the opportunity to progress steadily toward independence, maturity, and confident responsibility, while gaining unhurried individual growth, good health, and happiness along the way. This important work is accomplished today as it was then: by offering diverse in-camp programs, an extensive wilderness trip program, and meaningful work on the farm and in the camp community. Children choose and plan most of their own activities beyond the required swimming and riding classes. A work program in which staff members and campers all participate emphasizes collaboration and community accomplishment. Treetops continues to enroll campers and hire staff members from varying racial, religious, national, economic, and geographic backgrounds.

PROGRAM OFFERINGS

The waterfront: Waterfront activities are offered on Round Lake, which is on the camp property. Skills are taught for their intrinsic value as well as to prepare children for longer trips or more challenging conditions.

Swimming: Each child is placed in an appropriate American Red Cross swim class and attends a swim class for one period every day except Sunday. Swim classes are taught with an emphasis on safety, skill development, and fun. In addition to instructional classes, general swims are part of the daily schedule.

Canoeing and kayaking: Most children learn basic safety and paddling skills on Round Lake. As children become proficient, they may participate in day and overnight trips on the many lakes and rivers in the Adirondack Park.

Sailing: Expert instruction is available. Many of the sailboats are moved to the Saranac Lakes in midsummer to provide greater challenges and the opportunity for the campers to go on day and overnight sailing trips.

English riding: Treetops owns its own stable and horses. In addition to the required weekly lesson, many children choose to ride more often. Campers have two riding rings to choose from, plus the

camp's own trails and nearby Clifford Falls, where Treetops has the use of another barn, a corral, and trails that lead into the backwoods. When campers have learned to saddle, bridle, and care for their mounts and have demonstrated adequate equestrian skills, they are eligible for an overnight riding trip to Clifford Falls.

Hiking and rock climbing: Treetops' unique location offers a wide variety of mountains and trails to hike and excellent places for rock climbing. Treetops offers a range of trips, from short, easy hikes for beginners to more challenging hikes for the most rugged and adventurous camper.

Overnight trips: Overnight trips last from two to five days. They vary widely in difficulty in order to accommodate beginners, seasoned veterans, and all those in between. In addition to the hiking, climbing, and riding trips, children paddle or sail in nearby lakes and rivers, swim in little-known prime swimming holes, explore, or gather flora and fauna for the nature rooms.

Crafts and the arts: Both Junior and Senior Camp divisions have a well-equipped ceramics studio, a woodshop, and a weaving room. Children participate in batik, photography, knitting, candle making, painting, drawing, and other crafts. Campers make their own music, whether by singing before mealtimes, practicing instruments, or performing in informal concerts. They enjoy participating in plays, practicing their own dance and gymnastics routines, and square dancing.

Work program: The Treetops experience includes gaining a sense of community through fun activities and meaningful individual contributions that foster responsibility. The community work program involves all children in daily chores and the physical care of the gardens and animals. Although barn chores may be the most arduous and demanding assignments, they are usually the most popular jobs.

The farm and gardens: The barn provides incredible opportunities for fun and learning. Not only do children see firsthand the ways of horses, ponies, cows, pigs, chickens, llamas, sheep, and goats, they also care for them. Children have the opportunity to nurture the farm animals and learn about them in a hands-on environment. For example, children may knit a hat with wool from the same sheep they help herd and care for. The 3 lush acres of camp gardens do far more than contribute fresh lettuce, beans, and strawberries to the camp table—the gardens help children see how every bit of food they eat derives from soil, sun, and water and requires planting, cultivating, weeding, and harvesting. They learn about soil by participating in the extensive composting program. Nothing is wasted. All of the food scraps are recycled to the compost pile or fed to the pigs.

ENROLLMENT

The camp community is diverse. Children come from throughout the United States and represent a wide range of economic, racial, religious, and social backgrounds. Routinely, children attend from such countries as Guatemala, Mexico, Korea, France, Germany, Canada, Israel, Russia, and Indonesia. Treetops is usually fully enrolled with 75 junior campers and 90 senior campers.

DAILY SCHEDULE

7:00	Barn chores
8:00	Breakfast
8:45	Clean-up and morning council
9:45	Morning activities
12:15	Lunch
1:00	Afternoon council and rest hour
2:45	Afternoon activities
5:00	Work jobs
6:00	Dinner
7:00	Evening activities

One evening each week is set aside for square dancing. On a second evening, campers gather to sing, watch drama productions, or listen to musical pieces on which children have been working.

EXTRA OPPORTUNITIES AND ACTIVITIES

The camp program is complemented by field trips to places like the Lake Placid Horse Show, a nearby fish hatchery, the fort at Crown Point, the Paul Smith's Visitors Interpretive Center, the Wild Center natural history museum, and the Onchiota Native American Museum. Professional artists and craftspeople are brought in as artists in residence. For 15- to 17-year-olds, Treetops Expeditions offers wilderness programs in small groups that have teens canoeing, backpacking, climbing, hiking, and kayaking in the Canadian

Rockies, the south Pacific, Alaska, Spain, Scotland, Ecuador, and France. Treetops also offers an English Enrichment Program for campers who would like to improve their English speaking skills.

FACILITIES

Treetops has access to the library and other facilities of North Country School, the junior boarding school that shares its campus during the fall, winter, and spring. Children live in large platform tents, lean-tos, or small cabins.

STAFF

The Camp Treetops counselor-camper ratio of 1:3 offers an exceptional environment for the attention and care of children and teens. Treetops' multigenerational staff includes professional educators and others with outstanding experience. The youngest staff members are terrifically energetic 18-year-olds, normally with a year of college behind them. Treetops attracts seasoned veterans, many of whom are parents themselves; many have been at Treetops for several summers. The staff return rate is typically 75 to 80 percent, and many former campers return to work as staff members. Treetops' summer staff typically totals about 75.

MEDICAL CARE

Treetops employs 2 full-time nurses, 1 each in the Junior and Senior Camps. The camp doctor has offices 7 miles away at the Lake Placid Hospital. Because Lake Placid—one of two Olympic Training Centers in the United States—attracts world-class athletes, the medical facilities are excellent. In addition, there is a strong emphasis on nutrition at Treetops. The camp grows much of its own food and bakes its own bread. No soda, candy, or junk food is served. Care packages from home are carefully screened.

RELIGIOUS LIFE

Treetops is nondenominational. The camp staff works to make arrangements for children who wish to attend services in Lake Placid.

COSTS

The camp fee for the 2008 season is $6800. A $1000 deposit is required with registration and is applied to tuition. The fee is all-inclusive, with the exception of transportation to and from camp and incidentals. No spending money is needed, and incidentals are billed to campers' accounts.

FINANCIAL AID

To make the camp experience available to as many families as possible, Treetops awards need-based scholarships; applications are available on request. About 25 percent of the campers receive varying levels of financial aid.

TRANSPORTATION

Counselors accompany children on buses from Manhattan. Children are also picked up at the Albany Airport and the Saranac Lake Airport. Driving time from New York City is approximately 5½ hours.

APPLICATION TIMETABLE

Although applications are accepted beginning in September, there is often a waiting list until all of the returning campers have been heard from. The return rate is routinely more than 80 percent, which limits openings, especially for the older age groups.

FOR MORE INFORMATION, CONTACT

Karen Culpepper, Director
Camp Treetops
P.O. Box 187
Lake Placid, New York 12946

Phone: 518-523-9329 Ext. 112
Fax: 518-523-4858
E-mail: karenc@nct.org
Web site: http://www.nct.org

PARTICIPANT/FAMILY COMMENTS

"I would like to take this opportunity to tell you what a successful stay Ted had at Treetops. I recognize a great deal of personal growth in him and the proud acquisition of many new skills and areas of interest."

CAREER EXPLORATIONS

▼▲▼▲▼▲▼▲▼▲▼▲▼▲▼▲▼▲▼▲▼▲▼▲▼▲▼▲▼▲▼▲▼

SUMMER INTERNSHIPS IN NEW YORK AND BOSTON FOR HIGH SCHOOL STUDENTS

NEW YORK, NEW YORK, AND BOSTON, MASSACHUSETTS

TYPE OF PROGRAM: Summer internship and career exploration program for residential and day students; optional SAT preparation and college-preparatory track

PARTICIPANTS: Coeducational, ages 16–18

ENROLLMENT: 60–80 in New York City, 40–60 in Boston

PROGRAM DATES: July 2008

HEADS OF PROGRAM: Margot Jackler, M.Ed., Executive Director; Josh Flowerman, New York Director; Todd Aronson, Boston Director

LOCATION

Career Explorations (CE) offers internships in New York City and Boston. New York interns live in the Meredith Willson Residence Hall at the Juilliard School in the midst of Lincoln Center on the Upper West Side of Manhattan. Boston program participants live in the Little Building on the campus of Emerson College across the street from the Boston Common in the heart of downtown Boston. Career Explorations makes full use of the diverse cultural, educational, and recreational resources that place New York City and Boston among the most exciting cities in the world.

BACKGROUND AND PHILOSOPHY

Founded in 2003 by the Flowerman family, Career Explorations is designed to provide opportunities for highly motivated high school students to gain valuable insight into possible career goals and courses of study in a nurturing and supervised environment. Career Explorations makes available a healthy

balance of work, culture, social life, and entertainment as participants embrace the transition from high school to college.

PROGRAM OFFERINGS

Career Explorations presents a unique opportunity for high school students to sample the professional world thorough monthlong internships, to experience city life and culture, and to interact with like-minded students from around the world. Working alongside practicing professionals, students experience the day-to-day realities in a chosen career field. Interns gain real-world work experience, learn new skills, make industry contacts, obtain letters of recommendation, and become better prepared to make important decisions about college and the future.

Internships: Career Explorations offers internships in a variety of fields, including public relations, theater, film, politics and government, physical therapy, veterinary medicine, medicine, real estate, finance, museum education, journalism, fashion design and marketing, professional sports, general and entertainment law, music, photography, advertising, and event planning, among others. For guidance on choosing an internship, students should contact Career Explorations, who pride themselves on matching each applicant with an internship customized to meet his or her interests.

SAT: Through partnership with Vertex Academic Services (http://www.vertexacademic.com), a premier provider of standardized test preparation, Career Explorations is pleased to offer interns the opportunity to receive expert SAT tutoring. Students receive a balance of classroom-style and one-on-one instruction. SAT tutoring is scheduled during evening and weekend free time and does not conflict with CE's extensive calendar of activities.

ENROLLMENT

Enrollment is competitive and based on merit, application, and recommendations.

EXTRA OPPORTUNITIES AND ACTIVITIES

In addition to a glimpse into a professional field, Career Explorations offers a fun, activity-packed summer that includes supervised activities and opportunities to explore New York City and Boston. Students experience live theater, concerts, sporting events, museums, group dinners, shopping, and everything else that the city has to offer. Career Explorations also offers seminars on the college admissions process and optional tours of college campuses in the area.

FACILITIES

New York interns and staff members reside at the Juilliard School's Meredith Willson residence hall in world-renowned Lincoln Center, which is located in midtown Manhattan. Boston interns live in Emerson College's Little Building, which is adjacent to the Boston Common. Both residence halls provide 24-hour security, and all rooms are air conditioned. Juilliard's residence hall includes a lounge area with television, a pool table, a computer center, and a card-operated laundry room. The Little Building includes Emerson College's main cafeteria, the Emerson College bookstore, a convenience store, a snack bar, and a fitness center (18 and over).

Both residence halls provide dining options for program participants in their modern cafeterias. On weekdays, students and staff members have breakfast and dinner available while taking responsibility for their own lunches. On weekends, brunch and dinner are available in both cafeterias.

STAFF

In both New York and Boston, CE staff members are on call 24 hours a day. Each intern is assigned to a Group Advisor (GA), who acts as a friend, mentor, dorm parent, and internship liaison. Group Advisors are an integral part of the Career Explorations experience. The student-staff ratio is 7:1, not including the directors, who also live with the students.

MEDICAL CARE

All participants are required to have health insurance, including benefits for emergency care and hospitalization. In New York, emergency and urgent care is available at St. Luke's Hospital, seven blocks from Juilliard at 59th Street and Amsterdam Avenue. In Boston, the Tufts University–New England Medical Center is located at 750 Washington Street, just over a quarter mile from the Little Building.

COSTS

Tuition for both four-week residential programs for 2007 was $5795. This includes tuition, housing, breakfast and dinner, a one-month pass for public transportation within New York City or Boston, group activities, special events, and weekend excursions. Transportation to and from New York City and Boston, lunch during the week, medical insurance, optional trips, personal laundry, and incidentals are not included.

Early enrollment discounts are available. Students should contact Career Explorations for more details.

TRANSPORTATION

Interns are responsible for making their own travel arrangements to Boston and New York City. Transportation is provided to and from local airports (Logan for Boston and LaGuardia and Newark for New York) and train and bus stations in each location.

APPLICATION TIMETABLE

Admission to both Career Explorations Boston and New York programs are made on a rolling basis. Initial inquiry is welcome year-round. Career Explorations encourages prospective interns to apply early, as internships are selective

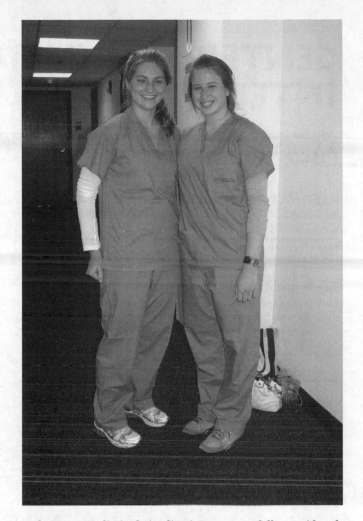

and spaces are limited. Applications are carefully considered, and students are notified of the admission decision within three weeks of receipt of all application materials. Applications and schedules are available online at the Career Explorations Web site: http://www.ceinternships.com.

FOR MORE INFORMATION, CONTACT

NYC Program:
Director: Josh Flowerman
Phone: 973-455-1478

Boston Program:
Director: Todd Aronson
Phone: 973-559-3261

Career Explorations
18 Exeter Lane
Morristown, New Jersey 07960
Phone: 973-455-1478
Fax: 973-539-8370
E-mail: info@careerexplorations.com
Web site: http://www.ceinternships.com

PARTICIPANT/FAMILY COMMENTS

"I expected this internship to be good, but to me it was golden. I've loved, learned, and enjoyed every aspect of it, and it definitely will help me choose the right college, and maybe even career."

"We had lots of laughs and shared great memories. I will remember this summer forever!"

CENTER FOR CULTURAL INTERCHANGE

▼▲▼▲▼▲▼▲▼▲▼▲▼▲▼▲▼▲▼▲▼▲▼▲▼▲▼▲▼▲

DISCOVERY ABROAD

DESTINATIONS THROUGHOUT EUROPE, ASIA, AFRICA, SOUTH AMERICA, AUSTRALIA, NEW ZEALAND, AND MEXICO

TYPE OF PROGRAM: Language School Programs (homestay), Independent Homestay Programs, and High School Abroad (homestay)

PARTICIPANTS: Coeducational, ages 14–18

ENROLLMENT: Approximately 150 outbound students

PROGRAM DATES: Two-, three-, and four-week programs available year-round; three-, five-, and ten-month programs available beginning in the fall and winter

HEAD OF PROGRAM: Juliet Jones, Outbound Programs Director

LOCATION
The Center for Cultural Interchange (CCI) offers American youth the chance to experience the life and language of many countries around the world. Eligible participants can take part in homestay, high school, or language programs in Argentina, Australia, Belgium, Brazil, Chile, Costa Rica, Denmark, England, Finland, France, Germany, Ireland, Italy, Japan, Mexico, New Zealand, Norway, Poland, Spain, Sweden, Switzerland, and Taiwan.

BACKGROUND AND PHILOSOPHY
The Center for Cultural Interchange is a nonprofit student exchange organization founded in 1985. CCI's goals are to promote cultural understanding, academic development, and world peace. CCI focuses primarily on the homestay experience, as it is by far the best way for participants to get a firsthand understanding of another culture. By becoming a member of a family in another country, participants are given the opportunity to share in meals, conversation, and the daily life and traditions of the country visited.

CCI organizes academic-year, semester, and short-term homestay programs for Americans abroad as well as academic-year, semester, and short-term homestay programs for international students in the United States. More than 1,300 American students and host families participate in CCI programs each year. CCI welcomes participants and hosts of every race, nationality, creed, and religion.

CCI is listed by the Council on Standards for International Educational Travel (CSIET) and is designated by the USIA as a J-1 Exchange Visitor Program Sponsor. CCI is also a member of the Federation of International Youth Travel Organizations (FIYTO).

PROGRAM OFFERINGS
CCI offers a wide range of summer, semester, and academic-year programs in Europe, Asia, Africa, South America, Australia, New Zealand, and Mexico. CCI provides each student with comprehensive orientation materials, full medical insurance coverage, and a well-structured network of support in the U.S. and abroad.

Students may choose from Language School Programs, Independent Homestay Programs, or High School Abroad in many parts of the world.

Language School Programs For students who want to live with a host family while participating in fun language classes and activities, CCI offers a variety of Language School Programs. All Language School Programs emphasize language study and provide the opportunity to participate in planned cultural/sport activities while sharing in the daily life of a host family. Junior Language School Programs in Costa Rica, Mexico, Spain, and France cater specifically to students ages 14–16.

Independent Homestay Programs CCI's Independent Homestay Programs focus exclusively on the homestay experience. Welcoming host families provide room and board and consider participants full members of the family. This program is perfect for the mature student who desires full immersion in the culture and language.

Summer Group Programs CCI also coordinates group homestay programs to exciting destinations around the globe. Students may travel with a group organized from their own school or can join a CCI group with other students from around the United States. Group programs are escorted by a trained adult American leader and vary in length from ten days to four weeks.

High School Abroad CCI's High School Abroad focuses on the importance of complete linguistic and cultural immersion. Participants attend high schools abroad, make new international friends, share time with host families, and learn a great deal about themselves during this three-, five-, or ten-month program.

ENROLLMENT
More than 1,300 American and international students participate in CCI programs each year. Language requirements vary by destination and program length; in some cases, there is no language requirement.

EXTRA OPPORTUNITIES AND ACTIVITIES
Many of CCI's programs offer optional activities that the student can choose to participate in for an extra fee. These

activities may be weekend excursions to historical sites, sports activities, or local cultural events.

STAFF

The CCI National Office is located in Chicago, Illinois. The national office staff is composed of caring individuals with extensive experience in student exchange, most of whom are former homestay participants themselves. CCI also maintains a network of nine regional offices across the United States. These regional offices are responsible for the screening, recruitment, and orientation of American students and host families and provide ongoing support. The CCI Board of Directors is composed of volunteer educational professionals who maintain the direction for CCI's mission of global cross-cultural understanding.

MEDICAL CARE

All programs include comprehensive medical insurance for the duration of the program.

COSTS

The 2006 program fees for CCI short-term programs (two weeks to three months) began at $820 and varied depending on the length of stay, country, and type of program. The 2006 program fees for long-term programs (three, five, or ten months) began at $5000.

All CCI programs include orientation materials, the support of the CCI U.S. National Office and partner offices abroad, support of a local representative while abroad, housing, airport transfers, and comprehensive medical insurance. Program fees do not include international airfare, optional activities, passport/visa fees, or spending money.

FINANCIAL AID

The Center for Cultural Interchange prides itself on providing interesting and affordable opportunities to all American students interested in cultural exchange. To that end, CCI offers

several possibilities for students to offset the cost of participating in a cultural exchange program.

Applicants for the High School Abroad program may apply for a $1000 scholarship.

CCI also encourages U.S. host family members to expand on their cultural experience by participating in the Host Family Circle, a program that provides partial scholarships to host family members interested in studying abroad.

CCI also offers an annual essay contest to its academic-year or semester host brothers and sisters (14–17 years) through which they can win a free program abroad.

TRANSPORTATION

International airfare arrangements are generally the responsibility of the participants, but CCI is happy to provide assistance, if necessary. Transfers to and from the major airport nearest the host family are included in most teen program fees.

APPLICATION TIMETABLE

U.S. students interested in applying are required to submit a complete application with a $250 deposit for short-term programs and a $500 deposit for High School Abroad programs. Applications for short-term programs are due no later than six weeks prior to departure. High School Abroad applications are due no later than April 15 for the fall semester and September 15 for the spring semester.

FOR MORE INFORMATION, CONTACT

Outbound Department
Center for Cultural Interchange
746 N. LaSalle Drive
Chicago, Illinois 60610
Phone: 312-944-2544 (in Chicago area)
      866-684-9675 (toll-free)
Fax: 312-944-2644
E-mail: info@cci-exchange.com
Web site: http://www.cci-exchange.com

PARTICIPANT/FAMILY COMMENTS

"I am really happy I decided to take this year to be here in Spain. I love it! I am really glad I am here with CCI. I am so pleased with the amount of support I'm getting. I never want (it) to end!"—Eve Pulver, former CCI student to Spain

"Our experience was perfect!"—Julie Vedvick, Spanish teacher and CCI group leader to Mexico

CHESHIRE ACADEMY

SUMMER PROGRAMS

CHESHIRE, CONNECTICUT

TYPE OF PROGRAM: English as a second language (ESL); Writing, Reading, and Study Skills (WRSS); select college-prep courses
PARTICIPANTS: Coeducational, grades 7–12
ENROLLMENT: Approximately 150
PROGRAM DATES: Five weeks, from the first week of July until the first week of August
HEAD OF PROGRAM: Marisa Faleri, Director

LOCATION

The 120-acre wooded campus is located in the center of an attractive New England town of 30,000 residents. The Academy is 2 hours from New York City and Boston. The surrounding cities, such as the state capital, Hartford (22 miles away), and the home of Yale University, New Haven (14 miles away)—along with Boston and New York City—offer a wide range of cultural opportunities for Summer Programs students.

BACKGROUND AND PHILOSOPHY

Founded in 1794, Cheshire Academy is a highly regarded co-educational college-preparatory school with an academic tradition of preparing young men and women for rewarding college experiences, careers, and personal lives. Graduates from around the world include many highly respected and successful people in all fields of endeavor.

Since 1911, Cheshire Academy Summer Programs has been offering a challenging academic program that meets the educational interests of a variety of students. Program success is accomplished in a structured, stimulating, and supportive family-like environment, created by small classes (an average of 7 students) and a close, personal working relationship between teachers and students.

Academic courses are continually monitored by the individual teachers and the Director of the Summer Programs. Each student receives a weekly progress report that, with a comment from the classroom teacher, is sent to the parents or guardian. This allows the teachers, students, and parents to remain informed of the student's progress throughout the summer.

PROGRAM OFFERINGS

Writing, Reading, and Study Skills Program The WRSS Program is designed to help students improve their academic skills, independence, self-confidence, and achievement in a classroom setting. Students learn to develop healthy habits and strategies that support learning and that have a direct bearing on the students' success in all academic disciplines. Students are placed in the appropriate level of the program after taking diagnostic tests to assess their verbal and study skills.

English as a Second Language Program Cheshire Academy's English as a Second Language Program has served the Academy since 1911. The program is practically oriented and challenging, providing ESL classes that increase English proficiency for beginning, intermediate, and advanced students. The ESL curriculum stresses writing, vocabulary, grammar,

speaking, and reading. Students take a placement test and are assigned according to their levels in each of the basic skills. Small classes and the sensitivity of highly committed, caring, experienced faculty members make it possible for students to develop their new-found English skills and knowledge quite rapidly. In addition to general course work, class groups participate in local and regional field trips that build on the curriculum.

College Prep The College-Prep Program is designed for high school students who are seeking academic enrichment in two specific areas of study. The students can concentrate on one or two courses and really focus on the subject matter for five weeks. It is hoped that the students are able to embrace a subject and be rewarded by a real sense of accomplishment at the end of the summer. Course offerings, subject to enrollment, are algebra I, algebra II, geometry, precalculus, chemistry, biology, physics, Spanish I, and U.S. history. Advanced Placement test preparation courses are also offered in several subjects.

ENROLLMENT

The average enrollment is 150 students, with close to a 1:1 ratio of girls to boys. Most students board, and twenty different countries and ten states are represented in the student body.

DAILY SCHEDULE

7:30– 8:15	... Breakfast
8:30–12:30	... Academics
12:30– 1:30	... Lunch
1:30– 4:30	... Afternoon activities
5:30– 6:30	... Dinner
7:30– 9:00	... Study hall
10:30	... Lights out

On Saturday and Sunday, brunch is served from 10:30 to 12. Dinner is served from 5:30 to 6:30. Students are expected to follow all of the rules and regulations outlined in the *Student Handbook*. Stealing, possession or use of alcohol or illegal drugs, visiting the rooms of students of the opposite sex, or any activity that compromises the good name of Cheshire Academy will result in dismissal from Summer Programs.

EXTRA OPPORTUNITIES AND ACTIVITIES

Afternoon Activities The Afternoon Activities Program offers a variety of athletic, art, and alternative activities designed to encourage all students. Because each student's interest in activities varies, they may select from a variety of afternoon activities on a weekly basis. The activities are designed for students of all abilities and levels to participate in, providing fun and a proper foundation to excel to a higher level. Cheshire Academy athletic facilities accommodate swimming in its six-lane pool, basketball on two full-size courts, tennis on eight courts, and soccer on five playing fields. It also has two baseball diamonds; an outdoor track; a weight-training room for strength, endurance, and aerobic conditioning; and one of the best ropes and challenge courses in all of New England. Other Afternoon Activity options include computers, fine arts, crime scene investigation, Dance Dance Phenomenon, Ultimate Frisbee, fencing, rocketry, photography, Discover Connecticut field trips, and creative writing/journalism, with the end product being one or more issues of a Summer Programs newspaper or literary magazine.

Weekend Recreation Program The Weekend Recreation Program is chaperoned by faculty members and designed to involve students in a variety of social and recreational activities on and off campus. On-campus activities typically include student dances, swimming, and recreational sports. Examples of off-campus trips include a three-day discovery trip to Washington, D.C., and Saturday excursions to Boston's Quincy Market, Broadway plays and other New York City attractions, and major amusement parks.

FACILITIES

Bowden Hall (1796), the original school building, now houses various administrative offices. Horton Hall (1946) and the New Dorm (2001) are residence halls for girls, and von der Porten Hall (1959) is a residence hall for boys. The Student Health Center is located on campus in the Richmond Building. Two additional houses, Walters and Skilton, are smaller residences. The John J. White Science Center provides science facilities and a lecture hall. Music classes are conducted in the Charles Harwood Student Center (1988). The student center houses recreational rooms and lounges, a snack bar, and the Academy's bookstore. Art classes are held in the Arthur N. Sheriff Field House, which also provides extensive athletic facilities and additional classrooms. The Gideon Welles Dining Commons provides excellent dining facilities. A humanities building and library were added to the campus in 2003.

The 120-acre campus includes eight athletic fields, eight tennis courts, a quarter-mile track, woodlands, and a stream. The indoor athletic facilities include two basketball courts, an exercise room, and a swimming pool.

STAFF

The majority of the Summer Programs teaching staff are members of the Academy's school year program.

MEDICAL CARE

The Student Health Center is a recently renovated state-of-the-art facility. It is located in the Richmond Building in the center of campus. The nursing staff collaborates with a multispecialty physician group within walking distance of campus. The nursing staff is on-site or on call 24 hours a day. The Academy is conveniently located approximately 20 minutes from both Yale–New Haven Hospital and Midstate Medical Center.

RELIGIOUS LIFE

Cheshire Academy is not affiliated with any religion, but it is within walking distance of churches of several denominations and a synagogue.

COSTS

The boarding tuition for the 2007 five-week program was $5660; day tuition was $3080.

TRANSPORTATION

Cheshire Academy is 45 minutes from Bradley International Airport in Hartford, 20 minutes from Tweed–New Haven Airport, and 1½ hours from New York City airports. All are easily reached by Connecticut Limousine service, which has a terminal in New Haven. Private limousine service is also available.

APPLICATION TIMETABLE

Cheshire Academy's Summer Programs have a rolling admissions policy. Students are urged to submit their application as early as possible, due to limited boarding space.

FOR MORE INFORMATION, CONTACT

Marisa Faleri, Director
Summer Programs
Cheshire Academy
10 Main Street
Cheshire, Connecticut 06410
Phone: 203-272-5396
Fax: 203-250-7209
E-mail: summer@cheshireacademy.org
Web site: http://www.cheshireacademy.org

PARTICIPANT/FAMILY COMMENTS

"I would like the person in charge of last summer's program to see the enclosed report from my son's middle school principal and from his skills teacher, both commenting on the positive effects of the Cheshire Academy summer program. I spoke to the parents of his friend who attended last summer and they were also thrilled with the program. My son has attended some academic-oriented programs every summer, but this is the only one that had a noticeable effect. I certainly intend to send him to the summer program this year, regardless of where he attends high school."—Parent of a Summer Programs student

CHOATE ROSEMARY HALL

INTERNATIONAL SUMMER PROGRAMS

CHINA, FRANCE, AND SPAIN

TYPE OF PROGRAM: Academic and cultural enrichment

PARTICIPANTS: Coeducational; students must have completed grade 9

PROGRAM DATES: Five to six weeks, typically beginning the third Monday in June

HEADS OF PROGRAM: Carol Chen-Lin, Beijing; Nancy Burress, Santander and La Coruña, Spain; Carl Hermey and Elizabeth Jannot, Paris

LOCATION

Choate Rosemary Hall Summer Programs Abroad offer students the opportunity to spend an exciting summer in a faraway place, immersed in the language and culture of China, France, or Spain. All programs begin with a two-day (three-day for Spain) on-campus orientation in Wallingford, Connecticut.

China program students reside in a college dormitory for the first two weeks, followed by a two-week homestay with Chinese families. French program students live with Parisian families, either singly or with a roommate. Students going to Spain live with families in either Santander of La Coruña, picturesque ocean cities on the northern coast. These students are always placed one to a family.

BACKGROUND AND PHILOSOPHY

The goal of the programs is to help students develop fluency in the written and spoken language in a secure, structured, and caring environment. Students enhance their language skills for school—and for life!

PROGRAM OFFERINGS

Language instruction and placement testing begin at orientation, where students are introduced to the country they are about to experience firsthand. All three programs immerse students in the culture of the host country, helping them to increase their skill level—sometimes dramatically—in four essential areas: listening, speaking, reading, and writing.

Students who clearly demonstrate progress and proficiency in the major language skills at the end of the program abroad may be eligible for higher placement in their home schools. A detailed written report is sent home to parents at the end of the program. A copy of the report, along with appropriate supporting materials, is sent to the student's school upon request. Choate Rosemary Hall students have the opportunity to accelerate as much as one year in language study, as determined by their degree of improvement.

ENROLLMENT

Participants must have completed grade 9 before the start of the program. Two years study of French or Spanish is the usual requirement, but exceptions may be made for strong students who have completed only one year. The China program welcomes students who would like to begin their study of Chinese. All participants are expected to show sufficient maturity and the self-discipline to avoid inappropriate behavior. The program director has the right to send home (at the parents' expense) any student whose behavior jeopardizes the safety or viability of the group.

DAILY SCHEDULE

In the European programs, students take 3 hours of classes each morning. In Paris, four courses—French language, French literature, art history, and French history—comprise the academic program, along with an independent research project on an artistic or cultural topic, which each student carries out using the libraries, galleries, or museums of Paris. Afternoons are devoted to exploring the historic and artistic treasures of the city. These visits are thematically linked to the morning art history class and are led by two Parisian teachers. Free time in the city precedes dinner with the French family; homework for the next day follows dinner.

In the China program, students attend four hour-long classes each weekday. The curriculum for beginning and intermediate students includes grammar, conversation, and writing. Advanced students take the same course load plus newspaper reading and literature. Twice each week, students participate in afternoon activities such as calligraphy, painting, and dancing and have an opportunity to attend such cultural events as the Beijing Opera.

In Spain, students are divided into three distinct levels: primary, intermediate, and advanced. Students at the first two levels study grammar, art history and architecture, and Spanish history. Instead of grammar, the advanced students take Spanish literature. One or two afternoons per week, the group visits local points of interest. Saturdays are the occasion of day trips to more distant attractions. Most weekdays, after the main meal in the early afternoon, students may head for the beach. They return home for curfew and supper at 9 p.m.

EXTRA OPPORTUNITIES AND ACTIVITIES

In Paris, midway through the summer, students spend three days in the Loire Valley, touring well-known châteaux and exploring the cities of Tours and Amboise. En route back to Paris, they visit the Chartres cathedral or the château of Vaux-le-Vicomte. Additional excursions have included Versailles and Monet's house and gardens at Giverny.

In Spain, at the end of the homestay, the group from Santander joins the students from La Coruña, and the combined group travels from the Northwest back to Madrid. Stops include Santiago de Compostela, Salamanca, Segovia, Toledo, and finally Madrid. The last afternoon in the capital provides a few hours of free time in which students may go shopping or return to the Museo del Prado. The final elegant dinner on the last evening of the program is always a memorable occasion.

On weekends, Summer in China students visit historical sites and local points of interest such as the Great Wall, the Ming Tomb, the Forbidden City, and the Summer Palace. The highlight of this program, at the end of the academic session, is a six-day excursion. Past itineraries have included Shanghai, Nanjing, Suzhou, Hangzhou, and Xi'an. This is an experience of a lifetime for students who are eager to explore the Chinese language and culture.

FACILITIES

The program in Spain rents space in modern, private schools close to the beach. Classroom facilities in Paris are located in the Sixth Arrondissement, not far from Saint Germain. Both facilities have spacious classrooms that are equipped for audiovisual presentations.

The host for the China program, the Beijing Chinese Language Institute, is widely recognized for its strong faculty and students. The school is located between the fourth and fifth ring road of Beijing, with convenient access to all parts of the city via subway, bus, and taxi.

All of Choate's programs abroad take place in modern cities with modern medical facilities. All participants are required to offer proof of medical insurance with coverage abroad or to purchase such insurance through Choate for the duration of the program.

STAFF

In Spain, each city's program is run by a staff of 2 American teachers from Choate and 2 Spaniards. The American teachers stay in regular contact with the host families. Nancy Burress, a senior member of the Spanish faculty at Choate, administers the program in the U.S., and Luis Bao oversees the staffing and the in-country operations of the program in Spain.

Carl W. Hermey, a senior member of Choate's French faculty, administers the Paris program in the U.S., and Elizabeth Jannot, a longtime resident of France, leads the program in Paris. At least 1 other Choate French teacher accompanies the group to Paris. All classes are taught in French by a team of native speakers whose combined experience with Choate students totals more than forty years.

The China program is organized, led, and directed by Dr. Carol S. Chen-Lin, a senior member of Choate Rosemary Hall's language faculty and an experienced teacher of Chinese. In China, Yue Hui oversees the teacher training and host family arrangements. Classes are taught by experienced native speakers who are trained to teach Chinese as a second language.

COSTS

Programs cost approximately $6500. This includes airfare, transportation abroad, tuition, all meals and lodging, books, and entrance fees for group activities. Expenses not included in the fee are a passport, transportation to the Choate campus, transportation after return to the U.S., and personal expenses such as telephone calls and spending money. Expenses are based on the exchange rate effective September 1, 2007. Prices are subject to equitable adjustment should there be a significant change in the rate of exchange or in the airfare prior to the start of the program.

FINANCIAL AID

A limited amount of need-based financial aid is allocated for each program.

APPLICATION TIMETABLE

All candidates must submit an application, the $60 application fee, an official transcript, and teacher recommendations. Since the number of candidates for these programs exceeds the available spaces, early applications are recommended. Some applications are received in early fall before the desired summer of entry. Last minute applicants, if accepted, are placed in families and classes in accordance with availability.

FOR MORE INFORMATION, CONTACT

International Summer Programs
Choate Rosemary Hall
333 Christian Street
Wallingford, Connecticut 06492
Phone: 203-697-2365
E-mail: cchen-lin@choate.edu (Summer in China)
        chermey@choate.edu (Summer in Paris)
        nburress@choate.edu (Summer in Spain)
Web site: http://www.crhsummerabroad.org

CHOATE ROSEMARY HALL

SUMMER ARTS CONSERVATORY

WALLINGFORD, CONNECTICUT

TYPE OF PROGRAM: Intensive arts conservatory, emphasizing performance, playwriting, and exhibitions
PARTICIPANTS: Coeducational, entering grades 7–12
ENROLLMENT: 50
PROGRAM DATES: June 29 to August 1
HEAD OF PROGRAM: Paul J. Tines, Executive Director

LOCATION

Choate Rosemary Hall's 450-acre campus is located in the center of Wallingford, a town 12 miles north of New Haven and 20 miles south of Hartford. It is a 2-hour drive from Boston and New York City.

BACKGROUND AND PHILOSOPHY

The five-week Arts Conservatory offers programs in theater, playwriting, choral music, stringed instruments, and the visual arts. Arts Conservatory students create together, live together, and play together. Each morning begins as students gather in the Chase-Bear Experimental Theater for physical warm-ups and the day's announcements.

Several characteristics make the Arts Conservatory unique. It offers a truly interdisciplinary approach to arts education and embraces the philosophy that the student must first understand the process of creating art. Students are given the tools to understand how to create. In all five programs, students consistently work on the techniques and skills of painting, drawing, singing, dancing, acting, playing an instrument, or playwriting.

PROGRAM OFFERINGS

Theater In this program, 30 students explore and experience all phases of theatrical expression. The curriculum consists of classes in acting, acting style, stage movement, and musical theater—voice and dance. Students perform in both new works and previously published plays.

Playwriting/Screenwriting The Student Playwriting/Screenwriting Program is developed to nurture 10 young writers and to provide a solid foundation for both stage plays and film. The curriculum consists of classes in elements of scriptwriting, film analysis, screenplay development, and film and play labs. Students have public readings of their works.

Visual Arts The Visual Arts Program is a rare opportunity for 10 students to explore the creative process and challenge their artistic potential under the instruction of professional artists who are also teachers. The curriculum consists of painting, ceramics, drawing, portfolio discussions, and open studio time.

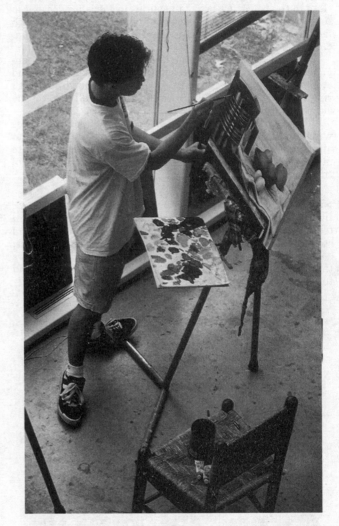

ENROLLMENT

Each summer, 50 students from all over the country participate in the Arts Conservatory.

DAILY SCHEDULE

During the day, students attend classes, open studio sessions, and play, choral, and string rehearsals. Students take field trips to museums, theaters, outdoor musical concerts, and art openings.

EXTRA OPPORTUNITIES AND ACTIVITIES

Time is set aside for leisure activities, including swimming, tennis, volleyball, or relaxing in the Student Activities Center. Students spend one weekend (optional trip) during the program in New York City, where they attend Broadway and off-Broadway shows, visit museums and galleries, explore Shubert Alley, and shop in SoHo and Greenwich Village.

FACILITIES

The Paul Mellon Arts Center, designed by world-renowned architect I. M. Pei, houses two theaters, a recital hall, music classrooms and practice rooms, art studios, dance facilities, and a large art gallery/lounge area. Students live in campus dormitories and have access to Choate Rosemary Hall's recreational and athletic facilities.

STAFF

Classes are taught by experienced arts educators from Choate Rosemary Hall's faculty and from other private and public schools around the country. Faculty members also serve as dormitory advisers.

Paul Tines, Director of the Paul Mellon Arts Center, is head of the arts department at Choate Rosemary Hall. Mr. Tines, who received his master's degree from Johns Hopkins University and a Certificate of Advanced Studies from Wesleyan University, has studied at the American Academy of Dramatic Arts in New York and the Royal Academy of Dramatic Arts in London. He was a member of Choate's theater department from 1982 to 1992 and then served as the Director of the Ward Center for the Arts and Chair of the Arts Department at the St. Paul's Schools in Baltimore before returning to Wallingford.

MEDICAL CARE

The Pratt Health Center is staffed 24 hours a day. Overnight care in the health center is provided when necessary, but there is an additional charge. Each student is required to submit health forms before registration. All students must have proper immunizations and provide complete medical information on these forms. By Connecticut law, failure to submit the proper medical forms or to have immunizations (or to get them immediately upon arrival at Choate) obligates the school to dismiss the student. Each student is also required to submit proof of medical insurance before registration. Failure to submit proof of medical insurance upon arrival at Choate obligates the school to dismiss the student.

RELIGIOUS LIFE

A synagogue and various denominational churches (Congregational, Baptist, Roman Catholic, and Episcopalian) are within walking distance of the campus.

COSTS

The charge for resident students, including room, board, and field trips, is $4975. Linen service is available at an additional fee. The fee for day students is $3975. The fee for the optional weekend trip to New York City is $595.

TRANSPORTATION

Transportation is provided to students. Ground transportation upon arrival to and departure from the program is an additional fee.

APPLICATION TIMETABLE

A $60 nonrefundable application fee payable to Choate Rosemary Hall is required. The Summer Arts Conservatory's application deadline is May 30.

FOR MORE INFORMATION, CONTACT

Randi Joseph Brandt, Admission Director
Choate Rosemary Hall Summer Arts Conservatory
Paul Mellon Arts Center
333 Christian Street
Wallingford, Connecticut 06492

Phone: 203-697-2423
Fax: 203-697-2396
E-mail: rbrandt@choate.edu
Web site: http://www.choate.edu/pmac

PARTICIPANT/FAMILY COMMENTS

"I learned more in five weeks than I did in two years of drama classes back home. I will always look back and remember Choate as a very special and wonderful time in my life."

CHOATE ROSEMARY HALL

▼▼▼▼▼▼▼▼▼▼▼▼▼▼▼▼▼▼▼▼▼▼▼▼▼▼▼▼▼▼▼▼

SUMMER PROGRAMS

WALLINGFORD, CONNECTICUT

TYPE OF PROGRAM: College-preparatory academic enrichment/credit for residential and day students
PARTICIPANTS: Coeducational, students who have completed grades 6–8 and 9–12
ENROLLMENT: 500
PROGRAM DATES: June 29 to August 1, 2008
HEAD OF PROGRAM: James Irzyk, Director

LOCATION
The 450-acre campus of Choate Rosemary Hall is in the center of Wallingford, a town 12 miles north of New Haven and 20 miles south of Hartford. It is a 2-hour drive from Boston and New York City.

BACKGROUND AND PHILOSOPHY
The Choate Rosemary Hall Summer Programs were established in 1916. The mission is to encourage, support, and challenge each student's potential while making the learning experience productive, rewarding, and enjoyable. This is accomplished not only in the classroom, but also in the dormitory, through sports and social activities, and by sharing life in a residential community.

PROGRAM OFFERINGS
Students in each program are fully integrated into all athletic, extracurricular, and social activities on campus.

FOR HIGH SCHOOL STUDENTS (GRADES 9–12)
Summer Session Course offerings give students the opportunity for advancement, credit, and preparation for courses for the next school year. All courses stress skills in reading, writing, computation, and analytical thought. The average class size is 12.

English Language Institute A program designed to help students improve their English in a supportive yet challenging academic environment. Students develop their ability in language skills, including writing, speaking, listening, and reading.

John F. Kennedy Institute in Government Students take three courses on the formation of political ideas, the foundation and workings of the American government, and current domestic issues. A trip to Washington, D.C., is a highlight of the program, as students meet members of Congress, lobbyists, and journalists.

The Writing Project In this intensive two-week program (offered in two different sessions), students receive daily writing and reading assignments and an introduction to computer-assisted writing and gain confidence in their writing skill.

Immersion Courses Students may enroll in one of the following courses: first-year French, Latin, or Spanish; algebra I; geometry; trigonometry/precalculus; or physics. Credit is granted by the student's school.

Math and Science Workshops Similar to the Writing Project, these two-week programs aim to give students a "leg up" on the material for regular-year classes. Classes include Algebra Review, Topics in Algebra II, Topics in Precalculus, Topics in Calculus, Topics in Chemistry, and Topics in Physics.

FOR MIDDLE SCHOOL STUDENTS (GRADES 6–8)
FOCUS Program This four-week program parallels the Summer Session but stresses cooperative learning, the use of technology in the classroom, problem-solving skills, effective communication, hands-on projects, and research skills. Small classes and experienced dorm advisers encourage personal growth and self-awareness. Enrollment is limited to 75 students.

Math/Science Institute for Girls (CONNECT) (for students completing grades 6–8) Experiments, building models, developing and testing hypotheses, and using technology are integral components of the curriculum. This four-week program is an opportunity for students to discover the natural and logical relationship between math and science.

Beginning Writers Workshop (for students competing grades 5 or 6) Interactive assignments, fun, camaraderie, peer support, and individual conferences are integral teaching strategies in this program. The workshop develops and builds skills for effective reading, writing, and speaking.

Young Writers Workshop This two-week workshop uses both the critical and creative writing methods to instill confidence, develop understanding, and suggest strategies to improve writing skills. Class discussions, exercises, and individual conferences develop a supportive, cohesive group in which students can produce their best writing.

FOCUS English Language Institute Similar to the ELI program, this four-week program is open to students who have studied English for at least two years in their home school. Social activities are planned with the other grade 6–8 program. Enrollment is limited to 30 students.

ENROLLMENT

Each summer, 500 students from nearly fifty-five states and countries attend the summer programs. Students come from such countries as France, Japan, Spain, Switzerland, Germany, Korea, Turkey, and Argentina. Adding strength to the student body are 30 highly motivated students (Connecticut Scholars) from Connecticut's urban public school systems.

DAILY SCHEDULE

Classes meet Monday, Tuesday, Thursday, and Friday from 8:15 a.m. to 2:40 p.m. and Wednesday and Saturday from 8:15 a.m. to 12:45 p.m. Athletics are held from 3:30 to 5:30 p.m. All programs have 2 hours of evening study.

EXTRA OPPORTUNITIES AND ACTIVITIES

A variety of activities are offered on and off campus. Trips are scheduled on Wednesday afternoons and on weekends and usually include visits to Boston, New York City, shopping malls, movie theaters, professional sporting events, and nearby college campuses.

FACILITIES

Choate's academic and athletic facilities are among the best in the country. The campus resembles those of many small liberal arts colleges. The Science Center includes twenty-two air-conditioned classrooms and laboratories and a 150-seat auditorium. The Humanities Center houses thirty air-conditioned classrooms, an audiovisual viewing room, a computer center, and photographic studios. The dining hall is air conditioned.

The Andrew Mellon Library has more than 60,000 volumes, 6,750 reels of microfilm, more than 2,100 CDs, English and foreign language periodicals and newspapers, and the latest library research technology, as well as wireless Internet access. The Archives hold school memorabilia, including the papers of such distinguished alumni as John F. Kennedy '35, Adlai Stevenson '18, Alan Jay Lerner '36, Glenn Close '65, Jamie Lee Curtis '76, and Michael Douglas '63.

The International Learning Center includes a thirty-two-station language laboratory and allows for individual instruction and practice for the English Language Institute and foreign language classes. The Paul Mellon Arts Center houses two theaters, a recital hall, music classrooms and practice rooms, art studios, dance and film facilities, and an art gallery. The renovated Johnson Athletic Center houses three basketball and three volleyball courts and weight-training and Nautilus rooms. There are twenty outdoor tennis courts, thirteen athletic fields, and a 25-meter, eight-lane indoor swimming pool with an electronic timing system. The social hub is the John Joseph Activities Center, which has games, a snack shop, and several televisions with VCRs.

STAFF

Many of the faculty members are teachers in Choate Rosemary Hall's regular session. Additional faculty members come from other independent secondary and public schools and from colleges and universities. Thirty teaching interns from select colleges and universities complement the program.

MEDICAL CARE

The infirmary is open daily, and overnight care is available. The school physician is in residence and can be paged for emergencies. Parents must have some form of insurance for their child. Each student is required by Connecticut law to submit a health form before enrolling.

COSTS

In 2007, tuition, room, and board for the summer session were $5400. Day student costs ranged from $900 to 1650. Costs for the Kennedy Institute were $5400, with an additional $455 for the Washington, D.C., trip. Costs for the English Language Institute were $6000, with an additional $400 for the long weekend trip. Boarding students in the two-week Writing Project paid $2220, and day students paid $1620. Boarding students in the CONNECT program paid $4600, and day students paid $3320. For the Young Writers Workshop, boarding students paid $2220, and day students paid $1680. Students boarding in Beginning Writers Workshop paid $2220; day students paid $1680. Boarding students in the Immersion Courses paid $5200, and day students paid $3900.

FINANCIAL AID

Need-based financial aid is available; applications should be submitted by March 10. Candidates are notified of their acceptance and financial aid awards by April 1.

APPLICATION TIMETABLE

Early application is encouraged. Students are strongly encouraged to apply by May 11. Admission is on a rolling basis. Acceptance decisions are made within two weeks of receiving a completed application.

FOR MORE INFORMATION, CONTACT

Mariann Arnold, Director of Admissions
Choate Rosemary Hall Summer Programs
Wallingford, Connecticut 06492

Phone: 203 697-2365
Fax: 203-697-2519
E-mail: marnold@choate.edu
Web site: http://www.choate.edu/summer

CLEARWATER CAMP FOR GIRLS

SUMMER CAMP

MINOCQUA, WISCONSIN

TYPE OF PROGRAM: Traditional camping, sailing, water-skiing, aquatic sports and horseback-riding programs, overnight wilderness trips, extended trips

PARTICIPANTS: Girls, ages 8–16

ENROLLMENT: 120 per session

PROGRAM DATES: Two 3½-week sessions, June 18 to July 12 and July 14 to August 7, or a full seven-week session, June 18 to August 7, 2008

HEADS OF PROGRAM: Sunny Moore, Executive Director; Laurie and Perry Smith, Codirectors

LOCATION
Clearwater Camp is located in north-central Wisconsin on Tomahawk Lake, 3 miles south of Minocqua off U.S. 51. It is about 340 miles northwest of Chicago, 220 miles northeast of Minneapolis, and 200 miles north of Madison.

BACKGROUND AND PHILOSOPHY
Clearwater was founded in 1933 by Mrs. John P. Sprague, who owned and directed the camp for thirty-eight years. The current director was a camper during this period. Sunny Moore, who has directed Clearwater since 1970, became the principal owner in 1975.

The camp is dedicated to providing an environment that will stimulate the most healthy and purposeful growth toward maturity possible. It is a place where a camper may learn to interact with her peers, to develop new skills, to venture into the unknown, and to succeed in her pursuit of new goals. Considerable effort goes into structuring the program to ensure a proper balance between scheduled activity instruction and the free use of time to enjoy the beauty of the Northwoods with new friends. The wonders of a summer at Clearwater are many and varied, but perhaps the greatest of all is the joy of learning to know oneself.

PROGRAM OFFERINGS
Campers participate in 18 hours of instruction per week in the following camp activities: archery, arts and crafts, campcraft, canoeing and canoe trips, drama, English riding, kayaking, nature lore, pioneer camping, photography, sailing, swimming, tennis, tumbling, waterskiing, and windsurfing. Each week, every girl receives a new schedule of activities. Each girl's program, built upon activity preferences and parent requests, makes the best use of staff members' skills and available equipment.

The activity program at Clearwater is designed to allow for the growth of the camper not only at the activity level but also in her relationships with others and with herself. Weeks in camp are a time to explore, to develop new hobbies, to have fun, and to learn the satisfying use of nonscheduled time.

Clearwater does not have awards for achievement in activities. Instead, if competition is to develop among campers, it is the decision of the campers to compete. Clearwater relies on a camper's natural enthusiasm, on its staff, and on its flexible yet determined program to provide the initiative that leads to success in and mastery of activities.

Each activity is governed by rules and procedures designed for the safety of the campers and for the proper learning of the activity. Water safety is a very important element in the camp's many water-oriented activities. Each camper must pass a swimming safety test before she may go out in any boat without a counselor or participate in sailing or waterskiing activities.

ENROLLMENT
Recent campers represent more than twenty states and four other countries. Enrollment is open to any girl who meets the age requirements.

DAILY SCHEDULE
Clearwater Camp's daily schedule features four instructional periods as well as scheduled portions of free-choice time. Three times per week, larger blocks of time are left unscheduled; these time blocks may be used to pursue individual nonscheduled interests, to clean cabins, or to spend extra time perfecting skills in the principal activities.

EXTRA OPPORTUNITIES AND ACTIVITIES
The out-of-camp trip program fulfills an important and unique role in the total Clearwater experience. Trip groups are small, usually consisting of 8 girls and 2 counselors. Trips are unhurried, as it sometimes takes a slower pace to respond to the beauty of nature and to realize that a person can cope and be comfortable in an environment markedly different from any

encountered before. Such discoveries build self-confidence and expand a girl's knowledge of herself.

The type of trip, its destination, and its length are determined by camper desire, skill, and previous experience. Some trips are by canoe for two or three days along one of the many northern Wisconsin waterways.

For the skilled, older campers, trips of up to ten days are taken with backpacks or by canoe to Isle Royale or the Boundary Waters Canoe Area Wilderness (BWCAW).

FACILITIES

Campers live in three main cabin units: Harbor, Cape, and Point. These are organized according to age. Many cabins are enclosed, while many, especially for the older girls, have 3½-foot canvas flaps over screens on four sides. For younger campers, each cabin is equipped with bathroom facilities. The two older units have central toilet and shower facilities.

The three units are geographically separate from one another. The youngest girls live near main camp buildings such as the dining room, the office area, and general meeting areas; the Cape and Point girls live out on the 5-acre island, which is reached by a footbridge and walk along wooded trails from which the lake is always visible.

For the sailing program, Clearwater has twelve boats—seven C-scows, three X-boats, and two Sunfish. The Sunfish are excellent training boats because of their small size, while the X's and C's can accommodate larger classes for teaching and require greater skill from the sailors.

STAFF

Each member of the Clearwater staff is selected not only for her maturity and skills in an activity area but also for her commitment to young people and her belief in the value of a camp experience. On the staff are counselors who have previously been campers at Clearwater as well as returning and new counselors. Each summer a few staff members are 19 years old; the majority are older, with all having completed college work. The ratio of campers to staff members is 4:1.

A registered nurse is a full-time member of the staff. She determines when it would be in the best interest of a camper to be in the infirmary or to be seen by one of the physicians in Minocqua, 10 minutes away.

COSTS

Clearwater's tuition for the 2008 season is $5900 for the full seven-week session, $3200 for the first 3½-week session, and $3400 for the second 3½-week session. When 2 or more children from the same family register, a reduction of $100 is allowed for each full-season registration, $75 for each single session. Tuition includes all phases of the camp program in which a camper is able to participate, including living expenses, laundry, out-of-camp trips in Wisconsin, sailing and basic riding instruction, and use of all equipment. Not included are transportation to and from camp, strictly personal expenses, and extended trips.

For campers who enjoy more riding and want to perfect horsemanship, an extended program is offered with more riding hours, more advanced instruction, and trail rides. The charge is $375 per session. An extended waterskiing program for campers in grades 7–10 is also available for $350 per session.

APPLICATION TIMETABLE

Inquiries and enrollment applications are welcome year-round.

FOR MORE INFORMATION, CONTACT

Sunny Moore
Clearwater Camp
7490 Clearwater Road
Minocqua, Wisconsin 54548
winter
Phone: 715-356-5030
      800-399-5030 (toll-free)
summer
Phone: 715-356-5030
Fax: 715-356-3124
E-mail: clearwatercamp@newnorth.net
Web site: http://www.clearwatercamp.com

PARTICIPANT/FAMILY COMMENTS

"My daughter and I think of camp often. She is quick to tell a camp story or sing a favorite song. Without doubt, her experience at Clearwater will be with her forever. She tells everyone it was the best summer of her life. Words just can't explain all the wonderful feelings and experiences that she gained at camp."

"She has a confidence I've never seen before—she is still radiating! Please save a place for her next year."

COLORADO COLLEGE

▶▶▶▶▶ PRE-COLLEGE SUMMER PROGRAMS

COLORADO SPRINGS, COLORADO

TYPE OF PROGRAM: Academic enrichment
PARTICIPANTS: Young men and women entering their junior or senior year of high school
ENROLLMENT: 120
PROGRAM DATES: Early June through early August
HEAD OF PROGRAM: Kendra Henry, Director of Summer High School Programs

LOCATION
Colorado College is located on a 94-acre campus in downtown Colorado Springs near the base of the 14,110-foot Pikes Peak and about an hour from Denver.

BACKGROUND AND PHILOSOPHY
A private, four-year liberal arts and sciences college, Colorado College is consistently ranked in the top tier in *U.S. News & World Report* for academic excellence. Best known for its innovative Block Plan, where students take only one course at a time, Colorado College offers a new perspective on core classes and standard curriculum. Small and supportive learning communities give students the time to participate fully—without distractions. At Colorado College, the goal is to provide the finest liberal arts education in the country. Drawing upon the adventurous spirit of the Rocky Mountain West, the College challenges students, one course at a time, to develop those habits of intellect and imagination that will prepare them for learning and leadership throughout their lives.

PROGRAM OFFERINGS
Colorado College hosts a number of special precollege programs throughout the summer, including the Summer Session High School Program, the College Ahead! Summer Enrichment Program, and the Southwest High School Scholars Program.

Summer Session High School Program A wide range of college-credit courses are open to high school students who are prepared for college-level work. Students must submit a letter of recommendation from a teacher or counselor, a high

school transcript, and a completed application. A limited amount of financial aid is available to high school students. Students are not required to live on campus but may do so in a residence hall specifically for high school students who are at least 16 years old. Students take courses in the College's unique academic scheduling system called the Block Plan, which entails taking one class at a time for an intensive three-week period. College-preparatory programming, which includes special sessions on the college admissions process, college application essay writing, and career opportunities, is available at no extra cost. Students are offered excursions in the Colorado Springs vicinity and other extracurricular opportunities.

College Ahead! is a full-scholarship summer-enrichment program for rising high school juniors from the American Southwest (Arizona, Colorado, New Mexico, Oklahoma, and Texas). The program is designed to help students prepare for higher education by providing a stimulating and supportive introduction to collegiate academic and social life. This two-week program encourages students to explore options after high school, particularly opportunities available at a small liberal arts college. Students choose between a social science and a natural science course. In addition, students learn how to better prepare for the college application process and beyond.

Southwest High School Scholars Program is a full-scholarship opportunity for a limited number of exceptionally talented and highly motivated rising high school seniors from the American Southwest (Arizona, Colorado, New Mexico, Oklahoma, and Texas) to participate in the Summer Session High School Program described above. The program is designed to demonstrate the value of a liberal arts education and to help students prepare for college work. Students must live on campus and participate in the college-preparation programming.

ENROLLMENT
Class sizes remain small in the summer, often with a range of 7 to 25 students in each course. Students are open-minded, motivated, and curious about college opportunities.

DAILY SCHEDULE

While class times vary by subject and instructor, most courses meet for about 3 hours each weekday, often from 9 a.m. to noon. Many of the science courses include afternoon laboratories, which typically run from 1 to 3 p.m., depending on the subject and the instructor. Many courses throughout the curriculum include field trips; course descriptions specify whether any extensive field study takes place away from the campus.

EXTRA OPPORTUNITIES AND ACTIVITIES

Summer at Colorado College provides a tantalizing array of activities to accompany academic studies. Whether one wants to listen to wonderful music during the Summer Festival of the Arts, climb Pikes Peak, explore hip-hop or Brazilian dance, or just lie in the grass and think, the perfect complement to the summer academic program exists at Colorado College.

FACILITIES

High school students may live in on-campus housing during their participation in Summer Session. Students live in traditional residence hall facilities and eat meals on campus, as well. The College provides a single bed, a chest of drawers, a desk and a chair, a mirror, a mattress protector, a wastebasket, a wall or ceiling light, a live jack for telephone and Ethernet service, and, for a nominal fee, a small refrigerator in the rooms. Housing is available to upcoming high school juniors and seniors only. Students must be at least 16 years of age to live in the residence halls.

STAFF

Colorado College employs 208 faculty members, 82 percent of whom are full-time.

MEDICAL CARE

Colorado College offers limited health services to all students enrolled in credit courses in the summer. Students may waive these services. Those students who do not waive these services must submit a student health record and Colorado Alternative Certificate of Immunization for College Students. These forms are available in PDF format on the Boettcher Health Center Web site.

COSTS

The cost of tuition for study during the summer at Colorado College is exceptionally competitive—a summer course is approximately one-half the tuition charged during the regular year—and reflects the College's commitment to support a broad range of educational needs. Tuition is the same for Colorado residents and out-of-state students and covers instruction in all academic courses. In 2007, tuition was $575 per 1 semester hour of credit. Tuition is billed in May, and final payment is due at the time of registration, unless other arrangements have been made with the business office. In addition, some courses require supplementary program fees, which cover additional costs such as travel, food, lodging, and other expenses. These extra program costs are listed with the course description. Program fees are charged and due at the same time as tuition for the course. The cost for room and board ranged from $985 for a single room for three weeks to $1820 for a double room for nine weeks.

FINANCIAL AID

A limited amount of merit-based financial aid is available for qualifying high school students in the Summer Session courses. The College Ahead! and Southwest High School Scholars Programs are full-scholarship programs. More information is available by contacting the office of the Director of Summer High School Programs.

TRANSPORTATION

From the Colorado Springs airport, there are taxis that bring students directly to Colorado College's Loomis Hall. In addition, the TNM&O bus service comes into the downtown bus terminal, which is about 1 mile from the campus. Students can then take a taxi to the College. For additional information, students may contact the office of the Director of Summer High School Programs or visit the Web site.

APPLICATION TIMETABLE

To sign up for a Summer Session class, high school students must send a completed application form, the $50 application fee, a letter of recommendation from a teacher or counselor, and a current high school transcript. The Director of Summer High School Programs makes the admission decision. Applicants for the College Ahead! and Southwest High School Scholars programs must be from Arizona, Colorado, New Mexico, Oklahoma, or Texas. The College Ahead! application deadline is April 27 and the Southwest High School Scholars application is due April 6, but students should apply early.

FOR MORE INFORMATION, CONTACT:

Kendra Henry, Director of Summer High School Programs
Colorado College
14 East Cache La Poudre Street
Colorado Springs, Colorado 80903

Phone: 719-389-6935
E-mail: khenry@coloradocollege.edu
Web site: http://www.coloradocollege.edu/SummerPrograms/
SummerSession/HSstudents.asp

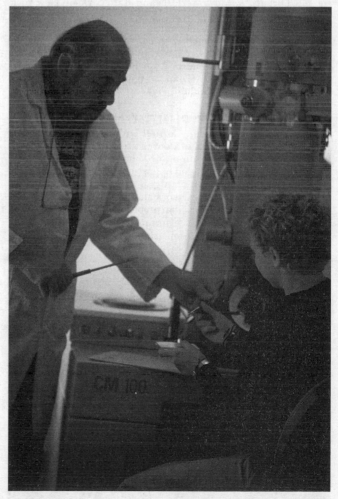

CORNELL UNIVERSITY SUMMER COLLEGE

Cornell University

SUMMER PROGRAM

ITHACA, NEW YORK

TYPE OF PROGRAM: Academic course work
PARTICIPANTS: Coeducational, students who have completed the sophomore, junior, or senior year of high school
ENROLLMENT: 600 juniors and seniors; 200 sophomores
PROGRAM DATES: Six-week session: June 21 to August 5, 2008; three-week session I: June 21 to July 12, 2008; three-week session II: July 13 to August 2, 2008
HEAD OF PROGRAM: Abby H. Eller, Director

LOCATION

Cornell University is located in the heart of the Finger Lakes region of central New York State, one of the Northeast's most spectacular summer vacation areas. The 740-acre campus overlooks Cayuga Lake and is surrounded by rolling hills. Some of the most breathtaking waterfalls and state parks in New York are a short bike or bus ride away.

Ithaca is a small, cosmopolitan city with a population of 30,000. Ithaca can be reached by car from Boston in 7 hours, from Buffalo in 3 hours, from Cleveland in 7 hours, from Manhattan in under 5 hours, from Philadelphia in 4 hours, and from Washington, D.C., in 7 hours; Syracuse and Binghamton are within an hour's drive.

BACKGROUND AND PHILOSOPHY

Now in its forty-sixth year, Cornell University Summer College provides academically talented students who have completed their sophomore, junior, or senior year in high school by June 2008 an unparalleled opportunity to experience what it is like to live and learn at a great Ivy League university, take real university courses, work closely with Cornell's world-renowned faculty members, earn college credit, explore majors and career options, get a jump on successful college applications, make friends from around the world, and much more.

PROGRAM OFFERINGS

Through outstanding one-, three-, four-, and six-week programs, Summer College students focus on areas that include architecture; art; business; college success; computing and information science; engineering; humanities; law and politics; life, environmental, agriculture, and applied social sciences; media; medicine, science, and biological research; psychology; veterinary medicine; and writing. Although academics are a crucial component of Summer College, learning extends far beyond the classroom walls.

Sophomores are eligible for five programs, including four 3-week options, Body, Mind, and Health: Perspectives for Future Medical Professionals; Freedom and Justice: The Law in Theory and Practice; Leadership Through Managerial Communication; and On Camera: Studies in Film Analysis, and the six-week option, CollegeSuccess: Critical Reading and Thinking. Juniors and seniors can participate in all (more than twenty-five) options.

ENROLLMENT

Summer College students are part of an international, multicultural community, with members coming from all over the United States and the world.

DAILY SCHEDULE

Students in the six-week session spend mornings in classes (roughly 2½ hours each weekday, with laboratory courses requiring an additional 2 to 3 hours a day). Most afternoons are devoted to career-exploration activities, such as field trips, experiments, simulations, lectures, or discussions. The academic course work is rigorous; students should plan to spend 2 hours a day in preparation for every hour in class. The nightly check-in is 11 p.m. Sunday through Thursday and midnight Friday and Saturday.

Students in the three-week session spend weekday mornings in class (roughly 2½ hours each day) and afternoons in a seminar and in meetings with teaching assistants and the faculty director. The nightly check-in is 11 p.m. Sunday through Thursday and midnight Friday and Saturday.

EXTRA OPPORTUNITIES AND ACTIVITIES

Sessions about the college application process are offered throughout the summer, with information on the art of filling out applications, the value of campus visits, and the nitty-gritty of college interviews. Cornell's Undergraduate Admissions staff answers questions about applying to selective colleges. Juniors and seniors may also take part in a half-day crash course in college study skills before classes begin and in math, study skills, and writing workshops throughout the summer.

Students enjoy theater parties; athletic activities, including basketball, volleyball, aerobics, yoga, and intramural sports; weekend dances; a student-organized show; and get-togethers with faculty members to discuss current topics. They also produce Summer College's weekly newspaper and its literary supplement. Free concerts and lectures are offered throughout the summer.

FACILITIES

Students are housed in residence halls and eat and relax together in on-campus dining halls and student community centers. They have full access to Cornell's academic facilities, including the Cornell library system (which holds more than 6 million volumes), numerous computer laboratories (with Internet access), an astronomical observatory, an extensive botanical garden, and an art museum. Students may also use the athletics facilities on campus, including tennis courts, swimming pools, gyms, and an eighteen-hole golf course. Cornell University is famed for the spacious beauty of its campus. Students enjoy hiking in the gorges that cut through the campus and exploring the spectacular waterfalls and geological formations.

STAFF

Most courses are taught by Cornell University faculty members. The residence halls are staffed by head residents, residential community advisers, and program assistants, all of whom work to ensure that the students' experiences in the residence halls are good ones.

MEDICAL CARE

Gannett Health Center is open for general and emergency health care. Students complete the Health History Form prior to registration.

RELIGIOUS LIFE

Cornell University is a secular institution. Cornell United Religious Work coordinates religious activities on campus, and services for many religious groups are held during the summer.

COSTS

The cost for the 2007 six-week Summer College program was $7975, the cost for the four-week program was $6100, the cost for the three-week sessions was $4810, and the cost for the one-week session was $1600. These amounts cover tuition, room, board, and all fees, including those for courses and activities at Cornell. They do not include the cost of books, supplies, or travel.

FINANCIAL AID

Summer College offers a limited number of partial scholarships to gifted students from the U.S., Canada, or Mexico who could not otherwise attend. Summer College's limited financial aid is awarded to students whose academic performance has been outstanding and who demonstrate financial need, and it is reserved primarily for participants in the six-week session. Financial aid decisions are made on a rolling basis after the student has been accepted into a program. The deadline for applying for aid is early April.

TRANSPORTATION

The Ithaca Tompkins Regional Airport (10 minutes from the campus) is served by Northwest Airlines and US Airways. Syracuse (Hancock International) is served by most major airlines, including Northwest, United, and US Airways/America West.

APPLICATION TIMETABLE

Inquiries are welcome throughout the year. In 2008, the admissions application deadline for most programs is May 2. Admissions are made on a rolling basis for most programs, so it is to the student's advantage to apply early. Students should visit the Summer College's Web site for more details.

FOR MORE INFORMATION, CONTACT

Cornell University Summer College
B20 Day Hall
Ithaca, New York 14853-2801
Phone: 607-255-6203
Fax: 607-255-6665
E-mail: summer_college@cornell.edu
Web site: http://www.summercollege.cornell.edu

CUSHING ACADEMY

SUMMER SESSION

ASHBURNHAM, MASSACHUSETTS

TYPE OF PROGRAM: Academic enrichment
PARTICIPANTS: Coeducational, ages 12–18
ENROLLMENT: 350
PROGRAM DATES: July to August
HEAD OF PROGRAM: Dr. James Tracy, Headmaster

LOCATION
Located in the hills of north-central Massachusetts, 60 miles from Boston, Cushing Academy's 162-acre campus offers a rural atmosphere with the cultural advantages of a major city only an hour's drive away. The school is situated in and overlooks the picturesque New England town of Ashburnham.

BACKGROUND AND PHILOSOPHY
Established in 1865, Cushing Academy is an accredited boarding school for boys and girls in grades 9 through 12. The Summer Session, offering programs for boys and girls ages 12 to 18, continues the school's approach to education into the summer. The mission of the Summer Session is to allow young people to grow and learn by facing challenges in a secure and supportive environment, thereby successfully developing self-esteem. Cushing strives to develop happy, fair-minded, and productive human beings, and all of its programs are directed toward this goal. The focus is always on the potential of the adolescent, and Cushing helps students discover, develop, and appreciate their own uniqueness and value.

PROGRAM OFFERINGS
Each student is enrolled in one of six major programs: College Prep–Secondary School Level; Critical Skills Across the Curriculum in English, Mathematics, and Study Techniques; English as a Second Language; the Prep for Success Program; or Studio Art. The average class contains 8–12 students, with a purposeful yet friendly atmosphere that encourages questions and discussion. Faculty members prepare two formal evaluations on each student, one in the middle and one at the end of the summer. Written evaluations highlight the progress made by the individual student relative to his or her own needs and placement, and a grade of honors, pass, or fail is given.

College Prep–Secondary School Level For students ages 14–18, this program offers a choice of Critical and Creative Writing, A Literary Tour of New England, Research and Technology, Geometry, Algebra I and II, Precalculus, Calculus, U.S. History, Biology, Chemistry, Physics, and Theater Workshop. The courses taught in this program prepare students to meet the challenge of a college-level curriculum confidently and successfully. Each of these courses is the equivalent of a year of secondary school course work, and Cushing awards a full year of secondary school academic credit upon successful completion of the program.

Critical Skills Across the Curriculum in English, Mathematics, and Study Techniques This program is for students ages 14–18. It encompasses four key components: English, Mathematics, Study Techniques, and Technology. Each student is given placement tests to assess skills and learning styles and an individualized learning program is developed. Students are assigned to classes structured to meet their specific learning needs. Each student learns at his or her own pace, mastering progressively higher levels of skills. The schedule is flexible enough to allow a focus on either English or mathematics development or both. Study Techniques and Technology are taught within the context of the subject matter.

English as a Second Language (ESL) is offered for students ages 14–18. Within the ESL program, classes enhance skills in reading, writing, speaking, and listening. Students can dramatically increase their proficiency in English through this three- or six-week immersion experience. Students are tested at the beginning of the program and placed in a class appropriate to their skill level. Up to fourteen levels ensure that each student's needs are met. Preparation for the Test of English as a Foreign Language (TOEFL) is offered, and the opportunity to take the official TOEFL is offered to students of advanced and high intermediate levels during the final weeks of the program.

Prep for Success For students ages 12–13, this program offers a choice of science, English, mathematics, study skills, and ESL. The courses taught in this program prepare students for the academic experiences that lie ahead in secondary school. Featuring hands-on learning, each course has a dual focus on the subject matter and on the skills needed for academic success, including reading comprehension strategies, vocabulary development, word analogies, time management, organizational techniques, and test-taking strategies.

Studio Art This program, for students ages 13–18, is taught in Cushing's state-of-the-art Emily Fisher Landau Center for the Visual Arts, a beautiful facility with five advanced studios and a gallery. Both experienced and beginning art students are provided with opportunities to explore a variety of media, including painting and drawing, pottery, silversmithing, and photography.

ENROLLMENT
Approximately 350 students, representing more than thirty countries and as many states, attend the session.

DAILY SCHEDULE

Classes in the major programs take place for 4 hours, Monday through Friday, beginning at 8 a.m. Each afternoon, students participate in academic, athletic, and fine arts electives, of which Cushing offers a wide variety. Writing workshop, SAT preparation, computer design, and Algebra I are just a few academic electives offered. Fine arts electives include painting and drawing, photography, silversmithing, pottery, dance, theater, and videomaking, while athletic activities include aerobics, basketball, golf, soccer, swimming, tennis, and volleyball.

EXTRA OPPORTUNITIES AND ACTIVITIES

Each week brings a variety of activities to campus, including dances, sports events, and performances by musical groups and entertainers. Optional excursions are scheduled every Saturday and Sunday to shopping centers, amusement parks, beaches, Red Sox games, local community service opportunities, and other activities that take advantage of recreational and cultural offerings in the Boston area and throughout New England.

On Wednesdays, a variety of class field trips to sites such as Plimoth Plantation, the New England Aquarium, and Mystic Seaport are organized. These excursions are included in the comprehensive fee and are chaperoned by faculty members. College counseling and secondary school placement counseling are available for students who want assistance with educational planning.

During each week, Cushing offers a special all-school activity, including a trip to High Meadow resort and a dinner/dance cruise around Boston Harbor. Among the special events is International Evening, a celebration of the rich cultural diversity present at the Summer Session. In preparation the students bring from home traditional clothing, flags, posters, and recipes. Cushing's dining hall is transformed into an international bazaar, where students view displays and sample foods from other cultures. The evening concludes with student-created performances of songs, dances, and skits representative of their culture. The Cushing Cabaret, a night dedicated to short programs and entertainment by the Cushing community, has also become a well-loved summer tradition. Students and faculty members show off their talent through comedy, music, poetry, skits, and more.

FACILITIES

The campus combines the charm of nineteenth-century buildings with the graceful contemporary style of Cushing's award-winning library. Boys and girls live in separate dormitories with roommates, supervised by members of the faculty. Two or three students are assigned to each room. The Joseph R. Curry Academic Center, an outstanding new facility for the study of science, mathematics, and the performing arts, includes a large theater and dance practice rooms and music studios. The spacious dining hall accommodates the entire Cushing community for relaxed and congenial mealtimes. The Student Center, part of the student commons complex, houses the student post office, student bank, bookstore, snack bar, and lounge. Athletic facilities include playing fields, tennis courts, a gymnasium with weight room, and a world-class ice arena.

STAFF

Teachers are experienced professionals educated in the theories and methods of teaching. They are also supportive, insightful, caring, good-humored, and kind. A diverse group, they share a willingness to spend their lives with young people. Most have master's degrees, and some have doctorates; all have experience teaching in this country or abroad. The faculty-student ratio is approximately 1:8. In their roles as dorm parents, athletic coaches, and chaperones, Cushing teachers are in an excellent position to know when to offer support, enforce discipline, mediate a dispute, or let students work things out among themselves.

MEDICAL CARE

The Health Center is fully equipped to handle all routine medical needs. Nurses and doctors are available at all times. Cushing uses the Henry Heywood Hospital in nearby Gardner for nonroutine needs.

COSTS

Program tuitions vary, but the six-week fee of $5650 covers the following: tuition for all courses, academic electives, and athletic activities; meals and dormitory housing; required trips and excursions; special all-school activities; books and supplies; athletic uniform; on-campus social activities; dormitory-room supplies; and limited accident insurance. In addition, students have use of the Academy's communications system, which includes a private telephone, voice mail, and Internet access for each student.

TRANSPORTATION

The staff meets flights and provides free transportation between Cushing and Logan International Airport (Boston) on scheduled arrival and departure dates. Parents may also wish to secure personalized transportation assistance through Concierge Services for Students LTD, at 617-523-8686 or http://www.conciergeforstudents.net.

APPLICATION TIMETABLE

The application form should be completed and mailed with the nonrefundable processing fee of $60 as early as possible. Admissions decisions are made as soon as these materials are in hand. Within four weeks of acceptance, a nonrefundable enrollment deposit of $500 is due. The remainder of the tuition is due on or before May 15.

FOR MORE INFORMATION, CONTACT

Cushing Academy Summer Session
39 School Street
Ashburnham, Massachusetts 01430-8000

Phone: 978-827-7700
Fax: 978-827-6927
E-mail: summersession@cushing.org
Web site: http://www.cushing.org

CYBERCAMPS

cybercamps
by giant campus

SUMMER COMPUTER CAMPS

MORE THAN FIFTY LOCATIONS NATIONWIDE

TYPE OF PROGRAM: Coed summer technology program for youths and teens; day and residential summer camp with a focus on computers

PARTICIPANTS: Coeducational, ages 7–18

ENROLLMENT: Open enrollment, with class sizes between 30 and 40

PROGRAM DATES: Weekly sessions, from June 11 to August 31 (varies by location)

HEAD OF PROGRAM: Kathleen Fitzgerald, National Camp Director

LOCATION

Cybercamps is the summer computer camp destination for youths and teens across the country. With more than fifty locations in eighteen states, campers are able to find a Cybercamps location nearby. Students have the option for day or residential camp, and there is adult supervision at all locations.

Camp locations in California include Concordia University, DeAnza College, Stanford University, and the University of California, Berkeley, Los Angeles, and San Diego; in Connecticut, the University of Bridgeport and the University of Hartford; in Florida, Barry University, Nova Southeastern University, the University of Central Florida, and the University of Miami; in Georgia, Georgia State University, Oglethorpe University, and Southern Polytechnic University; in Illinois, Benedictine University, Concordia University, and Loyola University; in Maryland, Towson University and the University of Maryland; in Massachusetts, Bentley College, Dana Hall School, Massachusetts Institute of Technology, and Merrimack College; in Michigan, the University of Michigan; in Minnesota, the University of Minnesota; in Missouri, Webster University; in New Jersey, Caldwell College, the College of Saint Elizabeth, and Rutgers; in New York, Adelphi University, the New School, and New York Institute of Technology; in North Carolina, Duke University and the University of North Carolina at Chapel Hill; in Oregon, Lewis & Clark College; in Pennsylvania, Bryn Mawr College; in Virginia, George Mason University, Oak Marr Recreation Center, and Northern Virginia Community College, Alexandria; in Washington, Bellevue Community College, Trinity Lutheran College, and the University of Washington, Bothell and Tacoma; and in Washington, D.C., American University.

BACKGROUND AND PHILOSOPHY

Cybercamps, the summer computer camp for youths, is part of the Giant Campus family of youth programs. It has established itself as the most innovative national summer computer camp available. After more than a decade of summers, Cybercamps is still regarded as the premier summer program for kids who are interested in computers and technology, thanks to its dedication to innovation.

Cybercamps' philosophy has guided the program since its start more than a decade ago—human brains learn more when they're having fun™. This simple concept has been a driving force for Cybercamps and has kept it true to its values as a company.

PROGRAM OFFERINGS

Gamer Campers who like playing video games will definitely enjoy Cybercamps' gaming courses, which are filled with fun projects in game design, game modding, and 3-D modeling for games. The Cybercamps game design courses offer campers the chance to create their own video games, modify games they already have, and create game environments and graphics using industry-leading software. These courses are not just for game players. They are also for anyone who wants to be a part of the emerging fields of game design, narrative media, technology education, and interactive software design.

User Campers' lives are filled with technology. They take digital photos, maybe have their own Web site, and use IM and text messages to chat. Cybercamps' multimedia courses give campers the chance to use technology in a way that gives them the ability to customize it to their personal style. These courses allow students to build a Web site, master digital photography, and design graphics that show off their creativity and style. These courses offer a focus in graphic design, flash animation, and Web design.

Coder Through Cybercamps' programming series of courses, students learn to control the brains of their computer by writing programs in a language that it can understand. All courses are customized to match the campers' level of interest and the speed at which they learn. These are ideal courses for campers who want to program a robot (robotics), write computer programs (C++ programming), or write software packages (Java scripting).

EXTRA OPPORTUNITIES AND ACTIVITIES
In addition to its courses and special interest projects, Cybercamps offers a variety of activities—both indoor and outdoor—that its participants love, including Capture the Flag, Ultimate Frisbee, Dance-Dance-Revolution®, board games, and videos. Cybercamps also offers a number of traditions, including Wild Water Wednesdays, Friday Awards Ceremony, Robot Rivalries, Game Testing, Movie Mania, and Campus Tours.

STAFF
Cybercamps teaching staff members are parents, educators, technology professionals, and experts—adults who provide a safe and nurturing environment that helps campers have a great summer. They are cool people that youths feel comfortable around, and they are passionate about helping kids experience technology in a safe and productive way. The camper-staff ratio is 5:1, the lowest for a national program. On average, more than 80 percent of the camp directors return each year to lead Cybercamps programs.

MEDICAL CARE
Cybercamps maintains more than 300 standards of health and safety in all camp locations. These standards cover various aspects of a camp's operations in ten specific areas, including health care (staff and facility requirements, medication management, required health information, and recordkeeping) and staffing (staff qualifications,

training, ratios, supervision, and behavior management guidelines). In addition, Cybercamps' standards go beyond these basic requirements to include a comprehensive staff training program for all camp staff members, from the camp director through counselors, covering emergency management plans, health care, and overall program management. Cybercamps' staff members are trained in first aid and CPR, and each staff member has been through its rigorous screening system.

COSTS
Cybercamps offers day camps, extended day camps, and residential camps. Weekly tuition rates vary by location. Day camp ranges from $599 to $749, with variations to personalize each camper's program. For specific tuition and fees, students may call 888-904-2267 (toll-free) or visit Cybercamps' Web site (http://www.cybercamps.com).

APPLICATION TIMETABLE
Cybercamps accepts registrations on a rolling basis beginning in September. Courses fill up quickly, and early registration and multiweek discounts are available.

FOR MORE INFORMATION, CONTACT
Camp Consultant
Cybercamps
3101 Western Avenue, Suite 100
Seattle, Washington 98121
Phone: 206-442-4500
        888-904-2267 (toll-free)
Fax: 206-442-4501
E-mail: info@cybercamps.com
Web site: http://www.cybercamps.com

DUKE UNIVERSITY
TALENT IDENTIFICATION PROGRAM (TIP)

Duke
TIP

PRECOLLEGE, FIELD STUDIES, AND INSTITUTES

DURHAM, NORTH CAROLINA

TYPE OF PROGRAM: Academic (general), gifted and talented

PARTICIPANTS: Coeducational, grades 9–12 (varies by program)

ENROLLMENT: PreCollege Program: 50–100 participants; Field Studies: 18 to 22 students per program; Institutes: 28 to 36 students per program

PROGRAM DATES: PreCollege Program: one 6-week session; Field Studies and Institutes: multiple two-week sessions; all programs are held between June and mid-August

HEAD OF PROGRAM: Hollace Selph, Director of Educational Programs

LOCATION

Locations vary by program. The Duke University PreCollege Program takes place at Duke University in Durham, North Carolina. Each individual domestic or international Field Study involves travel to an exciting location chosen specifically to enhance the academic content of the program. In 2007, locations included the mountains of North Carolina or Virginia, California, New Mexico, England, France, Italy, China, and Costa Rica. Each Institute is held on the campus of a top university, such as Duke University and Wake Forest University.

BACKGROUND AND PHILOSOPHY

The Duke University Talent Identification Program (Duke TIP) is a national leader in identifying academically talented students and providing innovative programs to support the development of their optimal educational potential. Duke TIP, a nonprofit educational organization, conducts two annual talent searches, offers a variety of educational programs, and provides additional services to students, teachers, and parents. Since 1980, Duke TIP has served more than 1.6 million students.

PROGRAM OFFERINGS

The Duke University PreCollege Program takes place each summer from July through mid-August and provides the opportunity for rising high school seniors to earn Duke University credit. Students attend Duke's summer session courses along with Duke undergraduate students, following the University's course and exam schedule. Duke TIP provides a structured residential program with trained staff members. During the six-week program, students have access to a variety of activities, community service opportunities, and educational seminars. This program is available exclusively to rising high school seniors.

Domestic and International Field Studies and Institutes vary each year. Prospective students should visit the Duke TIP Web site for complete program descriptions, dates, pricing, and current offerings. Duke TIP Field Studies and Institutes are much more than just a science or humanities class. Each is an authentic academic experience, similar to a college field course. Although these programs are only two weeks long, the academic material offered in these courses can satisfy the intellectual hunger of the most ardent learner.

Students selected for admission into one of these programs participate in a variety of activities, such as discussions, research projects, fieldwork, and/or presentations. Each instructor's personal combination of methods has been developed to maximize student achievement while drawing from the unique features of each site. Duke TIP Field Studies and Institutes are noncredit, and no grades are awarded. Upon completion, each student receives a rubric and narrative assessment from the instructor, detailing his or her individual performance throughout the course. While it is very likely that any motivated student can succeed in these courses, they have been established specifically for academically gifted students.

Offerings for 2007 included *Above and Beyond: Astronomy, Physics, and Astrobiology* (North Carolina); *A Writer's Art: Creative Writing* (New Mexico); *Off the Beaten Path: Field Ecology and Mountain Geology* (Virginia); *Reel Expressions: Filmmaking* (California); *Art and Soul: Architecture and Art History* (Rome and Florence, Italy); *China: A Leader in the Global Economy* (Shanghai, Xian, and Beijing, China); *Philosophic Quest: Paris Through the Eyes of its Greatest Minds* (Paris, France); *World Politics: A Diplomat's Perspective* (London, England); *Tropical Ecology* (Costa Rica); *Tropical Medicine and Ethnobiology* (Costa Rica); *International Affairs Institute: The Ethics of War* (Wake Forest University); *Great Debates Institute: For the Sake of Argument* (Duke University); and *Leadership Institute: Theory and Practice* (Duke University).

EXTRA OPPORTUNITIES AND ACTIVITIES

Opportunities, excursions, and activities vary by site. While students should expect a large amount of structured academic time, staff members also organize a variety of supplemental activities. Examples include trips to local museums, movie theaters, or shopping centers; outdoor hiking or canoe trips; community service opportunities; and soccer or Ultimate Frisbee tournaments on the quad.

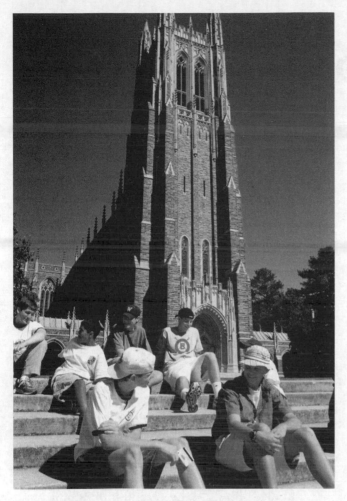

FACILITIES

Facilities vary by site. Students are housed in single-sex rooms of university residence halls, hotels, international schools, or field stations. Specific information is available in the *Student and Parent Guide,* which is sent to students when they are accepted into the program. The guide for each program is also available on the Duke TIP Web site.

STAFF

Instructors for the PreCollege Program are Duke University faculty members, guest instructors, or advanced doctoral students. Each full-time residential staff member serves as a mentor, tutor, and role model and has training in leadership and residence hall advising. Students should expect 1 staff member for each group of approximately 10 to 12 students.

Instructors for the Field Studies and Institutes may be professors or doctoral students from leading universities or exceptional teachers from schools across the country. The teaching/residential assistants are usually highly skilled graduate or undergraduate students who possess experience in both the course content and student educational programs. Students should expect 1 staff member for each group of approximately 8 to 10 students.

MEDICAL CARE

All participants are required to carry current health insurance. Students in need of medical care are transported by Duke TIP staff members to the medical facilities at or near each site.

COSTS

The cost for the 2007 PreCollege Program was $6900 (airfare and books not included). Program costs for the 2007 Field Studies and Institutes ranged from $2300 to $3900 (airfare and books not included).

At this time, need-based financial aid is available for the domestic Field Studies and Institutes only.

TRANSPORTATION

Field Study and Institute participants meet Duke TIP staff members at the airport indicated in the program description, and PreCollege participants check in after they arrive on Duke's campus. Exact transportation details vary by program and are outlined in the *Student and Parent Guide.* To ensure the safety of each student and that of the group, participants in the International Field Studies are required to travel with Duke TIP staff members from the gateway airport as part of the group reservation secured by Duke TIP.

APPLICATION TIMETABLE

Application materials for Duke TIP are available online, and the review process of the application portfolios begins in January. Applications are reviewed as they are received, and participants are notified within three weeks of the status of their application. The final application deadline is mid-March, and final payments are due by mid-April.

FOR MORE INFORMATION, CONTACT

Duke University TIP
1121 West Main Street
Durham, North Carolina 27701

Phone: 919-668-9100
Fax: 919-681-7921
Web site: http://www.tip.duke.edu

DUKE YOUTH PROGRAMS

▼▲▼▲▼▲▼▲▼▲▼▲▼▲▼▲▼▲▼▲▼▲▼▲▼▲▼▲▼▲

SUMMER ENRICHMENT PROGRAMS

DURHAM, NORTH CAROLINA

TYPE OF PROGRAM: Summer enrichment programs for academically motivated students in the areas of writing, science, drama, performing arts, and college selection/admissions

PARTICIPANTS: Middle school and high school students

ENROLLMENT: 40–150 participants per program; varies by program

PROGRAM DATES: Duke Young Writers' Camp: three 2-week sessions, June through July; Duke Action Science Camp for Young Women: one 2-week session in June; Duke Expressions! Performing Arts Camp: one 2-week session in June; Duke Creative Writers' Workshop: one 2-week session in July; Duke Biosciences & Engineering Camp: one 2-week session in June; Duke Drama Workshop: one 2-week session in July; Duke Constructing Your College Experience: one 1-week session in July

LOCATION
Duke University is located in Durham, North Carolina. Duke is a 20-minute drive from Raleigh-Durham International Airport, 15 minutes from the University of North Carolina at Chapel Hill, and 10 minutes from North Carolina Central University.

BACKGROUND AND PHILOSOPHY
Duke Youth Programs is a part of Duke University Continuing Studies and has offered summer enrichment programs for more than twenty years. Young people from around the country attend to engage in interactive, innovative, and transformative learning experiences. Programs are designed to meet the needs of motivated students who desire intellectual experiences beyond the traditional academic setting. The programs provide a supportive atmosphere of active learning. Cocurricular social and recreational activities are planned to complement the instructional day. Participants also experience life in a college setting and the responsibilities of independent living with supervision.

PROGRAM OFFERINGS
Duke Young Writers' Camp (grades 6–11 in 2007–08 school year) The Duke Young Writers' Camp provides participants the opportunity to explore and refine writing skills through a diverse curriculum of short story, poetry, journalism, playwriting, mystery writing, and more. Students develop creative and analytical processes of writing in self-selected courses under the guidance of professional educators and published writers. Classes are small and the learning environment is supportive yet challenging. Each instructional day begins with a morning gathering period, a time for large-group instruction and guest speakers, followed by classes and concludes with a readers' forum, a time for students to share their work with their peers.

Duke Action Science Camp for Young Women (grades 5–7 in 2007–08 school year) Duke Action promotes scientific discovery through field and laboratory experiences in a forest environment. Participants examine ecological and biological principles through explorations of terrestrial and aquatic life, chemical and physical properties of the environment, and the impact of human activities on ecosystems. Learning activities include trips to outdoor field sites, educational games and simulations, and laboratory experiments. Opportunities are provided for students to interact with women in careers in the physical, biological, and environmental sciences. Applicants should have a genuine enthusiasm for science and a willingness to engage in outdoor exploration of scientific concepts through hands-on activities.

Duke Expressions! Performing Arts Camp (grades 5–8 in 2007–08 school year) Duke Expressions! provides an intense, hands-on exploration of the performing arts, with offerings in drama,

dance, vocal training, and musical theater. Participants and staff members work together to encourage and support participants as they develop their creativity and expand their talents. The instructional day includes three classes, studio time, and a gallery period. Studio time provides an opportunity for participants to work on individual and group projects. The gallery period provides a forum for participants to share their work with their peers. The session concludes with a final performance and gallery to showcase campers' work.

Duke Creative Writers' Workshop (grades 10–11 in 2007–08 school year) The Duke Creative Writers' Workshop provides advanced writers who are committed to refining their skills and building a community of writers an intensive creative writing experience. Instructors and peers work collaboratively to assist participants in reaching their self-defined workshop goals. The interactive format allows participants to share work in small groups and receive constructive written and verbal feedback in a supportive environment. Students select a primary instructor based on the genre in which they wish to work for the duration of the camp. Other learning experiences include participation in mini-lessons, individual conferences, forums, writing exercises, and readings.

Duke Biosciences & Engineering Camp (grades 6–8 in 2007–08 school year) Through laboratory experiments and other related activities, participants increase their knowledge of the human body as a system of biological components ranging from cells to organs. Participants are introduced to mechanics, sensing, communication and energy, tissue engineering, and robotics. There are also opportunities for participants in the program to develop their critical-thinking and problem-solving skills through group and individual assignments. To further enhance their experience, participants visit other laboratories on campus and nearby university laboratories.

Duke Drama Workshop (grades 9–11 in 2007–08 school year) The Duke Drama Workshop offers high school students an intense drama experience, which culminates with a final performance. The workshop provides a supportive environment for students who are committed to refining their skills and building a community of actors. Participants attend daily acting classes to learn the creative and technical processes of acting. They also attend rehearsal periods of selected scenes from plays under the direction of professional educators, actors, and artists. Based on their individual areas of interest, students select from several acting classes and rehearsal periods representing drama, musical theater, and comedy.

Duke Constructing Your College Experience (grades 10–11 in 2007–08 school year) Constructing Your College Experience is designed to empower college-bound students in their exploration of college options and navigation of the college application process. Participants learn to evaluate colleges relative to their needs and interests, understand the multidimensional application process, and discover the challenges and opportunities of university life. In addition to small-group instruction, each student receives individualized guidance from an experienced college admissions counselor. Students sample college life by living, eating, and attending class on the Duke campus.

ENROLLMENT
Enrollment varies by program and ranges from 40 to 150 participants per program.

DAILY SCHEDULE
Specific program schedules vary. The average instructional day is from 9 a.m. to 4 p.m.

EXTRA OPPORTUNITIES AND ACTIVITIES
A variety of cocurricular social and recreational activities are offered during afternoons, evenings, and weekends. Each afternoon, students participate in elective activities, such as arts and crafts, sports and games, drama, or community service. Additional evening and weekend activities include dances, talent shows, karaoke, movies, and more.

FACILITIES
All participants live, dine, and attend class on Duke University's East Campus. Some programs have class on West Campus. All participants have an opportunity to visit West Campus during their stay.

STAFF
The instructional staff includes professional educators, published writers, and talented artists. Each camp has an academic director, who coordinates the academic life and advises instructional staff members. The residential staff members are mature, talented, and enthusiastic graduate and undergraduate students, who supervise campers in the residential hall and at other out-of-class times, such as meals, free times, and special events. The residential counselors also plan and lead a variety of social and recreational activities. A professional educator directly supervises the residential staff members and their activities.

MEDICAL CARE
Medical care is available at Duke University Wellness Center and the Medical Center.

RELIGIOUS LIFE
The Duke University Chapel offers nondenominational services on Sunday mornings. Residential staff members are available to escort participants to these services as well as Friday evening temple services. Requests for other services are handled individually and are accommodated if possible.

COSTS
Tuition for 2007 was $825 to $915 for day participants, $900 to $1055 for extended day participants, and $1150 to $1705 for residential participants.

Residential tuition covers instruction, instructional supplies, room, board, recreational activities, a camp T-shirt, and a notebook. Day and extended day camper tuition covers Monday-through-Friday instruction, instructional supplies, lunch, a camp T-shirt, and a notebook. Extended day camper tuition also includes Monday-through-Friday dinner and afternoon/evening academic and recreational activities until 9 p.m. Students are encouraged to bring spending money for optional activities and souvenirs.

FINANCIAL AID
Limited need-based financial assistance is available. The financial aid application is available on the Youth Programs Web site or by calling the program. Applications are due by March 16.

TRANSPORTATION
Duke University is 20 minutes from Raleigh-Durham International Airport and 10 minutes from the Durham Amtrak Station. Duke Youth Programs transports students to and from the airport and train station during designated times. The program cannot meet and escort unaccompanied minors from the gates. Only participants who meet airline requirements to travel alone and are comfortable making their way to the baggage area should plan to fly and use the shuttle provided.

APPLICATION TIMETABLE
Inquiries are always welcome. Registration begins on December 3, 2007, and remains open as long as space is available. A $300 nonrefundable deposit is required at the time of registration. All balances must be paid by May 17, 2008.

FOR MORE INFORMATION, CONTACT
Duke Continuing Studies
Duke Youth Program
Box 90700
201 Bishop's House
Durham, North Carolina 27708
Phone: 919-684-6259
Fax: 919-681-8235
E-mail: youth@duke.edu
Web site: http://www.learnmore.duke.edu/youth

PARTICIPANT/FAMILY COMMENTS

"I remember how amazing the teachers and counselors were, and all the wonderful new friends I made. Everyone was so nice, and it gave me so much confidence."

DUNNABECK AT KILDONAN

LANGUAGE TRAINING PROGRAM

AMENIA, NEW YORK

TYPE OF PROGRAM: Residential program focusing on language training for students with dyslexia or language-based learning difficulties
PARTICIPANTS: Coeducational, ages 8–16
ENROLLMENT: 85
PROGRAM DATES: End of June through middle of August
HEADS OF PROGRAM: Ronald A. Wilson, Headmaster; Ben Powers, Camp Director

LOCATION

Located on a hillside of woodlands, fields, and a pond, the 325-acre campus of Kildonan School, which includes school facilities and athletic fields, is in a spacious rural setting 90 miles north of New York City.

BACKGROUND AND PHILOSOPHY

Dunnabeck at Kildonan was established in 1955 by Diana Hanbury King to meet the needs of normal, intelligent boys and girls who are failing or underachieving in their academic work because of specific difficulties in reading, writing, and spelling. The Orton-Gillingham Approach is used throughout the program. Standardized diagnostic tests are given at the beginning of the season to plan the student's program and at the end to assess progress. Keyboarding and word processing form an integral part of the program. The recreational program is designed to supplement rather than compete with the academic program.

PROGRAM OFFERINGS

During the six-week summer program, all tutoring is done on an individual basis. Each student receives a 1-hour lesson daily. In addition, students are taught to study independently and to make the best possible use of group study periods. From the tutor, the student learns to set high standards, to work confidently, and to take pride in achievement. Considerable emphasis is placed on the student's writing. Stimulating and interesting material is provided for leisure reading. Math tutoring is available on a limited basis for an additional cost. Word processing classes are taught using an alphabetical keyboarding approach. Both the camp and the school are accredited by

the Academy of Orton-Gillingham Practitioners and Educators (AOGPE). They are also a certified/accredited training site by the AOGPE.

ENROLLMENT

Dunnabeck can accommodate 85 boys and girls ranging in age from 8 to 16. Students are admitted to the program without regard to race, creed, or color. Enrollment is for the full six weeks.

DAILY SCHEDULE

A typical day of activities may include:

6:40	Wake up
7:10	Leave dorms
7:15– 8:40	Breakfast
7:50– 8:50	Period One
8:55– 9:55	Period Two
10:00	Snack
10:00–11:00	Period Three
11:05–12:05	Period Four
12:15– 1:15	Lunch
1:20– 2:20	Period Five
2:30– 3:30	Study hall
3:45– 5:45	Afternoon group activity
6:00– 6:45	Dinner
7:00– 8:30	Mixed group activity
8:30– 9:30	Quiet time in dorms
9:30	Bedtime

EXTRA OPPORTUNITIES AND ACTIVITIES

Archery, camping, canoeing, ceramics, crafts, hiking, horseback riding, multimedia, painting, photography, sailing, soccer, softball, swimming, tennis, waterskiing, and woodworking are all offered.

FACILITIES

Kildonan's campus features a schoolhouse with a computer center and gymnasium, the Francis St. John Library, Simon Art Studios, two stables, a woodworking facility, and an elementary building with a computer center. There are also three dormitories.

STAFF

Ronald A. Wilson, Headmaster, was educated in New York and Connecticut. He holds a B.S. in psychology from SUNY at Brockport and an M.S. in counselor education from Western Connecticut State University.

Ben Powers, Camp Director, is currently completing his Master of Arts degree in language education at Indiana University. He holds a B.A. in Russian/French from LaSalle University and has a Certificate from the University of Paris Sorbonne IV in French studies. He has also been a language training tutor at Kildonan School for the past four years.

Diana Hanbury King, Founder and Director Emeritus, was educated in England and Canada. She holds a B.A.Hons. degree from the University of London and an M.A. from George Washington University. Mrs. King was the 1990 recipient of

at Dunnabeck come from the Kildonan Language Training Department and, therefore, have extensive experience in this specialized tutoring.

Since the success of the program is dependent on its staff, great care is taken in selecting mature and imaginative men and women who enjoy working with young people. Most of the counselors come from Europe, Australia, New Zealand, and England through the Camp America and CCUSA programs.

The Dunnabeck staff-camper ratio is 1:2. A number of tutors also work at Kildonan during the school year.

MEDICAL CARE

There is a fully equipped infirmary on campus with full-time nursing coverage, and local physicians serve as the school doctors. Sharon (Connecticut) Hospital is approximately 5 miles away.

COSTS

Tuition for the 2007 session was $8350 for residential students, $6600 for day students, and $4725 for half day students. Additional expenses include fees for transportation, laundry, and special trips. Financial aid is available. Students should contact Admissions for the appropriate form.

TRANSPORTATION

Arrangements can be made for students to be transported from LaGuardia and Kennedy International Airports in New York or Bradley Airport in Hartford. Harlem Valley Line train service is available from Grand Central Station in New York City to Wassaic.

APPLICATION TIMETABLE

Applications should be received by March 1. A $30 fee should accompany the initial application. A $1000 deposit is due upon acceptance.

FOR MORE INFORMATION, CONTACT

Director of Admissions
Dunnabeck at Kildonan
425 Morse Hill Road
Amenia, New York 12501
Phone: 845-373-8111
Fax: 845-373-2004
E-mail: admissions@kildonan.org
Web site: http://www.Dunnabeck.org

the Samuel T. Orton Award, the highest honor bestowed by the International Dyslexia Association.

The Academic Dean is Dr. Robert A. Lane. Dr. Lane received his doctorate in learning disabilities from Teachers College, Columbia University. As an instructor in Columbia's Department of Curriculum and Teaching, he taught graduate-level courses in the Learning dis/Abilities Program, coordinated the student-teaching program, and was Clinical Supervisor at the Center for Educational and Psychological Services. His career in education began at Kildonan, where he taught literature and language training and supervised from 1992 to 1995. Before returning to Kildonan, Dr. Lane was also a diagnostic clinician at a private clinic in Connecticut.

Theresa L. Collins, Director of Language Training at the Kildonan School, completed a B.A. in psychology at Colgate University and holds an M.S. in educational psychology from SUNY at Albany. She has been involved with Camp Dunnabeck since 1986 and with the Kildonan School since 1987. A Fellow of the Academy of Orton-Gillingham Practitioners and Educators, she plays a major role in training and supervising teachers at both Dunnabeck and Kildonan.

Karen Leopold holds a Master of Science in Education degree and New York State permanent certifications in reading, special education, and English 7–12. She is also a certified member and Fellow-in-Training in the Academy of Orton-Gillingham Practitioners and Educators. For the past eight years, Karen has taught in one-on-one and small-group settings. In addition to acting as the K–12 Multisensory Language Consultant for various public school districts, she has been evaluating Kildonan tutors and helping them meet the individual needs of their students for the past two years.

All tutors are trained in the Orton-Gillingham Approach by Fellows of the Orton-Gillingham Academy. Many of the tutors

EASTERN U.S. MUSIC CAMP

AT COLGATE UNIVERSITY

HAMILTON, NEW YORK

TYPE OF PROGRAM: Music performance and instruction
PARTICIPANTS: Coeducational, ages 10–19
ENROLLMENT: 200
PROGRAM DATES: Two-, three-, and four-week sessions, June 29 through July 26, 2008
HEADS OF PROGRAM: Thomas and Grace Brown, Directors

LOCATION

Eastern U.S. Music Camp, Inc., established in 1976, is conducted at Colgate University in Hamilton, New York. The University is ideally situated on a 1,100-acre hillside campus. This magnificent campus shares a valley with the quaint village of Hamilton. The peaceful countryside surrounding Hamilton has gently rolling hills in a tranquil rural setting.

Hamilton is a village of 2,500 people. Shops, homes, and the Colgate Inn front a green in the center of this friendly town. The campus adjoins the village, and the shops and services are within easy walking distance.

BACKGROUND AND PHILOSOPHY

For thirty-three years, Thomas and Grace Brown have designed and directed a program to provide students with opportunities and enrichment in all areas of music. Each summer, students who attend are happy to be an integral part of the music program and exciting campus life. They are offered a professional, well-balanced music program of high standards and an opportunity to pursue musical studies through class, individual, and group in-

struction; to perform a wide range of instrumental and choral works in ensemble and concert; and to participate in supervised sports (optional) and other informal recreational activities. The program is designed to complement the growth and development of young people. Such musical training teaches concentration, offers social opportunities, and helps develop sensitivity to, and pride in, the beautiful things in life. Careers in music are not necessarily the goals of students attending the Camp; the experience is one that is remembered and valued throughout life in any career. The total musical and social experience has made the Camp one of the most highly regarded music programs in the country.

Enrollment is limited to ensure ample opportunity for both individual and group instruction. Highly individualized instruction in a friendly atmosphere is stressed by the professional, nationally known staff, including college faculty members.

PROGRAM OFFERINGS

Performing Groups Each student may participate in several groups and on more than one instrument and/or voice. Original compositions by students studying composition are developed and rehearsed for possible performance. Music ranges from classical to modern and traditional to rock.

Each of the following thirteen groups performs in a public concert on campus every week:

Symphonic Band is open to all competent wind, brass, and percussion players. Major works of all periods are performed.

Symphony Orchestra Symphonic works of all periods are performed.

Concert Choir includes all students. Choral works from all periods of composition are presented.

Jazz Ensembles are open to all competent players.

Jazz-Rock and Jazz Combos are open to all jazz players.

Vocal Jazz features modern choral arrangements accompanied by a rhythm section.

Chamber Orchestra is open to all string players.

Studio Orchestra is open to all competent string players, who perform special arrangements with Jazz Ensemble.

Wind Ensemble is a select ensemble open to all competent players.

Madrigal Choir is a select voice ensemble.

Women's Choir, Men's Choir, and **Chamber Choir** are also offered.

Ensembles and Workshops Opportunities are available in ensemble performances that emphasize individualized instruction. Rehearsals are daily. Ensembles and workshops are available in Piano, Brass, Improvisation, Percussion, Guitar, String, Woodwind, Harp, Flute, Jazz Combos, Composition and Arranging, Vocal Techniques/Repertoire, Vocal Jazz, Piano Techniques/Repertoire, Madrigal Choir, Women's Choir, Men's Choir, Chamber Choir, and Electronic Music.

Classes Each student selects one of the following daily classes: Beginning Theory, Theory, Harmony, Composition and Arranging, Conducting, and Improvisation (high school credit).

Private Instruction Private lessons are offered weekly on all instruments, plus voice, piano, guitar, harp, and pipe organ, and can be arranged for a nominal fee.

Concerts are held Saturdays at 8 p.m. and Sundays at 3 p.m. Recitals are held Wednesdays at 7:30 p.m. All concerts and recitals are open to the public and take place in the air-conditioned Dana Arts Center on the Colgate University campus.

ENROLLMENT

Eastern U.S. Music Camp offers two-, three-, and four-week sessions from June 29 to July 26, 2008. Students can select from the following sessions: June 29 to July 26 (four weeks), June 29 to July 20 (three weeks), July 6 to July 26 (three weeks), June 29 to July 13 (two weeks), July 6 to July 20 (two weeks), and July 13 to July 26 (two weeks).

Students are encouraged to stay for the full four weeks or may enroll for the two- or three-week sessions. Each week, a new concert program is prepared. Musical and social benefits are greater with longer sessions. Tape auditions are not required. Students may earn high school credit when enrolled for the full four weeks.

EXTRA OPPORTUNITIES AND ACTIVITIES

Students enjoy numerous recreational and sports facilities, such as an indoor/outdoor Olympic-size pool, a gym, a golf course, tennis courts, a track, and a fully equipped fitness center. They often enjoy walks into the quaint village of Hamilton to see movies and visit an old fashioned ice-cream shop. There are also picnics on the Student Union patio; a trip to nearby Cooperstown, New York; games; softball; volleyball; golf; basketball; and a pizza party Saturday evenings after the concert. There are informal workshops, lectures, and opportunities to question faculty members and instructors. Colgate-sponsored performances are also held. This is a wonderful opportunity to meet talented and interesting people from around the country and other countries. The friendly faculty and staff members coach the students daily and are always available to share their talents with the students. This is an ideal place to grow.

FACILITIES

The campus is accented by a spring-fed lake with swans, wild and domestic ducks, and tree-lined walks and drives. Several buildings date to the nineteenth century. The quad on the hill includes modern residence halls, Memorial Chapel, O'Connor Campus Center, and a blend of old and new academic buildings. Also on the hill and overlooking scenic mountains are the Observatory, Cultural Center, and dining hall. Down from the hill are Case Library, Dana Arts Center, Sanford Field House, and well-manicured athletic fields.

Rehearsals, classes, concerts, private lessons, and recitals are held in the air-conditioned Dana Arts Center. Resident students live in modern boys' and girls' dorms, 2 per room by age, that include laundry facilities, lounges, and TVs. Three well-balanced meals, including a full and varied salad bar and vegetarian options, are served daily by the Marriott Corporation in a modern stone facility with an intimate atmosphere. Wooden tables next to the windows overlook the beautiful valley and hills below.

STAFF

Faculty and staff members are carefully selected professional certified educators, solo artists, composers, and conductors, including members of the Colgate Music Department, area college music faculties, and symphony orchestras. Nationally renowned guest artists and clinicians are on campus for master classes and concerts. The counseling staff members, including carefully selected and qualified counselors plus 2 dorm directors who are certified teachers, reside in the same living areas with the students, with a ratio of approximately 1:4.

COSTS

The resident student cost for instruction, room, and board for 2008 is as follows: two weeks, $1760; three weeks, $2640; and four weeks, $3445. The day student cost for instruction and complete program (lunch included) is as follows: two weeks, $635; three weeks, $952; and four weeks, $1270. Costs cover lodging, meals, ensembles, workshops, class, participation in organizations, sports, recreational activities, personal guidance, recitals, special programs, and campus concerts. Weekly private music lessons offered by professional artist instructors are optional. A class workbook costs about $5. Use of the dorm washers and dryers costs $1.50 for each.

FINANCIAL AID

A financial aid form is available. Funds are limited.

TRANSPORTATION

Colgate University is about 30 miles southeast of Hancock International Airport in Syracuse, New York, and 25 miles from the Utica, New York, train station. Regular bus services stop on campus, next to the Dana Arts Center, each day. By car, the campus is 2½ hours west of Albany, New York.

APPLICATION TIMETABLE

To provide the highest quality music program, enrollment is limited. Admission is on a rolling basis, and the application should be mailed as soon as possible. Applications are available on the Web site or in the brochure. The balance is due June 12, 2008.

FOR MORE INFORMATION, CONTACT

Before June 27, 2008
Dr. Thomas Brown or Grace Brown
Eastern U.S. Music Camp
7 Brook Hollow Road
Ballston Lake, New York 12019

Phone: 518-877-5121
          866-777-7841 (toll-free)
E-mail: summer@EasternUSMusicCamp.com
Web site: http://EasternUSMusicCamp.com

After June 27 and until July 26, 2008
Eastern U.S. Music Camp
Colgate University
Hamilton, New York 13346

Phone: 315-228-7041
E-mail: summer@EasternUSMusicCamp.com
Web site: http://EasternUSMusicCamp.com
          http://www.colgate.edu

EDU-CULTURE INTERNATIONAL

▼▼▼▼▼▼▼▼▼▼▼▼▼▼▼▼▼▼▼▼▼▼▼▼▼▼▼▼▼▼▼▼▼

SUMMER LANGUAGE-IMMERSION PROGRAMS

SPAIN, FRANCE, AND COSTA RICA

TYPE OF PROGRAM: Summer language-immersion, study-abroad, and travel programs for high school students in France, Spain, and Costa Rica; summer language immersion in Costa Rica for middle school students and high school freshmen

PARTICIPANTS: Coeducational, students ages 14–18 (Spain and France); students ages 12–18 (Costa Rica)

ENROLLMENT: 450 students each summer in groups of 25 to 30

PROGRAM DATES: Varies according to program—from two to four weeks, mid-June through mid-August

HEAD OF PROGRAM: Phyllis O'Neill and Marie Harris, Managing Directors and Founders

LOCATION

Edu-Culture International's (ECI) unique language-immersion, study-abroad, and travel programs take place in Spain, France, and Costa Rica.

The language-study portions of ECI's Spain programs are located in the culturally rich Renaissance city of Salamanca, the lovely seaside towns of Nerja and San Sebastian, and in the lively Andalusian city of Granada. Travel destinations during these trips include Barcelona, Madrid, Toledo, Segovia, Cordoba, Seville, Bilbao, and more.

The France programs are based in the dynamic Rhône Valley city of Lyon, in the student-filled university of town of Aix-en-Provence, and in Toulouse, France's fourth-largest city, known as La Ville Rose. Portions of these programs take place in the beautiful Mediterranean towns of Nice and Montpellier, as well as in the Alpine village of Gap. All trips include visits to nearby villages and towns as well as three days in Paris. Students who have been to Paris in the past have the option of an alternative itinerary while there.

Programs in the safe, democratic country of Costa Rica are based in Heredia, Monteverde, and Flamingo Beach for high school students and in Grecia for middle school students and high school freshmen. Additional travel destinations include Arenal Volcano, Manuel Antonio National Park, and many more.

BACKGROUND AND PHILOSOPHY

Founded in 1998 by two experienced teachers with advanced degrees in education, Phyllis O'Neill and Marie Harris, Edu-Culture International is a nonprofit educational organization based in Berkeley, California, with additional offices in Boston, Europe, and Costa Rica.

ECI brings together a team of educational professionals dedicated to broadening the academic horizons of students and to creating well-rounded culturally aware student leaders. ECI's summer programs offer intensive small-group language learning, unique host family immersion experiences, team-building opportunities, travel excursions, and organized social/cultural/educational activities balanced with free time to explore the host community and develop personal friendships.

PROGRAM OFFERINGS

ECI's summer-abroad programs in Spain, France and Costa Rica all offer a different combination of the following components: language classes, activities/excursions, homestay, dorm, host-family immersion, travel within the host country, and university-credit option.

Most of ECI's summer study-abroad programs last from three to four weeks, with the first two to three weeks including language classes. The morning classes, lasting about 3 hours in total (Monday–Friday), are small, interactive, and usually include other international students. Verbal communication skills are stressed, and classes are taught by highly skilled, experienced professionals, always native speakers in the target language. After lunch, there are a variety of supervised activities, such as salsa dancing, kayaking, visits to nearby villages and towns, bike riding, hiking, swimming, cooking classes, and more. After dinner, participants enjoy concerts, dancing, movies, and other social activities. Each day is structured to include free time, facilitating the development of confidence, independence, and social skills. Students stay either with families who live near the language school or in a dormitory setting with ECI's chaperones.

All programs include up to one week of travel to some of the most beautiful destinations in Spain, France, and Costa Rica. ECI always chooses high-quality, centrally located hotels to give students the most exciting and enriching experience possible.

Edu-Culture's college-credit option is an invaluable asset in today's competitive realm of higher education. High school students who are planning on applying to college in the future know how important it is to have a strong application. Most of ECI's programs offer teens the opportunity to earn 3 semester units of credit in Spanish or French through an accredited U.S. university. These credits are transferable and are accepted by most universities in the United States.

ECI's immersion families typically host the students during the third week of their program and are carefully chosen and matched to participants by ECI staff members. Students usually stay one per family during the immersion week.

Edu-Culture has developed an extensive network of connections with superior high schools and teachers in Spain, France, and Costa Rica. Through these connections, ECI consistently finds wonderful host families, most of whom have teenagers of their own. High school travelers interact with the family, the family's children, and friends of the children. This is a great opportunity for students to live the life of a Spanish, French, or Costa Rican teenager. The students and immersion families write letters or e-mails prior to their visit to get to know each other, and they often remain friends for a lifetime.

To increase the amount of interaction between teens on the trips and local young people, each ECI trip includes the Language Partners Program. Energetic university students meet with small groups of students for a few hours each week. These young people work to enrich the total experience by providing participants with numerous opportunities for integration into the community and practice in the target language. In small groups, they explore the town, participate in a variety of activities, and discuss an assortment of topics, such as entertainment, school, politics, travel, vacations, and sports.

Designed to be fun as well as challenging, ECI's programs provide students with an unforgettable and exhilarating once-in-a-lifetime experiences.

ENROLLMENT

ECI's high school groups are limited to 30 participants each. The Grecia Costa Rica Program for middle school students and high school freshmen is limited to only 24 participants. Each group has 3 full-time chaperones, 1 of whom is always from the country in which the program is based.

EXTRA OPPORTUNITIES AND ACTIVITIES

ECI specializes in customizing its programs for students who would like specific activities not offered in the group itinerary. Extra dance or cooking classes, additional guided museum visits, extended host-family stays, surfing lessons, and music, culture, or history classes—these are just some of the ways ECI can personalize a participant's experience to make it as meaningful and enriching as possible.

FACILITIES

During the study portion of ECI's programs, participants live with host families or in small student residences chosen for safety, location, and exposure to other international students. During the organized travel portion, students stay in centrally located three-star hotels with their chaperones.

STAFF

ECI's chaperones are selected on the basis of language ability, maturity, patience, personal integrity, judgment, enthusiasm, and their ability to earn the respect and trust of teenage participants. Most of them are teachers who have traveled abroad extensively and who possess near-native fluency in the target language as well as an in-depth knowledge of local history and culture. All receive extensive training prior to departure, and many of ECI's best leaders return year after year to travel with the program.

Teachers in ECI's language schools are always native speakers of Spanish or French.

MEDICAL CARE

Fees include supplemental medical insurance. Students who need medical care are always escorted by ECI's staff members and/or host families to designated health-care facilities. Medical expenses are reimbursed when the students return home.

COSTS

The costs of the 2007 programs range from $3850 to $6400. The fees include airfare, most meals, all accommodations, group activities and excursions, language classes, and medical insurance. ECI also offers cancellation/interruption trip insurance for a nominal fee.

FINANCIAL AID

ECI is offering three scholarships of $3000 each to be applied toward the 2007 summer programs. One scholarship will be awarded for study in Spain, one for study in France, and one for study in Costa Rica. Scholarship recipients are chosen on the basis of their application, essay, and teacher recommendation form. Winners will be announced no later than March 1, 2007. Scholarship applications and information are available on ECI's Web site (http://www.educulture.org/) or are sent to families upon request.

APPLICATION TIMETABLE

Students may apply as early as September 1 for the following summer's programs. Initial applications can be done online with a $95 application fee. A teacher's recommendation form is required for final acceptance in the program. Students are encouraged to apply early, as the trips fill quickly. Admission is on a rolling basis.

FOR MORE INFORMATION, CONTACT

Phyllis O'Neill, Director
Edu-Culture International (ECI)
P.O. Box 2692
Berkeley, California 94702
Phone: 510-845-3925
      510-845-2230
      866-343-8990 (toll-free)
Fax: 510-845-2231
E-mail: info@educulture.org
Web site: http://www.educulture.org/

EF INTERNATIONAL LANGUAGE SCHOOLS

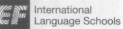

LANGUAGE STUDY

FRANCE, SPAIN, ITALY, GERMANY, ECUADOR, COSTA RICA, AND CHINA

TYPE OF PROGRAM: Language immersion courses

PARTICIPANTS: Coeducational, open to students and professionals 16 years of age and older

ENROLLMENT: Approximately 10–12 students per class (average)

PROGRAM DATES: Two- to fifty-two-week sessions every other Monday year-round. Semester courses and Academic Year Abroad courses are also available, as well as a new Multi-language Year program.

LOCATION

EF International Language Schools offers courses in France, Spain, Italy, Germany, Ecuador, Costa Rica, and China.

BACKGROUND AND PHILOSOPHY

EF International Language Schools believes that the most effective way to learn a language is by living it. With more than forty years of experience as a leader in language education, EF offers students a variety of programs to match their academic and professional needs while studying in an international environment and living among native speakers. Whether students are looking for a short intensive course to boost their language skills, an enriching summer-study vacation, or a full year of living and studying abroad, EF has a course that is right for them. Social, athletic, and cultural activities are available in addition to classroom instruction. Courses are taught by native speakers, and students have the opportunity to make friends from all over the world in an internationally diverse classroom. Teachers focus on grammar and conversation throughout instruction, with the aid of textbooks and language laboratory sessions. EF courses are suitable for students and professionals of all ability levels from beginner to advanced.

PROGRAM OFFERINGS

SPAIN

Barcelona Study in Spain's most dynamic city. EF Barcelona is located on Calle Calvet, a short walk from many of the city's most fashionable cafés and shops. Students have the choice of enjoying Spanish hospitality in a homestay (available year-round) or living in a University of Barcelona student residence in the summer. Excursions to Madrid, Seville, and the Pyrenees are among the many activities that may be offered by the School.

Malaga Soak up some sun along Spain's Costa del Sol. The EF school is situated just blocks from the sunny beaches in the Pedregalejo neighborhood and a short bus ride from the city center. Malaga is a great choice for students who want to learn Spanish in the relaxed environment of one of Spain's most popular beach destinations.

ECUADOR

Quito Quito has become one of the most popular destinations in which to learn Spanish. The EF Escuela Internacional de Espanol in Quito is a charming building with modern educational facilities, located in one of the city's best residential areas, just 5 minutes from the city center. Popular excursions allow students to visit and explore the Amazon, the equator, the foothills of the Andes, beautiful protected rain forests, and even the Galápagos Islands. There are also many volunteer opportunities available.

COSTA RICA

Tamarindo Beach Welcome to Costa Rica. EF's new school in Playa Tamarindo, one of Costa Rica's most attractive coastal towns, is the perfect place to combine Spanish language immersion with the laidback feel of Central America. Students can practice their language skills only steps away from beautiful surfing beaches and then spend the afternoon visiting the country's renowned cloud forests.

FRANCE

Nice Students spend the summer in sunny southern France. EF Ecole Internationale de Français stands just 100 yards from the beach and the famous Promenade des Anglais. Students can choose accommodations in a homestay or student residence. Popular excursions include day trips to Monaco and Cannes, visits to famous museums, and weekend trips to Paris and the Alps—not to mention endless opportunities for sports and outdoor activities.

Paris There's little that can't be found in Paris, France's largest and capital city. Students focus on conversation in French, with the option of taking special interest courses in areas such as literature, film, and business language. Programs include accommodation in a local Parisian homestay. Frequent excursions may include visits to the Palace of Versailles, the Louvre, Chartres, and Fontainebleau.

ITALY

Rome Rome is the perfect destination for students looking for cultural and historical treasures around every corner. The language school is located in an elegant building in the center of the city, convenient to the central train station. Learning facilities include a modern language laboratory and study center with well-equipped workstations to encourage language practice. Students may choose homestay or apartment accommodations, and weekend excursions may include visits to Italian cities such as Siena, Naples, Venice, and Florence.

GERMANY

Munich The EF Internationale Sprachschule is located in the lively Schwabing district of Munich, a favorite meeting place for students and artists. Occupying a four-story building in a quiet courtyard on Herzogstrasse, the EF School provides a stimulating international environment in which to study. In their homestay, students have

the chance to learn about the German way of life from inside its culture as their language ability naturally develops. The school staff organizes a variety of social activities for students throughout the year to destinations including Prague, Innsbruck, Salzburg, the majestic castles of Füssen, and Austrian alpine ski resorts.

CHINA

Shanghai Learn Mandarin Chinese in the city known as the Pearl of the Orient. Shanghai has transformed into a thriving metropolis with a perfect combination of modern development and ancient traditions. EF's language school is within walking distance of the premier shopping and entertainment districts and close to shopping malls, restaurants, bookstores, and banks. The city hosts the Shanghai International Arts Festival in September, The International Film Festival in June, and many other cultural and sporting events throughout the year.

Beijing Recently named the Official Language Training Services Supplier of the Beijing 2008 Olympic Games, EF is honored to be part of China's historic debut. Students can experience the excitement of a city preparing for the Summer Olympic Games and discover the great cultural and historical center of China that is Beijing. EF's newest study center for Mandarin Chinese is nestled in a central yet quiet neighborhood, making it the perfect place for students to improve their language skills. On the weekends, they can take advantage of excursions to famous temples and the Great Wall of China.

College Credit Students can work toward completion of an undergraduate degree while improving their language skills and experiencing a new culture. Through EF's partnership with Eastern Washington University, eligible students may earn up to 6 quarter language credits (equivalent to 4 semester credits) on the university level by advancing through EF proficiency levels with a minimum grade. Credit is available for 100- and 200-level language courses. More information is available by contacting the EF Admissions Office.

DAILY SCHEDULE

Classes are held Monday through Friday for approximately 3 or 4 hours per day. The following is a typical day at the EF Ecole Internationale de Français in Nice, France:

```
 9:00–10:20 . . . Grammar
10:45–12:05 . . . Reading and writing
12:30– 1:40 . . . Special interest class: French History
        2:00 . . . Excursion to the Musée Chagall
        7:00 . . . Mediterranean dinner and game of boules at
                   local outdoor café
```

ENROLLMENT

EF programs are open to students of ages 16 and older, including adults. The average age of an EF student is 18–25 years old. Previous language study experience is not required to attend a short-term course, EF Academic Year Abroad, or Multi-Language Year Abroad and beginner start dates are available. EF students come from countries all over the world, including Germany, Sweden, Canada, Australia, the United Kingdom, France, Spain, Japan, Korea, and Italy. Average class size is approximately 10–12 students.

STAFF

With more than 40 years of experience, EF believes that the selection and training of qualified teachers must be the first priority of any language school. All EF instructors are native speakers qualified to teach their own language to nonnative students. EF teachers have access to an extensive range of classroom material and equipment, including the latest in language-teaching technology.

COSTS

The cost of each program varies, depending on length of stay and course location. Interested students should contact the EF Admissions Office for specific program fees.

TRANSPORTATION

EF is able to book international airfare for students enrolling in EF International Language School courses. In addition, all course centers offer students the security and convenience of an EF-organized arrival transfer from the airport to their accommodation.

APPLICATION TIMETABLE

Applications are accepted at any time and are based on availability. Students are advised that many courses fill up quickly due to high demand; early application is strongly recommended. Applications are processed upon their receipt.

FOR MORE INFORMATION, CONTACT

EF International Language Schools
EF Center Boston
One Education Street
Cambridge, Massachusetts 02141

Phone: 800-992-1892 (toll-free)
Fax: 800-590-1125 (toll-free)
E-mail: ils@ef.com
Web site: http://www.ef.com

ELITE EDUCATIONAL INSTITUTE

SUMMER PROGRAM

CALIFORNIA, CANADA, SOUTH KOREA, AND THAILAND

TYPE OF PROGRAM: Academic enrichment and test preparation

PARTICIPANTS: Coeducational, grades 3 through 12

ENROLLMENT: Varies according to individual centers

PROGRAM DATES: Most programs are eight-week sessions from late June to late August. The fourteen-week 2100 Goal Program runs from late June until the national SAT testing date in October

HEAD OF PROGRAM: Ms. Wonna Kim, Program Director

LOCATION

Elite has twenty-three educational centers—eleven in Southern California; three in Northern California; four in Canada; four in Seoul, South Korea; and one in Bangkok, Thailand—and is continuing to grow. All Elite centers are in major cities or suburbs convenient to them.

BACKGROUND AND PHILOSOPHY

Founded in 1987, Elite has built its reputation by offering academic enrichment to motivated, goal-oriented students of all ability levels. Elite's flagship programs prepare students for successful performance on the SAT Reasoning Test for college admissions through a variety of course offerings and schedules. Younger students benefit from the disciplined, results-oriented environment and get a head start on the fundamental language arts and math skills they need for success in middle school, junior high, and high school.

Elite distinguishes itself in the field of SAT preparation by taking the test very seriously. Elite avoids the use of gimmicky shortcuts and misleading, get-smart-quick promises, focusing instead on developing those underlying skills actually measured by the SAT and other standardized tests: critical reading, math, writing proficiency, critical thinking, and sound reasoning. As a result, Elite's students are prepared not just for higher test scores but also for continued academic success in college and beyond.

In the last few years, more than a dozen Elite students have scored a perfect 1600 on the SAT, and countless others have scored in the high 1500s. Elite students' success on the SAT has continued with the introduction of the new SAT in March 2005, which has a maximum score of 2400 points. In just the first year of the administration of the new SAT, several Elite students scored a perfect 2400, and a multitude of others have scored in the high 2300s, putting them in the top 1 percent of students nationwide. Elite's younger students sign up to improve their performance in grade school, prepare for admission to private primary and secondary schools, or just to get an advance look at the subjects ahead.

PROGRAM OFFERINGS

Elementary Enrichment classes, intended for students about to enter grades 3 through 6, are kept small to foster confidence and participation. The academic emphasis is on reading, writing, and mathematics, with some initial work on critical thinking and analysis. Teachers emphasize the process of discovery, learning, and understanding so that all students finish the summer better prepared for the school year ahead, regardless of their present ability level.

Students can enroll in general classes for writing, vocabulary, reading, and math. Some centers also offer classes for specific middle school admissions tests.

Junior High Enrichment courses, recommended for the summer before grades 7 through 9, are intended to give students a head start on high school. The core of the Junior High Enrichment program is the **Elite Book Camp**. Focusing on developing students' critical reading, grammar, and writing skills, the Elite Book Camp caters to a range of abilities, from remedial to advanced. **Elite's Math Enrichment Program** provides students with a "preview" of the specific math class ahead, such as geometry, so they know what to expect.

Almost all of the Junior High Enrichment students are about to enter competitive high schools where enrollment in honors and AP classes is limited and want to get a head start on admission to the best courses their high schools offer.

Elite SAT Boot Camp is an extremely intensive and demanding program designed for high school students who want to commit most of their summer to raising their SAT scores. Students attend 5 hours of classes each day, Monday through Friday, mastering the definitions of thousands of common SAT words; sharpening their critical reading skills by reading and analyzing dozens of short stories, critical essays, and magazine articles; and developing their writing skills by writing numerous essays that are scored by instructors. Classes are kept varied and interesting, with a mixture of instructors and class materials throughout each day.

The Boot Camp program puts the summer to good use for students of all ability levels. The program is particularly useful for students whose critical reading skills lag behind their math skills.

The Elite 2100 Goal Program is a rigorous and extensive SAT test-preparation program that requires many hours of out-of-class work and preparation. The aims of the 2100 Goal Program are college-level reading and writing and a thorough mastery of high school mathematics, resulting in truly outstanding test scores in high school and academic success thereafter. This program is designed for high school students at the top of their game who successfully take AP and honors classes at their high schools and want to round out their college applications with superior test scores.

Admission to the 2100 Goal Program is very selective; students have to achieve minimum scores on Elite's diagnostic test, have a high GPA, and demonstrate the maturity and commitment the program demands. Acceptance to the program is always at the discretion of the center directors. Students should contact the directors of the center they plan to attend to determine eligibility. The fourteen-week 2100 Goal Program requires students to stay enrolled until the national SAT testing date in October.

The Elite Basic SAT Course offers students a package of five interlocking classes during the summer session: two critical reading classes, a math class, a writing class, and a practice test session. Students enrolled in the Basic SAT Course meet for a total of 11½ hours per week—each of the weekly classes meets for 2 hours, and the practice test lasts for 3½ hours.

A majority of the students who live near Elite's educational centers continue with the program after the summer. Elite's SAT preparation courses conducted during the school year consist of a practice test session followed by three classes to help students continue developing their critical reading, math, and writing skills. Classes are offered on weekday afternoons and Saturdays to give students the convenience of designing their own course schedules. Enrollment in Elite's SAT program during the school year is on a rolling basis, with students signing up for four-week sessions. The curriculum is intentionally designed to be useful for long-term students, with materials that are never exactly the same twice. Even the vocabulary is constantly updated and revised.

ENROLLMENT

The maximum number of students in each class at Elite is 15. The Summer Program at Elite attracts students from all over the United States, Canada, and Korea. Elite does not offer room or board, so students from other states and provinces typically spend the summer with relatives or family friends. Elite's students reflect a range of academic abilities and ethnic backgrounds.

DAILY SCHEDULE

Classes in elementary enrichment, junior high enrichment, basic SAT preparation, and the 2100 Goal Program meet for 2 hours each. All students in Elite's SAT programs are required to take a weekly practice SAT test, which lasts for 3½ hours.

At every center, Elite SAT Boot Camp, which runs from Monday through Friday, starts at 8:30 a.m. and ends at 2 p.m., with a half-hour break for lunch. All other summer programs at Elite are held at a variety of times and days to make it easy for students to fit their SAT work around their other plans for the summer, and program schedules may vary from center to center.

Students of all ages and abilities are expected to preserve Elite's productive, academically focused atmosphere. Elite has zero tolerance for academic dishonesty, truancy, or possession of any tobacco, alcohol, or drugs. Elite immediately expels students who violate its rules of conduct.

EXTRA OPPORTUNITIES AND ACTIVITIES

Elite does not sponsor activities outside of its core classroom offerings. However, because Elite's summer offerings are so rigorous and attract students with shared goals for success, satisfying and lasting friendships are formed each year.

FACILITIES

Elite has twenty-three educational centers worldwide.

Northern California's centers are in Fremont, San Francisco, and San Jose.

Southern California's centers are in Anaheim Hills, Arcadia, Cerritos, Fullerton, Irvine, downtown Los Angeles, Northridge, Rowland Heights, San Diego, Valencia, and West Los Angeles.

Canada's centers are in Vancouver, Coquitlam, and Richmond in British Columbia and Toronto, Ontario.

South Korea's centers are in Apgujung, Yeon Hee, Boon Dong, and Mok Dong.

Thailand's center is located in Bangkok.

STAFF

Elite's faculty is composed of instructors who have graduated from the most prestigious public and private colleges and universities. Many instructors are professionals in their respective areas of knowledge or hold advanced degrees from graduate schools. They have years of experience in sharing their expertise and enthusiasm with Elite's students in a presentation that is clear, coherent, and memorable.

Even though the atmosphere is informal, and many of the teachers are on a first-name basis with students, the focus is on work and making students smarter.

MEDICAL CARE

Elite does not provide on-site medical care.

RELIGIOUS LIFE

Elite is not affiliated with any religious organization.

COSTS

Tuition for Elite programs is as follows: **Elementary Enrichment,** $840 for eight weeks; **Junior High Enrichment,** $840 to $1200 for eight weeks; **Basic SAT Program,** $960 to $1200 for eight weeks; **Elite SAT Boot Camp,** $1900 to $2200 for eight weeks; **2100 Goal Program,** $2200 for fourteen weeks.

FINANCIAL AID

Financial aid is not available.

TRANSPORTATION

Elite does not provide transportation.

APPLICATION TIMETABLE

Elite encourages inquiries from both students and parents at any time, and students are accepted in the order of applications received. Early registration is advised, as space is limited. Registration cannot be considered unless accompanied by a diagnostic test report. Students should contact their nearest Elite center to schedule a free diagnostic test and academic counseling session.

FOR MORE INFORMATION, CONTACT

Ms. Wonna Kim
Program Director
Elite Educational Institute
4009 Wilshire Boulevard, Suite 200
Los Angeles, California 90010

Phone: 213-365-8008
Fax: 213-365-1253
Web site: http://www.ElitePrep.com

EMAGINATION COMPUTER CAMPS

SUMMER CAMP

ATLANTA, GEORGIA; LAKE FOREST, ILLINOIS; ROSEMONT/BRYN MAWR, PENNSYLVANIA; AND WALTHAM, MASSACHUSETTS

TYPE OF PROGRAM: Computer technology in a traditional summer camp setting

PARTICIPANTS: Boys and girls, ages 8–17

PROGRAM DATES: Four 2-week sessions, early June through mid-August. Overnight, day, extended-day, and full-day programs

HEAD OF PROGRAM: Michael Currence, Camps Director

LOCATION
Emagination Computer Camps operate at four locations around the country. Rosemont College, less than 10 miles west of the historic city of Philadelphia, offers a quiet suburban campus with impressive Gothic architecture.

Mercer University's beautiful campus is situated on 400 parklike acres in northeast Atlanta. Expansive outdoor fields, an indoor pool, and a gymnasium make Mercer an ideal location for Emagination's camp activities.

The Lake Forest Academy, in Lake Forest, Illinois, is situated on 160 parklike suburban acres, providing an idyllic location for summer camp. The campus occupies the former J. Ogden Armour estate, which was built in the early 1900s, and is located 30 miles from Chicago on the North Shore of Lake Michigan.

Bentley College's impeccably maintained, suburban campus is in Waltham, Massachusetts. Bentley, a business university, is a leader in integrating education and information technology and is less than 10 miles from the heart of historic Boston.

Overnight campers live in dorm rooms, grouped by age and gender, and counselors provide 24-hour supervision. Athletic facilities include a pool, playing fields, and a gymnasium.

BACKGROUND AND PHILOSOPHY
Emagination's mission is to educate, entertain, and help develop healthy kids. Emagination is a family-owned company with an experienced staff. The camps are about learning and having fun—in tech workshops and in recreation. Founded in 1982, Emagination understands kids who love computers and is proud that many campers return year after year—many becoming counselors.

At Emagination, campers can build a PC, swim, design a Web page, and play soccer. They advance computer skills, make friends, learn independence, and develop self-confidence. Campers from all across America and around the world come together in a community of kids like themselves—exploring workshops and doing things they like. Plus, they gain the social and emotional benefits of a traditional summer camp experience in a structured environment.

PROGRAM OFFERINGS
RPG Game Design: Here, students make an RPG game—creating stats and appearances for new party members, inventing challenging quests, making bosses and other enemy encounters, and placing them in a world they create.

Action Game Design/Advanced Action Games: Campers develop game-building skills as they create an action adventure game. They learn to program a fast-paced game that adds backgrounds, paths, and obstacles and also learn to import and create images, sprites, and sounds.

Strategy Game Design/Advanced Strategy Games: Students make a strategy/conquest game, build terrains, and generate enemy strongholds for their players to battle. They create special power-up items for their units to make their armies stronger and make original maps for multiplayer games that they play against their friends.

3-D Game Modding: Campers develop original 3-D models and import them into a popular game engine. They explore material ID and multisub object mapping while creating their own character and object models.

Sprite Comics: Campers rip, edit, and recolor popular video-game sprites using 2-D graphics software. They create original sprites and use believable backgrounds and exciting text to create fun comics.

3-D Animation: Students design, model, and animate their own 3-D environment. They create objects and text; make realistic scenes with textures, transparency, and mesh objects; and create cool effects using volume lights.

3-D Character Modeling: Using advanced animation tools, campers develop the design, model, and textures of a 3-D character; learn skeleton structure, mesh optimization, and UVW and XYZ texturing; and use animation principles such as timing, anticipation, arcs, and pose-to-pose action to animate their 3-D model.

3-D Texture Mapping: Campers create original textures and add surface texture using a library of predeveloped models. They explore polygons and object coordinates and learn wrapping techniques to enhance 3-D models.

Flash Web Animation/Advanced Flash Animation: Campers produce creative animations, illustrations, and navigation for Web sites. They first create simple objects and text and then try their hand at adjusting the color, size, and shape.

Computer Skills: Using PowerPoint and Excel, students create sizzling presentations, simple animations, and fun spreadsheets—all while exploring Microsoft Office Suite.

Windows Operating System: Campers install Microsoft Windows operating systems and set up wired and wireless networks. They learn about the registry and administrative tools, how to protect their system with a firewall and antivirus/spam/spyware utilities, and how to diagnose and troubleshoot common system problems.

Linux Operating System: Campers install a Linux-based operating system and set up multiple shells and GUIs. They add open-source software and network applications. They learn command line functionality and navigation and how to diagnose and troubleshoot common system problems.

Networks: Participants build a network and troubleshoot it, crimp the cables, install the routers and switches, and set up the security. They also discover how to make LINUX-based and Microsoft operating systems coexist. (Offered in Massachusetts only)

Radio-Controlled (RC) Cars: Each student builds his or her own RC car and races it with fellow campers, discovering the ins and outs of RC car construction. Campers can take their cars home.

Robotics: Campers build three robots and compete in contests with fellow campers. They discover touch sensors, photo interrupters, infrared rays, and nontrack movement. Campers take their robots home and may continue to explore their capabilities.

Programming BASICs: Participants write their first program using the BASIC programming language. They explore Boolean logic—an integral part of all programming—and create random generators, mad lib games, and other fun programs. This course sets the foundation and is a prerequisite for all other programming workshops.

Video Game Programming: Campers design and code their own playable action game. They control events with a game loop; create tables for races, special moves, enemies, and treasures; and learn to make enemies fight back with artificial intelligence programs.

C++/Advanced C++: Participants learn object-oriented programming rules and reusable code, write basic programs with if/then statements and while/for loop functions, build 2-D arrays and simple strings, and make their own version of a grid-style game, such as Battleship, checkers, or chess.

PERL: Participants develop Web-based applications using the powerful data-manipulation capabilities of the Perl programming language. File input/output, arrays, hashes, strings, and networking are just a few of the topics covered. (Offered in Massachusetts only)

Java: Students use recursive-programming techniques and learn the basics of making Java-based applications. They also find existing routines on the Web and put them together to create their first Java applications. (Offered in Massachusetts only)

Independent Study: Campers participate in a self-directed programming project that is overseen by an experienced counselor. Available advanced topics vary by location and may include C++, PERL, Visual Basic, C, and Java.

Popular Games: Participants play DDR or console games and test their skills in contests using X-Box, PlayStation, or Game Cube—learning strategy and having fun!

Retro Games: This is a chance for kids to play like they did before computers with kickball, Ultimate Frisbee, or soccer—a different activity every day. Campers can swim or play board games or discover the strategies of the hottest trading card games.

Basketball: Campers work on layups, jump shots, pick-and-rolls, drills, and skills and participate in tournaments. Basketball counselors lead a challenging and fun-filled two-week workshop. (Offered in Massachusetts only)

Soccer: Slide tackles, perfect crosses, crisp passing, incredible saves, and dynamic headers are just some of the skills developed in this fun, two-week structured workshop. (Offered in Massachusetts only)

EXTRA OPPORTUNITIES AND ACTIVITIES
The evening program offers a balance of technology and recreation. There are many fun events, such as a Saturday-night LAN party, weekend trips, Tech Talk, Carnival Night, and Fun Friday. Weekend day-trip destinations include museums, historical sites, professional baseball and soccer games, amusement parks, and more.

FACILITIES
Residential campers are housed in college dorm rooms by age and gender. Rooms accommodate 2 or 3 campers. On-site, mature resi-

dential counselors are available 24 hours a day to supervise campers. Air-conditioned computer rooms feature multiple bays of PCs and a bay of systems for games classes. Emagination Computer Camps has access to athletic fields, tennis courts, and gymnasiums for a variety of indoor sports.

STAFF
Emagination staff members are carefully hired after multiple interviews and reference and background checks, and they are extensively trained. Emagination selects counselors who embrace technology, enjoy being with kids, and want to teach, lead, and have fun. Many counselors began as campers and understand the important role computers play in growing up. The technology-savvy staff members (college/grad students and schoolteachers) are wonderful instructors, leaders, and mentors, and most stay with the camps for at least two summers. All counselors complete a full weeklong, on-site training program before campers arrive, covering such topics as child safety, CPR, and first aid.

MEDICAL CARE
Emagination Computer Camps are located within 3 miles of a hospital, with a health supervisor on premises. Staff members are certified in Red Cross First Aid and CPR. Parents and the camper's doctor must provide important information about the camper's medical conditions and needs as well as any dietary, activity, and other restrictions and limitations. Parents are encouraged to call or e-mail to ask questions or discuss any health-care-related issues.

COSTS
The total tuition for the overnight session in 2007 was $2245. Tuition for day campers was $1235 per session. The extended-day option (Monday–Friday, 8 a.m. to 6:15 p.m.) was $1285 per session. The full-day session (7:30 a.m. to 7:45 p.m.) was $1545. Parents should visit http://www.computercamps.com for any available discounts.

TRANSPORTATION
For overnight campers, transportation may be arranged to and from nearby airports, railroad stations, and bus terminals. For day campers, staff members can help make arrangements and contacts for car pooling or shuttle services. In Illinois and Pennsylvania, daily pick-up and drop-off at local train stations is available.

APPLICATION TIMETABLE
Applications are available beginning in late November. As courses are filled on a first-come, first-served basis, early application is highly recommended. Reservations are confirmed by mail and are accompanied by an information/orientation packet.

FOR MORE INFORMATION, CONTACT
Emagination Computer Camps
110 Winn Street, Suite 205
Woburn, Massachusetts 01801
Phone: 781-933-8795
    877-248-0206 (toll-free)
Fax: 781-933-0749
E-mail: camp@computercamps.com
Web site: http://www.computercamps.com

EMMA WILLARD SCHOOL

GirlSummer

▼▼▼▼▼▼▼▼▼▼▼▼▼▼▼▼▼▼▼▼▼▼▼▼▼▼▼▼▼▼▼▼▼▼▼

GIRLSUMMER

TROY, NEW YORK

TYPE OF PROGRAM: Academic enrichment
PARTICIPANTS: Girls entering grades 7–12
ENROLLMENT: 50–100 girls each session
PROGRAM DATES: Multiple two-week sessions in June, July, and August
HEADS OF PROGRAM: Doug Murphy, Executive Director

LOCATION
GirlSummer is located on 137 extraordinary acres atop Mount Ida amid the natural beauty of Troy, New York. The school is listed in the National Register of Historic Places and offers inspiring architecture and a state-of-the-art setting for learning and living. Just a little more than 2 hours by car from Manhattan, New York's historic Capital Region is the pride of the Hudson Valley and has been designated a National Heritage Area.

BACKGROUND AND PHILOSOPHY
Since 1814, Emma Willard School has been one of the nation's leading college-preparatory boarding and day schools for young women. As an extension of its successful and long-standing summer day program for elementary school–age girls, Emma Willard developed GirlSummer for middle and high school girls who want a taste of residential campus life in an all-girls environment.

The GirlSummer experience is a two-week-long immersion in a stimulating and fun on-campus academic environment. Designed to further scholastic aptitude and broaden academic interests within a dynamic, structured environment, GirlSummer's unique curriculum approach was developed specifically to pique each student's interests and challenge her abilities. GirlSummer combines rigorous yet interesting academic endeavors during the day with great evening and weekend activities.

PROGRAM OFFERINGS
College Prep & Preview GirlSummer College Prep & Preview gives high school girls a head start on the college admissions process. By the end of the session, each girl will have developed her own College Plan. Classes include SAT Prep, Writing for College—Applications and Essays, Writing for College—Academic Papers, Clubs and Volunteerism, Choosing a College, The College Admissions Process, and Social Life at College. Off-campus field trips might include visits to local colleges for college tours and visits with college admissions officers.

Foreign Language Study (Spanish or French) The program is designed for any ability level and is based not on rote memorization but rather on conversation. It offers a unique linguistic learning environment that provides students the opportunity to speak their selected language in a real-life setting. Cultural awareness is learned through teaching about traditional geographic regions, traditions, customs, and foods. In addition, campers enjoy an exploration of cultures, which may include learning folk dances, cooking dishes from specific

regions, or even taking a field trip to Manhattan for foreign language–themed productions on or off Broadway.

Fine Arts GirlSummer offers a dynamic program, investigating many fields and media of the fine arts. Moving from drawing and mixed media through painting and photography, fine arts students gain a broad view of modern working art. The program offers a review of the basics of proportion, lines, and shading while using charcoal, pencil, pastels, and markers to create an array of graphic presentations. Campers then move on to painting, implementing much of what has already been learned to focus on subject matter, use of color, and application of paint and style. The final topic of the session is digital photography, where students learn how to frame compositions and balance style, colors, and contrast.

Performing Arts Beginning with the building blocks of acting, students learn the tools professional actors use to create believable performances by working on scenes, monologues, and speeches. GirlSummer builds on this by allowing campers to study improv and musical theater. Girls are asked if they are comfortable in front of an audience, if they can be put on the spot, and what improv games they have tried. The weeks are then rounded out with dramatic acting, when everything the girls have learned is brought together. They can practice dialogue, monologue, emotional expression, voice, and more.

Writer's Workshops This program offers students who love to write and students who want to improve their writing abilities the opportunity to work in intensive writing workshops of limited size. Discussion and ideas abound; the course is a comprehensive education in the craft of writing, and the program outlines the lessons needed to be a good writer. Main topics covered include introduction to writing, the mechanics of creative writing, journaling, blogging, poetry, and fiction writing. Off-campus field trips might include a visit to a major publishing house and talks with writers, editors, and others in the field.

Mock Trial Mock Trial is one of the fastest-growing extracurricular activities among secondary school students. The Emma Willard School team was the Rensselaer County Champion last year and placed second this year under the able leadership of a popular faculty member, and attorney, Mr. Brendan Randall. Mr. Randall has designed a special two-week curriculum just for GirlSummer and leads this summer's innovative program for those who would like to learn how the American legal system works. Guided by a model that is used in most law schools around the country, students study the structure and process of dispute resolution and learn how to prepare and present mock trial cases as both attorneys and witnesses. This program covers the individual steps of a trial, from opening statements to closing arguments, and the fundamentals of the legal system, from pleadings to judgments. At each stage, the students videotape performances for individual and group evaluation.

Model UN The Model United Nations program presents a unique and engaging opportunity for students to learn about other cultures, current events, and international relations in a hands-on environment. From drafting resolutions in the General Assembly to resolving crises in the Security Council, students learn through doing. This summer, Emma Willard School's model UN adviser, Mr. Brendan Randall, leads an in-depth program for girls who currently participate in model UN programs or simply would like to learn more about the United Nations and international relations. In each session, students represent specific countries and prepare for a model United Nations. The experience culminates with an exciting mock session.

ENROLLMENT
To allow for small classes with individual attention, GirlSummer enrolls a maximum of 100 campers each session.

EXTRA OPPORTUNITIES AND ACTIVITIES
Each academic camp goes on unique and exciting field-trip adventures. Depending on the program, field trips might include visiting a major college or university in the area, science centers or planetariums, French- or Spanish-themed events or restaurants, or a major publishing house to meet authors and editors.

Each two-week session incorporates a Saturday excursion, known as Super Saturday, to local diversions and cultural attractions. Buses depart early Saturday morning for a variety of exciting destinations. Popular destinations include amusement parks, beaches, aquariums, music festivals, shopping malls, and Manhattan.

FACILITIES
All students stay overnight in the spectacular dormitory facilities located on campus and enjoy the first-rate services and

amenities that full-time Emma Willard School students do during the school year. Campers are supervised by adult and junior counselors who live in the dorms with them.

STAFF
Intelligent and energetic, the staff is the heart of the GirlSummer experience. From professional teachers to talented graduate and undergraduate students, all staff members participate in safety and training sessions. The maximum student-teacher ratio is 8:1.

MEDICAL CARE
Medical care is available 24 hours a day at nearby hospital facilities. All participants must submit comprehensive medical forms and proof of insurance.

COSTS
The tuition for each two-week session is $2395. This includes all instruction; instructional materials; a breakfast, lunch, and dinner each day; a dorm room with linens; self-service laundry facilities; all sports and recreational activities; transportation for sponsored trips; admission tickets to excursion destinations; and total 24-hour supervision for the duration of each camp session. In addition, there is a $100 field-trip account that allocates spending money for each student on their academic and nonacademic trips.

FINANCIAL AID
There is no financial aid available at this time.

TRANSPORTATION
Airport pick-up and drop-off are available for an additional fee.

APPLICATION TIMETABLE
Inquiries are welcome at any time. Applications are accepted until June 1. After June 1, acceptance to the program is based on availability.

FOR MORE INFORMATION, CONTACT
GirlSummer at Emma Willard School
285 Pawling Avenue
Troy, New York 12180
Phone: 866-EWS-CAMP (397-2267, toll-free)
Web site: http://www.emmawillard.org/summer/residential

ENFOREX INTERNATIONAL SUMMER SCHOOLS IN SPAIN

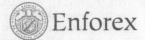

ENFOREX SUMMER PROGRAM

BARCELONA, GRANADA, MADRID, MARBELLA, SALAMANCA, AND VALENCIA, SPAIN; GUANAJUATO, MEXICO

TYPE OF PROGRAM: Spanish-language, educational, activities, sports, and cultural camp

PARTICIPANTS: Coeducational, ages 5–18

ENROLLMENT: 250 per session, in each school

PROGRAM DATES: Two-, three-, four-, six-, and eight-week sessions starting 2008

HEAD OF PROGRAM: Antonio Anadon, Director

LOCATION

Barcelona Summer School Barcelona is not only the capital of the region of Cataluña but also the Spanish center of fashion, art, architecture, and gastronomy and the most diverse and cosmopolitan city in Spain. The summer school is located between Plaza Cataluña and Plaza España. The center is in a safe, affluent neighborhood just a short walk from other famous areas of the city such as the Gran Vía, Las Ramblas, and the university. The Barcelona Junior Program offers residence stays, with students divided by age and gender in dormitory halls, and the option of living with a host family.

Granada Summer Camp With a profound history and the most visited attraction in Spain, La Alhambra, Granada is a modern city located at the foot of the Sierra Nevada, just 45 minutes from the Costa Tropical. The Granada Junior Program offers residence stays, with students divided by age and gender in dormitory halls, and the option of living with a host family.

Madrid Summer Camp Madrid, the capital of Spain, is located in the very center of the country. Its location allows visits to cities such as Barcelona, Seville, and Granada in less than 4 hours and other closer cities, such as Toledo, El Escorial, Salamanca, and Segovia, in less than 1 hour. The Summer Camp is located in one of the most prestigious private schools in the vicinity of one of Europe's largest universities. It is only 15 minutes from the city center and well equipped for many different sports.

Marbella Summer Camp (La Costa del Sol) Marbella (Málaga) is a beach resort located in the south of Spain, 20 minutes from Málaga and 1½ hours from Granada and Seville, the capital of Andalusia. An old town that still preserves most of its character, it has its own microclimate, white Mediterranean-style houses, and luxurious beaches. The three residential schools are located in areas of singular beauty and close to the beach. Nearby sites of special interest include the Nerja Caves, Granada, Gibraltar, and Seville.

Salamanca Summer Camp Salamanca, which is known as the "Golden City," is home to the second-oldest university in the world and some of the most fascinating architecture in Europe. Its Plaza Mayor, the most impressive in Spain, serves as the heart of the city and the region of Castile, where the purest of Spanish dialects is spoken. Located in the old walled city center, the school is in a five-floor, sixteenth-century Renaissance building recognized by UNESCO as a World Heritage Complex. The complex also has a classic cloister patio and an attached fifteenth-century church, one of the best examples of plateresque architecture in Salamanca.

Valencia Summer Camp Valencia, which is located on the Mediterranean coast of Spain, has a population of about 800,000. The region has become one of the most sought-after tourist destinations due to the large number of days of sunshine it receives each year and its temperate climate. The camp's residential facilities are integrated into the campus of the University of Valencia. It offers a friendly atmosphere where international students are welcomed by their Spanish peers.

Guanajuato Summer Camp, Mexico Guanajuato, located in central Mexico, is a picturesque, tranquil university city that serves as the capital of the Guanajuato state. The city is protected by UNESCO as a World Heritage Site. Guanajuato is the ideal setting for a summer camp. It is a very safe place to live and is characterized by winding pedestrian streets, plazas bordered by pastel-colored houses with iron balconies, and abundant flowers. The majority of the campers live with host families, who warmly welcome students and cook the best local dishes for them. The camp has excellent facilities for youngsters to practice sports and take part in cultural activities such as cooking and dance classes. On the weekends, excursions may include colonial cities such as San Miguel de Allende and Guadalajara.

Camp for Families An opportunity exists for families to come to camp together, with parents staying in an apartment or with host families, studying Spanish in the adult school while their children go to camp.

BACKGROUND AND PHILOSOPHY

The International Summer Camps were founded in 1989 by ENFOREX, Spanish in the Spanish World, designed and elaborated by professional educators. Spanish (60 percent) and international (40 percent from all over the world) teenagers enjoy an educational holiday at seven of the top residential schools in Spain. The program's main goals are to learn Spanish in an attractive environment and inculcate the basis of teamwork and individual responsibility in common tasks, study and play in direct contact with nature, build social relationships, and make new friends. In order to enhance the students' ability to handle daily tasks without the support and protection of their families, ENFOREX offers a wide range of enriching activities. The Summer Camp is also designed for Spanish students, creating an international atmosphere that is suitable for the development of languages and exchange of cultures. The School is CEELE-certified by the University of Alcala and is also accredited by the Instituto Cervantes.

PROGRAM OFFERINGS

The program offers facilities for families and is designed for students between 5 and 18 years of age. At the School, they are divided into four different groups: 5–10, 11–12, 13–14, and 15–18. Students receive four lessons of Spanish language and culture per day. Class size averages 5 students, with a maximum of 12. Each lesson is 45 minutes long. On the first day of school, a placement test is administered to determine the student's level of Spanish. There are six different levels in Spanish, from complete beginner to proficiency. Classes are designed specifically for each level and age group. The following language skills are taught at all levels: speaking, listening, writing, grammar, Spanish culture, and Spanish history. All students receive a certificate diploma at the end of the course.

Recreational sports are one the camp's most fun activities. Sports may be practiced individually or in groups and include swimming, horseback riding, archery, paddleball, tennis, water sports, jet skiing, camping, golf, basketball, aerobics, soccer, baseball, handball, and volleyball.

A day camp option is also available, allowing students to attend camp from 9 a.m. to 8 p.m. without living on the premises. Day camp students attend the academic program, Spanish classes, and cultural and sports program with the rest of the students from Monday to Friday.

EXTRA OPPORTUNITIES AND ACTIVITIES

The School offers a wide range of activities, including a nature workshop, handcrafts, theater, photography, computers and the Internet, radio, journalism, mural painting, and dance (jazz, flamenco and "Sevillanas") workshops, which are available for students who wish to experience one or more of these cultural activities. Students also have the option of staying with host families.

A wide range of fun social activities are organized in the afternoon or after dinner, indoors and outdoors, and include parties, concerts, entertaining games, competitions, picnics and camping, movies, camp dances, and talent shows. Students enjoy one full-day and two half-day trips every week to nearby sites of special interest around Granada (La Alhambra and other historic Moorish relics), Barcelona (Sagrada Familia, Modernistic Route, and Picasso Museo), Marbella (Granada, the Nerja Caves, the Banús Yacht Harbor, Gibraltar, and Seville), Madrid (El Prado, Toledo, El Escorial, Salamanca, Plaza Mayor, and Barcelona), Salamanca (Avila, Segovia, and Burgos and Castilla Cathedrals), and Valencia (Gandia, New Science, Art Museum, and Alicante).

DAILY SCHEDULE

8:00– 9:15	Wake up and breakfast
9:30– 1:00	Spanish lessons
1:00– 2:15	Sport, cultural activities, swimming
2:15– 3:15	Lunch
3:15– 4:00	Workshops
4:00– 8:30	Lunch
3:00 4:30	Workshops
4:30– 8:30	Sports, activities, afternoon snack, and games
9:00– 9:45	Dinner
10:30–11:30	To bed

FACILITIES

The School's main building has a dining room, classrooms, dormitories, a computer room, and a library. The campuses have a swimming pool, golf, archery, soccer fields, and a sports complex with a gymnasium and paddleball, tennis, basketball, and volleyball courts. The Marbella School has its own farm and a horseback riding school with more than 14 horses.

STAFF

Spanish lessons are taught by native Spanish teachers holding five-year college degrees in Spanish linguistics and teaching Spanish as a foreign language, plus the CAP (teachers' aptitude test). Some have master's degrees and doctorates in Spanish.

The School Director, the maximum authority in the program, supervises both a Coordinator for Social Activities and a team of group leaders. There is a group leader for approximately every 8

students. ENFOREX offers a free group-leader placement for minimum groups of 8 students. If a teacher or educational leader sends a group of 8 students and wishes to accompany them, he or she can stay for free for the duration of the group's stay.

MEDICAL CARE

Medical personnel are on 24-hour call at the School. The School has arrangements with Marbella's General Hospital, which is 5 minutes away, for emergency treatment. All students are covered with medical insurance; however, it is recommended that students take out a private insurance that covers repatriation.

COSTS

Full board with accommodation is €1095 for two weeks, € 1730 for three weeks , €2150 for four weeks, €3000 for six weeks, and €3955 for eight weeks; day camp is €535 for two weeks, €1070 for four weeks, €1605 for six weeks, and €2140 for eight weeks. These fees include twenty Spanish lessons per week, accommodation in the camp's dormitory, three meals a day, course material, two afternoon excursions every fortnight, one full-day excursion every fortnight, activities described, assistance of group leaders, health insurance, application and enrollment fees, and laundry service once every two weeks. There is also a homestay option. Optional fees include horseback riding classes (5 hours a week), €155; swimming, €85; tennis or paddle classes (6 hours a week), €155; and golf (9 hours a week), €235.

TRANSPORTATION

The Barcelona School is just a short ride from the Barcelona airport. The Marbella International School is located 20 minutes from Málaga airport and 6 hours from Madrid's airport, Barajas. Transfers are available from both airports. The Madrid and Salamanca International Schools are located 15 minutes and 2 hours from the Madrid airport, respectively. The Valencia School is just a short ride from the Valencia airport, and the Granada school is just 15 minutes from the Granada airport and 1½ hours from the Málaga airport. ENFOREX can arrange packages for international students to arrive from New York, Miami, Los Angeles, or other cities.

FOR MORE INFORMATION, CONTACT

ENFOREX Spanish in the Spanish World
c/ Alberto Aguilera, 26
28015 Madrid
Spain

Phone: +34-91-594-3776
Fax: +34-91-594-5159
E-mail: info@enforex.es
Web site: http://www.enforex.com
　　　　　http://www.enfocamp.com

PARTICIPANT/FAMILY COMMENTS

"This year, I told Mom I want to go back. I can't forget the good times we had, the friends I met, the fun activities we did and all I learned. It's going to be another great summer!"—Carlos Martí, Barcelona, Spain

ENSEMBLE THEATRE COMMUNITY SCHOOL

SUMMER PROGRAM

EAGLES MERE, PENNSYLVANIA

TYPE OF PROGRAM: Residential arts program
PARTICIPANTS: Coeducational, ages 14–18
PROGRAM DATES: June 28 to July 30
HEAD OF PROGRAM: Seth Orbach, Director

LOCATION

Eagles Mere is a small summer community in Pennsylvania's Allegheny Mountains. The town has a history of encouraging the performing arts and makes the community arts facility, the DeWire Center, available to the School. The beautiful surroundings—a lake, a supervised beach, and many hiking trails—offer a peaceful environment apart from the distractions of urban life.

BACKGROUND AND PHILOSOPHY

The Ensemble Theatre Community School (ETC), founded in 1984, is a five-week program that provides highly motivated students, ages 14 to 18, with a concentrated summer-training experience that is challenging and inspiring. At ETC, extraordinary people make exceptional theater. Students learn the craft of acting in classes and through performances. ETC emphasizes collaboration in a supportive environment. Self-discovery is encouraged—ETC's small size and experienced, professional faculty members ensure that a student's training is individualized.

A group is only as strong as each of its members; therefore, the contributions of every member of the community are essential. Learning to trust each other and to take creative risks are crucial aspects of the Ensemble Theatre Community School experience. ETC's intensive, group-oriented structure encourages the understanding that the ensemble process—both on stage and off—and is vital in the creation of meaningful theater. In learning to take responsibility for the day-to-day needs of a community, ETC students learn some of the most important elements of exciting theater—communication, commitment, spontaneity, self-discipline, hard work, and fun.

PROGRAM OFFERINGS

ETC is a school. During an ETC summer, course work is balanced with workshops and performances so that students can apply concepts learned in class to their work on stage. Each student takes core courses in acting, movement, and music. Instruction in technical theater occurs throughout the summer as students and instructors work together to build and paint the sets, construct costumes and props, and hang and focus the lights.

Acting is taught in sections of 7 to 9 students to ensure individual attention. Freeing the imagination, responding truthfully in imaginary circumstances, and learning to trust are key elements of the curriculum. Topics include theater games, textual analysis, improvisation, and voice and diction.

Movement class emphasizes the importance of physical control and expression for the student actor. Students explore their personal movement vocabularies in order to expand their awareness of their bodies and apply what they discover in their acting work. Creative improvisations are balanced with more traditional warm-ups and basic technique.

Music combines musical theory with practical exercises in singing, breathing, and listening. Students are encouraged to explore and expand their musical potential and to experiment vocally. An advanced class is available for those students who have already had substantial training in music.

Each student is cast in one major production and in a children's theater piece that involves all students and faculty members. Plays are chosen based on which works best for an acting ensemble rather than by which feature only one or two leading roles.

Some past productions have included *The Fantastics, Our Town, Antigone, As You Like It, The Crucible, To Kill a Mockingbird, Hay Fever, Great Expectations, Under Milkwood, The Dining Room, The Caucasian Chalk Circle, Peter Pan, Pericles,* and *Blood Wedding.* Scripts are often created by a playwright to meet ETC's specific requirements.

In addition, workshops are offered in directing, playwriting, musical theater, stage combat, makeup, scene painting, the Alexander technique, Shakespeare and his world, neutral mask, and sound design.

ENROLLMENT
Students who are between the ages of 14 and 18 come from a variety of backgrounds—from those who are seasoned veterans to beginners. Each student receives an evaluation at the end of the summer, which serves as the basis for a college recommendation written by the director. ETC students have gone on to study at such colleges and universities as Amherst, Barnard, Boston University, Brown, Carnegie-Mellon, Columbia, Davidson, Emerson, Georgetown, Harvard, Juilliard, Kenyon, Lewis & Clark, Oberlin, Penn State, Sarah Lawrence, Tisch School of the Arts at NYU, Tulane, University of North Carolina at Chapel Hill, Vassar, Wesleyan, and Yale. Some students have been awarded academic credit by their high schools for the work they do at ETC.

DAILY SCHEDULE
The weekly schedule allots time for study, rehearsal, relaxation, and household duties.

8:00	Breakfast
8:30	Household responsibilities
8:50	Warm-Ups
9:30	Class I: Acting or Program Time
11:00	Class II: Movement
1:30	Journal Writing or Reflective Time
1:50	Class III: Acting or Music
3:00	Rehearsal
5:00	Dinner Preparation or Rest
6:00	Dinner
7:45	Rehearsal or Tech Work
10:45	Group Unwinding
11:30	Bedtime

FACILITIES
Ensemble Theatre Community School makes its home in the Players' Lodge, across from the town green. Students live dormitory style, in the same house as the interns and faculty members.

STAFF
The unusual opportunity for students to live cooperatively in the same home with professional faculty members assures that the learning process is ongoing. Discoveries are made in class, on stage, and in the kitchen. The faculty is joined by college interns, who participate in all aspects of the program, and by visiting professionals, who conduct workshops in their specialties.

COSTS
The total cost, including room and board, is $4500. Financial aid may be provided in two forms—grants to the family (tuition remission) and extended payment plans. Most financial aid awards combine the two forms. Students should inquire about financial aid upon application. Resources are limited, so early application is recommended.

APPLICATION TIMETABLE
Both beginners and experienced students are encouraged to apply. Space is limited, so early application is advised. Any applications received by March 30, the early application deadline, are reviewed upon arrival, with admission notification by April 30. Applications received after March 30 may be accepted for any remaining openings.

FOR MORE INFORMATION, CONTACT
Seth Orbach, Director
Ensemble Theatre Community School
43 Lyman Circle
Shaker Heights, Ohio 44122
Phone: 216-464-1688
E-mail: info@etcschool.org
Web site: http://www.etcschool.org

PARTICIPANT/FAMILY COMMENTS

"I felt more a part of ETC than I've ever felt a part of anything. I felt like I had a special relationship with almost everyone, and that was wonderful. . . I also appreciated being treated as an equal, even though I had less experience than most of the people and was one of the youngest."—Kristina

"I worked on props, costumes, painting, and various other technical things. I learned a great deal about everything I worked on because the faculty members were so willing to help if there were any problems."—Eddie

"This program has given me a chance not only to be involved in wonderful theater but also to find things out about myself I never realized were in me before. I have more confidence and faith in myself because everyone has been supportive of me."—Danielle

"The sonnet classes are demanding, requiring a lot of commitment and imagination. This year, I came to love sonnet class, as it was helpful in giving me new places to go in my acting work."—Mike

"I feel like the whole world should function the way this community does; we're all so close and connected."—Ariel

EXCEL

SUMMER PROGRAMS

AMHERST, MASSACHUSETTS; PARIS AND PROVENCE, FRANCE; OXFORD, ENGLAND; FLORENCE, ITALY; MADRID AND BARCELONA, SPAIN; AND BEIJING, CHINA

TYPE OF PROGRAM: Precollege academic enrichment
PARTICIPANTS: Coeducational, students completing grades 9–12
ENROLLMENT: 100–150 per session, U.S.; 70, Europe and China
PROGRAM DATES: Three-, four-, and seven-week programs in June, July, and August
HEADS OF PROGRAM: Jeffrey Shumlin, Peter Shumlin, and Patrick Noyes, Directors

LOCATION
Excel at Amherst College is based on the campus of Amherst College, Amherst, Massachusetts. Located in the heart of the Pioneer Valley, Amherst College and the town of Amherst offer a picturesque setting for learning and adventure. The college campus and adjacent town common form the heart of the "Five-College Area."

Excel at Oxford/Tuscany is located at St. Hilda's College in Oxford, England, and at a sixteenth-century villa outside Florence, Italy. Each location serves as an ideal base for active, focused study of the history, archeology, literary traditions, and politics of the region. Excel at Madrid/Barcelona students explore the rich and varied culture of Spain from the modern campuses of universities.

Excel Paris/Provence begins with two weeks in Aix-en-Provence, a dynamic university town nestled between the small hill villages of the Lubéron to the north and the dramatic cliffs of the Mediterranean coast to the south. In Paris, the group stays in the Marais district in the center of the city, a short walk from the Place des Vosges, Île St-Louis, and Centre Pompidou.

Excel in China is based on the campus of the Capital University of Economics and Business in Beijing. Students can focus on studying Mandarin or can join active seminars on topics such as history, art, contemporary cinema, international relations, and economic development. During the third week, the entire program takes a week-long excursion to Hanzhou, Shanghai, and the island of Putuoshan.

BACKGROUND AND PHILOSOPHY
The Excel programs are sponsored by Putney Student Travel, now in its fifth decade of offering educational programs for high school students. Excel emphasizes growth and education through the challenges of hands-on learning by doing, exploring and adapting to new experiences, working cooperatively in small groups, and setting and achieving high personal expectations. Students select two areas of study and work in small seminars, undertaking extensive field trips and projects related to their subject areas. Each course culminates in a final project—a theatrical production, student newspaper, art and photography exhibit, mock trial, video, and debate forum are among the possibilities, depending on the course. Course work is intellectually challenging, but credit is not offered and

grades are not given, because Excel students typically attend high-pressure schools during the academic year and want to focus in a more informal context during the summer on subjects that genuinely interest them. Outside the classroom, Excel offers a variety of athletic and cultural activities, and many are organized by students themselves. Students who are best suited for the program are those who are motivated to stretch themselves intellectually, artistically, and physically and, in so doing, have fun.

PROGRAM OFFERINGS
Courses are divided into five categories: arts (drawing and painting, photography, architectural design, writing, theater production, music composition, fashion design, dance, ceramics, and video production), humanities (ethics, film studies, history, and philosophy), languages and rhetoric (journalism, French, Mandarin, and Spanish), social and natural sciences (archaeology, international relations, criminal justice, and behavioral and social psychology), and specialized courses, SAT preparation, and structured writing, which are offered on the domestic campuses only. There is also a program at Excel Amherst featuring college visits and small workshops to introduce students to the college admissions process.

ENROLLMENT
Enrollment at Excel Amherst ranges from 100 to 150 students, who are selected from across the country and around the world. International programs are generally limited to 70 students.

EXTRA OPPORTUNITIES AND ACTIVITIES
During afternoons and evenings, students choose from a wide variety of organized activities, ranging from swimming and Ultimate Frisbee to community service and from on-campus coffeehouses to off-campus visits to arts productions in the local area during the evenings. Instructional sports clinics in soccer, tennis, and golf are offered three late afternoons a week at Amherst. On weekends, all students and staff members participate in excursions to areas of local and regional interest, including Cape Cod, Montreal, the White Mountains, the Adirondacks, and Vermont. Excel at Oxford/

Tuscany allows students to explore the rich heritage of Europe with frequent day trips and a weekend interlude in Paris. Excel at Madrid/Barcelona includes day trips and small-group weekend excursions to Segovia, Toledo, and Salamanca, among others. Excel at Paris/Provence offers students the opportunity to explore the hills and coast of southern France and includes a weekend excursion to the beautiful and historic beaches of Normandy.

FACILITIES
Students are housed in residence halls of each campus. Meals are provided in one of each college's dining halls. In addition, students at each campus have access to college athletic facilities, libraries, art studios, computer rooms, and language labs.

STAFF
Excel faculty members are among the finest in their fields, drawn from some of the world's best colleges and universities. They are chosen for their extensive knowledge of and enthusiasm for the course material as well as for their dynamic teaching methods and their willingness and ability to work closely with their students. A complete set of biographies of Excel instructors from the summer of 2007 is available at http://www.goputney.com.

DAILY SCHEDULE
The daily schedules at Excel Oxford/Tuscany, Madrid/Barcelona, Paris/Provence, and China are flexible, allowing for frequent field trips and in-depth exploration of the surrounding regions. The community meeting is a crucial part of the daily schedule of all programs.

MEDICAL CARE
There are excellent medical facilities within easy reach of each campus. All students must provide a medical form completed by their physician and a medical treatment release form prior to the beginning of the program.

RELIGIOUS LIFE
Excel is nondenominational. Students may attend area religious services if they wish.

COSTS
The tuition fees in 2007 were as follows: Excel at Amherst College, $5190 for the four-week (July) program and $4390 for the three-week (August) program. The tuition for Excel at Oxford/Tuscany was $7590. Tuition for the Madrid/Barcelona

program was $7290. Tuition for Paris/Provence was $7590, and tuition for China was $5890. Tuition includes instructional programs, all regularly scheduled activities, room, board (two meals on the European programs), overnight excursions that are a part of the Excel program (including lodging, meals, and transportation), use of college facilities, afternoon and evening activities, and transportation to and from the local airport.

TRANSPORTATION
Amherst, Massachusetts, is within a 3-hour drive of New York City and Boston. The airports in Hartford, Connecticut, and Albany, New York, are nearby. Staff members pick up students at these airports and at nearby train and bus stations on the first day of the program and drop them off on the last.

Excel organizes group flights for its Oxford/Tuscany, Paris/Provence, China, and Madrid/Barcelona programs, in which students can participate if they so choose.

APPLICATION TIMETABLE
Admission to Excel is selective. Applications, which must be accompanied by a personal statement and two teacher references, are carefully considered by the Admissions Committee. Maturity, intellectual curiosity, integrity, and a cooperative spirit are all important admissions criteria. Students should apply early, as limited spaces in small classes are granted on a first-come, first-served basis.

FOR MORE INFORMATION, CONTACT
Patrick Noyes, Director
345 Hickory Ridge Road
Putney, Vermont 05346

Phone: 802-387-5000
Fax: 802-387-4276
E-mail: excel@goputney.com
Web site: http://www.goputney.com

PARTICIPANT/FAMILY COMMENTS

"This was, by far, the best summer of my entire life. The people I met were amazing. The places I went and the things I was exposed to made this experience one I will never forget. Thank you so much for letting me be part of Excel for my second year!"

THE EXPERIMENT IN INTERNATIONAL LIVING

OFFERED BY WORLD LEARNING

EXPERIMENT IN INTERNATIONAL LIVING

BRATTLEBORO, VERMONT

TYPE OF PROGRAM: International youth travel
PARTICIPANTS: Coeducational, high school students
ENROLLMENT: 900–1,100
PROGRAM DATES: Three to five weeks in the summer
HEAD OF PROGRAM: Tony Allen and John Meislin, Directors of the Experiment in International Living

LOCATION

The Experiment in International Living is offered by World Learning, which is located in southern Vermont, and by affiliated offices on six continents. These offices provide Experiment in International Living programs with full-time international support and up-to-the-minute information on local events in program countries.

BACKGROUND AND PHILOSOPHY

World Learning was founded in 1932 as the Experiment in International Living, a pioneer in people-to-people exchange. It is one of the oldest private nonprofit international educational services organizations in the world. For more than seventy-five years, it has sustained its founding concept—learning the culture and language of another country by living as a member of one of its families—while also pioneering new initiatives in response to a changing world.

The range of Experiment in International Living programs includes snorkeling with seals in lava grottoes while observing the ecology of Ecuador's Galapagos Islands, wandering through Samurai villages after language classes in Japan, and biking along the coast of Brittany while immersing oneself in French culture and history.

Each Experiment in International Living program begins with a cross-cultural orientation in the host country, usually in the capital of the country. During orientation, participants learn about the customs and characteristics of the society in which they will be living in order to help them fully experience and enjoy their new environment.

Experiment in International Living programs are especially suited to students who are inquisitive and highly motivated to learn about cultures other than their own. Essential personality traits are adaptability, responsibility, a spirit of cooperation, and a sense of humor.

PROGRAM OFFERINGS

Students can choose from extraordinarily diverse programs in any of twenty-six countries from Australia to South Africa. Some programs provide intense immersion in the language and culture of a single place and people; some engage students in a culture through community service; and others develop the global perspective necessary to tackle international ecological problems. Choices are based on participant preference and on the special program opportunities made available by the Experiment's overseas contacts. Homestay and Travel and Regional Exploration programs in such countries as Brazil, Chile, China, France, Ghana, Italy, Mexico, New Zealand, Poland, Spain, Switzerland, Thailand, Turkey, and the United Kingdom are popular. Ecological Adventure

programs in places like Argentina, Australia, Belize, Botswana, Brazil, Chile, Costa Rica, Ecuador, Mexico, the Navajo Nation, New Zealand, Spain, and Switzerland offer exciting learning opportunities. Community Service programs in Argentina, Belize, Botswana, Brazil, Chile, Costa Rica, Germany, Ghana, Mexico, the Navajo Nation, Poland, South Africa, Thailand, and Turkey attract students who want to make personal contributions to the well-being of the world community. Language Training programs are available in France, Japan, Italy, and Spain. Programs in the arts are available in France, Morocco, Spain, South Africa, and the United Kingdom.

The following programs were offered in 2007; students should contact the Vermont office for more details.

Homestay By living with a family, students absorb and experience not just the language but also the values, customs, and traditions of a new country. They participate in the everyday life of the host family and engage in regular, fun activities with the U.S. leader, other group members, and host families. Traveling with the group and leader, students journey to another part of the country, trying out communication and exploration skills. The group visits three or four places, taking in the main sights while still having time to interact with local people.

Ecological Adventure Students examine rich natural and cultural resources through an adventurous travel program that is sensitive to environmental needs. As they tour historic, cultural, and scenic areas, the students explore ecological diversity firsthand, with the leader keeping the focus on the extraordinary balance of nature in the host country. Through camping, canoeing, snorkeling, or sailing, students embark on adventurous exploration into rural areas to appreciate a culture's spiritual and economic relationships to its environment. Students learn the value of being a global citizen and understanding the impact of ecological issues from a local and global perspective.

Community Service Students can make a peaceful, personal contribution to the well-being of the common planet by working on a Community Service program. Students gain invaluable hands-on experience in the process and discover how community service lets them learn from, as well as about, people in another culture. Students gain an understanding of how much can be accomplished with very few resources and of the cultural variations in approaches to problem solving. Students travel with their group and leader during the last part of the program to explore other parts of the country.

Language Training Focusing on verbal communications skills, students benefit from the highly skilled, experienced teachers and the community-based interactive learning of the Language Training programs. Participants work hard, but the rewards are extraordinary. Students can apply their lessons every minute of every day and can learn with an astonishing speed and ease. The Language Training programs require one year of French and one year of Spanish for the France and Spain programs, respectively. The Japan and Italy Language Training programs have no language prerequisites.

Travel and Regional Exploration Participants discover famous cultural and historical sights, interpreting them from the enriched perspective gained by living with a local family and taking part in the daily life of a community. They may journey to bustling port cities; hike through animal sanctuaries; travel by horse; sail, swim, and snorkel; or visit native markets.

The Arts Students explore theater, film, photography, or folklore to enrich the understanding of the host culture. Whether engaging in a photography project in the streets of Paris, flamenco dance lessons in southern Spain, or performing theater in the land of Shakespeare, a participant's creativity and talent provide a palette for a remarkable summer.

ENROLLMENT

Experiment in International Living programs are open to high school students. The majority are sophomores, juniors, and recently graduated seniors. Previous study of the host country language is required for some programs. Each participant is part of a group of travel companions for the duration of the Experiment in International Living program. Groups represent a broad spectrum of interests and personalities, encouraging the development of warm and lasting friendships.

STAFF

Leaders provide the support each participant needs to learn and to discover what international understanding means. The Experiment in International Living chooses its group leaders for their language fluency, maturity, emotional balance, experience in group leadership, and skill in working with young people. From the in-country orientation to the return to the United States, both the group and the leader serve as valuable resources for personal support, idea exchange, and activity planning.

COSTS

Fees for Experiment in International Living programs are determined by the chosen program's components, length of stay, and host country. Prices range from about $3700 to $6200. These all-inclusive fees cover round-trip international transportation; orientation and language training; meals, lodging, and transportation throughout the program; admission to the program's scheduled events; costs related to the group leader; and health and accident insurance. Not included in the program fees are round-trip transportation to and from the program's U.S. starting point, personal spending money (usually $400 to $600), and costs of required travel documents and immunizations.

A $100 nonrefundable application fee must accompany the initial application, along with a $300 space reservation deposit, which is applied to the program fee. Full payment is required before the program start date. VISA and MasterCard are accepted.

FINANCIAL AID

Some awards are based on merit, most on need, and some on a combination of the two. Annually, more than 35 percent of Experiment in International Living participants receive scholarships from the Experiment. Awards typically range from 10 to 50 percent of the individual's program fee. Scholarships are awarded on a rolling first-come, first-served basis. Program applicants are sent financial aid information and applications upon request.

APPLICATION TIMETABLE

Initial inquiries are welcome throughout the year. Detailed information and application forms are available early in the fall. May 1 is the deadline for the initial application. The Experiment's Admission Committee reviews an individual's application as soon as all of the application materials have been received. The candidate is contacted in writing soon after the committee has reached a decision. Students are accepted into Experiment in International Living programs on a rolling basis beginning in the fall. Applicants may choose any program for which they meet the minimum age and language study requirements.

FOR MORE INFORMATION, CONTACT

The Experiment in International Living
Kipling Road
Brattleboro, Vermont 05302-0676
Phone: 802-257-7751
        800-345-2929 (toll-free)
Fax: 802-258-3428
E-mail: eil@worldlearning.org
Web site: http://www.usexperiment.org

THE FESSENDEN SCHOOL

ESL SUMMER PROGRAM

WEST NEWTON, MASSACHUSETTS

TYPE OF PROGRAM: Total-immersion English as a second language, international residential living
PARTICIPANTS: Coeducational, ages 10–15
ENROLLMENT: 45
PROGRAM DATES: June 29 to August 1

LOCATION
The Fessenden School, established in 1903, is located on a beautiful 41-acre campus just 12 miles from the historic and cultural center of Boston.

BACKGROUND AND PHILOSOPHY
The five-week Fessenden English as a Second Language (ESL) Summer Program has had more than twenty-five countries represented since its inception in 1992. What makes the Fessenden ESL Summer Program so special is its small size, personal attention, blend of academics, cultural interactions, language projects, travel experiences, summer camp activities, and total language immersion. Students attend academic

classes, use the English language in a variety of projects and enrichment classes, play together in the pool and on the athletic fields, travel to New York City, camp in the woods of Maine, and learn how to work and live in a global society. Students use their English language skills while learning to work as a team. The School places a strong emphasis upon respect for the individual and cultural differences that each student brings to the community.

Community life at the Fessenden ESL Summer Program is also an integral part of the Fessenden experience. Children of the same gender and similar age groups but different nationalities live together in the same dormitory. Great friendships develop from living in a multinational, multilingual environment using English as a common language. Family-style dining encourages English language development, while students sample American and international cuisine.

PROGRAM OFFERINGS
The Language Classroom All morning classes emphasize the four basic skills of listening, speaking, reading, and writing. Classes taught by Fessenden's team of language specialists are small enough to offer consistent individual attention to each student. The student-teacher ratio is 5:1. The Summer ESL Program's multilevel curriculum serves to enhance the students' understanding of cultural events, excursions, and weekend trips while helping them to demonstrate progressively greater competence in English.

The academic objective of Fessenden's Summer ESL Program is to make learning English language skills a positive and valuable experience for each student regardless of his or her prior knowledge of English. Students are placed in small classes based on the results of comprehensive language assessments. Fessenden offers many levels of language instruction, ranging from beginning to advanced. Teachers take into consideration each student's linguistic needs when planning lessons. The girls and boys leave the program with greatly improved skills in speaking, listening, writing, and reading English.

Afternoon Enrichment Program Students also gain English skills while participating in less formal but carefully planned afternoon activities. These activities include computer skills, language lab, arts and crafts, hands-on science, video production, and International Day.

The purpose of the enrichment program is to integrate English language learning into real-life situations as well as to have fun in a relaxing and creative setting. Teachers provide situations that require students to use English while gaining knowledge and skill in diverse activities.

EXTRA OPPORTUNITIES AND ACTIVITIES

The Summer ESL Program offers a wide variety of experiences through field trips and weekend excursions. Two of the biggest "traveling classrooms" are the day trip to New York City and the four-day camping trip in the woods of Maine. Other events include trips to historic downtown Boston, a July 4 Independence Day celebration, barbecues, fireworks, a Boston Red Sox baseball game, the Big Apple Circus, a whale watch, a trip to the beach, and International Day presentations.

COSTS

For 2007, the total cost of the five-week program was $5975. The cost of the program includes all class and material fees, weekend and evening trips, meals, transportation, laundry service, and required health insurance. Personal spending money is not included in the cost of the program. The School recommends $400 in personal spending money be kept in an account for each student by the director.

APPLICATION TIMETABLE

Interested applicants and their families should contact the Fessenden School Summer ESL Program at the address, phone numbers, or Web site listed in this description. Applicants who access the School's Web site should select "summer."

FOR MORE INFORMATION, CONTACT

Mark Hansen
Director of the Fessenden ESL Summer Program
250 Waltham Street
West Newton, Massachusetts 02465

Phone: 617-678-2978 or 617-630-2318
Fax: 617-630-2317
E-mail: esl@fessenden.org
Web site: http://www.fessenden.org

FUTURE LEADER CAMP AT NORWICH UNIVERSITY

CHALLENGE—TEAMWORK—ADVENTURE

NORTHFIELD, VERMONT

TYPE OF PROGRAM: Leadership development
PARTICIPANTS: Coeducational; students who have completed grades 9, 10, and 11; have been accepted to Norwich University for the fall class; and are in good academic standing
ENROLLMENT: Limited to 80 per session
PROGRAM DATES: Two 2-week sessions in July
HEAD OF PROGRAM: Lieutenant Colonel "Skip" Davison, Director of Future Leader Camp

LOCATION

Future Leader Camp (FLC) is conducted at Norwich University, which is located in the rugged Green Mountains of central Vermont. The campus is located in the small town of Northfield, 10 miles south of the state capital of Montpelier and 50 miles from Burlington, the largest city in Vermont. Both Montpelier and Burlington are cultural centers for the arts and the Burlington International Airport is within an hour's drive. Vermont is world-renowned as one of America's most beautiful states, and some of the nation's most popular resorts, such as Stowe, Sugarbush, and Killington, are located within an hour's drive. Vermont is an outdoor paradise for those who like rock climbing, hiking, camping, mountain biking, swimming, canoeing, kayaking, fishing, and more. In addition, the cities of Boston and Montreal are only a 3-hour drive from the campus.

BACKGROUND AND PHILOSOPHY

FLC's mission is to enable dedicated youths to become decisive, caring, and disciplined leaders in a challenging environment and to instill confidence and courage through hands-on adventure, survival, and physical training while fostering in each the moral integrity and flawless character required of responsible citizens and future leaders.

FLC is designed for students who wish to further develop their leadership skills or for those are already serving in leadership positions within their school, community, or place of employment. The camp staff members take participants to the next level of leadership while providing a fun and worthwhile camp experience.

Using a combination of adventure training, group discussions, and hands-on training, the goal of FLC is to instill the basic principles of small-group leadership techniques, ethics, effective communications, problem solving, and teamwork, while developing in each participant a sense of self-confidence, self-respect, and self-discipline. The leadership philosophy emanates from the camp Director who believes that "leadership is an art . . . acquired over time . . . by those with the strength of character . . . to master its form."

Training includes physical fitness, rappelling, climbing wall, rifle range, land navigation, leadership reaction course, wilderness and water survival, paintball, rock climbing, hiking, rope bridging, and a three-day overnight Survival Course.

Camp participants are issued uniforms as part of the program to facilitate training and create an atmosphere of camaraderie. FLC is not a military boot-camp and only those with demonstrated leadership potential, a proven academic record, and a desire to excel need apply. The professional staff members are trained, certified, and qualified to instruct all courses taught.

PROGRAM OFFERINGS

The first phase of Future Leader Camp begins with daily instruction in rappelling, rope bridging, climbing and survival techniques, paintball, rifle and archery range, water survival, and physical fitness training. Physical fitness training is conducted by ability groups and instructs participants on how to properly exercise. Most evenings, participants find themselves in the classroom learning about the basic principles and traits of leadership. Group discussions are held and an in-depth study of Sir Ernest Shackleton's leadership abilities is examined. Other topics include effective communications, how to conduct briefings and coordinate events, and CPR certification. The next phase requires participants to face two physical challenges: hiking to the top of Vermont's second-highest peak, Camels Hump, and then climbing and rappelling the cliffs of Dear Leap Mountain in Killington, Vermont. Phase three finds participants on a three-day "in the woods" overnight survival exercise where the team's individual and collective skills are put to the test. The exercise includes extensive wilderness survival skills training and land navigation.

All participants are required to hold the position of Team Leader at least once during the camp. The Team Leader position is rotated daily and each participant receives a performance evaluation from his or her counselor and their peers.

Finally, the camp ends with a physical fitness test, drill competition, and Olympics Challenge course. The physical fitness test measures individual ability, while the drill competition measures the team's ability to work together as a team. The Olympic Challenge is all about fun and includes such events as the Tired Relay, the Litter Press, the Run-Dodge and Jump, and Log Toss. The last day is one of rest and relaxation at Lake Elmore, one of Vermont's most beautiful lakes for a day of swimming, canoeing, kayaking, hiking, and some really good chow.

ENROLLMENT

Camp is conducted in two sessions. Enrollment is limited to the first 80 qualified applicants. Interested individuals must submit an application, a letter of recommendation, health form, medical waiver form, and travel form to be considered.

DAILY SCHEDULE

First call is at 5:30 a.m., followed by physical fitness training the first week from 6 to 7. During the first week, there are morning, afternoon, and evening training sessions. Evenings are generally reserved for group discussions or recreational activities. The training schedule is full and participants are kept busy from sunup to sundown. Midweek and week two are filled with training events that last all day and the schedule changes from day to day. Lights go out by 10 p.m. except during the overnight field exercise.

EXTRA OPPORTUNITIES AND ACTIVITIES

During the course, all participants earn their Adult CPR and Basic First Aid certification. Those who arrive already certified are asked to assist the instructor and receive appropriate recognition for their assistance.

FACILITIES

Participants stay in dorm rooms on campus and dine in the university's dining facility. Participants must supply their own linen and washing machines are available in the dorms. The dining facility is operated by SODEXHO food service and meals are served cafeteria style, offering a wide variety of choices. The university campus consists of 1,200 acres and has numerous athletic and classroom facilities. Participants also consume Meals Ready to Eat (MREs) on days when training prevents them from going to the dining facility. Accommodations are made for those with food allergies, although individuals must take responsibility for readings menus. The medical release and waiver form should clearly state the participant's type of food allergy.

STAFF

The director is a full-time employee of Norwich University and is retired from the military with more than thirty years of experience working with young people. The camp training officer is also a full-time employee and holds a master's degree in outdoor leadership education and is certified to conduct all training. The operations officer is CPR instructor certified and is qualified to oversee all training events. Camp counselors are junior and senior cadets who attend Norwich University. They must apply and be interviewed for the counselor positions. In addition, a number of faculty and staff members from the university contribute to training and classes.

MEDICAL CARE

All staff members and counselors are CPR certified. An EMT first responder is on call during all training. Green Mountain Medical Clinic is located across the street from the university and provides basic health care. Central Vermont Hospital is located less than 10 miles from the campus.

RELIGIOUS LIFE

Due to a tightly packed training schedule, times to attend services during the two-week camp cannot be provided.

COSTS

The camp costs $1455. This includes room, meals, uniforms, and all camp activities.

FINANCIAL AID

Financial aid is not generally available. Families who have financial need should contact the program office at 802-485-2531.

TRANSPORTATION

Participants provide their own transportation to the camp. Included with every information packet is a travel brochure outlining how to get to Vermont by air, train, bus, or privately owned vehicle. The Burlington International Airport (BTV) is located an hour from the campus in Burlington, Vermont. The bus and train station are located in Montpelier, Vermont, only 10 miles from the campus. For a minimum charge the FLC staff will make arrangements to have participants who arrive by air, train, or bus picked up and dropped off. The round trip price to and from the airport is $50; Amtrak and the bus station are $25. Participants who arrive by privately owned vehicle will be provided with a parking pass.

APPLICATION TIMETABLE

The office begins accepting applications January 1. Applications are submitted with a letter of recommendation, medical form, and $25 nonrefundable application fee. A $250 nonrefundable deposit must be received upon acceptance to guarantee the applicants seat in the camp and order their uniforms. The entire cost of the camp is due by June 1, unless the family has made other arrangements with the camp director. Last year the program filled and a waiting list started the last week in April.

FOR MORE INFORMATION, CONTACT

Future Leader Camp at Norwich University
27 I. D. White Avenue
Northfield, Vermont 05663

Phone: 802-485-2531
Fax: 802-485-2739
E-mail: flc@norwich.edu
Web site: http://www.norwich.edu/flc

GEORGETOWN UNIVERSITY

▼▼▼▼▼▼▼▼▼▼▼▼▼▼▼▼▼▼▼▼▼▼▼▼▼▼▼▼

SUMMER PROGRAMS FOR HIGH SCHOOL STUDENTS

WASHINGTON, D.C.

TYPE OF PROGRAM: Academic enrichment and college preparation

PARTICIPANTS: Coeducational, grades 10–12, depending upon program

ENROLLMENT: 400–500

PROGRAM DATES: College Prep Program, one 5-week session in June and July; Summer College for High School Students, two 5-week sessions, June to July and July to August; Gateway to Business for High School Students, one 5-week session in July and August; International Relations Program, one week in July; American Politics, one week in July; Journalism Workshop, one week in July

HEAD OF PROGRAM: Veronica DiConti, Associate Dean of Summer Programs

LOCATION

The programs take place on the Georgetown University campus in Washington, D.C. Participants take advantage of the cultural, recreational, and educational opportunities abounding in the nation's capital.

PROGRAM OFFERINGS

Summer College for High School Students Outstanding high school students are offered the opportunity to expand their studies with college courses taken in an intensive yet supportive college environment. Students live on campus and attend classes with undergraduate Georgetown students. A limited number of students are accepted for each session.

A student enrolls in one or two courses appropriate to his or her interests, background, and previous academic achievement. Courses include business administration, biology, computer science, economics, English, fine arts, government, history, languages, math, philosophy, physics, psychology, sociology, and theology. A typical full-time course load for a five-week session is 6 credits. Students may enroll for both sessions with the approval of the director.

To be admitted into the program, nonnative speakers of English must send evidence of sufficient English language ability (TOEFL, CELT, ALIGU, or other standardized test scores).

Gateway to Business for High School Students This program gives students the opportunity to explore the area of business through an intensive five-week, 3-credit course. Participants in the program are treated as college students and receive college credit on successful completion of the course. Areas covered include finance, marketing, accounting, management, communications, strategy, planning, organizational behavior, information systems, and business law. There are field trips to businesses in the area to provide participants with hands-on knowledge of a working industry. The program ultimately allows students to gain a better understanding of the business world and enables them to determine whether business school is something they would like to pursue.

International Relations Program This program provides an opportunity for high school students to acquire intercultural awareness through an exploration of the complex nature of international relations and the ethical implications of foreign-policy decisions. The program is designed to take advantage of Georgetown University's resources as a leading center of international studies located in the nation's capital. This challenging program combines lectures by members of Georgetown's faculty and distinguished guest speakers; visits to governmental departments, agencies, or international organizations; small-group discussions; and an international crisis simulation. This approach helps students develop conceptual tools for understanding complex issues.

College Preparatory Program The Georgetown University College Preparatory Program helps high school students solidify and advance English and math fundamentals and prepare for the SAT and college admissions process. It is designed to help students improve their academic performance while in high school and get a jump start on getting into the college of their choice. Included are SAT test-taking workshops and practice exams that cover all sections, in addition to diagnostic tests and personalized reports. Students also learn to improve their critical thinking and composition and writing skills, develop their math expertise, and enhance their research and study skills. Students are immersed in the full Georgetown experience—living, sharing meals, socializing, and exchanging ideas with fellow students and faculty members.

American Politics and Public Affairs Program Washington, D.C., is all about power and politics, and there is no better place to study them than Georgetown. The American Politics and Public Affairs Program gives students a distinctively Georgetown view of the people, the institutions, and the processes that shape the nation's policies. The program helps students examine the interaction among Congress, the president, and the courts and visit the places where they work. Participants put what they have learned into practice through a simulated political campaign.

Journalism Workshop Students who want to make their voices heard participate in the Journalism Workshop. Participants choose photojournalism, print journalism, or both and learn about the special challenges a Washington journalist faces. Students explore topics such as ethics, media, and law and craft strategies to develop sources. A body of work is produced that is displayed on a Web site that students develop in the media lab.

ENROLLMENT
Georgetown University's summer programs enroll students from across the United States and from several other countries.

EXTRA OPPORTUNITIES AND ACTIVITIES
Many trips and activities are organized by program counselors, including area sightseeing and cultural and sports events.

FACILITIES
In addition to the University dormitories for residential participants, all students have access to the University library and to the sports/gym complex.

STAFF
Courses are taught by Georgetown University faculty members, and there is a full-time staff of trained counselors who live in the dormitories.

COSTS
For the 2007 College Prep Program, tuition was $3100. Room and board cost $2215 for an air-conditioned double room. Pay-as-you-go dining is also available. Provisions should be made for approximately $75 per course for books. Costs are subject to change for the 2008 program year.

For the Summer College for High School Juniors, tuition in 2007 was $965 per credit. Room and board cost $2215 for an air-conditioned double room. Food is also available on a pay-as-you-go basis. Books and personal expenses are not included. Costs are subject to change for the 2008 program year.

Tuition, room, board, and selected recreational activities for the International Relations Program in 2007 cost $1575 for resident students; commuting students paid $1100. (Costs are subject to change for the 2008 program year.

FINANCIAL AID
A limited number of partial tuition scholarships are available for the College Prep Program and the Summer College for High School Students.

APPLICATION TIMETABLE
Applications are available now. Interested students may request a catalog by visiting http://www.summer.georgetown. edu.

FOR MORE INFORMATION, CONTACT
Summer Programs for High School Students
Georgetown University
Box 571006
Washington, D.C. 20057-1006
Phone: 202-687-8700
Fax: 202-687-8954
E-mail: scsenrollment@georgetown.edu
Web site: http://www.summer.georgetown.edu

THE GEORGE WASHINGTON UNIVERSITY SUMMER SCHOLARS PROGRAM

THE GEORGE
WASHINGTON
UNIVERSITY
WASHINGTON DC

EXPERIENCE GW! DISCOVER D.C.!

WASHINGTON, D.C.

TYPE OF PROGRAM: Precollege program and minicourses
PARTICIPANTS: Coeducational, grades 9–11
ENROLLMENT: 120 students
PROGRAM DATES: Mid-June through mid-August
HEAD OF PROGRAM: Barbara Frank, Director

LOCATION

The George Washington University (GW) is the largest private university located in Washington, D.C. Situated in the heart of the city, GW offers an academic community that is uniquely enriched by its seamless coexistence with the rich variety of historic, cultural, and educational resources in the nation's capital. Summer Scholars experience two distinctly different campus environments. Students take classes at the downtown Foggy Bottom campus, which is located just blocks from the White House and within easy walking distance of historic Georgetown, the Kennedy Center for the Performing Arts, the Department of State, and many other government and cultural institutions. The Metro-accessible campus is an ideal place to study while exploring the nation's history, international communities, and the inner workings of organizations that shape national and international policy.

Summer Scholars reside 3 miles from the Foggy Bottom campus at the more intimate Mount Vernon campus in northwest Washington, D.C., located in a peaceful, wooded residential neighborhood and in proximity to parks and biking and hiking trails. A 15-minute shuttle ride links the two campuses and offers a view of the Potomac waterfront and the historic Watergate Hotel.

BACKGROUND AND PHILOSOPHY

GW Summer Scholars has two residential programs for high school students: a six-week precollege program for high school juniors and ten-day minicourses for students in grades 9–11. The six-week residential program offers a unique opportunity for high school juniors to accelerate their college career and earn credit in a college-level course at a top-ranked university. In addition to complete integration in an intensive course with undergraduate students, Summer Scholars enroll in a writing course and participate in academic exploration semi-

nars. The ten-day noncredit minicourses are intensive and highly interactive seminars that introduce students to possible fields of academic interest.

The GW Summer Scholars Program draws upon the wealth of cultural and educational opportunities unique to Washington, D.C., and the greater metropolitan area to expand upon the range of enrichment and recreational activities available to participants. The program introduces students to the experience of independent living, while offering important educational resources and programs that enhance their understanding of college life.

PROGRAM OFFERINGS

The GW Summer Scholars six-week precollege program for juniors offers academic exploration and personal enrichment. Students enroll in credit-bearing courses. Course offerings represent a variety of academic disciplines and are taught by University faculty members.

A writing course integrates cultural exploration with the process of writing a college-level paper, developing critical writing and research skills that are applicable to any area of study. Academic Exploration seminars encourage students to explore the range of their academic interests and the variety of specialized learning communities within the university setting.

A practical focus on college readiness is addressed through weekly seminars that range from the college admissions process to career paths, study skills, and research strategies, promoting confidence and self-sufficiency in balancing the academic and social demands of college life. Enrichment opportunities extend beyond the classroom to include the cultural and educational resources of the Washington, D.C., area.

Noncredit minicourses are available to students in grades 9–11. These faculty-taught intensive seminars and workshops allow students to explore complex issues in potential fields of interest. The courses are highly interactive, engaging students in applied learning through in class activities and field trips to relevant sites around Washington, D.C.

ENROLLMENT

The Summer Scholars Program is a coeducational program that draws upon a diverse group of students from across the nation and around the world. Admission to the six-week precollege program is open to high school juniors with a B average or better. Minicourse programs are open to students in grades 9–11. Enrollment is limited.

DAILY SCHEDULE

A typical weekday in the Summer Scholars six-week program begins with breakfast in Ames Dining Hall. Students spend the day taking classes, studying, or attending a special program or seminar. On Friday mornings, students attend a required laboratory that is part of the Summer Scholars Writing Seminar. In the afternoon, students have the option of visiting an area college or exploring the sights. Saturdays include recreational activities, such as touring Baltimore Harbor, paddling the Potomac, or visiting the Kennedy Center of the Performing Arts. On Sundays, students are free to relax, social-

ize, and study. The schedule is flexibly structured so that students have sufficient time for study and recreation.

The noncredit minicourses are highly structured programs. Following breakfast, students are in classes from 9 a.m. to 4 p.m. Lunch breaks and short breaks are included. Students regularly accompany the course instructor on course-related field trips around the city. In the evenings, students enjoy a variety of organized recreational activities and special programs.

EXTRA OPPORTUNITIES AND ACTIVITIES

The program's location in Washington, D.C., provides students with a unique opportunity to enjoy the vibrant international and multicultural community of the nation's capital. Students discover that life in Washington, D.C., appeals to every possible interest, such as history, government, the arts, and entertainment. Summer Scholars have the opportunity to go shopping in Georgetown or to enjoy ethnic cuisine in Adams Morgan. Summer Scholars also participate in organized outings to a variety of destinations, such as national and historic sites, the Smithsonian, the Library of Congress, the U.S. Capitol, area universities, and recreational parks.

FACILITIES

Summer Scholars reside on the beautiful grounds of the Mount Vernon campus. Students have access to the campus facilities, including the library, computer labs, swimming pool, tennis courts, and top-notch recreational facilities. Students share double rooms on floors that are staffed by a Resident Advisor. Each room is furnished with beds, dressers, desks, a mini-refrigerator, and a microwave. Rooms are also cable ready and come equipped with phone jacks and Internet access. Vending machines, a TV, and a community lounge, complete with a kitchen, are available in the residence hall. Laundry facilities are also located inside the building. Entrance to the residence hall is secure, and the Mount Vernon campus is gated and staffed with on-site security 24 hours a day.

STAFF

A dedicated, on-site team coordinates the Summer Scholars Program, emphasizing a high degree of individual attention for every student. The Summer Scholars office is located less than a block from the residence halls. A full-time director manages the day-to-day activities. Highly trained, live-in Resi-

dent Advisors staff the residence halls and provide guidance and support 24 hours a day. Staff members accompany all planned group activities. The courses are taught by GW faculty members with years of experience teaching students at all levels of learning.

MEDICAL CARE

Although a very safe and healthy summer is anticipated, the GW Summer Scholars staff is prepared to handle emergencies. In the event of an illness or a medical emergency, Student Health Services is staffed and equipped to deal with most routine situations that require medical attention. If a situation requires hospital treatment, program staff members accompany the student to the nearest hospital and parents are immediately contacted.

COSTS

In 2007, the six-week precollege program costs were approximately $6100 for residential students. This included tuition for credit-bearing courses, a writing course, Academic Exploration, room, and partial board. Costs for students who commute were approximately $4200. Minicourses cost approximately $2400 per course and included tuition, room, and board; the commuter option cost approximately $1900. Textbooks, notebooks, and supplies are additional. Participants should plan to bring spending money for laundry, recreation, and incidental expenses. Tuition and fees for 2008 are available on the program Web site.

FINANCIAL AID

Limited need-based scholarship assistance is available for qualified applicants for the six-week precollege program only. Applicants for need-based scholarship assistance are required to fill out the Summer Scholars financial aid form and provide supporting documents.

TRANSPORTATION

Leaving on the half hour and operating until 7 p.m., the GW Shuttle links the two campuses with a scenic 15-minute ride down the hill to Foggy Bottom. The Foggy Bottom campus also has its own stop on the D.C. Metro, and both campuses are on Metro bus lines. The Mount Vernon campus is conveniently located near Washington-Dulles International Airport, Reagan National Airport, and Union Station. The Summer Scholars program is able to provide detailed information about transportation to and from these locations.

APPLICATION TIMETABLE

Applications are accepted on a rolling basis up until late May. Priority consideration is given to early applicants. Space is limited, and late applications are accepted pending space availability.

FOR MORE INFORMATION, CONTACT

GW Summer Scholars Program
The George Washington University
2100 Foxhall Road, NW
Washington, D.C. 20007
Phone: 202-242-6802
E-mail: scholars@gwu.edu
Web site: http://www.summerscholars.gwu.edu

GIRLS FIRST AT MADEIRA SCHOOL

SUMMER RESIDENTIAL ACADEMIC PROGRAM

MCLEAN, VIRGINIA

TYPE OF PROGRAM: Academic enrichment
PARTICIPANTS: Coeducational, ages 11 to 16
ENROLLMENT: Approximately 100 students per session
PROGRAM DATES: Two 2-week sessions from July 8 to August 3
HEAD OF PROGRAM: Douglas Murphy, Director

LOCATION
Madeira's 100-year history educating girls in grades 9–12 in the Washington, D.C., area has allowed the school to develop strong relationships with some of the capital's most influential professionals in order to provide girls with fresh intellectual possibilities. The 376-acre campus is just 12 miles from Washington, D.C., and the world-class array of cultural and historic destinations the United States' capital city has to offer.

BACKGROUND AND PHILOSOPHY
Girls First at Madeira School gives rising seventh to eleventh grade girls the chance to supplement their school-year studies with rigorous and fun class work and benefit from experiential learning through the guidance of successful women in a wide range of careers. Girls First students pursue a scholastic adventure of their choice while participating in a variety of enjoyable daily and nightly activities in a beautiful riverside setting 20 minutes from the nation's capital. Young women who attend Girls First don't just read textbooks; they engage in layered learning where classroom experiences are never removed from real-world applications.

PROGRAM OFFERINGS
Writer's Workshop. Imagination is welcomed and fostered in this workshop. However, as the participants learn, inspiration is only the beginning. Girls First also makes sure girls gain the ability to express themselves in a powerful and elegant way by exposing them to the technical side of the English language, feedback from a passionate audience, and the simple practice of writing regularly. The teachers are young creative writing professionals who are familiar with the classics of poetry and fiction, as well as essential contemporary works. Sylvia Plathe and Franz Kafka share time with Joshua Beckman and Sharon Olds. Girls First believes that a necessary step to becoming a good writer is learning to pay attention to the surrounding world; frequent field trips and outdoor exercises are an enjoyable and rewarding part of the curriculum.

Chinese Conversation and Culture. China is well on its way to becoming a global superpower, yet its culture and language are understood by few outside of the Far East. The Chinese conversation and culture class introduces girls to a society that has produced many of the world's technological and cultural achievements and a language, Mandarin, that is spoken by more people than any other. No past experience with Chinese is required for students in this class. Girls first learn the fundamentals of tonal languages, practicing pronunciation with their instructors and each other. Then they add vocabulary and grammar skills, all in the course of learning how to have basic conversations with Mandarin speakers. The teachers incorporate original ideas into a well-founded approach to language as well as the large Madeira campus and its multimedia capabilities, making the curriculum far more than just a traditional classroom experience.

Forensic Science. Many Americans have seen popular programs and movies showcasing forensic science—but how is crime scene investigation really accomplished? Girls First invites inquisitive minds to join its experienced instructors in its forensic science class. No previous experience is needed. The instructors start from scratch, teaching skills that, by the end of the course, allow the students to examine a mock crime scene and solve a realistic case.

One of the reasons Girls First teaches forensics is that it applies a broad spectrum of sciences toward answering fascinating questions about crime. By grappling with the intriguing mysteries of forensics, students acquire skills that they can apply in many analytic endeavors. Students gain experience with a number of scientific fields, like chemistry, biology, and physics—an experience that not only gives them a head start on their school year, but may blossom into a lifelong interest.

Veterinary Science. As recent disease scares have illustrated, the field of veterinary medicine is not only vital to animals, but also to human health. Veterinary scientists help ensure the safety of food supplies, protect humans from animal epidemics, and provide holistic care for some mankind's most beloved assistants and companions, be they dogs, horses, birds, or other, more exotic species. The course introduces girls to this fascinating, expanding field and its variety of advanced diagnostic and therapeutic methods. Learning about these techniques exposes students to medical study and treatment methods in general—an exposure that serves as a great leg up on any future medical or life science courses they may take. The teachers provide hands-on projects that immerse the students in the details of a specific veterinary issue, helping them learn far more than they would through abstract textbook learning. In demanding but fun laboratory examinations, students tackle real veterinary problems, and, in the process, gain a deep understanding of many different topics in biology and chemistry.

Performing Arts. Girls First invites girls of all ages and levels to its performing arts workshop, where they are challenged, supported, and taught in an open but demanding program. Girls study acting, singing, and dancing techniques, from classical to contemporary. They perform dramatic and comedic scenes as well as improvisations. The young, talented instructors use focused personal exercises and flexible group experiments to build strong skills. Girls discover that great acting is possible from anyone with the willingness to succeed, since it follows as much from education and preparation as natural talent. The immersive course creates an accepting and encouraging community of performers who are learning together, helping each other, and having a great time together. The small class size allows for frequent one-on-one tutoring tailored to each student's specific talents and needs. The program is designed to help students develop a wide range of skills that will serve them well when they leave the stage and participate in other experiences. Learning to be comfortable in front of an audience, to control one's body and voice, and to improvise assists in future public speaking situations and increases overall confidence and social skills.

Fashion Design. Fashion design is an exciting, fast-paced field in which some of America's most intelligent artists work. Girls First's talented instructors show girls that fashion design makes use of a great deal of academic knowledge as well as creativity and talent. They present scholarly material in a creative, hands-on environment and allow girls to immerse themselves in the tasks of designing a space or piece of clothing. No previous design or drawing experience is required, just eagerness to learn and the desire to create. The fashion design curriculum helps girls identify and respond to clothing trends, with the end result of planning their own themed clothing line and designing a garment. The classroom experience is supplemented by many on- and off-campus field trips where girls look at famous spaces and clothes and talk to professionals who give them an insider's view of the fashion and interior design industries. Girls leave the program with the ability and courage to explore their unique design concepts as well as with a sound understanding of the design process in general, one that will help them in an array of creative pursuits.

Architecture. Architecture is known as the science and art of designing buildings and structures, but it is so much more. A wider definition includes the design of the total built environment from the microlevel of furniture to the grand stage of urban planning. Throughout history the study has grown from the dynamics between needs—such as shelter, safety, and community areas—to the Bauhaus school and, ultimately, to postmodernism. Architecture is a fascinating blend of social science, art, technology, engineering, politics, history, and philosophy, and the resulting structures seek to manipulate light, space, volume, and texture in addressing abstract and functional needs. Girls who enroll in this course are introduced to the basic principles, modern questions, and history of the subject while also building models, designing landscapes, and visiting relevant structures in the area.

International Politics and Global Issues. It is more apparent today than ever before that America does not exist in a vacuum—events and conflicts in foreign countries have become just as important to Americans as domestic or local issues. Yet many people have little or no understanding of the complex international forces, religious factions, and ethnic groups that share and shape the world. The goal of the international politics and global issues course is not just to introduce students to the absorbing fields of international relations, political science, and diplomacy, but to make them informed, thoughtful, and influential global citizens. The instructors craft a curriculum that makes the discovery of international politics stimulating and enjoyable. World cultures and issues come alive through historical material, contemporary accounts, and multimedia presentations. Classroom teaching and individual research projects go hand-in-hand with lively group discussions and problem-solving sessions.

ENROLLMENT
There are approximately 100 students in each session.

DAILY SCHEDULE

7:30– 8:30 . . .	Breakfast
8:45– 9:00 . . .	Morning Meeting
9:15–10:15 . . .	Class Session 1
10:30–11:45 . . .	Class Session 2
12:00– 1:00 . . .	Lunch
1:15– 2:30 . . .	Class Session 3
2:45– 4:00 . . .	Class Session 4
4:15– 5:15 . . .	Activities/Sports/Free Time
5:30– . . .	Dinner
6:45– 8:00 . . .	Evening Options
8:15–11:00 . . .	Free Time/Entertainment

Each program's schedule may vary from the sample given above.

EXTRA OPPORTUNITIES AND ACTIVITIES
Girls First takes full advantage of the long summer days and Madeira's lovely, expansive campus in creating both organized and optional activities for the afternoons and evenings. Staff members' ideas, as well as student suggestions, contribute to forming a wide range of options, emphasizing social interaction, fun, and relaxation. Popular activities include a starlight tour of the Washington monuments, dining at ethnic restaurants in Georgetown, going to an WNBA Mystics game, seeing a show at the Wolf Trap Performing Arts Center, or visiting the Kennedy Center.

FACILITIES
Girls live in double rooms in Madeira's six attractive dormitories that combine modern conveniences with turn-of-the-century architectural charm. Each 25–30 girl house at Madeira has its own technology center, laundry room, and lounge. Students eat thoughtfully prepared, healthy, gourmet meals in a spacious, newly renovated dining hall. The forty-six classrooms at Madeira include a broad range of laboratory, computer, and multimedia features suited for the instructors' innovative educational purposes and the students' educational needs.

STAFF
Intelligent and energetic, the staff is the heart of the Girls First experience. From professional teachers to talented graduate and undergraduate students, all staff members participate in safety and training sessions. The maximum student-teacher ratio is 8:1. The staff members are not only experts in their disciplines but also have extensive backgrounds in teaching and working with teens.

MEDICAL CARE
Medical care is available 24 hours a day at nearby hospital facilities. All participants must submit comprehensive medical forms and proof of insurance.

COSTS
The tuition for each two-week session is $2395.

FINANCIAL AID
No financial aid is available at this time.

TRANSPORTATION
Airport pick-up and drop-off are available at either Washington-Reagan National Airport (DCA) or Washington-Dulles International Airport (IAD) for an additional fee.

APPLICATION TIMETABLE
Inquiries are welcome at any time. Applications are accepted until June 1. After June 1, acceptance to the program is based on availability, and applications must include a late fee of $100.

FOR MORE INFORMATION, CONTACT
Girls First at Madeira School
Madeira School
8328 Georgetown Pike
McLean, Virginia 22102

Phone: 800-883-4159 (toll-free)
E-mail: girlsfirst@madeira.org
Web site: http://www.madeira.org/girlsfirst

GLOBAL LEADERSHIP ADVENTURES

SUMMER PROGRAM

SOUTH AFRICA, COSTA RICA, BRAZIL, GHANA, INDIA

TYPE OF PROGRAM: International community service and leadership development
PARTICIPANTS: Coed, ages 15–18
ENROLLMENT: Rolling admission
PROGRAM DATES: Three-week sessions, June–August
HEAD OF PROGRAM: Andrew H. Motiwalla, Executive Director

LOCATION
Global Leadership Adventures (GLA) offers programs in Brazil, South Africa, Costa Rica, India, and Ghana. Fortaleza, Brazil, is best known for its stunning beaches and is one of the most diverse nations in the world. Cape Town is located on the coast of South Africa, a dynamic nation and one of the most inspirational on the continent. The country's 45 million people speak eleven official languages, and its cultural traditions come from Europe, Africa, and Asia. Costa Rica, with its spectacular rain forests and beautiful beaches, remains one of the few countries in Central America that has been free of armed conflict for decades. India has a fast-growing economy and is deeply rooted in tradition and spirituality. Ghana is Africa's first democracy and rich in traditional culture and music.

BACKGROUND AND PHILOSOPHY
In November 2004, Fred Swaniker founded the Summer Academy at Cape Town as part of the larger institution of the African Leadership Academy, a high school designed to train future political, social, and economic leaders of Africa. Believing that the lack of ethical leadership in Africa is at the root of the continent's greatest challenges that have prevented countries from realizing their full potential, he wanted to develop an effective training ground for future leaders and establish a strong network between these students, who—much like Nelson Mandela in South Africa or Mahatma Gandhi in India—could transform entire nations.

Because the focus of the African Leadership Academy is with African students, the Summer Academy at Cape Town was established to provide student leaders worldwide a space to learn together, challenge one another, and develop lifelong bonds. The

academy immediately became an effective model for bringing high school students worldwide together to study abroad in a meaningful way and affect lives through community service projects. To share this powerful experience and expand its global reach, the organization was renamed Global Leadership Adventures.

GLA is more than a high school summer camp or a community service program. Its main objective is to provide an avenue for future leaders of the world to obtain a more global view and a deeper understanding of the issues facing the planet. While the focus of the program is community service, it also combines travel, adventure, intellectual stimulation, discussion about world events and problems, and volunteer community service in a way that is safe and secure for teenagers who are in high school or just graduating. Its vision is to empower youth to be agents of positive change across borders. It provides students worldwide with exceptional programming in a caring environment that instills values of leadership through safe and integrated cultural experiences, including meaningful community service, an international student body, discussions about leadership and global issues, access to local leaders, and exciting excursions.

GLA believes that leaders are made and not born and that leadership is a critical life skill that can be developed. The program nurtures and develops teenagers, with these influential experiences preparing them for a lifetime of principled, ethical leadership.

PROGRAM OFFERINGS
GLA offers high school students around the world a challenging opportunity to develop and mature into global citizens and young leaders through experiential learning, volunteer work, and in-depth cultural interactions. All GLA programs are thoughtfully designed for students to experience the richness of each location's distinct culture. At the core of every program is a safe GLA experience that combines hands-on service opportunities, thought-provoking seminars, meetings with dynamic local leaders, cultural excursions, and connections with students from around the world. Ultimately, GLA offers students an exciting avenue for global learning and personal growth in a safe environment under the guidance of caring mentors.

All GLA volunteer projects are part of a greater plan to improve community life as a whole. Past projects include caring at a daycare center for infants and toddlers affected or infected by HIV/AIDS, planting community food gardens to provide fresh vegetables to local families, uplifting battered women's spirits by painting beautiful murals at their shelter and mentoring their children, running sports camps and activities for local youth, and preparing food for a soup kitchen that helps impoverished youth.

ENROLLMENT
GLA seeks curious and energetic students ages 15–18 from around the world who are eager to do community service, interact with people from different backgrounds, and learn about other cultures, histories, and languages. Participants in GLA come from all over the world, many from the United States and the United Kingdom. Over the last three years, thirty five countries and more than 150 of the world's top schools have been represented in the program.

DAILY SCHEDULE
The daily schedule includes a Language & Culture and Global Issues class in the morning and community service work every afternoon. Friday, Saturday, and Sunday are reserved for excursions to places of natural, cultural, and historical significance and include meeting leaders at NGOs.

EXTRA OPPORTUNITIES AND ACTIVITIES
The programs include excursions to each destination's most beautiful and culturally historic sites. Excursions range from hiking up Table Mountain in Cape Town and white-water rafting in Costa Rica to capoiera workshops on the beach in Brazil to visiting a temple in India or meeting a traditional healer in Ghana. In addition, students have the extraordinary opportunity to see leadership in action and visit project sites where individuals are making a difference in their communities. Every excursion is carefully selected, so students return home with memories to last a lifetime and a more holistic country experience.

FACILITIES
Students live together on a campus of a local private high school. In all campuses there are many amenities, including hot and cold water, library, Internet, and sports facilities. GLA aims to provide a great campus environment with comfortable housing, discussion rooms, and eating and recreational facilities in a self-contained area. Men's and women's residential areas are always separate.

STAFF
Each GLA program has a dedicated on-site leadership team comprising a director, an assistant director, and one mentor for every 10 students. Mentors are educators from some of the best high schools around the world. These passionate teachers facilitate rich discussions and reflection sessions that transform the students' experiences into lessons about leadership. Through their guidance in all non-classroom-related activities, mentors challenge students to think critically about world issues and to build strong friendship. As a role model, friend, and guide, each mentor helps students achieve their best.

MEDICAL CARE
Safety always comes first at GLA. Prior to the start of any program, all safety precautions, such as developing extensive emergency procedures, researching the best area hospitals, and hiring round-the-clock security personnel, are attended to and reevaluated. Once the program begins, on-site staff members prioritize the welfare and best interest of the students. All staff members are trained in first aid.

RELIGIOUS LIFE
The program is unable to provide avenues for worship but can accommodate some personal time on campus for spiritual reflection.

COSTS
GLA programs are all inclusive—the fee covers housing, in-country transportation, three full meals a day, health insurance, and entrance fees to all scheduled program activities. In 2007,

the fee is $4395—program fees are expected to increase moderately in 2008. Limited financial aid is available. Scholarship recipients are selected based on financial need.

TRANSPORTATION
Because a large number of participants travel from the United States and the United Kingdom, there are designated GLA flights from these countries to program destinations. Once students are accepted, they can choose to purchase tickets on these flights, which are accompanied by GLA a chaperone, or make their own arrangements to meet GLA staff members at destination airports. GLA has contracts with experienced local bus companies to transport staff members and students together for all official off-campus activities.

APPLICATION TIMETABLE
Students must complete the online application, submit one teacher recommendation, and pay a $395 application deposit. Admissions decisions are made on a rolling basis, usually within forty-eight hours, and spaces fill quickly. The deposit is refundable only if the student is not admitted.

FOR MORE INFORMATION, CONTACT:
Global Leadership Adventures
2633 Lincoln Boulevard #427
Santa Monica, California 90405

Phone: 860-927-0047 (toll-free)
Fax: 866-612-3697 (toll-free)
E-mail: info@globalleadershipadventures.com
Web site: http://www.globalleadershipadventures.com

PARTICIPANT/FAMILY COMMENTS

"I came to identify myself with and become close to people from other countries and backgrounds, while at the same time I learned to appreciate and admire their differences in culture and lifestyle. I feel not only more globally aware, but also more self-aware."—Katherine F., New York

"I have been inspired to continue reaching out to others. I am positive that I will come back to Africa some day to contribute what I can."—Ashley S., California

"The GLA experience forced me to challenge my views by exposing me to individuals with worldwide views. The enlightening debate provoked during the program has continued to influence my perspective, especially on matters of global relevance."—Mike C., England

GLOBAL WORKS

SUMMER PROGRAMS

COSTA RICA, FRANCE, ECUADOR AND THE GALAPAGOS ISLANDS, PUERTO RICO, IRELAND, SPAIN, FIJI ISLANDS/NEW ZEALAND, YUCATAN/MEXICO, CENTRAL MEXICO, MARTINIQUE, ARGENTINA, PERU, AND PANAMA

TYPE OF PROGRAM: International travel combining environmental and community service, cultural and language immersion, and outdoor adventure activities
PARTICIPANTS: Coeducational, high school students
ENROLLMENT: 13–18
PROGRAM DATES: Two to four weeks in the summer
HEAD OF PROGRAM: Erik Werner, Director/Owner

LOCATION
Global Works summer programs are located all over the world. Students live in places that range from small village homes in the mountains of Fiji to dormitories located just outside of the French Alps. Several Global Works programs offer homestays with families to increase language learning and cultural exchange. The Global Works home office is located in State College, Pennsylvania, but will soon be relocating to Boulder, Colorado.

BACKGROUND AND PHILOSOPHY
Global Works strives to provide high school students with rewarding community service and adventure travel programs that foster personal growth and promote social and cultural awareness for them and the communities they serve. Today's community- and service-minded youths make a difference in the global community as they live with and touch the lives of the people they serve. Days filled with meaningful projects, travel, and exposure to different cultures, are rounded out with just the right amount of adventure, fun, and play.

PROGRAM OFFERINGS
Costa Rica: Global Works offers several programs to Costa Rica, with various starting dates, durations, language learning options, and a multitude of adventure activities. All seven trips uncover the country's many treasures, from 12,000-foot mountain peaks to lush cloud forests and beautiful, pristine beaches. Service projects represent 60 percent of the experience. In cooperation with local community members, participants build health centers, community centers, school playgrounds, and bridges. They may assist in reforestation, help with conservation projects, or perform similar service. Nonproject time is spent white-water rafting, hiking through the cloud forests of Monteverde, swimming at the beach, playing soccer, or visiting new friends. All of the programs to Costa Rica include a ten- to twelve-day homestay with a village family, which encourages serious language learning. Homestays are carefully arranged, allowing participants to experience different customs, traditions, and foods and practice their language skills. All staff members are bilingual.

Fiji Islands: This trip captures the magic of these exotic South Pacific Islands. From the welcoming ceremonies of each village to the environmental and community-service projects, participants are treated to sun-filled days reminiscent of another time. Traditional Fijian hospitality is unsurpassed. Projects may include constructing *bures* (thatched huts), building a tree nursery, developing reforestation zones, and restoring community buildings. Participants truly feel as if they are part of each community. Adventure activities include SCUBA diving, snorkeling through beautiful reefs, hiking, swimming, and dancing. Participants experience island time and a beautifully different culture.

Puerto Rico: Global Works offers several trips to Puerto Rico, all of which focus on service and adventure. One of these trips has the added focus of Spanish language learning and a homestay. Projects always meet a community need and tend to focus on small construction projects. Adventure activities include SCUBA diving, hikes in the rain forest, snorkeling, sea kayaking, swimming, and visits to Old San Juan and Spanish forts. This is the trip for students looking for service, adventure, sun, and sand.

France: This journey takes students to three different regions of France for service projects and adventure activities. This is also a language program with a ten- to twelve-day homestay. French is spoken 80 percent of the time. Projects such as castle restoration, reforestation, and interpretive trail blazing, are cooperatively worked on by both the local community and Global Works members. When the group is not working on projects, time is spent rock climbing, biking, rafting, hiking, and visiting museums, chateaux, and medieval fortresses.

Ireland: The warm hospitality of Irish culture opens its doors to students through community projects. Projects include reforestation, painting playgrounds for elementary schools, and working with peace and reconciliation centers. Students participate in gaelic football, sightseeing, traditional Irish music nights, hiking, surfing, biking, and numerous other activities. Irish culture is filled with music, writers, warm hospitality, and wit. Western Ireland quenches the eyes with dramatic landscapes, seaside cliffs, lush green farms, and beautiful mountains. Participants experience the magic of the Emerald Isle.

Ecuador: Few countries compare to Ecuador in geographic and cultural diversity. The Andean highlands, mountain villages, dormant volcanoes, thermal baths, and cloud forest biospheres provide majestic settings for community projects, nature preserve construction, adventure activities, and friendly homestays. Homestays with village friends last ten to twelve days and provide a unique opportunity for serious language learning and cultural immersion. Students travel to the Galapagos Islands to see incredible wildlife

and visit Parque Nacional and the Darwin Stations, which are isolated biological preserves with numerous unique and threatened species. Participants contribute to projects assisting local communities and the environment.

Mexico–Yucatan: This is a journey through the Yucatan peninsula that most tourists never encounter. Participants sleep in a seventeenth-century Spanish hacienda, swim in an underground pool or *cenote*, live and interact with Mayan families during a ten day homestay, eat home-cooked Mexican meals, learn traditional dances, work on community projects, and snorkel on a small rustic island. Students experience the warmth of the people, Mexico's rich history, and the brilliant colors and flavors found in this beautiful country while also contributing to meaningful service projects in small communities.

Spain: Students are invited on a journey through Spain that combines old world charm; visits to renowned sites; homestays with warm, friendly families; and cultural and language immersion. Projects include working with a self-sustaining community on construction and greenhouse needs as well as helping in Senior Centers or group homes for individuals with physical challenges. Activities blend water sports, day excursions to the mountains, soccer, sightseeing in Madrid, and day hikes. A four-week college-credit Spanish language course is also offered in Spain, combining classroom language study, homestays, adventure activities, and service opportunities.

Panama: Students enjoy the beauty and diversity of Panama and its island beaches while learning Spanish and participating in community and environmental projects. This program includes a ten-to twelve-day homestay, during which time students improve their Spanish language skills and enjoy cultural exchange with the host family. Adventure activities include snorkeling, water sports, hiking, sightseeing, and visits to national parks and market towns.

Martinique: Surrounded by the exquisite waters of the Atlantic Ocean to the east and the Caribbean Sea to the west, this island is a portrait of paradise. The program includes a ten-day homestay where students will practice their French with warm families while working alongside local youth and taking in the culture and adventure activities available, such as snorkeling, SCUBA, hiking to waterfalls, cooking lessons, soccer, and much more.

Central Mexico: This program is highlighted with language study at the Cemenahuac Language School where students will spend approximately 5 to 7 hours per day in appropriate-level language classes as well as intercambios with local high school students. Other highlights include an Acapulco beach excursion, exploring the historic district of Mexico City, white water rafting on the Amacuzac River, exploring the mystical pyramids of Teotihuacan, and more.

Peru: Students should check with the home office regarding the Peru program.

Argentina: Participants experience an adventure that takes them through the buzz of Buenos Aires to the gaucho plains of the pampas and up to the mountains of the Andes. Students work on projects with local agencies in the historic neighborhood of La Boca, followed by a ten-day homestay in Posadas, where everyone practices their Spanish while staying with local families. An overnight trip to Igazu Falls will amaze, and then it's off to Mendoza and the Central Andes for skiing, snowboarding, sled rides, and more before relaxing and reminiscing in Buenos Aires and returning home.

ENROLLMENT
Global Works programs are open to participants who are 13 to 18 years old; several trips are divided into age-appropriate groups. Some trips require two years of secondary language study in French or Spanish. No special construction skills are needed—just a desire to have fun, participate, and be part of a community.

EXTRA OPPORTUNITIES AND ACTIVITIES
Serious language learning is available on the language-immersion programs to Argentina, Central Mexico, Martinique, Peru, France, Costa Rica, Puerto Rico, Ecuador, Panama, Spain, and Mexico. Global Works also provides certificates of participation after the completion of each program, which documents the service work completed. Students generally receive 40 to 70 hours of service credit.

FACILITIES
Depending on the day and the trip, students may stay in hostels, university dormitories, lodges in the wilderness, local villagers' homes, or tents on the beach.

STAFF
Skilled, knowledgeable, friendly, mature, and detail-oriented staff members are hired for Global Works programs. Leaders are chosen for their language skills, experience working with youth, flexibility, responsibility, organization, and ability to have fun. The staff-student ratio is 1:5, and each program has an on-site director who works closely with the home base in Pennsylvania.

COSTS
In 2007, tuition ranged from $2995 to $4995 for two to four weeks, depending on the destination. Airfare is additional; a group fare is offered when possible with staff accompanying the group.

TRANSPORTATION
Students are met and returned to designated airports on the opening and closing days of each program. Staff members travel with students on all international trips.

APPLICATION TIMETABLE
A $600 deposit (nonrefundable after March 1 and credited toward tuition) is due at the time of application. Applications are accepted on a rolling basis until programs fill. Most participants apply during the months of January, February, and March.

FOR MORE INFORMATION, CONTACT
Global Works, Home Office
1113 South Allen Street
State College, Pennsylvania 16801

Phone: 814-867-7000
Fax: 814-867-2717
E-mail: info@globalworkstravel.com
Web site: http://www.globalworkstravel.com

THE GOW SCHOOL SUMMER PROGRAM

CAMPING, ACADEMICS, AND WEEKEND OVERNIGHT TRIPS

SOUTH WALES, NEW YORK

TYPE OF PROGRAM: Academics, traditional camping activities, and weekend trips
PARTICIPANTS: Coeducational, ages 8–16
ENROLLMENT: 125
PROGRAM DATES: June 22 to July 26, 2008
HEAD OF PROGRAM: David Mendlewski, Director

LOCATION
South Wales is a rural community in the western part of New York State, approximately 25 miles southeast of Buffalo and a short drive from Niagara Falls and Toronto.

BACKGROUND AND PHILOSOPHY
The Gow School Summer Program was created for girls and boys who are experiencing academic difficulties and have learning differences but possess the potential for success. The programs are composed of a carefully considered balance between academics, traditional camp activities, and weekend overnight trips. At summer's end, camper-students go home confident, relaxed, and prepared for the coming school year.

The academic program provides young people with an opportunity to improve their academic skills and achieve personal victories over those things that stand in the way of their success. A summer at Gow not only provides remediation and enrichment in the academic program but also allows for a fun and engaging summer full of new experiences, opportunities, and friendships. The Gow School is dedicated to providing camper-students with a balance between academics and traditional camp activities.

PROGRAM OFFERINGS
The program is one of balance—solid academics and strong athletic, social, cultural, and recreational activities. The weekly program combines structure and focus with flexibility and choice. Gow strives to develop the skills and natural abilities of each person while encouraging a sense of enthusiasm and positive self-image.

Academic program Since all the students have experienced past academic difficulties or learning differences, the democ-

racy of common problems begins to erase self-consciousness, and self-esteem increases. Classes have an average enrollment of 3 to 6 students and meet five days per week. An optional postlunch tutorial supervised by faculty members, many focus programs, a word processing/computer literacy course, and a comprehensive language course are offered.

Daily drills and written work are stressed, and all classes focus on motivation, positive mental attitude, organization, study skills, social growth, confidence, and self-esteem.

Traditional camp and weekend trips Camping can contribute to a young person's life in a way that few other experiences can. The program goals are for each camper to have a pleasant, fun-filled summer; improve skills; and develop confidence, self-control, inner discipline, good sportsmanship, and self-esteem. Campers unskilled in particular activities are channeled into special instruction so that they may become more proficient and develop a feeling of adequacy. As they continue to grow in confidence, they are able to take their place with their peers and contribute successfully. Character development and citizenship are stressed at all times.

Activity Instruction Clinics (AICs) are one-week individually chosen options that offer more focus, skill, and individual attention. Optional Period activities include creative arts and individual and team sports, with an emphasis on playing sports over instruction in the sport.

In addition to daily activities, campers take advantage of the rich geographical setting with overnight trips on weekends, including educational, cultural, pioneering, and canoe trips.

ENROLLMENT
Campers come from all over the United States and the world and are generally language disabled, underachieving, and/or experiencing academic difficulty.

DAILY SCHEDULE

7:30	Wake-up
8:00	Breakfast
8:30–12:45	Four academic periods
12:45	Lunch and rest period
2:00– 5:00	Three camp activity periods
6:00	Group meetings and camp lineup
6:10	Dinner
7:15	Evening activity
8:30	In dorms
8:45– 9:45	Late-night activity
10:00–11:00	Lights-out

EXTRA OPPORTUNITIES AND ACTIVITIES
Special events include a carnival, Icky Olympics, a softball league World Series, casino night, big/little-brother and big/little-sister activities, campfires, talent shows, and the last-night banquet and rock ceremony. There is also a counselor-in-training (CIT) program for older campers.

FACILITIES

The buildings include the Main Building (1926), which houses classrooms, the Health Center, and the Govian Book Store. The library contains a reading room, book stacks capable of storing 10,000 volumes, and classrooms. Orton Hall contains classrooms, a science laboratory, a spacious study hall, and a state-of-the-art computer resource center. There are six comfortable dormitories on campus. The recently renovated Thompson Building (1980 and 2005) contains the Simms Family Theater, a painting and drawing studio, a ceramics and 3-D art studio, a digital lab, and a metal shop for the applied technology class. In 2002, the Gow Center opened. It contains three squash courts, a basketball court, an indoor tennis/lacrosse facility, a 3,000-square-foot weight room, locker rooms, and a social/recreation area. The physical plant is valued at more than $7 million. The school has facilities for tennis, basketball, volleyball, baseball, softball, soccer, lacrosse, weight lifting, archery, golf, wrestling, floor hockey, ceramics, painting, arts and crafts, trail hiking, a ropes course, and fishing. The swimming program makes use of a nearby natatorium. The equestrian program makes use of a local riding stable.

STAFF

Most of the camp's academic instructors come from the Gow School's regular faculty. The dorm counselors and coaches are college students, graduate students, and teachers, some of whom are alumni of the Gow School and Summer Programs. The staff members are selected on the basis of character, stability, interest in working with young people, warmth, personality, education, and the ability to teach a skill. An extensive orientation period is held. Emphasis is given to the development of friendships, regard for others, and a sense of community.

MEDICAL CARE

The resident camp nurse works with the local physician. There is a 24-hour ambulatory center about 15 minutes away, and Buffalo hospitals are about 30 minutes away.

COSTS

Tuition for the 2008 program is $5975 (for those who register before May 1, the cost is $5700). This charge is comprehensive and includes the cost of instruction, lodging in dormitories, all meals, course materials, and transportation to and from the airport. It also includes day trips and all weekend excursions and tours. The tuition should be paid in full by May 15.

FINANCIAL AID

Scholarships are available on a limited basis, according to need and are granted on a first come, first served timetable.

TRANSPORTATION

Campers are met by counselors at the Buffalo International Airport, the Greyhound station, or the Amtrak station on opening day and dropped off accordingly on the final day.

APPLICATION TIMETABLE

The Summer Program has a rolling admission policy. Students should submit their application with two school recommendations, a current grade report, and a handwritten letter from the camper. Personal interviews and tours of the campus are encouraged and available year-round. The application form should be completed and returned as soon as possible.

FOR MORE INFORMATION, CONTACT

David Mendlewski, Director
The Gow Summer Programs
South Wales, New York 14139
Phone: 716-652-3450
Fax: 716-687-2003
E-mail: summer@gow.org

THE GRAND RIVER ACADEMY

SUMMER ACADEMY

AUSTINBURG, OHIO

TYPE OF PROGRAM: Residential academic program, enrichment and credit, and English as a second language
PARTICIPANTS: Coeducational; ages 14–18, grades 9–12
ENROLLMENT: Maximum of 100
PROGRAM DATES: June 24 to August 3, 2007
HEAD OF PROGRAM: Randy Blum, Headmaster

LOCATION
The Grand River Academy is located on a 200-acre campus in the rural town of Austinburg, in northeastern Ohio's Western Reserve. The campus is 1 hour east of Cleveland and 2 hours west of Pittsburgh.

BACKGROUND AND PHILOSOPHY
The Academy is nationally recognized as one of the few remaining nonmilitary, nonsectarian boys' boarding schools in the United States. Although the Grand River Academy is committed to single-sex education, in response to parents' requests that their daughters also have an opportunity to benefit from the Academy's unique program, the six-week summer academy is a coeducational boarding program.

The summer program is fundamentally designed as an extension of the Academy's winter school. The goal is to prepare students, including those not working to their potential, for a successful college education. During summer, as in the winter session, attention is paid to physical, emotional, and social growth in a community where concern for each individual's needs is emphasized. Each day is structured in order to provide students with a harmonious blend of academics and fun activities.

PROGRAM OFFERINGS
During the six-week summer academy, a student can strengthen an academic area or investigate a new subject. The program emphasizes small classes (2–5 students per class) and individual attention.

The Academy typically offers most college-preparatory courses each summer. Students may complete only 1 credit

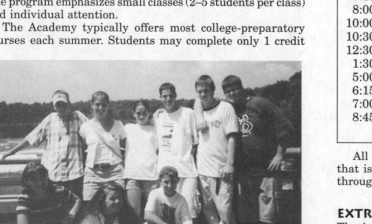

each summer. Written reports from teachers, with percentage grades, summarize individual student progress every week.

Students attend class for 4 hours each morning; several activity options are available each afternoon. As in the regular school year, all teachers live on campus and are available for extra help in the afternoon and during a supervised evening study period.

ENROLLMENT
Students enroll from throughout the United States and several other countries. The Academy offers a diverse population with roughly an equal number of boys and girls. Applicants of any race, color, or national or ethnic origin are welcome.

DAILY SCHEDULE

7:15– 7:45	Breakfast
8:00–10:00	Class
10:00–10:30	Morning break
10:30–12:30	Class
12:30– 1:15	Lunch
1:30– 5:00	Recreational activities
5:00– 6:00	Free time
6:15– 7:00	Family-style dinner
7:00– 8:45	Free time
8:45–10:45	Study period
11:00	Lights-out

All accepted students receive a handbook. The structure that is a cornerstone of the Academy's educational program throughout the year continues in the summer.

EXTRA OPPORTUNITIES AND ACTIVITIES
The Academy's North Coast location offers an impressive array of social and cultural options. Students may enjoy professional baseball games, paintball games, local amusement parks, concerts, Lake Erie beaches, regular Friday night

dances, and Saturday night movies at a local theater. All activities and field trips are carefully scheduled and supervised by a faculty member.

FACILITIES
Everyone makes use of the Academy's abundant facilities, which include classroom buildings, five dormitories, an air-conditioned library, a fine arts area, the student union, a gymnasium, a weight room, tennis courts, soccer, baseball, and paintball fields, and a beach volleyball court. An excellent golf course is also available nearby for recreation.

STAFF
The summer faculty comprises members of the winter school staff.

MEDICAL CARE
A licensed nurse is on staff and on call at all times to respond to student health needs from the Academy's well-equipped infirmary.

COSTS
Tuition, room, and board for the 2007 summer academy were $3500 for seven-day boarding students and $3300 for five-day boarding students. In addition, parents should plan on ap-

proximately $500 for such things as laundry, books, and entertainment. An allowance account can be set up at the parents' request.

TRANSPORTATION
The Academy is easily accessible by car or bus. Transportation is available to campus from the Cleveland Hopkins International Airport. There is an extra charge for this service.

APPLICATION TIMETABLE
Applications should be accompanied by a nonrefundable $25 processing fee. Upon notification of acceptance, a nonrefundable $500 deposit is due to hold a place in the program. Upon receipt of the deposit, an I-20 Certificate of Eligibility is sent to foreign nationals for U.S. immigration purposes.

A visit to campus is not required but may be arranged with the admissions office.

FOR MORE INFORMATION, CONTACT
Office of Admission
The Grand River Academy
3042 College Street, P.O. Box 222
Austinburg, Ohio 44010

Phone: 440-275-2811
Fax: 440-275-3275
E-mail: academy@grandriver.org
Web site: http://www.grandriver.org

PARTICIPANT/FAMILY COMMENTS

"I have made ties with people all over the world . . . an unforgettable experience."—Rachel Kroner, Geneva, Ohio

"GRA not only helped me pass a class, but I also learned about different cultures."—Will Modic, Cleveland, Ohio

"GRA Summer School is even better than Burger King."—Sergei Timofeev, Moscow, Russia

"Summer School was great . . . but I like the food better in Puerto Rico."—Jose Luis "Bubba" Morales, San Juan, Puerto Rico

"I learned how to have fun and get my work done."—Jackson Robb, Charleston, South Carolina

HARVARD SECONDARY SCHOOL PROGRAM

SUMMER SCHOOL

CAMBRIDGE, MASSACHUSETTS

TYPE OF PROGRAM: College-level academic
PARTICIPANTS: Coed residential or commuter students who are completing grade 10, 11, or 12 and are fluent in English
ENROLLMENT: 1,000
PROGRAM DATES: June 21–August 15, 2008

LOCATION

Harvard University Summer School is in Cambridge, Massachusetts. By subway, Harvard is only minutes from downtown Boston. Cambridge is popular with young people and is considered the ultimate college town. There are bookstores, music stores, sidewalk cafés, shops, and ethnic restaurants.

BACKGROUND AND PHILOSOPHY

The Harvard Summer School, the oldest summer session in the United States, was founded in 1871. The Harvard Secondary School Program was developed to offer academically motivated high school students a college experience, enabling them to make better-informed decisions about their academic future.

PROGRAM OFFERINGS

Secondary school students take college courses along with college students, and they earn college credit. During the eight- or four-week summer sessions, Harvard offers nearly 300 courses in more than sixty liberal arts fields. Areas of study include anthropology, computer science, foreign languages, astronomy, natural sciences, classics, expository and creative writing, drama, economics, fine arts, studio arts, government, history, linguistics, literature, mathematics, and music, among others. Most Summer School faculty members have Harvard affiliations during the academic year, but instructors also are recruited from other universities.

ENROLLMENT

Harvard's academic resources and distinguished reputation attract people of all ages, backgrounds, and nationalities. Last year, more than 5,000 students from all areas of the United States and ninety other countries attended Harvard Summer School. Selected on the basis of their high school grades, school recommendations, and College Board scores, secondary school men and women who have finished the tenth, eleventh, or twelfth grade make up one fifth of the Summer School population. Approximately 90 percent of the secondary school participants live in dormitories on campus; the remaining 10 percent commute.

DAILY SCHEDULE

Secondary school resident students must enroll in eight units of credit; 4- and 8-unit courses are offered. Sophomores must take a writing or math class; they choose a second class from a selected list. Four-unit courses meet either daily for 1 hour or twice weekly for 2½ hours. Eight-unit courses meet for 2 or more hours per day. Commuting students take either 4 or 8 units of study. Summer school students eat meals together in a campus dining hall three times a day, seven days a week. Students are given freedom and responsibility to establish their own priorities and manage their own time.

EXTRA OPPORTUNITIES AND ACTIVITIES

Harvard Summer School, Cambridge, Boston, and the New England region offer a multitude of summer activities. The Summer School sponsors movies, concerts, dances, social gatherings, and day trips in Boston and around New England. The College Choices Program offers tours of other New England colleges, a workshop on writing college applications, and a college fair attended by thirty colleges. Students may audition to join the Summer School Chorus, or Orchestra; all students may join the Pops Band. Students can join intramural sports teams, learn to row, attend professional sports events, perform in the talent show or the trivial bowl, or volunteer for community service projects in the area.

FACILITIES

Harvard University's resources are exceptional. A distinguished faculty, well-equipped laboratories, fine museums, many athletic facilities, and the largest university library system in the world are available to Summer School students.

Secondary school students live with other secondary school students in dormitories in and near Harvard Yard. Several of the dormitories are more than a century old, and the furnishings are simple.

STAFF

A carefully chosen resident proctor (a Harvard College undergraduate) serves as an adviser during the summer to provide support and guidance—suggesting activities, helping students find their way around Cambridge and Boston, and inviting students to weekly study breaks. Proctors are assigned an average of 20 students each.

Each proctor serves under the guidance of an assistant dean. Assistant deans live in dormitories and work with their proctors to develop a sense of community and to guarantee appropriate conditions for study.

The director of the Secondary School Program, along with her staff and 3 assistant deans, is responsible for the campus life and academic welfare of Secondary School Program students. There is always a Secondary School Program dean on call.

MEDICAL CARE

All Summer School students are required to have health insurance against major illnesses and accidents. Students who do not have such coverage with an American carrier must buy it through the Summer School. The outpatient facilities of the University Health Services are available 24 hours a day for urgent care needs. The Stillman Infirmary, an on-campus hospital facility, is available for acute inpatient care.

RELIGIOUS LIFE

Harvard University has no religious affiliation, but opportunities for worship are available on or near campus for members of many faiths.

COSTS

In 2007, costs per 4-unit course were as follows: application fee, $50; tuition, $2275 ($4550 for 8 units); room and board, $3975 for the eight-week session, $2020 for the four-week session; health insurance, $110. Late fees also apply after payment deadlines.

TRANSPORTATION

Harvard University is located approximately 6 miles from Logan International Airport in Boston. Transportation to and from the airport is available by taxi or public transportation.

APPLICATION TIMETABLE

Applicants are admitted to the Secondary School Program and notified on a rolling basis until the program fills—i.e., there is no specific application deadline. The Secondary School Program welcomes inquiries at any time throughout the year.

FOR MORE INFORMATION, CONTACT

Harvard Secondary School Program
51 Brattle Street
Cambridge, Massachusetts 02138-3722

Phone: 617-495-3192
E-mail: ssp@hudce.harvard.edu
Web site: http://www.ssp.harvard.edu

HAWAI'I PREPARATORY ACADEMY

SUMMER SESSION

WAIMEA, HAWAII (BIG ISLAND)

TYPE OF PROGRAM: Academic enrichment, boarding and day

PARTICIPANTS: Boys and girls entering grades 6–12

ENROLLMENT: 120

PROGRAM DATES: Mid- to late June to mid- to late July

HEAD OF PROGRAM: Shirley Ann K. Fukumoto

LOCATION

Hawaii Preparatory Academy (HPA) is one of the premier college-preparatory boarding and day schools in the Pacific region. The school has two campuses in Waimea on the island of Hawaii. The Upper Campus, which hosts the Summer Session program, is located on 220 acres at the foot of the Kohala Mountains, in the heart of Hawaii's ranching country. The Village Campus is housed on a separate 8-acre campus just 2 miles away.

A special aspect of HPA is its use of Hawaii's unique geographical and social setting. Through many courses and activities, the school gives students a strong sense of Hawaii and its culture.

HPA is a 45-minute drive from the Kona International Airport. There are many daily, direct flights to Kona from the Honolulu International Airport. Flight time is about 40 minutes.

BACKGROUND AND PHILOSOPHY

The HPA Summer Session, which was established in 1974, offers enrichment and unique study opportunities in English, science, and culture for boarding students and a limited number of day students entering grades 6–12. The program, which enrolls boys and girls from throughout the world, runs for four weeks, from late June to late July.

Summer Session offers new and prospective HPA students an excellent introduction to the school's program and instructors. Many students return every summer to take advantage of the outstanding program and staff and to meet students from around the world.

PROGRAM OFFERINGS

Upper School students can select from the following 2-hour academic and elective courses: algebra I, analytical college reading, art explorations, ceramics, college planning, creative writing, culture of Hawaii, drivers education, electronics, environmental art, golf, hands-on science, marine biology, mixed-media production, photography, prealgebra, reading/study skills, SAT preparation (math and verbal), service learning, and 3-D art. ESL courses include discussion through film, grammar (beginning, intermediate, and advanced), introduction to science, and writing (intermediate and advanced).

Middle School offerings include algebra I, art explorations, ceramics, creative writing, electronics, environmental art, exploring the Big Island, hands on Hawaii, marine biology, mixed-media production, photography, prealgebra, problem solving in math, and reading/study skills. ESL courses include art/writing, grammar (beginning, intermediate, and advanced), performing arts, and writing (intermediate and advanced).

These courses are predominantly for enrichment and do not offer credit. Many courses—particularly in the sciences—include field trips as part of the curriculum.

ENROLLMENT

HPA's diverse students come predominantly from the Hawaiian Islands, the U.S. mainland, and the Pacific Rim nations.

DAILY SCHEDULE

On Monday through Friday, students attend three courses (two 2-hour morning courses and one 2-hour afternoon course). There are afternoon sports until 5 p.m. A 1-hour study hall follows the buffet dinner and ends with a social period and then lights out. Weekend excursions include trips to state and national parks such as Volcanoes National Park, cultural sites, snorkel cruises, and ocean sports.

EXTRA OPPORTUNITIES AND ACTIVITIES

Optional sports include instruction in horseback riding, scuba certification, movement/dance, and tennis. On Saturday, buses take students to the beach and shopping areas. Students can also go to the movies or on camping excursions.

During the last few afternoons of the Summer Session sports program, students participate in the "mini Olympics," which includes many nonathletic and athletic team events. The final summer and Olympics event is the talent show, which is presented on the last evening of the Summer Session program. Parents are encouraged to come to the campus a day early to join their children at this event.

FACILITIES

Ten buildings on the Upper Campus house multiple classrooms, the Kono Institute of English Studies, Castle Lecture Hall, the Science and Technology Center, and Davenport Music Center and rehearsal rooms. Other academic facilities include the Gates Performing Arts Center, the Dyer Memorial Library, the Gerry Clark Art Center, Davies Chapel, and a 4,100-square-foot student union.

Athletic facilities include the award-winning Rutgers Tennis Center, Castle Gymnasium, the Nakamaru Fitness Center, Dowsett Swimming Pool, a cross-country course, a track, a tack room, and football, baseball, soccer, and polo fields.

Three residence halls on the Upper Campus house students in double and sometimes triple rooms. Each room has beds and built-in closets, shelves, desks, and dressers. The rooms are equipped with telephone connections and computer access to the campuswide computer network and the Internet. Each building has a central lounge and laundry facilities. Faculty members and residential assistants provide supervision.

The recently renovated restaurant-style dining facilities are located in the Taylor Commons. Also located in this building are the Academics and Student Life Center, Accounting/Business Office, Auxiliary Programs/Summer Sessions Office, Health Services, and digital audio/visual laboratory.

STAFF

The teaching staff consists of regular school faculty members as well as teachers from Hawaii and around the world. Teachers take a personal interest in every student and often serve as advisers and dorm parents.

Faculty and staff members, most of whom are regular school faculty members or college students who are HPA alumni, supervise the dormitories and excursions.

MEDICAL CARE

Students must have a physical examination and a TB test prior to arrival. HPA has a fully equipped Health Services Center, and a nurse is on duty or on call at all times. For more serious emergencies, the North Hawaii Community Hospital is located 3 miles from the campus.

COSTS

Tuition covers instruction, room, board, books, most group activities, and excursions. Airfare and ground transportation, optional sports, and personal expenses are extra. Costs in 2007 included a $30 application fee ($25 when applying online), tuition ($4000), an equestrian program ($450), tennis instruction ($375), and scuba certification ($425).

TRANSPORTATION

Participants fly directly into Kona International Airport from Honolulu, the U.S. mainland, or Japan. For students flying into Honolulu first, the school can assist with travel arrangements to Kona (additional fees apply). The school also can arrange for transportation to and from Kona International Airport at the beginning and end of the summer session (additional fees apply).

APPLICATION TIMETABLE

Applications are accepted from January 1 until April 15. Late applications are considered on a space-available basis. Notification of acceptance starts March 15. Upon acceptance, students are required to pay a $500 nonrefundable reservation deposit and return the registration materials with course selections.

FOR MORE INFORMATION, CONTACT

Shirley Ann Fukumoto
Auxiliary Programs Office
Hawai'i Preparatory Academy
65-1692 Kohala Mountain Road
Kamuela, Hawaii 96743

Phone: 808-881-4088
Fax: 808-881-4071
E-mail: summer@hpa.edu
Web site: http://www.hpa.edu

HUMANITIES SPRING IN ASSISI

HUMANITIES SPRING IN ASSISI
Santa Maria di Lignano, 206081 Assisi ITALY

HUMANITIES SPRING IN ASSISI

ASSISI, ITALY

TYPE OF PROGRAM: Arts and academic travel-study program based in Assisi, Italy
PARTICIPANTS: Coeducational, students completing grades 9–12
ENROLLMENT: 12
PROGRAM DATES: Late June through late July
HEAD OF PROGRAM: Jane R. Oliensis, Director

LOCATION

Humanities Spring in Assisi (HSIA) is based in a turn-of-the-century schoolhouse in the hills outside Assisi, Umbria, but students also travel widely in Italy—as far north as Florence and Venice and south to Pompeii, Paestum, and the Amalfi Coast—to experience firsthand some of the best art and architecture of all time. For the program's core 2½ weeks, Assisi becomes home, with its fairy-tale castle; grass-filled Roman amphitheater; *infiorata* (festival of flowers); piazza del commune, with its impromptu concerts, classical and jazz; ice-cream cafés; and the Basilica of St. Francis, bursting with sunlight and its joyful, experimental frescoes. Students live in double or single rooms with views of fields, plum trees, and mountains. In afternoon and day trips, students get to know many nearby Umbrian cities, including Perugia, a lively university town where students see a frescoed Renaissance wall street, climb down a monumental Etruscan well, and then sit on the Duomo steps and listen to jazz at Perugia's famous Umbria Jazz Festival; Bevagna, with its Roman bath, sparkling mosaics, and ancient Romanesque churches; and Spoleto, where students see a cyclopic wall and watch a contemporary ballet, performed outside in Spoleto's Roman Theater. Whether they are in Assisi; off on a six-day trip to Florence and Venice to learn about Michelangelo, listen to opera in the Bobili gardens, visit the Doge's palace, or ride the traghetto down the grand canal; or on a weeklong trip to the breathtaking Amalfi Coast, with its lemon groves, beaches with spectacular views, Doric temples, and ancient Greek and Roman cities, students always have a quiet and pleasant home base to come back to, where they can relax and absorb what they've studied and what they've seen on trips.

BACKGROUND AND PHILOSOPHY

Humanities Spring's methods are hands-on and site-specific. Ms. Oliensis founded HSIA in 1991 to bring Classical and Italian Renaissance art and literature to life for American students. Students constantly experience great art and literature in situ, in their original historical and artistic contexts—Propertius in Assisi, Michelangelo in Florence, or fairy-tale Gothic architecture in Venice. HSIA is committed to the belief that great art and literature can make students' lives happier and more complete, help students to solve problems, and understand themselves better. From the very first day, students write about and/or sketch what they see and learn to use great art and literature—from classical to contemporary—as a springboard for journals, poems, sketches, and their own individual development.

Conversation is the keynote at Humanities Spring. Students learn inside the classroom and out. Trips illuminate classes, just as classes help students connect more deeply with what they see on trips. The method at Humanities Spring is interdisciplinary and experiential. Students study Ruskin on the history of Venice's whimsical Gothic arches and then are on the lookout for signature (number 4) arches as they ride Venice's traghetto down the Grand Canal, or they pick a symbol they especially love from one of Ravenna's sparkling Byzantine mosaics and then decipher it back at the Humanities Spring library loft. They may also compare Robert Browning's *Fra Lippo Lippi* with their own reactions to Lippi's rainbow-colored fresco cycle in Spoleto. In the pastoral poetry class, students

use observation and mythology to explain why the Venus's mirror, a wildflower growing in the fields around Humanities Spring, is named after that goddess.

As a community, HSIA fosters the spirit of collaboration, both in and out of the classroom. Conversation is at the heart of the HSIA experience. Students do homework and chores together and comment on each other's paintings-in-progress, sketches, or poems they are writing. There are no grades at Humanities Spring (except for a frequent *bravo!* or *bravissima!*). Students have occasionally obtained credit at their high schools for HSIA courses.

PROGRAM OFFERINGS

Students at HSIA create their own individual curricula. Most students take two or three morning classes and at least one afternoon activity. All classes are based on discussion of the literature they read, the art they study and see on trips, and student work.

Italian 1: Intensive grammar, syntax, and conversation offer students full immersion. Students write short compositions from day one, memorize conversations, and read everything from short contemporary poems to comic medieval fables.

Italian 2: Students read and discuss (in Italian!) a different text each year. The HSIA 2007 text is Calvino's wonderful imaginary travelogue *Città Invisibili*. The class also studies vocabulary and grammar in the context of Calvino, and students write at least one *città invisibile* of their own.

Cities—A History of Public and Private Space: Students travel to see Greek, Roman, medieval, and Renaissance cities; study different ideas of public buildings and of home; and write short compositions, often using their hometowns as a point of departure.

The Italian Renaissance: Age of Experiment—Poetry, Painting, and Architecture: The 2007 theme is From Medieval to Renaissance, and the course concentrates on the discovery of imagination in the pivotal (and experimental!) Renaissance figures of St. Francis, Dante, and Giotto. Assisi, a city that was so important to all three, is the program's primary textbook. Students also make many study-trips and keep a journal and/or sketchbook for this course.

Classical Poetry in Context: In the **Latin Unit,** students read Propertius's poems in relation to the archaeology of Assisi, his hometown, with its Latin inscriptions, Roman amphitheaters, temples, beautiful *casa di Properzio,* and more. In the **Greek Unit,** students make the connection of Homer's *Iliad* and *Odyssey* with Greek (and related Etruscan) paintings and vase paintings all over Italy; students travel to see wonderful Perugia, Tarquinia, Florence, Pompeii, and Paestum.

ENROLLMENT
Humanities Spring in Assisi is for students who are interested in poetry and art, classics, ice cream, adventure, and the Italian language and culture. Students do not need to have any previous or background knowledge of art history, Latin, Greek, Italian, or archaeology to get a lot out of their Humanities Spring experience. The only essentials for HSIA students are enthusiasm and the desire to learn. Humanities Spring finds that diverse backgrounds and interests make the summer more fruitful and stimulating for everyone. Students come from all over the United States and Italy.

DAILY SCHEDULE
A day at Humanities Spring:

```
      9:00 . . . breakfast
 9:30–10:30 . . . classes
10:30–10:55 . . . merenda (snack), IISIA favorites include peach
                  tea and Italian animal crackers
11:00–12:30 . . . classes
      1:00 . . . Italian lunch (pranzo)—un primo, un secondo,
                  ed un dolce—dessert!
 3:30– 4:00 . . . trip prep—students read (in Italian) about
                  what they are going to see that day
 4:00– 7:30 . . . trip or activities
      8:00 . . . dinner
```

Students also do their half-hour chores (making dog pasta, gardening, sweeping, and others) some time in the morning before lunch.

Evening Activities: Two or three evenings a week, HSIA goes out to jazz concerts, operas, festivals, ballets, local processions, or puppet shows. HSIA usually meets before events in a piazza or ice-cream caffè to read program notes and discuss plots and musical motifs to help students get oriented and experience more directly what they are going to see. One night a week, usually on Fridays, wonderful Italian cakes are served at Serate: play readings, films (Passolini's Decameron is an HSIA favorite), or guest lecturers. Students take turns choosing cakes at the extraordinary Sensi Pasticceria.

Other evenings, students go into Assisi for open-air concerts—improvised or scheduled, for ice cream, and for the gentle hum of piazza life, or they stay at home to do homework, stargaze, take a long walk, or just talk with other students, staff members, and HSIA visitors.

EXTRA OPPORTUNITIES AND ACTIVITIES
Students spend three days in bungalows near the Venetian Lido. Canals, bridges, whimsical Gothic facades—all of Venice is a fairy tale. Students tour the city on foot and by vaporetto and experience firsthand Venice's sparkling mosaics, peach- and raspberry-colored palazzi, and wonderful Renaissance paintings.

Students also spend three days in Florence, studying Michelangelo and the Boboli gardens, Botticelli and the Duomo, Giotto's bell tower, and all the wonderful bridges. They get a sense of the extraordinary aesthetic at the core of the Renaissance. During the

evenings, they watch street theater in the Piazza della Signoria. Students stay in a pretty (air-conditioned) bed-and-breakfast near Santa Croce.

HSIA also goes south for a week to tour Pompeii (both the domus and the public buildings); Paestum, the ancient Greek city with its three extraordinary Greek temples; Naples' archaeological museum; and the breathtaking Amalfi Coast, famous for its pottery, lemon groves, Roman villas, and beautiful medieval cities with their exotic Saracen flavor. Students stay at the Hotel Mandetta in Paestum, a small elegant hotel with a beautiful private beach.

FACILITIES
Humanities Spring in Assisi is in Santa Maria di Lignano in the midst of the breathtaking national park of Monte Subasio, its home base for 2½ weeks. Students swim in the waterfalls at the Humanities Spring near the school and go for walks and bike rides all over Santa Maria di Lignano. Students may also go horseback riding through the woods and fields at a nearby agriturismo.

Students may also help Elia and Vittorio, HSIA's wonderful neighbors, feed the chickens or make hay at the beautiful working farmhouse next to Humanities Springs. Students may also garden in the HSIA vegetable garden and small herb garden. Students who take the herb and flower afternoon activity sometimes brew interesting medieval teas for the rest of the group.

STAFF
The Humanities Spring staff of 7 includes art historians and painters, poets, and archaeologists. All hold degrees from distinguished universities in the United States and in Europe. The staff members at Humanities Spring all wear several different hats. The staff is always available to help students with everything from Italian homework to a misunderstanding with a roommate to how to order hazelnut ice cream. Conversation is nonstop; students and staff members all learn together.

MEDICAL CARE
HSIA uses the medical services of the Assisi Hospital, an excellent small hospital 20 minutes away. Routine first aid is provided free of charge. All students are required to come to HSIA with medical coverage.

RELIGIOUS LIFE
Interested students may attend Sunday services at the local Santa Maria di Lignano church (with its recently restored blue ceiling and sparkling hand-painted gold stars) or at any of the churches in Assisi.

COSTS
HSIA 2008 runs from June 25 to July 23. The program costs $3400, which includes everything (airport pickup and return, all traveling expenses within Italy, all tickets to Spoleto Festival events, all museum fees, all hotel expenses, room, board, and tuition) except for the occasional meal out (typically one lunch and/or one dinner each week). Students pay their own airfare. Some small work-study scholarships are available to high school students (awarded on the basis of merit and need); college students may apply for more extensive work-study aid.

Graduate students may apply for HSIA teaching internships. Undergraduates are occasionally accepted as interns. Interested students should include two HSIA-related course proposals with the standard HSIA application form.

APPLICATION TIMETABLE
Applications are accepted on a rolling basis until all spots are filled. HSIA recommends that interested students apply by March 15.

FOR MORE INFORMATION, CONTACT
Jane R. Oliensis, Director
Humanities Spring in Assisi
Santa Maria di Lignano, 2
06081 Assisi (PG) Italy

Phone: 011-39-075-802400
Fax: 011-39-075-802400
E-mail: info@humanitiesspring.com
Web site: http://www.humanitiesspring.com

PARTICIPANT/FAMILY COMMENTS

"This experience was beyond amazing. I learned so much about myself and about the world around me."

"I've never laughed so much in my whole life."

THE HUN SCHOOL OF PRINCETON

▼▲▼▲▼▲▼▲▼▲▼▲▼▲▼▲▼▲▼▲▼▲▼▲▼▲▼▲▼▲▼▲▼

SUMMER ACADEMIC SESSION/AMERICAN CULTURE AND LANGUAGE INSTITUTE (ACLI)/SUMMER THEATRE CLASSICS

PRINCETON, NEW JERSEY

TYPE OF PROGRAM: Academic enrichment classes and/or full-credit classes in a variety of subjects (math, English, science, SAT), including intensive English language courses in grammar and reading and opportunities for American cultural and historical enrichment

PARTICIPANTS: Coeducational, ages 12 to 18 (12-year-olds may be accepted into enrichment courses). Must be 13 to board.

ENROLLMENT: Approximately 180 students in the Summer Academic Session; maximum of 30 in ACLI

PROGRAM DATES: One 5-week session, June 23 to July 25

HEADS OF PROGRAM: Mr. William McQuade, The Hun School of Princeton Upper School Head; Donna O'Sullivan, Director of Auxiliary Services; LeRhonda Greats, Director of Summer Academic Session; Dianne Somers, Director, ESL Program

LOCATION

The Hun School of Princeton, located in historical Princeton, New Jersey, is a private coeducational school for grades 6–12. The five-week summer session complements and follows the curriculum, standards, and philosophy of The Hun School. The greater Princeton area is available to students with its many resources. Resident students frequently take trips into town for ice cream or shopping or to enjoy the sights of Princeton University.

BACKGROUND AND PHILOSOPHY

The Hun School Summer Session offers students an ideal setting to explore new areas of learning while building on basic foundations of knowledge. At the Hun School, a dedicated and experienced faculty helps students gain confidence in their scholastic abilities as they guide them to appreciate their talents. Students' efforts are supported by programs that adhere to the highest standards of excellence while helping them achieve their specific goals. The incorporation of innovative learning technologies within the summer curriculum completes what can be the road map to success. Summer at Hun represents a special time when friendships are made and horizons are expanded. During its summer session, Hun welcomes students from surrounding communities and from around the world.

PROGRAM OFFERINGS

There are three main programs offered at Hun:

The Summer Academic Session serves students in grades 6–12. Some enrichment courses are appropriate for students entering sixth, seventh, or eighth grade. Small-group instruction, traditional grading standards, and individual attention are hallmarks of the Summer Academic Session. Students may choose 2½-hour courses or full-credit (comprehensive) courses, which meet 5 hours per day. There are two class periods. Comprehensive course work is for students wishing to accelerate their curriculum, enhance their high school transcripts for college admission, or make up a class. Enrollment in one comprehensive course, 120 hours, constitutes a full academic load for the five-week session. Preview/review classes or other 2½-hour

classes are designed for students wishing to make up incomplete problems in a particular subject. Students may choose a course that reviews work they have previously taken in order to reinforce material covered, or they may select a course that prepares them for work they will undertake in the fall. Students may select one or two courses from this category. Each course is 60 hours.

Comprehensive courses offered include Algebra I, Algebra II, Geometry, Precalculus, and Chemistry. Enrichment courses are Algebra I Preview or Review, Algebra II Preview or Review, Calculus, Precalculus, Geometry, Reading and Writing, Middle School Creative Writing, Middle School Literature, Middle School Math, Middle School Pre-Algebra, English Literature, American Literature, Biology, Physics, Chemistry, Computer Technology, Tennis, and SAT Prep. Additional courses may be added if there is sufficient student interest. Courses are subject to cancellation due to lack of enrollment. Students may be day students or board on campus (must be 13 years of age to reside at the School). Students do not have to be Hun School students.

The American Culture and Language Institute (ACLI) is designed specifically for international students who wish to study English at an American school. Students from the Princeton area may also attend as day students and can be as young as age 11. However, most students in the program board at the School and are from outside the United States. Balancing academic classroom work with cultural enrichment, the program offers students an ideal environment in which to improve their English language skills while learning more about the history of the United States and American customs and society. International students interested in making the transition from schools in their home country to college-preparatory study in America find the ACLI program to be ideally suited to their needs (must be 13 years of age to reside at the School). Students may be 11 years old and can participate in all activities and trips except the overnight trips.

ENROLLMENT

There are approximately 180 students in the Summer Academic Session, both boarding and day, and about 25 to 30 students in the American Culture and Language Institute. Students come from all over the United States and the world and, in 2007, represented the countries of Bahrain, China, Italy, Korea, Russia, Saudi Arabia, Taiwan, Turkey, and the United States.

DAILY SCHEDULE

Resident Students

7:00– 7:45	Breakfast
8:00–10:30	Period 1
10:30–10:50	Break
10:50–12:20	Period 2
12:20– 1:00	Lunch
1:00– 2:00	Period 2 (continued)
2:00– 2:45	Extra Help
3:00– 5:00	Intramurals/Activities
5:30– 6:00	Dinner
6:00– 7:15	Free Time
7:30– 9:30	Study Hall
9:45	On Corridor
10:30	Lights Out

(Day students follow the same schedule from Period 1 through Extra Help)

EXTRA OPPORTUNITIES AND ACTIVITIES

The Student Activities Center and Game Room are open to all summer students for enjoyment. A Snack Bar opens after classes and remains open into the evening. The Game Room houses Ping-Pong tables and a Foosball table. Boarding students participate in weekday activities from 3 to 5 p.m. They include miniature golf, bowling, swimming, shopping, ice skating, and other activities. During that time, the computer lab is open, as is the game room and, on designated days, the Fitness Center and gym facilities. In addition, movies are shown on the big-screen TV. Weekend activities for boarders include trips to amusement parks, the New Jersey shore, Philadelphia, white-water rafting, movies off campus, and other organized trips. The Hun School also organizes tournaments in Ping-Pong, pool, and volleyball. The students in the American Culture and Language Institute follow a trip schedule that includes outings each Wednesday and a weekend trip to Washington, D.C.

FACILITIES

Classes are held in air-conditioned classrooms in the Chesebro Academic Center. The Bookstore, Snack Bar, and Game Room are located in the Buck Activities Center. Students who choose to reside on campus live in dormitory-style housing. The new Athletic Center Complex is available. Students may use the gymnasium, tennis courts, basketball courts, and weight room facility at designated times. Students eat meals in the School's air-conditioned dining hall. Boarding students have access to the Internet in their dorm rooms.

STAFF

Instructors are chosen for their ability to motivate and communicate with students and for their love of teaching. A core of Hun School faculty members is the heart of the program, in addition to local teachers who come highly recommended. The residential staff consists of Hun School alumni and members of the faculty and staff.

MEDICAL CARE

The Hun School Clinic is staffed by the School's nurse who is available from 9 a.m. to 3 p.m. on school days. The nurse is on call 24 hours a day, including weekends and evenings. In addition, the Medical Center of Princeton is approximately 2 miles from the Hun campus. Resident students who become seriously ill are sent home to be cared for by their parents or guardian.

RELIGIOUS LIFE

The Hun School welcomes students from all faiths and religions. Students may attend nearby religious services on weekends.

COSTS

In 2007, the cost for the Summer Academic Program was $5023 for boarding students, $1248 for a 2½-hour course as a day student, $2165 for a comprehensive course, and $2830 for two 2½-hour courses. For the American Culture and Language Institute, boarding students' tuition was $6540 and day students paid $2900.

TRANSPORTATION

Parents or guardians of resident students must arrange transportation from nearby airports (Kennedy International Airport and Newark International Airport) to the Hun School of Princeton on the day of registration, Sunday, June 22, 2008. Other students arrive by car or train and are escorted by their guardian or family friend.

APPLICATION TIMETABLE

The School accepts students on a rolling admission basis beginning in December and continuing until the start of the summer session. Applicants are urged to apply by May 1 in order to ensure a placement in the resident program or to maximize their placement possibilities in a popular class. The Hun School cannot guarantee space availability in all classes. Classes may be cancelled due to a lack of enrollment. Applications are available on the School's Web site at http://www.hunschool.org.

Academic questions should be directed to Ms. LeRhonda Greats at 609-921-7600 Ext. 2258 or lgreats@hunschool.org.

FOR MORE INFORMATION, CONTACT

Mrs. Donna O'Sullivan
Director of Auxiliary Services
The Hun School of Princeton
176 Edgerstoune Road
Princeton, New Jersey 08540
Phone: 609-921-7600 Ext. 2265
Fax: 609-924-2170
E-mail: dosullivan@hunschool.org
Web site: http://www.hunschool.org

PARTICIPANT/FAMILY COMMENTS

"Thank you once again for providing another year of summer learning and fun for my son. I continue to feel that spending part of his summer at Hun is part of the reason he is growing up and maturing into a caring and refined young man."

iD TECH CAMPS–HANDS-ON TECHNOLOGY FUN!

HIGH-TECH COMPUTER CAMPS FOR THE DIGITAL GENERATION

LOCATED AT 50 PRESTIGIOUS UNIVERSITIES NATIONWIDE IN 22 STATES AND SPAIN

TYPE OF PROGRAM: Summer technology and computer camps (categories: academics, computers, computer programming, computer science, Web page design, arts, animation, cartooning, cinematography, digital media, film, film editing, film production, graphic arts, photography, special interests, computer game design, computer graphics, robotics)

PARTICIPANTS: Coeducational, ages 7–17

PROGRAM DATES: Weeklong and multiweek day and overnight programs, June to August

LOCATION

iD Tech Camps provides hands-on, weeklong day and overnight technology camps for students ages 7–17 at fifty prestigious universities nationwide in twenty-two states and Spain. Campers learn the latest technology with instructors who make learning fun.

Camp locations are as follows: in Arizona, Arizona State University; in California, Cal Lutheran University, Pepperdine University, St. Mary's College of California, Santa Clara University, Stanford University, the Tiger Woods Learning Center in Anaheim, and the University of California, Berkeley, Davis, Irvine, Los Angeles, San Diego, and Santa Cruz; in Colorado, Colorado College and the University of Denver; in Connecticut, Sacred Heart University; in Florida, the University of Central Florida and the University of Miami; in Georgia, Emory University; in Illinois, Lake Forest College and Northwestern University; in Massachusetts, Merrimack College, MIT, and Smith College; in Michigan, the University of Michigan; in Minnesota, the University of Minnesota; in Missouri, Washington University; in New Jersey, Rider University and Seton Hall University; in New York, Columbia University and Vassar College; in North Carolina, the University of North Carolina at Chapel Hill and Wake Forest University; in Ohio, Case Western Reserve University; in Pennsylvania, Carnegie Mellon University and Villanova University; in Rhode Island, Brown University; in Tennessee, Vanderbilt University; in Texas, Southern Methodist University, the University of Houston, and the University of Texas at Austin; in Virginia, the College of William and Mary, the University of Virginia, and Virginia Tech; in Washington, the University of Washington; and in Washington, D.C., Georgetown University.

BACKGROUND AND PHILOSOPHY

With one computer per student and an average of 5 students per instructor, campers are given the attention they need to excel. Each program immerses campers in a creative and fun learning environment, enabling them to harness the power of technology while having a blast and completing a final project with leading products that industry professionals use.

iD Tech Camps does not have Counselors-in-Training (CITs), hiring only trained adult counselors to teach the courses and supervise the camps. A high return rate for the staff indicates how the camps are run. This also means that students see familiar faces each summer. A mandatory, comprehensive in-person staff training program covers safety, supervision, and

curriculum and instills the passion for technology in children. Regional Managers, who manage a set of camps, have daily contact with their Directors and evaluate their staff each week. Multiple unannounced site visits from the corporate office throughout the summer allow staff members to complete detailed evaluations and provide feedback to the camp staff. Background checks and reference checks are completed on all staff members. All Directors and Lead Instructors must be certified in CPR and first aid.

iD Tech Camps is accredited by the ACA at various locations. All iD Tech Camps locations meet and surpass many of the criteria set forth by the ACA. Camps are located at prestigious universities, which helps set high standards for campers to pursue a college degree. Instructors teach hands-on instead of depending on online tutorials to teach students. iD Tech Camps offers an in-depth, focused, project-based curriculum instead of having students dabble in a variety of areas. Consequently, students come away with solid skill sets, using hardware and software that professionals use in the industry.

PROGRAM OFFERINGS

Students create 2-D and 3-D video games, experience game modding, improve their gaming skills with the Gaming Athletes course, build robots to compete, design Web sites with Flash® animations, film and edit digital movies, create a comic book with zany digital photos, learn programming, and more. Campers take home a project at the end of the weeklong course. In addition, teens can travel to Spain for the documentary filmmaking program or participate in iD Gaming Academy for an intensive three weeks of game development. There are also a unique Sports & Tech program at Stanford University and a Surf & Tech program at Pepperdine University and UC Santa Cruz.

Courses include:

Adventures in Comic Creation, ages 7–10 (http://www.internaldrive.com/art-camp/index.htm)

Adventures in Game Design, ages 7–10 (http://www.internaldrive.com/multimedia)

Video Game Creation, ages 10–17 (http://www.internaldrive.com/video-game/)

Video Game Creation Xtreme, ages 10–17 (http://www.internaldrive.com/gaming-camp/)

3-D Game Design, ages 13–17 (http://www.internaldrive.com/3D-game-design/)

3-D Character Modeling, ages 13–17 (http://www.internaldrive.com/3D-game-design/)

Game Modding, ages 13–17 (http://www.internaldrive.com/game-modding/)

Gaming Athletes, ages 13–17 (http://www.internaldrive.com/cyber-athlete/)

Digital Video Editing, ages 10–17 (http://www.internaldrive.com/digital-video/)

Special F/X Editing, ages 13–17 (http://www.internaldrive.com/film-camp/)

Web Design & Flash Animation, ages 10–17 (http://www.internaldrive.com/web-design/)

RoboContenders, ages 10–17 (http://www.internaldrive.com/robotics/)

Programming, ages 12–17 (http://www.internaldrive.com/programming-camp/)

Programming v2.0, ages 13–17 (http://www.internaldrive.com/programming/)

Sports & Tech with Stanford Athletics, ages 11–14 (http://www.internaldrive.com/sports-camp/)

Surf & Tech at UC Santa Cruz or UC San Diego, ages 11–17 (http://www.internaldrive.com/surf-camp/)

Documentary Filmmaking and Cultural Immersion in Spain, ages 14–17 (http://www.internaldrive.com/spain/)

iD Gaming Academy, ages 13–17 (http://www.idgamingacademy.com/).

EXTRA OPPORTUNITIES AND ACTIVITIES

During Family Showcase, iD Tech Camps cordially invites family and friends to tour its labs and meet with iD staff members. Evening activities play a prominent role at the camp. The overnight campus boarding experience promotes new friendships and more time with instructors. Campers join in evening sessions that include gaming tournaments, Dance-Dance-Revolution, karaoke singing, chess, and short programs.

STAFF

A blend of spirit, energy, dedication, and desire to work with kids and teens is something that iD Tech Camp staff members all share. Each instructor is personally interviewed and carefully selected. Because the camp tries to hire the best, they also pay the best, which means that the instructors are enthusiastic, energetic, and knowledgeable about technology.

MEDICAL CARE

iD Tech Camps directors and instructors are trained in first aid and CPR and have gone through company training sessions. All students have 24-hour access to on-campus emergency health facilities as well as to local hospitals and emergency centers.

COSTS

Tuition in 2007 was $729 for day students and $1129 for boarding students per weekly session. In 2007, the Documentary and Filmmaking and Cultural Immersion in Spain program cost $3999, not including airfare. iD Gaming Academy tuition was $3999. Discounts are available, including multiweek and sibling discounts.

APPLICATION TIMETABLE

Applications are accepted on a rolling basis, starting in November. Since courses are filled on a first-come, first-served basis, early and multiple-week applications are highly recommended.

FOR MORE INFORMATION, CONTACT

iD Tech Camps
42 West Campbell Avenue, Suite 301
Campbell, California 95008
Phone: 888-709-TECH (8324) (toll-free)
Fax: 408-871-2228
E-mail: info@internalDrive.com
Web site: http://www.internalDrive.com

PARTICIPANT/FAMILY COMMENTS

"Of all the many camps my son has attended, this is by far the best. As an educator, I'm extremely impressed with the quality of this program."—Connie Ryan, Parent

"iD Tech Camps is a fun and educational experience that helped me look deeper into a subject that I really enjoy."—Kristian, Student

"This is our seventh year at iD Tech Camps, which is a good indicator that something's working!"—Maureen Everett, Parent

"My daughter never experienced computer science or video gaming before, but the knowledge she acquired is priceless."—Brian Rountree, Parent

IDYLLWILD ARTS SUMMER PROGRAM

‹‹‹‹‹‹‹‹‹‹‹‹‹‹‹‹‹‹‹‹‹‹‹‹‹‹‹‹‹‹‹‹‹‹

SUMMER ARTS PROGRAM

IDYLLWILD, CALIFORNIA

TYPE OF PROGRAM: Summer arts program
PARTICIPANTS: Coeducational, ages 5–adult
ENROLLMENT: 1,850
PROGRAM DATES: June 28–August 17, 2008
HEAD OF PROGRAM: Steven Fraider, Director

LOCATION

Nestled at the mile-high level in the San Jacinto Mountains of southern California, the 205-acre Idyllwild Arts campus is located in one of the most spectacular natural settings in the western U.S. This tranquil site is far removed from urban distractions and offers students a unique learning environment. The campus is surrounded by 20,000 acres of protected woodland, making it a gateway for wilderness activities. Idyllwild is approximately 110 miles southeast of Los Angeles and northeast of San Diego. The village of Idyllwild supports a year-round population of approximately 2,500 in addition to many weekend and holiday visitors. The towns nearest to Idyllwild are Palm Springs, Hemet, and Banning.

BACKGROUND AND PHILOSOPHY

The Idyllwild Arts Foundation was incorporated in 1946 "for the purpose of promoting and advancing artistic and cultural development in Southern California and primarily for the advancement of instruction in music and the arts." Founder Dr. Max Krone, then Dean of the Institute of the Arts at the University of Southern California, and his wife, Beatrice, envisioned a beautiful and harmonious atmosphere that would provide opportunities for a wide variety of artistic experiences to students of all ages and levels of ability. In 1950, the first students enrolled in the Idyllwild School of Music and the Arts (ISOMATA) Summer Program. Today, the mission of the Idyllwild Arts Summer Program—the name was updated by the Board of Trustees in 1995—is to provide for students of all ages and abilities the opportunity to benefit from arts instruction of the highest caliber.

Students enrolled in the Idyllwild Arts Summer Program receive intensive, hands-on arts experience in a competition-free environment that emphasizes individual growth. Students enroll in one course per session that becomes the primary focus of their participation in the Summer Program. Students are expected to attend every class meeting or rehearsal. If a student is unable or unwilling to participate fully in the program, he or she may be asked to leave the program. Students should be prepared to work hard and learn a great deal. Although many optional recreational activities are scheduled, the requirements of a student's chosen course, whether a rehearsal, class, or lecture, always take first priority. If a student feels the need for additional help or instruction, he or she can feel comfortable about asking an instructor for more time and attention.

PROGRAM OFFERINGS

The Summer Program consists of courses in creative writing, dance, film/video, music, theater, and visual arts. Specific

course offerings are organized into art centers according to age. Courses are available to both boarding and day students.

Children's Center (ages 5–12): The minimum boarding age is 9. Courses include Multi-Arts, a one-week day program for students ages 5–8. For students ages 9–12, there are one- and two-week programs in dance, music (piano), theater, visual arts, and creative writing. Professional artist-educators use age-appropriate materials and methods to convey the excitement and discipline necessary for accomplishment in the arts. Small classes and a low student-teacher ratio, approximately 9:1, ensure that students receive a great deal of individual attention and support. An important goal of the Children's Center is for students to gain an enthusiasm and excitement for the arts and a basic foundation of technical knowledge.

Junior Artist's Center (ages 11–13): Workshops include one- and two-week offerings in theater, visual arts, and creative writing. In addition, students in this age range may participate in selected Youth Arts Center music and dance courses based on experience and ability.

Youth Arts Center (ages 13–18): Courses are two weeks in length with the exception of the Summer Theatre Festival, which is offered in two 3-week sessions. The Youth Arts Center comprises the largest segment of the Summer Program, with seventy-three weeks of course offerings in all of the visual and performing arts. Courses include art exploration, two bands, ceramics, chamber music, choir, computer animation, dance, fiction writing, filmmaking, harp, jazz, jewelry making, musical theater, two orchestras, painting and drawing, photography, piano, poetry, screenwriting, and theater.

Family Week: A one-week session is offered. Families live together and have the opportunity to explore the visual and performing arts in a relaxed setting. Adults and children choose from a variety of arts and outdoor activities. Evening events are for the whole family.

ENROLLMENT

The Idyllwild Arts Summer Program enrolls approximately 1,800 students per summer, consisting of 350 children, 900 teenagers, 450 adult and college students, and 100 family campers. About 75 percent of students are from California, with the remaining 25 percent from the rest of the U.S. and abroad. Approximately 60 percent of summer students are female.

DAILY SCHEDULE

In general, Youth and Junior Artist students can expect to be involved in course-related activities a minimum of 6 hours per day, six days per week. Individual course schedules vary according to the needs and requirements of each discipline. Instruction begins at 9 a.m. and may continue into the evening in some programs. Children's Center courses meet Monday through Saturday, with recreational activities for boarding students on Sundays.

Fostering respect for individuals, for the arts, and for education are the foundations upon which expectations of student behavior are based. A few policies pertaining to safe and cooperative communal living and adherence to state and federal laws, including student use of tobacco, drugs, and alcohol, along with vandalism, violence, and leaving campus without permission, are enforced rigorously.

EXTRA OPPORTUNITIES AND ACTIVITIES

A variety of evening and weekend activities, including dances, game nights, art playgrounds, pool parties, talent shows, and field games, are organized by the counseling staff and offered to students. In the Children's Center, all boarding students participate in an extensive program of recreational activities offered each evening from 7 to 9 p.m. On weekends, longer and more extensive activities, including art projects, informal drama productions, and field games, are scheduled.

FACILITIES

The Idyllwild Arts campus has more than one hundred buildings, including an air-conditioned concert hall, a modern library, an exhibition center, a sound stage, two recital halls, three outdoor theaters, numerous art studios, classrooms and practice rooms, an air-conditioned dining hall, a health center, a swimming pool, residence halls for faculty members and adult students, three large college-style dormitories for Youth students, and four small dormitories for Children's Center and Junior Artist students. Students are housed with 3 or 4 roommates per room. Each room has a private bathroom with a shower.

STAFF

Faculty members are dedicated artist-teachers who look forward to the challenge of working with a diverse student body. The Summer Program provides students with the opportunity to work directly with professional artists, dancers, directors, musicians, and writers who are committed to the process of arts education and to their own arts discipline. Approximately 275 faculty members participate in the Summer Program. The summer staff of 55 consists of deans, counselors, teaching assistants, lifeguards, and nurses. Students are supervised in the dormitories by resident counselors. Most counselors are college students or recent graduates with a major or strong interest in the arts. Counselor applicants are rigorously screened and interviewed.

MEDICAL CARE

Health services are administered by 3 resident nurses. There is a medical clinic in the village of Idyllwild that treats students who require the services of a physician. Idyllwild also has a pharmacy and fire department paramedics. The nearest hospital is located in Hemet, approximately 25 miles from the campus.

COSTS

Fees vary by art center and by course. In 2007, the cost of a two-week Youth, Junior Artist, or Children's Center program, including tuition, meals, housing, application fee, and lab fee, ranged from $2115 to $2355, depending on the course. The all-inclusive cost of a one-week Family Camp program ranged from $1725 for 2 people to $3650 for a group of 6. An initial deposit of $250 is required with all applications. All fees are payable in full thirty days before a program begins. Students who pay in full by March 15 receive a 10 percent discount. It is recommended that boarding students keep $25 per week in the student bank to pay for snacks, art supplies, and postcards.

FINANCIAL AID

A significant part of the school's mission is to provide financial aid where needed for talented young artists from diverse backgrounds. In 2006, nearly 300 students received financial aid totaling more than $300,000. All financial aid is in the form of scholarships. Scholarships are awarded based on the financial need of the student, the talent of the student in a specific discipline, and the enrollment needs of the school.

TRANSPORTATION

Idyllwild is approximately 2½ hours by car from Los Angeles or San Diego. Students flying to southern California should arrange a flight to the Ontario International Airport, 75 miles from Idyllwild, or the Palm Springs Airport, 60 miles from the campus. The school offers van pick-up service to and from either airport for a fee of $100 each way. There is no public transportation to Idyllwild.

APPLICATION TIMETABLE

Enrollment begins February 1. Inquiries are welcome anytime. Families interested in touring the campus may do so by contacting the school at the address listed below. Most courses maintain open enrollment. Visual arts classes are small, so early enrollment is encouraged.

FOR MORE INFORMATION, CONTACT

Idyllwild Arts Summer Program
P.O. Box 38
Idyllwild, California 92549
Phone: 951-659-2171 Ext. 2365
Fax: 951-659-4552
E-mail: summer@idyllwildarts.org
Web site: http://www.idyllwildarts.org

INTERLOCHEN

INTERLOCHEN ARTS CAMP

INTERLOCHEN, MICHIGAN

TYPE OF PROGRAM: Coeducational summer arts program
PARTICIPANTS: Girls and boys, ages 8–18
ENROLLMENT: More than 2,100
PROGRAM DATES: June to August
HEAD OF PROGRAM: Jeffrey S. Kimpton, President

LOCATION
Interlochen Arts Camp is located on a wooded 1,200-acre campus situated between Duck Lake and Green Lake in rural northwest lower Michigan. It is approximately 4 hours from the Detroit area and 6 hours from Chicago. It is close to Lake Michigan, the Sleeping Bear Dunes National Lakeshore, and Traverse City, a popular year-round tourist destination.

BACKGROUND AND PHILOSOPHY
The mission of Interlochen Center for the Arts, of which the camp is a part, is to engage and inspire people worldwide through excellence in educational, artistic, and cultural programs, enhancing the quality of life through the universal language of the arts. Founded in 1928, the camp provides arts education at its highest level, not just for the young artist, but for the growth of the complete individual, preparing them well for today's demanding and changing society. High school, intermediate, and junior campers learn as much about themselves as they do about their art, meeting young people from different environments, backgrounds, and cultures. Through individualized attention from counselors and instructors and exposure to famous conductors and guest artists, students are encouraged to explore and reach for their dreams.

PROGRAM OFFERINGS
Specific class offerings vary in each of the three divisions: junior (grades 3–6), intermediate (grades 6–9), and high school (grades 9–12). Each student's schedule is determined individually.

Dance: Offerings include beginning through advanced levels in both ballet and modern dance technique.

Music: Offerings include band, orchestra, jazz ensemble, piano and organ, beginning through advanced instrument instruction, chorus, music theory, chamber music, computer music, jazz improvisation, vocal technique, classical guitar, and composition. Four-week Advanced High School String Quartet and three-week Advanced Vocal and Choral Programs are also offered.

Theater Arts: Courses include theater production, theater workshop, acting studio, musical theater, Shakespeare, and playwriting.

Visual Arts: Courses include art exploration, drawing, painting, ceramics, fiber arts, metalsmithing, printmaking, sculpture, and photography.

Creative Writing: Offered in the intermediate and high school divisions, a special intensive course is offered in each three-week session. Students work under the apprenticeship of professional writers and teachers on an individual basis. A creative writing class is also offered at the intermediate level.

Motion Picture Arts: Dedicated to exposing students to filmmaking as a truly collaborative art form, the emphasis is placed on all aspects of the medium—from the written word to the moving image, from the aesthetics of film art to the basics of practical filmmaking.

ENROLLMENT
Interlochen Arts Camp enrolls more than 2,100 campers each summer. Members of minority groups and international students represent 15 percent of the population. Students come from all fifty states and more than forty other countries.

DAILY SCHEDULE
Arts instructional classes are held Tuesday through Saturday from approximately 8 a.m. to 5 p.m. Sunday's schedule includes ecumenical and religious services as well as concerts. Rehearsals and recreational and divisional activities take place on Mondays.

EXTRA OPPORTUNITIES AND ACTIVITIES

Extracurricular activities include recreation, picnics, camp-fires, dances, arts and crafts, off-campus trips, and other planned activities.

FACILITIES

Campers live with a counselor and 10–18 other campers in one of the 120 rustic cabins located in each division. There are 450 buildings on the Interlochen campus, including the cabins, fourteen performance sites, and seventeen practice studios, which hold more than 275 individual practice rooms. The camp can seat more than 12,500 in its performance venues. Performance sites include Corson Auditorium (1,000), Kresge Auditorium (4,000), and the historic Interlochen Bowl (6,000). Michael P. Dendrinos Chapel/Recital Hall, Hildegarde Lewis Dance Building, Harvey Theatre, and Phoenix Theatre each seat up to 200 people comfortably.

STAFF

Faculty members at Interlochen Arts Camp include distinguished artists and educators from colleges, universities, and secondary schools around the world. Guest artists also enhance instruction by providing master classes.

MEDICAL CARE

A team of doctors and nurses is on staff throughout the summer. There is an infirmary for each division. Interlochen is within minutes of a large regional medical center in Traverse City.

RELIGIOUS LIFE

Interlochen is not affiliated with any particular religion. The camp provides campers with the opportunity to attend a variety of religious and ecumenical services on campus.

COSTS

The average cost for the high school six-week session in 2007 is $5890. The average three-week session is $3431. Tuition varies, based on the student's division and major as well as the length of time at camp.

The fees include general expenses such as room, board, most classes and group instruction, camp uniform, all recreational facilities, and admission to faculty and student performances. Any additional fees for supplies or laboratory costs are listed within the camp schedule. Students should contact Interlochen for rates for 2008.

High school division programs run for three, four, or six weeks. Junior and intermediate division sessions run from two to four weeks, and campers may attend subsequent sessions for a discount.

Private lessons are available for an additional fee.

It is recommended that students maintain a personal account of $400 for the six-week session and $250 for the two- and three-week sessions to cover miscellaneous expenses.

A $1000 deposit is required at the time of acceptance. Full payment is due by June 1.

FINANCIAL AID

The purpose of Interlochen's financial aid program is to help provide outstanding young performers the means to further their artistic development. Interlochen is able to provide some degree of assistance to approximately 25 percent of its campers. Financial aid is based on one or a combination of three criteria: the financial need of the family, the artistic ability of the student, and the enrollment needs of the camp.

In addition, the Emerson Scholars Program provides a full music scholarship for 52 students from across the United States.

TRANSPORTATION

Interlochen is approximately 16 miles southwest of Traverse City and is easily accessible by any mode of transportation. The camp is served by Cherry Capital Airport in Traverse City via direct flights from Chicago, Detroit, Milwaukee, and Minneapolis. Interlochen staff members pick up campers at the airport.

APPLICATION TIMETABLE

Complete applications (application; audition/portfolio materials, if required; application fee; and tax forms, if applying for Financial Aid) are reviewed on a rolling basis. Early application is highly recommended. The preferred application deadline is February 1. The application fee is $25 for an online application and $50 for a paper application. For more information, prospective students and their families should visit http://www.interlochen.org/camp.

FOR MORE INFORMATION, CONTACT

Office of Admissions
Interlochen Center for the Arts
P.O. Box 199
Interlochen, Michigan 49643
Phone: 231-276-7472
E-mail: admissions@interlochen.org
Web site: http://www.interlochen.org

INTERNATIONAL SUMMER CAMP MONTANA, SWITZERLAND

SUMMER PROGRAMS

CRANS-MONTANA (VALAIS), SWITZERLAND

TYPE OF PROGRAM: Sports and language camp
PARTICIPANTS: Coeducational, ages 8–17
ENROLLMENT: 330 (maximum)
PROGRAM DATES: June 29 to July 19, July 20 to August 9, and August 10 to August 30
HEADS OF PROGRAM: Philippe Studer and Erwin Mathieu, Camp Owners/Directors

LOCATION

Crans-Montana, an internationally known health and sports resort area in the heart of the Swiss Alps, is located 1,500 meters above sea level in the French-speaking part of Switzerland. Known as "The Sun Terrace of Switzerland," Crans-Montana is situated on a sun-drenched plateau that enjoys an average of 13 hours of sunshine every day in the summer. Rising above the vineyards and orchards of the Rhone Valley, the camp is surrounded by magnificent pine tree forests and is protected from wind by a snow-peaked mountain range. Campers enjoy miles of beautiful trails that traverse meadows of alpine flowers, leading to majestic views of forests, lakes, mountains, and glaciers.

BACKGROUND AND PHILOSOPHY

For more than forty years, International Summer Camp Montana (ISCM) has strived to develop in its campers physical and intellectual achievement through an American-style camping experience employing European traditions. The camp's fundamental philosophy is to provide a healthy outdoor-living experience through sports and fellowship in a creative and wholesome environment. Campers develop both their minds and their bodies through a myriad of activities, broadening their outlook and enriching their lives through the opportunity to meet people of different backgrounds from all over the world. Through its combination of cooperative living with recreational, educational, and social activities, ISCM enables each young man and woman to acquire the maturity and independence that are essential to his or her well-being. Respect for others' views, understanding of democratic ideals, and responsible citizenship are stressed in this unique program, which provides an unforgettable opportunity for campers to gain self-understanding while interacting with others in an environment of beauty, joy, and learning. At ISCM, the emphasis is on cooperation, not competition; creativity, not conformity.

International Summer Camp Montana is a member of the Crans-Montana and Valais Tourist Offices, the Swiss Hotel Association, the Swiss Ski Federation, and the Association for Horsemanship Safety and Education.

PROGRAM OFFERINGS

Just a sampling of the numerous activities offered at ISCM includes sailing, rafting, swimming, English riding instruction, dressage, jumping and vaulting, trail riding, tennis, summer skiing and snowboarding in Saas Fee and Zermatt, fencing, mountain hiking, campcraft, overnight hikes, rock climbing, golf, circus skills, mountain biking, basketball, volleyball, softball, soccer, touch football, cricket, table tennis,

floor hockey, fitness training, performing arts, drawing, painting, screen printing, creative nature crafts, weaving, macramé, modelling, nature collecting, scrapbook making, aerobics, archery, badminton, billiards, Frisbee, a fitness course, gymnastics, mini golf, trampolining, track and field, outdoor games, and various educational talks and videos covering Swiss history and culture, classical and modern music, and nature study.

Activities are directed toward both personal and group development, and, while enjoyable and interesting, they challenge each camper to exercise his or her intelligence and promote the emergence of abilities and insight. Campers may participate in the activities of their choice during free time and are always under the supervision and guidance of the staff.

Campers are divided into three groups: Juniors, ages 8–10; Pioneers, ages 11–13; and Seniors, ages 14–17. Programs for each section are commensurate with the ability, endurance, and resourcefulness of its age level. The average Junior group size is 6 campers; the average Pioneer and Senior group size is 8.

Although ISCM is a coeducational camp, boys and girls generally pursue programs separately; experience has shown that wholesome contact during selected activities—excursions, hikes, games, and entertainment—is beneficial to all.

English is the main language spoken at camp, although French, Italian, and German are also spoken. Upon request, campers may be grouped with others who speak a specific language.

ENROLLMENT

Since 1961, boys and girls from all over the world have come to ISCM. Each year, campers represent more than fifty countries in North America, South America, Europe, North Africa, and Asia, with the majority coming from the United States, Canada, Mexico, Italy, France, Great Britain, the Netherlands, Scandinavia, Germany, Belgium, Spain, and the Middle East. Only boys and girls of outstanding moral character are accepted; for this reason, a letter of recommendation from each camper's teacher is required.

DAILY SCHEDULE

Because of the great deal of individual choice, particularly for older campers, no day at ISCM is exactly the same as any other. Meal times, evening program schedules, and lights-out are determined by age group.

EXTRA OPPORTUNITIES AND ACTIVITIES

In addition to exploring neighboring mountain areas through day and overnight hikes, campers participate in two excursions, included in the camp fee, during each period. One excursion visits places of interest in the Central Valais: Zermatt, the mountain village at the foot of the Matterhorn; Saas Fee, the village of the glaciers; the St. Bernard Pass; the Rhone Glacier; and Sierre, with its manor, art exhibitions, and various museums. The second excursion is to other parts of Switzerland, such as the Lake Geneva area, with the towns of Geneva, Lausanne, and Montreux and the castles of Chillon and Gruyère; Bern, the medieval town and capital of Switzerland; the Bernese Oberland; Thun; and Interlaken.

ISCM also features traditional activities such as campfires, sing-a-longs, stunt nights, theater groups, folk dancing, shopping trips, a camp horse show, storytelling, and birthday parties.

An optional language program is offered in English, French, Spanish, and German at beginner, intermediate, and advanced levels. Five 50-minute lessons are taught each week in the native language of the instructors.

FACILITIES

ISCM's main building is the solidstone Moubra House, which overlooks spacious playing fields, forests, a lake, and the Rhone Valley and includes camper and staff living quarters, a dining room, a rec room, a living room, a theater, a game room, and six classrooms. Camp also features four additional buildings, including a large chalet. Campers are housed by gender on separate floors of Moubra House or in the chalet. Rooms are sunny and well-equipped with all modern conveniences; most have wide balconies. Each floor has a large number of bathrooms.

STAFF

The camp staff comprises 2 camp directors, each in charge of his or her own sector (programming and educational supervision, catering, and administration); 3 head counselors, each responsible for one of the age groups; counselors; sports instructors; language teachers; and office staff members. A trained dietitian supervises the preparation of excellent French-style food with an international flavor. The program staff consists of approximately 80 multilingual members.

Each member of the International Summer Camp Montana staff is carefully chosen on the basis of age, education, camping experience, emotional maturity, and the ability to work with growing children. Experienced counselors from previous seasons provide stability to the counseling group. All counselors have experience in American or European camps.

MEDICAL CARE

The health, safety, and general welfare of each camper are meticulously guarded. Three resident nurses and an on-call physician are responsible for the good health of campers and staff members. There is a fully equipped hospital nearby in Sierre.

COSTS

The camp fee for each three-week session is 5600 Swiss francs (US$4667). This fee includes all living expenses, excursions and overnight hikes, activities and sports, infirmary service, laundry service, and instruction in riding, tennis, swimming, and other activities. Not included in this cost are travel to and from camp, personal allowances, medical treatment and medical prescriptions, the optional language program (250 Swiss francs), and fees for ski lifts and transportation during skiing trips. All fees are payable in Swiss francs.

International Summer Camp Montana gladly assumes full responsibility for the program arrangements made and will do its best to fulfill these. However, International Summer Camp Montana is not liable for events or transportation organized or carried out for it by third parties. Therefore, International Summer Camp Montana cannot be held responsible for any extra costs, injuries, damages, delays, or inconveniences caused during these proceedings. In the event of litigation, the court of original jurisdiction is in Sierre.

TRANSPORTATION

ISCM representatives meet and escort campers traveling by air to and from Geneva Airport on arrival and departure days and facilitate check-in and customs formalities. The fee for this service is 80 Swiss francs for a one way trip and 160 Swiss francs for a round-trip; transportation is provided by deluxe bus and includes a snack or meal as well as confirmation of return flight. Arrangements for this service must be made at least two weeks before the camper's arrival.

APPLICATION TIMETABLE

The number of places is limited; parents, particularly those who wish to enroll their children in the second session, are advised to make reservations early. Campers may enroll for one, two, or all three sessions. Extensions of camp sessions are accepted only on a space-available basis.

A nonrefundable and nontransferable deposit of 1000 Swiss francs is required with registration. The balance of tuition is payable in full before May 1. Various cancellation policies apply.

A camp DVD is available free of charge.

FOR MORE INFORMATION, CONTACT

Philippe Studer and Erwin Mathieu, Directors
International Summer Camp Montana
La Moubra
CH-3963 Crans-Montana 1
Switzerland

Phone: +41 27 486 86 86
Fax: +41 27 486 86 87
E-mail: info@campmontana.ch
Web site: http://www.campmontana.ch

INTERN EXCHANGE INTERNATIONAL

▼▼▼▼▼▼▼▼▼▼▼▼▼▼▼▼▼▼▼▼▼▼▼▼▼▼▼▼▼▼▼▼▼

SUMMER INTERNSHIP/TRAVEL PROGRAM

LONDON, ENGLAND

TYPE OF PROGRAM: Residential career internship program
PARTICIPANTS: Coeducational, ages 16–18
ENROLLMENT: 150–220 participants per session
PROGRAM DATES: One session per year, thirty days in June and July
HEADS OF PROGRAM: Nina Miller Glickman, M.Ed., and Lynn Ann Weinstein, Directors

LOCATION
Intern Exchange International (IEI) participants live in London, a dynamic, safe, world-class city without language barriers. Students reside in the University of London residence halls in the heart of Bloomsbury, the historic literary district where Virginia Woolf and Charles Dickens once lived. The British Museum, Soho, Oxford Street, and the West End theatres are just minutes away.

BACKGROUND AND PHILOSOPHY
Nina Glickman and Lynn Weinstein established Intern Exchange International in 1987 as a way to encourage high school students to make an informed career choice. IEI's exciting summer internships in London offer students a hands-on experience in a profession that interests them. In addition to career exposure and the opportunity to obtain prestigious references for college, this monthlong peek into the day-to-day rhythms of the working world provides a wonderful growth experience. Day trips, weekend excursions, and special touring events are an integral part of the summer.

IEI is a bridge between high school and college, where students experience tremendous social, academic, and personal growth; their newfound sense of independence will serve them well in college. Because of the unique nature of this program, the interns experience freedom as young, responsible adults within established boundaries. IEI students are self-directed, responsible individuals who enjoy learning in a real-world environment and who are excited by this outstanding opportunity to learn and live in London for the summer.

PROGRAM OFFERINGS
In this program, students gain exposure to a promising career at the side of a practicing professional. Work is combined with interesting and fun evening and weekend activities and excursions.

Internships give students a chance to participate firsthand in a field of interest by doing meaningful work with a preceptor. They might help prepare cases for trial with prominent barristers and solicitors, conduct research in the clinics of well-known physicians, or unearth underground ruins with archaeologists. Internship programs include Archaeology, Art Gallery and Auction House, Business/Finance, Community Service/Social Services, Culinary Arts, Genealogy, Hotel Management, Information Technology, Law, Medicine (Medical Research, Veterinary Medicine), Public Relations/Marketing, Publishing, Retail Sales, and Strategic Studies. New internships are always being developed.

Career Plus-Programmes take students into the real world, where they get the background and skills they need to pursue their chosen path. Accomplished professionals serve as mentors and tutors in a variety of project-based workshops. Video Production students work with professionals to create their own documentaries, Journalism interns team up with journalists to publish their own newspaper, and those in the Theatre Programme study The Method with experienced actors and then test their skills on scenes and improvisation. Plus-Programmes include Fashion and Design; Journalism; Digital, Documentary, and Special Processes Photography; Video Production; and Theatre.

All Career Plus-Programme participants are eligible to receive three college credits upon successful completion of their entire programme. These credits will be issued by Cavendish College and are transferable for high school or college credit and to bolster college applications.

Interns maintain a weekly journal in which they reflect on a subject of their own choice or pick from a wide range of suggested topics. The journal can be used as a valuable resource for writing high school essays and preparing for college entrance essays.

ENROLLMENT
The program accepts high school students, including graduating seniors, ages 16 to 18. Between 150 and 220 students are enrolled each session.

EXTRA OPPORTUNITIES AND ACTIVITIES
After a full week of internships, theatre, concerts, and special dinners out on the town, weekends are split between "pick and choose" days in London and daylong excursions into the country. Interns enjoy exploring the historic sites of Stonehenge, Bath, the Cotswolds, Brighton, Greenwich, and Cambridge. London itself has much to offer, including afternoon tea with scones and cream at Harrods, Madame Tussaud's, Piccadilly, and the street musicians in Leicester Square. Past interns have seen Usher, Tina Turner, Red Hot Chili Peppers, Simon and Garfunkel, and Oasis in concert. Opportunities abound for the free evenings.

An Intern Exchange exclusive offers interns a special college planning programme entitled The IEI Advantage. The series of three workshops helps interns use their IEI summer experience to maximum advantage in the college application and interview process and beyond.

FACILITIES
Interns live in two comfortable, secure, University of London residence halls—Hughes Parry Hall and Canterbury Hall. These

adjacent modern dormitories, with single rooms, shared baths, common rooms, and TV lounges, face an elegant Georgian crescent with lovely gardens. Tennis and squash courts and a pool are available for the interns' use. Reception desks are manned 24 hours a day; public telephones and laundry facilities are available. A full English breakfast and a three-course evening meal (with vegetarian options) are provided in the spacious, self-service dining rooms. The surrounding Russell Square neighborhood, friendly and cozy, offers all the conveniences of home—cleaners, restaurants, a supermarket, a chemist, a movie theatre, and a health food store. Three tube stations are within easy walking distance.

STAFF

The program staff includes Directors Nina M. Glickman, M.Ed., and Lynn Ann Weinstein, who founded Intern Exchange International nineteen years ago and have personally supervised its growth and development ever since. IEI prides itself on always having appropriate supervision for its interns. The program is one of the few in which a Director lives with the students. The summer staff members are experienced and mature. The Dorm Leader, who has experience working with teens, serves as a liaison between the students, Resident Assistants (RAs), and Directors. The Career Plus-Programme Administrator works with the Tutors in the day-to-day operations of these programs. The Resident Assistants are experienced teachers. They assume responsibility for a group of students and provide support, encouragement, and guidance. All IEI staff members live in the dorms with the interns and are available 24 hours a day, seven days a week.

MEDICAL CARE

IEI is affiliated with experienced physicians who are available to see the interns and on call 24 hours a day in the event of an emergency.

COSTS

Program tuition in 2007 is $6945 plus group airfare. Included in the tuition is housing, breakfast and dinner daily, linens and towels, and housekeeping services. Also included are special dinner events, group activities (scheduled theatre, weekend trips, and excursions), a Tube Pass, and luggage tags. Not included in the fee are transportation to and from London from the students' home cities, lunches, laundry, souvenirs, personal spending money, health club, and optional trip cancellation and medical insurance.

TRANSPORTATION

IEI interns are routed to London from major airports convenient to their homes. All flights are on regularly scheduled commercial airlines. Interns on IEI group flights are met at London's Heathrow Airport and transferred to IEI's housing in London. To facilitate well-organized departures and arrivals, all travel is arranged by IEI's Travel Coordinator. Students need a valid passport to enter the United Kingdom; visas are not required for holders of U.S. passports.

APPLICATION TIMETABLE

Admission to the internship program is on a rolling basis and is extremely limited in certain programs. There is no final date for registration; the final date depends on the availability of internships and housing. Students who apply after April 1 should telephone the IEI office to confirm availability of places in the program. Completed applications are reviewed promptly. After acceptance, Interns receive a BritKit (IEI's summer guide), travel information, medical forms, and other important information.

FOR MORE INFORMATION, CONTACT

Nina Miller Glickman, M.Ed., and Lynn Ann Weinstein, Directors
Intern Exchange International
2606 Bridgewood Circle
Boca Raton, Florida 33434-4118

Phone: 561-477-2434
Fax: 561-477-6532
E-mail: info@internexchange.com
Web site: http://www.internexchange.com

PARTICIPANT/FAMILY COMMENTS

"Thank you for another fabulous summer! I had so much fun in London. I really got a taste of behind-the-scenes gallery work."

"I've had a great time on this program with the friends I've made as well as at my medical internship. I wish I could do this every summer!"

INTERNSHIP CONNECTION

SUMMER INTERNSHIPS FOR HIGH SCHOOL AND COLLEGE STUDENTS

BOSTON, MASSACHUSETTS

TYPE OF PROGRAMS: Internship programs
PARTICIPANTS: High school and college students from Boston and the surrounding areas
PROGRAM DATES: Four to six weeks, flexible schedule, June through August
HEAD OF PROGRAM: Carole Jabbawy, Ed.D., Founder and Director

LOCATION

Internship Connection provides high school and college students with customized internships matched to their career interests in downtown and Greater Boston. Students must live at home or have their own housing.

BACKGROUND AND PHILOSOPHY

As a college professor, administrator, and parent of three grown sons, Dr. Carole Jabbawy learned first-hand the advantages experienced by students who sought out internships starting in high school and continuing through college. She established Internship Connection as a comprehensive school-to-career program that simplifies the time-consuming process of finding an internship. The program provides students with career counseling, practical tools for creating a resume, interview preparation, and a match to a mentor in the student's field of interest. Individualized internships provide opportunities for personal growth, networking contacts for the future, and a competitive advantage when applying to colleges and jobs. A key component of the program is a carefully crafted mentor's letter of recommendation designed for college and job applications that confirms and describes the student's in-depth academic and career interests and how they relate to their internship.

Often students must choose a college major by sophomore year, and if the student is applying to a specialized college program such as engineering, they need to know by their senior year of high school. Experiencing a summer internship confirms to students and parents that the career interest is a good match, or it may lead to another area of interest. Students have the advantage of "trying on" a career before committing to years of preparation and a significant financial investment. The Internship Connection program fosters independence and responsibility and helps students connect to their own unique strengths, interests, and talents. Students gain confidence and acquire maturity and life skills through career experience.

PROGRAM OFFERINGS

Becoming a sports reporter at a local newspaper, caring for patients at a walk-in medical clinic for the homeless in Boston, working in the news division of a cable TV station, interning at an arts non-profit, or working for a local congressman at the Massachusetts State House are just a few opportunities students have experienced through the Internship Connection.

Program components include: guidance relating academic interests and talents to career possibilities; assistance with creating a resume and preparing for a workplace interview; educational school-to-career materials on topics such as qualities that employers seek, professionalism, and how to ask for a letter of recommendation; journals designed for reflection; feedback on journal entries; a letter of recommendation from the workplace mentor; and community service documentation.

Internships are unpaid, and students work part-time for an approximate total of 60 hours, usually over a four- to six-week period during the summer. The schedule is flexible, determined by the needs of both student and mentor. The process usually begins sometime between October and April, with an initial meeting between the student and the program director to discuss the student's academic and extracurricular interests and special talents. Career options are explored, and primary and secondary career interests are identified. The student receives instructions for creating a resume and is then coached through the process by e-mailed drafts and revisions. In addition, the student is prepared, via telephone, for the upcoming workplace interview. Typical interview questions are asked and tips are provided.

At the same time, members of the Internship Connection staff research and establish contacts with potential mentors and placement sites. Special searches are conducted when a student identifies a unique talent or combined career interests. In all cases, a placement is selected that best matches the individual interests and geographical preferences of the student as well as the needs of the mentoring organization.

Then, sometime between March and May, when a potential match is made, the student is put in contact with the placement site. Once the internship is confirmed, the student establishes goals and a schedule with the workplace mentor. Most students work part-time, allowing them to incorporate other activities, jobs, or downtime. During the internship, the student e-mails and receives feedback on a brief, weekly journal entry sent to Internship Connection. Often students refer to their journals when preparing for college interviews and essays.

Upon successful completion of the internship, the workplace mentor writes a letter of recommendation that focuses on not only the student's personal qualities, but also the connection between the internship and the student's academic and career interests. The Internship Connection also provides documentation for 60 hours of community service credit for those students choosing to intern at nonprofit organizations.

DAILY SCHEDULE

The student and workplace mentor coordinate a schedule to suit both of their needs and the particular demands of the internship. Because each internship is part-time, students have the advantage of being able to take classes or work other jobs during the summer. Sometimes, however, college students prefer a full-time schedule, which can also be arranged.

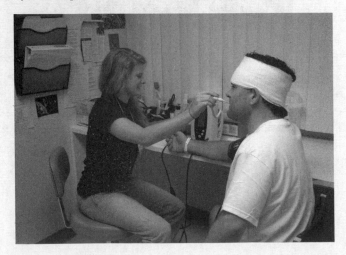

ENROLLMENT

The program is open to high school and college students. Students are encouraged to apply by February to assure proper time for a placement. Applications after April 1 will be accepted as time and space allow.

STAFF

Carole Jabbawy, Ed.D., the Director of Internship Connection, holds a doctorate in education from Boston University in educational leadership and curriculum development. Her career in education spans more than thirty years, including teaching middle and high school students, training and supervising classroom teachers, and advising high school and college students about career opportunities. Leading workshops for teachers and parents, she focuses on bringing out the unique strengths and talents of each student. She is an educational consultant to museums with respect to museum/school collaborations and to businesses relating to the development and implementation of on-site internship programs for high school and college students.

The program's staff members are carefully chosen for both their experience in working with students as well as for their contacts in a wide variety of career fields. They work with experts in various areas to provide students with the life skills and materials they need to take part in a successful, positive internship.

COSTS

The cost of a summer or school-year internship is $1500. This covers the initial student assessment meeting, administrative costs, career counseling, a portfolio of educational materials, resume assistance, preparation for the workplace interview, securing and coordinating the placement, and supervision and feedback on the portfolio journal assignment.

TRANSPORTATION

Students convey their location preferences for their internship. They are responsible for their own transportation to and from their internships.

APPLICATION TIMETABLE

Members of the Internship Connection staff enjoy talking to students who would like to learn more about the program before enrolling. To enroll, students are encouraged to visit the Internship Connection Web site, http://www.internshipconnection.com, where they can print out their application and the consent and release form and later mail them with the $500 deposit. The deposit holds space in the program and initiates the process that secures an internship that matches the student's specific interests. The balance of the cost is due April 1 for summer interns and must be paid before the internship begins. Admission is on a rolling basis. Students who apply after April 1 are admitted as time and space allow. Students are contacted after their application materials and deposit are received.

FOR MORE INFORMATION, CONTACT

Dr. Carole Jabbawy
Internship Connection
17 Countryside Road
Newton, Massachusetts 02459

Phone: 617-796-9283
Fax: 617-796-9283
E-mail: carole@internshipconnection.com
Web site: http://www.internshipconnection.com/

PARTICIPANT/FAMILY COMMENTS

"During all of my college interviews, I talked about my summer internship at a political action non-profit. The college admissions counselors seemed impressed that I already had gained this type of experience in high school."— Eric M., former IC intern, now a freshman at Stanford University

"I valued the independence and how much the station trusted me to go out on my own with a $10,000 camera! Too often interns don't get much responsibility. I wasn't copying papers and getting coffee. I had an amazing experience and was able to learn about the communications field and what goes into being a successful journalist." —Amanda K., interned in the news division of a local cable TV station during her junior summer of high school

"I just went to the Jug squad...a group of inner-city kids my age who are training to be peer leaders relating to health issues in their community. I have the privilege to watch, learn, and sometimes teach. My mentor is involving me in everything. I've helped manage several training sessions and became the leader on my last day." —Nikki S., interned at The Medical Foundation during her sophomore summer of high school

THE JOHNS HOPKINS UNIVERSITY PRE-COLLEGE PROGRAM

SUMMER ACADEMIC ENRICHMENT

BALTIMORE, MARYLAND

TYPE OF PROGRAM: Academic enrichment, residential and commuter

PARTICIPANTS: Coeducational, high school students finishing their sophomore, junior, or senior year

PROGRAM DATES: Term I (commuters only), June; Term II, July

LOCATION

The Johns Hopkins University Homewood campus in Baltimore is home to 4,100 undergraduates, 1,600 graduate students, and 400 faculty members. Not all stay for the summer, but many do, making the campus a lively place for summer study and exploration. Closed to automobiles, the 140-acre campus, located in a residential area north of downtown, offers a bucolic summer atmosphere. Students meet new friends and walk to class along meandering brick paths. They study under spreading trees and on sunlit benches found throughout the park-like campus.

BACKGROUND AND PHILOSOPHY

During the Pre-College Summer Program, Hopkins opens a wide range of undergraduate courses to outstanding high school students age 15 and older who come to campus to earn transferable college credit while they test the University as a possible college choice. Rigorous courses promise academic challenge, while many planned activities, field trips, and social events make the program a highly structured and unforgettable experience, no matter where students finally choose to attend college.

PROGRAM OFFERINGS

The Johns Hopkins Pre-College Summer Program courses offer students a rare glimpse into a unique institution. Participants select up to two college-level courses offered during one of two 5-week terms for commuting students. Residential students, on campus during the second term, also experience (supervised) residence-hall living. Some students choose to explore wide-ranging interests; others concentrate in specific academic disciplines. All participants study in small classes taught by outstanding faculty members and receive an exhilarating introduction to the renowned Hopkins learning experience. Extracurricular activities broaden the experience even more. Participants may follow a student at the medical school, explore computer music at the Peabody Conservatory, observe astronomers at work on Hubble and FUSE, or enjoy a reading by an award-winning author.

Students apply for different reasons: to get ahead on college requirements, to try a new subject of interest, to complete a college-level course, or to reach beyond high school curricula. They choose from such wide-ranging classes as Calculus, Tutankhamen and His Time, and Introduction to Oceanography. Tours to Hopkins centers and research facilities, meetings with physicians and specialists at the Bloomberg School of Public Health, guidance from experienced advisers, firsthand exposure to the latest data from the Space Telescope Science Institute, a visit to an embassy in nearby Washing-

ton, D.C.—such activities extend the benefits of this prestigious program far beyond the classroom.

Students may obtain 1 college credit in the following new programs:

Health Studies—Molecular Biology and Bioethics: This program is offered in the first two weeks in July.

Earth and Planetary Studies—Natural Disasters and Global Change: This program is available during the middle two weeks in July.

History—The American Civil War: This program is offered during the last week in July and the first week in August.

ENROLLMENT

High school students at least 15 years old who are finishing their sophomore, junior, or senior year of high school with a minimum grade point average of 3.0 (on a 4.0 scale) are eligible to apply for admission.

DAILY SCHEDULE

Residential participants spend five weeks of their summer testing out the life of a full-time Johns Hopkins student. They live on campus in residence halls, eat with their new friends in dining halls, burn the midnight oil in the computer labs, and relax in the social lounges—all while earning college credit in real Hopkins undergraduate courses. As residential students, they make the 140-acre Homewood campus their home. Residential and commuter students alike experience the very best of college life: small, challenging classes taught by an exceptional faculty.

EXTRA OPPORTUNITIES AND ACTIVITIES

Summer may seem relaxed, but a wealth of activities keep after-class schedules bustling with fun and enrichment. Participants take trips to Baltimore's Inner Harbor, Gettysburg, or Washington, D.C. On campus, they swim or work out in the O'Connor Recreation Center, run on the outdoor track, tour the Lacrosse Hall of Fame, or play on an intramural sports team. The Mattin Center offers music practice rooms and the Digital Media Center. Students show off to new friends at the Pre-College Talent Show, enjoy great art at the Baltimore

Museum of Art next door to campus, relax with friends at coffee houses, hang out on the quad, and much more.

FACILITIES
The state-of-the-art facilities on the Homewood campus—including many new classrooms and laboratories for languages, science, and computers; a comprehensive research library; and a recreation center with a climbing wall, indoor and outdoor tracks, fields, and a pool—are all open to program participants. Residential facilities include wired (and wireless) residence-hall rooms.

STAFF
Experienced residential staff members help students discover the many learning opportunities available inside and outside the classroom. They guide students toward the right academic and personal advising. They oversee extracurricular activities and social events, and they help each program participant get the most from a rich and varied program.

MEDICAL CARE
Residential advisers help students obtain health services, available through the campus Center for Health and Wellness, which is open from 8:30 until 5, Monday through Friday, and through Campus Security on weekends for emergencies and referrals. Students needing special medication should bring a five-week supply. The Health Center requires several immunizations for students living in campus housing.

RELIGIOUS LIFE
The Office of the Chaplain publishes a Faith Community Directory that is included in each orientation packet. The directory lists more than twenty-five different religious denominations that hold services in Baltimore, many within walking distance of the campus. Transportation to and from most religious services is available.

COSTS
Commuter Program (Terms I & II) Students living with a parent or legal guardian in the Baltimore area may commute to classes during Term I or II. The tuition is $590 per credit. Commuter students must also pay an activities fee of $100. Books and pocket expenses are not included in the program fee. Approximately $50 per week, or $250 total, is recommended for pocket expenses.

Residential Program (Term II only) The Term II residential program fee of $5990 includes tuition for two courses, room and board, and activities. Books and pocket expenses are not included in the program fee. Approximately $50 per week, or $250 total, is recommended for pocket expenses.

TRANSPORTATION
Residential students live on the campus in residence halls. Commuter students provide their own transportation to and from the campus.

APPLICATION TIMETABLE
The early application deadline is March 21. Applications accompanied by financial aid forms are due by February 15. Applications for the Term II residential program are due by March 30. Term I commuter applications are due by May 16. Term II commuter applications are due by June 20.

FOR MORE INFORMATION, CONTACT
Summer Programs Office
100 Whitehead Hall
The Johns Hopkins University
3400 North Charles Street
Baltimore, Maryland 21218-2685
Phone: 410-516-4548
    800-548-0548 (toll-free)
Fax: 410-516-5585
E-mail: summer@jhu.edu
Web site: http://www.jhu.edu/summer

THE JUNIOR STATESMEN SUMMER SCHOOL

GEORGETOWN, PRINCETON, STANFORD, AND YALE UNIVERSITIES

TYPE OF PROGRAM: Political education and leadership training

PARTICIPANTS: Coeducational, ages 14–18, entering grades 9–12

ENROLLMENT: Varies by session

PROGRAM DATES: Georgetown Session I, June 16–July 7; Georgetown Session II, July 14–August 4; Princeton and Yale, June 23 to July 18; Stanford, June 30 to July 25

HEAD OF PROGRAM: Jessica Brow, Associate Director of Summer Programs

LOCATION
There are six sessions of the Junior Statesmen Summer School: Session I is held in the San Francisco Bay Area at Stanford University; Session II is held at Yale University in Connecticut; Sessions III and IV are held in Washington, D.C., at Georgetown University; and Session V is held at Princeton University in New Jersey. Each locale is within minutes of famous historical and cultural attractions.

BACKGROUND AND PHILOSOPHY
For more than seventy years, the Junior Statesmen Summer School has prepared students for responsible leadership in a democratic society. The goals of the Summer School are to develop an appreciation and understanding of American democratic history and government; to encourage the natural idealism of youth while confronting them with the realities of practical politics and helping them learn that a just and democratic society requires adherence to certain ethical principles; to help create an atmosphere, a challenge, and a stimulus for the intellectual awakening of high school students; to help students develop leadership skills; to teach students techniques of oral communication, argumentation, and persuasion; to confront a diverse group of young people with the challenge of living together in an independent environment; to encourage logical and critical thinking; to help students discover the joy and excitement of independent research; to

develop students' self-confidence, which is essential to effective leadership; to develop an appreciation of freedom of speech; and to help students develop time-management skills and a sense of personal responsibility.

PROGRAM OFFERINGS
The Junior Statesmen Summer School offers a rigorous academic challenge to outstanding high school students. The curriculum at all sessions includes an Advanced Placement course in U.S. government and politics, an honors course in speech communication, an exciting high-level political speakers program, and debates on current issues. Students at the Junior Statesmen Stanford Summer School may take AP Economics, Constitutional Law, or AP Comparative Government instead of AP American Government. Students at the Yale session may take Constitutional Law. Students at the Georgetown session may take U.S. Foreign Policy or Constitutional Law. Princeton University students may take AP U.S. History, AP Comparative Government, Political Philosophy, or U.S. Foreign Policy. Students entering ninth grade may participate in the Freshman Scholars program at Princeton and take AP U.S. Government and Public Speaking.

Students may obtain high school credit for their course work at the Summer School. These courses are offered as Advanced Placement and/or honors classes. If high school credit is desired, students must make preliminary arrangements with their school prior to the session.

Speakers Program The Summer School is enriched by a high-level, nonpartisan speakers program that is closely integrated with classroom instruction. Free-wheeling question-and-answer sessions allow students to examine the institutions and processes of American government with controversial policy makers.

Students at the Georgetown session question national leaders in the Capitol Building, the Pentagon, the State Department, the White House, and the Supreme Court Chambers. Yale and Princeton session students question ambassadors in the United Nations building. During the Stanford Summer School speakers program, students question outstanding scholars on campus as well as national and state leaders who join the students for in-depth examinations of politics in the "Golden State."

ENROLLMENT
About 1,400 outstanding high school students attend the five Summer School sessions. Enrollment at Yale is 250 students; at Stanford, 300 students; at each Georgetown session, 250 students; and at Princeton, 350 students. At the Georgetown session, most students are entering their senior or junior year in high school. At the other sessions, incoming high school sophomores may also participate. Students in the Freshman Scholars program at Princeton are incoming ninth graders. The age range is from 14 to 18.

DAILY SCHEDULE
At the Stanford, Yale, and Princeton sessions, government classes are held in the morning, speech classes in the afternoon, and student debates in the evening. Students taking AP

U.S. History at Princeton take the class in the morning and afternoon. Students in the Freshman Scholars program at Princeton have class in the morning and afternoon, with study time in the evening. At the Georgetown session there is no set schedule, owing to an extensive speakers program. Classes are held six days a week at various times during the day and evening. No classes are held on Sunday. There is a curfew, at which time students must be in the dorm. High school field trip rules apply. Expulsion, without refund, is the penalty for serious rule violations.

EXTRA OPPORTUNITIES AND ACTIVITIES
At each session, university admissions officials discuss their institution's admission policies, financial aid, housing, student life, and academic offerings.

Parties and dances are held on Saturday. A talent show is held during each session. On Sunday, students and faculty members may visit nearby cultural and historical attractions. In Washington, trips to the Smithsonian museums and other landmarks are encouraged. Stanford session students go to San Francisco; Yale and Princeton students enjoy attractions in New York City. Students may take advantage of recreational facilities on each campus; some incur a fee. Available recreation may include swimming, tennis, basketball, racquetball, and volleyball.

FACILITIES
Students use university classrooms, libraries, and recreational facilities and live in residence halls.

STAFF
The Junior Statesmen Summer School faculty members, resident assistants, and staff members are drawn from universities around the country. Government and history professors are political scientists or historians who hold a doctorate. Speech instructors have at least a master's degree and are dedicated to excellence in their own classroom teaching and in the oral and written work of their students. Resident Assistants are college students (or recent college graduates) who have attended a previous session of the Summer School.

Faculty and staff members and resident assistants live in the university residence near the students and are responsible around the clock for student supervision and academic and personal counseling.

COSTS
For the 2007 session, tuition, room, and board were $4150, which included transportation to the speakers program. Not covered were school supplies, souvenirs, access to recreational facilities (if the university charges a fee), laundry, and some meals off campus on speaker program days. Up to $250 is recommended for spending money. A $100 nonrefundable deposit is required upon acceptance. The tuition balance is due one month before the program. All tuition paid by the student's parents is refundable until two weeks before the start of the Summer School.

FINANCIAL AID
The Junior Statesmen Foundation has a $450,000 scholarship fund to assist students who find tuition to be a barrier. Scholarships ranging from $50 to $2700 are awarded on the basis of academic merit and financial need. More than half of the students receive a scholarship. Parents fill out a financial aid form, which can be requested from The Junior Statesmen Foundation. Staff members assist students who want to try to raise funds in their community.

APPLICATION TIMETABLE
Students may request a Summer School catalog from the Junior Statesmen Foundation. Applicants submit an application form, a three-page essay, a high school transcript, and one teacher recommendation. Students are accepted on a rolling basis. The admission season begins in January and ends in June. There is no application fee.

FOR MORE INFORMATION, CONTACT
Admissions Director
The Junior Statesmen Summer School
400 South Camino Real, Suite 300
San Mateo, California 94402
Phone: 650-347-1600
　　　　800-334-5353 (toll-free)
Fax: 650-347-7200
Web site: http://www.jsa.org

KENT SCHOOL

SUMMER WRITERS CAMP

KENT, CONNECTICUT

TYPE OF PROGRAM: Educational program
PARTICIPANTS: Coed, grades 7–10
ENROLLMENT: 50
PROGRAM DATES: July 6–25, 2008
HEAD OF PROGRAM: Todd Marble, Founder

LOCATION

The Kent School campus is surely one of the most beautiful in the country. Its idyllic western Connecticut setting in the foothills of the Berkshires offers campers the best of natural living. Nestled along the winding Housatonic River at the foot of dramatic Mount Algo, the 1,200-acre campus is a short walk from the picturesque town of Kent and near the Appalachian Trail.

BACKGROUND AND PHILOSOPHY

Whether a poem, a play, or a piece of science fiction, writing is a powerful way to express ideas and passions. At Kent School Summer Writers Camp, young writers come from all over the world to find their voices, hone their craft, and gain the confidence to share their work in a fun, supportive atmosphere.

In a small Morning Workshop taught by a professional writer, students explore their own voice through a variety of written forms. They have the opportunity to delve more deeply into a genre of their choice in an Afternoon Writing Studio led by a writer with expertise in that particular form. They also have the chance to share their work in camp publications and spoken-word venues.

When students are not writing or making new friends, they are enjoying a variety of art forms and athletic activities from soccer to rowing.

Kent School Summer Camp accepts students without regard to race, color, creed, or national or ethnic origin and so administers its educational policies, admissions policies, scholarships and loan programs, athletic policies, and other school-administered policies.

PROGRAM OFFERINGS

Each day is divided into three general activity periods—Morning Workshop, Afternoon Writing Studio, and recreational activities—followed by an optional swim in Kent School's indoor pool to help cool down in late afternoon. Throughout the day, there is plenty of time for snacks, visiting, and downtime.

In Morning Workshop, students explore a variety of genres, including poetry, short story, essay, memoir, and science fiction. In Afternoon Writing Studio, there is a more intensive concentration in the writing form of choice. Recent offerings have included songwriting, journalism, poetry, fantasy, playwriting, and personal essay/memoir.

In Workshops and Writing Studios, which are limited to 10, students investigate all stages of the creative writing process—from the first spark of an idea to a finished piece worthy of an audience. They learn techniques for generating ideas and how to organize their thoughts and polish their work. In an environment of trust and exploration, they discover and refine individual writing practice through daily writing exercises. These range from spontaneous, 5-minute "flash fiction" pieces to work that calls on a deeper level of thought and feeling, such as a poem cycle or a personal essay about an earliest memory. As the program progresses, students have the opportunity to develop or complete, with a teacher's guidance, any longer work they may have already begun. Through it all, constructive feedback from teachers and peers helps students become stronger, more confident writers.

The Visiting Artists Series introduces students to other artistic disciplines through a four-part series of performances and workshops. The visiting artists explore with students the creative process and connections among the arts. Working in a variety of art

forms, including music, dance, and visual arts, they challenge students to take creative risks, experiment, and improvise.

On Visiting Writers Day, campers have the unique opportunity to meet and learn from several dynamic authors. These professional writers spend the day at Kent working with campers in small groups. Each writer leads an interactive seminar during Morning Workshop, and in the afternoon, visiting writers and students participate together in a reading for the camp community.

As students develop as writers over the course of three weeks, they may want to share their work. One great venue for doing this is Café Kent, the School's on-campus evening coffee house series, where the young writers show friends and teachers what they have created. In addition to spoken word, Café Kent showcases individual and group performances that may include music, comedy, dance, and theater.

Students also have the opportunity to publish their creative writing in the camp's literary journal, *Paper Café,* as well as the camp newspaper and individual and class chapbooks and on the camp's Web site.

Students choose one sport or art activity for each of two 8-day sessions. These 1-hour afternoon recreational activities are co-ed and noncompetitive and include basketball, soccer, water sports, rowing, and tennis. The camp provides all equipment except tennis rackets. Art activities have included painting, drawing, and performing arts. Students are encouraged to bring musical instruments, and all campers have access to Kent School's abundant resources.

ENROLLMENT

There are 50 girls and boys participating in the Summer Writers Camp, entering grades 7–10.

One of the best parts of life for students at Kent Writers Camp is making friends with people they might otherwise never meet. Here, the sounds of many accents and regional dialects blend into the communal voice of a writers' colony, because in addition to most of the fifty U.S. states, young writers come from such countries as Aruba, Brazil, Canada, China, England, France, Germany, Guam, Italy, Japan, Mexico, Portugal, Saudi Arabia, South Korea, Spain, and Thailand.

EXTRA OPPORTUNITIES AND ACTIVITIES

On the second and third Sundays of camp, students hop a bus for an exciting day trip to a nearby theater or other recreational venue. Recent summer performances have included productions at

Shakespeare & Co. in Lennox, Massachusetts, and the Powerhouse Summer Theater at Vassar College in Poughkeepsie, New York.

During the week, students head to such local attractions as Lake Waramaug State Park. Saturday evenings are filled with dances and trips to an inline skating rink and video arcade. And of course, campfires and storytelling round out the communal fun.

DAILY SCHEDULE

6:45 . . .	Wake-up exercises (optional)
7:15 . . .	Rising bell
7:30 . . .	Breakfast
8:00– 8:15 . . .	Nurse's office hours
8:30– 9:30 . . .	Morning Workshop
9:45 . . .	Snack break
10:15–11:15 . . .	Morning Workshop
11:45 . . .	Lunch
12:15– 1:15 . . .	Reading/computer lab/extra help
1:30– 2:30 . . .	Writing Studio
3:00– 4:30 . . .	Recreational activities
4:30– 5:30 . . .	Rest period
5:00– 6:00 . . .	Nurse's office hours
5:30 . . .	Dinner
6:15– 7:15 . . .	Visiting Artist Workshop/group activities
7:30– 8:30 . . .	Study hall
9:15 . . .	Dorm meetings/student readings
9:30 . . .	Dorm closing
9:45 . . .	Lights out for grades 7–9
10:00 . . .	Lights out for grade 10

FACILITIES

Through camp dorm life, students get to know the independence, responsibility, and excitement of a boarding school experience. Comfortable and modern boys' and girls' dorms are supervised by experienced resident faculty members and college-aged teaching fellows. Each dorm has a common area where campers can meet and hang out with friends. Rooms are furnished with writing desks and bureaus, and all are equipped with bedding and linens.

Classes are held in air-conditioned Foley Hall. Computer writing labs are available for writing and research. The John Gray Park Library has 50,000 volumes and 125 periodicals. Recreational facilities include a 25-yard, six-lane pool; the Fitness Center; thirteen outdoor clay tennis courts; four indoor tennis courts; two basketball courts, three squash courts, and a state-of-the-art rowing center.

STAFF

Summer program faculty members are drawn from Kent and other top independent schools and universities. As published authors, poets, and journalists, they know how to help students grow as writers. And because each teacher is aided by a teaching assistant (many of whom are English majors at top U.S. colleges) students receive lots of individual attention throughout the program. Since

teachers and their assistants live on campus during the program, they are available throughout the day and evening for questions and conversation.

Todd Marble, the camp's founder and director, received his B.A. from Colby College and his M.A. from Trinity College. Mr. Marble is Kent School's Athletics Director and Director of Summer Programs as well as a coach. He developed the Kent School Summer Writers Camp and has directed it since its inception in 1996. He taught mathematics for seven years at Kingswood-Oxford School, where he was the third-form master and served on the admissions staff. Mr. Marble is an avid outdoorsman and sports enthusiast.

Julia Bolus, the camp's academic director and teacher, received her B.A. from Connecticut College. Ms. Bolus, in her eleventh year as the camp's Academic Director, is a writer who also works with the Arthur Miller Literary and Dramatic Property Trust. A play based on her collection of poems, *Circus of Infinite Attractions*, premiered off-Broadway at the International Fringe Festival. Ms. Bolus also works with the Inge Morath Foundation and has participated as a visiting writer in public schools and as a presenter for the Connecticut Commission on the Arts.

MEDICAL CARE

Around-the-clock security is provided to ensure Kent School's safe, friendly atmosphere. A registered nurse is available daily throughout the program, and a local doctor is always on call. Excellent hospital facilities are within easy reach in nearby Sharon and New Milford. Emergency calls to or from students are channeled through the director's office. Pay phones, located in dorm hallways, are available for student use. All emergency and dorm phone numbers are mailed to parents before the start of camp.

COSTS

The inclusive fee for boarding students is $2800. Before students arrive, they are advised to establish a student bank account for their discretionary use during camp. The suggested amount for an account is $125, and limited withdrawals are allowed, provided the account has a balance.

APPLICATION TIMETABLE

Potential campers can apply online at http://www.writerscamp.org. In addition to the application, students should send a handwritten writing sample (no more than one page), a school transcript, and a recommendation from the school principal, guidance counselor, or current teacher. There is a $25 application fee, with the check made payable to Kent School Summer Writers Camp.

FOR MORE INFORMATION, CONTACT

Meredith Schipani
Summer Writers Camp Admissions Director
Kent School
1 Macedonia Road
Kent, Connecticut 06757
Phone: 860-538-KENT (5368)
Fax: 860-927-6109
E-mail: schipanim@kent-school.edu
Web site: http://www.writerscamp.org

KILLOOLEET

SUMMER PROGRAM

HANCOCK, VERMONT

TYPE OF PROGRAM: Traditional summer camp
PARTICIPANTS: Coeducational, ages 9–14
ENROLLMENT: 100 campers per summer
PROGRAM DATES: June 29 to August 17
HEADS OF PROGRAM: Kate Seeger and Dean Spencer, Directors

LOCATION
Located on the edge of the Green Mountain National Forest—which extends for hundreds of square miles to the north, west, and south—Killooleet's 300 acres feature woods, meadows, rolling hills, and a private lake. Most campers bring or rent bicycles to explore Killooleet's expansive ½-mile campus. Camp is just 35 miles northeast of Rutland, in the center of Vermont.

BACKGROUND AND PHILOSOPHY
Killooleet is run by educators who believe that a supportive environment emphasizing community, group dynamics, and respect for individual freedom promotes happiness and helps everyone achieve more. Killooleet campers find an atmosphere in which they can invest their energy in growth, learning as they explore new challenges. They come to value their contributions, believe in themselves, enjoy life, develop close friendships, and, ultimately, stand on their own two feet. Self-confidence blossoms as campers acquire skills and discipline in activities in which they are personally interested. Through its noncompetitive program, Killooleet removes winning as a motivation and replaces it with the pleasures of participation, challenge, and accomplishment. Killooleet has little need for hierarchy and has only a few educational rules: scapegoating, rudeness, put-downs, and breaking group concentration are not allowed.

Killooleet is coeducational, understanding that, in childhood, youths need to define their own masculinity or femininity. Realistic relationships between the sexes, rather than segregation, are nurtured at all ages in camp. While cabin groups are assigned by age and gender, girls and boys share meals, hikes, and activities.

There is respect for the value of work. Days begin with cabin cleanup, and periods include time for getting out and putting away materials. On overnight trips, campers do everything to make a campsite livable. During Crew Time, campers work in the kitchen, garden, and horse barn or bike to town for the mail. The oldest campers assist the staff and run tables, games, and activities.

Founded in 1927, Killooleet has been under the direction and ownership of the Seeger family—John, Eleanor, and Kate—since 1949. The camp is accredited by the American Camping Association.

PROGRAM OFFERINGS
Killooleet believes in the value of a full camp season, which enables children to face issues and work through them. Summers at Killooleet begin slowly, as each child becomes a respected member of his or her cabin group. During the first ten days, each group is scheduled for every activity. Middle weeks find campers developing individual interests through afternoon choice periods or "checking in" to a favorite activity. The final week is full of performances and closing activities.

Visual Arts The camp provides facilities for woodwork, stained glass, jewelry, silversmithing, batik, drawing, painting, silk screen, sculpture, sewing, weaving, knitting, and ceramics.

Performing Arts The dramatics program is based on improvisation and creative dramatics, and each summer features a musical and several cabin productions. Campers use Killooleet's video studio, cameras, and editing equipment to produce essays, skits, parodies, and short movies. Music is an integral part of camp. Singing and lessons on guitar, five-string banjo, bass, drums, and harmonica are offered. The R&B band and various music ensembles practice regularly.

Sports and Skills Killooleet offers horseback riding, soccer, tennis, basketball, bicycling, swimming, canoeing, sailing, archery, riflery, Ultimate Frisbee, volleyball, and softball. Dance, gymnastics, windsurfing, fencing, karate, lacrosse, and track are often available. The nature room has an array of tools for collecting and examining finds. Electronics and rockets are also available.

Outdoor Exploration Campers explore the beauty of Vermont during day hikes and overnight trips. On these days, everyone is out of camp, climbing a mountain and enjoying the view, bicycling, caving, canoeing, horseback riding, rock climbing, exploring a local brook, or strolling with frequent stops to sketch and photograph the scenery.

ENROLLMENT
Children of every faith, race, and nationality are welcome. Although the majority of campers come from metropolitan New York and Boston, campers and counselors represent many parts of the United States and, normally, six to eight other nations. Killooleet works to dispel prejudices, as every camper finds respected leaders and friends among people of different backgrounds.

DAILY SCHEDULE
Killooleet features four hour-long activity periods each day. Half-hour "recalls" between periods help keep the pace slow and allow campers to learn to use their free time wisely—swimming in the lake on a hot day, finishing a ceramics project, taking a guitar lesson, or just having time to get ready for the next scheduled period.

Ending times for evening programs vary with the activity. Bedtime includes time for winding down, chatting, independent reading, and reading aloud or singing.

Killooleet punctuates the week twice, with hikes on Wednesday and a Town Meeting on Sunday. The season features two 3-day camping trips.

COSTS
Camp costs in 2007 were $6600 for the full season. This fee covers all camp expenses except travel to and from camp. After the deposit, which is due upon enrollment, two payments are usually made to cover the remaining balance; other payment plans are available.

FINANCIAL AID
Some scholarships, based on need, are available. On average, 24 percent of campers do not pay full tuition.

APPLICATION TIMETABLE
Killooleet is glad to answer questions about camp over the phone and will arrange a personal interview with parents if possible. Applications are accepted until the program is full.

FOR MORE INFORMATION, CONTACT
winter
Kate Seeger
Killooleet
70 Trull Street
Somerville, Massachusetts 02145
Phone: 617-666-1484
       800-395-2221 (toll-free)
Fax: 617-666-0378
E-mail: kseeger@killooleet.com
Web site: http://www.killooleet.com

summer
Kate Seeger
Killooleet
Hancock, Vermont 05748
Phone: 802-767-3152

EXTRA OPPORTUNITIES AND ACTIVITIES
Cabins take turns planning Sunday afternoon's all-camp game or special event. Evening activities include sings, campfires, cabin evenings, and one or two evenings a week for special interest clubs such as cooking, dance, cartooning, and juggling.

FACILITIES
Killooleet's grounds include a private lake, tennis courts, softball and soccer fields, a basketball court, archery and riflery ranges, a garden, barns, and a horseback riding ring as well as a theater, band room, the Main House, and five arts buildings. The center room of the Main House features a library filled with books and music. Campers live in wooden cabins with screened, shuttered windows and doors. Groups of 8 to 12 live with 2 or 3 counselors. Campers eat in groups of 4 (with 1 counselor) on the screened porch of the Main House.

STAFF
Counselors run their cabins and activities in a manner consistent with their individual personalities and beliefs. From this, campers learn the value of individuality. Teachers anchor the staff; most staff members are in college or are recent college graduates (the minimum counselor age is 18). Each summer, about one half of the staff members return. Counselors are equally divided between men and women, and the camper-counselor ratio is 3:1.

MEDICAL CARE
A registered nurse oversees health care and a doctor is on call. The nearest hospital is just 25 miles away. The state of Vermont inspects and licenses Killooleet and approves sources of water and food.

RELIGIOUS LIFE
Killooleet's philosophy is partially based on Quaker principles, which teach that each person has an inner light and balance. Everyone is encouraged to speak specifically of their own faith and philosophy freely as occasion arises. There is no all-camp devotion.

PARTICIPANT/FAMILY COMMENTS

"Thanks for the two best summers of my life. I learned so much and grew so much as a person. I learned about kindness, respect for others, and human nature, not to mention many other things. More importantly I learned about confidence and believing in myself. The values that Killooleet has taught me will stay with me for the rest of my life ... it is truly a special place."

LANDMARK SCHOOL SUMMER PROGRAM

∨∨∨∨∨∨∨∨∨∨∨∨∨∨∨∨∨∨∨∨∨∨

SUMMER ACADEMIC PROGRAMS

PRIDES CROSSING, MASSACHUSETTS

TYPE OF PROGRAM: Academic skill development and recreation for students with language-based learning disabilities or dyslexia

PARTICIPANTS: Coeducational, ages 7–20, grades 1–12

ENROLLMENT: 160

PROGRAM DATES: Six-week session, from late June to early August

HEAD OF PROGRAM: Robert J. Broudo, M.Ed., Head of School

LOCATION

Landmark School has two beautiful campuses on the Atlantic coast just 25 miles north of Boston and close to beaches, fishing ports, and sailing centers. The location is ideal for educational, cultural, and recreational activities, and the School takes full advantage of its setting.

BACKGROUND AND PHILOSOPHY

Landmark's Summer Program offers a chance to learn, relax, and have fun in a supportive environment—whether it's gaining a jump start for the next grade or supplementing gaps in learning—for students with language-based learning disabilities. The program combines intensive, academic skill development with recreational activities and exploration along Boston's beautiful North Shore. Landmark provides a customized program for each student that is designed to improve reading, writing, spelling, and study skills. The program's daily one-to-one tutorial is the cornerstone of its individualized approach. Students are bright, motivated to learn, and emotionally healthy, but they need help to achieve academic excellence.

PROGRAM OFFERINGS

Full-Day Academic Program High school students receive two daily periods of one-to-one tutorial instruction within a program that concentrates on mastery of language arts skills. Reading, writing, spelling, and study skills are reinforced in small classes of 4 to 8 students. Math and elective classes are offered as well. In addition, high school students can choose an elective class in art or physical education.

Full-Day Combination Programs Students may choose to combine a morning of academics with one of several hands-on, outdoor afternoon activities. Classes are organized in groups of 4 to 8 students of similar age and achievement levels, with the focus on developing and improving reading, writing, and spelling skills. Each student receives a daily one-to-one tutorial before embarking on an afternoon of inspired creativity, supervised adventures, and group activities.

Marine Science Program Marine science education is offered to students in grades 8–12 who are comfortable around water and interested in the environment. Students spend their afternoon exploring local coastal and ocean ecosystems, working on research teams, and collecting data. As with all of Landmark's Combination/Recreation Programs, the other half of the day is spent in classes in which students develop their language skills through a one-to-one tutorial and in language

arts and math classes. The Marine Science Program provides experience in the field, the laboratory, and the classroom and includes overnight and weekend expeditions.

Adventure Ropes/Sea Kayaking Program Available to students in grades 8–12, the first stage of the Adventure Ropes/Sea Kayaking Program challenges and develops leadership and problem-solving skills, perseverance, and initiative with high-ropes course programming. The second stage, sea kayaking, focuses on paddling strokes, wet exits, and safety techniques. Students learn about seamanship, navigation, and coastal environments and explore group dynamics. The program's final challenge, an independent solo experience, tests each student's inner strength and resources and provides newfound perspectives.

Musical Theater Students in grades 8–12 may choose to perform onstage or develop technical theater skills behind the scenes in the Musical Theater Program. The program culminates in a full-scale theatrical production where performers learn to act, dance, and sing onstage as part of a musical company. Technical students try their hand at set design and building, sound, and lighting and produce the summer musical production.

Exploration Program For students in grades 3–7, Marine Science and Adventure Ropes activities are offered together in consecutive thirteen-day segments. Field trips, lab work, kayaking, an introduction to snorkeling, and exploration of the North Shore's ocean and coastal ecosystems are included. In Adventure Ropes, students engage in fun, problem-solving group activities; games; and confidence building on Landmark's low- and high-ropes courses.

Practical Arts An introduction to woodworking skills and the art of small-engine repair, the Practical Arts Program is offered to students in grades 3–7. The woodworking unit covers basic skills and culminates in building a boat as a final project. Repairing a single-cylinder small engine using common tools, researching parts, and rebuilding an engine with the help of a specialized computer program are highlights of the engine class.

Half-Day Academic Program for Day Students Day students in grades 1–12 may choose a half-day academic option, which is offered in the morning. This program builds language arts skills through small classes and a daily one-to-one tutorial. While the focus is on reading, writing, and spelling skills for all grade levels, a math class is also included for high school students.

ENROLLMENT

Landmark's Summer Program attracts students from across the United States and from many other countries. The program accepts bright students who have been diagnosed with a language-based learning disability such as dyslexia. Successful candidates should be emotionally healthy and motivated to learn but need remedial help with reading, writing, spelling, listening, speaking, or mathematics. Prior to admission, Landmark must receive a diagnostic evaluation as well as educational and medical records. Landmark offers day and residential programs to students in grades 9–12 and day programs to students in grades 1–12. Landmark admits grade 8 students to the residential program on a case-by-case basis.

DAILY SCHEDULE

The day is divided into two parts, from 8 to 11 a.m. and from 12:30 to 3 p.m. Academics are scheduled in the morning, while recreational activities (Marine Science, Adventure Ropes/Sea Kayaking, Musical Theater, Exploration, and Practical Arts) are offered in the afternoon. Students in the Full-Day Academic Program have classes in the morning and the afternoon. From 11 a.m. to 12:30 p.m., high school students have a study period and lunch, while younger students are involved in recreational activities and lunch. Boarding students complete their day with planned recreational activities, dinner, and a quiet hour. Bedtimes vary according to the student's age.

EXTRA OPPORTUNITIES AND ACTIVITIES

Afternoons and weekends offer opportunities for outdoor activities and trips (both day and overnight) to local points of interest, historic sites, and cultural programs. Free time, movies, and social events on campus complement these activities.

FACILITIES

Landmark has two campuses located on Boston's beautiful North Shore. The high school and administrative offices are located in the Prides Crossing section of Beverly, Massachusetts. The elementary/middle school is nestled in the woods on an estate in Manchester-by-the-Sea.

STAFF

Summer staff members are highly trained teachers and supervisors from the regular school year staff. A student-faculty ratio of 3:1 allows Landmark to provide a customized program for each student.

MEDICAL CARE

The Health Center attends to the medical needs of the Landmark community. The center is available on school days from 7 a.m. to 11 p.m.; the duty staff is in charge at other times. Student medications are dispensed from the Health Center. The school physician, other specialists, and the Beverly Hospital Emergency Room are available at all times for residential student appointments and emergencies. The state requires that immunization history forms be submitted at enrollment. In addition, counselors are available if necessary.

RELIGIOUS LIFE

Students who wish to attend religious services are provided with transportation.

COSTS

Tuition varies according to the program. Tuition for 2007 was as follows: Full-Day Academic Program, $8350 for residents and $6050 for day students; Marine Science, Adventure Ropes/Sea Kayaking, and Musical Theater Programs, $7950 for residents and $5650 for day students; elementary/middle school programs (Exploration and Practical Arts), $5650; and Half-Day Academic Program, $3975 (day students only).

TRANSPORTATION

Landmark is located about 25 miles from Boston's Logan Airport and within walking distance of the train from Boston. Scheduled transportation to and from Logan Airport is available.

APPLICATION TIMETABLE

Students are accepted in order of applications received. Early application is advised, as space is limited. Applicants cannot be considered without a full diagnostic report; the School is happy to answer questions about testing and to help guide parents or school counselors to diagnostic sources. A tuition deposit of $500 for day students and $1000 for boarding students must accompany the application.

FOR MORE INFORMATION, CONTACT

Director of Admission
Landmark School
429 Hale Street
P.O. Box 227
Prides Crossing, Massachusetts 01965-0227

Phone: 978-236-3000
Fax: 978-927-7268
E-mail: admission@landmarkschool.org
Web site: http://www.landmarkschool.org

LANDMARK VOLUNTEERS

YOUTH ACROSS AMERICA

ACROSS THE UNITED STATES

TYPE OF PROGRAM: Two-week summer and one-week spring service opportunities with leading nonprofit organizations

PARTICIPANTS: Coeducational: rising sophomores, juniors, and seniors

ENROLLMENT: 625

PROGRAM DATES: Two-week summer programs from June 16 to August 12; one-week spring programs

LOCATION

Every year, Landmark Volunteers is proud to work with more than fifty important and vital nonprofit organizations across the country. Each is dedicated to values that enrich society. Recent programs have included Glacier Institute, Montana; Shakespeare & Company, Massachusetts; Maine Coast Heritage Trust, Maine; Rocky Mountain Village, Colorado; Acadia National Park, Maine; Perkins School for the Blind, Massachusetts; Gould Farm, Massachusetts; Sawtooth National Recreation Area, Idaho; the Boston Symphony at Tanglewood, Massachusetts; the Hole in the Wall Gang Camp, Connecticut; Morgan Horse Farm, Vermont; Norman Rockwell Museum, Massachusetts; National Elk Refuge, Wyoming; Henry Coe State Park, California; Chico Basin Ranch, Colorado; and many others.

BACKGROUND AND PHILOSOPHY

Landmark Volunteers was founded in 1992 by a board of prominent educators and community leaders to provide teenagers with the opportunity to improve themselves by helping improve the world around them. Landmark's core philosophy is that young people are an integral part of society and that they have something unique and important to contribute if given the opportunity to do something meaningful. Those who acquit themselves well in their summer service are provided with letters of recommendation

and community-service credit. The other benefits of volunteering at Landmark are unique to each individual; the experience may plant the seed for a future career, produce a great friend or a lifelong mentor, or form a deep connection with a particular area of the country.

PROGRAM OFFERINGS

Landmark Volunteers works with more than fifty nonprofit organizations across the country—each dedicated to values that enhance society. Allowing students to participate in the missions of these important organizations enables them to effect positive change, both in their own lives and in the lives of others. As a volunteer with Landmark, a student has a distinct "Landmark experience"—an experience that extends through the programs regardless of the site or type of work involved. The Landmark experience is one of fun, hard work, cooperation, and a shared sense of purpose. It is one that has been successful for many years, is well organized by a full-time Landmark staff, and is expertly led in the field by dynamic team leaders. The experience is one of both giving and growth.

Depending on a student's interests, it is important to think about which programs are right for them. When applying to Landmark, volunteers are required to list six programs of interest.

The work of a Landmark volunteer helps further the missions of important organizations and makes a positive impact on society. The type of work varies with the needs and nature of each host organization. At most programs, the work is primarily manual—from clearing trails to painting and building projects to grounds maintenance. At other programs, volunteers may become directly involved in the host organization's mission or with its clientele. For specific descriptions of the work assignments at the various sites, students should visit Landmark's Web site at http://www.volunteers.com.

ENROLLMENT

Enrollment in 2007 was approximately 650 rising high school sophomores, juniors, and seniors.

DAILY SCHEDULE

Landmark teams work a full day and generally adhere to the normal hours of the staff members at their particular location.

EXTRA OPPORTUNITIES AND ACTIVITIES

Volunteers work as a team with 12 other high school students from around the country who want to make a real difference in the world around them. In this spirit of teamwork and dedication, hard work can quickly turn into fun. It is no wonder friendships take root easily, grow, and last a lifetime. After work, students may take advantage of activities unique to their host site.

FACILITIES

Housing is arranged in cooperation with the host organizations, and it therefore varies by site. Volunteers may be housed on-site in cabins, dorm, or tents or off-site at a local church, school, or college dorm. To get a better idea about housing at a particular site, students should visit Landmark Volunteers' Web site, select a program from the list, and click on the "housing" link.

STAFF

Volunteers serve in a team with up to 12 other students under the full-time leadership and supervision of an adult Landmark team leader. The team leaders are role models: college graduates, many with postgraduate degrees, who are socially conscious, responsible, and dynamic leaders in their communities.

A team is further supported by an "overseer," a senior member of the local community serving as a valuable community resource. A member of the host organization instructs volunteers, providing an inside look at the mission and workings of the organization.

MEDICAL CARE

Each team leader is required to know how to reach the local emergency room, to identify a local physician, and to have read the Red Cross first aid manual that is provided to them with their first aid kit. Parents must complete a medical form that advises of any relevant condition or medication and permits Landmark to authorize treatment in the event of an emergency.

COSTS

There is a tax-deductible contribution of $1250 for the two-week summer programs for applications postmarked before March 15 and $1300 for applications postmarked after March 15. The tax-deductible contribution for the one-week spring programs is $750. A $100 deposit is due with the application. Landmark Volunteers is a tax-exempt organization, and contributions are deductible to the extent provided by law.

TRANSPORTATION

Each volunteer is responsible for his or her personal travel arrangements and expenses. With more than fifty programs across the nation, students have the option to travel to a new part of the country or stay close to home. If a volunteer is traveling by air, a Landmark representative meets them at the airport and shuttles them to the site.

APPLICATION TIMETABLE

There are a limited number of Landmark volunteer positions available. Admission is based on the merits of the application, the references, and when the application materials are received by Landmark. It is important that applications are submitted as early as possible. The application process consists of filling out the application, completing the Landmark student essay, submitting the reference form and letter of evaluation from a teacher, and sending a $100 deposit along with other information. Interested students may visit the Web site to apply online, print an application, request a brochure, or learn more about the program.

FOR MORE INFORMATION, CONTACT

Landmark Volunteers
P.O. Box 455
800 North Main Street
Sheffield, Massachusetts 01257

Phone: 800-955-1178 (toll-free for brochure)
Fax: 413-229-2050
E-mail: landmark@volunteers.com
Web site: http://www.volunteers.com

PARTICIPANT/FAMILY COMMENTS

"I learned about nature, teamwork, friendship. . . . I couldn't have asked for a more exciting, challenging, or fun experience."

"My son had a fabulous time . . . his self-assurance grew a hundredfold."

"Our team leader was outstanding. He was there for us 24 hours a day with help, caring, and leadership."

LES ELFES–INTERNATIONAL SUMMER/WINTER CAMP

SPORTS, LANGUAGES, AND CULTURAL AND PERSONAL ENRICHMENT

VERBIER, SWITZERLAND, AND WHISTLER, BRITISH COLUMBIA, CANADA

TYPE OF PROGRAM: Wide variety of sports (including summer skiing), language study (French, Spanish, German, and English), cultural activities, and personal development
PARTICIPANTS: Coeducational, ages 8 to 18
ENROLLMENT: Maximum of 140 students per session
PROGRAM DATES: Summer: early June through end of August; winter: December through April
HEAD OF PROGRAM: Philippe and Nicole Stettler, Associate Directors

LOCATION
Verbier: In the heart of the Swiss Alps, Verbier, the home of Les Elfes–International Summer/Winter Camp, is a cosmopolitan resort. As the camp is located on a mountain meadow overlooking Verbier, the panorama from the camp is breathtaking. With more than 250 miles of connected trails, skiers in winter are served by ultramodern equipment and more than 120 ski lifts. The area provides all kinds of summer sports, including horseback riding, golf, swimming, tennis, rock climbing, paragliding, a ropes course, and mountain bike treks. Near Les Elfes is the sports center with an Olympic-size indoor swimming pool, an ice rink, and tennis and squash courts. A stable for horseback riding is nearby. Many cultural and historic sites are in the area. Campers enjoy the nearby streams, mountain meadows, and a lake with a private beach and waterskiing.

Whistler: The camp in Whistler, Canada, is located in the beautiful mountain range of British Columbia, in a spectacular environment surrounded by the Whistler Mountains. The facilities and accommodations in Whistler are the same as those in Verbier.

BACKGROUND AND PHILOSOPHY
Since 1987, Les Elfes–International Summer/Winter Camp has provided children and teens from around the world with holidays that combine the discovery and practice of new exciting sports with learning and perfecting languages (French, Spanish, German, and English). Children and teens discover other cultures and make new friends. Activities are designed to promote leadership and teamwork and to challenge students toward excellence in a way that maximizes both personal and group development and enhances self-confidence and interpersonal skills. Each child's program of activities reflects his or her personal aptitudes and choices. Children return home with the best of memories of their holidays, whether in summer or winter.

PROGRAM OFFERINGS
The summer camp experiences are organized into three-week sessions. When participants arrive (usually on a Sunday), they are introduced to the camp and are shown the sports installations and the town. The following day, the newcomers choose their various activities with the counselors.

Sports, Culture, and Activities The camp is focused mainly on outdoor sports activities. To complete their program, the students have the opportunity to discover sites outside Verbier and to water-ski on Lake Geneva. Youngsters are encouraged to try new activities with optimum safety and to improve their skills in those they already know. The International Summer Camp's program is extremely varied. Sports include badminton, basketball, football, miniature golf, ropes course, squash, table tennis, tennis, volleyball, and many others. There is also an eighteen-hole golf course in magnificent surroundings. Students enjoy hikes and mountain bike treks surrounded by alpine flora and fauna, rock climbing, figure skating, ice hockey, curling, swimming, and waterskiing. Cultural activities include weekly excursions to a town in Switzerland (such as Bern, Lausanne, or Geneva) or an interesting and entertaining site and concert outings (classical, blues, jazz, or rock).

The camp in Whistler offers the same outdoor activities as Verbier, plus additional ones that take advantage of the unique setting in Canada. These activities include sea kayaking, fly fishing, black bear watching, wild eagle viewing—and more.

Language Study The language program includes 8 hours per week of language courses (French, German, Spanish, or English), which are optionally expandable to 15 hours per week for an intensive course. The teachers are young, enthusiastic, and helpful college graduates. During their stay, the youngsters have a chance to practice the languages with their friends.

ENROLLMENT
The program serves groups of 140 students from more than forty-five nations. This international setting allows children and teens to experience and value other cultures and to make new worldwide friends.

DAILY SCHEDULE
The day begins at 7:45 a.m. with rising, washing, and getting ready for breakfast. A full breakfast is served at 8:15 with orange juice, hot and cold milk, hot chocolate, cereals, bread with ham and cheese, various jams, and fruit. At 9 a.m., students engage in their language activities, ski or snowboard, or take a tour depending on the day and individual program. At noon, campers enjoy a picnic lunch. Sports activities at 1 p.m. are followed by a snack at 4 p.m. At 4:30, the campers enjoy games and recreational activities, sports, or individual courses. Dinner prepared by the chef is served to students at the table beginning at 6:30 p.m. The menu includes American and European dishes and international foods. At 8 p.m., students participate in organized activities, play games, watch a video, or enjoy quiet time. Bedtime is at 10 p.m.

EXTRA OPPORTUNITIES AND ACTIVITIES
As extra-cost options, the students can take a beginner course in paragliding, enjoy horseback riding, or go summer skiing or snowboarding with professional instructors for three days per stay in Zermatt. A more intensive language study program is also available for an additional charge.

In addition to the activities program, it is possible to have private lessons in golf ($40 per hour), tennis ($40 per hour), and horseback riding ($40 per hour).

FACILITIES

Students live in two recently constructed (1995) chalets of wood and stone in the Swiss alpine tradition that offer charm and elegant comfort. Both chalets are situated in green, calm surroundings and are only 5 minutes from the center of Verbier. The chalets are completely equipped with a professionally equipped kitchen and a vast and sunny dining room, which opens onto a sitting room with a fireplace. There are classrooms, conference rooms, a library, a game hall, a film theater, a music hall (or discotheque), and a fitness room. The camp is fully equipped with all the equipment and accessories for indoor and outdoor games and sports. Campers live in rooms with two to four beds, a bathroom including a shower, and a radio and telephone. Maid service in the rooms is provided daily.

The menus are well balanced and adapted to the youngsters' needs and activities. The dietary needs of each individual are taken into consideration.

STAFF

A sports director and his assistant manage the instructors, the programs, and the smooth running of the camp. Three group leaders, their "second-in-command," and their assistants accompany the youngsters during activities organized into three independent age groups. All of the staff members (counselors, instructors, teachers, cooks, and camp and sports administrators) are dedicated young people trained for this kind of work. Most of the staff members are college graduates; they come from many nations and are fluent in both English and French. They are extremely enthusiastic and entirely committed. They give careful and effective supervision in order to direct the youngsters' energy and make their stay safe and enjoyable.

MEDICAL CARE

To avoid injury, the participants are trained by professional instructors or sports masters in all of their sports activities. Weather conditions are monitored by experienced mountain guides, and summer skiing and snowboarding, rock climbing, mountain biking treks, and hiking are only allowed under good weather conditions. In the event of a medical necessity other than the basic first aid, the camp offers around-the-clock nurses and doctors, an up-to-date clinic ¼-mile from the camp, three drugstores, and a regional hospital. By car, two University hospitals are 40 minutes and 1¼ hours away, respectively (10 minutes away by helicopter). These advantages and the reputation of Swiss medical treatment guarantee the best care in all situations. Parents are encouraged to provide their own health and accident insurance; otherwise, health and accident insurance provided by the camp is required at an additional cost of SF 80 ($55) per week.

RELIGIOUS LIFE

Arrangements for attendance at church can be made on an individual basis.

COSTS

Verbier: Costs for this extraordinary sports and educational program, including all living expenses, 8 hours per week of language study (in French, German, Spanish, or English), cultural excursions, and activities, are as follows: three-week summer sessions, SF 5300 ($4640); two-week winter sessions, SF 3370 ($2981); and one-week school-group ski camps, SF 1100–1450 ($870–$1150). These group programs include a minimum of 20 students and a maximum of 140 students. A deposit of $800 holds a student reservation; the balance must be paid prior to arrival. An additional health and accident insurance fee of SF 80 ($70) per week is required. An additional 7 hours of language study are available for $90 per week. Round-trip transportation by private bus is available to Geneva for $130 and to Martigny for $35. Personal expenses are not included. Full details are in the camp agreement, which can be obtained by request.

During the summer, optional sports expenses for skiing or snowboarding, including equipment and instructors (for six half-days per twenty-one-day session) are $370; horseback riding, including equipment, is six half-days for $314 per hour; and paragliding tandem flights at $150 per flight.

During the winter, optional sports expenses include full skiing plus equipment at $110 per week, full snowboarding plus equipment at $125 per week, and paragliding tandem flights at $150 per flight.

Whistler: The cost of this extraordinary sports and educational program includes all living expenses and 8 hours per week of English lessons. The two-week session costs Can$2995; the four-week session, Can$5990; and the six-week session costs Can$8900.

Optional themes of five mornings per week (with equipment, instruction, and coaching) include English as a second language (Can$150), skiing/snowboarding (Can$475), mountain biking (Can$475), or golf (Can$495).

Students may select from other activities such as horseback riding (Can$60/hour), private tennis lessons (Can$60/hour), fly fishing (Can$170/two hours), and Hummer 4WD tours (Can$250). Health insurance and accident insurance are compulsory and can be arranged through Les Elfes (Can$100/week). Personal expenses are not included. Full details are in the camp agreement, which is available upon request.

TRANSPORTATION

The camp in Verbier is located 105 miles from Geneva, 60 miles from Lausanne, 20 miles from Martigny, and 165 miles from Milan. Transportation by private bus to airports, bus stations, and trains in Geneva, Martigny, and other locations can be arranged.

The camp in Whistler is located 1.3 hours north of Vancouver. Arrangements can be made with Les Elfes for students to be picked up at the Vancouver airport. Roundtrip transportation by private bus from Vancouver is available for Can$150.

APPLICATION TIMETABLE

Applications are accepted year-round as long as session openings are available. A brochure is available upon request.

FOR MORE INFORMATION, CONTACT

Philippe and Nicole Stettler
Les Elfes International Summer and Winter Camps
P.O. Box 174
1936 Verbier
Switzerland
Phone: 41-27-775-35-90
Fax: 41-27-775-35-99
E-mail: info@leselfes.ch
Web site: http://www.leselfes.com

PARTICIPANT/FAMILY COMMENTS

"During six weeks with new friends from all the world, the children gained a new understanding of other people . . . enjoying beauty and freedom that only the Swiss Alps can provide."—Mr. Alexander W. K., Florida

LEYSIN AMERICAN SCHOOL IN SWITZERLAND

SUMMER IN SWITZERLAND

LEYSIN, SWITZERLAND

TYPE OF PROGRAM: Academic enrichment, language studies, SAT/ACT prep, I.B. prep, performing and visual arts, travel, leadership, sports, and recreation

PARTICIPANTS: Coeducational; Alpine Adventure (ages 9–12), Alpine Exploration (ages 13–15), Alpine Challenge (ages 16–19)

ENROLLMENT: 250–300 each session

PROGRAM DATES: First Session (2008): June 28 to July 18; Recreation and Culture Week: July 18 to July 26; Second Session: July 26 to August 15

HEAD OF PROGRAM: Tim Sloman

LOCATION

Summer in Switzerland (SIS) is located in the picturesque town of Leysin, overlooking the Rhone Valley 1,000 meters (3,000 feet) below and facing the majestic panorama of the southern Alps.

BACKGROUND AND PHILOSOPHY

SIS provides a special summer experience of academic enrichment, foreign language study, performing and visual arts, travel, leadership, sports, and recreation. The global community at SIS is warm and friendly, and all the students, from more than forty different countries, are appreciated for their uniqueness. SIS is a program of the Leysin American School in Switzerland (LAS) and takes place on the LAS campus. LAS is a coeducational, college-preparatory boarding school for American and non-American students in grades 9–12, with postgraduate and year-abroad programs.

PROGRAM OFFERINGS

There are three student groups: Alpine Adventure (AA), ages 9–12; Alpine Exploration (AE), ages 13–15; and Alpine Challenge (AC), ages 16–19. AA has a student-faculty ratio of 4:1 and is more of a camp setting. Activities are generally by group and are closely supervised. Both AE and AC students take 4 hours of morning classes, and all participate in afternoon activities. Their student-faculty ratio is 5:1. Curfews vary depending on age group. AE and AC students may also sign up for Leadership Adventure; Theatre International; intensive ESL; Alpine Chamber Music; Sat/ACT Prep Course; Highlight Tours to France, Italy, Germany, Austria, England, and within Switzerland; and Program Assistants (ages 18–19 years).

Enrichment and Academic Courses Students participate on weekday mornings in four periods of enrichment and academic courses. SIS offers American high school credit classes for those

enrolled in both the first and second sessions. Courses for AE and AC students include French, Spanish, algebra, geometry, computer science, English, TOEFL, International Baccalaureate (I.B.) prep (math, creative writing, and extended essay), SAT prep, photography, chorus, piano, acting, 2-D art, 3-D art (including ceramics), and visual and performing arts. Art students participate in a school-wide exhibition of painting, sculpture, writing, and photography. Many nonnative English speakers choose to enroll in comprehensive English as a second language (ESL) courses, which cover conversation, grammar, and written communication at all levels. AA students have the choice of taking either beginner's French or English as a second language. They also take environmental education, computer proficiency, arts and crafts, and theater classes together. In addition, they may sign up for a weeklong Recreation and Culture Week, based in Leysin for the week between the two sessions.

Recreation and Sports In the afternoon, students take part in various recreational, sports, and leadership activities. Recreation and sports include basketball, volleyball, soccer, Frisbee, hiking, open tennis and tennis lessons, ice skating, swimming, paragliding, white-water rafting, mountain biking, and horseback riding. AA participants typically do activities as a group.

Theatre International Theatre International students train in the mornings, improving skills in acting, improvisation, costuming, writing, directing, stage combat, and acting for film. In the afternoons, students prepare, publicize, rehearse, and stage a number of shows to the entire SIS community. Whenever possible, Theatre International offers students special excursions to theater productions.

Leadership Adventure This program alpine activities such as climbing, rappelling, white-water rafting, hydrospeeding, alpine hiking, ropes courses, and other outdoor activities. During school mornings, students participate in outdoor education and leadership classes, such as a first-aid and CPR class. They learn to develop their leadership styles, map-reading techniques, nature and conservation skills, and outdoor skills. Students learn to lead a climbing activity and learn about the different types of equipment and how to use them. Students also learn how to prepare an activity they will lead with younger students at SIS. Activities include overnight and longer trips out of Leysin. The program staff members are experienced, skilled, and certified outdoors instructors.

Alpine Chamber Music (ACM) (The program is subject to enrollment numbers; students should call for more information.) This new program provides an outstanding opportunity for talented young musicians to immerse themselves in the study and performance of music. There is focused private instruction with world-class musicians and chamber ensemble work with a repertoire that caters to many playing levels. The curriculum consists of classes in music theory, history, and the traditions of great performers. Students have the opportunity to attend numerous world-renowned music festivals in Switzerland and also join the regular SIS program for some activities and the weekend excursions. ACM students are encouraged to sign up for the weeklong Highlight Tour to Austria with its focus on the rich history of classical music.

SAT/ACT Preparation. This new program is taught by a trained teacher from a specialized company, Studyworks. Students review math content and learn techniques suited to the nature of the math questions. Verbal review comprises reading skills and techniques as well as vocabulary review. For the Writing section, students hone their essay-writing skills to ensure that they can meet the required standards and review the grammar fundamentals needed for the test. SAT Prep students have SAT classes all morning and three afternoons per session. The rest of the time they join the general program.

Excursions Students visit Swiss cities and cultural centers on weekend day trips. Outings are also taken to tourist attractions in the mountains and the countryside. Faculty guides accompany each trip. Students are given information and an orientation before the trips begin. Typically excursions are to Lausanne, Geneva, Berne, Lucerne, and Zermatt.

Evening Activities and Special Events Evening recreation includes attending theater productions, the Montreux Jazz Festival, talent shows, ice skating parties, casino night, eating special dinners like Swiss fondue, dancing at the disco, campfires, night hikes, and sports tournaments. Most of these activities take place on the campus, but some special events take place in Leysin and are chaperoned by faculty members.

DAILY SCHEDULE

8:00 . . .	Breakfast
9:00 . . .	Morning classes
12:10 . . .	Lunch for AA
12:25 . . .	Lunch for AE and AC
1:30 . . .	Quiet time and study hour
2:45 . . .	First activity period
4:15 . . .	Second activity period
6:00 . . .	Dinner, AC allowed off campus in Leysin village
6:30 . . .	Free time, AC/AE allowed off campus in Leysin
8:00 . . .	Evening activities
9:30 . . .	AA lights-out, Red Frog/on-campus open time
10:45 . . .	AE lights-out
11:15 . . .	AC lights-out

EXTRA OPPORTUNITIES AND ACTIVITIES

Leysin Recreation and Culture Week This exciting, fun-filled week is held between the first and second sessions and is designed with AA students in mind. Students attending either session may sign up. Days consist of half- and full-day trips, recreational opportunities, and cultural activities. Special emphasis is placed on teaching students about the host country, Switzerland, and sharing the beauty of their own cultures with one another.

Recreation and Culture Week Highlight Tours Optional weeklong tours to France, Germany, Austria, Italy, England, and within Switzerland are offered during Recreation and Culture Week for students in the AE and AC programs. The French Highlight Tour includes Paris, Versailles, and the Loire Valley. The Germany Tour visits the town of Munich and the scenic region of Bavaria. The Austrian tour emphasizes music and includes a visit to Salzburg. The Italian Highlight Tour offers visits to Florence, Venice, and Pisa. The England Highlight Tour visits popular sites in London as well as Stratford-upon-Avon and other places of interest. Faculty members supervise these tours.

FACILITIES

SIS uses the boarding facilities of the Leysin American School in Switzerland (LAS). Boys and girls are housed in different dormitories according to age group. The dormitories are safe, clean, and fully staffed by resident faculty members. All rooms have an en suite bathroom. Every effort is made to make the dorm a home away from home. LAS resources include music practice rooms, an art studio, and computer science labs. A well-equipped black-box theater is available for the dramatic arts. On-campus sports take

place in the LAS gymnasium, which has a basketball court, fitness center, and a squash court. Students also use the two sports centers in Leysin that contain an indoor swimming pool, squash and tennis courts, an ice-skating rink, a soccer field, and climbing walls.

STAFF
Faculty members are primarily from schools in the U.S. and Canada. Teachers are certified. Professional theater people with teaching experience supervise the theater department.

MEDICAL CARE
The school provides accident and health insurance coverage for students. A medical clinic is available in Leysin, and there are regional hospitals in Monthey and Lausanne. The school has a complete infirmary, and 2 full-time nurses are on staff.

RELIGIOUS LIFE
The school is nonsectarian, but provisions are made for students to attend Protestant and Roman Catholic services in Leysin on Sunday mornings and a Muslim mosque on Fridays when possible.

COSTS
Fees are all-inclusive and cover room, board, tuition, books, activities, and excursions. There is a minimal price increase each year. For 2007, costs were as follows: three-week session, €3350; three-week session plus Recreation and Culture Week, €4750; and both three-week sessions plus Recreation and Culture Week, €7600.

FINANCIAL AID
Up to four scholarships are awarded each session. Two are based on financial need, and the other two are merit-based awards: one for theater and one for leadership. Each scholarship is for no more than €1275.

TRANSPORTATION
The school provides all SIS participants with transportation on official arrival and departure dates to and from the airport in Geneva at no additional cost.

APPLICATION TIMETABLE
Students of all nationalities, ages 9–19, are eligible for admission to SIS. All specific information regarding tuition, fees, application forms, and supplementary data is provided in an annually updated flyer. Applications are accepted on a rolling basis. Students should note that SIS does apply a quota system for male and female applicants, age groups, nationalities, and spoken languages. Early applications are, therefore, more likely to receive a favorable response.

FOR MORE INFORMATION, CONTACT
Admissions Office
Leysin American School
CH 1854 Leysin
Switzerland

Phone: 603-431-7654 (United States)
888-642-4142 (toll-free in the U.S.)
+41-24-493-3777 (Switzerland)
Fax: +41-24-494-1585 (Switzerland)
E-mail: admissions@las.ch
Web site: http://www.las.ch/summer

LIFEWORKS INTERNATIONAL

LIFEWORKS

GLOBAL SERVICE-LEARNING PROGRAMS

BRITISH VIRGIN ISLANDS, COSTA RICA, THAILAND, CHINA, GALAPAGOS, AND AUSTRALIA

TYPE OF PROGRAM: Cultural, experiential, and adventure-based community-service programs. Students qualify for high school community-service credits.

PARTICIPANTS: Coeducational, ages 14–19, grouped by age

ENROLLMENT: Up to 15 students per group

PROGRAM DATES: Two- to four-week programs from June through August

HEAD OF PROGRAM: James Stoll

LOCATION

Lifeworks offers community-service programs in the British Virgin Islands (land- and sea-based voyage), Costa Rica, Thailand (outskirts of Bangkok and in the provinces), China, Galapagos (based on Santa Cruz island, with day and overnight trips to neighboring islands), and Australia (Sydney, Queensland, and Northern Territories).

BACKGROUND AND PHILOSOPHY

Backed by more than thirty years of offering experiential education for youth, Lifeworks has been developed as a service-learning opportunity. Based on the premise that every participant has something unique to offer, students are provided the opportunity to make their own ripple in this world through their involvement with Lifeworks. At the core of Lifeworks is the mission question "what mark would you like to leave because you were given the opportunity to walk the planet?"

Students work in collaboration with established local, national, and international service organizations. The symbiosis of such an arrangement enables students to share in knowledge specific to the region in which they are living and undertake significant local assignments. Skills and learning are fostered through hands-on participation in service projects. Each program location offers a distinctive focus so that students may gain insight into a new field of study or further develop an existing interest. Team-building, leadership, and self-reliance development are a natural part of living and working in a close community with a common goal.

At the completion of the program, a direct donation is made to the service organizations with which students have worked. This donation is included in the tuition cost and helps to fund ongoing projects. All participating students are enrolled in the President's Student Service Award—an initiative that recognizes young Americans for outstanding community service. This award scheme is also sponsored by the Corporation for National and Community Service.

Lifeworks programs are designed to focus on three levels of support: human, community, and global, each intrinsically linked. Service at the human level aims to transcend cultures and beliefs as participants work toward a broader common goal. Lifeworks looks for effective ways to reach individuals through their community, with health, education, environmental, or safety-based projects. It is the hope of Lifeworks that individual involvement will have an impact at the global level.

PROGRAM OFFERINGS

In the British Virgin Islands, Lifeworks participants assist with the BVI College and local schools, the Red Cross, the Conservation and Fisheries Department, the National Parks Trust, and the Marine Parks service organizations of the British Virgin Islands. This is a mobile, live-aboard service program based on a sailing yacht to enable multiple projects and marine-related work. Ongoing projects include the repropagation of mangrove systems and the monitoring of turtle populations and nesting. As part of a worldwide effort, students participate in the Darwin Initiative, which includes the tagging and monitoring of turtles and their nests, along with sea grass, water-quality, and beach monitoring around the islands. At intervals, Lifeworkers visit local schools and community centers to develop full days of activities and programming for children. Outside of project work, students also snorkel, hike, and sail throughout this island group.

Lifeworks Costa Rica is involved in a variety of community service projects with the Fundación Humanitaria. Students work with schools, health centers, and care facilities to help make a real difference in the community. Living with home-stay families offers a unique cultural exchange, which is enhanced with a formal Spanish language component. The program includes a trip to Tortuguero to see turtle nesting sites and to aid in beach clean up and travel to the Monteverde Rainforest and Arenal volcano.

In Thailand, Lifeworks teams up with the DPF Foundation for underprivileged children. DPF's Founder and Senator, Ms. Prateep Ungsongtham Hata, was awarded the prestigious 2004 World Children's Prize for the Rights of the Child in recognition of her work with Bangkok's disadvantaged children. Students work in the kindergartens and schools created by the foundation, with a focus on enhancing the children's self-esteem through team-building games, art projects, and teaching English.

During the China program, Lifeworks students work primarily with physically disabled children in privately funded orphanages. Students organize and implement sports and arts and crafts activities for the children, assist in providing direct care for the younger ones, and help in the construction of a playground. It is an opportunity to work as part of one of the most needed efforts in China. Between projects, students explore Beijing and visit the Great Wall, Forbidden City, and the Terracotta warriors.

In Galapagos, Lifeworks students work with the national parks on Santa Cruz and San Cristobal islands, assisting with maintenance of the giant tortoise hatchery facility and activities, signage, and general upkeep within the parks. Other projects are involved with local schools, cultural exchange, and ranger patrol programs. In addition, there are trips to St. Bartholomew, to the Plazas to snorkel with sea lions, and for a long weekend of exploring and horseback riding on the high volcanic island of Isabella.

In Australia, working with the Australian Red Cross, Lifeworks students participate primarily in aboriginal community projects. Beginning in Sydney, students have a cultural orientation as well as explore the city. Participants take an active role in learning about aboriginal history and customs, with a unique and rare opportunity to experience their culture firsthand. Students live within the aboriginal community of the Tiwi Islands offshore from Darwin, designing local youth projects and putting them into action. Students learn how aboriginals live with the land, use bush medicines, and preserve their ancient traditions and, in turn, offer the local children summer program activities. Students' interaction and education is furthered with travel to the National Parks of the Northern Territories and then to Queensland, where the reef and rain forest meet.

ENROLLMENT

Enrollment is limited to 15 students per group, with participants from all over the United States. International students are also encouraged to participate. All programs are coed.

EXTRA OPPORTUNITIES AND ACTIVITIES

Unique to Lifeworks is the Lifeworks Forum, which takes place at intervals throughout the program. Students take time to participate in a variety of discussions, focusing on assisting each student in identifying and moving toward making their own individual contribution to the world. The Lifeworks Forum focuses on that goal as well as discussing related subjects, including integrity dilemmas, goals and affirmations, and other life choices people make.

STAFF

The average age of staff members is 27 and up. A staff-to-student ratio of 1:6 is maintained throughout the programs. Lifeworks selects staff members who have good organizational skills, demonstrate ingenuity, have mature decision-making abilities, are responsible, and have experience working with teens. Desirable staff qualities include adaptability and an adventurous spirit.

COSTS

Program costs for 2007 ranged from $3670 to $4770, depending on location and duration chosen. Each program tuition includes a direct donation to be made by the students to the service organizations with which they work.

TRANSPORTATION

Students fly in small groups and staff assistance is available at arrival airports.

APPLICATION TIMETABLE

Applications are accepted at any time. Some programs are filled faster than others. Some fill in February, and most are full by April. Students should call for information on availability if applying late.

FOR MORE INFORMATION, CONTACT

Lifeworks International
P.O. Box 5517
Sarasota, Florida 34277
Phone: 941-924-2115
       800-808-2115 (toll-free)
Fax: 941-924-6075
E-mail: info@lifeworks-international.com
Web site: http://www.lifeworks-international.com

LINDEN HILL SUMMER PROGRAM

MORNING ACADEMICS, TRADITIONAL CAMP ACTIVITIES, AND WEEKEND OVERNIGHTS

NORTHFIELD, MASSACHUSETTS

TYPE OF PROGRAM: Morning academics with afternoon/evening traditional camp activities and weekend overnight trips

PARTICIPANTS: Coeducational, ages 7–17

ENROLLMENT: 45

PROGRAM DATES: June 28 to July 28

HEAD OF PROGRAM: James A. McDaniel, Summer Director and Headmaster

LOCATION
Linden Hill's rural campus is set on the side of a mountain overlooking the Connecticut River Valley, in the town of Northfield. The rural setting, with breathtaking scenery, is ideal for exploring on foot or mountain bike. The surrounding towns offer many diverse and exciting cultural and historical opportunities for all ages.

BACKGROUND AND PHILOSOPHY
Since 1961, Linden Hill School has served the needs of boys ages 9–16 with language-based learning differences in a traditional boarding school with a family setting. Linden Hill has developed a highly successful multisensory teaching program, which utilizes a child's senses to reinforce learning. Building upon the school's successful year-round formula, the Linden Hill Summer Program combines challenging, stimulating academic classes with exciting and extensive recreational opportunities. In a structured, supportive environment, participants are encouraged to grow in confidence and self-esteem, to make lasting friendships, and to develop as individuals. Linden Hill is accredited by the New England Association of

Schools and Colleges. It holds membership in the National Association of Independent Schools, the Association of Independent Schools in New England, and the New England League of Middle Schools.

PROGRAM OFFERINGS
A balanced program offers students solid academics and strong athletic, social, cultural, and recreational activities. The weekly program combines structure and focus with flexibility and choice. Linden Hill develops the skills and natural abilities of each person while encouraging a sense of enthusiasm and positive self-image. Campers go home feeling confident, relaxed, and ready for the coming school year.

Academic Programs Since all of the students have experienced past academic difficulties or learning differences, the democracy of common problems begins to erase self-consciousness, and self-esteem increases. Classes have an enrollment of 1 to 6 students and meet five days per week during the morning hours. Daily drills and written work are stressed, and all classes focus on motivation, a positive mental attitude, organization, study skills, social growth, confidence, and self-esteem.

Traditional Camp Program Camping can contribute to a young person's life in a way that few other experiences can. The program goals are for each camper to have a pleasant, fun-filled summer; improve skills; and develop confidence, self-control, inner discipline, good sportsmanship, and self-esteem. Campers who are unskilled in particular activities are channeled into special instruction so that they may become more proficient and develop a feeling of self-confidence. As they continue to grow in confidence, they are able to take their place with their peers and contribute successfully. Character development and citizenship are stressed at all times. In addition to daily activities, campers take advantage of the rich geographical setting with overnight trips on weekends, including educational, cultural, pioneering, and rafting trips.

ENROLLMENT
The Linden Hill Summer Program attracts campers from across the United States and from many other countries. Generally, the campers are underachieving and experiencing some academic difficulty, although they have average to above-average intelligence.

EXTRA OPPORTUNITIES AND ACTIVITIES
Weekend trips have included a Red Sox baseball game, Boston's Faneuil Hall and Quincy Market, and overnight camp trips. Talent shows, plays, and special guests are just a few of the many exciting events. There is also a counselor-in-training (CIT) program for older campers.

FACILITIES
The buildings include Bennett House, Haskell Hall, Hayes Hillside Dormitory, Duplex Dormitory, and the gymnasium. The newly renovated Bennett House, originally a farmhouse, accommodates the kitchen, dining room, reception room, spacious dorm rooms, and student center. Haskell Hall (1964)

houses the classrooms, art studio, science laboratory, comprehensive library, computer center, and spacious study hall. Hayes Hillside Dormitory (1961) sleeps 30 students. The full-sized gym, finished in 1998, is a multipurpose facility housing a full-sized basketball court and climbing wall. The school overlooks the Connecticut River and some of the most beautiful landscape in New England. There are nature walks and hikes on-site and at the nearby Northfield Mountain facility; these trails are also great for mountain bikes. A large pond provides entertainment for students. Linden Hill also has its own athletic field. Nearby, Northfield Mount Hermon School has many facilities that are made available to Linden Hill, including a swimming pool and tennis courts.

DAILY SCHEDULE

7:30	Wake-up
8:00	Flagpole honors assembly
8:10	Breakfast, followed by room inspection
9:00	Focus period one
10:00	Circle of Friendship with snack
10:30	Focus period two
11:30	Focus period three
12:30	Lunch and rest period
2:00– 3:00	First activity instruction clinic
3:00	Break and snack
3:10– 4:10	Second activity instruction clinic
4:15– 5:00	Optional period (hobby, creative arts, technology, special activity)
5:00– 6:00	Showers and relaxation
6:00	Flagpole honors assembly, followed by dinner
7:15	Special evening activity
8:30	Snack, return to dorm

STAFF

The majority of the program's academic instructors, along with the dorm parents and athletic director, are part of Linden Hill's regular faculty. Staff members are carefully chosen for their ability to relate to the student body, exceptional talents, warmth, personality, and ability to inspire. The staff-camper ratio is about 1:3. James A. McDaniel is the Headmaster and Summer Program Director.

MEDICAL CARE

Students are provided with medical services as required. The nurse resides on campus. In case of emergency, Linden Hill is just 10 minutes from the Northfield Mount Hermon Health Clinic and 20 minutes from Franklin Medical Center. Staff members are trained in first aid and CPR.

COSTS

Tuition for the 2007 season was $5850. This charge is comprehensive and included the cost of instruction, lodging in dormitories, all meals, course materials, and transportation to and from the airport. It also included day trips and all weekend excursions and tours. The tuition should be paid in full by May 15. An additional $250 should be deposited into the participant's campus bank account by June 28. This fee covers incidentals and all spending money.

FINANCIAL AID

Tuition loans and scholarships are available on a limited basis. Early payment discounts are available.

TRANSPORTATION

Linden Hill is located approximately 75 miles from Bradley International Airport in Hartford, Connecticut. Transportation can be provided to the airport.

APPLICATION TIMETABLE

The Linden Hill Summer Program has a rolling admissions policy. Students should submit their application with teacher evaluations, an official transcript, and a handwritten letter from the camper. Personal interviews and tours of the campus are encouraged and available year-round. The application form should be completed and returned as soon as possible.

FOR MORE INFORMATION, CONTACT

James A. McDaniel, Headmaster and Summer Program Director
Linden Hill Summer Program
154 South Mountain Road
Northfield, Massachusetts 01360
Phone: 413-498-2906
        888-254-6336 (toll-free)
Fax: 413-498-2908
E-mail: admissions@lindenhs.org
Web site: http://www.lindenhs.org

MARIANAPOLIS SUMMER SCHOOL

SUMMER PROGRAM

THOMPSON, CONNECTICUT

TYPE OF PROGRAM: Academic enrichment
PARTICIPANTS: Coeducational for grades 9–12 and post-graduate
ENROLLMENT: 50 students
PROGRAM DATES: Begins the second week of June and ends the third week of July. Applicants should visit the Web site for exact dates.
HEAD OF PROGRAM: Marilyn Ebbitt, Headmistress

LOCATION

Marianapolis Preparatory School sits on a 250-acre campus atop Thompson Hill. It is a Catholic boarding school situated in the heart of Connecticut's antique district in proximity to Boston (1 hour), Providence (45 minutes), and New York City (3 hours).

PROGRAM OFFERINGS

In the structured six-week summer program, students benefit from small classes while strengthening their academic abilities and creating lasting friendships. There are a number of

events that take students off campus to explore all New England has to offer. Marianapolis Summer Program emphasizes customized learning, individual growth, and renewed confidence in academics. Students enrolled in the Summer Program have the opportunity to take two (or, in some cases, three) courses of their choice. Teachers assign homework on a nightly basis, and students have a mandatory 2-hour study period in the evening. A sample of course offerings includes:

Art and Music Students are offered the opportunity to tap into their own creativity. Courses in the art department include photography, studio art, and woodworking. The history of music is explored through the genres of folk, blues, spiritual, and jazz, leading to the evolution of American popular music.

English as a Second Language (ESL) ESL courses help international students become masters of speaking, reading, and writing the English language. Faculty members in this program are professionally trained ESL specialists. Many have lived abroad themselves and understand the experience of leaving home to study in another country.

English Courses in English introduce students to the world of literature through the art of poetry and the short story, novel, and play. Students receive instruction on the writing process and learn to become more effective writers through grammar, usage, punctuation, sentence construction, paragraph organization, and vocabulary.

Courses in science, history, and mathematics are created on an as-needed basis.

DAILY SCHEDULE

8:00	Breakfast and announcements
9:00	Course
12:00	Lunch
1:00	Course
4:00– 5:00	Athletics or off-campus event
6:00– 7:00	Dinner
7:00– 9:00	Study
11:00	Lights out

EXTRA OPPORTUNITIES AND ACTIVITIES

Extra Excursions and Activities Weekends are devoted to planned activities. Whether it is a baseball game at Fenway Park in Boston, a trip to Central Park in New York City, or a visit to a local watering hole for a swim, the summer is filled with excitement. Hiking trails, lakes, and ponds are within easy reach for supervised trips, and Connecticut offers a wide variety of summer theater, music, and other attractions.

Athletics Each summer school student must participate in athletics during the weekday afternoons. The program is both recreational and instructional. Sports offered vary according to the interests of the students in the program; in past summers they have included tennis, softball, volleyball, soccer, basketball, aerobics, cross-country running, biking, and lacrosse.

tial to developing an atmosphere that is conducive to learning. Recreational lounges within the dorms offer Internet, television, board games, and table tennis.

Summer school students also have access to the Internet and to e-mail in the dormitories, library, and the computer lab. Students eat daily meals and weekend brunches in the dining room or on the patio.

MEDICAL CARE

A nurse is on call 24 hours a day. Emergency medical service is available at Day Kimball Hospital, which is located less than 10 minutes from the campus.

COSTS

Summer school runs in one session, from the second week of June to the third week of July for grades 9–12. The boarding program costs $6000, which covers tuition, room and board, and most organized activities. The day program costs $1000 per course (offered to students living in proximity to the school). This cost includes tuition, lunch, and most organized activities. Financial aid is not available for the summer program.

FOR MORE INFORMATION, CONTACT

Admissions Office
Marianapolis Preparatory School
26 Chase Road
P.O. Box 304
Thompson, Connecticut 06277

Phone: 860-923-9565
Fax: 860-923-3730
Web site: http://www.marianapolis.org

FACILITIES

Bayer House and St. Albert's Hall are restored historic homes housing boarding students. Resident faculty members serve as advisers to students and staff the dormitories. Faculty members work to create an atmosphere in which serious study can take place and where friendships can be made. Rooms are equipped with beds, bureaus, desks, chairs, and overhead lights. Coin-operated washers and dryers are available on campus for students to do their laundry. While Marianapolis does have some single rooms, most students have a roommate. Though the basic organization of the dormitories is informal, structured study halls in the evening and constant faculty presence in the dormitories are recognized as essen-

THE MARVELWOOD SUMMER PROGRAM

KENT, CONNECTICUT

TYPE OF PROGRAM: Academic remediation, classes for credit or enrichment, and skill building
PARTICIPANTS: Coeducational, students entering grades 7–11
ENROLLMENT: A maximum of 60
PROGRAM DATES: July 7 to August 4, 2007
HEAD OF PROGRAM: Craig Ough, Director

LOCATION
The Marvelwood School is located on an 83-acre campus in the town of Kent in northwest Connecticut. Its rural hilltop setting makes it ideal for hiking, biking, camping, skiing, and field studies. The campus sits above the Housatonic River in the foothills of the Berkshire Mountains, in proximity to the Appalachian Trail. The school is 55 miles west of Hartford and 80 miles north of New York City.

BACKGROUND AND PHILOSOPHY
Begun in 1964 by Marvelwood's founder, Robert A. Bodkin, who adopted the successful methods of the Salisbury Summer School, the Marvelwood Summer Program provides a secure, supportive, and challenging environment in which a diverse group of young people can achieve academic and personal success. The staff members and teachers at Marvelwood recognize that each student walks a unique path toward success, one that is not always easily recognized in traditional learning environments. The curriculum is designed to accommodate all types of learning styles.

The unique program features course work supplemented by independent projects, a multi-tiered focus on study-skill development, afternoon seminars, and community service opportunities. The curriculum enables young people to manage their school work more effectively; apply their newly developed skills to reading, writing, and mathematics; and think of themselves as capable and successful learners.

Students thrive in small, structured classes that encourage interaction with other students. Marvelwood's teachers emphasize project-based learning, understanding that a hands-on approach to education is the best style for diverse learners.

PROGRAM OFFERINGS
The Marvelwood Summer Program offers small (student-faculty ratio of 4:1) structured classes and an interactive and creative curriculum.

Core Courses Each student enrolls in one core course, such as English, math, history, or English as a second language (ESL) for international students. Courses may be taken for enrichment or credit. The core course also incorporates the Personal Track program and Student Learning Partnership. Core courses involve a total of 30 hours of class time, plus 12 hours earned through the Personal Track Program.

The Personal Track Program The Personal Track Program helps students learn the importance of educational independence by applying what they are studying in the core course to an independent project that matches their personal interests. Project proposals are developed through discussion with the core course teacher. As part of each evening's study hall, 30 minutes is dedicated to completing a Personal Track project.

Student Learning Partnerships Program A Student Learning Partnership (SLP), as part of Dr. Mel Levine's School Attuned Program, is developed for each student, focusing specifically on the core course. Advisers assist students in identifying and understanding their strengths and weaknesses and developing strategies to guide them to greater academic achievement in all of their courses.

Strategies Course In the mandatory Strategies course, students work with their instructors to strengthen study skills, improve reading comprehension, develop effective time-management skills and test-preparation strategies, and organize notes and assignments. This class period may also be used for extra help from classroom teachers and work on the Student Learning Partnership.

Supplementary Courses and Electives The supplementary course is either a second core course or an elective class. Students may be given the opportunity to take a supplementary course for credit but must request this special arrangement well ahead of time.

Afternoon Seminars Students have their choice of two afternoon seminars. The Leadership Seminar uses nearby natural resources (the Appalachian Trail, the Housatonic River, natural cliff faces) to involve students in activities that help them build confidence, forge trusting relationships, discover leadership potential, and learn and master skills that will help them throughout their lives. This seminar employs team-building challenges, conflict resolution training, communication workshops, and community service activities.

The Theater Seminar covers all aspects of theater production, including scene study, playwriting, improvisation, stage movement, monologue preparation, and character development. Participants in the Theater Seminar work with accomplished director/playwright Jocelyn Beard, culminating in a public performance at the end of the session.

English as a Second Language Program ESL classes are offered at two levels. ESL 1 is an introductory course for the beginning English speaker; ESL 2 students should have had at least one year of experience speaking and writing in English. ESL students enroll in at least one ESL core course and the Strategies class and may choose either a second ESL course or an elective for their third class. They are typically paired with an American roommate.

ENROLLMENT

A maximum of 60 students from across the country and overseas, who have just completed the sixth through the tenth grades, are admitted to the program each summer. Typically, students are well-motivated boys and girls with deficits in the verbal area and in study discipline, who need an intensive, structured experience.

DAILY SCHEDULE

The daily schedule is followed Monday through Friday and on Saturday until noon. On Saturday afternoon and Sunday, there are supervised trips and a variety of activities throughout the day.

7:45– 8:15	Breakfast
8:30– 9:45	Core and Elective Classes
9:45–10:00	Break
10:00–10:11	Core and Elective Classes
12:00	Lunch
1:00	Afternoon Seminars convene
5:30	Dinner
6:00– 7:00	Free Time
7:00	Independent Study for Personal Track projects
7:30	Study Hall
9:00–10:00	Quiet hour in the dorms
10:00	Lights out

EXTRA OPPORTUNITIES AND ACTIVITIES

Marvelwood offers a broad range of fun and interesting activities each weekend, including white-water rafting, canoeing, and rock climbing; visits to local museums, restaurants, playhouses, and amusement parks; community service projects; and trips to New York City, Boston, and the Connecticut shoreline.

Students are invited to attend a two-week session at Ebner Camps (http://www.ebnercamps.com) in nearby Litchfield, Connecticut, before and/or after the Summer Program.

International students are also invited to participate in the Homestay Program on the Marvelwood campus after the completion of the Summer Program. Participants enjoy daily activities such as swimming, sports, canoeing, arts and crafts, cultural and sightseeing trips, and movies.

FACILITIES

The campus includes twenty buildings, eight tennis courts, four playing fields, two ponds, and large open spaces and woods. There are separate dormitories for boys and girls. The Robert A. Bodkin Library contains 10,000 volumes of print material, 300 nonprint media items, and ten computers for student use. A wireless network is monitored by the Information Technology Department.

STAFF

Most faculty members in the Summer Program are members of the Marvelwood School faculty, including specialists in study skills, remedial reading, English composition, literature, and mathematics. In addition, each student is assigned an adviser who oversees the student's progress in the program. Advisers are in daily contact with students and their teachers, and they meet once a week with the students to assess progress, discuss strategies, and set goals. Advisers call parents weekly to share progress reports.

MEDICAL CARE

A registered nurse holds infirmary hours each morning, and Sharon Hospital in Sharon, Connecticut, is 12 miles away. All students

must submit a standard health form before matriculating. Enrollment in a student accident insurance policy is required.

RELIGIOUS LIFE

There are weekly opportunities to attend Roman Catholic, Protestant, and Jewish services in the area, but attendance is not required.

COSTS

The boarding tuition for 2007 is $5150; tuition for day students is $3450. This charge is comprehensive and covers such costs as room and board, classes, books, and supplies. Students attending the Theater Seminar who do not participate in the rest of the program are charged $1200 for the session. There are additional fees for field trips and special activities as well as transportation. International students pay a $250 student fee. Spending money can be deposited at the Business Office; the recommended amount is $20 per week. Any unused portion is refunded at the end of the summer. A $1500 deposit is required upon acceptance. Tuition must be paid in full prior to the beginning of the program in June.

TRANSPORTATION

Flights are met at Bradley International Airport (Hartford/Springfield) and JFK and La Guardia Airports in New York, trains and buses in Hartford, as well as the Metro North train in Wingdale, New York.

APPLICATION TIMETABLE

Applications are accepted through the end of June, as long as space is available. Inquiries and campus visits are welcome at any time. In addition to the application, Marvelwood also requires a current school transcript, two teacher recommendations, and a nonrefundable application fee of $50. An interview and a campus tour are strongly encouraged but not mandatory. The Admissions Committee notifies applicants of their decision within two weeks of receiving all application materials.

FOR MORE INFORMATION, CONTACT

Caitlin Lynch
Director of Summer Admissions
The Marvelwood School
476 Skiff Mountain Road
P.O. Box 3001
Kent, Connecticut 06757

Phone: 860-927-0047 Ext. 1011
Fax: 860-927-0021
E-mail: summer@marvelwood.org
Web site: http://www.marvelwood.org/about/welcome_summer.asp

PARTICIPANT/FAMILY COMMENTS

"I have proven to myself I can do well . . . It gives me great satisfaction knowing that some hard work and a little extra push can go a long way. Marvelwood has taught me something valuable that will stay with me the rest of my life."

"We were so pleased with the program and what it did for our son. He continues to exhibit greatly improved study habits. Perhaps even more important, his attitude toward school work and learning responsibilities has become noticeably more serious and mature."

MASSACHUSETTS COLLEGE OF ART

mass art

SUMMER STUDIOS IN ART AND DESIGN

BOSTON, MASSACHUSETTS

TYPE OF PROGRAM: Visual arts
PARTICIPANTS: Coeducational, students entering grades 11 and 12
ENROLLMENT: Approximately 100 (about 50 residential)
PROGRAM DATES: Four weeks in July and August
HEAD OF PROGRAM: Liz Rudnick, K–12 Outreach Coordinator

LOCATION

On the Avenue of the Arts, Massachusetts College of Art (MassArt) is situated in the heart of Boston's cultural district. The Emerald Necklace weaves its way by, with the Museum of Fine Arts and the Isabella Stewart Gardner Museums each within one walking block. The Institute for Contemporary Art, the Museum of the National Center of Afro-American Artists, the Photographic Resource Center, and more than sixty other museums and art galleries make Boston a thriving urban cultural center.

Outside the city, Massachusetts offers the beautiful rocky coastline of the North Shore and the sweeping beaches that extend down through the South Shore toward Cape Cod. Inland, Massachusetts' rolling hills, mountains, and farmland extend out to the west toward Mass MOCA and the Berkshires.

BACKGROUND AND PHILOSOPHY

MassArt's precollege summer program is an intensive experience in artmaking and viewing designed specifically for students entering their junior and senior years in high school. Students develop work for their portfolios and develop work habits that encourage excellence in their artistic endeavors. Through the structured curriculum that combines foundation courses with electives, students are able to experience the rigors of higher education in the visual arts. Students attending MassArt's Summer Studios are well prepared to make decisions about their future education, whether it is a liberal arts education or an education focused on fine arts and design.

Summer Studios takes advantage of MassArt's extraordinary facilities. Printmaking, metal sculpting, photography, fashion, ceramics, filmmaking, and computer animation are some of the areas students can select to study. MassArt faculty members, graduate students, undergraduate students, and alumni return to the campus for the summer months to teach and share their knowledge with the students of Summer Studios.

Established in 1873, Massachusetts College of Art was the first and remains the only four-year independent public art college in the U.S. The College is nationally known for offering broad access to a high-quality professional arts education, accompanied by a strong general education in the liberal arts. A major cultural force in Boston, MassArt offers public programs of innovative exhibitions, lectures, and events.

PROGRAM OFFERINGS

There are four components to the Summer Studios program: the two morning foundation classes, electives, and Sneak Preview College Day. The morning foundation classes are 2D and 3D Fundamentals and Issues and Images.

2D and 3D Fundamentals All students study the fundamentals of design and composition while building a strong foundation in two- and three-dimensional work. Students develop their ability to observe through the practice of drawing and sculpting from the figure. Students receive a written evaluation from the faculty at the conclusion of the program.

Issues and Images Students study various questions concerning art, including what it is, why people look at and make it, and what the role of the artist is in society. This class emphasizes critical-thinking skills through the study of contemporary art, art history, and current events. Students receive a written evaluation from the faculty at the conclusion of the program. Issues and Images enables students to experience arts in the community through weekly field trips to artists' studios, galleries, and museums.

Electives All students attend two elective studios. Students receive a written evaluation from the faculty at the conclusion of the program. The Monday/Thursday choices are

Surreal Painting: Myth and Metaphor, Painting from the Figure, Architecture, Metalworking, Design and Composition, and Fashion Design. The Tuesday/Friday choices are Ceramics, Printmaking, Jewelry and Metals, Computer Animation, Comic Book Art, and Fundamentals in Filmmaking.

Sneak Preview College Day College Day is a full-day event that addresses the needs of students who are trying to understand college admissions policies and procedures. The morning of this event focuses on portfolio reviews. In the afternoon, several area colleges in the visual arts join MassArt to introduce students to their particular school's offerings.

ENROLLMENT
In past years, Summer Studios has had approximately 25 percent of its student body come from Boston and the surrounding area. Fifty-eight percent of the student body has come from western and central Massachusetts. Seventeen percent of the students have come from out of state and from other countries.

DAILY SCHEDULE
Monday, Tuesday, Thursday, and Friday:

8:30–11:20	2D and 3D Fundamentals
11:30–12:30	Issues and Images
12:30– 1:30	Lunch
1:30– 4:30	Electives

Wednesday (except for College Day):

8:30–12:00	Electives
1:30– 4:30	Issues and Images field trips

In addition to program activities, the staff of the residence hall plans additional activities for resident students on evenings and weekends. The following is a sampling of past activities and destinations that residents have visited: Arnold Arboretum, bookbinding workshop, Castle Island, Crane Beach Sand Castle Competition, DeCordova Museum and Sculpture Park, flea markets, George's Island, gym/team sports, hiking, Institute of Contemporary Art, MIT Science Park, Museum of African American Art, Museum of Fine Arts, New England Aquarium, Newburyport, Omni Theater at the Science Museum, open mike at the Student Center, outdoor picnics and barbecues, papermaking workshop, planetarium, poetry readings, Quincy Market and Faneuil Hall, running, science museum, sketching trips, and whale watching.

COSTS
Tuition for the 2007 Summer Studios was $1995. The residence fee, which includes room and board, was $2430. The program fee and residential fee were $4425. A $100 nonrefundable program deposit is required with all applications. Residential students must submit a $100 residence hall deposit.

FOR MORE INFORMATION, CONTACT
Liz Rudnick
Massachusetts College of Art
621 Huntington Avenue
Boston, Massachusetts 02115
Phone: 617-879-7174
E-mail: lizrudnick@massart.edu
Web site: http://www.massartplus.org

MISS PORTER'S SCHOOL SUMMER PROGRAMS

▼▼▼▼▼▼▼▼▼▼▼▼▼▼▼▼▼▼▼▼▼▼▼▼▼▼▼▼▼▼

SUMMER PROGRAMS FOR MIDDLE SCHOOL GIRLS

FARMINGTON, CONNECTICUT

TYPE OF PROGRAM: Leadership, arts, science, athletics, Chinese immersion

PARTICIPANTS: Girls entering grades 7–9 (athletics program begins with grade 6)

ENROLLMENT: 12 to 50 students per program; 150 total

PROGRAM DATES: Sarah Porter Leadership Institute Level 1: June 22–28; Sarah Porter Leadership Institute Levels 1 and 2: June 22–July 5; The Athletic Experience: June 29–July 5; Summer Challenge: July 6–18; Arts Alive!: July 6–18; Daoyun Chinese Summer Program: June 22–July 18

HEAD OF PROGRAM: Terry Armington

LOCATION

Miss Porter's School (MPS) Summer Programs take place on the campus of Miss Porter's School in the historic village of Farmington, 9 miles from Hartford, Connecticut.

BACKGROUND AND PHILOSOPHY

Miss Porter's School Summer Programs offer girls from across the United States and around the world the opportunity to explore and develop their interests and skills in leadership, science, the arts, or athletics and to try out boarding school life at Miss Porter's School. Started in 1995, Summer Challenge was developed in response to research on the importance of the middle school years to girls' continued interest and competency in mathematics, science, and technology. Arts Alive!, an interdisciplinary curriculum in the arts, and the Sarah Porter Leadership Institute were introduced in 2003, and The Athletic Experience was launched in summer 2005. A respected leader in girls' education since 1843, Miss Porter's School offers the demanding curriculum, collaborative environment, and diverse community that distinguish the finest boarding schools.

PROGRAM OFFERINGS

The **Sarah Porter Leadership Institute Level 1** (June 22–28; girls entering grades 7–9) develops girls' leadership potential as they learn about communication, goal setting, conflict resolution, and more. After participating in the Institute Level 1 curriculum during the first week, students who are accepted to the **Sarah Porter Leadership Institute Level 2** (June 29–July 5; girls entering grades 8 and 9) gain more extensive leadership experience through more advanced activities. More information is available at http://www.sarahporterinstitute.org.

The Athletic Experience (June 29–July 5; girls entering grades 6–9) is designed for beginning and experienced athletes to develop skills in three sports. Girls choose from basketball, field hockey, lacrosse, soccer, softball, squash, and volleyball. More information can be found at http://www.athleticexperience.org.

Summer Challenge (July 6–18; girls entering grades 7–9) students become forensic investigators of a mock crime through hands-on activities. For more information, interested students should visit http://www.summerchallenge.org.

Arts Alive! (July 6–18; girls entering grades 7–9) features writing, along with the visual and performing arts, to address the questions, "Who am I?", "What do I see and how do I see it?", and "How do I express myself?" Additional information about this program can be found online at http://www.mpsartsalive.org.

ENROLLMENT

Girls come to MPS Summer Programs from across the United States and around the world. Participants may choose one or more of the four programs; their stay on campus can vary from six days to a month.

EXTRA OPPORTUNITIES AND ACTIVITIES

Each of the programs offers special evening activities and field trips that support the program's goals. For example, participants in the Sarah Porter Leadership Institute Level 1 complete a ropes course and hear presentations by women who are leaders in their fields, and girls who stay on for Level 2 go on a camping trip and plan and execute a service project in a nearby community. Athletes who attend The Athletic Experience hear from a sports psychologist and attend a professional sporting event. Students in Arts Alive! and Summer Challenge may travel together to New York City or Boston for a weekend day of museum visits and exploration. Girls who attend more than one program enjoy time to relax and be with friends between the end of one program and the beginning of the next program. Girls have the chance to settle into their new dorm rooms, and activities are informal. There may be a trip to the movies or to play mini-golf.

FACILITIES

The Sarah Porter Leadership Institute, The Athletic Experience, Arts Alive!, and Summer Challenge all make extensive use of the wide range of Miss Porter's School facilities. The historic campus in Farmington Village, classrooms, theater, art studios, library, computer labs, and athletic facilities provide a resource-rich experience for Summer Programs girls.

Students live in small, homelike dormitories, most of which are former family residences. Meals are served in the Dining Hall in the Main building. The dorms are supervised by counselors, many of whom are recent graduates of Miss Porter's School, and by senior program faculty members and program directors.

A security officer monitors the MPS campus around the clock. Each MPS security officer, as well as several counselors, is trained in basic first aid and CPR. A security officer can respond to any campus emergency within minutes. Dormitories are kept locked; students gain access to their dorms by using the swipe card lock system.

STAFF

All of the program directors are Miss Porter's School teachers and administrators during the regular school year. Summer Programs teachers come from Miss Porter's School and other area independent schools, and most of the counselors are recent graduates of Miss Porter's.

MEDICAL CARE

Medical care is provided by the Miss Porter's School physician, who is on call 24 hours a day for consultations and to arrange office visits. For The Athletic Experience, a licensed athletic trainer is also on hand throughout the program. In an emergency, the student is taken to the Emergency Room of the Connecticut Children's Medical Center in Hartford. Parents (or guardians) are notified whenever contact is made with a physician regarding the health of their daughter. If an office visit is required, the family receives a bill from the physician. Enrolled students receive information regarding submitting a physical examination record, proof of health insurance (or purchasing health insurance), and medication authorization forms.

COSTS

In 2007, tuition was $750 for the Sarah Porter Leadership Institute Level 1, $950 for the Leadership Institute Level 2, $750 for The Athletic Experience, and $2200 for Arts Alive! or Summer Challenge (two-week programs). Tuition included the academic/program fee, room and board, course materials, field trips, and an MPS Summer Programs t-shirt. The application fee was $35. The Dormitory Damage Deposit of $100 (cash) is returned at the end of the program if no damage has been

done to the dorms or facilities. The suggested amount of spending money is $25 to $30 per week; spending money is deposited into personal accounts, from which students may make withdrawals as needed using their personal key/debit cards. Costs may be subject to change in 2008.

FINANCIAL AID

For the Sarah Porter Leadership Institute, Arts Alive!, and Summer Challenge, limited financial aid is available on a first-come basis for families who demonstrate financial need. Applicants who wish to apply for financial aid should contact the Summer Programs Office for a financial aid application, instructions, and an IRS Form 4506. Financial aid requests are reviewed when a student's application folder is complete and the financial aid application and all necessary tax forms have been submitted. Decisions about financial aid awards are made beginning on March 31.

APPLICATION TIMETABLE

For the Sarah Porter Leadership Institute, Arts Alive!, and Summer Challenge, students must submit an application form with a letter of recommendation from their school and teacher, an official school transcript, and a $35 nonrefundable application fee. Application and recommendation forms are available online at http://www.mpssummerprograms.org or by calling the Summer Programs Office. Admission decisions are made when all required forms and fees are received. To register for The Athletic Experience, students must submit the registration form with a $150 tuition deposit.

FOR MORE INFORMATION, CONTACT

Summer Programs Office
Miss Porter's School
60 Main Street
Farmington, Connecticut 06032
Phone: 860-409-3692
      800-HI SARAH (choose option 3) (toll-free)
Fax: 860-409-3515
E-mail: summer_programs@missporters.org
Web site: http://www.mpssummerprograms.org

MOUNT HOLYOKE COLLEGE

SummerAction
take the lead!

SUMMERACTION: TAKE THE LEAD!

SOUTH HADLEY, MASSACHUSETTS

TYPE OF PROGRAM: Leadership development
PARTICIPANTS: Young women, 9-11 grade
ENROLLMENT: 80
PROGRAM DATES: June 29 to July 12, 2008
HEADS OF PROGRAM: Susan Pliner, Ed.D., and Laurie Boucher, M.A.

LOCATION
SummerAction: Take the Lead! is held on the campus of Mount Holyoke College in western Massachusetts. Mount Holyoke is among the nation's top liberal arts colleges and is consistently named one of the most beautiful college campuses in the nation by *Princeton Review.*

BACKGROUND AND PHILOSOPHY
Mount Holyoke College has a proud tradition of cultivating powerful women leaders. Under the guidance of the Weissman Center for Leadership and the Liberal Arts, which is known for its innovative and effective work, the Take the Lead program has been developing leadership skills in young women for nearly a decade. Action projects by Take the Lead participants have generated national publicity in such magazines as *CosmoGIRL!, Seventeen, ym,* and *Teen People.* Take the Lead, a four-day fall program, is designed for 40 young women nominated by their high schools. Due to the program's extraordinary success, Take the Lead has been expanded to offer a two week SummerAction: Take the Lead! for 80 young women. SummerAction does not include a nomination process, and any qualified student is welcome to apply.

SummerAction is designed for idealistic, energetic young women who want to make a difference in the world. The program engages participants in fun, highly interactive workshops and activities that build leadership skills. It gives student leaders the chance to join a network of young action-oriented advocates who are passionate about important issues such as the environment, poverty, racism, sexism, animal rights, and school violence. Each participant learns about the critical elements needed to turn ideas into action and engages in a real community project to develop her skills. SummerAction is about building each student's capabilities to return home and implement a vision and plan for addressing an issue of importance in her school, in her community, and in the world.

PROGRAM OFFERINGS
Turning ideas into an action project. Before arriving for SummerAction, each student identifies an issue that she cares about. During the program, with the help of faculty members, a mentor, and peers, the student plans an action project to address the issue that she can implement back home.

Participating in a team-based community project. During the program, each student joins a team of committed peers for hands-on participation in a local community project of particular interest to her. This hands-on experience is a laboratory for putting new skills and knowledge into action.

During the two weeks, students attend workshops on public speaking, mentoring, publicity strategies, community organizing, leadership styles, and fund-raising. In addition, students participate in a daylong session with ACT NOW!, a highly regarded youth development program that empowers girls through improvisational moviemaking. Students also attend a video presentation by Hollywood producer *(The Princess Diaries, The*

Sisterhood of the Traveling Pants) and Mount Holyoke alumna Debra Martin Chase '77. There is also a workshop on applying to colleges and an opportunity to hear about the Five College Consortium and tour Mount Holyoke, Hampshire, and Amherst Colleges.

ENROLLMENT
The student body of around 80 participants is geographically and culturally diverse. Students are selected based on their potential for leadership and making a difference as demonstrated by their academic, extracurricular, or community involvement as well as their insight and motivation to take action on an issue.

DAILY SCHEDULE

7:30 . . .	Breakfast
8:30 . . .	Announcements and workshop assignments
9:00 . . .	Workshop
10:00 . . .	Break/snack
10:15 . . .	Workshop
11:45 . . .	Lunch
1:45 . . .	Yoga
2:45 . . .	Break/snack
3:00 . . .	Work on presentation with peers and mentor
4:00 . . .	Complete presentation
5:30 . . .	Dinner, free time
7:30 . . .	Change Agent Experience
8:30 . . .	Optional: West African dance workshop, origami workshop,
10:00 . . .	Optional: Visit the Thirsty Mind coffee shop
11:00 . . .	Room check-in

EXTRA OPPORTUNITIES AND ACTIVITIES
Students live in a Mount Holyoke residence hall, and the program is designed to give them a taste of college life. All meals are served at the newly renovated campus center overlooking Lower Lake. Each day there are recreational choices, including swimming, yoga, tennis, team sports, weight training, and dance. Other activities might include a talent show, a celebration banquet, jewelry making, and a scavenger hunt. On the weekend there are day trips to New England sites such as the Emily Dickinson House, the Berkshires, and the Connecticut beaches.

FACILITIES

Students have full access to the library, art museum, hiking trails, and athletic facilities on the 800-acre campus of Mount Holyoke. Classes take place on the campus. There is a visit to the Mount Holyoke Equestrian Center, which is home to one of the best collegiate riding programs in the nation. Community projects take place at local organizations and are fully supervised by the SummerAction faculty and staff.

STAFF

SummerAction faculty and staff members are drawn from the Mount Holyoke College community, including Take the Lead alumnae. Classes are taught by faculty members from Mount Holyoke's Weissman Center for Leadership and the Liberal Arts and other academic departments.

MEDICAL CARE

An on-site nurse provides 24-hour coverage.

COSTS

The fee for the SummerAction: Take the Lead program is $2950. The fee includes room, board, all program materials, event tickets, and local transportation.

FINANCIAL AID

A limited number of need-based scholarships are available.

TRANSPORTATION

Mount Holyoke is located 45 minutes from Bradley International Airport (Hartford/Springfield) and 30 minutes from the Springfield Amtrak station. The SummerAction transportation coordinator advises families on the easiest ways to reach the campus. Transportation can be arranged from Bradley Airport and local train and bus stations to the campus.

APPLICATION TIMETABLE

Applications are reviewed on a rolling basis, and prospective students are encouraged to apply early. Students must submit the following: the application form; a personal statement describing the student's reasons for applying to the SummerAction

program; a letter of recommendation from a teacher, guidance counselor, or religious or community leader; and a high school transcript. The final deadline for applications is May 1. Notification of acceptance is made within three weeks of receipt of the completed application. A $250 nonrefundable deposit is required upon acceptance. Application and recommendation forms are available online at http://www.mtholyoke.edu/summeraction or by calling 413-538-3500.

FOR MORE INFORMATION, CONTACT

Rosita Nunez, Associate Director, Take the Lead
Mount Holyoke College
South Hadley, Massachusetts 01075-1441
Phone: 413-538-3500
Fax: 414-538-2691
E-mail: summeraction-web@mtholyoke.edu
Web site: http://www.mtholyoke.edu/summeraction

PARTICIPANT/FAMILY COMMENTS

"Take the Lead was completely inspiring. I've never been in a room with so many powerful women. The energy level was electrifying!" —Blair Beuche, Take the Lead participant.

"The biggest thing for girls my age is that they are overwhelmed by the workload involved in starting a project. Mount Holyoke really empowered us with the idea that we do have the ability to pull off a project that is bigger than just one or two people—one that involves the whole community." —Alison Rogers, Take the Lead participant

"My mentor really helped me to think about ways to execute my action project. It was inspiring to work with someone who shares the desire to achieve goals that sometimes seem unattainable." —Lindsay Mecca, Take the Lead participant

MOUNT HOLYOKE COLLEGE

SUMMERMATH AND SEARCH PROGRAMS

SOUTH HADLEY, MASSACHUSETTS

TYPE OF PROGRAM: Academic enrichment
PARTICIPANTS: Young women, rising 9–12 grade
ENROLLMENT: Approximately 60 students
PROGRAM DATES: Four weeks in July
HEADS OF PROGRAM: Dr. Charlene Morrow, Psychology Department, and Dr. James Morrow, Mathematics Department

LOCATION

SummerMath and SEARCH take place concurrently on the campus of Mount Holyoke College in western Massachusetts. The area is known for its natural beauty, institutions of higher learning, and cultural offerings.

BACKGROUND AND PHILOSOPHY

SummerMath was initiated in 1982 with an emphasis on teaching and learning mathematics in a more conceptual and participatory manner. SummerMath works to increase the participation of women and members of minority groups in science, mathematics, engineering, and technology.

SummerMath focuses on understanding rather than just memorizing, on learning to be an independent learner without being isolated, and on doing mathematics in context. The program is neither competitive nor remedial; rather, it uses a problem-solving format in which students work on challenging problems, devise their own approaches for solving problems, and then give detailed explanations of their solutions. There are frequent interactions with teachers as the students learn to become more self-motivated and better able to direct their own learning.

The SEARCH program was initiated in 2004 to offer young women the opportunity to experience a mathematics research environment. This is an in-depth and intensive program for students who want to know about mathematics that is beyond what is seen in high school.

PROGRAM OFFERINGS

The SummerMath Program Students take three classes, each involving student activity, questioning, discussion, and discovery. Each class has the goal of helping students become powerful and effective problem solvers.

The three classes are Fundamental Mathematical Concepts, where students work and discuss ideas in pairs, with an instructor and an undergraduate assistant circulating about the classroom asking probing questions and leading small-group discussions; Computer Programming, where students work in pairs at a computer using Logo to solve problems of geometric design, learning to plan, organize, and revise their ideas by working on projects such as transformational geometry, tangram puzzles, patchwork quilt designs, and group murals; and Workshops, consisting of two 2-week workshops, with choices including robotics, statistics, architecture, economics, and geometric origami. Workshops are intended to give students a hands-on experience with ways in which mathematics can be applied.

The SEARCH Program This program is designed for students who have developed some confidence in mathematics but who have not seen mathematics beyond the high school curriculum. Students are given the opportunity for in-depth exploration guided by mathematics faculty members and in collaboration with other students. The environment is hands-on and lively, with an emphasis on students formulating and answering their own questions. Students are introduced to several pieces of software that are useful tools for mathematical explorations. There are several evening collaborative problem-solving sessions, as well as field trips.

ENROLLMENT

The SummerMath student body of around 50 students is academically, geographically, and racially diverse. Some students excel in math and some do not, but many experience a lack of confidence in their mathematical abilities that is still far too prevalent in young women. Virtually all past SummerMath students have expressed an increase in self-confidence upon completion of the program. SummerMath seeks students who are highly motivated and open to trying new methods of learning.

SEARCH is a smaller program, equally as diverse as SummerMath and housed in the same dormitory. The two programs share many activities.

EXTRA OPPORTUNITIES AND ACTIVITIES

Most students live in the dormitory, and the residential program is designed to give students a taste of college life. There are offerings from workshops on personal growth to colleges and careers to SAT preparation to jewelry making. Each afternoon, there are recreational choices, including swimming, team sports, weight training, and aerobic dance. Weekends include day trips to such places as the Boston Museum of Science or Shakespeare & Co. in the Berkshires.

DAILY SCHEDULE

A typical day at SummerMath:

8:00	Breakfast
8:45	Mathematics
10:15	Break
10:30	Computer Programming
12:00	Lunch
1:00– 2:30	Workshop
3:00	Recreation
4:30	Floor meeting with RA
5:30	Dinner, free time
7:00	College student panel
8:00	Social events, free time
11:00	Room Check-In

A typical day at SEARCH:

8:00	Breakfast
8:45–12:00	Classes and Problem Sessions (including a break)
12:00	Lunch
1:00– 2:30	Technology Workshop
3:00	Recreation
4:30	Floor meeting
5:30	Dinner, free time
6:30	Problem-Solving Session
8:00	Social events, free time
11:00	Room Check-In

FACILITIES

Students have full access to the library, art museum, hiking and biking trails, and athletic facilities on the 800-acre campus of Mount Holyoke. Classes take place on campus. One dormitory is used exclusively for SummerMath and SEARCH students. All meals are served at the newly renovated campus center overlooking Lower Lake.

STAFF

SummerMath staff members are drawn from Mount Holyoke and other colleges throughout the United States. SEARCH classes are taught by college mathematics faculty members. Resident assistants and teaching assistants are undergraduate students from Mount Holyoke and other colleges.

MEDICAL CARE

Free emergency and one-time medical coverage is provided through the University of Massachusetts Health Service.

COSTS

The fee for both programs is $4500, which includes room, board, all program materials, event tickets, and local transportation. For day students, the fee is $3500.

FINANCIAL AID

Need-based scholarships of up to $2000 are available.

TRANSPORTATION

The campus is located 45 minutes from Bradley International Airport (Hartford/Springfield) and 30 minutes from the Springfield Amtrak station. Transportation is provided to and from Bradley Airport and the Springfield bus and train stations.

APPLICATION TIMETABLE

Applications are due by May 2, with late acceptance on a space-available basis. Financial aid is awarded on a rolling basis, so early application is strongly advised.

FOR MORE INFORMATION, CONTACT

Charlene and James Morrow, Directors
SummerMath and SEARCH
Mount Holyoke College
South Hadley, Massachusetts 01075-1441

Phone: 413-538-2608
Fax: 413-538-2002
E-mail: summermath@mtholyoke.edu
Web site: http://www.mtholyoke.edu/proj/summermath
http://www.mtholyoke.edu/proj/search

PARTICIPANT/FAMILY COMMENTS

"I met so many wonderful and diverse people...most importantly, SummerMath improved my self-confidence in all areas tremendously! It's definitely an experience I will always carry with me."—SummerMath student

"I think our teachers have been keeping secrets from us...you will never see mathematics like this in high school! Now I can make connections between the real world and mathematics."—SEARCH student

"Of all the experiences that [our daughter] has had, SummerMath at Mount Holyoke was the most singular and the most influential in her development."—Parent

NATIONAL STUDENT LEADERSHIP CONFERENCE

CAREER-FOCUSED LEADERSHIP DEVELOPMENT PROGRAMS FOR HIGH-ACHIEVING HIGH SCHOOL STUDENTS

WASHINGTON, D.C.; COLLEGE PARK, MARYLAND; BERKELEY, CALIFORNIA; NEW YORK, NEW YORK; AND EUROPE

TYPE OF PROGRAM: Students develop key leadership skills while exploring careers in law, diplomacy, politics, medicine, engineering, business, national security, forensic science, journalism, community service, or the arts

PARTICIPANTS: Coeducational, ages 14–18

ENROLLMENT: Limited to approximately 100 to 150 per program session

PROGRAM DATES: Five- and ten-day programs in the winter/spring, fall, and summer

HEAD OF PROGRAM: Mike Sims, J.D., Executive Director

LOCATION

National Student Leadership Conference (NSLC) programs take place at many of the nation's outstanding educational institutions, including UC-Berkley in California, Fordham University in New York, the University of Maryland in College Park, and American University (AU) in Washington, D.C. Study-abroad programs travel to France and Switzerland.

BACKGROUND AND PHILOSOPHY

Since 1989, the National Student Leadership Conference has been preparing high-achieving high school students for leadership roles in high school and college and beyond. In these unique and exciting programs, young leaders from across the country and around the world do more than just explore careers—they live them. Participants learn by doing as they immerse themselves in the area they are studying and develop their abilities to think, analyze, and effectively make decisions. Because the NSLC believes that students can learn and have fun at the same time, these programs are highlighted with interesting activities, exciting field trips, and enriching social experiences.

PROGRAM OFFERINGS

Programs are offered year-round and emphasize leadership in different academic areas. Students learn communication skills and negotiation strategies through interactive workshops taught by a distinguished faculty. Guest speaker programs allow students to meet and learn from national and world leaders. Students also gain the added advantage of experiencing college life while living on university campuses.

Law & Advocacy provides students with the opportunity to study and experience the American judicial system through a comprehensive mock trial simulation.

International Diplomacy immerses participants in the study of world politics and international relations. In a United Nations (UN) simulation, students serve as delegates to the UN and debate controversial world issues.

Medicine & Health Care offers students the opportunity to explore the world of medicine through discussions with practicing physicians and leading medical researchers, site visits, and simulations designed to examine some of the most controversial issues facing the medical community. Special partnerships with the University of Maryland School of Medicine and the J. David Gladstone Institutes enable students to experience the medical profession firsthand.

Mastering Leadership lets students experience the excitement of the nation's capital while studying the principles and qualities of the world's greatest leaders. Special workshops and simulations

help students unlock their leadership potential. Students have the opportunity to create and run a community service project in Washington, D.C.

Entrepreneurship & Business presents students with a first-hand look at the challenges of modern business and the opportunity to learn from prominent business leaders. Working in management teams, students make tough decisions to build a growing business.

U.S. Policy & Politics gives students the opportunity to visit the halls of government, discuss current issues with leading political advisers and politicians, and return home with a real-world understanding of the roles played by the public, press, and leaders of the U.S. A presidential campaign simulation and mock senate are highlights of the program.

Engineering immerses students in the ever-changing world of aircraft, robotics, bridges, and biological and chemical engineering. The NSLC's partnerships with the University of Maryland and the University of California Schools of Engineering make this conference an extraordinary opportunity that puts the student on the path to becoming a leading engineer.

Forensic Science brings students into the world of crime-scene investigation (CSI). With their CSI team, students learn and practice the techniques of leading forensic scientists during a crime-scene analysis simulation. Students meet with leaders in the fields of medicine, law enforcement, and law while touring such facilities as crime labs and the FBI.

Globalization & International Business gives students the opportunity to learn about the global economic institutions that connect the world. During special briefings at the International Monetary Fund, the World Bank, and a variety of multinational corporations, as well as exciting hands-on simulations, students discover the complexities of international trade.

Journalism & Mass Communication enables students to learn about careers in the communication field during hands-on experiences with the American University School of Communication. Students learn from AU faculty members as they try their hand at broadcasting, scriptwriting, photography, filmmaking, or print journalism.

Study Abroad: Globalization & International Business gives students the opportunity to travel to Geneva, Switzerland, to learn about the global economic institutions that connect the world. Through special briefings at the World Trade Organization, the International Olympic Committee, the United Nations, and a variety of multinational corporations, students discover the complexities of international trade.

State Leadership Workshop: During the NSLC State Leadership Workshop, students gain essential leadership skills while learning to plan and manage a large-scale service project. Working with peers from across their state, students develop a service project they can implement in their own school and community when they return home.

At the end of each program, students receive a Certificate of Achievement and an official program transcript verifying their participation. The NSLC is sponsored and endorsed by American University. High school students participating in the NSLC have the option of earning college credit through American University, which is transferable to most institutions. This credit-bearing curriculum, which links theory to practice, recognizes the increasing importance of global approaches to leadership and to preparing leaders for the complexities and challenges of an increasingly interconnected world.

ENROLLMENT

The NSLC is open to students who have demonstrated academic excellence (B average or better), leadership potential, and a commitment to improving themselves and the world in which they live. Students must either be nominated by their school or make a merit application to NSLC. Last year, young men and women from throughout the United States and more than forty different countries participated in NSLC programs.

DAILY SCHEDULE

7:30– 8:30	... Breakfast
9:00–10:15	... Workshop
10:30–12:00	... Lecture/discussion
12:00– 1:30	... Lunch
1:30– 3:30	... Field trip
3:30– 5:00	... Leadership exercise
5:00– 6:30	... Dinner
7:00– 9:00	... Simulations: Mock trial/United Nations/Leadership in Action (depending on program)
9:00–11:00	... Social activity

EXTRA OPPORTUNITIES AND ACTIVITIES

Students in California enjoy educational and recreational trips to the San Francisco Bay Area, including visits to a crime lab, the J. David Gladstone Institutes for Medical Research, Pier 39, and Ghirardelli Square. In Washington, D.C., special tours, field trips, and briefings take students "inside" Washington, including foreign embassies, Capitol Hill, the Supreme Court, the Pentagon, the Smithsonian Institution, the FBI, the World Health Organization, the National Institutes of Health, and much more. Students in New York discover the financial, art, and diplomatic communities through special trips, including the United Nations, the Federal Reserve, the Harlem Arts Community, and much more.

FACILITIES

Students reside 2 to 4 to a room in university dormitories or hotel conference facilities. Experienced residential advisers and counselors live in halls with the students and are always available to answer questions and solve problems. All on-campus meals are taken in university or hotel dining rooms.

STAFF

Teaching faculty members include law professors, deans, judges, Ph.D.'s, graduate school professors, and respected academic schol-

ars. Faculty and staff members reside on-site. The faculty/staff–student ratio is approximately 1:12.

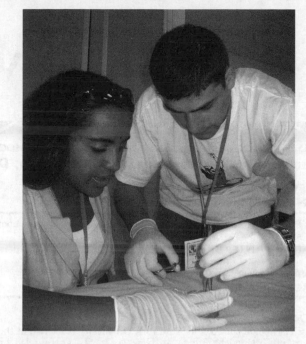

MEDICAL CARE

Students have access to 24-hour medical care at a nearby hospital. Students must have medical insurance to enroll and are responsible for medical expenses incurred during the program.

COSTS

Tuition is $2295 for ten-day programs and $1095 for the NSLC State Leadership Workshop. This includes housing, all on-campus meals, course materials, miscellaneous academic expenses, and activities. It also includes off-campus field trips, chartered bus transportation for educational tours, counselor supervision, and 24-hour access to medical treatment.

FINANCIAL AID

Need- and merit-based partial scholarships and financial assistance are available to qualified students. A scholarship application must be requested from the NSLC office. Scholarships are awarded on a rolling basis, so students should apply early.

TRANSPORTATION

Students are responsible for transportation to and from the programs. Airport pick-up and drop-off can be arranged through the NSLC for a $25 fee (each way).

APPLICATION TIMETABLE

Admission to NSLC is highly selective and the programs fill quickly, so early application is encouraged. Students nominated by their schools receive an invitation to apply for preapproved admission, based on space availability. A student making a merit application must complete an enrollment application and submit it with an educator recommendation. A deposit of $250 is required with all applications. Admission is granted on the basis of academic merit, extracurricular accomplishment, and leadership potential.

FOR MORE INFORMATION, CONTACT

National Student Leadership Conference
414 North Orleans Street, Suite LL8
Chicago, Illinois 60610-1087
Phone: 312-322-9999
         800-994-NSLC (6752) (toll-free)
Fax: 312-765-0081
E-mail: info@nslcleaders.org
Web site: http://www.nslcleaders.org

PARTICIPANT/FAMILY COMMENTS

"My time spent at the NSLC was unforgettable. With the exceptional skills and knowledge that I gained, I am certain that I am able to create positive change in the world."

NEW YORK UNIVERSITY

◣◣◣◣◣◣◣◣◣◣◣◣◣◣◣◣◣◣◣◣◣◣◣◣◣◣◣◣◣

TISCH SCHOOL OF THE ARTS SUMMER HIGH SCHOOL PROGRAMS IN ACTING, MUSICAL THEATRE PERFORMANCE, VIDEO NARRATIVE, ANIMATION, DRAMATIC WRITING, AND PHOTOGRAPHY AND IMAGING

NEW YORK, NEW YORK; DUBLIN, IRELAND; AND PARIS, FRANCE

TYPE OF PROGRAM: College-level training for high school students
PARTICIPANTS: Rising high school seniors and rising juniors of exceptional maturity
ENROLLMENT: 16–56 per program/course
PROGRAM DATES: Four weeks, July through August

LOCATION

Tisch School of the Arts at New York University is located in the heart of Greenwich Village, in New York City, surrounded by historic and intriguing neighborhoods such as the East Village, SoHo, Chinatown, and Union Square. Centers for the visual arts, contemporary music, and avant-garde theater are all close by. Within walking distance are the Astor Place Theater and productions at off-Broadway and experimental theaters such as Joseph Papp's Public Theater and La MaMa Experimental Theatre Club or at the performance spaces of TriBeCa and SoHo. Just a bus ride away are the Museum of Television and Radio, the International Center of Photography, the Metropolitan and Whitney museums, the Museum of Modern Art, the Shakespeare Festival in Central Park, and Lincoln Center. In the summer, the city becomes a festival of street fairs, alfresco concerts, and impromptu street performances.

BACKGROUND AND PHILOSOPHY

The Tisch School is internationally recognized as a premier center for the study of the performing and media arts, with programs in acting, cinema studies, dance, design, dramatic writing, film and television, interactive telecommunications, musical theater, performance studies, photography and imaging, and recorded music. The School has a faculty of more than 300 artist-teachers whose professional careers lend depth and insight to their teaching. Merging the artistic training of a professional school with the academic resources of a major university, the Tisch School provides young artists and scholars with a humanistic education, rigorous training in their discipline, and an invaluable opportunity to pursue their development as an artist.

Within the Tisch School of the Arts, the Department of Drama offers an undergraduate program that leads to the B.F.A. degree. Training the professionally focused actor is the Department of Drama's principal concern. The department offers one of the most prestigious and unique theater training programs in the country, combining rigorous studio classes offered at select professional New York City studios with academic course work at the NYU campus.

The Kanbar Institute of Film and Television offers an undergraduate program leading to the B.F.A. degree and provides a comprehensive education that includes the liberal arts as well as professional training. The program is designed to offer a broad range of exposure—from creative experiences in conceiving and producing works in film and television to theoretical studies that provide a historical frame of reference.

PROGRAM OFFERINGS

The Summer High School Programs at Tisch School of the Arts are for rising high school seniors (juniors entering their senior year). (Sophomores, or rising juniors, of exceptional maturity may be considered.) Programs are offered in New York, New York; Dublin, Ireland; and Paris, France. Students select one program, in one location, when applying.

The summer programs in acting, musical theater performance, dramatic writing, video narrative, animation, and photography and imaging are direct outgrowths of the professional training offered to B.F.A. students and reflect the same standards of excellence that characterize Tisch's degree programs. These are precollege training programs. Students earn 6 college credits upon successful completion of the program. Each program enrolls 16 to 56 students of top quality.

The Tisch summer programs help high school students learn more about themselves, about their talent, and about the standards of college training programs. Participants gain an enriching and enlightening experience as well as a sense of what a professional training program can offer them and their suitability for such study.

Acting (Strasberg) is an intensive introduction to college-level professional actor training. Training includes 28 hours of class work each week conducted at the Lee Strasberg Theatre Institute. The Strasberg Institute practices the acting technique commonly known as the "Method," one of the most renowned techniques in the world. The Method focuses on the connection between the actor's personal experience and emotions (called the "sense memory") and the experiences and emotions of the character. It is this personal spark that turns a skilled technician into a true artist. Classes include acting technique, scene study, tap, jazz, speech, movement, production rehearsal, acting for the camera, and singing. Students present a special workshop performance at the end of the session.

Musical Theatre Performance is an intense introduction to college-level professional musical theater performance training. The program strives for proficiency in acting, dance, and voice to produce a complete and well-rounded musical theater performer. All classes are aimed at developing the strength, stamina, discipline, and professionalism needed to compete and succeed as a professional. Students attend classes in tap, ballet, jazz, modern dance, acting, vocal technique, and vocal performance.

The **Experimental Theatre Workshop** (ETW) at the Experimental Theatre Wing has gained, since its inception in 1975, an international reputation as a hotbed for the creation of new theater artists and cutting-edge theater art. Based on the work of Jerzy Grotoski and Konstantin Stanislavski, the primary curriculum combines physically based acting, postmodern dance (including Viewpoints), extended vocal technique, and various approaches to improvisation and creating individual theater, with rigorous training in realistic acting, speech, and singing. Seeking playfulness, the goal of all classroom work is spontaneity inside of a disciplined approach in order for each student to discover and shape his or her own artistic vision. The faculty of ETW consists of professionals in contemporary theater, dance, and music. Studio training is composed of physically based acting and improvisation, speech, and vocal performance with a focus on freeing the voice and finding the uniqueness of each voice. Movement classes focus on heightening body awareness, with additional training in contact improvisation, postmodern dance, and hip-hop. There are also classes in self-scripting, giving the student an opportunity to explore his or her own artistic vision while creating original work.

Filmmakers Workshop: Video Narrative is designed to introduce students to the techniques and theory of developing and producing short-story ideas that they shoot on video and edit digitally on computer. As most students enter the program with little or no experience in film or video, early assignments are designed to familiarize them with equipment and to introduce documentary, experimental, and narrative approaches. Working in crews in the digital video medium, students learn directing, shooting, and editing skills as they produce pieces that are 3 to 5 minutes in length. Special emphasis is placed on visual language; early projects are produced entirely without sound. In addition, screenings of significant works and discussions with industry professionals and Tisch faculty members are held. Daily sessions are divided into lecture, lab, and screening periods.

The **Animation Filmmaker's Workshop** is an exciting and intensive course focusing on the basic techniques of animation. In each class, students explore a sampling of animation methods and view a variety of animated films from all over the world. Techniques include 2-D drawings, stop-motion puppets, pixilation, collage, paint on film, and 3-D computers. The course demonstrates how drawing and moving graphics relate, but students do not have to know how to draw in order to take this course. At the end of the course, students compile their animation exercises on DVD, digital video, or video reel.

Dramatic Writing provides an intensive introduction to writing for film and stage, using core classes taught in the bachelor's degree curriculum of the Department of Dramatic Writing. Students learn the fundamentals of dramatic structure in lecture and discussion sessions, develop their own scripts in writing workshop, and present their work in an afternoon colloquium. Theater games, improvisation, and writing exercises are employed to help students develop their writing and presentation skills.

Photography and Imaging focuses on using photo-based image making for communication, creative expression, and personal exploration. Participating students gain the visual and verbal vocabulary to further articulate their interests in relation to creating and discussing imagery. Designed for beginning and advanced students, this program is a rigorous combination of cultural, technical, and historical lectures; darkroom work; critiques of student work; critical discussions; and written responses to lectures, readings, and gallery visits. Taking full advantage of the many creative communities in New York City, this program includes many field trips. Students embark on photographic expeditions as well as visit major museums and gallery exhibitions and artist's studios.

International High School Programs offer students the opportunity to immerse themselves in the rich cultural and artistic offerings of Dublin and Paris. Students may study acting or video narrative in Dublin or acting in Paris.

ENROLLMENT

The person who best benefits from and contributes to the programs is disciplined, mature, and prepared to focus on the work at hand and brings an abiding respect for his or her fellow human beings. Prior accomplishment as an artist is not as important as an openness to the training and ideas being presented.

Tisch School of the Arts attempts to judge the suitability of applicants from their academic records, essays, resumes, and letters of recommendation.

FACILITIES

Students in all programs reside together in New York University housing located within walking distance of the classes. NYU housing includes front desk service and 24-hour security. Residential advisers share living space with the students and supervise activities outside of the studio. Evening and weekend time is scheduled to include a variety of group outings as well as class preparation and rehearsal time.

MEDICAL CARE

All students enrolled in the Tisch School of the Arts high school programs are considered to be officially enrolled New York University students and thus have access to the services of the NYU Health Center.

COSTS

The comprehensive fee for tuition, room, and board was $7413–$8894 for the 2007 program. This included tuition for 6 college credits, meals Monday through Friday and weekend dinners, accommodations, activities, and a fee for health services. Students in the Filmmakers Workshops were also assessed a lab and equipment insurance fee of approximately $450. Interested students should visit the programs' Web site for the current fees.

FINANCIAL AID

Some need-based scholarships are available. Students are also encouraged to speak to their guidance counselors about community sources of funding. For additional information, students should visit http://specialprograms.tisch.nyu.edu/object/SP_HSScholarship.html.

APPLICATION TIMETABLE

Tisch School of the Arts encourages students to apply early. Applications and related materials (personal statement, recommendation letters, resume, and transcripts) should be received no later than February 8, 2008. (This date may be subject to change. Interested students should call or check the Web site for updated information.) Applications received after this date will not be reviewed. The online application fee for 2007 was $60, and $80 for printed applications. Interested students should call or visit the Web site for 2008 fees.

FOR MORE INFORMATION, CONTACT

Programs are subject to change. When inquiring for more information, students should specify which program(s) they are interested in and clearly state that they are interested in high school programs.
Summer High School Programs
Tisch School of the Arts
New York University
721 Broadway, 12th Floor
New York, New York 10003-6807
Phone: 212-998-1500
Fax: 212-995-4578
E-mail: tisch.special.info@nyu.edu
Web site: http://www.nyu.edu/tisch/spsum08

PARTICIPANT/FAMILY COMMENTS

"The high school program at Tisch influenced me to make this career a part of my life. Every day the classes pushed us in ways that I never imagined."—High School Program participant and Tisch senior

NORTHFIELD MOUNT HERMON SCHOOL

NMH SUMMER SESSION

NORTHFIELD, MASSACHUSETTS

TYPE OF PROGRAM: Academic credit and enrichment
PARTICIPANTS: Coeducational, students entering grades 7–12
ENROLLMENT: 250
PROGRAM DATES: June 28 to August 2
HEAD OF PROGRAM: Gregory T. Leeds, Director

LOCATION

The 300-acre campus is located at the edge of the town of Northfield, overlooking the Connecticut River, in western Massachusetts. Although the setting is rural, field trips take students to nearby New England locales, such as Boston and Hampton Beach.

BACKGROUND AND PHILOSOPHY

In a supportive residential setting, NMH Summer Session provides a strong program to students from a wide variety of backgrounds and cultures.

PROGRAM OFFERINGS

College Prep—students entering grades 10–12
Middle School Program—students entering grades 7–9

College Prep This program is for capable, motivated high school students. Course offerings include Expository Writing, Academic Writing, Creative Writing, Literature and Composition, Psychology, American History, Algebra I and II, Geometry, Precalculus, Calculus, Chemistry, Biology, and English as a Second Language.

The average class size is 10 students. Academic classes meet in the morning six days a week. Each student chooses one class. Some classes may qualify for academic-year credit if students make prior arrangements with their own schools. In addition, there are afternoon sports and minor courses in art, music, drama, and various other subjects.

Middle School This program is designed to provide students with a taste of serious academic work in a boarding school setting. Each participant takes two courses that are intended

to help prepare him or her for the academic year. Offerings include Writing, Skills in Literature, Drama, Literature, Prealgebra, Algebra I, Field Biology, Beginning Spanish, Beginning French, and English as a Second Language.

There are two 75-minute morning sessions each day, six days a week, and afternoon sports and minor courses.

ENROLLMENT

There are about 250 students. Approximately 50 percent come from abroad, most notably from Europe, Latin America, and East Asia. In addition, the summer population includes minority students and students from all parts of the United States.

DAILY SCHEDULE

7:30– 8:15	Breakfast
8:30–11:30	Classes
11:30– 1:00	Lunch
1:30– 3:00	College Prep minors and labs, Middle School sports
3:30– 5:00	College Prep sports, Middle School minors
5:00– 6:30	Dinner
6:00– 7:30	Open
7:30–10:00	Study
10:30	Middle School students lights-out
11:00	College Prep students in rooms

EXTRA OPPORTUNITIES AND ACTIVITIES

NMH Summer Session regularly provides trips that range from visiting Boston and historic sites to fun excursions to Hampton Beach or Six Flags Amusement Park.

FACILITIES

The School's facilities include phone and computer network connections in student rooms; online access to a library and more than 100,000 volumes; computer and multimedia labs; specialty studios for painting, photography, and dance; and a music building with pianos and practice rooms. Athletic facilities include a gym with an indoor pool and a fitness center and outdoor playing fields and tennis courts.

STAFF
Teachers are drawn from Northfield Mount Hermon's school-year teaching staff and from other schools and colleges. In addition, 30 teaching interns from top colleges and universities assist with the on-campus program.

MEDICAL CARE
A resident physician and nurse are on call 24 hours a day.

COSTS
Tuition, room, and board for on-campus programs were $5700 to $5800 in 2007. About $400 should be enough for personal spending money. There is a $1500 nonrefundable deposit at the time of enrollment, which is applied to the tuition charge.

FINANCIAL AID
A financial aid program makes it possible for students from all economic levels to attend. Financial aid is based on demonstrated financial need.

APPLICATION TIMETABLE
Inquiries are welcome anytime. Although there is no application deadline (unless a student is applying for financial aid), students are encouraged to apply early, as some courses fill quickly. Financial aid applications must be submitted by March 15. Admission decisions are made as files are completed.

FOR MORE INFORMATION, CONTACT
Northfield Mount Hermon Summer Session
1 Lamplighter Way
Mount Hermon, Massachusetts 01354

Phone: 413-498-3290
Fax: 413-498-3112
E-mail: summer_school@nmhschool.org
Web site: http://www.nmhschool.org

NORTHWESTERN UNIVERSITY

⋁⋀⋁⋀⋁⋀⋁⋀⋁⋀⋁⋀⋁⋀⋁⋀⋁⋀⋁⋀⋁⋀⋁⋀

CENTER FOR TALENT DEVELOPMENT

EVANSTON, ILLINOIS

TYPE OF PROGRAM: Residential and commuter academic summer program for academically talented youth

PARTICIPANTS: Coeducational, students completing grades pre-K–12

ENROLLMENT: 1,000 per session

HEAD OF PROGRAM: Susie Hoffmann, Summer Program Coordinator

LOCATION

Northwestern University (NU) is located in Evanston, Illinois, approximately 12 miles north of downtown Chicago. On the shores of Lake Michigan, Northwestern University's 240-acre campus includes beaches, tennis courts, a lagoon, and a sports and aquatics center. The parklike campus also offers convenient access to Chicago's vibrant cultural life, famous architecture, and bustling metropolitan atmosphere. However, Northwestern is more than another pretty campus. Established in 1851, it is considered one of the premier universities in the United States, well known for its top-notch academic programs, world-class faculty members, and superbly qualified student body.

Center for Talent Development (CTD), part of NU's School of Education and Social Policy, provides services and resources to academically talented students and their families. The summer program also occurs at sites other than Evanston and the Chicago suburbs. They include the Civic Leadership Institute in downtown Chicago, and Equinox (for students completing grades 10–12) and Spectrum (for students completing grades 7–9) at Case Western Reserve University (CWRU). Spectrum and Equinox are joint programs of Northwestern University's Center for Talent Development and Case Western Reserve University.

Participants in the Civic Leadership Institute live on the campus of the University of Illinois at Chicago (UIC). This location, adjacent to Chicago's Loop, allows students access to educational and recreational opportunities throughout the city. Field studies and service projects take students to vibrant ethnic neighborhoods like Greektown, Chinatown, and Pilsen. On evenings and weekends, students visit the city's famous historical and cultural sites, as well as tourist attractions like Navy Pier, Millennium Park, and the Magnificent Mile. Living downtown provides students with an unparalleled opportunity to experience all that this incredible city has to offer.

CWRU, located in Cleveland, Ohio, is one of the nation's leading independent research universities. It occupies 550 acres in University Circle, a parklike concentration of approximately fifty cultural, medical, educational, religious, and social service institutions located at the eastern edge of the city center. University Circle attracts visitors from throughout the region to its concerts, theater performances, athletic events, art shows, public lectures, exhibits, and restaurants. Housing, shopping, and recreational facilities are all located in the area.

BACKGROUND AND PHILOSOPHY

Celebrating more than twenty years of summer programming, CTD has continued to expand its scope to provide high-quality academic enrichment and acceleration for gifted precollegiate students. The success of these programs stems from CTD's unique commitment to research on the psychology, sociology, and education of gifted and talented learners; the staff's experience of working with academically able students on a year-round basis; and the program's ability to attract innovative master teachers.

While academics come first, CTD summer programs also provide a rich, supervised setting for the social interactions and friendships so important to a student's developing self-concept. An added distinction of CTD is its accreditation by the North Central Association of Colleges and Schools. It is the only center for gifted education in the country to receive this distinction.

CTD's high academic standards and diverse student body ensure that students learn not only from their teachers but also from one another. While students share a passion for learning and discovering and the intellectual capacity for advanced academic work, they also possess unique backgrounds and experiences. In 2006, CTD students came to Northwestern from urban, suburban, and rural settings in forty-two states and twelve countries. About one half of the students return for a second year, and about 70 percent choose to reside on campus for their three-week class.

DAILY SCHEDULE

```
 7:30– 8:15 . . . Breakfast
 8:30–12:00 . . . Class
12:00– 1:00 . . . Lunch
 1:00– 2:45 . . . Class
 3:00– 5:00 . . . Afternoon activities
 5:00– 7:00 . . . Dinner/relax
 7:00– 9:00 . . . Evening activity or study session
 9:00–10:00 . . . Free time
      10:00 . . . Room check
      11:00 . . . Lights out
```

PROGRAM OFFERINGS

The Center for Talent Development offers four academic programs: Leapfrog (students completing pre-K–grade 3), Apogee (completing grades 4–6), Spectrum (completing grades 7–9), and Equinox (completing grades 10–12). Leapfrog is a commuter-only weekly program held for three 1-week sessions.

Apogee, Spectrum, and Equinox students at CTD enroll in one class for a three-week period. CTD offers more than ninety classes in the sciences, humanities, writing, mathematics, and more. Classes meet for 5¼ hours a day. Classes are not held on weekends, but study sessions for residential students are available on Saturdays and Sundays. In order to maximize personal attention to the learner, CTD summer courses are limited to 18 students per class, and each class has both a master teacher and a teaching assistant.

Equinox also offers the Civic Leadership Institute, which combines engaging academic work with community service and hands-on field experiences, in order to help young people develop the knowledge, experience, and leadership skills they need to make a positive impact on society.

Participants have opportunities to interact with intellectual peers and develop friendships, engage in recreational activities, and enjoy local events and resources, ranging from swimming in Lake Michigan to attending Chicago Symphony Orchestra concerts under the stars.

FACILITIES

Students have access to many campus facilities, including recreational sites, libraries, and student centers. CTD students have access to computer facilities owned by both CTD and the University, but hours are somewhat limited. In 2006, 60 percent of enrolled students reported that they brought their own computers to the campus. Students who own portable computers, especially those enrolled in writing-intensive classes, may find it convenient to have their computers with them while attending CTD. Students should note that CTD, Northwestern University, the University of Illinois at Chicago, and Case Western Reserve University cannot provide technical support for personal computers.

Residential students live in dormitories under the supervision of specially trained residential staff members. Male and female students may share a floor but have separate bathrooms. Students eat with residential staff members and other members of the University community in a dormitory dining room and, on weekends, enjoy a broad range of activities, such as off- and on-campus theater, concerts, movies, sports events, dances, and talent shows.

STAFF

Teaching staff members for CTD summer programs are drawn from premier schools throughout the country. Teachers are chosen for their mastery of subject matter, enthusiasm, ability to individualize their teaching, and skill in providing interesting, thought-provoking, and varied classroom experiences. Each class has a teaching assistant selected from students at university campuses across the United States. The residential staff is drawn from undergraduate campuses from around the country and consists of mature, responsible, well-trained undergraduates who exhibit both academic achievement and a love of learning.

MEDICAL CARE

The summer program fee covers basic health services at each of the campuses' fully staffed and equipped health centers. Students who require more extensive assistance are taken to nearby hospitals. The residential fee covers clinic services; it does not provide medical insurance coverage. All summer program participants must be covered by a major medical insurance policy.

COSTS

Residential tuition in 2007 was $2450 and commuter tuition was $1550. Leapfrog tuition was $220 per week for a half-day course and $450 for the all-day course (for students completing third grade only). In addition, a nonrefundable $50 application fee is required. Interested students should visit http://www.ctd.northwestern.edu/summer for 2008 fees. Financial aid is available.

APPLICATION TIMETABLE

Summer brochures are available in January. Students should call or e-mail CTD to request a brochure. Space is limited, and applicants are encouraged to apply early. Applications must be received by May 15, 2008.

FOR MORE INFORMATION, CONTACT

Center for Talent Development
617 Dartmouth Place
Evanston, Illinois 60208
Phone: 847-491-3782
E-mail: ctd@northwestern.edu
Web site: http://www.ctd.northwestern.edu

NORTHWESTERN UNIVERSITY

COLLEGE PREPARATION PROGRAM

EVANSTON, ILLINOIS

TYPE OF PROGRAM: College preparation

PARTICIPANTS: Coeducational; residential and commuter high school students between their junior and senior years; students between their sophomore and junior years are considered on a case-by-case basis

ENROLLMENT: Approximately 90

PROGRAM DATES: June 15 to July 26 (six-week courses), June 15 to August 9 (eight-week and intensive course sequences)

HEAD OF PROGRAM: Stephanie Teterycz, Director of Summer Session and Special Programs

LOCATION

Northwestern University is located along the shores of Lake Michigan, 12 miles north of Chicago. The 240-acre Evanston campus offers a private beach, lakefront jogging paths, sailing facilities, and playing fields. The quiet atmosphere of the surrounding neighborhood is truly conducive to study, while the proximity to the city of Chicago offers students access to cultural events, museums, and world-famous architecture.

BACKGROUND AND PHILOSOPHY

The College Preparation Program (CPP) offers high school students entering their senior year a truly unique college experience. The CPP combines the rigor of Northwestern courses and a challenging college-level writing tutorial with many exciting opportunities for summertime fun. Combined, these elements provide students with the knowledge and experience they need for a successful college career. The program is founded on the premise that college life is not simply an academic experience but a social and cultural one as well. CPP participants are encouraged to take full advantage of Northwestern University's diverse community of students by building mature social relationships as they explore new intellectual avenues. Although newly found freedom can be liberating, it can also be distracting—even frightening. This is why the College Preparation Program employs college-age resident advisers (RAs) who help students learn to manage their time, focus their energy, and balance their academic and social commitments.

PROGRAM OFFERINGS

College Preparation Program students may enroll in almost any of the freshman- and sophomore-level courses that Northwestern offers during the summer. Virtually every academic discipline is represented, from anthropology and French to physics and biology. Students may register for up to three courses, with many CPP participants choosing to take one of the popular three-course foreign language or science sequences. Summer Session staff members are always available for consultation during course selection.

In addition to those courses, an essential part of the College Prep experience is the College Writing Tutorial. This is a noncredit course taught by a Northwestern writing instructor and consists of weekly lectures, group activities, and instructor-led discussions about advanced writing techniques. Careful reading, textual analysis, and skills building are emphasized in an atmosphere of open interaction as students are introduced to strategies for building a focused argument, supporting a thesis, and constructing an annotated bibliography. The tutorial and related, individual sessions that are staffed by teaching assistants meet each week during the first six weeks of the program.

College is, however, far more than a purely academic enterprise. It is with this fact in mind that the College Preparation Program offers access to numerous social and cultural activities in Evanston and Chicago. Every summer, students visit some of Chicago's most famous cultural attractions, including the Art Institute and the Museum of Science and Industry. The program also organizes outings to ball games at Wrigley Field and numerous festivals throughout the city. Students may participate in any activities that interest them, with the understanding that their academic success is the first priority.

Life on Northwestern's Evanston campus is rich and diverse. Plays, concerts, sporting events, and picnics are planned throughout the summer. The College Prep residence hall is a true home away from home, where students share ideas, study, chat, relax, play games, and enjoy movie nights.

ENROLLMENT

Students who are between their junior and senior years in high school and who have a minimum 3.5 GPA (on a 4.0 scale) are eligible to apply. Admission is competitive, and all admitted students are academically talented, demonstrating exceptional skills in a variety of subjects. Approximately 70 students enroll as residents in the program, while another 20 enroll as commuters. Students who live in Evanston or the surrounding city and suburbs, or those who plan to live with relatives in the area during the summer, may apply as CPP Commuting Scholars. Both residential and commuting students enjoy the same program benefits, and everyone participates in the Writing Tutorial. The College Preparation Program embraces ethnic and cultural diversity and encourages students of all backgrounds to apply.

DAILY SCHEDULE

A College Prep student's daily schedule is very much like that of any other college student. A typical morning might consist of breakfast with a roommate and a 9 a.m. class. After lunch, students might spend their time researching a paper in the library, working in the lab, or attending the Writing Tutorial. A CPP participant might finish off the day with a jog along the lakefront, dinner and a movie with friends, or an evening of quiet study.

FACILITIES
Residential College Prep students share double rooms in a University residence hall and take their meals in a nearby dining hall. Students have access to Northwestern's sports and aquatics center, which includes an Olympic-size swimming pool; tennis, basketball, racquetball, and squash courts; an exercise room; and a large gym. There are also several other sports facilities on campus, including a sailing center. In the Norris Student Center, students can enjoy a crafts studio, a game room, a browsing library, a snack bar, an ice cream parlor, shops, and an art gallery. Students also have access to any of the state-of-the-art labs, studios, and theaters that are part of their course work.

MEDICAL CARE
Residential staff members have first aid and CPR training, and a student health service is located on campus. Evanston Hospital is located approximately 1 mile from the campus.

RELIGIOUS LIFE
The College Prep Program is secular and nonaffiliated. There are, however, a number of places of worship located on or near the campus.

COSTS
Students are encouraged to take two 6- or 8-week courses or one intensive sequence. The projected cost per course is $2867. The cost for the six-week program in 2007 was $5562, which included room, board, the program fee, and tuition for one course. The cost for the intensive sequence was $11,806, which included room, board, the program fee, and tuition for three courses. Use of University health services and athletic facili-

ties is included in the program fee. Students are responsible for paying for their own books and transportation.

FINANCIAL AID
A limited amount of financial aid is available. Those interested in applying for financial aid should visit the Northwestern University College Preparation Program Web site.

TRANSPORTATION
The city of Evanston is a suburb of Chicago and, as such, is easily accessible. Travel time to the campus is about 30 minutes from O'Hare International Airport and about 1 hour from Midway Airport. Shuttle buses run from both airports to Northwestern on the first day of the program. All students are responsible for arranging their own transportation home at the end of the program.

APPLICATION TIMETABLE
The early and international application deadline is March 7, 2008. The regular application deadline is April 11, 2008. Along with the application, students must submit one essay, an official high school transcript, a letter of recommendation from a teacher or counselor, and an application fee. Students are advised to apply as early as possible to ensure that all of their materials are received by the deadline.

FOR MORE INFORMATION, CONTACT
The College Preparation Program
Northwestern University
405 Church Street
Evanston, Illinois 60201-4558

Phone: 847-467-6703
Fax: 847-491-3660
E-mail: cpp@northwestern.edu
Web site: http://www.northwestern.edu/collegeprep/

NORTHWESTERN UNIVERSITY

▼▲▼▲▼▲▼▲▼▲▼▲▼▲▼▲▼▲▼▲▼▲▼▲▼▲▼▲▼▲▼▲▼▲

NATIONAL HIGH SCHOOL INSTITUTE

EVANSTON, ILLINOIS

TYPE OF PROGRAM: Summer enrichment and college preparation

PARTICIPANTS: Coeducational, high school students

ENROLLMENT: Approximately 700 students enrolled in six different programs

PROGRAM DATES: Approximately June 29 to August 2, 2008, for Theatre Arts, Film and Video Production, Journalism, and Music. Approximately July 13 to August 2, 2008, for Debate and July 13 to August 1, 2008, for Speech.

HEAD OF PROGRAM: Barbara Reeder, Administrative Director

LOCATION
Northwestern University is located 12 miles north of downtown Chicago on Lake Michigan.

BACKGROUND AND PHILOSOPHY
Since 1931, the National High School Institute (NHSI) has brought outstanding students to Northwestern University's Evanston campus for intense educational experiences. The oldest and largest university-based program of its kind, the NHSI allows students to experience aspects of "college life" while submerged in study. Students are affectionately known as "Cherubs," a name given to them in the 1930s by Northwestern Dean Ralph Dennis whose goal, "to bring together gifted young people and superior teachers in an atmosphere of affection, knowledge, and trust," is still upheld today.

PROGRAM OFFERINGS
Each of the six divisions has its own curricular goals and objectives but are all united in their educational philosophy to challenge and develop the potential of every student. Pro-

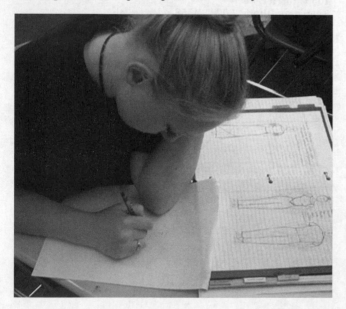

grams are enrichment based, and students are not graded and do not receive high school or college credit. An intense schedule of academics is accented with many of the opportunities that Evanston and Chicago have to offer.

Coon-Hardy Debate Program for High School Students
Modeled after the national championship Northwestern Debate Society, this program investigates how to apply argumentation, communication, and research skills to the study of the next year's national debate proposition. The curriculum is designed to teach principles that can be abstracted to many debating situations well beyond the study of this year's topic. Coon-Hardy is based on three complementary principles: interactive learning, teamwork, and curricular integration. An amazing faculty, led by Northwestern Professor and Director of Debate Scott Deatherage, completes an aggressive learning experience. The program runs for three weeks and is open to current high school freshman, sophomores, and juniors with debate experience.

Speech-Forensics This program offers complete curricula in four areas of high school speech: extemporaneous speaking, oral interpretation of literature, original oratory, and Lincoln-Douglas debate. Programs are three weeks and are open to current high school freshman, sophomores, and juniors.

Journalism This program is designed to sharpen journalistic skills as writers and editors for print or broadcast. In intensive lab sessions, students learn how to write news, feature, and editorial stories and television news; edit stories; write headlines; design newspaper pages; and report the news. College professors and practitioners evaluate writing assignments in one-on-one sessions. Workshops expose students to a variety of subjects, such as freelance writing, sports reporting, and journalistic ethics. The program runs for five weeks and is open to current high school juniors with a special interest in journalism.

Music As a Music Division participant, students may choose from among eight programs: Composition, Jazz Studies, Music Education, Piano, Strings, Voice, Winds/Percussion, and Guitar. All include private practice sessions and weekly seminars. The programs run for five weeks (guitar for two weeks) and are open to current eighth graders and high school freshmen, sophomores, and juniors.

Film and Video Production Students are introduced to the art and science of television, digital imagery, and writing through courses in camera, digital design, cinema history, and critical theory. The Media Arts Division simulates this process through two intensive concentrations: Production and Writing. The program runs for five weeks and is open to current high school juniors.

Production College-level instruction gives students the skills necessary to produce original projects in documentary video, narrative video, animated short, and interactive video (Web). NHSI students have access to the same new equipment as the Northwestern undergraduates.

Writing Daily writing labs and intensive instruction in story structure, dialog, and visual storytelling are supplemented by

a wide range of electives that provide students with thorough knowledge and practice in creating scripts.

Theatre Arts By experimenting with a multitude of crafts and disciplines, students discover that theater is a collaborative art and an emotionally, physically, and intellectually rigorous one. Two programs are offered within this division. The programs run for five weeks and are open to current high school juniors. The estimated program size is 150 students, with 10 students in the Design/Technical concentration.

General Theatre Curriculum Designed for students with a serious interest in theater, this program immerses students in the theater experience by delving into the essential concern of the theater process—the human condition. The student performs in one of ten production companies and studies with professional directors, choreographers, acting coaches, and designers. Core classes include acting, voice and movement, aesthetics of theater, text analysis, and production crew. Electives, guest lectures, and field trips to relevant productions supplement the core classes.

Design / Technical Concentration In addition to the core classes, students take special courses in the design process, enroll in a stage management workshop, and concentrate a portion of their time in the study of theater design and production.

Musical Theatre This program builds upon the instruction in the Theatre Arts program, furthering the study in acting and voice and movement, while adding relevant course work in musical theater scene study, dance, and voice master classes. Students must be accepted to and complete the full Theatre Arts Division curriculum before proceeding to the Musical Theatre extension. The program runs two weeks following Theater Arts and is open to high school juniors only. The estimated program size is fewer than 40 students.

ENROLLMENT

Criteria for acceptance into the programs include grades, letters of recommendation, PSAT (or SAT) scores, personal essays, and experience in the student's chosen concentration.

COSTS

The 2007 program costs were as follows: Coon-Hardy Debate, $2450; Speech-Forensics, $2450; Musical Theatre (includes Theatre Arts), $6300; Theatre Arts, Film and Video Production, Journalism, and Music, $4300; and Classical Guitar, $1850. All programs are residential. In addition to tuition, the fees include housing, meals, and tickets to all events and field trips. Additional costs are at the discretion of the student.

FINANCIAL AID

Each year, a large number of students receive scholarships and financial assistance. Awards are given based on academic achievement and financial need. Financial aid requests are included with the division applications.

APPLICATION TIMETABLE

Applications are usually due by early April; however, deadlines vary slightly, so students should verify dates with the current brochures. An early deadline date is usually available a few weeks prior to the regular deadline, usually in early March. This deadline serves as a planning opportunity for families and students and does not increase admission chances. There is a $50 application fee.

FOR MORE INFORMATION, CONTACT

Nick Kanel
National High School Institute (NHSI)
617 Noyes Street
Evanston, Illinois 60208
Phone: 800-662-NHSI (toll-free)
Fax: 847-467-1057
E-mail: nhsi@northwestern.edu
Web site: http://www.northwestern.edu/nhsi

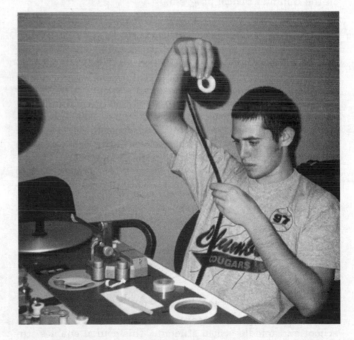

OAK CREEK RANCH SCHOOL

SUMMER SESSIONS

WEST SEDONA, ARIZONA

TYPE OF PROGRAM: Four-week summer school sessions. Students may earn ½ credit in two subjects per session. Traditional and experiential classes are offered.

PARTICIPANTS: Coed boarding school students, grades 7–12, ages 12–19

ENROLLMENT: 60–70 students per session

PROGRAM DATES: Three 4-week sessions are offered from June through mid-August

HEAD OF PROGRAM: David Wick Jr., J.D., Headmaster

LOCATION

Oak Creek Ranch School's 17-acre campus is located 15 miles west of beautiful Sedona, Arizona, adjoining the Coconino National Forest. The temperate climate of northern Arizona allows students to participate in a variety of outdoor activities, including hiking, rock climbing, camping, mountain biking, and horseback riding. Summer School students enjoy swimming, recreational sports, and fishing on campus. Excursions to the Grand Canyon and other points of interest are included in the Summer School program.

BACKGROUND AND PHILOSOPHY

Oak Creek Ranch School is a fully accredited, coed boarding school for teenagers ages 12–19 (grades 7–12). Founded in 1972 by David Wick, the School specializes in helping underachievers, undermotivated teens, and students with ADD or ADHD. Small classes, an experienced faculty, and individualized programs enable teenagers to realize their full potential. Self-discipline, responsibility, and commitment to self and others are important principles of the School's Leadership and Character Development program. All programs are designed to help teens build self-esteem and a strong desire to succeed. Experiential learning is used to stimulate intellectual curiosity and provide students with the opportunity to apply knowledge learned in the classroom to practical situations.

PROGRAM OFFERINGS

Oak Creek Ranch School is fully accredited by the North Central Association (NCA).

In 2007, the following Summer School classes were offered:

Science Through Mountain Biking: Designed for both high school and middle school students, this course enables students to learn the fundamentals of scientific theory while mountain biking through some of the most beautiful geological areas in the West.

Wilderness Literature: Students spend three weeks hiking and backpacking in wilderness areas of Yosemite and Redwoods National Parks while they read the literature created in these and similar areas. Students must be in good physical health, and they must be able to carry a 40-pound backpack.

Composition & Literature: This course is offered to middle school and high school students and is designed to help students achieve the required level of proficiency for their respective grades.

Middle School English: This course is designed to help middle school students achieve the required level of proficiency for their respective grades.

Social Studies: Topics include United States and world geography, history, and cultures. A study of the U.S. monetary and political system is covered.

Government/Economics: This course examines the role of the federal government and its impact on the economy and society. Students examine and compare differing forms of government throughout the world. Emphasis is placed on understanding how the federal government of the United States operates as a constitutional, federal, and democratic republic. Home economics, banking, budgeting, and microeconomic and macroeconomic principles are also covered in this course.

United States History: Students examine the events and people that have had an impact on the development of the United States. Students are expected to conduct research about current events using a variety of Internet news sources, newspapers, and magazines. Frequently, students are required to express their opinions of current events using factual data to support their arguments. Research, reading, writing, and group discussions are incorporated into this course work.

High School Math: This course is designed for students needing credit in prealgebra, algebra, algebra II, and advanced math. Individualized programs are designed to help students achieve their desired level of proficiency.

Middle School Math: This course is designed for students needing help in middle school math concepts. Individualized programs are designed to help students achieve their desired level of proficiency.

Conversational Spanish: This course is designed for both middle school and high school students. This class develops basic speaking skills and introduces the student to the Spanish culture.

Spanish I, II, and III: Conversational Spanish for high school students.

Computer Applications: This class is offered to both middle school and high school students and provides both individualized instruction and self-paced learning. Students may choose to master any of the following software applications: Word, Excel, and PowerPoint; Web programming tools: HTML or JavaScript; or Adobe graphics software: Illustrator and PhotoShop.

ENROLLMENT

Three 4-week summer sessions are available for credit or personal enrichment. Class sizes are fewer than 10 students, allowing students to receive one-on-one instruction. Students may take two classes per four-week session and earn ½ credit per class.

EXTRA OPPORTUNITIES AND ACTIVITIES

Recreational activities include swimming, rock climbing, mountain biking, horseback riding, overnight camping, trips to water parks, paintball games, movies, concerts, and shopping. Field trips to the Grand Canyon, Sedona's Slide Rock, the historical mining town of Jerome, a traditional rodeo in Prescott, and nearby Indian ruins are just a few of the many activities included in Oak Creek Ranch School's summer program.

FACILITIES

Oak Creek Ranch School's state-of-the-art Mac and PC labs enable students to utilize the latest technology and software applications in and out of the classroom. The Summer School facilities include dormitory residences, an administration building and dining room, multiple classrooms with audiovisual equipment, a library/study center, a recreation center, an outdoor pool, tennis courts, basketball courts, an equestrian center, and a playing field.

STAFF

Summer school is taught by members of the School's regular certified faculty. Each dormitory residence is supervised by a caring and supportive dorm adviser.

MEDICAL CARE

A registered nurse is on campus in the School's health center five days a week. Sedona Urgent Care in Sedona and the Verde Valley Medical Center in Cottonwood are utilized if students require additional medical attention. Emergency care is only minutes from the School—day or night. Medical authorization forms must be submitted to the School prior to the first day of school.

RELIGIOUS LIFE

Oak Creek Ranch School is not affiliated with any religious group. Students are invited to attend any church or religious service they desire. At the parent's request, the School can arrange transportation to and from these services.

COSTS

The 2007 tuition was $4100 per four-week session. This fee includes room, board, and most classes. Additional fees may be charged for special classes.

TRANSPORTATION

Students arrive the Sunday before classes begin. Transportation to and from the Phoenix Sky Harbor Airport is provided at the beginning and end of each Summer School session.

APPLICATION TIMETABLE

Inquiries are welcome all year. A current brochure is mailed upon request, and students are accepted from January through the summer, as space allows. An application form is available on the School's Web site. An application fee of $400 is required to secure enrollment. If the student is not accepted, the application fee is refunded.

FOR MORE INFORMATION, CONTACT

David Wick Jr., Headmaster
Oak Creek Ranch School
P.O. Box 4329
West Sedona, Arizona 86340
Phone: 928-634-5571
     877-554-OCRS (toll-free)
Fax: 928-634-4915
E-mail: admissions@ocrs.com
Web site: http://www.ocrs.com

OXBOW SCHOOL

OXBOW SUMMER ART CAMP

SUMMER ARTS PROGRAM

NAPA, CALIFORNIA

TYPE OF PROGRAM: Visual arts
PARTICIPANTS: Coeducational, ages 14 to 17
ENROLLMENT: 48 campers per session
PROGRAM DATES: Serious Art, Serious Fun: July 1–18; The Art of Digital Storytelling: July 26–August 12, 2007
HEAD OF PROGRAM: Barbara Bitner, Oxbow Summer Program Director

LOCATION

The campus is located in Napa, California, at the oxbow of the Napa River and within walking distance of cafes, shops, and theaters in downtown Napa. Napa Valley is renowned for such recreational activities as biking, hiking, and hot air ballooning. The Oxbow School is located 1 hour north of the many arts and cultural attractions of San Francisco and the Bay Area and within day-trip distance of the Sierras and the Pacific Coast.

BACKGROUND AND PHILOSOPHY

For the past eight years, the Oxbow School has offered a one-semester, visual arts–based program for high school juniors and seniors nationwide. Since 2003, it has added a summer camp program for youth ages 14-17. Oxbow was established on the belief that active involvement in the arts fosters flexible thinking and creative problem-solving skills that will serve students in all their future pursuits. The School is unique in this respect, as it is the only institution in the United States that educates all of its students through immersion in the visual arts and interdisciplinary academics.

Oxbow Summer Art Camp believes that there is no limit to what a student can achieve given high-level instruction in an inspiring and nurturing environment. To that end, Oxbow fosters a community of creative, inquiring minds where respect of self, others, and the environment; risk-taking; openness; and honesty in a nonjudgmental atmosphere are highly valued. Each individual's uniqueness is honored and "held" within the arena of the safety and unity of the camp community. It is an arena that promotes self-discovery, self-confidence, and creative expression. Students are encouraged to seek out their own artistic interests while learning at their own pace and being challenged to broaden their horizons. Students form potential lifelong bonds with like-hearted, like-minded fellow campers, and they have a lot of fun.

Campers spend roughly half their day in artistic pursuits via instruction or time in the studio, with the other half devoted to additional creative time or recreational activities with fellow campers, including field trips, sports, or projects with visiting artists.

PROGRAM OFFERINGS

The program offers two sessions. The first session, **Serious Art, Serious Fun** focuses on creating project-based art in a variety of media. Taught by professional artists and teachers, campers work in drawing, painting, sculpture, fabrication, and digital as well as black-and-white film photography to explore and develop their interests and creativity. The goal of this session is to inspire and nurture creativity, enhance art skills and produce a work that is personally significant to the camper.

The second session, **The Art of Digital Storytelling,** focuses on the art behind making live-action movies, comic books, children's books, and stop-motion animation. Through instruction from industry professionals, campers explore how to come up with great story ideas with compelling plots and memorable characters while learning the fundamentals of the visual arts

needed to express ideas. Then, working collaboratively, stories come to life in a variety of forms—acting, directing, stop-motion animation, filmmaking and editing, comics, including anime and manga, and more.

ENROLLMENT

The program enrolls a maximum of 48 campers per session. They represent a wide variety of geographic, demographic, and artistic backgrounds. Oxbow can accommodate both boarding and day campers.

DAILY SCHEDULE

7:30– 8:00 . . .	Wake-up
8:30 . . .	Breakfast
9:00–12:00 . . .	Studio sessions
12:00 . . .	Lunch
12:30– 3:00 . . .	Afternoon activities
3:00– 4:30 . . .	Studio session
4:30– 5:30 . . .	Bunk time
5:30 . . .	Dinner
6:30– 8:00 . . .	Studio time or recreational activities
8:00– 8:30 . . .	E-mail
8:30–10:00 . . .	Evening activity
10:30 . . .	Lights out

The studio sessions offer instructional sessions in all four studios for the first half of the session. In the second half, the students work independently on a large project of their own design. Afternoon activities include swimming, kayaking, field games, "art angel" time, or dorm activities. During bunk time, students have time to write, sketch, or spend time with their bunkmates. Recreational activities after dinner may include field games such as Ultimate Frisbee, soccer, touch football, and more.

Campers from the Napa/Sonoma region can choose the extended day option, which runs from 8:30 a.m. to 9:30 p.m.

EXTRA OPPORTUNITIES AND ACTIVITIES

Students may spend their afternoons playing sports or participating in other recreational activities. Their evenings are devoted to a wide variety of activities, including movie nights, camp fires, dancing, a party, talent shows, skits, costume making, and activities led by visiting artists. The evening before camp ends, there is a final show to highlight and celebrate the accomplishments of the campers. Families and friends are invited.

FACILITIES

The campus is located on a 3-acre site that includes dormitories, studios, a dining hall, faculty housing, and an organic garden. Boarding campers live in dorm suites that have three bedrooms, two baths, a common area, and laundry facilities. There are 2 or 4 campers per room, with a dorm counselor assigned to each suite. The award-winning studios with roll-up glass walls provide state-of-the art working facilities that are virtually outdoors.

STAFF

Oxbow Camp fosters a community of creative, inquiring minds where respect, tolerance, risk-taking, openness, and honesty are highly valued. The summer staff members are chosen for their commitment to these principals and are trained in how to share them with others. There are 14 instructors and counselors at the camp, leading to a student-counselor ratio of 4:1.

Dorm counselors function as "art angels" for the campers—they are friends and advisers. In addition, they ensure that camp rules are followed and that campers are healthy and safe and getting the most from their experience at the camp. The counselors are either college graduates or undergraduates in art or a related field. Many are alumni of the Oxbow Semester program.

The faculty members are drawn from the Bay Area's rich community of talented professional artists and teachers. They are carefully chosen for their years of experience working with youth as well as their expertise in their field. Outside of the studios, the faculty members continue to participate as an integral part of the camp community.

MEDICAL CARE

Medical care is available 24 hours a day at nearby hospital. Staff members accompany students to the medical facilities. After submitting the camp registration, students must submit a medical history and release form and a signed Physician's Medical Statement along with proof of insurance.

COSTS

In 2007, tuition plus room and board is $8100 per session. Day students pay $2500 per session, which includes all program fees and three meals per day. A $750 deposit is required before May 1 in order to reserve a space. Those students who register and pay a deposit before December 29 of the previous year receive a $250 discount on the program.

TRANSPORTATION

Oxbow provides free transportation via shuttle vans between the airport and Napa for students flying into either Oakland or San Francisco airports. The Sacramento Airport is another option, but pick-up service is not available, so other arrangements must be made. The campus is located off of Highway 29. Directions are available on the Web site at http://www.NoLanyardsCamp.org.

APPLICATION TIMETABLE

For registrations received before May 1, a $750 registration fee is required, with the full balance due on May 1. Registrations received after May 1 must include full tuition payment. For registrations to be considered complete, a signed Physician's Medical Statement and a completed Enrollment Agreement are required. These can be downloaded from the Web site.

FOR MORE INFORMATION, CONTACT

Oxbow Summer Art Camp
Oxbow School
530 Third Street
Napa, California 94559
Phone: 707-255-6000
E-mail: summercamp@oxbowschool.org
Web site: http://www.NoLanyardsCamp.org

PARTICIPANT/FAMILY COMMENTS

"Oxbow taught me to find the good in my art when I was ready to give up on it. Oxbow doesn't tell you, 'no, you can't do that.' They encourage and support all your art dreams. And, while you are at it, you meet tons of great new people." — Andreana, former camper

"Oxbow made me realize that it takes time and hard work to finish projects, but if you have a good idea and you stick to it, you are most likely to get the results you want. It definitely changed the way I think about others and myself. It was a life-changing experience." — Madison, former camper

"Oxbow encouraged me to take risks in my artwork. I love that everyone is so incredibly open-minded and respectful, as well as simply considerate of others. I feel inspired to do more after Oxbow." — Jenna, former camper

OXBRIDGE ACADEMIC PROGRAMS

▼▲

THE OXFORD TRADITION, THE CAMBRIDGE TRADITION, L'ACADÉMIE DE PARIS, L'ACADÉMIE DE FRANCE, LA ACADEMIA DE ESPAÑA, THE OXFORD PREP EXPERIENCE, AND THE CAMBRIDGE PREP EXPERIENCE

OXFORD AND CAMBRIDGE, ENGLAND; PARIS AND MONTPELLIER, FRANCE; AND BARCELONA, SPAIN

TYPE OF PROGRAM: Academic and cultural enrichment
PARTICIPANTS: Coeducational; grades 8–12
ENROLLMENT: The Oxford Tradition, 370; The Cambridge Tradition, 230; L'Académie de Paris, 170; L'Académie de France, 85; La Academia de España, 150; The Oxford Prep Experience, 140; The Cambridge Prep Experience, 190
PROGRAM DATES: The month of July; optional week in Paris in early August
HEAD OF PROGRAM: Professor James G. Basker, Director

LOCATION
Established more than fifteen years ago, Oxbridge Academic Programs offers academic summer programs at Oxford and Cambridge Universities in England; in Paris and Montpellier in France; and in Barcelona in Spain.

BACKGROUND AND PHILOSOPHY
Each program is designed to immerse students in two academic subjects or creative arts while taking advantage of the enormous cultural resources of Oxford, Cambridge, Paris, Montpellier, or Barcelona. All seven programs combine rigorous classroom activity with day trips, eminent guest speakers, cultural enrichment, and the experience of studying in one of the world's great centers of learning and history. The emphasis is on small classes, individual attention, and innovative teaching methods. Through the use of dynamic, caring, and imaginative teachers drawn from Oxford and Cambridge Universities, the Sorbonne, and other leading global institutions, coupled with a hands-on approach that creates an immediacy and excitement about learning, students are inspired to new levels of performance. The challenging academic program, a rich array of extracurricular activities, and a mixture of independence and structured living help students develop the best in themselves while building a foundation for their college years and beyond.

PROGRAM OFFERINGS
Oxbridge Academic Programs offers a wide range of courses in the sciences, humanities, social sciences, and creative arts. In Oxford, Cambridge, Paris, Montpellier, and Barcelona, each student selects two subjects, one as a Major and one as a Minor. Major courses meet five or six mornings a week and include in-class time for fieldwork, labs, workshops, writing, guest speakers, group discussion, and one-on-one attention. Major courses require homework and project and preparation time in the afternoons and evenings. Minor courses meet three afternoons a week, with all work contained within the class session.

All of the programs aim to provide each student with a unique and tangible interaction with his or her subject in a way that cannot be reproduced in any other location. Using the extensive history and cultural resources of their immediate surroundings, teachers create an environment in which the students learn not only through traditional class instruction but also from firsthand interaction with the famous landmarks, museums, sites, and research facilities that surround them. From molecular medicine and quantum physics to creative writing, drama, and English literature to war in world history, each of more than 100 courses is designed to combine the expertise of the faculty member with the enthusiasm and energy of the students. Combine this with the ancient and stimulating surroundings of Oxford, Cambridge,

Paris, Montpellier, or Barcelona, and it creates an unforgettable and often life-changing experience. At the end of each program, every student receives grades, reports from their teachers, and formal descriptions of their courses, which can be used to apply for high school and college credit and supplement college applications.

ENROLLMENT
The Oxford Tradition and the Cambridge Tradition are for students who have completed grades 10–12 and enroll 370 and 265 students respectively. L'Académie de Paris, L'Académie de France, and La Academia de España are for students completing grades 9–12 and enroll 165, 85, and 145 students, respectively. The Oxford Prep Experience and the Cambridge Prep Experience are exclusively for students completing grades 8 and 9 and enroll 140 and 190 students, respectively. The 2007 student body included participants from more than forty states, five provinces of Canada, and twenty countries, including China, South Africa, Russia, Japan, Singapore, Malaysia, Kuwait, Venezuela, South Korea, Austria, Hungary, and Germany. Students come from diverse ethnic backgrounds, from public and private schools, and from cities and rural areas. Participants represent an exceptional range of interests, ideas, and perspectives.

DAILY SCHEDULE
Days begin with breakfast in the college or school dining hall, followed by Major classes. After a lunch break, afternoons include Minor classes, museum and gallery visits, guest lectures, sports, walking tours, and time for private study. In the afternoons, students are offered a wide variety of elective options by a full-time activities staff, allowing them to pursue activities of particular interest to them either individually or in groups with their friends. Dinner is served at approximately 6. Evening activities include social events, concerts, films, literary talks, theater, and more. Students are required to sign in at their colleges by 11 p.m. (10 p.m. in the Oxford Prep Experience and the Cambridge Prep Experience.

EXTRA OPPORTUNITIES AND ACTIVITIES
Each program offers group field trips, theater and concert outings, and guest lectures. These include poetry readings by the Poet Laureate of England, Andrew Motion; a private tour of Broughton Castle by Lord Saye and Sele; and watching a play at Shakespeare's Globe Theatre in London. In addition, each class

features outings and cultural activities appropriate to its course of study. There is also a daily program of sports and recreational activities.

Students enrolled in the Oxford and Cambridge Traditions have the opportunity to extend their experience by participating in the Paris Connection. In the Paris Connection, students are introduced to major elements of French culture, to prominent features of Parisian society, and, of course, to the wonders of the City of Light for one week. While there are no formal class sessions, the participants are led through Paris by expert scholars and art historians, who give in-depth and informative presentations at many of the main historical and cultural sites.

FACILITIES

Students in the Oxford Tradition live in Pembroke and St. Peter's Colleges of Oxford University. Students in the Oxford Prep Experience live in Oxford's Corpus Christi College. Students in the Cambridge Tradition live in Jesus College, and Cambridge Prep Experience students live in the oldest college at Cambridge University, Peterhouse. The Lycée Notre Dame de Sion, one of the most prestigious girls' schools in the center of Paris, is the host of L'Académie de Paris. The 400-year-old private school Notre Dame de La Merci is the host of the L'Académie de France in Montpellier. The Residencia Universitària Josep Manyanet hosts La Academia de España in central Barcelona. All the students live in college rooms—singles and doubles—with shared bathroom facilities. In some cases students can pay a supplemental fee for their own private bathroom. Each facility has its own dining hall and communal recreation areas.

STAFF

The program faculties contain distinguished scholars from Oxford, Cambridge, the Sorbonne, and other leading universities from around the world as well as writers, artists, and other professionals in their fields. Each year, these select groups include Rhodes, Marshall, Fulbright, and Gates Scholars as well as university professors, senior research fellows, published writers, professional actors, and internationally recognized artists. Oxbridge Academic Programs employs faculty members who not only have the highest academic credentials but the personalities and passion to teach teenagers. Each program also has a full administrative staff of experienced deans (all with extensive secondary school experience), assistants, and activities coordinators. The programs are fully residential, and members of the administration and faculty live among the students to provide around-the-clock supervision and support.

All programs were founded by Professor James G. Basker. Still the Director of Oxbridge Academic Programs, he was educated at Harvard (A.B.), Cambridge (M.A.), and, as a Rhodes Scholar, Oxford (D.Phil.). He is currently the Ann Whitney Olin Professor of English at Barnard College, Columbia University, and President of the Gilder Lehrman Institute of American History in New York City.

MEDICAL CARE

Each program is affiliated with a local general practitioner who is available to see students who require care. Prior to the program, attendees submit information regarding allergies to food and medication and other health issues that the administration closely monitors and refers to.

The policy of Oxbridge Academic Programs is to forbid any behavior that is illegal, antisocial, or dangerous either to the student or to the group. All programs are nonsmoking and strictly forbid the use or possession of drugs or alcohol.

RELIGIOUS LIFE

The programs are nondenominational. Students interested in attending religious services may consult the staff in each program for information regarding local places of worship.

COSTS

The comprehensive fees for the programs in 2007 were as follows: the Oxford Tradition, $6150; the Cambridge Tradition, $6150; L'Académie de Paris, $6150; L'Académie de France, $6150; La Academia de España, $6150; the Oxford Prep Experience, $5650; and the Cambridge Prep Experience, $5650. These fees included all tuition and instruction, accommodation, breakfast and dinner daily, transportation to and from the airports, all books and course materials, guest lectures, workshops, field trips, sports and activities, theater tickets, museum and gallery admissions, and social events. Fees did not include airfare, lunch daily, unscheduled (elective) activities, lab fees (specific courses only), or personal expenses such as snacks, laundry, and souvenirs. The fee in 2007 for the optional Paris Connection was $1550.

A deposit of $750 ($825 with cancellation insurance) should accompany the application and is fully refundable until February 29, 2008. Families are invoiced for the balance, which is due by March 31.

FINANCIAL AID

A limited number of full scholarships are available based on financial need, academic excellence, and the ability to contribute to the program in the broadest sense. Those interested should call the office for the separate application forms and information about the process that accompanies the scholarship application. The deadline for scholarships is late February or March 2008.

TRANSPORTATION

Students are met by staff members at the local airports and transported on buses to their program. At the end of each program, they are chaperoned back to the airport and are supervised right up to the security gate that leads to the passenger departure area.

APPLICATION TIMETABLE

Inquiries are welcome all year. Students whose applications are postmarked by their program-specific course guarantee deadline (from January to early February) are guaranteed a place in their program and first choice of courses (subject to being admitted and to enrollment minimums). The programs fill very quickly, so early application is recommended.

Office hours are 9 a.m. to 6:30 p.m. EST, Monday through Friday, and 10 a.m. to 4 p.m. on Saturday. (During the summer, the local program office hours are usually 8 a.m. to midnight, local time, seven days a week. Staff members can also be reached 24 hours a day in case of emergencies.)

FOR MORE INFORMATION, CONTACT

Oxbridge Academic Programs
601 Cathedral Parkway, Suite 7R
New York, New York 10025-2186
Phone: 212-932-3049
        800-828-8349 (toll-free in the U.S. and Canada)
Fax: 212-663-8169
E-mail: info@oxbridgeprograms.com
Web site: http://www.oxbridgeprograms.com

PARTICIPANT/FAMILY COMMENTS

"I enjoyed it so much. I would feel that I was cheating people of the opportunity if I didn't tell anybody else about it. Thank everyone for the summer of my lifetime!"

OXFORD ADVANCED STUDIES PROGRAM

SUMMER IN OXFORD, ENGLAND

OXFORD, ENGLAND

TYPE OF PROGRAM: Academic enrichment and accelera-
tion, high school credit, cultural visits, recreation, and
theater
PARTICIPANTS: Coeducational, ages 16–18
ENROLLMENT: 100
PROGRAM DATES: July 1-26, 2008
HEAD OF PROGRAM: Ralph Dennison, B.A., PGCE, Direc-
tor, Oxford Tutorial College

LOCATION
The program takes place in the medieval city of Oxford, England, 60 miles northwest of London. Oxford is the oldest
university in the United Kingdom and is renowned throughout the world as a center of learning and education. Oxford
Advanced Studies uses the facilities of Somerville College,
one of the colleges of Oxford University, whose splendid buildings provide an excellent backdrop to many of the activities.

BACKGROUND AND PHILOSOPHY
The Oxford Advanced Studies Program is in its twenty-fifth
year. It offers American and other international students the
opportunity to combine an in-depth and inspiring educational
experience with an exciting and stimulating range of social
and cultural activities. Because accredited high school courses
are offered, work undertaken during the summer has relevance to education at home. Experienced British university
graduates teach students in small seminar groups, and an
outstanding feature of the course is the weekly individual
tutorial in each subject. Students are regularly set challenging academic assignments and are encouraged to develop tutorial-style relationships with their teachers, the hallmark of
the educational system at Oxford and Cambridge. The academic experience is balanced with visits around England and
a varied sports and social itinerary, which enables everyone to
have a recreational as well as an intellectually rewarding
experience. The goals of the program are achieved through
close individual attention and interaction.

PROGRAM OFFERINGS
The program combines academic study and cultural visits and
experiences. Students choose two major subjects and may select an optional third subject. The course offerings are broken
down into six areas: creative arts (Practical Drama, Film Studies, and Creative Writing), humanities (Art and Architecture,
Shakespeare, The Modern Novel, The Greeks, and The Dic-
tatorships in Europe), social sciences (Introduction to Economics, International Relations, Comparative Government,
Psychology, Philosophy in Literature and International Business Management), languages (French, Spanish, German, Russian, Italian, Greek, and Latin at levels III, IV, and V), mathematics (Algebra, Trigonometry, Pre-Calculus, Calculus AB,
Calculus BC, and Probability and Statistics), and sciences
(Medical Biology, Physics, and Chemistry).

Courses are offered in other subjects as requested. Recently, students have followed specially designed curricula in
cosmology, vector calculus, romantic poetry, Anglo-Saxon, Chinese, and Arabic.

Two course assignments are set in each subject, and final
grades and reports are based both on those and on all-round
classroom performance. Students are recommended to receive
half credit for work completed in each of their academic subjects and are requested to check with their school guidance
counselor regarding the transferability of credits earned during the course.

ENROLLMENT
Oxford Advanced Studies students are enrolled from throughout the United States and from international schools worldwide. The program is limited to students from public and
independent high schools who have completed sophomore year.

DAILY SCHEDULE
After breakfast, students attend classes from 9 to 1 and from
2 to 4 on two afternoons. For each subject studied, there are
daily seminars in small groups and one-on-one tutorials. Three
afternoons each week are devoted to optional workshops, visits, sports, and cultural activities, and there is some free time.
Dinner is at 6:30; evening activities take place from 7.30 to
10.30. Students are required to be back in college by 11.

EXTRA OPPORTUNITIES AND ACTIVITIES
Most afternoons and evenings are taken up with various cultural and social activities, some of which take place in Oxford
itself, including visits to other colleges, galleries and museums, and theatrical and musical events. In addition, students
are taken to visit historic and cultural sites, such as Stratford-

upon-Avon (to see a play at the Shakespeare Memorial Theatre), Blenheim Palace, Warwick Castle, and London, where visits include the South Bank, including the Tate Modern gallery, Kensington and its museums, and Covent Garden, including a West End theatre production. Guided tours are offered on weekends.

Sports are not neglected, and, if they wish, students can participate in soccer, basketball, baseball, tennis, swimming, and squash. The traditional river pastime of punting is popular with many students, and croquet games are held on the college lawns. The mysteries of the noble English sport of cricket are explained, culminating in a staff-student cricket match.

FACILITIES

The Oxford Advanced Studies Program takes place in Somerville College, Oxford. Founded in 1879, it was originally a women's college and includes Margaret Thatcher amongst its alumni. Students live in rooms within the college where they are supervised by residential staff members. Teaching takes place within the college. Students have breakfast and evening meals in the large, spacious college dining hall. Special dietary needs can be easily met. The accommodations are individual study bedrooms with separate dormitories for boys and girls, and common room areas for social gatherings and small group activities. Students have access to the college library, and there is Internet access in each room, a student JCR for evening activities, and a small student gym. Laundry facilities are available.

STAFF

The course is supervised by Ralph Dennison, Director of Oxford Tutorial College, one of Oxford's leading independent further education colleges. A gifted educationalist with more than thirty years' teaching experience, he has brought together an excellent team of tutors, all of whom are highly qualified academics and natural communicators. The majority of course tutors are Oxbridge graduates, and many are still actively engaged in academic research. Most have taught on the program for a number of years and are familiar with U.S. and international high school curricula and aware of the needs of students from the U.S. They offer a dynamic and enthusiastic approach, which engages students' interest and invites active participation and discussion. The staff-student ratio of 1:4 allows for close attention to each individual student and allows for a less formal teaching approach. The residential staff members work closely with students to create a vibrant, sympathetic community and keep a careful eye on student welfare.

MEDICAL CARE

Residential staff members may be consulted if a student is unwell, and appointments may be made with the college physician, as required. The renowned John Radcliffe Hospital is very close, in case of any emergency. Because of the English

National Health Service, all medical treatments are available at a reasonable cost. However, it is required that students take out a comprehensive medical policy before traveling to England.

RELIGIOUS LIFE

Oxford Advanced Studies Program is nondenominational, but provisions can be made for students to attend places of worship in the Oxford area.

COSTS

There is a registration fee of $350. The all-inclusive course fee for the four-week program is $8500, payable by May 31. This covers all the program costs, including single room, breakfast, and dinner daily, tuition in two subjects, extracurricular activities, transportation, and entrances. It does not cover airfare, lunches, and personal expenditure. A third academic course may be added for a fee of $900.

TRANSPORTATION

The program organizes chaperoned round-trip flights from New York to London at a cost of approximately $900. This includes transportation from Heathrow airport to Oxford. Students who wish to make their own travel arrangements may, of course, do so, and the college advises students of transportation arrangements between the airport and Oxford.

APPLICATION TIMETABLE

The program is open to students who have completed tenth grade. Early application is advised to increase the likelihood of being accepted. Applications are received from December 1 through May 31. In addition to an application form, students must submit a high school transcript and a letter of recommendation from a teacher. Applicants are notified of their acceptance immediately upon evaluation by the Admissions Director in Oxford, and a formal acceptance is then issued.

FOR MORE INFORMATION, CONTACT

The Registrar
Oxford Advanced Studies Program
P.O. Box 2043
Darien, Connecticut 06820
Phone: 203-966-2886
Fax: 203-966-0015
E-mail: oxedge@optonline.net

PARTICIPANT/FAMILY COMMENTS

"An enlightening academic program combined with a lively social schedule. I feel as though I really grew mentally and emotionally on this trip. Thanks for the wonderful adventure OASP!"—Forrest White

OXFORD FILM AND MEDIA SCHOOL

FILM SCHOOL/MASTER FILM CLASS/VIDEO JOURNALISM/DOCUMENTARY/ INWARD BOUND ADVENTURE LEARNING

OXFORD, ENGLAND

TYPE OF PROGRAM: Educational enrichment, individual expression, and creative experiences
PARTICIPANTS: Coeducational, ages 14–18
ENROLLMENT: 10–20 participants per program
PROGRAM DATES: Four-week program in July
HEAD OF PROGRAM: Desmond Smith; Nick Smith, Assistant Head

LOCATION
The Oxford Media School (OMS) is located at New College in Oxford, England. It is 44 miles (70 kilometers) from Heathrow Airport and 50 miles (80 kilometers) from London.

BACKGROUND AND PHILOSOPHY
The Oxford Media School program was developed to offer a creative introduction to the worlds of film, television journalism, documentary production, and the dramatic arts.

The School brings together a film school, a "newsroom in Europe" for young journalists, a basic course in how to make one's own documentaries, and drama as a second subject for all students. Young people work in a friendly environment where fun is part of the learning philosophy.

The course welcomes inventive spirits who are prepared for team effort and hard, stimulating work in an atmosphere that develops strong friendships and personal achievement.

PROGRAM OFFERINGS
The Film School The School's main requirements are enthusiasm, dedication, and an ability to spend long hours on the set or at the editing table. Filmmaking is fun, but it's also teamwork. Students should be adaptable in group situations in order to take this course.

Introduction to Film In Week One, the team works in film and video exactly as Hollywood does today. Students both shoot digital video and edit on Apple's award-winning Final Cut Pro Software. The basics include how to write, direct, and shoot a script. Preproduction commences during Week Two. Movies are cast. Locations are scouted and costumes are arranged. Instructions are given on location shooting. Students work as part of the film crew, rotating key jobs. Camera and sound test rolls shot during the first week are checked. During Week Three, students learn the process of digital nonlinear editing for the final edits. Everyone works late during this week. In Week Four, the most hectic period, postproduction means adding music, sound effects, and preparation for the all-important screen credits.

Film Making: The Master Class (maximum of 10 students) This advanced film class is for film students who have already attended a first-year film school, such as Oxford, and wish to make films in a small unit, with a focus on script writing, developing dialogue, and advanced sound and lighting workshops. During the course, work is divided between hands-on learning, writing, shooting, and screening and discussing films with faculty members for their visual and narrative content.

The Documentary School The program teaches the basics of documentary filmmaking and television journalism. Subjects can be serious or light-hearted. Film deals with fiction; documentary makers find their material in the reality around them.

Introduction to the Documentary In this course, students get the basics of handling camera and sound alongside the film-school students. By the week two, students are researching and shoot-

ing segments for the School documentary. Students work in teams of two, one directing and the other shooting, then swap roles as they move through their stories. Together, the class makes a documentary about Oxford and how the city is changing in the twenty-first century. The group also goes to London to visit the foreign news bureaus of CBS News and the *New York Times*.

Documentary Making: The Master Class This program is designed for students who have already taken the first-year documentary or film course. This is a senior class that enhances the skills already gained in a first-year course. Students who have not attended OMS previously should send a reference and a copy of their prior work. This one-month workshop gives students more editing and shooting time and the ability to write and produce a longer documentary. In addition to advanced camera and editing workshops, students learn how to set up and use lights, how to make a budget, and ways to finance their first documentary.

The Television Documentary While a news story runs less than 3 minutes, a documentary can be as short as 6 minutes or as long as 6 hours. What makes documentaries different from daily news is the point of view of the director. Passion, intensity, and a sense of justice underscore the best documentary making. In this course, students get the basics of how to find a subject, how to write the outline, and how to then work as part of a team that actually makes a documentary in Oxford. In week one, the topic of the documentary is chosen, along with learning the basics of camera and sound recording. In week two, shooting of the documentary begins. In weeks three and four, students write, record, and edit.

Field work is an essential component of all courses, and related excursions include visits to the news bureaus of ABC News, CBS News, and the Canadian Broadcasting Corporation. Additional visits to the BBC and Independent Television allow students to watch television programs in the making.

ENROLLMENT
Oxford Media School sessions are limited to 40 students or fewer. The small group size (limited to 10–20 students) encourages friendly, noncompetitive teamwork.

The media revolution involves the world. Oxford Media School wants to attract people of different backgrounds, cultures, and nationalities. Past experience suggests that students are equally divided between girls and boys.

DAILY SCHEDULE

The School runs by Oxford rules. Students go to the Great Hall for breakfast between 8 and 9 a.m. Classes start at 9 a.m. Students meet in the Common Room for coffee or tea at 10 a.m. Classes then resume until noon.

After a break for lunch, students return to their assignments for 3 to 4 hours in the afternoon. Participants spend 5 to 6 hours each day working with faculty members. Dinner is at 6 p.m., followed by tea or coffee in the Common Room. Most nights, students watch some of the world's best movies in the projection room.

EXTRA OPPORTUNITIES AND ACTIVITIES

The School arranges weekend picnics and, of course, that most Oxford of all activities—punting on the Cherwell. On weekends, there are trips to London, both to see the sights and to sample the British capital's incomparable shopping. Included in the School fee is a unique, supervised London and Stratford theater program that takes students each weekend to some of the best new plays of the London season and often features stage-door visits. Everyone enjoys a staff versus summer students barbecue and sports night on the New College sports grounds.

Students can enjoy Shakespeare on the college lawn most evenings and at many colleges. The Sheldonian—where Handel played—offers classical music most summer nights. Tennis with both grass and Har-Tru surfaces is available. On a glorious midsummer's eve, there is the Farewell Dinner and Graduation Ceremony to which all parents are invited.

FACILITIES

The Oxford Media program shares New College, Oxford, with several other summer schools, including Duke University, during the month of July. Founded in the fourteenth century, it is one of Oxford's founding colleges. Students have there own rooms with ensuite bathrooms. Most rooms offer high-speed Ethernet connections. Linen is supplied, and there is daily maid service, except on weekends.

STAFF

Desmond Smith, the School's founder and director, has been a writer, teacher, and television producer all his working life. He spent nearly twenty years working for three of the American networks. Oxford Media's teachers consist of skilled film, drama, and journalism teachers who have been members of the summer faculty for many years. The School maintains a 5:1 ratio of students to staff members.

MEDICAL CARE

New College has both a nurse and a medical doctor on call. In case of an emergency, the nearest hospital is less than 1 mile away. Students are requested to bring medical insurance with them.

RELIGIOUS LIFE

Within easy walking distance of student accommodations are opportunities for worship for members of many faiths.

COSTS

The comprehensive fees for 2007 were $6500. Master Class students paid $7000. The cost includes fees for theater and trips, digital lab costs, equipment damage insurance, room and board, and transportation to and from Heathrow Airport. The fees do not cover airfare, lunches, and personal expenditures.

FINANCIAL AID

Financial aid is not offered.

TRANSPORTATION

Transportation to and from the airport is provided.

APPLICATION TIMETABLE

Applications are due by June 1, 2008.

FOR MORE INFORMATION, CONTACT

Desmond Smith, Director
Oxford Media School
110 Pricefield Road
Toronto, Ontario M4W 1Z9
Canada
Phone: 416-964-0746
Fax: 416-929-4230
E-mail: newsco@sympatico.ca
Web site: http://www.oxfordmediaschool.com

PARTICIPANT/FAMILY COMMENTS

"I learned so much over the four weeks, and now I can't watch television or a movie without looking critically at the technical aspects, such as lighting and editing, as well as the story. Your staff members were some of the best teachers I've ever had, guiding me and letting me discover things for myself, rather than telling me what's right and wrong."—Martha Jack

"Walter learned an incredible amount about the entire film making process. When I came to the 'graduation' night festivities, I was so impressed by the quality of his and his fellow students' work. When I asked Walter what the best part of the entire experience was, he said, 'The teachers, the teachers, the teachers!'"—Julie Haas

PERRY-MANSFIELD PERFORMING ARTS SCHOOL & CAMP

SUMMER PROGRAM

STEAMBOAT SPRINGS, COLORADO

TYPE OF PROGRAM: An intensive performing arts summer school. Classes are offered in theater, musical theater, dance, and dramatic writing, with electives in visual arts and equitation.

PARTICIPANTS: Coeducational, age 8–senior in college

ENROLLMENT: 350

PROGRAM DATES: One 2-week Junior Camp (entering grades 5–7) begins late June; one 4-week Intermediate Program (entering grades 8–9) begins mid-July; one 6-week High School/College Program (entering grade 10 and older) begins mid-June; one-week Equestrian Programs begin mid-June (ages 10–12) and early August (ages 13–16); one 1-week Discovery Day Camp (ages 8–10) begins early August. Shorter-length specialty programs in dramatic writing, musical theater composing, and theater study abroad are offered for high school and college students.

HEAD OF PROGRAM: June Lindenmayer, Executive Director

LOCATION

Perry-Mansfield is located in Steamboat Springs, Colorado, 150 miles northwest of Denver. Steamboat Springs, a small Rocky Mountain community of 10,000, is rich with Western charm and natural beauty, making it a popular vacation destination.

Nestled in the hills of beautiful Strawberry Park, Perry-Mansfield's rustic 75-acre campus provides students with a safe, nurturing environment in which to learn. Students spend their days in open-air studios, which are naturally landscaped with grassy meadows, aspen groves, and alpine ponds.

BACKGROUND AND PHILOSOPHY

In 1913, Charlotte Perry and Portia Mansfield fulfilled their dreams of creating a theater and dance camp in the mountains. Now, ninety years later, Perry-Mansfield is recognized as the oldest continuously operating performing arts school and camp in the nation. Throughout the years, a number of distinguished alumni, faculty members, and guest artists have passed through the doors of Perry-Mansfield. The list in-

cludes Robert Battle, Sammy Bayes, Jessica Biel, Ruthanna Boris, John Cage, Wally Cardona, Martha Clarke, Merce Cunningham, Harriette Ann Gray, Julie Harris, Dustin Hoffman, Hanya Holm, Lee Horsley, Doris Humphrey, José Limon, Agnes de Mille, Daniel Nagrin, Jason Raize, Lee Remick, Amala Shankar, Ton Simons, Frances Sternhagen, Helen Tamiris, Joan Van Ark, and Charles Weidman.

Today, students from all over the world take classes from a select group of accomplished and internationally renowned faculty members. The tradition of Perry-Mansfield remains unsurpassed as the camp continues to prepare emerging young artists for the stage. Recent alumni are performing with Ballet Hispanico, Munich Ballet, Paul Taylor, Nederlands Dans Theatre, and Battleworks Dance Company and on Broadway and television and in film. Students are invited to share in the magic of Perry-Mansfield.

PROGRAM OFFERINGS

At the high school/college level, the Theater Program offers classes in acting, advanced acting, scene study, voice and movement, acting Shakespeare, directing, production, stage combat, and audition workshop. The Musical Theater Program offers classes in musicianship, explorations in ear training, and rhythmic foundations. Core studies are offered in musical scene study and audition technique, original works (cabaret and songwriting), great shows, and great performers (learning the repertoire and movement for the singing actor). The Dance Program offers classes in ballet, modern, jazz, repertory, dance composition, pointe, tap, and trapeze. Students have the opportunity to learn to perform repertory from both faculty members and guest artists.

At the junior (grades 5–7) and intermediate (grades 8–9) levels, the Theater Program offers classes in creative dramatics for the juniors and intermediate acting for the intermediates. An accelerated class is available to the advanced intermediate by audition only. The Musical Theater Program offers classes in foundations in musical theater, performance skills for the young singing actor, and musical theater workshop. The Dance Program offers classes in ballet, modern, jazz, dance composition, tap, and trapeze.

Equestrian Camp is for students ages 10–12 (session one) and ages 13–16 (session two). The Equestrian Program teaches students horsemanship and provides riding instruction. Riders learn the fundamentals of horse care, training, dressage, and jumping. Students choose from either English or Western styles of riding.

ENROLLMENT

This community provides a safe, nurturing atmosphere for approximately 350 residential and day students.

EXTRA OPPORTUNITIES AND ACTIVITIES

Students can take private voice, piano, guitar, and riding lessons. Students also have the opportunity to enjoy the Rocky Mountains with planned hiking and rafting trips and trips to the hot springs and pool. Local events, including the Balloon Rodeo, Art in the Park, and the Fourth of July Parade, are all a part of the summer experience at Perry-Mansfield.

FACILITIES

There are four dance studios, two theaters, an art studio, rehearsal spaces, a dramatic writing studio, a music composition lab, an infirmary, a dining hall, a scene shop, a cantina, a camp store, stables, a barn, and riding arenas. All buildings are equipped with fire extinguishers and smoke alarms. Students and staff members are informed of fire evacuation plans and a fire drill is conducted at the beginning of each camp session.

STAFF

Perry-Mansfield prides itself on its renowned faculty members, who come from all over the United States and abroad. Counselors are selected based on their experience with children and must participate in a weeklong training program. Faculty and staff members must pass a background check before being hired. The staff-camper ratio is 1:2.

MEDICAL CARE

Two registered nurses reside on campus and are available 24 hours a day. Perry-Mansfield has an infirmary where all medication is stored and administered. Students are insured by Perry-Mansfield while at camp for accidents and illnesses; however, preexisting conditions are not covered. Yampa Valley Medical Center is located 7 miles from the campus.

COSTS

Tuition for residential students in the High School/College Program is $4000. The Intermediate Program is $3400, and the Junior Camp is $2200. The Equestrian Program is $875 for either session.

Day student rates vary, based on the number of classes taken. For the High School/College Program, the rate ranges from $575 to $1400, the Intermediate Program ranges from $450 to $1100, and the Junior Camp ranges from $300 to $620. Day student tuition for the equestrian program is $500. The Discovery Day Camp tuition is $500.

FINANCIAL AID

Scholarships are awarded in the areas of theater, musical theater, and dance. Scholarships are merit based. Those interested in applying for a scholarship can participate in a live audition or submit a video to be viewed by the appropriate departmental faculty members and directors.

Work-study is awarded based on need (for high school and college students only). Positions available are studio host, dining hall attendant, camp beautification, and equestrian wrangler. The equestrian wrangler positions are filled strictly with students having a strong background in equitation. For more information, prospective students should call the Perry-Mansfield office.

TRANSPORTATION

Arrangements for transportation from Denver International Airport can be arranged through Alpine Taxi, a Steamboat company providing shuttle service from the airport to Perry-Mansfield. Alpine Taxi's toll-free number is 800-343-7433. Students flying into Yampa Valley Regional Airport in Hayden (the closest airport to the camp) are picked up by a Perry-Mansfield staff member.

APPLICATION TIMETABLE

Inquiries are welcome throughout the year. Registrations are accepted on a first-come, first-served basis, beginning in September, until all available spaces are filled. Tuition is due in full no later than April 1. Enrollments after April 1 must be paid in full.

FOR MORE INFORMATION, CONTACT

Perry-Mansfield Performing Arts School and Camp
40755 RCR 36
Steamboat Springs, Colorado 80487
Phone: 800-430-2787 (toll-free)
Fax: 970-879-5823
E-mail: p-m@perry-mansfield.org
Web site: http://www.perry-mansfield.org

THE PHILLIPS ACADEMY SUMMER SESSION

▽△▽△▽△▽△▽△▽△▽△▽△▽△▽△▽△▽△

SUMMER SCHOOL

ANDOVER, MASSACHUSETTS

TYPE OF PROGRAM: Academic enrichment, precollege
PARTICIPANTS: Coeducational, boarding and day, rising grades pre-8–12
ENROLLMENT: 570
PROGRAM DATES: July 1 to August 6
HEAD OF PROGRAM: Paul D. Murphy, Director

LOCATION
The buildings and facilities of the Academy are located on 500 acres of landscaped campus. Andover, Massachusetts, incorporated in 1646, is an attractive elm-shaded community 25 miles north of Boston and close to historical sites, the mountains, and the seacoast locations of New England.

BACKGROUND AND PHILOSOPHY
Fostering a passion for lifelong learning, the Summer Session combines a full boarding (precollege) experience with small classes in a multicultural community. Innovative pedagogy complements traditional areas. The Summer Session offers its students five weeks of intensive academic and personal growth—growth that can certainly make a difference beyond the limits of this program and this campus.

The Summer Session program encompasses demanding classes, recreational afternoon activities, college counseling, engaging trips to colleges, social and cultural opportunities, and welcoming dormitories that prepare students for collegiate residential life in an environment designed for their age group.

Here for five weeks, students with impressive academic goals prepare for the rigors of the best colleges and for the rigors of thriving and serving in this complex world.

PROGRAM OFFERINGS
There are more than sixty course and program offerings in literature and writing, computer programming, computer animation, mathematics, the natural sciences, philosophy, the social sciences, languages, speech and debate, English as a second language, and SAT prep, as well as an Intensive Writing Workshop specifically for day students; the average class size is 14. In addition, there are courses in the visual and performing arts.

Interdisciplinary programs in math/biology, history/archaeology, and English/theater/film are offered to middle school-aged students. These three Lower School Institutes (LSI) focus on the younger student: pre-eighth and some pre-ninth graders. Students enrolled in these interdisciplinary institutes enjoy a team of teachers, an integrated curriculum, curricular trips off campus, and, if boarding, a residential experience tailored to younger students. A complementary course in effective learning skills is planned.

The Summer Session has an organized recreational activities program. Sports such as basketball, tennis, swimming, soccer, softball, volleyball, instructional skating, dance, physical fitness, and squash are offered. All activities are coed. The numerous Academy music studios, playing fields and tennis courts, the gymnasium, and the six-lane swimming pool provide excellent facilities for both scheduled and informal activities.

Of additional interest are a number of activities, such as Outdoor Adventure, that are not always available in secondary schools.

ENROLLMENT
Summer Session students represent an extraordinary diversity of geography, religion, race, and economic circumstances. They represent approximately forty-five states, the District of Columbia, Puerto Rico, and the U.S. Virgin Islands and more than thirty-nine countries; approximately 15 percent are granted financial aid.

The Admission Committee looks for evidence that the applicant has the intellectual ability, the industry, and the character to make the most of the Summer Session opportunity. The Committee expects the applicant to have a strong school record and a serious desire to spend the summer in challenging, disciplined study.

DAILY SCHEDULE
Classes meet Monday through Saturday, and the daily schedule depends on the courses or program selected. Students mini-

mally spend 18 hours per week in class and can expect 3 to 4 hours of homework each evening.

College workshops are held Monday, Tuesday, Thursday, and Friday afternoons, and individual meetings with the college counselor are available. Academic resource areas, including the Math Center, Writing Center, library, photo lab, art studio, music studios, and all computer labs, are available for use by all students. Study hours are kept in dormitories and academic resource areas.

EXTRA OPPORTUNITIES AND ACTIVITIES

Special trips and tours offer travel to museums, amusement parks, the beach, a whale-watching expedition, shopping malls, and other activities. There are also trips to nearby colleges in addition to the regularly scheduled college counseling workshops.

Weekly colloquia provide the opportunity to hear and discuss ideas on a range of contemporary topics with scholars, artists, activists, and other speakers. The diversity of the community is highlighted in international celebrations, and students share their talents in self-initiated shows.

FACILITIES

In addition to six classroom buildings, the campus encompasses a 120,000-volume library, an impressive athletic complex, the Addison Gallery of American Art, the Gelb Science Center, the Peabody Museum of Archaeology, the Moncrieff Cochran Bird Sanctuary, the Elson Art Center, Isham Health Center, a computer center, a theater complex, and forty-three dormitories. All students are assigned an Andover e-mail address for the summer, and all boarding students have Internet access in their dormitory rooms.

STAFF

The teaching faculty members, from private and public schools and colleges as well as Phillips Academy, are selected for their excellence in the classroom and their understanding of young people. The senior teaching staff is augmented by a corps of some 25 teaching assistants, recent college graduates, and strong college juniors whose enthusiasm for learning serves as a model for serious but joyful intellectual inquiry.

MEDICAL CARE

The Isham Health Center is licensed as a hospital by the Commonwealth of Massachusetts. Registered nurses are on duty at all times, and, in addition to having usual office hours, a physician and consulting psychologist are always on call.

RELIGIOUS LIFE

In the town of Andover, there are Protestant churches of several denominations, a Roman Catholic church, and a Jewish Reform temple, all of which welcome students of the Summer Session for worship.

COSTS

In 2007, the $5800 charge for boarding students included tuition, board, room, and linens. The day-student charge of $4000 covered tuition, supplemental medical insurance, and all meals.

The Lower School Institute and the ESL Institute tuition for boarding students was $5950, and the day student tuition was $4150, which included similar amenities. The nonrefundable application fee ($50 for U.S. students, $100 for international students) must accompany the application. Within two weeks of acceptance, the student must pay a nonrefundable $1500 deposit, which is credited toward the tuition charge.

Expenditures for books, trips, tours, and extras (such as spending money) should be approximately $500–$700.

FINANCIAL AID

Financial aid is awarded according to financial need. The Summer Session Financial Aid Form must be requested, completed as directed, and postmarked no later than March 1.

TRANSPORTATION

The Academy provides transportation upon arrival and departure to and from Boston's Logan International Airport and the Manchester–Boston Regional Airport (Manchester, New Hampshire) at specified times. Train and bus access is also available.

APPLICATION TIMETABLE

Catalogs containing application forms may be obtained in November. Courses often fill quickly; it is therefore advantageous to apply as early as possible. The suggested deadline is April 7.

All application materials—the recommendations, transcript, autobiographical statement, other required forms, and fee—should be placed in the envelope provided and mailed to the Phillips Academy Summer Session.

FOR MORE INFORMATION, CONTACT

Maxine S. Grogan, Dean of Admission
The Phillips Academy Summer Session
Phillips Academy
180 Main Street
Andover, Massachusetts 01810-4166
Phone: 978-749-4400
Fax: 978-749-4415
E-mail: summer@andover.edu
Web site: http://www.andover.edu/summersession

PARTICIPANT/FAMILY COMMENTS

"He had a wonderfully enriching academic and social experience that profoundly affected him."—parent

"There seems to have been on campus a wonderful atmosphere of encouragement that fostered both independence and cooperation, and our daughters came back to us with a good sense of value of their work that combined imagination, discipline, and—not least—fun."—parent

"Thanks mostly to Andover, I have better time management, study habits, higher goals, and more open opinions."—student

PHILLIPS EXETER ACADEMY

SUMMER SCHOOL

EXETER, NEW HAMPSHIRE

TYPE OF PROGRAM: Academic enrichment
PARTICIPANTS: Coeducational, grades 8–12 and postgraduate year
ENROLLMENT: 650
PROGRAM DATES: Five-week program; July 1–August 4, 2007
HEAD OF PROGRAM: Ethan W. Shapiro, Director

LOCATION
The 400-acre Phillips Exeter Academy campus is located in the town of Exeter, the Colonial capital of New Hampshire, which is in the heart of the state's seacoast area. Boston, Newburyport, Portsmouth, and the White Mountains are all within easy access for excursions.

BACKGROUND AND PHILOSOPHY
Every summer, Phillips Exeter Academy welcomes to the campus some 700 students for five weeks of academic study, athletics, and exploration that carry participants far beyond the classrooms and the playing fields. Typically, students come from more than forty states; Puerto Rico; Washington, D.C.; and several dozen other nations. Most reside in campus dormitories; others travel daily from their homes in the New Hampshire seacoast area. Together they embody a rich diversity of language, culture, religion, and race. They come to Exeter with that particular mix of intellectual curiosity and adventurous spirit that holds the promise of glimpsing new horizons and making new discoveries.

PROGRAM OFFERINGS
Exeter's Upper School offers programs of study for high school students entering grades 10 and beyond. Students create their own academic programs by selecting three courses from the more than 100 offered in a wide range of disciplines. Students may choose to concentrate on a specific academic area, taking science courses such as Introduction to Physics, Marine Biology, and Animal Behavior or arts courses such as Photography, Sculpture, and Architecture. More often, however, they elect to balance the arts and sciences, enrolling in Creative Writing,

American Government, and Problem Solving in Algebra or Writing Nature, Video Production, and Introduction to Chemistry. Whatever their academic choices, students find themselves working in small classes with highly experienced, dedicated teachers. During the five-week term, they have full access to the Academy's exceptional facilities, including the state-of-the-art Phelps Science Center and the Class of 1945 Library, the largest secondary school library in the world.

Younger students, those entering grades 8 and 9, may apply for the Access Exeter program, which offers accelerated studies in six different academic clusters. Each cluster consists of three courses organized around a central theme: The American Experience in War, The Land and the Sea, Problem Solving: An Odyssey of the Mind, A Global Community, The Creative Arts, and Exeter: C.S.I. Crime Scene Investigation. Each cluster emphasizes hands-on learning, or participatory education, both in and beyond the classroom. Students in The Land and the Sea program, for example, venture out to Appledore Island on the Isles of Shoals and go whale-watching along Jeffreys Ledge off the coast of Massachusetts. At midterm, all Access Exeter students and their teachers depart the campus for a two-night/three-day excursion; students in the Global Community program travel to Montreal, Quebec, where they immerse themselves in the French-speaking Canadian culture.

Complementing the academic curriculum, the Summer School offers a physical education program that is an essential part of the student's Exeter experience. For two 12-day sessions, students participate in a variety of physical activities that include tennis, soccer, softball, basketball, track and field, lacrosse, aerobics, weight training, and water polo. Upper School students may also apply for the crew or squash program.

ENROLLMENT
Students come to the Summer School from about thirty countries and more than forty states. Students of all racial, religious, and social backgrounds are welcome.

DAILY SCHEDULE
Academic and athletics classes are required appointments. When students do not have required appointments, they are expected to use their time productively. Dormitory check-in is at 9 p.m. (11 p.m. on Saturday), and the dorm is expected to be conducive to study after this time. Students should be mature enough to regulate their behavior; antisocial behavior may result in disciplinary action. Disciplinary procedures are designed to teach the student the value of integrity. The daily schedule for students enrolled in Access Exeter varies slightly from the schedule observed by older students.

EXTRA OPPORTUNITIES AND ACTIVITIES
Educational and recreational excursions are a regular feature of Wednesday afternoons and weekends, when there are no required appointments. Such excursions are optional and may consist of a hike in the White Mountains, tours of New England colleges, a Boston museum visit, or a whale watch. Extracurricular activities include theater, music, and various sports. Students are encouraged to enjoy the cultural and ethnic diversity that is at the heart of the Exeter Summer School experience.

FACILITIES

Exeter is proud of its outstanding academic and athletic facilities. The centerpiece of the campus is Louis Kahn's architectural landmark, the Phillips Exeter Library, which has a capacity of 250,000 volumes and can seat 400 students. The collection currently consists of 150,000 volumes in addition to an extensive collection of tapes, albums, and compact discs. The library houses one of the academy's six computer labs. Equally imposing is the Love Gymnasium, with its five basketball floors, two ice rinks, two pools, fifteen squash courts, a weight-training room, a dance room, and a training room. Outside there are acres of baseball diamonds, soccer fields, tennis courts, an all-weather 400-meter track, and a cross-country course through the nature preserve.

The Forrestal-Bowld Music Center is a state-of-the-art facility with more than 24,000 square feet of space dedicated to the study of music. In addition to three large rehearsal rooms, there are eleven teacher studios, eight of them equipped with grand pianos, and sixteen practice rooms with upright pianos. New to the campus in fall 2001 was the Phelps Science Center, a $38-million complex that offers students and teachers outstanding facilities for scientific investigation and study. Other highlights of the campus are the two-stage Fisher Theater, the Frederick R. Mayer Art Center and Lamont Gallery, and the Grainger Observatory.

STAFF

The majority of the Summer School's instructors are Phillips Exeter Academy faculty members. Additional qualified instructors are recruited from other schools and universities, and many have made long-term commitments to teaching Summer School.

MEDICAL CARE

The infirmary is staffed 24 hours a day. Exeter Hospital, which is just minutes away, offers emergency medical service. Enrollment in the Summer School Group Insurance Plan is included in the tuition.

RELIGIOUS LIFE

The Summer School is nondenominational; students may attend religious services at nearby churches and synagogues if they wish.

COSTS

Boarding tuition for the 2007 Summer School was $5995 for Upper School students. The Access Exeter boarding tuition was $6195 (including the required excursion fee). A nonrefundable $1500 deposit is due at the time of enrollment, with the balance due on May 15. The 2007 tuition for day students was $995 per course. It was $3995, including the required excursion fee, for Access Exeter day students.

FINANCIAL AID

Limited financial aid is available. The deadline for financial aid application is March 1.

APPLICATION TIMETABLE

Admission to the Phillips Exeter Academy Summer School is competitive and is based on academic achievement and motivation. There is a rolling admission procedure, and only completed applications can be considered. Since many courses fill rapidly, it is in the candidate's best interest to complete the application as early as possible. Application and teacher reference forms are to be found in the Summer School catalog. A separate application form is required for those students who wish to participate in Access Exeter.

FOR MORE INFORMATION, CONTACT

Ethan W. Shapiro, Director
Phillips Exeter Summer School
20 Main Street
Exeter, New Hampshire 03833-2460
Phone: 603-777-3488
      800-828-4325 Ext. 3488 (toll-free)
Fax: 603-777-4385
E-mail: summer@exeter.edu
Web site: http://www.exeter.edu/summer

PORTSMOUTH ABBEY SCHOOL

PORTSMOUTH
ABBEY
SCHOOL

SUMMER ENGLISH PROGRAM

PORTSMOUTH, RHODE ISLAND

TYPE OF PROGRAM: Academic enrichment in English
PARTICIPANTS: Coeducational, grades 7–11, ages 12–16
ENROLLMENT: 90
PROGRAM DATES: Four weeks, two sessions beginning first week in July
HEAD OF PROGRAM: Dr. Michael R. Bonin, Director

LOCATION
The Portsmouth Abbey School is located on 500 acres on the shores of Narragansett Bay in Portsmouth, Rhode Island. It is several miles north of Newport, Rhode Island; 25 miles from Providence, Rhode Island; 65 miles from Boston, Massachusetts; and 190 miles from New York, New York.

BACKGROUND AND PHILOSOPHY
The Summer English Program provides each student with a talented and dedicated faculty, excellent facilities, and a sound program of studies that is faithful to the moral and intellectual ideals that Benedictine communities have been passing on to youths for more than 1,500 years.

PROGRAM OFFERINGS
The Summer English Program offers intensive enrichment in reading, writing, and speaking. The courses offered are Composition, Literature/Reading, Public Speaking, ESL, Latin, Study Skills, and Creative Writing.

Most courses meet one period per day. Classes are very small, and a faculty-student ratio of 1:5 ensures personal attention. There are also daily reading periods and an evening study hall.

Afternoons are set aside for recreational activities and athletics, including basketball, journalism, soccer, squash, studio art, tennis, volleyball, and weight training.

ENROLLMENT
About 90 boys and girls from the United States and other countries attend the Summer Session.

DAILY SCHEDULE
Classes meet Monday through Saturday from 8:25 a.m. to 12:45 p.m. The athletic and recreational programs are in the afternoons. The evening study hall is from 7:30 to 9:30 p.m.

EXTRA OPPORTUNITIES AND ACTIVITIES
There are afternoon trips to the beach or local destinations as well as evening movies and coffeehouse performances. On the weekends, day trips are to Boston and Newport.

FACILITIES
All Summer School participants have access to the modern facilities of the School, including wireless Internet access; the St. Thomas More Library; audiovisual facilities; complete indoor and outdoor athletic facilities for tennis, soccer, basketball, volleyball, weight training, and squash; and an all-weather track. Students live in two houses. Resident faculty and staff members supervise each house.

STAFF
The Summer Session is fortunate to have a loyal staff, many of whom have been returning for ten years or more. The staff includes both regular faculty members from the Portsmouth Abbey School and dedicated teachers from other independent and public schools.

MEDICAL CARE
The School Infirmary is open each day at specific and published times, and a registered nurse is on duty. At times when the infirmary is closed, a registered nurse is always on call.

The School physician has daily clinic hours at the School as needed. For emergency cases, Newport Hospital is a few minutes away.

The School physician must have a complete health history of every student. The forms for the health history are mailed to parents when the student is enrolled.

RELIGIOUS LIFE

Portsmouth Abbey School is a Catholic school in the Benedictine tradition. All boarding students attend Mass weekly in the School church.

COSTS

The fee for boarding students in 2007 was $4800 for both sessions (four weeks) or $2500 for one session (two weeks). This included tuition, room, board, textbooks, and all weekend activities. For day students, the fee was $2700 for both sessions or $1400 for one session.

FINANCIAL AID

Financial aid is both limited and competitive. Requests for financial aid should be submitted by April 15.

TRANSPORTATION

Parents should make transportation arrangements for arrival to and departure from Portsmouth Abbey School. A list of local bus and livery services is available from the Summer English Program office.

APPLICATION TIMETABLE

Inquiries are welcome at any time; interested students should contact the Director. Applications are processed on a rolling basis but some programs fill early, so the Summer School recommends filing materials as soon as possible. The application fee is $55.

FOR MORE INFORMATION, CONTACT

Summer English Program
Portsmouth Abbey School
285 Cory's Lane
Portsmouth, Rhode Island 02871

Phone: 401-643-1225
Fax: 401-683-5888
E-mail: summer@portsmouthabbey.org
Web site: http://www.portsmouthabbey.org

PRATT INSTITUTE

SUMMER PRE-COLLEGE PROGRAM

BROOKLYN/MANHATTAN, NEW YORK

TYPE OF PROGRAM: College-credit bearing precollege program in art, design, and architecture
PARTICIPANTS: Coeducational; students who have completed grades 10–12
ENROLLMENT: 400
PROGRAM DATES: Four weeks: July 7 to August 1
HEAD OF PROGRAM: Special Programs Administrator

LOCATION
Pratt Institute, one of the world's leading schools of art, design, and architecture has campuses in Brooklyn and Manhattan. Each site is located in the heart of museums, theaters, galleries, and culture and design centers. Pratt Institute's Brooklyn campus setting provides ample space for student enrichment and the pursuit of artistic endeavors.

BACKGROUND AND PHILOSOPHY
Founded in 1887 by industrialist and philanthropist Charles Pratt, Pratt Institute offers precollege programs in art, design, architecture, and creative writing for high school students considering careers in those fields. The Pre-College Program is an intense learning experience; 4 college credits are earned upon successful completion. Students develop their creative talents and skills and build an effective portfolio for college admission.

PROGRAM OFFERINGS
The Brooklyn campus accommodates residential and commuter students. The Manhattan campus is for commuter students only. The curriculum is comprised of six mandatory courses or activities: an elective, a foundation course, an art history appreciation course, a portfolio development course, a lecture series, and cultural-insights activities.

Elective Courses Students may choose one course from the following sixteen majors: architecture, creative writing, fashion design, fine arts/painting and drawing, graphic design, illustration (digital), illustration (traditional), industrial design, interior design, jewelry/metal arts, photography, and sculpture as well as 2-credit electives: art and design discovery, art history, cultural studies, and media arts/video.

Architecture New York City, with its wealth of architectural treasures, provides the ideal setting for this intensive hands-on workshop. Students learn to think about an architectural problem, develop a solution, produce sketches, draft plans, and build models.

Art and Design Discovery* (Brooklyn only) This course allows students to experience different disciplines in art, design, and architecture. Through hands-on projects and lectures, students sample areas of study such as fine arts/painting and drawing, illustration, graphic design, interior design, industrial design, and architecture.

Art History* This course offers an introductory historical survey of Western art and examines the major artistic movements of the last 600 years within their social, political, and cultural contexts. Students can develop their skills in both visual analysis and critical thinking. They learn to recognize the distinct hands of individual artists as well as understand fundamental concepts. Painting, sculpture, architecture, and graphic art are explored as well.

Creative Writing This elective offers opportunities to develop writing skills in one or more genres and helps students prepare for college. Students begin with an examination of written language, the composing process, and voice, followed by exposure to various genres, including poetry, essay, fiction, writing for film, magazine writing, and text for Web sites.

Cultural Studies* This course draws its inspiration from the social sciences and humanities. This elective is an introduction to the relation between cultural practices and their various social contexts in the contemporary world. Through their explorations, students begin to develop the skills necessary to intervene in the production of culture. At the final Pre-College Art Exhibit, students present their critical analysis of a chosen aspect of culture.

Fashion Design (Brooklyn only) New York, a leading fashion capital, is the ideal setting to study fashion design. Students learn key aspects of the design process, including sketching, pattern making, and clothing construction. Participants apply real-world knowledge to their work after studio visits of successful designers and exposure to the industry's many career options.

Fine Arts/Painting and Drawing This studio course enhances perceptual and aesthetic awareness through the creation of fine art. Instruction in drawing and painting incorporates various techniques, media, and subject matter. On-site work is an essential element of this course.

Graphic Design This course shows how and when to use photography, illustration, typography, and computer graphics to design logos, Web pages, books, video spots, exhibits, posters, and packaging. Field trips to great graphic design showcases and studios around New York City are included.

Illustration (Digital) In this elective, students analyze the style trends used in today's illustration field and explore the trends of the future. Participants incorporate and develop their illustration skills while experimenting with scanning, digital photography, and software such as PhotoShop and Illustrator. Study combines technology and traditional illustration. Students are expected to produce professional-level work. The only deviation from established illustration is that the final outcome is digital.

Illustration (Traditional) In this course, participants explore ways to create pictures that communicate new ideas. Students develop their technical and artistic skills in drawing and painting and learn how photographic and digital media can enhance their art.

Industrial Design (Brooklyn only) Industrial design is the thoughtful creation of forms to find solutions needed in everyday life. This course examines how embracing today's social, physical, and ecological needs presents opportunities for creative design. Through drawing and model making, students explore and redefine society's forms and inventions.

Interior Design (Brooklyn only) New York City is the world center for interior design and is the perfect setting for this course, where space is shaped, planned, and furnished. There is emphasis on the impact of the interior space on the individual as well as various groups. Students work with the classic elements of light, color, form, and space in this exciting studio course. Students visit some of New York's outstanding interior spaces and commercial showrooms.

Jewelry/Metal Arts (Brooklyn only) In this course, students design wearable art in silver, copper, and brass. This elective involves basic metal arts and jewelry-making techniques. Students learn basic techniques through demonstration and projects, including sawing, texturing, riveting, chain masking, and stone setting.

Media Arts/Video* (Brooklyn only) This elective is an introduction to the craft and aesthetic of video. Students explore perception, motion, composition, and sequence in order to develop the language and grammar of video before engaging in actual videomaking exercises and creative projects. The course utilizes lightweight cameras. Preproduction planning and postproduction digital editing are introduced.

Photography Participants achieve a broad-based knowledge of black and white photography by studying 35mm camera operations, lighting techniques, and darkroom procedures. Making contact prints, enlarging and finishing photographs, and techniques of shooting are explored. Introduction to color and digital photography is included. Students must have access to a 35mm camera. This studio course entails extensive fieldwork.

Sculpture (Brooklyn only) This course concentrates on the creation of three-dimensional art. It offers an in-depth examination of the materials and processes used in sculpture. It explores subtractive methods such as carving stone and additive methods such as construction with wire.

Foundation Courses Students enrolling in an art, design, or architecture elective automatically are enrolled in Foundation of Art and Design. Students enrolling in the creative writing elective are automatically enrolled in Foundation Writing Studio. Students enrolling in the cultural studies elective are automatically enrolled in Foundation–Cultural Studies. Each Foundation course is worth 2 credits.

Foundation of Art and Design Students develop their skills in using color, shape, and other formal concepts basic to professional study of art and design. Modeled after Pratt's first-year Foundation program and taught by professional artists and designers, this course expands participants' visual thinking, strengthens their portfolio, and provides a basis for further study.

Foundation Writing Studio This course introduces students to the three traditional forms of creative writing, offers them opportunities to develop their writing skills in each of the genres, and helps them prepare for college. Through reading assignments, writing exercises, workshops, and critical analysis of readings, students develop basic skills in expository and creative writing. Genres covered include poetry, fiction, and plays.

Foundation–Cultural Studies (Brooklyn only) This new course introduces essential skills and methods of the analysis of culture. Students draw examples of concrete objects of study from specific design, media, arts, communications, and popular culture sources for class exercises. Students gain familiarity with computer applications of data analysis and use of video for data collection.

Art History Appreciation (noncredit) Mostly through guided visits at New York's museums, students gain appreciation of a wide range of chronological and geographic periods, media, and disciplines. Students explore the many functions of art and the stylistic differences and similarities across historical periods. The course also serves as a complement to studio classes.

Portfolio Development (noncredit) In this course, students learn how to select what to include in their portfolio, based on standards set by top colleges, as well as develop the basic technical skills for creating a professional portfolio. Upon conclusion, students can have their portfolios reviewed by a Pratt admissions counselor to help them gain first-hand understanding of what might be expected by colleges.

Lecture Series (noncredit; Brooklyn only) The Pre-College lecture series invites successful artists, industrial design professionals, and architects to share their individual perspectives on the path they have chosen. Presenters speak for 20 minutes then answer students' questions.

Cultural Insights (noncredit; Brooklyn only) Cultural insights are activities that allow students to explore the many offerings available in New York City. Students participate in social and cultural activities such as plays, museums, and studio visits. The activities are chaperoned, typically last 3 to 4 hours, and take place on the weekend.

DAILY SCHEDULE

There are about 30 hours of class per week. Weekends consist mostly of free, unsupervised time during the day, except for Sunday afternoon, and Friday and Saturday evenings, which include a mandatory Cultural Insights activity. The following is the daily schedule, Monday through Friday:

9:00–12:15	Class (mandatory)
12:15– 1:30	Lunch break
1:30– 4:50	Class (mandatory)
5:00– 6:00	Dinner
6:00–10:30	Homework space available (optional) or evening activity on Friday (mandatory)
11:00	Curfew

ENROLLMENT

American and international high school students enroll in Pratt's Summer Pre-College Program; some students have extensive backgrounds, whereas others have had less training. Students who have completed grades 10–12 may apply. Generally, students who demonstrate the ability to benefit from the program are admitted.

EXTRA OPPORTUNITIES AND ACTIVITIES

Weekend social and cultural activities are open to all Pre-College Program students and are mandatory for Brooklyn resident students. These activities offer further opportunities to explore art and New York City.

FACILITIES

The Pratt Brooklyn campus has twenty-three buildings, including an athletics center with a track, tennis courts, a sauna, and a weight room. The campus has centrally located air-conditioned residence halls, dining rooms, spacious studios, an extensive library, and art galleries. Both campuses have numerous state-of-the-art computer labs.

STAFF

Pratt's Center for Continuing and Professional Studies provides the leadership for the program. The faculty members for the Pre-College Foundation Program and electives are recognized writers, architects, artists, and designers. Expert guest lecturers and critics are also an essential part of the program. The Office of Residential Life oversees the residential portion of the program; a director and several advisers live in the residence halls. The staff members check curfews, organize small social activities, and monitor the living environment. All residents are expected to follow curfew.

MEDICAL CARE

All students must fill out health forms included in their Pre-College package. Staffed by a full-time nurse and counselor, Pratt's on-campus Office of Counseling and Health Services is available to Pre-College students.

COSTS

Tuition for the program is $2145. Other costs are as follows: student administration fee, $200; housing, $665; meal plan for residents, $625; local transportation for residents, $76; and optional commuter board plan, $150. Spending money of $300 for the purchase of art supplies is suggested. Prices are subject to change. The campus residence package includes breakfast, lunch, and dinner during the week and brunch and supper on weekends. Residence halls are available only in Brooklyn.

FINANCIAL AID

Merit-based scholarships are available for qualified students. The deadline for applications and slides is April 1 (postmark). Late applications are not accepted. All scholarships are for tuition only; they do not cover supplies, room, or board. The Black Alumni at Pratt sponsors a full scholarship program (for New York State resident students of minority groups only). Interested students should call 718-636-3479 for further information. Scholarship applications and instructions for submitting slides of work can either be sent upon request or downloaded from the Web site.

APPLICATION TIMETABLE

The registration deadline is April 1. Full payment deadline is May 15, by which time all tuition and fees are due. Applications are accepted as early as October. Since many classes fill quickly, students should apply early. A campus tour or overnight stay as a Pratt guest can be arranged through the Admissions Office (telephone: 718-636-3514). All applications must be accompanied by a $200 deposit, a $25 application fee, and a letter of recommendation from the student's guidance counselor or art teacher. International students are required to submit a letter from their English teacher that states their level of spoken and written comprehension.

FOR MORE INFORMATION, CONTACT

Center for Continuing and Professional Studies
Summer Pre-College Program, Pratt Institute
200 Willoughby Avenue, ISC 205
Brooklyn, New York 11205

Phone: 718-636-3453
Fax: 718-399-4410
E-mail: precollege@pratt.edu
Web site: http://www.pratt.edu/ccps-precollege

THE PUTNEY SCHOOL

SUMMER PROGRAMS

PUTNEY, VERMONT

TYPE OF PROGRAM: Visual and Performing Arts, Creative Writing, and EFL/ESL

PARTICIPANTS: Coeducational, ages 14–17

ENROLLMENT: 145 boarding and 15 day students

PROGRAM DATES: Session I: Sunday, June 24, through Saturday, July 14; Session II: Sunday, July 15, through Saturday, August 4

HEAD OF PROGRAM: Thomas D. Howe, Director

LOCATION
The Putney School campus is located in southeastern Vermont on a 500-acre hilltop farm near the Connecticut River. The campus offers beautiful views, miles of trails, a pond, a nature preserve, and a working dairy and animal farm.

BACKGROUND AND PHILOSOPHY
The Putney School Summer Programs offer students the opportunity for in-depth exploration in visual arts, performing arts, creative writing, and English as a second language (ESL) while learning the value and responsibility of working in a community and living close to the land. The Summer Programs highlight successful academic-year programs at The Putney School in the arts, writing, and international education and share the school's emphasis on self-discovery and inner growth, independent inquiry and initiative, and community exchange.

The goal of the program is for students to grow through enjoyable, productive, and safe experiences. Students are asked to agree to certain expectations to ensure the safety of the community and mutual respect of all individuals. The use of alcohol or illegal drugs is strictly prohibited and results in dismissal.

PROGRAM OFFERINGS
Each program provides 6 hours of hands-on instruction per day. All programs share community, residential, and recreational activities.

Summer Arts Workshops Designed for students seriously interested in the arts, these workshops offer students the opportunity to work in depth with professional artists, writers, and performers in two chosen areas. Offerings include drawing, painting, sculpture, ceramics, glass arts, modern and jazz dance, book arts, chamber music, vocal ensemble, jazz ensemble, songwriting, music composition, filmmaking, printmaking, photography, wearable arts, weaving, woodworking, jewelry, theater, animation, and other fields.

The Program for International Education (EFL/ESL) This program is designed for international students who wish to build confidence in using English as a living language in academic and social situations as well as increase their awareness of other cultures.

The Writing Program This program offers students guidance and instruction in all aspects of the written word. It gives students a chance to look at writing as a craft and a tool for self-expression, heightened observation, analytic thinking, problem solving, and

reflection. Writing workshops include a full-day Writing Intensive and half-day workshops in fiction, poetry, and playwriting.

ENROLLMENT
The enrollment figures for each session are as follows: Arts and Writing Programs, 130 and the Program for International Education, 15.

Students attend the summer programs from all areas of the United States and from countries in Eastern and Western Europe, Asia, Latin America, and Africa.

DAILY SCHEDULE

8:00 . . .	Breakfast
9:00 . . .	Morning workshops
12:00 . . .	Lunch
12:40 . . .	Assembly
1:15 . . .	Afternoon workshops
4:15 . . .	Outdoor activities
6:00 . . .	Dinner
7:15 . . .	Evening workshops
9:00 . . .	Visiting hour
10:00 . . .	In dorms

EXTRA OPPORTUNITIES AND ACTIVITIES
Afternoon outdoor activities include, but are not limited to, supervised swimming, basketball, hiking, soccer, ultimate Frisbee, volleyball, fencing, yoga, gardening, and work on the farm. Organized evening activities in the arts and off-campus cultural excursions are offered. Weekends are devoted to camping trips, recreational activities, and local field trips.

FACILITIES
Putney has superb facilities for the arts, including fully equipped studios for printmaking, welding, woodworking, photography, weaving, painting, ceramics, dance, and theater; a 250-seat concert hall; and art galleries. The computer lab provides support for writing programs and Internet access. The campus includes the 70-acre Garland Pond Nature Preserve, a protected wildlife area. The school library contains more than 25,000 volumes. Dormitories are small (10 to 25 students), and each is supervised by 2 or 3 adult dorm heads. Outdoor facilities include miles of riding and biking trails, an outdoor basketball court, extensive playing fields, and a working farm.

STAFF

The staff consists of 50 faculty members, some of whom are members of the academic-year faculty and all of whom are highly qualified instructors, equally experienced in teaching and the practice of their field. Twenty college-age resident staff members assist in the program. Staff members are caring, supportive, and deeply involved in the welfare and growth of participants.

MEDICAL CARE

A registered nurse is on staff and available for office hours during the week and on-call during the evenings and weekends. An urgent-care clinic and a fully equipped hospital are each 20 minutes away. Residential staff members are trained in emergency first aid. Each student submits a medical examination and release form before arriving on campus. The program requires family medical insurance for all participants.

RELIGIOUS LIFE

The program has no religious affiliation but provides transportation for students who wish to attend local services.

COSTS

Costs for tuition, room, and board in 2007 were $3200 for each three-week session; two sessions were $6000. Tuition, room, and board for international students were $3400 for one session, which included health insurance; two sessions were $6400. Tuition for day students was $1200 for one session; two sessions were $2050. There is an additional materials fee for some workshops. Students should bring no more than $150 for spending money.

FINANCIAL AID

Financial aid is offered based on need, as assessed from a family financial statement. Most qualified applicants receive some financial assistance. Financial aid applications are due March 1.

TRANSPORTATION

Putney is about 2½ hours from Boston and 3½ hours from New York City, just off Exit 4 of Interstate 91 in southeastern Vermont. The nearest airport is Bradley International Airport (BDL) in Hartford, Connecticut. The program provides transportation to and from the airport on arrival and departure days, for an additional fee. Transportation to and from any other airport must be arranged by family.

APPLICATION TIMETABLE

Inquiries and visits to campus are welcome throughout the year. Students are accepted to the programs on a rolling basis beginning in December. Early application is encouraged; some workshops fill early, and students are only placed in workshops after they have submitted a full application.

FOR MORE INFORMATION, CONTACT

Thomas D. Howe, Director of Summer Programs
The Putney School
Elm Lea Farm
Putney, Vermont 05346
Phone: 802-387-6297
Fax: 802-387-6216
E-mail: summer@putneyschool.org
Web site: http://www.putneyschool.org/summer

PARTICIPANT/FAMILY COMMENTS

"It is the only place in the world that I know of that puts you in an entirely creative environment and allows you to express yourself artistically in totally new ways ... I came home a better, happier, and more artistically aware person than I had ever known I could be."

"We were all so favorably impressed with Putney, and it turned out to be just the experience she/we were hoping for. What impressed us most was the seriousness and quality of the programs and yet, the lack of a "competitive" atmosphere. All these kids are obviously talented and motivated and that translated into an atmosphere of work AND fun. Whatever you are doing, you are doing right."

"He is in a safe, nurturing, friendly, and fun environment when he is at Putney. The various courses he has taken have been well taught and interesting and given him room to grow. The instructors have all been great, and the feedback they give is real, honest, and valuable. The students really look happy and friendly and willing to open up their groups to new arrivals, which is very impressive. The students are respectful of each other's work and really seem to be proud of each other's accomplishments. Putney has built his confidence and given him a little taste of what college will be like when he can concentrate more fully on what he loves."

"This was her first summer camp experience, and it surpassed all her hopes and expectations."

"After Putney, he is confident, driven, focused, and on a personal mission to do well in school and get into college. I got a matured, focused child back from your program. He loves to write—in fact he was just chosen to write with about 20 other students for a new newspaper that is being published for young adults. You guys gave him space, let him write, accepted him, and gave him beauty to look at with his eyes and to feel in his heart about himself."

"The instructors provided unmatched enthusiasm, encouragement, instruction, and guidance, bringing out the best in my daughter. She is confident in making art and felt that Putney is special, which it is. The friendships will be lasting ones, too, I feel."

"Perhaps more impressive than the variety of offerings is the happiness the students seem to derive from classes. Every class was filled with engaged, smiling, and animated students."—New England Association of Schools and Colleges report

PUTNEY STUDENT TRAVEL

▼▲▼▲▼▲▼▲▼▲▼▲▼▲▼▲▼▲▼▲▼▲▼▲▼▲▼▲▼▲▼

SUMMER PROGRAMS

PUTNEY, VERMONT

TYPE OF PROGRAM: Community service, global action, language learning, cultural exploration, foundations, and campus-based precollege enrichment (Excel). For more details regarding the Excel programs, students should see the separate listing in this section.

PARTICIPANTS: Coeducational, students completing grades 7–12

ENROLLMENT: 16–18 per group except Excel programs, which range from 50 to 150

PROGRAM DATES: Programs of three to seven weeks in June, July, and August

HEADS OF PROGRAM: Jeffrey and Peter Shumlin, Directors

LOCATION

Putney Student Travel offers **Community Service** programs in Alaska, Bali, Brazil, Costa Rica, Dominica, Dominican Republic, Ecuador, Grenada, Hawaii, India, Nicaragua, and Tanzania. **Global Awareness in Action** programs begin and end at Yale University, with separate units offered in Cambodia, India, Madagascar, Malawi, El Salvador, and the U.S. Gulf Coast. **Language Learning** programs are offered in Argentina, Costa Rica, France, and Spain. **Cultural Exploration** programs visit Australia/New Zealand and Europe. **Foundations** is a three-week program based in Costa Rica specifically designed for students finishing the seventh and eighth grades. **Excel** campus-based programs are held at Amherst College, Madrid/Barcelona, Oxford/Tuscany, Paris/Provence, and China. Putney Student Travel's year-round home is a converted barn surrounded by the hills and forests of Putney, Vermont.

BACKGROUND AND PHILOSOPHY

Putney Student Travel was founded in 1952 by George and Kitty Shumlin, devoted educators and parents of the present Directors, Peter and Jeffrey Shumlin. Over the course of five decades, the mission has remained unchanged—to enable young people to learn firsthand about the lives and cultures of people in the United States and other nations, to establish communication and friendship with them, to learn other languages, to pursue academic interests in an active and fun environment, to give of themselves, and, through these experiences, to enhance their confidence, skills, perspectives, and values.

Putney Student Travel programs are special. They emphasize doing, having fun, getting off the beaten track, making friends, and being involved with people rather than just touring, sightseeing, or studying. Participants are encouraged to take responsibility and to help develop group spirit. All programs are designed for motivated, inquisitive students who are mature and responsible. Admission is selective.

PROGRAM OFFERINGS

Community Service Programs: Students in these programs give of themselves to people in need. They spend four weeks living as a group in small, rural communities, where they join local people to work on small-scale construction projects, teach local children, and help villagers with maintenance, farming, and environmental projects. Each group of 16 students and 2 leaders has the opportunity to provide useful help to communities in need and to understand another culture at a level far beyond what tourists or short-term visitors experience. On weekends, there is time to relax at the beach, take wilderness and cultural excursions, and join in community life. One need not be a skilled laborer to apply. Students must possess sensitivity to-

ward others, a sense of humor and adventure, and a desire to work hard and to make the most of simple living conditions.

Global Awareness in Action Programs: War and terrorism dominate the headlines, but the long-term issues of lagging economic development, environmental degradation, erosion of traditional community structures, and inadequate resources for health care and children's services underlie today's crises and demand attention. One of the greatest challenges for the next generation of world leaders and decision makers is to devise workable strategies for improving conditions in the developing world. Global Action programs begin and end with three-day group forums at Yale University. For three weeks, participants pursue research and service in relation to a particular subject focus while on location in Cambodia, India, Madagascar, Malawi, El Salvador, or the U.S. Gulf Coast.

Language Learning Programs: The Putney way of learning a language emphasizes having fun in Argentina, Costa Rica, France, or Spain while speaking French or Spanish in natural, everyday living situations. Over the past half century, Putney has learned that sitting passively in a classroom with other Americans does not enhance language learning. Putney's dramatic oral/conversational exercises and games are combined with carefully planned itineraries that allow students to immerse themselves in the local life and culture, encouraging students to discard their inhibitions and speak freely. The atmosphere in each language group is noncompetitive. These four- to six-week programs explore cultural sites in cities and out-of-the-way regions of Argentina, Costa Rica, France, and Spain and engage students in short-term internships in rural areas and in recreational activities, including hiking and skiing. Each program includes a one-week, carefully selected homestay.

Cultural Exploration Programs: These programs either follow travel-based itineraries or focus on intensive, hands-on involvement in arts-related activities. Participants in travel-based programs learn about the countries they visit by joining in local life rather than touring as part of an isolated group of Americans. Each program includes a series of extended stays, avoiding hectic short hops, and brings students into close contact with local people while exploring history, traditions, the physical environment, and contemporary life. Arts-based programs encourage students with a special interest in creative writing or theater to expand and develop their skills and to engage their creativity through daily activities.

Foundations: The Foundations program is designed for creative, energetic, and engaged seventh and eighth grade students who want to transition from a traditional camp setting into a program that incorporates elements of Putney's exciting, educational offerings for older students around the world. Using a beautiful, beachside village in Costa Rica as a base, students participate in activities including Spanish language learning, community service, environmental studies, and recreation.

Excel at Amherst College, Oxford/Tuscany, Madrid/Barcelona, Paris/Provence, and China: These three-, four-, and seven-week programs provide students with an experience that is very different from traditional summer school. In small, seminar-style classes without the pressure of grades, students interact with outstanding instructors and motivated peers, participate in hands-on activities, and incorporate local resources in their learning. *Interested students should see the separate listing for the Excel program.*

ENROLLMENT
Putney groups (other than Excel and Foundations) are generally limited to 16 to 18 students. Students completing grades 7 and 8 are eligible for the Foundations program. Students completing grade 8 are eligible for some Language Learning programs. Students completing grades 9–12 are eligible for most other programs, though a few are limited to students completing grades 10–12.

FACILITIES
Putney accommodations are simple but comfortable and safe. In the Language Learning and Cultural Exploration programs, students stay in small inns and chalets and at student centers, where they have a chance to make friends with young people from other countries. Putney trips do not involve camping, unless specified in the brochure. Meals are taken in small restaurants, inns, and residences. On Community Service and Global Action projects, students live in small, rural villages in a school or other community building that is not in use during the summer. There are separate spaces for boys and girls and simple bathroom facilities. Helpers from the community take primary responsibility for meals, but students assist with preparation and cleanup.

STAFF
Putney Student Travel leaders are selected on the basis of their maturity, enthusiasm, patience, judgment, and ability to win the trust and respect of participants. Many are graduate students or

instructors who have lived, studied, and traveled abroad and who speak foreign languages. Leaders are given extensive preparation and training in Putney before departure. Brief bios of each of Putney's leaders from 2007 are available on the Web site at http://www.goputney.com/about/bios/allPST.htm.

COSTS
Tuition fees of $4000 to $9000, depending upon the program, cover all regular expenses, including meals, accommodations, excursions, and entertainment. Most tuition fees also include round-trip airfare from New York, Miami, or Los Angeles, depending on the destination. There are no hidden expenses. A $700 deposit must be submitted with the application; this fee is credited to the total tuition fee and is refunded in full if the application is not accepted.

TRANSPORTATION
Putney groups travel by air, train, bus, boat, and bicycle and on foot.

APPLICATION TIMETABLE
In forming each group, attention is given to the age and school year of applicants. Applications are carefully considered by the Admissions Committee, and participants are selected on the basis of their readiness for the Putney experience. Each year, Putney receives more applications than it is able to accept, so early application is encouraged. Admission is on a rolling basis.

FOR MORE INFORMATION, CONTACT
Jeffrey Shumlin, Admissions Director
Putney Student Travel
345 Hickory Ridge Road
Putney, Vermont 05346
Phone: 802-387-5000
Fax: 802-387-4276
E-mail: info@goputney.com
Web site: http://www.goputney.com

PARTICIPANT/FAMILY COMMENTS

"I was expecting to meet new people, have fun, and experience different cultures, and all of this happened. It was the best month of my life."

RANDOLPH-MACON ACADEMY

SUMMER PROGRAMS

FRONT ROYAL, VIRGINIA

TYPE OF PROGRAM: Academic/academic enrichment
PARTICIPANTS: Coeducational, grades 6–12
ENROLLMENT: 200 students
PROGRAM DATES: End of June to end of July (4 weeks)
HEAD OF PROGRAM: Maj. Gen. Henry M. Hobgood, USAF (Ret.), President

LOCATION
Randolph-Macon Academy's 135-acre campus is located 70 miles west of Washington, D.C., in picturesque Front Royal, Virginia. The town is nestled along the banks of the south fork of the Shenandoah River, at the head of the beautiful Skyline Drive.

BACKGROUND AND PHILOSOPHY
Founded in 1892, Randolph-Macon Academy (R-MA) is affiliated with the United Methodist Church and has separate Middle and Upper School campuses. R-MA's summer program provides a structured environment in which students are inspired to become lifelong learners.

Throughout the four weeks of the program, students from around the United States and the world immerse themselves in academics while participating in learning and extracurricular activities that contribute to their development and growth. At the high school level, students choose between one new course and two repeat courses. Students who have the desire to improve their grades or to get ahead for the coming school year benefit most from this program.

R-MA is fully accredited by the Virginia Association of Independent Schools and the Southern Association of Colleges and Schools. R-MA is also a member of the National Association of Independent Schools and the Association of Boarding Schools.

PROGRAM OFFERINGS
R-MA's Summer School Program offers a low student-teacher ratio, supervised study periods, Saturday classes, air-conditioned facilities, a full sports complex, and outstanding afternoon and weekend activities.

The Middle School program offers advancing sixth- through eighth-grade students the opportunity to focus on math, English, computer applications, study skills, world events, and a hands-on history course, History in Action. Classes are held in the morning. In the afternoons, students participate in mentoring groups and then have the opportunity to go on short recreational trips or participate in various sports and games. Academic field trips are taken on Wednesdays.

The Upper School program offers English (grades 8–12), prealgebra, algebra I, algebra II, geometry, Spanish I and II, biology, chemistry (all include laboratory work), U.S. government, U.S. history, world history II, and study skills. Students may take one new course or two repeat courses.

The average class size is 12 students. In the Upper School, students are graded on the following scale: A (90–100 percent), B (80–89 percent), C (70–79 percent), D (60–69 percent), and F (0–59 percent). Middle School students receive an E for excelling, an S for satisfactory progress, and an N for not working up to grade-level standards.

R-MA also offers a unique summer flight-training program that provides the aspiring aviator with ground school, approximately 15 hours of aircraft time, an FAA medical examination, and transportation to and from the airport. Flight time is logged in one of the Academy's single-engine Cessna 152 airplanes. Students who already have a single-engine private pilot rating may work toward their instrument rating. Students must turn 16 during or before the summer program in order to participate in the flight program.

The English as a Second Language (ESL) Program is designed for the non-English-speaking student who has some basic English preparation. The course combines classroom group sessions, cultural experiences, and other activities to provide a total-immersion program. The program includes Beginner ESL, Intermediate ESL, and Advanced ESL.

ENROLLMENT
Approximately 200 students enroll in R-MA's Summer Program each year—140 at the Upper School, 50 at the Middle School, and 8 in the flight program. More than 50 percent of the students are from Virginia and Maryland, 10–15 percent are from outside the U.S., and the rest of the students come from approximately twenty states all over the country.

DAILY SCHEDULE
A typical day at the Upper School may include the following:

6:30	Wake-up
7:15	Breakfast
8:00–12:15	First period
12:20–12:45	Lunch
1:00– 5:15	Second period
5:20– 6:00	Study hall
6:00– 6:45	Dinner
7:00– 9:00	Activity period
9:00–10:00	Free time
10:00–10:30	CQ'd to room
10:30	Lights-out

A typical day at the Middle School may include:

6:45	Wake-up
7:45– 8:15	Breakfast
8:20	Flag ceremony/announcements
8:30– 9:45	First period
9:50–11:05	Second period
11:10–12:25	Third period
12:40– 1:20	Lunch
1:25– 2:05	Mentoring
2:15	Afternoon announcements
2:20– 3:20	Intramurals/homework lab
3:20– 4:40	Free time
4:45– 5:30	Study hall
5:50– 6:30	Dinner
7:00– 9:00	Recreational activities
9:30	Prepare for bed
9:45	Lights-out

EXTRA OPPORTUNITIES AND ACTIVITIES
Weekend activities may include trips to King's Dominion, Busch Gardens, Hersheypark, Half Moon Beach, Splashdown Water Park, golf and batting cages, local movie theaters, bowling, swimming, and paintball competitions.

The Middle School academic trips on Wednesdays may include trips to the White House, Arlington National Cemetery, Luray Caverns, the Steven F. Udvar-Hazy Center, Monticello, Manassas Battlefield Park, Antietam Battlefield Park/ Harpers Ferry, or Shenandoah National Park.

FACILITIES
All classes and dorm rooms are air conditioned and wired for Internet capability. Two students share a room; roommates are determined by grade and/or age. Each floor is supervised by a dorm counselor.

The R-MA pool is open to students during free time, as are the gymnasium and the weight room. Two soccer fields, five tennis courts, a football field, a lacrosse field, a softball field, a baseball field, and an outdoor basketball court are available for student use.

The Middle School students are housed on a separate campus from the Upper School, with their own classrooms, spacious dorm rooms, cafeteria, and gymnasium. They share the Upper School weight room, pool, and chapel throughout the week.

MEDICAL CARE
Registered nurses are on staff. Students requiring additional medical care may go to Warren Memorial Hospital, which is located less than a mile from the campus. Each student is required to submit immunization records and a copy of their last physical before registration day.

COSTS
Tuition, room, and board costs for 2007 are $2479, plus a recommended personal account of $850 and an application fee of $75. Tuition, room, and board for international students are $3265, plus a recommended personal account of $900, an ESL lab fee of $250, and an application fee of $200. For day students, costs are $775 per new Upper School course and $385 for repeat Upper School courses. The cost of the Middle School day program is $875.

Lunch for the entire four weeks is $95 for Upper School day students taking repeat courses. The cost of lunch is included in the tuition for all other students.

Miscellaneous charges include $15 for telephone rental and $100 in lab fees. Cost for the flight program is $2479 plus flying time per hour and $750 for the personal account.

APPLICATION TIMETABLE
Inquiries into the summer programs are welcomed year-round; updated information is published in December of each year. Tours of the campus are available Monday through Saturday. Interviews are not required for the summer program. Applications are accepted until classes are full but should be turned in no later than one week before the summer program begins. The application fee is $75. Applicants are notified of the admissions decision a few days after the admissions office has received all the required paperwork.

FOR MORE INFORMATION, CONTACT
Admissions Office
200 Academy Drive
Front Royal, Virginia 22630

Phone: 800-272-1172 (toll-free)
Fax: 540-636-5419
E-mail: admissions@rma.edu
Web site: http://www.rma.edu

RASSIAS
Student Programs

RASSIAS LANGUAGE PROGRAMS

FRANCE, SPAIN, ITALY, AND CHINA

TYPE OF PROGRAM: French, Spanish, Italian, and Mandarin Chinese language studies; homestays, community service, and travel

PARTICIPANTS: Coeducational, grades 9–12

ENROLLMENT: 175 students in groups of 20 to 25

PROGRAM DATES: Four to six weeks from late June through early August

HEADS OF PROGRAM: Bill Miles and Helene Rassias-Miles, Directors

LOCATION
Rassias Language Programs offers language studies, homestays, and travel in France, Spain, Italy, and China.

BACKGROUND AND PHILOSOPHY
Rassias has been offering language study immersion experiences to students since 1985.

Rassias Language Programs sprang from Helene Rassias' childhood experiences in France. There she accompanied her father, a renowned professor at Dartmouth College and developer of the Rassias Method® of language instruction. All Rassias language programs use the Rassias Method—an approach that provides a dynamic, uninhibited cultural and linguistic immersion. The approach is widely used at Dartmouth and many other institutions worldwide.

The homestay programs benefit from the directors' personal contacts, which they have developed over twenty-five years of traveling and studying abroad. Working closely with local sources who are friends of the directors, Rassias carefully selects families for the homestay program. Students continue to speak, write, and read in the foreign language even after departing for the travel portion of their trip.

PROGRAM OFFERINGS
Rassias Programs—France (grades 9–11) Rassias French language programs, offered in Tours and Arles, combine French language studies with travel and cultural immersion. Courses are taught by a master teacher and 2 assistants. Group size varies from 20 to 25 participants, with orientation taking place in Normandy and Brittany (Tours) or the Pyrenees (Arles).

Tours (four weeks) Students with two or more years of French can expand their language skills while living with host families in Tours, a town located on the banks of the Loire River. Once in Tours, students attend French language classes in the morning. Afternoons are devoted to planned group activities or excursions. During this

time, students live with host families. Visits to a Brittany coastal town, Normandy beaches, and Paris round out the experience.

Arles (five weeks) Students with two or more years of French study the language while living with host families in Arles, a town located in the beautiful region of Provence. Classes are held in the morning. Afternoons are devoted to planned group activities or excursions. During this time, students live with host families. During the final weeks of the program, students tour the Riviera, the Loire Valley, and Paris.

Rassias Programs—Spain (grades 9–11) These three 4-week Spanish language and family-stay programs are designed for students with two or more years of Spanish. They are based in Gijón, Segovia, and Pontevedra and are taught by a master teacher and 2 or 3 assistants. Group size varies from 20 to 25 students.

Gijón (four weeks) The family-stay and classes unfold in Gijón, a beach resort city of 250,000 inhabitants, which lies on Spain's North Atlantic coast. Classes are held in Gijón's famous sports club where afterwards students can play basketball and volleyball, swim, or take an aerobics class—all in Spanish. Orientation and a bit of tourism start the program in Segovia and Madrid. The final weeks are spent on a day kayak near the Pikos Mountains and a visit to the famed Guggenheim museum in Bilbao and end with exploration of fabulous Barcelona.

Segovia (four weeks) The ancient city of Segovia is the core of this program, where classes, excursions both in Segovia and to the castle towns that surround it, visits with local artists and politicians, and the family-stay all take place. The program starts with orientation in Toledo, where students not only explore this city, which on Spain's national historical register in its entirety, but also spend time getting acquainted and moving away from English to Spanish. The group then travels through Andalusia (while continuing to speak Spanish) to amazing Granada, the classic beaches of the south, ancient Cordoba, and lively Sevilla. From Sevilla they head to Segovia and their 2½-week homestay. The program ends with several days in Madrid.

Pontevedra (four weeks) The program begins with orientation in the beautiful walled city of Avila. Here, students relax, explore, and start practicing Spanish. Students then travel to vibrant Sevilla and then to Extremadura, the land of the conquistadors. Here, students visit Mérida, Cáceres, the Yuste Monastery, and the beautiful valley of the Jerte River. On the way to Pontevedra, they stop in Salamanca. The sights, sounds, and overall urban quality of the city make this a favorite stop among students and staff members.

The homestay and classes take place in coastal Pontevedra. With a name dating back to time of the Roman Empire (Pontus Veteri), Pontevedra has been a central point of travel for pilgrims along the southern leg of the Camino de Santiago since medieval times. Located in Galicia, in a region known as Rías Bajas, Pontevedra is off the beaten track of foreign tourists, offering an advantage to those students who wish to speak only Spanish. While in Pontevedra, students visit beach resorts, small fishing villages, inland medieval sites, and the protected islands just off the coast, as well as more well-known places, such as Santiago de Compostela, Bayone, and Tuy.

Rassias Program–Orte, Italy (grades 9 to 11) This four-week Italian language and family-stay program is designed for students who are beginners in Italian as well as those with one to two years of Italian studies. Students currently taking Latin (or another Romance language) are encouraged to attend.

The adventure starts on the coast of Tuscany, which is an area rich in history and also renowned for its natural beauty. Talamone, the medieval picturesque fishing village that is home for the first few days, is one of the entrances to the beautiful Natural Park of the Maremma. Students then travel by sailboat to Elba Island, returning to the mainland to another wonderful area of provincial Tuscany, Siena and the medieval town of San Gimignano, before finally arriving at Florence.

During the homestay, students become members of the small and hospitable community of Orte. Weekday mornings are spent learning and practicing Italian, and evenings and one weekend are spent with the families. Various activities keep afternoons busy: short trips to learn about the provincial area around Orte, which is rich in archeological (Tarquinia, Ferento), historical (Viterbo, Caprarola), artistic (Tuscania, Bomarzo, Orvieto), and natural sites (the protected areas around the Lakes Vico and Bolsena); visits to nearby Rome, only 40 minutes by train from Orte; sport activities and socializing with members of the community in the popular open swimming pool fed by natural hot springs and located in a beautiful valley (about 1 kilometer from Orte).

The final days of the program are spent on the beautiful Amalfi coast with its picturesque villages; Pompeii, one of the most famous ancient cities in the world; and the exuberant splendor of Naples.

Rassias Program–Gyalthang, Yunnan Province, China This program is a forty-day language, community service, and trekking program in Yunnan Province, located east of the Himalayas and one of China's least visited and most intriguing provinces. One week of travel and trekking is followed by eighteen days of homestay, classes, and community service work and ends with one week at the Baima Snow Mountain School. It is designed by Dartmouth graduate, Rassias friend, and native Tibetan Pasang Tashi and his nephew, owner of Forbidden Frontier, for trekking in Yunnan. It is for students who are beginners in Chinese as well as those with one to two years of Chinese studies.

The trip begins in Kunming, the capital of Yunnan. In Kunming, students hike the Dragon Gate, with its gorgeous view of Dian Chi Lake, which is a source of inspiration to many local poets. Students also visit the Bamboo Temple, Green Lake Park, and a lively area of tea houses and cafes, which is also a cultural center for Tai Chi, Chikung, Peking opera, and western dance. After exploring

Kunming, the group heads north to Dali. Dali is situated on a fertile green plain that is watered by eighteen streams cascading down from the symmetrical nineteen peaks of the Canshan Mountain Range. Students visit Xizhou, an ancient village famous for its delicate Bai Minority architecture and the batik heritage, go on a boat cruise on Erhai Lake, and then head 2 hours north to the ancient village of Shaxi. Shaxi Village is the only surviving example of a Southern Silk Road trade center and is listed as one of the 100 most endangered sites in the world.

The Homestay in Gyalthang (2½ weeks) Students climb 6 hours by bus to the Tibetan town of Gyalthang, situated at 10,820 feet. In Gyalthang, students combine study of the Mandarin Chinese language with a great deal of exploration. They meet the host students from No. 5 Middle School of Gyalthang, where the classes are held. Over this two-week period, students visit Tibetan monasteries as well as sacred pilgrimage sites as well as enjoy cultural performances, typical food, and a day of biking and picnicking through beautiful villages. Students also participate with the host students in a three-day community service project at the Bita Lake Nature Reserve, under the direction of Nature Conservancy U.S.A.

The group then travels to the Baima Snow Mountain School. Situated at 9,180 feet in the Baima Nature Reserve, the school was founded by the Wildlife Fund and a Tibetan lama for the education of orphans from the region and children from the mountains. Here, students continue their Chinese language courses as well as help teach the local children. Rassias students live with local families in a very rural environment and go with them to cultural performances and festivities, community service, and hikes to Lijiang, a World Heritage Site protected by UNESCO at the foot of the Jade Dragon Snow Mountain. Students visit a 500-year-old village and Black Dragon Spring before returning to Kunming the following day.

STAFF

The language programs are taught by a master teacher and teaching assistants. Many have had prior teaching experience using the Rassias Method. All attend teacher workshops at the Rassias Foundation at Dartmouth College.

All staff members have studied and have usually lived in the region that they will tour with students; many possess a near-native understanding of a country's language and culture.

COSTS

The fees, including airfare, range from $7200 to $8000 for the language programs.

APPLICATION TIMETABLE

Starting November 30 each year, all completed applications are reviewed during the first fifteen days of the following month. Programs are usually full following the March 31 deadline.

FOR MORE INFORMATION, CONTACT

Bill Miles
Rassias Programs
P.O. Box 5456
Hanover, New Hampshire 03755

Phone: 603-643-3007
Fax: 603-643-4249
E-mail: info@rassias.com
Web site: http://www.rassias.com

REIN TEEN TOURS

▼▲▼▲▼▲▼▲▼▲▼▲▼▲▼▲▼▲▼▲▼▲▼▲▼▲▼▲▼▲

SUMMER TRAVEL PROGRAMS AND COMMUNITY SERVICE PROGRAMS

UNITED STATES, CANADA, HAWAII, ALASKA, ENGLAND, FRANCE, SWITZERLAND, ITALY, AND SPAIN

TYPE OF PROGRAM: Active travel, community service
PARTICIPANTS: Coeducational, ages 12–17
ENROLLMENT: 42 per group
PROGRAM DATES: End of June through August; tours vary from twenty-one to forty days
HEAD OF PROGRAM: Norman Rein, Owner

BACKGROUND AND PHILOSOPHY

Rein Teen Tours was founded in 1986 with the objective of offering teenagers activity-oriented, supervised travel in places throughout North America and Europe. The Rein Teen Tour staff, with more than thirty-six years of experience in organizing teen travel, works diligently throughout the year to promote creativity in its tour planning and to guarantee a safe, educational, productive summer for its participants. Since its inception, Rein Teen Tours has shown a commitment to supervision, safety, and worthwhile programming.

Believing that the composition of the group is crucial to the success of the tour, great energy is invested in assembling the tour groups, emphasizing age compatibility and geographic diversity among the members of each group. Many teenagers choose to join on their own, as the program is specifically designed to promote interaction and to keep social pressure to a minimum. The professional tour staff specializes in promoting socialization and minimizing "cliqueness" among tour members. Teenagers come to Rein Teen Tours with positive attitudes, anxious to make many new friends, visit many great places, and participate in a variety of activities that ultimately exceed their greatest expectations.

A Rein Teen Tours summer is appropriate for any teenager with a desire to participate in a variety of unforgettable activities while enjoying the excitement of traveling throughout North America. When teenagers outgrow traditional camp, the ever-changing daily events on a Rein Teen Tour hold their interest while maintaining their enthusiasm throughout the trip.

PROGRAM OFFERINGS

Rein Teen Tours offers a wide variety of tour itineraries for travel throughout North America and Europe.

A variety of tours that visit the western United States and western Canada are offered. Western options include three-week, four-week, and six-week tours. Three-week tours begin in Salt Lake City and travel to Bryce Canyon and Zion Canyon National Parks, Grand Canyon National Park, Las Vegas, San Diego, Los Angeles, Lake Tahoe, and San Francisco. Four-week trips add to the excitement with visits to the Black Hills of South Dakota, Mount Rushmore, and the Badlands, Yellowstone, and Grand Teton National Parks. Six-week tours visit all the same great spots in the western United States and add the thrill of visiting western Canada and the Pacific Northwest. This includes the excitement of Calgary and the Calgary Stampede, the beauty of Banff and Jasper National Parks, and the majesty of Lake Louise, Vancouver, Whistler, British Columbia, and Seattle.

The Eastern Adventure, limited to junior high school–age teenagers, visits many beautiful scenic areas, including Niagara Falls, the White Mountains of New Hampshire, and Acadia National Park. Action-packed city stops include Toronto, Montreal, Quebec City, Boston, and Washington, D.C. The tour also includes two sun-drenched days at an Atlantic Ocean beach resort. This twenty-eight-day trip is a great first tour for young teenagers who are anxious to travel.

The Hawaiian/Alaskan Adventure allows teenagers to visit the farthest and most exotic reaches of the United States. Alaskan highlights include a seven-day Inside Passage luxury liner cruise. Three of the Hawaiian Islands—Oahu, the "Big Island of Hawaii," and Maui—are visited and allow for fun activities, including a snorkel cruise; Hawaiian surfing, with instruction; and a memorable journey to Hawaii Volcanoes National Park. The tour also visits Vancouver, Whistler, British Columbia, Seattle, Portland, Mount Hood National Park, Lake Tahoe, and San Francisco. In these areas, participants enjoy summer snow skiing, sand dune buggy rides, jet boating, whale watching, and sea kayaking.

Rein Europe offers an exciting thirty-two-day opportunity for teenagers to visit England, France, Switzerland, Italy, and Spain. While in Europe, teens stay at charming three- and four-star hotels, enjoy fun European cuisine, and experience the cultures of the visited countries. Some highlights of Rein Europe include summer snow skiing and snowboarding on the Matterhorn, a gondola ride on Venice's Grand Canal, visits to Mediterranean beaches on the French and Spanish Riviera, white-water rafting on the Reuss River in Switzerland, London theater, and a thrilling glacial excursion and cave exploration. Sightseeing highlights include Buckingham Palace, the Eiffel Tower, the Sistine Chapel, the Louvre, the Tower of Pisa, and the Roman Colosseum.

Rein's Project Hawaii presents teenagers with the opportunity to perform meaningful volunteer work and earn a certificate documenting performance of 80 hours of community service. Participants live on the Big Island of Hawaii in the comfortable dormitories of the University of Hawaii. During this 26-day program, teens choose from a variety of volunteer projects where they have the opportunity to work with local youth, senior citizens, and homeless animals. Participants enjoy recreational trips to several Hawaiian Islands on the weekends, where they can snorkel, surf, and enjoy magnificent Hawaiian beaches and resorts.

ENROLLMENT

Rein Teen Tours attracts teenagers from all over the United States, Canada, and the world. Over the past several summers, international participants from Europe, South America, and Asia have added to the geographic diversity of the tour groups.

EXTRA OPPORTUNITIES AND ACTIVITIES

Each teenager is treated as an individual, as the flexibility of the programs allows participants to choose from a variety of activities in the areas visited. In scenic areas and national parks, teenagers are encouraged to try new activities and benefit from professional instruction. Examples include snorkeling at Catalina Island, waterskiing on Lake Tahoe, and summer snow skiing in Whistler, British Columbia. While visiting major cities, such as Los Angeles and San Francisco, tours attend circus school, comedy clubs, teen dance clubs, major-league baseball games, local theater, and theme parks. Past travelers have remarked that there is never a dull moment on a Rein Teen Tour. They compliment Rein Teen Tours on its innovative, up-to-date activities, citing examples such as high-energy dragster racing, summer snow skiing, off-road Jeep trips, and hands-on sessions with sea lion and dolphin trainers at the Rein Teen Tours marine life encounter.

FACILITIES

Rein Teen Tours believes that tour members should enjoy the most convenient accommodations in all areas visited. Safety and security are top priorities when choosing facilities. A variety of facilities, chosen because of their proximity to many local activities, vary between scenic campgrounds, fun college dorms, and exciting resort hotels. Camping highlights include waterfront resort campgrounds in California, tranquil campground settings in the mountains of the Canadian Rockies, and picturesque camping near the rim of the Grand Canyon. All campgrounds feature modern bathroom facilities with hot water, private showers, flush toilets, and electricity. When camping, a great night's sleep is certain on a self-inflating Thermorest camping mattress and cot inside a custom-designed cabin tent, all provided by Rein Teen Tours. Three nutritious meals featuring a wide variety of food, as well as fun snacks, are provided when camping.

Fun campus stays at popular universities include UCLA, University of Michigan, University of Alaska, University of Toronto, and University of Minnesota. Dynamic hotels include the Hyatt at Fisherman's Wharf in San Francisco, the Planet Hollywood Resort in Las Vegas, the Doubletree Guest Quarters Suite Resort in Orlando, the Hilton Waikoloa Village in Hawaii, and the Canyons Resort in Park City, Utah. Tour members are always provided individual beds in university dormitories and hotels. On hotel and dormitory days, three meals are provided at varied restaurants, with teenagers ordering directly from regular menus. Dining accommodations include fun dinner parties at trendy Hard Rock Cafes, Planet Hollywoods, Bubba Gump's, California Pizza Kitchens, and Rainforest Cafes in various cities.

STAFF

The summer tour staff comprises teachers, graduate students, and college graduates who are experienced campers and travelers. Each tour operates with a ratio of 1 adult for every 7 teenagers. The tour directors, all certified by the American Red Cross for basic first aid training and CPR, are among the most experienced in the teen tour industry. Staff members receive extensive training prior to the tour, as their leadership qualities consistently play a major role in the success of the summer tours. Rein Teen Tours summer staff members are frequently commended for their mature and responsible attitude as well as their sense of humor and compassion for the needs of the teenagers.

MEDICAL CARE

The safety and health of the tour members are the most important aspect of the operation of the tours. To promote tour wellness, tours are planned to allow time for leisure, relaxation, nutritious meals, and adequate sleep. In the event that medical services are needed, Rein Teen Tours has established relationships with an extensive network of medical facilities, including hospitals, 24-hour emergency medical clinics, and local physicians, who are available to treat teenagers requiring medical attention at any time or place during the tour.

COSTS

Trips range in price from $4999 to $8999 and include all lodging, three meals daily, all recreation and entertainment admissions, gratuities, and taxes.

TRANSPORTATION

Travel arrangements for all teenagers are made by the Rein Teen Tours travel staff and provide for getting teenagers from their home area to tour start points and back home upon completion of the tour.

APPLICATION TIMETABLE

Tour enrollment is on a rolling basis, and early inquiry is suggested as tour spaces are limited. A $350 deposit is required with the enrollment application.

FOR MORE INFORMATION, CONTACT

Rein Teen Tours
30 Galesi Drive
Wayne, New Jersey 07470
Phone: 800-831-1313 (toll-free)
Fax: 973-785-4268
E-mail: summer@reinteentours.com
Web site: http://www.reinteentours.com

PARTICIPANT/FAMILY COMMENTS

"My parents and I investigated many summer options and decided Rein Teen Tours offered the most. Boy, did we make the right decision! Not only did I visit the most amazing sights, but also in a relatively short period of time, I made wonderful and lasting friendships. Highest marks to the Rein Teen Tour staff for providing me with the best accommodations, an incredible itinerary (full of activity everyday!), and a dynamic staff who made me their number one priority. Everyone was terrific! Thank you for giving me a summer of excellent memories!"

"My husband and I just want to thank you for the wonderful experience you have given our son. Jayson went on this trip not knowing anyone, and came home with wonderful friends and lifetime relationships! He has not stopped raving about the marvelous things that he was exposed to. Each and every place was an 'awesome' adventure for him. The trip was well organized and relevant to the interests of teens. All of the pre-planning was obvious in the smooth manner in which the trip ran. We highly recommend Rein Teen Tours!"

RENSSELAER POLYTECHNIC INSTITUTE

SUMMER@RENSSELAER

TROY, NEW YORK

TYPE OF PROGRAM: Academic enrichment programs and sport camps
PARTICIPANTS: Post-K–12
ENROLLMENT: Varies by program
PROGRAM DATES: Various sessions in May, June, July, and August
HEAD OF PROGRAM: Mike Gunther, Program Manager for Recruitment

LOCATION

Rensselaer is located in the northeastern United States, in the heart of New York's Capital Region. The region, which includes the cities and suburbs of Albany, Schenectady, and Troy, has a combined population of approximately 870,000 and is an important business, governmental, industrial, and academic hub.

Overlooking the city of Troy and the historic Hudson River, Rensselaer's 275-acre campus blends recently constructed facilities with a cluster of classical-style, ivy-covered brick buildings dating from the turn of the century. A program of extensive renovation has equipped the campus with ultramodern teaching facilities while preserving the traditional elegance of its historic buildings.

Rensselaer retains the quiet and natural beauty of a parklike setting while offering many conveniences of an urban campus. Students enjoy easy access to Boston (3 hours), New York City (2½ hours), and Montreal (4 hours). The Adirondacks, the Berkshires, and the Catskills, all within an hour of Troy, offer hundreds of areas for camping, hiking, and skiing.

BACKGROUND AND PHILOSOPHY

The oldest degree-granting technological university in North America, Rensselaer Polytechnic Institute (RPI) was founded in 1824 "for the purpose of instructing persons in the application of science to the common purposes of life."

Rensselaer has become one of the world's premier technological research universities, offering more than 100 programs and 1,000 courses that lead to bachelor's, master's, and doctoral degrees.

Summer is an exciting time to be at Rensselaer, a place where enthusiasm and innovation are the very hallmarks of its programs and classes. Rensselaer invites elementary, middle, and high school students to enroll in summer enrichment programs and sports camps. In addition, summer credit courses are available to academically talented and qualified high school students.

PROGRAM OFFERINGS

Summer@Rensselaer offers many programs. For more information about all opportunities that are offered, including specific dates and costs, students are encouraged to visit the Web site (http://summer.rpi.edu). Any program applications or registrations that are needed can also be downloaded at the Web site.

SUMMER ENRICHMENT PROGRAMS

Summer enrichment day programs allow elementary, middle, and high school students the chance to participate in noncredit programs that stimulate their minds and exercise their bodies. Day programs available in summer 2007 include the Architecture Career Discovery Program (high school students), the ASM Materials Camp (rising juniors and seniors), the LEGO® Robotics Engineering Academy (ages 11–14), The Magical World of Flight (middle and high school students), Nature's Treasure Hunt (elementary and middle school students), the Samaritan-Rensselaer Children's Center RPI Summer Day Camp (kindergarten graduates through age 12), the VEX Robotics Engineering Academy (ages 13–15), Video Production: Through the Eyes of the Lens (high school students), Whodunit? The Science of Crime Scenes (middle school students), Why Plastics? (elementary and middle school students), Young Actors Guild (ages 8–18), the PREFACE Program (high school sophomores), and Rensselaer Science and Technology Entry Program (STEP) (middle and high school students in five area schools).

An overnight summer enrichment program, the Computer Game Development Academy for rising and graduating seniors, is offered for two sessions, June 25–July 6 and July 16–August 27.

Questions about application and registration for summer enrichment programs may be directed to Mike Gunter at 518-276-8351.

CREDIT COURSES

Summer courses for college credit provide students with an opportunity to pursue more rigorous course work than may be available in high school. For example, the School of Engineering offers Introduction to Engineering Electronics, Engineering Graphics and CAD, and Introduction to Engineering Analysis. Such courses as The Graphic Novel, Methods of Reasoning, General Psychology, and introductions to economics and logic are offered by the School of Humanities and Social Sciences. The School of Science offers a variety of courses in calculus and computer science. Students can find more information on the Web (http://summer.

rpi.edu/update.do?artcenterkey=28), and the Admissions Office (518-276-6216, admissions@rpi.edu) will answer any questions about applying for the courses.

SPORTS CAMPS
With Rensselaer fielding twenty-three varsity teams, Summer@Rensselaer offers numerous sports camps each summer. Interested students can find sport camp information on the Web (http://summer.rpi.edu/update.do?catcenterkey= 5). Students with questions about sports camps are encouraged to call Mike Gunter (518-276-8351).

ENROLLMENT
Summer@Rensselaer programs serve a variety of students in kindergarten through high school.

DAILY SCHEDULE
The schedules vary by program. Students should check online for specifics.

Sample Day Schedule for the Computer Game Development Academy

9:00–12:00	Game Development Studio
12:00– 1:00	Lunch
1:00– 3:00	Programmer/Arts Studio
2:00– 3:30	Break
3:30– 6.00	Programmer/Arts Studio

Sample Evening Schedule for the Football Camp

6:00– 6:15	Arrive/Register/Dress
6:30– 6:45	Stretch
6:45– 7:45	Offense Practice
7:45– 7:50	Break
7:50– 8:50	Defense Practice
8:50– 9:00	"Football Talk"
9:00	Depart

FACILITIES
Studio classrooms and laboratories around the campus use the latest educational technologies and encourage collaboration and team learning among students.

STAFF
Approximately 400 tenured and tenure-track faculty members call Rensselaer home. Ninety-six percent of the faculty members have earned a Ph.D., first professional, or other terminal degree in their fields. Some enrichment programs employ Rensselaer students, who are organized, personable, detail oriented, good team members, and effective problem solvers.

MEDICAL CARE
The Student Health Center is a comprehensive, nationally accredited, physician-directed center providing outpatient ambulatory health care. The center is open during the summer. Staff members include a full-time physician, two part-time physicians, four licensed Ph.D. psychologists, two full-time physician assistants, a health educator, registered nurses, and a part-time nurse practitioner.

COSTS
Credit courses in 2007 for undergraduate students are $1019 per credit hour. Each summer enrichment program and sports camp is individually priced. The program listing on the Summer@Rensselear Web site has additional information.

TRANSPORTATION
All students must furnish their own transportation to and from campus.

APPLICATION TIMETABLE
Applicants for credit courses are required to submit a current high school transcript, inclusive of all current-year marking periods. Any available SAT or ACT scores, a high school profile, and college counselor contact information should be submitted as well.

For other programs, students must fill out a registration form that is available online. Students should apply early as space is limited in many enrichment programs and sports camps.

FOR MORE INFORMATION, CONTACT
Mike Gunther, Program Manager for Recruitment
Outreach Programs
Rensselaer Polytechnic Institute
110 8th Street, CII Suite 4011
Troy, New York 12180-3590
Phone: 518-276-8351
E-mail: gunthm@rpi.edu
Web site: http://summer.rpi.edu

RHODE ISLAND SCHOOL OF DESIGN

▼△▼△▼△▼△▼△▼△▼△▼△▼△▼△▼△▼△▼△▼△▼

PRE-COLLEGE PROGRAM

PROVIDENCE, RHODE ISLAND

TYPE OF PROGRAM: Visual arts study
PARTICIPANTS: Coeducational, students between ages 16 and 18 (born between August 9, 1989, and June 28, 1992)
ENROLLMENT: About 550
PROGRAM DATES: June 28–August 9, 2008

LOCATION
Rhode Island offers some of New England's most scenic coastline, beautifully preserved colonial villages, and the cultural richness of Providence and Newport. Rhode Island School of Design's (RISD) main campus is on College Hill, on Providence's East Side, which is home to both RISD and Brown University. Additional facilities are located in downtown Providence's up-and-coming arts enclave. The elegantly restored homes and gardens of College Hill offer students the relaxed ambience of neighborhood life, while Providence Place Mall, Thayer and Wickenden Streets, and the historic downtown area provide easy access to numerous restaurants, bookstores, specialty shops, and cultural activities. In addition, Waterplace Park, adjacent to RISD's campus, is home to the acclaimed waterfront festival WaterFire.

BACKGROUND AND PHILOSOPHY
The Pre-College Program accepts high school students into an intensive six-week college-like art and design program. In the setting of an internationally renowned design school, a structured curriculum gives each student a strong foundation of skills and understanding in the visual arts. The intensity and focus of the program provide students with the opportunity to experience art as a major academic priority before investing in a college program. Many students create a portfolio for college admissions, while others explore art and design to complement their liberal arts background. Although a previous background in art or design is not necessary, all students should be strongly motivated and ready to commit to a rigorous schedule of study. Students should be prepared to undertake and complete a considerable amount of out-of-class work.

PROGRAM OFFERINGS
All students are required to take three foundation courses: Foundation Drawing, Basic Design, and Art History. In addition, students may choose one of the following major areas of concentration: architecture, ceramics, comic book art, computer animation, drawing, fashion design, furniture design, game design, graphic design, illustration, industrial design, interior design, jewelry, painting, photography (digital), photography (traditional), printmaking, sculpture, textile design, video, or Web design.

The required Foundation Drawing and Basic Design courses each meet one full day per week. Another two days each week are spent working intensively in the major area. Two hours of the fifth weekday are devoted to art history, with the remaining time available for completion of homework assignments.

ENROLLMENT
High school students who have reached their sixteenth birthday as of June 28, 2008, and have enrolled as a junior or senior by September 2008 may apply for admission to the 2008 Pre-College Program. Graduating seniors are welcome, as long as they do not turn 19 before August 9, 2008. Other than these age restrictions, all applicants who show promise of being able to benefit from the program are admitted. The approximately 550 students enrolled in the program usually represent thirty to forty states and more than twenty countries.

DAILY SCHEDULE

7:30– 8:30	Breakfast
9:00	Classes begin
12:00– 1:00	Lunch
4:00	Classes end
5:00– 6:00	Dinner
7:00–10:00	Open studio, social and recreational activities
11:00	Curfew (Sunday–Thursday)
12:00	Curfew (Friday and Saturday)

Students should know all of the regulations of the Pre-College Program. A handbook, which clearly describes these and other rules, is provided to all students and their parents. Violation of Pre-College Program policies or regulations is taken seriously by the college administration; students may be subject to various sanctions or dismissal if they disregard them.

For example, students are required to be in the dormitories by curfew. They are not permitted to sign out from their dormitory overnight unless previous written permission from a parent or guardian is on file in the office of the resident director. Resident students are not allowed to possess or drive motor vehicles, including motor scooters and motorcycles.

EXTRA OPPORTUNITIES AND ACTIVITIES
Students in the program may take part in a full schedule of evening and weekend activities. Trips are planned to popular Rhode Island landmarks, including Newport and Narragansett beaches. At RISD's Tillinghast Farm, a 33-acre expanse

on Narragansett Bay, students may enjoy sailing, sunbathing, kite flying, picnicking, and relaxing in the outdoors. At least one trip to Boston and/or a prominent New England museum of art is organized. Excellent theater productions are sponsored by neighboring Brown University. There are also school-sponsored concerts, films, dances, and other social events. In the evenings, students are able and encouraged to work in open studios.

FACILITIES

The RISD campus is one of this country's largest and best-equipped centers for the study of art and design. Its forty-two restored campus buildings house studios, classrooms, a library, an auditorium, an excellent museum, galleries, and book and supply stores. The school's dining and residence facilities are near the center of the campus. College housing has quiet study areas, recreational facilities, and work areas.

STAFF

Members of the faculty are drawn from RISD's regular academic-year faculty, RISD alumni, professionals in the field, and instructors from colleges and universities throughout the country.

The residence staff is made up of RISD's year-round professional staff members and resident assistants—RISD students who are carefully selected, trained, and supervised. RISD's Public Safety Department also monitors dormitories.

MEDICAL CARE

RISD's on-campus Health Services is staffed by a registered nurse and on-call physicians. If students have emergency medical problems requiring treatment at the local hospital, they are escorted there and their parents are notified. Health forms are included in the application package. Medical insurance is required.

COSTS

The 2007 tuition and fees were as follows: a $5900 program fee for boarding students (includes tuition, activities fee, housing, and dining) and a $3825 program fee for commuting students (tuition and activities fee only). Boarding students are required to pay a nonrefundable deposit of $500, and commuting students pay a nonrefundable deposit of $350. These deposits are applied to the total program fee. The meal contract is mandatory for all residential students. Students may need to spend as much as $800 for art supplies, depending on their major. In addition, there are equipment rental fees in certain majors.

For the 2008 summer session, applications submitted on or before April 9 must be accompanied by a nonrefundable deposit or payment in full. The deadline for full payment is April 25. Applications submitted after April 9 must include payment in full of all tuition and fees. If the application is not accepted or registration is closed, tuition and fees are refunded promptly.

APPLICATION TIMETABLE

Early application is highly recommended. All of the major courses have a limited number of spaces, and students are assigned to each on a first-come, first-served basis.

To apply, students must return a completed Pre-College Program Application Form, a short statement of interest, and one letter of recommendation from either an art instructor or a guidance counselor.

Non-U.S. citizens must submit special paperwork by March 31. RISD holds a Pre-College Pre-View in March for students and their families. Details should appear on the RISD Web site in December 2007.

FOR MORE INFORMATION, CONTACT

Pre-College Program
Rhode Island School of Design
Two College Street
Providence, Rhode Island 02903-2787

Phone: 800-364-7473 Ext. 1 (toll-free)
Fax: 401-454-6218
Web site: http://www.risd.edu/precollege.cfm

RUMSEY HALL SCHOOL

SUMMER SESSION

WASHINGTON DEPOT, CONNECTICUT

TYPE OF PROGRAM: Academic enrichment or review
PARTICIPANTS: Coeducational; boarding, grades 5–9; day, grades 3–9
ENROLLMENT: 75 students
PROGRAM DATES: Five-week program
HEAD OF PROGRAM: Dave Whiting, Director

LOCATION

Situated in the southern foothills of northwestern Connecticut's Berkshire Mountains, Rumsey Hall is 43 miles from Hartford, Connecticut, and 80 miles northeast of New York City. The 147-acre campus is surrounded by beautiful wooded hills and the scenic Bantam River.

BACKGROUND AND PHILOSOPHY

Rumsey Hall School was established in 1900 and is noted for high academic standards and individual attention. Since its inception, the School has retained its original philosophy, "to help each child develop to his or her maximum stature as an individual, as a family member, and as a contributing member of society." Students are constantly exposed to the idea that success comes through the application of steady effort. The Summer Session is an extension of the Rumsey philosophy. Working with a limited enrollment in a relaxed, sensibly structured, and informal atmosphere, experienced Rumsey faculty members provide intensive academic review or give students a head start for the coming year.

PROGRAM OFFERINGS

Normal class size ranges from 8 to 10 students, and individual attention and help are available. Special emphasis is placed on English, mathematics, study skills, and computer skills. Students who need language skills or developmental reading help are given individual attention from trained specialists. English as a second language (ESL) is offered to international students. Rumsey Hall students have access to state-of-the-art personal computers and software. Each classroom is equipped with at least one station, and there are sixteen terminals in the computer lab. All terminals are linked to a schoolwide information system, and students have appropriate access to the Internet. Each student has an e-mail address for easy communication with home and friends.

The close relationship between teachers and students is a special part of boarding school. Opportun-ities for support and encouragement are abundant, and renewed self-confidence is often the most outstanding product of a summer at Rumsey. Most students have roommates, and life in a dormitory teaches valuable lessons about getting along with others and being part of a community. All meals are family-style, with faculty members and their families in attendance.

Report cards are mailed at midterm and at the end of the term. Written reports, which include grades for each subject and teacher comments regarding academic and social progress, are provided at the end of the session. Each student is discussed individually at weekly faculty meetings. Parental input is encouraged.

ENROLLMENT

Students come from a variety of states, countries, and local communities. There are 75 students: 25 boarding boys, 25 boarding girls, and 25 day students.

DAILY SCHEDULE

7:45	Wake up
8:00– 8:30	Breakfast
8:45–10:30	Classes
10:30–11:00	Recess and snack
11:00– 1:10	Classes
1:15	Lunch
2:00– 4:30	Activities/recreation
5:00– 6:00	Reading period
6:00	Dinner
7:00– 8:00	Study hall
8:00– 9:30	Free time
9:30–10:00	Lights out

EXTRA OPPORTUNITIES AND ACTIVITIES

Great emphasis is placed on providing a variety of recreational and enrichment activities to ensure a balanced, happy, and productive Summer Session. Every afternoon, students select from a variety of activities, such as swimming, hiking, tennis, fishing, horseback riding, baseball, soccer, lacrosse, and basketball. Occasional off-campus school trips are planned to museums, concerts, amusement parks, and sporting events. A considerable effort is made to cultivate students' interests and to expose them to new experiences.

Weekends begin on Friday after classes. Livery service to and from train stations, bus depots, and airports is easily arranged if enough notice is given to the School office. Students are free to leave with parental permission but must return by 7 p.m. Sunday evening. For students who choose to remain on

campus, there is a range of on- and off-campus activities available with close faculty supervision at all times. Students may attend church service in Washington and nearby towns.

FACILITIES

Buildings include a new art room, music room, and science lab. Traditional-style classrooms, a library, and a study hall encompass the academic setting. Boys' and girls' dorms allow for both single and double rooms. Two beautiful on-campus ponds supply fishing and nature activities. There are three newly renovated indoor tennis courts, a large gym for basketball and volleyball, and a spacious dining hall that allows for family-style meals.

STAFF

Both full- and part-time staff members make up the Rumsey Hall Summer Session faculty. The faculty members instruct classes, supervise afternoon activities, and are dorm parents for the boarding students. Students live with supportive dorm parents and become a part of their dorm parents' families.

COSTS

Tuition, room, and board totaled $5600 for boarding students, $2000 for day students, and $1300 for half-day students for the 2007 summer session. A deposit of $500 for boarders and $200 for day students is required to secure a space for the summer and is used as a drawing account for student expenses. Any money remaining in the drawing account is returned at the end of the summer session. There is an additional fee of $550 for individual tutoring in language skills, and an additional $850 is required for enrollment in ESL.

FINANCIAL AID

Financial aid is available through the School's financial aid office and is based on need. A copy of the previous year's tax return is required.

TRANSPORTATION

Livery service to and from train stations, bus depots, and airports can be easily arranged with advance notice.

APPLICATION TIMETABLE

Inquiries are welcome at any time of the year, with most families beginning the admissions process in the winter or early spring in anticipation of summer enrollment. Admissions interviews and tours are scheduled throughout the year. Applications are accepted on a rolling basis, and decisions are made within two weeks of receiving the completed application package. Families are asked to respond to an offer of acceptance in a similar time frame due to the limited space available.

FOR MORE INFORMATION, CONTACT

Matthew S. Hoeniger, Director of Admission
Rumsey Hall School
201 Romford Road
Washington Depot, Connecticut 06794

Phone: 860-868-0535
Fax: 860-868-7907
E-mail: admiss@rumseyhall.org

PARTICIPANT/FAMILY COMMENTS

"One of the things I enjoy most about summer life at Rumsey is the range of experiences available to students. We are not watchers, we are doers. The question is not whether we'll participate. The question is which activity we will participate in."

"The faculty and students are very close at Rumsey. That should be a given at any boarding school for children this age, but there is something special about this community that surpasses your expectations."

RUSTIC PATHWAYS

INTERNATIONAL COMMUNITY SERVICE, ADVENTURE TRAVEL, AND FOREIGN LANGUAGE TRAINING

AUSTRALIA, NEW ZEALAND, THE FIJI ISLANDS, THAILAND, COSTA RICA, AFRICA, INDIA, CHINA, VIETNAM, AND THE U. S.

TYPE OF PROGRAM: International community service, adventure travel, and foreign language training

PARTICIPANTS: Middle and high school students, 10–18 years old

ENROLLMENT: Differs from program to program, but generally 14–16 students per program departure date

HEADS OF PROGRAM: David Venning, Chairman; Evan Wells, President

LOCATION

Rustic Pathways serves Australia, New Zealand, the Fiji Islands, Thailand, Costa Rica, Africa, India, China, Vietnam, and the United States. Programs operate in a variety of locations within each country. Whatever types of programs students are looking to participate in, whether it be community service in the rainforests of Costa Rica, Thailand, or the Fiji Islands; working with wildlife in Australia, Thailand, and Costa Rica; summiting Mount Kilimanjaro or crossing the Himalayas in India; immersing themselves in the Spanish or Chinese language; or skiing the slopes of New Zealand, Rustic Pathways has a program to take them there.

BACKGROUND AND PHILOSOPHY

Rustic Pathways is an international travel organization with year-round operations in many of the countries it serves. Focused in safe, clean, friendly, and culturally diverse destinations, its programs offer students an array of overseas travel opportunities. Rustic Pathways' combination of international program options allows students to easily custom design a summer adventure that suits their needs.

Rustic Pathways also offers interesting and economical customized excursions for families, teacher-led groups, and special interest groups throughout the year.

Rustic Pathways began operations twenty-four years ago. The Chairman, David Venning, initially set the tone for the company by taking small groups of high school students into the Australian outback via four-wheel-drive vehicles. Over the years, the list of destinations and programs has expanded, and the personal attention and emphasis on safety, learning, and growing has continued.

As the company has grown throughout the years, so have its myriad of exotic destinations. David still leads trips himself, but he now has a fantastic team of well-traveled, highly respected, intelligent individuals who continue to promote the ideals of Rustic Pathways through their own program leadership. Adventure travel is still an integral part of the company's offerings, but community service and foreign language instruction have taken on a vital role within the company's global operations.

Rustic Pathways offers exciting and worthwhile community service projects that help students explore and understand the local flavor and unique lifestyles of remote village communities in several of the countries it serves. Rustic Pathways also proudly offers students the opportunity to immerse themselves in foreign language programs in both Costa Rica and China. Among other objectives, these community service, language, and adventure programs seek to bridge cultural gaps by allowing students to donate time, energy, and resources to helping others while experiencing life in a different cultural environment.

PROGRAM OFFERINGS

More than forty diverse, unique programs make up the list of choices for students and parents interested in traveling with Rustic Pathways. Each program generally has several departure dates through-

out the summer, and programs are designed to easily interconnect, allowing a student to customize the summer of their dreams.

Australia Students escape to the Land Down Under to participate in Rustic Pathway's Community Service School. This program is designed for students that really want to make a difference through learning how various service initiatives can positively impact the areas in which they are implemented. In addition to the Community Service School, students can dive into community service head first with the Sydney Reef and Rainforest Program, which takes them from the opera house of Sydney to the tip of the Daintree Rainforest, with a stop on the Great Barrier Reef to snorkel and study dwarf minke whales with professional marine biologists.

New Zealand Rustic Pathways offers remarkable ski and snowboard programs as well as their North Island Adventure, a high-adrenaline, action-packed adventure program that takes students from one extreme to the next as they raft, rappel, snorkel, skydive, and zorb their way through wild New Zealand.

The Fiji Islands The Fiji Islands are the home of some of the most hospitable and friendly people on the planet, and they welcome Rustic Pathways with open arms into their villages and their hearts. In this breathtaking island nation, students can take part in specialized service programs from marine conservation to medical assistance while living at Rustic Pathways' Eco-Lodge Base House. They can also be adopted by a Fijian mother and father, teach in the local schools, and get involved in ongoing construction and maintenance projects while being rewarded with well-earned community service hours. Participants in the Big Fiji Explorer Program can also sail through the Yasawa Islands, swim beside thundering waterfalls, and snorkel over colorful coral reefs. Students go for the service, the culture, and the friendships, and stay for the sunshine, clear skies, pristine waters, and smiling faces.

Thailand Sawat-de Krup, and welcome to the land of smiles. Rustic Pathways has an enormous operation in Thailand, with their Ricefields' Base House at its heart. The Ricefields' Base House is the hub for unbelievable community service opportunities, like Meals on Flip Flops, preparing and delivering nutritional Thai meals to the elderly and disadvantaged, and Coloring Books and Kiddies, working alongside teachers and village parents in the local co-op kindergarten. There is also the Come With Nothing, Go Home Rich Program, a dramatic, advanced-service project in three remote villages, where students give from their hearts and get an extraordinary experience in return. For more adventure, these wonderful service projects can be combined with any Rustic Pathways Chairman's Programs, such as Photography or the Wonders and Riches of Asia, as well as the two newest adventure programs: Island Hopping and Diving (exploring the southern jewels of Thailand through SCUBA diving, rock climbing, and sea kayaking) and Hill

Tribe Trekking Adventure (a rare opportunity to trek deep into the heart of Thailand's northern jungles and remote villages).

Costa Rica For those who like the sounds of monkeys chattering in the rainforest, white water rushing down a river, and scarlet macaws singing overhead, Costa Rica is the place to visit. Students can choose from language immersion, community service, and all-out-adventure programs. Students can start the summer by taking Spanish classes in the Spanish Language Immersion Program and then test their new language skills at a gratifying service project, like the Maleku Tribe Immersion and Service Program, or they can help on one of the many projects around Rustic Pathways' Volcanoes and Rainforests Community Service Base located near the incredible Arenal Volcano. After their work is done, they can reward themselves with an extraordinary adventure program, like the Costa Rica Adventurer or Natural Wonders Extreme. Or they can chill out and catch some waves at Rustic Pathways' world-famous surf house. They should bring their flip flops and a positive attitude to Costa Rica, where the motto is Pura Vida.

Africa Can Kili be conquered? Participants find out on this amazing journey to the "rooftop of Africa." Grabbing backpacks and hiking boots, they join Rustic Pathways in Tanzania to ascend the highest peak on the continent and one of the most famous mountains on the planet. They use the longest, least-technical route, the Marangu, to increase their chances of reaching the summit of the tallest freestanding volcano in the world. Rustic Pathways' Service and Safari Program offers the opportunity to work on local environmental and community-based projects with villages nestled between the Serengeti and Ngorongoro Crater National Parks and to see the majestic African wildlife on a three-day safari. Students get in-depth exposure to Tanzanian culture and way of life while providing meaningful community service.

India Students step out of reality and into the clouds at McLeod Gange. Nestled at the base of the Himalaya Mountains, McLeod Gange is a peaceful and happy place, where prayer flags wave and cows walk down the street as though they have somewhere to be. Participants take some time to teach in the elementary school, learn Tibetan cooking techniques, and live with a Tibetan family to discover their way of life. To see another side of this massive subcontinent, they travel through mountains and valleys and rivers and streams on the Himalayan Traveler or the Buddhist Caravan Programs. On these explorations of magical lands, students follow their guide through monasteries, temples, and mountain passages as they experience this one-of-a-kind land.

Vietnam From the Northern Highlands to the Southern Delta, Rustic Pathways takes participants on a breathtaking, nonstop journey highlighting the very best this stunning country has to offer. Students check out some of the country's rich history by exploring places like Ha Long Bay, the northern city of Hanoi, the ancient capitol of Hue, the buzzing metropolis of Saigon, and the Mekong Delta. Whether one's interests are in learning the past, discovering the present, or seeing the future of Vietnam, this program offers the chance to do it all.

China The newest additions to Rustic Pathways' global operations explore the highlights and wonders of vast and magnificent China or immerse students in the language of Mandarin in the mountains of Yunnan Province. Participants explore the hidden secrets of the cities and villages of China on the Wonders of China Program as they crisscross the country on an unforgettable journey that open their eyes to the beauty and mystery of this great country. The language immersion program, set in the breathtaking village of Dali, is the top choice for students looking to develop their Mandarin through hands-on cultural immersion and intensive language instruction through the highly respected Dali University— one of the most prestigious Chinese language training centers in the whole country

U.S.A. Rustic Pathways' Spring Break Service Project in New Orleans and its New Orleans Summer Rebuilding Program enable students to help victims of Hurricane Katrina. Through a partnership with Habitat for Humanity, students help to build a musicians' village in a neighborhood that was destroyed by the storm. Eighty brand new homes and a musical center are being built, and students assist in every phase of the construction process. They can also take in the sights and sounds of New Orleans on a tour of the French Quarter or cruise though a swamp on an airboat and feast on Creole cuisine.

ENROLLMENT

Rustic Pathways draws students from nearly all fifty states as well as from many countries around the world, creating groups that learn from each other while growing together during their international experiences. Rustic Pathways summer programs are designed for positive, level-headed students with a keen interest in experiential learning and international travel.

FACILITIES

Because of the diverse nature of Rustic Pathways' programs, facilities differ considerably from program to program and country to country. Students find themselves sleeping in a thatched hut in a remote village in Asia, aboard a large sailing boat in the south Pacific, camping beneath the Southern Cross in the middle of the Australian Outback, or tucked in the warm bed of a luxurious five-star hotel. To provide culturally unique and diverse travel experiences, Rustic Pathways utilizes local facilities and resources. Program participants regularly have the opportunity to avail themselves of local customs, foods, and facilities as they travel.

STAFF

Rustic Pathways is a rich and diverse company full of sincere, committed professionals with wide-ranging experience in their various fields. Taken together, team members speak more than twenty languages, have traveled across more than 130 countries, and have led countless groups of students and adult clients across some of the world's most interesting, exotic places. In terms of diversity, the full-time staff includes international sportsmen and sportswomen, champion snowboarders, accomplished musicians, teachers, authors, published songwriters, competitive surfers, and former Buddhist monks.

MEDICAL CARE

Student safety is a top priority for Rustic Pathways. Its staff commonly includes Wilderness First Responders, EMTs, Wilderness EMTs, Surf Life Guards, staff with St. John's Certificates, and staff with Red Cross First Aid and CPR training. Rustic Pathways periodically runs staff CPR courses, First Aid training, First Aid refresher courses, and Wilderness First Responder courses.

APPLICATION TIMETABLE

Admission to Rustic Pathways programs is by application only. Students and their parents must file an application through Rustic Pathways' Web site or by mail. Applications are accepted as early as September and are accepted up to two weeks prior to a scheduled trip departure if there is space available on the requested program. Applications are processed on a first-come, first-served basis. There is a $100 application fee for each participant ($200 after April 15), which is returned to students who are not accepted into the program. There is no application fee for returning students. Programs are popular, and participants are encouraged to apply as early as possible to ensure a departure date that suits their summer schedule.

Between January and April, Rustic Pathways staffing teams tour the United States, visiting schools, summer camp fairs, and interested parents and students. Staff members enjoy and appreciate the opportunity to meet with parents and prospective students during this time. Students should contact the Rustic Pathways Home Office to schedule a home visit while staff members are in their area.

FOR MORE INFORMATION, CONTACT

Rustic Pathways
P.O. Box 1150
Willoughby, Ohio 44096
Phone: 440-975-9691
        800-321-4353 (toll-free)
Fax: 440-975-9694
E-mail: rustic@rusticpathways.com
Web site: http://www.rusticpathways.com

SAINT THOMAS MORE SCHOOL

SUMMER ACADEMIC CAMP

OAKDALE, CONNECTICUT

TYPE OF PROGRAM: Summer academic camp
PARTICIPANTS: Boys, grades 7–12
ENROLLMENT: 100
PROGRAM DATES: Five-week session, July 1 to August 3
HEAD OF PROGRAM: Bridget Autencio

LOCATION
Saint Thomas More School is located in Oakdale, Connecticut, which is midway between Boston and New York, about 10 miles north of the Long Island Sound. The 100-acre campus is situated along 4,000 feet of waterfront on Gardner Lake, the largest lake in eastern Connecticut.

BACKGROUND AND PHILOSOPHY
Saint Thomas More School was founded in 1962 by Headmaster James F. Hanrahan to assist the young person with no social, emotional, or behavioral problems who is not living up to his academic potential. The Saint Thomas More School way of life is based on the belief that young people need structure, order, clear expectations, close personal attention, and consequences that are appropriate to their behavior.

Boys attend the summer program for a combination of academics and summer fun. Some students come for make-up credit and some for enrichment; international students come to improve their English. It is possible for each student's goals to be attained.

The average class size in the summer is 6. Students are given close personal attention by dedicated teachers who are drawn from the regular School faculty.

PROGRAM OFFERINGS
There are three class periods from 8:25 a.m. to 12:05 p.m., Monday through Saturday. Students take three courses.

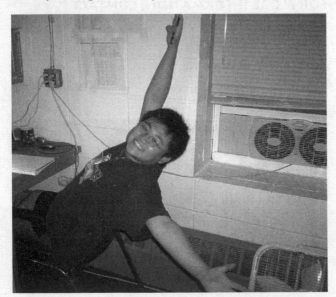

Courses include English I, II, and III; world history; U.S. history; arithmetic; prealgebra; algebra I and II; geometry; general science; physical science; biology; chemistry; Spanish I and II; computer science; art; reading I and II; ESL reading and writing I and II; SAT preparation; and TOEFL iBT preparation.

ENROLLMENT
About 100 boys attend the five-week session. The program is open to boys entering grades 7–12. Students come from many states and from all over the world.

DAILY SCHEDULE
All students attend classes from 8:25 a.m. to 12:05 p.m. from Monday through Saturday. From lunch until 7 p.m., the School transforms into a summer camp. After lunch, there is a structured activity period, during which campers play in an organized intramural program. This is followed by a period in which the boys can choose their own recreation. Options include, but are not limited to, tennis, swimming, boating, basketball, and weight lifting. On rainy days, the indoor pool is available. After dinner, there is a mail call, then free time until study hall begins at 7:15 p.m. At that time, all students return to their rooms for a 2½-hour, teacher-supervised study period. At 10:30 p.m., lights go out.

EXTRA OPPORTUNITIES AND ACTIVITIES
There are eleven field trips over the five weeks. Every Wednesday, after lunch, campers go by bus to one of the nearby attractions, including museums, beaches, roller-skating arenas, and the Mystic Aquarium. On Sunday, there are full-day trips to amusement parks, ocean beaches, Mystic Seaport, and the Boston Museum of Science. Also, there is a trip every Saturday night, usually to a movie theater.

FACILITIES
The summer program has the use of all the facilities at Saint Thomas More School. For academic use, this includes three classroom buildings, science laboratories, a language laboratory, a computer room, and a library. For housing, boys live 1 or 2 to a room in three modern dormitories. Teachers live in the boys' dorms to monitor and supervise their lives. All dorms are carpeted and oak-paneled. For athletics, a full-size gymnasium includes a basketball court and a large, twenty-station weight room equipped with cardiovascular machines and free weights. The student recreation area includes pool, Ping-Pong, and a TV room. The School's 100 acres include 4,000 feet of waterfront on Gardner Lake. The boathouse holds numerous canoes, sailboats, windsurfers, paddle boats, and rowboats for recreational use. Many campers enjoy the high-quality fishing in the lake, which is stocked with game fish. Other outdoor facilities include a running track, two soccer fields, two baseball fields, a lacrosse practice field, four outdoor tennis courts, and six outdoor basketball courts.

STAFF
The staff is drawn from the regular School faculty. Every teacher has a minimum of a bachelor's degree; many have

their master's. With 15 teachers for 100 student campers, there is a great amount of close personal attention for each student.

MEDICAL CARE

A nurse is a member of the staff and is available for regular office hours from Monday to Saturday. In addition, a second nurse is on call for health-related needs. The School physician is on call as needed. There is a local ambulance service 5 minutes away, and a modern hospital is 12 miles from the campus.

Students are required to have had a recent physical examination and to have medical insurance.

RELIGIOUS LIFE

Saint Thomas More School is Catholic in philosophy. All students attend mass once a week.

COSTS

Tuition, room, and board cost for the five-week session in 2007 totaled $5495 for domestic campers and $5995 for international campers. This cost also covered books, fees, laundry, and trips. Extra costs include travel to and from the camp and a weekly spending allowance of $20 per week.

TRANSPORTATION

The campus is approximately midway between Boston and New York, about 10 miles north of New London, and less than 10 minutes from Exit 80 off I-395 in Norwich. Students traveling from great distances can fly into Bradley (Hartford-Springfield) Airport or JFK International Airport.

Arrangements for a driver service to pick up a camper at an airport can be made through the School. The School can also arrange for campers to be escorted back to the airport for return flights at the end of the program.

APPLICATION TIMETABLE

Applications are accepted until the session is full. To ensure the availability of courses, early application is encouraged. Interviews and campus tours can be arranged throughout the year. The application fee is $50 for domestic campers and $75

for international campers. An admission decision is made within one week of the School's receiving the required forms and application.

FOR MORE INFORMATION, CONTACT

Timothy Riordan
Office of Admissions
Saint Thomas More School
45 Cottage Road
Oakdale, Connecticut 06370

Phone: 860-823-3861
Fax: 860-823-3863
E-mail: triordan@stmct.org
Web site: http://stmct.org

PARTICIPANT/FAMILY COMMENTS

"Colin has already asked me if he can come back next year. How can a parent say 'No' to a child who wants to go to summer school?"

"It was more fun than I expected, and it felt good to finally start getting good grades."

ST. TIMOTHY'S SCHOOL

▼▲▼▲▼▲▼▲▼▲▼▲▼▲▼▲▼▲▼▲▼▲▼▲▼▲▼

SUMMER PROGRAMS

STEVENSON, MARYLAND

TYPE OF PROGRAM: Leadership training and political education; English as a second language (ESL) with American culture
PARTICIPANTS: Coeducational, ages 13–18
PROGRAM DATES: July 1 to July 28, 2008
HEAD OF PROGRAM: Anne Esposito, Business Manager

LOCATION
St. Timothy's School is located in Stevenson, Maryland. Its large rural campus provides students with a beautiful and safe environment that is ideally located near a number of major cities. The School is approximately 20 minutes by car from downtown Baltimore; 45 minutes from Washington, D.C.; 1½ hours from Philadelphia; and 3 hours from New York City. The closest airport, Baltimore/Washington International (BWI), is about a 20-minute drive from the campus.

BACKGROUND AND PHILOSOPHY
The Summer Programs at St. Timothy's School provide an exciting and stimulating experience in a fun environment. Students from around the country and the globe come to the campus to learn, experience new ideas and places, develop strong friendships, and grow as individuals. The School's programs, committed faculty members, campus resources, unique location, and student body combine to create one of the best summer programs available today.

St. Timothy's academic sessions are open to students entering grades 8 through 11. The average class size ranges from 5 to 15, with a student-teacher ratio of 7:1. These small classes offer individual attention and allow the School to develop a tight-knit community where each student's intellectual curiosity is kindled and new ideas are embraced. Students divide their time between classroom instruction and field trips, including the Smithsonian, the United Nations, and meetings with acclaimed authors.

Afternoons and weekends are a time for a wide variety of athletic, recreational, and cultural activities. The residential life staff plans a variety of outings to appeal to students, including soccer, basketball, Ultimate Frisbee, canoeing, ceramics, theme park visits, and theatrical performances. St. Timothy's goal is to offer programs and activities that enhance and enrich every student's summer experience.

PROGRAM OFFERINGS
International Leadership Program The International Leadership Program exposes students to many issues confronting the world today while helping them to strengthen their leadership skills. Students spend four weeks learning about international relations, the U.S. government, public policy, and various global challenges. Students go behind the scenes to learn how different governmental and nongovernmental organizations work; meet with policy experts, political leaders, and historians to discuss global problems; and eventually develop their own plans about new ways to address these challenges. Students also work to develop their own leadership skills, including communication and public speaking, conflict resolution, team building, group dynamics, and management techniques. The program is intensive and hands on.

St. Timothy's proximity to Washington, D.C., allows students to regularly visit and meet with foreign policy experts, government leaders, foreign service workers, news correspondents, and other important figures in world politics. Students are involved in simulations, case studies, research, seminar discussions, and

lectures led by both St. Timothy's faculty members and outside experts. Academic sessions run from Monday to Saturday. Sundays are a time for relaxing, recreation, and visits to area attractions.

Intensive English Language Program The Intensive English Language Program is a four-week ESL program stressing the academic skills of reading, writing, and speaking and listening. Students are also involved in an American culture course, which emphasizes an experiential approach to American culture. This intensive program strengthens students' practical English skills, helps them gain an appreciation of U.S. history and culture, and prepares them for the Test of English as a Foreign Language (TOEFL). Students are placed into three instructional groups based on the results of the Secondary Level English Proficiency (SLEP) test and oral interviews. The groups consist of basic proficiency (limited exposure to previous English instruction), intermediate proficiency (good comprehension and grammatical skills), and advanced proficiency (a strong capability with the English language, requiring only polishing in idioms, conversation styles, and formal writing). Students spend time in three different instructional classes five mornings a week. These consist of reading, writing, and speaking and listening. Two afternoons a week and all day on Saturday, students spend their time in the American culture class. Students in American culture spend most of their time learning about American history and culture via field trips to important American sites and cultural touchstones. Three afternoons a week, students are involved in afternoon recreation and athletic programs. Sundays include time for optional shopping trips, excursions to recreational and amusement sites, and other visits that take advantage of the beautiful Maryland countryside.

EXTRA OPPORTUNITIES AND ACTIVITIES

St. Timothy's Summer Programs offer students the chance to be involved in a wide range of social and recreational activities. When students are not in class or on a field trip, they may be playing a recreational soccer game, hiking along the Appalachian Trail, watching a Baltimore Orioles baseball game, or shopping in Georgetown. All of the activities and trips are led by the residential and summer program staff. Unlike other programs, there is no additional cost for these activities. Soccer, basketball, swimming, Frisbee, canoeing, hiking, and weight lifting are just some of the athletic activities students can look forward to during the summer. Students might visit a Six Flags amusement park or Hersheypark, sail on Chesapeake Bay, canoe on the Potomac River, shop, visit Water Country Water Park, play mini golf, attend a theatrical production, or go to the cinema.

FACILITIES

The 145-acre rural campus features twenty-two buildings, including the Hannah More Arts Center, which houses a 350-seat theater and dance studio, and the Art Barn, with facilities for two- and three-dimensional art, photography, graphic design, and ceramics. Fowler House, the main academic building, contains the 22,000-volume Ella R. Watkins Library. Students live in two dorms: Carter House, a stately 1930s mansion, and Heath House, a more contemporary residence, both of which contain faculty apartments, living rooms, study areas, computer labs, and student lounges.

Athletic facilities include six all-weather tennis courts, an outdoor swimming pool, and a state-of-the-art athletic complex with basketball courts, locker rooms, a fitness center, and a training room. The School's extensive riding program is facilitated by indoor and outdoor riding rings, five fenced fields, and a twenty-four-stall barn.

The campus has a gated entrance; after-hours visitors are required to check in before entering.

STAFF

St. Timothy's is proud of the faculty and staff members who work with students in the summer. They are some of the brightest, most talented, and fun people working in schools today. Students always find someone with his or her door open, willing to talk. In addition, each student has an adviser to provide guidance and support throughout the summer. Faculty and staff members are on duty around the clock to make sure that the summer is both fun and safe.

MEDICAL CARE

A nurse is available, and the School is in proximity to Johns Hopkins Medicine as well as an outpatient clinic.

RELIGIOUS LIFE

Churches of various denominations, as well as temples and synagogues, are located within 15 minutes of the campus. Transportation for students who wish to attend services is provided on request.

COSTS

The cost for the International Leadership Program is $4500, which includes all meals, books and materials, local transportation, use of campus facilities, housing, class-related trips, and entertainment fees.

The cost for the Intensive English Language Program is $5000 and includes all meals, books and materials, local transportation, use of campus facilities, housing, class-related trips, and entertainment fees.

TRANSPORTATION

Transportation to and from the campus is provided from Baltimore/Washington International Airport, Baltimore's Penn Station, and the Baltimore Bus Station. Transportation from Reagan International Airport and Dulles Airport may be arranged for an additional fee. More detailed travel information is provided upon enrollment.

APPLICATION TIMETABLE

For the International Leadership Program and Intensive English Language Program, admission is rolling. Students should fill out an application form, including a recommendation from a teacher, a copy of their transcript, and a deposit check of $950 (once the student is enrolled, this deposit is nonrefundable). Space is limited, and students are enrolled on a first-come, first-served basis. Students are required to have medical insurance while enrolled in the Summer Programs. Students may purchase insurance through St. Timothy's or provide proof of their insurance at the time of application. International students are required to purchase insurance coverage through St. Timothy's School for the duration of the camp. The final balance is due no later than May 1.

FOR MORE INFORMATION, CONTACT

Dan Casella
Director of Summer Program
St. Timothy's School
8400 Greenspring Avenue
Stevenson, Maryland 21153

Phone: 410-486-7400 Ext. 3125
Fax: 410-486-1167
E-mail: sttsummerprog@stt.org
Web site: http://www.stt.org

SALEM SPOTLIGHT AT SALEM ACADEMY AND COLLEGE

SUMMER ACADEMIC CAMPS

WINSTON-SALEM, NORTH CAROLINA

TYPE OF PROGRAM: Academic enrichment
PARTICIPANTS: Girls entering grades 8–12
ENROLLMENT: 75 students each session
PROGRAM DATES: Multiple two-week sessions in June, July, and August
HEAD OF PROGRAM: Douglas Murphy, Program Coordinator

LOCATION
Salem Spotlight at Salem Academy and College is located in beautiful Winston-Salem, North Carolina. Spotlight takes full advantage of Salem Academy and College's historic campus as well as the bustling neighboring areas. Located 80 miles northeast of Charlotte, Winston-Salem is one of the most culturally active cities in the nation, and Salem Spotlight students enjoy—and often participate in—many of the special offerings in town. Within a few hours of the campus are mountains for skiing, camping, or hiking; rivers for white-water rafting; and the beautiful beaches of North and South Carolina for sun and fun.

BACKGROUND AND PHILOSOPHY
Salem Academy and College created Spotlight as a premier summer academic enrichment program for young women, a natural extension of its rich heritage and institutional commitment dating back 233 years. Salem Academy and College, which was founded in 1772 in Winston-Salem, North Carolina, is the oldest girls' school in continuous operation in the nation and shares an exquisite, historic 64-acre campus with Salem College, a liberal arts college for women. Spotlight is an opportunity for bright, intellectually curious young women from around the country to live and learn together in a place where extraordinary moments in ordinary days become treasured memories.

PROGRAM OFFERINGS
Forensic Science In this program, students explore one of the fastest-growing and most exciting fields in science. From popular TV shows to Academy Award–winning movies, criminal investigations have become a national obsession. This course is an introduction to crime-scene investigation and the techniques and tools that are critical to analysis, operation, and gathering of evidence. The course re-creates the history of forensics, and students learn through case studies, fingerprinting, and the incredible variety of other tools and technology available to criminologists and investigators. At the conclusion of each course, students get to tackle a mock crime scene, collect evidence, link clues, and solve the mystery.

Writer's Workshop Writing skills are essential to success in learning environments such as Salem Academy and College. By honing and improving her written voice, a student can enhance her ability to communicate with the world and to change it. The workshop focuses on mechanics, fiction, journalism, blogging, poetry, and journaling. This program is a comprehensive education in the craft of writing, and it outlines the lessons students need in order to be good writers. With careful attention to the development of each student, the Writer's Workshop can improve the quality of writing for girls of all ages and skill levels.

Fine Arts Regardless of a student's skill level when she arrives, Salem Spotlight staff members challenge her abilities to excel. The instructors understand that many fine arts students already have a favorite medium or style. Students in a chosen area of study can continue to develop those skills—in addition to participating in the other art modules—while identifying new talents and interests and broadening their artistic horizons. The course includes photography, painting, drawing, mixed media, collage, and more. Each session concludes with a student-run gallery exhibition showing the best of each girl's work.

Journalism Spotlight's journalism course trains girls in a wide range of analytic thinking and writing skills. Students leave this course equipped with the tools needed for successful journalism—tools that are also of great benefit in essay and nonfiction writing. Students can apply abilities gained in this class to anything from college application essays to blog entries; well-trained writers are increasingly in demand and appreciated in today's rapidly growing information society. Students learn the techniques of interviewing and reporting though fun, real-world projects. Part of the excitement of journalism is its variety of field assignments; students have many opportunities to get out of the classroom and discover stories for themselves. Instructors also provide a solid background in basic journalistic practices, with a focus on the unique structures of journalistic essays and house styles, as well as techniques used in specific subject fields such as feature, sports, and editorial writing.

Spanish Language and Culture Most students who are learning Spanish read books, work on grammar, and study vocabulary; however, few get the chance to immerse themselves in the culture, food, customs, or vernacular that make the language unique. Salem Spotlight's Spanish program is designed to pick up where a student's traditional Spanish class ends. Rote memorization can ultimately drive students away from foreign-language study; the goal of this program is to immerse students in the Spanish language and culture. Personal interviews with each student determine the level of individualized study and expectations for their two weeks. In each session, Spanish students can look forward to a special evening out with their friends and teacher hosted by an authentic Spanish restaurant, and there are additional academic trips to important Spanish-speaking locations.

Environmental Studies Environmental science introduces students to the study of the interactions among the physical, chemical, and biological components of the environment, with a special focus on the pressing current issues of global warming, the food system, and environmental degradation. This interdisciplinary field draws upon knowledge from areas such as economics, ethics, and social sciences; instructors take advantage of its breadth in order to offer girls avenues into a number of disciplines, making the class much more than a straightforward science course. The course's flexibility allows girls who are interested in specific areas, such as biodiversity, renewable energy, or hydrogen technologies, to investigate them deeply. On field trips around Winston-Salem to fields, streams, and other natural areas, students explore a variety of interrelated topics in environmental policy, economics, and ethics and come to see

the hidden mechanisms that affect the Earth. Innovative, interesting lab work supplements the students' field studies.

Business and Leadership A complicated and necessary responsibility of citizens involves identifying a need for change, participating in creating that change, and leading one's community to the successful expression thereof. It takes enormous courage to accept the responsibility of leadership. This course explores various dimensions of business and leadership, including the intersection of the pragmatic, such as economics, with the personal. It also examines major themes and concepts in business, such as marketing strategies and long-term financial stability. The group creates a mock business and then devises a cohesive business plan for the company. In addition, the course focuses on the nature of leadership through self-expression and personal growth.

Performing Arts Spotlight's Performing Arts program has something for everyone—from students who are newly interested in acting to those who are in every school play and are looking to improve their skills. Students can learn the most valuable "tricks of the trade," including how to get up on stage for the first time without freezing. Tips for quickly memorizing lines and improving improvisational skills for those unforeseeable mid-play goofs are also favorite topics. Through one-on-one work with her teacher and collaborating with new friends, each student develops her skills from a platform of three critical performing arts building blocks: acting, improvisation, and dramatic acting. Spotlight's ideal location allows participants to visit some of the city's top performing arts groups, including the Winston-Salem Symphony, the Wachovia Little Symphony, the Piedmont Opera Theatre, the Little Theatre, and the Piedmont Chamber Singers.

Psychology This course is perfect for students who are fascinated by or curious about the inner workings of the mind. It begins with the themes central to the study of psychology. It then delves deeper into two of the most fascinating areas of study: social psychology and abnormal psychology. The curriculum is designed to give students broad exposure to the many areas of study in psychology, and course work is pursued both in the classroom and in real-world settings. The focus on social psychology uses both the classroom and unique social experiments to explore this topic: how will other members of the campus community react to various staged situations—and why?

DAILY SCHEDULE
Though actual schedules may vary, the following is a typical schedule for program participants.

```
7:45–8:45 . . . Breakfast
9:00–10:15 . . . Classroom Session I
10:15–10:30 . . . Morning break
10:30–11:45 . . . Classroom Session II
12:00–1:00 . . . Lunch
1:15–3:15 . . . Afternoon activities
3:30–4:45 . . . Classroom session III
5:00–6:00 . . . Dinner
6:15–7:30 . . . Evening Seminar
8:00–10:30 . . . Movies, games, free time
11:00 . . . Students in rooms (most nights)
```

EXTRA OPPORTUNITIES AND ACTIVITIES
Every year, all Salem Spotlight students go on two fun and exciting field trips. Staff members are always working on new and stimu-

lating field trips for Salem Spotlight in order to create the most rewarding excursions possible. This year, plans include trips to an amusement park and a concert or a day trip to one of the great neighboring areas.

Course-specific off-campus field trips are organized to make the most of North Carolina and its surrounding attractions. Living History students spend time at Old Salem, while the young entrepreneurs from Business and Leadership head straight to Charlotte for a meeting with top executives at Wachovia Corporation's world headquarters.

FACILITIES
All girls live in the newly remodeled McMichael Residence Hall, which adjoins Salem Academy's housing. It features modern suite-style rooms and common study and social lounges. Students are supervised by teachers who live in the dorms with the students.

STAFF
The heart and soul of Spotlight is its incredible staff. Outgoing and intelligent, the teachers are both great role models and caring, compassionate mentors. They are present at all times, live in the dorms with the students, and encourage every girl to make friends, have fun, and learn. The maximum student-teacher ratio is 8:1, ensuring each student receives the most of her time spent at Spotlight.

MEDICAL CARE
Medical care is available 24 hours a day at nearby hospital facilities. All participants must submit comprehensive medical forms and proof of insurance.

COSTS
The tuition for each two-week session is $2395. This includes all instruction, instructional materials, breakfast, lunch, and dinner each day; a dorm room with linens; self-service laundry facilities; all sports and recreational activities; transportation for sponsored trips; admission tickets to excursion destinations; and total 24-hour supervision for the duration of each camp session. In addition, there is a $100 field-trip account that allocates spending money to each student for field trips.

FINANCIAL AID
No financial aid is available at this time.

TRANSPORTATION
Airport pick-up and drop-off are available from Greensboro Airport (GSO) for an additional fee.

APPLICATION TIMETABLE
Inquiries are welcome at any time. Applications are accepted until June 1. After June 1, acceptance to the program is based on availability, and applications must include a late fee of $100.

FOR MORE INFORMATION, CONTACT
Salem Spotlight
Salem Academy and College
P.O. Box 10578
Winston-Salem, North Carolina 27108-0578

Phone: 800-883-1753 (toll-free)
E-mail: spotlight@salem.edu
Web site: http://spotlight.salem.edu

SALISBURY SUMMER SCHOOL

▼▲▼▲▼▲▼▲▼▲▼▲▼▲▼▲▼▲▼▲▼▲▼▲▼▲▼▲▼▲▼

ACADEMIC ENRICHMENT PROGRAM

SALISBURY, CONNECTICUT

TYPE OF PROGRAM: Study skills development
PARTICIPANTS: Coeducational, ages 13–18
ENROLLMENT: 108
PROGRAM DATES: June 28 to August 2, 2008
HEAD OF PROGRAM: Ralph J. Menconi, Director

LOCATION

Salisbury School is set on a hilltop surrounded by more than 600 acres of extensive woodlands, fields, streams, and lakefront in the foothills of the Berkshire Mountains. The campus is bordered by the Appalachian Trail to the west, and the Twin Lakes to the north. While seemingly rural, Salisbury is only an hour to Hartford, 2 hours to New York City, and 3 hours to Boston.

BACKGROUND AND PHILOSOPHY

Founded in 1946 as a unique program for students in need of academic assistance, the Salisbury Summer School of Reading and English continues to be recognized by educational consultants and educators from the United States and abroad as the finest resource for helping students whose lack of motivation, language skills, and/or self-confidence have prevented them from achieving their full potential.

The Salisbury Summer School of Reading and English provides the comfortable environment needed to learn the most important lesson in all of schooling: how to learn. In a nongraded curriculum, the teachers at Salisbury Summer School are trained to make young people become better students or true students for the first time. Skills training focuses on the study of English through reading, writing, vocabulary development, time management, and note-taking, with an optional algebra review or creative writing course. The skills learned also transfer easily to disciplines other than English and math. Course credits for English and math are available by prior arrangement with the Director.

PROGRAM OFFERINGS

While many summer schools offer reading and study skills courses, only Salisbury immerses students in a curriculum and academic environment structured exclusively to promote better organization and improved reading and writing. Minimizing distractions and maximizing student-teacher contact (a ratio of 4:1), Salisbury employs experienced teachers who also serve as dorm monitors and academic advisers. Students become part of a five-week summer boarding school in which teachers get to know students in all facets of their lives.

All students are required to take the three core courses: reading and study skills, composition, and word skills (outlined below). In addition, students may choose from electives in creative writing or mathematics review. Math offerings cover prealgebra, algebra 1 and 2, with some geometry. Students in the Creative Writing classes write poems, short stories, and journals for peer review and discussion under the guidance of faculty members who are trained in these areas. Classes in verbal areas and math include SAT preparation as part of the curriculum.

Reading and Study Skills The core of the Summer School program, the skills course integrates proven reading comprehension techniques and study methods that are designed to help students work more accurately and efficiently in their winter school courses. All students are trained to use a plan book to take assignments, to maintain an organized notebook, and to use a study schedule to plan their time. Outlining provides essential training for the development of skills of logic, discrimination, and orderly thought. Since reading must have lasting value, strategies to reinforce recall and improve memory are presented together with a variety of study systems, in order to synthesize the total study process. The double period course also emphasizes application of the various comprehension techniques. Sentences, paragraphs, and longer articles are analyzed for their underlying structure. Common paragraph patterns such as cause-and-effect, comparisons, examples, and analysis are studied. Other exercises seek to develop discrimination between main ideas and supporting details. The course concludes with how to prepare for and take examinations. Developmental reading classes are given three days per week to all students with the aim of significantly improving each student's reading rate and comprehension. Reading outside the curriculum is also required of each student, using books of his or her own selection.

Composition This class seeks to give students the writing skills necessary to perform well on the kinds of academic essays and tests they encounter during the school year. Writing practice is given every day, with assignments structured along the lines of English papers, history essays, or even science laboratory reports. Other composition assignments include book reports or book reviews, dramatic criticism, and, for older students, timed writings required for the SAT. Peer evaluation, in the form of oral readings, forms part of each class and most papers are revised and rewritten to correct errors. This class also stresses grammatical accuracy and proofreading skills. In coordination with the study skills class, composition class reinforces note taking, outlining, and other organizational skills. Class texts include a book of writing models, a grammar exercise workbook, and other basic writing sourcebooks. Every composition class has 2 instructors and meets for two periods every day.

Word Skills Diagnostic tests determine the placement of each student in different sections of this course, each of which includes varying amounts of vocabulary, spelling, and word analysis, depending on individual needs. In word analysis, the student examines the structure of language from a phonetic and structural viewpoint; those in need of more remedial instruction focus on decoding skills. In spelling, rules and their exceptions are presented in a systematic manner and commonly misspelled words are routinely examined. Vocabulary study is based upon the study of affixes, roots, word families, word histories, and words in context. Emphasis is placed not only on the acquisition of a larger vocabulary over the summer, but also on the fostering of the student's curiosity about words and their definitions. Word Skills classes also help prepare students for the SAT.

ENROLLMENT
Most students come from across the U.S., with others coming from such countries as Argentina, China, Germany, Korea, Mexico, Spain, and Turkey.

DAILY SCHEDULE

8:00– 8:30	Breakfast
8:45–12:55	Classes (each class is 35 minutes in length with a midmorning break)
1:00	Lunch
1:30– 2:30	Adviser/advisee conferences, reading time, or town trips
3:00– 4:00	Recreational sports and activities program
4:00– 5:00	Free time
5:00	Quiet reading and study period
6:00	Dinner, followed by free time
7:30– 9:00	Study period
9:00– 9:45	Free time
10:00–11:00	Quiet time in dormitories

EXTRA OPPORTUNITIES AND ACTIVITIES
As part of the boarding school experience, the school offers a number of options for the afternoon portion of the day. A shopping trip to town is offered two afternoons each week. On Mondays, Wednesdays, and Fridays, every student is required to attend an athletic or activities commitment from 3 to 4 p.m. During weekends, activities include games, swimming, theater trips, movies, and shopping trips. Also on weekends, Salisbury School offers cycling and hiking trips and waterfront activities at a nearby lake and waterfalls.

FACILITIES
All classes are held in the new, 40,000-square-foot Humanities Center that is located on campus. The new building is a state-of-the-art facility, which also houses the library and computer lab. Students are separated into six dorms by age

and gender. Access to numerous indoor and outdoor athletic facilities contributes to a diverse afternoon schedule.

STAFF
Many teachers have come long distances to teach at Salisbury, and most of them return for many summers, showing their confidence in the school's program. The faculty of Salisbury Summer School is a diverse group of professional educators who come from both public and private schools. Many are department chairs or division heads at other schools. In recent years, Salisbury School, Suffield Academy, Loomis Chaffee School, and the Gunnery in Connecticut have been represented, as have Tampa Preparatory School in Florida, the Ojai Valley School in California, the Newman School in New Orleans, and the Langley School in Virginia. Salisbury has also drawn teachers from the American School in London; the Maret School in Washington, D.C.; and Robert Moses Junior High School in New York. A small number of teaching interns who plan careers in education have the opportunity to work with experienced educators at Salisbury Summer School.

MEDICAL CARE
Medical services are available to all students on a 24-hour basis and under the supervision of an RN and the school physician. Sharon Hospital, located in Sharon, Connecticut, is a well-equipped community hospital with a full complement of board-certified specialists. Students are referred to the emergency room or to a medical specialist when necessary. Students may come to the school's health Center for evaluation and treatment of illness and injuries, as well as for dispensing of medications.

COSTS
Tuition for the 2007 program was $6750, which included all textbooks, classroom supplies, entertainment fees, and town trip expenses. Room and board are included in the tuition fee. A nonrefundable tuition deposit of $750, payable upon acceptance, is required. The balance of the tuition is due before June 15. Charges for medical needs and transportation, if any, are billed separately.

FINANCIAL AID
Financial aid from the Harold Corbin Summer School Scholarship Fund is available on a limited basis. Inquiries should be addressed to the Summer School Admissions Office.

APPLICATION TIMETABLE
Applications, accompanied by a $30 application fee ($100 for international students), are accepted on a rolling basis. Interviews and tours are given throughout the school year. Acceptances are also sent out on a rolling basis, usually within two weeks of a completed application, including interview and recommendations.

FOR MORE INFORMATION, CONTACT
Summer School Office
Salisbury Summer School
251 Canaan Road
Salisbury, Connecticut 06068
Phone: 860-435-5700
Web site: http://www.salisburysummerschool.org

SARAH LAWRENCE COLLEGE

SUMMER PROGRAMS FOR HIGH SCHOOL STUDENTS

BRONXVILLE, NEW YORK

TYPE OF PROGRAM: Residential and evening intensive courses in eight fields of study
PARTICIPANTS: High school students entering grades 10, 11, and 12 and graduating seniors
PROGRAM DATES: Six-week courses beginning in late June and three-week courses beginning in July. Other programs offered in fall and spring.
HEAD OF PROGRAM: Liz Irmiter, Director of Special Programs

LOCATION
The College is located in southern Westchester County, bordering the communities of Yonkers and Bronxville, New York, and just 15 miles north of midtown Manhattan. The Sarah Lawrence College campus occupies 41 wooded acres. Ivy-covered, Tudor-style, and contemporary buildings house classrooms, faculty offices, and students.

BACKGROUND AND PHILOSOPHY
The Sarah Lawrence College Programs for High School Students give young people the opportunity to enhance their academic experience and explore their passions in a supportive, noncompetitive environment. Students enjoy individual meetings with their instructors; a distinguishing component of the unique Sarah Lawrence education.

PROGRAM OFFERINGS
Course offerings vary each year, and classes are limited in size so that students can receive individual attention, meeting one-on-one with their instructors. Offerings in 2008 include the following courses:

Sarah Lawrence College & The International Film Institute of New York's Six-Week Summer Filmmaking Intensive (Six-week residential, June 22–August 2) Students gain hands-on experience and instruction in all aspects of filmmaking, focusing on four core elements: writing for the screen, directing, production, and postproduction. Classroom lectures feature hands-on camera work augmented by special guest speakers and behind-the-scenes visits to Manhattan production studios and editing facilities. Classwork concludes with a seminar on the topic of "What's Next," fea-

turing one-on-one career guidance. After students shoot three film exercises focused on different filmmaking techniques, they are ready to write, direct, produce, shoot, and edit their own short videos. They choose the format—narrative, documentary, or experimental—and may choose to stick to a script (with actors, costumes, and a controlled set) or approach their shoot with the spirit of improvisation. They are the director; they call the shots. The final product—to which they own the exclusive rights—is a completed short that is ready for their professional portfolio, graduate school application, or Web distribution. This program is open only to students who are entering their junior or senior years as well as graduating seniors.

Sarah Lawrence College's Summer in the City (Three-week residential, July 13–August 2) Using New York City as the backdrop, students take classes about the history, literature, science, and theater of New York. This exciting new program provides an opportunity to discover the city that 8 million people call home while living just 30 minutes away on the beautiful Sarah Lawrence College campus. Throughout the three weeks, students travel into the city, visiting theaters, neighborhoods, and landmarks that give them a deeper understanding of the subjects they study in history, theater, creative writing, and literature. (The final class descriptions will be available online in March 2008.)

Young Artists Summer Music Intensive (Three-week residential, July 13–August 2) Expanding upon existing skills while exploring new concepts, students are organized into ensembles and assigned a faculty member coach. Students hone their performance skills in daily master classes and a final concert experience. Classes in jazz improvisation, composition, and keyboard skills promote the kind of creative musical thinking necessary for today's musicians. There are also introduction to music theory, aural skills, and sight reading classes.

Concentrating on the Visual: Painting, Sculpture, Watercolor (Three-week residential, July 13–August 2) Students focus on either sculpture or painting. Courses are offered in painting

(experimental painting, variations in aqua media) and sculpture (techniques, methods, and concepts). In addition, each day begins with a drawing class. Whether working to build a portfolio for college admission or examining their artistic spirit, this course challenges students to learn, explore, and create. There is a class trip to a local museum in the first week of the program.

Creation and Invention: Summer Theatre Intensive (Three-week residential, July 13–August 2) Students participate in an exciting and rigorous program that includes acting, movement, playwriting, and creating original work. In acting, students discover the creative state where the individual actor feels free to explore, take risks, and make mistakes in an environment free of judgment. They delve into the craft of the playwright through a series of exercises that experiment with form, character, and conflict. They also take part in the dynamics of a creative ensemble that works toward the development of a "work in progress" performance piece. If students love the theater, this course gives them the concentration and freedom they need. There is a class trip to the Museum of Modern Art in the first week of the course.

Telling Stories for the Screen (Three-week nonresidential, July 14–July 31, Mondays and Thursdays, 6–8:30 p.m.) Students introduce themselves to the craft of screenwriting by telling an original story from their own unique perspective. They examine concepts and techniques relevant to screenwriting for features or shorts, including three-act structure, characters, dialogue, action, and format. In addition to exploring different approaches to narrative screenwriting, the course emphasizes individual development. Through lectures, screenings, writing exercises, and one-on-one sessions, student are given the tools to develop their writer's voice and to begin work on their own screenplay.

Free Verse Poetry: Reining In and Letting Loose (Three-week nonresidential, July 14–July 31, Mondays and Thursdays, 6–8:30 p.m.) Students discover the uniqueness of contemporary American free-verse poetry. Workshops focus on how to use essential components of the poem, from emotional impulse and tone to metaphor and transitions, in their own work. Through readings, in-class writing exercises, and workshopping, they learn how to clear a path to transform their personal views into creative, effective poetry.

Precise Stories and Creative Essays: Writing Across Your Life (Three-week nonresidential, July 14–July 31, Mondays and Thursdays, two sessions: 4–6:30 p.m. and 7–9:30 p.m.) Students are introduced to a new way of thinking about creative, expository, and exploratory writing while polishing and refining what they already know. They discover how to build an essay through its component parts and how to read with more care, argue with more persuasiveness, and realize their more creative "writerly" self.

ENROLLMENT

The number of students enrolled in each program varies. Sarah Lawrence College's Summer in the City enrolls 15 students. Summer Filmmaking Intensive has 32 students, 16 per section. Summer Music Intensive registers 30 students total, split into classes. Painting, Sculpture, Watercolor enrolls 36 students total, 12 per medium. Summer Theatre Intensive has 32 students total, 16 per instructor. Telling Stories for the Screen accommodates 15 students. Free Verse Poetry enrolls 15 students. Precise Stories and Creative Essays works with 30 students total, 15 per section.

DAILY SCHEDULE

Daily schedules vary according to the individual programs. Interested students should visit the Web site at http://www.sarahlawrence.edu/summer for tentative daily schedules.

EXTRA OPPORTUNITIES AND ACTIVITIES

Students living on campus enjoy evening and weekend programs and trips coordinated and run by a staff of residential counselors living on campus. Evening programs include community-building activities, film viewings, and other social events. Weekend trips include visits to museums, parks, concerts, and New York City neighborhoods (Chinatown, Greenwich Village, Harlem, Lincoln Center, Little Italy, Times Square, and more).

On the final Friday of the program, all of the programs celebrate the completion of their summer intensives with a recital, exhibition, and performance of their work to take place throughout the day. Parents and friends are welcome to attend these activities.

FACILITIES

In addition to the round-tabled classrooms, Sarah Lawrence has outstanding library, performing arts, music, art, science, computing, and sports facilities as well as a new 60,000-square-foot visual arts center.

STAFF

Courses are taught by faculty members who are chosen for their intellectual excellence, their unqualified commitment to helping students discover and develop their potential, and their understanding of adolescent development, needs, and abilities.

COSTS

The application fee for all high school courses is $25. For residential programs, a deposit of $250 is due by the registration deadline. Other costs vary by course, though all meal plans include breakfast, lunch, and dinner.

For the six-week residential program, housing is $1700, and the meal plan is $1150. For the three-week residential programs, housing and meals cost $1450.

Tuition is $5250 for Summer Filmmaking Intensive. Tuition is $2450 for the Summer in the City, Summer Music Intensive and Summer Theatre Intensive programs and $2500 (including supplies) for the Summer Visual Arts Intensive. Tuition for the three-week nonresidential Telling Stories, Free Verse Poetry, and Precise Stories and Creative Essays programs is $1500.

TRANSPORTATION

Sarah Lawrence College is accessible from train and bus stations as well as by car.

APPLICATION TIMETABLE

Spaces are assigned on a first-come, first-served basis. The registration deadline is June 20, 2008.

FOR MORE INFORMATION, CONTACT

Liz Irmiter
Director of Special Programs
Sarah Lawrence College
1 Mead Way
Bronxville, New York 10708-5999
Phone: 914-395-2693
E-mail: specialprograms@sarahlawrence.edu

PRE-COLLEGE SUMMER STUDIO

BOSTON, MASSACHUSETTS

TYPE OF PROGRAM: Arts program
PARTICIPANTS: Coeducational, ages 15–18 (must have completed sophomore year of high school)
ENROLLMENT: 75
PROGRAM DATES: June 29–August 1, 2008
HEAD OF PROGRAM: Debra Samdperil, Director of Continuing Education and Artist's Resource Center

LOCATION
The School of the Museum of Fine Arts, Boston, is located in Boston's Fenway cultural district, and the Pre-College Summer Studio will be held from June 29 to August 1, 2008. There is no better time to come to Boston than in the summer. Boston comes alive in June and July—whether one is strolling along the banks of the Charles River, taking in a free outdoor concert or theater performance, catching a baseball game at Fenway Park, or participating in the nation's largest Fourth of July celebration.

Boston's vibrant local art scene is always evident in the many fine art galleries from Newbury Street to the South End to the Fort Point area. Museums, such as the Institute of Contemporary Art, the Harvard University Art Museums, Massachusetts Institute of Technology Museums, and the Isabella Stewart Gardner Museum, are easily accessible using the city's extensive public transportation system. The Museum of Fine Arts, Boston, is just across the street.

BACKGROUND AND PHILOSOPHY
The School of the Museum of Fine Arts, Boston (SMFA), recognizes that disciplines converge and influence each other and that contemporary art is truly interdisciplinary. The School encourages all students to build solid foundations and acquire skill sets in numerous disciplines in order to create new possibilities and forms of artmaking.

SMFA, one of the oldest and most distinguished fully accredited professional art schools in the country, is a division of the Museum of Fine Arts, Boston, and is one of the most comprehensive art museums in the world. The SMFA and Tufts University have partnered in educating artists for more than sixty years. The SMFA also recently formed a partnership with Northeastern University. SMFA undergraduate and graduate students take studio art courses at the SMFA and academic courses at Tufts or Northeastern and graduate with a degree from Tufts or Northeastern.

PROGRAM OFFERINGS
Pre-College Summer Studio students are a diverse group of young artists who are devoted to the evolution of their artwork. The SMFA's five-week Pre-College Summer Studio is a unique and rigorous program focused on making art, sharing art, and living art. Students explore painting, drawing, printmaking, sculpture, installation, video, and digital photography, as well as sound art and performance, so that they may take their artmaking to the next level. These core courses encompass basic skills, experimentation, conceptual thinking, problem solving, critique, and discussions. The full credit value of the Pre-College Summer Studio is 5 credits.

Pre-College Summer Studio features individual-focused instruction. Highly skilled and experienced artists/teachers instruct students in studio work and lead them in discussions about the artmaking process. The SMFA's unusually low student-faculty ratio (6:1) ensures that students get the attention they need as they evolve their artwork. Students are also matched with a graduate-student mentor from SMFA's Master of Fine Arts program who, during regular meetings throughout the Pre-College Summer Studio, helps them further develop their individual vision.

Inspiring and encouraging, the program's dedicated faculty members, teaching assistants, and graduate-student mentors create a space in which students have the opportunity to experience the intersection of disciplines as part of the artmaking process, advance their technical skills in all subjects, learn to work both independently and collaboratively, experience how artists engage through interaction with each other and the wider community, gain self-confidence around their own creative process, and develop critical thinking skills by learning how to ask questions and productively critique themselves and others. Every week, students engage in each of the curriculum areas below.

Art Jamming Sessions: The program begins and ends each week by bringing together the entire Summer Studio community: all students, faculty members, teaching and resident assistants, graduate mentors, and program staff members. These sessions include discussions, activities, and presentations that explore the interdisciplinary process, current art topics, culture and art, and student influences.

2-D: Painting, Drawing, and Printmaking: The two-dimensional area emphasizes both traditional foundations and contemporary issues of drawing, painting, and printmaking.

3-D: Sculpture: During sculpture sessions, students explore a variety of simple materials and techniques for realizing three-dimensional form while developing a vocabulary for understanding its relationship to meaning.

Digital Studio: Video, Digital Photography, and Sound Art: The Digital Studio area provides students with opportunities to explore digital art using video, digital photography, and sound art.

Artists in Action: Collaboration and Performance: This section focuses on the creation of a collaborative project—a chance to discover the classroom group as a community.

Professional Practices: During the final week of the program, students participate in Professional Practices sessions. The SMFA's Admissions Office and Artist's Resource Center provide presenta-

tions, resources, and one-on-one guidance in regard to portfolio building, career paths in the arts, and the college application process.

ENROLLMENT
Students may enroll as residential students or as commuters. Residential student stay in the state-of-the-art Artist's Residence Hall (see Facilities below). Local participants who choose not to stay in the Artists' Residence Hall may enroll in the program as commuters. Commuters are required to attend all class sessions, Monday through Friday, as well as gallery, studio, and museum visits and artist talks. Studio space may be available for commuters to work in during the evenings. While on campus, commuters must follow the same rules and guidelines as residential students, including check-in and checkout procedures.

FACILITIES
The strong sense of community that develops between students is an important part of the Summer Studio program. That spirit of creativity and collaboration continues in the Artist's Residence Hall (ARH) at the end of each day and during the weekends. The state-of-the-art residence hall, located one block from the School, is custom made for artists, with shared studios on each floor. The ARH offers 24-hour security, full-time residence life staff members, first-floor laundry facilities, elevators, seminar rooms, outdoor courtyards, gallery space, a convenience store, and a smoke-free living environment. Each two-story studio has floor-to-ceiling windows, worktables and easels, temporary storage space, special ventilation, work sinks, and an Internet connection.

EXTRA OPPORTUNITIES AND ACTIVITIES
In addition to unlimited access to the permanent collections of the Museum of Fine Arts, Boston, which is just across the street from the SMFA, students also enjoy presentations by Museum professionals working in conservation and exhibitions, as well as behind-the-scenes tours of special collections such as rare books and prints.

Boston is an extended classroom for the program. Visits from renowned artists and excursions in the Boston area provide opportunities for direct engagement with the local art and culture scene. Students participate in off-site interactive tours at several area college museums such as the Massachusetts Institute of Technology and Harvard University. They also attend special programs at local studios and galleries, including GASP (Gallery Artists Studio Projects) and the Berwick Research Institute. Just a short shuttle ride away, the collections of the Tufts University Art Gallery/ Aidekman Arts Center are available.

During the weekends and in the evenings, students have the opportunity to use their assigned studio space to pursue independent work and class projects. They also participate in organized outings that complement the program's curriculum. Sample outings include First Fridays gallery openings, city tours of Boston, public art walking tours, open studios, performance events, film screenings, and some exciting day-long adventures. In addition to organized activities on weekends, students also have free time.

STAFF
One of the Museum School's strongest assets is its faculty of working artists and professional teachers who bring a wealth of experience and background to the classroom. These teachers encourage students to push themselves to their limits and engage with their work, while helping them develop an ongoing dialogue with materials, content, and process that will continue long after they have finished the program. Graduate-student mentors provide additional support in the form of one-on-one advising.

The experienced residence life staff members who live in the Artist's Residence Hall foster a sense of community and lead weekend activities and field trips.

MEDICAL CARE
All students must have proof of health insurance to participate in the Pre-College Summer Studio program.

COSTS
The cost of the 2007 Pre-College Summer Studio for residential students was $6500, which includes tuition ($3500), room ($1725), board ($1275), and student life and activity fees. The cost for commuters was $3700, which includes tuition and student life and activity fees. Commuters may purchase individual meals and snacks with cash. Students should visit http://www.smfa.edu/precollege for 2008 costs.

FINANCIAL AID
All applicants to the Pre-College Summer Studio are eligible to apply for scholarships. Need- and merit-based partial- and full-tuition scholarships are available. Applications for scholarships must be received by April. For exact deadlines, students should visit http://www.smfa.edu/precollege. To request a scholarship application, students should call 617-369-3644.

TRANSPORTATION
The School of the Museum of Fine Arts, Boston, can be easily reached by public transportation or car. Students who are flying into Logan Airport can take a 20–25 minute cab ride to the School.

APPLICATION TIMETABLE
Applications are accepted on a rolling basis, with all applications due in April. Acceptance decisions are mailed within ten days of receipt of application. For exact deadlines, students should visit http://www.smfa.edu/precollege.

All applicants must submit the application form and nonrefundable $50 application fee, one letter of recommendation from an art teacher or guidance counselor, a typewritten essay (2–3 pages) on why the student wants to attend the Summer Studio, and at least eight images (slides, photographs, or digital images) of the student's recent artwork (completed within the last year) sent on a DVD, CD-ROM, or VHS tape (NTSC format only). International applicants should visit the Web site for additional requirements.

FOR MORE INFORMATION, CONTACT:
School of the Museum of Fine Arts, Boston
230 The Fenway
Boston, Massachusetts 02115

Phone: 617-369-3644
Fax: 617-369-3679
E-mail: coned@smfa.edu
Web site: http://www.smfa.edu/precollege

SEACAMP

BIG PINE KEY, FLORIDA

TYPE OF PROGRAM: Marine science, scuba, sailing, windsurfing, environmental, and recreational program
PARTICIPANTS: Coeducational, ages 12–17
ENROLLMENT: 140–160 per session
PROGRAM DATES: June 24 to July 11, July 14 to July 31, and August 3 to August 20
HEADS OF PROGRAM: Irene Hooper, Executive Director; Grace Upshaw, Camp Director

LOCATION

Seacamp's tropical location on Newfound Harbor in the beautiful lower Florida Keys, just minutes from the only living coral reef in the United States, enables campers to participate in a truly one-of-a-kind marine studies program. Campers investigate the Atlantic Ocean, the Gulf of Mexico, and Florida Keys National Marine Sanctuary, moving among clear blue waters, coral canyons, sandy and grassy areas, mud flats, and natural tide pools—all abundant with a variety of invertebrates, fish, and mammals. All of this is offered just 120 miles south of Miami and 30 miles east of Key West.

BACKGROUND AND PHILOSOPHY

Founded in 1966, Seacamp, the first program dedicated to the education of youth in marine sciences, is the result of a cooperative effort of parents, scientists, businessmen, and camp leaders. Conservation practices and a respect for the marine environment are at the core of the Seacamp philosophy: "For all the sea has to teach us and all the fun of learning it."

Seacamp is accredited by the American Camping Association.

PROGRAM OFFERINGS

Marine Science The Marine Science Program is the heart of Seacamp. Young scientists participate in a variety of courses under the guidance of academically trained marine science instructors, biologists, geologists, and oceanographers. Campers work at their own level of interest while learning basic ecological principles that are pertinent both to the study of marine science and to the future of our natural resources. Designed to appeal to all campers, this comprehensive program is coordinated in a number of 21-hour course offerings that are selected each summer based on responses elicited from the current year's participants. Courses may include general marine sciences, marine communities, animal behavior, marine invertebrates, marine botany, marine vertebrates, marine geology, and marine aquaria. Advanced studies are offered in reef fish ecology, coral reef ecology, independent studies, and underwater field research using scuba. All science activities include studies in both the field and the laboratory. Boat trips take place on 10-foot by 25-foot trimaran-type hulls that accommodate 12–15 participants; all boats carry Coast Guard-approved safety equipment. On-board radios are constantly monitored by Seacamp's base station. During boat trips, campers investigate various marine environments and species, including 400 varieties of algae, coral, and fishes. Onshore trips vary, depending upon the weather, the tide, and areas of camper interest. In the past, such trips have included a geological survey of the keys, visits to the Key Deer Refuge, zonation studies of the intertidal areas, and investigations of canals and the mangrove fringe area. Upon completion, campers receive a Seacamp Certification describing courses taken.

Independent Research Projects Campers may pursue an independent research project of their choice through arrangements

with the science staff, the culmination of which may be published in *The Seacamp Journal of Research*.

Scuba Seacamp offers several courses in scuba diving to qualified participants. Scuba courses are designed to give the camper the appropriate skills for safely using scuba as an underwater research tool. In order to participate in scuba, campers should have no history of heart, lung (including asthma), sinus, or ear troubles. Seacamp's Scuba I course is a basic certification class that is offered to campers 13 and older. Satisfactory course completion earns the camper a nationally recognized certificate. Marine investigation courses (Scuba II) using scuba techniques for certified divers are offered at introductory, intermediate, and advanced levels. Scuba III is offered to campers 15 and older. Successful completion of Scuba III earns the camper a Master Diver Certification. Scuba IV is an ongoing research class that publishes a paper in *The Seacamp Journal of Research*.

Aquatic Programs Exploration of the ocean's surface is guided by winds, tides, and currents. Campers taking sailing and windsurfing receive instructions on how to operate their vessels based on these factors. While here, campers seeking to further their knowledge about sailing may choose to enroll in Seacamp's more in-depth sailing class and obtain their certification in light air sailing from the U.S. Sailing Association. Windsurfing courses start campers on a dry-land simulator; they learn the basic aspects of rigging, tacking, jibing, rules of the road, board control, and more and progress to racing and freestyle techniques. Canoeing and kayaking classes explore the natural resources of the Coupon Bight Aquatic Preserve. Certification in American Red Cross lifeguarding is also offered.

ENROLLMENT

Each session, 140 to 160 campers come to Seacamp, mostly from the U.S., but also from across the world. There are about 30 international campers each summer from an average of twelve countries. Many Seacamp program graduates have gone on to prominent careers as environmental educators and marine scientists.

DAILY SCHEDULE

One of Seacamp's unique aspects is that campers create their schedules. In addition to science and scuba classes, campers choose from a variety of programs to ensure that there is something interesting and exciting for everyone. Typically, the day starts at 7 a.m., with breakfast at 7:30. Campers enjoy free time before the morning program, which runs from 9 until noon. Lunch is at 12:30, after which campers rest or explore the area. The afternoon program runs from 2:15 until 5:20, after which there is just enough time to dry off and get ready for dinner at 6. After dinner there is free time until 8:30, during which campers enjoy a swim, volleyball, or basketball and talk about the day's excitement. The evening program begins at 8:30 and comprises anything from dancing with friends to hearing a visiting scientist talk about current international scientific issues to playing blackjack at Seacamp's version of a Caribbean casino to sitting by the campfire next to the open ocean, singing and laughing. Lights-out is at 10:30, by which time campers can hardly wait for the next exciting day.

EXTRA OPPORTUNITIES AND ACTIVITIES

Campers interested in journalism may work on the camp newspaper, *SEASCOPE,* which is published periodically during camp sessions. Arts and crafts activities include ceramics, copper enameling, stone carving, tie-dyeing, driftwood art, macramé, and painting. Photography allows campers to take home memories of friends, wildlife, and underwater experiences.

Activities are planned to incorporate the needs of all of the campers, so no one is ever left out. Seacamp's enthusiastic and gregarious staff members go out of their way to include everyone in the fun.

FACILITIES

Campers and staff members are housed by age in dormitories. Seacamp honors cabinmate requests, if possible, when both families are in agreement.

Seacamp's lab facilities include a running seawater circulation system that serves two 250-gallon display tanks, two 50-gallon aquaria, twenty 20-gallon aquaria, and two 600-gallon tanks, which campers and science staff members use for research and observation. A preparation room is stocked with charts, illustrations, stereo and compound microscopes, preserving jars and solutions, water analysis kits, seines, and oceanographic equipment. A man-made lagoon serves as a temporary habitat for larger live specimens.

Other camp facilities include a dining hall, a kitchen, a recreation hall, an arts and crafts building, a health center, a sailing shelter, several teaching shelters, a staff lounge, and administration offices.

STAFF

Seacamp receives more than 1,000 requests for applications, from all over the world, for 55 program staff positions. Staff members are chosen for their expertise as program directors, marine science instructors, nationally certified scuba instructors, and American Red Cross–certified water safety instructors and their overall ability. Before campers arrive, program staff members go through an intensive three-week training session in which they are certified in American Red Cross lifeguarding, first aid, CPR, and National Association of Underwater Instructors (NAUI) skin diving instruction. If arriving staff members are scuba certified, Seacamp also certifies them as NAUI rescue divers. In addition to all of these certifications, staff members are also trained extensively in boat-handling skills through Seacamp's Captain's Workshop and in consistent leadership skills. Most staff members come from across the U.S.; however, there have been staff members from places as far away as New Zealand, England, South Africa, Scotland, and Russia. The overall resident camper–staff member ratio is 3:1. The close relationships developed between staff members and campers because of this small ratio encourage individuality and provide for small-group instruction.

MEDICAL CARE

An in-residence registered nurse manages the health center. A camp physician from Big Pine Key is on call, and ambulance service is available around the clock. Complete hospital facilities are in nearby Marathon and Key West. First aid equipment and supplies are kept on all motor boats.

A general health certificate form and a scuba health certificate must be submitted at least three weeks prior to each camper's arrival. All campers are covered by Seacamp's health insurance while at camp; this policy is limited, however, and parents are encouraged to carry their own insurance for their children.

COSTS

Costs for the 2007 program were $3150. Extra fees for scuba were $375 per course. Costs are subject to change. All campers must have masks, fins, and snorkels to participate in Seacamp's programs; these can be bought in the camp's Ship's Store. Other optional equipment, T-shirts, treats, and toiletries are also available at the Ship's Store.

Campers who are enrolled for more than one session stay at camp between sessions at no extra charge. During this time, they participate in a variety of supervised programs, get a chance to do their laundry, and take advantage of opportunities to visit historic Key West. About $75 spending money is suggested for this time.

TRANSPORTATION

Parents may bring campers by car to Big Pine Key. Counselors also meet participants at the Miami International Airport on the opening day of camp and escort them to Big Pine Key on a chartered bus (about 120 miles). The fee for round-trip service is $90 (subject to change).

APPLICATION TIMETABLE

To join the Seacamp adventure, interested campers should contact Seacamp for an application. Off-season tours of the facilities are available, and all are welcome to visit. Completed applications must include a $350 deposit (refundable until May 1) and a letter of recommendation from the camper's science teacher or principal. Parents and campers receive a Seacamp information packet, with articles on transportation, what to bring, camp store credit, permission forms, and health forms.

FOR MORE INFORMATION, CONTACT

Seacamp
1300 Big Pine Avenue
Big Pine Key, Florida 33043-3336
Phone: 305-872-2331
Fax: 305-872-2555
E-mail: snorkel+scuba@seacamp.org
Web site: http://www.seacamp.org

SERVICE LEARNING IN BARCELONA

▼▲▼▲▼▲▼▲▼▲▼▲▼▲▼▲▼▲▼▲▼▲▼▲▼▲

CULTURAL IMMERSION THROUGH COMMUNITY SERVICE

BARCELONA, SPAIN

TYPE OF PROGRAM: Community service, academic study, and language intensive
PARTICIPANTS: Coeducational, international, from age 16
ENROLLMENT: 15 or more
PROGRAM DATES: July 2–31, 2008
HEAD OF PROGRAM: John Nissen, Director

LOCATION

The 2008 site for the International Seminar Series' (ISS) Service Learning program in Spain is Barcelona.

BACKGROUND AND PHILOSOPHY

The International Seminar Series' (ISS) vision is to give thoughtful and accomplished young people an opportunity for immersion in another culture through active participation in community service work and focused study. Daily, ongoing service projects distinguish this program from the more usual study-and-travel approach to summer programs. From this engagement, each participant can derive richness of experience, depth of understanding, and reflective interaction with a greater world.

PROGRAM OFFERINGS

Community Service: Participation in community service is at the core of the program. For the entire month, students explore the everyday aspects of contemporary Spanish culture through direct participation in it, offering assistance to a specific community outside their own and carefully considering what the offering and receipt of such assistance can mean. Students work 3 to 4 hours a day, five days a week, during their month in Barcelona. Assignments with established organizations are made according to the student's interest and experience, the skills required by the organization, and the student's ability in Spanish. Specific activities vary according to the needs of the organization.

The Intellectual Engagement: The seminar is the academic complement to community service work. It gives grounding to the students' daily experience as they work and go about Barcelona. The goal is to understand the city and its people through study, observation, and interaction. For their academic class, students choose one course—Art and Architecture, Politics and History, or Writing and Literature.

Spanish Language Use and Instruction: Students speak and study Spanish from the first day. They are tested and grouped into four sections, from beginners (no previous experience in Spanish) to advanced (mostly students who have taken or will be taking Advanced Placement Spanish). Class size does not exceed 10. The emphasis of the work is oral expression. Speaking Spanish outside academic classes is the norm—at home and meals with host families, at the Service Learning Centro, and in daily conversation.

Study Travel and Cultural Explorations: During the month, a significant amount of time is devoted to visiting traditional places within Barcelona, such as La Sagrada Familia, Parc Guell, Montjuic, the Barri Gotic, and the harbor and beaches, and outside the city to such places as Montserrat and the Benedictine monastery as well as sites that are more closely related to the work done in community service and the seminar. Barcelona is defined as much by its multicultural population as by its famous architecture.

FACILITIES

Students are housed with local families who speak Spanish, rather than Catalan, at home. Breakfast and dinner are provided each day. Students are responsible for their own lunches. Many share a meal with people at the community service site. Others stop for tapas or meet friends for an inexpensive meal at local restaurants.

STAFF

Faculty and staff members are thoughtful, experienced teachers drawn from Barcelona and elsewhere. They teach individual courses, oversee community service work, and conduct study travel, but they also act as mentors to the students and links to the community beyond. Faculty and staff members work hard in helping students become thoughtful observers and active participants in the larger host culture. During the winter, they work collaboratively to develop the content of the program.

COSTS

The program fee for 2008 is $7000, which includes a $50 application fee and a $1500 enrollment deposit. Additional expenses to be anticipated are transportation to and from Barcelona, lunch costs, and personal expenses for laundry, individual purchases, and other incidentals.

FINANCIAL AID

A modest amount of need-based financial aid is available. A separate application is sent on request.

TRANSPORTATION

Students are responsible for making their own travel arrangements to and from Barcelona. They are met at their point-of-arrival airport, train station, or bus terminal and accompanied to the homes of their host families. The procedure is reversed on departure.

APPLICATION TIMETABLE

Students must complete a formal application (either on paper or through the ISS Web site) and submit transcripts and teacher or counselor recommendations. Admission is selective and places are limited. The recommended deadline is April 15, and students are encouraged to apply early.

FOR MORE INFORMATION, CONTACT

John Nissen, Director
International Seminar Series
P.O. Box 1212
Manchester, Vermont 05254-1212

Phone: 802-362-5855 (telephone and fax)
E-mail: iss@study-serve.org
Web site: http://www.study-serve.org

SERVICE LEARNING IN PARIS

CULTURAL IMMERSION THROUGH COMMUNITY SERVICE

PARIS, FRANCE

TYPE OF PROGRAM: Community service, academic study, and language intensive

PARTICIPANTS: Coeducational, international, from age 16

ENROLLMENT: 40 or more

PROGRAM DATES: July 2–31, 2008

HEAD OF PROGRAM: John Nissen, Director

LOCATION

The 2008 Service Learning in Paris program is its tenth summer. The program is based in the 15th arrondissement.

BACKGROUND AND PHILOSOPHY

The International Seminar Series' (ISS) vision is to give thoughtful and accomplished young people an opportunity for immersion in another culture through active participation in community service work and focused study. Daily, ongoing service projects distinguish this program from the more usual study-and-travel approach to summer programs. From this engagement, each participant can derive richness of experience, depth of understanding, and reflective interaction with a greater world.

PROGRAM OFFERINGS

Community Service Participation in Community Service is at the core of the program. For the entire month, students explore the everyday aspects of contemporary French culture through direct participation in it, offering assistance to a specific community

outside their own and carefully considering what the offering and receipt of such assistance can mean. Students work 3 to 4 hours a day, five days a week, during their month in Paris. Assignments with established organizations are made according to the student's interest and experience, the skills required by the organization, and the student's ability in French. Specific activities vary according to the needs of the organization.

The Intellectual Engagement The seminar is the academic complement to community service work. It gives grounding to the students' daily experience as they work and go about Paris. The goal is to understand the city and its people through study, observation, and interaction. For their academic class, students choose one course—Art and Architecture (in English or French), French Politics and History, or Writing and Literature.

French Language Use and Instruction Students speak and study French from the first day. They are tested and grouped into four sections, from beginners (no previous experience in French) to advanced (mostly students who have taken or will be taking Advanced Placement French). Class size does not exceed 10. The emphasis of the work is oral expression. Speaking French outside academic classes is the norm—at meals, in the office, and in daily conversation.

Study Travel and Cultural Explorations During the month, a significant amount of time is devoted to visiting traditional places such as Chartres, Versailles, Vaux-le-Vicomte, and sites that are more closely related to the work done in Community Service and the seminar. Modern Paris is defined as much by its new towns and ethnic suburbs as by the Champs Elysées.

FACILITIES

Students and staff members are housed in the Foyer, a residence hall complex in the 15th arrondissement, with dining facilities and classrooms. Breakfast and dinner are provided each day. Students are responsible for their own lunches. Many share a meal with people at the Community Service site. Others may buy the quintessential baguette and cheese sandwich at a patisserie or meet friends for an inexpensive plat du jour at local restaurants. Students are also able and encouraged to use the kitchen at the Foyer.

STAFF

Faculty and staff members are thoughtful, experienced teachers drawn from Paris and elsewhere. They teach individual courses, oversee community service work, and conduct study travel, but they also act as mentors to the students and links to the community beyond. Faculty and staff members work hard in helping students become thoughtful observers and active participants in the larger host culture. During the winter, they work collaboratively to develop the content of the program.

COSTS

The program fee for 2008 is $7000, which includes a $50 application fee and a $1500 enrollment deposit. Additional expenses to be anticipated are transportation to and from Paris, lunch costs, and personal expenses for laundry, individual purchases, and other incidentals.

FINANCIAL AID

A modest amount of need based financial aid is available. A separate application is sent on request.

TRANSPORTATION

Students are responsible for making their own travel arrangements to and from Paris. They are met at their point-of-arrival airport, train station, or bus terminal and accompanied to the seminar housing site. The procedure is reversed on departure.

APPLICATION TIMETABLE

Students must complete a formal application (either on paper or through the ISS Web site) and submit transcripts and teacher or counselor recommendations. Admission is selective and places are limited. The recommended deadline is April 15, and students are encouraged to apply early.

FOR MORE INFORMATION, CONTACT

John Nissen, Director
P.O. Box 1212
Manchester, Vermont 05254-1212
Phone: 802-362-5855 (telephone and fax)
E-mail: iss@study-serve.org
Web site: http://www.study-serve.org

SKIDMORE COLLEGE PRE-COLLEGE PROGRAM IN THE LIBERAL AND STUDIO ARTS

SUMMER PROGRAM

SARATOGA SPRINGS, NEW YORK

TYPE OF PROGRAM: Credit-bearing, first-year college courses in the liberal and studio arts
PARTICIPANTS: Coeducational, grades 10–undergraduate
ENROLLMENT: 114–120
PROGRAM DATES: Five weeks, July to early August
HEAD OF PROGRAM: Dr. James Chansky, Director of Summer Special Programs

LOCATION

Saratoga Springs is a small, cosmopolitan town in upstate New York, well-known as a summer resort town and for its Victorian heritage, famed spas, thoroughbred racing, and commitment to the arts. The lively summer season at Skidmore College receives national recognition for the rich diversity of its programs in the liberal, fine, creative, and performing arts and for the public offerings that fill Skidmore's theater, gallery, and recital and lecture halls.

BACKGROUND AND PHILOSOPHY

Since the late 1970s, Skidmore has been bringing bright high school students to campus for a summer experience of college life and learning. Through the combination of first-year college-level courses, dormitory living, and the rich and varied intellectual, cultural, artistic, and social life of the summer campus, the program is designed to offer high school students a true college experience.

PROGRAM OFFERINGS

Pre-College students enroll in two credit-bearing courses, and some college-level noncredit courses, selected from among a range of offerings in the humanities, social sciences, natural sciences, and mathematics, as well as a robust array in the studio arts. They may focus on a particular area or explore more broadly. Courses are taught primarily by full-time Skidmore faculty members, known for their attention to students and to student learning. Students working in the studio arts can take full advantage of exceptional studio space and a strong arts program, reflecting the College's strengths in this

area in particular. In addition to faculty support, the Academic Coordinator assists students in their course work, managing their time, and acclimating to the pace of college life. Special sessions help Pre-College students think about what they want to study in college, what sort of college they want to attend, how to negotiate the college application process, how to compose admissions essays, and how to prepare portfolios for applications in studio art. The art exhibits and lecture-demonstrations and evening lectures, readings, recitals, and performances offered by the concurrently running summer programs further enhance students' intellectual and cultural life, and the extracurricular activities put together by the residence hall staff inject an element of pure fun into the program.

ENROLLMENT

Program students come from all over the United States as well as from abroad, the majority coming from the Northeast and mid-Atlantic states. They reflect a very wide diversity of social, economic, ethnic, and racial backgrounds.

DAILY SCHEDULE

Pre-College students enroll in two courses, equivalent to full-time enrollment in a typical college semester. Preparation time averages about 2 hours daily for each class. Free time is spent engaging in the many public events held on campus and in more relaxing and fun program-sponsored events, including swimming, working out in the gym, walking downtown to a coffeehouse, socializing with new friends on campus and in the dormitory, and attending the many performances, films, lectures, and other events happening across the campus.

EXTRA OPPORTUNITIES AND ACTIVITIES

Among the larger challenges facing Pre-College students is finding the time to take advantage of all the activities and events on campus: jazz concerts offered by the nationally known Jazz Institute faculty members and visiting artists; fiction, nonfiction, and poetry readings and discussions by the prize-winning writers in the New York State Summer Writers Institute; great movies shown in the International Film Festival; lecture-demonstrations and art openings through the Summer Studio Art Programs; and more.

Events organized by the dorm staff specifically for high school students include regular get-togethers following evening events, movie nights, volleyball games, study breaks, and other activities. Weekend off-campus events include attending a performance of the New York City Ballet at the Saratoga Performing Arts Center, spending a day at the Six Flags Great Escape Amusement Park (among the largest in the U.S.), taking a day trip to New York City, and exploring the downtown area of Saratoga Springs.

FACILITIES

Students are housed in a dormitory and dine in the College's recently renovated dining hall. The library provides lots of space for study and group work, a substantial collection of books and journals, and state-of-the-art computers. The sports and recreation center includes weight rooms; racquetball, squash, and basketball courts; a competition-sized swimming pool; an all weather outdoor track and artificial turf field; and several tennis courts. A running path winds its way around the perimeter of the campus, and numerous hiking trails zigzag through the woods to the north of the campus.

STAFF

The Pre-College Program is one among the many summer academic programs administered by Skidmore's Office of the Dean of Special Programs, the office bearing responsibility for all summer programs. The teaching faculty members and the academic coordinator are members of the Skidmore faculty and community and are all seasoned educators selected on the basis of their ability to teach first-year-level courses. The residential staff consists of an adult professional Residential

Director and a staff of well-trained and experienced college students who serve as residential assistants.

MEDICAL CARE

Emergency and critical care for program participants is available through the College's Office of Health Services and the Saratoga Hospital, which is 5 minutes from the campus. All students are required to submit a medical and release form prior to their arrival.

COSTS

The total program cost for a residential student is approximately $4800–$5600 and includes tuition for two courses, room, board, and an activity fee. Books and supplies carry additional charges.

FINANCIAL AID

Some full and partial scholarships are awarded annually on the basis of need and merit. As aid is limited, early application is advisable.

TRANSPORTATION

Skidmore College is half an hour from the Albany County Airport and 45 minutes from the Albany-Rensselaer Amtrak station. Major bus lines also deliver service directly to Saratoga Springs. Taxi and limousine service is available to take students to campus.

APPLICATION TIMETABLE

Students are encouraged to make their inquiries in the late fall and to apply as soon as they receive application materials. Admission decisions are made on a rolling basis, usually within two weeks of receipt of a completed application. To ensure a place in the program, applications are best received by May 1, though applications are reviewed up to mid-June on a space-available basis.

FOR MORE INFORMATION, CONTACT

Dr. James Chansky, Director of Summer Special Programs
Pre-College Program in the Liberal and Studio Arts
Office of the Dean of Special Programs
Skidmore College
815 North Broadway
Saratoga Springs, New York 12866
Phone: 518-580-5590
Fax: 518-580-5548
E-mail: jchansky@skidmore.edu
Web site: http://www.skidmore.edu/summer

PARTICIPANT/FAMILY COMMENTS

"This was one of my greatest summers . . . Skidmore had so much to offer me, from friends in the dorm, a big and comfortable library, great trips, college life, friendly professors . . . an overall great place away from home."

SMITH COLLEGE

SMITH SUMMER SCIENCE AND ENGINEERING PROGRAM

NORTHAMPTON, MASSACHUSETTS

TYPE OF PROGRAM: Enrichment programming in science and engineering for girls
PARTICIPANTS: Girls, grades 9–12
PROGRAM DATES: June 29 to July 26
HEAD OF PROGRAM: Dr. Gail E. Scordilis, Director

LOCATION
Smith College is located in Northampton, Massachusetts, in the scenic Pioneer Valley of western New England. The 125-acre Smith campus is situated a short walk from downtown Northampton (population 31,000), and it is bordered by the natural beauty of the Connecticut River, the Holyoke Mountain Range, and the foothills of the Berkshire Mountains.

BACKGROUND AND PHILOSOPHY
Girls in high school with dreams of pursuing a career in science, engineering, or medicine should make the 2008 Smith College Summer Science and Engineering Program (SSEP) part of their plan. A month in the summer at Smith gives students an exceptional opportunity to do science and engineering, enhance their skills, boost their confidence, and connect with professionals who support their efforts. Students also make great new friends from all over the world who share their interests. Since 1990, more than 1,400 high school girls from representing forty-six U.S. states, the District of Columbia, Puerto Rico, and forty-seven other countries have participated in this innovative program. After the program, participants report that they return to high school better prepared to tackle tough science courses and better informed about what to expect in college.

Smith College is one of the top-rated liberal arts colleges in the U.S. and the nation's largest college dedicated solely to the education of women. Housed in the multi-building Clark Science Center, the Smith science faculty includes some of the finest researchers and teachers in the country. Smith undergraduates don't just hear and read about scientific research, they are active participants. As a result, for more than seventy-five years, Smith has ranked in the top 3 percent of 519 private colleges in the number of graduates who have gone on to earn Ph.D.'s in science. In 1999, Smith became the first women's college in the nation to establish its own program in engineering science, the Picker Program in Engineering.

Students don't have to wait until college to experience the benefits of a Smith education. The summer of 2008 marks the nineteenth year of the Smith College Summer Science and Engineering Program. The SSEP extends the benefits of Smith's strong traditions to girls still in high school. Participants in the summer program are taught by Smith faculty members, live in a college house alongside Smith undergraduate interns, and have access to all campus facilities. Central to the program is a learning community that is rich in role models, cooperative, hands-on, minds-on, investigative, and challenging—where girls get all of the faculty's attention, all of the opportunities, and all of the encouragement to achieve their best.

PROGRAM OFFERINGS
The 2008 SSEP runs from Sunday, June 29, through Saturday, July 26. All SSEP participants give two oral presentations of their work, one at the midpoint of the program (Friday, July 11, and Saturday, July 12) and a second presentation at the conclusion of the program (Friday, July 25, and Saturday, July 26). At the conclusion of the program, parents and family members arriving to pick up their daughters attend the final student presentations and share in their accomplishments. The presentations are followed by a family/student/faculty lunch that concludes the summer program.

Unlike regular school classes, SSEP research courses emphasize asking questions and learning by doing, not listening and watching. During their monthlong stay on campus, students take two 2-week-long courses. A maximum of 16 students work alongside a Smith faculty member, who is assisted by an undergraduate intern. Informal lectures in the laboratory and field provide students with the basis for asking experimental questions; then they learn how to do real experiments. Most of the work is carried out as a cooperative team effort, with ample opportunities for individual contributions. SSEP participants learn how scientists and engineers formulate questions, work on some amazingly sophisticated scientific instruments, and develop valuable critical-thinking and analytical skills.

Research courses for the 2008 program include investigations in architecture, astronomy, biology, biochemistry, chemistry, engineering and design, women's health, and writing. SSEP courses are designed to be relevant and interesting. In courses such as Your Genes, Your Chromosomes: A Laboratory Course in Human Genetics, The Music in Engineering, and Women and Exercise: A Biochemical Investigation, SSEP participants explore their world in new and intriguing ways. In addition, Experiment and Exploration: A Laboratory for Writers, is an intensive SSEP course that offers students individualized instruction to strengthen their writing skills. Participants in the 2008 SSEP may also choose to join a group of researchers from Smith, the YWCA, and Mt. Sinai Adolescent Health Center who are investigating young women's health issues. These student researchers will contribute to the Web site ByGirlsForGirls.org and help to disseminate important information about teen health to girls around the world.

ENROLLMENT
Enrollment in the program is limited to 100 to ensure the quality of the academic experience offered. Eligible candidates are academically talented girls who will be entering grades 9–12 in fall 2008. In all of its programming, Smith is committed to reaching a diverse student body. In the 2007 SSEP, approximately 40 percent of participants identified themselves as members of minority groups.

DAILY SCHEDULE
On a typical weekday, students eat breakfast from 7:30 to 8:30 a.m., are involved in 2 to 3 hours of investigation in the morning, break for lunch at noon, and then return to their research for 2 to 3 hours in the afternoon. On average, participants spend 120 contact hours working with faculty members.

Dinner each evening is scheduled from 5:30 to 7 p.m. Throughout the program, discussions occur with faculty members on exploring career opportunities in science, engineering, and medicine. In addition, the Smith Office of Admission sponsors workshops that support students at different stages of the college planning process.

EXTRA OPPORTUNITIES AND ACTIVITIES
In addition to doing great science, the SSEP is about making new friends and getting a taste of college life. Smith's 125-acre campus is beautiful, with traditional ivy-covered buildings, magnificent gardens, and a pond named Paradise. SSEP participants live together in one college house along with SSEP interns, who serve as supervisors, advisers, and teaching/research assistants, and SSEP residential directors, who are in charge of all aspects of students' residential life. All meals are served in the house dining room. During free time, participants can choose from organized sport, recreational, and cultural activities or be on their own with friends from the program. Smith's superb athletic facilities include two gymnasiums, an indoor pool, indoor and outdoor track and tennis facilities, squash courts, a horseback-riding arena, a dance studio, a croquet court, a climbing wall, and a state-of-the-art fitness center. Weekend activities include local arts festivals, museums, and theatrical performances throughout the Pioneer Valley. Participants enjoy hikes to local nature preserves, movie nights, and the annual SSEP talent show. Also located within easy walking distance of the campus in downtown Northampton are a varied selection of shops, restaurants, and movies. The program fee covers the costs of all organized program activities and field trips.

STAFF
The Program Director is Dr. Gail E. Scordilis, an alumna of Smith and a member of the Department of Biological Sciences. Dr. Leslie Jaffe, Director of Smith College Health Services, is the SSEP Health Consultant. Smith College faculty and academic staff members instruct participants in the SSEP. For every 10 students enrolled, there is a Smith undergraduate intern who serves as a residential counselor and research/teaching assistant to the faculty. Two residential directors, who are trained in residential life management, live on-site and supervise the undergraduate staff.

MEDICAL CARE
Upon acceptance, all SSEP participants are required to submit a prescription medication form and a medical information form detailing their relevant medical histories, insurance information, and parental consent for care. Medical care is provided for program participants by a group of local physicians who specialize in pediatric and adolescent medicine. In addition, Smith is only a few miles from Northampton's Cooley Dickinson Hospital and convenient to Springfield's extensive Bay State Medical Center.

COSTS
The fee for participation in the 2008 Smith Summer Science and Engineering Program is $4350 and covers the cost of all program materials and activities.

FINANCIAL AID
Partial to full financial aid is available to a limited number of participants and is awarded solely on the basis of demonstrated financial need. The SSEP is supported in part by grants to Smith College from the Bechtel Foundation; Ford Motor Company Fund; Howard Hughes Medical Institute; Motorola Foundation; Osram Sylvania, Inc.; S. D. Bechtel, Jr. Foundation; and Young Women's Leadership Foundation. More than 40 percent of 2007 participants received financial aid. Students requesting financial aid must complete the financial aid application, found on the reverse side of the SSEP application.

TRANSPORTATION
Smith College is located in Northampton in the Connecticut River valley of western Massachusetts. From I-91, students should take Exit 18 and follow the signs to Route 9, which leads directly to the campus. Bradley International Airport, 33 miles south of Northampton on I-91, is the nearest airport. Major train and bus lines also serve the area.

APPLICATION TIMETABLE
The 2008 SSEP is open to academically talented girls who will enter grades 9–12 in fall 2008. Enrollment in the program is limited to ensure the quality of the academic experience. Admission to the SSEP is selective and is based on academic performance in middle and/or high school, teacher recommendation, and a written essay. Applications from students with all levels of previous science training are welcome. Students need not have taken advanced science courses, but they must have a strong record of academic achievement, a high level of motivation, and willingness to explore. There are two deadlines for application, an early admission date of March 1 and a regular admission date of May 1. The program receives approximately three times the number of applicants needed to fill the 100 program slots, so early application is urged.

FOR MORE INFORMATION, CONTACT
Gail E. Scordilis, Ph.D., Director
Educational Outreach
Clark Hall
Smith College
Northampton, Massachusetts 01063
Phone: 413-585-3060
Fax: 413-585-3068
E-mail: ccooke@smith.edu
Web site: http://www.smith.edu/summerprograms/ssep/

SOUTHERN METHODIST UNIVERSITY

SMU. SCHOOL OF EDUCATION & HUMAN DEVELOPMENT

SUMMER PROGRAMS

DALLAS, TEXAS

TYPE OF PROGRAM: Academic enrichment and acceleration

PARTICIPANTS: Coeducational, students who have completed grades 7–11

ENROLLMENT: Approximately 100 per program

PROGRAM DATES: Two sessions: Talented and Gifted, July 8–27, 2007; College Experience, July 1–August 1, 2007

HEAD OF PROGRAM: Marilyn Swanson, Director of Programming, Gifted Students Institute

LOCATION
The programs are held on the campus of Southern Methodist University (SMU), a private coeducational institution located in University Park, a district surrounded by the city of Dallas. The 164-acre campus, replete with Georgian architecture, is home to numerous theaters, concert halls, and a library collection of more than 2 million volumes.

BACKGROUND AND PHILOSOPHY
SMU programs began in 1978 and are designed to provide students with intellectual challenges and exciting learning experiences. Many students establish mentor relationships and develop friendships that last a lifetime. Programs encour-

age students to mature socially as well as intellectually and foster the development of maturity and self-confidence.

PROGRAM OFFERINGS
Southern Methodist University offers two summer residential programs. The Talented and Gifted Program (TAG) is for academically talented and gifted youths completing grades 7, 8, and 9. College Experience (CE) is planned for rising high school juniors and seniors who are motivated and capable of successfully completing college-credit courses. In all programs, small classes ensure that students develop strong relationships with faculty members, and residence hall life provides a warm, supportive environment. In addition, a variety of educational and recreational experiences are offered.

Talented and Gifted TAG is open to students entering grades 8–10 in 2007–08. During this three-week residential program, students participate in two stimulating classes chosen from a wide selection of SMU credit and noncredit courses. Cultural enrichment activities are provided for all TAG students. Three-hour credit courses include mathematical sciences, economics, political science, mechanical engineering, psychology, philosophy, and ethics. Noncredit courses include poetry writing, engineering, Shakespeare, theater arts, film, public discourse, mathematics, photography, physics, geography, rocketry, and paleontology.

College Experience Academically talented high school students can get a head start on college and a taste of campus life during this exciting five-week summer program at SMU. The selection of college-credit subjects for morning classes includes philosophy, English, math, psychology, history, and government. In the afternoon, all College Experience students participate in a "core" class or humanities overview class for 3 hours of college credit. Students who elect to live in the CE residence hall participate in special cultural, educational, and recreational activities.

ENROLLMENT
Enrollment for the College Experience program is limited to 40 students. Applicants must have completed the tenth or eleventh grade. Enrollment for TAG is limited to 75 students. Applicants must have completed the seventh, eighth, or ninth grade.

Participants are selected on the basis of academic ability and motivation, as demonstrated by grades, SAT or ACT test scores, teacher recommendations, and other application requirements.

SMU does not discriminate on the basis of race, color, national or ethnic origin, sex, or disability.

DAILY SCHEDULE
Students attend morning and afternoon classes. Evenings are spent in study and recreation.

EXTRA OPPORTUNITIES AND ACTIVITIES
In addition to challenging course work, students take advantage of campus libraries, museums, the student center, and computer labs. Both programs offer planned activities for both

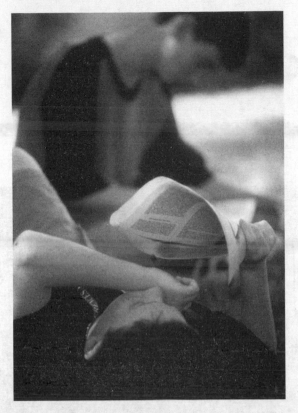

individuals and small and large groups. Activities include evening seminars, movies, musical and dramatic performances, picnics, athletics events, talent shows, guest lectures, special programs, and parties and dances. During free time, students decide individually whether to study or just to relax with their friends.

FACILITIES

Students for both programs live in air-conditioned residence halls near the center of the campus. For both programs, the hall is reserved exclusively for program students, their hall director, and resident advisers (RAs). Students are housed 2 to a room, with adjoining or hall bathrooms. Boys and girls are separated. Meals are served cafeteria style and feature a salad bar, a sandwich bar, hot entrees and vegetables, and a variety of desserts.

STAFF

TAG students are supervised in every activity by the faculty and staff. College Experience students experience life as college students. The residence hall staff is carefully selected and qualified to provide academic and nonacademic guidance. College Experience faculty members are SMU professors. TAG teachers are both SMU faculty members and secondary school teachers with training and an interest in working with gifted students.

MEDICAL CARE

Students in both programs are covered by group medical insurance while enrolled. They are treated for illness or injury at the SMU Health Center or at a local hospital, if necessary, during their program participation.

RELIGIOUS LIFE

Religious services are held on campus.

COSTS

Tuition for College Experience is approximately $2200. The cost for CE room and board is $1400. The total cost for TAG is $2500. All costs are estimated.

FINANCIAL AID

Limited financial aid is available and is awarded on the basis of need. Early application is highly recommended.

TRANSPORTATION

Students are responsible for their own transportation to and from the programs, but students who arrive in Dallas by air, bus, or train can make arrangements to be picked up by program staff members.

APPLICATION TIMETABLE

Application forms are available in January and are accepted on a rolling basis until all available spaces are filled. SAT or ACT scores are highly recommended. College Experience and TAG applicants complete an application that includes recommendations, a brief essay, transcripts, and test scores.

FOR MORE INFORMATION, CONTACT

Marilyn Swanson, Director of Programming
Gifted Students Institute–College Experience
Gifted Students Institute–TAG
Southern Methodist University
P.O. Box 750383
Dallas, Texas 75275-0383

Phone: 214-768-0123
E-mail: gifted@smu.edu
Web site: http://www.smu.edu/giftedyouth

PARTICIPANT/FAMILY COMMENTS

"A day of TAG is equivalent to a week of life outside the world of TAG. My two summers gave birth to new knowledge and new friendships; I finally found my 'niche.'"

"Her time at TAG has been the most positive educational experience she has ever had."

SOUTHWESTERN ACADEMY

▼▼▼▼▼▼▼▼▼▼▼▼▼▼▼▼▼▼▼▼▼

SOUTHWESTERN SUMMER ADVENTURES

SAN MARINO, CALIFORNIA

TYPE OF PROGRAM: Academic enrichment, credit, and English as a second language
PARTICIPANTS: Boys and girls in grades 6–12
ENROLLMENT: 50
PROGRAM DATES: Four-, seven-, and fourteen-week programs, from June 9 to September 12
HEAD OF PROGRAM: Kenneth Veronda, Headmaster

LOCATION
The San Marino campus is located in one of the most beautiful neighborhoods in Southern California, minutes away from Pasadena and Los Angeles. The campus sprawls over more than 8 acres in a quiet and serene community, making this a perfect location for Middle School and high school students to board, study, and enjoy the summer.

BACKGROUND AND PHILOSOPHY
Southwestern Academy offers a warm, friendly, safe, and supportive environment for boys and girls to grow toward success. Founded in 1924, Southwestern is an accredited, not-for-profit, independent school for students from across the United States and around the world. Southwestern offers classes for grade 6 through high school. Small classes promote individual interaction with teachers and encourage the pursuit of interests beyond course requirements. Southwestern Academy's vision is to offer American and international students personalized, stimulating classes and supportive nurturing care that allows individual student success and an understanding of diverse cultures.

PROGRAM OFFERINGS
The Southwestern Summer Adventures program consists of two components: an Intensive English as a Second Language (ESL)/American Culture Program and traditional college-prep classes. Courses range from four weeks to a full semester and are offered on the campuses in San Marino, California, and in Beaver Creek, Arizona. Depending on the length of the program, students can earn academic credit.

The San Marino campus offers two English language programs. The **Intensive ESL Program** is designed to help students improve their English skills. There are three ability levels: beginning, intermediate, and advanced. Students improve their skills through listening and conversation, writing and grammar, and reading and vocabulary. There is also an SAT/TOEFL preparation component. Students who enroll in the seven-week or fourteen-week program can earn half- or full-semester credit. The **American Culture Program** teaches English-speaking skills, but it also incorporates field trips in the region. Course work includes 20 hours of English per week, developing reading, vocabulary, and conversation skills. Students receive a certificate at the end of the program.

Students who do not need ESL can select from a wide range of core courses, such as math, science, history, and English.

ENROLLMENT
Each program enrolls an average of 10 to 12 students, ages 11 through 18, who wish to improve their English skills and/or participate in a number of recreational and cultural activities in the region. Students are exposed to a multicultural learning atmosphere and gain a fresh perspective on academics. Students may commute to the program, or they can live in a dormitory at the school.

EXTRA OPPORTUNITIES AND ACTIVITIES
Weekly educational and entertaining field trips are offered to a variety of popular attractions throughout Southern California. Such trips include Disneyland, Griffith Park, Huntington Library, the Los Angeles County Museum of Art, and the Getty Museum. For boarding students, there are three additional trips offered each weekend.

FACILITIES
All dorms are of modern, masonry construction and have TVs, VCRs, and computers with Internet and e-mail access. Each dormitory is supervised by a resident counselor who has an apartment adjacent to the dormitory. Boarding students are provided with a buffet-style cooked breakfast and a family-style lunch and dinner. Commuting students have a hot lunch with the whole school group at no additional charge. Teachers and staff members eat with the students.

STAFF
The San Marino campus staff consists of the school's Headmaster, Dean of ESL, Director of Admissions, and approximately 25 teachers and dorm counselors. Counseling, testing, and crisis-intervention services are provided by the school psychologist.

MEDICAL CARE
The application includes authorization for the school to coordinate any medical procedures that may be necessary during the program.

COSTS

For 2007, the fourteen-week program (June 18 to September 7) cost $15,900. The seven-week program (June 18 to July 27) was $8250. The four-week programs (June 18 to July 13, July 16 to August 10, or August 13 to September 7) were $5500 for each session. Students also needed an additional amount of money in their student spending account.

APPLICATION TIMETABLE

The completed application includes an application form, an emergency medical form, a health statement, and the $100

application fee. The school accepts applications throughout the year and accepts students as long as space is available. On acceptance, the contract reserves space in the school.

FOR MORE INFORMATION, CONTACT

Director of Admissions
Southwest Academy
2800 Monterey Road
San Marino, California 91108

Phone: 626-799-5010 Ext. 5
Fax: 626-799-0407
E-mail: admissions@southwesternacademy.edu
Web site: http://www.southwesternacademy.edu

SOUTHWESTERN ADVENTURES

SUMMER ADVENTURES

RIMROCK, ARIZONA

TYPE OF PROGRAM: Academic enrichment, ESL courses, outdoor recreation, environmental education, field trips, and academic credit courses

PARTICIPANTS: Coeducational, ages 12–18

ENROLLMENT: 45

PROGRAM DATES: Four- and eight-week sessions, from June 23 to August 15

HEAD OF PROGRAM: Rob Bufton, Head of Campus

LOCATION

Southwestern Academy's Beaver Creek Ranch Campus is in a secluded red sandstone canyon that was carved by the creek around it. The Coconino National Forest surrounds the 180-acre campus. The campus rests at an elevation of 4,000 feet and is located 15 miles from Sedona, 45 miles south of Flagstaff, and 100 miles north of Phoenix, Arizona.

BACKGROUND AND PHILOSOPHY

Summer Adventures at Southwestern Academy offers students entering Upper or Middle School a four- or eight-week program that uniquely combines college-preparatory, academic enrichment, and language skills with the fun and exciting activities that the season presents.

PROGRAM OFFERINGS

Students enroll in classes that provide opportunities to link academics with some of the most popular hot spots of the area. Students also discover that the Summer Adventures program enables them to develop self-reliance and confidence while making new friendships with other students from around the world. The low teacher-student ratio provides a nurturing and supportive environment, establishing a sense of community and trust that embraces the school's core values. Field trips and scholastics are designed to be achievement based, with individual attention made available to each student as needed—all surrounded by an energetic and spirited atmosphere.

The Summer Adventures program includes a core curriculum with comprehensive courses in English, history, science,

math, Spanish, and art. Courses are selected individually to meet each student's academic needs. English as a second language is offered to international students who need to improve their skills in reading, writing, and speaking. Afternoons are left open for study time, enrichment through arts and crafts, elective course work, and travel. Electives also include outdoor and wilderness skills.

High school course credit and Lower School letters of achievement can be earned to make up credits for deficiencies, or students can gain a head start on the coming school year. Southwestern Academy is accredited by the Western Association of Schools and Colleges.

ENROLLMENT

Campers and counselors generally come from the Southwest area and are joined by other students from the U.S. and around the world. Southwestern Academy's programs are open to all qualified students without regard to race, creed, or national origin.

DAILY SCHEDULE

7:00– 7:30	Breakfast
7:30– 9:00	Period 1
9:10–10:40	Period 2
10:50–12:20	Period 3
12:20– 1:00	Lunch
1:30– 2:30	Study hall
3:00– 6:00	Activities
6:00– 6:45	Dinner
7:00–10:00	Programs

EXTRA OPPORTUNITIES AND ACTIVITIES

The canyon setting of the Beaver Creek Ranch Campus provides creek and pool swimming, archaeological and geological field trips, backpacking, rock climbing, and the exploration of nearby caves containing prehistoric remains. There is trout fishing in the creek as well as bass fishing in the campus ponds. The nights are clear for star gazing.

Recreational activities include basketball, softball, swimming, volleyball, horseback riding, hiking, billiards, table tennis, horseshoes, mountain biking, weight training, camping, and indoor games. A golf course is also nearby.

Weekend activities include overnight travel to Sunset Crater, the Grand Canyon, Lake Powell, Navajo and Hopi reservations, Petrified Forest, and Canyon de Chelly. Camping skills are learned and applied during these trips. In addition, there are organized studies at each site that provide hands-on learning in history, geology, ecology, economics, and geography.

FACILITIES

Campus buildings include classic dorms with double and triple rooms; river-stone cottages for faculty members; classrooms and study assembly; a science lab; recreation halls; natural and man-made swimming pools; indoor tennis, basketball, and volleyball courts; weight and fitness rooms; an art build-

ing; and sports fields. There is a full gymnasium on campus. Computers and computer instruction are available to all students.

Surrounded by large sycamores and cottonwoods, two ponds and a trout stream are located on campus.

STAFF

Southwestern Academy is an accredited college-preparatory school with a noncompetitive program. Teachers from the school's regular term instruct the summer program classes. Resident teachers supervise all afternoon and evening travel and activities.

COSTS

In 2007, tuition, room, and board were $5500 for the four-week session and $8950 for the eight-week session. A deposit of $500 was required for the student's personal expenses.

FINANCIAL AID

Limited financial aid is available. Special grants are based on financial need.

TRANSPORTATION

Beaver Creek Ranch Campus is 7 hours from Los Angeles by car and 1½ hours from Phoenix. A private airstrip is nearby. Unless other arrangements are made, students fly into Phoenix Sky Harbor Airport and take a shuttle to Camp Verde, where they are greeted by a Southwestern Academy staff or faculty member and escorted to the campus.

APPLICATION TIMETABLE

Southwestern's year-round campuses are always open for tours, interviews, and/or admission information. Applications are accepted throughout the year. Summer applications are due by May 15.

FOR MORE INFORMATION, CONTACT

San Marino Campus
Southwestern Academy
2800 Monterey Road
San Marino, California 91108
Phone: 626-799-5010 Ext. 5
Fax: 626-799-0407
E-mail: admissions@southwesternacademy.edu

Beaver Creek Ranch Campus
Southwestern Academy
Rimrock, Arizona 86335
Phone: 928-567-4581

PARTICIPANT/FAMILY COMMENTS

"Summer Adventures at Southwestern Academy is a place where everyone can find success."

"It was a good summer—the best of my life. The studying was difficult, but I'm so glad my parents sent me, or I never would have had this experience. You work for the teachers and counselors, and they work for you. There's not anything in the world they wouldn't do for us. They're just fantastic."

"Everybody works together as a unit. You know the teachers personally and respect their knowledge. But they're more than teachers, they're people who care. They teach you more than lessons—they teach you about life."

SPOLETO STUDY ABROAD

SUMMER ARTS AND HUMANITIES PROGRAM

SPOLETO, ITALY

TYPE OF PROGRAM: Visual arts, photography, film studies, dance, and vocal music

PARTICIPANTS: Coeducational, ages 15–19

ENROLLMENT: 40 per session

PROGRAM DATES: Summer Session I: June 20 to July 11 (Visual Arts, Photography, and Vocal Music) Summer Session II: July 16 to August 8 (Film Studies and Dance)

HEADS OF PROGRAM: Jill and Lorenzo Muti, Co-Directors

LOCATION

The Spoleto Valley in Central Italy is an ideal setting for students interested in an in-depth exploration of the visual and historical heritage of Italy. Cities like Assisi, Siena, Arezzo, or Orvieto, all filled with incredible artistic treasures, are easily reached by car or by train, and major centers like Rome or Florence are less than 2 hours away. This region is emblematic of Central Italy, both historically and artistically.

BACKGROUND AND PHILOSOPHY

The Spoleto Study Abroad Summer Sessions 2008 for Students is a collaborative community of artists and scholars gathered to explore deeply the rich cultural heritage of central Italy while fostering individual artistic, intellectual, and personal growth.

This program takes place in Trevi, in the Spoleto Valley, one of the most beautiful areas of Central Italy. It offers students, ages 15–19, who are interested in visual arts, photography, film, dance, and vocal music, a challenging and innovative experience. Students will be immersed in this diverse, vibrant culture and surrounded by talented and motivated peers and faculty members.

Spoleto Study Abroad is an international program cosponsored by a consortium of selective independent schools. Spoleto Study Abroad is celebrating its eleventh year of cultivating the arts and humanities in students from around the world.

PROGRAM OFFERINGS

Visual Arts Students explore the philosophical, intellectual, and technical aspects of art through art history, studio classes, and hands-on field trips. Courses include instruction and practice in drawing, painting, and two-dimensional design. The theoretical aspects of the course are then illustrated with visits to and examinations of works of art found throughout the town and the region. Students are encouraged to take risks, to experiment with new media, and to incorporate new subject matter in order to develop a stronger portfolio. Final projects are exhibited at the art show.

Photography Students study a selection of historical and contemporary photographers while developing a personal style of their own. The course focuses on a variety of photographic techniques, such as portraiture, landscape, night photography, documentary photography, and hand-coloring Polaroid dye transfers. Final projects are exhibited at the art show.

Vocal Music Emphasizing artistic and technical growth, students are immersed in a wealth of vocal musical offerings. Throughout the course of study, students are exposed to the history and influence of Italian opera from its inception through four centuries of transformations to the present day. Students receive both private and group instruction with leading musicians in the field, exploring a gamut of musical compositions from the early baroque to the contemporary. This course takes into consideration the developmental level of individual singers. With this in mind, prior to the start of the session, students are encouraged to bring or request music that would be of particular interest to them. Several concerts are given throughout the session, giving the students the opportunity to perform in Spoleto, Trevi, and in neighboring towns in the Spoleto Valley.

Film Exploring the emergence of post-WWII Italian cinema and the directors whose work and influence changed the way movies are made, students in this course view, discuss, and analyze films by DeSica, Fellini, Rosellini, Bertolucci, and Antonioni. Students are also invited to compare these seminal films to excerpts from the works of other European and American directors. This course teaches students how to "read" a film and provides a thorough introduction to essential cinematic vocabularies.

Taking advantage of the Spoleto program's extraordinary setting, as well as opportunities for location shooting elsewhere in Umbria and Tuscany, students produce a short (5–8 minute) digital film, developing their concept from treatment to screenplay to shooting script and edited footage.

ENROLLMENT

Students must have finished the ninth grade and demonstrate marked proficiency in either instrumental/vocal music or drama through an audition process or through submission of a portfolio. There is no language requirement.

DAILY SCHEDULE

Classes are scheduled four days a week and follow a typical Italian pace of life.

8:00	Breakfast
9:00	Classes
1:15	Lunch
3:00– 5:00	Free time/organized activities
5:00	Studio workshops and rehearsals
8:00	Dinner

EXTRA OPPORTUNITIES AND ACTIVITIES

Throughout the session, the faculty team plans interdisciplinary units of study that are enriched by excursions to such cultural centers as Florence, Siena, Assisi, Rome, Urbino, and other medieval hill towns throughout Umbria and Tuscany.

Recreational activities are planned throughout the session. The city also offers facilities for swimming, soccer, basketball, and tennis.

FACILITIES

Classes take place in the gorgeous sixteenth-century Villa Fabbri. The building, which takes its name from the local family responsible for its original construction, is situated right in the middle of town and is surrounded by a beautiful park. The Villa offers breathtaking views of the Spoleto Valley and the crest of hills covered with olive trees that encircle it. The rooms in the building offer abundant and luminous space for art and music classes. One of the most dazzling aspects of the Villa is the first-floor area, which is completely adorned with sixteenth-century frescoes still reverberating with vibrant colors.

Students are also lodged in the Villa. The second floor of the main structure and its adjacent nineteenth-century wing have been refurbished and offer double or triple bedrooms with a view either onto the park or the open valley.

Just across the street from the Villa is a nineteenth-century theater, a spectacular little jewel that is used for master classes, concerts, and the normal daily activity of the drama program.

STAFF

Faculty members at Spoleto Study Abroad are distinguished artists and educators from colleges, universities, and secondary schools from the United States and Italy. They are chosen for their extensive knowledge and enthusiasm, their dynamic teaching methods, and their ability to work closely with students.

MEDICAL CARE

Spoleto Study Abroad is affiliated with a medical staff that is available to see students who require care. Students needing emergency attention are taken to the closest hospital.

COSTS

The comprehensive fee for Spoleto Study Abroad is $5800 per session. This fee includes tuition, all meals, lodging, books, materials, entrance fees for group activities, and all transportation in Italy. Expenses not included are round-trip airfare to Rome, passport fees, travel insurance, and such personal expenses as laundry, snacks, telephone calls, and spending money. Fees are set based on the exchange rate on September 20 of each year. Spoleto Study Abroad reserves the right to make equitable tuition adjustments if the exchange rate varies significantly by June 1 preceding the summer sessions.

TRANSPORTATION

Specific flights are announced at the time of acceptance into the program. Staff members meet all participants to escort them to Rome on the same international flight. Students are met at Fiumicino Airport in Rome by Spoleto Study Abroad staff members. At the end of the program, students are chaperoned back to the program's gateway city.

APPLICATION TIMETABLE

Inquiries about the program are welcome anytime. Applications can also be downloaded from the Web site. Applications are due on February 1, 2008. Spoleto Study Abroad accepts late applications as long as space remains available.

FOR MORE INFORMATION, CONTACT

Nancy Langston, Marketing Director
Spoleto Study Abroad
P.O. Box 13389
Charleston, South Carolina 29422-3389

Phone: 843-822-1248
E-mail: spoleto@mindspring.com
Web site: http://www.spoletostudyabroad.com

PARTICIPANT/FAMILY COMMENTS

"Traveling to Italy to pursue my passion for art while working in an atmosphere where everyone is also striving to fulfill their insatiable hunger for learning is truly ideal. What an opportunity!"—Whitner B., Charlotte, North Carolina

"The classes and teachers are amazing! Such dedication! Such skill and talent do these wonderful people possess that I don't feel as if I am in school . . . no, I truly love waking up and going to class."—Alex M., Princeton Junction, New Jersey

"I have learned more about being an actor throughout the summer session than I would in a semester course at home. The faculty is intense, demanding, and fun."—Zoe S., San Francisco, California

"I will leave Spoleto Study Abroad with new drawing skills, a deeper appreciation for the beautiful art here, a more informed understanding of Italy's history and culture, and a different outlook on others and myself."— Michael M., Knoxville, Tennessee

"I have found my Spoleto Study Abroad experience to essentially be the catalyst in bringing out the true artist from within me."— Matthew V., Glendale, California

SQUAW VALLEY ACADEMY

SQUAW VALLEY ACADEMY

SUMMER SCHOOL

LAKE TAHOE, CALIFORNIA

TYPE OF PROGRAM: Academic enrichment and credit, outdoor athletics

PARTICIPANTS: Boys and girls entering grades 6 through 12

ENROLLMENT: 65

PROGRAM DATES: Two 3-week semesters, June 24–August 3, 2007

HEAD OF PROGRAM: Donald Rees, Cofounder and Headmaster

LOCATION

Squaw Valley Academy (SVA) is nestled in a valley at the edge of the Tahoe National Forest in California, within 5 miles of Lake Tahoe and 2 miles from Squaw Valley USA, the site of the 1960 Winter Olympics. At an elevation of 6,200 feet, the campus experiences a full range of seasonal climate and enjoys 300 days of sunshine each year. Temperatures range from 20°F in winter to 85°F in summer. Reno/Tahoe International Airport is the closest airport for arrivals and departures.

SVA is near Tahoe City and the historic town of Truckee, California. Sacramento is 100 miles to the west, Reno is 45 miles to the east, and San Francisco is about 200 miles west, or about 4 hours by car.

BACKGROUND AND PHILOSOPHY

Squaw Valley Academy was founded in 1978 to offer a combination of college-preparatory learning, outdoor education, and sports opportunities for sixth through twelfth graders. SVA has strong preparation for college and university as its central focus and also incorporates outdoor sports and activities as a catalyst for personal growth and achievement.

Each day, students participate in outdoor sports to foster real accomplishment and a strong student community. SVA provides opportunities for mountain

biking, hiking, river and sea kayaking, white-water rafting, swimming, summer ice skating, and rock climbing. Students may also take weekend trips to Virginia City, Reno, Sacramento, and other nearby cities.

A typical day includes morning classes to earn credit for a semester or full-year course. Teachers integrate study and organizational skills in specific subject areas. Although the program is international, it readily accepts students who may be struggling academically. These students benefit from small class sizes and experienced, patient teachers.

PROGRAM OFFERINGS

Most core academic courses are offered: algebra I, algebra II, biology, chemistry, creative writing, economics, English 9–12, ESL, geometry, government, physics, prealgebra, precalculus, Spanish I–IV, studio art, U.S. history, world geography, world history, and more middle school core courses. A minimum of 3 students must be enrolled to offer a course.

The English as a Second Language Program (ESL) is available for students ages 10 through 17, in all levels of English. Students participate in English immersion by also attending classes with American students, sharing a dormitory room with an American student, and participating in all outdoor sports. Group discounts are available for this program.

Most core academic and some elective courses are offered for credit. Students may earn credit either for one semester in the three-week session or for a full-year course in the six-week session.

Participants enroll in two academic courses per session plus an outdoor activity in the afternoon. Each course is 2 hours per day.

ENROLLMENT

Typically, SVA hosts 65 summer school boys and girls from many countries and the United States.

DAILY SCHEDULE

```
 7:30 . . . Breakfast
 8:15 . . . Course one
10:15 . . . Break
10:30 . . . Course two
12:30 . . . Lunch
 1:00 . . . Afternoon activity
 5:15 . . . Dinner
 5:45 . . . Dinner crew clean-up
 6:00 . . . Free time
 7:30 . . . Mandatory study hall
 9:30 . . . Free time
10:00 . . . Lights out
```

EXTRA OPPORTUNITIES AND ACTIVITIES

The Academy offers three different activities each day, from which students select one option. Activities include swimming, mountain biking, tennis, hiking, miniature golf, ice skating, fly fishing, kayaking, horseback riding, and trips to nearby museums. On weekends, all students participate in one designated activity, such as a boat cruise, white-water rafting, or a beach picnic party. Costs for these activities are deducted from the student account.

FACILITIES

Two separate residential buildings accommodate students and staff. Four students live in each room, which includes a private bathroom and shower. Common rooms and laundry facilities are located in each building. There are adult staff members on duty 24 hours per day, seven days a week.

STAFF

The Academy's staff and faculty members believe self-esteem is enhanced through real accomplishment in the academic, athletic, and social aspects of life at a boarding school. The faculty members teach a project-based curriculum to meet the California state standards within the state framework.

Most full-time teachers have a current teaching credential and a minimum of two years' teaching experience prior to SVA. About half the staff members have advanced degrees in their subject areas. In addition, many teachers offer an elective based on their experience and expertise outside their academic subject(s).

MEDICAL CARE

Medical staff members hold all medications in a locked cabinet and distribute as necessary. Sick students stay in the on-campus infirmary after a visit to the nearby doctor's office. The Truckee Tahoe Forest Hospital is 10 miles north.

RELIGIOUS LIFE

Religious services are held at local churches that serve a number of faiths, but attendance at these services is not required by SVA.

COSTS

In 2007–08, boarding students pay $7980 for the two-semester program, which covers tuition, room, board, and education. Day students pay $3500, which covers education only. Boarding students are required to pay a $525 room deposit plus an additional $2000 into a student account. All textbooks and uniforms are purchased separately. The tuition for the one-semester, three-week program is half the six-week tuition.

TRANSPORTATION

SVA is located 2 miles east of Squaw Valley USA and 10 miles south of Truckee, California. Students who fly to SVA from other areas should arrive at the Reno/Tahoe International Airport, and SVA staff members will transport them to the campus, or the student may take a taxi or private shuttle for the 45-minute ride.

APPLICATION TIMETABLE

Applicants are required to submit a completed summer school application along with a teacher recommendation, a principal/counselor recommendation, a copy of the student's most recent transcript and/or report card, a copy of the student's disciplinary/behavioral records (or confirmation that the student has no disciplinary history at the school), and copies of standardized aptitude or achievement tests. There is no application deadline, but students should apply as early as possible to guarantee placement in the program.

FOR MORE INFORMATION, CONTACT

Summer School Admissions
Squaw Valley Academy
235 Squaw Valley Road
P.O. Box 2667
Olympic Valley, California 96146
Phone: 530-583-9393 Ext. 14
Fax: 530-581-1111
E-mail: info@sva.org
Web site: http://www.sva.org/index.php?click1=
　　　　　summerterm

STAGEDOOR MANOR PERFORMING ARTS CENTER

SUMMER THEATER/DANCE CAMP

LOCH SHELDRAKE IN THE CATSKILL MOUNTAINS, NEW YORK

TYPE OF PROGRAM: Theater, dance camp
PARTICIPANTS: Boys and girls, ages 10–18
ENROLLMENT: 265
PROGRAM DATES: Three-, six-, or nine-week sessions; June 18–July 8, July 9–29, and July 30–August 19
HEADS OF PROGRAM: Cynthia Samuelson, Owner and Producer; Barbara Fine Martin, Director

LOCATION

Located in the heart of the famous "Catskills on Broadway" vacation area, Stagedoor Manor is in a woodland setting just 95 miles northwest of New York City. Thirty-one years ago, the Samuelson family bought and converted a small resort hotel into a multispace theater complex.

BACKGROUND AND PHILOSOPHY

Stagedoor Manor combines all the excitement of theater with all the fun of a great summer camp.

Stagedoor Manor is the only summer theater program of its kind in the world, a complete community where all of the kids and staff members are in love with the theater, dance, and the performing arts. Stagedoor believes that each boy and girl should be guided to choose his or her own schedule, with a flexibility that encourages them to stretch and grow and discover new capabilities.

No previous experience is required. Many of the campers are beginners or have been in school plays. Others have already appeared on Broadway, in films, or on television. Each camper is given the opportunity at his or her experience level to study and grow at his or her own pace.

Stagedoor Manor teaches theater, dance, and voice extremely well, but much more important is its goal to nurture and care for its campers.

PROGRAM OFFERINGS

At Stagedoor Manor, time is divided into thirds.

Classes: Taught in almost every aspect of performance, classes include theater, dance, voice, and technical arts; technique and improvisation; acting for film and television; comedy; moviemaking; Shakespeare; modeling and makeup; speech and diction; costuming, lights, and technical theater; ballet (all levels), tap, jazz, and modern dance; and choreography and styles. Advanced master classes are available for those ready to go beyond the beginner levels. Guest workshops on all subjects are taught by working leaders in the industry. More than fifty different classes are offered in all skill levels. Each camper chooses an individual class program with faculty guidance and mentoring.

Performances: Every camper is in a show at all times. Nobody is left out. Stagedoor produces eight musicals and five dramas in every session. To ensure individual attention and coaching, musicals are cast with 24 to 26 campers per show and dramas with 10 to 15 campers per show. Many agents, managers, and casting directors attend rehearsals and performances searching for fresh talent.

Stagedoor alumni include film star Natalie Portman, singer/actress Mandy Moore, *Scrubs* star Zach Braff, Robert Downey Jr., *2½ Men* star Jon Cryer, Helen Slater, Mary Stuart Masterson, *The Village* star Bryce Dallas Howard, and writer/director Todd Graff, who created the movie *CAMP* based on his memories of Stagedoor Manor and filmed it at the camp in 2003. Many famous alumni return each summer to share their experiences with current campers.

Recreation: Activities include swimming (an outdoor pool for hot summer days and a heated indoor pool for rainy days and evenings), tennis (coach on staff), volleyball, basketball, dee-jay dances, open-microphone coffeehouse and canteen, game nights, trips off camp to movies and dinner, camper-organized showcases, and themed parties every session. All sports are noncompetitive for those who want to join in.

ENROLLMENT

Boys and girls, ages 10–18, come to Stagedoor Manor from every state and all over the world. They attend for three weeks, six weeks, or nine weeks. No audition is required, but Stagedoor seeks campers who love performance and want to be totally immersed in the world of theater.

FACILITIES

At Stagedoor Manor's private former resort hotel, campers live (4–6 in a room) dormitory style in regular hotel rooms with private bathrooms. All rooms are fully carpeted, with bunks, full-size clothing chests, and closets. Landscaped grounds and cozy walkways give the camp a campus atmosphere. Adding on through the years, the site now houses seven theaters, twenty-two class-rooms, video studios, outdoor and indoor heated pools, an air-conditioned dining room, and dance and rehearsal studios. Two major theaters are also air conditioned.

STAFF

Teachers at Stagedoor Manor are mature professionals who are active in the theatrical industry and teach at leading universities. A separate counseling staff (all age 21 or over), with no junior counselors or counselors in training, provides close supervision and support. The staff numbers 160 members for 265 campers.

Guest workshop and Master Class visitors include Broadway, movie, and television stars, along with agents, casting directors, and behind-the-scenes creative talent. Recent guests include Broadway duo Richard Maltby and David Shire, CBS series star Yancy Arias, Rockette dance captain Kim Calore, commercial actor and author Aaron Marcus, Broadway musical director and conductor Kim Grigsby, Tony-nominated actor Gavin Creel, Tony award–winning Broadway composer Jeanine Tesori, *Wicked* star Michelle Federer, and multiple-Tony costume designer Ann Hould-Ward. Representatives from Nickelodeon, Disney, Wilhelmina, Brookside Artists, Carson Adler, Warner Brothers, MTV, and many others visit, looking for tomorrow's stars. Former Stagedoor alumni, now working on film, TV, and stage, join the camp on show weekends to share their experiences and give advice to current campers.

MEDICAL CARE

Stagedoor provides a health center staffed by registered nurses, paramedics, and emergency medical technicians 24 hours a day. There are separate rooms, with television and air conditioning, for those who require isolation and rest. A nearby medical group is on call, with Catskill Medical Center only 10 minutes away.

RELIGIOUS LIFE

Stagedoor Manor is nonsectarian. Campers who wish may attend services at nearby churches and temples. Escort and transportation are provided.

COSTS

Sessions at Stagedoor are three weeks. Tuition starts at $4445 for one session, with consideration for additional sessions. This tuition includes room and board, use of all facilities, rental of scripts and costumes, and any technical support required for productions. A full preview of fees is listed on the enrollment contract.

TRANSPORTATION

Campers fly into Newark Airport, just outside New York, where they are met by Stagedoor staff members and taken to the camp in large air-conditioned coaches. Return to the airport is provided if required.

APPLICATION TIMETABLE

Rolling enrollment begins in September and continues to late spring the next year. Some sessions and age groups fill up faster than others, and early registration is advised.

FOR MORE INFORMATION, CONTACT

Cynthia Samuelson and Barbara Fine Martin
8 Wingate Road
Lexington, Massachusetts 02421
Phone: 888-STAGE-88 (toll-free)
E-mail: stagedoormanor@aol.com
Web site: http://www.stagedoormanor.com/

PARTICIPANT/FAMILY COMMENTS

"Stagedoor Manor was a wonderful way to be introduced to the world of acting. It was great groundwork into musical theater, dance, and most importantly, acting."—Actress Helen Slater (as quoted in the *New York Times*)

"I was born at Stagedoor Manor. The camp is like Oz. Your real life is in black and white, but the minute you step off the bus, everything is in color."—Writer/director Todd Graff (*CAMP*)

"We will never be able to tell you what your camp has meant to us and our son . . . he has carried the pride and new found confidence with him all year long!"—Stagedoor parent

"Solid educational and administrative foundation, a history of success, and an overriding concern for the character development of the children entrusted to them."—*Town and Country* magazine

"Thank you so very much for a summer filled with wonderful memories and so much joy. I learned so much about myself as an artist, in an environment filled with unconditional love and support. Stagedoor made me who I am."—Stagedoor camper

"The only thing wrong with Stagedoor Manor is it's only for kids. This truly ticks me off. Every time I go, I want to stay!"—Actor Richard Dreyfuss

STANFORD UNIVERSITY

SUMMER COLLEGE FOR HIGH SCHOOL STUDENTS

STANFORD, CALIFORNIA

TYPE OF PROGRAM: College preparation

PARTICIPANTS: Coeducational; for students who have completed their junior or senior year of high school. Applications from accomplished and mature high school sophomores are also considered.

ENROLLMENT: 300–325 students

PROGRAM DATES: One 8-week session from the end of June through the middle of August

HEAD OF PROGRAM: Patricia Brandt, Associate Dean for Summer Session

LOCATION
Stanford University is located approximately 35 miles south of San Francisco, California.

BACKGROUND AND PHILOSOPHY
Stanford admits to the summer session exceptional high school students who are ready to explore a challenging university environment. This includes enrolling in regular Stanford courses, living together in Stanford student residences, and interacting with members of the Stanford faculty and student community. Students gain an inside perspective on life at a major university and begin to shape the college study skills that will prepare them for their freshman year.

PROGRAM OFFERINGS
Selected Stanford undergraduate courses for which the student has met the prerequisites are open to Summer College students. Subjects include anthropology, art, astronomy, athletics, biological sciences, chemistry, classics, communications, comparative literature, computer science, drama, economics, engineering, English, foreign languages, history, mathematics, music, philosophy, physics, political science, psychology, sociology, and statistics. The recommended and minimum course load for residential Summer College students is 8 units, which consists of two or three elective courses. The maximum course load is 12 units. As is expected at a preeminent university, course work expectations are demanding and grading is far more difficult than in high school. All summer course work completed by high school students in the Stanford Summer College may be applied toward a Stanford degree should the student subsequently be admitted to a regular degree program. Credit for work at Stanford may be transferred to other universities at the discretion of those institutions.

A special Success Series program has been developed for residential Summer College participants. College Admission 101 is an opportunity to meet with Stanford admission officers and gain an inside perspective on the college admission process. Participants identify the skills that will help them research and select the colleges and universities that are appropriate for them. They learn how to secure recommendations and understand the role extracurricular activities play in their admission package. Working Smarter is a course that teaches strategies in time management, reading, speaking, writing, and test preparation. Participants explore learning preferences and develop techniques to optimize their education. Writing Well at the College Level is a course designed to improve participants' critical-thinking skills, encourage them to feel comfortable expressing themselves, and strengthen their writing techniques. SAT Preparation Class is a workshop in which participants build skills and confidence for taking the SAT. Instruction focuses on test-taking strategies to enhance performance on the exam.

While it is recommended that all high school students take part in the residential program, students from the Bay Area who live within manageable commuting distance may participate in the program as commuter students. Commuter students are required to take a minimum of 3 units of course work.

ENROLLMENT
Approximately 300 to 325 high school students from across the country and around the world participate in the Summer College.

EXTRA OPPORTUNITIES AND ACTIVITIES
While it is true that students spend a large portion of their free time studying, there are many opportunities for out-of-classroom learning and fun. Some activities are organized by the program staff, while others are initiated and planned by the students themselves. Past activities have included intramural sports teams, dorm yearbook, talent show, house discussions with Stanford professors and undergraduate admission staff members, visits to San Francisco and Monterey, and public service projects.

FACILITIES

Located on a stunning 8,100-acre campus, Stanford University is renowned for its dedication to scholarly pursuits. All Summer College students live together in historic Lagunita Court, which is located within 5 minutes' walking or biking distance of most classrooms and is equipped with computer lounges and quiet areas perfect for late-night study and conversations. In addition, students have access to the Stanford Libraries, with more than 2.4 million volumes in their humanities and social sciences collections, as well as Stanford's extensive athletic facilities, including fully equipped gymnasiums, an Olympic-size pool, and an eighteen-hole golf course.

STAFF

An experienced and carefully chosen group of Stanford students serve as mentors in the dorm, providing students with advice on how to make a successful transition to college life. An adult program director is also in residence to provide supervision. Students are trained to be their own educational advocates, forming a house government and organizing house programs and activities.

MEDICAL CARE

Vaden Student Health Center has a full-time staff of physicians, nurses, and mental health professionals. Students must have health insurance to register at Stanford University. They may purchase insurance from the University, if necessary.

COSTS

The cost for 8 units of university course work, room, board, textbooks, and program fee was approximately $9500 for the eight-week session in 2007.

FINANCIAL AID

A limited amount of scholarship aid is available.

TRANSPORTATION

The San Francisco Bay Area is served by international airports in San Francisco and San Jose. Students can take a shuttle directly from any of the airports to the Stanford campus.

APPLICATION TIMETABLE

Summer brochures and applications are available in the beginning of January; applications are due late April. Admission is selective but is designed to be more open than the Stanford undergraduate admission process. Students are encouraged to apply as early as possible, as enrollment is limited. Students who wish to be admitted as commuters submit the same application as the residential students and are evaluated by the same standards as residential applicants. Admission decisions are made on a rolling basis to accommodate early applications.

A completed application consists of the application form; an official high school transcript; SAT, PSAT, or ACT test scores; an essay; one letter of recommendation from a high school teacher or counselor; and a $50 application fee. Admission to the Stanford Summer College for High School Students does not imply later admission to one of Stanford's regular degree programs.

FOR MORE INFORMATION, CONTACT

Stanford Summer Session
482 Galvez Street
Stanford, California 94305-6079

Phone: 650-723-3109
Fax: 650-725-6080
E-mail: summersession@stanford.edu
Web site: http://summer.stanford.edu

SUMMER AT DELPHI™

THE DELPHIAN SCHOOL™

SHERIDAN, OREGON

TYPE OF PROGRAM: Residential and day private academic camp with personalized student programs, challenging activities, fun weekend trips, and traditional camping; also an English as a second language (ESL) program
PARTICIPANTS: Coeducational; day, ages 5–18; boarding, ages 8–18
ENROLLMENT: 300 students
PROGRAM DATES: June 23 to August 2
HEAD OF PROGRAM: Rosemary Didear, Headmistress

LOCATION
The Delphian School's 800-acre campus is set among rolling hills in the Oregon Coastal Range. The expanses of meadows and forestland support many outdoor activities. The recreational resources of the city of Portland, Mount Hood, and the Pacific Coast are nearby.

BACKGROUND AND PHILOSOPHY
Delphi was founded in 1976 by a group of educators and parents who were concerned about the decline that they perceived in the standards of American education. Delphi uses the innovative study methods developed by American philosopher and educator L. Ron Hubbard. These methods are recognized worldwide as a breakthrough in education; with them, students develop the confidence and know-how to tackle even the most challenging subjects. Students become increasingly able to take responsibility for their own education. The Delphian School is licensed to use Applied Scholastics™ educational services.

PROGRAM OFFERINGS
Delphi is so much more than a summer camp. It is a challenging environment for anyone who wants to learn, thrive, and grow. Students are challenged every day with improving their study skills as well as their understanding of basic subjects such as math, science, English, and computer technology.

Delphi is one of the only summer camps to give students instruction in the subject of how to study. This vital instruction, which is missing in many school systems today, can greatly increase any student's enthusiasm for learning. As they learn these study methods, students find they are able to understand and apply the data they are studying in school. The result is that many students realize they can succeed in today's competitive environment, and their enthusiasm for learning soars.

The School offers more than 250 academic courses ranging from math and writing to nutrition and photography. At the same time, students are challenged with a wide range of sports and outdoor activities that all take advantage of the beautifully scenic Pacific Northwest and all it has to offer. Activities include horseback riding, archery, sports, drama, art and music, and tennis, as well as exciting weekend trips like whitewater rafting, camping, exploring Seattle, trips to the beach, hiking, and more. Students should visit http://www.SummerAtDelphi.com for a complete list of activities and weekend trips.

The purpose of the Summer at Delphi program is to challenge young people in and out of the classroom and help them discover that their potential for success is unlimited. It truly is a once-in-a-lifetime experience.

ENROLLMENT
Delphi enrolls 300 boys and girls, ages 5–18, for the Summer Session. Students who are 8 years or older may board. Summer

at Delphi is an international experience—students come from across the United States and from various other countries. Delphi admits students of any race, color, and national or ethnic origin.

DAILY SCHEDULE
In the Upper School, mornings and evenings are devoted to classroom academics. Afternoons are spent on a variety of activities, such as sports, archery, swimming, horseback riding, ceramics, or computer studies.

Middle School students spend their mornings and late afternoons on academic subjects. Afternoons include such activities as art, ceramics, music, horseback riding, swimming, computer studies, and a variety of sports, including archery. Evenings are reserved for group activities such as crafts and games.

In the Lower School, there is even greater emphasis on the outdoors and on recreational activities that have educational value. Students go on field trips and other outings. In general, the mornings are devoted to basic reading and math studies.

All students who are 12 or older participate in the school's student services program. Through the program, students contribute 50 minutes a day to the operation and maintenance of the school, gaining a greater appreciation and responsibility for the workings of a large organization.

EXTRA OPPORTUNITIES AND ACTIVITIES
Regular weekend excursions can include anything from whitewater rafting to exploring Seattle. There is a swimming or bowling trip one afternoon a week and several off-campus full-weekend excursions, including at least one camping trip. Upper School students can travel to Ashland for the world-renowned Oregon Shakespeare Festival. On-campus activities include dances, movies, a model rocket launch, and sports tournaments. Upper School and older Middle School students may participate in their

choice of five different camps: tennis, soccer, volleyball, chess, and horsecare/riding–all offered as part-time one- to two-week-long camps.

FACILITIES

All academic facilities are located in the large main building. There is a chemistry/biology lab as well as a state-of-the-art audio/visual lab. There are more than 100 computers with Internet access available throughout the school; a library with more than 10,000 volumes; a theater; music practice rooms; art, ceramics, and photography studios; a career center; and a woodshop. There are also a student lounge, a recreation room, and a snack bar.

Student dormitories are located in both the main building and another building overlooking the Willamette Valley.

Athletics facilities include a 13,500-square-foot gymnasium with basketball, volleyball, and racquetball courts and a room for weight lifting and gymnastics. There are athletics fields for soccer, baseball, and softball and four outdoor lighted tennis courts.

STAFF

Rosemary Didear became the third Head of School in the year 2000. She is a graduate of Columbia University's Barnard College; before her appointment, she served as the school's Dean.

The faculty is composed of more than 40 experienced educators and 50 additional staff members who instruct, provide dorm supervision, coach, and generally advise students outside of the classroom in the afternoons and evenings. Faculty members have a broad range of practical and professional experience, and many have been at the Delphian School for more than twenty years. All faculty and staff members are chosen for their ability to work closely with students, and most live on campus with their families.

MEDICAL CARE

A Medical Liaison on campus is able to give immediate first aid for injuries and accidents and arrange for emergency or specialized medical care when necessary.

Not all injuries and illnesses call for treatment by a physician, and care may be carried out at Delphi following guidelines developed with the school's consulting physician.

Doctors are in the nearby towns of Sheridan and McMinnville; the nearest hospital is 30 minutes away in McMinnville.

RELIGIOUS LIFE

The neighboring towns have religious services for most major faiths; the school arranges for transportation so that students may attend.

COSTS

The Delphian School offers many different programs (day school, seven-day boarding, five-day boarding, English as a second language, and summer boarding and day programs); each has its own price structure. Participants should inquire online (http://www.SummerAtDelphi.org) or call the Admissions Office at 800-626-6610 to request a price sheet.

TRANSPORTATION

Transportation between the school and the Portland airport and train station is provided on scheduled enrollment and departure days.

APPLICATION TIMETABLE

An initial inquiry is welcome at any time. On-campus interviews are conducted from 9 a.m. to 5 p.m. Monday through Friday. Because space is limited, early applications are encouraged. There is a nonrefundable $50 application fee.

FOR MORE INFORMATION, CONTACT

Sharon Fry, Director of Admissions
The Delphian School
20950 Southwest Rock Creek Road
Sheridan, Oregon 97378
Phone: 503-843-3521
       800-626-6610 (toll-free)
E-mail: summer@delphian.org
Web site: http://www.summeratdelphi.org

PARTICIPANT/FAMILY COMMENTS

"I've learned more about responsibility and integrity, and I've gained more confidence in myself. The wholesome learning environment has made me enthusiastic about education again."

"I'm really excited that I finished this course (algebra) because now I feel like I will be much better prepared for geometry, which is the class that I will be taking this year at my school. It was hard, but feels very rewarding now."

"Learning How to Learn by L. Ron Hubbard really helped me understand why, at times, even when I was interested in a subject, I would want to stop learning. Now I am able to learn whatever I want, and if I start to feel bad about learning, I will know what to do, which is really exciting!"

SUMMERBERG AT HEIDELBERG COLLEGE

Heidelberg College

▼▲▼▲▼▲▼▲▼▲▼▲▼▲▼▲▼▲▼▲▼▲▼▲▼▲▼▲▼▲▼▲▼▲

SUMMER RESIDENTIAL ACADEMIC PROGRAM FOR BOYS AND GIRLS ENTERING EIGHTH THROUGH TWELFTH GRADES

TIFFLIN, OHIO

TYPE OF PROGRAM: Academic enrichment program
PARTICIPANTS: Coeducational, ages 12 to 17
ENROLLMENT: Approximately 100 students per session
PROGRAM DATES: Two 2-week sessions from July 15 to August 10
HEADS OF PROGRAM: Douglas Murphy, Director

LOCATION

Heidelberg College lies on a beautiful 110-acre campus in Tiffin, Ohio. The surrounding area is lovely, and the charming town of Tiffin is the social center for the farming and academic community. The downtown area is a safe, short walk from campus and features cafes, a bookstore, shops, music, cultural and historic attractions, and more.

BACKGROUND AND PHILOSOPHY

SummerBerg is designed to keep students engaged through hands-on classroom projects, fun activities, and personal coaching. Courses are designed to be challenging, but also clear and accessible. SummerBerg's team of talented teachers and resident advisers (RAs) are trained to serve students not only as educators, but also as counselors, mentors, and friends. During each two-week session, students live together in a modern residence hall on Heidelberg's idyllic campus.

PROGRAM OFFERINGS

Broadcast Journalism In this exciting program, students have the opportunity to learn first-hand about television journalism. The program focuses both on the technical aspects of television production and on the skills required of TV reporters, including reporting, interviewing techniques, story writing, and editing news stories into compelling narratives. Students work in the studios of WHEI, a television station owned and operated by Heidelberg College, which telecasts programming that is entirely produced, written, and directed by Heidelberg College students. The students learn how to put together field reports and full broadcasts with weather, news, and sports. Because the classes are small, each student has a chance to participate in all of the major roles of a TV broadcast, including acting as anchorperson, director, and camera operator. No experience is necessary.

Chinese SummerBerg's Chinese course introduces students to the Mandarin language as well as to the Chinese culture and customs. No past experience with Chinese is required for students in this class; the fluent instructors take students step-by-step through the

process of language learning, keeping assignments always fun and collaborative. Students first learn the fundamentals of tonal languages, practicing pronunciation with their instructors and each other. Then they add vocabulary and grammar skills, all in the course of learning how to have basic conversations with Mandarin speakers. SummerBerg teachers incorporate original ideas into a well-founded approach to language, and they take advantage of the Heidelberg campus and its multimedia capabilities. The class also presents the Mandarin language in a cultural context, exposing students to the fascinating complexities of Chinese society. Regions and cities are discussed alongside art, politics, and religion. A class-related field trip near the end of the session allows students to speak Chinese in a real-world setting.

Creative Writing Creative Writing Workshop offers guidance to all aspiring writers, regardless of experience. Students read a variety of texts and are encouraged to write every day and share their work in a relaxed and supportive environment. Whether meeting at the library, in the classroom, or on a shady spot on the campus, this program is about helping students find their voice and articulate their ideas in written formats. Creative Writing Workshop is also a good choice for students who need to work on their writing skills and mechanics; students gain the ability to express themselves more clearly and elegantly through exposure to the technical side of the English language. Imagination is welcomed and fostered, helping students discover their inner voice through whatever style they choose. The teachers are young creative writing professionals who are familiar with the classics of poetry and fiction, as well as essential contemporary works. Each session includes a mix of activities and programs, ranging from poetry readings to improvisational free writes to open mics with readings by professional writers, including the course's own teachers.

Film Studies At SummerBerg, students learn to understand television and movies in novel ways. Through an exploration of the history of the medium, as well as exposure to theories and schools of film, students gain a new appreciation for film and a more sophisticated critical eye. Students first become familiar with the basic tools of filmmaking, including screen writing, directing, and editing; they also discuss the implications of digital media in film's evolution. Class work is composed of discussion, lectures, research in the library and online, and, of course, lots and lots of movies. Students read Pauline Kael and understand why she is both highly regarded and scorned. They watch and learn how Leni Reifenstahl used shadows and colors to serve her purpose. And they appreciate the subtlety and genius of Hitchcock, Kubrik, Scorcese, and other legends. Film Studies exposes students to a wide range of artists and techniques and gives them a greater foundation for appreciating and critiquing film arts.

Forensic Science Many Americans have seen the popular television programs and movies that showcase forensic science, but how is crime scene investigation really accomplished? SummerBerg invites students with inquisitive minds to join its experienced instructors in their Forensic Science class. No previous science experience is needed, as the instructors start with the basics. Using simulated and authentic data, students collect and examine fingerprints, analyze bloodstain patterns, and learn to reconstruct and solve crimes. Students may learn to process biological evidence, trace evidence, and impression evidence (such as fingerprints, shoe prints, and tire tracks), and analyze ballistics information. SummerBerg's creative instructors ensure that the presentation of material is never dry and that it is always connected to a compelling crime story. The multidisciplinary approach encompasses not only biology, physics, and other sciences, but also art, law, and writing. Students also consider the legal aspects of forensics, including constitutional issues related to forensic science.

German *Sprechen Sie Deutsch?* German is one of the most important languages in the twenty-first century, spoken by approximately 100 million native speakers and another 20 million non-native speakers around the world. It is used widely in business, politics, and culture across Europe and beyond. Heidelberg is rich in Germanic history and has many strong European ties though modern exchange programs. During this course, students are acquainted with the basics of German grammar, as well as the vocabulary needed to carry on a conversation. Classes incorporate games and interactive participation to make lessons fun and engaging. In addition to the language, students also learn about the unique culture and geography of Germany and other German-speaking nations, including the Bavarian Alps, the Black Forest, and the Rhine River. SummerBerg also examines German history and culture, which has produced such figures as Johann Sebastian Bach, Ludwig van Beethoven, and Johann Wolfgang von Goethe.

Prelaw and Criminal Justice For students curious about becoming a lawyer, judge, legislator, or a law enforcement official, SummerBerg is proud to offer this prelaw and criminal justice course for the first time this year. This exciting course provides students with a broad look at the criminal justice system, in part through a tour of an active law enforcement or criminal facility. The prelaw and criminal justice class spans issues related to constitutional rights, corrections, and criminology. Students gain a deeper understanding of the U.S. legal system and how it is different from systems in other nations. They not only learn about the criminal justice process, but also are afforded an opportunity to discuss some of the more pressing ethical issues facing the justice system in the twenty-first century, such as the death penalty, prison reform, and the rights of convicted criminals. SummerBerg's prelaw and criminal justice course combines history, sociology, political science, psychology, social work, and law.

Spanish Spanish is one of the world's most widely spoken languages; it is growing rapidly in importance in the United States. SummerBerg's Spanish program is designed to improve students' written and oral skills, including both grammar basics and the nuances of the language. Students discuss and participate in aspects of Spanish and Latin American cultural traditions, modern customs, and artistic expression. They also explore culture through learning about a variety of Spanish-speaking countries, examining popular media, enjoying music and original films in Spanish, and even cooking traditional dishes. At SummerBerg, fun is an important aspect of learning. Rather than focus on rote memorization of vocabulary and verb forms, instructors adopt a novel approach, offering students a cultural perspective while making the language come alive through interactive games and participation.

Sports Management Sports Management students learn what it takes to manage and market professional and collegiate athletic organizations, own and manage a sports-related business, or serve as an agent, lawyer, coach, or other member of a major sports organization. Teachers draw upon real-world examples to showcase the fascinating world of sports management, a unique profession that combines knowledge of athletics with business, journalism, communications, and social psychology. Students gain an understanding of the fundamental skills required to manage a sports team and individual players, including the math used in statistics and accounting. As part of the course, students also take a field trip to visit with representatives of a professional sports team.

DAILY SCHEDULE

7:30– 8:30	Breakfast
8:45– 9:00	Morning Meeting
9:15–10:15	Class Session 1
10:30–11:45	Class Session 2
12:00– 1:00	Lunch
1:15– 2:30	Class Session 3
2:45– 4:00	Class Session 4
4:15– 5:15	Activities/Sports/Free Time
5:30– 6:30	Dinner
6:45– 8:00	Evening Options
8:15–11:00	Free Time/Entertainment

Each program's schedule may vary from the sample given above.

EXTRA OPPORTUNITIES AND ACTIVITIES
SummerBerg takes full advantage of the long summer days and the expansive, beautiful Heidelberg campus by offering a fun mix of organized and optional activities for the afternoons and evenings. Staff members collaborate with students to organize activities, both athletic and nonathletic, that emphasize social interaction and simple fun and relaxation. Activities are always safe and supervised, and they allow students from different program tracks to meet and get to know each other.

FACILITIES
Heidelberg is regarded as one of the best private liberal arts colleges in the Midwest and has been featured in numerous publications. During the academic year, Heidelberg College hosts a diverse community of 1,500 students and 83 full-time faculty members. SummerBerg offers students access to the College's amenities, including state-of-the-art computer centers and campuswide wireless access; tennis courts, athletic fields, and library. The integrated wired classrooms, the brand new Science Center with modern science equipment, and the other academic buildings are all within easy walking distance of the residence halls. All students live in Williard Hall, a recently constructed, fully air-conditioned, sixty-five-bed residence hall. Students are assigned roommates by age and gender. Boys and girls live on separate floors, and RAs live on each hall to provide 24-hour supervision. Students eat most meals in the College dining hall, but they also head outside for a BBQ on nice summer evenings.

STAFF
Intelligent and energetic, the staff is the heart of the SummerBerg experience. From professional teachers to talented graduate and undergraduate students, all staff members participate in safety and training sessions. The maximum student-teacher ratio is 8:1.

MEDICAL CARE
Medical care is available 24 hours a day at nearby hospital facilities. All participants must submit comprehensive medical forms and proof of insurance.

COSTS
The tuition for each two-week session is $2395.

FINANCIAL AID
No financial aid is available at this time.

TRANSPORTATION
Airport pick-up and drop-off are available at Detroit International Airport for an additional fee.

APPLICATION TIMETABLE
Inquiries are welcome at any time. Applications are accepted until June 1. After June 1, acceptance to the program is based on availability, and applications must include a late fee of $100.

FOR MORE INFORMATION, CONTACT
Summerberg at Heidelberg College
310 E. Market Street
Tiffin, Ohio 44883

Phone: 866-686-3012
E-mail: summerberg@heidelberg.edu
Web site: http://www.heidelberg.edu/summerberg

SUMMER INSTITUTE FOR THE GIFTED

SUMMER PROGRAMS

STAMFORD, CONNECTICUT

TYPE OF PROGRAM: Three-week coeducational, residential and day summer program for academically gifted students in grades 1K–11. Combines a challenging academic program with traditional summer camp activities

PARTICIPANTS: Gifted students in grades 1K–11

ENROLLMENT: 2,000; each session has approximately 100–275 students

PROGRAM DATES: June 24 to July 14, June 25 to July 15, July 2 to July 22, July 16 to August 5, July 23 to August 12, July 30 to August 19

HEAD OF PROGRAM: Barbara Swicord

LOCATION

The Summer Institute for the Gifted (SIG) is held at some of the most beautiful campuses in the United States, including the University of California at Berkeley and Los Angeles, Vassar College (Poughkeepsie, New York), Princeton University (Princeton, New Jersey), Amherst College (Amherst, Massachusetts), the University of Texas at Austin (Austin, Texas), the University of Michigan (Ann Arbor, Michigan), Emory University (Atlanta, Georgia), and Bryn Mawr College (Bryn Mawr, Pennsylvania). Day campuses include Fairfield University (Fairfield, Connecticut), Stuart Country Day School (Princeton, New Jersey), Bryn Mawr College (Bryn Mawr, Pennsylvania), Moorestown Friends School (Moorestown, New Jersey), and Manhattanville College (Purchase, New York).

BACKGROUND AND PHILOSOPHY

Since its founding in 1984, the Summer Institute for the Gifted has provided academically talented young people with an important enrichment supplement to their regular education. The Summer Institute blends a strong academic program of

introductory and college-level courses, an opportunity for cultural exposure, social growth, and traditional summer camp activities. Although the program is held at several different locations, the sessions at each site are identical in purpose and structure.

The Summer Institute for the Gifted enables enthusiastic and capable students to become involved in a challenging academic program that is designed to engage students at a level commensurate with their abilities. The academic program is central to the spirit of SIG. Students are expected to perform at the upper level of their capabilities.

Varied cultural opportunities, educational evening entertainment performances, weekend off-campus trips, a full recreational program, and social activities address all the needs of the academically talented student.

This mixture of offerings allows the participants to be in a stimulating intellectual atmosphere as well as an enjoyable social setting. Most importantly, it provides them the opportunity to engage with their intellectual peers—students who have similar interests and abilities.

PROGRAM OFFERINGS

Academic offerings: The curriculum combines traditional subjects with courses that are meant to introduce new topics to students. There is a wide range of course offerings geared for highly motivated students of all ages. Course offerings for younger students range from Foundations of Mathematics to Introduction to Robotics to The Wonders and Mysteries of Ancient Egypt. Classes available to students in grades 7–9 include selections such as Introduction to Veterinary Medicine, Mock Trials and the Justice System, and Psychology. Older students may choose anything from an Introduction to Genetics to the Art of Debate.

PSAT/SAT mathematics and verbal preparatory courses are available to prepare students for standardized exams. High school students may take some courses for college credit. The courses are taught by selected college professors and experts in the fields in which they teach. Counselors are regularly available to assist and tutor students. A final grade report is sent to each student's home at the conclusion of the program, and, upon written request, a grade report is sent to the student's school.

Cultural offerings: There are a number of cultural courses available to students, regardless of age. The classes are meant to introduce areas of study that may not be available in the student's current local school. Architecture, Modern Dance, Painting and Drawing, Photography, Sculpture, and Theater and Drama are just a few of the cultural courses that a student can choose from at the Summer Institute for the Gifted.

Recreational offerings: SIG offers a wide range of recreational courses. Tennis, squash, fencing, chess, lacrosse, soccer, swimming, archery, and other recreational courses are available to be learned and enjoyed. Each course is taught by an experienced professional, who works with the beginners as well as the more advanced. A free recreational hour each day gives the SIG student a chance to participate in sports and recreation in a noninstructional environment.

EXTRA OPPORTUNITIES AND ACTIVITIES

In the Residential Program, special off-campus trips are planned for Saturdays (Saturday Get-Away Trips). Some of the previous years' trips included hiking the Appalachian Trail, canoeing or rafting down the Delaware River, a relaxing day at the lake, historical trips to New York City and Philadelphia, caving, and trips to the South Street Seaport; Radio City Music Hall; the Museum of Broadcasting; the Intrepid Air-Sea-Space Museum; the Franklin Institute; an archaeological expedition; Hersheypark; Renaissance Faires; the Kutztown Folk Festival; Washington, D.C.; Baltimore's Inner Harbor; the Rock and Roll Hall of Fame/Playhouse Square Center; Sea World; the Cleveland Museum of Art; the Cleveland Museum of Natural History; the Great Lakes Science Center; and Dover Lake Waterpark.

FACILITIES

Sites for SIG include some of the country's most prestigious academic institutions. Each campus is carefully selected on the basis of its academic facility, its outstanding reputation, and its capability to assist with the accomplishment of SIG goals and purposes. Complete use of the academic and research facilities on all campuses is available to all students.

STAFF

SIG's faculty and staff members are carefully chosen to ensure that only the most qualified people work with the students. They are selected not only on the basis of their credentials, but also on their enthusiasm and interest in working with younger students. All staff members, counselors, faculty members, and directors are well-trained, highly motivated, and responsible individuals who demonstrate a genuine interest in the educational and social growth of young people.

COSTS

The cost of the Summer Institute for the Gifted three-week residential program for 2007 started at $3795. This amount included tuition for the academic program; all room and board charges, including three meals each day; recreational program costs; evening entertainment program expenses; Saturday Get-Away Trip costs, including transportation and admission fees; and all special program costs. An additional nonrefundable application processing fee of $150 is due with the application. Some financial aid is offered to students on a need basis. The deadline for financial aid applications is April 1.

APPLICATION TIMETABLE

Inquiries are always welcome. The information office is open Monday through Friday from 9 a.m. to 8 p.m., Eastern time.

Students who meet one of the following criteria are invited to apply to SIG programs: all participants in recognized talent searches, students who score in the 95th percentile or higher on standardized tests (administered locally or by their schools), students who have been identified as gifted and/or who have participated successfully in a local or school gifted program, and students providing strong letters of recommendation from teachers or counselors citing their academic gifted ability and performance.

Students should apply as early as possible, as only a limited number of students can be accepted and accommodated by each session of the Summer Institute for the Gifted. In past seasons, qualified applicants have been turned away due to space limitations. Applications are accepted at any time but should be postmarked no later than May 15. Qualified applicants are accepted and enrolled on a first-come, first-served basis, according to the postmarked date on the application envelope.

FOR MORE INFORMATION, CONTACT

Summer Institute for the Gifted
River Plaza
9 West Broad Street
Stamford, Connecticut 06902-3788

Phone: 866-303-4744 (toll-free)
Fax: 203-399-5598
E-mail: sig.info@aifs.com
Web site: http://www.giftedstudy.com

SUMMER PROGRAMS AT BRYN MAWR COLLEGE

WRITING FOR COLLEGE, SCIENCE FOR COLLEGE, AND WOMEN OF DISTINCTION: PERSONALIZING THE COLLEGE ADMISSIONS PROCESS

BRYN MAWR, PENNSYLVANIA

TYPE OF PROGRAM: Precollege academic programs in writing and science as well as a college admissions preparation program

PARTICIPANTS: Young women completing their freshman, sophomore, junior, or senior year in high school

ENROLLMENT: Varies with each program

PROGRAM DATES: Writing for College and Science for College (residential or commuter): three weeks, last week of June through second week of July; Women of Distinction: one week, third week of July (residential or commuter)

HEAD OF PROGRAM: Varies with each program

LOCATION

The College's 135-acre campus is located 11 miles west of Philadelphia, in a suburban town with a population of 9,000. The town is an easy 5-minute walk from the campus and offers a movie theater, several cafés and restaurants, and a drugstore, a bookstore, and a variety of other stores.

BACKGROUND AND PHILOSOPHY

Since 1993, Bryn Mawr's Writing for College program has prepared high school–aged young women to write well for college in a program that is intensive, supportive, and fun. The academic, recreational, and college-preparatory dimensions are interwoven to create an integrated experience whose aim is to build a community of writers. All experiences, including seminars, workshops, tutorials, student readings, field trips, college visits, guest writers/speakers, and personal interactions, together challenge and stimulate the community.

In 2004, Bryn Mawr expanded its summer offerings to include the one-week Women of Distinction program. It added the three-week Science for College program in 2005.

PROGRAM OFFERINGS

Writing for College Students apply to participate in one of the following writing-intensive strands:

Creative Writing Modeled on undergraduate creative writing programs, the creative writing strand helps participants balance the solitary act of writing with the artistic, academic, and peer interaction that nourishes and supports it. The strand links the study of the art and craft of literature to a workshop approach to creative writing that offers a range of experiences, from free writing to radical revision, in a supportive, encouraging community. As readers and writers, participants explore approaches to three genres—poetry, short fiction, and creative nonfiction—as well as cross-genre writing, literary essay, and portfolio preparation.

Urban Studies In this strand, students investigate the spatial and sociopolitical dimensions of American cities as well as the larger environmental contexts in which cities are situated. Using the historically rich and culturally diverse city of Philadelphia as the principal site of investigation, participants apply readings and views drawn from a range of disciplines to such critical questions as what makes urban landscapes so compelling and also so complex, what can be learned from investigating the uses of space and the diversity of cultures as dimensions of life in the city, and how the role of nature in an urban environment can be understood. Participants also look at how life in cities is represented in both historical and more contemporary contexts through literature, photography, music, and film. Assignments are designed to enhance students' descriptive, creative, and analytical writing skills.

Science for College This interdisciplinary program is designed for students who are interested in analyzing the natural world and better understanding science as an interplay of language, experiments, and processing information to discover new concepts. The program is structured to provide opportunities for students to explore a wide variety of subspecialties in the sciences, including biology, chemistry, geology, physics, and psychology, as well as to work closely with a faculty member in each of those subspecialties. Students are encouraged to learn about each subspecialty and to make connections between core concepts and practices across all of them, with discussions of technology and its place in science woven throughout. A hands-on preparation for college science, the program draws on Bryn Mawr's extensive resources in the sciences: world-renowned science faculty members, state-of-the-art laboratories, and dedicated, creative teachers. The program interweaves academic, recreational, and college-preparatory dimensions to create an integrated experience. All aspects of the Science for College program, including seminars, guest lectures by Bryn Mawr science faculty members, labs, tutorials, field trips, and personal interactions, work together to support a community of experienced and novice scientists.

Women of Distinction: Personalizing the College Admissions Process This program is designed to assist students in navigating the college admissions process. Through interactive workshops and personality-assessment tools, such as the Myers-Briggs Type Indicator, students gain a better understanding of

themselves and what is important to them in selecting a college. Students spend time learning about their motives and styles and what makes them unique. They receive coaching on how to express their personal story effectively in an essay and in an interview. Finally, armed with more information about themselves, students learn what distinguishes one college from another as well as what to expect in their first year. By the end of the week, students have enhanced their ability to select colleges that are a good match for their interests and preferences, and they can better communicate their strengths in the admissions process. Students who previously participated in the program recorded a significant improvement in their ability to articulate their strengths and explain what makes them unique. They also increased their optimism and reduced their anxiety about the college admissions process.

The weeklong workshop is taught jointly by professionals from the Bryn Mawr Admissions Office and LEADERSHIP Philadelphia, the Philadelphia region's premier leadership development organization. This program is designed for both residential and commuting participants.

ENROLLMENT

The Writing for College program enrolls 45 students per year, with 15 students per instructor and teaching assistant. The Science for College program enrolls 15 students, and the Women of Distinction program enrolls approximately 25 students.

DAILY SCHEDULE

The daily schedule varies with each program.

FACILITIES

Residential students live in a Bryn Mawr College residence hall with their resident advisers. Participants can take advantage of all of Bryn Mawr's facilities, including the campus center, computing center, libraries, gymnasium, tennis courts, and playing fields.

STAFF

The program staff for the Writing for College and Science for College programs includes a coordinator, an academic director, instructors, teaching assistants, and resident advisers who are Bryn Mawr or Haverford College seniors or recent graduates. The faculty/teaching assistant–student ratio is typically 1:8, and the resident adviser–student ratio is 1:10. The Dean of Admissions at Bryn Mawr College directs the Women of Distinction program, carrying out the program with admissions staff members and personnel from LEADERSHIP Philadelphia, a leadership development organization in Philadelphia.

COSTS

The all-inclusive cost for tuition, dormitory, meals, activities, and materials for the three-week Writing for College and Science for College programs is $3000 for residential students and $2200 for commuters; the one-week Women of Distinction program costs $1100 for the residential program and $900 for commuters. In addition, participants in the Writing for College and Science for College programs can stay on for a fourth week to take part in the Women of Distinction program at a reduced cost.

FINANCIAL AID

A limited amount of need-based financial aid is available for the Writing for College and Science for College programs.

TRANSPORTATION

The Bryn Mawr College campus is 30 minutes by car from the Philadelphia International Airport. It is also accessible by commuter train.

APPLICATION TIMETABLE

Applications are accepted on a rolling basis until May 1.

FOR MORE INFORMATION, CONTACT

Ann Brown, Coordinator
Writing for College
Bryn Mawr College
101 North Merion Avenue
Bryn Mawr, Pennsylvania 19010-2899

Phone: 610-526-5376 (year-round)
E-mail: summer@brynmawr.edu
Web site: http://www.brynmawr.edu/summerprograms

PARTICIPANT/FAMILY COMMENTS

"Writing for College was absolutely wonderful. I feel that I have truly grown as a writer. I am eager to use my new techniques at school. The people here were all so enthusiastic (especially the professors)—there was just an absolutely wonderful atmosphere pervading the program."

SUMMER STUDY PROGRAMS

UNIVERSITY PARK, PENNSYLVANIA; BOULDER, COLORADO; AND PARIS, FRANCE

TYPE OF PROGRAM: College credit and/or enrichment courses; Kaplan SAT/ACT review; athletic, recreational, outdoor, and cultural activities; and weekend trips

PARTICIPANTS: Coeducational, students completing grades 9–12

ENROLLMENT: 125 to 400 students, depending on the location

PROGRAM DATES: Three to 6½ weeks, late June through mid-August

HEADS OF PROGRAM: Bill Cooperman, Executive Director; Mike Sirowitz, David Wolk, Brett Goodman, Jason Thaw, Diane Strumlauf, Erin Flaherty, and Tom Cook, Directors

LOCATION

Penn State Situated in the center of Pennsylvania and surrounded by the Appalachian Mountains, Penn State's University Park campus is located in what has been called the "ultimate college town" and is one of the nation's most beautiful campuses. The campus includes two golf courses, forty-eight tennis courts, and a 72-acre lake, as well as Beaver Stadium, a 106,500-seat football complex that is home to the Nittany Lions. Participants in Summer Study at Penn State find themselves immersed in the quaint, yet upscale, atmosphere of State College. The town revolves around the University and caters to the needs of its student population. There are restaurants, shops, fashion boutiques, bookstores, playhouses, movie theaters, video arcades, and dance clubs across the street.

University of Colorado Recently rated the number one Recreation and Outdoor Town in America by *Outdoor Magazine,* Boulder, Colorado, offers students 200 miles of biking and hiking trails and 30,000 acres of open space. The university's location at the base of the majestic Rocky Mountains means white-water rafting, backpacking, hiking, and rock climbing are easily accessible to students. Summer Study students at CU-Boulder find themselves immersed in a beautiful Western college town featuring concert halls, restaurants, art galleries, shops, dance clubs and bookstores.

Summer Study in Paris at the Sorbonne Located in the center of Paris in the heart of the famous Latin Quarter, the Sorbonne lies in the shadow of the Eiffel Tower, a few blocks from the Seine. The central location permits Paris to be an extension of the classroom and the city itself to be the campus. The buildings on the University's campus are all within a short walk of one another. The central city location puts the Eiffel Tower, Place de la Concorde, the Champs-Elysees, the Arc de Triomphe, Napoleon's Tomb, and many other major points of interest within a short walking distance. All the other sights and sounds of Paris are visited on daily excursions.

BACKGROUND AND PHILOSOPHY

Summer Study programs offer high school students completing grades 9–12 the opportunity to experience college life in a relaxed summertime atmosphere. With the pressure off, summer academic life permits time for personal growth and maturation and the successful development of study, time management, and community living skills; motivation; and independence. Students enjoy a unique summer filled with stimulating academic challenges and fun.

PROGRAM OFFERINGS

Students opting to join the 6½-week program at Penn State or the five-week program in Boulder attend freshman-level college courses with college students. At these locations, the distinguished university faculty members teach all college-credit classes. Most courses offered to Summer Study students award 3 college credits. Participants may choose a summer curriculum of college credits, an enrichment class, or the Kaplan SAT/ACT review.

Students opting to join the 3½-week program at Penn State, the three-week program in Boulder, or the programs in Paris attend two or three enrichment courses or the Kaplan SAT/ACT review. Enrichment classes are taught by Summer Study instructors and are designed to assist precollege students by offering opportunities not generally given as part of the regular high school curriculum. Students should call Summer Study's office or visit its Web site for a complete listing of college and enrichment courses that are offered.

DAILY SCHEDULE

Weekdays start with breakfast, followed by a morning class. College-credit courses (if applicable) and enrichment classes are held after lunch. The balance of the afternoon permits plenty of time for organized events, excursions, sports, outdoor activities, individual exploration, art, theater, and music. Dinner is followed by exciting planned evening activities at all campus locations.

EXTRA OPPORTUNITIES AND ACTIVITIES

Penn State Summer Study's College Counseling Center is a professional advisory service offered to all students. Students electing this option are scheduled for a series of seven private half-hour sessions, matching the students' academic abilities, social maturity, and career aspirations with the college that best suits those interests. Private instruction in tennis, golf, and speed-reading is also available. Intensive soccer, basketball, volleyball, and lacrosse clinics are offered for students who want to improve their skills and techniques. Students may also join Body Works Fitness Center, a 20,000-square-foot, state-of-the-art fitness facility. Evenings include rock concerts, shows, dance clubs, ice skating, movies, broomball, skit night, video game night, Arts Festival concerts, and a banquet/awards night. Three weekends are spent visiting universities in nearby cities, including Cornell, Syracuse, the University of Maryland, and Johns Hopkins. First-class hotels and major attractions are featured during these weekends, including Hersheypark, Harbor Place in Baltimore, and water slides in upstate New York.

University of Colorado Amid the splendor of the Rocky Mountains, University of Colorado at Boulder students may enroll in instructional sports clinics in tennis, basketball, soccer, or volleyball. Specialty clinics in rock climbing, pottery, and yoga are also available. Evening activities include rock concerts, movies, shows, dance clubs, street fairs, amusement parks, a Colorado Rockies baseball game, theater productions, and skit nights. Exciting weekend trips include action-packed adventure trips, whitewater rafting, hiking, horseback riding, and visits to Vail, Breckinridge, Colorado Springs, Pikes Peak, and Rocky Mountain National Park.

Summer Study in Paris Cultural excursions and recreational outings are the special features of the five- and three-week Paris programs. Excursions include visits to many famous sites in Paris and hot-air balloon rides. Students also enjoy browsing through high-fashion Parisian boutiques, people-watching at Parisian cafés, and shopping at open-air markets. Nightly planned events include going to dance clubs, Bastille Day fireworks, movies, the Latin Quarter, the Gardens of Tuileries, the Fireman's Ball, the opera, and Planet Hollywood and taking a Seine cruise. Weekend excursions include visits to the Palace of Versailles, the Loire Valley chateau country, and Disneyland Paris. Students interested in learning French can enroll in the French Immersion portion of the program, featuring speak-only-French roommates and groups for day/night excursions and French classes. As English is the working language of the program, Summer Study students do not need to have any working knowledge of French to join the program.

FACILITIES

All Summer Study participants fill out a roommate survey form for careful roommate matching according to students' ages and interests.

At Penn State and CU-Boulder, students live in one residence hall, 2 students per room. A telephone, refrigerator, freezer, microwave oven, and Internet access are available in each room. Television and laundry facilities are available in the residence. Students have full use of all athletic facilities and computer/word processing labs.

Participants in Paris are housed in an all-suites hotel, with 3 or 4 students sharing a two-bedroom, private-bath suite (including a kitchen with a refrigerator, freezer, and microwave; cable television; and telephone service). Breakfast is served at the hotel. Dinner is served at six local restaurants that cooperate in the program's unique dine-around plan. Students have full access to a computer and word processing center, e-mail, and the Internet.

STAFF

All of the campuses are rated among the top universities in the world. Professors, graduate students, and upper-level undergraduate students teach enrichment courses. All staff members are dedicated professionals who live in the residence halls with the students. They are available at all times to facilitate activities and help with student guidance.

COSTS

Program tuition for the 2007 summer was as follows: 6½-week program at Penn State, $6495; 3½-week program at Penn State, $4195; five-week program in Colorado, $6495; three-week program in Colorado, $3895; five-week program in Paris, $6495; and three-week program in Paris, $4995.

FINANCIAL AID

Limited partial-tuition scholarships are available for those who are academically qualified but financially needy.

TRANSPORTATION

Summer Study provides round-trip motorcoach transportation from centrally located points for the Penn State programs. For full coordination, Creative Travel International, Inc., an affiliate of Summer Study, arranges all air-travel arrangements and transfers for out-of-town and international students. Students flying to Denver or Paris or connecting in New York are met by Summer Study staff members upon arrival.

APPLICATION TIMETABLE

Enrollment is limited, and applications are reviewed on a rolling admissions basis.

FOR MORE INFORMATION, CONTACT

Bill Cooperman, Executive Director
Summer Study Programs
900 Walt Whitman Road
Melville, New York 11747
Phone: 631-424-1000
       800-666-2556 (toll-free)
Fax: 631-424-0567
E-mail: info@summerstudy.com
Web site: http://www.bestsummerever.com

SUMMER THEATRE INSTITUTE–NYC 2008
YOUTH THEATRE OF NEW JERSEY'S
RESIDENTIAL TEEN THEATRE TRAINING PROGRAM

SUMMER PROGRAM

NEW YORK, NEW YORK

TYPE OF PROGRAM: Professional theater training program for actors, dancer-actors, musical-theater actors, directors, and playwrights

PARTICIPANTS: Coeducational, ages 14 (or entering their freshman year in fall 2008) to 19 years

ENROLLMENT: 30–40 students for the full four-week residential program

PROGRAM DATES: Four-week residential theater training program: June 15 to July 11, 2008

HEAD OF PROGRAM: Allyn Sitjar, Artistic Director

LOCATION
Summer Theatre Institute–NYC (STI–NYC) is on a campus located in the heart of one of the greatest cultural cities in the world—New York City. For STI 2006 and 2007, students were housed in the Meredith Wilson Residence Hall in the Rose Building on the campus of The Juilliard School in Lincoln Center. The 2008 campus housing location in New York City will be announced in late December. In addition to the intense theater training program, students have an opportunity to experience a variety of shows and concerts, museums, and the creatively inspiring energy of New York City.

BACKGROUND AND PHILOSOPHY
Summer Theatre Institute–NYC is Youth Theatre of New Jersey's preprofessional summer theater training program for teens. Now in its twenty-third year, this nonprofit arts organization, based in Sparta, New Jersey, specializes in training kids, teens, and young adults in a broad range of theater skills. Students of all levels are taught by professional theater artists. STI–NYC auditions students of all levels from across the country and overseas. Youth Theatre of New Jersey continuously trains young artists year-round in New York and New Jersey, and it also produces new American plays and musicals. It is a member of the American Alliance for Theatre & Education and Artpride.

The Summer Theatre Institute–NYC program is open to teen actors, musical theater actors, dancer-actors, directors, and playwrights. STI–NYC offers an exciting total theater experience for young aspiring theater artists. The program concentrates on developing the total instrument of the young performer/actor—body, mind, and creativity. It is a chance for teens and young adults to learn new physical theater skills, explore their creativity, expand their imaginations, and celebrate the performing artist in themselves.

Summer Theatre Institute–NYC is a conservatory theater program whose main goal is to create an atmosphere in which young theater artists can explore, experience, and process a variety of theater skills without pressure or competition. For the beginning student, it is a chance to learn, explore, and create a dynamic and accessible repertoire of theater skills. For students who have had some exposure to doing shows or taking some classes, it is a chance to discover new methods and techniques, and to strengthen, deepen, and explore their artistic muse as well as their physical skills.

The program is also designed to reinforce personal confidence, performance technique, and ensemble work. Ensemble

work is emphasized to develop a sense of total group cooperation while still maintaining a sensitivity to individual needs. Through the ensemble work, the young artists discover the true meaning of theater as a collaborative art form. In addition to the theater training and creative process, social and communication skills are nurtured, and the development of strong friendships is common.

PROGRAM OFFERINGS
The Summer Theatre Institute program offers a full process experience in multidisciplinary performance skills. With enthusiastic and experienced professional theater artists, young actors, dancer-actors, musical-theater actors, directors, and playwrights immerse themselves in their particular craft, developing both the physical/mental sharpness and fluidity that only comes with intensive process work. They are then given the practical experience of making their work come alive through several final projects and showcases.

The program exposes the young theater artist to the inner workings of a true conservatory program and prepares precollege and college students for the rigors and joys of the top theater conservatory programs in the country. Having this experience in their portfolio has proven to be a big plus for many alumni, who have gone on to professional theater careers and top college programs, such as Boston University, Carnegie Mellon University, New York University's Tisch School of the Arts, Syracuse University, the University of Southern California, and others. For young artists who are new to the experience, it is a chance to discover the joys of true process work in classes that challenge their physical prowess, explode their imagination, focus their creative energy, and are just plain fun.

The four-week residential program of the Summer Theatre Institute is designed to offer the maximum experience of being part of a theater company of young artists who are completely immersed in honing their craft and working on process. Students enrolled in the full four-week residential program can take advantage of the full training program, performance opportunities, campus life, and field trips. The residential experience is also an opportunity to experience living on a college campus, make friends with fellow artists, and experience the mentoring of professional theater artists and teachers who all share a love of theater.

Core Classes Core ensemble classes are taught in acting, improvisation, mime/theater movement, dance, voice, and speech. In addition to core classes and specialized workshops, informational guests give practical advice on show business.

Actors The acting program consists of a wide variety of skills, including scene study, improvisation, theater movement, mime, mask improvisation, audition technique, stage combat, monologue and scene projects, showcase collaborations, and more.

Musical-Theater Actors and Dancer-Actors Special workshops for young performers who have been busy honing their song and dance skills help to focus, integrate their training, and stretch their imagination in such classes as acting, dance/theater improvisation, choreography, movement styles, styling the song, musical theater movement, musical theater history, audition technique, and more.

Playwrights Writers are able to stretch their skills and challenge their imaginations in workshops such as writing through theater games, elements of playwriting, dramatic structure, the playwright's voice, staged readings, and more.

Directors In this program, directors hone their craft through script analysis, open scenes, the director's tools, language and imagery, the collaborative imperative, performance projects, and more.

ENROLLMENT
Summer Theatre Institute currently accepts 30 to 40 students between the ages of 14 and 19 from across the country and overseas for the full four-week residential program. It is important to fill out the application and set audition appointments early. Auditions are held in New York and New Jersey between February and May. Out-of-town and overseas students may submit their auditions on videotape or DVD and have their interview by telephone after their tape/DVD has been received and viewed. Audition requirements are specific and it is recommended that students contact STI before sending in their tapes/DVDs so that they are clear on the requirements and there are no delays.

EXTRA OPPORTUNITIES AND ACTIVITIES
Enhancing the training at Summer Theatre Institute is the experience of living in one of the greatest cultural cities in the world. Students are a part of the pulse, energy, and variety of New York City. Included in the program are field trips to the Metropolitan Museum of Art and a variety of theatergoing experiences, from dance, comedy, and cabaret to Broadway and Off-Broadway. In addition to the various field trips, the campus is a beehive of activity, including concerts on the lawn, weekly movies, lectures, and exhibitions.

STAFF
Summer Theatre Institute's staff consists of 2 full-time faculty members available and living on campus with the students and 2 full-time graduate student teaching assistants. Professional theater teachers from the New York and New Jersey area come in every day for classes and workshops. All teaching theater artists are professionally involved in theater projects all over the country. Many of the teaching artists hold faculty positions at some of the major college theater programs, such as the Mason Gross School of the Arts at Rutgers University, New York University, Juilliard, Hunter College, University of North Carolina, and more.

COSTS
Tuition for the full four-week residential program is $5450 for students applying before May 20. Tuition increases after the May 20 deadline.

TRANSPORTATION
Students arrange their own airport transportation from the three major airports to the campus. Students can choose from a variety of transportation options, including buses, cabs, or reservations made with limousine companies or airport shuttle companies. The Summer Theatre Institute is happy to provide more detailed information. Students fly into either Newark International Airport in New Jersey or La Guardia Airport in New York. Students flying from outside of the United States fly into either JFK Airport in New York or Newark International Airport.

APPLICATION TIMETABLE
Initial inquiries from students of all levels can be made in August for the following year. Students should apply and schedule their audition early. Staff members are happy to answer any questions students may have regarding audition requirements.

Priority consideration is given to students who complete the application and audition process by April 25. Auditions are required, and they are held in New York and New Jersey between February and May. Students from out of town or overseas who cannot audition in person can send a videotaped audition; once their tapes/DVDs have been received and viewed, they are interviewed by telephone. The deadline for videotaped auditions is May 18. The final application/audition deadline is May 25.

The application fee is $55. An early enrollment discount is available until May 18.

Interested students should call or e-mail their mailing address to Summer Theatre Institute at the Institute address to receive the complete 2008 application packet. The Web site for the program is http://www.youththeatreinstitutes.org. Additional information can be found online at http://www.summeroncampus.com.

FOR MORE INFORMATION, CONTACT
Allyn Sitjar, Artistic Director
Summer Theatre Institute–NYC
Youth Theatre of New Jersey
23 Tomahawk Trail
Sparta, New Jersey 07871
Phone: 201-415-5329 (cell)
        212-258-2110 (weekday evenings)
        973-729-6026 (weekends)
Fax: 973-726-8926
E-mail: youththeatreallyn@yahoo.com
Web site: http://www.youththeatreinstitutes.org

SYRACUSE UNIVERSITY SUMMER COLLEGE

▼▲▼▲▼▲▼▲▼▲▼▲▼▲▼▲▼▲▼▲▼▲▼▲▼▲▼▲▼▲▼

SUMMER PROGRAM

SYRACUSE, NEW YORK

TYPE OF PROGRAM: Academic programs
PARTICIPANTS: Coeducational; high school sophomores, juniors, and seniors
ENROLLMENT: 185 to 225
PROGRAM DATES: June 30 to August 8, 2008
HEAD OF PROGRAM: Anne Shelly, Executive Director of Syracuse's Summer College for High School Students

LOCATION
The program takes place on the Syracuse University (SU) campus, with offices at 111 Waverly Avenue, Suite 240. The University is on a hill on the east side of downtown Syracuse, at the crossroads of upstate New York. Syracuse is in the western foothills of the Adirondack Mountains and at the eastern edge of the Finger Lakes region, which is renowned for its scenic lakes, vineyards, and vacation areas. It is within a 5-hour drive of New York City, Toronto, Philadelphia, and Boston.

BACKGROUND AND PHILOSOPHY
Syracuse University began its Summer College for academically talented high school students in 1961 to offer teenagers the opportunity to start college study early and to test career interests firsthand before making crucial decisions about the future. Students can choose from one of eleven programs and attend college-level, credit-bearing preprofessional and academic courses over six weeks, or they can choose to enroll in a two-week noncredit art studio or a one-week noncredit music workshop. Whether the student chooses a credit or noncredit program, he or she lives the life of a college student—on campus in a regular residence hall, sharing experiences and living space with other high school students from a variety of backgrounds.

PROGRAM OFFERINGS
The 2008 credit-bearing curriculum options include acting and musical theater, architecture, engineering and computer science, fashion and textile design, forensic science, interior and environmental design, law, liberal arts, management, public communications, and theater production. Credits earned through Summer College are accepted at Syracuse and most other colleges and universities upon matriculation and credit-transfer request. It is the student's college of matriculation that determines credit transfer. Noncredit programs are available in art and music. Students should visit http://www.summercollege.syr.edu for specific information.

The typical class meets Monday through Thursday (plus Friday in some programs) for 4 to 6 hours per day, depending on the program. Students participate in field trips and campus activities. Supervised residence hall living includes special weekend events. The residence hall staff is trained for supervising, not only in the residence hall but also outside the classroom as mentors.

ENROLLMENT
There are between 185 and 225 participants in Summer College, with an average of 25 students per program. Many are from New York State, Pennsylvania, New Jersey, and New England. Some come from as far as Florida, Texas, California, and Puerto Rico or internationally from St. Croix, Turkey, and Ukraine. Students come from all socioeconomic levels and ethnic backgrounds. Successful applicants are in good academic standing and demonstrate maturity and self-discipline. Eligibility is determined by

completed applications, which include high school transcripts, a student essay, national test scores, and letters of recommendation.

DAILY SCHEDULE
A typical day in Summer College at Syracuse University mirrors a day in the life of a first-year college student: breakfast in a residence dining hall in time to get to class, a class schedule that varies according to the academic program, and lunch and dinner with fellow students in the dining hall. Special activities typically include academic field trips, an ice cream social, a talent show, a semiformal dance, field trips to amusement parks and beaches, and picnics. In addition to planned group activities, Summer College students have access to the University's swimming pools, tennis courts, computer clusters, gyms, game rooms, and ice rink.

EXTRA OPPORTUNITIES AND ACTIVITIES
Extra opportunities vary by academic program. Acting and musical theater students perform in a grand finale production. Architecture students travel to study buildings designed by prominent architects such as Frank Lloyd Wright, Louis Kahn, and I. M. Pei. Their course projects are critiqued by professors from SU's School of Architecture. All students participate in an end-of-program celebration attended by parents and faculty members. As part of the end celebration, portfolios and design projects are exhibited and mock trials and scenes from the final theater production are performed, among other exciting activities.

The University's faculty and staff members and summer student population enjoy traditional summer weekday events that take advantage of fine weather and the beautiful campus location.

FACILITIES
Summer College students live in an undergraduate residence hall on the Syracuse campus. Athletic facilities on the campus include the well-known Carrier Dome. The Schine Student Center is centrally located near the residence halls, dining centers, and classroom buildings and next door to the Bird Library.

STAFF
The Summer College Office is staffed year-round. In the summer, Syracuse University professors and instructors teach all credit courses. The Summer College residential staff lives in the residence hall and includes 3 living-learning coordinators (LLCs) and 10 to 12 resident advisers (RAs). LLCs and RAs are mature, trained graduate and undergraduate students who supervise and plan activities.

MEDICAL CARE
In addition to its Health Services Center, the University shares its "hill" with University Hospital and Crouse-Irving Memorial Hospital. As part of the application process, students supply complete medical information, and a parent or guardian signs an authorization form for medical treatment and provides insurance information.

RELIGIOUS LIFE
Summer College students have the option of attending religious services within walking distance of the campus. There are no services that are a part of Summer College.

COSTS
The cost of tuition, room, board, activities, and insurance is between $5800 and $6245 for credit-bearing programs, depending on the program of study. The cost of the noncredit programs ranges from $750 (for one-week music workshops) to $1400 (for the two-week art studio). Textbooks and supplies are not included in the cost of the program. Upon acceptance, admittance is guaranteed into the program of the student's choice by submitting a $1500 deposit within three weeks of receipt of the letter of acceptance. Applicants must be paid in full on or before June 20.

FINANCIAL AID
A limited number of partial scholarships are awarded based solely on financial need. No full scholarships are available.

TRANSPORTATION
Syracuse University is 15 minutes from Hancock International Airport, 10 minutes from the east-west Amtrak interstate railway, and adjacent to north-south Route 81, which connects with the New York State Thruway, about 6 miles north of the campus.

APPLICATION TIMETABLE
Inquiries are welcome at any time, and applications are accepted throughout the year. Tours and interviews may be arranged at the student's convenience. Offices are open from 8:30 a.m. to

5 p.m. September through mid-May and from 8 a.m. to 4:30 p.m. in the summer. The postmark deadlines for completed applications are as follows: all six-week credit programs, May 15, 2008, and financial aid, April 15, 2008.

FOR MORE INFORMATION, CONTACT
Syracuse University Summer College
for High School Students
111 Waverly Avenue, Suite 240
Syracuse University
Syracuse, New York 13244-2320

Phone: 315-443-5297
Fax: 315-443-3976
E-mail: sumcoll@syr.edu
Web site: http://www.summercollege.syr.edu

PARTICIPANT/FAMILY COMMENTS

"I have made lots of new friends, learned to set up my own schedule, and have become more self-reliant."

"We put in a lot of hours on projects, but the work was interesting and the time flew by."

"Summer College is a respectful, mature environment in which everyone comes together for the same reason—to learn."

"I like the Syracuse campus. The buildings are beautiful, and, while the campus is very big, it's fairly compact and almost everything is convenient."

"My son enjoyed the summer program tremendously. It has had a profound and lasting impression on him."

TABOR ACADEMY

SUMMER PROGRAM

MARION, MASSACHUSETTS

TYPE OF PROGRAM: Sports and arts instruction, academic enrichment
PARTICIPANTS: Coeducational, ages 8–15
ENROLLMENT: 165 boarding program, 250 day program
PROGRAM DATES: June 30–August 11; two-, four-, or six-week sessions
HEAD OF PROGRAM: Noel Pardo, Director

LOCATION

Situated directly on the shore of Sippican Harbor, Buzzards Bay, in Marion, Massachusetts, the Tabor Academy Summer Program makes full use of the residential, academic, and athletic facilities of Tabor Academy, an independent, coeducational boarding school founded in 1876.

BACKGROUND AND PHILOSOPHY

Established in 1917, the Tabor Academy Summer Program gives young people the opportunity to develop to their full potential as athletes, students, and individuals. Under the guidance of highly qualified counselors, coaches, and teachers, the program encourages young people to take pride in their personal achievements in the classroom, on the playing fields, and on the waterfront. Tabor provides the option of doing summer schoolwork without losing any of the joys of a summer program.

PROGRAM OFFERINGS

Each of the activities offered in the program is carefully supervised, with special attention to the individual. Instruction is a major part of each activity, and emphasis is placed on personal achievement, rather than competitive "success." Each camper creates his or her own recreational program by choosing among these activities: art, baseball, basketball, ceramics, crafts, drama, field hockey, junior sports, lacrosse, sailing, soccer, squash, softball, swimming, tennis, and volleyball.

Because of Tabor's oceanfront location and extensive waterfront facilities, sailing is among the most popular activities. Tabor's fleet includes Capris, Lasers, Optimists, and four 20s. Sailing lessons are provided by certified instructors who

offer basic lessons for beginners and more challenging opportunities for experienced sailors.

Campers may also take advantage of academic offerings. Although academic courses are not required, most participants in the program choose to take one or two of the following classes: computers, creative writing, developmental reading, English, English as a foreign language, exploratory science, French, Latin, mathematics (including algebra and geometry), oceanography, photography, SAT prep, Spanish, SSAT prep, study skills, and theater arts. Whether the course is taken for purposes of review or enrichment, classes are kept small so that teachers may work closely with individual students. Classes meet five times a week and do not require homework, as both instruction and practice exercises are completed during the 70-minute class periods.

Tabor's waterfront oceanography laboratory is a state-of-the-art facility for the study of marine biology, and oceanography is the most popular course selection in the summer program. Field trips to local beaches and wetlands, as well as to the New England Aquarium and the Woods Hole Oceanographic Institute, complement the hands-on experience in Tabor's oceanography lab.

DAILY SCHEDULE

7:00– 8:30	Rising, breakfast, and room inspection
8:30–12:25	Periods A, B, and C for academics and activities
12:25– 1:00	Buffet lunch
1:00– 2:20	Rest period
2:20– 2:30	Afternoon meeting
2:30– 5:00	Periods D and E for activities
5:00– 6:00	Showers and clean-up
6:00– 6:45	Family-style dinner
6:45– 7:00	Evening meeting
7:00– 9:00	Evening activities
9:00–10:00	Lights out

Sundays are reserved for special programs and trips to local attractions in Boston, Providence, and Cape Cod.

ENROLLMENT

While the vast majority of campers come to Tabor from the New England and mid-Atlantic states, others come from around the nation and the world. In a typical summer, 20 or 30 international students, representing twelve or thirteen different countries, join the 120–130 American participants in the program.

FACILITIES

Tabor Academy provides first-class facilities for academics, the fine and performing arts, and outdoor sports (with nine playing fields, seven all-weather tennis courts, and access to a golf course). The athletic center offers an indoor skating rink, a gymnasium, a multipurpose field house, a fitness center, and nine squash courts. Campers live in the well-equipped dormitories of the Academy, and they enjoy the full services of the school's health center and dining hall.

STAFF

The program's staff includes more than eighty teachers, coaches, and counselors, many of whom are faculty members at Tabor Academy or similar schools. In a typical summer, several staff members are Tabor Academy graduates or former participants in the Summer Program.

MEDICAL CARE

Basic medical care is provided by Tabor Academy's Baxter Health Center, which is supplemented by local community health and hospital services. This includes 24-hour/seven-day-a-week nurses who live on campus. In addition, pediatricians stop by every morning and are on-call when needed. Campers are required to have medical insurance, and parents are asked to submit a detailed medical form before registration day.

COSTS

Residential tuition for the two-week session is $2400, tuition for the four-week session (including two academic courses) is $4700, and tuition for the six-week session (including two academic courses) is $6000. Linen and laundry service is also included in the tuition. The program recommends establishing a $200 "bank account" for a camper's spending money; campers may make withdrawals from this account only with the Director's permission, and the balance is returned to the parents at the end of the session. Day tuition is $280 per week for half day and $440 per week for full day (not including academic courses, $650 per course).

TRANSPORTATION

On opening and closing days, the program provides transportation between Logan International Airport, Boston, and Tabor Academy, Marion.

APPLICATION TIMETABLE

Applications are welcome throughout the year. The residential application deadline is May 1 for the $1200 deposit and June 1 for the full amount. The day application deadline is June 1, and the full amount must be paid. Tours of Tabor's campus and meetings with summer program administrators occur during scheduled information sessions.

FOR MORE INFORMATION, CONTACT

Noel Pardo, Director, or
Anny Candelario, Summer Program Coordinator
Tabor Academy Summer Program
Tabor Academy
66 Spring Street
Marion, Massachusetts 02738

Phone: 508-748-2000 Ext. 2242
Fax: 508-291-8392
E-mail: summer@taboracademy.org
Web site: http://www.taboracademy.org/summer

TAFT SUMMER SCHOOL

ON-CAMPUS PROGRAM

WATERTOWN, CONNECTICUT

TYPE OF PROGRAM: Academic enrichment
PARTICIPANTS: Coeducational, grades 7–12
ENROLLMENT: 150
PROGRAM DATES: June 24 to July 28, 2007
HEAD OF PROGRAM: Stephen J. McCabe Jr., Director

LOCATION
The Taft School, which was founded in 1890 by Horace Taft, is located in Watertown, Connecticut, a community of 20,000 residents close to the city of Waterbury. Watertown is 45 minutes from Hartford, 1½ hours from New York City, and 2½ hours from Boston.

BACKGROUND AND PHILOSOPHY
The Taft Summer School, which was established in 1982, provides an opportunity for motivated students entering grades 7–12 to review course material, prepare for future courses, or enrich their academic experience by taking courses that are not normally available to them. The school offers intensive study in a residential, independent school environment—one in which boys and girls can learn how best to realize their potential as students. Teachers from Taft's faculty join teachers from other fine public and private schools to provide an exciting and varied academic program. While the Summer School's primary focus is academic, an extensive athletic program and a varied schedule of weekend activities round out the residential experience.

PROGRAM OFFERINGS
Young Scholars Program Aimed at younger men and women (those completing the sixth through eighth grades) who in-

tend to take on the challenges of rigorous public and private secondary schools, this program focuses on building essential skills and instilling students with greater confidence as they look ahead to seventh, eighth, and ninth grades and further down the road, to the demands of a college-preparatory program.

Liberal Studies Program This program offers major courses and electives in a variety of disciplines to students entering the tenth, eleventh, and twelfth grades. Each student is required to take four courses: two 100-level majors and two 200-level electives.

Major course offerings include English, mathematics, biology, physical science, French, Spanish, ESL, history, studio art, and photography. Elective course offerings include creative writing, photography, acting, drawing and painting, printmaking, art history, testing, reading and study skills, current events, public speaking, psychology, research paper, and SAT/SSAT verbal and math preparation.

DAILY SCHEDULE

```
 7:00– 8:15 . . . Breakfast
 8:30–10:00 . . . First period
10:00–10:30 . . . Break or assembly
10:30–12:00 . . . Second period
12:00– 1:00 . . . Lunch
 1:00– 1:40 . . . Third period
 1:45– 2:25 . . . Fourth period
 3:15– 4:30 . . . Sports
 5:00– 6:30 . . . Dinner
 6:30– 7:30 . . . Free time/Extracurricular activities
 7:30– 9:30 . . . Supervised evening study hall
       10:15 . . . Students in dormitories
       10:30 . . . Lights out
```

EXTRA OPPORTUNITIES AND ACTIVITIES
On weekends and Wednesday afternoons, activities and off-campus trips are available to students. In the past, students have visited New York City, Boston, and Mystic Seaport. Broadway shows, dances, movies, shopping, barbecues, and a trip to

an amusement park are common outings. Optional trips include museums, beaches, and the ballpark. Sports competitions and a rock concert are two samples of on-campus activities.

Art students' work is exhibited at the end of the program during the arts festival.

FACILITIES
Taft's 220-acre campus includes six separate dormitories; the 53,000-volume Hulbert Taft, Jr. Library; the Ivy Kwok Wu Science and Mathematics Center; a modern infirmary; and the Bingham Auditorium. The Modern Language Learning and Resource Center uses a sophisticated combination of computer hardware and software to facilitate learning a foreign language. The Arts and Humanities Center contains classrooms, faculty offices, the Student Union, spacious art rooms, and a black-box experimental theater. The Cruikshank Athletic Center contains a field house for basketball and volleyball and indoor tennis and squash courts. In addition to Taft's athletic fields, twelve tennis courts and a running track are available to Summer School students.

STAFF
Faculty members at Taft are selected on the basis of their excellence in teaching, their commitment to young people, and their desire to instill enthusiasm for learning. The Summer School faculty is chosen primarily from the regular school-year faculty and from other independent and public schools. In addition, Taft selects several outstanding college seniors and recent graduates who are interested in a career in education to assist faculty members. Interns work in the classroom with a senior teacher, live in the dormitories, assist in the afternoon sports, and serve as advisers to Summer School students.

MEDICAL CARE
The Martin Infirmary is a fully equipped facility with a registered nurse on duty at all times. A physician visits the school on a regular basis and is on call throughout the day. Local hospitals are nearby for medical service.

RELIGIOUS LIFE
While Taft is a nonsectarian school, students are encouraged to attend the religious institution of their choice. Churches of various denominations are within walking distance of the campus. Students with special needs can be accommodated.

COSTS
The charge for all boarding students in the on-campus program is $5500. This amount covers tuition, room and board, and all trips and activities. Tuition for a full-time day student living in Watertown or the immediate vicinity is $3400. The tuition for part-time day students is $950 per course. An additional fee to cover books, supplies, incidentals, and spending money is placed in each student's bank account—$450 for boarding students and $250 for day students. An independent laundry service is available.

FINANCIAL AID
Limited financial aid is available to deserving boarding and day students.

TRANSPORTATION
Taft provides transportation, free of charge, to and from Bradley International Airport in Windsor Locks, Connecticut, and JFK Airport in New York. Additional fees are charged to escort unaccompanied minors and to arrange pick-up at other locations. There is train and bus transportation into Waterbury.

APPLICATION TIMETABLE
Applications are accepted beginning December 1. As there is a rolling admissions process and applications are reviewed as soon as they are received, it is wise to submit an application early to secure a boarding space and classroom choices before they fill. An application fee of $50 must accompany the application. Upon enrollment, which secures a place, a nonrefundable deposit of $1000 is required. The balance of tuition is due by June 1. The application may be downloaded from the Web site.

FOR MORE INFORMATION, CONTACT
Taft Summer School
110 Woodbury Road
Watertown, Connecticut 06795
Phone: 860-945-7961
Fax: 860-945-7859
E-mail: summerschool@taftschool.org
Web site: http://www.taftschool.org/summer

TASIS—THE AMERICAN SCHOOL IN ENGLAND

THE TASIS SPANISH SUMMER PROGRAM, SALAMANCA
LES TAPIES ARTS AND ARCHITECTURE, FRANCE

ENGLAND: SUMMER SCHOOL; SPAIN: SUMMER LANGUAGE PROGRAM; FRANCE: ARTS AND ARCHITECTURE PROGRAM

THORPE, SURREY, ENGLAND
SALAMANCA AND COSTA DEL SOL, SPAIN
LES TAPIES, FRANCE

TYPE OF PROGRAM: *England:* Academic enrichment courses, theater workshops, sports, and travel; *Spain:* Intensive immersion in Spanish language; *France:* Intensive workshops in painting, drawing, printmaking, photography, and architecture

PARTICIPANTS: *England:* Coeducational, ages 12–18, *Spain:* Coeducational, ages 13–17; *France:* Coeducational, ages 14–18

ENROLLMENT: *England:* 250; *Spain:* 75; *France:* 18

PROGRAM DATES: *England:* Four weeks in June and July, three weeks in August; *Spain:* July 3–August 1; *France:* Three weeks in June and July

HEADS OF PROGRAM: Jeff Barton, Chris Tragas, and John Smalley, Directors

LOCATION

England The School's beautiful 43-acre rural campus, in the heart of a small English village, is only 8 miles from Royal Windsor, 18 miles from the city of London, and 6 miles from Heathrow International Airport. Rich in natural leisure and cultural resources, this prime residential area is also a popular tourist destination. King John sealed the Magna Carta in the nearby fields of Runnymede, and the Royal Shakespeare Theatre and Stratford-upon-Avon attract classical drama lovers the world over. The program takes full advantage of its proximity to London.

Spain The TASIS Spanish Summer Language Program offers students a means to broaden their linguistic and cultural horizons by bringing them to the ancient learning center of Salamanca, 2 hours

from Madrid. Students reside in a beautifully restored fourteenth-century building, which is just a 5-minute walk from the famous Plaza Mayor. For the final week of the program, students relocate to a luxury resort on the Costa del Sol, with faculty and student housing, classrooms, a swimming pool, and immediate access to the beach.

France Nestled in the mountains of the Massif Central in southern France, Les Tapies is a picturesque seventeenth-century hamlet that has been carefully restored to retain its original character and serves as an ideal base for a creative arts program. The six stone buildings form a harmonious unit that blends into the landscape and provides spectacular views of the Rhône Valley and the French Alps in the distance.

BACKGROUND AND PHILOSOPHY

TASIS–The American School in England was founded in 1976, and the Summer School was inaugurated that same year to offer an intensive credit-based learning experience for students new to Europe or those seeking to strengthen skills or knowledge in one particular area.

PROGRAM OFFERINGS

England Each course provides a minimum of 4 hours of classroom work every day, and students are taught in small classes with individualized instruction. Students choose an elective course in addition to one major course. Major courses include English Literature and Composition/IB Prep; High School Skills; Middle School Skills; Archaeology and Architecture; Shakespeare's Theatre; ShakespeareXperience; Theatre in London; Biology/IB Prep; Chemistry/IB Prep; Algebra I and II; Geometry; Precalculus; Economics/International Business; Lights, Camera, Action!; Movie Animation; Art in London; SAT Review; English as a Second Language; Speed Reading; and TOEFL Review.

Theatre in London With a focus on reading and analyzing plays, this course's major objective is to enjoy as many productions as possible in London and Stratford-upon-Avon. Recent plays and musicals seen include *Phantom of the Opera, Les Misérables, The Lion King, Chicago,* and *Billy Elliot.*

ShakespeareXperience Through intensive study, students discover the meaning of Shakespeare's words and poetry, the background of Elizabethan history and theater, theater culture and etiquette, modern and traditional theatrical techniques, and movement, voice, and acting skills. This course offers a unique opportunity to learn a Shakespearean play and perform it publicly at the Globe Education Centre Theatre, part of the modern reproduction of Shakespeare's legendary Globe Theatre in London.

Art in London London provides unforgettable opportunities for students to view contemporary art alongside work from the great masters. Studio drawing and painting classes on campus allow students to experiment with the techniques used in the works of art they see exhibited in London museums and galleries. By the end of the course, students will have completed at least two pieces to portfolio standard.

English Language Program ESL courses are offered in four- and three-week sessions, as are TOEFL preparation classes.

Lights, Camera, Action! is designed to provide the hands-on experience of writing, shooting, and producing a film. Students write and produce short films and learn and practice the basics of operating cameras, setting lights, and recording clean audio.

Movie Animation is a fast-paced introduction to creating animated movies. Students are guided through the steps of the animated movie process and learn to operate camera equipment and computer software for compiling and editing their own original movies.

Spain The daily schedule includes four language classes and Language in Life activities, using Salamanca as the classroom. There is an average of 10 students in each class and six levels, ranging from beginning to advanced. All classes are conducted entirely in Spanish. Students may earn one academic credit upon completion of the course. Excursions to Madrid, Segovia, Toledo, and other places of historic and cultural interest take place on the weekends.

France Students enroll in one of the major courses, Architecture, Drawing, Painting and Printmaking, or Photography, as well as an elective in an area of interest that strengthens their creative and presentation techniques or develops manual skills through restoration projects. Students meet 4 hours daily for the major courses and 2 hours per day for the elective courses. Excursions to nearby historic towns take place on weekends.

ENROLLMENT

In **England,** 250 students enroll each summer, with approximately 30 percent originating from the United States. Students enrolled in intensive English as a second language classes represent thirty different countries.

In **Spain,** 75 students enroll each summer, with approximately 80 percent from the United States.

In **France,** 18 students enroll, with approximately 50 percent from the United States.

EXTRA OPPORTUNITIES AND ACTIVITIES

England On-campus extracurricular activities include photography, drama, music, journalism, and art as well as social activities such as picnics, barbecues, dances, and movie nights. All students participate in the off-campus travel program each weekend by choosing from the wide variety of overnight and day trips available. These include trips to Oxford, Cambridge, Brighton, and Bath and frequent trips to Windsor and London. Optional weekend trips are offered to destinations such as Edinburgh, Wales, and Paris at extra cost. Sports such as horseback riding, waterskiing, fitness and aerobics, basketball, tennis, golf, and baseball are all included in the schedule each day. Some require additional cost.

Spain Students explore the Spanish heritage by visiting the towns of La Alberca, Toledo, Segovia, and Madrid, where they see the famous El Prado Museum. Students participate in sports during the afternoon, including swimming, aerobics classes, flamenco dancing, soccer, and tennis.

France The ideal location of Les Tapies just north of Provence provides extensive opportunities to draw on the cultural riches of such historic sites as Avignon, Nîmes, Arles, and Aix-en-Provence. Visits to the local Chestnut Museum and the Wool Mill, picnic walks in the mountains, kayaking down the Ardèche Gorge, and fishing or swimming provide relaxing breaks from the intense studio work and opportunities to discover the beauty of the Ardèche countryside.

FACILITIES

England TASIS–The American School in England is a coeducational boarding and day school for 700 students during the academic year. The programs draw on the full facilities of the year-round boarding program, which includes two late-Georgian

mansions that serve as the main student residences and house dining rooms and a 12,000-volume library. Other facilities include three computer centers, an art/music complex, two modern gymnasiums, a fitness center, and a 350-seat theater. There are also outdoor tennis and basketball courts, three athletics fields, and a regulation baseball diamond. Off-campus facilities are used for swimming, horseback riding, golf, and waterskiing.

Spain The program makes full use of a beautifully restored fourteenth-century convent that contains classrooms, a vaulted dining room, a student lounge, an interior courtyard, and accommodations. The off-campus sports facilities include a swimming pool, a fitness center, tennis courts, volleyball and basketball courts, soccer fields, and ample green space for running and jogging. The final week is spent in a luxury resort on the Costa del Sol in southern Spain, which offers faculty and student accommodations, classrooms, and a swimming pool as well as sports facilities and immediate access to the beach.

France Students reside and study in fully restored stone buildings, which enjoy stunning views of one of France's most unspoiled regions. The facilities include an art studio for drawing, painting, and printmaking; an architecture studio; a darkroom; a spacious dining room and lounge; and residential accommodation for 18 students and 6 staff members. Outdoor terraces provide extensions to the living spaces and ideal settings for barbeques and informal dining. The hamlet also has a games room for pool, table soccer, Ping-Pong, darts, and board games. The swimming pool is popular for cooling off from the hot Ardèche sun.

STAFF

England The faculty consists of 40 qualified and experienced members, and the student-faculty ratio is 6:1.

Spain The faculty consists of 10 qualified and experienced administrators and teachers. The student-faculty ratio is approximately 10:1.

France The faculty consists of 3 full-time teachers, with additional visiting artists. The student-faculty ratio is approximately 6:1.

COSTS

England The all-inclusive 2007 cost for four-week enrichment courses is $5300; for three-week enrichment courses, $4200; and for six-week academic courses, $7100

Spain The all-inclusive 2007 cost for one month is $5400.

France The all-inclusive 2007 cost for the three-week program is $4600.

FOR MORE INFORMATION, CONTACT

The TASIS Schools, U.S. Office
1640 Wisconsin Avenue, NW
Washington, D.C. 20007
Phone: 202-965-5800
            800-442-6005 (toll-free)
Fax: 202-965-5816
E-mail: usadmissions@tasis.com
Web site: http://www.tasis.com

TASIS–THE AMERICAN SCHOOL IN SWITZERLAND

TASIS

▼▲▼▲▼▲▼▲▼▲▼▲▼▲▼▲▼▲▼▲▼▲▼▲▼▲▼▲▼▲▼▲▼▲▼▲

LANGUAGES, ART HISTORY, PHOTOGRAPHY, ENGINEERING, AND PAINTING TICINO

LUGANO AND CHÂTEAU D'OEX, SWITZERLAND

TYPE OF PROGRAM: *Lugano:* Intensive foreign language study, art history, digital photography, engineering, and painting Ticino; *Château d'Oex:* Intensive French language instruction

PARTICIPANTS: Coeducational, *Lugano:* ages 6–18; *Château d'Oex:* ages 13–17

ENROLLMENT: *Lugano:* 300; *Château d'Oex:* 65

PROGRAM DATES: *Lugano:* Four weeks, June–July; three weeks, July–August; *Château d'Oex:* Four weeks in July, plus one optional week in August

HEADS OF PROGRAMS: Betsy Newell, Dean Topodas, Jim Haley, Vincent Clarke, David Damico, and Margaret Blackburn

LOCATION

Lugano, Switzerland: Nestled in the foothills of the southern Swiss Alps, with spectacular views, the TASIS campus is a compact cluster of historic buildings and new facilities. It overlooks the attractive resort town of Lugano and is 2 miles from Agno International Airport and less than an hour's drive from Milan (Malpensa) International Airport in Italy. The idyllic setting allows for a wide range of enjoyable activities, including windsurfing, pleasure cruises to lakeside hamlets, picnics, and hiking to picturesque villages.

Château d'Oex, Switzerland: Located in the French-speaking canton of Vaud, the area offers outstanding opportunities for French language learning and an appreciation of the area's natural beauty.

BACKGROUND AND PHILOSOPHY

Founded in 1956 by Mrs. M. Crist Fleming, TASIS is a coed college-preparatory American boarding school for students in grades 6–12 and postgraduates.

The Summer Programs began thirty-two years ago and were designed to offer American and international students an opportunity to study abroad and a chance to live in a truly international environment. The French Language Program, located in Château d'Oex, was founded thirteen years ago.

PROGRAM OFFERINGS

Four- and three-week courses in English as a second language, French, and Italian are offered during the months of June, July, and August. Students who have attended Italian classes during the first session are welcome to join the one-week Home-Stay in Italy option. Engineering and art history are offered during the first session; painting Ticino and digital photography are offered during the second session only. The age range is 14–18, and the average class size is 11. Courses such as drama, video making, art, and computer language learning programs complement intensive classroom work, offering creative options for the practice of oral communication skills. Progress reports are mailed home to parents at the end of the session.

Middle School Program (MSP): This program is specifically designed to cater to the needs of preadolescents, ages 11–13. The program offers intensive French and English as a second language.

Le Château des Enfants (CDE): An international summer camp for students ages 6–10, Le Château des Enfants offers English, French, and Italian instruction. Emphasis is placed on acquiring oral skills in the target language through music, drama, games, excursions, and activities as well as classroom study.

TASIS French Language Program (TFLP): This program in Château d'Oex offers intensive language instruction for 13- to 17-year-olds and an optional six days at the end of the four weeks in the south of France.

ENROLLMENT

In Lugano, 300 students represent as many as forty different countries. In Château d'Oex, approximately 65 students enroll from all over the world, including the Americas, Europe, and Asia.

EXTRA OPPORTUNITIES AND ACTIVITIES

Lugano: All students participate in afternoon sports and activities. Students choose from a variety of sports, including swimming, aerobic dance, basketball, cross-country running, soccer, softball, tennis, and volleyball. The afternoon activities include art, photography, and computer club. Weekend excursions provide ample opportunity for students to explore local areas of interest. Full-day excursions to Como and Milan, Lucerne, and Valley Verzasca and half-day excursions to nearby places of interest, such as Swiss Miniature in Melide and the antique street markets in Como, are organized. Optional weekend travel destinations (at an extra cost) include such cities as Florence, Nice, Paris, Venice, and Verona.

Château d'Oex: Hiking, rock climbing, tennis, swimming, basketball, and soccer are offered. Weekend destinations include Geneva, Interlaken, Zermatt, and Gstaad.

FACILITIES

Lugano: The program uses all of the boarding school facilities of the American School in Switzerland. The historic Villa de Nobili houses the administrative offices, dining rooms/terraces, classrooms, and dormitory areas. Villa Monticello contains classrooms, a computer center, and dormitories. Hadsall House houses an audiovisual lab, a recreation center, and a snack bar, as well as dormitory accommodations. The art and photography studios are adjacent. The new M. Crist Fleming Library holds 20,000 volumes.

On-campus sports facilities include a new gymnasium, an outdoor pool, a fitness center, and two multipurpose hard courts.

Château d'Oex: The historic wood-carved chalets, set in the heart of the village, are home to TASIS students. They house dormitories, classrooms, a dining room, and recreation areas. There are a tennis/basketball court and Ping-Pong tables in the garden of the main chalet. Nearby facilities include a swimming pool, soccer field, and beach-volley. Tennis players of intermediate and advanced ability can enroll in the intensive tennis offering to improve their skills under the guidance of certified tennis instructors. (Spaces are limited and an additional fee of $350 applies.)

STAFF

There are 60 full-time summer staff members (the staff-student ratio is 1:5). Qualified classroom teachers also undertake supervisory responsibilities, including coaching sports, chaperoning trips, dormitory coverage, and the "in loco parentis" role. Counselors work alongside teachers in the dorms, on excursions, on the sports fields, and in recreational activities to help provide a caring environment for students.

Many of the staff members are current or former TASIS faculty members, and counselors are alumni from all TASIS programs.

COSTS

For Lugano and Château d'Oex, Switzerland, the all-inclusive cost for a four-week session in 2007 was $5300. The cost for the three-week session was $4300. The TASIS French Language Program, with the additional optional week to Nice, South of France, amounted to $6350. There are no additional fees, with the exception of long-haul airfare, the optional European weekend travel costs, personal spending money, and health insurance and medical expenses.

FOR MORE INFORMATION, CONTACT

U.S. Office
The TASIS Schools
1640 Wisconsin Avenue, NW
Washington, D.C. 20007
Phone: 202-965-5800
        800-442-6005 (toll-free)
Fax: 202-965-5816
E-mail: usadmissions@tasis.com
Web site: http://www.tasis.com

TREETOPS EXPEDITIONS (TTX)

▼▲▼▲▼▲▼▲▼▲▼▲▼▲▼▲▼▲▼▲▼▲▼▲▼▲▼▲▼▲

ADIRONDACK FIELD ECOLOGY (AFE); GLACIER AND ROCK CLIMBING, SAILING, SEA KAYAKING, TRAIL BUILDING

LAKE PLACID, NEW YORK; ALASKA; VANUATU; MINNESOTA; MONTANA

TYPE OF PROGRAM: Wilderness-based, academic, and adventure expeditions

PARTICIPANTS: Coeducational, ages 14–17 (TTX); ages 17–20 (AFE)

PROGRAM DATES: July 1–28, 2007 (most programs)

HEAD OF PROGRAM: Chad Jemison, TTX Director

LOCATION

Treetops eXpeditions (TTX) is based out of North Country School, which sits on a 200-acre sustainable farm on beautiful Round Lake in the Adirondack Mountains near Lake Placid, New York. The area provides many opportunities for hiking and backpacking, climbing (rock and ice), horseback riding, skiing (Nordic, Alpine, and Telemark), snowboarding, snowshoeing, canoeing, bicycling, and swimming. Although the main basecamp for TTX is in the Adirondack Mountains, the courses range across North America and even around the world to the South Pacific.

BACKGROUND AND PHILOSOPHY

Whether in Alaska or Vanuatu, climbing a mountain trail, or working on a trail, Treetops eXpeditions programs are about learning how to give back to the land and to communities. It is about pushing through the mental and physical challenges of hard work and strenuous hikes and paddles. It is about leaving the comforts of home for the adventure of a new and rugged experience. It is about the satisfaction of a job well done, the elation of reaching a destination, the warmth of relaxing around a fire with new friends, and the confidence gained from overcoming challenges. Treetops eXpeditions is about creating change in the world and in one's self—and having fun doing so.

PROGRAM OFFERINGS

Treetops eXpeditions of Lake Placid, New York, offers safe, fun, wilderness-based expeditions. For summer 2007, there are five teen expeditions (TTX trips) for 14–17 year olds, and there is also Adirondack Field Ecology (AFE)—a college-level course for students ages 17–20 for college credit.

TTX: Expeditions for Adventurous Teens: For more than thirty years, North Country School and Camp Treetops have offered exceptional summer adventure travel trips for teens. This summer the tradition continues, with transformative monthlong wilderness trips to the following exciting destinations: Vanuatu, Alaska, Boundary Waters (Minnesota), Glacier National Park (Montana), top-notch rock-climbing crags in the Northeast, and the wilds of the Adirondacks. These trips thoughtfully extend the guiding philosophy and values of North Country School and Camp Treetops beyond the 200-acre campus to the far reaches of North America and the world. Caring adults, strong communities, responsibility for self and others, embracing diversity, and environmental sustainability are at the foundation of all TTX trips. (http://www.ttexpeditions.org)

AFE: Real Experience, Real College Credit: Why sit for hours in a lecture hall this summer? Through AFE, education comes alive! This course has a major emphasis on learning ecology in the field through hands-on projects. AFE is one of the few opportunities for students in this age group to earn college credit while working in the field. Students work side by side with professors from Paul Smith's College, "the college of the Adirondacks," collecting data on professional studies. AFE's research director, Dr. Ken Baker, is a tenured biology professor whose passion for fieldwork is contagious. For AFE's final project, students conduct a weeklong authentic research project of their own making that can help prepare them for their undergraduate capstone/thesis. After all this fascinating work, a five-day wilderness canoe trip tops off a summer of expeditionary learning.

Students who complete Adirondack Field Ecology with a grade of B or higher receive full credit for the Paul Smith's College course Field Ecology 232. Students receive an official Paul Smith's College transcript, and the credits may be transferred to other universities. Although this course has a far more cooperative than competitive approach to learning, there are high expectations for students' commitment to their learning. The course depth is comparable to challenging AP-level or intro college-level science courses. (http://www.adkecology.org)

ENROLLMENT

TTX: Students ages 14 to 17 (including any rising ninth graders) can enroll.

AFE: Students ages 17 to 20 (including any rising twelfth graders) can enroll.

DAILY SCHEDULE

Although the schedule varies greatly, a typical day of activities may include:

7:00 . . .	Wake up
7:15 . . .	Breakfast
8:00 . . .	Community meeting
8:30 . . .	Morning field activity
12:00 . . .	Deli sandwich lunch
1:00 . . .	Afternoon field activity
4:30 . . .	Free choice time/make dinner
6:00 . . .	Dinner and clean up
7:30 . . .	Evening activity
10:30 . . .	Quiet time in tents

FACILITIES

Both TTX and AFE courses are primarily "car camping" or wilderness based. The trips seek to tread lightly on the land; therefore, students sleep in tents and cook and eat their meals outside. The beauty and challenges of the natural world define the program's playground and classroom.

STAFF

The Treetops eXpeditions and Adirondack Field Ecology program leaders are all first-rate—most have led trips like this for many years, and all are passionate about the wilderness. Renowned faculty members from Paul Smith's College are involved in many aspects of the teaching and research projects during the AFE course. On each team, all leaders have CPR and Wilderness First Aid training, and at least one has Wilderness First Responder Certification for trips with backcountry sections. The instructor-student ratio is between 1:3 and 1:4. The staff is fully committed to making each student's summer exciting and transforming.

MEDICAL CARE

TTX and AFE staff members are well qualified to care for day-to-day medical issues that arise and set plans for seeking professional medical attention at the nearest hospital or clinic should the need arise.

COSTS

AFE tuition is $4800, and tuition for TTX trips ranges from $4800 to $5900. This fee includes food and lodging on all course activities as well as transportation to and from the airport and during the course. A $1000 deposit is due with the application. Students must supply their own clothing and backpacking gear. Group gear (tent, stove, cooking gear, first aid kit, etc.) is provided. A limited amount of scholarship assistance is available for each summer. For further information, students and families should contact Chad Jemison at chad.jemison@nct.org; 518-523-9329 Ext. 149; or visit the TTX Web site at http://www.ttexpeditions.org.

TRANSPORTATION

Students typically arrive at and depart the course by plane, bus, or car at a specific airport closest to the course area.

APPLICATION TIMETABLE

Applications are available on the TTX Web site at http://www.ttexpeditions.org, and it is possible to apply online. Applications are accepted until April 15. Students and their families should call after April 15, as space may still be available. A $1000 deposit is due with the application. The tuition balance is due one month prior to the beginning of the course, although other arrangements can be made.

FOR MORE INFORMATION, CONTACT

Chad Jemison, TTX and AFE Director
Treetops eXpeditions
P.O. Box 187
Lake Placid, New York 12946

Phone: 518-523-9329 Ext. 149
E-mail: chad.jemison@nct.org
Web site: http://www.ttexpeditions.org

UNION COLLEGE

FIVEPOINTS ACADEMIC CAMP

SCHENECTADY, NEW YORK

TYPE OF PROGRAM: Academic enrichment
PARTICIPANTS: Boys and girls entering grades 8–12
ENROLLMENT: 100 students per session
PROGRAM DATES: Multiple two-week sessions in July
HEAD OF PROGRAM: Douglas Murphy, Program Coordinator

LOCATION

FivePoints is Union College's premier summer academic program. Located only a few hours from New York City, FivePoints students live on a historic campus in the newly renovated College Park Hall. Each student can look forward to the exciting New York City Adventure as well as unique and educational field trips.

BACKGROUND AND PHILOSOPHY

Drawing on Union College's excellence in teaching and commitment to cutting-edge instruction, FivePoints is one of the most innovative and fun summer academic programs in the country. With exciting courses, such as Forensic Science and Digital Creative Arts, FivePoints is Union College's answer for bright young minds searching for amazing summer experiences. Students from around the country make the most of their summer vacation by living, laughing, and learning in one of America's best colleges. Experiencing life on a college campus and academic immersion in one chosen field of study are the central pillars of the FivePoints program. The program is academically stimulating and socially enriching. Academics are extremely important, but FivePoints is first and foremost a summer program. Staff members spend the entire winter preparing and organizing for each summer. The goal is to fill every day and dedicated free time with fun activities designed to bring FivePoints students together and make the most of the vast campus resources.

PROGRAM OFFERINGS

Business, Economics, and Entrepreneurship Economics and business courses are among the most popular with undergraduates, even with students who have no plans to major in these disciplines. The FivePoints program is designed for anyone with an interest in learning about business models and real-world applications. This course is designed to give students an excellent grasp of the fundamentals for creating a business, backed with basic economic theory.

Digital Creative Arts: Photography, Music, Animation, and Design This project-based course is designed for students of all levels to explore their creativity through a wide variety of digital media. Students learn how to use and combine elements of digital photography, film, music, animation, and graphic design.

Toy and Entertainment Engineering Toys and games, the rides at amusement parks, and the special effects in movies are becoming increasingly technically sophisticated. Yet the concepts that make them work are relatively simple. Collectively, the creation of these technological wonders falls under

the heading "entertainment engineering." In this course, students learn the basic design principles behind entertainment products, principles that will assist them in this class as well as in their future engineering or multimedia studies.

Forensic Science Forensic science is defined as the application of science to questions of law. With one primary aim—establishing whether there is any scientific evidence to link a person or item to an apparent outcome, usually a crime scene—forensic science is a multidisciplinary enterprise that incorporates the basic principles of biology, chemistry, and physics. Through a variety of unique experiments and testing procedures, students utilize all three fields, providing them with valuable insight and experience for future studies. The course examines important laboratory equipment, the limitations of particular methodologies, and how to prioritize information that is critical to criminal investigation and prosecution.

Improv Comedy Improvisational comedy, or improv, asks students to discover unpredictable, real-time ways to make others laugh. The study of improv develops intellectual and social skills that build communication abilities and self-confidence. The challenge of performing without lines or cues exhilarates students and provides opportunities to create zany characters and outlandish situations. Through games like Newscasters, Head in a Bucket, and Hoedown, students learn to think on their feet and develop a close-knit community. Because risk and camaraderie are such important aspects of improv, instructors foster a safe environment full of supportive fellow students, where both praise and advice are offered to every member of the class.

Psychology This is the perfect course for students who are fascinated by or curious about the inner workings of the mind. The course begins with the themes central to the study of psychology. It then delves deeply into three of the most fascinating areas of study: social psychology, abnormal psychology, and cognitive psychology. The curriculum is designed to give students broad exposure to the many areas of study in psychology, and the course work is pursued both in the classroom and in real-world settings.

Mass Media: Communications and Journalism Communications and journalism professionals seek to inform, educate, and entertain their audience through a wide variety of media, including newspapers, television, and radio. In this unique FivePoints program, students study the foundation of skills necessary for success in communications and learn to differentiate factual reporting from sensationalism and editorial content. Students discover whether what is heard and read is accurate reporting or if it is designed to shape individuals' perceptions of culture.

ENROLLMENT
FivePoints enrolls a maximum of 100 students per session to allow for small classes with individualized attention.

DAILY SCHEDULE
FivePoints staff members work year-round to design and organize a variety of exciting activities and adventures for students' free time. While some students are planning for a trip into town with their new friends, another group might choose to participate in one of the online tournaments. Students who enjoy swimming can check out the pool—classmates may need another player for their water polo match. Regardless of a student's interests, FivePoints offers each student a variety of free-time options.

7:45– 8:45	Breakfast
9:00–10:15	Class Session I
10:15–10:30	Morning break
10:30–11:45	Class Session II
12:00– 1:00	Lunch
1:15– 3:15	Afternoon activities
3:30– 4:45	Class Session III
5:00– 6:00	Dinner
6:15– 7:30	Evening Seminar
8:00–10:30	Evening activities
11:00	Check-in

EXTRA OPPORTUNITIES AND ACTIVITIES
Every student can look forward to a course-specific destination upon arrival in New York City, where they are immersed in a real-world learning environment. Following the individualized field trips, every FivePoints student participates in an organized New York City adventure. The coach bus is fully loaded with movies, reclining seats, and air conditioning. Sitting next to their new friends, students enjoy the ride as they look forward to a full day in the greatest city in the world.

FACILITIES
FivePoints students stay in College Park Hall. This outstanding facility, which opened in fall 2004, features 110 single rooms and sixty doubles, with bathrooms in every unit. Col-

lege Park Hall is air-conditioned and complete with laundry facilities, large common areas on each floor, a game room, and vending rooms. It even has its own fitness center with a variety of cardio and other exercise equipment. FivePoints students reside in the doubles, with a roommate of the same age range but from a different academic track. In addition to College Park Hall, FivePoints students have complete access to the wide variety of amazing facilities Union College has to offer.

STAFF
The highly trained staff members are outgoing, intelligent, and energetic; they define this unique residential experience. From the classroom to the dorm room, they serve as exceptional role models, guides, and mentors. The small student-teacher ratio of 8:1 allows staff members to get to know each student, focus on his or her experience and abilities, and learn to make the best of each individual's potential.

COSTS
The tuition for each two-week session is $2395. Tuition includes all instructional materials and complete room and board. Students stay in College Park Hall and enjoy three great meals a day in Union College's first-rate dining hall. Tuition also includes the following facilities and activities: a fully furnished dorm room with linens, self-service laundry facilities, all organized sports and recreational activities, transportation for sponsored trips, admission tickets for all recreational events, and 24-hour supervision for the duration of each camp session. In addition, there is a $100 field-trip account, which allocates spending money to each student for field trips.

TRANSPORTATION
For an additional fee, airport pick-up and drop-off are available for all students choosing to fly through Albany Airport (ALB). Parents are welcome to drive students to the campus, and all international students are met at the airport by FivePoints staff members.

APPLICATION TIMETABLE
Inquiries are welcome at any time. Applications are accepted until June 1. After June 1, acceptance to the program is based on availability, and applications must include a late fee of $100.

FOR MORE INFORMATION, CONTACT
FivePoints
Office of Special Events
Union College
807 Union Street
Schenectady, New York 12308

Phone: 800-883-2540 (toll-free)
E-mail: fivepoints@union.edu
Web site: http://www.union.edu/fivepoints

UNIVERSITY OF CHICAGO
GRAHAM SCHOOL OF GENERAL STUDIES

SUMMER PROGRAMS FOR HIGH SCHOOL STUDENTS

CHICAGO, ILLINOIS

TYPE OF PROGRAM: Academic enrichment, college credit
PARTICIPANTS: Coeducational, rising sophomores, juniors, and seniors in high school
ENROLLMENT: 225
PROGRAM DATES: Session I begins June 16, end dates vary
HEAD OF PROGRAM: Cary Nathenson, Associate Dean

LOCATION
The University of Chicago is located in the historic Hyde Park neighborhood of Chicago, 7 miles south of the Loop, as the city's downtown is called. Hyde Park has been home to artists and writers throughout the last century, and 60 percent of the University's faculty members live in the neighborhood. Diverse and vibrant, Hyde Park offers all the amenities of a small college town—bookstores, restaurants, cafés, and shops—but is only a quick train, bus, or bike ride from the treasures of downtown Chicago, America's third-largest city. The beaches and biking and jogging paths of Lake Michigan are a short walk away.

BACKGROUND AND PHILOSOPHY
The University of Chicago was founded in 1892 to inspire excellence in liberal arts education as well as in a variety of professions. A leader in higher education since its inception, the University College (for undergraduates) focuses on a broad liberal education in the humanities, the sciences, the social sciences, and the arts. The University's Summer Programs for High School Students, offered through the Graham School of General Studies, reflect the University's overall emphasis on a commitment to intellectual challenge, critical thinking, and personal discovery. The programs also offer a college-preparatory environment in which students can test their intellectual limits, live like a college student, and learn to make thoughtful and informed decisions about their academic future. All courses are offered for college credit.

PROGRAM OFFERINGS
High school students have four program options.

Summer Quarter Undergraduate Course Offerings In this program, students take regular undergraduate courses alongside University of Chicago students. They may take one, two, three, or four courses that are three to ten weeks in length, depending on the schedule they choose.

Insight This program consists of three-week, intensive courses in which students can explore a discipline in depth and in a hands-on environment. Topics include law, writing, Egyptology, psychology, and urban studies.

Research in the Biological Sciences This two-course program offers intensive theoretical and practical experience with current research techniques, in and out of the laboratory, in the biological sciences.

Stones and Bones This two-course program provides students with an opportunity to join a paleontological expedition. After studying geology and evolutionary biology at the Field Museum of Natural History, students apply their knowledge at an expedition site in Wyoming. After the dig, students return to Chicago to analyze and conserve their finds.

The Traveling Academy Interdisciplinary courses in Western civilization are offered overseas. In summer 2007, the program focused on classical Greek drama, with travel to Athens, Delphi, Mycenae, and the Isle of Spetses.

ENROLLMENT
Students are drawn from throughout the United States. Students who complete their freshman, sophomore, or junior year before the summer are welcome to apply. Admission is competitive and administered on a rolling basis. The University is committed to a diverse student body, and that commitment is reflected in the summer programs.

DAILY SCHEDULE
Students in the Summer Quarter for High School Students program who live on campus take two courses simultaneously. Weekly classroom and lab hours vary depending on the length of the course—the shorter the course, the more intensive the work. Courses are offered on the Hyde Park main campus. Courses can be scheduled anytime from 9 a.m. to 8 p.m., and students choose their own course schedule. There are a variety of possible course combinations; courses are three to ten weeks in length, and students take a total of two to four courses in a summer.

Students in all other programs can expect to be in class-related activities—whether in the classroom, the lab, the field, tutorials, or small-group work—all day.

Residential students take their meals together in the dormitory dining hall three times a day, and there are many other cafés, coffee shops, and cafeterias on campus.

EXTRA OPPORTUNITIES AND ACTIVITIES

In the evening and on weekends, a full program of social and recreational events is available, and students can participate as they have interest. Dances, concerts, movies on the quads, lectures, a fine arts festival, DOC Films (the oldest student-run film organization in the country), barbecues, study breaks, and more are normally planned. Excursions to Six Flags Great America Amusement Park, Ravinia Music Festival, Chicago Cubs or White Sox games, and Chicago's world-class museums are also part of the extracurricular schedule. Students are encouraged to organize their own events with the help of the Resident Advisers who live in the dormitory with students.

The Reynolds Club is the hub of student activity in the summer. Students play pool, discuss current events with friends, get a snack, study, read, or just relax among the Gothic gargoyles.

The city of Chicago offers something for everyone and is especially attractive and active in the summer. Summer participants can explore ethnic neighborhoods, discover the wonders of the Shedd Aquarium or the Adler Planetarium, admire the Impressionists' works at the Art Institute, shop along the Magnificent Mile, take a Ferris-wheel ride on Navy Pier, cruise the Chicago River on an architectural tour, hear outstanding jazz and blues, or savor the many cuisines of the city's restaurants.

FACILITIES

The University's facilities are open to all summer students. Computing clusters (including one in the dormitory), e-mail and Internet access, the libraries, the laboratories (if related to a student's course work), and athletic facilities are among the resources available for study, research, and recreation.

On campus, Robie House, considered Frank Lloyd Wright's finest creation, is open for tours; the Smart Museum of Art houses the University's collection of fine arts that span a period of 5,000 years; the Oriental Institute museum is home to the University's collection of ancient Near Eastern artifacts; and the gallery of the Renaissance Society fosters an understanding of contemporary art and introduces international artists to Chicago audiences.

Residential students live in a University dormitory in a double room with a roommate.

STAFF

Courses are taught by University faculty members and advanced graduate students, many of whom are nationally and internationally recognized in their fields. Insight courses may be taught by other professionals from the University or the Chicago area because of their recognized expertise in a particular discipline.

A staff of trained Resident Advisers (RAs), who are University of Chicago undergraduates or graduate students, live in the dormitory with summer students. They are available to provide advice and guidance as students acclimate themselves to college living, the campus, and the city. They are responsible for fostering a comfortable and supportive residential environment for all students. In addition, they plan, implement, and attend all of the social and recreational activities. The RA staff is supervised by a Residential Program Director and an Assistant Director, who are graduate students or other adults. They, in turn, report to the Associate Dean.

MEDICAL CARE

All students are required to have adequate health insurance coverage for injury, accident, or major illness. Students who are not covered are required to purchase health insurance, which is available through the University. In addition, all students pay a health services fee that entitles them to care through the Primary Care Group at the University of Chicago Hospitals. A physician and a therapist are on call 24 hours a day. Students must have required immunizations (including two vaccinations against measles, consistent with state of Illinois law) before classes begin.

RELIGIOUS LIFE

The University maintains no religious affiliation. Rockefeller Chapel is the center of religious life at the University, and weekly ecumenical services are held there in the summer. Centers for a number of other faiths are available to students.

FINANCIAL AID

Partial tuition scholarships are awarded on the basis of financial need and academic merit. Awards are made on a rolling basis, and early application is encouraged. A completed Tuition Scholarship Form as well as the parents' most recent tax return are required for consideration. Awards can be applied toward tuition costs only; there is no aid available for room and board or other fees.

COSTS

Tuition costs vary from program to program. In 2007, the Summer Quarter for High School Students tuition was $2425 per course. Insight tuition was $2425 per course. Research in the Biological Sciences tuition was $5039 for two courses. Room and board for all these programs cost $450 per week. Stones and Bones tuition was $4850 for two courses plus $2790 for room, board, and transportation. The Traveling Academy was $6995, all costs included.

TRANSPORTATION

The city of Chicago is served by Chicago–O'Hare International Airport and Midway Airport. Students are advised of airport shuttle services upon their acceptance to the program, and students must make their own transportation arrangements to and from the airport at both the beginning and the conclusion of the program.

APPLICATION TIMETABLE

Applications are accepted through April 15 for Traveling Academy and May 15 for all other programs. Admission decisions are made on a rolling basis. Because admission is selective and limited, early application is encouraged. In addition to the application form, students must submit a personal essay, two letters of recommendation from teachers, and a current transcript. Online applications are available on the Web site at http://summer.uchicago.edu.

FOR MORE INFORMATION, CONTACT

Sarah López, Administrative Assistant
Summer Session Office
Graham School of General Studies
University of Chicago
1427 East 60th Street
Chicago, Illinois 60637

Phone: 773-834-3792
Fax: 773-702-6814
E-mail: uc-summer@uchicago.edu
Web site: http://summer.uchicago.edu

UNIVERSITY OF CONNECTICUT

AMERICAN ENGLISH LANGUAGE INSTITUTE

STORRS, CONNECTICUT

TYPE OF PROGRAM: English immersion
PARTICIPANTS: International students, ages 13–17 (SEE); ages 16 and up (IEP)
ENROLLMENT: 30 students per session
PROGRAM DATES: SEE Session I: June 24 to July 13; SEE Session II: July 22 to August 10; IEP, June 18 to August 10
HEAD OF PROGRAM: Kristi Newgarden, Director

LOCATION
Nestled in rural New England, the University of Connecticut campus provides a safe, yet exciting location for English language and cultural studies. Storrs is a scenic, agricultural area about 25 miles northeast of Hartford, the state capital, and is midway between New York and Boston, each of which is about 1½ to 2½ hours away.

BACKGROUND AND PHILOSOPHY
Since 1991, the University of Connecticut American English Language Institute (UCAELI) has provided English instruction to more than 2,000 students from countries throughout the world. UCAELI supports all students in pursuit of their goals by providing high-quality instruction and access to the University's academic, professional, social, and cultural resources. Founded in 1990, the institute is a member of the American Association of Intensive English Programs (AAEIP). The IEP program is accredited by the Commission on English Language Program Accreditation (CEA).

PROGRAM OFFERINGS
The action-packed three-week **Summer English Experience Program (SEE)** is designed specifically for teenagers. It combines English study with sightseeing, recreation, and cultural learning. Course work and a variety of activities and trips offer students a great way to learn about the history and culture of both New England and the United States. SEE offers students a safe introduction to university life. The program's location on a major

public university campus enhances the learning experience. The uniquely designed curriculum features experiential learning, and the immersion in English leads to maximum improvement in the shortest time. Learning with international peers fosters tolerance and cultural understanding in program participants—not to mention self-knowledge and self-confidence.

The **Intensive English Program (IEP)** is for adult students who wish to concentrate on developing their English skills while experiencing the rich culture of a university community. Many students enrolled in this program are preparing for further study in the United States. All levels of instruction, from beginner through advanced, are offered each session. A variety of activities and trips complement the classroom work. The session runs for eight weeks during the summer.

Conversation Partners play an important role in UCAELI students' English education. These local volunteers include middle school and high school students, University students and staff members, and other members of the community. They provide SEE and IEP students with the informal, fluent English conversation that is an important aspect of learning the language. Not only do the students improve their English-speaking skills, they also form lasting friendships with the Conversation Partners.

ENROLLMENT
International students ages 13 to 17 participate in the SEE program. Many countries are represented in each UCAELI program. In the IEP, most students come from Korea (40 percent), Japan (20 percent), South America (10 percent), Turkey (5 percent), and other countries (25 percent). There are generally 8 to 12 students in each class.

DAILY SCHEDULE
SEE Program: English classes are held in the mornings Monday through Friday, with conversation classes held Monday, Wednesday, and Friday afternoons. All levels of instruction are offered. Students take English classes for about 3 to 4 hours each weekday. Other afternoon activities include arts and crafts, outdoor games, and trips to museums.

IEP Program: Prospective students should visit the Web site for the daily class schedule (http://www.ucaeli.uconn.edu/english/programs/iep/prog.php). The program consists of 22 hours of study per week.

EXTRA OPPORTUNITIES AND ACTIVITIES

SEE Program: Students take full-day trips to New York City and Boston to visit museums, historic sites, and parks as well as other attractions. Other planned excursions include a trip to Providence, Rhode Island, for a baseball game and trips to area parks and beaches. At the end of the program, students have a fun day at the Six Flags New England Amusement Park in Springfield, Massachusetts.

IEP Program: Typical summer activities include barbecues, outdoor sports, trips to the beach, and a full-day trip to New York City or Boston.

FACILITIES

SEE Program: SEE students stay in double rooms with private bathrooms on campus and take their meals in a University dining hall. There is also a homestay option.

IEP Program: IEP students may choose to live on campus in a dormitory or in an off-campus apartment. There is also a homestay option. Students are able to use the University's main library and computer labs and the gym in the Field House where they can enjoy the basketball and racquetball courts, indoor track, swimming pool, and exercise equipment.

STAFF

SEE Program: SEE instructors are experienced secondary-level teachers, most of whom have a degree in bilingual education or teaching English as a second language. Counselors have international experience and have worked with teenagers in camp or recreational settings.

IEP Program: All current UCAELI instructors in the Intensive English Program hold master's degrees in either Teaching English to Speakers of Other Languages (TESOL) or in English. Instructors' overseas experience includes teaching in China, Taiwan, Japan, Korea, and Chile. All UCAELI instructors share a love of teaching, the English language, and working with international students. Students find their instructors and counselors to be experienced and enthusiastic.

Kristi Newgarden has been the Director of UCAELI since 1999. She is responsible for all aspects of program management and development. Kristi holds a master's degree in TESOL and

has taught extensively in intensive English programs overseas and in the United States. As director, Kristi makes an effort to have regular contact with UCAELI students. She assists students with applications, meeting faculty members, and creating transitional study programs. She also teaches part-time in the Intensive English Program. Arthur Galinat, Program Coordinator, joined UCAELI in 2003. He handles admissions and student services and helps students adjust to life on campus. Arthur also leads many trips and activities. Lena Dillman, Financial Assistant, has been with UCAELI since 2004. She assists students with payments and questions about the program and life at the University. Neena Kapoor, Program Aide, joined UCAELI in 2005. She assists with admissions, the Conversation Partner Program coordination, and other student services.

MEDICAL CARE

IEP Program: The University Infirmary, located on campus, is available to all students. Facilities include a women's clinic, an advice nurse, and counseling services. All students are required by the University to maintain health insurance coverage. Students may purchase their own insurance coverage, or the Bailey Agency provides insurance for students who have not purchased their own coverage plan. More information about the University-sponsored insurance program can be found at http://www.shs.uconn.edu/insuran1.html.

COSTS

SEE Program: Tuition for the three-week SEE program is $2850, which includes instruction, lodging, meals, trips, and activity fees. A discount is available for groups of 10 or more. It is recommended that students bring some personal money for miscellaneous items, souvenirs, trips, and other expenses.

IEP Program: IEP tuition and fees total about $2900 for the eight-week summer session. Room and board fees are additional and average $2200.

For both programs, tuition should be paid in full prior to the start of classes. Tuition and fees may be paid in cash in person or by check, money order, wire transfer, or credit card. For additional information, students should visit the Web site at http://ucaeli.uconn.edu/english/costs/.

For those students who wish to stay with a local family, single rooms are available in nearby homes. Meals are negotiated; the fee includes the cost of three meals per day. Transportation to the campus may or may not be provided by the host family. Students should request a UCAELI Homestay Application if interested in this option.

TRANSPORTATION

The University is located 1 hour from Bradley International Airport.

APPLICATION TIMETABLE

SEE Program: SEE applicants must submit the fully completed application to the UCAELI office by May 1, 2007 for Session I. Applications must be received by June 1, 2007 to be considered for Session II.

IEP Program: IEP applicants must submit the fully completed application, an affidavit of support, financial certification, the $75 application fee, the $100 tuition deposit, and the $100 on-campus housing deposit. Applications and the $100 tuition deposit for the Summer English Experience are accepted up to one month prior to the start of the program.

FOR MORE INFORMATION, CONTACT

University of Connecticut American English Language Institute
843 Bolton Rd., Unit 1198
Storrs, Connecticut 06269-1198

Phone: 860-486-2127
Fax: 860-486-3834
E-mail: register-ucaeli@uconn.edu
Web site: http://ucaeli.uconn.edu/

UNIVERSITY OF CONNECTICUT

UCONN MENTOR CONNECTION

STORRS, CONNECTICUT

TYPE OF PROGRAM: Mentorship program; provides students with hands-on experience and academic enrichment in a focused interest area

PARTICIPANTS: Coeducational, students currently in grades 10–11

ENROLLMENT: 80

PROGRAM DATES: July 7–July 25, 2008

HEAD OF PROGRAM: Dr. Joseph Renzulli, Director, Neag Center for Gifted Education and Talent Development, University of Connecticut

LOCATION

UCONN Mentor Connection is located in the heart of New England on the University of Connecticut's Storrs campus. Storrs is approximately 40 minutes southeast of Hartford, 2 hours southwest of Boston, and 2½ hours northeast of New York City. UConn is less than an hour from historic Mystic Seaport and the Connecticut shoreline and less than 2 hours from Newport, Rhode Island.

BACKGROUND AND PHILOSOPHY

UCONN Mentor Connection was founded on the belief that it is essential for students to have the opportunity to manifest their talents in high levels of creative productivity. The program's goals are to recruit highly motivated, academically talented teenagers from throughout the nation who can benefit from a stimulating summer program; to allow students to achieve their highest potential by participating in unique, real-world mentorship experiences; to increase students' awareness of their personal strengths and options; and to nurture their talents.

Creative productivity results from the interaction of above-average ability, creativity, and task commitment (motivation), and each of these can be developed and nurtured through authentic opportunities to conduct real research. The university setting provides an especially promising context for creative productivity, because firsthand inquiry is the core of almost all daily work. The purpose of Mentor Connection is to allow students to participate in real-life experiential research and creative projects.

PROGRAM OFFERINGS

UCONN Mentor Connection offers approximately twenty-five different mentorship sites in many areas of the arts and sciences. Each site provides direct, apprentice-based involvement with faculty members and advanced graduate students at the University. Sites include archaeology, biological research, chemistry, communications, creative writing, education, engineering, mathematics, molecular and cell biology, pharmacy research, physics, psychology, puppetry, and Web page design.

Participants in the UCONN Mentor Connection program take on the role of a practicing professional, experience real-world problem solving, and develop a collaborative relationship with a researcher in their area of interest. Participants also have the opportunity to earn 3 college credits through the University of Connecticut, provided certain requirements are met.

ENROLLMENT

UCONN Mentor Connection welcomes applications from a wide variety of students. Motivated, creative, resourceful, enthusiastic, inquisitive, and academically inclined are only a few of the adjectives that describe UCONN Mentor Connection students. Students must be willing to engage in exciting challenges, learn how to conduct investigations in an area of interest, and sustain a long-term commitment to a project.

Roughly half of the students are Connecticut residents, and the rest come from out of state. Participants have the opportunity to make friends with other students who share similar interests, but who come from very different backgrounds than they do.

DAILY SCHEDULE

9:00– 4:00	Work on-site with mentors
4:00– 5:00	Special-topic presentations
5:30	Dinner
7:00	Meeting for staff members and students
7:00–10:00	Evening activities

EXTRA OPPORTUNITIES AND ACTIVITIES

There are optional group activities every evening and organized field trips every weekend. UCONN Mentor Connection celebrates students' projects with a formal dinner and a research and humanities symposium at the end of the program.

FACILITIES

Students are housed in dormitories at the University of Connecticut, and they receive three meals a day in a University dining hall. While at UCONN Mentor Connection, students can take advantage of the University library and the University computer center.

COSTS

Tuition is $3100 and includes room, board, field trips, activities, and the option to earn 3 credits. Students should not bring more than $50–$100 spending money for the three-week program. Tuition is due July 1, 2008.

FINANCIAL AID

A limited number of need-based full- and partial-tuition scholarships are available for applicants from the state of Connecticut who demonstrate financial need.

APPLICATION TIMETABLE

Initial inquiries are welcome after February 1, 2008. The application deadline is May 2, 2008. The application packet must include three essays, two teacher recommendations, applicable test scores, and a current school transcript.

FOR MORE INFORMATION, CONTACT

Heather Spottiswoode, Program Manager
UCONN Mentor Connection
University of Connecticut
2131 Hillside Road, Unit 3007
Storrs, Connecticut 06269-3007

Phone: 860-486-0283
Fax: 860-486-2900
E-mail: mentorconnection@uconn.edu
Web site: http://www.gifted.uconn.edu

PARTICIPANT/FAMILY COMMENTS

"This program is not summer school. It doesn't teach basic, boring stuff over and over again. This program is hands-on. It is an experience in life. Students get to actively participate in a project or in research in which they choose to be involved. The people at the program are unbelievable. The mentors are fascinating and interesting. Everyone has a different background and a different life story. . . .This program has changed my life. I know what college will be like, I have decided on my future major, I have broadened my interests, and I have made 80 new friends."

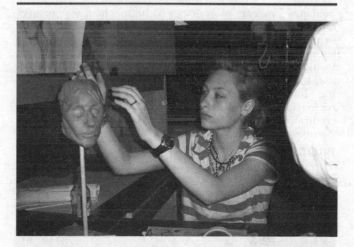

UNIVERSITY OF MARYLAND
Young Scholars Program

░░░░░░░░░░░░░░░░░░░░░░░░░░░░░░░░

SUMMER PROGRAM

COLLEGE PARK, MARYLAND

TYPE OF PROGRAM: College preparation
PARTICIPANTS: Coeducational, current high school sophomores and juniors
ENROLLMENT: Approximately 300 students
PROGRAM DATES: July 13–August 1, 2008
HEAD OF PROGRAM: Eric Johnson, Program Coordinator, Office of Extended Studies

LOCATION

The program is held at the University of Maryland, College Park, the leading public research institution in the mid-Atlantic region. The University ranked eighteenth nationwide among public universities in the 2006 *U.S. News & World Report* "America's Best Colleges." The University is a Metro ride from the sights and culture of Washington, D.C., and a 45-minute trip by rail or car from Baltimore, Maryland.

BACKGROUND AND PHILOSOPHY

The University of Maryland's Young Scholars Program is a great way to test academic interests and explore career opportunities while learning about college life. The Young Scholars Program offers current high school sophomores and juniors three weeks of academic discovery and career exploration—the chance to meet students who share similar interests, study with some of the University's best faculty members in a dynamic classroom environment, and benefit from the University's vast resources, including libraries, computer and instructional labs, and recreational facilities. Participants earn 3 Maryland credits by choosing one 3-credit course.

PROGRAM OFFERINGS

The Young Scholars Program offers the following courses: Introduction to Architecture, American Studies, Creative Writing Workshop, Drawing I, Environmental Biology, Introduction to Engineering Design, Materials Science

and Engineering, Business and Entrepreneurship, Mock Trials, International Political Relations, Introduction to Journalism, Introduction to Kinesiology, Math and Games, Introduction to Music Technology, and Contemporary Social Problems.

ENROLLMENT

Each course has an enrollment limit ranging from 15 to 40 students.

DAILY SCHEDULE

Residential participants begin their day with breakfast at 7:30 a.m. Classes meet Monday through Friday, 9 a.m. to 4 p.m.; this schedule may vary depending on the particular course requirements. Lunch is from noon to 1:30 p.m. Residential students go to dinner around 6 p.m.

EXTRA OPPORTUNITIES AND ACTIVITIES

Scheduled social events include mixers, Terp Zone, karaoke night, talent night, a trip to Washington, D.C., and more.

FACILITIES

Participants may reside in on-campus housing or commute. Residence halls are air-conditioned dormitory or suite-style accommodations. All participants have access to the University's computing labs.

Students have breakfast and lunch on campus; dinner is enjoyed at various eateries in the city of College Park. All residential students receive meal cards that provide for breakfast, lunch, and dinner; commuter students receive a meal card for daily weekday lunches.

STAFF

Courses are taught by highly qualified faculty members who have both teaching expertise and real-world experience.

MEDICAL CARE

Students who become ill or injured are taken to the Campus Health Center, a nationally accredited ambulatory health-care facility located on campus, or to the nearest hospital, depending on the severity of the injury or illness.

COSTS

Course package fees—residential or commuter—for 2008 are still being determined. There is a nonrefundable application processing fee of $55 and a nonrefundable confirmation deposit of $150 that is credited toward the total course package. The course package fee includes most course and program expenses. Students should expect to purchase books, class packets, and classroom supplies. Approximately $50 to $75 per week should cover most miscellaneous personal expenses. Additional infor-

mation about fees and costs is available on the Web site at http://www.summer.umd.edu.

TRANSPORTATION
The University of Maryland is located between two major airports, Baltimore/Washington International Thurgood Marshall Airport in Baltimore and Ronald Reagan International Airport in Washington, D.C. Subway and train stations are connected to the University by the Shuttle-UM bus service. The Shuttle-UM service route also offers transportation service within the vicinity of the campus at predetermined locations, five days a week.

APPLICATION TIMETABLE
Applicants to the Young Scholars Program must be current high school sophomores or juniors in good academic standing, have a grade point average of 3.0 or better, and demonstrate maturity, self-discipline, motivation, and a desire to succeed.

The application process begins February 18. All applications must be accompanied by a $55 nonrefundable processing fee and a $150 confirmation deposit that is credited toward the total course package fee. Com-

pleted applications include a signed application form, a copy of the student's high school transcript, and a letter of recommendation. Only completed applications are considered, so students are advised to follow the instructions carefully. Admissions are made on rolling and space-available basis. Course enrollment is limited; early applicants are more likely to receive their first choice.

FOR MORE INFORMATION, CONTACT
Eric Johnson, Program Coordinator
Office of Extended Studies
0132 Main Administration Building
University of Maryland
College Park, Maryland 20742-5015
Phone: 301-405-1027
E-mail: johnsone@umd.edu
Web site: http://www.summer.umd.edu

PARTICIPANT/FAMILY COMMENTS

"This program provides a rare opportunity for a young person to see a career 'up close.' My daughter loved it."

"An exceptional experience. We would highly recommend this program to other parents and students."

"My son had a great time and was so busy he never had time to call home."

"The program was a good opportunity for my daughter to experience away-from-home life, which was very positive."

"A great opportunity at a great school!"

"This is a great program. I was very pleased with the communication, and the instructor was excellent."

UNIVERSITY OF MIAMI

UNIVERSITY OF
Miami

SUMMER SCHOLAR PROGRAMS

CORAL GABLES, FLORIDA

TYPE OF PROGRAM: Academic enrichment, college credit
PARTICIPANTS: Coeducational, rising high school juniors and seniors
ENROLLMENT: 150–180
PROGRAM DATES: June 22–July 11, 2008
HEAD OF PROGRAM: Dana Render, Assistant Director of High School Programs, Division of Continuing and International Education

LOCATION
The University of Miami (UM) undergraduate campus is nestled in the heart of Coral Gables, a picturesque suburb that blends tropical splendor with Mediterranean-inspired architecture. Walkways link the flora-filled campus courtyard, plazas, arboretums, and quadrangles. Lake Osceola, located in the center of the campus, is surrounded by a red brick sidewalk and feeds into the canals that wander through the lush grounds. Enjoyment of nature, sports, water, and outdoor life are possible year-round in south Florida.

BACKGROUND AND PHILOSOPHY
The University of Miami is the largest private research university in the Southeast. Established in 1925, UM is known for its outstanding faculty, groundbreaking research, diverse student body, and history of excellence in athletics. The University's Summer Scholar Programs (SSP) were established in 1991. Taught by outstanding University of Miami faculty members, these programs present a unique opportunity for students to earn college credit in specific areas of concentration. The programs offer intensive three-week studies. Students learn firsthand what college is like by living and studying on campus. Students also take laboratory classes and have the opportunity to learn about their particular interests by visiting local sites that are relevant to their fields of study.

PROGRAM OFFERINGS
High school students have the opportunity to choose from a variety of programs to meet their interests and should contact the University for specific program offerings. Fieldwork and laboratory research enhance the academic teachings and help students explore potential careers. Previous summer scholars studying broadcast journalism have visited local television studios and produced their own segments; marine science students have completed oceanic studies on the coral reefs of south Florida; film students have produced their own films; and health and medicine students have visited the medical campus and talked with medical experts. Programs scheduled for 2007 included Art, Broadcast Journalism, Engineering, Filmmaking, Forensic Investigation, Global Politics, Health and Medicine, Marine Science, Sports Management, and Studio and Communication Arts.

ENROLLMENT
Students are drawn from areas throughout the United States and abroad. Admission is competitive and administered on a rolling basis. Any student who has completed their sophomore or junior year of high school is welcome to apply. To be accepted, students must demonstrate high academic standards, with a minimum B average. In order to participate in the health and medicine program, students must also have completed two science courses, one of which must be a biology course, with a competitive grade point average. The rich cultural diversity of the University of Miami is reflected in all of the Summer Scholar Programs.

DAILY SCHEDULE
Summer scholars enroll in two courses that meet daily. The length of each class varies depending on lab work, field trips, and lectures; however, summer scholars are in class-related activities all day. All students live in campus residential housing, which is supervised by trained staff members. Three meals each day during the week and two meals each day during the weekend are provided. All programs have evening curfews. With the exception of students walking to shops across the street from the campus, students are not to leave the campus on their own during their stay. Several evening and weekend activities are planned, and anyone may participate.

EXTRA OPPORTUNITIES AND ACTIVITIES
Though the Summer Scholar Programs are challenging academic programs for students, evening and weekend activities are also scheduled, which allow students the time to enjoy the camaraderie of fellow scholars and experience the tropical flavor of the region. Excursions to local hot spots, a snorkeling trip, and the opportunity to take advantage of the University's facilities, such as the wellness/fitness center, are available during the students' free time.

FACILITIES
The University of Miami's facilities, including the Richter Library and the Smathers Wellness Center, are available for student use during the program. During free time, students have access to the University's billiards tables, fitness room, and tennis, volleyball, and basketball courts. Computer facili-

ties are accessible when required for class projects, and the residence hall rooms also have Internet access for those who bring their own computer. Students share an air-conditioned room with another scholar in on-campus residence halls that are staffed with program resident assistants.

STAFF

Classes are led by UM faculty members, who engage students in discovery through discussion, debate, lab experiments, and field trips as appropriate to the program. They are available for questions, addressing concerns, or assistance.

University of Miami undergraduate and graduate students, as well as recent graduates, live in the residential halls and serve as teaching assistants in the classroom. Many have served as UM resident advisers during the academic year and are available to promote a comfortable learning environment for the scholars.

MEDICAL CARE

All students are required to have adequate health insurance coverage for injury, accident, or major illness. There is a health center on campus that can handle injuries, illnesses, and prescriptions. In addition, Doctors Hospital is directly across from the University, in case of serious injury or medical emergency.

RELIGIOUS LIFE

The University has no religious affiliation; however, opportunities for worship are available on campus for members of a variety of faiths.

COSTS

The cost of attending the Summer Scholar Programs in 2007 was $4600, which included tuition, textbooks, instructional supplies, residence hall lodging, the meal plan, field trips, access to the Student Health Center and the Smathers Well-

ness Center, all planned excursions, and some extracurricular activities. A nonrefundable application fee of $100 and deposit of $500 (due within two weeks of acceptance into the program) are applied toward the final cost of the program.

FINANCIAL AID

A limited number of partial scholarships may be available for students who demonstrate high academic performance. Information regarding scholarships for 2008 may be found on the programs' Web site.

TRANSPORTATION

For those who plan to arrive by air, Miami International Airport is near the University. Upon arrival at the airport, students are met by a Community Assistant, who directs students to the baggage claim and guides them to transportation that will deliver them directly to the residence hall on campus. Flight arrangements are the responsibility of the student and are not included in the cost of the program.

APPLICATION TIMETABLE

Applications for admission to the Summer Scholar Programs are accepted through the middle of May. Required materials include a current transcript, a letter of introduction and interest, a letter of recommendation from a teacher, and a nonrefundable $100 application fee. Because admission is selective and space is limited, applicants are encouraged to apply early. When a particular program becomes full, applicants are considered for their second choice if they desire or are placed on a waiting list. A deposit of $500 must be received within two weeks of acceptance. Students who withdraw from the program after May 11, 2007, forfeit their $500 deposit. The University reserves the right to cancel any program due to insufficient enrollment or events beyond its control. In such cases, applicants are considered for their program of second choice or given a refund of all fees and deposits. All programs are subject to change without notice.

FOR MORE INFORMATION, CONTACT

Ms. Dana Render
Assistant Director of High School Programs
Summer Scholar Programs
Division of Continuing Studies
P.O. Box 248005
Coral Gables, Florida 33124-1610
Phone: 305-284-6107
    800-STUDY-UM (toll-free)
Fax: 305-284-2620
E-mail: ssp.cstudies@miami.edu
Web site: http://www.miami.edu/summerscholar

UNIVERSITY OF PENNSYLVANIA

▼▲▼▲▼▲▼▲▼▲▼▲▼▲▼▲▼▲▼▲▼▲▼▲▼▲▼▲

PENN PRE-COLLEGE PROGRAM, PENN SUMMER SCIENCE ACADEMY, PENN SUMMER ART STUDIOS, AND PENN SUMMER THEATRE WORKSHOP

PHILADELPHIA, PENNSYLVANIA

TYPE OF PROGRAM: Credit and noncredit summer programs for academically talented high school students

PARTICIPANTS: Coeducational, students who are rising juniors and seniors

ENROLLMENT: Approximately 400 students

PROGRAM DATES: (2007) Penn Pre-College Program: June 30 to August 11; Penn Summer Science Academy, Penn Summer Arts Studio, and Penn Summer Theatre Workshop: June 30 to July 28

HEAD OF PROGRAM: Dr. John S. Ceccatti, Associate Director of Natural Science Programs; Heather Haseley, Youth Programs Coordinator

LOCATION

The University of Pennsylvania's Summer High School Programs take place on its historic, tree-lined, 260-acre campus. The campus is home to the largest open-stack library in the nation, state-of-the-art laboratories, a leading museum of archeology and anthropology, the Hospital of the University of Pennsylvania, and the Annenberg Center for the Performing Arts.

BACKGROUND AND PHILOSOPHY

Founded by Benjamin Franklin in 1740, Penn was the fourth college of the colonies. Among the ten largest research complexes in the U.S and member of the Ivy League, Penn is known for its academic excellence and groundbreaking research.

PROGRAM OFFERINGS

Penn's summer programs are intended for academically talented, committed students. Each program provides many academic, cultural, and recreational activities for residential and day students.

Penn Pre-College Program Students in the Penn Pre-College Program get a head start on college by earning undergraduate credit for the courses they take alongside Penn undergraduates. The credits earned are generally transferable to other colleges and universities. Courses are intense, demanding, and fast-paced. Students are encouraged to enroll in two courses, a full-time summer course load. Numerous social, intellectual, and cultural activities are available to Pre-College students.

Successful applicants to this program must have completed their sophomore or junior year of high school by June, have an outstanding record of achievement, and demonstrate maturity, discipline, and the ability to undertake course work at Penn. PSAT, SAT, or ACT scores are required, along with a letter of recommendation, official high school transcript, personal resume, and an essay.

Penn Summer Science Academy (PSSA) The Penn Summer Science Academy offers high-achieving high school students the opportunity to pursue in-depth study in one of three areas: biomedical research, physics, or forensic science. This noncredit program consists of both guided and independent

lab and field projects, lectures and workshops, and computer labs and seminars, taught by Penn scientists, graduate students, and outside professionals. Intensive study and lab work (9 to 4 every day) is supplemented by a wide range of additional academic and social opportunities.

Applicants must have completed their sophomore or junior year in high school by June, have outstanding records, and demonstrate the ability to do academic work. Teacher recommendations; a transcript; PSAT, SAT, or ACT scores; a personal resume; and an essay are required.

Penn Summer Arts Studios (PSAS) Penn Summer Art Studios is an intensive, noncredit program consisting of studios in the following areas of concentration: animation, architecture, digital video, drawing and painting studio, ceramics, and photography. Instruction by Penn faculty members is both technical and conceptual.

Applicants must have completed their sophomore or junior year in high school by June. All applicants must have strong academic records and show evidence of ability to do creative work. A high school transcript; PSAT, SAT, or ACT scores; teacher recommendations; a personal resume; and an essay are required. It is recommended that students submit a portfolio in any format (CD, slides, Web site, or the actual work) with their applications.

Penn Summer Theatre Workshop (PSTW) Penn Summer Theatre Workshop is an intensive immersion into the study and practice of theater. This noncredit program, developed and directed by members of Penn's theater arts faculty, includes performance-related courses in acting, scene study, and the Alexander Technique, along with academic preparation in dramaturgy and criticism.

Applicants must have completed their sophomore or junior year in high school by June, have outstanding records, and demonstrate the ability to do academic work. Teacher recommendations; a transcript; PSAT, SAT, or ACT scores; a personal resume of work and/or training in theater; and an essay are required.

ENROLLMENT

Pre-College and Summer Academy programs include a talented, international, and multicultural group of students.

While the majority of students come from throughout the U.S., about 15 percent are international students.

DAILY SCHEDULE
The daily schedule is varied. Breakfast, lunch, and dinner are served in the Commons or Houston Market. Before and after classes, students may avail themselves of a variety of recreational and social activities that are offered each day. The course work is very rigorous, so students should expect to spend approximately 4 to 6 hours each day in study and class preparation. There are evening chat sessions, student groups, and floor and program activities each evening. Curfew during the week is 10 p.m., and on weekends, 12 a.m. Students are able to leave campus with written permission from their parents.

EXTRA OPPORTUNITIES AND ACTIVITIES
Students enjoy an extraordinary range of activities, including trips to the beach; the mountains; New York City; Washington, D.C.; restaurants; museums; theaters; and concerts. Penn has two indoor pools and gyms, track and football fields, and tennis and basketball courts.

Students may also participate in a series of college study skills, preprofessional workshops, and a college admissions preparation program that includes workshops in SAT preparation and application building. They also enjoy field trips and guided tours of professional and other sites, such as the Children's Hospital of Philadelphia and Penn's Veterinary Hospital.

FACILITIES
Residential students are housed in the Quad, the traditional first-year student residence. All rooms are air conditioned and wired for Internet service, telephone, and cable television.

STAFF
Residence halls are supervised by Residential Counselors (RCs), outstanding Penn undergraduates who also act as counselors, tutors, and guides around the campus and the city to help students adjust to university life. The ratio of RCs to students is about 1 to 10. The College House Dean, Residential Director, and senior residential staff are also in residence.

MEDICAL CARE
All summer school students are required to have health insurance. Emergency or urgent care is provided by the Children's Hospital of Philadelphia or by the Hospital of the University of Pennsylvania Emergency Room, and routine care is provided through Student Health Services.

RELIGIOUS LIFE
The University of Pennsylvania is a secular institution. The University chaplain coordinates many programs and is available to all students at any time. Numerous religious centers are also available to students, both on and around the campus.

COSTS
Pre-College Program costs are estimated at $7360 to $8635 for residential students and $3300 to $5850 for day students (depending on the number of courses taken). PSSA, PSAS, and PSTW costs are estimated at $3045 for day students and $5105 for residential students. Residential costs include housing, dining, program fees, and instruction.

TRANSPORTATION
A variety of transportation options are available within Philadelphia and from Philadelphia International Airport to the Quad.

APPLICATION TIMETABLE
Applications are available in January. Students should visit the Web site for more information about application deadlines (http://www.upenn.edu/summer/highschool).

FOR MORE INFORMATION, CONTACT
Summer High School Programs
University of Pennsylvania
3440 Market Street, Suite 100
Philadelphia, Pennsylvania 19104-3335
Phone: 215-746-6901
Fax: 215-573-2053
Web site: http://www.upenn.edu/summer/highschool

UNIVERSITY OF SOUTHERN CALIFORNIA

EXPLORATION OF ARCHITECTURE

LOS ANGELES, CALIFORNIA

TYPE OF PROGRAM: Intensive academic introduction
PARTICIPANTS: Coeducational; ages 15–18, grades 10–12
ENROLLMENT: 100
PROGRAM DATES: Two- or four-week programs beginning in July.
HEADS OF PROGRAM: Paul R. Tang, AIA, Assistant Professor, USC School of Architecture

LOCATION

The University of Southern California (USC) is located in downtown Los Angeles, which is situated between the southern California mountain ranges and the Pacific Ocean. The campus is located just north of the Museum of Natural History, near where the I-10 and I-110 freeways meet. Hollywood, Los Angeles International Airport (LAX), and the Pacific coast are no more than 20–30 minutes from campus. The University currently occupies 155 acres. The wide variety of urban and environmental conditions in the area make Los Angeles an excellent laboratory for the study of architecture, from hillside housing in Hollywood to high-rise office towers and recreational centers such as the newly constructed Staples Center.

USC is close to the various cultural and historical districts of Los Angeles such as Chinatown, Olivera Street, Koreatown, and Old Pasadena. Students can visit film studios, hear music at the Hollywood Bowl, or visit world-class museums such as the Los Angeles County Museum of Art and the Norton Simon Museum. Through joint programs with the University's neighbors and campus safety programs, USC has become one of the safest urban campuses in the United States. In fact, USC's Department of Public Safety is one of the largest private security forces in the world today.

BACKGROUND AND PHILOSOPHY

One of the most comprehensive and rewarding programs of its kind in the country, USC's Exploration of Architecture high school program was begun in 1985. Today, students can choose to participate in the two- or four-week programs. The four-week program offers 3 units of college credit. The programs are intended to provide high school students from across the country and around the world with an intensive, in-depth, and "hands-on" introduction to the design of the built environment and the experience of architectural studies at the university level. The ultimate goal is to help students make a highly informed decision regarding their college and career direction while at the same time exposing them to the ethnic, cultural, and artistic diversity of one of the country's largest metropolitan centers.

Previous architectural study is not a requirement for admission; all students need is their enthusiasm and an interest in architecture. Participants benefit from the involvement of several full- and part-time faculty members, teaching assistants, and resident advisers. Participating students experience firsthand what it is like to approach design projects in a real studio setting.

Outside of the classroom, students tour various architectural points of interest, including important historical and contemporary structures and museums. Students have the opportunity to explore the full spectrum of Los Angeles' built environment, from downtown high-rises to the houses of Frank Lloyd Wright.

PROGRAM OFFERINGS

The design studio experience is the focus of the program, emphasizing the basic skills of drawing and model building. Studio projects explore the design of cities, furniture, landscapes, and buildings. At the end of each week, students present their projects to faculty members and visitors for a discussion of their ideas, intentions, and execution. Each week builds upon the lessons and projects of the previous week. All students participating are advised on how to use their work from the program to produce a portfolio for college admission. Students also learn about the restoration of historic architecture by visiting structures like Frank Lloyd Wright's Freeman House and the Gamble House by Greene & Greene. Participants attend lectures and studios with USC architecture faculty members and get assistance from upper-division architecture students. Finally, while living at a USC residence hall, students receive an important introduction to college life. Furthermore, participants have the chance to meet and make friends with other students from around the country and around the world.

ENROLLMENT

The Exploration of Architecture program can accommodate up to 100 students. Students from nearly all cultural and socioeconomic backgrounds have participated in this program. Typically, about 5 percent of students are international, while approximately 40 percent of domestic students are from outside California.

DAILY SCHEDULE

After breakfast, the day's activities begin at 9 a.m. and continue until 9 p.m. No two days follow the same schedule; one day may begin with studio time or lecture, while another may begin right away with a tour. Lunch and dinner breaks are typically taken at noon and 5 p.m., respectively. Students must observe a strict curfew of 10:30 p.m.

FACILITIES

Studios and lectures take place in Watt and Harris Halls. In 2007, students were housed in Marks Tower on the USC campus. Students are able to purchase some supplies at the Pertusati Bookstore. Health and fitness facilities are open to students over 16 years of age.

MEDICAL CARE

Exploration of Architecture requires that all students pay the weekly student health fee, which was $14 per week for summer 2007. This fee is subject to change.

COSTS

Costs for the 2007 program were $2700 for two weeks and $4485 for four weeks. The cost covered tuition, meals, housing, and transportation during the program. Prices are subject to change. Additional costs include lab fees, supply fees, and personal spending money.

FINANCIAL AID

Financial aid is offered to students on the basis of financial need. Students who wish to be considered for financial aid must submit copies of their parents' tax returns along with the financial aid application.

TRANSPORTATION

Transportation is provided for all field trips and off-campus activities. Students arriving at LAX are provided with shuttle service to and from the campus for a nominal fee.

APPLICATION TIMETABLE

Applications are processed as they are completed on a rolling basis until all spaces are filled.

FOR MORE INFORMATION, CONTACT

Director of Admissions
USC School of Architecture
Watt Hall 204
Los Angeles, California 90089-0291
Phone: 800-281-8616 (toll-free)
Fax: 213-740-8884
E-mail: uscarch@usc.edu
Web site: http://arch.usc.edu

THE UNIVERSITY OF THE ARTS

PRE-COLLEGE SUMMER INSTITUTE

PHILADELPHIA, PENNSYLVANIA

TYPE OF PROGRAM: Visual and performing arts; media and communications

PARTICIPANTS: Students entering their junior or senior year of high school, as well as recent graduates, ages 16–19

ENROLLMENT: Approximately 400

PROGRAM DATES: July 7 through August 1, 2008

HEADS OF PROGRAM: Erin Elman, Director of Pre-College Programs; Melissa DiGiacomo, Assistant Director of Pre-College Programs

LOCATION

The University of the Arts (UArts) is unlike any other university. It is the only university in the nation teaching a broad range of visual, performing, and communication arts and focusing exclusively on the arts. The University comprises three colleges and a liberal arts division. Summer program courses are offered in each college of the University: College of Art and Design, College of Media and Communication, and College of Performing Arts.

UArts is located in the heart of Center City Philadelphia on the Avenue of the Arts (South Broad Street). It is in the center of the arts and culture district and within walking distance of museums, galleries, theaters, and the cultural life of the city.

BACKGROUND AND PHILOSOPHY

The Pre-College Summer Institute was created as an opportunity for students who have had varying interests and backgrounds in the visual and performing arts to study together in a university environment. Some participants enroll to discover their individual talents. Others want to build on their education. Still others seek to learn about specific careers in the arts. The programs are flexible enough to address all of these various needs.

PROGRAM OFFERINGS

The ArtsSmart program allows high school students to explore their individual talents and interests, learn new art and design skills, and develop a better, more comprehensive portfolio. The program provides students with an arts education experience that is comparable to one at the college level. It is also a great opportunity for young artists to experiment with new materials and art forms as they develop their portfolios. Students in the ArtsSmart program choose two concentrations as well as two electives.

The media workshops provide students with intensive study in animation, screen directing, digital filmmaking, or writing for film and television, using state-of-the-art equipment and facilities.

Performing arts programs include the four-week process-oriented acting and musical theater programs, as well as a two-week intensive dance and jazz performance program for instrumentalists and/or vocalists.

Interested students should visit the UArts Web site (http://www.uarts.edu/precollege) for the complete list of concentrations and electives that are offered.

ENROLLMENT

The Pre-College Summer Institute enrolls students from all over the world. A letter of recommendation from an art instructor or guidance counselor, school transcripts, and a portfolio or audition tape are required for a scholarship.

DAILY SCHEDULE

	9:00 . . . Classes begin
12:00–	1:00 . . . Lunch
	5:00 . . . Classes end
	7:00 . . . Social activities
	10:30 . . . Curfew (Sunday–Thursday)
	12:00 . . . Curfew (Friday and Saturday)

EXTRA OPPORTUNITIES AND ACTIVITIES

Activities include museum visits, concerts, films, sports events, trips to the New Jersey shore, barbecues, and other social events. At the end of the program, there are a reception and an exhibition of works created by the visual arts students and a showcase presentation by the performing arts students.

FACILITIES

The University of the Arts campus comprises ten buildings with classrooms, studios, theaters, galleries, lounges, residential apartments, and administrative offices.

Visual arts students work in recently renovated studios with fully equipped shops for working in ceramics and jewelry/metals, photography labs, and state-of-the-art multimedia labs.

The facilities used by performing arts students reflect the growing range of tools available to professional composers, artists, and performers. They include a music technology studio, a recording studio, editing suites, practice rooms, and light-filled dance studios with mirrors and resilient floors with 4-inch suspension for safety and comfort.

STAFF

The staff includes a year-round Director, Erin Elman, and Assistant Director, Melissa DiGiacomo.

Faculty members are expert, practicing professionals in the visual and performing arts. They provide instruction and direction to developing student artists who are serious about academic study. The faculty members understand the demands of their respective professions and are expert at imparting knowledge, technique, energy, and discipline.

MEDICAL CARE

The University's Health Services Office is open weekdays, 8 a.m. to 7 p.m., and is professionally staffed. In instances of medical emergencies, students are taken to Thomas Jefferson Hospital for care.

COSTS

For 2008 tuition and housing pricing information, students should contact the precollege department directly. Information is also available on the Web at http://www.uarts.edu/precollege.

FINANCIAL AID

A limited number of partial-tuition scholarships are available for visual and performing arts students. Interested students should apply early. The deadline is in March.

TRANSPORTATION

The University is easily accessible by public transportation from New Jersey and suburban Philadelphia via the regional rail lines of PATCO and SEPTA, respectively. UArts is also convenient to Amtrak and Greyhound stations and to the Philadelphia International Airport.

APPLICATION TIMETABLE

Scholarship and registration deadlines are in March.

FOR MORE INFORMATION, CONTACT

Pre-College Programs
The University of the Arts
320 South Broad Street
Philadelphia, Pennsylvania 19102

Phone: 215-717-6430
     800-616-ARTS (toll-free outside Pennsylvania)
Fax: 215-717-6433
E-mail: precollege@uarts.edu
Web site: http://www.uarts.edu

VALLEY FORGE MILITARY ACADEMY

SUMMER CAMP

WAYNE, PENNSYLVANIA

TYPE OF PROGRAM: Traditional outdoor challenge
PARTICIPANTS: Boys and girls, ages 6–17
ENROLLMENT: 320
PROGRAM DATES: Overnight Camp: Monday, June 23, to Friday, July 18, 2008; Day Camp: Monday, June 16, to Friday, July 25, 2008
HEADS OF PROGRAM: COL Thad A. Gaebelein, Commandant of Cadets; MAJ Jeff Bond, Director of Summer Camp

LOCATION
Valley Forge is located on 120 acres of beautifully maintained grounds in Wayne, Pennsylvania, just 15 miles west of Philadelphia and minutes from Valley Forge National Park.

BACKGROUND AND PHILOSOPHY
The Valley Forge Summer Camp is operated by the Valley Forge Military Academy (VFMA) Foundation and maintains the same high standards that have made that institution internationally famous.

PROGRAM OFFERINGS
There are several options for a fantastic camp experience. Boys can choose from an overnight adventure camp, Senior Ranger overnight or day camp, and overnight band camp. Day-only options for boys and girls include a coed day camp and a coed band camp.

The camps are divided into age-appropriate groups consisting of Pathfinders (ages 6–7), Pioneers (ages 8–9), Junior Rangers (ages 10–11), Raiders (ages 12–13), and Senior Rangers (ages 14–17).

The Senior Ranger overnight and day camp is a physical-fitness camp designed to build self-confidence and leadership. Through the positive experience of physical exercise and success, the camper builds an awareness of his or her own abilities and talents.

Each camp has several activity periods each day to challenge and build self-confidence in the campers' lives. The camp's uniqueness lies in its ability to enhance the lives of the campers through team building, esteem building, and helping all the campers realize their own innate ability to succeed. During these periods, campers participate in sports, swimming, go-carts, low ropes and high ropes courses, rappelling tower, wall climbing, drill, orienteering, and more. A Boy Scout can attend and earn merit badge requirements. There are at least five trips during the four-week stay that all campers participate in, depending on their ages. Some of these trips include Dorney Park, a paintball park, canoeing, state parks, a minor-league baseball game, and a Philadelphia Phillies baseball game.

There are several special activities to enhance the camping experience. For an extra fee, the academic program provides each camper with the opportunity to improve his skills in reading, English, or math on the elementary and middle school levels. A new program beginning this year is an SAT Prep class for the high school age campers. The faculty

members of VFMA conduct classes in a relaxed and informal atmosphere. Class size varies between four and ten campers.

Sessions are held five mornings each week for two weeks and are scheduled so as not to interfere with afternoon camp activities. There are other optional activities available on a first-come, first-served basis. Space is limited and an additional fee is charged. These programs include Competitive Marksmanship Training, Karate, SCUBA, and a horsemanship program. The Band Camp offers an excellent program through individual lessons, theory classes, concert band techniques, and camper/staff recitals for youths with one or more years of instrumental experience. Afternoons and evenings are rounded out with fun activities, such as sports, canoeing, swimming, and trips.

DAILY SCHEDULE

7:00	Reveille
8:00	First mess (Breakfast)
9:00–10:15	First activity
10:15–10:30	Break to next challenge
10:30–11:45	Second activity
11:45–12:15	Break to second mess
12:15	Second mess (Lunch)
13:15–14:30	Third activity
14:30–14:45	Break to next challenge
14:45–16:00	Fourth activity
16:00–16:15	Break to next challenge
16:15–17:30	Fifth activity
17:30–18:15	Break to third mess
18:15	Third mess (Supper)
19:15–20:15	Sixth activity
20:15–20:30	Break to next challenge
20:30–21:30	Seventh activity
21:30	Back to barracks
22:15	Taps

The day campers participate in all the activities of the overnight camp as well as the trips available on the week of attendance. Day campers begin their day at 9 a.m. and conclude at 4 p.m. The Academy offers extended care from

7 a.m. till 6 p.m. for working moms and dads at no charge. The day campers also have lunch provided for them in the mess hall.

The schedule varies on weekends and during field trips. Campers are required to follow the school rules, which include a code of conduct. Counselors receive conflict-resolution training and work individually with their campers to resolve individual problems. The Director of Summer Camp handles special circumstances.

ENROLLMENT

Approximate numbers are as follows: 40 each in Band and Pioneers, and 100 each in Junior Rangers, Raiders, and Senior Rangers. Participants in Band Camp must already play a concert band instrument at the middle school level or better with a minimum of two years' experience. Valley Forge Military Academy summer campers represent more than twenty-two states and fourteen other countries.

FACILITIES

Campers stay on campus in one of five cadet barracks. The 120-acre campus has every facility necessary to ensure that each camper has an enjoyable and safe place to live and have fun.

STAFF

The staff of 130 men and women includes counselors, Assistant Camp Commandants, Camp Commandants, food service staff members, medical staff members, teaching faculty members, sports coordinators, and other personnel. The camp maintains an 8:1 camper-counselor ratio. The youngest campers, ages 6–7, have a 5:1 camper-counselor ratio. All counselors and other professional staff members enjoy working with school-age children and receive special training to enhance the experience for each of the campers.

MEDICAL CARE

The Academy Health Center is staffed during camp. Minor ailments are treated promptly. Local hospitals are used for medical support beyond the capabilities of the Health Center.

RELIGIOUS LIFE

The Valley Forge Military Academy Summer Camp Chapel service is held every Sunday and is a nondenominational

service that campers are required to attend. It is an essential part of their character development at Valley Forge. Arrangements can be made for campers of particular faiths to attend services locally.

COSTS

Charges for 2006 were $3300 each for Pioneer Camp, Raider/Ranger Camp, and Band Camp. Day camp was $350 per week, for up to six weeks. Fees included the cost of room and board; use of all athletic facilities; instruction in athletics, leadership, camp-crafts, and basic scouting skills; and camp uniforms. There was an additional fee of $175 for each camper's spending and activities allowance. The additional fees for specialty programs ranged from $250 to $900 and are available on a first-come, first-served limited basis until June 1.

TRANSPORTATION

Valley Forge Military Academy is approximately 40 minutes from both the Philadelphia International Airport and 30th Street Station. Valley Forge provides pickup and drop-off services for the start and end of the Overnight Camp.

APPLICATION TIMETABLE

Initial inquiries are welcome at anytime. Appointments to visit the campus are made on a daily basis. Invitations are sent for special campus visitation programs. It is recommended that parents and prospective campers schedule a visit at their earliest convenience. Camp applications are accepted starting in January and must include a nonrefundable $125 deposit. Character and medical references are required, and acceptance letters are sent promptly. The balance of the fees is due on or before the reporting date to camp.

FOR MORE INFORMATION, CONTACT

Valley Forge Military Academy and College
1001 Eagle Road
Wayne, Pennsylvania 19087
Phone: 610-989-1253
          610-989-1262
Fax: 610-688-1260
E-mail: summercamp@vfmac.edu
Web site: http://www.vfmac.edu

VISIONS

COMMUNITY SERVICE, CROSS-CULTURAL LIVING AND LEARNING, AND ADVENTUROUS EXPLORATION

NORTH AMERICA, CENTRAL AND SOUTH AMERICA, ASIA, AND THE CARIBBEAN AND WEST INDIES

TYPE OF PROGRAM: Community service, cross-cultural immersion, and adventurous exploration
PARTICIPANTS: Coeducational, ages 14–18 (grades 9–12)
ENROLLMENT: 350 total in twelve locations
PROGRAM DATES: Four weeks in July; three weeks in August
HEADS OF PROGRAM: Joanne Pinaire and Teena Beutel

LOCATION
VISIONS offers summer residential experiences based in Alaska, the Mississippi Gulf Coast, Montana, the British Virgin Islands, Costa Rica, Dominica, Guadeloupe, the Dominican Republic, Ecuador and the Galapagos, Nicaragua, Peru, and Vietnam. Housing is in a school or community building in the heart of each community. Some sites offer short-term home stays.

BACKGROUND AND PHILOSOPHY
Established in 1988, VISIONS offers uniquely integrated summer experiences for teenagers. Community service work is the focus of the programs, which also feature an intentional blend of cross-cultural immersion experiences and intimate exploration of the program site. Students and staff leaders live and work together as a team. VISIONS emphasizes cooperative living in a supportive setting. Weekly circle meetings keep lines of communication open through focused reflection and listening. Under staff guidance, participants play the central role in building the trusting foundation of their program environment.

At every VISIONS site, projects encompass construction as well as other kinds of service, such as tutoring or volunteering with children, the elderly, or the handicapped; environmental work in national parks and wilderness areas; agricultural work; and apprenticeships with local vendors, artisans, or health professionals. Participants learn carpentry skills from staff carpenters. Local maestros teach adobe or cinder-block construction techniques. Past projects include ground-up construction of low-income housing, schools, medical clinics, youth centers, playground structures, log bridges, and irrigation canals, and the rehabilitation of housing and community buildings.

Time is always set aside for exploration. Depending on the location, recreation includes rock climbing, ice climbing, backpacking, rafting, snorkeling, sea kayaking, scuba diving, horseback riding, and sight seeing. Participants work and socialize with residents, attend ceremonies and cultural festivities. Relationships with local people provide the important contexts for understanding and learning about other cultures.

PROGRAM OFFERINGS
Alaska VISIONS has sites on the northern boundary of south-central Alaska, roughly 4 hours from Fairbanks, along the Wrangell St. Elias National Park. Projects in native villages include building playgrounds and recreation facilities, renovating community buildings and elders' homes, and supervising children's activity programs. Participants learn about Athabascan culture and a unique frontier heritage. Recreation includes day hikes, extended backpacking trips in the Wrangell Mountains, an ice-climbing adventure, trips to neighboring towns, and wildlife viewing.

Montana Participants live and work on Plains Indian reservations surrounded by abundant natural resources and stunning landscapes. Projects include renovation and construction of tribal buildings and elders' homes, ceremonial structures, and playgrounds for schools and communities; organizing day camp activities for children; and trail work in primitive wilderness. Renowned for its

beauty, the "Last Best Place" offers backpacking, rock climbing, horseback riding, rafting, attending powwows, and sharing a sweat lodge with native friends. Participants learn firsthand about native traditions and history that has shaped life on and off the reservations.

Mississippi Gulf Coast: Hurricane Relief VISIONS supports Katrina Relief in coastal Mississippi. The unprecedented devastation requires a rebuilding effort that will take up to a decade. VISIONS is home-based in North Gulfport and Turkey Creek, communities rooted in African American history. Purchased by newly emancipated African Americans in 1866, these few acres of swamp land grew into vibrant, self-sufficient neighborhoods with farms, homesteads, businesses, and the first African American school in the Gulfport region. Turkey Creek is a strategic, vital watershed that has come under threat from developers, a threat that intensified in the aftermath of Katrina. The service work in Mississippi will vary to include construction, renovation, debris clean-up, and work with the elderly and children.

Vietnam VISIONS Vietnam blends the bustle of historic Hanoi with serene landscapes of rice paddies, rolling hills and mountains, jungles, and the coast. In the older generation's faces are reflected centuries of perseverance and loyalty to tradition while the youthful majority of Vietnamese seek to embrace Western, market-based principles. (Sixty percent of Vietnam's 84 million people are under of thirty years old.) Service includes improvements to housing for those disadvantaged and disabled by the long-term, cross-generational effects of chemicals such as Agent Orange and assisting English-language and craft classes for children. Participants work and recreate with Vietnamese teenagers. In cooperation with the Vietnam American Society, VISIONS Vietnam participants witness war's remnant legacy while simultaneously experiencing the optimistic, forgiving, forward-looking character of the Vietnamese. Exploration will be often and fascinating—historical sites, perhaps in Ho Chi Minh City; Ha Long Bay, the World Heritage Site renowned for its beauty and geology; and restaurants, shops, museums, and more.

The Dominican Republic This program offers service work and language immersion in a Spanish-speaking Third-World country. Past participants have built a medical clinic, homes, and schools. Every summer, participants build houses and organize an extensive day camp for Dominican children. During free time, students experience the vibrant culture and beauty in and around Santo Domingo. Swimming, snorkeling, hiking excursions into the interior, and evenings of merengue dancing are some of the recreation activities offered. This program has a minimum requirement of two years of high school Spanish.

British Virgin Islands In the Caribbean British Virgin Island (BVI), VISIONS groups work on community projects in collaboration with the Ministry of Health and Welfare, National Parks Trust, Red Cross, Disaster Relief Services, and BVI Services. One group lives on Tortola, the largest of the British Virgin Islands; a second group lives on Virgin Gorda, a smaller neighboring island. Construction is the focus—housing from the ground up, public buildings, structures, and trails for the National Parks Trust. VISIONS also works with public school summer programs, the elderly, and subsistence farmers. The classic Caribbean beaches and coves are perfect for snorkeling and scuba diving.

Guadeloupe Guadeloupe is a French language-immersion experience on a Caribbean island blending French and Caribbean cultures. VISIONS works in communities on either mainland Basse Terre or on Terre de Bas, one of Les Saintes—tiny islands off the southern tip of the mainland. VISIONS participants undertake joint renovation projects on parks and preservation endeavors designated by local governments and apprentice with local fishermen and artisans. Besides swimming and snorkeling, the group explores the rainforests and mountains of Guadeloupe; the small outer lying islands; colorful, fragrant open air markets; and the exquisite countryside. This program has a minimum requirement of two years of high school French.

Dominica The "Nature Island" of the Lesser Antilles, with its lush, unspoiled beauty, stands apart from other Caribbean islands. A rainforest mountain range is the north-south spine of Dominica, alive with rare tropical birds and flowers. Whales and dolphins swim the coastal waters. The volcanic island soil is rich, rainfall is abundant, and hundreds of rivers and streams drain the island. Despite its natural beauty, Dominica's economy is strictly Third World. VISIONS participants live and work on the Carib Reserve, home to the surviving original inhabitants of the Caribbean Islands. Service focus on pressing needs in Carib Territory, such as reforestation, supervising enrichment activities for children, renovating housing and community buildings, and constructing schools, cisterns, roads, and shelters.

Peru VISIONS Peru combines service work in a southeastern Andean village with discovery of ancient Inca and colonial Spanish cultures. Participants live in a highland community while accomplishing adobe construction projects, environmental work, and volunteering in local schools. Students explore Peru's majestic landscapes by hiking and traveling to centuries-old marketplaces and resplendent historic sites, including Machu Picchu. Groups learn local customs and sometimes participate in cultural traditions. They work with and meet Andean farmers, educators, politicians, musicians, and artisans. This program has a minimum requirement of two years of high school Spanish.

Ecuador and the Galapagos Mitad del Mundo offers Spanish language and indigenous culture immersion on the Galapagos Islands and in a mainland Andean community. This program combines group living and a home-stay experience. Half the program unfolds on the Galapagos, the other half in the Andean village of Chaupiloma. Projects mix construction, agriculture/farming, and ecological and environmental work. Participants actively explore a "megadiverse" World Heritage Site (the Galapagos) and the diverse beauty and culture of Ecuador's Andean highlands. Recreation includes snorkeling, wildlife viewing, and hiking; treks to waterfalls and lakes; visits to marketplaces and thermal baths; and learning about folkloric music, arts, and dancing. This program has a minimum requirement of two years of high school Spanish.

Costa Rica This is a language immersion program in one of the most lush of Central American countries. Half the program is on a sea turtle preservation reserve on the Caribbean coast, accessed by boat through winding canals—a quiet, safe sanctuary with 3 kilometers of beach to patrol. Participants assist with turtle patrols and data collection, and in development projects on this remote reserve. Home base during the second half of the program is Quebrada, a farming community nestled in lush green mountains in central Costa Rica. In partnership with local associations, participants undertake construction and other work to improve community resources. Participants must have a minimum of two years of high school Spanish.

Nicaragua A stunning medley of mountains, craters, lakes, plains, bustling towns, open-hearted people, and scenic bus rides, Nicaragua leaves travelers floored by its breathtaking beauty. Nicaragua, which has been stable for well over a decade, leads Central America's self-sustaining development evidenced throughout the country by solar and other 'green' energy initiatives; effectively functioning cooperatives in agriculture, coffee, and women's crafts; and community resources development. VISIONS is home-based in the northern mountain town of Jinotega, the strategic coffee production area, a *tranquillo* city encircled by out-lying small villages. Participants engage in intensely focused community work—from construction to agriculture to apprenticeships—with Nicaraguan artisans, farmers, and others. No trip to Nicaragua is complete without an excursion to Central America's oldest city, of Granada, an inviting metropolis featuring old stately colonial-era buildings painted in an array of pastels, great restaurants, Spanish schools, and a four-star hotel on the plaza. This program has a minimum requirement of two years of high school Spanish.

ENROLLMENT

There is a maximum of 25 students and 6 adult leaders and a minimum of 16 students and 4 leaders in any program. All programs are coed. The general age range of participants is from 14 to 18; a few programs have a minimum age of 16.

STAFF

The backbone of a safe, high-quality program is the leadership. VISIONS maintains a staff-student ratio of 1:4. The average age of leaders is mid-to-late 20s and upward. Roughly 50 percent of the leaders return each season. They are returned Peace Corps volunteers, outdoor wilderness experts, Ph.D. candidates and graduate students, teachers and other educators, and, sometimes, professionals from the host community. Experienced carpenters teach building skills. Program directors have proven leadership abilities and are veterans of previous VISIONS summers. All VISIONS leaders hold minimum First Aid and CPR certification; the majority hold advanced certifications (Wilderness First Aid, Wilderness First Responder, Lifeguard Training, Wilderness EMT). Some sites require these higher certifications.

COSTS

Tuition ranges from $3100 to $4900, depending on location and length of the program.

FINANCIAL AID

VISIONS offers both partial and full scholarships. Applications for financial assistance are accepted until April 15.

APPLICATION TIMETABLE

VISIONS accepts applications starting in October. Because enrollment in each program is limited, students are advised to inquire and apply early.

FOR MORE INFORMATION, CONTACT

VISIONS
P.O. Box 220
Newport, Pennsylvania 17074
Phone: 717-567-7313
      800-813-9283 (toll-free)
Fax: 717-567-7853
E-mail: info@visionsserviceadventures.com
Web site: http://www.VisionsServiceAdventures.com

WASHINGTON UNIVERSITY IN ST. LOUIS

HIGH SCHOOL SUMMER SCHOLARS PROGRAM

ST. LOUIS, MISSOURI

TYPE OF PROGRAM: Residential academic precollege program awarding college credit

PARTICIPANTS: Coeducational, rising high school seniors ages 16 and older

ENROLLMENT: 70–80 per session

PROGRAM DATES: Two 5-week sessions, June 8 to July 12 and July 13 to August 15, 2008

HEAD OF PROGRAM: Marsha Hussung, Director

LOCATION

Washington University is located in a quiet, tree-lined suburban neighborhood 7 miles west of downtown St. Louis. It is circled by the city's Central West End and the suburban communities of University City and Clayton. Directly across the street is Forest Park, one of the largest urban parks in the country and home to the St. Louis Art Museum, the St. Louis Zoo, the Science Center, and more.

BACKGROUND AND PHILOSOPHY

Founded in 1988, Washington University's High School Summer Scholars Program (HSSP) provides academically talented rising seniors with a rare and special experience— five weeks of a rewarding academic challenge, serious fun, and the excitement of living and bonding with fellow students from around the globe. The best possible introduction to college life and a chance to earn college credit are offered in an atmosphere that values excellence in teaching and personal attention to each student. Participants get a head start on college courses (and learn the study skills required to do well), garner helpful hints on college admissions and financial aid, and experience the independence of college life through residence hall living.

PROGRAM OFFERINGS

In this small, selective program, participants can earn up to 7 semester units of college credit. Nearly sixty stimulating introductory college courses from two dozen departments are offered, ranging from the arts and humanities to science and social science. Courses include French, German, Italian, Spanish, Russian, dance, fiction writing, music, biology, chemistry, earth and planetary science, mathematics, physics, art history, English literature and composition, history, philosophy, archaeology, economics, political science, psychology, and religious studies. Most courses carry 3 credits, and participants usually take two courses during a session. Participants study with undergraduates from Washington University and other colleges and universities.

Weekly Exploratory Seminars provide information on college life and financial and career planning. Sessions are led by University staff members and representatives of the Schools of Architecture, Art, Arts and Sciences, Business, and Engineering.

ENROLLMENT

In 2006, 144 students came to HSSP from every part of the United States and from around the world, including France, Turkey, Bulgaria, and China. To be eligible, participants must be at least 16 years old and a current high school junior. HSSP seeks strong students with academic averages of at least B+ who are capable of succeeding in college classes, with a combined SAT score of at least 1800, a PSAT selection index of 180, or an ACT or PLAN composite score of at least 25. International students should have a TOEFL score of at least 213 or the equivalent.

EXTRA OPPORTUNITIES AND ACTIVITIES

Weekly meetings, trips, and social events are planned, but plenty of unscheduled time is also allotted for participants to get to know Washington University and the other students who are there for the summer. Ozark float trips and visits to Six Flags and a St. Louis Cardinals baseball game are especially popular with Summer Scholars. On campus, the Holmes Lounge provides jazz, blues, and folk music throughout the summer. The Gateway Festival Orchestra presents free concerts on several Sunday evenings in the Washington University Quadrangle. A free international and American film series is offered throughout the summer sessions.

FACILITIES

Students live in a modern, air-conditioned campus residence hall occupied only by other members of the program and are supervised by experienced resident advisers (RAs) and a Residential Program Supervisor, who hold weekly meetings to share concerns and help plan the social life and outings. The residence hall is equipped with a computer lab, laundry facilities, study and lounge areas, and additional amenities.

Summer students may use the University's general library or any of the twelve department and school libraries located on campus. All libraries offer a wide variety of electronic resources, including access to the Internet. The Washington University Computing and Communications

Center provides a variety of computer resources and services; campus computer labs are equipped with Macintoshes and PCs.

The Athletic Complex provides a variety of recreational opportunities such as racquetball, squash, tennis, track, weight training, and swimming. The Campus Y also sponsors exercise classes and programs.

STAFF

The Program Director oversees all logistical and residential aspects of the Summer Scholars Program, providing informal academic counseling and enrollment assistance and also working closely with the residential staff. Living in the residence hall with the Summer Scholars are a Residential Program Supervisor and specially selected and trained Resident Advisers (RAs) who are Washington University students or recent graduates.

Washington University faculty members, graduate students, and subject specialists teach the regular college courses in which Summer Scholars enroll. On average, the summer instructor–student ratio is 1:10.

MEDICAL CARE

The University Health Services Center is staffed with a physician and a nurse Monday through Friday. Emergency care is available through Barnes-Jewish Hospital, part of the Washington University Medical Center. All participants must be covered by medical insurance and must complete medical forms prior to enrollment.

COSTS

The program fee for 2007 was $5365, which covered tuition, housing, meals, use of the Athletic Complex, and participation in special workshops and social activities. Books, supplies, travel, and personal and incidental expenses are not covered by the program fee. All program fees are due three weeks prior to the start of the desired session.

FINANCIAL AID

Scholarship aid, which is based on financial need and academic performance, ranges from $500 to $4000. Financial aid applications must be included with program application forms.

TRANSPORTATION

Washington University is centrally located in the St. Louis metropolitan area and is readily accessible by major highways (I-44, I-55, I-64, I-70), bus (Greyhound), rail (Amtrak), and air (Lambert–St. Louis International Airport). Within the city, there is extensive public transportation by bus and light rail. Students should contact their travel agency for advice on travel arrangements.

APPLICATION TIMETABLE

Admissions are made on a rolling basis. The application deadline for Session A is May 2; the deadline for Session B is June 6. For international applicants, the deadline for Session A is March 24, and the deadline for Session B is April 28. Applications must include a nonrefundable $35 application fee ($70 for international applicants), recommendations from a school guidance counselor and a teacher, and the applicant's official high school transcript. The application fee is waived for applications received by March 1. Applications are available in late January.

FOR MORE INFORMATION, CONTACT

Marsha Hussung, Director
High School Summer Scholars Program
Campus Box 1145
One Brookings Drive
Washington University in St. Louis
St. Louis, Missouri 63130-4899

Phone: 866-209-0691 (toll-free)
Fax: 314-935-4847
E-mail: mhussung@wustl.edu
Web site: http://ucollege.wustl.edu/hssp

PARTICIPANT/FAMILY COMMENTS

"HSSP is an extraordinary opportunity to stay up all night debating philosophy, eat frozen yogurt in a hammock, define yourself, determine what you want in a college, discover hope for something better than high school, and have the time of your life!"—Kathleen, Idaho

WASHINGTON UNIVERSITY IN ST. LOUIS

SAM FOX SCHOOL OF DESIGN AND VISUAL ARTS, COLLEGE OF ART

PORTFOLIO PLUS

ST. LOUIS, MISSOURI

TYPE OF PROGRAM: Credit and noncredit art classes
PARTICIPANTS: High school students
ENROLLMENT: Limited
PROGRAM DATES: Mid-June–mid-July
HEAD OF PROGRAM: Cris Baldwin and
    Mauricio Bruce

LOCATION

Set amid a thriving metropolitan region of 2.6 million residents, Washington University in St. Louis benefits from the vast array of social, cultural, and recreational opportunities offered by the St. Louis area. Bordered on the east by St. Louis's famed Forest Park and on the north, west, and south by well-established suburbs, the 169-acre Hilltop Campus features predominantly Collegiate Gothic architecture, including a number of buildings on the National Register of Historic Places.

BACKGROUND AND PHILOSOPHY

Washington University in St. Louis is among the world's leaders in teaching and research. The College of Art was established in 1879, the first in the nation to become a part of a university. In 125 years, the Washington University College of Art has gone from 30 students in a cramped attic to a well-respected professional school whose faculty comprises practicing artists, whose talented students are drawn from all over the world, and whose alumni star in every area of art. The College of Art is strongly committed to the development and success of young artists.

Students are constantly reminded that the study of art is on a broader plane than may at first be supposed. The mind, as well as the eye and hand, must be trained. The broader the general education of the student, the more likely the success of the student in later years.

PROGRAM OFFERINGS

Portfolio Plus is the College of Art's summer program for high school students interested in visual arts. This curriculum is open to students who have completed their sophomore, junior, or senior years of high school. It offers portfolio preparation in the studios of one of the top universities in the country, the opportunity to earn college credit (6 credits for the morning and afternoon sessions), the documentation of work in slide form, and letters of recommendation for college admission upon successful completion of the program.

The morning session includes a drawing class that emphasizes both observational drawing and the figure and a class that explores both 2-dimensional and 3-dimensional design. During the afternoon session, students may choose from animation, painting, ceramics, digital photography, printmaking, advanced drawing in color, fashion design, and sculpture. Field trips to local museums are also scheduled.

Drawing: Students learn to recognize and manipulate fundamental elements of line, tone, texture, volume, and plane with relation to representational drawing. Students work in a

wide variety of media and techniques (charcoal, pencil, pastels, and wet media) from the figure, still life, and the environment.

2-D/3-D Design: This course is an introduction to basic design principles and their applications on the 2-dimensional surface and in 3-dimensional form.

Ceramics: This course is an introduction to the design and making of functional pottery as well as sculptural objects. Students learn the basic forming processes of the wheel, coil, and slab construction.

Animation: In this introduction to animation, students design and build 3-D models and environments using Maya. After creating a storyboard, students animate their creations and develop a movie output to DVD at broadcast quality. Particle dynamics, special effects, lip-syncing, sound, and compositing are also explored.

Fashion Design: This course familiarizes students with techniques and materials used in drawing illustrations for fashion designs. Problems associated with designing groups, collections, and lines of apparel for popular and selected consumption are included.

Painting: Students explore traditional and nontraditional techniques both on-site as well as in the studio. Students look at examples from art history as well as from contemporary artists.

Advanced Drawing in Color: This is a technique-driven course that teaches students how to draw realistically using color pastels. Compositional skills are emphasized. Value, temperature, and intensity of color are explored using figure, still life, and landscape.

Digital Photography: This course explores digital technology for capturing, enhancing, and producing still lens-based images. The course addresses basic digital camera operations, the visual language of camera-generated images, and computer overflow. Students must supply their own digital camera.

Printmaking: Students learn various mixed-media approaches to printmaking, including collagraph, pronto plate lithography, etching, and other contemporary processes. There is a focus on making editions as well as one-of-a-kind prints.

Sculpture: Students explore contemporary sculptural concepts and processes in various media, including plaster, wax, plastics, metal, and wood fabrication, with an emphasis on the development of technical skills.

ENROLLMENT
Studio sizes are limited. Minimum enrollment is required for all classes. Students must be at least 16 years of age and have completed their sophomore year of high school to be eligible for the program.

DAILY SCHEDULE
Portfolio Plus classes meet both in the morning from 9 a.m. to noon and in the afternoon from 1 to 4 p.m. All classes run Monday through Friday.

FACILITIES
The Sam Fox School of Design and Visual Arts at Washington University, a $56.8-million complex, serves as a campuswide umbrella organization for the study and promotion of visual culture. The center allows for greater collaboration between the participating units and the development of new and interdisciplinary programs, while also preserving the integrity of the distinct disciplines of architecture, art, and art history and archaeology. In addition, it brings students and faculty members in the College of Art together in two adjacent buildings on the Danforth Campus.

Students live in one of the secure, modern residence halls on the South Forty (the undergraduate residential area) with other members of the program and the residential staff. In addition, there are students from other precollege programs at the University living in the dormitories. The dormitories are secure and are kept locked 24 hours a day. Resident advisers (RAs) living in the halls provide advice, information,

social planning, and assurance that the rules and regulations of the program are maintained. There are planned activities for the evenings and weekends.

STAFF
All classes are taught by College of Art faculty members.

MEDICAL CARE
All students attending the program have access to the health-care facility, which is on campus. In addition, major medical centers are located throughout the St. Louis area.

COSTS
The estimated cost for the program in 2008 is $4900. This includes tuition and lab fees for 6 hours of college credit, housing, meals, access to student health services, student ID, use of library facilities, use of the Athletic Complex, and an e-mail account. Individual art supplies as well as personal and other items are not included. The tuition for commuting students is estimated at $2470 for the program.

FINANCIAL AID
At least one full scholarship is offered. Students wishing to be considered for this award must submit with their application materials eight slides and a high school transcript showing a minimum B average. The deadline to apply for the scholarship is April 1.

TRANSPORTATION
Students need to provide their own transportation to the University. Those students who are traveling by air should contact Mauricio Bruce at 314-935-4643 or by e-mail at mbruce@art.wustl.edu.

APPLICATION TIMETABLE
To apply, students must submit an application form, which can be found online, along with a one-page essay on why they would like to study art, a letter of recommendation from a high school teacher, and a check for $250 before April 1. Of this charge, $30 is an application fee and is not applied toward tuition.

FOR MORE INFORMATION, CONTACT
Mauricio Bruce
College of Art
Campus Box 1031
Washington University in St. Louis
One Brookings Drive
St. Louis, Missouri 63130-4899

Phone: 314-935-4643
E-mail: mbruce@art.wustl.edu
Web site: http://art.wustl.edu

WEISSMAN TEEN TOURS

SUMMER PROGRAMS

UNITED STATES/WESTERN CANADA, HAWAII, AND EUROPE

TYPE OF PROGRAM: Activity-oriented travel

PARTICIPANTS: Coeducational, ages 13–18 (grouped compatibly by age)

ENROLLMENT: Europe, 45 per group; United States/Western Canada 40 Day and 30 Day, 40 per group; Hawaii (two and three week), 30 per group

PROGRAM DATES: Europe, late June through early August; United States/Western Canada 40 Day, early July through mid-August; 30 Day, early July through early August; Hawaii, three-week: late July through mid-August, two week: early August through mid-August

HEADS OF PROGRAM: Eugene, Ronee, Adam, and Ilana Weissman, Founders/Owners/Directors

BACKGROUND AND PHILOSOPHY

"We're family . . . not just another teen tour" clearly defines the degree of warmth and caring that best describes the Weissman Experience. Each tour is personally escorted by Ronee, Eugene, Adam, or Ilana Weissman and their experienced staff. From the inception of their program thirty-three years ago, the Weissmans have devoted themselves to providing tours that are the most personalized in the student travel field. The Weissmans stress quality, not quantity, allowing them to direct their attention to each teen as an individual and to guarantee a personally customized experience for everyone. Despite a waiting list every year, the program is limited to one European tour group, two United States/Western Canadian tour groups, and two Hawaiian tour groups.

Students develop friendships and a genuine respect for themselves, their natural surroundings, and the people they come in contact with wherever they go. Ronee, Eugene, Adam, and Ilana have given the Weissman Student Tour its unique, family-oriented style and unusual togetherness that all its members share.

PROGRAM OFFERINGS

Weissman Tours offers two Hawaiian, one European, and two U.S. itineraries, which provide high-quality, action-packed—yet leisurely—experiences that are among the best in student travel. The domestic program focuses on the national parks, big cities, and resort activity centers located in the far western portion of the U.S. and Canada. The three-week Aloha Hawaii tour includes a magnificent Carnival cruise to Ensenada, Mexico (also included

as part of the U.S./Western Canadian tours), in addition to beautiful Hawaiian oceanfront resorts. The European Experience encompasses England, Holland, Belgium, France, Switzerland, and Italy, combining the exploration of the culture and history of the cities with the recreation and outdoor adventure found in some of the most magnificent resorts in Europe.

The Weissman Tours are incredibly active, with planned activities every day and evening. Since they are not wasting time setting up and taking down tents, everyone has more time to explore the cities and to enjoy all of the fabulous adventures travel has to offer. The Weissmans personally lead their groups on hikes, bicycling adventures, white-water rafting, kayaking, sailing, parasailing and waterskiing, horseback riding, snowboarding, skiing, snorkeling, scuba diving, surfing, golfing, and organized sports. The resorts also provide health clubs and fitness centers with the most up-to-date equipment and classes in aerobics and calisthenics. Every evening, teens enjoy dance clubs, TV tapings, concerts, shows, cruises, skating, campfires, comedy clubs, and much more. Since the program's jet flights are longer and the bus rides are shorter than those on other student tours, students on a Weissman Teen Tour have more time to experience, appreciate, and enjoy the cities and parks and all they have to offer.

ENROLLMENT

Weissman Teen Tours attracts students from the United States, Canada, Latin America, Europe, and Asia. Teens who travel with the Weissmans live together, work together, share responsibilities, and learn while having fun, enabling each tour member to develop lasting friendships within a warm family atmosphere.

EXTRA OPPORTUNITIES AND ACTIVITIES

Having the owner lead the tours fosters spontaneity and affords the group special opportunities that they would never have otherwise experienced. The Weissman Tour has often dined at restaurants that are "off the beaten trail" in Europe, where English is not spoken and the food and ambience are local and incredible. If a meaningful adventure should suddenly present itself, the Weissmans jump at the chance to participate. Groups have, for example, joined the North American Indian Council meeting in Montana, witnessing tribal dances as well as making new pen pals. The European group has dined at a magnificent villa overlooking the Tuscan countryside as guests of friends of the Weissmans, joined a "Sweet 16" party at an Italian dance club by invitation of the owner of an exquisite European hotel, challenged some Swiss friends to a game of tennis in Zermatt, and participated in a special presentation at the Anne Frank House in Amsterdam planned especially for the Weissman group.

FACILITIES

The Weissmans prepare throughout the year, personally visiting hotels, restaurants, and activities prior to booking groups. Teens are welcomed warmly, as if part of the hotel "family," upon their arrival. The U.S./Western Canadian itinerary features a well-balanced combination of centrally located deluxe and first-class hotels in the major cities, such as Hiltons, Marriotts, Hyatts, and Sheratons; a four-night Carnival Paradise Cruise; national park lodges; and resort activity centers. In addition, the Aloha Hawaii tour includes magnificent, activity-oriented, deluxe oceanfront resorts, plus a four-day Carnival Cruise. In Europe, the superior four- and five-star hotels are all selected for their location, strictly European ambience, excellent facilities, and safety regulations. Students awaken each morning to all the city has to offer. There is definitely an advantage to sleeping in a dry, safe, and beautiful hotel with plenty of great facilities, including pools, Jacuzzis, health clubs, and tennis courts—all waiting for the Weissman group to relax in after a busy day of activity.

STAFF

Weissman Tours is the only student travel program with all tours personally escorted in the United States and Europe by both the owner/directors and leaders who are experienced, well-trained, and committed to providing a safe and fun environment. All staff members are over 21, college graduates, nonsmokers, and certified in CPR and first aid. European staff members are proficient in French and/or Italian and have backgrounds in art history. They are required to live and work at the home/office of the Weissmans and to participate in extensive training sessions prior to the departure of the tours. Since many of the staff members are Weissman Teen Tour alumni, they understand the significance of the bond that is established between the teens and their leaders. The Weissmans believe that when teens travel so far from home, they should be with people with whom they can communicate, feel secure, and have fun.

Eugene Weissman has a master's degree in mathematics and has completed postgraduate work in administration, group dynamics, and child guidance. He has extensive experience as a high school educator, College Bound coordinator and administrator, teacher/consultant for the College Board SAT, camp director, and youth director. Ronee Weissman graduated Phi Beta Kappa, magna cum laude, and holds a master's degree in speech pathology. She has been elected to *Who's Who of American Women*, *Who's Who in the World*, and *Who's Who of Emerging Leaders in America*, as well as other biographical publications, for her outstanding achievement as a teen tour director and New York State–licensed, ASHA-certified speech pathologist. Adam Weissman, a graduate of the University of Pennsylvania, is a fourth-year Ph.D. student in clinical psychology, pursuing a career in adolescent psychology. Adam spent two postgraduate years conducting research for the Treatment Research Institute at Penn. Ilana Weissman, a gifted artist, is the Writing/Visual Arts Coordinator for the Ella Baker School, a progressive alternative school in New York City. She has created and implemented a multimedia arts/writing program and produced a benefit concert in celebration of ten years of freedom from apartheid in South Africa, combining the emerging talents of her students with those of professional artists. Ilana graduated with her B.A. and M.S. from Sarah Lawrence College and studied in the Juilliard precollege program, where she played French horn and performed in concerts at Carnegie Hall and Lincoln Center. With their diversified and well-rounded backgrounds, the Weissmans are able to provide leadership that combines knowledge, warmth, and genuine concern with all aspects of the development of a healthy, well-rounded teenager.

MEDICAL CARE

The Weissman family is committed to the health, safety, and security of all of its tour members. They have an extensive network

of medical facilities and doctors in every city, both in the United States and abroad. In Europe, the list includes many American hospitals as well as U.S. trained doctors. Parents are always contacted when a student receives medical treatment. All staff members are certified in CPR and first aid.

COSTS

The U.S./Western Canadian 40 Day tour is $9299, the 30 Day tour is $7599, the Hawaiian three-week tour is $6699, the two-week Hawaiian tour is $4799, and the European tour is $10,699. All first-class and deluxe accommodations, three healthy and nutritious meals daily, and extensive day and evening activities are included in the price. The lowest available scheduled APEX airfare is extra.

APPLICATION TIMETABLE

Students are welcome to inquire at any time. Enrollment is on a rolling basis. The brochure and U.S./European DVD may be requested. Due to the limited number of openings each season, early registration is recommended. Ronee and Eugene Weissman are available to speak to all interested students and their families.

FOR MORE INFORMATION, CONTACT

Ronee and Eugene Weissman
Weissman Teen Tours
517 Almena Avenue
Ardsley, New York 10502
Phone: 914-693-7575
        800-942-8005 (toll-free outside New York State)
Fax: 914-693-4807
E-mail: wtt@cloud9.net
Web site: http://www.weissmantours.com

PARTICIPANT/FAMILY COMMENTS

"Perhaps the most unique quality of the Weissman Teen Tour is the caring found there. Through your caring, you encouraged others to give of themselves. Never before had I met 2 people interested in whatever I had to say. It's very difficult to achieve such a special relationship between tour members and leaders, but you have more than succeeded! Maybe that's why we say, 'We're family . . . not just another teen tour!'"

"When Evan went to Europe three years ago with your group, I thought I had heard every superlative in the world, but Erica found a few new ones. Not only did she have a fantastic time meeting new people, but the reuniting with her former counselor and your continuing care and concern made this the premiere event of her life."

WESTCOAST CONNECTION TRAVEL

▼▼▼▼▼▼▼▼▼▼▼▼▼▼▼▼▼▼▼▼▼▼▼▼

SUMMER TRAVEL PROGRAMS

UNITED STATES, CANADA, EUROPE, AUSTRALIA, BELIZE, AND COSTA RICA

TYPE OF PROGRAM: Teen travel experiences, including touring groups, multisport adventures (including golf, skiing, and snowboarding), community service, and language study

PARTICIPANTS: Coeducational, ages 13–18 (grouped compatibly by age); separate group for those 17 and older

ENROLLMENT: Multisport and service groups are 10–22 students; touring and language groups are 35–50 students

PROGRAM DATES: Vary from eight to forty-two days from the end of June to August

HEADS OF PROGRAM: Mark Segal, Stan Browman, Fran Grundman, Mitch Lerner, Ira Solomon, and Jason Tanner, Directors

BACKGROUND AND PHILOSOPHY

Westcoast Connection was founded in 1982. Programs give students the opportunity to discover new and exciting places; to develop greater self-confidence, a respect for others, and new skills; and to make new friends.

No prior experience is necessary, just the desire to participate. On all adventures, the experienced staff ensures that everyone is comfortable and welcome right from day one.

PROGRAM OFFERINGS

Programs explore many regions of the United States, Canada, and Europe as well as Australia, Belize, and Costa Rica and generally run for one to six weeks.

On the East Coast, programs are in New England, Florida, the Mid-Atlantic, Quebec, and Ontario. In the southwestern United States, participants travel to California, Arizona, Nevada, and Utah. In the Pacific Northwest, locations offered are in Washington and Oregon, along with the Canadian Rockies and Whistler. Other locations include Colorado, Wyoming, Montana, Hawaii, and Alaska.

Trip settings encompass many of the most naturally beautiful locations in the world. Some of the spectacular national parks visited include Yellowstone, Grand Canyon, Bryce, Zion, Banff, and Jasper. Other natural settings are in the San Juan Islands and overseas in the Swiss Alps or at Australia's Great Barrier Reef.

Adventures offer an increased emphasis on challenging oneself, developing skills, and gaining a sense of accomplishment. Activities include surfing, rafting, snow skiing, snowboarding, rock climbing, mountain biking, kayaking, canoeing, ropes courses, caving, and hiking. Smaller groups enable students to form a unique trust and a tight bond with their peers. Professional guides instruct and lead specialty activities.

Active Tours Trips combine the natural wonders of the great outdoors with the attractions of major cities, including Los Angeles, San Francisco, Las Vegas, and Seattle in North America. Students participate in recreational activities, including surfing, rafting, snowboarding, snow skiing, horseback riding, mountain biking, and hiking. Evenings include baseball games,

dance clubs, comedy clubs, and more. These trips combine stays at hotels, resorts, and college dorms, and some tours include campsites.

European Programs Countries visited include France, Italy, Switzerland, Belgium, Holland, and England. Trips balance sightseeing and touring in major cities, along with recreation and entertainment as well as outdoor activities such as rafting and skiing/snowboarding in the Alps. Restful beach stays on the French and Adriatic Rivieras help relax the pace and enable students to enjoy a truly special experience in Europe.

Australia This action-packed trip includes scuba diving at the Great Barrier Reef, learning from the Aborigines in the outback, surfing lessons, touring Sydney, hiking in the rain forest, petting koalas and kangaroos, and an optional fantastic final stop in Hawaii.

On Tour These programs are for students completing grades 11 and 12 and provide older participants with more independence within a group program.

Florida and California Swing Junior Touring Golf Camps For golf enthusiasts, these trips feature play on top-rated courses, instructional clinics, and exciting touring highlights.

Skiing and Snowboarding at Mt. Hood and Whistler This program offers professional instruction and touring in the Pacific Northwest.

Major League Baseball Tour For baseball fanatics, this tour combines fifteen professional games, twelve stadium visits, and the Hall of Fame induction ceremony with other touring highlights.

Community Service Teens participate in life-changing experiences by combining volunteering and travel in Alaska, Belize, Costa Rica, or Hawaii.

Spanish and French Language Programs These unique programs integrate language study and travel within a country so that students can really experience the country visited.

ENROLLMENT

One outstanding aspect of Westcoast Connection's enrollment is its international flavor and geographic diversity. Approximately 85 percent of the students come from different regions of the United States, and 15 percent are from Canada and overseas. International participants have come from Aruba, Austria, Belgium, Brazil, China, Colombia, England, France, Honduras, India, Israel, Italy, Japan, Korea, Peru, Russia, South Africa, and Venezuela. This diversity ensures a well-balanced geographic mix and helps prevent cliques.

FACILITIES

All accommodations are selected for safety, cleanliness, facilities, and location. They include college dorms, hotels, resorts, chalets, inns, and, on some trips, campsites. (Adventure trips are mostly camping.) The Hawaiian, European, and Australian tours and the sports programs feature all-indoor stays. Private campsites have indoor washrooms with hot water, private showers, flush toilets, and electricity and recreational facilities. Camping is on mats in spacious tents. On the Active Tours, camping cots are also provided. On indoor stays, every student has an individual bed. Special dietary requests (including vegetarian, food allergies, and religious) are accommodated.

STAFF

Experienced, fun, exciting, patient, and sensitive leaders are selected for their ability to relate to, care for, and support teenagers. Directors and staff members complete CPR and

first aid training and are committed first and foremost to the health and safety of their students. All staff members are personally interviewed. Leaders participate in several pretrip orientation sessions and workshops to ensure the highest level of preparation in student travel.

Directors are generally teachers, social workers, coaches, or graduate students. All directors and staff members are nonsmokers.

MEDICAL CARE

Westcoast Connection's number-one priority is the health and safety of every participant. Each trip director is equipped with an extensive listing of local hospitals and clinics to visit as needed.

COSTS

Tuition ranges from $1500 to $8500. Fees include all activities, meals, accommodations, gratuities, and taxes. Airfare is not included.

APPLICATION TIMETABLE

Enrollment is on a rolling basis; initial inquiries are welcome at any time. Brochures and DVDs are available in October. Early enrollment is advised to secure trip preference. Discounts are available for early enrollment.

FOR MORE INFORMATION, CONTACT

United States
Westcoast Connection
154 East Boston Post Road
Mamaroneck, New York 10543

Phone: 914-835-0699
        800-767-0227 (toll-free outside New York State)
Fax: 914-835-0798
E-mail: usa@westcoastconnection.com
Web site: http://www.westcoastconnection.com
          http://360studenttravel.com

Canada
Westcoast Connection
5585 Monkland, Suite 140
Montreal, Quebec H4A 1E1
Canada
Phone: 514-488-8920

WILDERNESS VENTURES

▼▲▼

WILDERNESS EDUCATION AND EXPEDITIONS

THE AMERICAS, CANADA, AUSTRALIA, EUROPE, AND THE SOUTH PACIFIC

TYPE OF PROGRAM: Wilderness expeditions, leadership training, cultural immersion, and community service

PARTICIPANTS: Coeducational, ages 13–20, grouped by age

ENROLLMENT: More than thirty different expeditions with 10 to 15 participants each; multiple sections grouped by age are offered for each expedition

PROGRAM DATES: Sixteen- to thirty-nine-day expeditions in June, July, and August

HEADS OF PROGRAM: Mike and Helen Cottingham

LOCATION

Wilderness Ventures offers expeditions throughout the western United States, Hawaii, Alaska, Canada, Europe, Australia, Central America, South America, and the South Pacific. The expeditions are multienvironmental, enabling the participants to experience a variety of some of the most beautiful wilderness areas in the world.

BACKGROUND AND PHILOSOPHY

With more than thirty-five years of experience, Wilderness Ventures has become one of the most recognized and experienced multienvironmental wilderness programs for young adults.

Each summer, a variety of expeditions embark upon sixteen- to thirty-nine-day programs designed to teach the acquisition of wilderness skills, leadership techniques, and respect for the natural landscape. These goals are accomplished within a noncompetitive, nurturing, and fun environment in which students gain self-confidence through challenging activities, learn about themselves and others, and attain a lifelong appreciation for the spectacular beauty of wilderness.

Wilderness Skills All Wilderness Ventures expeditions teach a variety of wilderness skills, including, but not limited to, expedition planning; backcountry safety; meal planning, purchasing, and preparation; navigation; minimum-impact camping; and landscape and natural history interpretation. Specific programs also include instruction in sea kayaking, rock climbing, mountaineering, snow and ice climbing, canoeing, surfing, white-water rafting, white-water kayaking, mountain biking, road biking, canyoneering, sailing, snorkeling, surfing, and scuba diving. The acquisition of these skills develops self-confidence and prepares young adults for a lifetime of enjoyment in the outdoors.

Leadership Wilderness Ventures believes that leadership involves much more than leading a group safely through a wilderness or to the summit of a peak. All Wilderness Ventures expeditions emphasize the importance of learning how to make decisions and solve problems within a group. These skills are useful throughout life and well beyond the wilderness environment. The small-group format and the emphasis on the group experience require that all expedition members learn to place their personal needs behind the needs of the group. This group focus creates intimate bonding among expedition members and provides each individual with a valuable understanding of group cooperation that enhances social skills for success in life.

Wilderness Appreciation In 1973, access to the most spectacular wilderness environments was still available. It is a privilege for Wilderness Ventures expeditions to visit these natural treasures. Travel through these wilderness areas instills in students a responsibility for their future survival. On the expeditions, students not only learn the methods of minimum-impact camping, but also gain a love for these places and a burning desire to see them saved so that future generations might someday have a similar experience.

PROGRAM OFFERINGS

Students may choose an expedition based upon age appropriateness, level of prior experience, degree of physical challenge desired, and geographical areas of interest. The expeditions are divided into four distinct categories: Domestic Wilderness Adventures, International Adventures, Advanced Leadership Programs, and Service Adventures.

Domestic Wilderness Adventures Conducted for the past thirty-five years, these classic adventures range from two to six weeks and offer varying degrees of challenge in a variety of outdoor environments. Participants do not need prior experience for any program. Those who do have experience still find challenging offerings. Backcountry trips range from three to eight days, depending on the program.

International Adventures These exciting adventures range from two to four weeks, offering varying degrees of challenge in a variety of exotic wilderness and outdoor environments around the globe. They are excellent choices for both beginners and experienced students who thrive on outdoor adventure and cultural immersion.

Advanced Outdoor Leadership Programs Ranging from two to four weeks in length, these wonderful programs offer the highest degree of challenge and are conducted in only one or two environments. The programs are open to both beginning and experienced students seeking extended wilderness travel with a thorough focus on outdoor skills.

Service Adventures Students can complete between 40 and 80 hours of community service by working with local communities and assisting in environmental projects while adventuring in some of the most spectacular outdoor settings found in North America, Central America, South America, and the South Pacific. These service adventures combine the elements of adventure, cultural immersion, and service for high school students.

ENROLLMENT

Participants enroll from almost every state and several countries each year, with an even distribution of students coming from the Eastern Seaboard, the Midwest, the South, and the West. All expeditions are coeducational. A thorough screening process allows students to travel with others who are highly motivated to

STAFF

Wilderness Ventures staff members average 26 years of age, with a minimum age of 21. All are experienced leaders and educators. When not working with Wilderness Ventures, many teach at the secondary school or university level or pursue full-time careers in other environmental or outdoor occupations. All staff members are certified Wilderness First Aid Providers, Wilderness First Responders, or EMTs. All expeditions operate with low student-to-staff ratios, allowing for the highest level of personal attention. A man and a woman accompany each trip. Every summer, Wilderness Ventures averages a 60 percent return rate for staff members.

COSTS

Tuition ranges from $2600 to $6700, depending on the length and location of the expedition, the activities engaged in, and the geographical region. Tuition covers all expenses for the entire expedition except airfare to and from staging cities.

TRANSPORTATION

All expeditions begin or end in Anchorage, Alaska; Juneau, Alaska; Los Angeles, California; San Francisco, California; Denver, Colorado; Kona, Hawaii; Honolulu, Hawaii; Portland, Oregon; Salt Lake City, Utah; Seattle, Washington; Jackson, Wyoming; Miami, Florida; San Jose, Costa Rica; Quito, Ecuador; Barcelona, Spain; and Paris, France. Staff members meet participants at a central location in the airport on arrival day and accompany them back to the airport and remain with them until their flights depart.

APPLICATION TIMETABLE

Applications are accepted after September 1. Expeditions fill at varying rates, depending on the number of spaces available; many fill by January 1 and most are full by March 1. Students should call for information on program availability, especially if applying late. To receive an extensive catalog describing all of the adventures, interested students can contact Wilderness Ventures.

FOR MORE INFORMATION, CONTACT

Mike and Helen Cottingham, Directors
Wilderness Ventures
P.O. Box 2768
Jackson Hole, Wyoming 83001

Phone: 800-533-2281 (toll-free)
E-mail: info@wildernessventures.com
Web site: http://www.wildernessventures.com

PARTICIPANT/FAMILY COMMENTS

"Carson had an amazing trip this summer with Wilderness Ventures. We developed his photos immediately and he dove into remarkable detail about each day and what the group accomplished together and personally. He enjoyed his leaders and appreciated their expertise and leadership. We feel this trip was a real passage for him and definitely a highlight of his life."

succeed and who will contribute positively to the group experience. Each expedition offers multiple sections, which are grouped by age and experience compatibility.

DAILY SCHEDULE

The majority of time is spent in the backcountry. Because Wilderness Ventures holds so many wilderness permits throughout the United States and several other countries, expeditions are able to offer a variety of backcountry experiences and activities with minimal travel between areas. The daily schedule is flexible and varied, depending upon the expedition. Besides learning a wide variety of outdoor skills, participants have opportunities to relax by cooling off in a refreshing lake, soaking in a natural hot spring, basking in the mountain sunlight, or photographing or sketching wildlife.

EXTRA OPPORTUNITIES AND ACTIVITIES

Each expedition is conducted in a specific geographical region. During the brief travel between wilderness areas within each region, itineraries are planned to take advantage of worthwhile scenic, cultural, and historic sites. The leaders' knowledge of the areas traveled through prompts frequent informal discussions dealing with each region's particular history, economy, and geography. These discussions, together with the evening campfire programs and the comprehensive mobile libraries, enable students to gain a better understanding of local regions and instill within them a sense of place.

FACILITIES

When not sleeping under the stars, participants use lightweight mountaineering tents. Participants enrolled in international expeditions may also spend some evenings sleeping in hostels or high alpine huts or aboard a boat.

THE WINCHENDON SCHOOL

SUMMER SESSION

WINCHENDON, MASSACHUSETTS

TYPE OF PROGRAM: Academic remediation, makeup, and enrichment
PARTICIPANTS: Coeducational, grades 8–12
ENROLLMENT: 50
PROGRAM DATES: June 29 to August 9, 2008
HEAD OF PROGRAM: Elliot C. Harvey, Director

LOCATION
The Winchendon School is located in north central Massachusetts just 65 miles west of Boston. Its rural setting in the foothills of Mt. Monadnock is peaceful and secure. Situated advantageously, the School is able to offer wide-ranging field trips to museums, historic locations, mountains, and the seashore.

BACKGROUND AND PHILOSOPHY
Throughout its existence the Winchendon School Summer Session has provided students with an opportunity to make up lost credits, improve study skills, and generally strengthen their academic standing in a caring, structured setting. A multisensory, multiactivity approach characterizes the small classes (averaging 6 students), which place emphasis on individual needs.

PROGRAM OFFERINGS
Winchendon offers two distinct programs during its summer session. The first is a skills-based program for English-speaking college-bound students who need to make up courses. English, mathematics, and U.S. history courses are regularly available, as are courses in SAT preparation (both verbal and math sections). During the six-week summer session, students receive 13 hours of weekly instruction in each course. Credit can be given if the student has made arrangements before starting the summer program.

Winchendon also offers an ESL program for international students who wish to familiarize themselves with the language, life, and customs of the United States. In the formal ESL classes, emphasis is placed on spoken English, listening comprehension, reading, and writing. Three levels of instruction are available: beginning, intermediate, and advanced. Preparation for the TOEFL is a major objective of the intermediate and advanced levels.

Also available to ESL students is an American Culture course, which gives international students an opportunity to learn about American history and society in a hands-on field trip–oriented program that is highly conducive to a successful understanding and appreciation of the history and culture of the United States.

Of advantage to all students are the integrated afternoon sports/activities offerings. Students engage daily in such sports as golf, tennis, swimming, horseback riding, basketball, baseball, and soccer. Professional golf lessons are available at a small fee.

ENROLLMENT
Of the approximately 50 students on campus during the six-week summer experience, about 25 are from various parts of the United States. Class size averages 6 students per class.

DAILY SCHEDULE

7:00– 7:30	Breakfast
7:35	Room inspection
7:40– 8:40	Class
8:45– 9:45	Class
9:45–10:00	Break
10:05–10:45	Study hall/special help
10:50–11:50	Class
11:50–12:15	Lunch
12:20– 1:20	Class
1:30– 3:00	Sports/activities
5:00– 5:30	Work program
5:30– 6:15	Dinner
7:00– 7:30	Dorm cleanup
7:30– 9:00	Dorm study hours
10:00	In room
10:30	Lights out

All students are expected to meet all School appointments and follow rules of acceptable behavior.

EXTRA OPPORTUNITIES AND ACTIVITIES

Field trips to historic, cultural, and recreational areas are regularly available. On weekends, a variety of activities designed to enhance the students' learning experience are also scheduled.

FACILITIES

All School facilities, including an 18-hole golf course, are available to students on a daily basis. Other facilities located on the 250-acre campus are a swimming pool, ice arena, tennis courts, a gymnasium, an arts studio, several dormitories, a library, and three classroom buildings.

STAFF

Most teachers in the summer session are members of The Winchendon School faculty. When necessary, the staff is supplemented by qualified teachers from other private and public schools. The director of the program is a Winchendon School administrator during the regular academic year.

MEDICAL CARE

A nurse is available throughout the session. Less than 5 minutes from campus is a medical clinic that is fully staffed throughout the day and into the evening. The Henry Heywood Hospital is in Gardner, which is less than 10 minutes away.

RELIGIOUS LIFE

The Winchendon School is nondenominational. A variety of local churches are within easy reach of the campus.

COSTS

The cost for the 2008 summer session is $5900, including all field trips and books. Golf and horseback riding instruction are available for an extra fee.

APPLICATION TIMETABLE

Applications are accepted throughout the year, but it is recommended that they be forwarded by early May. Students wishing to visit the campus before enrolling are encouraged to do so. Appointments can be arranged by calling the Admissions Office.

FOR MORE INFORMATION, CONTACT

J. William LaBelle
Headmaster
The Winchendon School Summer Session
172 Ash Street
Winchendon, Massachusetts 01475

Phone: 800-622-1119 (toll-free)
Fax: 978-297-0911
E-mail: admissions@winchendon.org
Web site: http://www.winchendon.org

WOLFEBORO

THE SUMMER BOARDING SCHOOL

WOLFEBORO, NEW HAMPSHIRE

TYPE OF PROGRAM: Academic
PARTICIPANTS: Coeducational, ages 11–18
ENROLLMENT: 200
PROGRAM DATES: June 25–August 9, 2008
HEAD OF PROGRAM: Edward A. Cooper, Head of School

LOCATION

The School is situated 3 miles from the center of Wolfeboro, a resort town in the Lakes Region of central New Hampshire. The School's 128 acres include a quarter mile of shoreline on Rust Pond. The pond is approximately 2 miles long.

BACKGROUND AND PHILOSOPHY

Since 1910, Wolfeboro has exclusively been a summer boarding school, providing a highly structured supportive environment for girls and boys entering grades 6–12. With a staff of approximately 100 adults serving a student population of 200, the School's priorities include the development of effective study and organizational skills, academic accountability, confidence, and the establishment of habits that are conducive to academic success. The entire academic and nonacademic program is designed to support the attainment of individual goals in an exceptional outdoor environment. Courses are offered in all core subject areas for the purpose of review, preview, or credit.

PROGRAM OFFERINGS

The primary purpose of Wolfeboro is to provide constructive scholastic work for girls and boys ages 11–18 in an atmosphere of healthy outdoor living combined with summer recreation.

Parents are typically referred to Wolfeboro by educational consultants, directors of admissions, and heads of schools for the following purposes: to experience a traditional boarding school routine; improve core academic skills in preparation for the upcoming school year; strengthen organizational and study skills; complete course work for credit purposes, advanced or remedial; enhance academic confidence; elevate levels of academic responsibility and enthusiasm; receive SAT preparation (both mathematics and critical reading); improve skills in English as a second language (ESL); and immerse the student in an outdoor, academic, and away-from-home residential setting.

The program emphasizes effective and efficient study skills, organization, motivation, and confidence. The program is individualized to meet each student's needs. All courses may be taken

for credit. Students may make up failures; review or preview work in specific academic subjects; strengthen skills in English, grammar, writing, vocabulary, reading, mathematics, science, history, study skills, and foreign language; and take new courses for credit by special arrangement with the student's school. All students attend three academic periods six days per week.

The School serves as a valuable transitional experience for students who are about to enter a boarding school for the first time. Individual goals and a "Goals Document" are established for each student prior to arrival, after discussions with parents, schools, and counselors and a review of available standardized test scores, transcripts, and teachers' reports.

Classes are small (2–6 students per class), so student programs can be individualized within a given section. Credit courses are adjusted to satisfy the requirements of the student's school.

Weekly written teacher reports are made to the Head of School and to the student. Parents receive comprehensive reports after the first three weeks and at the end of the session. A final summary report is also provided.

DAILY SCHEDULE

6:45 . . .	Rising bell
7:15 . . .	Breakfast
7:45 . . .	Daily chores and inspection
8:05 . . .	Class bell
8:10 . . .	First period
9:00 . . .	Second period
9:50 . . .	Third period
10:40 . . .	Recess—morning snacks
10:50 . . .	Fourth period
11:40 . . .	Fifth period
12:30 . . .	Short swim
1:00 . . .	Dinner
2:00– 5:00 . . .	Programmed activities and sports
5:15 . . .	Mail call
6:00 . . .	Supper
6:40 . . .	Intramural league play
7:20 . . .	Prepare for study period
7:30 . . .	Study period
8:30 . . .	Study break
8:45 . . .	Study period
9:30 . . .	End of evening study
9:45 . . .	Prepare for lights-out
10:00 . . .	Lights-out

Sunday

7:30 . . .	Rising bell
8:00 . . .	Breakfast
9:00 . . .	Tent inspection
9:45 . . .	Trips depart
10:00 . . .	Recreation
1:00 . . .	Dinner
2:15 . . .	Recreation
6:00 . . .	Picnic supper
6:40–10:00 . . .	Same as daily schedule

Transportation is available on weekends to attend religious services.

Wolfeboro provides a structured, no-nonsense approach to both scholastic work and the quality of student life. The School be-

lieves that a student functions best in an environment in which all expectations are clearly understood. For this reason, the School has a detailed statement of required student conduct and methods of operation, which is mailed to each individual requesting information about the School.

Attendance at the School implies a sincerity of purpose and a sense of responsibility and cooperation. Students are assigned daily chores necessary to maintain a neat and clean school. Work assignments change every nine days.

ENROLLMENT
There are 200 students, who come from nearly all of the fifty states and several other countries. Wolfeboro does not discriminate on the basis of race, color, and national and ethnic origin in the administration of its educational policies, admission policies, financial assistance, and athletics and other School-administrated programs.

EXTRA OPPORTUNITIES AND ACTIVITIES
Weekend trips are made to the White Mountains and Maine beaches. There are overnight camping trips each weekend and numerous other weekend trips to places of special interest, such as water parks, amusement parks, and state parks.

FACILITIES
The administrative core of the campus is located near the entrance. The Gertrude Johnson Center accommodates offices and the central reception area. Jousson Lodge, with an excellent view of the main campus, the lake, surrounding woodland, and neighboring mountains, contains the dining room, kitchen, and Health Center. Near Jousson Lodge is the Student Center, site of many student functions and activities and the campus store and weight-training room. The academic core occupies the north periphery of the central campus and includes thirty-six classrooms. Complementing the academic area are three study halls and the faculty center.

The boys' residential area is between the administrative core and the lakefront. Middle School boys enjoy a separate residential campus. Waterfront facilities include a sandy beach, two large docks, six swimming lanes, sailboats, rowboats, patrol boats, lifeguard apparatus, and related safety equipment. The girls' residential area is beyond the playing fields at the opposite end of the campus.

Students live in sturdy 7-foot-high tents with screen doors mounted on 10-foot by 12-foot permanent wooden platform bases. Most tents are shared by 2 students. All are equipped with electric lighting, outlets, beds, shelves, and desks. Residential areas include modern bathroom and shower facilities. Each residential area is under the direction of a residential division head. Students are grouped by age into five-tent clusters, each of which is supervised by a faculty member living in an adjacent cottage. Dotted along the shoreline and periphery of the campus are cottages that house other faculty and staff members and their families.

The dining hall is more than a facility in which good food is served. By intent, mealtimes provide an opportunity to gather the whole community together in an atmosphere that reflects and affirms the very essence of the Wolfeboro experience. All meals, except Sunday's picnic supper, are served family-style at tables of 10 that include students, faculty members, and faculty families. Seating assignments and student-waiter assignments are rotated, which provides enriching and supportive social interaction for all. Each table is headed by a faculty member who ensures the observation of good eating habits and gracious social manners. All meals in the dining room begin with a blessing.

MEDICAL CARE
The ratio of students to staff members enables Wolfeboro to place top priority on health and safety. The School is fortunate to have a large, fully equipped hospital 2 miles away. Students are under the direct supervision of a local physician. A registered nurse is always on duty and routinely attends to students in the Health Center.

COSTS
A $3000 deposit must accompany the application; if the applicant is accepted, the deposit is credited toward the fee for room, board, and tuition. For current fee information, interested families should contact the School.

FINANCIAL AID
Limited financial assistance is occasionally available. Grants are made on a case-by-case basis.

TRANSPORTATION
Travel to Wolfeboro is quite simple. Staff members meet planes at both the Manchester (New Hampshire) Boston Regional Airport and Boston's Logan International Airport on opening day and transport students to Wolfeboro by chartered bus. The process is reversed on closing day.

APPLICATION TIMETABLE
Inquiries concerning Wolfeboro may be made at any time. Interviews and visits to the School are welcome and may be arranged by contacting the School.

FOR MORE INFORMATION, CONTACT
Edward A. Cooper, Head of School
Wolfeboro Camp School
P.O. Box 390
Wolfeboro, New Hampshire 03894-0390

Phone: 603-569-3451
Fax: 603-569-4080
E-mail: school@wolfeboro.org
Web site: http://www.wolfeboro.org

WORCESTER POLYTECHNIC INSTITUTE

WPI FRONTIERS PROGRAM

WORCESTER, MASSACHUSETTS

TYPE OF PROGRAM: Academic enrichment
PARTICIPANTS: Coeducational, students entering grades 11 and 12
ENROLLMENT: 125–150
PROGRAM DATES: July 2008
HEAD OF PROGRAM: Julic Chapman, Associate Director of Admissions

LOCATION
WPI is situated on 80 acres in Worcester, Massachusetts, New England's second-largest city. The campus, which is surrounded by parks and residential neighborhoods, is located 1 mile from downtown. Students have full access to WPI's facilities, including the Gordon Library, state-of-the-art laboratories and equipment, athletic facilities, and the university computer system.

BACKGROUND AND PHILOSOPHY
WPI Frontiers was founded twenty-five years ago to allow high school students to further explore their interests in science, mathematics, technology, and engineering. WPI Frontiers exposes students to current research problems and methods and encourages pursuit of careers in science and technology.

PROGRAM OFFERINGS
Aerospace Engineering Students explore the science of flight and learn how wings and aircraft create lift to fly. Basic concepts in aerodynamics—including drag, streamlining, airfoil stall, and aircraft design—are studied. They conduct wind- and water-tunnel experiments to visualize the flow over aircraft, then run simulations on laptop computers. Using what they have learned, students design and build a simple model aircraft, test it in the wind tunnel, and see it soar in free flight.

Biology and Biotechnology This program allows students to explore this science, from molecules and cells to ecology and evolution. They cut, splice, and insert DNA to engineer new bacteria; eavesdrop on their own nerves and muscles with computer-based technology; prepare and view cells in an electron microscope; meet a tiny roundworm that is the new favorite of geneticists; use DNA fingerprinting and antibodies to track genes and the proteins they code for; and study reproduction, ecology, anatomy, and scientific contributions (including a Nobel Prize) of the ancient horseshoe crab.

Chemistry In this program, students explore how life functions at the molecular level. They combine the newest technologies in the fields of chemistry and biochemistry to explore what happens when molecules collide, peel apart proteins and DNA, discover how enzymes work, and use computer modeling to see what biomolecules look like in 3-D. Students learn how chemistry makes color, fire, light, and electricity, using the latest genetic and biochemical techniques to create organisms that glow.

Computer Science Students journey into the world of object-oriented and Web programming. They explore at their own pace the world of programming as it is used in the World Wide Web and object-oriented languages, such as Java. Students have the opportunity to incorporate the work as part of effective multimedia interfaces for content that is of interest to them. In addition, special topics in computer science are discussed according to student interest.

Electrical and Computer Engineering Students discover the fascinating world of analog and digital electronics through classroom exercises and laboratory hands-on activities. They learn to use lab equipment, including power supplies, function generators, and oscilloscopes, to test circuits that they build. Students apply this knowledge to a design project that they work on throughout the course. Topics include audio amplification, light-wave transmission, analog signal processing, and digital circuitry. The prerequisites for students are a good attitude, an open mind, and a desire to learn.

Interactive Media and Game Development Students combine technology with art to create an interactive experience, taking on the role of programmer or artist and working on a team to bring a game to life. They draw their environment, model characters, record dialogue, mix sound effects, and tell their story. At WPI, students break down their idea into simple rules, write their algorithm, use powerful scripting languages, and publish their game on the Web.

Mathematics Students in this program learn how a mix of classical mathematics and modern technology can be used to solve current problems and open new areas. They use this background to examine encryption of numbers on the Internet via the RSA Algorithm and analysis of human voice patterns and musical instruments through Fourier methods. Specific problems of current information technology that these address include the need for secure transmission of data such as credit card numbers over the Internet, voice-print technology, and storage and use of music in digital format (WAV versus MP3 files, for example).

Mechanical Engineering Mechanical engineering is a broad discipline that includes many areas of interest, such as energy production and transfer, mechanical design, materials science, biomechanics, and fluid flow. Students explore the breadth of this discipline through a mixture of fundamental concepts and experimentation. Their focus is on the design of a device and the integration of mechanics and thermofluids.

Physics Students investigate selected fields and tools of modern physics—such as interplanetary travel, atomic spectroscopy, MRI (magnetic resonance imaging), and black holes—through a combination of lectures, audiovisual presentations, hands-on laboratory experiments, and visits to research facilities.

Robotics Students discover the science and technology of recreational robot design and operation. (This session is particularly useful in preparing participants for entry into or leadership within the FIRST robotics team in their high schools.) Students learn about driveline design, sensor operations, programming, pneumatics, and manufacturing techniques. They use this information to solve a challenging robotics problem. Each subgroup in the session brainstorms, designs, builds, and tests its own creation. The chance for each subgroup to show its team's design superiority comes when robots meet for the climactic end-of-session tournament.

In addition to the major areas of study, students also participate in a communication workshop of their choosing. These workshops include speech, creative writing, music, theater, elements of writing, and American history through film and the Internet.

ENROLLMENT

WPI Frontiers seeks students who have demonstrated superior ability and interest in science and mathematics. It is recommended that applicants be enrolled in a college-preparatory curriculum in which they have completed (or will complete) 4 units of English, 4 units of mathematics (including trigonometry and analytical geometry), and 2 units of a lab science. A letter of recommendation from a science or mathematics teacher or guidance counselor is also required.

DAILY SCHEDULE

```
 7:30– 8:30 ... Breakfast
 8:30–10:30 ... Academic programs
10:30–12:30 ... Communication workshops
12:30– 1:30 ... Lunch
 1:30– 4:30 ... Academic programs
 5:00– 6:00 ... Dinner
 6:30–10:30 ... Extracurricular activities
11:00 ... Check in
12:00 ... Lights out
```

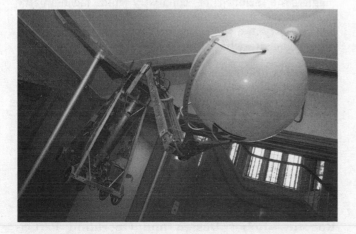

EXTRA OPPORTUNITIES AND ACTIVITIES

In addition to attending the academic programs and workshops, participants enjoy a full schedule of activities. Field trips, movies, performances, and tournaments enable participants to interact with each other and help develop leadership skills and friendships.

FACILITIES

Students are housed in one of WPI's supervised residence halls and attend classes in modern facilities. Students have access to the athletic facilities, including a fitness center, gymnasium, softball diamond, and tennis courts, and computer labs.

STAFF

Each course and workshop is taught by a WPI faculty member. In addition, residence halls and program activities are supervised by WPI upperclass students as well as members of the WPI administrative staff. Student staff members are selected based on leadership skills, academic achievement, enthusiasm, and demonstrated responsible behavior.

MEDICAL CARE

Frontiers staff members, campus police, and EMTs, in cooperation with local hospitals, handle any medical needs or emergencies that may arise.

COSTS

The tuition cost for the 2007 Frontiers program was $2100. This covered tuition, books, meals, housing, field trips, and activities.

TRANSPORTATION

Worcester is centrally located in New England, with access to four airports within an hour of the city: Logan (Boston, Massachusetts), T. F. Green (Providence, Rhode Island), Bradley International (Hartford, Connecticut), and Manchester (Manchester, New Hampshire). Worcester also has an Amtrak station located within 10 miles of the campus. Students traveling from outside of Worcester are provided information on traveling and transportation to the campus.

APPLICATION TIMETABLE

The application deadline is May 31. Students are notified of acceptance on a rolling basis.

FOR MORE INFORMATION, CONTACT

WPI Frontiers Program
100 Institute Road
Worcester, Massachusetts 01609-2280

Phone: 508-831-5286
Fax: 508-831-5875
E-mail: frontiers@wpi.edu
Web site: http://www.wpi.edu/+frontiers

WORCESTER POLYTECHNIC INSTITUTE

WPI LAUNCH PROGRAM

WORCESTER, MASSACHUSETTS

TYPE OF PROGRAM: Academic enrichment

PARTICIPANTS: Coeducational, students entering grades 9 and 10

ENROLLMENT: 50–75

PROGRAM DATES: July and August 2007 (Exact dates to be announced)

HEAD OF PROGRAM: Julie Chapman, Associate Director of Admissions

LOCATION

WPI is situated on 80 acres in Worcester, Massachusetts, New England's second-largest city. The campus, which is surrounded by parks and residential neighborhoods, is located 1 mile from downtown. Students have access to WPI's facilities, including the Gordon Library, campus center, and state-of-the-art laboratories and equipment.

BACKGROUND AND PHILOSOPHY

For the past twenty years, WPI summer programs have been enthusiastically attended by hundreds of young people. WPI Launch is distinguished from the school's other programs by its focus on current laboratory techniques and unsolved problems in biology, chemistry, computer science, and robotics. This program challenges students to explore the outer limits of knowledge in these fields. Students attend workshops and do lab work in their chosen area of study. With classmates, they work on projects and assemble their findings. Students learn from outstanding WPI instructors and students and use state-of-the-art experimental, analytical, and computer technology.

PROGRAM OFFERINGS

Biology—Homegrown Biotech: Biotechnology in Everyday Life Students explore the ways in which the field of biotechnology affects their everyday lives. Working in WPI's biotechnology lab, students have a chance to conduct a forensic investigation, create root beer using fermentation, or analyze the foods they eat to see if they have been genetically modified. Students carry out their own scientific investigations and share their findings in a presentation at the end of the week.

Chemistry—The Magic of Chemistry This is the program for those who have wanted to be mad scientists, with bubbling flasks of colored concoctions spread before them; or those who want to engineer DNA or proteins. In WPI's chemistry lab, students alter liquids at the flick of a wrist, change ordinary pennies into gold, and cut and splice genes to create creatures that glow. While this might sound like magic, the science of chemistry and biochemistry makes it possible. Students learn about chemistry and biochemistry and then prepare their own "magic show" to demonstrate what they have learned.

Computer Science—Computer Games Students who are interested in how computer game are made find this to be the right program for them. They learn how to use a computer language to create programs with graphics, sound, and animation. Working in teams, they undertake hands-on lab exercises to understand important computer science topics. By the end of the week, students will have created a project demonstrating their newfound skills with cool graphics and amazing animation, complete with a soundtrack.

Robotics—Robot Design and Operation Participants discover the science and technology of the exciting field of robotics during this program. They learn about mechanical design, sensors, and programming and build designs using Vex robots and program them using EasyC. Challenging robotics problems culminate in a competition between student groups at the end of the week.

ENROLLMENT
WPI's Launch program is offered to incoming high school freshmen and sophomores only.

DAILY SCHEDULE

8:00– 9:00	Student drop-off
9:00–12:30	Academic programs
12:30– 1:30	Lunch
1.30– 3.30	Academic programs
4:00– 5:00	Student pick-up

STAFF
Each academic program is taught by a WPI instructor, with assistance from WPI undergraduate and graduate students.

MEDICAL CARE
WPI's Launch staff members, campus police, and EMTs, in conjunction with local hospitals, handle any medical needs or emergencies that may arise.

COSTS
The tuition cost for the 2007 Launch program is $495. This covers all equipment and lunch.

TRANSPORTATION
Students need to arrange for transportation to and from the campus.

APPLICATION TIMETABLE
The registration deadline is July 15.

FOR MORE INFORMATION, CONTACT
WPI Launch Program
100 Institute Road
Worcester, Massachusetts 01609-2280

Phone: 508-831-5286
Fax: 508-831-5875
E-mail: launch@wpi.edu
Web site: http://www.wpi.edu/+launch

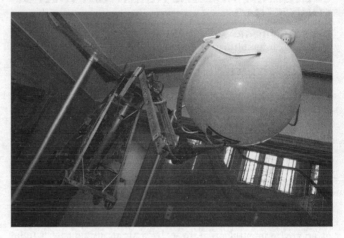

WORLD HORIZONS INTERNATIONAL

SERVICE AND ARTS PROGRAMS

COSTA RICA; ECUADOR; ENGLAND; ENGLISH-SPEAKING CARIBBEAN ISLAND OF DOMINICA; FIJI; ICELAND; INDIA; ITALY; KANAB, UTAH (IN CONJUNCTION WITH BEST FRIENDS ANIMAL SANCTUARY); NORTHRIDGE, CALIFORNIA; AND THE NORTHWEST HILLS OF CONNECTICUT

TYPE OF PROGRAM: Community service, cross-cultural exchange, intercultural language and learning, photography, and other visual and performing arts

PARTICIPANTS: Coeducational programs for high school students, college students, adults, and families

ENROLLMENT: 10–12 students per group, under the supervision of 2 adult leaders

PROGRAM DATES: Two- to five-week sessions beginning in the middle of June, spring-break trips, Christmas break trips, and more

HEAD OF PROGRAM: Stuart L. Rabinowitz, Director

LOCATION

World Horizons International, LLC, offers programs for Spanish-speaking students in Costa Rica and Ecuador. In addition, there are also intercultural travel-learning programs that involve work at an environmental program in Iceland; an orphanage in India and an orphanage in Rome, Italy; a program working with animals at Best Friends Animal Sanctuary in Utah; and a riding-for-the-handicapped facility in Northridge, California. Participants can choose to work in small-village settings in Fiji, in Nokoru Kulu on the island of Viti Levu, or in Dominica, an English-speaking island in the Caribbean. A photography trip to England and Iceland and a visual and performing arts camp in the northwest hills of Connecticut are also offered.

BACKGROUND AND PHILOSOPHY

World Horizons International is an organization founded in 1987 by Judy Manning, a former Peace Corps administrator, to sponsor programs for students interested in cross-cultural community service. From her nineteen years of working in the international field, Judy Manning established, developed, and ran summer programs in the Caribbean and Central America that provided volunteer opportunities for thousands of high school students. In 1988, World Horizons started with projects on English-speaking islands in the Caribbean, Alaska, and Central America. Now, after nineteen years, a very strong World Horizons presence has continued in these areas and also in Iceland, India, Italy, and additional domestic loca-

tions around the U.S. In addition, World Horizons has added visual and performing arts trips and camps to round out the program offerings.

World Horizons, under the leadership of Stuart L. Rabinowitz since 2001, continues to offer cross-cultural community service opportunities for teenage participants who wish to expand their knowledge of themselves and the world in which they live. In addition, new photographic tours and instruction are taught by Stuart Rabinowitz, a professional photographer for more than thirty years. In 2008, World Horizons plans to expand its' program offerings by offering a visual and performing arts camp in the northwest hills of Connecticut.

Every aspect of the World Horizons program is designed to enable each participant to enter into the life and culture of the local community. The immediate rewards of a summer with World Horizons come from the relationships that students build with people from the local community and other members of their World Horizons group and from the success of the community service involvement. One student on the program to Central America described her experience as "having assisted me in redirecting my academic concentrations and also helping me to transform my thoughts and feelings on life in general. World Horizons allows one to see what is really important in life." Another student who went on a program to Ecuador remarked," I returned with a different perspective of myself and American society. I brought home the knowledge that happiness does not rely on material possessions as our society seems to indicate, but rather it relies on the love we share with friends and families."

PROGRAM OFFERINGS

World Horizons volunteers live, work, and travel in groups of 10 to 12 students led by 2 highly qualified World Horizons staff members. Local representatives arrange housing for the group to live together in a local home, school, or community facility; the organization does not offer homestays. On community service trips, participants spend part of each day on a group project identified by the local host organization. These involvements might find the student painting and repairing homes of senior citizens; teaching arts and crafts, dance, music, or sports to children in a day-camp setting; or building a school, medical clinic, or community hall. On a continuation of the concept of community service, a portion of the afternoon may be devoted to an individual internship program, selected by the student when possible. These are unique involvements that are focused on learning more about the local people and their culture. Individual internships that former World Horizons volunteers have chosen include tutoring children, participating in an environmental awareness program, assisting a local physician, hosting a call-in radio show, helping in a dairy, and working in a fishery that cultivates giant clams and exotic fish. Individual internships are available in Costa Rica and Dominica and may possibly be available in other locations also.

California This is an opportunity to work with a therapeutic riding program called Strides, located in Northridge, California. Here, students assist with riding programs for the handicapped—spotting and leading riders and learning how to train horses. Students also have the opportunity to ride if they are interested.

Caribbean The community service offering on the island of Dominica in the eastern Caribbean involves the painting and repair of homes of senior citizens, painting murals on classroom walls, working with preschools and day-care centers, helping at a small orphanage, and assisting with local environmental issues. Individual internships are varied and interesting, and weekends are set aside for expeditions to nearby islands, hiking in the countryside, enjoying the local beaches, sightseeing, or taking part in festivals, such as Carnival, or regatta boat races.

Connecticut The World Horizons visual and performing arts program will take place in the beautiful northwest hills of Connecticut. International performers from around the world will teach one-week workshops in mime, mask making and performance, marionette making and performance, hand puppetry, photography, metal sculpture, and much more.

Costa Rica The World Horizons program in Costa Rica is designed to improve Spanish-speaking skills through cultural immersion. The site, about 3 hours south of San Jose, is in the region of San Ignacio de Acosta, which is popular with World Horizons volunteers who want to participate in community service and, at the same time, use their Spanish skills within the total immersion of a small Central American village. Participants work alongside local counterparts in painting homes and schools and refurbishing community facilities. In addition, they establish a day camp for children and have the opportunity to teach activities such as sports, arts and crafts, dance, and music. Afternoon internships are unique and diversified and may include picking coffee beans on a coffee plantation, assisting at the local health center, tutoring at an orphanage, working with the elderly, writing for the local newspaper, or learning the art of Costa Rican cooking in a local restaurant.

An alternative in Costa Rica is working in conjunction with the "Global Classroom." This environmental program involves working in the rainforest and helping with a reforestation project.

Ecuador The World Horizons program in Ecuador is located in the beautiful northern part of Ecuador, in the town of Cayambe, with a population of approximately 30,000. World Horizons participants go into the native Ecuadorian schools in the Andes Mountains to help teach the children, run activities and sports programs for the children, do repairs on the local schools, and participate in individual internships in Cayambe, which may include working in an orphanage, a local store, pharmacy, doctor's office, or health clinic. On weekends the students have the opportunity to visit a local market in Otavalo, take sightseeing trips to other areas of Ecuador, and hike up "El Cayambe" to historic Inca ruins.

England and Iceland (photography instruction): Stuart L. Rabinowitz, a professional photographer since 1976, takes students on a tour of fascinating sites in the north of England and Iceland. There is photography instruction, and students have the opportunity to use some large-format photographic equipment. The sites included are York, Howarth (where the Bronte sisters lived), Knaresborough, Robin Hood's Bay, and London. Then the students move on to Reykjavik to photograph Gulfoss, glaciers, and the fantastic landscape of Iceland.

Fiji Participants work in conjunction with the senior education officer on the island of Viti Levu. Located in the village of Nokoru Kulu, students work with the children of the area—teaching in the schools, tutoring, and running day camp activities. They also do painting and building projects for the people of the village. Weekends are spent seeing the sights of Fiji—waterfalls and the capital, Suva—and in activities such as snorkeling and swimming.

Iceland: The Land of the Midnight Sun Summers in Iceland are light and promote nightlife with coffee houses and plenty of recreational facilities, including whale watching and the "swimming pool and steam bath culture" of the north. The group is based in the capital city of Reykjavik and spends the working day planting trees in the government-sponsored reforestation project. At night there is lots of fun in the high north. This area is famous for its geothermals and accompanying horticulture. Internships may include working at the horticultural college and also with horticultural businesses in the region. The highlight of the trip is a two-day horse trek into the interior to see more beautiful and unusual scenery.

India This is a fabulous trip to assist in an orphanage in India. The program known as "Say Yes Now" and "Ramana's Garden" is located in Tapovan, Laxman Jhula, in the Tehri district of India. Students help with the gardens, tutor children, do repair work on the facilities, and help prepare the children for the future.

Italy Located in the heart of Italy, this group works with a local orphanage and program for children in Rome. Students involved with this program tutor children, run activities and sports programs, and mentor local, underprivileged children.

Utah Working in conjunction with Best Friends Animal Sanctuary, participants work alongside staff members in the daily care of the animals, many of which have been abused or abandoned. The group helps to feed, exercise, observe behavior, and work with animals with special needs. At any given time, there are more than 1,500 dogs, cats, birds, rabbits, goats, horses, and burros that have to be nursed back to health and are craving TLC. Weekend trips may include hiking, backpacking, canoeing, and visits to the Grand Canyon, Zion National Park, Lake Powell, and Bryce Canyon.

STAFF

Leaders are college graduates with extensive experience working with students as teachers in teenage-related programs. Many have worked, lived, and traveled abroad as Peace Corps volunteers. Assistant leaders are at least juniors in college. In addition, a facilitator from the local community assists with the programs.

COSTS

The all-inclusive fees for the 2007 programs, including roundtrip airfare from the departure point, ranged from $2995 to $5450.

FINANCIAL AID

World Horizons has limited scholarship assistance to students with financial need. Individual fund-raising information is also available upon request.

TRANSPORTATION

Programs begin with students departing as a group from New York, Miami, and Los Angeles area airports on regularly scheduled flights.

APPLICATION TIMETABLE

World Horizons accepts applications year-round. Enrollment is limited, so participants are encouraged to apply as early as possible to secure a spot in the program of their choice. Students are required to complete an application and supply the names of two references, a teacher, and their guidance counselor or adviser. A decision is made within two weeks of receiving a completed application. Some programs have deadlines for applying, so students should check each particular program for deadlines.

FOR MORE INFORMATION, CONTACT

World Horizons International, LLC.
P.O. Box 662
Bethlehem, Connecticut 06751
Phone: 203-266-5874
        800-262-5874 (toll-free)
Fax: 203-266-6227
E-mail: worldhorizons@att.net
Web site: http://www.world-horizons.com

WYOMING SEMINARY

SUMMER AT SEM 2007: THE COLLEGE PREP INSTITUTE, ENGLISH AS A SECOND LANGUAGE INSTITUTE, PERFORMING ARTS INSTITUTE

KINGSTON, PENNSYLVANIA

TYPE OF PROGRAM: Academic enrichment, English as a second language, and performing arts
PARTICIPANTS: Coeducational, through grade 12
ENROLLMENT: 400
PROGRAM DATES: Late June, July, and August; length of each program varies
HEAD OF PROGRAM: John R. Eidam, Director

LOCATION

Wyoming Seminary, founded in 1844, is one of the nation's oldest continuously coeducational college-preparatory schools. During the regular school year, it enrolls more than 400 students in pre-kindergarten through grade 8 on the Lower School campus in Forty Fort and 443 students in grade 9 through the postgraduate year on the Upper School campus in Kingston. Summer programs attract more than 400 students each year.

Summer programs are held on the 18-acre Kingston campus, set in a small-town residential area of northeastern Pennsylvania. Campus activities include concerts, films, picnics, and sports. The school is close to the recreational advantages of the Pocono region: mountains, lakes, and open space. Nearby cultural resources include professional performing arts venues, museums, and historic sites. Movie theaters, shopping, and restaurants are within walking distance. Kingston is approximately 2 hours from Philadelphia and New York City.

BACKGROUND AND PHILOSOPHY

Summer at Sem 2007 offers a seven-day-per-week boarding program for high school students. The College Prep Institute is led by experienced teachers who lead monthlong classes in a variety of secondary subject areas. The English as a Second Language Institute is recognized worldwide and helps prepare international students for boarding school life in the United States. It combines focused classroom learning with travel and cultural and social opportunities. The Institute is designed for students who have either studied some English as a foreign language or who have had some exposure to the English language. The Performing Arts Institute (founded in 1998) attracts extraordinarily talented students who work with world-renowned faculty members and conductors.

The school's faculty, recreational facilities, library resources, and small-town setting provide outstanding opportunities for growth in a safe and supportive environment.

PROGRAM OFFERINGS

Summer at Sem's three institutes are intended for academically talented, committed students. Each institute provides many academic, cultural, and recreational activities for residential and day students.

College Prep Institute Under the guidance of members of Sem's seasoned teaching staff, the College Prep Institute offers students a summer of enrichment and academic challenge in courses ranging from American History on Film to Public Speaking to Studio Art. Many of the courses are also offered in the Wyoming Seminary school-year curriculum. The content of courses taught over the summer is equivalent to that of trimester courses. Students can combine courses to meet their own interests; they can register for either one or two half-day courses. Courses are 2½ hours, five days each week for four weeks.

English as a Second Language Institute Now in its sixteenth year, this program attracts students from Asia, South America, and Europe. Students may enroll for four, five, or nine weeks depending on their own school's calendar. Along with intensive study of the English language, students travel with teachers and chaperones to New York City, Philadelphia, and Maine. Exposure to American culture is an important part of Summer at Sem's English as a Second Language Institute. Three sessions, taken separately or together, offer families flexibility in summer planning.

Performing Arts Institute (PAI) Students, teachers, and conductors from all over the world are attracted to this program. Intended for especially gifted musicians, actors, and dancers, PAI of Wyoming Seminary is a haven for young performing artists who are serious about developing their talents and who seek high-quality performance opportunities. Institute Director Nancy Sanderson brings twenty-four years of experience, talented faculty members, and professional associates to this creative endeavor. PAI for instrumentalists and vocalists is available to students from ages 12 to 18; PAI Dance for ages 10 to 18; PAI Musical Theater for ages 12 to 18; Young Artists Musical Theater for ages 10 to 13; Music Makers for ages 7 to 9; and Junior PAI for instrumentalists in grades 5 to 8.

ENROLLMENT

Summer programs enroll more than 400 boarding and day students: day students in grades 1–8 and boarding and day students in grades 9–12, including U.S. and international students. Students of all ethnic, racial, religious, and social backgrounds are welcome. Summer at Sem's tradition of internationalization makes the Performing Arts Institute (PAI) especially appealing to musicians and dancers from around the world.

EXTRA OPPORTUNITIES AND ACTIVITIES

Field trips and travel opportunities using the resources of the Wyoming Valley and northeastern Pennsylvania—parks, museums, recreational facilities, and historical sites—are important to the summer program. Campus cookouts, films, dances, sports, and the many concerts and shows of the Performing Arts Institute play a key role in campus life.

FACILITIES

Campus facilities include four residence halls; fully equipped Macintosh computer labs; two performing arts centers, including music practice rooms, a 400-seat theater, a concert hall, and a scene shop; a science center with five laboratories; a 21,000-volume library that provides access to many Pennsylvania libraries; two gymnasiums with a fitness room and pool; a stadium, a new artificial turf field, and tennis courts; studio art rooms and dance facilities; and a student center with lounges, games, and a wide-screen television.

STAFF

Regular Wyoming Seminary faculty members are joined by adjunct faculty members from regional and international schools, colleges, and universities. More than 30 faculty members live on campus year-round in residence halls and school housing; they provide a 24-hour presence on campus. Dormitories are supervised by the director of residence. College students, most of them Seminary graduates, serve as resident assistants and tutors. Performing Arts Institute faculty members perform with symphony orchestras and/or teach at universities and conservatories during the year. Throughout the summer, they perform in recitals, coach chamber groups, and play side-by-side with students in large ensembles.

MEDICAL CARE

The school is served by an on-staff nurse and school physician and is less than 10 minutes away from a fully accredited medical center. Students must complete health and health insurance forms prior to enrollment.

RELIGIOUS LIFE

Wyoming Seminary, affiliated with the United Methodist Church, welcomes students of all denominations. During the summer session, no religious services are scheduled; churches and synagogues are, however, within walking distance of the campus.

COSTS

In 2007, the application fee for secondary school academic programs was $50; the application fee for the English as a Second Language Institute was $100. Instructional fees were $575 for a four-week academic course. Boarding fees for four weeks were $2300 (seven days per week).

English as a second language course fees were as follows: Session I (four weeks), $3800; Session II (four weeks), $3600; and Session III (one week), $2000.

Performing Arts Institute fees for day students were $900 (three weeks), $1300 (four weeks), and $1800 (six weeks). For residential students, fees were $2425 (three weeks), $3350 (four weeks), and $4600 (six weeks). PAI Junior Division was $425, Young Artists Musical Theater was $425, and Music Makers was $425.

FINANCIAL AID

Financial aid is available on a limited basis for summer school programs.

TRANSPORTATION

The Wilkes-Barre/Scranton International Airport (AVP) at Avoca is served by USAir, United, Delta, and Northwest airlines. Limousine service is available for the 20-minute ride to Wyoming Seminary. The school is 1 mile from downtown Wilkes-Barre, which is served by national bus lines and is easily accessible from Interstates 80 and 81 and the Pennsylvania Turnpike.

APPLICATION TIMETABLE

Applications and publications for the new season are available in early January, and applications are accepted until registration in June.

FOR MORE INFORMATION, CONTACT

John R. Eidam
Dean of Admission and Director of Summer and International Programs
Wyoming Seminary
201 North Sprague Avenue
Kingston, Pennsylvania 18704-3593

Phone: 570-270-2186
Fax: 570-270-2198
E-mail: summeratsem@wyomingseminary.org
Web site: http://www.wyomingseminary.org/summer

INDEXES

lieves that a student functions best in an environment in which all expectations are clearly understood. For this reason, the School has a detailed statement of required student conduct and methods of operation, which is mailed to each individual requesting information about the School.

Attendance at the School implies a sincerity of purpose and a sense of responsibility and cooperation. Students are assigned daily chores necessary to maintain a neat and clean school. Work assignments change every nine days.

ENROLLMENT
There are 200 students, who come from nearly all of the fifty states and several other countries. Wolfeboro does not discriminate on the basis of race, color, and national and ethnic origin in the administration of its educational policies, admission policies, financial assistance, and athletics and other School-administrated programs.

EXTRA OPPORTUNITIES AND ACTIVITIES
Weekend trips are made to the White Mountains and Maine beaches. There are overnight camping trips each weekend and numerous other weekend trips to places of special interest, such as water parks, amusement parks, and state parks.

FACILITIES
The administrative core of the campus is located near the entrance. The Gertrude Johnson Center accommodates offices and the central reception area. Jousson Lodge, with an excellent view of the main campus, the lake, surrounding woodland, and neighboring mountains, contains the dining room, kitchen, and Health Center. Near Jousson Lodge is the Student Center, site of many student functions and activities and the campus store and weight-training room. The academic core occupies the north periphery of the central campus and includes thirty-six classrooms. Complementing the academic area are three study halls and the faculty center.

The boys' residential area is between the administrative core and the lakefront. Middle School boys enjoy a separate residential campus. Waterfront facilities include a sandy beach, two large docks, six swimming lanes, sailboats, rowboats, patrol boats, lifeguard apparatus, and related safety equipment. The girls' residential area is beyond the playing fields at the opposite end of the campus.

Students live in sturdy 7-foot-high tents with screen doors mounted on 10-foot by 12-foot permanent wooden platform bases. Most tents are shared by 2 students. All are equipped with electric lighting, outlets, beds, shelves, and desks. Residential areas include modern bathroom and shower facilities. Each residential area is under the direction of a residential division head. Students are grouped by age into five-tent clusters, each of which is supervised by a faculty member living in an adjacent cottage. Dotted along the shoreline and periphery of the campus are cottages that house other faculty and staff members and their families.

The dining hall is more than a facility in which good food is served. By intent, mealtimes provide an opportunity to gather the whole community together in an atmosphere that reflects and affirms the very essence of the Wolfeboro experience. All meals, except Sunday's picnic supper, are served family-style at tables of 10 that include students, faculty members, and faculty families. Seating assignments and student-waiter assignments are rotated, which provides enriching and supportive social interaction for all. Each table is headed by a faculty member who ensures the observation of good eating habits and gracious social manners. All meals in the dining room begin with a blessing.

MEDICAL CARE
The ratio of students to staff members enables Wolfeboro to place top priority on health and safety. The School is fortunate to have a large, fully equipped hospital 2 miles away. Students are under the direct supervision of a local physician. A registered nurse is always on duty and routinely attends to students in the Health Center.

COSTS
A $3000 deposit must accompany the application; if the applicant is accepted, the deposit is credited toward the fee for room, board, and tuition. For current fee information, interested families should contact the School.

FINANCIAL AID
Limited financial assistance is occasionally available. Grants are made on a case-by-case basis.

TRANSPORTATION
Travel to Wolfeboro is quite simple. Staff members meet planes at both the Manchester (New Hampshire) Boston Regional Airport and Boston's Logan International Airport on opening day and transport students to Wolfeboro by chartered bus. The process is reversed on closing day.

APPLICATION TIMETABLE
Inquiries concerning Wolfeboro may be made at any time. Interviews and visits to the School are welcome and may be arranged by contacting the School.

FOR MORE INFORMATION, CONTACT
Edward A. Cooper, Head of School
Wolfeboro Camp School
P.O. Box 390
Wolfeboro, New Hampshire 03894-0390

Phone: 603-569-3451
Fax: 603-569-4080
E-mail: school@wolfeboro.org
Web site: http://www.wolfeboro.org

WORCESTER POLYTECHNIC INSTITUTE

▼▲▼▲▼▲▼▲▼▲▼▲▼▲▼▲▼▲▼▲▼▲▼▲▼▲▼▲▼▲▼

WPI FRONTIERS PROGRAM

WORCESTER, MASSACHUSETTS

TYPE OF PROGRAM: Academic enrichment
PARTICIPANTS: Coeducational, students entering grades 11 and 12
ENROLLMENT: 125–150
PROGRAM DATES: July 2008
HEAD OF PROGRAM: Julie Chapman, Associate Director of Admissions

LOCATION
WPI is situated on 80 acres in Worcester, Massachusetts, New England's second-largest city. The campus, which is surrounded by parks and residential neighborhoods, is located 1 mile from downtown. Students have full access to WPI's facilities, including the Gordon Library, state-of-the-art laboratories and equipment, athletic facilities, and the university computer system.

BACKGROUND AND PHILOSOPHY
WPI Frontiers was founded twenty-five years ago to allow high school students to further explore their interests in science, mathematics, technology, and engineering. WPI Frontiers exposes students to current research problems and methods and encourages pursuit of careers in science and technology.

PROGRAM OFFERINGS
Aerospace Engineering Students explore the science of flight and learn how wings and aircraft create lift to fly. Basic concepts in aerodynamics—including drag, streamlining, airfoil stall, and aircraft design—are studied. They conduct wind- and water-tunnel experiments to visualize the flow over aircraft, then run simulations on laptop computers. Using what they have learned, students design and build a simple model aircraft, test it in the wind tunnel, and see it soar in free flight.

Biology and Biotechnology This program allows students to explore this science, from molecules and cells to ecology and evolution. They cut, splice, and insert DNA to engineer new bacteria; eavesdrop on their own nerves and muscles with computer-based technology; prepare and view cells in an electron microscope; meet a tiny roundworm that is the new favorite of geneticists; use DNA fingerprinting and antibodies to track genes and the proteins they code for; and study reproduction, ecology, anatomy, and scientific contributions (including a Nobel Prize) of the ancient horseshoe crab.

Chemistry In this program, students explore how life functions at the molecular level. They combine the newest technologies in the fields of chemistry and biochemistry to explore what happens when molecules collide, peel apart proteins and DNA, discover how enzymes work, and use computer modeling to see what biomolecules look like in 3-D. Students learn how chemistry makes color, fire, light, and electricity, using the latest genetic and biochemical techniques to create organisms that glow.

Computer Science Students journey into the world of object-oriented and Web programming. They explore at their own pace the world of programming as it is used in the World Wide Web and object-oriented languages, such as Java. Students have the opportunity to incorporate the work as part of effective multimedia interfaces for content that is of interest to them. In addition, special topics in computer science are discussed according to student interest.

Electrical and Computer Engineering Students discover the fascinating world of analog and digital electronics through classroom exercises and laboratory hands-on activities. They learn to use lab equipment, including power supplies, function generators, and oscilloscopes, to test circuits that they build. Students apply this knowledge to a design project that they work on throughout the course. Topics include audio amplification, light-wave transmission, analog signal processing, and digital circuitry. The prerequisites for students are a good attitude, an open mind, and a desire to learn.

Interactive Media and Game Development Students combine technology with art to create an interactive experience, taking on the role of programmer or artist and working on a team to bring a game to life. They draw their environment, model characters, record dialogue, mix sound effects, and tell their story. At WPI, students break down their idea into simple rules, write their algorithm, use powerful scripting languages, and publish their game on the Web.

Mathematics Students in this program learn how a mix of classical mathematics and modern technology can be used to solve current problems and open new areas. They use this background to examine encryption of numbers on the Internet via the RSA Algorithm and analysis of human voice patterns and musical instruments through Fourier methods. Specific problems of current information technology that these address include the need for secure transmission of data such as credit card numbers over the Internet, voice-print technology, and storage and use of music in digital format (WAV versus MP3 files, for example).

Mechanical Engineering Mechanical engineering is a broad discipline that includes many areas of interest, such as energy production and transfer, mechanical design, materials science, biomechanics, and fluid flow. Students explore the breadth of this discipline through a mixture of fundamental concepts and experimentation. Their focus is on the design of a device and the integration of mechanics and thermofluids.

Physics Students investigate selected fields and tools of modern physics—such as interplanetary travel, atomic spectroscopy, MRI (magnetic resonance imaging), and black holes—through a combination of lectures, audiovisual presentations, hands-on laboratory experiments, and visits to research facilities.

Robotics Students discover the science and technology of recreational robot design and operation. (This session is particularly useful in preparing participants for entry into or leadership within the FIRST robotics team in their high schools.) Students learn about driveline design, sensor operations, programming, pneumatics, and manufacturing techniques. They use this information to solve a challenging robotics problem. Each subgroup in the session brainstorms, designs, builds, and tests its own creation. The chance for each subgroup to show its team's design superiority comes when robots meet for the climactic end-of-session tournament.

In addition to the major areas of study, students also participate in a communication workshop of their choosing. These workshops include speech, creative writing, music, theater, elements of writing, and American history through film and the Internet.

ENROLLMENT

WPI Frontiers seeks students who have demonstrated superior ability and interest in science and mathematics. It is recommended that applicants be enrolled in a college-preparatory curriculum in which they have completed (or will complete) 4 units of English, 4 units of mathematics (including trigonometry and analytical geometry), and 2 units of a lab science. A letter of recommendation from a science or mathematics teacher or guidance counselor is also required.

DAILY SCHEDULE

7:30– 8:30	Breakfast
8:30–10:30	Academic programs
10:30–12:30	Communication workshops
12:30– 1:30	Lunch
1:30– 4:30	Academic programs
5:00– 6:00	Dinner
6:30–10:30	Extracurricular activities
11:00	Check in
12:00	Lights out

EXTRA OPPORTUNITIES AND ACTIVITIES

In addition to attending the academic programs and workshops, participants enjoy a full schedule of activities. Field trips, movies, performances, and tournaments enable participants to interact with each other and help develop leadership skills and friendships.

FACILITIES

Students are housed in one of WPI's supervised residence halls and attend classes in modern facilities. Students have access to the athletic facilities, including a fitness center, gymnasium, softball diamond, and tennis courts, and computer labs.

STAFF

Each course and workshop is taught by a WPI faculty member. In addition, residence halls and program activities are supervised by WPI upperclass students as well as members of the WPI administrative staff. Student staff members are selected based on leadership skills, academic achievement, enthusiasm, and demonstrated responsible behavior.

MEDICAL CARE

Frontiers staff members, campus police, and EMTs, in cooperation with local hospitals, handle any medical needs or emergencies that may arise.

COSTS

The tuition cost for the 2007 Frontiers program was $2100. This covered tuition, books, meals, housing, field trips, and activities.

TRANSPORTATION

Worcester is centrally located in New England, with access to four airports within an hour of the city: Logan (Boston, Massachusetts), T. F. Green (Providence, Rhode Island), Bradley International (Hartford, Connecticut), and Manchester (Manchester, New Hampshire). Worcester also has an Amtrak station located within 10 miles of the campus. Students traveling from outside of Worcester are provided information on traveling and transportation to the campus.

APPLICATION TIMETABLE

The application deadline is May 31. Students are notified of acceptance on a rolling basis.

FOR MORE INFORMATION, CONTACT

WPI Frontiers Program
100 Institute Road
Worcester, Massachusetts 01609-2280

Phone: 508-831-5286
Fax: 508-831-5875
E-mail: frontiers@wpi.edu
Web site: http://www.wpi.edu/+frontiers

WORCESTER POLYTECHNIC INSTITUTE

WPI LAUNCH PROGRAM

WORCESTER, MASSACHUSETTS

TYPE OF PROGRAM: Academic enrichment

PARTICIPANTS: Coeducational, students entering grades 9 and 10

ENROLLMENT: 50–75

PROGRAM DATES: July and August 2007 (Exact dates to be announced)

HEAD OF PROGRAM: Julie Chapman, Associate Director of Admissions

LOCATION

WPI is situated on 80 acres in Worcester, Massachusetts, New England's second-largest city. The campus, which is surrounded by parks and residential neighborhoods, is located 1 mile from downtown. Students have access to WPI's facilities, including the Gordon Library, campus center, and state-of-the-art laboratories and equipment.

BACKGROUND AND PHILOSOPHY

For the past twenty years, WPI summer programs have been enthusiastically attended by hundreds of young people. WPI Launch is distinguished from the school's other programs by its focus on current laboratory techniques and unsolved problems in biology, chemistry, computer science, and robotics. This program challenges students to explore the outer limits of knowledge in these fields. Students attend workshops and do lab work in their chosen area of study. With classmates, they work on projects and assemble their findings. Students learn from outstanding WPI instructors and students and use state-of-the-art experimental, analytical, and computer technology.

PROGRAM OFFERINGS

Biology—Homegrown Biotech: Biotechnology in Everyday Life Students explore the ways in which the field of biotechnology affects their everyday lives. Working in WPI's biotechnology lab, students have a chance to conduct a forensic investigation, create root beer using fermentation, or analyze the foods they eat to see if they have been genetically modified. Students carry out their own scientific investigations and share their findings in a presentation at the end of the week.

Chemistry—The Magic of Chemistry This is the program for those who have wanted to be mad scientists, with bubbling flasks of colored concoctions spread before them; or those who want to engineer DNA or proteins. In WPI's chemistry lab, students alter liquids at the flick of a wrist, change ordinary pennies into gold, and cut and splice genes to create creatures that glow. While this might sound like magic, the science of chemistry and biochemistry makes it possible. Students learn about chemistry and biochemistry and then prepare their own "magic show" to demonstrate what they have learned.

Computer Science—Computer Games Students who are interested in how computer game are made find this to be the right program for them. They learn how to use a computer language to create programs with graphics, sound, and animation. Working in teams, they undertake hands-on lab exercises to understand important computer science topics. By the end of the week, students will have created a project demonstrating their newfound skills with cool graphics and amazing animation, complete with a soundtrack.

Robotics—Robot Design and Operation Participants discover the science and technology of the exciting field of robotics during this program. They learn about mechanical design, sensors, and programming and build designs using Vex robots and program them using EasyC. Challenging robotics problems culminate in a competition between student groups at the end of the week.

ENROLLMENT
WPI's Launch program is offered to incoming high school freshmen and sophomores only.

DAILY SCHEDULE

8:00– 9:00	Student drop-off
9:00–12:30	Academic programs
12:30– 1:30	Lunch
1:30 3:30	Academic programs
4:00– 5:00	Student pick-up

STAFF
Each academic program is taught by a WPI instructor, with assistance from WPI undergraduate and graduate students.

MEDICAL CARE
WPI's Launch staff members, campus police, and EMTs, in conjunction with local hospitals, handle any medical needs or emergencies that may arise.

COSTS
The tuition cost for the 2007 Launch program is $495. This covers all equipment and lunch.

TRANSPORTATION
Students need to arrange for transportation to and from the campus.

APPLICATION TIMETABLE
The registration deadline is July 15.

FOR MORE INFORMATION, CONTACT
WPI Launch Program
100 Institute Road
Worcester, Massachusetts 01609-2280

Phone: 508-831-5286
Fax: 508-831-5875
E-mail: launch@wpi.edu
Web site: http://www.wpi.edu/+launch

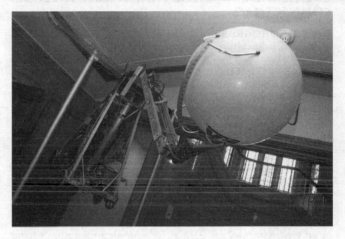

WORLD HORIZONS INTERNATIONAL

SERVICE AND ARTS PROGRAMS

COSTA RICA; ECUADOR; ENGLAND; ENGLISH-SPEAKING CARIBBEAN ISLAND OF DOMINICA; FIJI; ICELAND; INDIA; ITALY; KANAB, UTAH (IN CONJUNCTION WITH BEST FRIENDS ANIMAL SANCTUARY); NORTHRIDGE, CALIFORNIA; AND THE NORTHWEST HILLS OF CONNECTICUT

TYPE OF PROGRAM: Community service, cross-cultural exchange, intercultural language and learning, photography, and other visual and performing arts

PARTICIPANTS: Coeducational programs for high school students, college students, adults, and families

ENROLLMENT: 10–12 students per group, under the supervision of 2 adult leaders

PROGRAM DATES: Two- to five-week sessions beginning in the middle of June, spring-break trips, Christmas break trips, and more

HEAD OF PROGRAM: Stuart L. Rabinowitz, Director

LOCATION

World Horizons International, LLC, offers programs for Spanish-speaking students in Costa Rica and Ecuador. In addition, there are also intercultural travel-learning programs that involve work at an environmental program in Iceland; an orphanage in India and an orphanage in Rome, Italy; a program working with animals at Best Friends Animal Sanctuary in Utah; and a riding-for-the-handicapped facility in Northridge, California. Participants can choose to work in small-village settings in Fiji, in Nokoru Kulu on the island of Viti Levu, or in Dominica, an English-speaking island in the Caribbean. A photography trip to England and Iceland and a visual and performing arts camp in the northwest hills of Connecticut are also offered.

BACKGROUND AND PHILOSOPHY

World Horizons International is an organization founded in 1987 by Judy Manning, a former Peace Corps administrator, to sponsor programs for students interested in cross-cultural community service. From her nineteen years of working in the international field, Judy Manning established, developed, and ran summer programs in the Caribbean and Central America that provided volunteer opportunities for thousands of high school students. In 1988, World Horizons started with projects on English-speaking islands in the Caribbean, Alaska, and Central America. Now, after nineteen years, a very strong World Horizons presence has continued in these areas and also in Iceland, India, Italy, and additional domestic loca-

tions around the U.S. In addition, World Horizons has added visual and performing arts trips and camps to round out the program offerings.

World Horizons, under the leadership of Stuart L. Rabinowitz since 2001, continues to offer cross-cultural community service opportunities for teenage participants who wish to expand their knowledge of themselves and the world in which they live. In addition, new photographic tours and instruction are taught by Stuart Rabinowitz, a professional photographer for more than thirty years. In 2008, World Horizons plans to expand its' program offerings by offering a visual and performing arts camp in the northwest hills of Connecticut.

Every aspect of the World Horizons program is designed to enable each participant to enter into the life and culture of the local community. The immediate rewards of a summer with World Horizons come from the relationships that students build with people from the local community and other members of their World Horizons group and from the success of the community service involvement. One student on the program to Central America described her experience as "having assisted me in redirecting my academic concentrations and also helping me to transform my thoughts and feelings on life in general. World Horizons allows one to see what is really important in life." Another student who went on a program to Ecuador remarked," I returned with a different perspective of myself and American society. I brought home the knowledge that happiness does not rely on material possessions as our society seems to indicate, but rather it relies on the love we share with friends and families."

PROGRAM OFFERINGS

World Horizons volunteers live, work, and travel in groups of 10 to 12 students led by 2 highly qualified World Horizons staff members. Local representatives arrange housing for the group to live together in a local home, school, or community facility; the organization does not offer homestays. On community service trips, participants spend part of each day on a group project identified by the local host organization. These involvements might find the student painting and repairing homes of senior citizens; teaching arts and crafts, dance, music, or sports to children in a day-camp setting; or building a school, medical clinic, or community hall. On a continuation of the concept of community service, a portion of the afternoon may be devoted to an individual internship program, selected by the student when possible. These are unique involvements that are focused on learning more about the local people and their culture. Individual internships that former World Horizons volunteers have chosen include tutoring children, participating in an environmental awareness program, assisting a local physician, hosting a call-in radio show, helping in a dairy, and working in a fishery that cultivates giant clams and exotic fish. Individual internships are available in Costa Rica and Dominica and may possibly be available in other locations also.

California This is an opportunity to work with a therapeutic riding program called Strides, located in Northridge, California. Here, students assist with riding programs for the handicapped—spotting and leading riders and learning how to train horses. Students also have the opportunity to ride if they are interested.

Caribbean The community service offering on the island of Dominica in the eastern Caribbean involves the painting and repair of homes of senior citizens, painting murals on classroom walls, working with preschools and day-care centers, helping at a small orphanage, and assisting with local environmental issues. Individual internships are varied and interesting, and weekends are set aside for expeditions to nearby islands, hiking in the countryside, enjoying the local beaches, sightseeing, or taking part in festivals, such as Carnival, or regatta boat races.

Connecticut The World Horizons visual and performing arts program will take place in the beautiful northwest hills of Connecticut. International performers from around the world will teach one-week workshops in mime, mask making and performance, marionette making and performance, hand puppetry, photography, metal sculpture, and much more.

Costa Rica The World Horizons program in Costa Rica is designed to improve Spanish-speaking skills through cultural immersion. The site, about 3 hours south of San Jose, is in the region of San Ignacio de Acosta, which is popular with World Horizons volunteers who want to participate in community service and, at the same time, use their Spanish skills within the total immersion of a small Central American village. Participants work alongside local counterparts in painting homes and schools and refurbishing community facilities. In addition, they establish a day camp for children and have the opportunity to teach activities such as sports, arts and crafts, dance, and music. Afternoon internships are unique and diversified and may include picking coffee beans on a coffee plantation, assisting at the local health center, tutoring at an orphanage, working with the elderly, writing for the local newspaper, or learning the art of Costa Rican cooking in a local restaurant.

An alternative in Costa Rica is working in conjunction with the "Global Classroom." This environmental program involves working in the rainforest and helping with a reforestation project.

Ecuador The World Horizons program in Ecuador is located in the beautiful northern part of Ecuador, in the town of Cayambe, with a population of approximately 30,000. World Horizons participants go into the native Ecuadorian schools in the Andes Mountains to help teach the children, run activities and sports programs for the children, do repairs on the local schools, and participate in individual internships in Cayambe, which may include working in an orphanage, a local store, pharmacy, doctor's office, or health clinic. On weekends the students have the opportunity to visit a local market in Otavalo, take sightseeing trips to other areas of Ecuador, and hike up "El Cayambe" to historic Inca ruins

England and Iceland (photography instruction): Stuart L. Rabinowitz, a professional photographer since 1976, takes students on a tour of fascinating sites in the north of England and Iceland. There is photography instruction, and students have the opportunity to use some large-format photographic equipment. The sites included are York, Howarth (where the Bronte sisters lived), Knaresborough, Robin Hood's Bay, and London. Then the students move on to Reykjavik to photograph Gulfoss, glaciers, and the fantastic landscape of Iceland.

Fiji Participants work in conjunction with the senior education officer on the island of Viti Levu. Located in the village of Nokoru Kulu, students work with the children of the area—teaching in the schools, tutoring, and running day camp activities. They also do painting and building projects for the people of the village. Weekends are spent seeing the sights of Fiji—waterfalls and the capital, Suva—and in activities such as snorkeling and swimming.

Iceland: The Land of the Midnight Sun Summers in Iceland are light and promote nightlife with coffee houses and plenty of recreational facilities, including whale watching and the "swimming pool and steam bath culture" of the north. The group is based in the capital city of Reykjavik and spends the working day planting trees in the government-sponsored reforestation project. At night there is lots of fun in the high north. This area is famous for its geothermals and accompanying horticulture. Internships may include working at the horticultural college and also with horticultural businesses in the region. The highlight of the trip is a two-day horse trek into the interior to see more beautiful and unusual scenery.

India This is a fabulous trip to assist in an orphanage in India. The program known as "Say Yes Now" and "Ramana's Garden" is located in Tapovan, Laxman Jhula, in the Tehri district of India. Students help with the gardens, tutor children, do repair work on the facilities, and help prepare the children for the future.

Italy Located in the heart of Italy, this group works with a local orphanage and program for children in Rome. Students involved with this program tutor children, run activities and sports programs, and mentor local, underprivileged children.

Utah Working in conjunction with Best Friends Animal Sanctuary, participants work alongside staff members in the daily care of the animals, many of which have been abused or abandoned. The group helps to feed, exercise, observe behavior, and work with animals with special needs. At any given time, there are more than 1,500 dogs, cats, birds, rabbits, goats, horses, and burros that have to be nursed back to health and are craving TLC. Weekend trips may include hiking, backpacking, canoeing, and visits to the Grand Canyon, Zion National Park, Lake Powell, and Bryce Canyon.

STAFF
Leaders are college graduates with extensive experience working with students as teachers in teenage-related programs. Many have worked, lived, and traveled abroad as Peace Corps volunteers. Assistant leaders are at least juniors in college. In addition, a facilitator from the local community assists with the programs.

COSTS
The all-inclusive fees for the 2007 programs, including roundtrip airfare from the departure point, ranged from $2995 to $5450.

FINANCIAL AID
World Horizons has limited scholarship assistance to students with financial need. Individual fund-raising information is also available upon request.

TRANSPORTATION
Programs begin with students departing as a group from New York, Miami, and Los Angeles area airports on regularly scheduled flights.

APPLICATION TIMETABLE
World Horizons accepts applications year-round. Enrollment is limited, so participants are encouraged to apply as early as possible to secure a spot in the program of their choice. Students are required to complete an application and supply the names of two references, a teacher, and their guidance counselor or adviser. A decision is made within two weeks of receiving a completed application. Some programs have deadlines for applying, so students should check each particular program for deadlines.

FOR MORE INFORMATION, CONTACT
World Horizons International, LLC.
P.O. Box 662
Bethlehem, Connecticut 06751
Phone: 203-266-5874
      800-262-5874 (toll-free)
Fax: 203-266-6227
E-mail: worldhorizons@att.net
Web site: http://www.world-horizons.com

WYOMING SEMINARY

▼▲▼▲▼▲▼▲▼▲▼▲▼▲▼▲▼▲▼▲▼▲▼▲▼▲▼▲▼▲

SUMMER AT SEM 2007: THE COLLEGE PREP INSTITUTE, ENGLISH AS A SECOND LANGUAGE INSTITUTE, PERFORMING ARTS INSTITUTE

KINGSTON, PENNSYLVANIA

TYPE OF PROGRAM: Academic enrichment, English as a second language, and performing arts
PARTICIPANTS: Coeducational, through grade 12
ENROLLMENT: 400
PROGRAM DATES: Late June, July, and August; length of each program varies
HEAD OF PROGRAM: John R. Eidam, Director

LOCATION

Wyoming Seminary, founded in 1844, is one of the nation's oldest continuously coeducational college-preparatory schools. During the regular school year, it enrolls more than 400 students in pre-kindergarten through grade 8 on the Lower School campus in Forty Fort and 443 students in grade 9 through the postgraduate year on the Upper School campus in Kingston. Summer programs attract more than 400 students each year.

Summer programs are held on the 18-acre Kingston campus, set in a small-town residential area of northeastern Pennsylvania. Campus activities include concerts, films, picnics, and sports. The school is close to the recreational advantages of the Pocono region: mountains, lakes, and open space. Nearby cultural resources include professional performing arts venues, museums, and historic sites. Movie theaters, shopping, and restaurants are within walking distance. Kingston is approximately 2 hours from Philadelphia and New York City.

BACKGROUND AND PHILOSOPHY

Summer at Sem 2007 offers a seven-day-per-week boarding program for high school students. The College Prep Institute is led by experienced teachers who lead monthlong classes in a variety of secondary subject areas. The English as a Second Language Institute is recognized worldwide and helps prepare international students for boarding school life in the United States. It combines focused classroom learning with travel and cultural and social opportunities. The Institute is designed for students who have either studied some English as a foreign language or who have had some exposure to the English language. The Performing Arts Institute (founded in 1998) attracts extraordinarily talented students who work with world-renowned faculty members and conductors.

The school's faculty, recreational facilities, library resources, and small-town setting provide outstanding opportunities for growth in a safe and supportive environment.

PROGRAM OFFERINGS

Summer at Sem's three institutes are intended for academically talented, committed students. Each institute provides many academic, cultural, and recreational activities for residential and day students.

College Prep Institute Under the guidance of members of Sem's seasoned teaching staff, the College Prep Institute offers students a summer of enrichment and academic challenge in courses ranging from American History on Film to Public Speaking to Studio Art. Many of the courses are also offered in the Wyoming Seminary school-year curriculum. The content of courses taught over the summer is equivalent to that of trimester courses. Students can combine courses to meet their own interests; they can register for either one or two half-day courses. Courses are 2½ hours, five days each week for four weeks.

English as a Second Language Institute Now in its sixteenth year, this program attracts students from Asia, South America, and Europe. Students may enroll for four, five, or nine weeks depending on their own school's calendar. Along with intensive study of the English language, students travel with teachers and chaperones to New York City, Philadelphia, and Maine. Exposure to American culture is an important part of Summer at Sem's English as a Second Language Institute. Three sessions, taken separately or together, offer families flexibility in summer planning.

Performing Arts Institute (PAI) Students, teachers, and conductors from all over the world are attracted to this program. Intended for especially gifted musicians, actors, and dancers, PAI of Wyoming Seminary is a haven for young performing artists who are serious about developing their talents and who seek high-quality performance opportunities. Institute Director Nancy Sanderson brings twenty-four years of experience, talented faculty members, and professional associates to this creative endeavor. PAI for instrumentalists and vocalists is available to students from ages 12 to 18; PAI Dance for ages 10 to 18; PAI Musical Theater for ages 12 to 18; Young Artists Musical Theater for ages 10 to 13; Music Makers for ages 7 to 9; and Junior PAI for instrumentalists in grades 5 to 8.

ENROLLMENT

Summer programs enroll more than 400 boarding and day students: day students in grades 1–8 and boarding and day students in grades 9–12, including U.S. and international students. Students of all ethnic, racial, religious, and social backgrounds are welcome. Summer at Sem's tradition of internationalization makes the Performing Arts Institute (PAI) especially appealing to musicians and dancers from around the world.

EXTRA OPPORTUNITIES AND ACTIVITIES

Field trips and travel opportunities using the resources of the Wyoming Valley and northeastern Pennsylvania—parks, museums, recreational facilities, and historical sites—are important to the summer program. Campus cookouts, films, dances, sports, and the many concerts and shows of the Performing Arts Institute play a key role in campus life.

FACILITIES

Campus facilities include four residence halls; fully equipped Macintosh computer labs; two performing arts centers, including music practice rooms, a 400-seat theater, a concert hall, and a scene shop; a science center with five laboratories; a 21,000-volume library that provides access to many Pennsylvania libraries; two gymnasiums with a fitness room and pool; a stadium, a new artificial turf field, and tennis courts; studio art rooms and dance facilities; and a student center with lounges, games, and a wide-screen television.

STAFF

Regular Wyoming Seminary faculty members are joined by adjunct faculty members from regional and international schools, colleges, and universities. More than 30 faculty members live on campus year-round in residence halls and school housing; they provide a 24-hour presence on campus. Dormitories are supervised by the director of residence. College students, most of them Seminary graduates, serve as resident assistants and tutors. Performing Arts Institute faculty members perform with symphony orchestras and/or teach at universities and conservatories during the year. Throughout the summer, they perform in recitals, coach chamber groups, and play side-by-side with students in large ensembles.

MEDICAL CARE

The school is served by an on-staff nurse and school physician and is less than 10 minutes away from a fully accredited medical center. Students must complete health and health insurance forms prior to enrollment.

RELIGIOUS LIFE

Wyoming Seminary, affiliated with the United Methodist Church, welcomes students of all denominations. During the summer session, no religious services are scheduled; churches and synagogues are, however, within walking distance of the campus.

COSTS

In 2007, the application fee for secondary school academic programs was $50; the application fee for the English as a Second Language Institute was $100. Instructional fees were $575 for a four-week academic course. Boarding fees for four weeks were $2300 (seven days per week).

English as a second language course fees were as follows: Session I (four weeks), $3800; Session II (four weeks), $3600; and Session III (one week), $2000.

Performing Arts Institute fees for day students were $900 (three weeks), $1300 (four weeks), and $1800 (six weeks). For residential students, fees were $2425 (three weeks), $3350 (four weeks), and $4600 (six weeks). PAI Junior Division was $425, Young Artists Musical Theater was $425, and Music Makers was $425.

FINANCIAL AID

Financial aid is available on a limited basis for summer school programs.

TRANSPORTATION

The Wilkes-Barre/Scranton International Airport (AVP) at Avoca is served by USAir, United, Delta, and Northwest airlines. Limousine service is available for the 20-minute ride to Wyoming Seminary. The school is 1 mile from downtown Wilkes-Barre, which is served by national bus lines and is easily accessible from Interstates 80 and 81 and the Pennsylvania Turnpike.

APPLICATION TIMETABLE

Applications and publications for the new season are available in early January, and applications are accepted until registration in June.

FOR MORE INFORMATION, CONTACT

John R. Eidam
Dean of Admission and Director of Summer and International Programs
Wyoming Seminary
201 North Sprague Avenue
Kingston, Pennsylvania 18704-3593
Phone: 570-270-2186
Fax: 570-270-2198
E-mail: summeratsem@wyomingseminary.org
Web site: http://www.wyomingseminary.org/summer

INDEXES

A bold page number indicates an In-Depth Description.

Aboriginal Studies
LIFEWORKS with the Australian Red Cross, Australia

Academics (General)
Academic Camps at Gettysburg College, PA

Academic Study Associates–ASA at the University of California, Berkeley, CA

Academic Study Associates–ASA at the University of Massachusetts Amherst, MA

Academic Study Associates–Florence, Italy

Academic Study Associates–Nice, France

Academic Study Associates–Royan, France

Academic Study Associates–Spanish in España, Spain

Academy by the Sea, CA

Asheville School's Summer Academic Adventures, NC

Cambridge College Programme, United Kingdom

The Cambridge Experience, United Kingdom

The Cambridge Prep Experience, United Kingdom

The Cambridge Tradition, United Kingdom

Center for Cultural Interchange–Australia High School Abroad, Australia

Center for Cultural Interchange–Brazil High School Abroad, Brazil

Center for Cultural Interchange–Denmark High School Abroad, Denmark

Center for Cultural Interchange–Finland High School Abroad, Finland

Center for Cultural Interchange–France High School Abroad, France

Center for Cultural Interchange–Germany High School Abroad, Germany

Center for Cultural Interchange–Ireland High School Abroad, Ireland

Center for Cultural Interchange–Italy High School Abroad, Italy

Center for Cultural Interchange–Japan High School Abroad, Japan

Center for Cultural Interchange–Netherlands High School Abroad, Netherlands

Center for Cultural Interchange–Norway High School Abroad, Norway

Center for Cultural Interchange–Spain High School Abroad, Spain

Center for Cultural Interchange–Sweden High School Abroad, Sweden

Center for Cultural Interchange–Taiwan High School Abroad, Taiwan

Center for Talent Development Summer Academic Program, IL

Cheshire Academy Summer Program, CT

Choate Rosemary Hall Focus Program, CT

Choate Rosemary Hall Summer Session, CT

Colorado College Summer Session, CO

Cornell University Summer College Programs for High School Students, NY

Crossroads School–Summer Educational Journey, CA

Cushing Academy Summer Session, MA

Darlington Summer Programs, GA

Duke TIP Domestic Field Studies

Duke TIP International Field Studies

Duke University PreCollege Program, NC

Dunnabeck at Kildonan, NY

Eaglebrook Summer Semester, MA

Eagle Hill School Summer Session, MA

Excel at Amherst College, MA

Excel at Madrid/Barcelona, Spain

Excel at Oxford/Tuscany

Excel at Paris/Provence, France

Excel China, China

Fairfax Collegiate School Summer Enrichment Program, VA

FivePoints, NY

Georgetown University Gateway to Business Program for High School Students, D.C.

Georgetown University Summer College for High School Students, D.C.

George Washington University Summer Scholars Mini-courses, D.C.

George Washington University Summer Scholars Pre-college Program, D.C.

Girls First, VA

GirlSummer at Emma Willard School, NY

Global Leadership Adventures–Cape Town: Community Service and Leadership, South Africa

The Gow School Summer Program, NY

The Grand River Summer Academy, OH

Hargrave Summer Leadership Program, VA

The Harker Summer Institute, CA

Harker Summer Programs, CA

Harvard University Summer School: Secondary School Program, MA

Hawaii Preparatory Academy Summer Session, HI

The Hun School of Princeton–Summer Academic Session, NJ

Internship Connection, MA

Johns Hopkins University Zanvyl Krieger School of Arts and Sciences Summer Programs, MD

La Academia de España, Spain

L'Académie de France, France

L' Académie de Paris, France

Linden Hill Summer Program, MA

Marvelwood Summer Program, CT

Miami University Junior Scholars Program, OH

Northfield Mount Hermon Summer Session, MA

Northwestern University's College Preparation Program, IL

Northwestern University's National High School Institute, IL

Oak Creek Ranch School–Summer Academic Program, AZ

Oxford Advanced Studies Program, United Kingdom

The Oxford Experience, United Kingdom

The Oxford Prep Experience, United Kingdom

The Oxford Tradition, United Kingdom

Phillips Academy Summer Session, MA

Phillips Exeter Academy Summer School, NH

Portsmouth Abbey Summer School, RI

Randolph-Macon Academy Summer Programs, VA

Saint Thomas More School–Summer Academic Camp, CT

Salem Spotlight, NC

Skidmore College–Pre-College Program in the Liberal & Studio Arts for High School Students, NY

Southern Methodist University–College Experience, TX

Southern Methodist University TAG (Talented and Gifted), TX

Southwestern Adventures–Arizona, AZ

Squaw Valley Academy Summer School, CA

► ACADEMICS (GENERAL)

Stanford University High School
Summer College, CA
Summer at Delphi, OR
summer@rectory, CT
Summer@Brown, RI
The Summer Institute for the Gifted
at Amherst College, MA
The Summer Institute for the Gifted
at Bryn Mawr College, PA
The Summer Institute for the Gifted
at Emory University, GA
The Summer Institute for the Gifted
at Fairfield University, CT
The Summer Institute for the Gifted
at Manhattanville College, NY
The Summer Institute for the Gifted
at Moorestown Friends School, NJ
The Summer Institute for the Gifted
at Princeton University, NJ
The Summer Institute for the Gifted
at UCLA, CA
The Summer Institute for the Gifted
at University of California,
Berkeley, CA
The Summer Institute for the Gifted
at University of Michigan, Ann
Arbor, MI
The Summer Institute for the Gifted
at University of Texas, Austin, TX
The Summer Institute for the Gifted
at Vassar College, NY
Summer in Switzerland, Switzerland
Summer Study at Penn State, PA
Summer Study at The University of
Colorado at Boulder, CO
Summer Study in Paris at The
Sorbonne, France
Syracuse University Summer College,
NY
Tabor Academy Summer Program,
MA
Taft Summer School, CT
TASIS England Summer Program,
United Kingdom
UCLA Summer Experience: College
Level Courses, CA
University of Connecticut Mentor
Connection, CT
University of Maryland Young
Scholars Program, MD
University of Southern California
Summer Seminars, CA
Wolfeboro: The Summer Boarding
School, NH
Wyoming Seminary–Sem Summer
2008, PA

Acting
ACTeen August Academy, NY
ACTeen July Academy, NY
ACTeen June Academy, NY

ACTeen Summer Saturday Academy,
NY
American Academy of Dramatic Arts
Summer Program at Los Angeles,
California, CA
American Academy of Dramatic Arts
Summer Program at New York, NY
Choate Rosemary Hall Summer Arts
Conservatory–Theater, CT
Duke Drama Workshop, NC
Ensemble Theatre Community
School, PA
IEI–Theatre Plus Programme, United
Kingdom
Summer Theatre Institute–NYC,
2008, NY
UCLA Summer Experience:
Institutes, CA
University of Pennsylvania–Penn
Summer Theatre Workshop, PA

Aerobics
Camp California Fitness, CA

Animal Care
RUSTIC PATHWAYS–THE THAI
ELEPHANT CONSERVATION
PROJECT, Thailand
RUSTIC PATHWAYS–THE TURTLE
CONSERVATION PROJECT,
Costa Rica
World Horizons International–Kanab,
Utah, UT

Arabic
AFS-USA–Homestay Language
Study–Egypt, Egypt

Archaeology
ACADEMIC TREKS–Shipwrecks and
Underwater Archaeology in
Bermuda, Bermuda
Landmark Volunteers: New Mexico,
NM

Architecture
BAC Summer Academy, MA
Exploration of Architecture, CA
Pratt Institute Summer Pre-College
Program for High School Students,
NY
Summer@Rensselaer, NY
TASIS Arts and Architecture in the
South of France, France
University of Pennsylvania–Penn
Summer Art and Architecture
Studios, PA

Area Studies
World Affairs Seminar, WI

Art
Rhode Island School of Design
Pre-College Program, RI
TASIS Arts and Architecture in the
South of France, France

Art (Advanced Placement)
The Putney School Summer Arts
Program, VT

Art (Folk)
AFS-USA–Homestay Plus–Hungary,
Hungary

Art History/Appreciation
Academic Study Associates–Florence,
Italy
Humanities Spring in Assisi, Italy
Summer Advantage Study Abroad–
Cambridge University, United
Kingdom
Summer Advantage Study Abroad–
London, United Kingdom
Summer Advantage Study Abroad–
Rome, Italy, Italy
Summer Advantage Study Abroad–St.
Petersburg, Russia, Russian
Federation
Taft Summer School Abroad–France,
France
Taft Summer School Abroad–Spain,
Spain

Arts
Appel Farm Summer Arts Camp, NJ
Barat Foundation Summer Program
in Provence, France
Belvoir Terrace, MA
California State Summer School for
the Arts/Inner Spark, CA
The Cambridge Prep Experience,
United Kingdom
The Cambridge Tradition, United
Kingdom
Choate Rosemary Hall Summer Arts
Conservatory–Visual Arts
Program, CT
Excel at Amherst College, MA
The Experiment in International
Living–France, Five-Week Art and
Adventure in Provence, France
The Experiment in International
Living–Morocco Four-Week Arts
and Culture Program, Morocco
The Experiment in International
Living–South Africa Homestay and
Community Service, South Africa
EXPRESSIONS! Duke Fine Arts
Camp, NC
Fenn School Summer Day Camp, MA
GirlSummer at Emma Willard School,
NY
Interlochen Arts Camp, MI

La Academia de España, Spain
L'Académie de France, France
L' Académie de Paris, France
Massachusetts College of Art/Creative Vacation, MA
Massachusetts College of Art/Summer Studios, MA
Miss Porter's School Arts Alive!, CT
National Student Leadership Conference: Inside the Arts–New York City, NY
92nd Street Y Camps–Camp Yaffa for the Arts, NY
Northwestern University's National High School Institute, IL
Oxbow Summer Art Camp, CA
The Oxford Prep Experience, United Kingdom
The Oxford Tradition, United Kingdom
Perry-Mansfield Performing Arts School and Camp, CO
Pratt Institute Summer Pre-College Program for High School Students, NY
Rhode Island School of Design Pre-College Program, RI
School of the Museum of Fine Arts, Boston–Pre-College Summer Studio, MA
Southwestern Adventures–California, CA
TASIS Arts and Architecture in the South of France, France
TASIS Tuscan Academy of Art and Culture, Italy

Backpacking
AAVE–Boot/Saddle/Paddle
AAVE–Rock & Rapid
AAVE–Ultimate Alaska, AK
AAVE–Ultimate Alps
AAVE–Wild Coast Discovery
Adventure Treks–Alaska Adventures, AK
Adventure Treks–California Adventures, CA
Adventure Treks–Canadian Rockies Adventures, Canada
Adventure Treks–Montana Adventures, MT
Adventure Treks–Oregon Adventures, OR
Adventure Treks–Pacific Northwest Adventures, WA
Adventure Treks–Wilderness Adventures
Cheley Colorado Camps, CO
The Experiment in International Living–Thailand Homestay, Thailand

Treetops eXpeditions–Glacier/ Boundary Waters
Wilderness Ventures–Alaska College Leadership, AK
Wilderness Ventures–Alaska Expedition, AK
Wilderness Ventures–Alaska Southcentral, AK
Wilderness Ventures–Alaska Southeast, AK
Wilderness Ventures–Australia, Australia
Wilderness Ventures–California, CA
Wilderness Ventures–Cascade-Olympic, WA
Wilderness Ventures–Costa Rica, Costa Rica
Wilderness Ventures–European Alps
Wilderness Ventures–Grand Teton, WY
Wilderness Ventures–Great Divide
Wilderness Ventures–Hawaii, HI
Wilderness Ventures–High Sierra, CA
Wilderness Ventures–Jackson Hole, WY
Wilderness Ventures–Northwest
Wilderness Ventures–Oregon, OR
Wilderness Ventures–Pacific Northwest
Wilderness Ventures–Puget Sound, WA
Wilderness Ventures–Rocky Mountain
Wilderness Ventures–Spanish Pyrenees, Spain
Wilderness Ventures–Teton Crest
Wilderness Ventures–Washington Alpine, WA
Wilderness Ventures–Washington Mountaineering, WA
Wilderness Ventures–Wyoming Mountaineering, WY
Wilderness Ventures–Yellowstone
Wilderness Ventures–Yellowstone Fly Fishing
Wilderness Ventures–Yellowstone Wilderness

Band
Valley Forge Military Academy Summer Band Camp, PA

Bicycle Trips
AAVE–Bike Amsterdam-Paris
The Experiment in International Living–France, Biking and Homestay, France

Biology
Michigan Technological University American Indian Workshop, MI
University of Chicago–Research in the Biological Sciences, IL

University of Chicago–Stones and Bones, WY

Biology (Advanced Placement)
Adirondack Field Ecology, NY

Biomedical Research
University of Pennsylvania–Penn Summer Science Academies, PA

Boating
Wilderness Ventures–Ecuador and Galapagos Community Service, Ecuador

Body Boarding
Camp Pacific's Recreational Camp, CA
Camp Pacific's Surf and Bodyboard Camp, CA

Business
Georgetown University Gateway to Business Program for High School Students, D.C.
Milwaukee School of Engineering (MSOE)–Focus on Business, WI
National Student Leadership Conference: Entrepreneurship and Business–New York City, NY
National Student Leadership Conference: Entrepreneurship and Business–Washington, D.C.
National Student Leadership Conference: Globalization and International Business–Study Abroad
National Student Leadership Conference: Globalization and International Business–Washington, D.C.

Canoe Trips
Adventure Treks–Canadian Rockies Adventures, Canada
Keewaydin Dunmore, VT
Keewaydin Temagami, Canada
Songadeewin of Keewaydin, VT

Canoeing
Treetops eXpeditions–Glacier/ Boundary Waters

Career Exploration
Barnard's Summer in New York City: Young Women's Leadership Institute, NY
Career Explorations–Boston, MA
Career Explorations–New York, NY
IEI Student Travel–Internship Program in London, United Kingdom
Internship Connection, MA

Landmark Volunteers: Michigan, MI

Landmark Volunteers: Minnesota, MN

Landmark Volunteers: Rhode Island, RI

Landmark Volunteers: Vermont, VT

Landmark Volunteers: Washington, WA

National Student Leadership Conference: Medicine and Health Care–San Francisco, CA

National Student Leadership Conference: Medicine and Health Care–Washington D.C., MD

Childcare
LIFEWORKS with the China Little Flower Foundation in China, China

World Horizons International–Rome, Italy, Italy

World Horizons International–Tapovan, Laxman Jhula, India, India

Chinese Languages/Literature
ACADEMIC TREKS–Immersion China, China

AFS-USA–China Summer Homestay Language Study Program, China

Center for Cultural Interchange–Taiwan High School Abroad, Taiwan

Choate Rosemary Hall Summer in China, China

EF International Language School–Beijing, China

EF International Language School–Shanghai, China

Excel China, China

The Experiment in International Living–China North and East Homestay, China

The Experiment in International Living–China South and West Homestay, China

Miss Porter's School Daoyun Chinese Summer Program, CT

Rassias Programs–China, China

RUSTIC PATHWAYS–INTENSIVE CHINESE LANGUAGE, China

Summer Advantage Study Abroad–Nanjing, China, China

Classical Languages/Literatures
Humanities Spring in Assisi, Italy

College Planning
Bryn Mawr College–Women of Distinction: Personalizing the College Admissions Process, PA

College InSight, PA

Constructing Your College Experience, NC

Elite Educational Institute SAT and Subject Test Preparation, CA

Elite Educational Institute SAT Bootcamp–Korea, Republic of Korea

Elite Educational Institute SAT Preparation–Korea, Republic of Korea

Elite Educational Institute SAT Summer Bootcamp, CA

Elite Educational Institute–University of Oklahoma College Courses, CA

College Tours
College InSight, PA

Summer Study at Penn State, PA

Communications
Georgetown University Journalism Workshop for High School Students, D.C.

National Student Leadership Conference: Journalism and Mass Communication, D.C.

Summer Action–Take the Lead, MA

Community Service
AAVE–Africa

AAVE–Costa Rica Clásica, Costa Rica

AAVE–Costa Rica Spanish Intensive, Costa Rica

AAVE–Ecuador and Galapagos, Ecuador

AAVE–Surf Scuba Safari, Mexico

Academic Study Associates–Costa Rica, Costa Rica

ACADEMIC TREKS–Adventure Peru, Peru

ACADEMIC TREKS–Dolphin Studies in Belize, Belize

ACADEMIC TREKS–French Immersion in France, France

ACADEMIC TREKS–French Immersion in the French West Indies, Guadeloupe

ACADEMIC TREKS–Immersion China, China

ACADEMIC TREKS–Immersion Mexico, Mexico

ACADEMIC TREKS–Pacific Whale Treks, Canada

ACADEMIC TREKS–Sea Turtle Studies, Costa Rica

ACADEMIC TREKS–Shipwrecks and Underwater Archaeology in Bermuda, Bermuda

ACADEMIC TREKS–Spanish Language Immersion in Ecuador, Ecuador

ACADEMIC TREKS–Wilderness Emergency Medicine, Belize

AFS-USA–Community Service–Argentina, Argentina

AFS-USA–Community Service–Costa Rica, Costa Rica

AFS-USA–Community Service–Panama, Panama

AFS-USA–Community Service–Paraguay, Paraguay

AFS-USA–Community Service–Thailand, Thailand

AFS-USA–Homestay Plus–New Zealand, New Zealand

AFS-USA–Homestay Plus–Panama, Panama

AFS-USA–Team Mission–Ghana, Ghana

Asheville School's Summer Academic Adventures, NC

The Experiment in International Living–Argentina Homestay, Community Service, and Outdoor Ecological Program, Argentina

The Experiment in International Living&Argentina Visual Arts, Photography, and Service, Argentina

The Experiment in International Living–Belize Homestay, Belize

The Experiment in International Living–Botswana Homestay, Botswana

The Experiment in International Living–Brazil Homestay, Arts, and Community Service, Brazil

The Experiment in International Living–Costa Rica Homestay, Costa Rica

The Experiment in International Living–Germany, Four-Week Homestay, Travel, Community Service, Germany

The Experiment in International Living–Ghana Homestay, Ghana

The Experiment in International Living–Mexico–Community Service, Travel, and Homestay, Mexico

The Experiment in International Living–Morocco Four-Week Arts and Culture Program, Morocco

The Experiment in International Living–Navajo Nation, NM

The Experiment in International Living–New Zealand Homestay, New Zealand

The Experiment in International Living–Poland, Homestay, Community Service, and Travel, Poland

The Experiment in International Living–South Africa Homestay and Community Service, South Africa

The Experiment in International Living–Spain–Multiculturalism and Service, Spain

The Experiment in International Living–Thailand Homestay, Thailand

The Experiment in International Living–Turkey Homestay, Community Service, and Travel, Turkey

Global Leadership Adventures–Brazil: Community Service and Leadership, Brazil

Global Leadership Adventures–Cape Town: Community Service and Leadership, South Africa

Global Leadership Adventures–Costa Rica: Community Service and Leadership, Costa Rica

Global Leadership Adventures–Ghana: Community Service and Leadership, Ghana

Global Leadership Adventures–India: Community Service and Leadership, India

GLOBAL WORKS–Cultural Exchange and Service–Costa Rica-3 weeks, Costa Rica

GLOBAL WORKS Cultural Exchange and Service–Ireland-4 weeks, Ireland

GLOBAL WORKS–Cultural Exchange and Service–New Zealand and Fiji Islands-4 weeks

GLOBAL WORKS–Cultural Exchange and Service–Puerto Rico-2 or 4 weeks, Puerto Rico

GLOBAL WORKS–Cultural Exchange–Fiji Islands-4 weeks, Fiji

GLOBAL WORKS–Language Immersion, Cultural Exchange and Service–Argentina, Argentina

GLOBAL WORKS–Language Immersion, Cultural Exchange and Service–Costa Rica, Costa Rica

GLOBAL WORKS–Language Immersion, Cultural Exchange and Service–Ecuador and the Galapagos-4 weeks, Ecuador

GLOBAL WORKS–Language Immersion, Cultural Exchange and Service–France-4 weeks, France

GLOBAL WORKS–Language Immersion, Cultural Exchange and Service–Martinique-4weeks, Martinique

GLOBAL WORKS–Language Immersion, Cultural Exchange and Service–Mexico–3 weeks, Mexico

GLOBAL WORKS–Language Immersion, Cultural Exchange and Service–Panama/Costa Rica

GLOBAL WORKS–Language Immersion, Cultural Exchange and Service–Peru, Peru

GLOBAL WORKS–Language Immersion, Cultural Exchange and Service–Puerto Rico-4 weeks, Puerto Rico

GLOBAL WORKS–Language Immersion, Cultural Exchange and Service–Spain-4 weeks, Spain

GLOBAL WORKS–Language Immersion, Cultural Exchange and Service–Yucatan Peninsula, Mexico-4 weeks, Mexico

Landmark Volunteers: Arizona, AZ

Landmark Volunteers: California, CA

Landmark Volunteers: Colorado, CO

Landmark Volunteers: Connecticut, CT

Landmark Volunteers: Idaho, ID

Landmark Volunteers: Maine, ME

Landmark Volunteers: Massachusetts, MA

Landmark Volunteers: Michigan, MI

Landmark Volunteers: Minnesota, MN

Landmark Volunteers: Montana, MT

Landmark Volunteers: New Jersey, NJ

Landmark Volunteers: New Mexico, NM

Landmark Volunteers: New York, NY

Landmark Volunteers: Oregon, OR

Landmark Volunteers: Pennsylvania, PA

Landmark Volunteers: Rhode Island, RI

Landmark Volunteers: Vermont, VT

Landmark Volunteers: Virginia, VA

Landmark Volunteers: Washington, WA

Landmark Volunteers: Wyoming, WY

LIFEWORKS with the Australian Red Cross, Australia

LIFEWORKS with the British Virgin Islands Marine Parks and Conservation Department, British Virgin Islands

LIFEWORKS with the China Little Flower Foundation in China, China

LIFEWORKS with the DPF Foundation in Thailand, Thailand

LIFEWORKS with the Fundación Humanitaria in Costa Rica, Costa Rica

LIFEWORKS with the Galapagos Islands' National Parks, Ecuador

National Student Leadership Conference: Mastering Leadership, MD

National Student Leadership Conference: State Leadership Workshops, IL

92nd Street Y Camps–The TIYUL

Putney Student Travel–Community Service–Alaska, AK

Putney Student Travel–Community Service–Argentina, Argentina

Putney Student Travel–Community Service–Costa Rica, Costa Rica

Putney Student Travel–Community Service–Dominican Republic, Dominican Republic

Putney Student Travel–Community Service–Dominica, West Indies, Dominica

Putney Student Travel–Community Service–Ecuador, Ecuador

Putney Student Travel–Community Service–Hawaii, HI

Putney Student Travel–Community Service-India, India

Putney Student Travel–Community Service-Nicaragua, Nicaragua

Putney Student Travel–Community Service–Nusa Penida and Bali, Indonesia

Putney Student Travel–Community Service–Senegal, Senegal

Putney Student Travel–Community Service–Tanzania, United Republic of Tanzania

Putney Student Travel–Community Service–Vietnam, Vietnam

Putney Student Travel–Cultural Exploration–Thailand and Cambodia

Rassias Programs–China, China

Rein Teen Tours–Project Hawaii, HI

RUSTIC PATHWAYS–COME WITH NOTHING, GO HOME RICH, Thailand

RUSTIC PATHWAYS–COMMUNITY SERVICE SCHOOL IN AUSTRALIA, Australia

RUSTIC PATHWAYS–EXTENDED FIJI VILLAGE SERVICE, Fiji

RUSTIC PATHWAYS–FIJI ISLANDS COMMUNITY SERVICE, Fiji

RUSTIC PATHWAYS–INTRO TO COMMUNITY SERVICE IN FIJI, Fiji

RUSTIC PATHWAYS–INTRO TO COMMUNITY SERVICE IN THAILAND, Thailand

▶ COMMUNITY SERVICE

RUSTIC PATHWAYS–MALEKU TRIBE IMMERSION PROGRAM–COSTA RICA, Costa Rica
RUSTIC PATHWAYS–NEW ORLEANS SUMMER REBUILDING PROGRAM, LA
RUSTIC PATHWAYS–REMOTE HIGHLANDS COMMUNITY SERVICE IN FIJI, Fiji
RUSTIC PATHWAYS–RICEFIELDS, MONKS & SMILING CHILDREN, Thailand
RUSTIC PATHWAYS–SERVICE IN THE CLOUDS–INDIA, India
RUSTIC PATHWAYS–SERVICE LEARNING EXTREME
RUSTIC PATHWAYS–SOCCER AND SERVICE EXTREME
RUSTIC PATHWAYS–SOCCER AND SERVICE IN COSTA RICA, Costa Rica
RUSTIC PATHWAYS–SOCCER AND SERVICE IN FIJI, Fiji
RUSTIC PATHWAYS–SOCCER AND SERVICE IN THAILAND, Thailand
RUSTIC PATHWAYS–SURF & SERVICE–COSTA RICA, Costa Rica
RUSTIC PATHWAYS–THE CANO NEGRO SERVICE PROJECT, Costa Rica
RUSTIC PATHWAYS–THE THAI ELEPHANT CONSERVATION PROJECT, Thailand
RUSTIC PATHWAYS–THE TURTLE CONSERVATION PROJECT, Costa Rica
RUSTIC PATHWAYS–VOLCANOES AND RAINFORESTS, Costa Rica
RUSTIC PATHWAYS–WORLD SERVICE EXTREME
Service Learning in Barcelona, Spain
Service Learning in Paris, France
Studies Abroad for Global Education (SAGE), Summer SAGE Program, India
Summer Action–Take the Lead, MA
Treetops eXpeditions–Alaska Community Service, AK
Treetops eXpeditions–Vanuatu, Vanuatu
Visions–Alaska, AK
Visions–British Virgin Islands, British Virgin Islands
Visions–Costa Rica, Costa Rica
Visions–Dominica, Dominica
Visions–Dominican Republic, Dominican Republic
Visions–Ecuador, Ecuador
Visions–Guadeloupe, Guadeloupe
Visions–Mississippi, MS

Visions–Montana, MT
Visions–Nicaragua, Nicaragua
Visions–Peru, Peru
Visions–Vietnam, Vietnam
Volunteers for Peace International Voluntary Service–Estonia, Estonia
Volunteers for Peace International Voluntary Service–France, France
Volunteers for Peace International Voluntary Service–Germany, Germany
Volunteers for Peace International Voluntary Service–Italy, Italy
Westcoast Connection–Community Connections Alaska, AK
Westcoast Connection–Community Service Belize, Belize
Westcoast Connection–Community Service Costa Rica, Costa Rica
Westcoast Connection–Community Service–Habitat for Humanity, WA
Westcoast Connection–Community Service Hawaii, HI
Wilderness Ventures–Alaska Southeast Community Service, AK
Wilderness Ventures–Costa Rica Service, Costa Rica
Wilderness Ventures–Ecuador and Galapagos Community Service, Ecuador
Wilderness Ventures–Fiji Community Service, Fiji
Wilderness Ventures–Peru Community Service, Peru
Wilderness Ventures–Southwest Community Service
World Horizons International–Cayambe, Ecuador, Ecuador
World Horizons International–Costa Rica, Costa Rica
World Horizons International–Dominica, Dominica
World Horizons International–Fiji, Fiji
World Horizons International–Iceland, Iceland
World Horizons International–Kanab, Utah, UT
World Horizons International–Northridge, California, CA
World Horizons International–Rome, Italy, Italy
World Horizons International–Tapovan, Laxman Jhula, India, India

Computer Game Design
iD Gaming Academy–Stanford University, Palo Alto, CA
iD Gaming Academy–UC Berkeley, Berkeley, CA

iD Gaming Academy–UCLA, Westwood, CA
iD Gaming Academy–Villanova University, Villanova, PA

Computer Programming
Mount Holyoke College SummerMath Program, MA

Computers
Brewster Academy Summer Session, NH
Cybercamps–Adelphi University, NY
Cybercamps–American University, D.C.
Cybercamps–Barry University, FL
Cybercamps–Bellevue Community College, WA
Cybercamps–Benedictine University, IL
Cybercamps–Bentley College, MA
Cybercamps–Bryn Mawr College, PA
Cybercamps–Caldwell College, NJ
Cybercamps–College of St. Elizabeth, NJ
Cybercamps–Concordia University, Chicago, IL
Cybercamps–Concordia University, Irvine, CA
Cybercamps–Dana Hall School, MA
Cybercamps–DeAnza College, CA
Cybercamps–Duke University, NC
Cybercamps–Fordham University, NY
Cybercamps–George Mason University, VA
Cybercamps–Georgia State University, GA
Cybercamps–Lewis and Clark College, OR
Cybercamps–Loyola University, IL
Cybercamps–Merrimack College, MA
Cybercamps–MIT, MA
Cybercamps–New York Institute of Technology, NY
Cybercamps–Northern Virginia Community College, VA
Cybercamps–Nova Southeastern University, FL
Cybercamps–Oak Marr Rec Center, VA
Cybercamps–Oglethorpe University, GA
Cybercamps–Rutgers University, NJ
Cybercamps–St. John's University, NY
Cybercamps–Southern Polytechnic State University, GA
Cybercamps–Stanford University, CA
Cybercamps–The New School, NY
Cybercamps–Towson University, MD
Cybercamps–Trinity Lutheran College, WA
Cybercamps–UCLA, CA

Cybercamps–UC San Diego (UCSD), CA

Cybercamps–UNC, Chapel Hill, NC

Cybercamps–University of Bridgeport, CT

Cybercamps–University of California at Berkeley, CA

Cybercamps–University of Central Florida, FL

Cybercamps–University of Hartford, CT

Cybercamps–University of Maryland, MD

Cybercamps–University of Miami, FL

Cybercamps–University of Michigan, MI

Cybercamps–University of Minnesota, MN

Cybercamps–University of Washington, WA

Cybercamps–University of Washington, Bothell, WA

Cybercamps–Webster University, MO

Emagination Computer Camps–Georgia, GA

Emagination Computer Camps–Illinois, IL

Emagination Computer Camps–Massachusetts, MA

Emagination Computer Camps–Pennsylvania, PA

Frontiers Program, MA

iD Gaming Academy–Stanford University, Palo Alto, CA

iD Gaming Academy–UC Berkeley, Berkeley, CA

iD Gaming Academy UCLA, Westwood, CA

iD Gaming Academy–Villanova University, Villanova, PA

iD Tech Camps–Arizona State University, Tempe, AZ

iD Tech Camps–Brown University, Providence, RI

iD Tech Camps–Cal Lutheran University, Thousand Oaks, CA

iD Tech Camps–Carnegie Mellon University, Pittsburgh, PA

iD Tech Camps–Case Western Reserve University, Cleveland, OH

iD Tech Camps–College of William and Mary, Williamsburg, VA

iD Tech Camps–Colorado College, Colorado Springs, CO

iD Tech Camps–Columbia University, New York, NY

iD Tech Camps–Documentary Filmmaking and Cultural Immersion in Spain, Spain

iD Tech Camps–Emory University, Atlanta, GA

iD Tech Camps–Fordham University, Bronx, NY

iD Tech Camps–Georgetown University, Washington, D.C.

iD Tech Camps–Lake Forest College, Evanston, IL

iD Tech Camps–Merrimack College, North Andover, MA

iD Tech Camps–MIT, Cambridge, MA

iD Tech Camps–Northwestern University, Chicago, IL

iD Tech Camps–Pepperdine University, Malibu, CA

iD Tech Camps–Rider University, Lawrenceville, NJ

iD Tech Camps–Sacred Heart University, Fairfield, CT

iD Tech Camps–St. Mary's College of California, Moraga, CA

iD Tech Camps–Santa Clara University, Santa Clara, CA

iD Tech Camps–Smith College, Northampton, MA

iD Tech Camps–Southern Methodist University, Dallas, TX

iD Tech Camps–Stanford University, Palo Alto, CA

iD Tech Camps–Tiger Woods Learning Center, Anaheim, CA

iD Tech Camps–UC Berkeley, Berkeley, CA

iD Tech Camps–UC Davis, Davis, CA

iD Tech Camps–UC Irvine, Irvine, CA

iD Tech Camps–UCLA, Westwood, CA

iD Tech Camps–UC San Diego, La Jolla, CA

iD Tech Camps–UC Santa Cruz, Santa Cruz, CA

iD Tech Camps–University of Central Florida, Orlando, FL

iD Tech Camps–University of Denver, Denver, CO

iD Tech Camps–University of Houston, Houston, TX

iD Tech Camps–University of Miami, Coral Gables, FL

iD Tech Camps–University of Michigan, Ann Arbor, MI

iD Tech Camps–University of Minnesota, Minneapolis, MN

iD Tech Camps–University of North Carolina at Chapel Hill, Chapel Hill, NC

iD Tech Camps–University of Virginia, Charlottesville, VA

iD Tech Camps–University of Washington, Seattle, WA

iD Tech Camps–UT Austin, Austin, TX

iD Tech Camps–Vanderbilt University, Nashville, TN

iD Tech Camps–Vassar College, Poughkeepsie, NY

iD Tech Camps–Villanova University, Villanova, PA

iD Tech Camps–Virginia Tech, Blacksburg, VA

iD Tech Camps–Wake Forest University, Winston-Salem, NC

iD Tech Camps–Washington University in St. Louis, St. Louis, MO

Michigan Technological University American Indian Workshop, MI

Michigan Technological University Summer Youth Program, MI

Milwaukee School of Engineering (MSOE)–Focus on Technical Communication, WI

University of Vermont Summer Engineering Institute for High School Students, VT

Conservation Projects

ACADEMIC TREKS–Sea Turtle Studies, Costa Rica

AFS-USA–Community Service–Paraguay, Paraguay

Landmark Volunteers: Maine, ME

Landmark Volunteers: New York, NY

Landmark Volunteers: Pennsylvania, PA

Putney Student Travel–Global Awareness–Madagascar, Madagascar

RUSTIC PATHWAYS–THE TURTLE CONSERVATION PROJECT, Costa Rica

RUSTIC PATHWAYS–VOLCANOES AND RAINFORESTS, Costa Rica

Treetops eXpeditions–Alaska Community Service, AK

Construction

RUSTIC PATHWAYS–NEW ORLEANS SUMMER REBUILDING PROGRAM, LA

Creative Writing

Bryn Mawr College–Writing for College, PA

Choate Rosemary Hall Writing Project, CT

Choate Rosemary Hall Young Writers Workshop, CT

Duke Creative Writers' Workshop, NC

Girls First, VA

Kent School Summer Writers Camp, CT

The Putney School Summer Writing Program, VT

Putney Student Travel–Cultural Exploration-Creative Writing in Argentina, Argentina

▶ CREATIVE WRITING

Salem Spotlight, NC
Sarah Lawrence College Summer
　High School Programs, NY
Tisch School of the Arts–International
　High School Program–Dublin,
　Ireland
Tisch School of the Arts–International
　High School Program–Paris,
　France
Visions–Nicaragua, Nicaragua
Visions–Vietnam, Vietnam

Criminal Justice
National Student Leadership
　Conference: Forensic Science, D.C.

Cross-Cultural Education
AAVE–Bold Europe
AAVE–China, China
AAVE–Thailand, Thailand
ACADEMIC TREKS–Adventure Peru,
　Peru
ACADEMIC TREKS–Immersion
　China, China
ACADEMIC TREKS–Immersion
　Mexico, Mexico
ACADEMIC TREKS–Shark Studies
　in Fiji, Fiji
ACADEMIC TREKS–Spanish
　Immersion in Oaxaca, Mexico,
　Mexico
ACADEMIC TREKS–Spanish
　Language Immersion in Ecuador,
　Ecuador
ACADEMIC TREKS–Wilderness
　Emergency Medicine, Belize
AFS-USA–Homestay Plus–Hungary,
　Hungary
AFS-USA–Team Mission–Ghana,
　Ghana
BROADREACH Fiji Solomon Quest
BROADREACH Red Sea Scuba
　Adventure, Egypt
Center for Cultural Interchange–
　Australia High School Abroad,
　Australia
Center for Cultural Interchange–
　Brazil High School Abroad, Brazil
Center for Cultural Interchange–
　Denmark High School Abroad,
　Denmark
Center for Cultural Interchange–
　Finland High School Abroad,
　Finland
Center for Cultural Interchange–
　France High School Abroad,
　France
Center for Cultural Interchange–
　Germany High School Abroad,
　Germany
Center for Cultural Interchange–
　Ireland High School Abroad,
　Ireland

Center for Cultural Interchange–Italy
　High School Abroad, Italy
Center for Cultural Interchange–
　Japan High School Abroad, Japan
Center for Cultural Interchange–
　Netherlands High School Abroad,
　Netherlands
Center for Cultural Interchange–
　Norway High School Abroad,
　Norway
Center for Cultural Interchange–
　Spain High School Abroad, Spain
Center for Cultural Interchange–
　Spain Sports and Language Camp,
　Spain
Center for Cultural Interchange–
　Sweden High School Abroad,
　Sweden
Center for Cultural Interchange–
　Taiwan High School Abroad,
　Taiwan
Choate Rosemary Hall Summer in
　China, China
Choate Rosemary Hall Summer in
　Paris, France
Choate Rosemary Hall Summer in
　Spain, Spain
GLOBAL WORKS–Cultural Exchange
　and Service–Ireland-4 weeks,
　Ireland
Hawaii Preparatory Academy
　Summer Session, HI
Intensive English Language Program,
　MD
Miss Porter's School Daoyun Chinese
　Summer Program, CT
The Putney School Summer Program
　for International Education (ESL),
　VT
Putney Student Travel–Cultural
　Exploration-Creative Writing in
　Argentina, Argentina
Putney Student Travel–Cultural
　Exploration–Thailand and
　Cambodia
Putney Student Travel–Global
　Action–El Salvador, El Salvador
Putney Student Travel–Global
　Action–India, India
Putney Student Travel–Global
　Action–Malawi, Malawi
Putney Student Travel–Global
　Action–South Africa, South Africa
Putney Student Travel–Global
　Awareness–China, China
Putney Student Travel–Global
　Awareness in Action–Cambodia,
　Cambodia
Putney Student Travel–Global
　Awareness–Madagascar,
　Madagascar

RUSTIC PATHWAYS–COME WITH
　NOTHING, GO HOME RICH,
　Thailand
RUSTIC PATHWAYS–FACES AND
　PLACES OF VIETNAM, Vietnam
RUSTIC PATHWAYS–INDIAN
　HIMALAYA TRAVELER, India
RUSTIC PATHWAYS–INTENSIVE
　CHINESE LANGUAGE, China
RUSTIC PATHWAYS–INTENSIVE
　SPANISH LANGUAGE, Costa Rica
RUSTIC PATHWAYS–OFF THE MAP
　BURMA AND CAMBODIA
RUSTIC PATHWAYS–
　PHOTOGRAPHY ADVENTURE
　IN THAILAND AND ANGKOR
　WAT
RUSTIC PATHWAYS–
　PHOTOGRAPHY ADVENTURE
　IN THAILAND AND BURMA
RUSTIC PATHWAYS–
　PHOTOGRAPHY ADVENTURE
　IN THAILAND AND VIETNAM
RUSTIC PATHWAYS–SERVICE AND
　SAFARI IN AFRICA, United
　Republic of Tanzania
RUSTIC PATHWAYS–SERVICE IN
　THE CLOUDS–INDIA, India
RUSTIC PATHWAYS–SOCCER AND
　SERVICE EXTREME
RUSTIC PATHWAYS–THE ART OF
　MUAY THAI, Thailand
RUSTIC PATHWAYS–THE
　BUDDHIST CARAVAN, India
RUSTIC PATHWAYS–THE
　WONDERS OF CHINA, China
Service Learning in Barcelona, Spain
TASIS Le Château des Enfants,
　Switzerland
TASIS Middle School Program,
　Switzerland
Treetops eXpeditions–Vanuatu,
　Vanuatu
Visions–Alaska, AK
Visions–British Virgin Islands,
　British Virgin Islands
Visions–Costa Rica, Costa Rica
Visions–Dominica, Dominica
Visions–Dominican Republic,
　Dominican Republic
Visions–Ecuador, Ecuador
Visions–Guadeloupe, Guadeloupe
Visions–Mississippi, MS
Visions–Montana, MT
Visions–Peru, Peru
Wilderness Ventures–Alaska
　Southeast Community Service, AK
World Horizons International–Costa
　Rica, Costa Rica
World Horizons International–
　Dominica, Dominica

World Horizons International–Fiji, Fiji

World Horizons International–Iceland, Iceland

Culinary Arts
The Experiment in International Living–France, Homestay, Language Training, and Cooking, France

The Experiment in International Living–Italy Biodiversity, Cooking, and Culture, Italy

The Experiment in International Living–Mexico Cooking and Culture, Mexico

Dance
Brant Lake Camp's Dance Centre, NY

Ensemble Theatre Community School, PA

The Experiment in International Living–Brazil Homestay, Arts, and Community Service, Brazil

EXPRESSIONS! Duke Fine Arts Camp, NC

Idyllwild Arts Summer Program–Children's Center, CA

Idyllwild Arts Summer Program–Family Week, CA

Idyllwild Arts Summer Program–Junior Artists' Center, CA

Idyllwild Arts Summer Program–Youth Arts Center, CA

92nd Street Y Camps–Camp Yaffa for the Arts, NY

Stagedoor Manor Performing Arts Training Center/Theatre and Dance Camp, NY

Danish Language/Literature
Center for Cultural Interchange–Denmark High School Abroad, Denmark

Design
BAC Summer Academy, MA

IEI–Print and Broadcast Journalism, United Kingdom

Massachusetts College of Art/Summer Studios, MA

Pratt Institute Summer Pre-College Program for High School Students, NY

Rhode Island School of Design Pre-College Program, RI

Washington University in St. Louis, College of Art–Portfolio Plus, MO

Digital Media
FivePoints, NY

School of the Museum of Fine Arts, Boston–Pre-College Summer Studio, MA

UCLA Summer Experience: Institutes, CA

Drawing
University of Pennsylvania–Penn Summer Art and Architecture Studios, PA

Washington University in St. Louis, College of Art–Portfolio Plus, MO

Dutch Language
Center for Cultural Interchange–Netherlands High School Abroad, Netherlands

Ecology
Adirondack Field Ecology, NY

BROADREACH Honduras Eco-Adventure, Honduras

The Experiment in International Living–Australia Homestay, Australia

The Experiment in International Living–Belize Homestay, Belize

The Experiment in International Living–Costa Rica Homestay, Costa Rica

The Experiment in International Living–Ecuador Homestay, Ecuador

LIFEWORKS with the Galapagos Islands' National Parks, Ecuador

Economics
Junior Statesmen Summer School–Stanford University, CA

National Student Leadership Conference: Globalization and International Business–Study Abroad

Engineering
Frontiers Program, MA

Michigan Technological University Explorations in Engineering Workshop, MI

Michigan Technological University Summer Youth Program, MI

Michigan Technological University Women in Engineering Workshop, MI

Milwaukee School of Engineering (MSOE)–Discover the Possibilities, WI

Milwaukee School of Engineering (MSOE)–Focus on the Possibilities, WI

MIT MITES (Minority Introduction to Engineering and Science), MA

National Student Leadership Conference: Engineering–San Francisco, CA

National Student Leadership Conference: Engineering–Washington D.C., MD

The Renaissance Scholar Program, TX

Smith College Summer Science and Engineering Program, MA

Summer@Rensselaer, NY

University of Vermont Summer Engineering Institute for High School Students, VT

Worcester Polytechnic Institute–Launch, MA

English as a Second Language
The Fessenden School Summer ESL Program, MA

Harker Summer English Language Institute, CA

The Hun School of Princeton American Culture and Language Institute, NJ

Intensive English Language Program, MD

Marianapolis Summer Program, CT

The Putney School Summer Program for International Education (ESL), VT

Southwestern Adventures–Arizona, AZ

Southwestern Adventures–California, CA

Summer English Experience, CT

The Winchendon School Summer Session, MA

Wyoming Seminary–Sem Summer 2008, PA

English Language/Literature
Choate Rosemary Hall English Language Institute, CT

Choate Rosemary Hall English Language Institute/Focus Program, CT

Elite Educational Institute–University of Oklahoma College Courses, CA

Georgetown University College Prep Program, D.C.

Rumsey Hall School Summer Session, CT

Summer Advantage Study Abroad–Cambridge University, United Kingdom

Environmental Science
ACADEMIC TREKS–Caribbean Marine Reserves

Landmark Volunteers: Massachusetts, MA

▶ ENVIRONMENTAL SCIENCE

Landmark Volunteers: Montana, MT
Landmark Volunteers: Wyoming, WY
92nd Street Y Camps–The TIYUL
World Horizons International–
  Iceland, Iceland

Equestrian Sports
World Horizons International–
  Northridge, California, CA

Farming
Camp Treetops, NY

Fashion Design/Production
IEI–Fashion and Design Plus
  Programme, United Kingdom

Field Research/Expeditions
Adirondack Field Ecology, NY
Asheville School's Summer Academic
  Adventures, NC
BROADREACH Marine Biology
  Accredited, Bahamas
Landmark Volunteers: Oregon, OR
LIFEWORKS with the British Virgin
  Islands Marine Parks and
  Conservation Department, British
  Virgin Islands
Putney Student Travel–Global
  Action–El Salvador, El Salvador
Putney Student Travel–Global
  Action–India, India
Putney Student Travel–Global
  Action–Malawi, Malawi
Putney Student Travel–Global
  Action–South Africa, South Africa
Putney Student Travel–Global
  Awareness–China, China
Putney Student Travel–Global
  Awareness in Action–Cambodia,
  Cambodia
University of Chicago–Insight, IL
University of Chicago–Stones and
  Bones, WY
Visions–Vietnam, Vietnam

Field Trips (Arts and Culture)
L'Académie de France, France
L' Académie de Paris, France
BAC Summer Academy, MA
Cambridge College Programme,
  United Kingdom
The Cambridge Prep Experience,
  United Kingdom
The Cambridge Tradition, United
  Kingdom
La Academia de España, Spain
Marianapolis Summer Program, CT
Miss Porter's School Summer
  Challenge, CT
Oxford Advanced Studies Program,
  United Kingdom

The Oxford Prep Experience, United
  Kingdom
The Oxford Tradition, United
  Kingdom
Service Learning in Paris, France
Summer Advantage Study Abroad–
  London, UKnited Kingdom
Summer Advantage Study Abroad–
  Paris, France, France

Film
The Experiment in International
  Living–United Kingdom
  Filmmaking Program and
  Homestay, United Kingdom
iD Tech Camps–Arizona State
  University, Tempe, AZ
iD Tech Camps–Brown University,
  Providence, RI
iD Tech Camps–Cal Lutheran
  University, Thousand Oaks, CA
iD Tech Camps–Carnegie Mellon
  University, Pittsburgh, PA
iD Tech Camps–Case Western
  Reserve University, Cleveland, OH
iD Tech Camps–College of William
  and Mary, Williamsburg, VA
iD Tech Camps–Colorado College,
  Colorado Springs, CO
iD Tech Camps–Columbia University,
  New York, NY
iD Tech Camps–Emory University,
  Atlanta, GA
iD Tech Camps–Fordham University,
  Bronx, NY
iD Tech Camps–Georgetown
  University, Washington, D.C.
iD Tech Camps–Lake Forest College,
  Evanston, IL
iD Tech Camps–Merrimack College,
  North Andover, MA
iD Tech Camps–MIT, Cambridge, MA
iD Tech Camps–Northwestern
  University, Chicago, IL
iD Tech Camps–Pepperdine
  University, Malibu, CA
iD Tech Camps–Rider University,
  Lawrenceville, NJ
iD Tech Camps–Sacred Heart
  University, Fairfield, CT
iD Tech Camps–St. Mary's College of
  California, Moraga, CA
iD Tech Camps–Santa Clara
  University, Santa Clara, CA
iD Tech Camps–Smith College,
  Northampton, MA
iD Tech Camps–Southern Methodist
  University, Dallas, TX
iD Tech Camps–Stanford University,
  Palo Alto, CA
iD Tech Camps–Tiger Woods
  Learning Center, Anaheim, CA

iD Tech Camps–UC Berkeley,
  Berkeley, CA
iD Tech Camps–UC Davis, Davis, CA
iD Tech Camps–UC Irvine, Irvine, CA
iD Tech Camps–UCLA, Westwood, CA
iD Tech Camps–UC San Diego, La
  Jolla, CA
iD Tech Camps–UC Santa Cruz,
  Santa Cruz, CA
iD Tech Camps–University of Central
  Florida, Orlando, FL
iD Tech Camps–University of Denver,
  Denver, CO
iD Tech Camps–University of
  Houston, Houston, TX
iD Tech Camps–University of Miami,
  Coral Gables, FL
iD Tech Camps–University of
  Michigan, Ann Arbor, MI
iD Tech Camps–University of
  Minnesota, Minneapolis, MN
iD Tech Camps–University of North
  Carolina at Chapel Hill, Chapel
  Hill, NC
iD Tech Camps–University of
  Virginia, Charlottesville, VA
iD Tech Camps–University of
  Washington, Seattle, WA
iD Tech Camps–UT Austin, Austin,
  TX
iD Tech Camps–Vanderbilt
  University, Nashville, TN
iD Tech Camps–Vassar College,
  Poughkeepsie, NY
iD Tech Camps–Villanova University,
  Villanova, PA
iD Tech Camps–Virginia Tech,
  Blacksburg, VA
iD Tech Camps–Wake Forest
  University, Winston-Salem, NC
iD Tech Camps–Washington
  University in St. Louis, St. Louis,
  MO
Oxford Media School–Film, United
  Kingdom
Oxford Media School–Film Master
  Class, United Kingdom
Oxford Media School–Newsroom in
  Europe, United Kingdom
Oxford Media School–Newsroom in
  Europe, Master Class, United
  Kingdom
Stagedoor Manor Performing Arts
  Training Center/Theatre and
  Dance Camp, NY
Summerberg at Heidelberg College,
  OH
Tisch School of the Arts–International
  High School Program–Dublin,
  Ireland

Finnish Language/Literature
Center for Cultural Interchange–
Finland High School Abroad,
Finland

First Aid
ACADEMIC TREKS–Wilderness
Emergency Medicine, Belize

Fishing
TASC Canadian Wilderness Fishing
Camps, Canada

Flamenco
Spanish Language and Flamenco
Enforex–Granada, Spain
Spanish Language and Flamenco
Enforex–Madrid, Spain
Spanish Language and Flamenco
Enforex–Marbella, Spain
Spanish Language and Flamenco
Enforex–Sevilla, Spain

Fly Fishing
Wilderness Ventures–Yellowstone Fly
Fishing

Forensic Science
FivePoints, NY
Summerberg at Heidelberg College,
OH
University of Pennsylvania–Penn
Summer Science Academies, PA

French Language/Literature
AAVE–France Classique, France
Academic Study Associates–Nice,
France
Academic Study Associates–Royan,
France
ACADEMIC TREKS–French
Immersion in France, France
ACADEMIC TREKS–French
Immersion in the French West
Indies, Guadeloupe
AFS-USA–Homestay–France, France
Barat Foundation Summer Program
in Provence, France
Canoe Island French Camp, WA
Center for Cultural Interchange–
France High School Abroad,
France
Center for Cultural Interchange–
France Language School, France
Choate Rosemary Hall Summer in
Paris, France
Edu-Culture International (ECI)–Aix-
en-Provence/Gap Host Family
Immersion, France
Edu-Culture International (ECI)–
Lyon Host Family and Travel
Program, France

Edu-Culture International (ECI)–
Toulouse/Montpellier Host Family
Immersion, France
EF International Language School–
Nice, France
EF International Language School–
Paris, France
Excel at Paris/Provence, France
The Experiment in International
Living–France, Biking and
Homestay, France
The Experiment in International
Living–France, Five-Week Art and
Adventure in Provence, France
The Experiment in International
Living–France, Four-Week
Brittany Discovery, France
The Experiment in International
Living–France, Four-Week
Homestay and Photography,
France
The Experiment in International
Living–France, Four-Week
Homestay and Theatre, France
The Experiment in International
Living–France, Four-Week
Homestay and Travel–Southern
France and Northern Spain,
France
The Experiment in International
Living–France, Four-Week
Homestay and Travel through
Alps, France
The Experiment in International
Living–France, Homestay,
Language Training, and Cooking,
France
The Experiment in International
Living–France, Three-Week
Camargue Homestay, France
The Experiment in International
Living–France, Three-Week
Homestay and Travel–Borders,
France
The Experiment in International
Living–Switzerland French
Language Immersion, Homestay,
and Alpine Adventure, Switzerland
GLOBAL WORKS–Language
Immersion, Cultural Exchange and
Service–France-4 weeks, France
GLOBAL WORKS–Language
Immersion, Cultural Exchange and
Service–Martinique-4weeks,
Martinique
Les Elfes–International Summer/
Winter Camp, Switzerland
Putney Student Travel–Language
Learning–France, France
Rassias Programs–Arles, France,
France

Rassias Programs–Tours, France,
France
Service Learning in Paris, France
Summer Advantage Study Abroad–
Paris, France, France
Summer Study in Paris at The
Sorbonne, France
Taft Summer School Abroad–France,
France
TASIS French Language Program in
Château–d'Oex, Switzerland,
Switzerland
Westcoast Connection–French
Language and Touring, France

General Camp Activities
Alford Lake Camp, ME
Alford Lake Family Camp, ME
Applejack Teen Camp, NY
Brewster Academy Summer Session,
NH
Camp Airy, MD
Camp Berachah Ministries–Camps
and Conferences, WA
Camp Greenbrier for Boys, WV
Camp Holiday Trails, VA
Camp La Junta, TX
Camp Lincoln for Boys/Camp Lake
Hubert for Girls, MN
Camp Lincoln for Boys/Camp Lake
Hubert for Girls Family Camp,
MN
Camp Louise, MD
Camp Pacific's Recreational Camp,
CA
Camp Regis, NY
Camp Rio Vista for Boys, TX
Camp Sierra Vista for Girls, TX
Camp Treetops, NY
Canoe Island French Camp, WA
Cape Cod Sea Camps–Monomoy/
Wono, MA
Cheshire Academy Summer Program,
CT
Crossroads School–Summer
Educational Journey, CA
Darlington Summer Programs, GA
Eagle Hill School Summer Session,
MA
Enforex Residential Youth Summer
Camp–Granada, Spain
Enforex Residential Youth Summer
Camp–Guanajuato, Mexico, Mexico
Enforex Residential Youth Summer
Camp–Madrid, Spain
Enforex Residential Youth Summer
Camp–Marbella Albergue College,
Spain
Enforex Residential Youth Summer
Camp–Marbella Alboran College,
Spain

▶ GENERAL CAMP ACTIVITIES

Enforex Residential Youth Summer
Camp–Marbella Aleman College,
Spain
Enforex Residential Youth Summer
Camp–Salamanca, Spain
Enforex Residential Youth Summer
Camp–Valencia, Spain
Fenn School Summer Day Camp, MA
Forest Ridge Summer Program, WA
The Gow School Summer Program,
NY
Harker Summer Programs, CA
The Hun School of Princeton–
Summer Day Camp, NJ
International Summer Camp
Montana, Switzerland, Switzerland
Kamp Kohut, ME
Keewaydin Dunmore, VT
Killooleet, VT
Linden Hill Summer Program, MA
Lochearn Camp for Girls, VT
92nd Street Y Camps–Camp Bari Tov,
NY
92nd Street Y Camps–Camp Kesher,
PA
92nd Street Y Camps–Camp Tevah
for Science and Nature, NY
92nd Street Y Camps–Camp Tova,
NY
92nd Street Y Camps–Camp Yomi,
NY
92nd Street Y Camps–Trailblazers,
NY
Pine Island Camp, ME
Saint Thomas More School–Summer
Academic Camp, CT
Songadeewin of Keewaydin, VT
Southwestern Adventures–Arizona,
AZ
Tabor Academy Summer Program,
MA
Talisman Summer Camp, NC
TASIS Le Château des Enfants,
Switzerland
TASIS Middle School Program,
Switzerland
Valley Forge Military Academy
Summer Camp for Boys, PA
Valley Forge Military Academy
Summer Coed Day Camp, PA

Geology/Earth Science
University of Chicago–Stones and
Bones, WY

German Language/Literature
Center for Cultural Interchange–
Germany High School Abroad,
Germany
Center for Cultural Interchange–
Germany Language School,
Germany

EF International Language School–
Munich, Germany
The Experiment in International
Living–Germany, Four-Week
Homestay, Travel, Community
Service, Germany

Global Issues
International Leadership Program,
MD

Golf
Camp Lincoln for Boys/Camp Lake
Hubert for Girls Golf Camp, MN
Enforex Spanish and Golf, Spain
Westcoast Connection–California
Swing Junior Touring Golf Camp,
CA
Westcoast Connection–Florida Swing
Junior Touring Golf Camp, FL

Government and Politics
Choate Rosemary Hall John F.
Kennedy Institute in Government,
CT
The Experiment in International
Living–Poland, Homestay,
Community Service, and Travel,
Poland
Georgetown University American
Politics and Public Affairs, D.C.
Girls First, VA
International Leadership Program,
MD
Junior Statesmen Symposium on
California State Politics and
Government, CA
Junior Statesmen Symposium on Los
Angeles Politics and Government,
CA
Junior Statesmen Symposium on New
Jersey State Politics and
Government, NJ
Junior Statesmen Symposium on
Ohio State Politics and
Government, OH
Junior Statesmen Symposium on
Texas Politics and Leadership, TX
Junior Statesmen Symposium on
Washington State Politics and
Government, WA
National Student Leadership
Conference: U.S. Policy and
Politics, D.C.
World Affairs Seminar, WI

Government and Politics (Advanced Placement)
Junior Statesmen Summer School–
Georgetown University, D.C.
Junior Statesmen Summer School–
Princeton University, NJ

Junior Statesmen Summer School–
Stanford University, CA
Junior Statesmen Summer School–
Yale University, CT

Health Sciences
Milwaukee School of Engineering
(MSOE)–Focus on Nursing, WI

Hiking
AAVE–España Clásica, Spain
AAVE–Peru and Machu Picchu, Peru
ACADEMIC TREKS–French
Immersion in France, France
ACADEMIC TREKS–French
Immersion in the French West
Indies, Guadeloupe
ACADEMIC TREKS–Spanish
Immersion in Oaxaca, Mexico,
Mexico
ACTIONQUEST: Galapagos
Archipelago Expeditions, Ecuador
ACTIONQUEST: Leeward and
French Caribbean Island Voyages
BROADREACH Adventures Down
Under, Australia
BROADREACH Arc of the Caribbean
Sailing Adventure
BROADREACH Costa Rica
Experience, Costa Rica
BROADREACH Fiji Solomon Quest
BROADREACH Yucatan Adventure,
Mexico
Cheley Colorado Camps, CO
The Experiment in International
Living–France, Four-Week
Homestay and Travel–Southern
France and Northern Spain,
France
The Experiment in International
Living–Spain–The Road to
Santiago, Spain
The Experiment in International
Living–Switzerland French
Language Immersion, Homestay,
and Alpine Adventure, Switzerland
Keewaydin Dunmore, VT
Landmark Volunteers: New Mexico,
NM
RUSTIC PATHWAYS–CLIMBING
KILI, United Republic of Tanzania
Songadeewin of Keewaydin, VT
Wilderness Ventures–Yellowstone-
Teton Family Adventure, WY

History
Summer Advantage Study Abroad–
Cambridge University, United
Kingdom
Summer Advantage Study Abroad–
Granada, Spain, Spain
Summer Advantage Study Abroad–
Nanjing, China, China

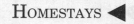
Summer Advantage Study Abroad–
Rome, Italy, Italy

Homestays
AAVE–España Clásica, Spain
AFS-USA–Community Service–
Argentina, Argentina
AFS-USA–Community Service–
Paraguay, Paraguay
AFS-USA–Homestay–Argentina,
Argentina
AFS-USA–Homestay–Chile, Chile
AFS-USA–Homestay–Ecuador,
Ecuador
AFS-USA–Homestay–Finland,
Finland
AFS-USA–Homestay–France, France
AFS-USA–Homestay Language
Study–Costa Rica, Costa Rica
AFS-USA–Homestay Language
Study–Egypt, Egypt
AFS-USA–Homestay Language
Study–Japan, Japan
AFS-USA–Homestay Language
Study–Latvia, Latvia
AFS-USA–Homestay Language
Study–Panama, Panama
AFS-USA–Homestay–Paraguay,
Paraguay
AFS-USA–Homestay Plus–Australia,
Australia
AFS-USA–Homestay Plus–Costa
Rica, Costa Rica
AFS-USA–Homestay Plus–Hungary,
Hungary
AFS-USA–Homestay Plus–Italy, Italy
AFS-USA–Homestay Plus–New
Zealand, New Zealand
AFS-USA–Homestay Plus–Panama,
Panama
AFS-USA–Homestay Plus–Paraguay
Soccer, Paraguay
AFS-USA–Homestay Plus–Spain,
Spain
AFS-USA–Homestay–Thailand,
Thailand
AFS-USA–Homestay–Turkey, Turkey
AFS-USA–Team Mission–Ghana,
Ghana
Center for Cultural Interchange–
Argentina Independent Homestay,
Argentina
Center for Cultural Interchange–
Brazil High School Abroad, Brazil
Center for Cultural Interchange–
Chile Independent Homestay,
Chile
Center for Cultural Interchange–
France Independent Homestay,
France

Center for Cultural Interchange–
Germany Independent Homestay,
Germany
Center for Cultural Interchange–
Ireland Independent Homestay
Program, Ireland
Center for Cultural Interchange–
Japan High School Abroad, Japan
Center for Cultural Interchange–
Spain Independent Homestay,
Spain
Center for Cultural Interchange–
United Kingdom Independent
Homestay, United Kingdom
Choate Rosemary Hall Summer in
Paris, France
Choate Rosemary Hall Summer in
Spain, Spain
Edu-Culture International (ECI)–Aix-
en-Provence/Gap Host Family
Immersion, France
Edu-Culture International (ECI)–
Andalusion Total Immersion, Spain
Edu-Culture International (ECI)–CPI
Costa Rica, Costa Rica
Edu-Culture International (ECI)–
Granada Homestay, Spain
Edu-Culture International (ECI)–
Granada Homestay or Dorm Plus
Southern Host Family Immersion,
Spain
Edu-Culture International (ECI)–
Granada-Nerja Homestay Combo,
Spain
Edu-Culture International (ECI)–
Lyon Host Family and Travel
Program, France
Edu-Culture International (ECI)–
Nerja Homestay Plus Southern
Host Family Immersion, Spain
Edu-Culture International (ECI)–
Nerja Homestay with Optional
Southern Host Family Immersion,
Spain
Edu-Culture International (ECI)–
Salamanca Dorm Plus Southern
Host Family Immersion, Spain
Edu-Culture International (ECI)–
Salamanca Homestay, Spain
Edu-Culture International (ECI)–
Salamanca Homestay Plus
Northern Host Family Immersion,
Spain
Edu-Culture International (ECI)–
Salamanca Homestay (Short
Version), Spain
Edu-Culture International (ECI)–San
Sebastian Homestay Plus Southern
Host Family Immersion, Spain
Edu-Culture International (ECI)–
Toulouse/Montpellier Host Family
Immersion, France

Enforex Homestay Program–Alicante,
Spain
Enforex Homestay Program–
Barcelona, Spain
Enforex Homestay Program–Granada,
Spain
Enforex Homestay Program–Madrid,
Spain
Enforex Homestay Program–Malaga,
Spain
Enforex Homestay Program–
Marbella, Spain
Enforex Homestay Program–
Salamanca, Spain
Enforex Homestay Program–Sevilla,
Spain
Enforex Homestay Program–Tenerife,
Spain
Enforex Homestay Program–Valencia,
Spain
The Experiment in International
Living–Argentina Homestay,
Community Service, and Outdoor
Ecological Program, Argentina
The Experiment in International
Living–Australia Homestay,
Australia
The Experiment in International
Living–Belize Homestay, Belize
The Experiment in International
Living–Botswana Homestay,
Botswana
The Experiment in International
Living–Brazil–Community Service
and Soccer, Brazil
The Experiment in International
Living–Brazil Homestay, Arts, and
Community Service, Brazil
The Experiment in International
Living–Chile North Homestay,
Community Service, Chile
The Experiment in International
Living–Chile South Homestay,
Chile
The Experiment in International
Living–China North and East
Homestay, China
The Experiment in International
Living–China South and West
Homestay, China
The Experiment in International
Living–Costa Rica Homestay,
Costa Rica
The Experiment in International
Living–Ecuador Homestay,
Ecuador
The Experiment in International
Living–France, Biking and
Homestay, France
The Experiment in International
Living–France, Five-Week Art and
Adventure in Provence, France

▶ HOMESTAYS

The Experiment in International Living–France, Four-Week Brittany Discovery, France

The Experiment in International Living–France, Four-Week Homestay and Photography, France

The Experiment in International Living–France, Four-Week Homestay and Theatre, France

The Experiment in International Living–France, Four-Week Homestay and Travel–Southern France and Northern Spain, France

The Experiment in International Living–France, Four-Week Homestay and Travel through Alps, France

The Experiment in International Living–France, Homestay, Language Training, and Cooking, France

The Experiment in International Living–France, Three-Week Camargue Homestay, France

The Experiment in International Living–France, Three-Week Homestay and Travel–Borders, France

The Experiment in International Living–Germany, Four-Week Homestay, Travel, Community Service, Germany

The Experiment in International Living–Ghana Homestay, Ghana

The Experiment in International Living–Italy Biodiversity, Cooking, and Culture, Italy

The Experiment in International Living–Italy Homestay, Language, Culture, and Travel, Italy

The Experiment in International Living–Japan Homestay, Japan

The Experiment in International Living–Mexico–Community Service, Travel, and Homestay, Mexico

The Experiment in International Living–Mexico Cooking and Culture, Mexico

The Experiment in International Living–Mexico Homestay, Sustainable Development and Fair Trade, Mexico

The Experiment in International Living–Mexico–Mayan Arts and Culture, Mexico

The Experiment in International Living–Morocco Four-Week Arts and Culture Program, Morocco

The Experiment in International Living–Navajo Nation, NM

The Experiment in International Living–New Zealand Homestay, New Zealand

The Experiment in International Living–Poland, Homestay, Community Service, and Travel, Poland

The Experiment in International Living–Scotland, United Kingdom

The Experiment in International Living–South Africa Homestay and Community Service, South Africa

The Experiment in International Living–Spain, Five-Week Homestay, Language Immersion, Spain

The Experiment in International Living–Spain, Four-Week Language Training, Travel, and Homestay, Spain

The Experiment in International Living–Spain–Multiculturalism and Service, Spain

The Experiment in International Living–Spain–Spanish Arts and Culture, Spain

The Experiment in International Living–Spain–The Road to Santiago, Spain

The Experiment in International Living–Spanish Culture and Exploration, Spain

The Experiment in International Living–Switzerland French Language Immersion, Homestay, and Alpine Adventure, Switzerland

The Experiment in International Living–Thailand Homestay, Thailand

The Experiment in International Living–Turkey Homestay, Community Service, and Travel, Turkey

The Experiment in International Living–United Kingdom Filmmaking Program and Homestay, United Kingdom

The Experiment in International Living–United Kingdom Theatre Program, United Kingdom

GLOBAL WORKS–Language Immersion, Cultural Exchange and Service–Ecuador and the Galapagos-4 weeks, Ecuador

GLOBAL WORKS–Language Immersion, Cultural Exchange and Service–France-4 weeks, France

GLOBAL WORKS–Language Immersion, Cultural Exchange and Service–Peru, Peru

GLOBAL WORKS–Language Immersion, Cultural Exchange and Service–Spain-4 weeks, Spain

Rassias Programs–Arles, France, France

Rassias Programs–China, China

Rassias Programs–Gijón, Spain, Spain

Rassias Programs–Pontevedra, Spain, Spain

Rassias Programs–Segovia, Spain, Spain

Rassias Programs–Tours, France, France

Taft Summer School Abroad–France, France

Taft Summer School Abroad–Spain, Spain

Horseback Riding

AAVE–Boot/Saddle/Paddle

AAVE–Colorado Discovery, CO

Cheley Colorado Camps, CO

Clearwater Camp for Girls, WI

Teton Valley Ranch Camp–Boys Camp, WY

Teton Valley Ranch Camp–Girls Camp, WY

Treetops eXpeditions–Horseback Riding

Humanities

The Renaissance Scholar Program, TX

University of Chicago–Insight, IL

Ice Climbing

AAVE–Ultimate Alaska, AK

Adventure Treks–Alaska Adventures, AK

Ice Hockey

Tabor Hockey School, MA

Intercultural Studies

AAVE–France Classique, France

Barat Foundation Summer Program in Provence, France

Excel at Oxford/Tuscany

Global Leadership Adventures–Cape Town: Community Service and Leadership, South Africa

GLOBAL WORKS–Cultural Exchange and Service–New Zealand and Fiji Islands-4 weeks

GLOBAL WORKS–Cultural Exchange–Fiji Islands-4 weeks, Fiji

The Putney School Summer Program for International Education (ESL), VT

Studies Abroad for Global Education (SAGE), Summer SAGE Program, India
University of Chicago–The Traveling Academy, Greece
Weissman Teen Tours–European Experience
Wilderness Ventures–European Alps

International Relations
Georgetown University International Relations Program for High School Students, D.C.
National Student Leadership Conference: Globalization and International Business–Washington D.C.
National Student Leadership Conference: International Diplomacy–Washington, D.C.
Summer Advantage Study Abroad–London, United Kingdom

Internships
Career Explorations–Boston, MA
Career Explorations–New York, NY
IEI Student Travel–Internship Program in London, United Kingdom
Internship Connection, MA

Italian Language/Literature
Center for Cultural Interchange–Italy High School Abroad, Italy
Center for Cultural Interchange–Italy Language School, Italy
EF International Language School–Rome, Italy
The Experiment in International Living–Italy Biodiversity, Cooking, and Culture, Italy
The Experiment in International Living–Italy Homestay, Language, Culture, and Travel, Italy
Humanities Spring in Assisi, Italy
Summer Advantage Study Abroad–Rome, Italy, Italy

Japanese Language/Literature
AFS-USA–Homestay Language Study–Japan, Japan
The Experiment in International Living–Japan Homestay, Japan

Jewish Studies
92nd Street Y Camps–The TIYUL

Journalism
Georgetown University Journalism Workshop for High School Students, D.C.
IEI–Print and Broadcast Journalism, United Kingdom

Junior Statesmen Symposium on Los Angeles Politics and Government, CA
National Student Leadership Conference: Journalism and Mass Communication, D.C.
Oxford Media School–Newsroom in Europe, United Kingdom
Oxford Media School–Newsroom in Europe, Master Class, United Kingdom

Kayaking
Mad River Glen Naturalist Adventure Camp, VT

Language Study
Choate Rosemary Hall Immersion Program, CT
GLOBAL WORKS–Language Immersion, Cultural Exchange and Service–Yucatan Peninsula, Mexico-4 weeks, Mexico
Summerberg at Heidelberg College, OH
Visions–Dominican Republic, Dominican Republic
Visions–Ecuador, Ecuador
Visions–Guadeloupe, Guadeloupe
Visions–Peru, Peru

Leadership Training
ACTIONQUEST: PADI Divemaster Voyages, British Virgin Islands
Barnard's Summer in New York City: A Pre-College Program, NY
Barnard's Summer in New York City: One-Week Liberal Arts Intensive, NY
Barnard's Summer in New York City: Young Women's Leadership Institute, NY
BROADREACH Arc of the Caribbean Sailing Adventure
Camp Greenbrier for Boys, WV
Duke TIP Institutes, NC
Future Leader Camp, VT
Global Leadership Adventures–Brazil: Community Service and Leadership, Brazil
Global Leadership Adventures–Costa Rica: Community Service and Leadership, Costa Rica
Global Leadership Adventures–Ghana: Community Service and Leadership, Ghana
Global Leadership Adventures–India: Community Service and Leadership, India
International Leadership Program, MD
Junior Statesmen Summer School–Princeton University, NJ

Junior Statesmen Symposium on California State Politics and Government, CA
Junior Statesmen Symposium on New Jersey State Politics and Government, NJ
Junior Statesmen Symposium on Ohio State Politics and Government, OH
Junior Statesmen Symposium on Texas Politics and Leadership, TX
Junior Statesmen Symposium on Washington State Politics and Government, WA
National Student Leadership Conference: Engineering–San Francisco, CA
National Student Leadership Conference: Engineering–Washington D.C., MD
National Student Leadership Conference: Entrepreneurship and Business–New York City, NY
National Student Leadership Conference: Entrepreneurship and Business–Washington, D.C.
National Student Leadership Conference: Forensic Science, D.C.
National Student Leadership Conference: Globalization and International Business–Study Abroad
National Student Leadership Conference: Globalization and International Business–Washington, D.C.
National Student Leadership Conference: Inside the Arts–New York City, NY
National Student Leadership Conference: Intelligence and National Security, D.C.
National Student Leadership Conference: International Diplomacy–Washington, D.C.
National Student Leadership Conference: Journalism and Mass Communication, D.C.
National Student Leadership Conference: Law and Advocacy–San Francisco, CA
National Student Leadership Conference: Law and Advocacy–Washington, D.C.
National Student Leadership Conference: Mastering Leadership, MD
National Student Leadership Conference: Medicine and Health Care–San Francisco, CA

National Student Leadership Conference: Medicine and Health Care–Washington D.C., MD

National Student Leadership Conference: State Leadership Workshops, IL

National Student Leadership Conference: U.S. Policy and Politics, D.C.

The Sarah Porter Leadership Institute, CT

Summer Action–Take the Lead, MA

Summer in Switzerland, Switzerland

Wilderness Ventures–Alaska College Leadership, AK

Wilderness Ventures–Washington Alpine, WA

Wilderness Ventures–Washington Mountaineering, WA

Wilderness Ventures–Wyoming Mountaineering, WY

Marine Studies

ACADEMIC TREKS–Caribbean Marine Reserves

ACADEMIC TREKS–Dolphin Studies in Belize, Belize

ACADEMIC TREKS–Pacific Whale Treks, Canada

ACADEMIC TREKS–Sea Turtle Studies, Costa Rica

ACADEMIC TREKS–Shark Studies in Fiji, Fiji

Acadia Institute of Oceanography, ME

ACTIONQUEST: Advanced PADI Scuba Certification and Specialty Voyages, British Virgin Islands

ACTIONQUEST: Junior Advanced Scuba with Marine Biology, British Virgin Islands

ACTIONQUEST: Tropical Marine Biology Voyages, British Virgin Islands

BROADREACH Adventures in Scuba and Sailing–Underwater Discoveries

BROADREACH Adventures in the Grenadines–Advanced Scuba, Saint Vincent and The Grenadines

BROADREACH Adventures in the Windward Islands–Advanced Scuba

BROADREACH Adventures Underwater–Advanced Scuba

BROADREACH Baja Extreme–Scuba Adventure, Mexico

BROADREACH Honduras Eco-Adventure, Honduras

BROADREACH Marine Biology Accredited, Bahamas

BROADREACH Yucatan Adventure, Mexico

Science Program for High School Girls, CA

Science Program for Middle School Boys on Catalina, CA

Science Program for Middle School Girls on Catalina, CA

Seacamp, FL

Martial Arts

RUSTIC PATHWAYS–THE ART OF MUAY THAI, Thailand

Mathematics

Choate Rosemary Hall Math and Science Workshops, CT

Choate Rosemary Hall Math/Science Institute for Girls–CONNECT, CT

Elite Educational Institute Elementary Enrichment, CA

Elite Educational Institute Elementary Enrichment–Korea, Republic of Korea

Elite Educational Institute–University of Oklahoma College Courses, CA

Georgetown University College Prep Program, D.C.

Johns Hopkins University Zanvyl Krieger School of Arts and Sciences Summer Programs, MD

Michigan Technological University American Indian Workshop, MI

Michigan Technological University Explorations in Engineering Workshop, MI

Michigan Technological University Women in Engineering Workshop, MI

Miss Porter's School Summer Challenge, CT

Mount Holyoke College SEARCH (Summer Explorations and Research Collaborations for High School Girls) Program, MA

Mount Holyoke College SummerMath Program, MA

Rumsey Hall School Summer Session, CT

University of Vermont Summer Engineering Institute for High School Students, VT

Medicine

National Student Leadership Conference: Medicine and Health Care–San Francisco, CA

National Student Leadership Conference: Medicine and Health Care–Washington D.C., MD

Mountain Biking

AAVE–Ultimate Hawaii, HI

Adventure Treks–Montana Adventures, MT

Wilderness Ventures–Colorado/Utah Mountain Bike

Mountaineering

Adventure Treks–Wilderness Adventures

RUSTIC PATHWAYS–CLIMBING KILI, United Republic of Tanzania

Wilderness Ventures–Cascade-Olympic, WA

Wilderness Ventures–European Alps

Wilderness Ventures–Northwest

Wilderness Ventures–Washington Mountaineering, WA

Music

Appel Farm Summer Arts Camp, NJ

Belvoir Terrace, MA

Boston University Tanglewood Institute, MA

Buck's Rock Performing and Creative Arts Camp, CT

Camp Encore-Coda for a Great Summer of Music, Sports, and Friends, ME

Eastern U.S. Music Camp, Inc. at Colgate University, NY

Idyllwild Arts Summer Program–Children's Center, CA

Idyllwild Arts Summer Program–Family Week, CA

Idyllwild Arts Summer Program–Junior Artists' Center, CA

Idyllwild Arts Summer Program–Youth Arts Center, CA

Spoleto Study Abroad, Italy

summer@rectory, CT

UCLA Summer Experience: Institutes, CA

Music (Folk)

Summer Advantage Study Abroad–Salamanca, Spain, Spain

Music (Instrumental)

Valley Forge Military Academy Summer Band Camp, PA

Music (Jazz)

Atelier des Arts, Switzerland

Crossroads School–Jazz Workshop, CA

Music (Piano)

Ithaca College Summer Piano Institute, NY

Musical Productions

University of Pennsylvania–Penn Summer Theatre Workshop, PA

Musical Theater
Summer Theatre Institute–NYC, 2008, NY

Native American Culture
The Experiment in International Living–Navajo Nation, NM
Landmark Volunteers: Arizona, AZ

Natural Resource Management
Landmark Volunteers: Colorado, CO
Landmark Volunteers: Montana, MT

Nature Study
ACTIONQUEST: Galapagos Archipelago Expeditions, Ecuador
Edu-Culture International (ECI)–Grecia Costa Rica, Costa Rica
The Experiment in International Living–New Zealand Homestay, New Zealand
LIFEWORKS with the Galapagos Islands' National Parks, Ecuador
Mad River Glen Naturalist Adventure Camp, VT
92nd Street Y Camps–Camp Tevah for Science and Nature, NY

Nautical Skills
ACTIONQUEST: British Virgin Islands–Sailing and Scuba Voyages, British Virgin Islands
ACTIONQUEST: British Virgin Islands-Sailing Voyages, British Virgin Islands
ACTIONQUEST: Mediterranean Sailing Voyage

Norwegian Language/Literature
Center for Cultural Interchange–Norway High School Abroad, Norway

Oceanography
Science Program for High School Girls, CA
Science Program for Middle School Boys on Catalina, CA
Science Program for Middle School Girls on Catalina, CA

Outdoor Adventure
AAVE–Bold Europe
AAVE–Wild Isles
AFS-USA–Homestay Plus–Australia, Australia
AFS-USA–Homestay Plus–New Zealand, New Zealand
Center for Cultural Interchange–Spain Sports and Language Camp, Spain

Fenn School Summer Day Camp, MA
Future Leader Camp, VT
GLOBAL WORKS–Cultural Exchange and Service–Costa Rica-3 weeks, Costa Rica
GLOBAL WORKS–Cultural Exchange and Service–Ireland-4 weeks, Ireland
GLOBAL WORKS–Cultural Exchange and Service–Puerto Rico-2 or 4 weeks, Puerto Rico
GLOBAL WORKS–Language Immersion, Cultural Exchange and Service–Argentina, Argentina
GLOBAL WORKS–Language Immersion, Cultural Exchange and Service–Costa Rica, Costa Rica
GLOBAL WORKS–Language Immersion, Cultural Exchange and Service–Martinique-4weeks, Martinique
GLOBAL WORKS–Language Immersion, Cultural Exchange and Service–Mexico-3 weeks, Mexico
GLOBAL WORKS–Language Immersion, Cultural Exchange and Service–Panama/Costa Rica
GLOBAL WORKS–Language Immersion, Cultural Exchange and Service–Yucatan Peninsula, Mexico-4 weeks, Mexico
Michigan Technological University Summer Youth Program, MI
Putney Student Travel–Community Service–Alaska, AK
Putney Student Travel–Cultural Exploration–Australia, New Zealand, and Fiji
Putney Student Travel–Cultural Exploration–Switzerland, Italy, France, and Holland
Rein Teen Tours–California Caper
Rein Teen Tours–Crossroads
Rein Teen Tours–Eastern Adventure
Rein Teen Tours–Grand Adventure
Rein Teen Tours–Hawaiian/Alaskan Adventure
Rein Teen Tours–Hawaiian Caper
Rein Teen Tours–Western Adventure
RUSTIC PATHWAYS–ASIAN PACIFIC EXTREME
RUSTIC PATHWAYS–BIG FIJI EXPLORER, Fiji
RUSTIC PATHWAYS–CLIMBING KILI, United Republic of Tanzania
RUSTIC PATHWAYS–COSTA RICA ADVENTURER, Costa Rica
RUSTIC PATHWAYS–EDGE OF THE MAP EXTREME
RUSTIC PATHWAYS–ELEPHANTS & AMAZING THAILAND, Thailand

RUSTIC PATHWAYS–HILL TRIBE TREKKING ADVENTURE, Thailand
RUSTIC PATHWAYS–INDIAN HIMALAYA TRAVELER, India
RUSTIC PATHWAYS–ISLAND HOPPING AND DIVING–THAILAND, Thailand
RUSTIC PATHWAYS–NEW ZEALAND NORTH ISLAND ADVENTURE, New Zealand
RUSTIC PATHWAYS–SERVICE LEARNING EXTREME
RUSTIC PATHWAYS–SOCCER AND SERVICE IN THAILAND, Thailand
RUSTIC PATHWAYS–SOUTH PACIFIC EXTREME
RUSTIC PATHWAYS–SUN, SAND & INTERNATIONAL SERVICE–FIJI, Fiji
RUSTIC PATHWAYS–SYDNEY, REEF & RAINFOREST, Australia
RUSTIC PATHWAYS–THE AMAZING THAILAND ADVENTURE, Thailand
RUSTIC PATHWAYS–THE WONDERS & RICHES OF SOUTHEAST ASIA
RUSTIC PATHWAYS–ULTIMATE JUNGLE ADVENTURE–COSTA RICA, Costa Rica
RUSTIC PATHWAYS–WORLD SERVICE EXTREME
Studies Abroad for Global Education (SAGE), Summer SAGE Program, India
Visions Alaska, AK
Visions–British Virgin Islands, British Virgin Islands
Visions–Costa Rica, Costa Rica
Visions–Dominica, Dominica
Visions–Mississippi, MS
Visions–Montana, MT
Weissman Teen Tours–U.S. and Western Canada, 40 Days
Weissman Teen Tours–U.S. and Western Canada, 30 Days
Westcoast Connection–American Voyageur
Westcoast Connection–Australian Outback Plus Hawaii
Westcoast Connection–Californian Extravaganza
Westcoast Connection–California Sprint, CA
Westcoast Connection–Community Connections Alaska, AK
Westcoast Connection–Community Service Belize, Belize
Westcoast Connection–Community Service Costa Rica, Costa Rica

▶ OUTDOOR ADVENTURE

Westcoast Connection–Community
Service–Habitat for Humanity, WA
Westcoast Connection–Community
Service Hawaii, HI
Westcoast Connection–Hawaiian
Spirit
Westcoast Connection/On Tour–
Australian Outback, Australia
Westcoast Connection–Spanish in
Costa Rica, Costa Rica
Westcoast Connection Travel–
Adventure California, CA
Westcoast Connection Travel–
California and the Canyons
Westcoast Connection Travel–
Canadian Mountain Magic,
Canada
Westcoast Connection Travel–
Eastcoast Encounter
Westcoast Connection Travel–Great
West Challenge
Westcoast Connection Travel–
Northwestern Odyssey
Westcoast Connection Travel–Quebec
Adventure, Canada
Westcoast Connection Travel–Western
Canadian Adventure, Canada
Westcoast Connection–U.S. Explorer

Pack Animal Trips
Teton Valley Ranch Camp–Boys
Camp, WY
Teton Valley Ranch Camp–Girls
Camp, WY

Painting
Oxbow Summer Art Camp, CA

Peace Education
World Affairs Seminar, WI

Performing Arts
Eastern U.S. Music Camp, Inc. at
Colgate University, NY
Perry-Mansfield Performing Arts
School and Camp, CO
The Putney School Summer Arts
Program, VT
World Horizons International–
Connecticut, CT
Wyoming Seminary–Sem Summer
2008, PA

Photography
The Experiment in International
Living–Argentina Visual Arts,
Photography, and Service,
Argentina
The Experiment in International
Living–France, Four-Week
Homestay and Photography,
France

IEI–Photography Plus Programme,
United Kingdom
RUSTIC PATHWAYS–
INTRODUCTION TO
PHOTOGRAPHY–SNAPSHOTS
IN THE LAND OF SMILES
RUSTIC PATHWAYS–OFF THE MAP
BURMA AND CAMBODIA
RUSTIC PATHWAYS–
PHOTOGRAPHY ADVENTURE
IN THAILAND AND ANGKOR
WAT
RUSTIC PATHWAYS–
PHOTOGRAPHY ADVENTURE
IN THAILAND AND BURMA
RUSTIC PATHWAYS–
PHOTOGRAPHY ADVENTURE
IN THAILAND AND INDIA
RUSTIC PATHWAYS–
PHOTOGRAPHY ADVENTURE
IN THAILAND AND VIETNAM
University of Pennsylvania–Penn
Summer Art and Architecture
Studios, PA
World Horizons International–United
Kingdom

Photojournalism
Georgetown University Journalism
Workshop for High School
Students, D.C.

Physical Fitness
Camp California Fitness, CA

Physics
University of Pennsylvania–Penn
Summer Science Academies, PA

Piano
Ithaca College Summer Piano
Institute, NY

Playwriting
Choate Rosemary Hall Summer Arts
Conservatory–Playwriting, CT
The Putney School Summer Writing
Program, VT
Summer Theatre Institute–NYC,
2008, NY

Precollege Program
Barnard's Summer in New York City:
A Pre-College Program, NY
Barnard's Summer in New York City:
One-Week Liberal Arts Intensive,
NY
Bryn Mawr College–Science for
College, PA
Bryn Mawr College–Writing for
College, PA
Cambridge College Programme,
United Kingdom

Colorado College Summer Session,
CO
Cornell University Summer College
Programs for High School
Students, NY
Duke University PreCollege Program,
NC
Ithaca College Summer College for
High School Students:
Minicourses, NY
Ithaca College Summer College for
High School Students: Session II,
NY
MIT MITES (Minority Introduction to
Engineering and Science), MA
Northwestern University's College
Preparation Program, IL
Pre-College Summer Institute, The
University of the Arts, PA
The Renaissance Scholar Program,
TX
Skidmore College–Pre-College
Program in the Liberal & Studio
Arts for High School Students, NY
Southwestern Adventures–California,
CA
Stanford University High School
Summer College, CA
The Summer Institute for the Gifted
at Amherst College, MA
The Summer Institute for the Gifted
at Bryn Mawr College, PA
The Summer Institute for the Gifted
at Emory University, GA
The Summer Institute for the Gifted
at Fairfield University, CT
The Summer Institute for the Gifted
at Manhattanville College, NY
The Summer Institute for the Gifted
at Moorestown Friends School, NJ
The Summer Institute for the Gifted
at Princeton University, NJ
The Summer Institute for the Gifted
at UCLA, CA
The Summer Institute for the Gifted
at University of California,
Berkeley, CA
The Summer Institute for the Gifted
at University of Michigan, Ann
Arbor, MI
The Summer Institute for the Gifted
at University of Texas, Austin, TX
The Summer Institute for the Gifted
at Vassar College, NY
Summer Study at Penn State, PA
Summer Study at The University of
Colorado at Boulder, CO
Summer Study in Paris at The
Sorbonne, France
Syracuse University Summer College,
NY

University of Chicago–Research in the Biological Sciences, IL

University of Chicago–Summer Quarter for High School Students, IL

University of Maryland Young Scholars Program, MD

University of Miami Summer Scholar Programs, FL

University of Pennsylvania–Pre-College Program, PA

Washington University High School Summer Scholars Program, MO

Prelaw

Junior Statesmen Summer School–Georgetown University, D.C.

Junior Statesmen Summer School–Yale University, CT

National Student Leadership Conference: Law and Advocacy–San Francisco, CA

National Student Leadership Conference: Law and Advocacy–Washington, D.C.

Rafting

AAVE–Africa

AAVE–Bold West

AAVE–Boot/Saddle/Paddle

AAVE–Colorado Discovery, CO

AAVE–Peru and Machu Picchu, Peru

AAVE–Rock & Rapid

Wilderness Ventures–Alaska Southcentral, AK

Wilderness Ventures–Alaska Southeast, AK

Wilderness Ventures–Costa Rica/Belize

Wilderness Ventures–Costa Rica Service, Costa Rica

Wilderness Ventures–Costa Rica Surfing, Costa Rica

Wilderness Ventures–Pacific Northwest

Wilderness Ventures–Peru Community Service, Peru

Wilderness Ventures–Southwest Community Service

Reading

Choate Rosemary Hall Beginning Writers Workshop, CT

Choate Rosemary Hall English Language Institute, CT

Choate Rosemary Hall English Language Institute/Focus Program, CT

Choate Rosemary Hall Writing Project, CT

Dunnabeck at Kildonan, NY

Elite Educational Institute Elementary Enrichment, CA

Elite Educational Institute Elementary Enrichment–Korea, Republic of Korea

Elite Educational Institute Junior High/PSAT Program, CA

Elite Educational Institute Junior High/PSAT Program–Korea, Republic of Korea

Landmark School Summer Academic Program, MA

Salisbury Summer School, CT

Robotics

Cybercamps–Bellevue Community College, WA

Cybercamps–Towson University, MD

iD Tech Camps–Arizona State University, Tempe, AZ

iD Tech Camps–Brown University, Providence, RI

iD Tech Camps–Cal Lutheran University, Thousand Oaks, CA

iD Tech Camps–Carnegie Mellon University, Pittsburgh, PA

iD Tech Camps–Case Western Reserve University, Cleveland, OH

iD Tech Camps–College of William and Mary, Williamsburg, VA

iD Tech Camps–Colorado College, Colorado Springs, CO

iD Tech Camps–Columbia University, New York, NY

iD Tech Camps–Emory University, Atlanta, GA

iD Tech Camps–Fordham University, Bronx, NY

iD Tech Camps–Georgetown University, Washington, D.C.

iD Tech Camps–Lake Forest College, Evanston, IL

iD Tech Camps–Merrimack College, North Andover, MA

iD Tech Camps–MIT, Cambridge, MA

iD Tech Camps–Northwestern University, Chicago, IL

iD Tech Camps–Pepperdine University, Malibu, CA

iD Tech Camps–Rider University, Lawrenceville, NJ

iD Tech Camps–Sacred Heart University, Fairfield, CT

iD Tech Camps–St. Mary's College of California, Moraga, CA

iD Tech Camps–Santa Clara University, Santa Clara, CA

iD Tech Camps–Smith College, Northampton, MA

iD Tech Camps–Southern Methodist University, Dallas, TX

iD Tech Camps–Stanford University, Palo Alto, CA

iD Tech Camps–Tiger Woods Learning Center, Anaheim, CA

iD Tech Camps–UC Berkeley, Berkeley, CA

iD Tech Camps–UC Davis, Davis, CA

iD Tech Camps–UC Irvine, Irvine, CA

iD Tech Camps–UCLA, Westwood, CA

iD Tech Camps–UC San Diego, La Jolla, CA

iD Tech Camps–UC Santa Cruz, Santa Cruz, CA

iD Tech Camps–University of Central Florida, Orlando, FL

iD Tech Camps–University of Denver, Denver, CO

iD Tech Camps–University of Houston, Houston, TX

iD Tech Camps–University of Miami, Coral Gables, FL

iD Tech Camps–University of Michigan, Ann Arbor, MI

iD Tech Camps–University of Minnesota, Minneapolis, MN

iD Tech Camps–University of North Carolina at Chapel Hill, Chapel Hill, NC

iD Tech Camps–University of Virginia, Charlottesville, VA

iD Tech Camps–University of Washington, Seattle, WA

iD Tech Camps–UT Austin, Austin, TX

iD Tech Camps–Vanderbilt University, Nashville, TN

iD Tech Camps–Vassar College, Poughkeepsie, NY

iD Tech Camps–Villanova University, Villanova, PA

iD Tech Camps–Virginia Tech, Blacksburg, VA

iD Tech Camps–Wake Forest University, Winston-Salem, NC

iD Tech Camps–Washington University in St. Louis, St. Louis, MO

Rock Climbing

AAVE–Bold West

AAVE–Colorado Discovery, CO

AAVE–Rock & Rapid

AAVE–Wild Coast Discovery

Mad River Glen Naturalist Adventure Camp, VT

Wilderness Ventures–Grand Teton, WY

Wilderness Ventures–Great Divide

Wilderness Ventures–High Sierra, CA

Wilderness Ventures–Jackson Hole, WY

Wilderness Ventures–Oregon, OR

Wilderness Ventures–Teton Crest

► ROCK CLIMBING

Wilderness Ventures–Wyoming Mountaineering, WY

Wilderness Ventures–Yellowstone/ Teton Adventure, WY

Russian Language/Literature

AFS-USA–Homestay Language Study–Latvia, Latvia

Summer Advantage Study Abroad– St. Petersburg, Russia, Russian Federation

Safari

AAVE–Africa

BROADREACH Red Sea Scuba Adventure, Egypt

RUSTIC PATHWAYS–SERVICE AND SAFARI IN AFRICA, United Republic of Tanzania

Sailing

AAVE–Sail Dive Greece, Greece

ACTIONQUEST: Advanced PADI Scuba Certification and Specialty Voyages, British Virgin Islands

ACTIONQUEST: Australian and Great Barrier Reef Adventures, Australia

ACTIONQUEST: British Virgin Islands–Sailing and Scuba Voyages, British Virgin Islands

ACTIONQUEST: British Virgin Islands-Sailing Voyages, British Virgin Islands

ACTIONQUEST: Junior Advanced Scuba with Marine Biology, British Virgin Islands

ACTIONQUEST: Leeward and French Caribbean Island Voyages

ACTIONQUEST: Mediterranean Sailing Voyage

ACTIONQUEST: PADI Divemaster Voyages, British Virgin Islands

ACTIONQUEST: Rescue Diving Voyages, British Virgin Islands

ACTIONQUEST: Tahiti and French Polynesian Island Voyages, French Polynesia

ACTIONQUEST: Tropical Marine Biology Voyages, British Virgin Islands

Adventure Treks–California Adventures, CA

Adventure Treks–Oregon Adventures, OR

BROADREACH Adventures in Scuba and Sailing–Underwater Discoveries

BROADREACH Adventures in the Grenadines–Advanced Scuba, Saint Vincent and The Grenadines

BROADREACH Adventures in the Windward Islands–Advanced Scuba

BROADREACH Adventures Underwater–Advanced Scuba

BROADREACH Arc of the Caribbean Sailing Adventure

Cape Cod Sea Camps–Monomoy/ Wono, MA

Clearwater Camp for Girls, WI

LIFEWORKS with the British Virgin Islands Marine Parks and Conservation Department, British Virgin Islands

Putney Student Travel–Cultural Exploration–Australia, New Zealand, and Fiji

RUSTIC PATHWAYS–ESCAPE TO FIJI, Fiji

Treetops eXpeditions–Sailing and Marine Ecology, FL

Westcoast Connection–Belize and Costa Rica Water Adventure

Wilderness Ventures–Fiji Community Service, Fiji

Wilderness Ventures–Hawaii, HI

Wilderness Ventures–Tahiti, Fiji, and New Zealand

SAT/ACT Preparation

Academic Study Associates–ASA at the University of California, Berkeley, CA

Academic Study Associates–ASA at the University of Massachusetts Amherst, MA

The Cambridge Experience, United Kingdom

College InSight, PA

Elite Educational Institute Junior High/PSAT Program, CA

Elite Educational Institute Junior High/PSAT Program–Korea, Republic of Korea

Elite Educational Institute SAT and Subject Test Preparation, CA

Elite Educational Institute SAT Bootcamp–Korea, Republic of Korea

Elite Educational Institute SAT Preparation–Korea, Republic of Korea

Elite Educational Institute SAT Summer Bootcamp, CA

The Oxford Experience, United Kingdom

Science (General)

Bryn Mawr College–Science for College, PA

Choate Rosemary Hall Math and Science Workshops, CT

Choate Rosemary Hall Math/Science Institute for Girls–CONNECT, CT

Duke Action: Science Camp for Young Women, NC

Frontiers Program, MA

Ithaca College Summer College for High School Students: Session I, NY

Johns Hopkins University Zanvyl Krieger School of Arts and Sciences Summer Programs, MD

Michigan Technological University Explorations in Engineering Workshop, MI

Michigan Technological University Women in Engineering Workshop, MI

Miss Porter's School Summer Challenge, CT

MIT MITES (Minority Introduction to Engineering and Science), MA

92nd Street Y Camps–Camp Tevah for Science and Nature, NY

Science Program for High School Girls, CA

Science Program for Middle School Boys on Catalina, CA

Science Program for Middle School Girls on Catalina, CA

Smith College Summer Science and Engineering Program, MA

Summer@Rensselaer, NY

University of Connecticut Mentor Connection, CT

Worcester Polytechnic Institute– Launch, MA

Screenwriting

Choate Rosemary Hall Summer Arts Conservatory–Playwriting, CT

Scuba Diving

AAVE–Australia, Australia

AAVE–Sail Dive Greece, Greece

AAVE–Surf Scuba Safari, Mexico

ACADEMIC TREKS–Caribbean Marine Reserves

ACADEMIC TREKS–Dolphin Studies in Belize, Belize

ACADEMIC TREKS–Shark Studies in Fiji, Fiji

ACADEMIC TREKS–Shipwrecks and Underwater Archaeology in Bermuda, Bermuda

ACTIONQUEST: Advanced PADI Scuba Certification and Specialty Voyages, British Virgin Islands

ACTIONQUEST: Australian and Great Barrier Reef Adventures, Australia

ACTIONQUEST: British Virgin Islands–Sailing and Scuba Voyages, British Virgin Islands

ACTIONQUEST: Junior Advanced Scuba with Marine Biology, British Virgin Islands

ACTIONQUEST: PADI Divemaster Voyages, British Virgin Islands

ACTIONQUEST: Rescue Diving Voyages, British Virgin Islands

ACTIONQUEST: Tropical Marine Biology Voyages, British Virgin Islands

BROADREACH Adventures Down Under, Australia

BROADREACH Adventures in Scuba and Sailing–Underwater Discoveries

BROADREACH Adventures in the Grenadines–Advanced Scuba, Saint Vincent and The Grenadines

BROADREACH Adventures in the Windward Islands–Advanced Scuba

BROADREACH Adventures Underwater–Advanced Scuba

BROADREACH Baja Extreme–Scuba Adventure, Mexico

BROADREACH Fiji Solomon Quest

BROADREACH Honduras Eco-Adventure, Honduras

BROADREACH Marine Biology Accredited, Bahamas

BROADREACH Red Sea Scuba Adventure, Egypt

BROADREACH Yucatan Adventure, Mexico

RUSTIC PATHWAYS–ESCAPE TO FIJI, Fiji

Seacamp, FL

Westcoast Connection–Belize and Costa Rica Water Adventure

Wilderness Ventures–Australia, Australia

Wilderness Ventures–Fiji Community Service, Fiji

Wilderness Ventures–Maui/Kauai, HI

Wilderness Ventures–Tahiti, Fiji, and New Zealand

Sculpture

School of the Museum of Fine Arts, Boston–Pre-College Summer Studio, MA

Sea Kayaking

AAVE–Ultimate Alaska, AK

ACADEMIC TREKS–Pacific Whale Treks, Canada

Adventure Treks–Alaska Adventures, AK

Adventure Treks–Pacific Northwest Adventures, WA

Wilderness Ventures–Alaska College Leadership, AK

Wilderness Ventures–Alaska Expedition, AK

Wilderness Ventures–Alaska Southcentral, AK

Wilderness Ventures–Alaska Southeast, AK

Wilderness Ventures–Cascade-Olympic, WA

Wilderness Ventures–Costa Rica, Costa Rica

Wilderness Ventures–Costa Rica Service, Costa Rica

Wilderness Ventures–Grand Teton, WY

Wilderness Ventures–Hawaii, HI

Wilderness Ventures–Northwest

Wilderness Ventures–Pacific Northwest

Wilderness Ventures–Puget Sound, WA

Wilderness Ventures–Rocky Mountain

Wilderness Ventures–Spanish Pyrenees, Spain

Wilderness Ventures Yellowstone

Wilderness Ventures–Yellowstone/Teton Adventure, WY

Wilderness Ventures–Yellowstone-Teton Family Adventure, WY

Wilderness Ventures–Yellowstone Wilderness

Skiing (Downhill)

AAVE–Ultimate Alps

AAVE Wild Coast Discovery

International Summer Camp Montana, Switzerland, Switzerland

RUSTIC PATHWAYS–SKI AND SNOWBOARD ADVENTURE IN NEW ZEALAND, New Zealand

Westcoast Connection Travel–Ski and Snowboard Sensation

Snorkeling

AAVE–Ecuador and Galapagos, Ecuador

AAVE–Ultimate Hawaii, HI

ACTIONQUEST: British Virgin Islands-Sailing Voyages, British Virgin Islands

ACTIONQUEST: Galapagos Archipelago Expeditions, Ecuador

ACTIONQUEST: Tahiti and French Polynesian Island Voyages, French Polynesia

The Experiment in International Living–Australia Homestay, Australia

GLOBAL WORKS–Cultural Exchange and Service–New Zealand and Fiji Islands-4 weeks

Putney Student Travel–Cultural Exploration–Australia, New Zealand, and Fiji

Seacamp, FL

Wilderness Ventures–Costa Rica/Belize

Snowboarding

AAVE–Ultimate Alps

RUSTIC PATHWAYS–SKI AND SNOWBOARD ADVENTURE IN NEW ZEALAND, New Zealand

Westcoast Connection Travel–Ski and Snowboard Sensation

Soccer

AFS-USA–Homestay Plus–Paraguay Soccer, Paraguay

Britannia Soccer Camp, CA

The Experiment in International Living–Brazil–Community Service and Soccer, Brazil

RUSTIC PATHWAYS–SOCCER AND SERVICE EXTREME

RUSTIC PATHWAYS–SOCCER AND SERVICE IN COSTA RICA, Costa Rica

RUSTIC PATHWAYS–SOCCER AND SERVICE IN FIJI, Fiji

RUSTIC PATHWAYS–SOCCER AND SERVICE IN THAILAND, Thailand

Social Science

University of Chicago–Insight, IL

Social Services

Landmark Volunteers: Colorado, CO

Landmark Volunteers: Connecticut, CT

Landmark Volunteers: Maine, ME

Landmark Volunteers: Massachusetts, MA

Landmark Volunteers: Minnesota, MN

Landmark Volunteers: New York, NY

Landmark Volunteers: Virginia, VA

Sociology

Summer Advantage Study Abroad–St. Petersburg, Russia, Russian Federation

Spanish Language/Literature

AAVE–Costa Rica Clásica, Costa Rica

AAVE–Costa Rica Spanish Intensive, Costa Rica

AAVE–España Clásica, Spain

Academic Study Associates–Barcelona, Spain

Academic Study Associates–Costa Rica, Costa Rica

Academic Study Associates–Spanish in España, Spain

ACADEMIC TREKS–Adventure Peru, Peru

ACADEMIC TREKS–Immersion Mexico, Mexico

ACADEMIC TREKS–Spanish Immersion in Oaxaca, Mexico, Mexico

ACADEMIC TREKS–Spanish Language Immersion in Ecuador, Ecuador

AFS-USA–Community Service–Argentina, Argentina

AFS-USA–Homestay Language Study–Costa Rica, Costa Rica

AFS-USA–Homestay Language Study–Panama, Panama

AFS-USA–Homestay–Paraguay, Paraguay

AFS-USA–Homestay Plus–Paraguay Soccer, Paraguay

AFS-USA–Homestay Plus–Spain, Spain

AFS-USA–Language Study–Spain, Spain

Center for Cultural Interchange–Costa Rica Language School, Costa Rica

Center for Cultural Interchange–Mexico Language School, Mexico

Center for Cultural Interchange–Spain High School Abroad, Spain

Center for Cultural Interchange–Spain Language School, Spain

Center for Cultural Interchange–Spain Sports and Language Camp, Spain

Choate Rosemary Hall Summer in Spain, Spain

Edu-Culture International (ECI)–Andalusion Total Immersion, Spain

Edu-Culture International (ECI)–CPI Costa Rica, Costa Rica

Edu-Culture International (ECI)–Granada Homestay, Spain

Edu-Culture International (ECI)–Granada Homestay or Dorm Plus Southern Host Family Immersion, Spain

Edu-Culture International (ECI)–Granada-Nerja Homestay Combo, Spain

Edu-Culture International (ECI)–Grecia Costa Rica, Costa Rica

Edu-Culture International (ECI)–Nerja Homestay Plus Southern Host Family Immersion, Spain

Edu-Culture International (ECI)–Nerja Homestay with Optional Southern Host Family Immersion, Spain

Edu-Culture International (ECI)–Salamanca Dorm Plus Southern Host Family Immersion, Spain

Edu-Culture International (ECI)–Salamanca Homestay, Spain

Edu-Culture International (ECI)–Salamanca Homestay Plus Northern Host Family Immersion, Spain

Edu-Culture International (ECI)–Salamanca Homestay (Short Version), Spain

Edu-Culture International (ECI)–San Sebastian Homestay Plus Southern Host Family Immersion, Spain

EF International Language School–Barcelona, Spain

EF International Language School–Malaga, Spain

EF International Language School–Playa Tamarindo, Costa Rica

EF International Language School–Quito, Ecuador

Enforex–General Spanish–Alicante, Spain

Enforex–General Spanish–Barcelona, Spain

Enforex–General Spanish–Granada, Spain

Enforex–General Spanish–Madrid, Spain

Enforex–General Spanish–Malaga, Spain

Enforex–General Spanish–Marbella, Spain

Enforex–General Spanish–Salamanca, Spain

Enforex–General Spanish–Sevilla, Spain

Enforex–General Spanish–Tenerife, Spain

Enforex–General Spanish–Valencia, Spain

Enforex Hispanic Culture: Civilization, History, Art, and Literature–Alicante, Spain

Enforex Hispanic Culture: Civilization, History, Art, and Literature–Barcelona, Spain

Enforex Hispanic Culture: Civilization, History, Art, and Literature–Granada, Spain

Enforex Hispanic Culture: Civilization, History, Art, and Literature–Madrid, Spain

Enforex Hispanic Culture: Civilization, History, Art, and Literature–Malaga, Spain

Enforex Hispanic Culture: Civilization, History, Art, and Literature–Salamanca, Spain

Enforex Hispanic Culture: Civilization, History, Art, and Literature–Sevilla, Spain

Enforex Hispanic Culture: Civilization, History, Art, and Literature–Tenerife, Spain

Enforex Hispanic Culture: History, Art, and Literature–Valencia, Spain

Enforex Homestay Program–Alicante, Spain

Enforex Homestay Program–Barcelona, Spain

Enforex Homestay Program–Granada, Spain

Enforex Homestay Program–Madrid, Spain

Enforex Homestay Program–Malaga, Spain

Enforex Homestay Program–Marbella, Spain

Enforex Homestay Program–Salamanca, Spain

Enforex Homestay Program–Sevilla, Spain

Enforex Homestay Program–Tenerife, Spain

Enforex Homestay Program–Valencia, Spain

Enforex Residential Youth Summer Camp–Barcelona, Spain

Enforex Residential Youth Summer Camp–Granada, Spain

Enforex Residential Youth Summer Camp–Guanajuato, Mexico, Mexico

Enforex Residential Youth Summer Camp–Madrid, Spain

Enforex Residential Youth Summer Camp–Marbella Albergue College, Spain

Enforex Residential Youth Summer Camp–Marbella Alboran College, Spain

Enforex Residential Youth Summer Camp–Marbella Aleman College, Spain

Enforex Residential Youth Summer Camp–Salamanca, Spain

Enforex Residential Youth Summer Camp–Valencia, Spain

Enforex Spanish and Golf, Spain

Enforex Spanish and Tennis, Spain

Enforex Study Tour Vacational Program–Alicante, Spain

Enforex Study Tour Vacational Program–Barcelona, Spain

Enforex Study Tour Vacational Program–Granada, Spain

Enforex Study Tour Vacational Program–Madrid, Spain

Enforex Study Tour Vacational Program–Malaga, Spain

Enforex Study Tour Vacational Program–Marbella, Spain

Enforex Study Tour Vacational Program–Salamanca, Spain

Enforex Study Tour Vacational Program–Sevilla, Spain

Enforex Study Tour Vacational Program–Tenerife, Spain

Enforex Study Tour Vacational Program–Valencia, Spain

Excel at Madrid/Barcelona, Spain

The Experiment in International Living–Argentina Homestay, Community Service, and Outdoor Ecological Program, Argentina

The Experiment in International Living–Argentina Visual Arts, Photography, and Service, Argentina

The Experiment in International Living–Chile North Homestay, Community Service, Chile

The Experiment in International Living–Chile South Homestay, Chile

The Experiment in International Living–Ecuador Homestay, Ecuador

The Experiment in International Living–Mexico Cooking and Culture, Mexico

The Experiment in International Living–Mexico Homestay, Sustainable Development and Fair Trade, Mexico

The Experiment in International Living–Mexico–Mayan Arts and Culture, Mexico

The Experiment in International Living–Spain, Five-Week Homestay, Language Immersion, Spain

The Experiment in International Living–Spain, Four-Week Language Training, Travel, and Homestay, Spain

The Experiment in International Living–Spain–Multiculturalism and Service, Spain

The Experiment in International Living–Spain–Spanish Arts and Culture, Spain

The Experiment in International Living–Spain–The Road to Santiago, Spain

The Experiment in International Living–Spanish Culture and Exploration, Spain

Global Leadership Adventures–Brazil: Community Service and Leadership, Brazil

Global Leadership Adventures–Costa Rica: Community Service and Leadership, Costa Rica

Global Leadership Adventures–Ghana: Community Service and Leadership, Ghana

Global Leadership Adventures–India: Community Service and Leadership, India

GLOBAL WORKS–Cultural Exchange and Service–Costa Rica-3 weeks, Costa Rica

GLOBAL WORKS–Cultural Exchange and Service–Puerto Rico-2 or 4 weeks, Puerto Rico

GLOBAL WORKS–Language Immersion, Cultural Exchange and Service–Costa Rica, Costa Rica

GLOBAL WORKS–Language Immersion, Cultural Exchange and Service–Ecuador and the Galapagos-4 weeks, Ecuador

GLOBAL WORKS–Language Immersion, Cultural Exchange and Service–Mexico-3 weeks, Mexico

GLOBAL WORKS–Language Immersion, Cultural Exchange and Service–Panama/Costa Rica

GLOBAL WORKS–Language Immersion, Cultural Exchange and Service–Peru, Peru

GLOBAL WORKS–Language Immersion, Cultural Exchange and Service–Puerto Rico-4 weeks, Puerto Rico

GLOBAL WORKS Language Immersion, Cultural Exchange and Service–Spain-4 weeks, Spain

iD Tech Camps–Documentary Filmmaking and Cultural Immersion in Spain, Spain

Les Elfes–International Summer/ Winter Camp, Switzerland

LIFEWORKS with the Fundación Humanitaria in Costa Rica, Costa Rica

Putney Student Travel–Language Learning–Argentina, Argentina

Putney Student Travel–Language Learning–Costa Rica, Costa Rica

Putney Student Travel–Language Learning–Spain, Spain

Rassias Programs–Gijón, Spain, Spain

Rassias Programs–Pontevedra, Spain, Spain

Rassias Programs–Segovia, Spain, Spain

RUSTIC PATHWAYS–INTENSIVE SPANISH LANGUAGE, Costa Rica

RUSTIC PATHWAYS–MALEKU TRIBE IMMERSION PROGRAM– COSTA RICA, Costa Rica

RUSTIC PATHWAYS–RAMP UP YOUR SPANISH, Costa Rica

RUSTIC PATHWAYS–SPANISH LANGUAGE IMMERSION, Costa Rica

Service Learning in Barcelona, Spain

Spanish Language and Flamenco Enforex–Granada, Spain

Spanish Language and Flamenco Enforex–Madrid, Spain

Spanish Language and Flamenco Enforex–Marbella, Spain

Spanish Language and Flamenco Enforex–Sevilla, Spain

Summer Advantage Study Abroad– Granada, Spain, Spain

Summer Advantage Study Abroad– Salamanca, Spain, Spain

Taft Summer School Abroad–Spain, Spain

TASIS Spanish Summer Program, Spain

Visions–Nicaragua, Nicaragua

Westcoast Connection–Spanish in Costa Rica, Costa Rica

Westcoast Connection–Spanish Language and Touring, Spain

World Horizons International–Costa Rica, Costa Rica

Speech/Debate

Choate Rosemary Hall Beginning Writers Workshop, CT

Junior Statesmen Summer School– Georgetown University, D.C.

Junior Statesmen Summer School– Princeton University, NJ

Junior Statesmen Summer School– Stanford University, CA

Junior Statesmen Summer School Yale University, CT

Junior Statesmen Symposium on California State Politics and Government, CA

Junior Statesmen Symposium on Los Angeles Politics and Government, CA

Junior Statesmen Symposium on New Jersey State Politics and Government, NJ

Junior Statesmen Symposium on Ohio State Politics and Government, OH

Junior Statesmen Symposium on Texas Politics and Leadership, TX

Junior Statesmen Symposium on Washington State Politics and Government, WA

Sports (General)

Camp Chikopi for Boys, Canada

Crossroads School–Sports Camps, CA

Darlington Summer Programs, GA

Hargrave Summer Leadership Program, VA

▶ SPORTS (GENERAL)

International Summer Camp Montana, Switzerland, Switzerland
Les Elfes–International Summer/Winter Camp, Switzerland
Miss Porter's School Athletic Experience, CT
Weissman Teen Tours–U.S. and Western Canada, 40 Days
Weissman Teen Tours–U.S. and Western Canada, 30 Days

Studio Arts
Miss Porter's School Arts Alive!, CT
Skidmore College–Pre-College Program in the Liberal & Studio Arts for High School Students, NY

Study Skills
Brewster Academy Summer Session, NH
Eaglebrook Summer Semester, MA
Georgetown University College Prep Program, D.C.
Landmark School Summer Academic Program, MA
Marvelwood Summer Program, CT
Rumsey Hall School Summer Session, CT
Salisbury Summer School, CT
Summer at Delphi, OR
summer@rectory, CT
The Winchendon School Summer Session, MA

Surfing
AAVE–Australia, Australia
AAVE–Bold West
AAVE–Surf Scuba Safari, Mexico
AAVE–Ultimate Hawaii, HI
AAVE–Wild Isles
BROADREACH Adventures Down Under, Australia
BROADREACH Baja Extreme–Scuba Adventure, Mexico
BROADREACH Costa Rica Experience, Costa Rica
Camp Pacific's Recreational Camp, CA
Camp Pacific's Surf and Bodyboard Camp, CA
RUSTIC PATHWAYS–ESCAPE TO FIJI, Fiji
RUSTIC PATHWAYS–SURF & SERVICE–COSTA RICA, Costa Rica
RUSTIC PATHWAYS–SURF THE SUMMER–COSTA RICA, Costa Rica
Westcoast Connection–Belize and Costa Rica Water Adventure
Wilderness Ventures–California, CA
Wilderness Ventures–Costa Rica Surfing, Costa Rica

Wilderness Ventures–Maui/Kauai, HI
Wilderness Ventures–Tahiti, Fiji, and New Zealand

Swedish Language/Literature
Center for Cultural Interchange–Sweden High School Abroad, Sweden

Swimming
Crossroads School–Aquatics, CA

Team Building
Future Leader Camp, VT
Landmark Volunteers: Arizona, AZ
Landmark Volunteers: Idaho, ID

Technology
Emagination Computer Camps–Georgia, GA
Emagination Computer Camps–Illinois, IL
Emagination Computer Camps–Massachusetts, MA
Emagination Computer Camps–Pennsylvania, PA
Worcester Polytechnic Institute–Launch, MA

Television/Video
ACTeen August Academy, NY
ACTeen July Academy, NY
ACTeen June Academy, NY
ACTeen Summer Saturday Academy, NY
iD Gaming Academy–Stanford University, Palo Alto, CA
iD Gaming Academy–UC Berkeley, Berkeley, CA
iD Gaming Academy–UCLA, Westwood, CA
iD Gaming Academy–Villanova University, Villanova, PA
iD Tech Camps–Documentary Filmmaking and Cultural Immersion in Spain, Spain
IEI–Video Production Plus Programme, United Kingdom
Ithaca College Summer College for High School Students: Session II, NY
Oxford Media School–Newsroom in Europe, United Kingdom
Oxford Media School–Newsroom in Europe, Master Class, United Kingdom
Tisch School of the Arts–Summer High School Programs, NY

Tennis
Camp Lincoln for Boys/Camp Lake Hubert for Girls–Tennis Camp, MN

Enforex Spanish and Tennis, Spain
TASIS French Language Program in Château-d'Oex, Switzerland, Switzerland

Thai Language
LIFEWORKS with the DPF Foundation in Thailand, Thailand

Theater/Drama
ACTeen August Academy, NY
ACTeen July Academy, NY
ACTeen June Academy, NY
ACTeen Summer Saturday Academy, NY
Belvoir Terrace, MA
Buck's Rock Performing and Creative Arts Camp, CT
Choate Rosemary Hall Summer Arts Conservatory–Theater, CT
Duke Drama Workshop, NC
Ensemble Theatre Community School, PA
The Experiment in International Living–France, Four-Week Homestay and Theatre, France
The Experiment in International Living–United Kingdom Theatre Program, United Kingdom
EXPRESSIONS! Duke Fine Arts Camp, NC
Idyllwild Arts Summer Program–Children's Center, CA
Idyllwild Arts Summer Program–Family Week, CA
Idyllwild Arts Summer Program–Junior Artists' Center, CA
Idyllwild Arts Summer Program–Youth Arts Center, CA
IEI–Theatre Plus Programme, United Kingdom
Ithaca College Summer College for High School Students: Session I, NY
Ithaca College Summer College for High School Students: Session II, NY
92nd Street Y Camps–Camp Yaffa for the Arts, NY
Northwestern University's National High School Institute, IL
Oxford Media School–Film, United Kingdom
Oxford Media School–Film Master Class, United Kingdom
Putney Student Travel–Cultural Exploration–Theatre in Britain, United Kingdom
Salem Spotlight, NC
Sarah Lawrence College Summer High School Programs, NY
Spoleto Study Abroad, Italy

Stagedoor Manor Performing Arts Training Center/Theatre and Dance Camp, NY
Summer in Switzerland, Switzerland
TASIS England Summer Program, United Kingdom
Tisch School of the Arts–International High School Program–Dublin, Ireland
Tisch School of the Arts–International High School Program–Paris, France
Tisch School of the Arts–Summer High School Programs, NY
University of Pennsylvania–Penn Summer Theatre Workshop, PA

TOEFL/TOEIC Preparation
Academic Study Associates–ASA at the University of California, Berkeley, CA
Intensive English Language Program, MD

Touring
AAVE–Australia, Australia
AAVE–Bike Amsterdam-Paris
AAVE–Bold Europe
AAVE–China, China
AAVE–Ecuador and Galapagos, Ecuador
AAVE–France Classique, France
AAVE–Peru and Machu Picchu, Peru
AAVE–Thailand, Thailand
AAVE–Wild Isles
Academic Study Associates–Barcelona, Spain
Academic Study Associates–Costa Rica, Costa Rica
Academic Study Associates–Florence, Italy
Academic Study Associates–Nice, France
Academic Study Associates–Royan, France
Academic Study Associates–Spanish in España, Spain
ACTIONQUEST: Australian and Great Barrier Reef Adventures, Australia
ACTIONQUEST: Leeward and French Caribbean Island Voyages
ACTIONQUEST: Mediterranean Sailing Voyage
ACTIONQUEST: Tahiti and French Polynesian Island Voyages, French Polynesia
AFS-USA–Community Service–Costa Rica, Costa Rica
AFS-USA–Homestay–Ecuador, Ecuador
AFS-USA–Homestay Language Study–Costa Rica, Costa Rica

AFS-USA–Homestay Language Study–Egypt, Egypt
AFS-USA–Homestay Language Study–Panama, Panama
AFS-USA–Homestay–Paraguay, Paraguay
AFS-USA–Homestay Plus–Spain, Spain
ATW: Adventure Roads
ATW: American Horizons
ATW: California Sunset
ATW: Camp Inn 42
ATW: Discoverer
ATW: European Adventures
ATW: Fire and Ice
ATW: Mini Tours
ATW: Pacific Paradise
ATW: Skyblazer
ATW: Sunblazer
ATW: Wayfarer
The Cambridge Experience, United Kingdom
Career Explorations–New York, NY
Choate Rosemary Hall Summer in China, China
Edu-Culture International (ECI)–Aix-en-Provence/Gap Host Family Immersion, France
Edu-Culture International (ECI)–Andalusion Total Immersion, Spain
Edu-Culture International (ECI)–CPI Costa Rica, Costa Rica
Edu-Culture International (ECI)–Granada Homestay, Spain
Edu-Culture International (ECI)–Granada Homestay or Dorm Plus Southern Host Family Immersion, Spain
Edu-Culture International (ECI)–Granada-Nerja Homestay Combo, Spain
Edu-Culture International (ECI)–Grecia Costa Rica, Costa Rica
Edu-Culture International (ECI)–Lyon Host Family and Travel Program, France
Edu-Culture International (ECI)–Nerja Homestay Plus Southern Host Family Immersion, Spain
Edu-Culture International (ECI)–Nerja Homestay with Optional Southern Host Family Immersion, Spain
Edu-Culture International (ECI)–Salamanca Dorm Plus Southern Host Family Immersion, Spain
Edu-Culture International (ECI)–Salamanca Homestay, Spain
Edu-Culture International (ECI)–Salamanca Homestay Plus Northern Host Family Immersion, Spain

Edu-Culture International (ECI)–Salamanca Homestay (Short Version), Spain
Edu-Culture International (ECI)–San Sebastian Homestay Plus Southern Host Family Immersion, Spain
Edu-Culture International (ECI)–Toulouse/Montpellier Host Family Immersion, France
Enforex Study Tour Vacational Program–Alicante, Spain
Enforex Study Tour Vacational Program–Barcelona, Spain
Enforex Study Tour Vacational Program–Granada, Spain
Enforex Study Tour Vacational Program–Madrid, Spain
Enforex Study Tour Vacational Program–Malaga, Spain
Enforex Study Tour Vacational Program–Marbella, Spain
Enforex Study Tour Vacational Program–Salamanca, Spain
Enforex Study Tour Vacational Program–Sevilla, Spain
Enforex Study Tour Vacational Program–Tenerife, Spain
Enforex Study Tour Vacational Program–Valencia, Spain
The Experiment in International Living–Chile North Homestay, Community Service, Chile
The Experiment in International Living–Chile South Homestay, Chile
The Experiment in International Living–China North and East Homestay, China
The Experiment in International Living–China South and West Homestay, China
The Experiment in International Living–France, Four-Week Brittany Discovery, France
The Experiment in International Living–France, Four-Week Homestay and Travel through Alps, France
The Experiment in International Living–France, Three-Week Homestay and Travel–Borders, France
The Experiment in International Living–Ghana Homestay, Ghana
The Experiment in International Living–Italy Homestay, Language, Culture, and Travel, Italy
The Experiment in International Living–Mexico–Community Service, Travel, and Homestay, Mexico

The Experiment in International Living–Mexico Homestay, Sustainable Development and Fair Trade, Mexico

The Experiment in International Living–Mexico–Mayan Arts and Culture, Mexico

The Experiment in International Living–Scotland, United Kingdom

The Experiment in International Living–Spain, Four-Week Language Training, Travel, and Homestay, Spain

The Experiment in International Living–Spain–Spanish Arts and Culture, Spain

The Experiment in International Living–Turkey Homestay, Community Service, and Travel, Turkey

The Experiment in International Living–United Kingdom Filmmaking Program and Homestay, United Kingdom

The Experiment in International Living–United Kingdom Theatre Program, United Kingdom

The Fessenden School Summer ESL Program, MA

LIFEWORKS with the Australian Red Cross, Australia

LIFEWORKS with the China Little Flower Foundation in China, China

LIFEWORKS with the DPF Foundation in Thailand, Thailand

LIFEWORKS with the Fundación Humanitaria in Costa Rica, Costa Rica

Linden Hill Summer Program, MA

The Oxford Experience, United Kingdom

Rassias Programs–Arles, France, France

Rassias Programs–Gijón, Spain, Spain

Rassias Programs–Pontevedra, Spain, Spain

Rassias Programs–Segovia, Spain, Spain

Rassias Programs–Tours, France, France

Rein Europe

Rein Teen Tours–California Caper

Rein Teen Tours–Crossroads

Rein Teen Tours–Eastern Adventure

Rein Teen Tours–Grand Adventure

Rein Teen Tours–Hawaiian/Alaskan Adventure

Rein Teen Tours–Hawaiian Caper

Rein Teen Tours–Project Hawaii, HI

Rein Teen Tours–Western Adventure

RUSTIC PATHWAYS–ASIAN PACIFIC EXTREME

RUSTIC PATHWAYS–BIG FIJI EXPLORER, Fiji

RUSTIC PATHWAYS–COSTA RICA ADVENTURER, Costa Rica

RUSTIC PATHWAYS–EDGE OF THE MAP EXTREME

RUSTIC PATHWAYS–ELEPHANTS & AMAZING THAILAND, Thailand

RUSTIC PATHWAYS–FACES AND PLACES OF VIETNAM, Vietnam

RUSTIC PATHWAYS–HILL TRIBE TREKKING ADVENTURE, Thailand

RUSTIC PATHWAYS–INDIAN HIMALAYA TRAVELER, India

RUSTIC PATHWAYS–INTRODUCTION TO PHOTOGRAPHY–SNAPSHOTS IN THE LAND OF SMILES

RUSTIC PATHWAYS–ISLAND HOPPING AND DIVING–THAILAND, Thailand

RUSTIC PATHWAYS–NEW ZEALAND NORTH ISLAND ADVENTURE, New Zealand

RUSTIC PATHWAYS–OFF THE MAP BURMA AND CAMBODIA

RUSTIC PATHWAYS–PHOTOGRAPHY ADVENTURE IN THAILAND AND ANGKOR WAT

RUSTIC PATHWAYS–PHOTOGRAPHY ADVENTURE IN THAILAND AND BURMA

RUSTIC PATHWAYS–PHOTOGRAPHY ADVENTURE IN THAILAND AND INDIA

RUSTIC PATHWAYS–PHOTOGRAPHY ADVENTURE IN THAILAND AND VIETNAM

RUSTIC PATHWAYS–SERVICE LEARNING EXTREME

RUSTIC PATHWAYS–SOUTH PACIFIC EXTREME

RUSTIC PATHWAYS–SUN, SAND & INTERNATIONAL SERVICE–FIJI, Fiji

RUSTIC PATHWAYS–SYDNEY, REEF & RAINFOREST, Australia

RUSTIC PATHWAYS–THE AMAZING THAILAND ADVENTURE, Thailand

RUSTIC PATHWAYS–THE BUDDHIST CARAVAN, India

RUSTIC PATHWAYS–THE WONDERS & RICHES OF SOUTHEAST ASIA

RUSTIC PATHWAYS–THE WONDERS OF CHINA, China

RUSTIC PATHWAYS–ULTIMATE JUNGLE ADVENTURE–COSTA RICA, Costa Rica

RUSTIC PATHWAYS–WORLD SERVICE EXTREME

TASIS Summer Program for Languages, Arts, and Outdoor Pursuits, Switzerland

Weissman Teen Tours–"Aloha–Welcome to Hawaiian Paradise", 3 weeks

Weissman Teen Tours–"Aloha–Welcome to Hawaiian Paradise", 2 weeks, HI

Weissman Teen Tours–European Experience

Weissman Teen Tours–U.S. and Western Canada, 40 Days

Weissman Teen Tours–U.S. and Western Canada, 30 Days

Westcoast Connection–American Voyageur

Westcoast Connection–Australian Outback Plus Hawaii

Westcoast Connection–Authentic Italy, Italy

Westcoast Connection–California Dreaming

Westcoast Connection–Californian Extravaganza

Westcoast Connection–California Sprint, CA

Westcoast Connection–Community Connections Alaska, AK

Westcoast Connection–Community Service Costa Rica, Costa Rica

Westcoast Connection–Community Service–Habitat for Humanity, WA

Westcoast Connection–European Escape

Westcoast Connection–French Language and Touring, France

Westcoast Connection–Hawaiian Spirit

Westcoast Connection–Major League Baseball Tour

Westcoast Connection/On Tour–Australian Outback, Australia

Westcoast Connection–Spanish in Costa Rica, Costa Rica

Westcoast Connection–Spanish Language and Touring, Spain

Westcoast Connection Travel–California and the Canyons

Westcoast Connection Travel–Eastcoast Encounter

Westcoast Connection Travel–European Discovery

Westcoast Connection Travel–Northwestern Odyssey

Westcoast Connection Travel/On Tour–European Escapade

Westcoast Connection Travel/On Tour–European Experience

Westcoast Connection–U.S. Explorer

Trail Maintenance
Landmark Volunteers: California, CA

Landmark Volunteers: Connecticut, CT

Landmark Volunteers: Idaho, ID

Landmark Volunteers: Michigan, MI

Landmark Volunteers: Oregon, OR

Landmark Volunteers: Pennsylvania, PA

Landmark Volunteers: Vermont, VT

Landmark Volunteers: Virginia, VA

Landmark Volunteers: Washington, WA

Landmark Volunteers: Wyoming, WY

Visual Arts
Atelier des Arts, Switzerland

Buck's Rock Performing and Creative Arts Camp, CT

Choate Rosemary Hall Summer Arts Conservatory–Visual Arts Program, CT

Oxbow Summer Art Camp, CA

The Putney School Summer Arts Program, VT

Spoleto Study Abroad, Italy

Washington University in St. Louis, College of Art–Portfolio Plus, MO

Waterskiing
ACTIONQUEST: Rescue Diving Voyages, British Virgin Islands

Weight Reduction
Camp California Fitness, CA

White-Water Trips
AAVE–Costa Rica Clásica, Costa Rica

Adventure Treks–California Adventures, CA

Adventure Treks–Canadian Rockies Adventures, Canada

Adventure Treks–Montana Adventures, MT

Adventure Treks–Oregon Adventures, OR

Adventure Treks–Pacific Northwest Adventures, WA

Adventure Treks–Wilderness Adventures

BROADREACH Costa Rica Experience, Costa Rica

Wilderness Ventures–Alaska Expedition, AK

Wilderness Ventures–Australia, Australia

Wilderness Ventures–California, CA

Wilderness Ventures–Colorado/Utah Mountain Bike

Wilderness Ventures–Costa Rica, Costa Rica

Wilderness Ventures–Costa Rica/ Belize

Wilderness Ventures–Ecuador and Galapagos Community Service, Ecuador

Wilderness Ventures–Great Divide

Wilderness Ventures–High Sierra, CA

Wilderness Ventures–Oregon, OR

Wilderness Ventures–Peru Community Service, Peru

Wilderness Ventures–Puget Sound, WA

Wilderness Ventures–Rocky Mountain

Wilderness Ventures–Southwest Community Service

Wilderness Ventures–Spanish Pyrenees, Spain

Wilderness Ventures–Teton Crest

Wilderness Ventures–Washington Alpine, WA

Wilderness Ventures–Yellowstone

Wilderness Ventures–Yellowstone Fly Fishing

Wilderness Ventures–Yellowstone/ Teton Adventure, WY

Wilderness Ventures–Yellowstone-Teton Family Adventure, WY

Wilderness Camping
Camp Treetops, NY

Keewaydin Temagami, Canada

Talisman Summer Camp, NC

Teton Valley Ranch Camp–Boys Camp, WY

Teton Valley Ranch Camp–Girls Camp, WY

Treetops eXpeditions–Alaska Community Service, AK

Treetops eXpeditions–Glacier/ Boundary Waters

Wilderness Ventures–Costa Rica Surfing, Costa Rica

Wilderness/Outdoors (General)
Camp Chikopi for Boys, Canada

Pine Island Camp, ME

Roaring Brook Camp for Boys, VT

Summer Study at The University of Colorado at Boulder, CO

Wilderness Ventures–Alaska Southeast Community Service, AK

Windsurfing
Wilderness Ventures–Maui/Kauai, HI

Work Camp Programs
Volunteers for Peace International Voluntary Service–Estonia, Estonia

Volunteers for Peace International Voluntary Service–France, France

Volunteers for Peace International Voluntary Service–Germany, Germany

Volunteers for Peace International Voluntary Service–Italy, Italy

Writing
Bryn Mawr College–Writing for College, PA

Choate Rosemary Hall Beginning Writers Workshop, CT

Choate Rosemary Hall English Language Institute, CT

Choate Rosemary Hall English Language Institute/Focus Program, CT

Choate Rosemary Hall Writing Project, CT

Choate Rosemary Hall Young Writers Workshop, CT

Duke Young Writers Camp, NC

Dunnabeck at Kildonan, NY

Elite Educational Institute Elementary Enrichment, CA

Elite Educational Institute Elementary Enrichment–Korea, Republic of Korea

Elite Educational Institute Junior High/PSAT Program, CA

Elite Educational Institute Junior High/PSAT Program–Korea, Republic of Korea

IEI–Print and Broadcast Journalism, United Kingdom

Ithaca College Summer College for High School Students: Session I, NY

Landmark School Summer Academic Program, MA

Miss Porter's School Arts Alive!, CT

Salisbury Summer School, CT

Tisch School of the Arts–Summer High School Programs, NY

AAVE–Journeys That Matter
AAVE–Africa
AAVE–Australia
AAVE–Bike Amsterdam-Paris
AAVE–Bold Europe
AAVE–Bold West
AAVE–Boot/Saddle/Paddle
AAVE–China
AAVE–Colorado Discovery
AAVE–Costa Rica Clásica
AAVE–Costa Rica Spanish Intensive
AAVE–Ecuador and Galapagos
AAVE–España Clásica
AAVE–France Classique
AAVE–Peak Four
AAVE–Peru and Machu Picchu
AAVE–Rock & Rapid
AAVE–Rock & Roll
AAVE–Sail Dive Greece
AAVE–Surf Scuba Safari
AAVE–Thailand
AAVE–Ultimate Alaska
AAVE–Ultimate Alps
AAVE–Ultimate Hawaii
AAVE–Wild Coast Discovery
AAVE–Wild Isles

Academic Study Associates, Inc. (ASA)
Academic Study Associates–ASA at the University of California, Berkeley
Academic Study Associates–ASA at the University of Massachusetts Amherst
Academic Study Associates–Barcelona
Academic Study Associates–Costa Rica
Academic Study Associates–Florence
Academic Study Associates–Nice
Academic Study Associates–Royan
Academic Study Associates–Spanish in España
The Cambridge Experience
The Oxford Experience

Academic Treks, the academic adventure and community service division of Broadreach
ACADEMIC TREKS–Adventure Peru
ACADEMIC TREKS–Caribbean Marine Reserves
ACADEMIC TREKS–Dolphin Studies in Belize
ACADEMIC TREKS–French Immersion in France
ACADEMIC TREKS–French Immersion in the French West Indies
ACADEMIC TREKS–Immersion China

ACADEMIC TREKS–Immersion Mexico
ACADEMIC TREKS–Pacific Whale Treks
ACADEMIC TREKS–Sea Turtle Studies
ACADEMIC TREKS–Shark Studies in Fiji
ACADEMIC TREKS–Shipwrecks and Underwater Archaeology in Bermuda
ACADEMIC TREKS–Spanish Immersion in Oaxaca, Mexico
ACADEMIC TREKS–Spanish Language Immersion in Ecuador
ACADEMIC TREKS–Wilderness Emergency Medicine

The Academy by the Sea/Camp Pacific
Academy by the Sea
Camp Pacific's Recreational Camp
Camp Pacific's Surf and Bodyboard Camp

Acadia Institute of Oceanography

ACTeen
ACTeen August Academy
ACTeen July Academy
ACTeen June Academy
ACTeen Summer Saturday Academy

ActionQuest
ACTIONQUEST: Advanced PADI Scuba Certification and Specialty Voyages
ACTIONQUEST: Australian and Great Barrier Reef Adventures
ACTIONQUEST: British Virgin Islands–Sailing and Scuba Voyages
ACTIONQUEST: British Virgin Islands-Sailing Voyages
ACTIONQUEST: Galapagos Archipelago Expeditions
ACTIONQUEST: Junior Advanced Scuba with Marine Biology
ACTIONQUEST: Leeward and French Caribbean Island Voyages
ACTIONQUEST: Mediterranean Sailing Voyage
ACTIONQUEST: PADI Divemaster Voyages
ACTIONQUEST: Rescue Diving Voyages
ACTIONQUEST: Tahiti and French Polynesian Island Voyages
ACTIONQUEST: Tropical Marine Biology Voyages

Adirondack Field Ecology
Adirondack Field Ecology

Adventure Treks, Inc.
Adventure Treks–Alaska Adventures
Adventure Treks–California Adventures
Adventure Treks–Canadian Rockies Adventures
Adventure Treks–Montana Adventures
Adventure Treks–Oregon Adventures
Adventure Treks–Pacific Northwest Adventures
Adventure Treks–Wilderness Adventures

AFS-USA
AFS-USA–China Summer Homestay Language Study Program
AFS-USA–Community Service–Argentina
AFS-USA–Community Service–Costa Rica
AFS-USA–Community Service–Panama
AFS-USA–Community Service Paraguay
AFS-USA–Community Service–Thailand
AFS-USA–Homestay–Argentina
AFS-USA–Homestay–Chile
AFS-USA–Homestay–Ecuador
AFS-USA–Homestay–Finland
AFS-USA–Homestay–France
AFS-USA–Homestay Language Study–Costa Rica
AFS-USA–Homestay Language Study–Egypt
AFS-USA–Homestay Language Study–Japan
AFS-USA–Homestay Language Study–Latvia
AFS-USA–Homestay Language Study–Panama
AFS-USA–Homestay–Paraguay
AFS-USA–Homestay Plus–Australia
AFS-USA–Homestay Plus–Costa Rica
AFS-USA–Homestay Plus–Hungary
AFS-USA–Homestay Plus–Italy
AFS-USA–Homestay Plus–New Zealand
AFS-USA–Homestay Plus–Panama
AFS-USA–Homestay Plus–Paraguay Soccer
AFS-USA–Homestay Plus–Spain
AFS-USA–Homestay–Thailand
AFS-USA–Homestay–Turkey
AFS-USA–Language Study–Spain
AFS-USA–Team Mission–Ghana

Alford Lake Camp
Alford Lake Camp
Alford Lake Family Camp

▶ AMERICAN ACADEMY OF DRAMATIC ARTS

American Academy of Dramatic Arts
American Academy of Dramatic Arts Summer Program at Los Angeles, California
American Academy of Dramatic Arts Summer Program at New York

American Institute for Foreign Study (AIFS)
Summer Advantage Study Abroad–Cambridge University
Summer Advantage Study Abroad–Granada, Spain
Summer Advantage Study Abroad–London, UK
Summer Advantage Study Abroad–Nanjing, China
Summer Advantage Study Abroad–Paris, France
Summer Advantage Study Abroad–Rome, Italy
Summer Advantage Study Abroad–St. Petersburg, Russia
Summer Advantage Study Abroad–Salamanca, Spain

American Trails West
ATW: Adventure Roads
ATW: American Horizons
ATW: California Sunset
ATW: Camp Inn 42
ATW: Discoverer
ATW: European Adventures
ATW: Fire and Ice
ATW: Mini Tours
ATW: Pacific Paradise
ATW: Skyblazer
ATW: Sunblazer
ATW: Wayfarer

Appel Farm Arts and Music Center
Appel Farm Summer Arts Camp

Asheville School
Asheville School's Summer Academic Adventures

Atelier des Arts
Atelier des Arts

Barat Foundation
Barat Foundation Summer Program in Provence

Barnard College/Columbia University
Barnard's Summer in New York City: A Pre-College Program
Barnard's Summer in New York City: One-Week Liberal Arts Intensive

Barnard's Summer in New York City: Young Women's Leadership Institute

Baylor University Honors College and School of Engineering/Computer Science
The Renaissance Scholar Program

Belvoir Terrace

Boston Architectural College
BAC Summer Academy

Boston University Tanglewood Institute
Boston University Tanglewood Institute

Brant Lake Camp
Brant Lake Camp's Dance Centre

Brewster Academy
Brewster Academy Summer Session

Britannia Soccer Camp

Broadreach
BROADREACH Adventures Down Under
BROADREACH Adventures in Scuba and Sailing–Underwater Discoveries
BROADREACH Adventures in the Grenadines–Advanced Scuba
BROADREACH Adventures in the Windward Islands–Advanced Scuba
BROADREACH Adventures Underwater–Advanced Scuba
BROADREACH Arc of the Caribbean Sailing Adventure
BROADREACH Baja Extreme–Scuba Adventure
BROADREACH Costa Rica Experience
BROADREACH Fiji Solomon Quest
BROADREACH Honduras Eco-Adventure
BROADREACH Marine Biology Accredited
BROADREACH Red Sea Scuba Adventure
BROADREACH Yucatan Adventure

Brown University
Summer@Brown

Bryn Mawr College
Bryn Mawr College–Science for College

Bryn Mawr College–Women of Distinction: Personalizing the College Admissions Process
Bryn Mawr College–Writing for College

Buck's Rock Performing and Creative Arts Camp

California State Summer School for the Arts/Inner Spark
California State Summer School for the Arts/Inner Spark

Cambridge College Programme
Cambridge College Programme

Camp Airy and Camp Louise Foundation, Inc.
Camp Airy
Camp Louise

Camp Berachah Ministries Christian Camps and Conferences
Camp Berachah Ministries–Camps and Conferences

Camp California Fitness

Camp Chikopi
Camp Chikopi for Boys

Camp Encore-Coda for a Great Summer of Music, Sports, and Friends
Camp Encore-Coda for a Great Summer of Music, Sports, and Friends

Camp Greenbrier for Boys
Camp Greenbrier for Boys

Camp La Junta
Camp La Junta

Camp Lincoln/Camp Lake Hubert
Camp Lincoln for Boys/Camp Lake Hubert for Girls
Camp Lincoln for Boys/Camp Lake Hubert for Girls–Family Camp
Camp Lincoln for Boys/Camp Lake Hubert for Girls–Golf Camp
Camp Lincoln for Boys/Camp Lake Hubert for Girls–Tennis Camp

Camp Regis, Inc.
Applejack Teen Camp
Camp Regis

Camp Treetops

Canoe Island French Camp
Canoe Island French Camp

Cape Cod Sea Camps, Inc.
Cape Cod Sea Camps–Monomoy/Wono

Career Explorations, LLC
Career Explorations–Boston
Career Explorations–New York

Center for Cultural Interchange
Center for Cultural Interchange–
Argentina Independent Homestay
Center for Cultural Interchange–
Australia High School Abroad
Center for Cultural Interchange–
Brazil High School Abroad
Center for Cultural Interchange–
Chile Independent Homestay
Center for Cultural Interchange–
Costa Rica Language School
Center for Cultural Interchange–
Denmark High School Abroad
Center for Cultural Interchange–
Finland High School Abroad
Center for Cultural Interchange–
France High School Abroad
Center for Cultural Interchange–
France Independent Homestay
Center for Cultural Interchange–
France Language School
Center for Cultural Interchange–
Germany High School Abroad
Center for Cultural Interchange–
Germany Independent Homestay
Center for Cultural Interchange–
Germany Language School
Center for Cultural Interchange–
Ireland High School Abroad
Center for Cultural Interchange–
Ireland Independent Homestay
Program
Center for Cultural Interchange–Italy
High School Abroad
Center for Cultural Interchange–Italy
Language School
Center for Cultural Interchange–
Japan High School Abroad
Center for Cultural Interchange–
Mexico Language School
Center for Cultural Interchange–
Netherlands High School Abroad
Center for Cultural Interchange–
Norway High School Abroad
Center for Cultural Interchange–
Spain High School Abroad
Center for Cultural Interchange–
Spain Independent Homestay
Center for Cultural Interchange–
Spain Language School

Center for Cultural Interchange–
Spain Sports and Language Camp
Center for Cultural Interchange–
Sweden High School Abroad
Center for Cultural Interchange–
Taiwan High School Abroad
Center for Cultural Interchange–
United Kingdom Independent
Homestay

Cheley Colorado Camps

Cheshire Academy
Cheshire Academy Summer Program

Choate Rosemary Hall
Choate Rosemary Hall Beginning
Writers Workshop
Choate Rosemary Hall English
Language Institute
Choate Rosemary Hall English
Language Institute/Focus Program
Choate Rosemary Hall Focus
Program
Choate Rosemary Hall Immersion
Program
Choate Rosemary Hall John F.
Kennedy Institute in Government
Choate Rosemary Hall Math and
Science Workshops
Choate Rosemary Hall Math/Science
Institute for Girls–CONNECT
Choate Rosemary Hall Summer Arts
Conservatory–Playwriting
Choate Rosemary Hall Summer Arts
Conservatory–Theater
Choate Rosemary Hall Summer Arts
Conservatory–Visual Arts Program
Choate Rosemary Hall Summer in
China
Choate Rosemary Hall Summer in
Paris
Choate Rosemary Hall Summer in
Spain
Choate Rosemary Hall Summer
Session
Choate Rosemary Hall Writing
Project
Choate Rosemary Hall Young Writers
Workshop

Clearwater Camp, Inc.
Clearwater Camp for Girls

Colorado College Summer Programs
Colorado College Summer Session

Cornell University
Cornell University Summer College
Programs for High School Students

Crossroads School for Arts and Sciences
Crossroads School–Aquatics
Crossroads School–Jazz Workshop
Crossroads School–Sports Camps
Crossroads School–Summer
Educational Journey

Cushing Academy
Cushing Academy Summer Session

Cybercamps–Giant Campus, Inc.
Cybercamps–Adelphi University
Cybercamps–American University
Cybercamps–Barry University
Cybercamps–Bellevue Community
College
Cybercamps–Benedictine University
Cybercamps–Bentley College
Cybercamps–Bryn Mawr College
Cybercamps–Caldwell College
Cybercamps–College of St. Elizabeth
Cybercamps–Concordia University,
Chicago
Cybercamps–Concordia University,
Irvine
Cybercamps–Dana Hall School
Cybercamps–DeAnza College
Cybercamps–Duke University
Cybercamps–Fordham University
Cybercamps–George Mason
University
Cybercamps–Georgia State University
Cybercamps–Lewis and Clark College
Cybercamps–Loyola University
Cybercamps–Merrimack College
Cybercamps–MIT
Cybercamps–The New School
Cybercamps–New York Institute of
Technology
Cybercamps–Northern Virginia
Community College
Cybercamps–Nova Southeastern
University
Cybercamps–Oak Marr Rec Center
Cybercamps–Oglethorpe University
Cybercamps–Rutgers University
Cybercamps–St. John's University
Cybercamps–Southern Polytechnic
State University
Cybercamps–Stanford University
Cybercamps–Towson University
Cybercamps–Trinity Lutheran College
Cybercamps–UCLA
Cybercamps–UC San Diego (UCSD)
Cybercamps–UNC, Chapel Hill
Cybercamps–University of Bridgeport
Cybercamps–University of California
at Berkeley
Cybercamps–University of Central
Florida

▶ CYBERCAMPS–GIANT CAMPUS, INC.

Cybercamps–University of Hartford
Cybercamps–University of Maryland
Cybercamps–University of Miami
Cybercamps–University of Michigan
Cybercamps–University of Minnesota
Cybercamps–University of Washington
Cybercamps–University of Washington, Bothell
Cybercamps–Webster University

Darlington School
Darlington Summer Programs

The Delphian School
Summer at Delphi

Duke University Talent Identification Program (Duke TIP)
Duke TIP Domestic Field Studies
Duke TIP Institutes
Duke TIP International Field Studies
Duke University PreCollege Program

Duke Youth Programs–Duke University Continuing Studies
Constructing Your College Experience
Duke Action: Science Camp for Young Women
Duke Creative Writers' Workshop
Duke Drama Workshop
Duke Young Writers Camp
EXPRESSIONS! Duke Fine Arts Camp

Eaglebrook School
Eaglebrook Summer Semester

Eagle Hill School
Eagle Hill School Summer Session

Eastern U.S. Music Camp, Inc. at Colgate University

Edu-Culture International (ECI)
Edu-Culture International (ECI)–Aix-en-Provence/Gap Host Family Immersion
Edu-Culture International (ECI)–Andalusion Total Immersion
Edu-Culture International (ECI)–CPI Costa Rica
Edu-Culture International (ECI)–Granada Homestay
Edu-Culture International (ECI)–Granada Homestay or Dorm Plus Southern Host Family Immersion
Edu-Culture International (ECI)–Granada-Nerja Homestay Combo
Edu-Culture International (ECI)–Grecia Costa Rica

Edu-Culture International (ECI)–Lyon Host Family and Travel Program
Edu-Culture International (ECI)–Nerja Homestay Plus Southern Host Family Immersion
Edu-Culture International (ECI)–Nerja Homestay with Optional Southern Host Family Immersion
Edu-Culture International (ECI)–Salamanca Dorm Plus Southern Host Family Immersion
Edu-Culture International (ECI)–Salamanca Homestay
Edu-Culture International (ECI)–Salamanca Homestay Plus Northern Host Family Immersion
Edu-Culture International (ECI)–Salamanca Homestay (Short Version)
Edu-Culture International (ECI)–San Sebastian Homestay Plus Southern Host Family Immersion
Edu-Culture International (ECI)–Toulouse/Montpellier Host Family Immersion

EF International Language Schools
EF International Language School–Barcelona
EF International Language School–Beijing
EF International Language School–Malaga
EF International Language School–Munich
EF International Language School–Nice
EF International Language School–Paris
EF International Language School–Playa Tamarindo
EF International Language School–Quito
EF International Language School–Rome
EF International Language School–Shanghai

Elite Educational Institute
Elite Educational Institute Elementary Enrichment
Elite Educational Institute Elementary Enrichment–Korea
Elite Educational Institute Junior High/PSAT Program
Elite Educational Institute Junior High/PSAT Program–Korea
Elite Educational Institute SAT and Subject Test Preparation

Elite Educational Institute SAT Bootcamp–Korea
Elite Educational Institute SAT Preparation–Korea
Elite Educational Institute SAT Summer Bootcamp
Elite Educational Institute–University of Oklahoma College Courses

Emagination Computer Camps
Emagination Computer Camps–Georgia
Emagination Computer Camps–Illinois
Emagination Computer Camps–Massachusetts
Emagination Computer Camps–Pennsylvania

Emma Willard School
GirlSummer at Emma Willard School

Enforex Spanish in the Spanish World
Enforex–General Spanish–Alicante
Enforex–General Spanish–Barcelona
Enforex–General Spanish–Granada
Enforex–General Spanish–Madrid
Enforex–General Spanish–Malaga
Enforex–General Spanish–Marbella
Enforex–General Spanish–Salamanca
Enforex–General Spanish–Sevilla
Enforex–General Spanish–Tenerife
Enforex–General Spanish–Valencia
Enforex Hispanic Culture: Civilization, History, Art, and Literature–Alicante
Enforex Hispanic Culture: Civilization, History, Art, and Literature–Barcelona
Enforex Hispanic Culture: Civilization, History, Art, and Literature–Granada
Enforex Hispanic Culture: Civilization, History, Art, and Literature–Madrid
Enforex Hispanic Culture: Civilization, History, Art, and Literature–Malaga
Enforex Hispanic Culture: Civilization, History, Art, and Literature–Salamanca
Enforex Hispanic Culture: Civilization, History, Art, and Literature–Sevilla
Enforex Hispanic Culture: Civilization, History, Art, and Literature–Tenerife
Enforex Hispanic Culture: History, Art, and Literature–Valencia
Enforex Homestay Program–Alicante

Enforex Homestay Program–Barcelona

Enforex Homestay Program–Granada

Enforex Homestay Program–Madrid

Enforex Homestay Program–Malaga

Enforex Homestay Program–Marbella

Enforex Homestay Program–Salamanca

Enforex Homestay Program–Sevilla

Enforex Homestay Program–Tenerife

Enforex Homestay Program–Valencia

Enforex Residential Youth Summer Camp–Barcelona

Enforex Residential Youth Summer Camp–Granada

Enforex Residential Youth Summer Camp–Guanajuato, Mexico

Enforex Residential Youth Summer Camp–Madrid

Enforex Residential Youth Summer Camp–Marbella Albergue College

Enforex Residential Youth Summer Camp–Marbella Alboran College

Enforex Residential Youth Summer Camp–Marbella Aleman College

Enforex Residential Youth Summer Camp–Salamanca

Enforex Residential Youth Summer Camp–Valencia

Enforex Spanish and Golf

Enforex Spanish and Tennis

Enforex Study Tour Vacational Program–Alicante

Enforex Study Tour Vacational Program–Barcelona

Enforex Study Tour Vacational Program–Granada

Enforex Study Tour Vacational Program–Madrid

Enforex Study Tour Vacational Program–Malaga

Enforex Study Tour Vacational Program–Marbella

Enforex Study Tour Vacational Program–Salamanca

Enforex Study Tour Vacational Program–Sevilla

Enforex Study Tour Vacational Program–Tenerife

Enforex Study Tour Vacational Program–Valencia

Spanish Language and Flamenco Enforex–Granada

Spanish Language and Flamenco Enforex–Madrid

Spanish Language and Flamenco Enforex–Marbella

Spanish Language and Flamenco Enforex–Sevilla

Ensemble Theatre Community School

The Experiment in International Living

The Experiment in International Living–Argentina Homestay, Community Service, and Outdoor Ecological Program

The Experiment in International Living, Argentina Visual Arts, Photography, and Service

The Experiment in International Living–Australia Homestay

The Experiment in International Living–Belize Homestay

The Experiment in International Living–Botswana Homestay

The Experiment in International Living–Brazil–Community Service and Soccer

The Experiment in International Living–Brazil Homestay, Arts, and Community Service

The Experiment in International Living–Chile North Homestay, Community Service

The Experiment in International Living–Chile South Homestay

The Experiment in International Living–China North and East Homestay

The Experiment in International Living–China South and West Homestay

The Experiment in International Living–Costa Rica Homestay

The Experiment in International Living–Ecuador Homestay

The Experiment in International Living–France, Biking and Homestay

The Experiment in International Living–France, Five-Week Art and Adventure in Provence

The Experiment in International Living–France, Four-Week Brittany Discovery

The Experiment in International Living–France, Four-Week Homestay and Photography

The Experiment in International Living–France, Four-Week Homestay and Theatre

The Experiment in International Living–France, Four-Week Homestay and Travel–Southern France and Northern Spain

The Experiment in International Living–France, Four-Week Homestay and Travel through Alps

The Experiment in International Living–France, Homestay, Language Training, and Cooking

The Experiment in International Living–France, Three-Week Camargue Homestay

The Experiment in International Living–France, Three-Week Homestay and Travel–Borders

The Experiment in International Living–Germany, Four-Week Homestay, Travel, Community Service

The Experiment in International Living–Ghana Homestay

The Experiment in International Living–Italy Biodiversity, Cooking, and Culture

The Experiment in International Living–Italy Homestay, Language, Culture, and Travel

The Experiment in International Living–Japan Homestay

The Experiment in International Living–Mexico–Community Service, Travel, and Homestay

The Experiment in International Living–Mexico Cooking and Culture

The Experiment in International Living–Mexico Homestqy, Sustainable Development and Fair Trade

The Experiment in International Living–Mexico–Mayan Arts and Culture

The Experiment in International Living–Morocco Four-Week Arts and Culture Program

The Experiment in International Living–Navajo Nation

The Experiment in International Living–New Zealand Homestay

The Experiment in International Living–Poland, Homestay, Community Service, and Travel

The Experiment in International Living–Scotland

The Experiment in International Living–South Africa Homestay and Community Service

The Experiment in International Living–Spain, Five-Week Homestay, Language Immersion

The Experiment in International Living–Spain, Four-Week Language Training, Travel, and Homestay

The Experiment in International Living–Spain–Multiculturalism and Service

▶ THE EXPERIMENT IN INTERNATIONAL LIVING

The Experiment in International Living–Spain–Spanish Arts and Culture

The Experiment in International Living–Spain–The Road to Santiago

The Experiment in International Living–Spanish Culture and Exploration

The Experiment in International Living–Switzerland French Language Immersion, Homestay, and Alpine Adventure

The Experiment in International Living–Thailand Homestay

The Experiment in International Living–Turkey Homestay, Community Service, and Travel

The Experiment in International Living–United Kingdom Filmmaking Program and Homestay

The Experiment in International Living–United Kingdom Theatre Program

Fairfax Collegiate School
Fairfax Collegiate School Summer Enrichment Program

The Fenn School
Fenn School Summer Day Camp

The Fessenden School
The Fessenden School Summer ESL Program

Forest Ridge School of the Sacred Heart
Forest Ridge Summer Program

Georgetown University
Georgetown University American Politics and Public Affairs

Georgetown University College Prep Program

Georgetown University Gateway to Business Program for High School Students

Georgetown University International Relations Program for High School Students

Georgetown University Journalism Workshop for High School Students

Georgetown University Summer College for High School Students

George Washington University
George Washington University Summer Scholars Mini-courses

George Washington University Summer Scholars Pre-college Program

Gettysburg College
Academic Camps at Gettysburg College

Global Leadership Adventures
Global Leadership Adventures–Brazil: Community Service and Leadership

Global Leadership Adventures–Cape Town: Community Service and Leadership

Global Leadership Adventures–Costa Rica: Community Service and Leadership

Global Leadership Adventures–Ghana: Community Service and Leadership

Global Leadership Adventures–India: Community Service and Leadership

GLOBAL WORKS
GLOBAL WORKS–Cultural Exchange and Service–Costa Rica-3 weeks

GLOBAL WORKS–Cultural Exchange and Service–Ireland-4 weeks

GLOBAL WORKS–Cultural Exchange and Service–New Zealand and Fiji Islands-4 weeks

GLOBAL WORKS–Cultural Exchange and Service–Puerto Rico-2 or 4 weeks

GLOBAL WORKS–Cultural Exchange–Fiji Islands-4 weeks

GLOBAL WORKS–Language Immersion, Cultural Exchange and Service–Argentina

GLOBAL WORKS–Language Immersion, Cultural Exchange and Service–Costa Rica

GLOBAL WORKS–Language Immersion, Cultural Exchange and Service–Ecuador and the Galapagos-4 weeks

GLOBAL WORKS–Language Immersion, Cultural Exchange and Service–France-4 weeks

GLOBAL WORKS–Language Immersion, Cultural Exchange and Service–Martinique-4weeks

GLOBAL WORKS–Language Immersion, Cultural Exchange and Service–Mexico–3 weeks

GLOBAL WORKS–Language Immersion, Cultural Exchange and Service–Panama/Costa Rica

GLOBAL WORKS–Language Immersion, Cultural Exchange and Service–Peru

GLOBAL WORKS–Language Immersion, Cultural Exchange and Service–Puerto Rico-4 weeks

GLOBAL WORKS–Language Immersion, Cultural Exchange and Service–Spain-4 weeks

GLOBAL WORKS–Language Immersion, Cultural Exchange and Service–Yucatan Peninsula, Mexico-4 weeks

The Gow School
The Gow School Summer Program

The Grand River Academy
The Grand River Summer Academy

Hargrave Military Academy
Hargrave Summer Leadership Program

The Harker School
Harker Summer English Language Institute

The Harker Summer Institute

Harker Summer Programs

Harvard University Summer School: Secondary School Program
Harvard University Summer School: Secondary School Program

Hawai'i Preparatory Academy
Hawaii Preparatory Academy Summer Session

Heidelberg College
Summerberg at Heidelberg College

Holiday Trails, Inc.
Camp Holiday Trails

Humanities Spring in Assisi
Humanities Spring in Assisi

The Hun School of Princeton
The Hun School of Princeton American Culture and Language Institute

The Hun School of Princeton–Summer Academic Session

The Hun School of Princeton–Summer Day Camp

iD Tech Camps
iD Gaming Academy–Stanford University, Palo Alto, CA

iD Gaming Academy–UC Berkeley, Berkeley, CA

iD Gaming Academy–UCLA, Westwood, CA

iD Gaming Academy–Villanova University, Villanova, PA

iD Tech Camps–Arizona State University, Tempe, AZ

iD Tech Camps–Brown University, Providence, RI

iD Tech Camps–Cal Lutheran University, Thousand Oaks, CA

iD Tech Camps–Carnegie Mellon University, Pittsburgh, PA

iD Tech Camps–Case Western Reserve University, Cleveland, OH

iD Tech Camps–College of William and Mary, Williamsburg, VA

iD Tech Camps–Colorado College, Colorado Springs, CO

iD Tech Camps–Columbia University, New York, NY

iD Tech Camps–Documentary Filmmaking and Cultural Immersion in Spain

iD Tech Camps–Emory University, Atlanta, GA

iD Tech Camps–Fordham University, Bronx, NY

iD Tech Camps–Georgetown University, Washington, D.C.

iD Tech Camps–Lake Forest College, Evanston, IL

iD Tech Camps–Merrimack College, North Andover, MA

iD Tech Camps–MIT, Cambridge, MA

iD Tech Camps–Northwestern University, Chicago, IL

iD Tech Camps–Pepperdine University, Malibu, CA

iD Tech Camps–Rider University, Lawrenceville, NJ

iD Tech Camps–Sacred Heart University, Fairfield, CT

iD Tech Camps–St. Mary's College of California, Moraga, CA

iD Tech Camps–Santa Clara University, Santa Clara, CA

iD Tech Camps–Seton Hall University, South Orange, NJ

iD Tech Camps–Smith College, Northampton, MA

iD Tech Camps–Southern Methodist University, Dallas, TX

iD Tech Camps–Stanford University, Palo Alto, CA

iD Tech Camps–Tiger Woods Learning Center, Anaheim, CA

iD Tech Camps–UC Berkeley, Berkeley, CA

iD Tech Camps–UC Davis, Davis, CA

iD Tech Camps–UC Irvine, Irvine, CA

iD Tech Camps–UCLA, Westwood, CA

iD Tech Camps–UC San Diego, La Jolla, CA

iD Tech Camps–UC Santa Cruz, Santa Cruz, CA

iD Tech Camps–University of Central Florida, Orlando, FL

iD Tech Camps–University of Denver, Denver, CO

iD Tech Camps–University of Houston, Houston, TX

iD Tech Camps–University of Miami, Coral Gables, FL

iD Tech Camps–University of Michigan, Ann Arbor, MI

iD Tech Camps–University of Minnesota, Minneapolis, MN

iD Tech Camps–University of North Carolina at Chapel Hill, Chapel Hill, NC

iD Tech Camps–University of Virginia, Charlottesville, VA

iD Tech Camps–University of Washington, Seattle, WA

iD Tech Camps–UT Austin, Austin, TX

iD Tech Camps–Vanderbilt University, Nashville, TN

iD Tech Camps–Vassar College, Poughkeepsie, NY

iD Tech Camps–Villanova University, Villanova, PA

iD Tech Camps–Virginia Tech, Blacksburg, VA

iD Tech Camps–Wake Forest University, Winston-Salem, NC

iD Tech Camps–Washington University in St. Louis, St. Louis, MO

Idyllwild Arts Foundation

Idyllwild Arts Summer Program–Children's Center

Idyllwild Arts Summer Program–Family Week

Idyllwild Arts Summer Program–Junior Artists' Center

Idyllwild Arts Summer Program–Youth Arts Center

Interlochen Center for the Arts

Interlochen Arts Camp

International Seminar Series

Service Learning in Barcelona

Service Learning in Paris

International Summer Camp Montana, Switzerland

International Summer Camp Montana, Switzerland

Intern Exchange International, Ltd.

IEI–Fashion and Design Plus Programme

IEI–Photography Plus Programme

IEI–Print and Broadcast Journalism

IEI Student Travel–Internship Program in London

IEI–Theatre Plus Programme

IEI–Video Production Plus Programme

Internship Connection

Internship Connection

Ithaca College Division of Continuing Education and Summer Sessions

Ithaca College Summer College for High School Students: Minicourses

Ithaca College Summer College for High School Students: Session I

Ithaca College Summer College for High School Students: Session II

Ithaca College Summer Piano Institute

The Johns Hopkins University

Johns Hopkins University Zanvyl Krieger School of Arts and Sciences Summer Programs

Junior Statesmen Foundation

Junior Statesmen Summer School–Georgetown University

Junior Statesmen Summer School–Princeton University

Junior Statesmen Summer School–Stanford University

Junior Statesmen Summer School–Yale University

Junior Statesmen Symposium on California State Politics and Government

Junior Statesmen Symposium on Los Angeles Politics and Government

Junior Statesmen Symposium on New Jersey State Politics and Government

Junior Statesmen Symposium on Ohio State Politics and Government

Junior Statesmen Symposium on Texas Politics and Leadership

Junior Statesmen Symposium on Washington State Politics and Government

Kamp Kohut

Kamp Kohut

▶ KEEWAYDIN FOUNDATION

Keewaydin Foundation
Keewaydin Dunmore
Keewaydin Temagami
Songadeewin of Keewaydin

Kent School
Kent School Summer Writers Camp

Kildonan School
Dunnabeck at Kildonan

Killooleet

Landmark School
Landmark School Summer Academic
Program

Landmark Volunteers, Inc.
Landmark Volunteers: Arizona
Landmark Volunteers: California
Landmark Volunteers: Colorado
Landmark Volunteers: Connecticut
Landmark Volunteers: Idaho
Landmark Volunteers: Maine
Landmark Volunteers: Massachusetts
Landmark Volunteers: Michigan
Landmark Volunteers: Minnesota
Landmark Volunteers: Montana
Landmark Volunteers: New Jersey
Landmark Volunteers: New Mexico
Landmark Volunteers: New York
Landmark Volunteers: Oregon
Landmark Volunteers: Pennsylvania
Landmark Volunteers: Rhode Island
Landmark Volunteers: Vermont
Landmark Volunteers: Virginia
Landmark Volunteers: Washington
Landmark Volunteers: Wyoming

**Les Elfes International
Summer/Winter Camp**
Les Elfes–International Summer/
Winter Camp

**Leysin American School in
Switzerland**
Summer in Switzerland

LIFEWORKS International
LIFEWORKS with the Australian
Red Cross
LIFEWORKS with the British Virgin
Islands Marine Parks and
Conservation Department
LIFEWORKS with the China Little
Flower Foundation in China
LIFEWORKS with the DPF
Foundation in Thailand
LIFEWORKS with the Fundación
Humanitaria in Costa Rica
LIFEWORKS with the Galapagos
Islands' National Parks

Linden Hill School
Linden Hill Summer Program

Lochearn Camp for Girls

The Madeira School
Girls First

Mad River Glen Cooperative
Mad River Glen Naturalist Adventure
Camp

**Marianapolis Preparatory
School**
Marianapolis Summer Program

The Marvelwood School
Marvelwood Summer Program

Massachusetts College of Art
Massachusetts College of Art/Creative
Vacation
Massachusetts College of Art/Summer
Studios

**Massachusetts Institute of
Technology**
MIT MITES (Minority Introduction to
Engineering and Science)

Miami University
Miami University Junior Scholars
Program

**Michigan Technological
University**
Michigan Technological University
American Indian Workshop
Michigan Technological University
Explorations in Engineering
Workshop
Michigan Technological University
Summer Youth Program
Michigan Technological University
Women in Engineering Workshop

**Milwaukee School of
Engineering**
Milwaukee School of Engineering
(MSOE)–Discover the Possibilities
Milwaukee School of Engineering
(MSOE)–Focus on Business
Milwaukee School of Engineering
(MSOE)–Focus on Nursing
Milwaukee School of Engineering
(MSOE)–Focus on Technical
Communication
Milwaukee School of Engineering
(MSOE)–Focus on the Possibilities

Miss Porter's School
Miss Porter's School Arts Alive!

Miss Porter's School Athletic
Experience
Miss Porter's School Daoyun Chinese
Summer Program
Miss Porter's School Summer
Challenge
The Sarah Porter Leadership
Institute

Mount Holyoke College
Mount Holyoke College SEARCH
(Summer Explorations and
Research Collaborations for High
School Girls) Program
Mount Holyoke College SummerMath
Program
Summer Action–Take the Lead

**National Student Leadership
Conference**
National Student Leadership
Conference: Engineering–San
Francisco
National Student Leadership
Conference: Engineering–
Washington, D.C.
National Student Leadership
Conference: Entrepreneurship and
Business–New York City
National Student Leadership
Conference: Entrepreneurship and
Business–Washington, D.C.
National Student Leadership
Conference: Forensic Science
National Student Leadership
Conference: Globalization and
International Business–Study
Abroad
National Student Leadership
Conference: Globalization and
International Business–
Washington, D.C.
National Student Leadership
Conference: Inside the Arts–New
York City
National Student Leadership
Conference: Intelligence and
National Security
National Student Leadership
Conference: International
Diplomacy–Washington, D.C.
National Student Leadership
Conference: Journalism and Mass
Communication
National Student Leadership
Conference: Law and Advocacy–
San Francisco
National Student Leadership
Conference: Law and Advocacy–
Washington, D.C.
National Student Leadership
Conference: Mastering Leadership

National Student Leadership Conference: Medicine and Health Care–San Francisco

National Student Leadership Conference: Medicine and Health Care–Washington, D.C.

National Student Leadership Conference: State Leadership Workshops

National Student Leadership Conference: U.S. Policy and Politics

New York University, Tisch School of the Arts
Tisch School of the Arts–International High School Program–Dublin
Tisch School of the Arts–International High School Program–Paris
Tisch School of the Arts–Summer High School Programs

92nd Street YM–YWHA
92nd Street Y Camps–Camp Bari Tov
92nd Street Y Camps–Camp Kesher
92nd Street Y Camps–Camp Tevah for Science and Nature
92nd Street Y Camps–Camp Tova
92nd Street Y Camps–Camp Yaffa for the Arts
92nd Street Y Camps–Camp Yomi
92nd Street Y Camps–The TIYUL
92nd Street Y Camps–Trailblazers

Northfield Mount Hermon School
Northfield Mount Hermon Summer Session

Northwestern University
Northwestern University's College Preparation Program
Northwestern University's National High School Institute

Northwestern University's Center for Talent Development
Center for Talent Development Summer Academic Program

Norwich University
Future Leader Camp

Oak Creek Ranch School
Oak Creek Ranch School–Summer Academic Program

The Oxbow School
Oxbow Summer Art Camp

Oxbridge Academic Programs
The Cambridge Prep Experience
The Cambridge Tradition
La Academia de España
L' Académie de France
L' Académie de Paris
The Oxford Prep Experience
The Oxford Tradition

Oxford Media School
Oxford Media School–Film
Oxford Media School–Film Master Class
Oxford Media School–Newsroom in Europe
Oxford Media School–Newsroom in Europe, Master Class

Oxford Tutorial College
Oxford Advanced Studies Program

Perry-Mansfield Performing Arts School and Camp
Perry-Mansfield Performing Arts School and Camp

The Phelps School
College InSight

Phillips Academy (Andover)
Phillips Academy Summer Session

Phillips Exeter Academy
Phillips Exeter Academy Summer School

Pine Island Camp
Pine Island Camp

Portsmouth Abbey School
Portsmouth Abbey Summer School

Pratt Institute
Pratt Institute Summer Pre-College Program for High School Students

The Putney School
The Putney School Summer Arts Program
The Putney School Summer Program for International Education (ESL)
The Putney School Summer Writing Program

Putney Student Travel
Excel at Amherst College
Excel at Madrid/Barcelona
Excel at Oxford/Tuscany
Excel at Paris/Provence
Excel China
Putney Student Travel–Community Service–Alaska

Putney Student Travel–Community Service–Argentina
Putney Student Travel–Community Service–Costa Rica
Putney Student Travel–Community Service–Dominican Republic
Putney Student Travel–Community Service–Dominica, West Indies
Putney Student Travel–Community Service–Ecuador
Putney Student Travel–Community Service–Hawaii
Putney Student Travel–Community Service–India
Putney Student Travel–Community Service–Nicaragua
Putney Student Travel–Community Service–Nusa Penida and Bali
Putney Student Travel–Community Service–Senegal
Putney Student Travel–Community Service–Tanzania
Putney Student Travel–Community Service–Vietnam
Putney Student Travel–Cultural Exploration–Australia, New Zealand, and Fiji
Putney Student Travel–Cultural Exploration–Creative Writing in Argentina
Putney Student Travel–Cultural Exploration–Switzerland, Italy, France, and Holland
Putney Student Travel–Cultural Exploration–Thailand and Cambodia
Putney Student Travel–Cultural Exploration–Theatre in Britain
Putney Student Travel–Global Action–El Salvador
Putney Student Travel–Global Action–India
Putney Student Travel–Global Action–Malawi
Putney Student Travel–Global Action–South Africa
Putney Student Travel–Global Awareness–China
Putney Student Travel–Global Awareness in Action–Cambodia
Putney Student Travel–Global Awareness–Madagascar
Putney Student Travel–Language Learning–Argentina
Putney Student Travel–Language Learning–Costa Rica
Putney Student Travel–Language Learning–France
Putney Student Travel–Language Learning–Spain

► RANDOLPH-MACON ACADEMY

Randolph-Macon Academy
Randolph-Macon Academy Summer
    Programs

Rassias Programs
Rassias Programs–Arles, France
Rassias Programs–China
Rassias Programs–Gijón, Spain
Rassias Programs–Pontevedra, Spain
Rassias Programs–Segovia, Spain
Rassias Programs–Tours, France

The Rectory School
summer@rectory

Rein Teen Tours
Rein Europe
Rein Teen Tours–California Caper
Rein Teen Tours–Crossroads
Rein Teen Tours–Eastern Adventure
Rein Teen Tours–Grand Adventure
Rein Teen Tours–Hawaiian/Alaskan
    Adventure
Rein Teen Tours–Hawaiian Caper
Rein Teen Tours–Project Hawaii
Rein Teen Tours–Western Adventure

Rensselaer Polytechnic Institute–Outreach Programs
Summer@Rensselaer

Rhode Island School of Design
Rhode Island School of Design
    Pre-College Program

Roaring Brook Camp for Boys

Rumsey Hall School
Rumsey Hall School Summer Session

Rustic Pathways
RUSTIC PATHWAYS–THE
    AMAZING THAILAND
    ADVENTURE
RUSTIC PATHWAYS–THE ART OF
    MUAY THAI
RUSTIC PATHWAYS–ASIAN
    PACIFIC EXTREME
RUSTIC PATHWAYS–BIG FIJI
    EXPLORER
RUSTIC PATHWAYS–THE
    BUDDHIST CARAVAN
RUSTIC PATHWAYS–THE CANO
    NEGRO SERVICE PROJECT
RUSTIC PATHWAYS–CHINESE
    LANGUAGE IMMERSION
RUSTIC PATHWAYS–CLIMBING
    KILI
RUSTIC PATHWAYS–COME WITH
    NOTHING, GO HOME RICH
RUSTIC PATHWAYS–COMMUNITY
    SERVICE SCHOOL IN
    AUSTRALIA

RUSTIC PATHWAYS–COSTA RICA
    ADVENTURER
RUSTIC PATHWAYS–EDGE OF THE
    MAP EXTREME
RUSTIC PATHWAYS–ELEPHANTS
    & AMAZING THAILAND
RUSTIC PATHWAYS–ESCAPE TO
    FIJI
RUSTIC PATHWAYS–EXTENDED
    FIJI VILLAGE SERVICE
RUSTIC PATHWAYS–FACES AND
    PLACES OF VIETNAM
RUSTIC PATHWAYS–FIJI ISLANDS
    COMMUNITY SERVICE
RUSTIC PATHWAYS–HILL TRIBE
    TREKKING ADVENTURE
RUSTIC PATHWAYS–INDIAN
    HIMALAYA TRAVELER
RUSTIC PATHWAYS–INTENSIVE
    CHINESE LANGUAGE
RUSTIC PATHWAYS–INTENSIVE
    SPANISH LANGUAGE
RUSTIC PATHWAYS–
    INTRODUCTION TO
    PHOTOGRAPHY–SNAPSHOTS
    IN THE LAND OF SMILES
RUSTIC PATHWAYS–INTRO TO
    COMMUNITY SERVICE IN FIJI
RUSTIC PATHWAYS–INTRO TO
    COMMUNITY SERVICE IN
    THAILAND
RUSTIC PATHWAYS–ISLAND
    HOPPING AND DIVING–
    THAILAND
RUSTIC PATHWAYS–MALEKU
    TRIBE IMMERSION PROGRAM–
    COSTA RICA
RUSTIC PATHWAYS–NEW
    ORLEANS SUMMER
    REBUILDING PROGRAM
RUSTIC PATHWAYS–NEW
    ZEALAND NORTH ISLAND
    ADVENTURE
RUSTIC PATHWAYS–OFF THE MAP
    BURMA AND CAMBODIA
RUSTIC PATHWAYS–
    PHOTOGRAPHY ADVENTURE
    IN THAILAND AND ANGKOR
    WAT
RUSTIC PATHWAYS–
    PHOTOGRAPHY ADVENTURE
    IN THAILAND AND BURMA
RUSTIC PATHWAYS–
    PHOTOGRAPHY ADVENTURE
    IN THAILAND AND INDIA
RUSTIC PATHWAYS–
    PHOTOGRAPHY ADVENTURE
    IN THAILAND AND VIETNAM
RUSTIC PATHWAYS–RAMP UP
    YOUR SPANISH

RUSTIC PATHWAYS–REMOTE
    HIGHLANDS COMMUNITY
    SERVICE IN FIJI
RUSTIC PATHWAYS–RICEFIELDS,
    MONKS & SMILING CHILDREN
RUSTIC PATHWAYS–SERVICE AND
    SAFARI IN AFRICA
RUSTIC PATHWAYS–SERVICE IN
    THE CLOUDS–INDIA
RUSTIC PATHWAYS–SERVICE
    LEARNING EXTREME
RUSTIC PATHWAYS–SKI AND
    SNOWBOARD ADVENTURE IN
    NEW ZEALAND
RUSTIC PATHWAYS–SOCCER AND
    SERVICE EXTREME
RUSTIC PATHWAYS–SOCCER AND
    SERVICE IN COSTA RICA
RUSTIC PATHWAYS–SOCCER AND
    SERVICE IN FIJI
RUSTIC PATHWAYS–SOCCER AND
    SERVICE IN THAILAND
RUSTIC PATHWAYS–SOUTH
    PACIFIC EXTREME
RUSTIC PATHWAYS–SPANISH
    LANGUAGE IMMERSION
RUSTIC PATHWAYS–SUN, SAND &
    INTERNATIONAL SERVICE–FIJI
RUSTIC PATHWAYS–SURF &
    SERVICE–COSTA RICA
RUSTIC PATHWAYS–SURF THE
    SUMMER–COSTA RICA
RUSTIC PATHWAYS–SYDNEY,
    REEF & RAINFOREST
RUSTIC PATHWAYS–THE THAI
    ELEPHANT CONSERVATION
    PROJECT
RUSTIC PATHWAYS–THE TURTLE
    CONSERVATION PROJECT
RUSTIC PATHWAYS–ULTIMATE
    JUNGLE ADVENTURE–COSTA
    RICA
RUSTIC PATHWAYS–VOLCANOES
    AND RAINFORESTS
RUSTIC PATHWAYS–THE
    WONDERS & RICHES OF
    SOUTHEAST ASIA
RUSTIC PATHWAYS–THE
    WONDERS OF CHINA
RUSTIC PATHWAYS–WORLD
    SERVICE EXTREME
RUSTIC PATHWAYS–YOUNG
    ADVENTURERS–COSTA RICA

Saint Thomas More School
Saint Thomas More School–Summer
    Academic Camp

St. Timothy's School
Intensive English Language Program
International Leadership Program

Salem Academy and College
Salem Spotlight

Salisbury Summer School
Salisbury Summer School

Sarah Lawrence College
Sarah Lawrence College Summer
  High School Programs

School of the Museum of Fine Arts, Boston
School of the Museum of Fine Arts,
  Boston–Pre-College Summer
  Studio

Seacamp

Skidmore College
Skidmore College–Pre-College
  Program in the Liberal & Studio
  Arts for High School Students

Smith College
Smith College Summer Science and
  Engineering Program

Southern Methodist University
Southern Methodist University
  College Experience
Southern Methodist University TAG
  (Talented and Gifted)

Southwestern Academy's Southwestern Adventures
Southwestern Adventures–Arizona
Southwestern Adventures–California

Spoleto Study Abroad
Spoleto Study Abroad

Squaw Valley Academy
Squaw Valley Academy Summer
  School

Stagedoor Manor Performing Arts Training Center/Theatre and Dance Camp

Stanford University Summer Session
Stanford University High School
  Summer College

Studies Abroad for Global Education (SAGE), Summer SAGE Program
Studies Abroad for Global Education
  (SAGE), Summer SAGE Program

Summer Institute for the Gifted
The Summer Institute for the Gifted
  at Amherst College
The Summer Institute for the Gifted
  at Bryn Mawr College
The Summer Institute for the Gifted
  at Emory University
The Summer Institute for the Gifted
  at Fairfield University
The Summer Institute for the Gifted
  at Manhattanville College
The Summer Institute for the Gifted
  at Moorestown Friends School
The Summer Institute for the Gifted
  at Princeton University
The Summer Institute for the Gifted
  at UCLA
The Summer Institute for the Gifted
  at University of California,
  Berkeley
The Summer Institute for the Gifted
  at University of Michigan, Ann
  Arbor
The Summer Institute for the Gifted
  at University of Texas, Austin
The Summer Institute for the Gifted
  at Vassar College

Summer Study Programs
Summer Study at Penn State
Summer Study at The University of
  Colorado at Boulder
Summer Study in Paris at The
  Sorbonne

Summer Theatre Institute New York City
Summer Theatre Institute–NYC,
  2008

Syracuse University
Syracuse University Summer College

Tabor Academy
Tabor Academy Summer Program
Tabor Hockey School

The Taft School
Taft Summer School
Taft Summer School Abroad–France
Taft Summer School Abroad–Spain

Talisman Summer Programs
Talisman Summer Camp

TASC for Teens, Inc.
TASC Canadian Wilderness Fishing
  Camps

TASIS The American School in England
TASIS Arts and Architecture in the
  South of France
TASIS England Summer Program
TASIS Spanish Summer Program

TASIS The American School in Switzerland
TASIS French Language Program in
  Château-d'Oex, Switzerland
TASIS Le Château des Enfants
TASIS Middle School Program
TASIS Summer Program for
  Languages, Arts, and Outdoor
  Pursuits
TASIS Tuscan Academy of Art and
  Culture

Teton Valley Ranch Camp Education Foundation
Teton Valley Ranch Camp–Boys
  Camp
Teton Valley Ranch Camp–Girls
  Camp

Treetops eXpeditions
Treetops eXpeditions–Alaska
  Community Service
Treetops eXpeditions–Glacier/
  Boundary Waters
Treetops eXpeditions–Horseback
  Riding
Treetops eXpeditions–Sailing and
  Marine Ecology
Treetops eXpeditions–Vanuatu

UCLA Summer Sessions and Special Programs
UCLA Summer Experience: College
  Level Courses
UCLA Summer Experience: Institutes

Union College
FivePoints

University of Chicago
University of Chicago–Insight
University of Chicago–Research in
  the Biological Sciences
University of Chicago–Stones and
  Bones
University of Chicago–Summer
  Quarter for High School Students
University of Chicago–The Traveling
  Academy

University of Connecticut American English Language Institute (UCAELI)
Summer English Experience

University of Connecticut Neag Center for Gifted Education and Talent Development
University of Connecticut Mentor Connection

University of Maryland, Office of Extended Studies
University of Maryland Young Scholars Program

University of Miami
University of Miami Summer Scholar Programs

University of Pennsylvania
University of Pennsylvania–Penn Summer Art and Architecture Studios
University of Pennsylvania–Penn Summer Science Academies
University of Pennsylvania–Penn Summer Theatre Workshop
University of Pennsylvania–Pre-College Program

University of Southern California–Office of Continuing Education and Summer Programs
Science Program for High School Girls
Science Program for Middle School Boys on Catalina
Science Program for Middle School Girls on Catalina
University of Southern California Summer Seminars

University of Southern California, School of Architecture
Exploration of Architecture

The University of the Arts
Pre-College Summer Institute, The University of the Arts

University of Vermont, College of Engineering and Mathematical Sciences
University of Vermont Summer Engineering Institute for High School Students

Valley Forge Military Academy and College
Valley Forge Military Academy Summer Band Camp
Valley Forge Military Academy Summer Camp for Boys

Valley Forge Military Academy Summer Coed Day Camp

Visions
Visions–Alaska
Visions–British Virgin Islands
Visions–Costa Rica
Visions–Dominica
Visions–Dominican Republic
Visions–Ecuador
Visions–Guadeloupe
Visions–Mississippi
Visions–Montana
Visions–Nicaragua
Visions–Peru
Visions–Vietnam

Vista Camps
Camp Rio Vista for Boys
Camp Sierra Vista for Girls

Volunteers for Peace International Voluntary Service
Volunteers for Peace International Voluntary Service–Estonia
Volunteers for Peace International Voluntary Service–France
Volunteers for Peace International Voluntary Service–Germany
Volunteers for Peace International Voluntary Service–Italy

Washington University in St. Louis
Washington University High School Summer Scholars Program

Washington University in St. Louis, College of Art
Washington University in St. Louis, College of Art–Portfolio Plus

Weissman Teen Tours
Weissman Teen Tours–"Aloha–Welcome to Hawaiian Paradise," 3 weeks
Weissman Teen Tours–"Aloha–Welcome to Hawaiian Paradise," 2 weeks
Weissman Teen Tours–European Experience
Weissman Teen Tours–U.S. and Western Canada, 40 Days
Weissman Teen Tours–U.S. and Western Canada, 30 Days

Westcoast Connection
Westcoast Connection–American Voyageur
Westcoast Connection–Australian Outback Plus Hawaii
Westcoast Connection–Authentic Italy

Westcoast Connection–Belize and Costa Rica Water Adventure
Westcoast Connection–California Dreaming
Westcoast Connection–Californian Extravaganza
Westcoast Connection–California Sprint
Westcoast Connection–California Swing Junior Touring Golf Camp
Westcoast Connection–Community Connections Alaska
Westcoast Connection–Community Service Belize
Westcoast Connection–Community Service Costa Rica
Westcoast Connection–Community Service–Habitat for Humanity
Westcoast Connection–Community Service Hawaii
Westcoast Connection–European Escape
Westcoast Connection–Florida Swing Junior Touring Golf Camp
Westcoast Connection–French Language and Touring
Westcoast Connection–Hawaiian Spirit
Westcoast Connection–Major League Baseball Tour
Westcoast Connection/On Tour–Australian Outback
Westcoast Connection–Spanish in Costa Rica
Westcoast Connection–Spanish Language and Touring
Westcoast Connection Travel–Adventure California
Westcoast Connection Travel–California and the Canyons
Westcoast Connection Travel–Canadian Mountain Magic
Westcoast Connection Travel–Eastcoast Encounter
Westcoast Connection Travel–European Discovery
Westcoast Connection Travel–Great West Challenge
Westcoast Connection Travel–Northwestern Odyssey
Westcoast Connection Travel/On Tour–European Escapade
Westcoast Connection Travel/On Tour–European Experience
Westcoast Connection Travel–Quebec Adventure
Westcoast Connection Travel–Ski and Snowboard Sensation
Westcoast Connection Travel–Western Canadian Adventure
Westcoast Connection–U.S. Explorer

Wilderness Ventures

Wilderness Ventures–Alaska College Leadership
Wilderness Ventures–Alaska Expedition
Wilderness Ventures–Alaska Southcentral
Wilderness Ventures–Alaska Southeast
Wilderness Ventures–Alaska Southeast Community Service
Wilderness Ventures–Australia
Wilderness Ventures–California
Wilderness Ventures–Cascade-Olympic
Wilderness Ventures–Colorado/Utah Mountain Bike
Wilderness Ventures–Costa Rica
Wilderness Ventures–Costa Rica/Belize
Wilderness Ventures–Costa Rica Service
Wilderness Ventures–Costa Rica Surfing
Wilderness Ventures–Ecuador and Galapagos Community Service
Wilderness Ventures–European Alps
Wilderness Ventures–Fiji Community Service
Wilderness Ventures–Grand Teton
Wilderness Ventures–Great Divide
Wilderness Ventures–Hawaii
Wilderness Ventures–High Sierra
Wilderness Ventures–Jackson Hole
Wilderness Ventures–Maui/Kauai
Wilderness Ventures–Northwest
Wilderness Ventures–Oregon

Wilderness Ventures–Pacific Northwest
Wilderness Ventures–Peru Community Service
Wilderness Ventures–Puget Sound
Wilderness Ventures–Rocky Mountain
Wilderness Ventures–Southwest Community Service
Wilderness Ventures–Spanish Pyrenees
Wilderness Ventures–Tahiti, Fiji, and New Zealand
Wilderness Ventures–Teton Crest
Wilderness Ventures–Washington Alpine
Wilderness Ventures–Washington Mountaineering
Wilderness Ventures–Wyoming Mountaineering
Wilderness Ventures–Yellowstone
Wilderness Ventures–Yellowstone Fly Fishing
Wilderness Ventures–Yellowstone/Teton Adventure
Wilderness Ventures–Yellowstone-Teton Family Adventure
Wilderness Ventures–Yellowstone Wilderness

The Winchendon School

The Winchendon School Summer Session

Wisconsin World Affairs Council, Inc.

World Affairs Seminar

Wolfeboro: The Summer Boarding School

Worcester Polytechnic Institute

Frontiers Program
Worcester Polytechnic Institute–Launch

World Horizons International

World Horizons International–Cayambe, Ecuador
World Horizons International–Connecticut
World Horizons International–Costa Rica
World Horizons International–Dominica
World Horizons International–Fiji
World Horizons International–Iceland
World Horizons International–Kanab, Utah
World Horizons International–Northridge, California
World Horizons International–Rome, Italy
World Horizons International–Tapovan, Laxman Jhula, India
World Horizons International–United Kingdom

Wyoming Seminary College Preparatory School

Wyoming Seminary–Sem Summer 2008

Academic Programs

AAVE–Costa Rica Clásica, Costa Rica

AAVE–Costa Rica Spanish Intensive, Costa Rica

AAVE–España Clásica, Spain

AAVE–France Classique, France

Academic Camps at Gettysburg College, PA

Academic Study Associates–ASA at the University of California, Berkeley, CA

Academic Study Associates–ASA at the University of Massachusetts Amherst, MA

Academic Study Associates–Barcelona, Spain

Academic Study Associates–Costa Rica, Costa Rica

Academic Study Associates–Florence, Italy

Academic Study Associates–Nice, France

Academic Study Associates–Royan, France

Academic Study Associates–Spanish in España, Spain

ACADEMIC TREKS–Adventure Peru, Peru

ACADEMIC TREKS–Caribbean Marine Reserves

ACADEMIC TREKS–Dolphin Studies in Belize, Belize

ACADEMIC TREKS–French Immersion in France, France

ACADEMIC TREKS–French Immersion in the French West Indies, Guadeloupe

ACADEMIC TREKS–Immersion China, China

ACADEMIC TREKS–Immersion Mexico, Mexico

ACADEMIC TREKS–Pacific Whale Treks, Canada

ACADEMIC TREKS–Sea Turtle Studies, Costa Rica

ACADEMIC TREKS–Shark Studies in Fiji, Fiji

ACADEMIC TREKS–Shipwrecks and Underwater Archaeology in Bermuda, Bermuda

ACADEMIC TREKS–Spanish Immersion in Oaxaca, Mexico, Mexico

ACADEMIC TREKS–Spanish Language Immersion in Ecuador, Ecuador

ACADEMIC TREKS–Wilderness Emergency Medicine, Belize

Academy by the Sea, CA

Acadia Institute of Oceanography, ME

ACTIONQUEST: Tropical Marine Biology Voyages, British Virgin Islands

Adirondack Field Ecology, NY

AFS-USA–China Summer Homestay Language Study Program, China

AFS-USA–Homestay–Argentina, Argentina

AFS-USA–Homestay–Chile, Chile

AFS-USA–Homestay–France, France

AFS-USA–Homestay Language Study–Egypt, Egypt

AFS-USA–Homestay Language Study–Latvia, Latvia

AFS-USA–Homestay–Paraguay, Paraguay

AFS-USA–Homestay–Thailand, Thailand

Asheville School's Summer Academic Adventures, NC

BAC Summer Academy, MA

Barat Foundation Summer Program in Provence, France

Barnard's Summer in New York City: A Pre-College Program, NY

Barnard's Summer in New York City: One-Week Liberal Arts Intensive, NY

Barnard's Summer in New York City: Young Women's Leadership Institute, NY

Brewster Academy Summer Session, NH

BROADREACH Honduras Eco-Adventure, Honduras

BROADREACH Marine Biology Accredited, Bahamas

Bryn Mawr College–Science for College, PA

Bryn Mawr College–Women of Distinction: Personalizing the College Admissions Process, PA

Bryn Mawr College–Writing for College, PA

Cambridge College Programme, United Kingdom

The Cambridge Experience, United Kingdom

The Cambridge Prep Experience, United Kingdom

The Cambridge Tradition, United Kingdom

Career Explorations–Boston, MA

Career Explorations–New York, NY

Center for Cultural Interchange–Australia High School Abroad, Australia

Center for Cultural Interchange–Brazil High School Abroad, Brazil

Center for Cultural Interchange–Costa Rica Language School, Costa Rica

Center for Cultural Interchange–Denmark High School Abroad, Denmark

Center for Cultural Interchange–Finland High School Abroad, Finland

Center for Cultural Interchange–France High School Abroad, France

Center for Cultural Interchange–France Language School, France

Center for Cultural Interchange–Germany High School Abroad, Germany

Center for Cultural Interchange–Germany Language School, Germany

Center for Cultural Interchange–Ireland High School Abroad, Ireland

Center for Cultural Interchange–Italy High School Abroad, Italy

Center for Cultural Interchange–Italy Language School, Italy

Center for Cultural Interchange–Japan High School Abroad, Japan

Center for Cultural Interchange–Mexico Language School, Mexico

Center for Cultural Interchange–Netherlands High School Abroad, Netherlands

Center for Cultural Interchange–Norway High School Abroad, Norway

Center for Cultural Interchange–Spain High School Abroad, Spain

Center for Cultural Interchange–Spain Language School, Spain

Center for Cultural Interchange–Spain Sports and Language Camp, Spain

Center for Cultural Interchange–Sweden High School Abroad, Sweden

Center for Cultural Interchange–Taiwan High School Abroad, Taiwan

Center for Talent Development Summer Academic Program, IL

Cheshire Academy Summer Program, CT

Choate Rosemary Hall Beginning Writers Workshop, CT

Choate Rosemary Hall English Language Institute, CT

Choate Rosemary Hall English Language Institute/Focus Program, CT

Choate Rosemary Hall Focus Program, CT

Choate Rosemary Hall Immersion Program, CT

► ACADEMIC PROGRAMS

Choate Rosemary Hall John F. Kennedy Institute in Government, CT

Choate Rosemary Hall Math and Science Workshops, CT

Choate Rosemary Hall Math/Science Institute for Girls–CONNECT, CT

Choate Rosemary Hall Summer in China, China

Choate Rosemary Hall Summer in Paris, France

Choate Rosemary Hall Summer in Spain, Spain

Choate Rosemary Hall Summer Session, CT

Choate Rosemary Hall Writing Project, CT

Choate Rosemary Hall Young Writers Workshop, CT

College InSight, PA

Colorado College Summer Session, CO

Constructing Your College Experience, NC

Cornell University Summer College Programs for High School Students, NY

Crossroads School–Summer Educational Journey, CA

Cushing Academy Summer Session, MA

Cybercamps–Adelphi University, NY

Cybercamps–American University, D.C.

Cybercamps–Barry University, FL

Cybercamps–Bellevue Community College, WA

Cybercamps–Benedictine University, IL

Cybercamps–Bentley College, MA

Cybercamps–Bryn Mawr College, PA

Cybercamps–Caldwell College, NJ

Cybercamps–College of St. Elizabeth, NJ

Cybercamps–Concordia University, Chicago, IL

Cybercamps–Concordia University, Irvine, CA

Cybercamps–Dana Hall School, MA

Cybercamps–DeAnza College, CA

Cybercamps–Duke University, NC

Cybercamps–Fordham University, NY

Cybercamps–George Mason University, VA

Cybercamps–Georgia State University, GA

Cybercamps–Lewis and Clark College, OR

Cybercamps–Loyola University, IL

Cybercamps–Merrimack College, MA

Cybercamps–MIT, MA

Cybercamps–The New School, NY

Cybercamps–New York Institute of Technology, NY

Cybercamps–Northern Virginia Community College, VA

Cybercamps–Nova Southeastern University, FL

Cybercamps–Oak Marr Rec Center, VA

Cybercamps–Oglethorpe University, GA

Cybercamps–Rutgers University, NJ

Cybercamps–St. John's University, NY

Cybercamps–Southern Polytechnic State University, GA

Cybercamps–Stanford University, CA

Cybercamps–Towson University, MD

Cybercamps–Trinity Lutheran College, WA

Cybercamps–UCLA, CA

Cybercamps–UC San Diego (UCSD), CA

Cybercamps–UNC, Chapel Hill, NC

Cybercamps–University of Bridgeport, CT

Cybercamps–University of California at Berkeley, CA

Cybercamps–University of Central Florida, FL

Cybercamps–University of Hartford, CT

Cybercamps–University of Maryland, MD

Cybercamps–University of Miami, FL

Cybercamps–University of Michigan, MI

Cybercamps–University of Minnesota, MN

Cybercamps–University of Washington, WA

Cybercamps–University of Washington, Bothell, WA

Cybercamps–Webster University, MO

Darlington Summer Programs, GA

Duke Action: Science Camp for Young Women, NC

Duke Creative Writers' Workshop, NC

Duke TIP Domestic Field Studies

Duke TIP Institutes, NC

Duke TIP International Field Studies

Duke University PreCollege Program, NC

Duke Young Writers Camp, NC

Dunnabeck at Kildonan, NY

Eaglebrook Summer Semester, MA

Eagle Hill School Summer Session, MA

Edu-Culture International (ECI)–Aix-en-Provence/Gap Host Family Immersion, France

Edu-Culture International (ECI)–CPI Costa Rica, Costa Rica

Edu-Culture International (ECI)–Granada Homestay, Spain

Edu-Culture International (ECI)–Granada Homestay or Dorm Plus Southern Host Family Immersion, Spain

Edu-Culture International (ECI)–Granada-Nerja Homestay Combo, Spain

Edu-Culture International (ECI)–Grecia Costa Rica, Costa Rica

Edu-Culture International (ECI)–Nerja Homestay Plus Southern Host Family Immersion, Spain

Edu-Culture International (ECI)–Nerja Homestay with Optional Southern Host Family Immersion, Spain

Edu-Culture International (ECI)–Salamanca Dorm Plus Southern Host Family Immersion, Spain

Edu-Culture International (ECI)–Salamanca Homestay, Spain

Edu-Culture International (ECI)–Salamanca Homestay Plus Northern Host Family Immersion, Spain

Edu-Culture International (ECI)–Salamanca Homestay (Short Version), Spain

Edu-Culture International (ECI)–San Sebastian Homestay Plus Southern Host Family Immersion, Spain

Edu-Culture International (ECI)–Toulouse/Montpellier Host Family Immersion, France

EF International Language School–Barcelona, Spain

EF International Language School–Beijing, China

EF International Language School–Malaga, Spain

EF International Language School–Munich, Germany

EF International Language School–Nice, France

EF International Language School–Paris, France

EF International Language School–Playa Tamarindo, Costa Rica

EF International Language School–Quito, Ecuador

EF International Language School–Rome, Italy

EF International Language School–Shanghai, China

Elite Educational Institute Elementary Enrichment, CA

Elite Educational Institute Elementary Enrichment–Korea, Republic of Korea

Elite Educational Institute Junior High/PSAT Program, CA

Elite Educational Institute Junior High/PSAT Program–Korea, Republic of Korea

Elite Educational Institute SAT and Subject Test Preparation, CA

Elite Educational Institute SAT Bootcamp–Korea, Republic of Korea

Elite Educational Institute SAT Preparation–Korea, Republic of Korea

Elite Educational Institute SAT Summer Bootcamp, CA

Elite Educational Institute–University of Oklahoma College Courses, CA

Emagination Computer Camps–Georgia, GA

Emagination Computer Camps–Illinois, IL

Emagination Computer Camps–Massachusetts, MA

Emagination Computer Camps–Pennsylvania, PA

Enforex–General Spanish–Alicante, Spain

Enforex–General Spanish–Barcelona, Spain

Enforex–General Spanish–Granada, Spain

Enforex–General Spanish–Madrid, Spain

Enforex–General Spanish–Malaga, Spain

Enforex–General Spanish–Marbella, Spain

Enforex–General Spanish–Salamanca, Spain

Enforex–General Spanish–Sevilla, Spain

Enforex–General Spanish–Tenerife, Spain

Enforex–General Spanish–Valencia, Spain

Enforex Hispanic Culture: Civilization, History, Art, and Literature–Alicante, Spain

Enforex Hispanic Culture: Civilization, History, Art, and Literature–Barcelona, Spain

Enforex Hispanic Culture: Civilization, History, Art, and Literature–Granada, Spain

Enforex Hispanic Culture: Civilization, History, Art, and Literature–Madrid, Spain

Enforex Hispanic Culture: Civilization, History, Art, and Literature–Malaga, Spain

Enforex Hispanic Culture: Civilization, History, Art, and Literature–Salamanca, Spain

Enforex Hispanic Culture: Civilization, History, Art, and Literature–Sevilla, Spain

Enforex Hispanic Culture: Civilization, History, Art, and Literature–Tenerife, Spain

Enforex Hispanic Culture: History, Art, and Literature–Valencia, Spain

Enforex Homestay Program–Alicante, Spain

Enforex Homestay Program–Barcelona, Spain

Enforex Homestay Program–Granada, Spain

Enforex Homestay Program–Madrid, Spain

Enforex Homestay Program–Malaga, Spain

Enforex Homestay Program–Marbella, Spain

Enforex Homestay Program–Salamanca, Spain

Enforex Homestay Program–Sevilla, Spain

Enforex Homestay Program–Tenerife, Spain

Enforex Homestay Program–Valencia, Spain

Enforex Spanish and Golf, Spain

Enforex Spanish and Tennis, Spain

Enforex Study Tour Vacational Program–Alicante, Spain

Enforex Study Tour Vacational Program–Barcelona, Spain

Enforex Study Tour Vacational Program–Granada, Spain

Enforex Study Tour Vacational Program–Madrid, Spain

Enforex Study Tour Vacational Program–Malaga, Spain

Enforex Study Tour Vacational Program–Marbella, Spain

Enforex Study Tour Vacational Program–Salamanca, Spain

Enforex Study Tour Vacational Program–Sevilla, Spain

Enforex Study Tour Vacational Program–Tenerife, Spain

Enforex Study Tour Vacational Program–Valencia, Spain

Excel at Amherst College, MA

Excel at Madrid/Barcelona, Spain

Excel at Oxford/Tuscany

Excel at Paris/Provence, France

Excel China, China

The Experiment in International Living–France, Homestay, Language Training, and Cooking, France

The Experiment in International Living–Spain, Four-Week Language Training, Travel, and Homestay, Spain

The Experiment in International Living–Spain–Multiculturalism and Service, Spain

Exploration of Architecture, CA

Fairfax Collegiate School Summer Enrichment Program, VA

The Fessenden School Summer ESL Program, MA

FivePoints, NY

Frontiers Program, MA

Georgetown University American Politics and Public Affairs, D.C.

Georgetown University College Prep Program, D.C.

Georgetown University Gateway to Business Program for High School Students, D.C.

Georgetown University International Relations Program for High School Students, D.C.

Georgetown University Journalism Workshop for High School Students, D.C.

Georgetown University Summer College for High School Students, D.C.

George Washington University Summer Scholars Mini-courses, D.C.

George Washington University Summer Scholars Pre-college Program, D.C.

Girls First, VA

GirlSummer at Emma Willard School, NY

Global Leadership Adventures–Brazil: Community Service and Leadership, Brazil

Global Leadership Adventures–Cape Town: Community Service and Leadership, South Africa

Global Leadership Adventures–Costa Rica: Community Service and Leadership, Costa Rica

Global Leadership Adventures–Ghana: Community Service and Leadership, Ghana

Global Leadership Adventures–India: Community Service and Leadership, India

The Gow School Summer Program, NY

The Grand River Summer Academy, OH

Hargrave Summer Leadership Program, VA

Harker Summer English Language Institute, CA

The Harker Summer Institute, CA

Harker Summer Programs, CA

Harvard University Summer School: Secondary School Program, MA

Hawaii Preparatory Academy Summer Session, HI

Humanities Spring in Assisi, Italy

The Hun School of Princeton American Culture and Language Institute, NJ

The Hun School of Princeton–Summer Academic Session, NJ

iD Gaming Academy–Stanford University, Palo Alto, CA

iD Gaming Academy–UC Berkeley, Berkeley, CA

iD Gaming Academy–UCLA, Westwood, CA

iD Gaming Academy–Villanova University, Villanova, PA

iD Tech Camps–Arizona State University, Tempe, AZ

iD Tech Camps–Brown University, Providence, RI

iD Tech Camps–Cal Lutheran University, Thousand Oaks, CA

iD Tech Camps–Carnegie Mellon University, Pittsburgh, PA

iD Tech Camps–Case Western Reserve University, Cleveland, OH

iD Tech Camps–College of William and Mary, Williamsburg, VA

iD Tech Camps–Colorado College, Colorado Springs, CO

iD Tech Camps–Columbia University, New York, NY

iD Tech Camps–Documentary Filmmaking and Cultural Immersion in Spain, Spain

iD Tech Camps–Emory University, Atlanta, GA

iD Tech Camps–Fordham University, Bronx, NY

iD Tech Camps–Georgetown University, Washington, D.C.

iD Tech Camps–Lake Forest College, Evanston, IL

iD Tech Camps–Merrimack College, North Andover, MA

iD Tech Camps–MIT, Cambridge, MA

iD Tech Camps–Northwestern University, Chicago, IL

iD Tech Camps–Pepperdine University, Malibu, CA

iD Tech Camps–Rider University, Lawrenceville, NJ

iD Tech Camps–Sacred Heart University, Fairfield, CT

iD Tech Camps–St. Mary's College of California, Moraga, CA

iD Tech Camps–Santa Clara University, Santa Clara, CA

iD Tech Camps–Seton Hall University, South Orange, NJ

iD Tech Camps–Smith College, Northampton, MA

iD Tech Camps–Southern Methodist University, Dallas, TX

iD Tech Camps–Stanford University, Palo Alto, CA

iD Tech Camps–Tiger Woods Learning Center, Anaheim, CA

iD Tech Camps–UC Berkeley, Berkeley, CA

iD Tech Camps–UC Davis, Davis, CA

iD Tech Camps–UC Irvine, Irvine, CA

iD Tech Camps–UCLA, Westwood, CA

iD Tech Camps–UC San Diego, La Jolla, CA

iD Tech Camps–UC Santa Cruz, Santa Cruz, CA

iD Tech Camps–University of Central Florida, Orlando, FL

iD Tech Camps–University of Denver, Denver, CO

iD Tech Camps–University of Houston, Houston, TX

iD Tech Camps–University of Miami, Coral Gables, FL

iD Tech Camps–University of Michigan, Ann Arbor, MI

iD Tech Camps–University of Minnesota, Minneapolis, MN

iD Tech Camps–University of North Carolina at Chapel Hill, Chapel Hill, NC

iD Tech Camps–University of Virginia, Charlottesville, VA

iD Tech Camps–University of Washington, Seattle, WA

iD Tech Camps–UT Austin, Austin, TX

iD Tech Camps–Vanderbilt University, Nashville, TN

iD Tech Camps–Vassar College, Poughkeepsie, NY

iD Tech Camps–Villanova University, Villanova, PA

iD Tech Camps–Virginia Tech, Blacksburg, VA

iD Tech Camps–Wake Forest University, Winston-Salem, NC

iD Tech Camps–Washington University in St. Louis, St. Louis, MO

IEI–Print and Broadcast Journalism, United Kingdom

IEI Student Travel–Internship Program in London, United Kingdom

Intensive English Language Program, MD

International Leadership Program, MD

Internship Connection, MA

Ithaca College Summer College for High School Students: Minicourses, NY

Ithaca College Summer College for High School Students: Session I, NY

Ithaca College Summer College for High School Students: Session II, NY

Johns Hopkins University Zanvyl Krieger School of Arts and Sciences Summer Programs, MD

Junior Statesmen Summer School–Georgetown University, D.C.

Junior Statesmen Summer School–Princeton University, NJ

Junior Statesmen Summer School–Stanford University, CA

Junior Statesmen Summer School–Yale University, CT

Junior Statesmen Symposium on California State Politics and Government, CA

Junior Statesmen Symposium on Los Angeles Politics and Government, CA

Junior Statesmen Symposium on New Jersey State Politics and Government, NJ

Junior Statesmen Symposium on Ohio State Politics and Government, OH

Junior Statesmen Symposium on Texas Politics and Leadership, TX

Junior Statesmen Symposium on Washington State Politics and Government, WA

Kent School Summer Writers Camp, CT

La Academia de España, Spain

L'Académie de France, France

L'Académie de Paris, France

Landmark School Summer Academic Program, MA

Les Elfes–International Summer/ Winter Camp, Switzerland

LIFEWORKS with the Fundación Humanitaria in Costa Rica, Costa Rica

Linden Hill Summer Program, MA

Marianapolis Summer Program, CT

Marvelwood Summer Program, CT

Miami University Junior Scholars Program, OH

Michigan Technological University American Indian Workshop, MI

Michigan Technological University Explorations in Engineering Workshop, MI

Michigan Technological University Summer Youth Program, MI

Michigan Technological University Women in Engineering Workshop, MI

Milwaukee School of Engineering (MSOE)–Discover the Possibilities, WI

Milwaukee School of Engineering (MSOE)–Focus on Business, WI

Milwaukee School of Engineering (MSOE)–Focus on Nursing, WI

Milwaukee School of Engineering (MSOE)–Focus on Technical Communication, WI

Milwaukee School of Engineering (MSOE)–Focus on the Possibilities, WI

Miss Porter's School Arts Alive!, CT

Miss Porter's School Daoyun Chinese Summer Program, CT

Miss Porter's School Summer Challenge, CT

MIT MITES (Minority Introduction to Engineering and Science), MA

Mount Holyoke College SEARCH (Summer Explorations and Research Collaborations for High School Girls) Program, MA

Mount Holyoke College SummerMath Program, MA

National Student Leadership Conference: Engineering–San Francisco, CA

National Student Leadership Conference: Engineering–Washington, D.C., MD

National Student Leadership Conference: Entrepreneurship and Business–New York City, NY

National Student Leadership Conference: Entrepreneurship and Business–Washington, D.C.

National Student Leadership Conference: Forensic Science, D.C.

National Student Leadership Conference: Globalization and International Business–Study Abroad

National Student Leadership Conference: Globalization and International Business–Washington, D.C.

National Student Leadership Conference: Inside the Arts–New York City, NY

National Student Leadership Conference: Intelligence and National Security, D.C.

National Student Leadership Conference: International Diplomacy–Washington, D.C.

National Student Leadership Conference: Journalism and Mass Communication, D.C.

National Student Leadership Conference: Law and Advocacy–San Francisco, CA

National Student Leadership Conference: Law and Advocacy–Washington, D.C.

National Student Leadership Conference: Mastering Leadership, MD

National Student Leadership Conference: Medicine and Health Care–San Francisco, CA

National Student Leadership Conference: Medicine and Health Care–Washington, D.C., MD

National Student Leadership Conference: State Leadership Workshops, IL

National Student Leadership Conference: U.S. Policy and Politics, D.C.

Northfield Mount Hermon Summer Session, MA

Northwestern University's College Preparation Program, IL

Northwestern University's National High School Institute, IL

Oak Creek Ranch School–Summer Academic Program, AZ

Oxford Advanced Studies Program, United Kingdom

The Oxford Experience, United Kingdom

Oxford Media School–Film, United Kingdom

Oxford Media School–Film Master Class, United Kingdom

Oxford Media School–Newsroom in Europe, United Kingdom

Oxford Media School–Newsroom in Europe, Master Class, United Kingdom

The Oxford Prep Experience, United Kingdom

The Oxford Tradition, United Kingdom

Phillips Academy Summer Session, MA

Phillips Exeter Academy Summer School, NH

Portsmouth Abbey Summer School, RI

Pratt Institute Summer Pre-College Program for High School Students, NY

The Putney School Summer Program for International Education (ESL), VT

The Putney School Summer Writing Program, VT

Putney Student Travel–Language Learning–Argentina, Argentina

Putney Student Travel–Language Learning–Costa Rica, Costa Rica

Putney Student Travel–Language Learning–France, France

Putney Student Travel–Language Learning–Spain, Spain

Randolph-Macon Academy Summer Programs, VA

Rassias Programs–Arles, France, France

Rassias Programs–China, China

Rassias Programs–Gijón, Spain, Spain

Rassias Programs–Pontevedra, Spain, Spain

Rassias Programs–Segovia, Spain, Spain

Rassias Programs–Tours, France, France

The Renaissance Scholar Program, TX

Rumsey Hall School Summer Session, CT

RUSTIC PATHWAYS–INTENSIVE CHINESE LANGUAGE, China

RUSTIC PATHWAYS–INTENSIVE SPANISH LANGUAGE, Costa Rica

RUSTIC PATHWAYS–MALEKU TRIBE IMMERSION PROGRAM–COSTA RICA, Costa Rica

RUSTIC PATHWAYS–RAMP UP YOUR SPANISH, Costa Rica

RUSTIC PATHWAYS–SPANISH LANGUAGE IMMERSION, Costa Rica

Saint Thomas More School–Summer Academic Camp, CT

Salem Spotlight, NC

Salisbury Summer School, CT

Sarah Lawrence College Summer High School Programs, NY

The Sarah Porter Leadership Institute, CT

Science Program for High School Girls, CA

Science Program for Middle School Boys on Catalina, CA

Science Program for Middle School Girls on Catalina, CA

Seacamp, FL

Service Learning in Barcelona, Spain

Service Learning in Paris, France

Skidmore College–Pre-College Program in the Liberal & Studio Arts for High School Students, NY

▶ ACADEMIC PROGRAMS

Smith College Summer Science and Engineering Program, MA
Southern Methodist University–College Experience, TX
Southern Methodist University TAG (Talented and Gifted), TX
Southwestern Adventures–Arizona, AZ
Southwestern Adventures–California, CA
Spanish Language and Flamenco Enforex–Granada, Spain
Spanish Language and Flamenco Enforex–Madrid, Spain
Spanish Language and Flamenco Enforex–Marbella, Spain
Spanish Language and Flamenco Enforex–Sevilla, Spain
Spoleto Study Abroad, Italy
Squaw Valley Academy Summer School, CA
Stanford University High School Summer College, CA
Studies Abroad for Global Education (SAGE), Summer SAGE Program, India
Summer Action–Take the Lead, MA
Summer Advantage Study Abroad–Cambridge University, United Kingdom
Summer Advantage Study Abroad–Granada, Spain, Spain
Summer Advantage Study Abroad–London, United Kingdom
Summer Advantage Study Abroad–Nanjing, China, China
Summer Advantage Study Abroad–Paris, France, France
Summer Advantage Study Abroad–Rome, Italy, Italy
Summer Advantage Study Abroad–St. Petersburg, Russia, Russian Federation
Summer Advantage Study Abroad–Salamanca, Spain, Spain
Summer at Delphi, OR
summer@rectory, CT
Summer@Rensselaer, NY
Summerberg at Heidelberg College, OH
Summer@Brown, RI
Summer English Experience, CT
The Summer Institute for the Gifted at Amherst College, MA
The Summer Institute for the Gifted at Bryn Mawr College, PA
The Summer Institute for the Gifted at Emory University, GA
The Summer Institute for the Gifted at Fairfield University, CT
The Summer Institute for the Gifted at Manhattanville College, NY

The Summer Institute for the Gifted at Moorestown Friends School, NJ
The Summer Institute for the Gifted at Princeton University, NJ
The Summer Institute for the Gifted at UCLA, CA
The Summer Institute for the Gifted at University of California, Berkeley, CA
The Summer Institute for the Gifted at University of Michigan, Ann Arbor, MI
The Summer Institute for the Gifted at University of Texas, Austin, TX
The Summer Institute for the Gifted at Vassar College, NY
Summer in Switzerland, Switzerland
Summer Study at Penn State, PA
Summer Study at The University of Colorado at Boulder, CO
Summer Study in Paris at The Sorbonne, France
Syracuse University Summer College, NY
Tabor Academy Summer Program, MA
Taft Summer School, CT
Taft Summer School Abroad–France, France
Taft Summer School Abroad–Spain, Spain
Talisman Summer Camp, NC
TASIS England Summer Program, United Kingdom
TASIS French Language Program in Château-d'Oex, Switzerland, Switzerland
TASIS Le Château des Enfants, Switzerland
TASIS Middle School Program, Switzerland
TASIS Spanish Summer Program, Spain
TASIS Summer Program for Languages, Arts, and Outdoor Pursuits, Switzerland
Tisch School of the Arts–International High School Program–Dublin, Ireland
Tisch School of the Arts–International High School Program–Paris, France
Tisch School of the Arts–Summer High School Programs, NY
UCLA Summer Experience: College Level Courses, CA
UCLA Summer Experience: Institutes, CA
University of Chicago–Insight, IL
University of Chicago–Research in the Biological Sciences, IL

University of Chicago–Stones and Bones, WY
University of Chicago–Summer Quarter for High School Students, IL
University of Chicago–The Traveling Academy, Greece
University of Connecticut Mentor Connection, CT
University of Maryland Young Scholars Program, MD
University of Miami Summer Scholar Programs, FL
University of Pennsylvania–Penn Summer Science Academies, PA
University of Pennsylvania–Pre-College Program, PA
University of Southern California Summer Seminars, CA
University of Vermont Summer Engineering Institute for High School Students, VT
Washington University High School Summer Scholars Program, MO
Westcoast Connection–French Language and Touring, France
Westcoast Connection–Spanish in Costa Rica, Costa Rica
Westcoast Connection–Spanish Language and Touring, Spain
The Winchendon School Summer Session, MA
Wolfeboro: The Summer Boarding School, NH
Worcester Polytechnic Institute–Launch, MA
World Affairs Seminar, WI
World Horizons International–United Kingdom
Wyoming Seminary–Sem Summer 2008, PA

Adventure Programs
AAVE–Africa
AAVE–Australia, Australia
AAVE–Bike Amsterdam-Paris
AAVE–Bold Europe
AAVE–Bold West
AAVE–Boot/Saddle/Paddle
AAVE–China, China
AAVE–Colorado Discovery, CO
AAVE–Costa Rica Clásica, Costa Rica
AAVE–Costa Rica Spanish Intensive, Costa Rica
AAVE–Ecuador and Galapagos, Ecuador
AAVE–España Clásica, Spain
AAVE–France Classique, France
AAVE–Peak Four
AAVE–Peru and Machu Picchu, Peru
AAVE–Rock & Rapid
AAVE–Rock & Roll, CO

AAVE–Sail Dive Greece, Greece
AAVE–Surf Scuba Safari, Mexico
AAVE–Thailand, Thailand
AAVE–Ultimate Alaska, AK
AAVE–Ultimate Alps
AAVE–Ultimate Hawaii, HI
AAVE–Wild Coast Discovery
AAVE–Wild Isles
ACADEMIC TREKS–Adventure Peru, Peru
ACADEMIC TREKS–Caribbean Marine Reserves
ACADEMIC TREKS–Dolphin Studies in Belize, Belize
ACADEMIC TREKS–French Immersion in France, France
ACADEMIC TREKS–French Immersion in the French West Indies, Guadeloupe
ACADEMIC TREKS–Immersion China, China
ACADEMIC TREKS–Immersion Mexico, Mexico
ACADEMIC TREKS–Pacific Whale Treks, Canada
ACADEMIC TREKS–Sea Turtle Studies, Costa Rica
ACADEMIC TREKS–Shark Studies in Fiji, Fiji
ACADEMIC TREKS–Shipwrecks and Underwater Archaeology in Bermuda, Bermuda
ACADEMIC TREKS–Spanish Immersion in Oaxaca, Mexico, Mexico
ACADEMIC TREKS–Spanish Language Immersion in Ecuador, Ecuador
ACTIONQUEST: Advanced PADI Scuba Certification and Specialty Voyages, British Virgin Islands
ACTIONQUEST: Australian and Great Barrier Reef Adventures, Australia
ACTIONQUEST: British Virgin Islands–Sailing and Scuba Voyages, British Virgin Islands
ACTIONQUEST: British Virgin Islands-Sailing Voyages, British Virgin Islands
ACTIONQUEST: Galapagos Archipelago Expeditions, Ecuador
ACTIONQUEST: Junior Advanced Scuba with Marine Biology, British Virgin Islands
ACTIONQUEST: Leeward and French Caribbean Island Voyages
ACTIONQUEST: Mediterranean Sailing Voyage
ACTIONQUEST: PADI Divemaster Voyages, British Virgin Islands

ACTIONQUEST: Rescue Diving Voyages, British Virgin Islands
ACTIONQUEST: Tahiti and French Polynesian Island Voyages, French Polynesia
ACTIONQUEST: Tropical Marine Biology Voyages, British Virgin Islands
Adventure Treks–Alaska Adventures, AK
Adventure Treks–California Adventures, CA
Adventure Treks–Canadian Rockies Adventures, Canada
Adventure Treks–Montana Adventures, MT
Adventure Treks–Oregon Adventures, OR
Adventure Treks–Pacific Northwest Adventures, WA
Adventure Treks–Wilderness Adventures
ATW: Adventure Roads
ATW: American Horizons
ATW: California Sunset
ATW: Camp Inn 42
ATW: Discoverer
ATW: European Adventures
ATW: Fire and Ice
ATW: Mini Tours
ATW: Pacific Paradise
ATW: Skyblazer
ATW: Sunblazer
ATW: Wayfarer
BROADREACH Adventures Down Under, Australia
BROADREACH Adventures in Scuba and Sailing–Underwater Discoveries
BROADREACH Adventures in the Grenadines–Advanced Scuba, Saint Vincent and The Grenadines
BROADREACH Adventures in the Windward Islands–Advanced Scuba
BROADREACH Adventures Underwater–Advanced Scuba
BROADREACH Arc of the Caribbean Sailing Adventure
BROADREACH Baja Extreme–Scuba Adventure, Mexico
BROADREACH Costa Rica Experience, Costa Rica
BROADREACH Fiji Solomon Quest
BROADREACH Honduras Eco-Adventure, Honduras
BROADREACH Red Sea Scuba Adventure, Egypt
BROADREACH Yucatan Adventure, Mexico
Cheley Colorado Camps, CO

The Experiment in International Living–Argentina Homestay, Community Service, and Outdoor Ecological Program, Argentina
The Experiment in International Living–Argentina Visual Arts, Photography, and Service, Argentina
The Experiment in International Living–Australia Homestay, Australia
The Experiment in International Living–Belize Homestay, Belize
The Experiment in International Living–Botswana Homestay, Botswana
The Experiment in International Living–Brazil–Community Service and Soccer, Brazil
The Experiment in International Living–Chile North Homestay, Community Service, Chile
The Experiment in International Living–China North and East Homestay, China
The Experiment in International Living–China South and West Homestay, China
The Experiment in International Living–Costa Rica Homestay, Costa Rica
The Experiment in International Living–Ecuador Homestay, Ecuador
The Experiment in International Living–France, Biking and Homestay, France
The Experiment in International Living–France, Four-Week Homestay and Photography, France
The Experiment in International Living–France, Four-Week Homestay and Theatre, France
The Experiment in International Living–France, Four-Week Homestay and Travel through Alps, France
The Experiment in International Living–France, Three-Week Homestay and Travel–Borders, France
The Experiment in International Living–Germany, Four-Week Homestay, Travel, Community Service, Germany
The Experiment in International Living–Morocco Four-Week Arts and Culture Program, Morocco
The Experiment in International Living–Navajo Nation, NM

► ADVENTURE PROGRAMS

The Experiment in International Living–Poland, Homestay, Community Service, and Travel, Poland

The Experiment in International Living–Scotland, United Kingdom

The Experiment in International Living–South Africa Homestay and Community Service, South Africa

The Experiment in International Living–Spain, Five-Week Homestay, Language Immersion, Spain

The Experiment in International Living–Spain–The Road to Santiago, Spain

The Experiment in International Living–Switzerland French Language Immersion, Homestay, and Alpine Adventure, Switzerland

The Experiment in International Living–Thailand Homestay, Thailand

The Experiment in International Living–United Kingdom Filmmaking Program and Homestay, United Kingdom

Future Leader Camp, VT

GLOBAL WORKS–Cultural Exchange and Service–Costa Rica-3 weeks, Costa Rica

GLOBAL WORKS–Cultural Exchange and Service–Ireland-4 weeks, Ireland

GLOBAL WORKS–Cultural Exchange and Service–New Zealand and Fiji Islands-4 weeks

GLOBAL WORKS–Cultural Exchange and Service–Puerto Rico-2 or 4 weeks, Puerto Rico

GLOBAL WORKS–Cultural Exchange–Fiji Islands-4 weeks, Fiji

GLOBAL WORKS–Language Immersion, Cultural Exchange and Service–Argentina, Argentina

GLOBAL WORKS–Language Immersion, Cultural Exchange and Service–Costa Rica, Costa Rica

GLOBAL WORKS–Language Immersion, Cultural Exchange and Service–Ecuador and the Galapagos-4 weeks, Ecuador

GLOBAL WORKS–Language Immersion, Cultural Exchange and Service–France-4 weeks, France

GLOBAL WORKS–Language Immersion, Cultural Exchange and Service–Martinique-4weeks, Martinique

GLOBAL WORKS–Language Immersion, Cultural Exchange and Service–Mexico-3 weeks, Mexico

GLOBAL WORKS–Language Immersion, Cultural Exchange and Service–Panama/Costa Rica

GLOBAL WORKS–Language Immersion, Cultural Exchange and Service–Peru, Peru

GLOBAL WORKS–Language Immersion, Cultural Exchange and Service–Puerto Rico-4 weeks, Puerto Rico

GLOBAL WORKS–Language Immersion, Cultural Exchange and Service–Spain-4 weeks, Spain

GLOBAL WORKS–Language Immersion, Cultural Exchange and Service–Yucatan Peninsula, Mexico-4 weeks, Mexico

Keewaydin Temagami, Canada

LIFEWORKS with the Australian Red Cross, Australia

LIFEWORKS with the British Virgin Islands Marine Parks and Conservation Department, British Virgin Islands

LIFEWORKS with the China Little Flower Foundation in China, China

LIFEWORKS with the DPF Foundation in Thailand, Thailand

LIFEWORKS with the Fundación Humanitaria in Costa Rica, Costa Rica

LIFEWORKS with the Galapagos Islands' National Parks, Ecuador

Putney Student Travel–Cultural Exploration–Australia, New Zealand, and Fiji

Putney Student Travel–Cultural Exploration–Switzerland, Italy, France, and Holland

Putney Student Travel–Global Awareness in Action–Cambodia, Cambodia

Rein Europe

Rein Teen Tours–California Caper

Rein Teen Tours–Crossroads

Rein Teen Tours–Eastern Adventure

Rein Teen Tours–Grand Adventure

Rein Teen Tours–Hawaiian/Alaskan Adventure

Rein Teen Tours–Hawaiian Caper

Rein Teen Tours–Western Adventure

RUSTIC PATHWAYS–THE AMAZING THAILAND ADVENTURE, Thailand

RUSTIC PATHWAYS–ASIAN PACIFIC EXTREME

RUSTIC PATHWAYS–BIG FIJI EXPLORER, Fiji

RUSTIC PATHWAYS–COMMUNITY SERVICE SCHOOL IN AUSTRALIA, Australia

RUSTIC PATHWAYS–COSTA RICA ADVENTURER, Costa Rica

RUSTIC PATHWAYS–ELEPHANTS & AMAZING THAILAND, Thailand

RUSTIC PATHWAYS–INTRODUCTION TO PHOTOGRAPHY–SNAPSHOTS IN THE LAND OF SMILES

RUSTIC PATHWAYS–ISLAND HOPPING AND DIVING–THAILAND, Thailand

RUSTIC PATHWAYS–NEW ZEALAND NORTH ISLAND ADVENTURE, New Zealand

RUSTIC PATHWAYS–OFF THE MAP BURMA AND CAMBODIA

RUSTIC PATHWAYS–SERVICE LEARNING EXTREME

RUSTIC PATHWAYS–SKI AND SNOWBOARD ADVENTURE IN NEW ZEALAND, New Zealand

RUSTIC PATHWAYS–SOCCER AND SERVICE IN COSTA RICA, Costa Rica

RUSTIC PATHWAYS–SUN, SAND & INTERNATIONAL SERVICE–FIJI, Fiji

RUSTIC PATHWAYS–SURF THE SUMMER–COSTA RICA, Costa Rica

RUSTIC PATHWAYS–SYDNEY, REEF & RAINFOREST, Australia

RUSTIC PATHWAYS–ULTIMATE JUNGLE ADVENTURE–COSTA RICA, Costa Rica

RUSTIC PATHWAYS–THE WONDERS & RICHES OF SOUTHEAST ASIA

RUSTIC PATHWAYS–WORLD SERVICE EXTREME

RUSTIC PATHWAYS–YOUNG ADVENTURERS–COSTA RICA, Costa Rica

Studies Abroad for Global Education (SAGE), Summer SAGE Program, India

TASC Canadian Wilderness Fishing Camps, Canada

Treetops eXpeditions–Glacier/Boundary Waters

Treetops eXpeditions–Sailing and Marine Ecology, FL

Treetops eXpeditions–Vanuatu, Vanuatu

Westcoast Connection–American Voyageur

Westcoast Connection–Australian Outback Plus Hawaii

Westcoast Connection–Belize and Costa Rica Water Adventure

Westcoast Connection–California Dreaming

Westcoast Connection–Californian Extravaganza

Westcoast Connection–California Sprint, CA

Westcoast Connection–Community Service Costa Rica, Costa Rica

Westcoast Connection–Hawaiian Spirit

Westcoast Connection/On Tour–Australian Outback, Australia

Westcoast Connection Travel–Adventure California, CA

Westcoast Connection Travel–California and the Canyons

Westcoast Connection Travel–Canadian Mountain Magic, Canada

Westcoast Connection Travel–Eastcoast Encounter

Westcoast Connection Travel–Great West Challenge

Westcoast Connection Travel–Northwestern Odyssey

Westcoast Connection Travel–Quebec Adventure, Canada

Westcoast Connection Travel–Western Canadian Adventure, Canada

Westcoast Connection–U.S. Explorer

Wilderness Ventures–Alaska College Leadership, AK

Wilderness Ventures–Alaska Expedition, AK

Wilderness Ventures–Alaska Southcentral, AK

Wilderness Ventures–Alaska Southeast, AK

Wilderness Ventures–Australia, Australia

Wilderness Ventures–California, CA

Wilderness Ventures–Cascade-Olympic, WA

Wilderness Ventures–Colorado/Utah Mountain Bike

Wilderness Ventures–Costa Rica, Costa Rica

Wilderness Ventures–Costa Rica/Belize

Wilderness Ventures–Costa Rica Service, Costa Rica

Wilderness Ventures–Costa Rica Surfing, Costa Rica

Wilderness Ventures–Ecuador and Galapagos Community Service, Ecuador

Wilderness Ventures–European Alps

Wilderness Ventures–Fiji Community Service, Fiji

Wilderness Ventures–Grand Teton, WY

Wilderness Ventures–Great Divide

Wilderness Ventures–Hawaii, HI

Wilderness Ventures–High Sierra, CA

Wilderness Ventures–Jackson Hole, WY

Wilderness Ventures–Northwest

Wilderness Ventures–Oregon, OR

Wilderness Ventures–Pacific Northwest

Wilderness Ventures–Peru Community Service, Peru

Wilderness Ventures–Puget Sound, WA

Wilderness Ventures–Rocky Mountain

Wilderness Ventures–Southwest Community Service

Wilderness Ventures–Spanish Pyrenees, Spain

Wilderness Ventures–Tahiti, Fiji, and New Zealand

Wilderness Ventures–Teton Crest

Wilderness Ventures–Washington Alpine, WA

Wilderness Ventures–Washington Mountaineering, WA

Wilderness Ventures–Wyoming Mountaineering, WY

Wilderness Ventures–Yellowstone

Wilderness Ventures–Yellowstone Fly Fishing

Wilderness Ventures–Yellowstone/Teton Adventure, WY

Wilderness Ventures–Yellowstone-Teton Family Adventure, WY

Wilderness Ventures–Yellowstone Wilderness

Arts Programs

Academic Study Associates–ASA at the University of Massachusetts Amherst, MA

ACTeen August Academy, NY

ACTeen July Academy, NY

ACTeen June Academy, NY

ACTeen Summer Saturday Academy, NY

AFS-USA–Homestay Plus–Hungary, Hungary

American Academy of Dramatic Arts Summer Program at Los Angeles, California, CA

American Academy of Dramatic Arts Summer Program at New York, NY

Appel Farm Summer Arts Camp, NJ

Atelier des Arts, Switzerland

Barat Foundation Summer Program in Provence, France

Belvoir Terrace, MA

Boston University Tanglewood Institute, MA

Brant Lake Camp's Dance Centre, NY

Buck's Rock Performing and Creative Arts Camp, CT

California State Summer School for the Arts/Inner Spark, CA

The Cambridge Prep Experience, United Kingdom

The Cambridge Tradition, United Kingdom

Camp Encore-Coda for a Great Summer of Music, Sports, and Friends, ME

Choate Rosemary Hall Summer Arts Conservatory–Playwriting, CT

Choate Rosemary Hall Summer Arts Conservatory–Theater, CT

Choate Rosemary Hall Summer Arts Conservatory–Visual Arts Program, CT

Crossroads School–Jazz Workshop, CA

Crossroads School–Summer Educational Journey, CA

Cushing Academy Summer Session, MA

Duke Drama Workshop, NC

Eastern U.S. Music Camp, Inc. at Colgate University, NY

Ensemble Theatre Community School, PA

Excel at Amherst College, MA

The Experiment in International Living–Brazil Homestay, Arts, and Community Service, Brazil

The Experiment in International Living–France, Five-Week Art and Adventure in Provence, France

The Experiment in International Living–France, Four-Week Homestay and Photography, France

The Experiment in International Living–France, Four-Week Homestay and Theatre, France

The Experiment in International Living–South Africa Homestay and Community Service, South Africa

The Experiment in International Living–Spain–Spanish Arts and Culture, Spain

The Experiment in International Living–United Kingdom Filmmaking Program and Homestay, United Kingdom

The Experiment in International Living–United Kingdom Theatre Program, United Kingdom

EXPRESSIONS! Duke Fine Arts Camp, NC

Fenn School Summer Day Camp, MA

FivePoints, NY

GirlSummer at Emma Willard School, NY

Humanities Spring in Assisi, Italy

Idyllwild Arts Summer Program–Children's Center, CA

Idyllwild Arts Summer Program–Family Week, CA

Idyllwild Arts Summer Program–Junior Artists' Center, CA

Idyllwild Arts Summer Program–Youth Arts Center, CA

IEI–Fashion and Design Plus Programme, United Kingdom

IEI–Photography Plus Programme, United Kingdom

IEI–Theatre Plus Programme, United Kingdom

IEI–Video Production Plus Programme, United Kingdom

Interlochen Arts Camp, MI

Ithaca College Summer Piano Institute, NY

La Academia de España, Spain

L' Académie de France, France

L' Académie de Paris, France

Massachusetts College of Art/Creative Vacation, MA

Massachusetts College of Art/Summer Studios, MA

Michigan Technological University Summer Youth Program, MI

Miss Porter's School Arts Alive!, CT

National Student Leadership Conference: Inside the Arts–New York City, NY

92nd Street Y Camps–Camp Yaffa for the Arts, NY

Northwestern University's National High School Institute, IL

Oxbow Summer Art Camp, CA

Oxford Media School–Film, United Kingdom

Oxford Media School–Film Master Class, United Kingdom

Oxford Media School–Newsroom in Europe, United Kingdom

Oxford Media School–Newsroom in Europe, Master Class, United Kingdom

The Oxford Prep Experience, United Kingdom

The Oxford Tradition, United Kingdom

Perry-Mansfield Performing Arts School and Camp, CO

Pratt Institute Summer Pre-College Program for High School Students, NY

Pre-College Summer Institute, The University of the Arts, PA

The Putney School Summer Arts Program, VT

The Putney School Summer Writing Program, VT

Putney Student Travel–Cultural Exploration–Creative Writing in Argentina, Argentina

Putney Student Travel–Cultural Exploration–Theatre in Britain, United Kingdom

Rhode Island School of Design Pre-College Program, RI

RUSTIC PATHWAYS–INTRODUCTION TO PHOTOGRAPHY–SNAPSHOTS IN THE LAND OF SMILES

RUSTIC PATHWAYS–PHOTOGRAPHY ADVENTURE IN THAILAND AND ANGKOR WAT

RUSTIC PATHWAYS–PHOTOGRAPHY ADVENTURE IN THAILAND AND BURMA

RUSTIC PATHWAYS–PHOTOGRAPHY ADVENTURE IN THAILAND AND INDIA

RUSTIC PATHWAYS–PHOTOGRAPHY ADVENTURE IN THAILAND AND VIETNAM

Salem Spotlight, NC

Sarah Lawrence College Summer High School Programs, NY

School of the Museum of Fine Arts, Boston–Pre-College Summer Studio, MA

Skidmore College–Pre-College Program in the Liberal & Studio Arts for High School Students, NY

Southwestern Adventures–California, CA

Spoleto Study Abroad, Italy

Stagedoor Manor Performing Arts Training Center/Theatre and Dance Camp, NY

Studies Abroad for Global Education (SAGE), Summer SAGE Program, India

Summer@Rensselaer, NY

Summer in Switzerland, Switzerland

Summer Theatre Institute–NYC, 2008, NY

Syracuse University Summer College, NY

TASIS Arts and Architecture in the South of France, France

TASIS England Summer Program, United Kingdom

TASIS Tuscan Academy of Art and Culture, Italy

Tisch School of the Arts–International High School Program–Dublin, Ireland

Tisch School of the Arts–International High School Program–Paris, France

Tisch School of the Arts–Summer High School Programs, NY

UCLA Summer Experience: Institutes, CA

University of Pennsylvania–Penn Summer Art and Architecture Studios, PA

University of Pennsylvania–Penn Summer Theatre Workshop, PA

Valley Forge Military Academy Summer Band Camp, PA

Washington University in St. Louis, College of Art–Portfolio Plus, MO

World Horizons International–Connecticut, CT

World Horizons International–United Kingdom

Wyoming Seminary–Sem Summer 2008, PA

Bible Camps

Camp Berachah Ministries–Camps and Conferences, WA

Community Service Programs

AAVE–Africa

AAVE–Bold West

AAVE–Costa Rica Clásica, Costa Rica

AAVE–Peak Four

AAVE–Peru and Machu Picchu, Peru

AAVE–Rock & Roll, CO

AAVE–Surf Scuba Safari, Mexico

AAVE–Wild Coast Discovery

Academic Study Associates–Costa Rica, Costa Rica

ACADEMIC TREKS–Adventure Peru, Peru

ACADEMIC TREKS–Caribbean Marine Reserves

ACADEMIC TREKS–Dolphin Studies in Belize, Belize

ACADEMIC TREKS–French Immersion in France, France

ACADEMIC TREKS–French Immersion in the French West Indies, Guadeloupe

ACADEMIC TREKS–Immersion China, China

ACADEMIC TREKS–Sea Turtle Studies, Costa Rica

ACADEMIC TREKS–Shark Studies in Fiji, Fiji

ACADEMIC TREKS–Shipwrecks and Underwater Archaeology in Bermuda, Bermuda

ACADEMIC TREKS–Spanish Language Immersion in Ecuador, Ecuador

ACADEMIC TREKS–Wilderness Emergency Medicine, Belize

ACTIONQUEST: British Virgin Islands-Sailing Voyages, British Virgin Islands

ACTIONQUEST: Galapagos Archipelago Expeditions, Ecuador

AFS-USA–Community Service–Argentina, Argentina

AFS-USA–Community Service–Costa Rica, Costa Rica

AFS-USA–Community Service–Panama, Panama

AFS-USA–Community Service Paraguay, Paraguay

AFS-USA–Community Service–Thailand, Thailand

AFS-USA–Homestay Plus–Panama, Panama

AFS-USA–Team Mission–Ghana, Ghana

Asheville School's Summer Academic Adventures, NC

Barat Foundation Summer Program in Provence, France

Center for Talent Development Summer Academic Program, IL

The Experiment in International Living–Argentina Homestay, Community Service, and Outdoor Ecological Program, Argentina

The Experiment in International Living–Argentina Visual Arts, Photography, and Service, Argentina

The Experiment in International Living–Belize Homestay, Belize

The Experiment in International Living Botswana Homestay, Botswana

The Experiment in International Living–Brazil–Community Service and Soccer, Brazil

The Experiment in International Living–Brazil Homestay, Arts, and Community Service, Brazil

The Experiment in International Living–Chile North Homestay, Community Service, Chile

The Experiment in International Living–Chile South Homestay, Chile

The Experiment in International Living–Costa Rica Homestay, Costa Rica

The Experiment in International Living–Germany, Four-Week Homestay, Travel, Community Service, Germany

The Experiment in International Living–Ghana Homestay, Ghana

The Experiment in International Living–Mexico–Community Service, Travel, and Homestay, Mexico

The Experiment in International Living–Morocco Four-Week Arts and Culture Program, Morocco

The Experiment in International Living–Navajo Nation, NM

The Experiment in International Living–New Zealand Homestay, New Zealand

The Experiment in International Living–Poland, Homestay, Community Service, and Travel, Poland

The Experiment in International Living–South Africa Homestay and Community Service, South Africa

The Experiment in International Living–Spain–Multiculturalism and Service, Spain

The Experiment in International Living–Thailand Homestay, Thailand

The Experiment in International Living–Turkey Homestay, Community Service, and Travel, Turkey

Global Leadership Adventures–Brazil: Community Service and Leadership, Brazil

Global Leadership Adventures–Cape Town: Community Service and Leadership, South Africa

Global Leadership Adventures–Costa Rica: Community Service and Leadership, Costa Rica

Global Leadership Adventures–Ghana: Community Service and Leadership, Ghana

Global Leadership Adventures–India: Community Service and Leadership, India

GLOBAL WORKS–Cultural Exchange and Service–Costa Rica-3 weeks, Costa Rica

GLOBAL WORKS–Cultural Exchange and Service–Ireland-4 weeks, Ireland

GLOBAL WORKS–Cultural Exchange and Service–New Zealand and Fiji Islands-4 weeks

GLOBAL WORKS–Cultural Exchange and Service–Puerto Rico-2 or 4 weeks, Puerto Rico

GLOBAL WORKS–Cultural Exchange–Fiji Islands-4 weeks, Fiji

GLOBAL WORKS–Language Immersion, Cultural Exchange and Service–Argentina, Argentina

GLOBAL WORKS–Language Immersion, Cultural Exchange and Service–Costa Rica, Costa Rica

GLOBAL WORKS–Language Immersion, Cultural Exchange and Service–Ecuador and the Galapagos-4 weeks, Ecuador

GLOBAL WORKS–Language Immersion, Cultural Exchange and Service–France-4 weeks, France

GLOBAL WORKS–Language Immersion, Cultural Exchange and Service–Martinique-4weeks, Martinique

GLOBAL WORKS–Language Immersion, Cultural Exchange and Service–Mexico-3 weeks, Mexico

GLOBAL WORKS–Language Immersion, Cultural Exchange and Service–Panama/Costa Rica

GLOBAL WORKS–Language Immersion, Cultural Exchange and Service–Peru, Peru

GLOBAL WORKS–Language Immersion, Cultural Exchange and Service–Puerto Rico-4 weeks, Puerto Rico

GLOBAL WORKS–Language Immersion, Cultural Exchange and Service–Spain-4 weeks, Spain

GLOBAL WORKS–Language Immersion, Cultural Exchange and Service–Yucatan Peninsula, Mexico-4 weeks, Mexico

Landmark Volunteers: Arizona, AZ

Landmark Volunteers: California, CA

Landmark Volunteers: Colorado, CO

Landmark Volunteers: Connecticut, CT

Landmark Volunteers: Idaho, ID

Landmark Volunteers: Maine, ME

Landmark Volunteers: Massachusetts, MA

Landmark Volunteers: Michigan, MI

Landmark Volunteers: Minnesota, MN

Landmark Volunteers: Montana, MT

Landmark Volunteers: New Jersey, NJ

Landmark Volunteers: New Mexico, NM

Landmark Volunteers: New York, NY

Landmark Volunteers: Oregon, OR

Landmark Volunteers: Pennsylvania, PA

Landmark Volunteers: Rhode Island, RI

Landmark Volunteers: Vermont, VT

Landmark Volunteers: Virginia, VA

Landmark Volunteers: Washington, WA

Landmark Volunteers: Wyoming, WY

▶ COMMUNITY SERVICE PROGRAMS

LIFEWORKS with the Australian Red Cross, Australia

LIFEWORKS with the British Virgin Islands Marine Parks and Conservation Department, British Virgin Islands

LIFEWORKS with the China Little Flower Foundation in China, China

LIFEWORKS with the DPF Foundation in Thailand, Thailand

LIFEWORKS with the Fundación Humanitaria in Costa Rica, Costa Rica

LIFEWORKS with the Galapagos Islands' National Parks, Ecuador

National Student Leadership Conference: Mastering Leadership, MD

National Student Leadership Conference: State Leadership Workshops, IL

92nd Street Y Camps–The TIYUL

Putney Student Travel–Community Service–Alaska, AK

Putney Student Travel–Community Service–Argentina, Argentina

Putney Student Travel–Community Service–Costa Rica, Costa Rica

Putney Student Travel–Community Service–Dominican Republic, Dominican Republic

Putney Student Travel–Community Service–Dominica, West Indies, Dominica

Putney Student Travel–Community Service–Ecuador, Ecuador

Putney Student Travel–Community Service–Hawaii, HI

Putney Student Travel–Community Service–India, India

Putney Student Travel–Community Service-Nicaragua, Nicaragua

Putney Student Travel–Community Service–Nusa Penida and Bali, Indonesia

Putney Student Travel–Community Service–Senegal, Senegal

Putney Student Travel–Community Service–Tanzania, United Republic of Tanzania

Putney Student Travel–Community Service–Vietnam, Vietnam

Rein Teen Tours–Project Hawaii, HI

RUSTIC PATHWAYS–THE BUDDHIST CARAVAN, India

RUSTIC PATHWAYS–THE CANO NEGRO SERVICE PROJECT, Costa Rica

RUSTIC PATHWAYS–COME WITH NOTHING, GO HOME RICH, Thailand

RUSTIC PATHWAYS–ELEPHANTS & AMAZING THAILAND, Thailand

RUSTIC PATHWAYS–EXTENDED FIJI VILLAGE SERVICE, Fiji

RUSTIC PATHWAYS–FIJI ISLANDS COMMUNITY SERVICE, Fiji

RUSTIC PATHWAYS–INTRO TO COMMUNITY SERVICE IN FIJI, Fiji

RUSTIC PATHWAYS–INTRO TO COMMUNITY SERVICE IN THAILAND, Thailand

RUSTIC PATHWAYS–NEW ORLEANS SUMMER REBUILDING PROGRAM, LA

RUSTIC PATHWAYS–REMOTE HIGHLANDS COMMUNITY SERVICE IN FIJI, Fiji

RUSTIC PATHWAYS–RICEFIELDS, MONKS & SMILING CHILDREN, Thailand

RUSTIC PATHWAYS–SERVICE IN THE CLOUDS–INDIA, India

RUSTIC PATHWAYS–SERVICE LEARNING EXTREME

RUSTIC PATHWAYS–SOCCER AND SERVICE EXTREME

RUSTIC PATHWAYS–SOCCER AND SERVICE IN COSTA RICA, Costa Rica

RUSTIC PATHWAYS–SOCCER AND SERVICE IN FIJI, Fiji

RUSTIC PATHWAYS–SOCCER AND SERVICE IN THAILAND, Thailand

RUSTIC PATHWAYS–THE THAI ELEPHANT CONSERVATION PROJECT, Thailand

RUSTIC PATHWAYS–THE TURTLE CONSERVATION PROJECT, Costa Rica

RUSTIC PATHWAYS–VOLCANOES AND RAINFORESTS, Costa Rica

RUSTIC PATHWAYS–WORLD SERVICE EXTREME

Service Learning in Barcelona, Spain

Service Learning in Paris, France

Studies Abroad for Global Education (SAGE), Summer SAGE Program, India

Summer Action–Take the Lead, MA

Treetops eXpeditions–Alaska Community Service, AK

Treetops eXpeditions–Vanuatu, Vanuatu

Visions–Alaska, AK

Visions–British Virgin Islands, British Virgin Islands

Visions–Costa Rica, Costa Rica

Visions–Dominica, Dominica

Visions–Dominican Republic, Dominican Republic

Visions–Ecuador, Ecuador

Visions–Guadeloupe, Guadeloupe

Visions–Mississippi, MS

Visions–Montana, MT

Visions–Nicaragua, Nicaragua

Visions–Peru, Peru

Visions–Vietnam, Vietnam

Volunteers for Peace International Voluntary Service–Estonia, Estonia

Volunteers for Peace International Voluntary Service–France, France

Volunteers for Peace International Voluntary Service–Germany, Germany

Volunteers for Peace International Voluntary Service–Italy, Italy

Westcoast Connection–Community Connections Alaska, AK

Westcoast Connection–Community Service Belize, Belize

Westcoast Connection–Community Service Costa Rica, Costa Rica

Westcoast Connection–Community Service–Habitat for Humanity, WA

Westcoast Connection–Community Service Hawaii, HI

Wilderness Ventures–Alaska Southeast Community Service, AK

Wilderness Ventures–Costa Rica Service, Costa Rica

Wilderness Ventures–Fiji Community Service, Fiji

Wilderness Ventures–Hawaii, HI

Wilderness Ventures–Peru Community Service, Peru

Wilderness Ventures–Southwest Community Service

World Horizons International–Cayambe, Ecuador, Ecuador

World Horizons International–Costa Rica, Costa Rica

World Horizons International–Dominica, Dominica

World Horizons International–Fiji, Fiji

World Horizons International–Iceland, Iceland

World Horizons International–Kanab, Utah, UT

World Horizons International–Northridge, California, CA

World Horizons International–Rome, Italy, Italy

World Horizons International–Tapovan, Laxman Jhula, India, India

Cultural Programs

AAVE–Africa

AAVE–Bike Amsterdam-Paris

SPECIALIZED PROGRAMS

AAVE–Bold Europe
AAVE–China, China
AAVE–Costa Rica Clásica, Costa Rica
AAVE–Ecuador and Galapagos, Ecuador
AAVE–España Clásica, Spain
AAVE–France Classique, France
AAVE–Peru and Machu Picchu, Peru
AAVE–Sail Dive Greece, Greece
AAVE–Surf Scuba Safari, Mexico
AAVE–Thailand, Thailand
AAVE–Ultimate Alps
AAVE–Wild Isles
Academic Study Associates–Barcelona, Spain
Academic Study Associates–Costa Rica, Costa Rica
Academic Study Associates–Florence, Italy
Academic Study Associates–Nice, France
Academic Study Associates–Royan, France
Academic Study Associates–Spanish in España, Spain
ACADEMIC TREKS–Adventure Peru, Peru
ACADEMIC TREKS–Immersion Mexico, Mexico
ACADEMIC TREKS–Spanish Immersion in Oaxaca, Mexico, Mexico
ACADEMIC TREKS–Spanish Language Immersion in Ecuador, Ecuador
ACADEMIC TREKS–Wilderness Emergency Medicine, Belize
ACTIONQUEST: Australian and Great Barrier Reef Adventures, Australia
ACTIONQUEST: Galapagos Archipelago Expeditions, Ecuador
ACTIONQUEST: Leeward and French Caribbean Island Voyages
ACTIONQUEST: Mediterranean Sailing Voyage
ACTIONQUEST: Tahiti and French Polynesian Island Voyages, French Polynesia
AFS-USA–China Summer Homestay Language Study Program, China
AFS-USA–Community Service–Argentina, Argentina
AFS-USA–Community Service–Costa Rica, Costa Rica
AFS-USA–Community Service–Panama, Panama
AFS-USA–Community Service–Paraguay, Paraguay
AFS-USA–Community Service–Thailand, Thailand

AFS-USA–Homestay–Argentina, Argentina
AFS-USA–Homestay–Chile, Chile
AFS-USA–Homestay–Ecuador, Ecuador
AFS-USA–Homestay–Finland, Finland
AFS-USA–Homestay–France, France
AFS-USA–Homestay Language Study–Costa Rica, Costa Rica
AFS-USA–Homestay Language Study–Egypt, Egypt
AFS-USA–Homestay Language Study–Japan, Japan
AFS-USA–Homestay Language Study–Latvia, Latvia
AFS-USA–Homestay Language Study–Panama, Panama
AFS-USA–Homestay–Paraguay, Paraguay
AFS-USA–Homestay Plus–Australia, Australia
AFS-USA–Homestay Plus–Costa Rica, Costa Rica
AFS-USA–Homestay Plus–Hungary, Hungary
AFS-USA–Homestay Plus–Italy, Italy
AFS-USA–Homestay Plus–New Zealand, New Zealand
AFS-USA–Homestay Plus–Panama, Panama
AFS-USA–Homestay Plus–Spain, Spain
AFS-USA–Homestay–Thailand, Thailand
AFS-USA–Homestay–Turkey, Turkey
AFS-USA–Language Study–Spain, Spain
AFS-USA–Team Mission–Ghana, Ghana
ATW: European Adventures
ATW: Mini Tours
Barat Foundation Summer Program in Provence, France
BROADREACH Arc of the Caribbean Sailing Adventure
BROADREACH Fiji Solomon Quest
BROADREACH Red Sea Scuba Adventure, Egypt
Cambridge College Programme, United Kingdom
The Cambridge Experience, United Kingdom
Canoe Island French Camp, WA
Center for Cultural Interchange–Argentina Independent Homestay, Argentina
Center for Cultural Interchange–Australia High School Abroad, Australia
Center for Cultural Interchange–Brazil High School Abroad, Brazil

Center for Cultural Interchange–Chile Independent Homestay, Chile
Center for Cultural Interchange–Costa Rica Language School, Costa Rica
Center for Cultural Interchange–Denmark High School Abroad, Denmark
Center for Cultural Interchange–Finland High School Abroad, Finland
Center for Cultural Interchange–France High School Abroad, France
Center for Cultural Interchange–France Independent Homestay, France
Center for Cultural Interchange–France Language School, France
Center for Cultural Interchange–Germany High School Abroad, Germany
Center for Cultural Interchange–Germany Independent Homestay, Germany
Center for Cultural Interchange–Germany Language School, Germany
Center for Cultural Interchange–Ireland High School Abroad, Ireland
Center for Cultural Interchange–Ireland Independent Homestay Program, Ireland
Center for Cultural Interchange–Italy High School Abroad, Italy
Center for Cultural Interchange–Italy Language School, Italy
Center for Cultural Interchange–Japan High School Abroad, Japan
Center for Cultural Interchange–Mexico Language School, Mexico
Center for Cultural Interchange–Netherlands High School Abroad, Netherlands
Center for Cultural Interchange–Norway High School Abroad, Norway
Center for Cultural Interchange–Spain High School Abroad, Spain
Center for Cultural Interchange–Spain Independent Homestay, Spain
Center for Cultural Interchange–Spain Language School, Spain
Center for Cultural Interchange–Spain Sports and Language Camp, Spain
Center for Cultural Interchange–Sweden High School Abroad, Sweden

► CULTURAL PROGRAMS

Center for Cultural Interchange–Taiwan High School Abroad, Taiwan

Center for Cultural Interchange–United Kingdom Independent Homestay, United Kingdom

Choate Rosemary Hall Summer in China, China

Choate Rosemary Hall Summer in Paris, France

Choate Rosemary Hall Summer in Spain, Spain

Edu-Culture International (ECI)–Aix-en-Provence/Gap Host Family Immersion, France

Edu-Culture International (ECI)–Andalusion Total Immersion, Spain

Edu-Culture International (ECI)–CPI Costa Rica, Costa Rica

Edu-Culture International (ECI)–Granada Homestay, Spain

Edu-Culture International (ECI)–Granada Homestay or Dorm Plus Southern Host Family Immersion, Spain

Edu-Culture International (ECI)–Granada-Nerja Homestay Combo, Spain

Edu-Culture International (ECI)–Grecia Costa Rica, Costa Rica

Edu-Culture International (ECI)–Lyon Host Family and Travel Program, France

Edu-Culture International (ECI)–Nerja Homestay Plus Southern Host Family Immersion, Spain

Edu-Culture International (ECI)–Nerja Homestay with Optional Southern Host Family Immersion, Spain

Edu-Culture International (ECI)–Salamanca Dorm Plus Southern Host Family Immersion, Spain

Edu-Culture International (ECI)–Salamanca Homestay, Spain

Edu-Culture International (ECI)–Salamanca Homestay Plus Northern Host Family Immersion, Spain

Edu-Culture International (ECI)–Salamanca Homestay (Short Version), Spain

Edu-Culture International (ECI)–San Sebastian Homestay Plus Southern Host Family Immersion, Spain

Edu-Culture International (ECI)–Toulouse/Montpellier Host Family Immersion, France

EF International Language School–Barcelona, Spain

EF International Language School–Beijing, China

EF International Language School–Malaga, Spain

EF International Language School–Munich, Germany

EF International Language School–Nice, France

EF International Language School–Paris, France

EF International Language School–Playa Tamarindo, Costa Rica

EF International Language School–Quito, Ecuador

EF International Language School–Rome, Italy

EF International Language School–Shanghai, China

Excel at Madrid/Barcelona, Spain

Excel at Oxford/Tuscany

Excel at Paris/Provence, France

Excel China, China

The Experiment in International Living–Argentina Homestay, Community Service, and Outdoor Ecological Program, Argentina

The Experiment in International Living–Argentina Visual Arts, Photography, and Service, Argentina

The Experiment in International Living–Australia Homestay, Australia

The Experiment in International Living–Belize Homestay, Belize

The Experiment in International Living–Botswana Homestay, Botswana

The Experiment in International Living–Brazil–Community Service and Soccer, Brazil

The Experiment in International Living–Brazil Homestay, Arts, and Community Service, Brazil

The Experiment in International Living–Chile North Homestay, Community Service, Chile

The Experiment in International Living–Chile South Homestay, Chile

The Experiment in International Living–China North and East Homestay, China

The Experiment in International Living–China South and West Homestay, China

The Experiment in International Living–Costa Rica Homestay, Costa Rica

The Experiment in International Living–Ecuador Homestay, Ecuador

The Experiment in International Living–France, Biking and Homestay, France

The Experiment in International Living–France, Five-Week Art and Adventure in Provence, France

The Experiment in International Living–France, Four-Week Brittany Discovery, France

The Experiment in International Living–France, Four-Week Homestay and Photography, France

The Experiment in International Living–France, Four-Week Homestay and Theatre, France

The Experiment in International Living–France, Four-Week Homestay and Travel–Southern France and Northern Spain, France

The Experiment in International Living–France, Four-Week Homestay and Travel through Alps, France

The Experiment in International Living–France, Homestay, Language Training, and Cooking, France

The Experiment in International Living–France, Three-Week Camargue Homestay, France

The Experiment in International Living–France, Three-Week Homestay and Travel–Borders, France

The Experiment in International Living–Germany, Four-Week Homestay, Travel, Community Service, Germany

The Experiment in International Living–Ghana Homestay, Ghana

The Experiment in International Living–Italy Biodiversity, Cooking, and Culture, Italy

The Experiment in International Living–Italy Homestay, Language, Culture, and Travel, Italy

The Experiment in International Living–Japan Homestay, Japan

The Experiment in International Living–Mexico–Community Service, Travel, and Homestay, Mexico

The Experiment in International Living–Mexico Cooking and Culture, Mexico

The Experiment in International Living–Mexico Homestay, Sustainable Development and Fair Trade, Mexico

The Experiment in International Living–Mexico–Mayan Arts and Culture, Mexico

The Experiment in International Living–Morocco Four-Week Arts and Culture Program, Morocco

The Experiment in International Living–Navajo Nation, NM

The Experiment in International Living–New Zealand Homestay, New Zealand

The Experiment in International Living–Poland, Homestay, Community Service, and Travel, Poland

The Experiment in International Living–Scotland, United Kingdom

The Experiment in International Living–South Africa Homestay and Community Service, South Africa

The Experiment in International Living–Spain, Five-Week Homestay, Language Immersion, Spain

The Experiment in International Living–Spain, Four-Week Language Training, Travel, and Homestay, Spain

The Experiment in International Living–Spain–Multiculturalism and Service, Spain

The Experiment in International Living–Spain–Spanish Arts and Culture, Spain

The Experiment in International Living–Spain–The Road to Santiago, Spain

The Experiment in International Living–Spanish Culture and Exploration, Spain

The Experiment in International Living–Switzerland French Language Immersion, Homestay, and Alpine Adventure, Switzerland

The Experiment in International Living–Thailand Homestay, Thailand

The Experiment in International Living–Turkey Homestay, Community Service, and Travel, Turkey

The Experiment in International Living–United Kingdom Filmmaking Program and Homestay, United Kingdom

The Experiment in International Living–United Kingdom Theatre Program, United Kingdom

The Fessenden School Summer ESL Program, MA

Global Leadership Adventures–Brazil: Community Service and Leadership, Brazil

Global Leadership Adventures–Cape Town: Community Service and Leadership, South Africa

Global Leadership Adventures–Costa Rica: Community Service and Leadership, Costa Rica

Global Leadership Adventures–Ghana: Community Service and Leadership, Ghana

Global Leadership Adventures–India: Community Service and Leadership, India

GLOBAL WORKS–Cultural Exchange and Service–Costa Rica-3 weeks, Costa Rica

GLOBAL WORKS–Cultural Exchange and Service–Ireland-4 weeks, Ireland

GLOBAL WORKS–Cultural Exchange and Service–New Zealand and Fiji Islands-4 weeks

GLOBAL WORKS–Cultural Exchange and Service–Puerto Rico-2 or 4 weeks, Puerto Rico

GLOBAL WORKS–Cultural Exchange–Fiji Islands-4 weeks, Fiji

GLOBAL WORKS–Language Immersion, Cultural Exchange and Service–Argentina, Argentina

GLOBAL WORKS–Language Immersion, Cultural Exchange and Service–Costa Rica, Costa Rica

GLOBAL WORKS–Language Immersion, Cultural Exchange and Service–Ecuador and the Galapagos-4 weeks, Ecuador

GLOBAL WORKS–Language Immersion, Cultural Exchange and Service–France-4 weeks, France

GLOBAL WORKS–Language Immersion, Cultural Exchange and Service–Martinique-4weeks, Martinique

GLOBAL WORKS–Language Immersion, Cultural Exchange and Service–Mexico-3 weeks, Mexico

GLOBAL WORKS–Language Immersion, Cultural Exchange and Service–Panama/Costa Rica

GLOBAL WORKS–Language Immersion, Cultural Exchange and Service–Peru, Peru

GLOBAL WORKS–Language Immersion, Cultural Exchange and Service–Puerto Rico 4 weeks, Puerto Rico

GLOBAL WORKS–Language Immersion, Cultural Exchange and Service–Spain-4 weeks, Spain

GLOBAL WORKS–Language Immersion, Cultural Exchange and Service–Yucatan Peninsula, Mexico-4 weeks, Mexico

Humanities Spring in Assisi, Italy

The Hun School of Princeton American Culture and Language Institute, NJ

iD Tech Camps–Documentary Filmmaking and Cultural Immersion in Spain, Spain

International Summer Camp Montana, Switzerland, Switzerland

LIFEWORKS with the Australian Red Cross, Australia

LIFEWORKS with the British Virgin Islands Marine Parks and Conservation Department, British Virgin Islands

LIFEWORKS with the China Little Flower Foundation in China, China

LIFEWORKS with the DPF Foundation in Thailand, Thailand

LIFEWORKS with the Fundación Humanitaria in Costa Rica, Costa Rica

LIFEWORKS with the Galapagos Islands' National Parks, Ecuador

Oxford Advanced Studies Program, United Kingdom

The Oxford Experience, United Kingdom

Putney Student Travel Community Service–Argentina, Argentina

Putney Student Travel–Community Service–Costa Rica, Costa Rica

Putney Student Travel–Community Service–Dominican Republic, Dominican Republic

Putney Student Travel–Community Service–Dominica, West Indies, Dominica

Putney Student Travel–Community Service–Ecuador, Ecuador

Putney Student Travel–Community Service–India, India

Putney Student Travel–Community Service–Senegal, Senegal

Putney Student Travel–Community Service–Tanzania, United Republic of Tanzania

Putney Student Travel–Community Service–Vietnam, Vietnam

Putney Student Travel–Cultural Exploration–Australia, New Zealand, and Fiji

Putney Student Travel–Cultural Exploration–Switzerland, Italy, France, and Holland

Putney Student Travel–Cultural Exploration–Thailand and Cambodia

Putney Student Travel–Global Action–El Salvador, El Salvador

Putney Student Travel–Global Action–India, India

Putney Student Travel–Global Action–Malawi, Malawi

Putney Student Travel–Global Action–South Africa, South Africa

Putney Student Travel–Global Awareness–China, China

Putney Student Travel–Global Awareness in Action–Cambodia, Cambodia

Putney Student Travel–Global Awareness–Madagascar, Madagascar

Putney Student Travel–Language Learning–Argentina, Argentina

Putney Student Travel–Language Learning–Costa Rica, Costa Rica

Putney Student Travel–Language Learning–France, France

Putney Student Travel–Language Learning–Spain, Spain

Rassias Programs–Arles, France, France

Rassias Programs–China, China

Rassias Programs–Gijón, Spain, Spain

Rassias Programs–Pontevedra, Spain, Spain

Rassias Programs–Segovia, Spain, Spain

Rassias Programs–Tours, France, France

Rein Europe

RUSTIC PATHWAYS–THE AMAZING THAILAND ADVENTURE, Thailand

RUSTIC PATHWAYS–ASIAN PACIFIC EXTREME

RUSTIC PATHWAYS–BIG FIJI EXPLORER, Fiji

RUSTIC PATHWAYS–THE BUDDHIST CARAVAN, India

RUSTIC PATHWAYS–THE CANO NEGRO SERVICE PROJECT, Costa Rica

RUSTIC PATHWAYS–COME WITH NOTHING, GO HOME RICH, Thailand

RUSTIC PATHWAYS–COMMUNITY SERVICE SCHOOL IN AUSTRALIA, Australia

RUSTIC PATHWAYS–COSTA RICA ADVENTURER, Costa Rica

RUSTIC PATHWAYS–ELEPHANTS & AMAZING THAILAND, Thailand

RUSTIC PATHWAYS–EXTENDED FIJI VILLAGE SERVICE, Fiji

RUSTIC PATHWAYS–FACES AND PLACES OF VIETNAM, Vietnam

RUSTIC PATHWAYS–FIJI ISLANDS COMMUNITY SERVICE, Fiji

RUSTIC PATHWAYS–HILL TRIBE TREKKING ADVENTURE, Thailand

RUSTIC PATHWAYS–INDIAN HIMALAYA TRAVELER, India

RUSTIC PATHWAYS–INTENSIVE CHINESE LANGUAGE, China

RUSTIC PATHWAYS–INTENSIVE SPANISH LANGUAGE, Costa Rica

RUSTIC PATHWAYS–INTRODUCTION TO PHOTOGRAPHY–SNAPSHOTS IN THE LAND OF SMILES

RUSTIC PATHWAYS–INTRO TO COMMUNITY SERVICE IN FIJI, Fiji

RUSTIC PATHWAYS–INTRO TO COMMUNITY SERVICE IN THAILAND, Thailand

RUSTIC PATHWAYS–ISLAND HOPPING AND DIVING–THAILAND, Thailand

RUSTIC PATHWAYS–MALEKU TRIBE IMMERSION PROGRAM–COSTA RICA, Costa Rica

RUSTIC PATHWAYS–NEW ORLEANS SUMMER REBUILDING PROGRAM, LA

RUSTIC PATHWAYS–NEW ZEALAND NORTH ISLAND ADVENTURE, New Zealand

RUSTIC PATHWAYS–OFF THE MAP BURMA AND CAMBODIA

RUSTIC PATHWAYS–PHOTOGRAPHY ADVENTURE IN THAILAND AND ANGKOR WAT

RUSTIC PATHWAYS–PHOTOGRAPHY ADVENTURE IN THAILAND AND BURMA

RUSTIC PATHWAYS–PHOTOGRAPHY ADVENTURE IN THAILAND AND INDIA

RUSTIC PATHWAYS–PHOTOGRAPHY ADVENTURE IN THAILAND AND VIETNAM

RUSTIC PATHWAYS–RAMP UP YOUR SPANISH, Costa Rica

RUSTIC PATHWAYS–REMOTE HIGHLANDS COMMUNITY SERVICE IN FIJI, Fiji

RUSTIC PATHWAYS–RICEFIELDS, MONKS & SMILING CHILDREN, Thailand

RUSTIC PATHWAYS–SERVICE AND SAFARI IN AFRICA, United Republic of Tanzania

RUSTIC PATHWAYS–SERVICE IN THE CLOUDS–INDIA, India

RUSTIC PATHWAYS–SERVICE LEARNING EXTREME

RUSTIC PATHWAYS–SOCCER AND SERVICE EXTREME

RUSTIC PATHWAYS–SOCCER AND SERVICE IN COSTA RICA, Costa Rica

RUSTIC PATHWAYS–SOCCER AND SERVICE IN FIJI, Fiji

RUSTIC PATHWAYS–SOCCER AND SERVICE IN THAILAND, Thailand

RUSTIC PATHWAYS–SPANISH LANGUAGE IMMERSION, Costa Rica

RUSTIC PATHWAYS–SUN, SAND & INTERNATIONAL SERVICE–FIJI, Fiji

RUSTIC PATHWAYS–SYDNEY, REEF & RAINFOREST, Australia

RUSTIC PATHWAYS–THE THAI ELEPHANT CONSERVATION PROJECT, Thailand

RUSTIC PATHWAYS–ULTIMATE JUNGLE ADVENTURE–COSTA RICA, Costa Rica

RUSTIC PATHWAYS–THE WONDERS & RICHES OF SOUTHEAST ASIA

RUSTIC PATHWAYS–THE WONDERS OF CHINA, China

RUSTIC PATHWAYS–WORLD SERVICE EXTREME

RUSTIC PATHWAYS–YOUNG ADVENTURERS–COSTA RICA, Costa Rica

Service Learning in Barcelona, Spain

Service Learning in Paris, France

Southwestern Adventures–Arizona, AZ

Spoleto Study Abroad, Italy

Studies Abroad for Global Education (SAGE), Summer SAGE Program, India

Summer Advantage Study Abroad–Cambridge University, United Kingdom

Summer Advantage Study Abroad–Granada, Spain, Spain

Summer Advantage Study Abroad–London, United Kingdom

Summer Advantage Study Abroad–Nanjing, China, China

Summer Advantage Study Abroad–
Paris, France, France

Summer Advantage Study Abroad–
Rome, Italy, Italy

Summer Advantage Study Abroad–St.
Petersburg, Russia, Russian
Federation

Summer Advantage Study Abroad–
Salamanca, Spain, Spain

Summer in Switzerland, Switzerland

Summer Study in Paris at The
Sorbonne, France

TASIS Le Château des Enfants,
Switzerland

TASIS Middle School Program,
Switzerland

TASIS Spanish Summer Program,
Spain

TASIS Summer Program for
Languages, Arts, and Outdoor
Pursuits, Switzerland

TASIS Tuscan Academy of Art and
Culture, Italy

Tisch School of the Arts–International
High School Program–Dublin,
Ireland

Tisch School of the Arts–International
High School Program–Paris,
France

Treetops eXpeditions–Alaska
Community Service, AK

Treetops eXpeditions–Vanuatu,
Vanuatu

University of Chicago–The Traveling
Academy, Greece

University of Connecticut Mentor
Connection, CT

Visions–Alaska, AK

Visions–British Virgin Islands,
British Virgin Islands

Visions–Costa Rica, Costa Rica

Visions–Dominica, Dominica

Visions–Dominican Republic,
Dominican Republic

Visions–Ecuador, Ecuador

Visions–Guadeloupe, Guadeloupe

Visions–Mississippi, MS

Visions–Montana, MT

Visions–Nicaragua, Nicaragua

Visions–Peru, Peru

Visions–Vietnam, Vietnam

Weissman Teen Tours–"Aloha–
Welcome to Hawaiian Paradise,"
3 weeks

Weissman Teen Tours–"Aloha–
Welcome to Hawaiian Paradise,"
2 weeks, HI

Weissman Teen Tours–European
Experience

Weissman Teen Tours–U.S. and
Western Canada, 40 Days

Weissman Teen Tours–U.S. and
Western Canada, 30 Days

Westcoast Connection–Authentic
Italy, Italy

Westcoast Connection–Community
Service Costa Rica, Costa Rica

Westcoast Connection–European
Escape

Westcoast Connection–French
Language and Touring, France

Westcoast Connection–Spanish in
Costa Rica, Costa Rica

Westcoast Connection–Spanish
Language and Touring, Spain

Westcoast Connection Travel–
European Discovery

Westcoast Connection Travel/On
Tour–European Escapade

Westcoast Connection Travel/On
Tour–European Experience

Wilderness Ventures–Australia,
Australia

Wilderness Ventures–Costa Rica,
Costa Rica

Wilderness Ventures–Costa Rica
Service, Costa Rica

Wilderness Ventures–Ecuador and
Galapagos Community Service,
Ecuador

Wilderness Ventures–European Alps

Wilderness Ventures–Fiji Community
Service, Fiji

Wilderness Ventures–Spanish
Pyrenees, Spain

World Affairs Seminar, WI

World Horizons International–
Cayambe, Ecuador, Ecuador

World Horizons International–Costa
Rica, Costa Rica

World Horizons International–
Dominica, Dominica

World Horizons International–Fiji,
Fiji

World Horizons International–
Iceland, Iceland

World Horizons International–Rome,
Italy, Italy

World Horizons International–
Tapovan, Laxman Jhula, India,
India

World Horizons International–United
Kingdom

Family Programs

Alford Lake Family Camp, ME

Camp Lincoln for Boys/Camp Lake
Hubert for Girls–Family Camp,
MN

Canoe Island French Camp, WA

Cheley Colorado Camps, CO

Idyllwild Arts Summer Program–
Family Week, CA

Wilderness Ventures–Yellowstone-
Teton Family Adventure, WY

Outdoor Programs

AAVE–Africa

AAVE–Australia, Australia

AAVE–Bike Amsterdam-Paris

AAVE–Bold Europe

AAVE–Bold West

AAVE–Boot/Saddle/Paddle

AAVE–China, China

AAVE–Colorado Discovery, CO

AAVE–Costa Rica Clásica, Costa Rica

AAVE–Ecuador and Galapagos,
Ecuador

AAVE–España Clásica, Spain

AAVE–France Classique, France

AAVE–Peak Four

AAVE–Peru and Machu Picchu, Peru

AAVE–Rock & Rapid

AAVE–Rock & Roll, CO

AAVE–Sail Dive Greece, Greece

AAVE–Surf Scuba Safari, Mexico

AAVE–Thailand, Thailand

AAVE–Ultimate Alaska, AK

AAVE–Ultimate Alps

AAVE–Ultimate Hawaii, HI

AAVE–Wild Coast Discovery

AAVE–Wild Isles

ACADEMIC TREKS–Adventure Peru,
Peru

ACADEMIC TREKS–Caribbean
Marine Reserves

ACADEMIC TREKS–Dolphin Studies
in Belize, Belize

ACADEMIC TREKS–Immersion
Mexico, Mexico

ACADEMIC TREKS–Pacific Whale
Treks, Canada

ACADEMIC TREKS–Sea Turtle
Studies, Costa Rica

ACADEMIC TREKS–Shark Studies
in Fiji, Fiji

ACADEMIC TREKS–Shipwrecks and
Underwater Archaeology in
Bermuda, Bermuda

ACADEMIC TREKS–Spanish
Immersion in Oaxaca, Mexico,
Mexico

ACADEMIC TREKS–Spanish
Language Immersion in Ecuador,
Ecuador

ACADEMIC TREKS–Wilderness
Emergency Medicine, Belize

ACTIONQUEST: Advanced PADI
Scuba Certification and Specialty
Voyages, British Virgin Islands

ACTIONQUEST: Australian and
Great Barrier Reef Adventures,
Australia

▶ OUTDOOR PROGRAMS

ACTIONQUEST: British Virgin Islands–Sailing and Scuba Voyages, British Virgin Islands

ACTIONQUEST: British Virgin Islands-Sailing Voyages, British Virgin Islands

ACTIONQUEST: Galapagos Archipelago Expeditions, Ecuador

ACTIONQUEST: Junior Advanced Scuba with Marine Biology, British Virgin Islands

ACTIONQUEST: Leeward and French Caribbean Island Voyages

ACTIONQUEST: Mediterranean Sailing Voyage

ACTIONQUEST: PADI Divemaster Voyages, British Virgin Islands

ACTIONQUEST: Rescue Diving Voyages, British Virgin Islands

ACTIONQUEST: Tahiti and French Polynesian Island Voyages, French Polynesia

ACTIONQUEST: Tropical Marine Biology Voyages, British Virgin Islands

Adirondack Field Ecology, NY

Adventure Treks–Alaska Adventures, AK

Adventure Treks–California Adventures, CA

Adventure Treks–Canadian Rockies Adventures, Canada

Adventure Treks–Montana Adventures, MT

Adventure Treks–Oregon Adventures, OR

Adventure Treks–Pacific Northwest Adventures, WA

Adventure Treks–Wilderness Adventures

AFS-USA–Homestay Plus–Australia, Australia

AFS-USA–Homestay Plus–New Zealand, New Zealand

AFS-USA–Homestay Plus–Spain, Spain

Asheville School's Summer Academic Adventures, NC

Brewster Academy Summer Session, NH

BROADREACH Adventures Down Under, Australia

BROADREACH Adventures in Scuba and Sailing–Underwater Discoveries

BROADREACH Adventures in the Grenadines–Advanced Scuba, Saint Vincent and The Grenadines

BROADREACH Adventures in the Windward Islands–Advanced Scuba

BROADREACH Adventures Underwater–Advanced Scuba

BROADREACH Arc of the Caribbean Sailing Adventure

BROADREACH Baja Extreme–Scuba Adventure, Mexico

BROADREACH Costa Rica Experience, Costa Rica

BROADREACH Fiji Solomon Quest

BROADREACH Honduras Eco-Adventure, Honduras

BROADREACH Marine Biology Accredited, Bahamas

BROADREACH Red Sea Scuba Adventure, Egypt

BROADREACH Yucatan Adventure, Mexico

Camp Berachah Ministries–Camps and Conferences, WA

Camp Chikopi for Boys, Canada

Camp Treetops, NY

Center for Cultural Interchange–Spain Sports and Language Camp, Spain

Cheley Colorado Camps, CO

Darlington Summer Programs, GA

The Experiment in International Living–Argentina Homestay, Community Service, and Outdoor Ecological Program, Argentina

The Experiment in International Living–Argentina Visual Arts, Photography, and Service, Argentina

The Experiment in International Living–Australia Homestay, Australia

The Experiment in International Living–Belize Homestay, Belize

The Experiment in International Living–Botswana Homestay, Botswana

The Experiment in International Living–Brazil–Community Service and Soccer, Brazil

The Experiment in International Living–Chile North Homestay, Community Service, Chile

The Experiment in International Living–Chile South Homestay, Chile

The Experiment in International Living–China North and East Homestay, China

The Experiment in International Living–Costa Rica Homestay, Costa Rica

The Experiment in International Living–Ecuador Homestay, Ecuador

The Experiment in International Living–France, Biking and Homestay, France

The Experiment in International Living–France, Four-Week Homestay and Travel–Southern France and Northern Spain, France

The Experiment in International Living–France, Four-Week Homestay and Travel through Alps, France

The Experiment in International Living–Navajo Nation, NM

The Experiment in International Living–New Zealand Homestay, New Zealand

The Experiment in International Living–Scotland, United Kingdom

The Experiment in International Living–South Africa Homestay and Community Service, South Africa

The Experiment in International Living–Spain, Five-Week Homestay, Language Immersion, Spain

The Experiment in International Living–Spain–The Road to Santiago, Spain

The Experiment in International Living–Switzerland French Language Immersion, Homestay, and Alpine Adventure, Switzerland

The Experiment in International Living–Thailand Homestay, Thailand

Fenn School Summer Day Camp, MA

The Fessenden School Summer ESL Program, MA

Future Leader Camp, VT

Hargrave Summer Leadership Program, VA

International Summer Camp Montana, Switzerland, Switzerland

Keewaydin Dunmore, VT

Keewaydin Temagami, Canada

Landmark Volunteers: Arizona, AZ

Landmark Volunteers: California, CA

Landmark Volunteers: Colorado, CO

Landmark Volunteers: Connecticut, CT

Landmark Volunteers: Idaho, ID

Landmark Volunteers: Maine, ME

Landmark Volunteers: Massachusetts, MA

Landmark Volunteers: Michigan, MI

Landmark Volunteers: Minnesota, MN

Landmark Volunteers: Montana, MT

Landmark Volunteers: New Jersey, NJ

Landmark Volunteers: New Mexico, NM

Landmark Volunteers: New York, NY

Landmark Volunteers: Oregon, OR

Landmark Volunteers: Vermont, VT

Landmark Volunteers: Virginia, VA

Landmark Volunteers: Washington, WA

Landmark Volunteers: Wyoming, WY

Les Elfes–International Summer/ Winter Camp, Switzerland

LIFEWORKS with the Australian Red Cross, Australia

LIFEWORKS with the British Virgin Islands Marine Parks and Conservation Department, British Virgin Islands

LIFEWORKS with the Fundación Humanitaria in Costa Rica, Costa Rica

LIFEWORKS with the Galapagos Islands' National Parks, Ecuador

Mad River Glen Naturalist Adventure Camp, VT

Michigan Technological University Summer Youth Program, MI

92nd Street Y Camps–Camp Tevah for Science and Nature, NY

92nd Street Y Camps–The TIYUL

Pine Island Camp, ME

Putney Student Travel–Community Service–Alaska, AK

Putney Student Travel–Global Awareness–Madagascar, Madagascar

Rein Europe

Rein Teen Tours–California Caper

Rein Teen Tours–Crossroads

Rein Teen Tours–Eastern Adventure

Rein Teen Tours–Grand Adventure

Rein Teen Tours–Hawaiian/Alaskan Adventure

Rein Teen Tours–Hawaiian Caper

Rein Teen Tours–Western Adventure

Roaring Brook Camp for Boys, VT

RUSTIC PATHWAYS–ASIAN PACIFIC EXTREME

RUSTIC PATHWAYS–BIG FIJI EXPLORER, Fiji

RUSTIC PATHWAYS–THE BUDDHIST CARAVAN, India

RUSTIC PATHWAYS–CLIMBING KILI, United Republic of Tanzania

RUSTIC PATHWAYS–COSTA RICA ADVENTURER, Costa Rica

RUSTIC PATHWAYS–FIJI ISLANDS COMMUNITY SERVICE, Fiji

RUSTIC PATHWAYS–HILL TRIBE TREKKING ADVENTURE, Thailand

RUSTIC PATHWAYS–INDIAN HIMALAYA TRAVELER, India

RUSTIC PATHWAYS–INTRODUCTION TO PHOTOGRAPHY–SNAPSHOTS IN THE LAND OF SMILES

RUSTIC PATHWAYS–ISLAND HOPPING AND DIVING–THAILAND, Thailand

RUSTIC PATHWAYS–SERVICE AND SAFARI IN AFRICA, United Republic of Tanzania

RUSTIC PATHWAYS–SOCCER AND SERVICE EXTREME

RUSTIC PATHWAYS–SOCCER AND SERVICE IN FIJI, Fiji

RUSTIC PATHWAYS–THE TURTLE CONSERVATION PROJECT, Costa Rica

RUSTIC PATHWAYS–ULTIMATE JUNGLE ADVENTURE–COSTA RICA, Costa Rica

RUSTIC PATHWAYS–VOLCANOES AND RAINFORESTS, Costa Rica

Seacamp, FL

Songadeewin of Keewaydin, VT

Southwestern Adventures–Arizona, AZ

Studies Abroad for Global Education (SAGE), Summer SAGE Program, India

Summer@Rensselaer, NY

Summer in Switzerland, Switzerland

Talisman Summer Camp, NC

TASC Canadian Wilderness Fishing Camps, Canada

TASIS French Language Program in Château–d'Oex, Switzerland, Switzerland

Teton Valley Ranch Camp–Boys Camp, WY

Teton Valley Ranch Camp–Girls Camp, WY

Treetops eXpeditions–Alaska Community Service, AK

Treetops eXpeditions–Glacier/ Boundary Waters

Treetops eXpeditions–Horseback Riding

Treetops eXpeditions–Sailing and Marine Ecology, FL

Treetops eXpeditions–Vanuatu, Vanuatu

University of Chicago–Stones and Bones, WY

Valley Forge Military Academy Summer Camp for Boys, PA

Valley Forge Military Academy Summer Coed Day Camp, PA

Visions–Alaska, AK

Visions–British Virgin Islands, British Virgin Islands

Visions–Costa Rica, Costa Rica

Visions–Dominica, Dominica

Visions–Dominican Republic, Dominican Republic

Visions–Guadeloupe, Guadeloupe

Visions–Mississippi, MS

Visions–Montana, MT

Visions–Peru, Peru

Weissman Teen Tours–"Aloha–Welcome to Hawaiian Paradise," 3 weeks

Weissman Teen Tours–"Aloha–Welcome to Hawaiian Paradise," 2 weeks, HI

Weissman Teen Tours–European Experience

Weissman Teen Tours–U.S. and Western Canada, 40 Days

Weissman Teen Tours–U.S. and Western Canada, 30 Days

Westcoast Connection–American Voyageur

Westcoast Connection–Californian Extravaganza

Westcoast Connection Travel–Adventure California, CA

Westcoast Connection Travel–Canadian Mountain Magic, Canada

Westcoast Connection Travel–Great West Challenge

Westcoast Connection Travel–Northwestern Odyssey

Westcoast Connection Travel–Quebec Adventure, Canada

Westcoast Connection Travel–Western Canadian Adventure, Canada

Westcoast Connection–U.S. Explorer

Wilderness Ventures–Alaska College Leadership, AK

Wilderness Ventures–Alaska Expedition, AK

Wilderness Ventures–Alaska Southcentral, AK

Wilderness Ventures–Alaska Southeast, AK

Wilderness Ventures–Australia, Australia

Wilderness Ventures–California, CA

Wilderness Ventures–Cascade-Olympic, WA

Wilderness Ventures–Colorado/Utah Mountain Bike

Wilderness Ventures–Costa Rica, Costa Rica

Wilderness Ventures–Costa Rica Service, Costa Rica

Wilderness Ventures–Costa Rica Surfing, Costa Rica

Wilderness Ventures–Ecuador and Galapagos Community Service, Ecuador

Wilderness Ventures–European Alps

Wilderness Ventures–Fiji Community Service, Fiji

Wilderness Ventures–Grand Teton, WY

Wilderness Ventures–Great Divide

Wilderness Ventures–Hawaii, HI

Wilderness Ventures–High Sierra, CA

Wilderness Ventures–Jackson Hole, WY

Wilderness Ventures–Maui/Kauai, HI

Wilderness Ventures–Northwest

Wilderness Ventures–Oregon, OR

Wilderness Ventures–Pacific Northwest

Wilderness Ventures–Peru Community Service, Peru

Wilderness Ventures–Puget Sound, WA

Wilderness Ventures–Rocky Mountain

Wilderness Ventures–Southwest Community Service

Wilderness Ventures–Spanish Pyrenees, Spain

Wilderness Ventures–Tahiti, Fiji, and New Zealand

Wilderness Ventures–Teton Crest

Wilderness Ventures–Washington Alpine, WA

Wilderness Ventures–Washington Mountaineering, WA

Wilderness Ventures–Wyoming Mountaineering, WY

Wilderness Ventures–Yellowstone

Wilderness Ventures–Yellowstone Fly Fishing

Wilderness Ventures–Yellowstone/ Teton Adventure, WY

Wilderness Ventures–Yellowstone-Teton Family Adventure, WY

Wilderness Ventures–Yellowstone Wilderness

Wolfeboro: The Summer Boarding School, NH

World Horizons International–Iceland, Iceland

World Horizons International–Kanab, Utah, UT

Special Needs Programs

Camp Berachah Ministries–Camps and Conferences, WA

Camp California Fitness, CA

Camp Holiday Trails, VA

Dunnabeck at Kildonan, NY

Landmark School Summer Academic Program, MA

Linden Hill Summer Program, MA

92nd Street Y Camps–Camp Bari Tov, NY

92nd Street Y Camps–Camp Tova, NY

Talisman Summer Camp, NC

Sports Camps

AFS-USA–Homestay Plus–Paraguay Soccer, Paraguay

Britannia Soccer Camp, CA

Camp Berachah Ministries–Camps and Conferences, WA

Camp Lincoln for Boys/Camp Lake Hubert for Girls–Golf Camp, MN

Camp Lincoln for Boys/Camp Lake Hubert for Girls–Tennis Camp, MN

Camp Pacific's Surf and Bodyboard Camp, CA

Center for Cultural Interchange–Spain Sports and Language Camp, Spain

Crossroads School–Aquatics, CA

Crossroads School–Sports Camps, CA

Darlington Summer Programs, GA

iD Tech Camps–Stanford University, Palo Alto, CA

iD Tech Camps–UC San Diego, La Jolla, CA

iD Tech Camps–UC Santa Cruz, Santa Cruz, CA

Miss Porter's School Athletic Experience, CT

RUSTIC PATHWAYS–THE ART OF MUAY THAI, Thailand

RUSTIC PATHWAYS–ESCAPE TO FIJI, Fiji

RUSTIC PATHWAYS–SOCCER AND SERVICE IN COSTA RICA, Costa Rica

RUSTIC PATHWAYS–SURF & SERVICE–COSTA RICA, Costa Rica

RUSTIC PATHWAYS–SURF THE SUMMER–COSTA RICA, Costa Rica

Summer@Rensselaer, NY

Tabor Hockey School, MA

Westcoast Connection–California Swing Junior Touring Golf Camp, CA

Westcoast Connection–Florida Swing Junior Touring Golf Camp, FL

Westcoast Connection–Major League Baseball Tour

Westcoast Connection Travel–Ski and Snowboard Sensation

Traditional Camps

Alford Lake Camp, ME

Alford Lake Family Camp, ME

Applejack Teen Camp, NY

Camp Airy, MD

Camp Berachah Ministries–Camps and Conferences, WA

Camp Chikopi for Boys, Canada

Camp Greenbrier for Boys, WV

Camp La Junta, TX

Camp Lincoln for Boys/Camp Lake Hubert for Girls, MN

Camp Louise, MD

Camp Pacific's Recreational Camp, CA

Camp Regis, NY

Camp Rio Vista for Boys, TX

Camp Sierra Vista for Girls, TX

Camp Treetops, NY

Canoe Island French Camp, WA

Cape Cod Sea Camps–Monomoy/ Wono, MA

Cheley Colorado Camps, CO

Cheshire Academy Summer Program, CT

Clearwater Camp for Girls, WI

Darlington Summer Programs, GA

Enforex Residential Youth Summer Camp–Barcelona, Spain

Enforex Residential Youth Summer Camp–Granada, Spain

Enforex Residential Youth Summer Camp–Guanajuato, Mexico, Mexico

Enforex Residential Youth Summer Camp–Madrid, Spain

Enforex Residential Youth Summer Camp–Marbella Albergue College, Spain

Enforex Residential Youth Summer Camp–Marbella Alboran College, Spain

Enforex Residential Youth Summer Camp–Marbella Aleman College, Spain

Enforex Residential Youth Summer Camp–Salamanca, Spain

Enforex Residential Youth Summer Camp–Valencia, Spain

Fenn School Summer Day Camp, MA

Forest Ridge Summer Program, WA

The Gow School Summer Program, NY

Harker Summer Programs, CA

The Hun School of Princeton–Summer Day Camp, NJ

Kamp Kohut, ME

Keewaydin Dunmore, VT

Killooleet, VT

Les Elfes–International Summer/ Winter Camp, Switzerland

Linden Hill Summer Program, MA

Lochearn Camp for Girls, VT

Mad River Glen Naturalist Adventure Camp, VT

92nd Street Y Camps–Camp Bari Tov, NY

92nd Street Y Camps–Camp Kesher, PA

92nd Street Y Camps–Camp Tevah for Science and Nature, NY

92nd Street Y Camps–Camp Tova, NY

92nd Street Y Camps–Camp Yaffa for the Arts, NY

92nd Street Y Camps–Camp Yomi, NY

92nd Street Y Camps–Trailblazers, NY

Pine Island Camp, ME

Saint Thomas More School–Summer Academic Camp, CT

Songadeewin of Keewaydin, VT

Summer at Delphi, OR

Summer in Switzerland, Switzerland

Tabor Academy Summer Program, MA

Talisman Summer Camp, NC

TASIS Le Château des Enfants, Switzerland

TASIS Middle School Program, Switzerland

TASIS Summer Program for Languages, Arts, and Outdoor Pursuits, Switzerland

Teton Valley Ranch Camp–Boys Camp, WY

Teton Valley Ranch Camp–Girls Camp, WY

Valley Forge Military Academy Summer Band Camp, PA

Valley Forge Military Academy Summer Camp for Boys, PA

Valley Forge Military Academy Summer Coed Day Camp, PA

Wilderness Programs

AAVE–Africa

AAVE–Australia, Australia

AAVE–Bold Europe

AAVE–Bold West

AAVE–Boot/Saddle/Paddle

AAVE–Colorado Discovery, CO

AAVE–España Clásica, Spain

AAVE–Peak Four

AAVE–Peru and Machu Picchu, Peru

AAVE–Rock & Rapid

AAVE–Rock & Roll, CO

AAVE–Surf Scuba Safari, Mexico

AAVE–Ultimate Alaska, AK

AAVE–Ultimate Alps

AAVE–Ultimate Hawaii, HI

AAVE–Wild Coast Discovery

AAVE–Wild Isles

Adirondack Field Ecology, NY

Adventure Treks–Alaska Adventures, AK

Adventure Treks–California Adventures, CA

Adventure Treks–Canadian Rockies Adventures, Canada

Adventure Treks–Montana Adventures, MT

Adventure Treks–Oregon Adventures, OR

Adventure Treks–Pacific Northwest Adventures, WA

Adventure Treks–Wilderness Adventures

BROADREACH Adventures Down Under, Australia

BROADREACH Costa Rica Experience, Costa Rica

BROADREACH Honduras Eco-Adventure, Honduras

Cheley Colorado Camps, CO

Keewaydin Temagami, Canada

Landmark Volunteers: New Mexico, NM

Landmark Volunteers: Oregon, OR

Michigan Technological University Summer Youth Program, MI

Putney Student Travel–Community Service–Alaska, AK

RUSTIC PATHWAYS–BIG FIJI EXPLORER, Fiji

RUSTIC PATHWAYS–CLIMBING KILI, United Republic of Tanzania

RUSTIC PATHWAYS–COSTA RICA ADVENTURER, Costa Rica

RUSTIC PATHWAYS–SERVICE AND SAFARI IN AFRICA, United Republic of Tanzania

RUSTIC PATHWAYS–ULTIMATE JUNGLE ADVENTURE–COSTA RICA, Costa Rica

TASC Canadian Wilderness Fishing Camps, Canada

Teton Valley Ranch Camp–Boys Camp, WY

Teton Valley Ranch Camp–Girls Camp, WY

Treetops eXpeditions–Glacier/Boundary Waters

Wilderness Ventures–Alaska College Leadership, AK

Wilderness Ventures–Alaska Expedition, AK

Wilderness Ventures–Alaska Southcentral, AK

Wilderness Ventures–Alaska Southeast, AK

Wilderness Ventures–Australia, Australia

Wilderness Ventures–California, CA

Wilderness Ventures–Cascade-Olympic, WA

Wilderness Ventures–Costa Rica, Costa Rica

Wilderness Ventures–Costa Rica Surfing, Costa Rica

Wilderness Ventures–European Alps

Wilderness Ventures–Grand Teton, WY

Wilderness Ventures–Great Divide

Wilderness Ventures–Hawaii, HI

Wilderness Ventures–High Sierra, CA

Wilderness Ventures–Jackson Hole, WY

Wilderness Ventures–Northwest

Wilderness Ventures–Oregon, OR

Wilderness Ventures–Pacific Northwest

Wilderness Ventures–Peru Community Service, Peru

Wilderness Ventures–Puget Sound, WA

Wilderness Ventures–Rocky Mountain

Wilderness Ventures–Spanish Pyrenees, Spain

Wilderness Ventures–Tahiti, Fiji, and New Zealand

Wilderness Ventures–Teton Crest

Wilderness Ventures–Washington Alpine, WA

Wilderness Ventures–Washington Mountaineering, WA

Wilderness Ventures–Wyoming Mountaineering, WY

Wilderness Ventures–Yellowstone

Wilderness Ventures–Yellowstone Fly Fishing

Wilderness Ventures–Yellowstone/Teton Adventure, WY

Wilderness Ventures–Yellowstone-Teton Family Adventure, WY

Wilderness Ventures–Yellowstone Wilderness

Travel Programs

Alaska
AAVE–Ultimate Alaska
Adventure Treks–Alaska Adventures
Adventure Treks–Wilderness
  Adventures
ATW: Fire and Ice
Rein Teen Tours–Hawaiian/Alaskan
  Adventure
Treetops eXpeditions–Alaska
  Community Service
Visions–Alaska
Westcoast Connection–Community
  Connections Alaska
Wilderness Ventures–Alaska College
  Leadership
Wilderness Ventures–Alaska
  Expedition
Wilderness Ventures–Alaska
  Southcentral
Wilderness Ventures–Alaska
  Southeast
Wilderness Ventures–Alaska
  Southeast Community Service

Antigua and Barbuda
ACTIONQUEST: Leeward and
  French Caribbean Island Voyages
BROADREACH Adventures in Scuba
  and Sailing Underwater
  Discoveries
BROADREACH Adventures
  Underwater–Advanced Scuba
BROADREACH Arc of the Caribbean
  Sailing Adventure

Argentina
The Experiment in International
  Living–Argentina Homestay,
  Community Service, and Outdoor
  Ecological Program
The Experiment in International
  Living–Argentina Visual Arts,
  Photography, and Service
GLOBAL WORKS–Language
  Immersion, Cultural Exchange and
  Service–Argentina

Arizona
AAVE–Boot/Saddle/Paddle
ATW: American Horizons
ATW: California Sunset
ATW: Camp Inn 42
ATW: Discoverer
ATW: Pacific Paradise
ATW: Skyblazer
ATW: Sunblazer
ATW: Wayfarer
Rein Teen Tours–California Caper
Rein Teen Tours–Crossroads
Rein Teen Tours–Grand Adventure
Rein Teen Tours–Western Adventure

Weissman Teen Tours–U.S. and
  Western Canada, 40 Days
Westcoast Connection–American
  Voyageur
Westcoast Connection–California
  Dreaming
Westcoast Connection–Californian
  Extravaganza
Westcoast Connection Travel–
  California and the Canyons
Westcoast Connection–U.S. Explorer
Wilderness Ventures Southwest
  Community Service

Australia
AAVE–Australia
ACTIONQUEST: Australian and
  Great Barrier Reef Adventures
BROADREACH Adventures Down
  Under
The Experiment in International
  Living–Australia Homestay
LIFEWORKS with the Australian
  Red Cross
Putney Student Travel–Cultural
  Exploration–Australia, New
  Zealand, and Fiji
RUSTIC PATHWAYS–COMMUNITY
  SERVICE SCHOOL IN
  AUSTRALIA
RUSTIC PATHWAYS–SERVICE
  LEARNING EXTREME
RUSTIC PATHWAYS–SOUTH
  PACIFIC EXTREME
RUSTIC PATHWAYS–SYDNEY,
  REEF & RAINFOREST
Westcoast Connection–Australian
  Outback Plus Hawaii
Westcoast Connection/On Tour–
  Australian Outback
Wilderness Ventures–Australia

Belgium
AAVE–Bike Amsterdam-Paris
Weissman Teen Tours–European
  Experience
Westcoast Connection Travel–
  European Discovery

Belize
ACADEMIC TREKS–Dolphin Studies
  in Belize
ACADEMIC TREKS–Wilderness
  Emergency Medicine
The Experiment in International
  Living–Belize Homestay
Westcoast Connection–Belize and
  Costa Rica Water Adventure
Westcoast Connection–Community
  Service Belize
Wilderness Ventures–Costa Rica/
  Belize

Bermuda
ACADEMIC TREKS–Shipwrecks and
  Underwater Archaeology in
  Bermuda

Botswana
The Experiment in International
  Living–Botswana Homestay

Brazil
The Experiment in International
  Living–Brazil–Community Service
  and Soccer
The Experiment in International
  Living–Brazil Homestay, Arts, and
  Community Service
Global Leadership Adventures–Brazil:
  Community Service and
  Leadership

British Virgin Islands
ACTIONQUEST: Advanced PADI
  Scuba Certification and Specialty
  Voyages
ACTIONQUEST: British Virgin
  Islands–Sailing and Scuba Voyages
ACTIONQUEST: British Virgin
  Islands-Sailing Voyages
ACTIONQUEST: Junior Advanced
  Scuba with Marine Biology
ACTIONQUEST: Leeward and
  French Caribbean Island Voyages
ACTIONQUEST: PADI Divemaster
  Voyages
ACTIONQUEST: Rescue Diving
  Voyages
ACTIONQUEST: Tropical Marine
  Biology Voyages
LIFEWORKS with the British Virgin
  Islands Marine Parks and
  Conservation Department
Visions–British Virgin Islands

California
AAVE–Bold West
Adventure Treks–California
  Adventures
Adventure Treks–Wilderness
  Adventures
ATW: American Horizons
ATW: California Sunset
ATW: Camp Inn 42
ATW: Discoverer
ATW: Fire and Ice
ATW: Pacific Paradise
ATW: Skyblazer
ATW: Sunblazer
ATW: Wayfarer
Duke TIP Domestic Field Studies
Rein Teen Tours–California Caper
Rein Teen Tours–Crossroads
Rein Teen Tours–Grand Adventure

► CALIFORNIA

Rein Teen Tours–Hawaiian/Alaskan Adventure
Rein Teen Tours–Hawaiian Caper
Rein Teen Tours–Western Adventure
Weissman Teen Tours–"Aloha–Welcome to Hawaiian Paradise," 3 weeks
Weissman Teen Tours–U.S. and Western Canada, 40 Days
Weissman Teen Tours–U.S. and Western Canada, 30 Days
Westcoast Connection–American Voyageur
Westcoast Connection–California Dreaming
Westcoast Connection–Californian Extravaganza
Westcoast Connection–California Sprint
Westcoast Connection–California Swing Junior Touring Golf Camp
Westcoast Connection–Hawaiian Spirit
Westcoast Connection Travel–Adventure California
Westcoast Connection Travel–California and the Canyons
Westcoast Connection Travel–Great West Challenge
Westcoast Connection–U.S. Explorer
Wilderness Ventures–California
Wilderness Ventures–High Sierra

Cambodia
RUSTIC PATHWAYS–ASIAN PACIFIC EXTREME
RUSTIC PATHWAYS–THE BUDDHIST CARAVAN
RUSTIC PATHWAYS–EDGE OF THE MAP EXTREME
RUSTIC PATHWAYS–INTRODUCTION TO PHOTOGRAPHY–SNAPSHOTS IN THE LAND OF SMILES
RUSTIC PATHWAYS–OFF THE MAP BURMA AND CAMBODIA
RUSTIC PATHWAYS–PHOTOGRAPHY ADVENTURE IN THAILAND AND ANGKOR WAT
RUSTIC PATHWAYS–THE WONDERS & RICHES OF SOUTHEAST ASIA

Canada
AAVE–Wild Coast Discovery
ACADEMIC TREKS–Pacific Whale Treks
Adventure Treks–Canadian Rockies Adventures
Adventure Treks–Wilderness Adventures
ATW: Adventure Roads

ATW: Camp Inn 42
ATW: Fire and Ice
ATW: Mini Tours
ATW: Pacific Paradise
ATW: Skyblazer
Rein Teen Tours–Crossroads
Rein Teen Tours–Eastern Adventure
Rein Teen Tours–Grand Adventure
Rein Teen Tours–Hawaiian/Alaskan Adventure
Weissman Teen Tours–U.S. and Western Canada, 40 Days
Weissman Teen Tours–U.S. and Western Canada, 30 Days
Westcoast Connection–American Voyageur
Westcoast Connection Travel–Canadian Mountain Magic
Westcoast Connection Travel–Eastcoast Encounter
Westcoast Connection Travel–Great West Challenge
Westcoast Connection Travel–Northwestern Odyssey
Westcoast Connection Travel–Quebec Adventure
Westcoast Connection Travel–Ski and Snowboard Sensation
Westcoast Connection Travel–Western Canadian Adventure
Westcoast Connection–U.S. Explorer

Chile
The Experiment in International Living–Chile North Homestay, Community Service
The Experiment in International Living–Chile South Homestay

China
AAVE–China
ACADEMIC TREKS–Immersion China
Duke TIP International Field Studies
EF International Language School–Beijing
EF International Language School–Shanghai
The Experiment in International Living–China North and East Homestay
The Experiment in International Living–China South and West Homestay
LIFEWORKS with the China Little Flower Foundation in China
Rassias Programs–China
RUSTIC PATHWAYS–ASIAN PACIFIC EXTREME
RUSTIC PATHWAYS–THE WONDERS OF CHINA
Summer Advantage Study Abroad–Nanjing, China

Colorado
AAVE–Boot/Saddle/Paddle
AAVE–Colorado Discovery
AAVE–Peak Four
AAVE–Rock & Rapid
AAVE–Rock & Roll
ATW: American Horizons
ATW: Discoverer
ATW: Skyblazer
ATW: Wayfarer
Treetops eXpeditions–Horseback Riding
Weissman Teen Tours–U.S. and Western Canada, 40 Days
Weissman Teen Tours–U.S. and Western Canada, 30 Days
Westcoast Connection–Californian Extravaganza
Wilderness Ventures–Colorado/Utah Mountain Bike
Wilderness Ventures–Southwest Community Service

Connecticut
92nd Street Y Camps–The TIYUL

Costa Rica
AAVE–Costa Rica Clásica
AAVE–Costa Rica Spanish Intensive
ACADEMIC TREKS–Sea Turtle Studies
BROADREACH Costa Rica Experience
Duke TIP International Field Studies
Edu-Culture International (ECI)–CPI Costa Rica
Edu-Culture International (ECI)–Grecia Costa Rica
EF International Language School–Playa Tamarindo
The Experiment in International Living–Costa Rica Homestay
Global Leadership Adventures–Costa Rica: Community Service and Leadership
GLOBAL WORKS–Cultural Exchange and Service–Costa Rica-3 weeks
GLOBAL WORKS–Language Immersion, Cultural Exchange and Service–Costa Rica
GLOBAL WORKS–Language Immersion, Cultural Exchange and Service–Panama/Costa Rica
LIFEWORKS with the Fundación Humanitaria in Costa Rica
RUSTIC PATHWAYS–COSTA RICA ADVENTURER
RUSTIC PATHWAYS–SOCCER AND SERVICE EXTREME
RUSTIC PATHWAYS–SOCCER AND SERVICE IN COSTA RICA

RUSTIC PATHWAYS–SURF & SERVICE–COSTA RICA
RUSTIC PATHWAYS–ULTIMATE JUNGLE ADVENTURE–COSTA RICA
Visions–Costa Rica
Westcoast Connection–Belize and Costa Rica Water Adventure
Westcoast Connection–Community Service Costa Rica
Westcoast Connection–Spanish in Costa Rica
Wilderness Ventures–Costa Rica
Wilderness Ventures–Costa Rica/ Belize
Wilderness Ventures–Costa Rica Service
Wilderness Ventures–Costa Rica Surfing

District of Columbia
ATW: Adventure Roads
Westcoast Connection–Major League Baseball Tour
Westcoast Connection Travel– Eastcoast Encounter

Dominica
BROADREACH Arc of the Caribbean Sailing Adventure
Visions–Dominica

Dominican Republic
Visions–Dominican Republic

Ecuador
AAVE–Ecuador and Galapagos
ACADEMIC TREKS–Spanish Language Immersion in Ecuador
ACTIONQUEST: Galapagos Archipelago Expeditions
EF International Language School– Quito
The Experiment in International Living–Ecuador Homestay
GLOBAL WORKS–Language Immersion, Cultural Exchange and Service–Ecuador and the Galapagos-4 weeks
LIFEWORKS with the Galapagos Islands' National Parks
Visions–Ecuador
Wilderness Ventures–Ecuador and Galapagos Community Service

Egypt
BROADREACH Red Sea Scuba Adventure

Fiji
ACADEMIC TREKS–Shark Studies in Fiji
BROADREACH Fiji Solomon Quest

GLOBAL WORKS–Cultural Exchange and Service–New Zealand and Fiji Islands-4 weeks
GLOBAL WORKS–Cultural Exchange–Fiji Islands-4 weeks
Putney Student Travel–Cultural Exploration–Australia, New Zealand, and Fiji
RUSTIC PATHWAYS–ASIAN PACIFIC EXTREME
RUSTIC PATHWAYS–BIG FIJI EXPLORER
RUSTIC PATHWAYS–FIJI ISLANDS COMMUNITY SERVICE
RUSTIC PATHWAYS–REMOTE HIGHLANDS COMMUNITY SERVICE IN FIJI
RUSTIC PATHWAYS–SERVICE LEARNING EXTREME
RUSTIC PATHWAYS–SOCCER AND SERVICE EXTREME
RUSTIC PATHWAYS–SOCCER AND SERVICE IN FIJI
RUSTIC PATHWAYS–SOUTH PACIFIC EXTREME
RUSTIC PATHWAYS–SUN, SAND & INTERNATIONAL SERVICE–FIJI
Wilderness Ventures–Fiji Community Service
Wilderness Ventures–Tahiti, Fiji, and New Zealand

Florida
ATW: Adventure Roads
ATW: Mini Tours
Rein Teen Tours–Eastern Adventure
Treetops eXpeditions–Sailing and Marine Ecology
Westcoast Connection–Florida Swing Junior Touring Golf Camp
Westcoast Connection Travel– Eastcoast Encounter

France
AAVE–Bike Amsterdam-Paris
AAVE–Bold Europe
AAVE–France Classique
AAVE–Ultimate Alps
ACADEMIC TREKS–French Immersion in France
ACTIONQUEST: Mediterranean Sailing Voyage
ATW: European Adventures
Barat Foundation Summer Program in Provence
Duke TIP International Field Studies
Edu-Culture International (ECI)–Aix-en-Provence/Gap Host Family Immersion
Edu-Culture International (ECI)– Lyon Host Family and Travel Program

Edu-Culture International (ECI)– Toulouse/Montpellier Host Family Immersion
EF International Language School– Nice
EF International Language School– Paris
Excel at Oxford/Tuscany
The Experiment in International Living–France, Biking and Homestay
The Experiment in International Living–France, Five-Week Art and Adventure in Provence
The Experiment in International Living–France, Four-Week Brittany Discovery
The Experiment in International Living–France, Four-Week Homestay and Photography
The Experiment in International Living–France, Four-Week Homestay and Theatre
The Experiment in International Living–France, Four-Week Homestay and Travel–Southern France and Northern Spain
The Experiment in International Living–France, Four-Week Homestay and Travel through Alps
The Experiment in International Living–France, Three-Week Camargue Homestay
The Experiment in International Living–France, Three-Week Homestay and Travel–Borders
GLOBAL WORKS–Language Immersion, Cultural Exchange and Service–France-4 weeks
National Student Leadership Conference: Globalization and International Business–Study Abroad
Putney Student Travel–Cultural Exploration–Switzerland, Italy, France, and Holland
Rassias Programs–Arles, France
Rassias Programs–Tours, France
Rein Europe
Summer Advantage Study Abroad– Paris, France
Taft Summer School Abroad–France
Weissman Teen Tours–European Experience
Westcoast Connection–European Escape
Westcoast Connection–French Language and Touring
Westcoast Connection Travel– European Discovery
Westcoast Connection Travel/On Tour–European Escapade

FRANCE

Westcoast Connection Travel/On
Tour–European Experience
Wilderness Ventures–European Alps

French Polynesia
ACTIONQUEST: Tahiti and French
Polynesian Island Voyages
Wilderness Ventures–Tahiti, Fiji, and
New Zealand

Georgia
ATW: Adventure Roads
92nd Street Y Camps–The TIYUL

Germany
EF International Language School–
Munich
The Experiment in International
Living–Germany, Four-Week
Homestay, Travel, Community
Service

Ghana
The Experiment in International
Living–Ghana Homestay
Global Leadership Adventures–
Ghana: Community Service and
Leadership

Greece
AAVE–Sail Dive Greece
ATW: European Adventures
University of Chicago–The Traveling
Academy

Grenada
BROADREACH Adventures in the
Windward Islands–Advanced
Scuba

Guadeloupe
ACADEMIC TREKS–Caribbean
Marine Reserves
ACADEMIC TREKS–French
Immersion in the French West
Indies
ACTIONQUEST: Leeward and
French Caribbean Island Voyages
BROADREACH Adventures in Scuba
and Sailing–Underwater
Discoveries
BROADREACH Adventures
Underwater–Advanced Scuba
BROADREACH Arc of the Caribbean
Sailing Adventure
Visions–Guadeloupe

Hawaii
AAVE–Ultimate Hawaii
ATW: Camp Inn 42
ATW: Fire and Ice
Rein Teen Tours–Hawaiian/Alaskan
Adventure

Rein Teen Tours–Hawaiian Caper
Rein Teen Tours–Project Hawaii
Weissman Teen Tours–"Aloha–
Welcome to Hawaiian Paradise,"
3 weeks
Weissman Teen Tours–"Aloha–
Welcome to Hawaiian Paradise,"
2 weeks
Westcoast Connection–Australian
Outback Plus Hawaii
Westcoast Connection–Community
Service Hawaii
Westcoast Connection–Hawaiian
Spirit
Wilderness Ventures–Hawaii
Wilderness Ventures–Maui/Kauai

Honduras
BROADREACH Honduras Eco-
Adventure

Iceland
World Horizons International–United
Kingdom

Idaho
Wilderness Ventures–Great Divide
Wilderness Ventures–Rocky Mountain
Wilderness Ventures–Teton Crest
Wilderness Ventures–Yellowstone Fly
Fishing

Illinois
ATW: American Horizons
ATW: Wayfarer
Rein Teen Tours–Crossroads
Westcoast Connection–Major League
Baseball Tour
Westcoast Connection–U.S. Explorer

India
Global Leadership Adventures–India:
Community Service and
Leadership
RUSTIC PATHWAYS–ASIAN
PACIFIC EXTREME
RUSTIC PATHWAYS–EDGE OF THE
MAP EXTREME
RUSTIC PATHWAYS–INDIAN
HIMALAYA TRAVELER
RUSTIC PATHWAYS–
PHOTOGRAPHY ADVENTURE
IN THAILAND AND INDIA
RUSTIC PATHWAYS–WORLD
SERVICE EXTREME
Studies Abroad for Global Education
(SAGE), Summer SAGE Program

Ireland
AAVE–Wild Isles
GLOBAL WORKS–Cultural Exchange
and Service–Ireland-4 weeks

Italy
AAVE–Bold Europe
AAVE–Ultimate Alps
ACTIONQUEST: Mediterranean
Sailing Voyage
ATW: European Adventures
Duke TIP International Field Studies
EF International Language School–
Rome
Excel at Oxford/Tuscany
The Experiment in International
Living–Italy Biodiversity, Cooking,
and Culture
The Experiment in International
Living–Italy Homestay, Language,
Culture, and Travel
Humanities Spring in Assisi
Putney Student Travel–Cultural
Exploration–Switzerland, Italy,
France, and Holland
Rein Europe
Summer Advantage Study Abroad–
Rome, Italy
Weissman Teen Tours–European
Experience
Westcoast Connection–Authentic Italy
Westcoast Connection–European
Escape
Westcoast Connection Travel–
European Discovery
Westcoast Connection Travel/On
Tour–European Escapade
Westcoast Connection Travel/On
Tour–European Experience
Wilderness Ventures–European Alps

Japan
The Experiment in International
Living–Japan Homestay

**Lao People's Democratic
Republic**
RUSTIC PATHWAYS–
INTRODUCTION TO
PHOTOGRAPHY–SNAPSHOTS
IN THE LAND OF SMILES

Maine
ATW: Mini Tours
92nd Street Y Camps–The TIYUL
Rein Teen Tours–Eastern Adventure
Westcoast Connection Travel–
Eastcoast Encounter

Martinique
BROADREACH Arc of the Caribbean
Sailing Adventure
GLOBAL WORKS–Language
Immersion, Cultural Exchange and
Service–Martinique-4weeks

Maryland
ATW: Mini Tours

Westcoast Connection–Major League
Baseball Tour

Massachusetts
ATW: Adventure Roads
ATW: Mini Tours
92nd Street Y Camps–The TIYUL
Rein Teen Tours–Eastern Adventure
Westcoast Connection Travel–
Eastcoast Encounter

Mexico
AAVE–Surf Scuba Safari
ACADEMIC TREKS–Immersion
Mexico
ACADEMIC TREKS–Spanish
Immersion in Oaxaca, Mexico
BROADREACH Baja Extreme–Scuba
Adventure
BROADREACH Yucatan Adventure
The Experiment in International
Living–Mexico–Community
Service, Travel, and Homestay
The Experiment in International
Living–Mexico Cooking and
Culture
The Experiment in International
Living–Mexico Homestay,
Sustainable Development and Fair
Trade
The Experiment in International
Living–Mexico–Mayan Arts and
Culture
GLOBAL WORKS–Language
Immersion, Cultural Exchange and
Service–Mexico–3 weeks
GLOBAL WORKS–Language
Immersion, Cultural Exchange and
Service–Yucatan Peninsula,
Mexico–4 weeks
Weissman Teen Tours–"Aloha–
Welcome to Hawaiian Paradise,"
3 weeks
Weissman Teen Tours–U.S. and
Western Canada, 40 Days
Weissman Teen Tours–U.S. and
Western Canada, 30 Days

Michigan
ATW: American Horizons
ATW: Wayfarer
Rein Teen Tours–Crossroads
Westcoast Connection–Major League
Baseball Tour
Westcoast Connection–U.S. Explorer

Minnesota
ATW: American Horizons
ATW: Wayfarer
Rein Teen Tours–Crossroads
Treetops eXpeditions–Glacier/
Boundary Waters
Westcoast Connection–U.S. Explorer

Mississippi
Visions–Mississippi

Missouri
ATW: American Horizons
Westcoast Connection–Major League
Baseball Tour

Monaco
ACTIONQUEST: Mediterranean
Sailing Voyage
Westcoast Connection–European
Escape
Westcoast Connection Travel–
European Discovery
Westcoast Connection Travel/On
Tour–European Escapade
Westcoast Connection Travel/On
Tour–European Experience

Montana
Adventure Treks–Montana
Adventures
Adventure Treks–Wilderness
Adventures
ATW: Camp Inn 42
ATW: Skyblazer
Rein Teen Tours–Grand Adventure
Treetops eXpeditions–Glacier/
Boundary Waters
Visions–Montana
Weissman Teen Tours–U.S. and
Western Canada, 40 Days
Weissman Teen Tours–U.S. and
Western Canada, 30 Days
Westcoast Connection–American
Voyageur
Westcoast Connection Travel–
Northwestern Odyssey
Wilderness Ventures–Great Divide
Wilderness Ventures–Rocky Mountain
Wilderness Ventures–Yellowstone
Wilderness Ventures–Yellowstone Fly
Fishing
Wilderness Ventures–Yellowstone
Wilderness

Morocco
The Experiment in International
Living–Morocco Four-Week Arts
and Culture Program

Myanmar
RUSTIC PATHWAYS–ASIAN
PACIFIC EXTREME
RUSTIC PATHWAYS–EDGE OF THE
MAP EXTREME
RUSTIC PATHWAYS–
INTRODUCTION TO
PHOTOGRAPHY–SNAPSHOTS
IN THE LAND OF SMILES
RUSTIC PATHWAYS–OFF THE MAP
BURMA AND CAMBODIA

RUSTIC PATHWAYS–
PHOTOGRAPHY ADVENTURE
IN THAILAND AND BURMA
RUSTIC PATHWAYS–THE
WONDERS & RICHES OF
SOUTHEAST ASIA

Namibia
AAVE–Africa

Netherlands
AAVE–Bike Amsterdam-Paris
Putney Student Travel–Cultural
Exploration–Switzerland, Italy,
France, and Holland
Weissman Teen Tours–European
Experience
Westcoast Connection Travel–
European Discovery

Netherlands Antilles
ACADEMIC TREKS–Caribbean
Marine Reserves
ACTIONQUEST: Leeward and
French Caribbean Island Voyages
BROADREACH Adventures in Scuba
and Sailing–Underwater
Discoveries
BROADREACH Adventures
Underwater–Advanced Scuba
BROADREACH Arc of the Caribbean
Sailing Adventure

Nevada
AAVE–Bold West
ATW: American Horizons
ATW: California Sunset
ATW: Camp Inn 42
ATW: Discoverer
ATW: Pacific Paradise
ATW: Skyblazer
ATW: Sunblazer
ATW: Wayfarer
Rein Teen Tours–California Caper
Rein Teen Tours–Crossroads
Rein Teen Tours–Grand Adventure
Rein Teen Tours–Western Adventure
Weissman Teen Tours–U.S. and
Western Canada, 40 Days
Westcoast Connection–American
Voyageur
Westcoast Connection–California
Dreaming
Westcoast Connection–Californian
Extravaganza
Westcoast Connection Travel–
California and the Canyons
Westcoast Connection–U.S. Explorer

New Hampshire
ATW: Mini Tours
Rein Teen Tours–Eastern Adventure

▶ NEW HAMPSHIRE

Westcoast Connection Travel–
Eastcoast Encounter

New Mexico
Duke TIP Domestic Field Studies
The Experiment in International
Living–Navajo Nation
Wilderness Ventures–Southwest
Community Service

New York
ATW: American Horizons
ATW: Mini Tours
ATW: Wayfarer
92nd Street Y Camps–The TIYUL
92nd Street Y Camps–Trailblazers
Rein Teen Tours–Crossroads
Rein Teen Tours–Eastern Adventure
Westcoast Connection–Major League
Baseball Tour
Westcoast Connection–U.S. Explorer

New Zealand
The Experiment in International
Living–New Zealand Homestay
GLOBAL WORKS–Cultural Exchange
and Service–New Zealand and Fiji
Islands-4 weeks
Putney Student Travel–Cultural
Exploration–Australia, New
Zealand, and Fiji
RUSTIC PATHWAYS–NEW
ZEALAND NORTH ISLAND
ADVENTURE
RUSTIC PATHWAYS–SKI AND
SNOWBOARD ADVENTURE IN
NEW ZEALAND
RUSTIC PATHWAYS–SOUTH
PACIFIC EXTREME
Wilderness Ventures–Tahiti, Fiji, and
New Zealand

Nicaragua
Visions–Nicaragua

North Carolina
Duke TIP Domestic Field Studies

Ohio
ATW: American Horizons
ATW: Wayfarer
Rein Teen Tours–Crossroads
Westcoast Connection–Major League
Baseball Tour
Westcoast Connection Travel–
Eastcoast Encounter

Oregon
Adventure Treks–Oregon Adventures
Adventure Treks–Wilderness
Adventures
ATW: Pacific Paradise
ATW: Skyblazer

Rein Teen Tours–Hawaiian/Alaskan
Adventure
Rein Teen Tours–Hawaiian Caper
Westcoast Connection–American
Voyageur
Westcoast Connection Travel–Great
West Challenge
Westcoast Connection Travel–
Northwestern Odyssey
Westcoast Connection Travel–Ski and
Snowboard Sensation
Wilderness Ventures–Great Divide
Wilderness Ventures–Northwest
Wilderness Ventures–Oregon
Wilderness Ventures–Pacific
Northwest

Panama
GLOBAL WORKS–Language
Immersion, Cultural Exchange and
Service–Panama/Costa Rica

Pennsylvania
ATW: Adventure Roads
ATW: American Horizons
ATW: Mini Tours
Rein Teen Tours–Eastern Adventure
Westcoast Connection–Major League
Baseball Tour

Peru
AAVE–Peru and Machu Picchu
ACADEMIC TREKS–Adventure Peru
GLOBAL WORKS–Language
Immersion, Cultural Exchange and
Service–Peru
Visions–Peru
Wilderness Ventures–Peru
Community Service

Poland
The Experiment in International
Living–Poland, Homestay,
Community Service, and Travel

Puerto Rico
GLOBAL WORKS–Cultural Exchange
and Service–Puerto Rico-2 or 4
weeks
GLOBAL WORKS–Language
Immersion, Cultural Exchange and
Service–Puerto Rico-4 weeks

Russian Federation
Summer Advantage Study Abroad–
St. Petersburg, Russia

Saint Kitts and Nevis
ACADEMIC TREKS–Caribbean
Marine Reserves
ACTIONQUEST: Leeward and
French Caribbean Island Voyages

BROADREACH Adventures in Scuba
and Sailing–Underwater
Discoveries
BROADREACH Adventures
Underwater–Advanced Scuba
BROADREACH Arc of the Caribbean
Sailing Adventure

Saint Lucia
BROADREACH Adventures in the
Windward Islands–Advanced
Scuba
BROADREACH Arc of the Caribbean
Sailing Adventure

Saint Vincent and The Grenadines
BROADREACH Adventures in the
Grenadines–Advanced Scuba
BROADREACH Adventures in the
Windward Islands–Advanced
Scuba
BROADREACH Arc of the Caribbean
Sailing Adventure

Solomon Islands
BROADREACH Fiji Solomon Quest

South Africa
AAVE–Africa
The Experiment in International
Living–South Africa Homestay and
Community Service
Global Leadership Adventures–Cape
Town: Community Service and
Leadership

South Carolina
ATW: Adventure Roads
Rein Teen Tours–Eastern Adventure

South Dakota
ATW: American Horizons
ATW: Discoverer
ATW: Skyblazer
ATW: Wayfarer
Rein Teen Tours–Crossroads
Rein Teen Tours–Grand Adventure
Rein Teen Tours–Western Adventure
Treetops eXpeditions–Glacier/
Boundary Waters
Westcoast Connection–U.S. Explorer

Spain
AAVE–Bold Europe
AAVE–España Clásica
Choate Rosemary Hall Summer in
Spain
Edu-Culture International (ECI)–
Andalusion Total Immersion
Edu-Culture International (ECI)–
Granada Homestay

Edu-Culture International (ECI)–
Granada Homestay or Dorm Plus
Southern Host Family Immersion
Edu-Culture International (ECI)–
Granada-Nerja Homestay Combo
Edu-Culture International (ECI)–
Nerja Homestay Plus Southern
Host Family Immersion
Edu-Culture International (ECI)–
Nerja Homestay with Optional
Southern Host Family Immersion
Edu-Culture International (ECI)–
Salamanca Dorm Plus Southern
Host Family Immersion
Edu-Culture International (ECI)–
Salamanca Homestay
Edu-Culture International (ECI)–
Salamanca Homestay Plus
Northern Host Family Immersion
Edu-Culture International (ECI)–
Salamanca Homestay (Short
Version)
Edu-Culture International (ECI)–San
Sebastian Homestay Plus Southern
Host Family Immersion
EF International Language School–
Barcelona
EF International Language School–
Malaga
The Experiment in International
Living–Spain, Five-Week
Homestay, Language Immersion
The Experiment in International
Living–Spain, Four-Week
Language Training, Travel, and
Homestay
The Experiment in International
Living–Spain–Multiculturalism
and Service
The Experiment in International
Living–Spain–Spanish Arts and
Culture
The Experiment in International
Living–Spain–The Road to
Santiago
The Experiment in International
Living–Spanish Culture and
Exploration
GLOBAL WORKS–Language
Immersion, Cultural Exchange and
Service–Spain-4 weeks
iD Tech Camps–Documentary
Filmmaking and Cultural
Immersion in Spain
Rassias Programs–Gijón, Spain
Rassias Programs–Pontevedra, Spain
Rassias Programs–Segovia, Spain
Rein Europe
Summer Advantage Study Abroad–
Granada, Spain
Summer Advantage Study Abroad–
Salamanca, Spain

Taft Summer School Abroad–Spain
Westcoast Connection–Spanish
Language and Touring
Wilderness Ventures–Spanish
Pyrenees

Switzerland
AAVE–Ultimate Alps
ATW: European Adventures
The Experiment in International
Living–Switzerland French
Language Immersion, Homestay,
and Alpine Adventure
National Student Leadership
Conference: Globalization and
International Business–Study
Abroad
Putney Student Travel–Cultural
Exploration–Switzerland, Italy,
France, and Holland
Rein Europe
Summer in Switzerland
Weissman Teen Tours–European
Experience
Westcoast Connection–European
Escape
Westcoast Connection Travel–
European Discovery
Westcoast Connection Travel/On
Tour–European Escapade
Westcoast Connection Travel/On
Tour–European Experience
Wilderness Ventures–European Alps

Thailand
AAVE–Thailand
The Experiment in International
Living–Thailand Homestay
LIFEWORKS with the DPF
Foundation in Thailand
RUSTIC PATHWAYS–THE
AMAZING THAILAND
ADVENTURE
RUSTIC PATHWAYS–ASIAN
PACIFIC EXTREME
RUSTIC PATHWAYS–THE
BUDDHIST CARAVAN
RUSTIC PATHWAYS–COME WITH
NOTHING, GO HOME RICH
RUSTIC PATHWAYS–EDGE OF THE
MAP EXTREME
RUSTIC PATHWAYS–ELEPHANTS
& AMAZING THAILAND
RUSTIC PATHWAYS–HILL TRIBE
TREKKING ADVENTURE
RUSTIC PATHWAYS–
INTRODUCTION TO
PHOTOGRAPHY–SNAPSHOTS
IN THE LAND OF SMILES
RUSTIC PATHWAYS–ISLAND
HOPPING AND DIVING–
THAILAND

RUSTIC PATHWAYS–
PHOTOGRAPHY ADVENTURE
IN THAILAND AND ANGKOR
WAT
RUSTIC PATHWAYS–
PHOTOGRAPHY ADVENTURE
IN THAILAND AND BURMA
RUSTIC PATHWAYS–
PHOTOGRAPHY ADVENTURE
IN THAILAND AND INDIA
RUSTIC PATHWAYS–
PHOTOGRAPHY ADVENTURE
IN THAILAND AND VIETNAM
RUSTIC PATHWAYS–SERVICE
LEARNING EXTREME
RUSTIC PATHWAYS–SOCCER AND
SERVICE EXTREME
RUSTIC PATHWAYS–THE
WONDERS & RICHES OF
SOUTHEAST ASIA
RUSTIC PATHWAYS–WORLD
SERVICE EXTREME

Trinidad and Tobago
BROADREACH Arc of the Caribbean
Sailing Adventure

Turkey
The Experiment in International
Living–Turkey Homestay,
Community Service, and Travel

United Kingdom
AAVE–Wild Isles
ATW: European Adventures
Cambridge College Programme
Duke TIP International Field Studies
Excel at Oxford/Tuscany
The Experiment in International
Living–Scotland
The Experiment in International
Living–United Kingdom
Filmmaking Program and
Homestay
The Experiment in International
Living–United Kingdom Theatre
Program
Rein Europe
Summer Advantage Study Abroad–
Cambridge University
Summer Advantage Study Abroad–
London, UK
Weissman Teen Tours–European
Experience
Westcoast Connection Travel–
European Discovery
Westcoast Connection Travel/On
Tour–European Experience
World Horizons International–United
Kingdom

United Republic of Tanzania
RUSTIC PATHWAYS–CLIMBING
KILI
RUSTIC PATHWAYS–EDGE OF THE
MAP EXTREME
RUSTIC PATHWAYS–SERVICE AND
SAFARI IN AFRICA
RUSTIC PATHWAYS–WORLD
SERVICE EXTREME

Utah
AAVE–Bold West
AAVE–Peak Four
AAVE–Rock & Rapid
ATW: American Horizons
ATW: Camp Inn 42
ATW: Discoverer
ATW: Skyblazer
ATW: Sunblazer
ATW: Wayfarer
Rein Teen Tours–California Caper
Rein Teen Tours–Crossroads
Rein Teen Tours–Grand Adventure
Rein Teen Tours–Western Adventure
Weissman Teen Tours–U.S. and
Western Canada, 40 Days
Weissman Teen Tours–U.S. and
Western Canada, 30 Days
Westcoast Connection–American
Voyageur
Westcoast Connection–California
Dreaming
Westcoast Connection–Californian
Extravaganza
Westcoast Connection Travel–
California and the Canyons
Westcoast Connection–U.S. Explorer
Wilderness Ventures–Colorado/Utah
Mountain Bike
Wilderness Ventures–Southwest
Community Service

Vanuatu
BROADREACH Fiji Solomon Quest
Treetops eXpeditions–Vanuatu

Vietnam
RUSTIC PATHWAYS–ASIAN
PACIFIC EXTREME
RUSTIC PATHWAYS–FACES AND
PLACES OF VIETNAM

RUSTIC PATHWAYS–
PHOTOGRAPHY ADVENTURE
IN THAILAND AND VIETNAM
RUSTIC PATHWAYS–THE
WONDERS & RICHES OF
SOUTHEAST ASIA
Visions–Vietnam

Virginia
ATW: Adventure Roads
ATW: Mini Tours
Rein Teen Tours–Eastern Adventure
Westcoast Connection Travel–
Eastcoast Encounter

Washington
AAVE–Wild Coast Discovery
Adventure Treks–Pacific Northwest
Adventures
Adventure Treks–Wilderness
Adventures
ATW: Camp Inn 42
ATW: Fire and Ice
ATW: Pacific Paradise
ATW: Skyblazer
Rein Teen Tours–Grand Adventure
Rein Teen Tours–Hawaiian/Alaskan
Adventure
Rein Teen Tours–Hawaiian Caper
Weissman Teen Tours–U.S. and
Western Canada, 40 Days
Weissman Teen Tours–U.S. and
Western Canada, 30 Days
Westcoast Connection–American
Voyageur
Westcoast Connection–Community
Service–Habitat for Humanity
Westcoast Connection Travel–Great
West Challenge
Westcoast Connection Travel–
Northwestern Odyssey
Westcoast Connection Travel–Ski and
Snowboard Sensation
Wilderness Ventures–Cascade-
Olympic
Wilderness Ventures–Northwest
Wilderness Ventures–Pacific
Northwest
Wilderness Ventures–Puget Sound
Wilderness Ventures–Washington
Alpine

Wilderness Ventures–Washington
Mountaineering

West Virginia
92nd Street Y Camps–The TIYUL

Wisconsin
ATW: American Horizons
ATW: Wayfarer

Wyoming
ATW: American Horizons
ATW: Camp Inn 42
ATW: Discoverer
ATW: Skyblazer
ATW: Wayfarer
Rein Teen Tours–Crossroads
Rein Teen Tours–Grand Adventure
Rein Teen Tours–Western Adventure
Treetops eXpeditions–Horseback
Riding
University of Chicago–Stones and
Bones
Weissman Teen Tours–U.S. and
Western Canada, 40 Days
Weissman Teen Tours–U.S. and
Western Canada, 30 Days
Westcoast Connection–American
Voyageur
Westcoast Connection–Californian
Extravaganza
Westcoast Connection Travel–
Northwestern Odyssey
Westcoast Connection–U.S. Explorer
Wilderness Ventures–Grand Teton
Wilderness Ventures–Great Divide
Wilderness Ventures–Jackson Hole
Wilderness Ventures–Rocky Mountain
Wilderness Ventures–Teton Crest
Wilderness Ventures–Wyoming
Mountaineering
Wilderness Ventures–Yellowstone
Wilderness Ventures–Yellowstone Fly
Fishing
Wilderness Ventures–Yellowstone/
Teton Adventure
Wilderness Ventures–Yellowstone-
Teton Family Adventure
Wilderness Ventures–Yellowstone
Wilderness

Special Needs Accomodations

AD/HD
Academy by the Sea, CA
Eagle Hill School Summer Session, MA
Oak Creek Ranch School–Summer Academic Program, AZ
Talisman Summer Camp, NC
The Winchendon School Summer Session, MA

Arthritis
Camp Holiday Trails, VA

Asthma
Camp Holiday Trails, VA

Burn Survivor
Cheley Colorado Camps, CO

Cancer
Camp Holiday Trails, VA

Cystic Fibrosis
Camp Holiday Trails, VA

Developmentally Challenged
California State Summer School for the Arts/Inner Spark, CA
Camp Berachah Ministries–Camps and Conferences, WA
92nd Street Y Camps–Camp Bari Tov, NY
92nd Street Y Camps–Camp Tova, NY

Diabetic
Camp Holiday Trails, VA

Eating Disorder
Camp California Fitness, CA

Emotionally Challenged
California State Summer School for the Arts/Inner Spark, CA
Cornell University Summer College Programs for High School Students, NY
Cybercamps–Adelphi University, NY
92nd Street Y Camps–Camp Tova, NY
Talisman Summer Camp, NC

Epileptic
Camp Holiday Trails, VA

Hearing Impaired
California State Summer School for the Arts/Inner Spark, CA
Camp Berachah Ministries–Camps and Conferences, WA
Camp Holiday Trails, VA

Colorado College Summer Session, CO
Cornell University Summer College Programs for High School Students, NY
The Experiment in International Living–Australia Homestay, Australia
The Experiment in International Living–Belize Homestay, Belize
The Experiment in International Living–Botswana Homestay, Botswana
The Experiment in International Living–Brazil Homestay, Arts, and Community Service, Brazil
The Experiment in International Living–Chile North Homestay, Community Service, Chile
The Experiment in International Living–Chile South Homestay, Chile
The Experiment in International Living–Germany, Four-Week Homestay, Travel, Community Service, Germany
The Experiment in International Living–Japan Homestay, Japan
Harvard University Summer School: Secondary School Program, MA
Johns Hopkins University Zanvyl Krieger School of Arts and Sciences Summer Programs, MD
Smith College Summer Science and Engineering Program, MA
Volunteers for Peace International Voluntary Service–Estonia, Estonia
Volunteers for Peace International Voluntary Service–France, France
Volunteers for Peace International Voluntary Service–Germany, Germany
Volunteers for Peace International Voluntary Service–Italy, Italy

Heart Defects
Camp Holiday Trails, VA

Hemophilia
Camp Holiday Trails, VA

HIV/AIDS
Camp Holiday Trails, VA

Kidney Disorders
Camp Holiday Trails, VA

Learning Disabled
Barnard's Summer in New York City: A Pre-College Program, NY
Barnard's Summer in New York City: One-Week Liberal Arts Intensive, NY

Barnard's Summer in New York City: Young Women's Leadership Institute, NY
Brewster Academy Summer Session, NH
California State Summer School for the Arts/Inner Spark, CA
Camp Berachah Ministries–Camps and Conferences, WA
Cheshire Academy Summer Program, CT
College InSight, PA
Cornell University Summer College Programs for High School Students, NY
Cushing Academy Summer Session, MA
Dunnabeck at Kildonan, NY
Eagle Hill School Summer Session, MA
Excel at Amherst College, MA
The Gow School Summer Program, NY
Harvard University Summer School: Secondary School Program, MA
Johns Hopkins University Zanvyl Krieger School of Arts and Sciences Summer Programs, MD
Landmark School Summer Academic Program, MA
Linden Hill Summer Program, MA
92nd Street Y Camps–Camp Tova, NY
Oak Creek Ranch School–Summer Academic Program, AZ
Rumsey Hall School Summer Session, CT
Saint Thomas More School–Summer Academic Camp, CT
Salisbury Summer School, CT
summer@rectory, CT
Talisman Summer Camp, NC
The Winchendon School Summer Session, MA

Organ Transplant Recipient
Camp Holiday Trails, VA

Physically Challenged
California State Summer School for the Arts/Inner Spark, CA
Camp Berachah Ministries–Camps and Conferences, WA
Camp Holiday Trails, VA
Center for Talent Development Summer Academic Program, IL
Colorado College Summer Session, CO
Cornell University Summer College Programs for High School Students, NY
Crossroads School–Aquatics, CA
Exploration of Architecture, CA

SPECIAL NEEDS ACCOMMODATIONS

▶ PHYSICALLY CHALLENGED

Harvard University Summer School: Secondary School Program, MA
Johns Hopkins University Zanvyl Krieger School of Arts and Sciences Summer Programs, MD
Smith College Summer Science and Engineering Program, MA
University of Vermont Summer Engineering Institute for High School Students, VT
Volunteers for Peace International Voluntary Service–Estonia, Estonia
Volunteers for Peace International Voluntary Service–France, France
Volunteers for Peace International Voluntary Service–Germany, Germany
Volunteers for Peace International Voluntary Service–Italy, Italy
World Affairs Seminar, WI

Sickle Cell Anemia
Camp Holiday Trails, VA

Visually Impaired
California State Summer School for the Arts/Inner Spark, CA
Camp Berachah Ministries–Camps and Conferences, WA
Camp Holiday Trails, VA
Colorado College Summer Session, CO
Cornell University Summer College Programs for High School Students, NY
The Experiment in International Living–Australia Homestay, Australia
The Experiment in International Living–Belize Homestay, Belize
The Experiment in International Living–Botswana Homestay, Botswana
The Experiment in International Living–Brazil Homestay, Arts, and Community Service, Brazil

The Experiment in International Living–Chile North Homestay, Community Service, Chile
The Experiment in International Living–Chile South Homestay, Chile
The Experiment in International Living–Germany, Four-Week Homestay, Travel, Community Service, Germany
The Experiment in International Living–Japan Homestay, Japan
Harvard University Summer School: Secondary School Program, MA
Johns Hopkins University Zanvyl Krieger School of Arts and Sciences Summer Programs, MD
Smith College Summer Science and Engineering Program, MA

Weight Reduction
Camp California Fitness, CA

Religious Affiliations

Christian
Camp Berachah Ministries–Camps and Conferences, WA
Hargrave Summer Leadership Program, VA

Episcopal
summer@rectory, CT

Jewish
Camp Airy, MD
Camp Louise, MD
92nd Street Y Camps–Camp Bari Tov, NY
92nd Street Y Camps–Camp Kesher, PA

92nd Street Y Camps–Camp Tevah for Science and Nature, NY
92nd Street Y Camps–Camp Tova, NY
92nd Street Y Camps–Camp Yaffa for the Arts, NY
92nd Street Y Camps–Camp Yomi, NY
92nd Street Y Camps–The TIYUL
92nd Street Y Camps–Trailblazers, NY

Roman Catholic
Portsmouth Abbey Summer School, RI
Saint Thomas More School–Summer Academic Camp, CT

Society Of Friends
Applejack Teen Camp, NY
Camp Regis, NY

Unitarian Universalist
Applejack Teen Camp, NY
Camp Regis, NY

United Methodist
Randolph-Macon Academy Summer Programs, VA
Wyoming Seminary–Sem Summer 2008, PA

NOTES

NOTES

Peterson's
Book Satisfaction Survey

Give Us Your Feedback

Thank you for choosing Peterson's as your source for personalized solutions for your education and career achievement. Please take a few minutes to answer the following questions. Your answers will go a long way in helping us to produce the most user-friendly and comprehensive resources to meet your individual needs.

When completed, please tear out this page and mail it to us at:

> Publishing Department
> Peterson's, a Nelnet company
> 2000 Lenox Drive
> Lawrenceville, NJ 08648

You can also complete this survey online at **www.petersons.com/booksurvey.**

1. **What is the ISBN of the book you have purchased? (The ISBN can be found on the book's back cover in the lower right-hand corner.)** _____

2. **Where did you purchase this book?**
   - ❑ Retailer, such as Barnes & Noble
   - ❑ Online reseller, such as Amazon.com
   - ❑ Petersons.com
   - ❑ Other (please specify) _____

3. **If you purchased this book on Petersons.com, please rate the following aspects of your online purchasing experience on a scale of 4 to 1 (4 = Excellent and 1 = Poor).**

	4	3	2	1
Comprehensiveness of Peterson's Online Bookstore page	❑	❑	❑	❑
Overall online customer experience	❑	❑	❑	❑

4. **Which category best describes you?**
   - ❑ High school student
   - ❑ Parent of high school student
   - ❑ College student
   - ❑ Graduate/professional student
   - ❑ Returning adult student
   - ❑ Teacher
   - ❑ Counselor
   - ❑ Working professional/military
   - ❑ Other (please specify) _____

5. **Rate your overall satisfaction with this book.**

Extremely Satisfied	Satisfied	Not Satisfied
❑	❑	❑

6. **Rate each of the following aspects of this book on a scale of 4 to 1 (4 = Excellent and 1 = Poor).**

	4	3	2	1
Comprehensiveness of the information	❑	❑	❑	❑
Accuracy of the information	❑	❑	❑	❑
Usability	❑	❑	❑	❑
Cover design	❑	❑	❑	❑
Book layout	❑	❑	❑	❑
Special features (e.g., CD, flashcards, charts, etc.)	❑	❑	❑	❑
Value for the money	❑	❑	❑	❑

7. **This book was recommended by:**
   - ❑ Guidance counselor
   - ❑ Parent/guardian
   - ❑ Family member/relative
   - ❑ Friend
   - ❑ Teacher
   - ❑ Not recommended by anyone—I found the book on my own
   - ❑ Other (please specify) _____

8. **Would you recommend this book to others?**

   Yes   Not Sure   No

   ❑   ❑   ❑

9. **Please provide any additional comments.**

   _____

   _____

   _____

   _____

Remember, you can tear out this page and mail it to us at:

Publishing Department
Peterson's, a Nelnet company
2000 Lenox Drive
Lawrenceville, NJ 08648

or you can complete the survey online at **www.petersons.com/booksurvey.**

Your feedback is important to us at Peterson's, and we thank you for your time!

If you would like us to keep in touch with you about new products and services, please include your e-mail address here: _____